Proceedings of the 2015 ACM International Conference on

ITS 2015

INTERACTIVE TABLETOPS AND SURFACES

Madeira, Portugal
15-18 November 2015

acm SIGCHI ITS 2015

hoto: Andrés Lucero | Design: Andrés Lucero, Rodrigo Zuloaga

Association for
Computing Machinery

Advancing Computing as a Science & Profession

The Association for Computing Machinery
2 Penn Plaza, Suite 701
New York, New York 10121-0701

Notice to Past Authors of ACM-Published Articles
ACM intends to create a complete electronic archive of all articles and/or other material previously published by ACM. If you have written a work that has been previously published by ACM in any journal or conference proceedings prior to 1978, or any SIG Newsletter at any time, and you do NOT want this work to appear in the ACM Digital Library, please inform permissions@acm.org, stating the title of the work, the author(s), and where and when published.

ISBN: 978-1-4503-3899-8 (Digital)

ISBN: 978-1-4503-4109-7 (Print)

Additional copies may be ordered prepaid from:

ACM Order Department
PO Box 30777
New York, NY 10087-0777, USA

Phone: 1-800-342-6626 (USA and Canada)
+1-212-626-0500 (Global)
Fax: +1-212-944-1318
E-mail: acmhelp@acm.org
Hours of Operation: 8:30 am – 4:30 pm ET

Printed in the USA

Welcome to ACM ITS 2015

We are pleased to welcome you to the ACM International Conference on Interactive Tabletops and Surfaces (ITS) 2015, held from 15-18 November 2015 in Funchal on the wonderful island of Madeira in Portugal, and organized with the support of the Madeira Interactive Technologies Institute (M-ITI). The island of Madeira is an autonomous region of Portugal located 310 miles from the African coast and 620 miles from continental Europe. Madeira is one of Europe's most longstanding holiday island destinations. Historical figures from Sisi (Empress Elisabeth of Austria) to Winston Churchill have enjoyed its mild climate. ACM ITS takes place in Portugal for the first time and is hosted by M-ITI, a research and innovation institute of the University of Madeira. M-ITI was established as an independent non-profit R&D organization founded by the University of Madeira, the Regional Government and Carnegie Mellon University. The institute operates in the interdisciplinary field of human-computer interaction and its vision is to become a world leading center of excellence in design for global change.

ITS 2015 marks the 10th anniversary of this series of annual research workshops and conferences that began in 2006 in Adelaide, Australia. Over the last ten years, the field of interactive tabletops and surfaces has seen significant change with low-cost touch-enabled surfaces in a wide range of form factors and sizes, that are now available off-the-shelf. Ideas from the community have gone from research prototypes to global consumer products and can be found in a wide variety of private and public spaces from museums, offices, schools and airports to hotels, medical centers and homes. To celebrate this, we are introducing a "10-year impact" award this year to recognise the research that was presented at the inaugural meeting of our community and has shown to be the most influential.

Sponsored by ACM SIGCHI and generously supported by SMART and Microsoft, the ACM Conference on Interactive Tabletops and Surfaces brings together researchers and practitioners from a variety of backgrounds and interest areas. The intimate size of this single-track symposium provides an ideal venue for leading researchers, practitioners, and students to share research results and experiences. As ever, our main goal has been to provide an engaging and high quality program. We have retained the successful format of previous years: a three-day conference event preceded by one day of workshops, tutorials and a doctoral symposium. This year we were delighted to receive 122 paper and note submissions of which we accepted 18 papers and 11 notes (resulting in a highly competitive overall acceptance rate of 24%). Submissions were assessed over the summer by a committee of program committee members, their reviewers, and finally at a remote PC meeting. The topics of this year's papers, notes, posters, and demos reflect the diversity of ideas and perspectives that comprise the ITS community, ranging from wall-sized surfaces to shape changing displays, from pen-and-paper to free-space interaction, and from education to projection systems for bike riding. What brings this all together is a commitment to innovation that expands our understanding of design considerations of ITS technologies and of their applications. The Doctoral Symposium (DS) accepted 7 doctoral students to present and discuss their research with both peers and a panel of experienced ITS researchers. The conference also includes an interactive hands-on reception that presents a juried selection of 26 posters and 12 demos. Finally, we have accepted 7 workshops that bring together researchers and practitioners in a focused setting to advance the state-of-the-art in specific areas related to interactive surfaces.

We are especially pleased to have two exciting keynote speakers this year. Charles Spence, head of the Crossmodal Research Laboratory at the University of Oxford, will open the conference with his talk "In Touch with the Future". Charles is interested in how we perceive the world around us, in particular, how our brains manage to process the information from each of our different senses (such as smell, taste, sight, hearing, and touch) to form the extraordinarily rich multisensory experiences that fill our daily lives. His research focuses on how a better understanding of the human mind will lead to the better design of multisensory foods, products, interfaces, and environments in the future. The conference will close with Jinha Lee's talk on "From Surface to Space". Jinha is a designer and engineer working at the boundary of the physical and digital world. He is exploring ways to weave digital information into physical space and material. Lee is currently on leave from his Ph.D. studies at MIT Media Lab directing the Interaction Group at Samsung Electronics. Jinha was named on MIT Technology Review's list of 35 young innovators and Fast Company's list of 32 greatest living designers.

As ever, a large number of people have contributed to the organization, reviewing, venue arrangement, web and media presence, and publicity for the ITS 2015, and we would like to express our deepest gratitude to the many dozens of volunteers whose efforts have contributed to what we hope will be a memorable event. We would in particular like to thank our student volunteers, the M-ITI staff, and our corporate sponsors for their continued support for this conference series.

Nuno Nunes
ITS '15 General Chair
Madeira Interactive Technologies Institute (M-ITI)
University of Madeira

Enrico Costanza
ITS '15 General Chair
Agents, Interaction and Complexity Group
University of Southampton

Patrick Olivier
ITS '15 Program Chair
Culture Lab
Newcastle University

Johannes Schöning
ITS '15 Program Chair
Expertise centre for Digital Media (EDM)
Hasselt University

Table of Contents

Table of Contents

Session 7: Development and Toolkits

Session Chair: Craig Anslow *(Middlesex University)*

Session 8: Back to the Future

Session Chair: Raimund Dachselt *(Technische Universität Dresden)*

Session 9: Latency and Shape Change

Session Chair: Andy Wilson *(Microsoft Research)*

Posters

Demos

Doctoral Symposium

Workshops

ITS 2015 Conference Organization

General Chairs: Nuno Nunes *(University of Madeira, Portugal)*
Enrico Costanza *(University of Southampton, UK)*

Program Chairs: Patrick Olivier *(Newcastle University, UK)*
Johannes Schöning *(Hasselt University, Belgium)*

Local Arrangements Chairs: Pedro Campos *(University of Madeira, Portugal)*
Evangelos Karapanos *(University of Madeira, Portugal)*

Proceedings Chair: Jo Vermeulen *(University of Birmingham, UK)*

Posters Chairs: Ahmed Kharrufa *(Diwan Software and Reflective Thinking, UK)*
David Kim *(Microsoft, USA)*
Monchu Chen *(University of Madeira, Portugal)*
Christian Holz *(Microsoft, USA)*

Demos Chairs: Tom Bartindale *(Newcastle University, UK)*
Ian Oakley *(Ulsan Institute of Science and Technology, South Korea)*
Valentina Nisi *(University of Madeira, Portugal)*
Pedro Branco *(University of Minho, Portugal)*

Web Chair and Logo Design: Andrés Lucero *(University of Southern Denmark, Denmark)*

Workshops Chairs: Nicolai Marquardt *(University College London, UK)*
Florian Block *(Harvard University, USA)*

Doctoral Symposium Chairs: Raimund Dachselt *(Technische Universität Dresden, Germany)*
Antonio Krüger *(Saarland University, Germany)*

Student Volunteers Chairs: José Luís Silva *(University of Madeira, Portugal)*
Betty Chang *(Waterloo University, Canada)*

Publicity Chairs: Craig Anslow *(Middlesex University, UK)*
Takuya Nojima *(University of Electro-Communications, Japan)*

Sponsorship and Industry Chairs: Edward Tse *(SMART Technologies, Canada)*
Miguel Peixoto de Oliveira *(Edigma, Portugal)*
Graham Cosier *(Tactable, USA)*

Madness Chair: Simon Völker *(RWTH Aachen, Germany)*

Steering Committee: *Chair:* Andy Wilson *(Microsoft Research, USA)*
Sheelagh Carpendale *(University of Calgary, Canada)*
Raimund Dachselt *(Technische Universität Dresden, Germany)*
Shahram Izadi *(Microsoft Research, USA)*
Miguel Nacenta *(University of St Andrews, UK)*
Stacey D. Scott *(University of Waterloo, Canada)*
Sriram Subramanian *(Sussex University, UK)*
Alumni:
Gerald Morrison *(SMART Technologies, Canada)*
Chia Shen *(Harvard University, USA)*
Bruce Thomas *(University of South Australia, Australia)*

Program Committee: Jason Alexander *(Lancaster University, UK)*
Craig Anslow *(Middlesex University, UK)*
Tom Bartindale *(Newcastle University, UK)*
Hrvoje Benko *(Microsoft, USA)*
Andrea Bellucci *(University Carlos III of Madrid, Spain)*
Florian Block *(Harvard University, USA)*
Anke Brock *(INRIA, France)*
Pedro Campos *(University of Madeira, Portugal)*
Florian Daiber *(DFKI, Germany)*
Raimund Dachselt *(Technische Universität Dresden, Germany)*
Hans Gellersen *(Lancaster University, UK)*
Nicholas Graham *(Queen's University, Canada)*
Mark Hancock *(University of Waterloo, Canada)*
Jonathan Hook *(University of York, UK)*
Petra Isenberg *(INRIA, France)*
Tobias Isenberg *(INRIA, France)*
Joaquim Jorge *(University of Lisbon, Portugal)*
Judy Kay *(University of Sydney, Australia)*
Ahmed Kharrufa *(Reflective Thinking, UK)*
David Kim *(Microsoft, USA)*
Gudrun Klinker *(TU Munich, Germany)*
Hideki Koike *(Tokyo Institute of Technology, Japan)*
Werner König *(University of Applied Sciences, Worms, Germany)*
Roberto Martinez-Maldonado *(University of Sydney, Australia)*
Nicolai Marquardt *(University College London, UK)*
Clemens Nylandsted Klokmose *(Aarhus University, Denmark)*
Alex Olwal *(Google X, USA)*
Harald Reiterer *(University of Konstanz, Germany)*
Yvonne Rogers *(University College London, UK)*
Anne Roudaut *(University of Bristol, UK)*
Stacey D. Scott *(University of Waterloo, Canada)*
Bruce Thomas *(University of South Australia, Australia)*
Edward Tse *(SMART, Canada)*
Simon Völker *(RWTH Aachen, Germany)*
Andy Wilson *(Microsoft, USA)*

Additional reviewers:

Daniel Afergan
Andrea Alessandrini
Florian Alt
Christopher Andrews
Caroline Appert
Shiri Azenkot
Felipe Bacim
Sriram Karthik Badam
Gilles Bailly
Jakob Bardram
Patrick Baudisch
David Benyon
Guillaume Besacier
Anastasia Bezerianos
Oliver Bimber
Rachel Blagojevic
Sebastian Boring
Doug Bowman
Jeremy Boy
Michael Boyle
Pedro Branco
Luca Brayda
Markus Bröcker
Judith Brown
Gerd Bruder
Emeline Brulé
Duncan Brumby
Stephanie Buisine
Melanie Buset
Diogo Cabral
Xiang Cao
Karina Caro
Luis Carriço
Lucila Carvalho
Alejandro Catala
Daniel Cernea
Matthew Chalmers
Y.-L. Betty Chang
Olivier Chapuis
Xiang 'Anthony' Chen
Christian Cherek
Victor Cheung
Sonia Chiasson
Ming Ki Chong
Irene-Angelica Chounta
Andrew Clayphan
Christian Corsten
Céline Coutrix
Joe Cutting
Prasun Dewan
Shalaka Dighe
Andreas Dippon
Gavin Doherty
Jonathon Doran
Jakub Dostal
Pierre Dragicevic
Ruofei Du
Carlos Duarte
Niklas Elmqvist
Steven Feiner
Andreas Fender
Tiare Feuchtner
Matthias Finke
Morten Fjeld
Sean Follmer
Eelke Folmer
Manuel Fonseca
Angus Forbes
Adrian Friday
Mathias Frisch
Kentaro Fukuchi
Steve Funke
Sarah Gallacher
Tovi Grossman
Jan Gugenheimer
Anhong Guo
Martin Hachet
Michael Haller
Nils Hammerla
Robert Hardy
Chris Harrison
Christin Henzen
Phil Heslop
Jens Heydekorn
Ken Hinckley
Uta Hinrichs
Axel Hösl
Tobias Höllerer
Christian Holz
Michael Horn

Additional reviewers (continued):

Eva Hornecker
Mona Hosseinkhani Loorak
Steven Houben
Takeo Igarashi
Pourang Irani
Daniel Jackson
Mikkel Jakobsen
Ghita Jalal
Yvonne Jansen
Hans-Christian Jetter
Jiepu Jiang
Ricardo Jota
Denis Kalkofen
Santosh Kalwar
Slim Kammoun
Hideaki Kanai
Shaun Kane
Bill Kapralos
Mustafa Karagozler
Arafeh Karimi
Abhijit Karnik
Frederic Kerber
Mohammadreza Khalilbeigi
Mohamed Khamis
Chang Min Kim
Jesper Kjeldskov
Daniel Klinkhammer
Khalil Klouche
Jarrod Knibbe
Søren Knudsen
Werner König
Per Ola Kristensson
Kai Kuikkaniemi
Marc Latoschik
Jeremy Laviole
Shaimaa Lazem
Bongshin Lee
Daniel Leithinger
Samantha LeVan
Vincent Levesque
David Lindlbauer
Stephen Lindsay
Lars Lischke
Agnes Lisowska Masson
Can Liu
Markus Löchtefeld
Paul Lubos
Zhihan Lv
Kent Lyons
Narges Mahyar
Sonja Maier
Sylvain Malacria
Regan Mandryk
Panos Markopoulos
Diego Martinez Plasencia
Fabrice Matulic
Daniel Mendes
Helena Mentis
Chulhong Min
Homei Miyashita
Meredith Morris
Annette Mossel
Stefanie Mueller
Joseph Mullenbach
Jörg Müller
Hani Murad
Lennart Nacke
Mathieu Nancel
Michael Nebeling
Hugo Nicolau
Takuya Nojima
Diana Nowacka
Andrea Nutsi
Kenton O'Hara
Eyal Ofek
Andrea Parker
Amanda Parkes
Fabio Paternò
Sharoda Paul
Nicole Percival
Lucas Pereira
Anthony Perritano
Florian Perteneder
Ulrike Pfeil
Ken Pfeuffer
Thomas Pietrzak
Katrin Plaumann
Bernd Ploderer
John Pollak
Kathrin Probst

Additional reviewers (continued):

Bradley Pursglove
Roman Rädle
Fateme Rajabiyazdi
Yosra Rekik
Jun Rekimoto
Jochen Rick
Kathryn Ringland
Marco Romano
Chris Rooney
Anne Roudaut
Thijs Roumen
Enrico Rukzio
Ramik Sadana
Alan Said
Munehiko Sato
Valkyrie Savage
Florian Schaub
Dieter Schmalstieg
Albrecht Schmidt
Benedikt Schmidt
Dominik Schmidt
Bertrand Schneider
Baris Serim
Teddy Seyed
Roy Shilkrot
Buntarou Shizuki
Beat Signer
Adalberto Simeone
Mathieu Simonnet
Rajinder Sodhi
Maurício Sousa
Oleg Spakov
Jürgen Steimle
Sophie Stellmach
Elizabeth Stobert
Wolfgang Stuerzlinger
Miriam Sturdee
Yusuke Sugano
Yuta Sugiura
Anthony Tang
Aneesh Tarun
Nick Taylor
Sara Tena
Kate Thompson
Eric Tobias
Cesar Torres
Melanie Tory
Dimitar Valkov
Jan Van den Bergh
Danniel Varona-Marin
Melodie Vidal
Daniel Vogel
Ulrich von Zadow
Chat Wacharamanotham
Philipp Wacker
Daniel Wagner
James Wallace
Jagoda Walny
Robert Walter
Na Wang
Yi Wang
Na Wang
Christian Weichel
Mark Whiting
Daniel Wigdor
Karl Willis
Raphael Wimmer
Paweł Woźniak
Min Wu
Mounia Ziat
Oren Zuckerman

ITS 2015 Sponsor & Supporters

ITS 2015 gratefully acknowledges our sponsoring SIG and the support of the following organizations:

Sponsor: SIGCHI

Silver Supporter: SMART™

Bronze Supporter: Microsoft

Friends of ITS: m·iti Madeira Interactive Technologies Institute; TURISMO DE PORTUGAL; madeira islands

In Touch with the Future

Charles Spence
Crossmodal Research Laboratory
Oxford University, UK
charles.spence@psy.ox.ac.uk

ABSTRACT

It was recently announced that there are now more than three billion touch screens in circulation [1]. What such a figure emphasizes, I think, is that touch is becoming an increasingly pervasive feature of our interaction with many technologies, from touch screen to vibrating cars all the way through to vibrating cutlery - really [2,3,6]! But what, exactly, is the advantage, or advantages of engaging this, our largest, sense? And what are the trade-offs? After all, a quick look at the history of the tactile stimulation of the skin surface resounds with promises that have gone unfulfilled: Anyone seen the tactile television, or bankers walking around with a vibrating belt communicating the latest stock market figures recently? I thought not! While I believe that effectively stimulating the skin surface holds many promises in the years to come, success in the real-world will only come from a proper understanding of the psychological limitations in tactile information processing, involving everything from tactile sensory suppression whenever we move (see [4]) through limits on multisensory perception and attention [2]. In this talk, I will highlight what I see as the biggest limitations of tactile stimulation/communication [5], before looking at some of the latest innovations that have really gotten me excited over the last couple of years in terms of showcasing what the world of digital tactile stimulation can potentially offer.

ACM Classification Keywords

H.5.2 User Interfaces: *Haptic I/O*.

Author Keywords: Touch; Tactile stimulation; Tactile communication; Information processing; Multisensory perception.

BIOGRAPHY

Professor Charles Spence is the head of the Crossmodal Research Laboratory at the University of Oxford. He is interested in how people perceive the world around them. In particular, how our brains manage to process the information from each of our different senses (such as smell, taste, sight, hearing, and touch) to form the extraordinarily rich multisensory experiences that fill our daily lives. His research focuses on how a better understanding of the human mind will lead to the better design of multisensory foods, products, interfaces, and environments in the future. His research calls for a radical new way of examining and understanding the senses that has major implications for the way in which we design everything from household products to mobile phones, and from the food we eat to the places in which we work and live.

In his keynote at ACM ITS, Charles will focus on "touch". Out of all the human senses, touch is the one that is most often unappreciated, and undervalued. Yet, the surface of the human body, the skin, is actually one huge sheet of tactile receptors. It provides us with the means to connect with our surroundings. Despite the important role that vision plays in our everyday lives, it is the skin that constitutes both the oldest, and by far the largest of our sense organs. The skin protects our body from the external world and, at the same time, informs us about what occurs on its surface.

ITS 2015, November 15–18, 2015, Funchal/Madeira, Portugal.
ACM 978-1-4503-3899-8/15/11.
DOI: http://dx.doi.org/10.1145/2817721.2817924

REFERENCES

1. Press release: The digital world has touch: Immersion's haptic technology reaches milestone of 3 billion devices. http://www.marketwatch.com/story/the-digital-world-has-touch-immersions-haptic-technology-reaches-milestone-of-3-billion-devices-2015-06-11 (downloaded on 17/08/2015).
2. Alberto Gallace and Charles Spence. 2014. *In touch with the future: The sense of touch from cognitive neuroscience to virtual reality*.
3. Cristy Ho and Charles Spence. 2008. *The Multisensory Driver: Implications for Ergonomic Car Interface Design*. Ashgate, Aldershot, England ; Burlington, VT.
4. Georgiana Juravle, Francis McGlone, and Charles Spence. 2013. Context-dependent changes in tactile perception during movement execution. *Cognition* 4: 913. http://doi.org/10.3389/fpsyg.2013.00913
5. Charles Spence. 2014. The Skin as a Medium for Sensory Substitution. *Multisensory Research* 27, 5-6: 293–312. http://doi.org/10.1163/22134808-00002452
6. Charles Spence and Betina Piqueras-Fiszman. 2014. *The Perfect Meal: The Multisensory Science of Food and Dining*. Wiley-Blackwell, Chichester, West Sussex, UK.

From Surface to Space

Jinha Lee
Samsung Electronics
lee.jinha@samsung.com

ABSTRACT

Humans have evolved to develop sophisticated skills to sense and interact with their physical surroundings; however, the majority of our interaction with digital information nowadays is confined to a single, small, flat screen. In this talk, I will discuss how we can leverage our kinesthetic skills and collaborative nature to enhance interaction with digital data, by representing the data in physical space or on multiple distributed devices. I will highlight some of my recent projects that demonstrate this vision including 3D spatial desktop, levitating interfaces, and a haptic wristwatch for the visually impaired.

ACM Classification Keywords

H.5.2 User Interfaces: *Haptic I/O*, *Interaction styles* (e.g., commands, menus, forms, direct manipulation).

Author Keywords: 3D interaction; Tangible interface; Haptic interface.

BIOGRAPHY

Jinha Lee is a Principal Engineer and Head of Interaction Group at Samsung Electronics. At the intersection of design and engineering, Lee explores ways to weave digital information into physical space and material, and how people can collaborate better in such environments. He also focuses on innovating software prototyping processes and developing experience-design driven business strategies. Previously, Lee has co-founded Eone [1] — a tactile watch brand for everyone including the visually impaired, and conducted research at SONY and Microsoft [2]. He has received his M.S. in Media Arts and Sciences from MIT and his B.E. in Electronic Engineering from the University of Tokyo. His works have been presented and exhibited at major academic conferences and museums, and have been recognized for design and innovation excellence; MIT Technology Review named him one of the "35 innovators under 35 (TR35)" [3]; FastCompany named him on one of 32 candidates for the greatest living designer in the world [4]; World Economic Forum named him a young global leader. In 2013, he gave a TED talk [5] about his inventions including 3D desktop that allows users to reach inside the screen [6] and a levitating interface [7].

ITS '15, November 15-18, 2015, Funchal, Portugal
ACM 978-1-4503-3899-8/15/11.
http://dx.doi.org/10.1145/2817721.2817925

REFERENCES

1. The Bradley Timepiece. Retrieved from http://leejinha.com/bradley. Retrieved October 3rd, 2015.
2. Jinha Lee and Cati Boulanger. 2012. Direct, spatial, and dexterous interaction with see-through 3D desktop. In *ACM SIGGRAPH 2012 Posters* (SIGGRAPH '12). ACM, New York, NY, USA, 1 page. http://doi.acm.org/10.1145/2342896.2342980
3. 35 Innovators Under 35. 2014. In *MIT Technology Review.* http://www.technologyreview.com/lists/innovators-under-35/2014/. Retrieved October 3rd, 2015.
4. Gus Wezerek. Co.Design Bracket Madness: Who is the World's Greatest Living Designer? 2014. http://www.fastcodesign.com/3027617/codesign-bracket-madness-who-is-the-worlds-greatest-living-designer. Retrieved October 3rd, 2015.
5. Jinha Lee. Reach into the computer and grab a pixel. 2013. In *TED Conference 2013.* http://www.ted.com/talks/jinha_lee_a_tool_that_lets_you_touch_pixels. Retrieved October 3rd, 2015.
6. Jinha Lee, Alex Olwal, Hiroshi Ishii, and Cati Boulanger. 2013. SpaceTop: integrating 2D and spatial 3D interactions in a see-through desktop environment. In *Proceedings of the SIGCHI Conference on Human Factors in Computing Systems* (CHI '13). ACM, New York, NY, USA, 189-192. http://doi.acm.org/10.1145/2470654.2470680
7. Jinha Lee, Rehmi Post, and Hiroshi Ishii. 2011. ZeroN: mid-air tangible interaction enabled by computer controlled magnetic levitation. In *Proceedings of the 24th Annual ACM Symposium on User Interface Software and Technology* (UIST '11). ACM, New York, NY, USA, 327-336. http://doi.acm.org/10.1145/2047196.2047239

The Influence of Multi-Touch Interaction on Procedural Training

Sarah Buchanan
University of Central Florida
Orlando, FL
sarahb@cs.ucf.edu

Jared Bott
University of Central Florida
Orlando, FL
jbott@cs.ucf.edu

Joseph J. LaViola Jr.
University of Central Florida
Orlando, FL
jjl@eecs.ucf.edu

ABSTRACT
This paper explores the use of multi-touch interaction in a 3D training environment as a way to enhance learning of sensorimotor skills as well as procedural knowledge. We present a between subjects experiment with 36 participants distributed into 3 groups that use multi-touch interaction, interaction with the physical apparatus, and a control group using basic mouse-based interaction. A post-training test carried out 3 days later evaluated performance in conducting the real world task from memory. Results show that the multi-touch interaction and the real world groups had significantly better performance scores than the mouse interaction group, with no significant difference between multi-touch and real world groups. Our results demonstrate that multi-touch interaction trained participants on the task as well as training on the actual equipment, indicating multi-touch interaction is a potential replacement for the physical apparatus when doing procedural training.

ACM Classification Keywords
H.5.2. Information Interfaces and Presentation (HCI): Miscellaneous

Author Keywords
Multi-touch; surface; procedural training; transfer learning; user study

INTRODUCTION
Multi-touch Tabletops and Surfaces have been used for a multitude of applications such as visualizing information [17] , inquiry-based learning [14], collaboration [6], neurorehabilitation [1], and strategic simulation training [2]. However, not much exploration has been done in leveraging multi-touch interaction for procedural training such as an industrial assembly tasks, mechanical repairs, or medical procedures. Industrial assembly or repairs are usually taught through video documentation, 2D mechanical drawings, or the explanation from an expert. Traditional medical education relies heavily on lectures for factual knowledge, observing professionals and treating patients under supervision. However, enactive learning and interfaces have been shown to be more effective than passive learning methods [10]. Enactive interfaces have been shown to be especially effective when optimizing affordances, or possible actions available to someone using the interface [16]. We aim to leverage the combined affordances of a multi-touch surface and a virtual environment to provide an effective replacement for their physical counterparts as a way to reduce cost and save time.

ITS '15, November 15 - 18, 2015, Funchal, Portugal

ACM 978-1-4503-3899-8/15/11:.$15.00.
DOI: http://dx.doi.org/10.1145/2817721.2817740

Figure 1: The motorized bicycle model in the virtual environment with the tools and parts on the table or in the tool bar for easy access.

Our goal is to evaluate the training benefits of a multi-touch training system that provides realistic affordances, by way of physical multi-touch gestures in a virtual environment. This paper focuses on the use of a multi-touch surface for learning a procedural task, specifically learning a repair and assembly task, and the transfer of knowledge to the real world task. Mechanical repair tasks, as well as medical procedures, are complex tasks which involve the knowledge of specific procedures, the location of parts, the interactions between parts, and the use of tools. We demonstrate realistic physical gestures and interaction techniques that aid in learning by creating realistic constraints that would be applicable to a variety of procedural tasks.

Specifically, we address the following research question: How does multi-touch interaction affect the learning of a procedural assembly task? To address this question, this paper presents a study evaluating the knowledge transfer acquired with multi-touch interaction technology compared to standard training methods. We compared multi-touch interaction to standard 2D mouse interaction and to actual physical training.

RELATED WORK

Multi-touch Interaction

There has been much work in interactive tabletops in education; for experiential learning [5], to enhance collaborative learning [13] or encourage inquiry-based learning [14], [15]. The Flow of Electrons [5] provides an augmented workspace for learning physical computing experientially. By allowing users to place electronics components on the surface and experiment with wiring and the outcomes, it allows users to make mistakes without fear of breaking anything. It bridges the gap between digital information and actual hardware components. Similarly, in [13] the affordances of study materials on the tabletop versus paper allowed for more playfulness and experimentation since the notes or drawings created were not permanent and were easily edited. In G-nome Surfer, a tabletop interface for learning genomics, users demonstrated a higher degree of cooperative behavior and higher test scores on tabletops compared to traditional GUI setups in genomics study. The ability for users to easily and immediately experiment and practice without the fear of making permanent mistakes is something that can benefit training applications as well, since users may be intimidated by expensive equipment or dangerous medical procedures.

Multi-touch interfaces have not been explored as much in the context of training. OrMiS [2], a tabletop interface for simulation-based training, where military officers use a map-based tool to carry out strategic maneuvers and combat, enabling large-scale training exercises without the cost of field deployment. OrMiS is designed to replace traditional PC-based simulation tools while improving ease of learning and better facilitating collaborative work. OrMis focuses on 2D map-based strategic tasks whereas we focus on training on a physical apparatus in a 3D environment using realistic gestures. For medical training SimMed implements a 3D simulation in an augmented tabletop environment to teach medical procedural skills for diagnosis and treatment [19]. They observed high levels of immersion and positive social aspects, as well as observations that suggest a significant learning effect. Their training was very open-ended in order to explore the diagnostic techniques trainees chose, whereas we are focused on training a specific step-by-step procedure. There are no other studies, that we are aware of, which evaluate the efficiency and effectiveness of procedural training using multi-touch interactive surfaces.

VR and AR Procedural Learning

Although there hasn't been much work with multi-touch systems in the areas of maintenance and medical training, there has been much work with VR and AR systems[8, 9, 11, 12]. There have been many studies evaluating the effectiveness of VR and AR compared to traditional methods, reporting in some cases that these methods perform as well as traditional hands-on methods. For instance, Ganier et al. compared tank

(a)

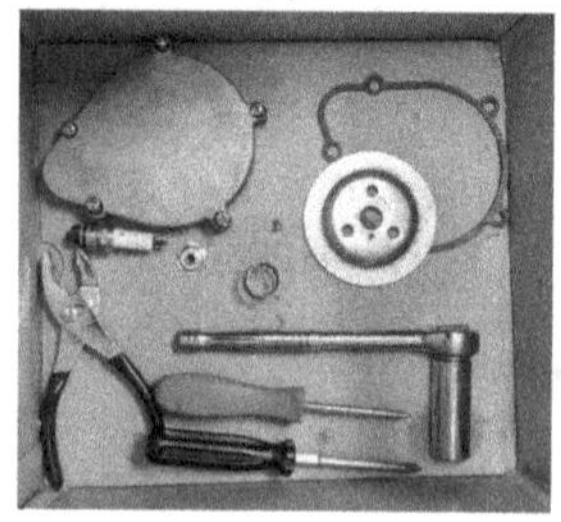

(b)

Figure 2: The physical motorized bicycle apparatus (2a) with the accompanying tools and parts (2b).

maintenance procedure performance after conventional training with a real tank and those trained in a virtual environment. Both training groups were also compared to a no-training control group who carried out the procedure using only job instructions [7]. No differences were found for the testing task completion times for the test groups, but significant differences were found between both test groups and the control group. Indicating that procedural knowledge learned in a virtual environment is transferred to real-world performance. Another study evaluated different Virtual Reality interaction technologies in learning an industrial maintenance task [18]. The four different interaction technologies were basic mouse, 2D mocap, 3D mocap, and a haptic device. They found negligible impact on the learning of assembly task when the focus is on transfer of procedural knowledge rather than the transfer of sensorimotor skills. In addition, users that trained with mouse and 2D mocap took significantly less time training.

Henderson and Feiner evaluate an augmented reality (AR) user interface designed to assist users in the psychomotor phase of procedural tasks [9]. Their user study showed participants completed the psychomotor aspects of the assembly task significantly faster and with greater accuracy than when using assistance on a stationary LCD screen. Another study examined VR and AR techniques compared with classic training techniques. The VR and AR methods showed no significant differences over control methods. In addition, they found AR training for industrial maintenance and assembly (IMA) tasks can reduce the number of unsolved errors [7]. One of the main differences with these AR and VR studies is they they make use of 3D spatial interfaces [3] while

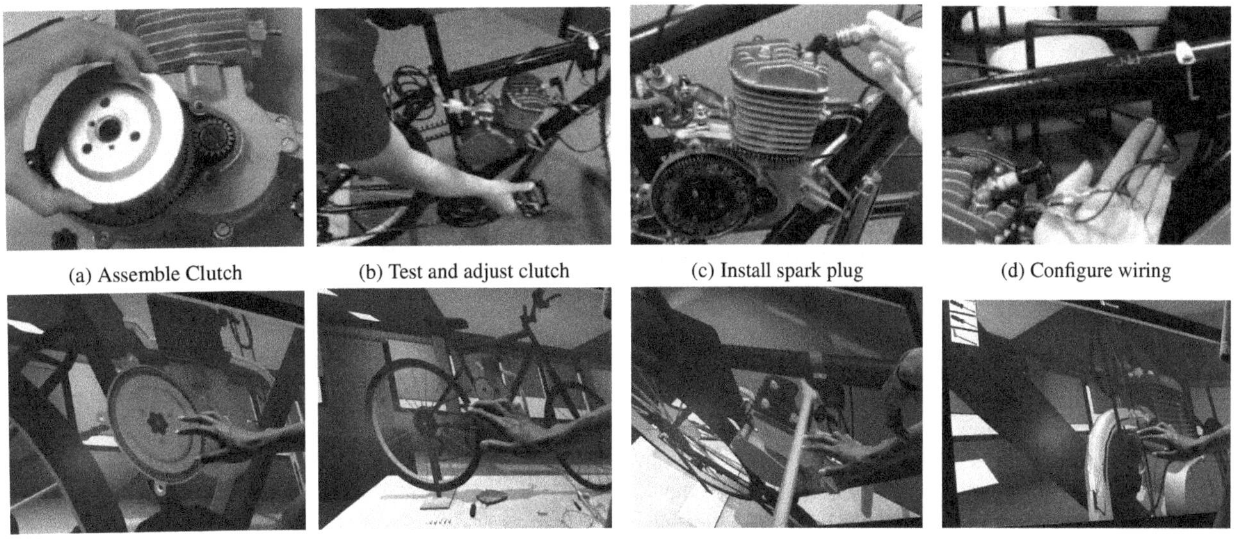

(a) Assemble Clutch (b) Test and adjust clutch (c) Install spark plug (d) Configure wiring

Figure 3: The four different sub-tasks (3a - 3d) shown on the physical bicycle apparatus (top), and in the virtual environment (bottom).

we focus on 2D multi-touch gestures. We aim to expand upon these results in virtual procedural training by exploring whether multi-touch interaction, which leverages realistic gestures, can perform as well as training on the real equipment.

TRAINING SYSTEMS AND TASK

The selected experimental task consisted of assembling and testing part of a 2-stroke bicycle-mounted engine (shown in Figure 2). The apparatus and task were selected based upon a number of constraints: (1) the task should use tools, parts and gestures that would be applicable to industrial, defense, or medical tasks, (2) the apparatus should be able to fit into our lab, (3) the task should be safe for all participants to perform, (4) the task should be significantly complex and non-obvious that a layman could not complete it without prior training. These constraints led us to repairing a 2-stroke bicycle engine where participants could assemble, test and adjust the clutch and other parts.

The overall task consisted of 22 steps grouped into 4 sub-tasks (shown in Figure 3): (1) clutch assembly, (2) clutch functionality testing and adjustments, (3) spark plug installation, and (4) wire configuration. Some examples of the operations participants had to perform are: tightening the clutch wheel nut to adjust the clutch plate, tightening screws with a screwdriver, installing the spark plug with a socket wrench, and plugging in wires. The task also required verifying the correct clutch plate tightness, where the engine needed to be disengaged with the clutch in and engaged with the clutch out. If either of these conditions are not true the clutch plate should be looser or tighter respectively. In total, participants had to manipulate roughly 25 parts, and use three different types of tools (shown in Figure 2b).

Motorized Bicycle

The physical apparatus was a motorized bicycle mounted on a small stand to allow pedaling the bike freely in place for testing purposes. The participants that trained on the physical bicycle had the advantage of experiencing the affordances provided by each of the tools and parts involved in the task. For instance, understanding the correct tightness of the clutch plate is an important step in the process. This can be experienced by tightening the nut about 80% of the way and making sure the clutch plate still has about 1/8" of movement. As described above, correct clutch plate tightness can be verified by pedaling the bike with both the clutch in and the clutch out. The user can verify the engine is disengaged visually by looking at the gears and observing the relative easiness of pedaling the bike. With the engine engaged, the user can feel that the bike is more difficult to pedal and hear the engine making a chugging sound. The ability to examine the parts and bike apparatus from any viewpoint or zoom level is also an advantage the physical model provides. As described above, the physical bicycle provides feedback in the form of opposing forces and aural and visual cues.

Virtual Model and Multi-touch Interaction

The virtual environment contained a detailed, working model of the bicycle, engine, components and tools involved (shown in Figure 1). A tool bar was also provided so that if a user was zoomed into a certain area of the bike they wouldn't have to zoom out to select a part from the table. Users could select the tool or part needed from the tool bar and it would hover next to the button. Each corresponding step in the task was replicated in the virtual model and required interaction. We ensured both the multi-touch and mouse interaction required the same number of steps to complete the task.

Previous work on user-defined multi-touch gestures for 3D objects influenced our multi-touch interaction model [4].

Based on this work, all objects, except for small screws, required two or more fingers to manipulate in order to make the interaction more realistic. The gestures incorporated were *double tap*, *translate*, *rotate*, *pressure*, *grasp*, *grip* and *hold*. *Double tap* zoomed in and out of the 5 main viewpoints of the bike. *Translate* was used to move parts and tools around. *Rotate* was used on the clutch plate to align it, and on the screwdrivers. *Pressure* was used to apply pressure when installing the spring and to attach the socket wrench to the spark plug. Pressure information was interpreted based off touch point size provided by the display device. *Grasp* was used on the clutch lever; multiple fingers had to push down on the lever while the thumb stayed on the handle grip. *Grip* was used on the socket wrench handle to grip it and rotate it around. *Hold* was used in 2-handed gestures where gravity or other forces would take over. For instance, if the user let go of the clutch plate before securing the clutch wheel nut with the other hand the plate would detach due to the force of the spring and fall to the table.

Where possible we aimed to replicate the affordances provided by the real model in the virtual model and multi-touch gestures. For example, the steps in the real task and the corresponding steps replicated in the virtual model follows and are shown in Figure 4. In the real model installing the clutch plate requires: (1) pressing and rotating the spring over the center bolt until it stays, (2) attaching the clutch plate by rotating it so it aligns with the three pegs, and then (3) holding and pressing the clutch plate over the spring while screwing on the clutch wheel nut. The corresponding multi-touch interaction required was identical, where the gestures required were: (1) translate and pressure rotate the spring, (2) translate, rotate and hold the clutch plate, (3) 2-handed interaction where one hand holds the clutch plate while the other hand translates and rotates the clutch wheel nut.

In the above example, even though the main gesture motions were identical, some affordances were not replicated due to the constraints of the interface. For instance, in the physical model you have to rotate and press on the spring until it clicks onto the center bolt, but sometimes this is tricky and can be hard understand how it feels when the spring attaches. Whereas in the multi-touch model, the user only needs to press and rotate 180 degrees and it will automatically connect. On the other hand, rotating and aligning the plate was more difficult in the multi-touch model since the user is required to exactly match up the plate with the three pegs and then press. In the physical model the same precision is not required. For step (3), the physical model's spring pushed back against the clutch plate reminding users to apply pressure to keep it in place. In the multi-touch environment, users had no such feedback and may forget that pressure is required to prevent the plate from detaching until the nut is secure.

We emphasized the model fidelity and interaction details even further to articulate any sensorimotor skills that wouldn't be found in the user manual alone. As for interaction details, the number of rotations required to rotate the clutch wheel nut, the screws with the screwdrivers, and the spark plug with socket wrench were the same for the actual bicycle apparatus and the virtual model. As for model fidelity, in order to get the clutch plate to the correct tightness, participants were directed to tighten the clutch wheel nut approximately 80% of the way and then perform the clutch testing procedure to verify it was working correctly. In the virtual model, 80% tightness also mapped to 1/8" of clutch plate movement so users could press on the clutch plate and see how much it depressed. We also indicated that it was harder to pedal the bicycle with the engine engaged by requiring 2 fingers and pressure to pedal when engaged and 1 finger versus no pressure threshold when disengaged.

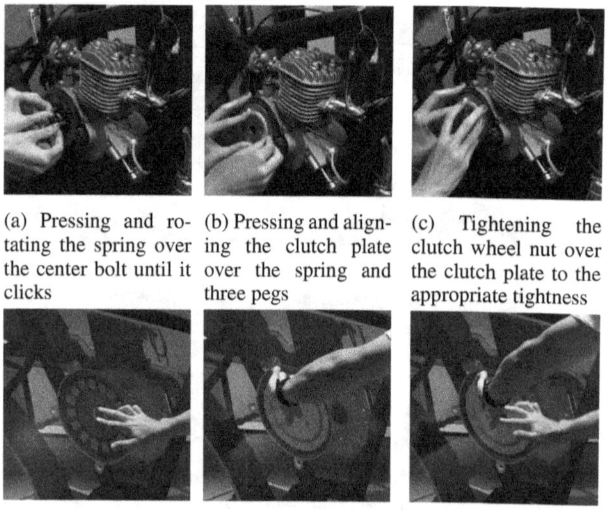

(a) Pressing and rotating the spring over the center bolt until it clicks

(b) Pressing and aligning the clutch plate over the spring and three pegs

(c) Tightening the clutch wheel nut over the clutch plate to the appropriate tightness

Figure 4: The three steps in assembling the clutch (4a - 4c) shown on the actual bicycle apparatus (top), and in the virtual environment (bottom).

Virtual Model and Mouse Interaction

The mouse interaction was intended as a control training group, providing only basic click and drag interaction. We implemented a simplified mouse condition over an optimized mouse condition to demonstrate that it's not only the number of steps the user completes, but the level of interaction that affects learning. We ensured both the multi-touch and mouse interaction required the same number of steps. With the mouse the user would drag the part or tool to the desired position and then when close enough it would snap to place. To perform rotations the user would click again and the part or tool would animate as it rotated into place. If a mistake was made, the user could click to uninstall and then move the part away. Since rotations only required one click to animate they could be completed much quicker than in the multi-touch interface where a user would have to perform multiple rotation gestures to install the part completely.

USER STUDY

We conducted a user study to explore the effectiveness of gesture-based multi-touch training. The study examined three different methods of training how to repair a 2-stroke bicycle engine. The three methods were using the actual equipment, using a virtual model with gesture based interaction, and using a virtual model with a mouse. All groups trained with the same paper manual and returned three days later for a post-training test. During the post-test participants were asked to perform the task on the actual equipment as quickly as possible from memory and were graded on correct steps and timed. Our hypotheses were:

H1 The participants trained using the gesture interface will score as well on the post-test as the participants trained with the actual equipment.

H2 The participants trained using the gesture interface will score better on the post-test than the participants trained using the mouse interface.

H3 Due to discrepancies between manipulating the actual components and the virtual model, the participants trained using the gesture interface will perform the post-test slower than the participants trained with the actual equipment.

H4 Since the gesture participants may have maintained some muscle memory of the task, participants trained using the gesture interface will perform the post-test faster than the participants trained using the mouse interface.

H5 The training time for the mouse participants will be faster than the bicycle and multi-touch groups since they don't have to go through the longer physical gestures.

Participants and Apparatus

There were 36 participants (13 female, 23 male) aged 18 to 37 ($\bar{x}$ = 23.6,σ = 4.58) randomly distributed into the three groups. The participants were recruited from a University setting from a wide variety of majors including Speech Pathology, Biology, Marketing, Business, Information Technology, and more. Participants rated their mechanical experience on a Likert scale from 1 to 7, ($\bar{x}$ = 3.06, σ = 2.04), and none of the participants had worked on a similar engine previously. Training was either conducted on the computer via a 55-inch Microsoft Perceptive Pixel multi-touch screen, or on the actual bicycle and engine. Post-tests were performed on the physical bicycle.

Study Design

The experiment follows a between-subjects design with 36 participants randomly divided into 3 experimental groups (each participant was assigned to a group in alternating order). Two groups trained in a virtual environment, one using multi-touch gestures or the other using mouse input. The third group was trained on the actual bicycle.

Participants were timed during training and testing and scored on the test. Participants were also asked to rate the following statements on a Likert scale from 1 (strongly disagree) to 7 (strongly agree), both post-training and post-testing:

Post-Training questions:

Q1 I feel prepared to complete the repair task after completing the training

Q2 I thoroughly understand the concepts that I learned during the training

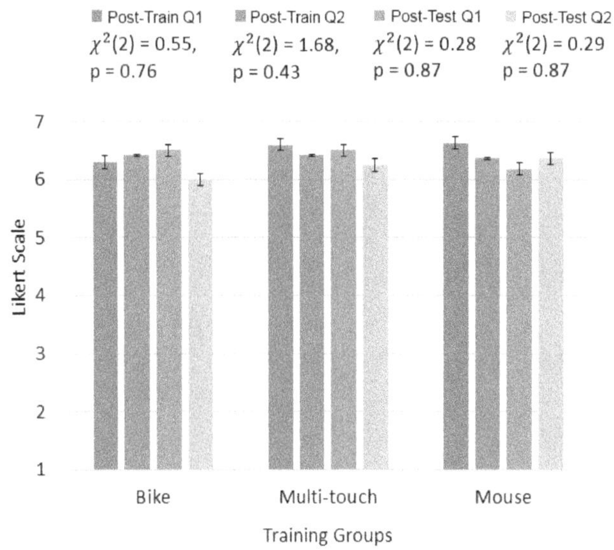

Figure 5: Average user Likert ratings on the preparedness and understanding questions asked after training and after testing.

Post-Testing questions:

Q1 I was sufficiently prepared to complete the repair task upon arrival today

Q2 I thoroughly understood the concepts that I learned during the training

Procedure

Testing occurred exactly 3 days after training to avoid short-term memory effects. For training, all groups followed the same protocol. First, participants were presented with the training apparatus (whether it be the computer or bicycle) and the paper manual. Second, they were familiarized either with the tools or the interaction model. Second, participants were asked to follow along with the paper manual as they conducted the task. They were told they could complete the training as many times as they wanted, so long as they could learn the task and describe the process back to the proctor correctly.

Three days later, participants returned to perform the task on the real bicycle engine. They were asked to perform the task correctly from memory without the user manual. They were scored on the steps shown in Table 1. One point was given for each step completed correctly and performed in the correct order, for a total of 22 points. If they skipped a step then later remembered and backtracked to complete it, they received a 1/2 point.

RESULTS

Training

Training Time

The participants could go through the training as many times as they wanted to learn the task and describe the process back to the proctor, the average total training time by group is

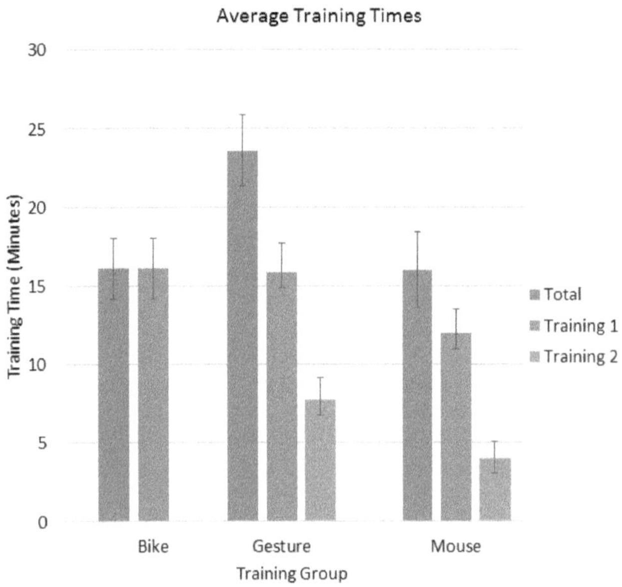

Figure 6: Average training times by training group. Participants could go through the training multiple times, however the participants in the physical bike group all opted to only perform the training once.

shown in Figure 6. We found that all of the participants in the Bike group only went through the process once, whereas all of the participants in the Multi-touch and Mouse groups went through the training twice. The bike trainees would have to wait on the proctor to dismantle the training model which may have discouraged them from going through it twice. Once the virtual users had learned the interface, they were able to quickly go through the training a second time. The virtual medium affords quickly repeating the training scenario as compared to the physical training apparatus.

	Steps		Steps
1	Clutch lever	11	Testing - clutch
2	Clutch button		down to adjust
3	Spring	12	Flathead screw
4	Clutch plate	13	Flathead screwdriver
5	Clutch wheel nut	14	Gasket
6	Begin testing	15	Gear case cover
7	Testing - pedal bicycle	16	5 screws
8	Testing - clutch down,	17	Phillips Screwdriver
	engine disengaged	18	Spark plug
9	Testing - clutch up,	19	Socket wrench
	engine engaged	20	CDI cap
10	Testing - diagnose	21	Connected wiring
	correct adjustment	22	Wiring correct

Table 1: Steps in the procedure that participants were scored on during the post-test.

An independent samples t-test did indicate the multi-touch group spent significantly more time than the bike group ($t_{22} = -2.42, p<0.025$) and the mouse group ($t_{22} = -2.96, p<0.007$) on the first training session. However, the bike and mouse groups training times were not significantly different ($t_{22} = 0.623, p = 0.540$). This result demonstrates that multi-touch participants had to perform detailed, realistic interactions and may have also spent extra time adjusting to new gestures.

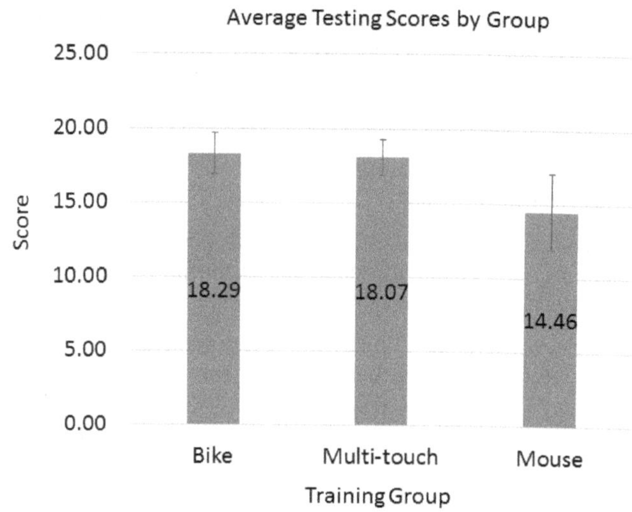

Figure 7: Average testing scores by training group.

Questionnaire

We performed a Kruskal-Wallis test (results are shown in Figure 5) which showed that there were no significant differences between the different groups for their responses to each of the 4 Likert questions (presented in the Participants and Apparatus section). These results indicate that participants from all groups felt that they were prepared after the training, and still felt that they were prepared after performing the actual post-test.

Testing

Testing Scores

When the participants returned for testing, they were asked to perform the task on the real bicycle and engine from memory. They were scored on number of steps completed correctly and timed. The average scores by group are shown in Figure 7. The scores were normally distributed for the Bike, Gesture, and Mouse groups as assessed by Shapiro-Wilk's test ($p > .05$). A one-way between-subjects analysis of variance (ANOVA) was run to compare the effect of the training method on the testing score. The main effect that training method had on the dependent variable, testing score, was found to be significant ($F(2,33) = 5.36$, $p < 0.010$). Independent samples t-tests indicated the gesture group scored significantly better than the mouse group ($t_{22} = 2.50, p<0.025$) and the bike group also scored significantly better than the mouse group ($t_{22} = 2.58, p<0.020$). However, the bike and gesture groups scores were not significantly different ($t_{22} = 0.240, p = 0.812$). This result demonstrates that participants that trained with Multi-touch performed as well as those trained on the actual apparatus and better than those trained on the Mouse.

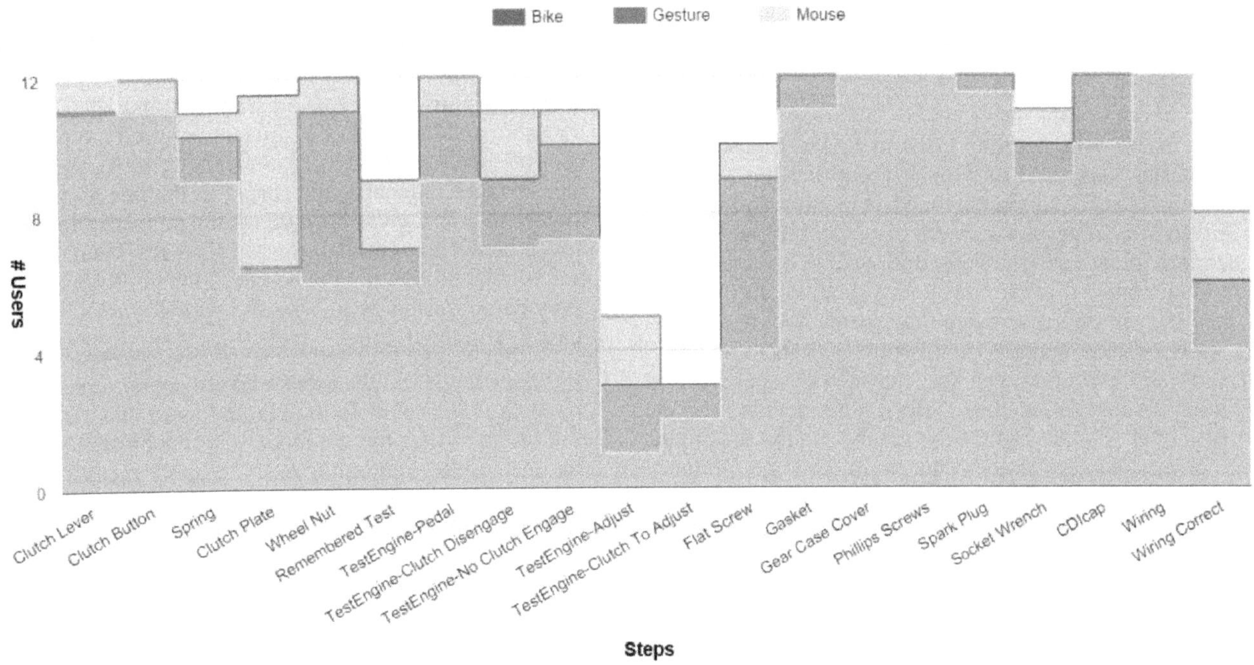

Figure 8: The number of users that completed each testing step correctly for each training group; the bike group in blue, the gesture group in red, and the mouse group in yellow. This graph also demonstrates on which steps users made the most errors by showing where the deficits are. For example, for the flat screw step only 4 of the mouse users performed the step correctly, whereas 9 gesture users and 10 bike users performed it correctly.

Testing Errors

Figure 8 shows each step of the testing process and how many users got the step correct, separated by testing groups. The errors occurred when a user forgot or skipped a step. If a user remembered to do a step, there was never a case where the user didn't know how to operate the tool or part in that step, but instead users completely forgot the process altogether.

Testing Scores

The testing times were also measured (shown in 9) and found to be normally distributed for the Bike, Gesture, and Mouse groups, as assessed by Shapiro-Wilk's test ($p > .05$). A one-way between-subjects analysis of variance (ANOVA) was run to compare the effect of the training method on the testing score. The main effect that training method had on the dependent variable, testing score, was not significant ($F(2,33) = 1.64$, $p = 0.209$).

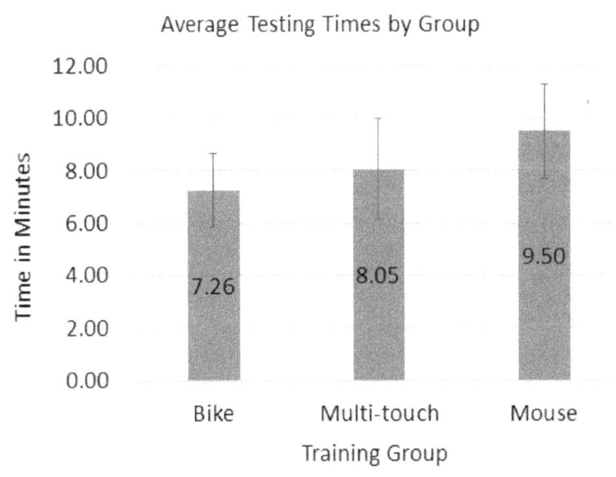

Figure 9: The average testing times by training group.

Discussion

The performance results (shown in Figure 7) demonstrate that participants trained with multi-touch interface scored as well as those trained on the actual apparatus and better than those trained on the mouse interface, confirming Hypotheses H1 and H2. However, the post-test times were not statistically significant and do not confirm Hypotheses H3 and H4. This could be due to a few reasons. It's possible incorrect steps could still lead to the same testing time as a test that was completed without errors. In addition, the inexperience of some participants using tools, causing them to be more cautious than others, may have lead to higher variance within groups. We believe that a few factors led to the multi-touch group scoring as well as the bike group. First, the affordances of the multi-touch model were closely mapped to the affordances of the real model, allowing multi-touch users to perform nearly the same physical gestures in the simulation as they would in real life. Secondly, strict constraints used in the multi-touch training (discussed in the Virtual Model and Multi-touch Interaction section) demanded more concentration allowing better memory of the steps as well as the physical motions required. Thirdly, users felt that repeating the training would be quick and easy since they could simply restart the environment to start again with the dismantled model versus undoing each step performed on the physical model.

Hypothesis H5 was partially confirmed, the Mouse group trained faster than the Multi-touch group but not the Bike group. We believe the gesture group had longer training times since there was a gesture learning curve and mistakes were made more often during training due some strict constraints. It could be argued that the multi-touch group performed better than the mouse group since they spent more time training. However, the majority of this time was spent learning, adjusting and executing gestures, not in additional training repetitions. Since the number of steps were identical and the virtual model was the same between the mouse and multi-touch groups, we believe the better multi-touch performance was due to the similarities of the multi-touch model affordances and physical gestures with the actual bicycle model and physical movements. Although the multi-touch training was not as efficient, time-wise, as the mouse training it was more effective.

The multi-touch interface provides the ability for users to manipulate tools and parts and perform realistic physical gestures as they would in a real-world procedure. Although our gesture set was somewhat small (7 gestures), it is still possible to achieve realistic actions; the gestures become more realistic when tied to physics forces and constraints. It is important for the physical motions and constraints within the procedural steps to be replicated where possible. For instance, consider a task in real life where one hand is required to hold a part in place while the other attaches it. The corresponding multi-touch interaction should also require a 2-handed gesture instead of objects snapping into to place or ignoring gravity. In some instances the stricter constraints in the multi-touch interaction may have led to more mistakes by users in training, but may have forced them to learn the steps better since they had to use more precise gestures.

For instance, a more complex 2-handed gesture was used for steps 4 and 5 (from Table 1) which required holding the clutch plate while tightening with the clutch wheel nut. As shown in Figure 8, more multi-touch users remembered the wheel nut step versus mouse users, potentially due to this increased amount of interaction. On the other hand it is interesting that approximately the same number of mouse and multi-touch users missed the clutch plate step. Some virtual users said this was because the shininess and/or shape of the plate in real life was not reflected in the virtual model and was hard to recognize.

In order to maintain the feeling of holding and manipulating the parts directly, or direct manipulation, we chose the viewpoints in the virtual environment carefully. A perceptual disconnect can occur when an object moves away from a user's touch and the object is no longer underneath the user's hand. This is particularly apparent when translating objects along multiple axes.

On a multi-touch interface, the user gets force feedback from the surface, however they don't get full 3DOF positional force nor any rotational force feedback. We chose to simulate applying force with pressure and use of more fingers. Pressure and the number of fingers required are good indicators of force but don't translate exactly to force in real life. For instance, attaching the spring to the bolt in the physical model requires pressing hard while rotating. In the multi-touch model users need to rotate 180 degrees and meet a pressure threshold. During the post-test, the multi-touch users expressed confusion as to why the spring wasn't attaching as easily as in the training.

For force feedback, the user could also be required to apply an opposing force in the form of more fingers and more pressure. For instance, the physical model's spring pushed back against the clutch plate reminding users to apply pressure to keep it in place. In the multi-touch environment, users had no such feedback and may forget that pressure is required to prevent the plate from detaching until the nut is secure. By requiring the user, in this instance, to apply pressure as an opposing force, they may learn the existence of force feedback in that action. Pressure could be improved upon by training users on how pressure is measured on a touch screen, calibrating pressure on a per user basis, or by providing visual and aural cues. Since forces cannot be felt by the user, visual and aural cues must compensate for that lost sense of force.

The realistic multi-touch gestures were tightly linked with physics in the virtual environment, procedural constraints, simulating forces, and carefully chosen viewpoints in order to create a convincing simulation of the physical actions within the maintenance procedure. Keeping in mind these considerations, multi-touch can provide a realistic and effective training environment for procedural tasks.

FUTURE WORK

In the future we would like to simulate more of the affordances provided by the physical model. For instance, we could add more pressure requirements to try to increase realism in the multi-touch condition. We could also provide aural cues to replace haptics or add tactile buzzing on the interaction surface to support better tactile feedback. In future experiments, examining how increasing the training time with each method affects learning would be interesting. Since we had the participants use a paper training manual we would like to incorporate training instructions and guidance into the virtual environment. We would also like to do a similar study comparing multi-touch gestures to Virtual Reality, full body gestures, and training on physical systems using Augmented Reality potentially on a more complex procedural task.

CONCLUSION

In this paper we presented the use of realistic multi-touch interaction in a 3D training environment as a way to enhance learning of sensorimotor skills a well as procedural knowledge. We conducted a between subjects experiment with 36 participants distributed into 3 groups in order to evaluate the effectiveness of multi-touch training. One group used multi-touch interaction in the 3D training environment, the second used basic mouse-based interaction, and the third trained on the real equipment. A post-training test carried out 3 days later evaluated performance in conducting the real task from memory. Results show that the multi-touch interaction and the real task groups had significantly better performance scores than the mouse interaction group, with no significant difference between multi-touch and real task groups. We demonstrated that multi-touch interaction trains participants on the task as well as training on the actual equipment, suggesting multi-touch interaction is a worthwhile training tool for procedural knowledge that requires sensorimotor skills.

ACKNOWLEDGMENTS

This work is supported in part by NSF CAREER award IIS-0845921 and NSF award CCF-1012056. Also, we would like to thank the members of ISUE lab for their support and the anonymous reviewers for their useful comments and feedback.

REFERENCES

1. Mirjam Augstein, Thomas Neumayr, and Irene Schacherl-Hofer. 2014. The Usability of a Tabletop Application for Neuro-Rehabilitation from Therapists' Point of View. In *Proceedings of the Ninth ACM International Conference on Interactive Tabletops and Surfaces (ITS '14)*. ACM, New York, NY, USA, 239–248.
2. Christophe Bortolaso, Matthew Oskamp, T.C. Nicholas Graham, and Doug Brown. 2013. OrMiS: A Tabletop Interface for Simulation-based Training. In *Proceedings of the 2013 ACM International Conference on Interactive Tabletops and Surfaces (ITS '13)*. ACM, New York, NY, USA, 145–154.
3. Doug A Bowman, Ernst Kruijff, Joseph J LaViola Jr, and Ivan Poupyrev. 2004. *3D user interfaces: theory and practice*. Addison-Wesley.
4. Sarah Buchanan, Bourke Floyd, Will Holderness, and Joseph J LaViola. 2013. Towards user-defined multi-touch gestures for 3D objects. In *Proceedings of the 2013 ACM international conference on Interactive tabletops and surfaces*. ACM, 231–240.
5. Bettina Conradi, Verena Lerch, Martin Hommer, Robert Kowalski, Ioanna Vletsou, and Heinrich Hussmann. 2011. Flow of electrons: an augmented workspace for learning physical computing experientially. In *Proceedings of the ACM International Conference on Interactive Tabletops and Surfaces*. ACM, 182–191.
6. Veronika Domova, Elina Vartiainen, and Marcus Englund. 2014. Designing a Remote Video Collaboration System for Industrial Settings. In *Proceedings of the Ninth ACM International Conference on Interactive Tabletops and Surfaces (ITS '14)*. ACM, New York, NY, USA, 229–238.
7. Franck Ganier, Charlotte Hoareau, and Jacques Tisseau. 2014. Evaluation of procedural learning transfer from a virtual environment to a real situation: a case study on tank maintenance training. *Ergonomics* 57, 6 (2014), 828–843.
8. Florian Gosselin, Sylvain Bouchigny, Christine Mgard, Farid Taha, Pascal Delcampe, and Cdric dHauthuille. 2013. Haptic systems for training sensorimotor skills: A use case in surgery. *Robotics and Autonomous Systems* 61, 4 (2013), 380 – 389. Models and Technologies for Multi-modal Skill Training.
9. S.J. Henderson and Steven K. Feiner. 2011. Augmented reality in the psychomotor phase of a procedural task. In *Mixed and Augmented Reality (ISMAR), 2011 10th IEEE International Symposium on*. 191–200.
10. DL Holton. 2010. Constructivism+ embodied cognition= enactivism: theoretical and practical implications for conceptual change. *Recuperado a partir de http://bit. ly/gVAOOu* (2010).
11. Sung Gu Kang, Byung Ju Ryu, Kyung Sook Yang, Young Hwii Ko, Seok Cho, Seok Ho Kang, Vipul R. Patel, and Jun Cheon. 2015. An Effective Repetitive Training Schedule to Achieve Skill Proficiency Using a Novel Robotic Virtual Reality Simulator. *Journal of Surgical Education* 72, 3 (2015), 369 – 376.
12. M. Kolesnikov, M. Zefran, A.D. Steinberg, and P.G. Bashook. 2009. PerioSim: Haptic virtual reality simulator for sensorimotor skill acquisition in dentistry. In *Robotics and Automation, 2009. ICRA '09. IEEE International Conference on*. 689–694.
13. Anne Marie Piper and James D Hollan. 2009. Tabletop displays for small group study: affordances of paper and digital materials. In *Proceedings of the SIGCHI Conference on Human Factors in Computing Systems*. ACM, 1227–1236.
14. Bertrand Schneider. 2012. Designing Tabletop Activities for Inquiry-based Learning: Lessons from Phylogenetics, Neuroscience and Logistics. In *Proceedings of the 2012 ACM International Conference on Interactive Tabletops and Surfaces (ITS '12)*. ACM, New York, NY, USA, 289–294.
15. Orit Shaer, Megan Strait, Consuelo Valdes, Taili Feng, Michael Lintz, and Heidi Wang. 2011. Enhancing genomic learning through tabletop interaction. In *Proceedings of the SIGCHI Conference on Human Factors in Computing Systems*. ACM, 2817–2826.
16. ThomasA. Stoffregen, BenotG. Bardy, and Bruno Mantel. 2006. Affordances in the design of enactive systems. *Virtual Reality* 10, 1 (2006), 4–10.
17. Nicole Sultanum, Sowmya Somanath, Ehud Sharlin, and Mario Costa Sousa. 2011. "Point It, Split It, Peel It, View It": Techniques for Interactive Reservoir Visualization on Tabletops. In *Proceedings of the ACM International Conference on Interactive Tabletops and Surfaces (ITS '11)*. ACM, New York, NY, USA, 192–201.

18. Yaiza Vélaz, Jorge Rodríguez Arce, Teresa Gutiérrez, Alberto Lozano-Rodero, and Angel Suescun. 2014. The Influence of Interaction Technology on the Learning of Assembly Tasks Using Virtual Reality. *Journal of Computing and Information Science in Engineering* 14, 4 (2014), 041007.

19. Ulrich von Zadow, Sandra Buron, Tina Harms, Florian Behringer, Kai Sostmann, and Raimund Dachselt. 2013. Simmed: combining simulation and interactive tabletops for medical education. In *Proceedings of the SIGCHI Conference on Human Factors in Computing Systems*. ACM, 1469–1478.

Training of Cognitive Performance in Complex Tasks with a Tabletop-Based Rehabilitation System

Mirjam Augstein
University of Applied Sciences Upper Austria
Hagenberg, Austria
mirjam.augstein@fh-hagenberg.at

Thomas Neumayr
University of Applied Sciences Upper Austria
Hagenberg, Austria
thomas.neumayr@fh-hagenberg.at

Isabel Karlhuber
LIFEtool gemeinnützige GmbH
Linz, Austria
isabel.karlhuber@lifetool.at

Sabine Dielacher
University of Applied Sciences for Health Professions Upper Austria
Linz, Austria
sabine.dielacher@fhgooe.ac.at

Sylvia Öhlinger
University of Applied Sciences for Health Professions Upper Austria
Linz, Austria
sylvia.oehlinger@fhgooe.ac.at

Josef Altmann
University of Applied Sciences Upper Austria
Hagenberg, Austria
josef.altmann@fh-hagenberg.at

ABSTRACT

As previously shown, tabletops can be used in neuro-rehabilitation to train different abilities that have been (temporarily) lost due to acquired brain injury, like motor skills or attention or visuo-constructive skills. However, complex skills like problem solving abilities have been considered only marginally in computer-based rehabilitation systems until now, partly because "complex skills" consist of a high number of distinct capabilities which makes it difficult to cover at least a large part. Nevertheless, the fun.tast.tisch. system has recently been extended by a module that aims at training complex skills. This paper describes therapeutic considerations underlying the design and implementation, discusses the interaction modalities used (e.g., the concept of pen-based interaction on tabletops in addition to touch and tangibles) and provides an overview on the module's interaction and graphic design. The module has already been tested with a small number of selected patients in the therapy setting. The findings of these initial tests are summarized and discussed.

Author Keywords

Tabletops; Neuro-Rehabilitation; Tangibles; Pens; Complex Skills

ACM Classification Keywords

H.5.2 Input devices and strategies: User Interfaces; H.5.2 Interaction styles: User Interfaces; H.5.2 User-centered design: User Interfaces

ITS'15, November 15–18, 2015, Funchal/Madeira, Portugal

ISBN 978-1-4503-3899-8/15/11...$15.00
DOI: http://dx.doi.org/10.1145/2817721.2817738

INTRODUCTION

The work described in this paper was conducted in the context of the fun.tast.tisch. project [6, 3, 4, 5], a multi-disciplinary[1] endeavor to support the process of neuro-rehabilitation. The project's focus is on the development of a tabletop application to be used as a supporting tool in conventional therapy sessions, thus we face patients and therapists as target groups. fun.tast.tisch. is not intended to replace conventional therapy, nor does it claim to be therapeutically more effective. It however aims at overcoming problems conventional approaches are facing as described in the following paragraphs.

In conventional neuro-rehabilitation, therapists have to do a lot of time-consuming additional work (e.g., computation of statistics or measuring a patient's performance at a specific exercise). Especially data collection was mentioned as exceptionally time-consuming if it has to be done manually. As time schedules are usually tight, this leads to a lot of therapy time being "lost" that could be better used for the patient. Further, therapists need to manually select and configure the exercises for the patient individually. This can be time-consuming as well but it can also lead to demotivation (e.g., when patients notice that the selected exercise was too difficult and the therapist is searching for an easier one). Another challenge is related to patients' attitude towards therapy. In order to improve skills, often a high number of repetitions in necessary. When variety of exercises is low, many patients who have been in therapy for a while are getting tired of it.

A computer-based setting has several advantages compared to conventional ones: first, the system can take over the time-consuming tasks mentioned above. Second, the system can offer means for more discreet adaptations to the exercise during the therapy session. Third, computer-based therapy is

[1]The project team consists of occupational therapists, software developers, interaction, graphic and object designers as well as assistive technology experts

often perceived as more exciting and offers more variation compared to conventional settings. Besides these general advantages involved with computer-based therapy, the tabletop setting offers additional benefit: it allows for tangible objects to be arranged on the surface which is important for the training of e.g., motor skills. Further, the table is a familiar object for patients which limits timidity towards technology (which is sometimes present in elderly patients) and many therapeutic tasks are designed to be done on a (traditional) table which makes them well transferable to the tabletop setting.

The fun.tast.tisch. therapy system consists of 16 so-called "modules" supporting patients to retrain skills that have (temporarily) been lost due to acquired brain injury (mostly caused by accident or stroke). A module contains a specific therapeutic exercise or series of similar exercises. Each module focuses on one or more concrete skills that should be trained, such as motor skills, specific memory or attention abilities, or visuo-constructive skills. An individual module is usually configured by the therapist according to the patient's current needs and then presents in a next step a certain task to the patient (e.g., to memorize goods to be "bought" from a digital shop, or rebuild a given shape using tangible objects).

The module described in this paper trains cognitive performance in complex tasks (further referred to as "complex skills") with a focus on problem solving and cognitive flexibility. It is specific (compared to the other modules) because i) it consists of a series of different tasks which have to be completed in a certain order, ii) in many cases this module requires much more time than most of the others and iii) it uses not only touch interaction and tangibles but also pen-based interaction (which is not the case for the other modules).

The technology used for the system builds upon the Microsoft PixelSense tabletop and was chosen due to several reasons. First, the table is able to recognize a high number of concurrent touch points, thus it can be used in multi-user settings (all our modules require a setting with a therapist and at least one patient). Second, it can, due to the optical display, recognize physical objects placed on the screen, which is also important as many of the modules involve interaction with tangibles. Third, the hardware should be affordable for rehabilitation centers and self-employed therapists, thus individually designed hardware solutions would have been too expensive.

This paper describes related work and presents the therapeutic background behind the complex skills module. Further, it provides an overview on the different interaction concepts before selected implementation challenges are shortly outlined. The results of initial user tests are presented before the paper concludes with a discussion and summary of findings.

RELATED WORK

Related work in the area of computer- and tabletop-supported rehabilitation in general has been discussed in detail in our earlier publications (see [5, 6, 3]). For example, Annett et al. [1, 2] describe a tabletop-based therapy system that has been applied for upper extremity motor rehabilitation (the target group is thus similar to ours). As our system, theirs aims at increasing patients' motivation and supporting therapists. Regarding therapy-related aspects it differs from ours significantly as it solely focuses on motor skills. In addition to therapeutic aspects, Annett et al. also focus on users' engagement and subjective impressions towards tabletop therapy. The related findings are partly similar to ours; they found that the benefit of technology lies not in technology itself but in its ability to provide responsive, dynamic content. In our studies, functionality like e.g., the provision of immediate automated feedback or changing the level of difficulty on the fly have been mentioned as most relevant. However, some of the patients in our studies also mentioned the modern technology itself as a motivating factor.

This section describes related work that provides evidence for the effect of complex skills training. Further, is discusses related work regarding tangible interaction in therapy settings and regarding general work on pen-usage on touch displays.

Complex Skills Training

The use of therapist-guided computer-assisted interventions as part of multimodal therapy approaches with clients with cognitive impairments relies on evidence-based recommendations [12]. Computer-assisted interventions support self-evaluation of cognitive dysfunctions, the development of cognitive flexibility and problem-oriented, methodical thinking [8], which, according to Müller et al. (see [18] and [17]) represent the most frequent dysfunctions in clients with dysexecutive syndrome. To the best of our knowledge, there is no other application for patients with impairment of executive functions that is as comprehensive as our complex skills module. Executive dysfunctions usually consist of several different kinds of dysfunctions[2] and most computer-based intervention approaches exclusively focus on one.

Within fun.tast.tisch., all exercises we implemented are rooted in traditional approaches that have proven to be therapeutically effective. The module described in this paper builds upon a traditional rehabilitation approach described in [22] (see later) and the following findings that provide evidence for the improvements of complex skills after therapeutic intervention.

Serino et al. [23] e.g., have found that patients with an impairment of the central executive system improved in all cognitive functions after a working memory program. Working memory is also in the focus of our complex skills module (see tasks 5, 7 and 8 described in Section Tasks in the Complex Skills Module).

Sammer et al. [21] describe that cognitive function often reveals deficits in executive functions, including maintenance and inhibition of attention, flexibility in thinking as well as planning. The aim of their study was to analyze the effect of cognitive training on cognitive performance patients (N=26). Half of the patients participated in a cognitive training exercise, while the other patients received standard treatment. The outcome showed improved performance of the group

[2]This is also the reason why the complex skills module consists of a set of tasks, each of them training specific functions in particular.

with cognitive treatment in two executive tasks after the training period, while no improvement was seen in the standard-treatment group. The results demonstrate that specific training is required for improvement of executive functions, while general rehabilitation is not sufficient. The tasks patients have to do in the complex skills module of fun.tast.tisch. are thus specifically designed for improving cognitive performance and cover different skills that should be trained (concentration and planning abilities).

von Cramon et al. ([26] and [25]) developed a specific problem-solving training and tested it in a small group study. Data revealed significant prepost effects in the planning test scores, all behavioral ratings and some intelligence subtests. Problem-solving abilities are also in the focus of our module.

Tangible Interaction in Therapy Systems

The fun.tast.tisch. system in general and also the complex skills module relies on interaction with tangible objects in addition to touch for therapeutic reasons. The following paragraphs outline related work in the area of tangible interaction in therapy settings.

Sharlin et al. [24] describe a tool (Cognitive Cubes) for assessment of 3D spatial cognitive ability that uses a Lego-like tangible UI for the description of a 3D shape. Users are shown a certain shape and have to rebuild it using the tangibles. One fun.tast.tisch. module (the spatial construction module, see [4]) contains a similar task. The complex skills module also includes tasks (tasks 1 and 3, see later) where the user has to re-construct a given, however two-dimensional, plan using tangible flat physical objects.

De la Guía [9] present the TraInAb rehabilitation system which is aimed at cognitive therapy (e.g., training memory skills). TraInAb uses a mobile device with an NFC reader and physical objects carrying NFC tags. Tasks 3, 5, 7 and 8 of the complex skills module also concentrate on (among others) memory. Additionally, fun.tast.tisch. contains a module focusing on memory abilities solely (the shopping module, see [4]). The recognition of physical objects however is different, being based on an optical analysis of the image of the screen captured by the tabletop (using the standard Microsoft PixelSense 256 byte tags or our own ones, see later).

Another rehabilitation system (Elements) is discussed by Wilson et al. [27]. The target group is the same as ours (acquired brain injury patients). Tangible objects are used for therapeutic tasks (simple three-dimensional shapes like a cylinder, similar to the ones fun.tast.tisch. uses for the spatial construction and spatial cognition modules, see [4]). The objects are placed on an horizontal LCD display and recognized by an additional camera tracking system. The object recognition approach is thus different from ours.

Pen Interaction in Touch-Based Systems

Although pen-based interaction in combination with common touch systems has been sufficiently researched and prototypes exist for different kinds of touch displays and pen technologies, there seem to be only a few real-world applications using it. This might be because there probably often is not as much added value as for our system. Here, we added the additional way of interaction not due to technological, but therapeutic reasons. This section summarizes related work on combining touch- and pen-based user interaction.

Brandl et al. [7] describe a prototypic system combining bimanual pen and touch interaction on horizontal surfaces. They present an experiment that demonstrated users to be faster and making fewer errors using pen and touch input compared to using either touch or pen. Although we did not aim at particularly facilitating two-handed interaction for the complex skills module (for many of the patients this is not possible due to hemiplegia), the analysis of Brandl et al. regarding advantages and disadvantages of touch-based and pen-based interaction in general is relevant to us, as well as the technologic approach (based on the Anoto[3] technology also used by Leitner et al. for the FLUX system [14]). The Anoto system was, however, no option for us as we rely on a standard tabletop system so that rehabilitation institutions could buy it without having to adapt it.

Another pen-based approach is described by Lee et al. [13], who introduce Haptic Pen, a tactile feedback stylus for touch screens. We generally find the idea of introducing haptic feedback to pen-based interaction particularly interesting, but decided it was not necessary for our system, as feedback is already provided along different sensory channels (visual and acoustic) by the table as well as by the therapist. Second, due to the optical display of the PixelSense, the pen needed to be based on an optical approach (e.g., infrared light) as well.

Qin et al. [20] outline an approach towards authenticated pen and touch interaction on tabletops. They use infrared pen technology to have the pen tip recognized by the table and suggest user authentication based on biometrics and pressure dynamics (both provided by their so-called pPen). Pen recognition is similar in fun.tast.tisch., authentication is however not necessary in our system. Therapists and patients log in via tagged cards in order to log the results of a therapy session for statistics computation and later discussion; no other users are involved in a therapy session.

To sum up, we found a lot of evidence for the potential positive effects of combining pen-based with touch-based interaction but few approaches that are technologically similar to ours, which is (to the best of our knowledge) among the first ones to involve usage of an infrared pen to interact with the Samsung SUR40 with Microsoft PixelSense tabletop system.

THERAPEUTIC CONSIDERATIONS

This section describes the therapeutic background behind the module and tasks a patient has to perform during the training.

Background

Managing everyday life and acquiring new skills requires executive functions (like e.g., anticipation, planning, targeted activity as well as monitoring, evaluation and inhibition). Literature provides different subdivisions of executive functions and dysfunctions (as can be found in e.g., [18] or [10]). Two core functions in connection with executive functions

[3]http://www.anoto.com, last access: 5th of Jan., 2015

are flexibility and persistency. Flexibility in this context is defined as the ability to adapt perceptual, cognitive and motor systems constantly; persistency corresponds to the ability to maintain engagement in "task-sets" withstanding distractions (see [19]). Müller et al. (see [18] and [17]) describe problems with i) working memory and monitoring, ii) cognitive flexibility and iii) planning and problem solving as the most common characteristics in clinical practice with clients suffering from dysexecutive syndrome.

As the manifestation of dysexecutive syndrome differs individually, it is necessary to consider heterogeneous patterns of symptoms, which result in a classification of three possible intervention paths [16]: cognitive training interventions, interventions with focus on behavioural management, and interventions with modification and manipulation of environment as core tasks. For the complex skills module, cognitive training approaches with a focus on improvement of problem solving, cognitive flexibility and working memory were chosen. According to [11], therapeutic interventions should be both disorder-specific and real-life orientated. Conventional therapy approaches as used as a basis for our module and described in the next section try to meet these requirements.

Considerations Behind the Complex Skills Module

The development of the complex skills module is based on practical exercises for clients with executive dysfunctions as suggested by Schweizer & Müller [22]. Neurotraining as a form of cognitive training requires patients' active participation and a basic ability to cope with cognitive challenges, willingness to cooperate and awareness of their specific disorder. In consideration of the first neurotraining principles listed by [22], our module is based on seven cornerstones:

- Versatility: a permanent change of required functions and training modalities (visual, verbal, tactile, auditory, etc.) is to be respected.
- Maintenance of functions: for keeping the clients motivation high, tasks which focus on remaining abilities are offered in the beginning of every training unit.
- Reduction of dysfunction: tasks are closely adjusted to the individual clients abilities and thus help to treat individual dysfunctions.
- Development of task solving strategies: the module offers the possibility to develop and directly apply task-solving strategies in cooperation with the therapist.
- Formulation of clearly designed task descriptions: to enable therapists to use the module in a client-centred way, different ways of task description are necessary.
- Promotion of cognitive flexibility: as a core of neurotraining, cognitive flexibility requires different, permanently changing conditions within each task.
- Self-regulation: the module supports clients in improving their self evaluation by enabling self-reliant error control.

As basic equipment for the different tasks of their neurotraining, Schweizer & Müller [22] use the "red mosaic" idea. Red mosaic involves a set of physical objects: 8x8cm squares made of red hard plastic as well as geometric parts of the square (diagonal and parallel halves and quarters). For the conceptualization of the complex skills module, the exercise "sports ground" (see [22]) was chosen for the following reason. As the sports ground task (see later) requires a maximum number of 12 pieces of the red mosaic it was considered suitable for the development of the module (the number of required tangible objects seemed technologically and therapeutically appropriate). Other tasks suggested by [22] require more red mosaic pieces and would thus have probably been too difficult to solve for some of the patients.

Schweizer & Müller propose the following tasks that were adapted for our module. Task 1 requires the reconstruction of a given object with parts of the red mosaic in order to train visuo-spatial perception and visuo-constructive skills. In task 2, in order to train visuo-constructive skills, the reconstructed object has to be copied by pencil. In order to train visuo-spatial memory and visuo-constructive skills, the object has to be reconstructed from memory in task 3. To train understanding of written or spoken texts, flexibility and visuo-spatial perception, a text is read to the patients by the therapist or by themselves in task 4. Word cards or picture cards illustrating specific words in the text are placed on the matching pieces of the red mosaic object constructed in the previous tasks. In task 5, picture cards or word cards have to be placed on the matching pieces of the object from memory. In task 6, concentration should be trained. It is important for therapists to focus on training concentration not memory. In order to train verbal or visual memory in task 7, patients are asked to recall the words or pictures learned in the previous tasks. In task 8, participants are asked to write the words they were able to recall in task 7 into the matching sections of the object drawn in task 2. Verbal and spatial memory is trained. Regarding the implementation of the complex skills module, no major changes to these tasks were made, except for task 8.

Tasks in the Complex Skills Module

Based on the therapeutic ideas described in the previous section, eight levels implemented by concrete tasks were defined for the complex skills module. The tasks have to be done one after another in the order provided by the system (some of the tasks are built on previous ones). In general, we followed the concept of a sports field where different sports activities are carried out at different locations (e.g., swimming, biking). The following paragraphs describe the tasks in more detail.

Task 1. This task requires a patient to rebuild a given template (showing squares representing the locations of the different sports activities) that is either shown in original size or scaled-down, depending on the level of difficulty the therapist selected. In case original size is used, the patient has to place tangible square objects (see Figure 3 (middle)) directly on digital squares that are shown on the display; if the scaled-down version is used, the template is shown in one area of the screen and the patient has to place the squares in another. The patient's solution is validated by the system.

Task 2. Here, a patient has to redraw a given template (again, the squares used by the template represent sports locations) using an infrared pen (see Figure 3 (right)). The patient's solution can be validated either by the system or by the therapist (the second option was introduced to increase user control as perceived by therapists because the systems validation is in many cases too sensitive to user mistakes or inaccuracy).

Task 3. This task requires a patient to rebuild the template used in tasks 1 and 2 from memory. The template is shown to the patient as long as necessary to memorize it, before it disappears. Again, the solution is then validated by the system.

Task 4. Here, a patient has to assign different sports activities to the correct areas shown on the screen via touch input (see Figure 3 (left)). A textual description provides information sufficient to determine the correct localization, e.g. "Next to the entrance, a man is swimming in the pond. Behind the pond, someone is playing tennis, [...]". The therapist can select the level of difficulty regarding the text, reaching from very simple wording to complex descriptions. The patient's solution is validated by the system.

Task 5. This task requires a patient to memorize the sports field and the locations of the different sports activities and then re-assign the activities to the empty sports locations from memory. The patient receives as much time to memorize the assignments as needed. The system validates the solution.

Task 6. This task mainly aims at training concentration skills. The patient is shown i) a detailed image section and ii) a number of images, and has to determine which image the section was taken from. This process is repeated 24 times with different image sections so that the overall task can take several minutes. The patient receives system feedback directly after each of the 24 repetitions.

Task 7. Here, the patient has to name from memory as many sports activities that were used in tasks 4 and 5 as possible. The therapist checks the named ones from a list provided by the system. After this task, a break of at least five minutes should be taken before the next task starts. The system thus reminds the therapist of the need of a break and offers a control to pause the module.

Task 8. This task again (as in task 5) requires a patient to assign from memory the correct sports activities to the empty sports locations in the arena. It differs from task 5 in that the correct assignments are not shown any more to give the patient time to memorize.

INTERACTION DESIGN AND CONCEPT

This section presents the interaction concepts behind the complex skills module and provides an overview on the different interaction modalities used.

Design Process

For the creation of the complex skills module we basically followed the same user-centered design process with our interdisciplinary team as for the other modules. In a first step the occupational therapists establish patients' requirements by describing an exercise and therapeutic backgrounds. Thereby, therapists focus on the question whether the introduction of an automated interactive system is likely to be time-saving, leads to easier adjustability, and could lead to higher motivation for patients to take part in often repetitive trainings, e.g., by introducing variety. Based on this description it is possible to create a Hierarchical Task Analysis which in turn is the basis for mock-ups that are next created by interaction designers. A consecutive Cognitive Walkthrough presenting these mock-ups is held where all different professionals of our team take part. If it is unclear how to solve some interaction scenario, occupational therapists do a quick evaluation within the target group using low-fidelity prototypes, e.g., paper-based ones. At some point there is a consensus in the interdisciplinary team on how to solve each interaction scenario so the mock-ups can be regarded as approved. The work of graphic designers and software developers uses the mock-ups to create interactive prototypes. Finally, these prototypes are used for early evaluations during the process and are incrementally improved. For the complex skill module there have been a number of interesting aspects regarding the screen organization which deviate from the other modules. These aspects are described in more detail below.

Screen Organization

We can distinguish between information that is displayed for the therapists and such that is displayed for patients. In the complex skills module, as the tasks themselves require a lot of space, most of the screen is used for patients' menus and task areas. The lack of space is also the reason why the seating arrangement for this module differs from most of the other modules. Mostly, the therapist sits at the short side of the table, often depending on the patient's more impaired side to either foster movements of the affected arm or to be better able to facilitate the training, e.g., passing the patient or adjusting physical objects, on the non-impaired side. At the complex skills module, the therapist is seated facing the patient.

The patient's part of the user interface consists of three areas: the template box, the construction area and the choice box (as marked by a, b and c in Figure 1) and was designed to display all necessary interaction elements in a consistent manner during the whole session. The functional division into three parts that are displayed at all times is intended to make it easier for patients to achieve orientation. According to the therapists in the project team, a user interface for this target group should not be too dynamic if not necessary. In the template box, a patient can find all instructions (often templates, i.e., arrangements of places or activities that need to be rebuilt by the patient in the construction area) throughout the different tasks. The construction area that takes up the largest part of the screen is the area where the patient's main interaction with the module takes place. In all tasks but task 6, the construction area shows a sports field. Finally, the choice box usually displays a collection of interactive elements that can be picked up and placed in the construction area by the patient. If one of the three areas is not needed for a task, this box remains empty.

As the boxes take up most of the screen, the therapist mainly interacts with the module via a cylindrical tagged object that can be placed anywhere on the screen at any time, e.g., to move on to the next task if a patient cannot solve the pre-

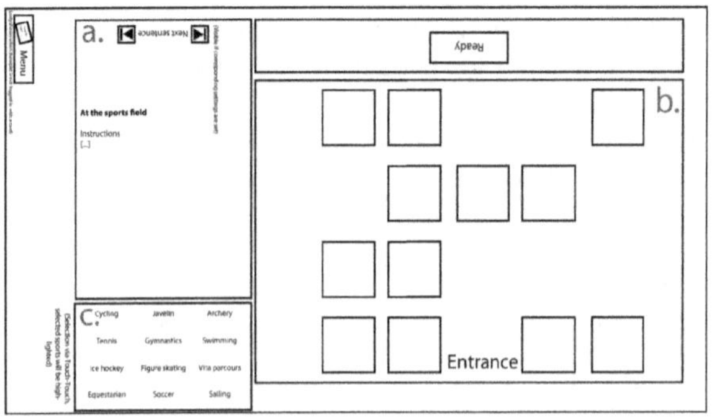

Figure 1. Screen organization in the complex skills module (non-functional interaction prototype). Three functional areas are depicted. a. marks the template box, b. the construction area, and c. the choice box.

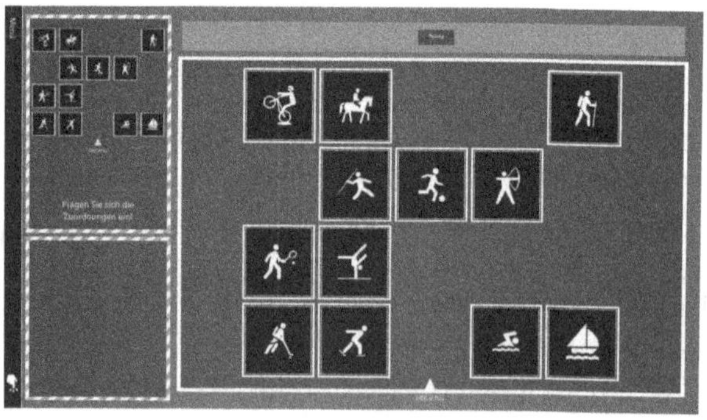

Figure 2. Screen design for task 5 in the complex skills module (playful version). The neutral version works with mono-colored background and without patterns but apart from that has the same structure.

vious one. This particular physical object is used by all fun.tast.tisch. modules to let the therapist re-configure the exercise the patient is currently interacting with at run-time. Re-configuration in most cases means changing the level of difficulty. When the cylinder is placed on the display, the module configuration menu is shown next to it. The cylinder was introduced because the selection of easier exercises during the process is often perceived as discouraging by patients in conventional settings. The cylinder object allows for more discreet adjustments without having to interrupt the session. Please refer to [6] for a detailed description and a picture.

The introduction of the cylinder has shown to greatly increase therapists' perceived user control. In contrast, therapists' menus (in the complex skills module there e.g., is a button aligned towards the therapist to tell the system that the patient has finished a task) are reduced to a minimum because this always bears the risk of unintended interactions by patients or even objects unwittingly sliding over the buttons.

Figure 2 shows the screen design for task 5. The design can be configured to be neutral or playful. The playful version is graphically more appealing but tests with other modules have shown that some patients perceive it as not adult-compatible. Also, patients with severe impairments could easily be distracted by the visual additions compared to the neutral view, hence the decision to include two different visual styles. In case the patient has problems reading the task instructions, the module can be configured to show them aligned towards the therapist (to read them out for the patient).

Input Modalities

Here we present the input methods used by the complex skills module (our system's general input modalities are described in [4], pen input has not been part of this description, yet).

Interaction via Touch

As for all our modules, touch input is used where therapeutically feasible (regarding patients' interaction), and for part of the configuration that has to be done by the therapist. For example, the patient has to assign the correct sports activities to the predefined locations on the screen in tasks 4, 5 and 8. This is done by touching first the activity and then the location spot where the activity takes place[4] (see Figure 3 (left)). Similarly, two activities can be swapped in case the patient has placed them wrongly first. In task 6, a patient has to choose from a number of pictures showing sports activities the one where a partial section (also shown in a picture) had been taken from. This is done via simple touch-based selection. In addition to simple touch, the module uses two-handed touch[5] for the therapist's menu[6]. Furthermore, the delayed touch[7] was also introduced to the complex skills module, mainly in order to avoid unintended input by the patient (e.g., if the patient has delayed response abilities).

Interaction via Tangible Objects

The complex skills module involves 12 semi-transparent squares made of acrylic glass that fit the size of the activity locations on the sports field, and one physical "privacy shield". The squares are recognized by tags that have been developed for this module specifically (see later). They have to be arranged on the sports field in task 1 (see Figure 3 (middle)) where a user has to rebuild a given arrangement that is shown either in the sports field directly or in the template box (downsized). Further, the patient later has to memorize the arrangements on the sports field and has to rebuild it from memory using the physical squares in task 3. As described earlier, task 7 requires a patient to memorize previously shown sports activities and recite them from memory.

During this task, the construction area is used for showing the list of sports activities aligned towards the therapist. The physical privacy shield is used to hide this information from

[4]It was not possible to use a Drag&Drop approach here because the patient could then have easily selected several activities at the same time unintendedly. Further, we do not consider the surface of the Samsung SUR40 with Microsoft PixelSense optimal for Drag&Drop operation as it is less smooth, compared to other touch displays (as those of most smartphones).

[5]Here, the patient has to perform two concurrent touches at two different positions on the screen; the two-handed touch is described in more detail in [4]

[6]The therapist's menu can be used to end a module before having finished it. In order not to activate it unintendedly, the therapist has to perform a two-handed touch.

[7]Here, the patient has to hold a touch for a predefined period of time before the system reacts; see a more detailed description of the delayed touch in [4]

Figure 3. The different input modalities used in the complex skills module: touch input (left), tangible objects (middle), and pen input (right).

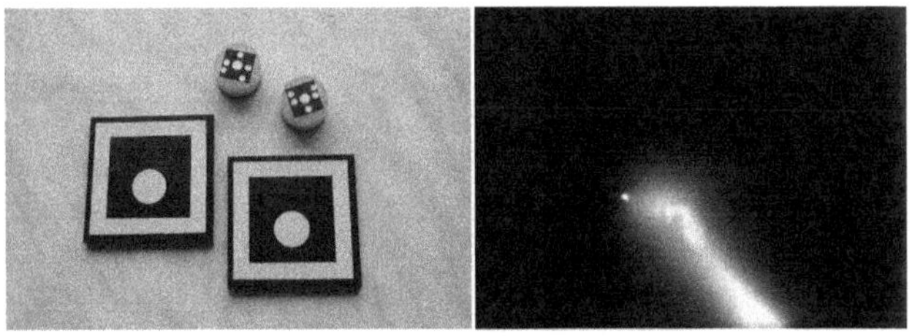

Figure 4. Comparison of our tags on the squares with the Microsoft PixelSense standard ones (left) and system's view of a user's hand placing an infrared pen on the screen (right).

the patient. The therapist is instructed by the system to place the shield at a certain position before the information is shown and can then select via touch all activities the patient named. In addition to the objects that have been introduced for the this module specifically, the cylinder used by our system to let the therapist adjust the module at runtime, as described before, is used also. Here, the cylinder helps e.g., to switch between textual or graphic representation of the different kinds of sports or among different levels of text complexity.

Interaction with a Pen
Task 2 requires a patient to redraw the sports field (i.e., the square areas that are placeholders for sports locations). We decided to use an infrared pen for this task mainly because firstly it is part of the intended therapeutic experience to use a pen and secondly using a finger on the SUR40 for drawing does not feel as smooth as we are used to on comparable devices like tables or smartphones. The table shows the patient's line at runtime (see Figure 3 (right)). The result can be evaluated in two ways. First, the table offers an automated evaluation of the picture, which can however be too sensitive to mistakes or inaccuracies in many cases. This is why second, the therapist can evaluate the result him- or herself and select from a given list of possible results (e.g., "solved" or "partly solved") the best-fitting one. Pen interaction is new to the system and has been introduced for this module particularly. The idea is based on conventional therapy tasks.

IMPLEMENTATION CHALLENGES
This section outlines selected technological and implementation challenges related to the complex skills module.

Reliable Tag Recognition
The first challenge is related to the tabletop's touch and tag recognition capabilities. Although the Samsung SUR40 with Microsoft PixelSense should in general be able to recognize over 50 concurrent touches, we found the reliable and smooth recognition of tags at runtime to be limited to approximately 10, when making use of the standard 256 byte tags provided by Microsoft PixelSense. Thus, we developed new tags with bigger and simpler designs (see a comparison of Microsoft's standard tags and ours in Figure 4 (left)), and introduced a new image recognition algorithm (using the AForge.NET[8] library) for our own tags to insure reliable program operation. Images of the surface are taken in short intervals (100 ms; this is sufficient for the complex skills module in order to achieve the desired results) and searched for quadrilaterals with a certain area and a circle included. We are able to detect the orientation of the tag, as the circle is not exactly placed in the middle. This is a common approach[9] if one does not want to depend on the conventional Microsoft-Tag mechanism [15].

Interaction with an Infrared Pen
Task 2 is to be operated by an infrared pen. The algorithm for the detection of the pen is similar to the one described in the previous section as it is also based on image analysis. In general, the system compares the drawn picture with the template that should have been drawn and determines whether the two versions match sufficiently or not. In order to, in the first place, check whether the infrared pen is currently used, the system analyzes the reflected current picture of the user interface and searches for a circle that matches the infrared pen tip (regarding its radius). A tolerance range for the size of the point was needed as the brightness of the pen may vary due to battery issues. Size variation was also the reason why the pen was preferred over the use of the finger (the size of the fingerprint varies drastically from person to person).

In order to identify the shape (here: circle), the number of vertices is determined; functionality provided by AForge.NET is then used to determine whether the vertices form a circle. Figure 4 (right) shows the system's view of the infrared pen placed on the screen. In order to follow the users drawn line, the system checks permanently the position of the pen by taking pictures of the user interface. The recognized positions are to be connected within a time frame of 300 milliseconds in order to display the drawn line. If the time frame is exceeded, the system concludes that the user has interrupted drawing the current line and the newly recognized dot (pen tip position) is interpreted as a newly started line.

Another challenge was related to the selection of an adequate infrared pen technology. Various pens have been tested during the implementation phase like e.g., the irpens Budget Infrared Pen[10], equipped with the top-rated Vishay TSAL6400 infrared LED and a manual control switch. This model was, however, not chosen for the project because the user needs to press a button for triggering the infrared radiation (which was not possible for many of the patients who tested the pen). We

[8] http://www.aforgenet.com/framework/samples/image_processing.html, last access: 23rd of Dec., 2014

[9] See also http://blogs.msdn.com/b/pixelsense/archive/2012/03/22/objecttracking.aspx, last access: 25th of June, 2015

[10] http://www.irpens.co/index.php/pens/budget/budget-infrared-pen.html, last access: 23rd of Dec., 2014

finally decided to work with the irpens Infrared Pen Djewel[11], a model equipped with TSAL infrared LED and dual control (nib pressure switch for hard surfaces as required for use on the tabletop and manual switch for more flexible surfaces). This pen was mainly chosen because its usage (i.e., pressing the pen on the surface in order to release the infrared radiation) seemed reasonable and practical in use for the patients.

USER TESTS AND FINDINGS

This section describes initial user tests that have been conducted with the complex skills module and related findings.

Aims and Method

The user tests were carried out with patients with cognitive deficits as a result of acquired brain injury. The tests were conducted by one of the occupational therapists in the project team. The method used was observation in combination with interview. The training was recorded for purposes of later analysis, additionally the video was used for a semi-structured interview with the creator of the conventional training idea behind the module (see later). As the intervention process described in [22] that was taken into account for our implementation, is well-structured and -defined, the intervention procedure itself was not object of the user test.

We wanted to analyze how the participants generally liked the training and aimed at gaining insights along several more concrete dimensions: we wanted to find out whether a) the *arm positioning* while working with the module was adequate for the patients, b) there was enough *freedom of movement* to position the tangible objects on the surface, c) the tangible objects were in general *easy to handle*, d) the objects used in tasks 1 and 3 were *recognized by the table in sufficient manner*, e) it was possible for the participants to *handle the infrared pen* used in task 2 well, f) the participants *noticed and correctly interpreted* the feedback (mostly: correct/incorrect) provided by the application, g) the *textual descriptions* (e.g., provided by task 4) were *easy to read* for patients with acquired brain injury, h) the *pictures and icons* showing the sports activities (tasks 4, 5 and 8) were *easy to understand and recognize* for the patients, and i) the patients were able to *manipulate via touch* (tasks 4, 5 and 8) the user interface (to assign the sports activities to the correct locations).

Participants

User tests were conducted with three carefully selected patients we considered representative for the target group. There were solely participants with mild cognitive impairment because the conventional complex skills training suggested by [22] was conceptualized for this target group (which excluded many patients with acquired brain injury from test participation). The participants also should not have severe motor impairments (not too much tone so as it must be possible to put the arm in position before the training starts) and should have awareness of their cognitive and motor skills; they further should be able to read and understand short texts and have no severe impairment in visual perception.

[11] http://www.irpens.co/index.php/infrared-pen-djewel.html, last access: 23rd of Dec., 2014

Participant 1 (male, 56) suffered a stroke five years ago. He is right-handed, hemiparesis is on the right side. P1 is capable of walking and still employed as a craftsman. He has mild cognitive impairment (slightly slowed down cognitive processing, mild lack of adaptation ability). P1 has awareness of his impairment and did not have experience with the system or multi-touch surfaces previous to the tests.

Participant 2 (male, 59) suffered a stroke six years ago. He is right-handed, hemiparesis is on the right side. P2 receives invalidity pension and has moderate impairment of planning activities and impulsion. P2 has awareness of his impairment and had already gained experience with the system earlier (no experiences with other multi-touch surfaces).

Participant 3 (male, 83) suffered a stroke two years ago. He is right-handed, hemiparesis is on the right side. P3 uses a walker and has moderate cognitive impairments, e.g., regarding planning activities, impulsion, concentration and adaptation ability. P3 has awareness of his impairment and did not have previous experience with any multi-touch surfaces.

Results

Each of the three participants found the training "exciting" (6 on a 6-item scale reaching from 1:repulsive to 6:exciting). All participants characterized the physical objects as easy to handle even if they had to handle them with their non-dominant hand. In the tested version, the squares shown in the construction area to be rebuilt using the objects (task 1) were as small as the squares in the template box. All participants expressed irritation about this circumstance, thus, as described earlier, the size of the digital squares in the construction area can now match the size of the physical ones. Because we intentionally did not provide related instructions before or during the training, handling the infrared pen was not possible for any of the participants, especially as all of them had to use their non-dominant hand (due to functional impairment of the dominant one). These problems led to the choice of a different pen, however, the challenges regarding pen-operation with the non-dominant hand remain. All participants noticed and recognized the application's feedback and waited for it after having solved a task. Two participants were not able to recognize the illustrations of the sports activities (icons), we thus increased the size of the presented pictures.

None of the participants was able to read the textual description of task 4, thus, the text size was increased meanwhile. Additionally, the module can be configured to show the textual task descriptions aligned towards the therapist. Regarding touch-based interaction as needed to assign the sports activities to the correct locations in tasks 4, 5 and 8, the following problems were reported. One of the participants kept too short contact with the surface (so that the action he wanted to take could not be identified by the table). All participants had difficulties understanding the process of swapping pictures in case they had placed them wrongly before and needed additional explanation. After these explanations and demonstrations all could handle the required touch-based input well.

To assure that our implementation complies with the original ideas behind the conventional training "sports ground", we conducted a semi-structured interview with Verena Schweizer, co-author of [22] and developer of the "sports ground" idea in Oct. 2014. The interview addressed the transferability of the original module and the moderate adaptations for our complex skills module (task 8). Schweizer expressed to consider our implementation according to the basic conceptualization of the original module as well as the formulation of intervention goals successful. In agreement with Schweizer, no further major modifications had to be made.

CONCLUSIONS

In this paper we provided a detailed description of designing and developing a tabletop-based system training cognitive performance in complex tasks. We discussed a series of coherent therapeutic exercises that have been approved by both occupational therapists and the developers of the original therapeutic concept our module is based on. We did not only describe the therapeutic considerations underlying the module but also a user interface and related interaction ideas considering the needs of therapists and patients. The general needs of both target groups regarding design and interaction have not only been analyzed in the small user tests described in this paper but also through continuous user involvement during the development process of the whole fun.tast.tisch. system and in larger-scale studies on other modules (see e.g., [6, 3]). The design and interaction concept of the complex skills module already consider these specific requirements and can thus be regarded a reference when developing similar tabletop-based exercises.

Regarding the therapeutic aspects, we also identified a potentially problematic aspect that remains (pen usage with the non-dominant hand for patients with hemiplegia). As a solution idea we implemented an opportunity for the therapist to overrule the system's feedback for task 2 – the therapist can lower the expectations for the desirable results at any time (this cannot be done by the system as it requires detailed knowledge of the patient's abilities and potential) and assess them according to the patient's individual prerequisites. Although this aspect is particularly important in the therapeutic area, we encourage increasing user-control in tabletop settings generally. Especially in cases where the system is intended to proceed to a subsequent task autonomously as a reaction to tangible interaction, user frustration is high when recognition does not work as expected.

Regarding user interface and interaction on a more general level, we presented a concept involving three different interaction modalities (touch, tangibles and pen). Especially pen usage is less common, compared to touch and tangibles. Using a pen to trace a line or draw a pre-defined shape could be interesting beyond rehabilitation purposes, e.g., for (learning) games with a haptic component. The pen recognition approach we introduced works reliably (given the lighting setting in general is suitable; this is however, not a pen-specific issue) and could be adapted for other settings.

Also, we (shortly, due to space issues) outlined technical challenges to be considered when setting up a tabletop environment for rehabilitation-purposed systems (most of them however apply to tabletop systems in other domains as well). The presented approach to overcome the issue of limited object recognition capabilities of the PixelSense is relevant for all systems that rely on a higher (i.e., more than 10) number of tags to be recognized concurrently. The concrete shape of individually developed tags can vary – we presented one possibility that works for all cases where tags do not need to be distinguishable (but their orientation must be identifiable).

Our menu reduction approach we introduced for therapists' configuration menus (that pop up only after placing a certain physical object on the display, also see [6]) to decrease the danger of unintended interaction by patients is not only transferable to settings where at least two users with different privileges interact with the tabletop at the same time. It also applies to all settings where a large screen area is needed for content representation (leaving little space left for menus).

As stated earlier, the complex skills module is part of fun.tast.tisch. which now contains 16 modules that have all been tested in clinical practice. The related findings already led to adaptations according to the target groups' needs. Thus, the main implementation phase is completed; we will now focus on technological considerations and supporting therapeutic institutions (who consider) using the system .

ACKNOWLEDGMENTS

The project fun.tast.tisch. acknowledges the financial support within the COIN program, managed by the Austrian Research Promotion Agency and funded by the Federal Ministry for Transport, Innovation and Technology and by the Federal Ministry of Economy, Family and Youth. Project partners: LIFEtool, ARTGROUP Advertising, University of Applied Sciences for Health Professions Upper Austria, University of Applied Sciences Upper Austria, Irene Schacherl-Hofer, software gmbh and TRANSPARENT DESIGN.

REFERENCES

1. Michelle Annett, Fraser Anderson, and Walter F. Bischof. 2010. Hands, Tables, and Groups Make Rehabilitation Awesome!. In *Proc. of the 15th Annual CyberTherapy & CyberPsychology Conf.* 3–8.
2. Michelle Annett, Fraser Anderson, and Walter F. Bischof. 2012. User Perspectives on Tabletop Therapy. In *Proc. of the 9th Int. Conf. on Disability, Virtual Reality & Associated Technologies*. Laval, France.
3. Mirjam Augstein and Thomas Neumayr. 2014a. Challenges and Opportunities of fun.tast.tisch. in Interactive Rehabilitation Settings. In *Proceedings of the 2nd International Workshop Collaboration meets Interactive Surfaces. Walls, Tables, Tablets, Phones, co-located with ITS2014*. Dresden, Germany.
4. Mirjam Augstein and Thomas Neumayr. 2014b. Touch and Tangibles – Interacting with fun.tast.tisch. Results of a Study with Non-Target-Group Users. In *Proceedings of the 2014 Workshop on Tactile/Haptic User Interfaces for Tabletops and Tablets (TacTT), held in conjuction with ITS2014*. Dresden, Germany.
5. Mirjam Augstein, Thomas Neumayr, Renate Ruckser-Scherb, Isabel Karlhuber, and Josef Altmann.

2013. The fun.tast.tisch. Project – A Novel Approach to Neuro-Rehabilitation Using an Interactive Multiuser Multitouch Tabletop. In *Proceedings of the ACM International Conference on Interactive Tabletops and Surfaces 2013*. St. Andrews, United Kingdom.

6. Mirjam Augstein, Thomas Neumayr, and Irene Schacherl-Hofer. 2014. The Usability of a Tabletop Application for Neuro-Rehabilitation from Therapists' Point of View. In *Proceedings of the 9th ACM International Conference on Interactive Tabletops and Surfaces*. Dresden, Germany.
7. Peter Brandl, Clifton Forlines, Daniel Wigdor, Michael Haller, and Chia Shen. 2008. Combining and Measuring the Benefits of Bimanual Pen and Direct-Touch Interaction on Horizontal Interfaces. In *Proc. of the Working Conf. on Advanced Visual Interfaces*. Italy.
8. Keith D. Cicerone, Cynthia Dahlberg, Kathleen Kalmar, Donna M. Langenbahn, James F. Malec, Thomas F. Bergquist, Thomas Felicetti, Joseph T. Giacino, Preston Harley, Douglas E. Harrington, Jean Herzog, Sally Kneipp, Linda Laatsch, and Philip A. Morse. 2000. Evidence-Based Cognitive Rehabilitation: Recommendations for Clinical Practice. *Archives of Physical Medicine and Rehabilitation* 81, 12 (2000), 1596–1615.
9. Elena de la Guiá, María D. Lozana, and Victor M.R. Penichet. 2014. Tangible User Interfaces applied to Cognitive Therapies. In *Proceedings of IUI 2014 Workshop: Interacting with Smart Objects*. Haifa, Israel.
10. Renate Drechsler. 2007. Exekutive Funktionen. Übersicht und Taxonomie. *Zeitschrift für Neuropsychologie* 18, 3 (2007).
11. Vorstand der GNP, Arbeitskreise der GNP, Wissenschaftlicher Beirat der GNP, Siegfried Gauggel, and Walter Sturm. 2005. Leitlinien der Gesellschaft für Neuropsychologie (GNP) für neuropschologische Diagnostik und Therapie. *Zeitschrift für Neuropsychologie* 16, 4 (2005), 175–199.
12. Sanna Koskinen and Jaana Sarajuuri. 2002. Computer-Administered Cognitive Remediation in a Frame of Holistic Neuropsychological Rehabilitation: FORAMENREAB Programs. *Acta Neurochirurgica. The European Journal of Neurosurgery* (2002).
13. Johnny C. Lee, Paul H. Dietz, Darren Leigh, William S. Yerazunis, and Scott E. Hudson. 2004. Haptic Pen: A Tactile Feedback Stylus for Touch Screens. In *Proceedings of the 17th Annual ACM Symposium on User Interface Software and Technology*. Santa Fe, USA.
14. Jakob Leitner, James Powell, Peter Brandl, Thomas Seifried, Michael Haller, Bernard Doray, and Paul To. 2009. FLUX - A Tilting Multi-Touch and Pen Based Surface. In *CHI '09 Extended Abstracts on Human Factors in Computing Systems*. Boston, USA.
15. Microsoft. 2012. Tagged Object Integration for Surface 2.0. Whitepaper. (2012).
16. Sandra Verena Müller, Sandy Harth, Helmut Hildebrandt, and Thomas F. Münte. 2006. Evidenzbasierte Therapie bei exekutiver Dysfunktion. *Fortschritte der Neurologie. Psychiatrie* 74, 1 (2006), 10–18.
17. Sandra Verena Müller, Sandy Harth, and Ulrike Klaue. 2008. *"Dann mache ich mir einen Plan". Arbeitsmaterialien zum planerischen Denken*. Verlag Modernes Lernen, Dortmund, Germany.
18. Sandra Verena Müller, Helmut Hildebrandt, and Thomas F. Münte. 2004. *Kognitive Therapie bei Störungen der Exekutivfunktionen: Ein Therapiemanual*. Hogrefe Verlag.
19. Sandra Verena Müller and Thomas F. Münte. 2009. Spektrum Akademischer Verlag, Chapter Störung von Exekutivfunktionen, 480–499.
20. Yongqiang Qin, Chun Yu, Hao Jiang, Chenjun Wu, and Yuanchun Shi. 2010. pPen: Enabling Authenticated Pen and Touch Interaction on Tabletop Surfaces. In *Proc. of the ACM Int. Conf. on Interactive Tabletops and Surfaces*. Saarbrücken, Germany.
21. Gebhart Sammer, Iris Reuter, Katharina Hullmann, Manfred Kaps, and Dieter Vaitl. 2006. Training of Executive Functions in Parkinson's Disease. *Journal of the Neurological Sciences* 248, 1–2 (2006), 115–119.
22. Verena Schweizer and Susanne Müller. 2012. *Neurotraining: Therapeutische Arbeit im kognitiven Bereich mit hirngeschädigten Erwachsenen*. Springer.
23. Andrea Serino, Elisa Ciaramelli, Anna Di Santantonio, Susanna Malagù, Franco Servadei, and Elisabetta Làvadas. 2007. A Pilot Study for Rehabilitation of Central Executive Deficits after Traumatic Brain Injury. *Brain Injury* 21, 1 (2007).
24. Ehud Sharlin, Yuichi Itoh, Benjamin Watson, Yoshifumi Kitamura, Steve Sutphen, and Lili Liu. 2002. Cognitive Cubes: a Tangible User Interface for Cognitive Assessment. In *Proceedings of the SIGCHI Conference on Human Factors in Computing Systems (CHI02)*. Minneapolis, Minnesota, USA, 347–354.
25. Yves von Cramon, Gabriele Mathes-von Cramon, and Norbert Mai. 1991. Problem-Solving Deficints in Brain-Injured Patients: A Therapeutic Approach. *Neuropsychological Rehabilitation* 1, 1 (1991), 45–64.
26. Yves von Cramon, Gabriele Mathes-von Cramon, and Norbert Mai. 2007. Problem-Solving Deficits in Brain-Injured Patients: A Therapeutic Approach. *Neuropsychological Rehabilitation* 1, 1 (2007), 45–64.
27. Peter H. Wilson, Jonathan Duckworth, Nick Mumford, Ross Eldridge, Mark Guglielmetti, Patrick Thomas, David Shum, and Heiko Rudolph. 2007. A Virtual Tabletop Workspace for the Assessment of Upper Limb Function in Traumatic Brain Injury (TBI). In *Proceedings of the International Workshop on Virtual Rehabilitation (ICVR)*. Venice, Italy, 14–19.

Blind People Interacting with Large Touch Surfaces: Strategies for One-handed and Two-handed Exploration

Tiago Guerreiro[1], Kyle Montague[2], João Guerreiro[3], Rafael Nunes[1], Hugo Nicolau[1], Daniel Gonçalves[3]
[1]LaSIGE, Faculdade de Ciências, Universidade de Lisboa , [2]University of Dundee,
[3]Instituto Superior Técnico, Universidade de Lisboa / INESC-ID
tjvg@di.fc.ul.pt, kmontague@dundee.ac.uk, joao.p.guerreiro@ist.utl.pt, rlnunes@di.fc.ul.pt, hmnicolau@fc.ul.pt, daniel.goncalves@inesc-id.pt

ABSTRACT
Interaction with large touch surfaces is still a relatively infant domain, particularly when looking at the accessibility solutions offered to blind users. Their smaller mobile counterparts are shipped with built-in accessibility features, enabling non-visual exploration of linearized screen content. However, it is unknown how well these solutions perform in large interactive surfaces that use more complex spatial content layouts. We report on a user study with 14 blind participants performing common touchscreen interactions using one and two-hand exploration. We investigate the exploration strategies applied by blind users when interacting with a tabletop. We identified six basic strategies that were commonly adopted and should be considered in future designs. We finish with implications for the design of accessible large touch interfaces.

Author Keywords
Blind; Large Surfaces; Tabletop; Strategies; Exploration.

ACM Classification Keywords
H.5.2. User Interfaces: User-centered design, Auditory (non-speech) feedback. Input devices and strategies, Interaction styles.

INTRODUCTION
In recent years, touchscreens have become ubiquitous in society, mostly due to their success in smartphones. Despite being an inherently visual technology, touchscreen devices are growing in popularity among blind users. The built-in accessibility features, such as Apple's VoiceOver or Android's Talkback, allow users to explore and control the device by providing audio feedback for touch actions (*Explore by Touch*). While these accessibility features have been shown to work for small touchscreens, it is not yet understood how practical they are for larger touchscreen interfaces such as interactive tabletop surfaces. The compact form factor of the mobile devices allows blind users to acquire spatial references from the physical corners and edges of the device. However, with large interactive tabletops and public displays it is not always possible to obtain these tactile reference points. As a result, exploration tasks become challenging. Furthermore, smartphone interfaces generally present a structured and populated grid of elements that can be used as cues to find the intended target; these are often not available in larger touch surfaces.

Previous work has proposed interface overlays that support non-visual target acquisition on tabletops. These include: linear lists of targets, combined touch-and-speech, and nearest neighbor with voice guidance to target [17]. While these solutions optimize the tasks of locating and counting targets, it is not clear whether participants were able to gain and leverage a spatial understanding of the interface.

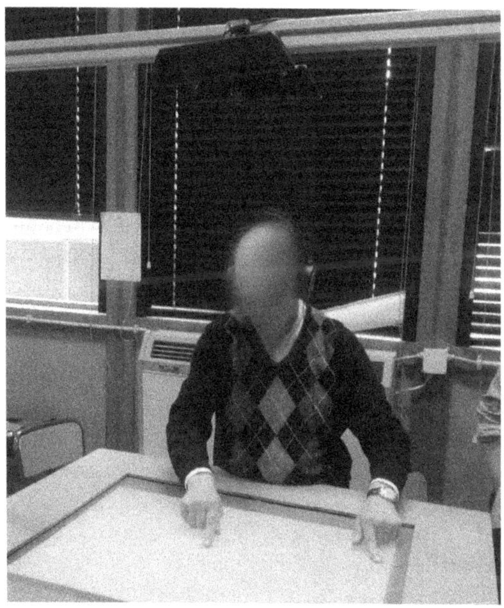

Figure 1. One blind participant using our interactive tabletop setup during a trial

This paper presents a user study with 14 blind participants aimed at understanding *how blind people interact with large touch surfaces* using the *Explore by Touch* approach. Motivated by the two-hand exploration behavior of blind users with physical objects [14] and braille reading [3],

ITS '15, November 15-18, 2015, Funchal, Portugal
© 2015 ACM. ISBN 978-1-4503-3899-8/15/11…$15.00
DOI: http://dx.doi.org/10.1145/2817721.2817743

alongside the emergence of such approaches in touchscreen interactions [13], we devised a two-hand alternative of *Explore by Touch.* To support simultaneous bimanual input from two hands, we developed an experimental screen reader using multiple sound sources to provide audio feedback. We combined the detailed touch interaction traces from the tabletop with annotated and coded observations of the recorded sessions, to identify and understand the strategies applied by blind participants with both one and two-hand interaction methods.

The contributions of this paper are: firstly, a user study examining tabletop **interaction strategies** of blind users; secondly, we define **touchscreen interaction metrics** to both identify the presence of, and rationale, for exploration strategies; and thirdly, we propose a set of **implications for the design of accessible large touchscreen interfaces**.

RELATED WORK

The related work reviewed in this section is three-fold: first, we discuss research on novel input and navigation techniques seeking to improve touchscreen accessibility for blind and visually impaired users; second, we address attempts to take advantage of non-visual multimodal feedback to improve spatial understanding; third, we present applications that explore the use of large touch surfaces for visually impaired people (maps, shapes and objects).

Touchscreen Accessibility

Touchscreen devices such as smartphones and tablets have built-in accessibility features (e.g. Apple's VoiceOver or Android's Talback) that allow visually impaired users to consume the content mainly through auditory feedback. These solutions rely both on gestures and direct exploration, where users drag their finger around the screen while the element in focus is read aloud by the system. Research has tried to improve these interfaces by leveraging gesture-based interaction, including understanding the preference and performance of both new and reference gestures [16], presenting new text-entry methods [12, 21] and browsing the interface using multitouch actions [15]. Other solutions took advantage of multitouch to input text, either using *Braille* (e.g. [2, 19, 24]), supporting two-handed exploration in *QWERTY* keyboards [13] or presenting new keyboard layouts [4].

Multimodal Feedback

While auditory feedback still dominates touchscreen interfaces for visually impaired users, other researchers have explored the use of haptics either alone or together with audio to provide a better spatial understanding. For instance, Giudice et al. [9] provide non-visual access to graphical information (graphs and shapes) on tablet devices by triggering tactile feedback through a single vibrating motor when an onscreen visual element is touched. Goncu et al [10] had a similar goal, but tried to take advantage of the multitouch capabilities of touchscreens, by allowing the simultaneous use of two fingers that could be used to define a line and hear the intersected shapes through sonified 3D audio. The tactile feedback was provided through vibrating motors attached to the fingers to allow the user to determine the elements positions and their geometric properties. Manshad and Manshad [18] presented a haptic glove that sends vibrations to each finger in order to direct the user to a graph on a grid, in the context of basic algebra.

Nevertheless, these techniques are targeted at very specific domains and do not generalize to all touchscreen interfaces.

Tabletops and Applications

While most research focused on small touchscreens, the knowledge about the accessibility features and research on touchscreens reduces considerably in larger touchscreen interfaces such as interactive tabletop surfaces.

In a first attempt to improve non-visual access to large touchscreens beyond *Explore by touch*, Kane et al. [17] proposed three novel input techniques to enhance the performance of tabletop interactions by blind users. Their proposed solutions decreased the error rates and times taken to complete tabletop interactions by removing the need for users to perform absolute spatial exploration. For example, *Edge Projection* linearized the targets from the fixed 2D positions on the surface into lists of targets that could be explored by sliding a finger along the horizontal or vertical edge of the screen. With this interface, it is possible for users to produce a mental model of targets from their sequence within the lists, as they would for menu navigation on a PC. This approach has strong advantages, as users do not need to accurately maintain a spatial location for each target; they can rely on the reading order of targets to relocate them. In the *Neighborhood Browsing* technique, the whitespace of the screen is divided between the sparse number of targets, and users can request voice guidance to the actual target location from these expanded regions. Voice guidance is also used within the *Touch-and-Speak* [17] condition, where the user can ask the system to read aloud the list of targets, then request directions to its screen position. While both of these interfaces require the user to perform spatial exploration, they are assisted with this interaction and led directly to the desired location.

A practical application that is most frequently associated with large touch surfaces for visually impaired people is interactive maps. Starting with NOMAD [22], several projects relied on tactile map overlays augmented with auditory feedback (detailed review in [7]). Brock et al. [6] later compared a classical raised-line map against an interactive map in a large touch surface with raised-line overlays and auditory output. While efficiency and user satisfaction improved significantly with the interactive map, effectiveness was dependent on the users' individual traits.

In the current study, we observe the natural interaction behaviors applied by blind users when presented with large touch surface exploration tasks. Through this study we uncover the underlying strategies adopted during both one and two-hand exploration. This evidence will support the development of technologies designed to ameliorate the barriers to non-visual interaction on large touch surfaces.

USER STUDY

This study focuses on identifying and understanding the strategies used by blind users to explore interactive large touch surfaces. We use a laboratory evaluation of tabletop exploration tasks, i.e. *locating, relocating* and *counting* targets, and describing the relative position between two targets. We then coded the video and interaction traces to develop an understanding of the characteristics of users' strategies and exploration patterns.

Research Questions

This user study aims to answer, on large touch surfaces, how do blind users:

1. …acquire targets with no prior screen knowledge?
2. …leverage prior screen knowledge when acquiring targets?
3. …spatially relate multiple objects on screen?
4. …gain an overview of all screen content?

Participants

Fourteen legally blind participants, three females, were recruited from a local social institution. Participants' age ranged from 23 to 62 (M=44.5, SD=12.1). Three participants were left-handed and five participants were experienced with touch phones. None reported having severe motor or hearing impairments. Three participants were congenitally blind. One participant lost sight in the last year. All others were considered legally blind for at least five years. All were screen reader users.

User Interfaces

We collected user interactions with the tabletop surface using our experimental screen reader (based on the current solutions available for mobile touchscreen devices i.e. *Talkback*[1] and *VoiceOver*[2]). The system was able to capture off-screen hand tracking [20], allowing us to identify which hand corresponds to the touch *id*, recorded by the tabletop. All users interacted with both one and two-hand conditions:

One-Hand is the *de facto* interaction technique for non-visual exploration of touchscreen devices as used by *VoiceOver* and *Talkback*, on mobile devices. Participants could interact by dragging their finger on the screen and the system would read aloud the name of the object as they entered it. The system would also perform a "click" sound when a participant's finger exited an object. Targets could be selected by performing a double tap gesture anywhere on the surface; the last target interacted with was then selected.

Two-Hand extends the basic functionality of the *one-hand* condition to provide support for simultaneous bimanual interactions. Independent speech feedback was provided for each hand. Based on the previous research investigating multiple sound sources [11] and non-visual exploration of interactive maps [5, 8], we restricted the number of simultaneous interactions to just one finger per hand. The optimal two-voice setup of the *Text-to-Speeches* spatial audio framework was used to support multiple sound sources [11], each hand was mapped to a specific voice (male or female) and location (left or right ear) to aid interaction feedback distinction.

These interface conditions allow the participants to explore the tabletop interfaces in a similar manner to tactile exploration. Moreover, by minimizing the restrictions on their interaction methods, we are able to observe their spontaneous behaviors and expressions of strategies [25].

Apparatus

This study was conducted using a Frustrated Total Internal Reflection (FTIR) tabletop computer with a 58 x 76cm screen dimension, a Kinect stereo camera positioned above the table, and stereo over-ear headphones were used to provide audio feedback (Figure 1). We used the TACTIC framework [20] to enable multitouch input on the tabletop surface and support hand/finger tracking. We developed a stimulus application to generate tabletop interfaces within a 9 x 12 grid (as used in [17]). We used sparse target layouts to produce screen locations with little or no possible interaction feedback, to both give the illusion of a freeform layout and observe the participants' behaviors under these challenging conditions. Participants were not informed that the targets were distributed in a grid layout or the number of targets in it. Target locations were randomly generated for each new task; all targets were 6cm x 6cm, to fill the cell. The stimulus application captured start and end timestamps, and the screen layout including *target names* and *locations* for each study trial. The interaction data was combined with the screen layout and saved to a log file.

Procedure

Users were invited to the laboratory to participate in the study. Before undergoing the tasks, participants were introduced to the interactive tabletop, provided with a short demonstration, and given time to try each interface condition for 10 minutes. Participants stood facing the tabletop, wearing headphones, as shown in Figure.

The following experimental tasks were used to expose interaction strategies and capture performance measurements for each of the two interface conditions:

1. *Locate.* Given the name (e.g. *Shoe)* of a target, participants were asked to explore the interface to find the target and select it. A single layout with five targets was generated, and participants were asked to locate three targets (one at a time). The second target was only asked once the first one was selected; and the same for the third one.

---

[1] http://developer.android.com/design/patterns/accessibility.html

[2] https://developer.apple.com/accessibility/ios/

2. *Relocate.* Having already complete the *locate* task for three targets, participants were then asked to relocate the same three targets in a random order.

3. *Count.* Participants were given a target name (and a new layout), and asked to count the number of instances of that target within the interface. The number of instances was restricted to a range of 3-5, and the overall number of objects onscreen was of 10. Unlike Kane *et al's* count task [17], each of our target instances had the same name and required the user to maintain awareness of the visited targets.

4. *Relate.* Participants were given the name of two targets and asked to state which target was topmost or leftmost. This required the participants to locate each of the named targets before they could answer the question. As with the *count* task, participants performed the *relate* tasks with different layouts with a screen density of 10 objects (this included the two named targets). To ensure that the *relate* tasks presented a consistent challenge to all participants we defined the following constraints to positioning of the two stimulus targets: in the vertical *relate* task, the targets are at most separated by two rows and at a distance of four columns or more; similar constraints applied to the horizontal *relate* task.

Participants selected the targets by performing a double tap gesture on the intended target. The system would start the task timer from the moment the participant touches the screen, and stop the timer when the task is complete and the participant removes their hands from the screen. The *one-hand* and *two-hand* interface conditions were counterbalanced across our participants. Once the participant performed all of the tasks for an interface condition, they were asked to complete a Single Ease Questionnaire [23] to obtain their perceived ease of use, along with their overall system opinions.

Design and Analysis

The study was a within-subjects design with one independent variable, interface condition. Each participant performed three *locate*, three *relocate*, two *count*, and two *relate* tasks for both interface conditions. We analyse user performance based on the following metrics:

Time Taken: Participants were instructed to remove their hand(s) from the tabletop when they completed each task; the time was then calculated from the difference between the participants' first and last interactions within the task.

Error Rate: An error occurred within *locate* or *relocate* tasks when the participant was unable to find the requested target. If the participant gave an incorrect answer for the *count* task, or wrong position for the *relate* tasks.

Coverage: Using the 9 x 12 grid locations defined above, we count the number of visits participants make to each location, per trial. We also compute the *New* and *Revisited Coverage* for between task analyses of *locate* and *relocate* trials. These values are used to quantify the levels of prior screen knowledge for the subsequent trials.

In addition to the aforementioned performance metrics, we analyzed the strategies that emerged from the exploration tasks. Logged data allowed us to generate animated gif files of the all screen interactions made by each participant (Figure). Effectively, we could replay the users' interactions for each task. These animated traces were then used to characterize and code exploration strategies applied for each task. Video recordings were used to support the coding where users' actions were unclear from the interaction traces. The strategies analysis comprised the coding of touchscreen interaction traces along the seven features shown in Table 1. To verify the reliability of the code set, we refined the characteristics through several phases, similar to the approach applied by Anthony et al. [1]. Initially, two researchers independently coded two sets of 10 randomly selected videos and traces, followed by discussion of the coding dimensions used. In the next phase, the researchers independently coded a set of 40 randomly selected videos and traces (14% of the dataset), the inter-rater reliability was then computed across the seven dimensions and the Cohen's kappa agreement was *k*=.89 (SD=.08). The remaining traces were then coded using the same schema independently by the two researchers. The full dataset of interaction traces, used for the coding, are publicly available at https://goo.gl/FIUqCU.

Name	***Description***
Started from the edge	Interaction traces that start from an edge of the screen; this also included the ones that started within the outer cells of the screen.
Structured Movements	Interactions where the trace movements appeared to have a form of organisation and arrangement.
Reference Points	Using other objects as relative location markers to help guide the exploration. One example is shifting direction towards a target when receiving feedback on another object.
Screen Symmetry	Traces where there is a horizontal or vertical axis of symmetry.
Hand Symmetry	Participant's hand movements were proportional in direction and distance.
Simultaneous Input	When the participant uses both hands simultaneously to explore the screen.
Equal Roles	If both hands perform the same operations.

Table 1. Features used to code the interaction traces, and definitions for each.

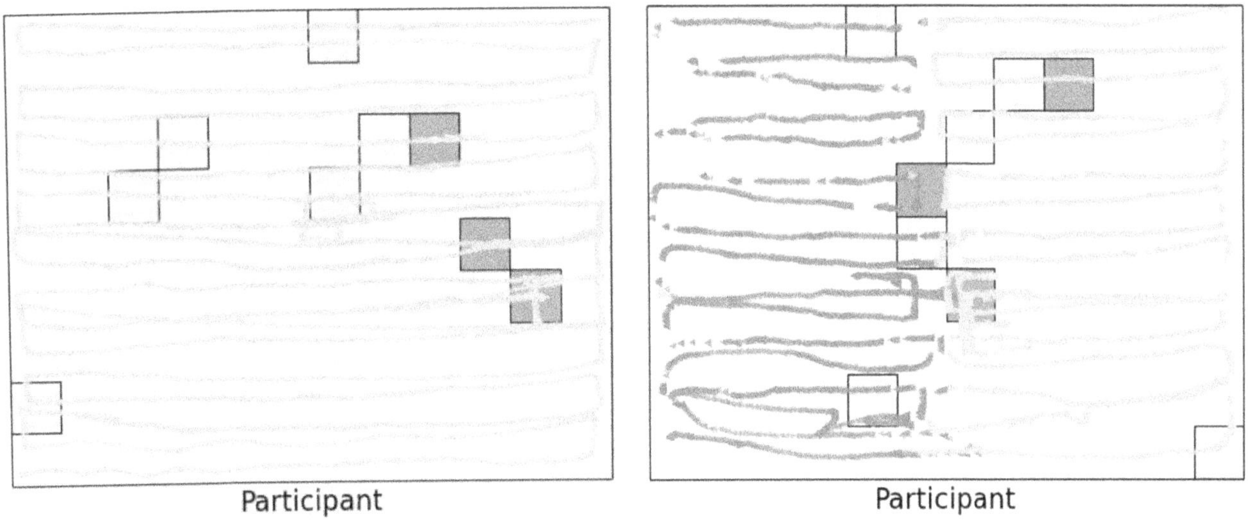

Figure 2. Interaction traces during one of the tasks showing a Path Scan strategy. Left: the participant performs a Count task with the One-Hand condition, Right: the same user performs the same task, but this time with Two-Hand. "Participant" indicates the location of the participant in relation to the tabletop.

FINDINGS

Analysis of the coded characteristics revealed the following usage patterns:

- In 85.71% of *count* tasks, independently from the condition, participants begin their explorations from the edges of the screen, and 55.36% used structured movements, ensuring the best possible coverage and exploration of the space.
- In 66.37% of all *Two-Hand* tasks, the participants used equal roles for each hand. Equal roles were most common in *count* tasks, with their use 89.29% of the time and lowest in the *relocate* tasks with only 38.10%. However, relocate tasks have a *simultaneous hand use* of 28.57%, making it less likely that both hands had equal roles in those tasks.

The coded interaction traces were clustered based on their similarity using the features outlined in Table 1. We will now discuss the characteristics and behaviors of the observed strategies, and how they were applied to the tasks.

Strategies

Originally, four strategy clusters were defined from the grouping of the features and manual inspection of the traces: *Path Scan, Focused, To-The-Point* and *Freeform.* The researchers then discussed the variance within these clusters and opted to divide the *Freeform* to include the *Freeform Symmetry* and *Finger Trailing* variations as their own strategies, giving six exploration strategies.

Path Scan exhibits similarities to the structured scanning paths already applied by screen readers and switch access assistive technologies. Users would start from the faraway edge or corner of the screen, and then drag their finger horizontally until that row has been covered. At which point they would drop a row and return along the horizontal axis in the opposite direction. This action is repeated until the user either locates the desired target, or reaches the end of the screen. When using *Two-Hand,* users leveraged the second hand by dividing the screen and shared the exploration between the hands. Users would mirror their moves, resulting in a well-structured, symmetrical trace, moving through the screen space row by row. Overall, participants applied this strategy 23.81% of the tasks for *One-Hand* and 30.06% with *Two-Hand.* Figure 2 illustrates a typical *Path Scan* trace in both the *One-Hand* and *Two-Hand* interface conditions.

Focused represents an extensive unstructured search of a small sub-section of the screen where the user believed the target to be. We observed this strategy in situations where the participant had prior knowledge of the target they were looking for. Specifically, the technique occurred during *relocate* tasks and, in some cases, *locate* tasks. However, this could only occur in *locate* tasks when the user had knowledge of that target from a previous *locate* task. Using their dominant hand only, the participant would start the touch exploration not from the edge of the screen, but in the

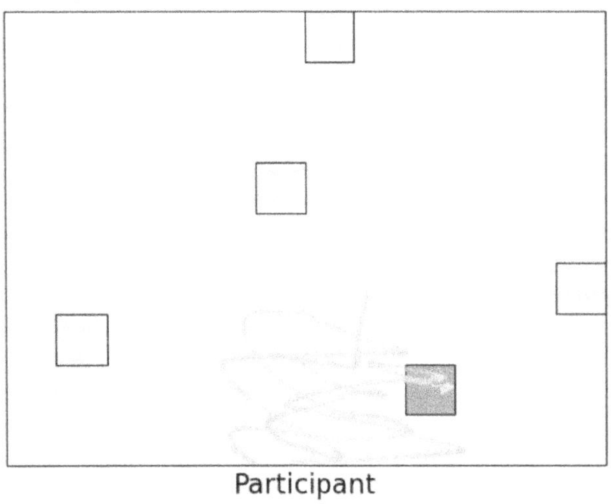

Figure 3. Focused strategy interaction traces of a Relocate task.

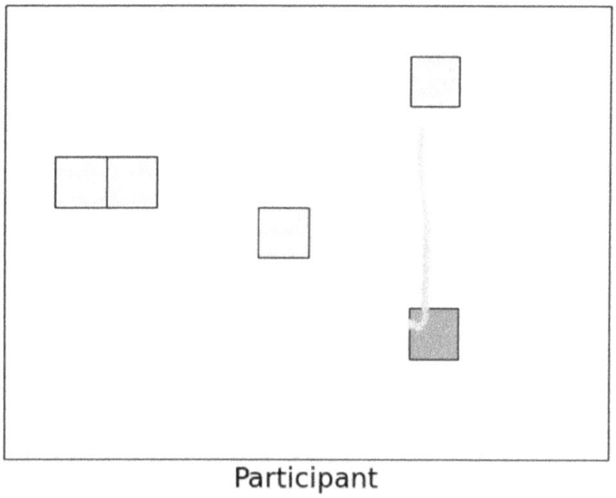

Figure 4. Interaction trace of a Relocate task presenting a To-the-point strategy.

area where they remembered hearing the target before. The movements traces were very close together, and would often overlap several times in a small area. If the participant was unsuccessful in locating the target within the initial sub-section, they would increase the search area slightly and continue with this technique - confident that the target was close by. While participants could explore with two hands simultaneously in the *Two-Hand* condition, they only performed this type of exploration with a single hand. Overall, participants applied this strategy 9.52% of the tasks for *One-Hand* and 5.95% with *Two-Hand. Figure 3* illustrates a trace applying a *Focused* strategy.

To-The-Point. As with the *Focused* search, this technique relied on participants having prior knowledge of target locations. Again, using the dominant hand, participants would start in an area of the screen close to the target. However, unlike the *Focused* technique, participants had no need to trace and retrace their steps in close proximity of the target. They appeared to know the exact location and could make very structured moves directly to it in a short amount of time. Again, within the *Two-Hand* condition participants did not use the second hand for this strategy. Overall, participants applied this strategy 24.4% of the tasks for *One-Hand* and 14.29% with *Two-Hand. Figure 4* illustrates the *To-The-Point* strategy, again only a single hand is used, and thus, the traces are the same for the *One-Hand* and *Two-Hand* interface conditions.

Freeform. We regarded this approach as more of an anti-strategy, where participants' movements appeared to be erratic, unpredictable, and without any discernable pattern. Within these traces, we see participants moving around the screen with no real understanding of what has been previously explored. When an object is heard, it is quickly revisited and then the unstructured search continues. Interestingly, in some cases participants were able to retain the spatial locations from this technique, and successful

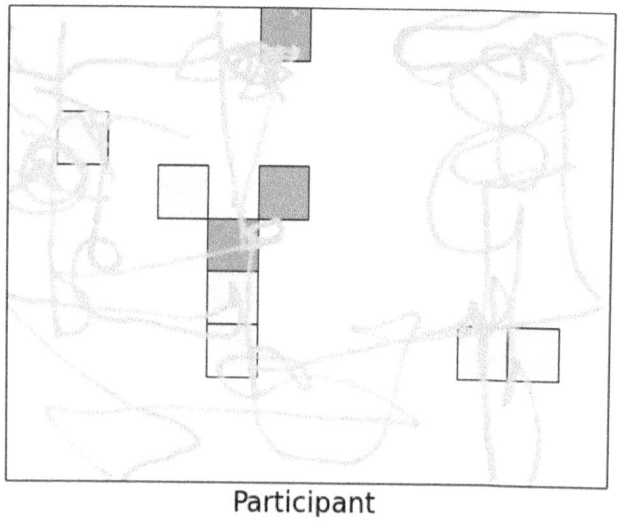

Figure 5. Interaction traces of a Count task showing a Freeform strategy.

apply them in the subsequent *locate* and *relocate* tasks using the *To-The-Point* strategy.

Overall, participants applied this strategy 29.17% of the tasks for *One-Hand.* One example of *Freeform* is show in *Figure* 5. Only interactions from the *One-Hand* condition were coded as *Freeform*, within the *Two-Hand* we refined this classification to include two variants: *Freeform Symmetry* and *Trailing Finger.*

Freeform Symmetry. As the name implies, this *Two-Hand* variant of the *Freeform* strategy (*Figure 6)*, leverages simultaneous input and hand symmetry to explore the screen in an unstructured manner. While some examples of this technique could be confused for the two hand *Path Scan* approach, they still exhibited an unpredictable nature of movement through the screen. Combining synchronized zigzags down the screen with loops and twists, resulting in horizontal symmetry of the screen. Participants applied this strategy in 15.77% of the tasks.

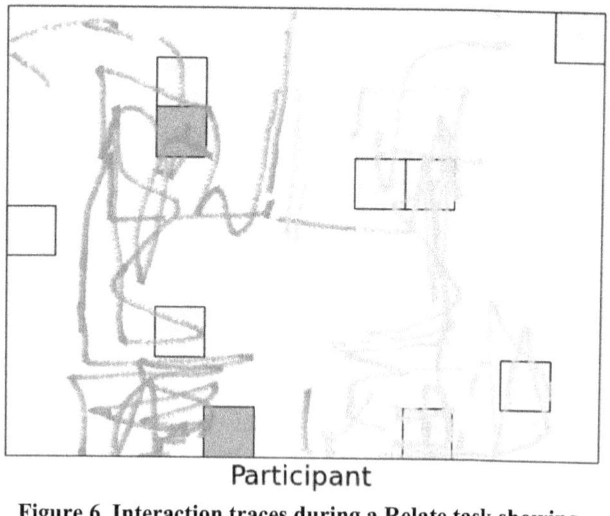

Figure 6. Interaction traces during a Relate task showing Freeform Symmetry strategy.

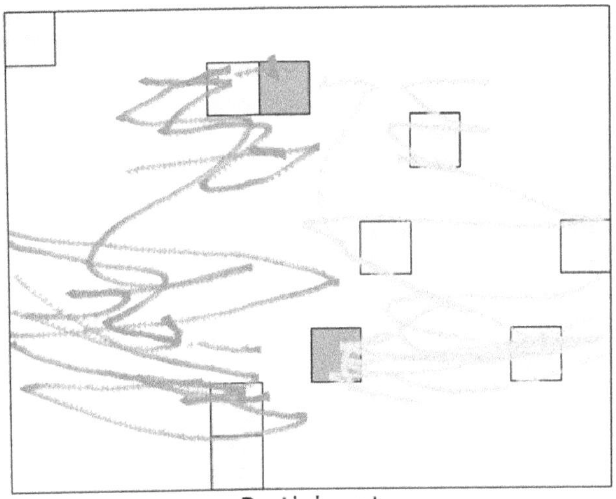

Figure 7. Interaction traces of a Relate task showing a Trailing Finger strategy.

Trailing Finger. With this variation of the *Freeform* strategy, participants used the second finger to search areas in parallel. Both hands shared similar movements but with a horizontal offset between them. Each hand would take in it turns to be the lead as the participants moved through the screen. Again, traces were unstructured and fingers moved quickly between different areas of the tabletop. Participants applied this strategy in 29.17% of the tasks. *Figure 7* shows the exploration trace where the user applied *Trailing Finger*, as captured by the *Two-Hand*. However, to understand this strategy the aforementioned animated gifs are needed, to see how the trace was created.

Quantitative Results

In what follows, we present a quantitative analysis for each task and describe how they fit with the strategies employed.

Finding targets without previous knowledge is inefficient. In the first task, participants were asked to search and select a target. This was done with three targets, in sequence, using the same layout and onscreen target disposition. All participants were able to identify the location of the target and only one user failed to accurately select it in the *Two-Hand* condition. They took an average total time to complete the task (search and select 3 targets) of 130.4 (SD=121.8) and 121.7 (SD=61.7) seconds in the *One-Hand* and *Two-Hand* conditions (n.s., Wilcoxon, Z=-.345, p=.730), respectively. Considering the first target only, when they had no previous knowledge of the layout, participants took an average of 62.1 (SD=82.4) and of 47.84 (SD=36.9) seconds (n.s., Wilcoxon, Z=-.220, p=.826), respectively. These results suggest that non-visually searching for a target on a large surface, without previous knowledge of its location, is a time consuming task.

The most common strategies applied by the users when performing searching for targets using *One-Hand,* were Path Scan (14.29%), Focused (19.05%) and To-The-Point (30.95%). 33.33% of the searching trials in this condition revealed a *Freeform* strategy. When two hands were supported - participants applied more structured searches (*Path Scan*, 26.19%) and decreased their use of focused searches (no *Focused* occurrences; *Straight-to-the-point*, 14.29%). 35.71% of the trials were dominated by an unstructured *Trailing Finger* strategy and 21.43% revealed no particular strategy (*Freeform).*

The high level of focused searches in the *One-Hand* setting derives from the design of this task: users performed the three trials sequentially in a grid with the same layout enabling them to acquire knowledge of target disposition for later recall. They were able to leverage that knowledge most of the times they had previously encountered it. Conversely, when using two hands, participants did not build on that knowledge. This could be either because they felt comfortable with the strategy they were using or because they retained less information due to the increased amount of feedback that was provided in this setting.

Considering just the first trial, the number of participants with a structured strategy was the same in both conditions (4). Other participants also opted for dividing the screen and applying a Symmetric strategy (unstructured); this happened only with *Two-Hand* (4 participants). Both structure and symmetry enabled participants to perform a wider coverage of the screen in their explorations with two hands as shown by the total percentage of screen areas covered (*One-Hand*, M=70.0%, SD=22.5%; *Two-Hand*, M=89% SD=12.0%; Wilcoxon, Z=-2.971, p=.003). However, due to a less focused strategy with *Two-Hand,* a significant difference was found in how people leverage previous coverage, i.e., *Unique Area Coverage*, (Z=-2.103, p=.035), between *One-Hand* (M=42.5%, SD=18.1%) and *Two-Hand* (M=31.2%, SD=12.5%). By using two hands, participants seem to have a better coverage of the screen but also to revisit more areas. Notice that using *Two-Hand*, participants cover a larger area and take approximately the same amount of time as when using *One-Hand.*

People can leverage previous screen knowledge. Users were provided with reusable screen knowledge in the locate tasks (the tasks were done in sequence over the same layout) and in the relocate ones, where they had to find previously identified targets. In the first trial, the users cover, in average, approximately, half of the screen in both conditions (*One-Hand*, M=51%, SD=31%; *Two-Hand*, M=53%, SD=38%; Wilcoxon, Z=-.596, p=.551). In the *One-Hand* condition, as mentioned above, the participants seem to get a good knowledge of the screen, applying focused searches when they have previously visited the targets. The amount of new screen area covered is significantly different from the first (M=51%, SD=31%) to the second (M=11%, SD=12%) tasks (Wilcoxon, Z=-2.512, p=.012) which then stabilizes at a low level of new coverage. With *Two-Hand*, this effect is only visible from the second (New coverage, M=30%, SD=30%) to the third (M=6%, SD=14%) task (Wilcoxon, Z=-2.358, p=.018).

Overall, the participants were able to gain knowledge of the targets on screen through prior explorations, then leverage that knowledge of the target locations by applying the *focused* strategy in the final task, in both conditions.

When people were asked to relocate targets they had located, they revealed to have a good notion of the whereabouts of the target, mostly applying a *To-the-point* (*One-Hand*, 66.7%; *Two-Hand*, 42.9%) or a Focused search (*One-Hand*, 19.1%; *Two-Hand*, 23.8%). In cases where participants lost the spatial awareness of the target position, they resorted mostly to a *Path Scan* strategy (*One-Hand*, 9.5%; *Two-Hand*, 11.9%) and only few trials showed no particular strategy (*One-Hand*, 4.8%; *Two-Hand*, 2.4%).

These results are corroborated by the percentage of total area covered in the three relocate trials (*One-Hand*, M=43%, SD=30%; *Two-Hand*, M=7%, SD=14%) that is significantly smaller than the one in the three *locate* tasks (One-Hand, M=70%, SD=22%; Two-Hand, M=89%, SD=12%), in *One-Hand* (Wilcoxon, Z=-2.534, p=.019) and even more so with *Two-Hand* (Wilcoxon, Z=-3.297, p=.001). The ability to leverage previous knowledge then translates in the overall performance to complete the tasks: users are significantly faster at relocating targets than at finding them in the first three searching tasks both in the *One-Hand* (Z=-1.977, p=.048) and *Two-Hand* conditions (Z=-2.354, p=.019). No significant differences were found between *One-Hand* (M=68.2, SD=63.4, seconds) and *Two-Hand* (M=66.9, SD=81.6, seconds) in the time to complete the relocate tasks (Wilcoxon, Z=.910, p=.363).

Relating targets requires additional aid. Locating and relating the position of two on screen targets showed to be a demanding task. Participants did not correctly relate the targets 46.4% (SD=30.78%) and 28.6% (SD=37.8%) of the times in the *One-Hand* and *Two-Hand* settings, respectively (a minor significant effect was found, Wilcoxon, Z=-1.890, p=.059). They took an average of 149.6 (SD=81.4) and 95.5 (SD=41.8) seconds to complete these tasks with *One-Hand* and *Two-Hand, respectively*. Using two hands revealed a significant effect on how fast people could find and relate both targets (Wilcoxon, Z=-1.977, p=.048). The main reason for this difference is that a second hand on the screen enabled the participants to maintain the position of a first target while searching for the second one. Even in the *One-Hand* condition, some participants used a second hand hovering the screen to *mark* where this target was. The strategies applied before locating a first target was very similar to the ones in the first task (*locate* a target) both in the *One-Hand* (*Path Scan*, 25.0%) and *Two-Hand* (*Path Scan*, 28.6%; *Trailing Finger*, 35.7%, *Freeform Symmetry*, 21.4%). No significant differences were found in the amount of coverage the participants did with both (*One-Hand*, M=75.8%, SD=18.9%; *Two-Hand*, M=80.0%, SD=17.5%; t(13)=-.790, p=.444).

Lack of understanding of visited space. Participants were asked to count the number of targets with a certain name on the screen. This task had two main requirements: perform a complete coverage of the screen and be aware of previously visited targets. They took an average time of 126.5 (SD=54.8) and 131.6 (SD=77.1) seconds (Wilcoxon, Z=-.031, p=.975) and had an error rate (answered with an incorrect number of targets) of 82.1% (SD=31.7%) and 64% (SD=36.3%) in the *One-Hand* and *Two-Hand* conditions, respectively. No significant differences were found between the two conditions regarding error rate.

Revisiting the aforementioned requirements, participants' performance show a slightly better coverage of the screen (Wilcoxon, Z=-1.712, p=.087, minor effect) when using two hands (M=93.6%, SD=6.3%) than with one hand (M=85.2%, SD=17.5%). Conversely, participants showed to visit target cells repeatedly and to do it significantly more so when using two hands (*Visits per Target Cell*; *One-Hand*, M=5.7, SD=3.4; *Two-Hand*, M=9.6, SD=4.7; t(13) = -3.181, p=.007). Although using two hands seems to provide the tools for a better coverage of the screen, at the same time users seem to repeatedly visit the same targets, and unknowingly treat those as new targets. These results are supported by the final counts presented: the participants tended to answer with a number below the actual count (average of -0.5 targets) in *One-Hand*, and a higher number in the *Two-Hand* (average of +0.5 targets) condition.

Participants employed a *Path Scan* strategy 46.3% (*One-Hand*) and 53.4% *(Two-Hand*) of the times. Additionally, when using two hands, participants also resorted to *Trailing Finger* (28.6%) and *Freeform Symmetry* (17.9%). The structured strategies enabled the participants to cover most of the screen, however, the participants have no extra cues to understand if they are revisiting a target, and in several cases, an entire line (*Figure* 2)

Subjective Feedback

We asked our participants to rate each interface condition using 7-point Likert scales for *ease of use* and *speed of use* upon completing the tasks. Wilcoxon signed-rank tests were applied to the Likert scale results. There were no significant differences between the interface conditions for *ease of use, z*=-.973, *p*=.331; or *speed of use*, *z* =-1.910, *p*=.056. When asked to state *which interface condition was preferred*, six participants selected *One-Hand*; six selected *Two-Hand*; and two thought that both interface conditions were similar.

The users that preferred *Two-Hand* referred to the larger dimensions of the tabletop, where the two-hand exploration allowed them to cover a larger area of the screen at the same time. One user that made use of the Path Scan strategy (Figure 2) responded, "*If you estimate the center of the screen and each finger explores half of it, it is way faster. You just have to pay attention*". Another user highlighted the role of two hands to provide a better spatial understanding of the screen and its targets, "*which is even more beneficial in Relate tasks*". The main reason for preferring *One-Hand* was a greater confidence in the auditory feedback, as it could only correspond to that particular finger. In *Two-Hand*, a few users revealed that sometimes they "*needed to move both fingers alternatively to understand which one touched a target*".

IMPLICATIONS FOR DESIGN

The results obtained enabled us to devise a set of implications for designing interfaces for large touchscreen interactive surfaces accessible to blind users.

Avoid spatial exploration in sparse grids. Nowadays, blind smartphone and tablet users are able to explore the screen with a *One-Hand* approach, which is also known as painless exploration. Our results showed that such exploration, when performed on a large surface, is anything but painless, particularly if the target density is low. Results showed that blind users may lose large amounts of time exploring areas without receiving any type of feedback or cue to direct them towards their intended goal which is time consuming and frustrating. Enabling users to use two hands to explore the screen did not improve their exploration abilities. These results support the need for interface layers that diminish the spatial load, as presented in [17] and allow users to grasp a relative mental model of the contents being.

Establish and maintain spatial models of screen content. In contrast to what was observed in previously unknown layouts, the users demonstrated efficiency in establishing a spatial model of the screen layout and relocating targets. They were able to leverage their spatial understanding to locate targets within previously explored areas. Looking at the preliminary studies performed by Kane et al [17], users were seen to store their items spatially ordered by relevance. They were also able to retrieve them. This ability can be leveraged in layouts that rely on spatial positioning, for example - enabling people to store and rearrange interface items for later recall.

Enable and provide richer feedback. One shortcoming that stood out in the evaluated settings was the inability for users to understand the state of the system, particularly of the explored areas and objects. Resorting to the hyperlink analogy, where previously visited links are presented differently to the sighted user, touch interfaces are falling short in providing feedback to the user about the history of the interaction taking place. While some actions could be detected automatically and feedback changed accordingly, users should also be allowed to enrich the exploration with their own cues and references (e.g., mark areas as visited or other context-related layers). In this paper, with *Two-Hand,* we gave a first step towards enriching the feedback on exploration, mostly by enabling the user to understand which hand touches each object. The design space of sound and/or other feedback channels (e.g., haptics) can be further explored to augment the information the user receives.

More permissive and flexible touch interfaces. As the size increases, so does the need of the user to explore. One of the limitations faced by blind people is that their options are to slide to the next elements or to "painlessly" explore the screen by finding and receiving feedback on each item. On the other hand, blind users are used to exploring physical surfaces and sheets of paper in search for objects or Braille dots. Some users were seen to leverage the usage of two fingers to split their screen or to assess relationships between objects. Allowing for more natural explorations, similar to the ones applied on physical surfaces, enables users to employ current abilities and thus improve their efficiency. Further research is needed to understand how to provide feedback without overloading the user.

Prioritized elements should be laid along screen edges. Participants were seen to resort to the screen edges as a starting point for their structured searches. This happened particularly when they were aware of the need to be thorough (Count, started from the edge in 85.71% of the trials). These results reinforce that the most relevant interaction contents should be placed along screen edges, particularly in the corners where the users are likely to start their exploration. Given that the most difficult task was locating targets without previous knowledge, the borders can be used as a bootstrap for creating a spatial model of the screen, including interactive contents that allow for accompanied learning of the layout.

Hand roles should be defined based on the task. When allowed to use two hands, users varied in how they utilized this ability. When looking for a good coverage of the screen, users applied equal roles to both hands (exploration) while when relating targets, users used one hand to mark a position and another one to explore. In other cases, like *relocating* targets with a focused search, users seemed to disregard their second hand. Hand roles seem to strongly relate with both the tasks being performed and the strategies applied and should be further explored creating and augmenting new bimanual interfaces for large surfaces.

Active strategy recognition. Current touchscreen interfaces are static and passive to the user's behavior. The results presented here revealed interaction patterns that speak clearly about the users' intentions and strategies (e.g., wandering around a target – Focused Search; starting from the edge and performing a structured search – Path Scan). In light of our results, such interfaces should consider adapting to the users' behaviors and support the interaction taking place e.g., apply Kane's [17] nearest neighbors, when a long focused search is detected; or provide relationship feedback when a *Relate* behavior is detected, instead of providing feedback of the independent touches.

CONCLUSION AND FUTURE WORK

Exploring the screen of a smartphone has become a common task for a great number of blind people. The onscreen items are linearized in a way that enables their users to quickly grasp an overview of the screen and build a good understanding of the content. Large touchscreen surfaces bring novel challenges to the exploration task. Not only is the exploration surface larger, but the interfaces built for these (e.g., interactive public displays or maps) often rely on interactions involving spatial positioning or reasoning. We examined how blind individuals interact with large touch surfaces (with a sparse number of targets) to *locate*, *relocate*, and *relate* targets, along with how well they are able to acquire a good spatial model of all screen contents in *count* tasks. Results revealed that the users employ different strategies depending on their goal but that these coping mechanisms are still ineffective. We investigated whether supporting bi-manual exploration would improve performance – which showed to be beneficial in some tasks, particularly to *relate* targets, and to provide better structure in the exploration task. Future work should build on the identified strategies and their shortcomings to develop effective exploration interfaces for blind people and large touch surfaces.

ACKNOWLEDGEMENTS

We thank Fundação Raquel e Martin Sain in Lisbon, and all the participants of the study. This work was supported by RCUK EP/G066019/1 and the Portuguese Foundation for Science and Technology, under grants UID/CEC/00408/2013, UID/CEC/50021/2013, and INCENTIVO/EEI/LA0021/2014.

REFERENCES

1. Anthony, L. et al. 2013. Analyzing user-generated youtube videos to understand touchscreen use by people with motor impairments. Proc. of CHI, ACM (2013), 1223-1232.
2. Azenkot, S., et al. 2012. Input finger detection for nonvisual touch screen text entry in *Perkinput*. Proc. of *GI '12*, ACM (2012), 121-129.
3. Bertelson, P., et al.. (1985). A study of braille reading: 2. Patterns of hand activity in one-handed and two-handed reading. The Quarterly Journal of Experimental Psychology, 37(2), 235-256.
4. Bonner, M. et al. 2010 No-Look Notes: Accessible Eyes-Free Multitouch Text-Entry. Proc. Pervasive '10, Springer (2010), 409-427.
5. Brock, A., et al. 2012. Kin'touch: understanding how visually impaired people explore tactile maps. In CHI Extended Abstracts, ACM (2012), 2471-2476.
6. Brock, A., et al. 2015. Interactivity Improves Usability of Geographic Maps for Visually Impaired People. Human–Computer Interaction, 30, 156-194.
7. Brock, A., et al. 2013. Map design for visually impaired people: past, present, and future research. Médiation et Information–Handicap et Communication, 36, 117–129.
8. Gardner, J., and Bulatov, V. 2006. Scientific Diagrams Made Easy with IVEO. Proc. of ICCHP, (2006) 1243–1250.
9. Giudice, N. et al. 2012. Learning non-visual graphical information using a touch-based vibro-audio interface. Proc. of ASSETS, ACM (2012), 103-110.
10. Goncu C., and Marriot K. 2011. Gravvitas: generic multitouch presentation of accessible graphics. Proc. of INTERACT, (2011), 30-48.
11. Guerreiro, J., Gonçalves, D. 2014. Text-to-Speeches: Evaluating the Perception of Concurrent Speech by Blind People. Proc. of ASSETS, ACM (2014),169-176.
12. Guerreiro, T. et al. 2008. A. From tapping to touching: Making touch screens accessible to blind users. IEEE Multimedia, 15, 4 (2008), 48-50.
13. Guerreiro, J., et al. 2015. TabLETS Get Physical: Non-Visual Text Entry on Tablet Devices. Proc. of CHI, ACM (2015), 39-42.
14. Hatwell, Y., et al.. (2003). Touching for knowing: cognitive psychology of haptic manual perception (Vol. 53). John Benjamins Publishing.
15. Kane, S., et al 2008. Slide rule: making mobile touch screens accessible to blind people using multi-touch interaction techniques. In Proc. of ASSETS, ACM (2008). 73-80,
16. Kane, S. K., et al.. 2011. Usable gestures for blind people: understanding preference and performance. Proc. of CHI. ACM (2011), 413-422.
17. Kane, S., et al. 2011. Access overlays: improving non-visual access to large touch screens for blind users. Proc. UIST, ACM (2011), 273-282.
18. Manshad, M., Manshad, A. 2008. Multimodal Vision Glove for Touchscreens. Proc. of ASSETS, ACM (2008), 251–252.
19. Nicolau, H., et al. 2014. B#: chord-based correction for multitouch braille input. Proc. of CHI, ACM (2014), 1705-1708.
20. Nunes, R., et al. 2015.TACTIC: An API for Touch and Tangible Interaction. Proc. of TEI, ACM (2015), 125-132.
21. Oliveira, J., et al. 2011. Blind people and mobile touch-based text-entry: acknowledging the need for different flavors. Proc. of ASSETS, ACM (2011), 179-186.
22. Parkes, D. 1988. "NOMAD":An audio-tactile tool for the acquisition, use and management of spatially distributed information by partially sighted and blind persons. Proc. of International Conference on Maps and Graphics for Visually Disabled People (1988), 24-29.
23. Sauro, J., & Dumas, J. S. 2009. Comparison of three one-question, post-task usability questionnaires. Proc. of CHI, ACM (2009), 1599-1608.
24. Southern, C. et al. 2012. An evaluation of BrailleTouch mobile touchscreen text entry for the visually impaired. Proc. of MobileHCI, ACM (2012), 317-326.
25. Thinus-Blanc, C., & Gaunet, F. (1997). Representation of space in blind persons: Vision as a spatial sense? *Psychological Bulletin*, *121*, 1 (1997), 20–42.

Knobology Revisited: A Comparison of User Performance between Tangible and Virtual Rotary Knobs

Simon Voelker[1], **Kjell Ivar Øvergård**[2], **Chat Wacharamanotham**[1], **Jan Borchers**[1]

[1] RWTH Aachen University
Aachen, Germany
{voelker, chat, borchers}@cs.rwth-aachen.de

[2] Buskerud and Vestfold University College
Tønsberg, Norway
Kjell.Oevergaard@hbv.no

ABSTRACT

We present an experimental comparison of tangible rotary knobs and touch-based virtual knobs in three output conditions: *eyes-on*, *eyes-free*, and *peripheral*. Twenty participants completed a simple rotation task on a interactive surface with four different input techniques (two tangibles and two virtual touch widgets) in the three output conditions, representing the distance from the locus of attention. We found that users were in average 20% faster using tangible knobs than using the virtual knobs. We found that tangible knobs retains performance even if they are not in the locus of attention of the users. We provide four recommendations of suitable choosing knobs based on tasks and design constraints.

Author Keywords

Tangible user interfaces; tabletop interaction; rotary widget

ACM Classification Keywords

H.5.2 Information Interfaces and Presentation: User Interfaces Input Devices and Strategies

INTRODUCTION

Rotary *tangible knobs* on multi-touch surfaces have be proposed for video navigation [3, 5, 13], menu selection [3], and interactive data exploration tasks [4, 7]. In comparison to touch-based *virtual knobs*, they provide haptic feedback that guides the user input. However, one drawback of tangibles is that they are not as dynamic as virtual controls, they cannot be created, modified, or removed as easily as *virtual controls* [11]. Also, tangibles need to be constructed and maintained. Because of these trade-offs, designers have to choose between using tangible knobs or virtual knobs. To make this decision, they need to better understand if, how, and in which scenarios the physicality of tangibles knobs improves the users' performance.

The literature does not provide a clear answer to these questions. The results of a study of SLAP Widgets favor tangible knobs [13], but the results from a study of CapWidgets suggest the opposite [5]. Although the tasks in both studies are similar (using the rotary knobs to navigate a video and mark outstanding frames) several other possible factors differ: SLAP Widgets were placed out of the users' sight (eyes-free input), CapWidgets were placed on top of the video (eyes-on input). They used different knob diameters (5 cm vs. 2 cm, respectively), and different tracking technologies (FTIR + DI vs. capacitive). Because of these different factors, it is difficult to identify why these two studies are contradicting each other.

ITS 2015, November 15–18, 2015, Funchal/Madeira, Portugal.

ACM 978-1-4503-3899-8/15/11 ...$15.00.
DOI: http://dx.doi.org/10.1145/2817721.2817725

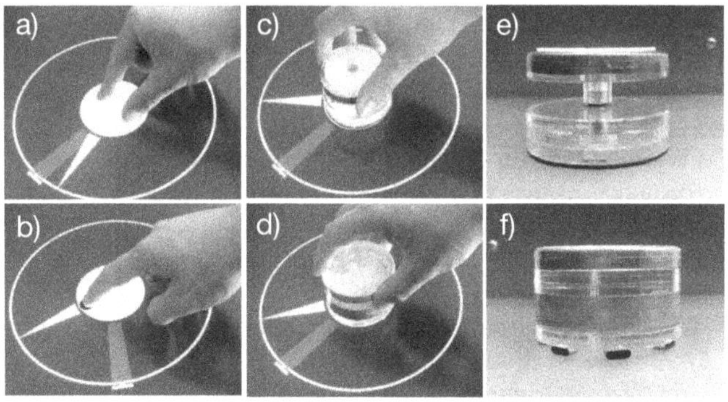

Figure 1. Four types of rotary widgets compared: (a) one- and (b) two-touch virtual knobs, (c,e) a tangible knob, of which rotor is independent of the base, and (d,f) a tangible puck: the entire widget is a rotor

We hypothesize that the main factor of these contradicting results was the difference of eyes-free vs eyes-on input. In an eyes-free task, the tangible knob provides haptic feedback that guides the users input. However, in an eyes-on task the tangible is blocking parts of the interface which makes it complicated for the user to see the target area. To verify this hypothesis we present the results of an experiment in which we compared two tangible knobs with two virtual knobs in terms of speed and accuracy in eyes-on and eyes-free tasks. To ensure that we only test these two factors we kept all other factors the same.

RELATED WORK

To use a virtual touch widget or a tangible widget, the user first *acquires* the widget with their hands and then *manipulates* the widget to a desired state [2, 11]. Fitzmaurice and Buxton [2] showed that space multiplexed input devices (e.g., tangibles) outperform time multiplexed input devices (e.g., a mouse) in acquisition task involving multiple objects. Tuddenham et al. [11] conducted a very similar experiment, but also included multi-touch as one condition. The results of their study showed that users are also more accurate using tangibles than using multi-touch in acquisition tasks. In these acquisition studies, the users need to constantly switch between multiple input widgets. Thus, the superiority of tangibles may not hold in tasks that focuses on manipulation, which requires more focused movements on single input widget.

As for manipulation phase, tangible sliders were found to be faster than virtual sliders [4, 11], although no notable difference in average tracking error as found [4]. Based on these findings, tangible sliders are preferable to virtual sliders. However, it is uncertain that these findings for sliders are are generalizable to knobs because muscle movements involved are more complex in knobs than in sliders [12]. A study by Tory and Kincaid [10] suggested that tangible knobs outperform virtual knobs. However, in their study both tangibles and output were collocated. To understand user performance in the rotary manipulation, we conduct an experiment to compare tangible knobs vs. virtual knobs.

THE EXPERIMENT

We have two main independent variables: *widget* type and *output* area. All widgets are 7 cm in diameter. All input was done on a horizontal touch screen. We compared four types of rotary widgets (Figure 1):

> *One-touch virtual knob* (a). Similar to an analog telephone dial, this knob can be rotated by dragging a small circle inside the knob to a desired angle.
>
> *Two-touch virtual knob* (b). This is similar to pinch-to-rotate gesture in touch screen phones. To rotate this knob, the user touches two finger inside the knob area. The orientation of the line connecting the two finger determines the knob orientation.
>
> *Tangible knob* (c, e) based on the SLAP knob design [13]. The rotor is attached to the base of the knob by a spindle. This allows rotational input without translating the base of the knob.
>
> *Tangible puck* (d, f) based on a design in from Photohelix [3]. This puck is a single rigid body. To rotate, the users manipulates the entire tangible, resulting in a coupling between translation and rotation.

For all four widget types, the user had to start each trial inside the output area. However, while turning touch knobs the users were able to drag outside of the input area, just like typical touch screen widgets.

We compared three output areas, representing the distance of the tangible from the locus of attention:

> *Eyes-on:* Visual feedback was displayed around the knob, providing single locus of attention. Nevertheless, the hand of the user may occlude the display during rotation.
>
> *Eyes-free:* Visual feedback was shown on a separate vertical display in front of the user, hence, no hand occlusion. However, the user cannot see the widget while looking at the visual output.
>
> *Peripheral:* In this condition, the output was display on the horizontal screen with 20 cm offset in front of the user. Although the widgets are outside of the locus of attention, they are still in the peripheral vision.

The size of the visual feedback was 7 cm diameter in all output conditions.

APPARATUS

During the experiment participants stand in front of a horizontal 55″ Microsoft capacitive touch display. The table surface is 90 cm high from the floor. The effective touch frame rate of our setup was 60 Hz.

A 46″ vertical display was placed directly behind the horizontal surface. Both displays had the resolution 1920 x 1080 pixels and were connected to a Mac Pro running the software for the experiments.

TASK

The experiment setup is shown in the Video Figure. We used the task from previous knobology study [8].

In each condition, the system display a gray circle (input area) and white ring with a blue target area and a white orientation indicator (visual output).

The widgets were already placed on the input area prior to each trial. Before each trial, the user turns the widget such that the white orientation indicator was inside a starting area, which is always at the 12:00 position ($= 0°$). After keeping the indicator one second inside the starting area, a blue static target area was displayed. The participants were asked to turn the knob until the indicator was inside the target area. The target area was randomly displayed at one of six predefined target areas, which are roughly equally-spaced around the knob, ($-150°$, $-100°$, $-50°$, $50°$, $100°$, and $150°$ from the starting area. To complete the trial, the used had to keep the indicator one second inside the target area.

DEPENDENT VARIABLES

We measured *movement time*, measured from when the indicator left the starting area until the trial was completed. For data analysis, we deducted the second that the users needed to wait inside the target area to complete the trial. For the accuracy, we count the *number of overshoots*, when the cursor exits the target area.

STUDY DESIGN

A $4 \times 3 \times 6 \times 5$ (input type $\times$ output area $\times$ target area $\times$ iteration) repeated measures experiment was used. All factors where within-subject independent factors, leading to a total of 360 trials per participants (on average, 30 minutes per participant). The experiment was divided into four blocks, one for each knob. All iterations in one block where done with the same knob. The order of blocks (hence also input devices) where determined by a Latin square that ensured counterbalancing.

The hypotheses tested in our experiment was as follows:

- H1: We expect that both tangibles will have faster movement times than the two virtual knobs.

Condition	Movement time	Number of overshoots
One-touch	1.47 [1.39, 1.54]	1.06 [0.91, 1.22]
Two-touch	1.83 [1.78, 1.88]	0.58 [0.49, 0.67]
Tangible Knob	1.21 [1.15, 1.28]	0.60 [0.50, 0.69]
Tangible Puck	1.14 [1.10, 1.18]	0.43 [0.37, 0.49]
Eyes-on	1.40 [1.32, 1.48]	0.66 [0.57, 0.75]
Peripheral	1.38 [1.31, 1.45]	0.67 [0.56, 0.78]
Eyes-free	1.45 [1.37, 1.53]	0.67 [0.55, 0.78]

Figure 2. Overall descriptive statistics by condition (mean [95% CI]

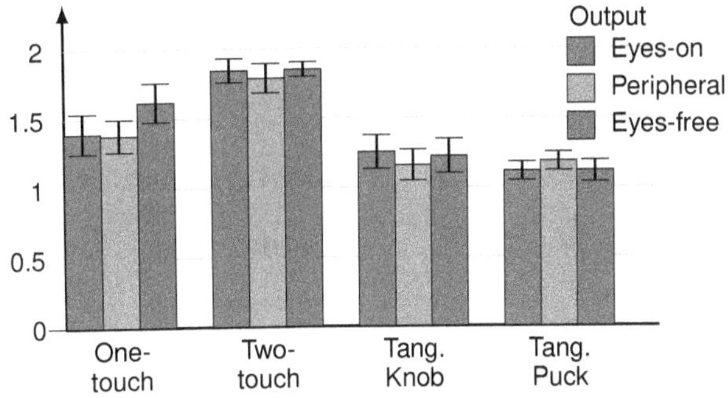

Figure 3. Movement time (mean and 95% CI)

- H2: The domination of tangible knobs will be particularly pronounced for the eyes-free condition.
- H3: We expect tangible knobs to have less errors associated with use (e.g. less overshooting) than virtual knobs.

PARTICIPANTS

20 participants (18 males; 2 females) aged 20 to 36 years ($M = 27$) volunteered for the study. All participants had normal or corrected-to-normal vision. 17 out of 20 participants were right-handed.

RESULTS

Results on iterations and different goal areas were aggregated into mean scores for movement and overshooting. For each multivariate test, we used 4 x 3 (widget × output) GLM repeated measures analysis [1]. Upon significant effects, post-hoc Bonferroni-corrected paired t-tests were performed (Familywise error rate $\alpha = .05$). Figure 2–4 show descriptive statistics with 95% CIs (unadjusted) Below, the CIs of mean differences were adjusted for paired design and Bonferroni-corrected. We provide extensive statistical results in the supplement.

Movement Time

We found a very large main effect of widget on movement time ($F_{1.68,31.91} = 43.81$, $p < .001$, $\eta_p^2 = .70$). As shown in Figure 2, the two-touch widget was slower than the one-touch widget ($M_{\text{two-one}} = 0.36$ s, $CI[0.22, 0.50]$). One-touch widget was again slower than puck and knob ($M_{\text{one-puck}} = 0.33$ s, $[0.07, 0.59]$; $M_{\text{one-knob}} = 0.26$ s, $[0.02, 0.49]$). The difference between the tangibles was negligible ($M_{\text{knob-puck}} = 0.07$ s, $[-0.06, 0.21]$).

[1]When Mauchly's sphericity test was significant, the Greenhouse-Geisser correction was used, resulting degrees of freedom with decimal points.

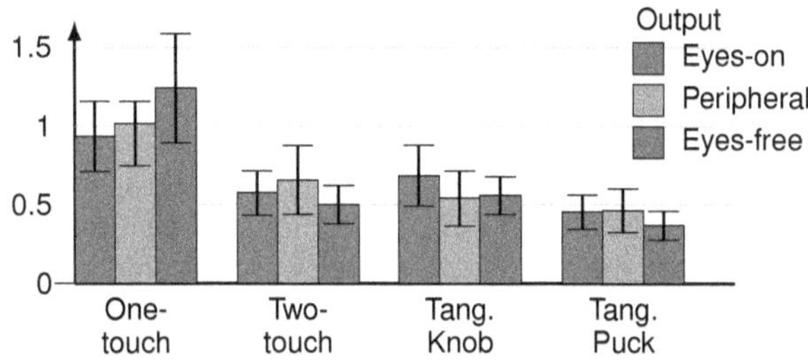

Figure 4. Number of overshoots (mean and 95% CI)

A large main effect of the output was also observed on movement time ($F_{1.18,22.50} = 6.26$, $p = .016$, $\eta_p^2 = .25$). The movements in the peripheral condition was faster than in the eyes-free condition ($M_{\text{free-perip.}} = 0.07$ s, $[0.05, 010]$). Other differences were negligible ($M_{\text{free-on}} = 0.05$, $[-0.01, 0.11]$), $M_{\text{on-perip.}} = 0.02$, $[-0.05, 0.10]$)).

A large interaction effect between widget and output was also evident ($F_{2.78,52.86} = 9.05$, $p < .001$, $\eta_p^2 = .32$). Figure 3 shows the overview of the interaction effect. In the eyes-free condition (H2), the simple effect of the widgets agreed with the main effect analysis above. In the eyes-on condition, we found that the tangible puck yielded faster movement time than one-touch widget ($M_{\text{one-puck}} = 0.29$ s, $[0.26, 0.54]$) (cf. [5]). In the one-touch widget, eyes-free output was slower than others ($M_{\text{free-on}} = 0.22$ s, $[0.10, 0.34]$, $M_{\text{free-perip.}} = 0.24$ s, $[0.20, 0.28]$).

Number of overshoots

There was a very large main effect of input devices ($F_{1.68,30.78} = 24.17$, $p < .001$, $\eta_p^2 = .560$). The one-finger widget was significantly more error prone than the others ($M_{\text{one-two}} = 0.49$ s, $[0.20, 0.77]$; $M_{\text{one-knob}} = 0.47$ s, $[0.22, 0.47]$; $M_{\text{one-puck}} = 0.64$ s, $[0.30, 0.97]$) However, the two-finger widget was comparable to both tangibles ($M_{\text{two-knob}} = -0.02$ s, $[-0.18, 0.14]$; $M_{\text{two-puck}} = 0.15$ s, $[-0.00, 0.30]$). The tangible knob was slightly more error-prone than the tangible puck ($M_{\text{knob-puck}} = 0.17$ s, $[0.02, 0.31]$).

No statistical or practical main effect of the location of information was found ($F_{2,38} = 0.22$, $p = .979$, $\eta_p^2 = .001$) and the mean number of overshooting was almost identical for all three output areas.

We found a large interaction effect between widget and output $F_{2.84,54,02} = 4.30$, $p = .01$, $\eta_p^2 = .18$). Figure 4 shows an overview of the interaction effect. When focusing on the eyes-free condition, however, the two-touch widget yielded more overshoots than the tangible puck ($M_{\text{two-puck}} = 0.13$ s, $[0.05, 0.21]$).

DISCUSSION

The results indicated that the tangibles (knob and puck) outperformed both touch widgets (one-touch and two-touch). Specifically, tangibles were faster across the board (supporting H1). For overshooting, the tangibles yielded fewer overshoots than the one-touch widget, but were comparable to the two-touch widget (partially supporting H3).

In the eyes-free condition, the performance of one-touch widget degraded more than others. The two-touch widget retained its performance in in the eyes-free condition. We surmise that the additional friction of the second finger slowed down the input, allowing users to better control the virtual knob. The accuracy of two-touch widget rivaled the tangible knob, but the two-touch widget was still worse than the tangible puck. Both tangibles were superior than touch widgets in terms of the movement time (supporting H2). The tangible knob performed slightly worse than then tangible puck, probably because of the friction from the rotary mechanics inside the tangible knob. This can be improved by a better manufacturing process.

The peripheral condition was faster than the eyes-free condition. We speculate that the awareness of hand movement allow the users to be more confident when manipulating the widgets. Since the speed were comparable between the peripheral and the eyes-on condition, we speculate that occlusion does not influence users' confidence in the rotation movements. For one-touch widget, both speed and accuracy were improved by placing the widget in peripheral vision instead of using it eyes-free.

Our results further support previous research: tangible controls are faster and less error-prone than touch-based controls [6, 9, 11, 13]. However, our data is contrary to the findings of Kratz et al. [5] as the tangible puck outperforms the one-touch widget in both movement time and overshoots. Of practical interest is the finding that differences between tangibles and touch-based interaction techniques are influenced by the locus of attention. This is especially interesting for evaluating the suitability for use of touch-interfaces in operative contexts where the human operator's visual attention must be directed towards an outside world, away from the controller [1].

CONCLUSION AND DESIGN IMPLICATIONS

In this paper, we present an experiment comparing tangible rotary knobs with virtual rotary knobs in eyes-on and eyes-free tasks. We found that tangible knobs are on average 20% faster then virtual knobs. In contrast to virtual knobs, tangibles did not perform significantly worse in eyes-free tasks compared to eyes-on tasks. The users were slower with the two-finger knob than with the one-finger knob, but they were more accurate using the two-finger knob.

Therefore, we draw the following design implications: (1) For the best performance in rotation tasks, we recommend using tangible puck over tangible knob and over virtual touch widgets. (2) If it is not possible to use tangibles, use two-touch widget for the tasks that require accuracy, and one-touch widget for the tasks that requires speed. (3) Design the user interface such that rotary widgets stays in peripheral vision of the users to increase manipulation confidence. (4) In eyes-free task, avoid using one-touch widget. We hope that these design implications help designer to make an informed decision if the should use tangible or virtual knobs for which kind of task and applications.

ACKNOWLEDGMENTS

This work was funded in part by the German B-IT Foundation and by the Norwegian Research Council through the MACS project (project number 217788).

REFERENCES

1. Bjelland, H. V., Hoff, Thomas Øvergård, K. I., and Bjørkli, C. A Case Study of a Touch-based Interface for In-car Audio Systems. *Design Journal 10*, 1 (2007), 24–34.
2. Fitzmaurice, G. W., and Buxton, W. An Empirical Evaluation of Graspable User Interfaces: Towards Specialized, Space-multiplexed Input. In *Proc. CHI '97*, ACM, 43–50.
3. Hilliges, O., Baur, D., and Butz, A. Photohelix: Browsing, Sorting and Sharing Digital Photo Collections. In *Proc. Tabletop 2007*, IEEE, 87–94.
4. Jansen, Y., Dragicevic, P., and Fekete, J.-D. Tangible Remote Controllers for Wall-Size Displays. In *Proc. CHI '12*, ACM, 2865–2874.
5. Kratz, S., Westermann, T., Rohs, M., and Essl, G. CapWidgets: Tangible Widgets versus Multi-touch Controls on Mobile Devices. In *Proc. CHI EA '11*, ACM, 1351–1356.
6. Lucchi, A., Jermann, P., Zufferey, G., and Dillenbourg, P. An Empirical Evaluation of Touch and Tangible Interfaces for Tabletop Displays. In *Proc. TEI '10*, ACM, 177–184.
7. Ma, J., Sindorf, L., Liao, I., and Frazier, J. Using a Tangible Versus a Multi-touch Graphical User Interface to Support Data Exploration at a Museum Exhibit. In *Proc. TEI '15*, ACM ,33–40.
8. Øvergård, K. I., Fostervold, K. I., Bjelland, H. V., and Hoff, T. Knobology in use: an experimental evaluation of ergonomics recommendations. *Ergonomics 50*, 5, Taylor & Francis, 694–705.
9. Terrenghi, L., Kirk, D., Sellen, A., and Izadi, S. Affordances for Manipulation of Physical Versus Digital Media on Interactive Surfaces. In *Proc. CHI '07*, ACM, 1157–1166.
10. Tory, M., and Kincaid, R. Comparing Physical, Overlay, and Touch Screen Parameter Controls. In *Proc. ITS '13*, ACM, 91–100.
11. Tuddenham, P., Kirk, D., and Izadi, S. Graspables Revisited: Multi-touch vs. Tangible Input for Tabletop Displays in Acquisition and Manipulation Tasks. In *Proc. CHI '10*, ACM, 2223–2232.
12. van der Vaart, A. *Arm movements in operating rotary controls*. PhD thesis, TU Delft, Delft University of Technology, 1995.
13. Weiss, M., Wagner, J., Jansen, Y., Jennings, R., Khoshabeh, R., Hollan, J. D., and Borchers, J. SLAP Widgets: Bridging the Gap Between Virtual and Physical Controls on Tabletops. In *Proc. CHI '09*, ACM, 481–490.

3D Tabletop User Interface with High Synchronization Accuracy using a High-speed Stereo Camera

Takumi Kusano
Saitama University
Saitama, Japan
kusano@is.ics.saitama-u.ac.jp

Takashi Komuro
Saitama University
Saitama, Japan
komuro@mail.saitama-u.ac.jp

ABSTRACT

In this paper, we try to compare standard and low latency mid-air 3D interactions in a tabletop user interface. For this purpose, we developed a 3D tabletop user interface that allows direct manipulation of 3D virtual objects presented on an autostereoscopic display. The system uses a high-speed stereo camera to synchronize real hands and virtual objects, both temporally and spatially, with a high degree of accuracy. In the developed system, we realized a processing speed resulting in a frame rate of 200 fps and a latency of 28.33 ms. We conducted a user study for evaluating the usability and sense of reality and the results showed that there was a significant difference in the time required to complete an object moving operation between the 200 fps and 30 fps cases.

Author Keywords

Tabletop UI; 3D interaction; direct manipulation; latency.

ACM Classification Keywords

H.5.2 [User Interfaces]: Graphical user interfaces, Interaction styles; I.3.7 [Three-Dimensional Graphics and Realism]: Virtual reality.

INTRODUCTION

In conventional touch panel interfaces, user operations and image presentation are restricted to a two-dimensional plane. Therefore, these interfaces suffer from the problems that the operational degree of freedom is low and that users lack a feeling of manipulating objects with a sense of reality. To overcome these problems, some studies have been conducted on user interfaces that allow users to manipulate 3D objects on a surface directly by hand.

Tangible user interfaces allow intuitive and various operations by making it possible to manipulate 3D real objects directly [5,7]. However, they lack versatility because they use physical objects, which require application-specific system design. On the other hand, studies on 3D tabletop interface systems that allow users to directly manipulate virtual 3D objects on a surface, which are presented by a head-mounted display [3], a 3D display [1,4] or a 3D projector [2], have been conducted. In these systems, high degree of freedom operations such as grasping and lifting virtual objects are possible.

However, most of these systems use a standard camera or a depth camera for hand detection and its low frame rate restricts the responsivity of the system. [1] uses 125 Hz tracker devices, but they did not conduct a comparative user study. It is reported that in direct touch input, latency as low as 5-10 ms can be perceived [6]. The study was conducted on 2D touch panel operation, but it would be important to reduce latency also in mid-air 3D operation. An interface system that uses a high-speed camera to recognize rapid motion of a hand [8], but it was not focused on latency.

With the background above, we developed a 3D tabletop user interface system that uses a high-speed stereo camera to synchronize real hands and virtual objects, both temporally and spatially, with a high degree of accuracy. The system allows users to perform a variety of operations (e.g., pushing, rotating, and lifting) by using 3D coordinates of hand edges calculated from stereo camera images.

The main contribution of this paper is that it is the first one that systematically tried to compare standard and low latency mid-air 3D interactions. From the results of a user study, we found that the operability of the system was significantly improved in low latency interaction.

SYSTEM

Hardware

The system we propose is a tabletop system that consists of an upwardly-oriented multi-view autostereoscopic display and a high-speed stereo camera installed above the display. An overview of the system is shown in Fig. 1.

The autostereoscopic display is used for presenting 3D images to users without them having to wear special glasses. It presents 3D images according to a fixed viewing point of a user in front of the system. The refresh rate of the display is 60 fps. The high-speed stereo camera is used for obtaining 3D positions of the user's hand. To reduce

ITS '15, November 15 - 18, 2015, Funchal, Portugal

ACM 978-1-4503-3899-8/15/11...$15.00
DOI: http://dx.doi.org/10.1145/2817721.2817724

camera latency, we used cameras having a frame rate of 200 fps (Grasshopper from Point Grey Research Inc.).

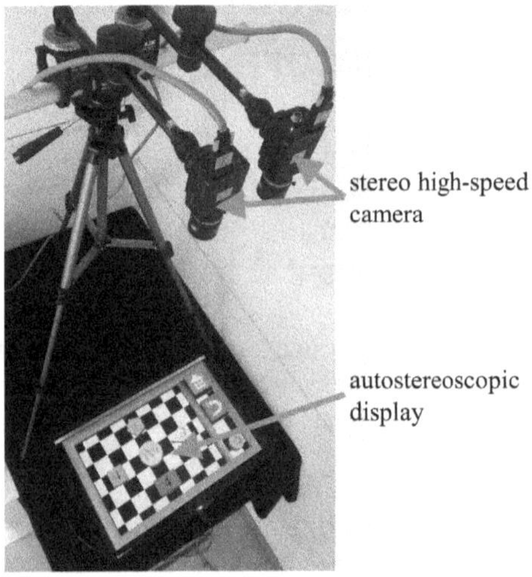

Figure 1. System configuration.

Calculating Hand Positions

For the calibration of the cameras, the system draws four markers on the display and obtains their positions in the camera image. Then the system finds the projection matrix P for each camera by solving the Perspective 4 Point (P4P) problem. By using the points on the display for calibration, 3D measurement becomes most accurate near the display, where users perform operations most often.

The system calculates 3D hand positions by an edge-based block matching method. First, the system finds all pixel points on hand edges from a left camera image. Next, the system finds the corresponding pixel points from a right camera image by the block matching method. Finally, the system calculates 3D coordinates of the hand edge points using the projection matrices for the left and right cameras.

To reduce the computational cost of hand recognition, regions of interest (ROIs) are set for the left and right cameras, and image processing is performed only in these ROIs. If a hand collides with a virtual object in 3D space, the hand and the object overlap in both the left and right camera images. Therefore, it is sufficient to set the ROIs around all virtual objects in the images. Figure 4 shows the left camera image and the processed image in the ROIs. By implementing this algorithm, we realized a processing speed giving a frame rate of 200 fps.

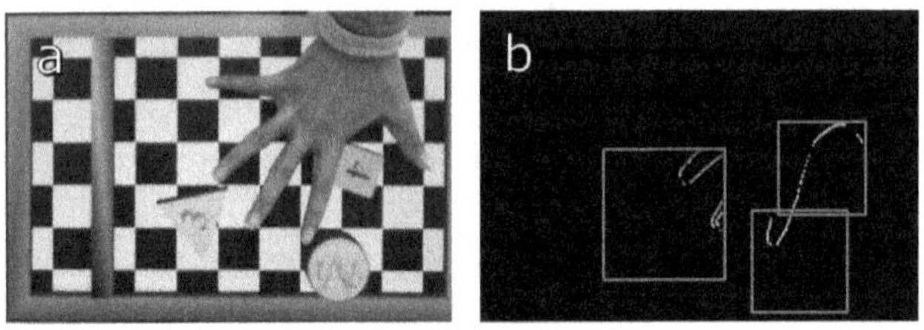

Figure 2. Image processing in ROIs. a: left camera image, b: depth map.

Since the processing time is almost proportional to the total area of ROIs, when the number of virtual objects or the sizes of virtual objects increase, the processing time may exceed the frame time (the inverse of the frame rate). In such a case, the effective frame rate decreases.

Manipulating Objects

In our system, collision detection is performed by assuming the shapes of virtual objects to be right prisms (triangular prisms, quadrangular prisms, pentagonal prisms, ...). With this assumption, we can use a single collision detection algorithm for a variety of objects. An object whose shape is not a right prism is approximated by a right prism. Collision between a hand and a virtual object is detected by checking if the 3D points of the hand edges are inside the object.

Various types of manipulation of virtual objects are realized by using the results of collision detection. In our system, different algorithms are applied for the case where an object is touched from one direction and for the case where it is touched from at least two opposing directions.

When an object is touched from one direction, the system moves and rotates the object according to the touched position and the penetration depth of the finger. Figure 3a shows the case where an object is pushed from the side, and Fig. 3b shows the case where a button object is pushed from above.

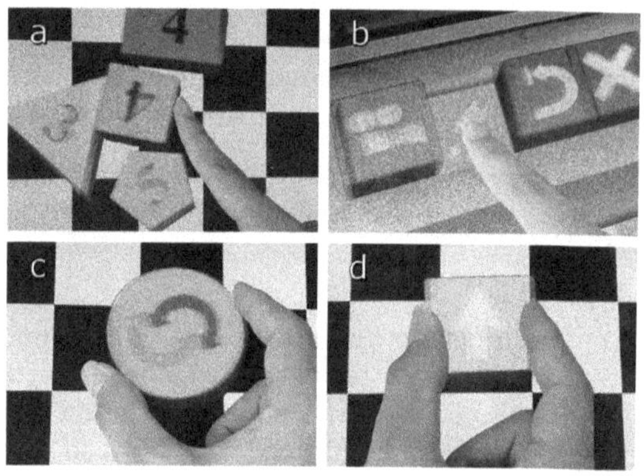

Figure 3. Various types of object manipulation. a: pushing an object from the side, b: pushing a button from above, c: turning a knob, d: lifting an object.

When an object is touched from at least two opposing directions, the object is regarded as being grasped. While an object is being grasped, the system moves and rotates the object using changes in the touched positions, as well as the penetration depths of the fingers.

Figure 3c shows the case where a knob object is turned with two fingers. The system rotates the object according to the moving directions of the touched positions. Figure 3d shows the case where an object is lifted. When an object is moved in the grasped state, the result of collision detection becomes unstable. Therefore we divide the grasped state into two states. If two fingers are inside the enlarged region of the object, the object is regarded as being grasped.

However, if one of the fingers is outside the object region, the object does not move. The object is movable only when both fingers are inside the object region.

EVALUATION

Latency and Positional Deviation

We measured the latency of the system and compared it with a system operating at a low frame rate of 30 fps. First, we took a video of a finger pushing an object from the side by using another camera at a frame rate of 200 fps. Then, we counted the number of frames from the frame in which the finger collided with the object to the frame in which the object started moving. This was repeated 15 times for each frame rate, and the mean value was regarded as the latency.

The results of latency measurements at 30 fps and 200 fps are summarized in Table I. The difference in latency between the two conditions was significant (p<<0.001). The positional deviation between the finger and the virtual object was reduced as shown in Fig. 4. This indicates that the reduction in latency improved not only the temporal synchronization accuracy between the hand and the virtual object, but also the spatial synchronization accuracy.

TABLE I. Measured latencies

	delay frames	latency [ms]
30 fps	9.800	49.00
200 fps	5.667	28.33

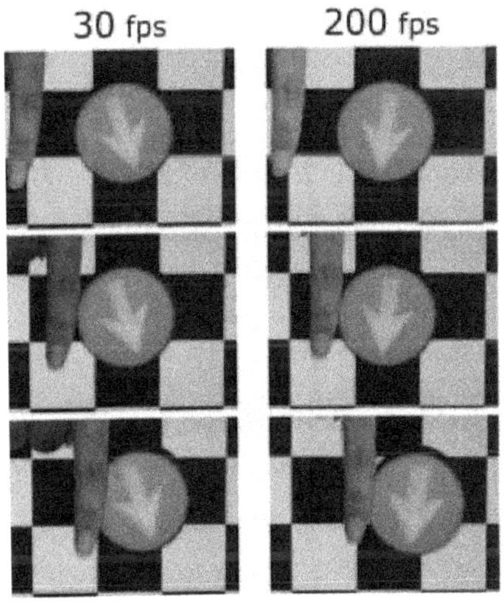

Figure 4. The positional gap between finger and virtual object.

User Study

We conducted an experiment to explore how the system's frame rate affects the usability and sense of reality in manipulating virtual objects. We recruited 25 participants (20 males and 5 females) from ages 18 to 27, and asked them to perform two tasks using our system. One task was to move a virtual object placed on the center of the screen to a designated position by pushing it from the side (Task 1). Figure 5a shows a photograph of this task. The participant was asked to move the object to inside a circle displayed on the screen. When the object reached the inside of the circle, the object returned to the center of the screen and the circle appeared in another position. The participant repeated this operation for eight different circle positions to complete one set. The participant was asked to repeat this set for three different circle sizes.

The other task was to push indicated button objects from above (Task 2). Figure 5b shows a photograph of this task. Three buttons were displayed on the screen, and the participant was asked to push one or more buttons indicated by arrows on the screen. When the correct buttons were pushed, the next indication appeared. The participant repeated this operation for ten different combinations of buttons to complete one set. The participant was asked to repeat this set three times.

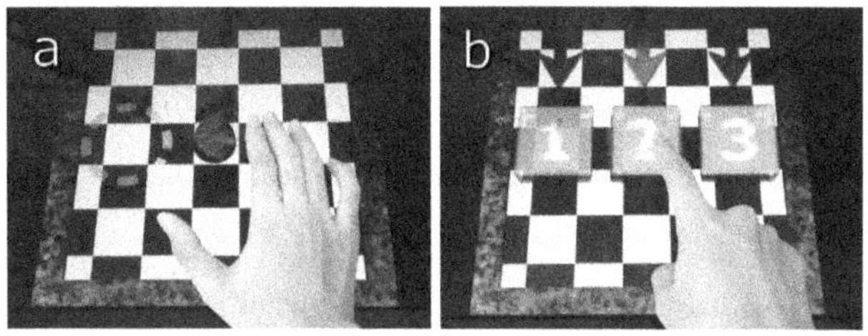

Figure 5. Tasks in evaluation experiment. a: Task 1, b: Task 2.

The participants performed Task 1 with frame rates of 200 fps and 30 fps in a randomized order for each participant, and then performed Task 2 also with these frame rates in a randomized order. The participants were given one-minute practice time before the measurements for each condition. The time from starting each task to finishing the task was measured and recorded.

After finishing each task, the participants were asked to answer the following questions.

- How much did you feel like you were manipulating a real object? (reality)
- How comfortably were you able to perform the operation? (comfort)
- How much did you enjoy the operation? (enjoyment)

Figure 6 shows the results of task completion times. For Task 1, the execution times for all target sizes were summed up for each participant. For Task 2, the execution times for three sets of trials were summed up for each participant.

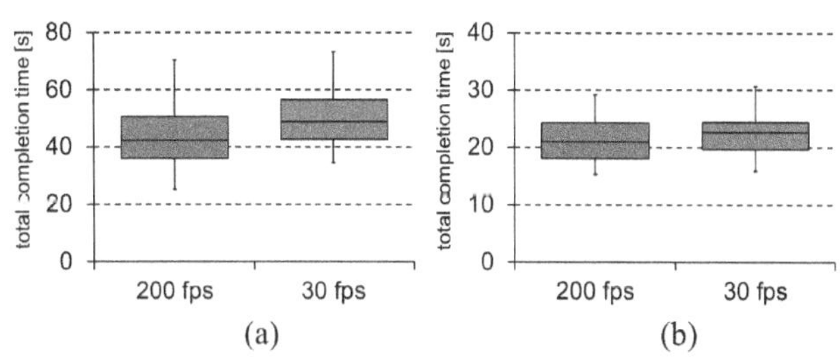

Figure 6. Task completion times. a: Task 1, b: Task 2

The results of a paired t-test showed that a significant difference was seen for Task 1 ($p<0.05$), and no significant difference was seen for Task 2, between the two frame rates. The mean scores of the questions on reality, comfort, and enjoyment for both tasks are shown in Fig. 7. The average scores at 200 fps were slightly higher for any item or either task than those at 30 fps, but the results of the paired t-test showed that there were no significant differences for any item or either task.

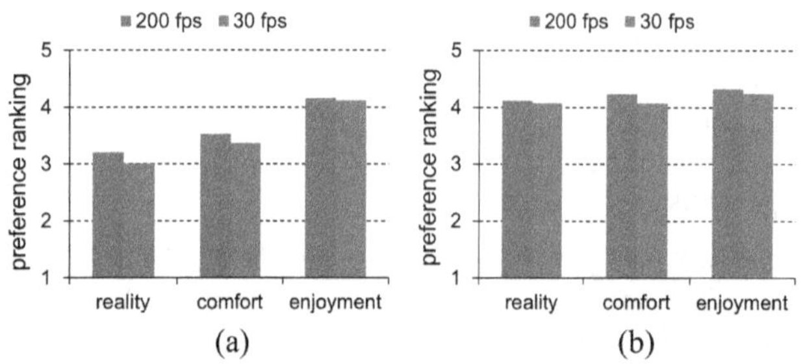

Figure 7. The results of the questionnaire. a: Task 1, b: Task 2

The reason for the significant difference in the completion time of Task 1 may be that collision detection was performed more frequently when the frame rate was set to 200 fps, and objects moved more smoothly, just as users intended, which reduced the errors in operation. For the button pushing task (Task 2), the operation was easy, and the participants just had to put their fingers on the indicated buttons. That may be why there was no difference in completion time.

The result of the questionnaire showed that there were no significant differences for any item or either task. Before this experiment, we had conducted a preliminary experiment with participants who were familiar with our system, and all participants answered that they felt a greater sense of reality in the operation at 200 fps than that at 30 fps. In the final experiment, the participants did not yet have any experience with the system and were not accustomed to the operation. In addition, we asked the participants to complete the tasks as quickly as possible, and so the participants did not notice any difference in the sense of reality. If the participants were given more training time, perhaps they would get accustomed to the operation and would notice a difference in the sense of reality.

APPLICATIONS

The proposed system can be used in many application fields such as designing, dynamic simulation, education, and amusement. We implemented some application examples to our system. In *Room Planner*, a user can design the layout of a room (Fig. 8a). In *Electronic Circuit Simulator*, a user can simulate an electronic circuit (Fig. 8b). *Magic Square* is an educational application for studying positive and negative numbers (Fig. 8c). *3D Space Seeker* is a 3D shooting game, in which a user can move a player character in 3D space (Fig. 8d).

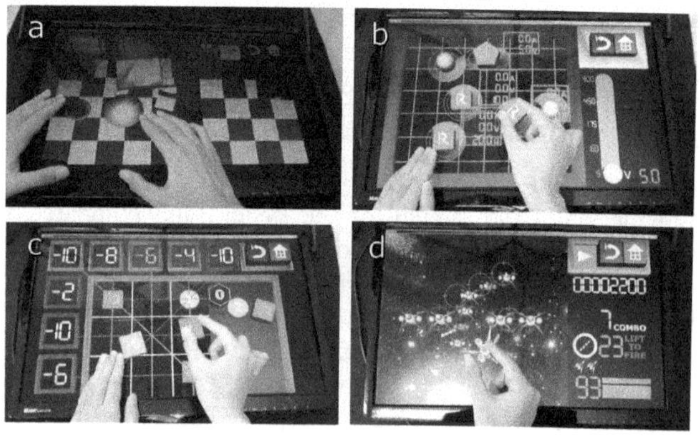

Figure 8. Application examples.

CONCLUSION

In this study, we proposed a tabletop user interface system in which users can manipulate 3D virtual objects. The system latency was significantly reduced by using a high-speed stereo camera and implementing a fast algorithm. The results of a user study showed that there was a significant difference in the time required to complete an object moving operation between the 200 fps and 30 fps cases.

Future work will include avoidance of hand occlusion, supporting multiple users for collaborative work, and considerations necessary for the practical use of the system.

REFERENCES

1. B. De Araùjo et al. 2012. Mockup builder: direct 3D modeling on and above the surface in a continuous interaction space, In *Proc.* GI '12, 173-180.
2. H. Benko et al. 2012. MirageTable: freehand interaction on a projected augmented reality tabletop. In *Proc.* CHI '12, pp. 199-208.
3. V. Buchmann et al. 2004. FingARtips - gesture based direct manipulation in augmented reality. In *Proc.* GRAPHITE '04, pp. 212-221.
4. O. Hilliges et al. 2009. Interactions in the air: adding further depth to interactive tabletops, In *Proc.* UIST '09, 139-148.
5. H. Ishii and B. Ullmer. 1997. Tangible bits: towards seamless interfaces, between people, bit and atoms, In *Proc.* CHI '97, pp. 234-241.
6. A. Ng et al. 2012. Designing for low-latency direct-touch input, In *Proc.* UIST '12, 453-464.
7. J. Patten et al. 2001. Sensetable: a wireless object tracking platform for tangible user interfaces. In *Proc.* CHI '01, 253-260.
8. T. Sato et al. 2006. OHAJIKI interface: flicking gesture recognition with a high-speed camera, In *Proc.* ICEC '06, 205-210.

Quantifying the Targeting Performance Benefit of Electrostatic Haptic Feedback on Touchscreens

Yang Zhang **Chris Harrison**
Carnegie Mellon University, Human-Computer Interaction Institute
5000 Forbes Avenue, Pittsburgh, PA 15213
{yang.zhang, chris.harrison}@cs.cmu.edu

ABSTRACT
Touchscreens with dynamic electrostatic friction are a compelling, low-latency and solid-state haptic feedback technology. Work to date has focused on minimum perceptual difference, texture rendering, and fingertip-surface models. However, no work to date has quantified how electrostatic feedback can be used to improve user performance, in particular targeting, where virtual objects rendered on touchscreens can offer tactile feedback. Our results show that electrostatic haptic feedback can improve targeting speed by 7.5% compared to conventional flat touchscreens.

Author Keywords
Electro-vibration; Friction; Haptic; Touch; Targeting.

ACM Classification Keywords
H.5.2. [User Interfaces]: Input devices and strategies.

INTRODUCTION
Owning to their intuitive direct manipulation interactions and general interface flexibility, touchscreens have become pervasive. However, their flat surfaces offer no programmable haptic feedback. Of course, touch is one of our most fundamental senses and plays a crucial role in our interactions with the physical world [22]. As a consequence, there is a significant literature on haptic feedback technologies and their performance impact on interactive experiences.

One such haptic technology is electrostatic feedback, first discovered in 1954 by Mallinckrodt [13] (then described as "electro-vibration"). Put simply, by oscillating an electric charge behind a thin insulator, a capacitive object (e.g., a fleshy finger) can be attracted to the surface, though only at very close distances. By controlling the oscillations, one can control the friction between a finger and the surface (see [2] for an extended discussion). More recently, electrostatic has been adapted for use on touchscreens. These initial efforts have chiefly explored the technology for interactive, assistive, and entertainment purposes [2,9,19,21].

ITS '15, November 15-18, 2015, Funchal, Portugal
© 2015 ACM. ISBN 978-1-4503-3899-8/15/11...$15.00
DOI: http://dx.doi.org/10.1145/2817721.2817730

In this work, for the first time, we quantitatively evaluate how electrostatic force feedback can be used to enhance targeting performance on touchscreens. This directly complements prior experimental work that has studied other haptic feedback means (see e.g., [3,4,12,16,18]). More specifically, we evaluated a series of haptic approaches in a head-to-head experiment. In addition to electrostatic feedback, we also tested designs with *actual* physical features, which serve as a gold standard. As a baseline control, we also included a plain (i.e., flat) touchscreen condition. Our main hypothesis was that electrostatic feedback would yield performance somewhere between no feedback and true physical feedback. The question was: where did electrostatic feedback lie within this spectrum?

RELATED WORK
Haptic Feedback on Touchscreens
Haptic feedback has been shown to make interactive experience more efficient and enjoyable [6,10]. The most common technique for providing haptic feedback is to use mechanical moving parts (i.e. vibration motor, piezo buzzer or solenoid). For example, many smartphones and Apple's "Force Touch" trackpads pulse or vibrate for certain events (e.g., key pressed). Lee et al. [11] created a pen instrumented with a solenoid that could, among many behaviors, simulate clicking, although the pen tip in actuality did not deform. Haptic pens of this nature have been evaluated in Fitts-style experiments previously (see e.g., [4,18]).

Another option is to overlay *physical* features onto a touchscreen, as seen in e.g., Touchplates [8] and SLAP Widgets [20]. However, this precludes dynamic button layouts and prevents the full screen space from being utilized. Thus research has also looked at transient physical elements, driven by pneumatics or hydraulics [6]. Harrison and Hudson evaluated such a "shape changing" display for targeting in an attention-saturated task [6]. There are also efforts to create texture "pixels" using micro-motor matrices [17], though these are challenging to scale.

There is also a class of ultrasonically-actuated haptic touch surfaces that modify friction through the squeeze film effect [1,3,5,12,15,16]. Interestingly, this effect *reduces* friction, which is opposite to electrostatic feedback. Studies similar to our own have been conducted on ultrasonic-based touchscreens [3,12], with results indicating that dynamic friction-reduction can be leveraged to improve users' pointing performance. Unfortunately, this result is not portable to electrostatic feedback, as the operating principle and sensation is rather different; hence this work directly compliments this prior work, filling a gap in the literature.

Experiments Using Electrostatic Force on Touchscreens

Most previous work on electrostatic force feedback touchscreens falls into one of two categories. First are efforts that attempt to model the fingertip-surface interface [5,14,15]. Special sensors were used for measuring the lateral frictional forces on a fingertip under well-controlled conditions. For example, Meyer et al. [14] modified the traditional ideal parallel plate model by considering the charge leakage through the *stratum corneum*. Such data can be used to better design and tune electrostatic feedback systems, for example, in generating more realistic textures.

A second significant body of literature studies how electrostatic forces can enable a variety of haptic feedback designs. For example, Bau et al. [2] investigated the perceptual characteristics of electro-vibration, in particular the minimum perception threshold and subjective evaluations of the electro-vibration by tuning the amplitude and frequency of the tactile signal. Later, electrostatic force feedback was explored for assistive technology for visually impaired users [21] and texture rendering [9]. Our work contributes to this literature by exploring and evaluating how electrostatic forces can aid users' targeting performance.

COMPARITIVE APPROACHES

At a high level, we wish to explore three *haptic modality* categories: *No Feedback, Physical,* and *Electrostatic* (see Figure 1). *No Feedback* is equivalent to most touchscreens today, and thus serves as our baseline. Achieving *Physical* feedback is considered by many to be the "holy grail" of touchscreen haptics. True physicality means zero latency and can stimulate our mechanoreceptors like real objects. However, achieving this in a manner that is as dynamic as a touchscreen display is to graphics remains elusive. Nonetheless, true physical feedback serves as a gold standard to which haptic technologies should aspire.

Once haptic feedback is introduced, either physically or electrostatically, there are different *haptic designs* that are possible. We include four designs in our evaluation, illustrated in Figure 1. *Line Leading Edge* places a haptic line at the leading edge of objects (relative to the direction of the incoming finger). This provides a cue that the finger has entered an object. *Line Center* is similar, but the haptic cue is provided in the middle of the object, conveying to the user that they are centered within an object. *Line Background* takes a different approach, and instead renders a line of feedback between objects, allowing for users to discern when they are crossing into a new object's area. And finally, we include a *Fill* design, where the whole object provides haptic feedback within its bounds.

Note that we provided haptic feedback on *all* objects in our experiment, instead of merely on the target for that trial. The reason is simple: in a real computing context, the users' destinations are not known *a priori*, and thus, haptic feedback must be equally applied to all applicable targets. These other, non-target objects are sometimes called "distractors" in the literature (see e.g., [12]).

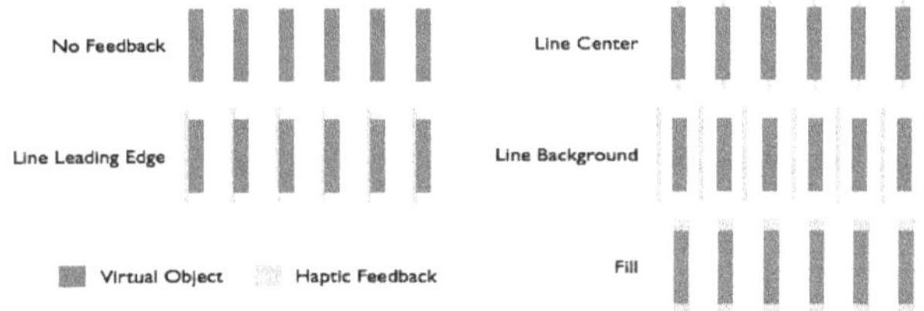

Figure 1. ***No Feedback*** **and four haptic feedback designs. The latter designs can be physical or provided electrostatically.**

USER STUDY

We used a Fitts-style dragging procedure [12], where each single trial had participants first select an object, drag the object to the target, and then lift their finger from the screen. This served as a metaphor for commonplace drag operations on touch devices – for example dragging a photo onto an email, selecting text, drag-and-dropping file and application icons, "swyping" over keyboard keys, scrolling a time selection widget, resizing an element with snapping points, etc. – all of which could be enhanced with haptic feedback.

Apparatus

We replicated the electrostatic setup described in Bau et al. [2]. Specifically, we used 3M MicroTouch capacitive panels mounted to a LCD screen (Figure 2). Our electrostatic feedback board used a 300 Hz signal to create haptic sensations and users were grounded using an antistatic wristband. A laptop, which ran the study and controlled the graphics on the LCD screen, sent commands to the board over USB.

As described in the Comparative Approaches section, we studied three haptic modalities. The *No Feedback* condition and all of the *Electrostatic* designs used the same area of our touchscreen monitor (Figure 2, right monitor, upper half). To create *Physical* feedback, we used two methods. For the line-based designs, we used thin transparent stickers adhered to the screen's surface. To switch between *Physical Line Center*, *Physical Line Leading Edge*, and *Physical Line Background* designs, the virtual objects were simply rendered in with different horizontal offsets. For *Physical Fill*, we covered the corresponding area in a loose grid of con-

Figure 2. Two monitors were used for the study. The left monitor contained three widths of the *Physical Fill* design. The right monitor hosted line-based designs (bottom half) and also the *electrostatic* and *No Feedback* designs (top half).

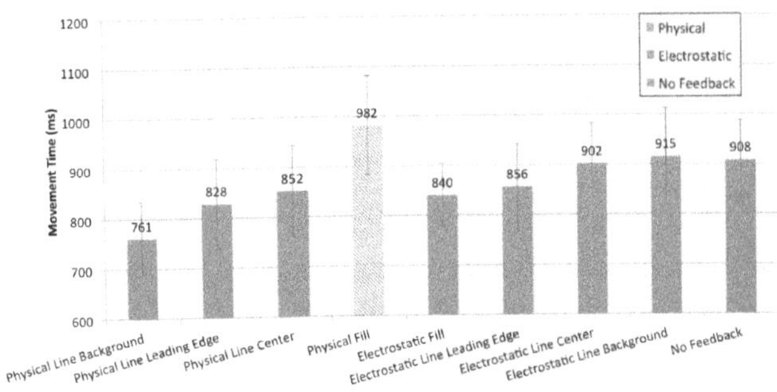

Figure 3. Average movement time cross feedback types. Error bars are standard error across participants.

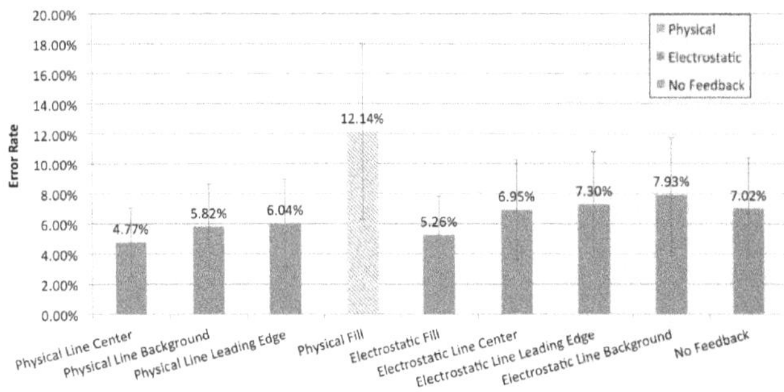

Figure 4. Average error rate cross feedback types. Error bars are standard error across participants.

ductive (copper-based) glue dots, which provided a slightly raised and matte texture, yet still passed touch events through to the 3M panel.

Participants

We recruited 20 participants (9 female), with a mean age of 24. All were regular computer users and right handed. The study took approximately 60 minutes and paid $10.

Design

The user study was a (2 × 4 + 1) × 3 × 5 within-subjects design. The independent variables and levels were:

Haptic Modality × Haptic Design + No Feedback baseline:

Physical Line Center, Physical Line Leading Edge, Physical Line Background, Physical Fill, Electrostatic Line Center, Electrostatic Line Leading Edge, Electrostatic Line Background, Electrostatic Fill, No Feedback.

Target Width (W): *16, 32, 64 pixels (0.26mm per pixel).*

Target Distance (D): *128, 256, 384, 512, 640 pixels.*

Participant completed five trials for each W-D combination, resulting in 75 trials for each haptic modality/design, which constituted one block. The order of blocks was randomized.

Procedure

For each trial, participants first touched the red object to select it. Participants then slid their finger across the distance and dropped the red object on the target, highlighted in green. Participants had to successfully lift their finger anywhere within the target area to move to the next trial. Trials where participants did not successfully lift their finger on the target on the first attempt were marked as errors and disregarded from analysis (i.e., a "one chance" procedure). Additionally, following the procedure in [4], we dropped one participant's data, which was greater than three standard deviations from the mean user performance.

Trials were combined into blocks, which contained all widths and distances for a given haptic modality/design pair. Participants could take breaks before starting each trial block. Each block started with a brief warm up, where participants were allowed to practice trials until they were comfortable with the new feedback (max. 3 minutes). After participants finished all blocks, they were asked to qualitatively rank nine cards representing the eight haptic modalities crossed by haptic design, plus *No Feedback*.

RESULTS AND DISCUSSION

Physical Fill

It became apparent during the study that *Physical Fill* was problematic, and indeed the condition was significantly worse in both movement time and errors than any other haptic modality/design (p<0.05). We believe this is not an effect of the design, but rather the physical implementation. More specifically, we suspect the copper glue dots interfered with the capacitive sensing of the 3M panel. Thus, we omit *Physical Fill* from subsequent analysis, though we include it in Figures 3 and 4 for reference.

Movement Time Analysis

Movement time (MT) is the time taken between when the object was selected and when it was successfully dropped on the target. The results in this section include only trials in which there were no errors. As illustrated in Figure 3, six techniques outperformed *No Feedback* (i.e., conventional touchscreens). A mixed-effects model ANOVA analysis showed a significant effect for modalities on movement time ($F(2,4.16)=69.7$ p<0.05). The average MT for the *Physical* modality was 813.7 (SD=38.5) ms, while the *Electrostatic* modality was 878.3 (SD=31.1) ms. This compares to 908 ms when *No Feedback* is provided. As expected, there were also significant effects on width ($F(2,38)=582.5$ p<0.05) and distance ($F(4,76)=301.6$ p<0.05).

The best haptic design provided by electrostatic force was *Electrostatic Fill*, which shortened the average movement time by 7.5% compared to *No Feedback*. The best haptic design within the physical modality was *Physical Line Background*, which shortened the average movement time by 16.2% compared with *No Feedback*. Post-hoc multiple means comparison tests showed that *Physical Line Background*, *Physical Line Leading Edge* and *Electrostatic Fill* were significantly better than *No Feedback* (p<0.05).

Error Rate Analysis

The result indicated no significant effect for modalities on error rate (see Figure 4). The factors which had significant effects on error rate were width ($F(2,38)=11.87$ p<0.05) and distance ($F(4,76)=4.69$ p<0.05). The best haptic design, with respect to errors, in the electrostatic modality was *Electrostatic Fill,* which lowered the mean error rate by 25.1%; and in the physical modality was *Physical Line Center*, which lowered the average error rate by 32.1% com-

Feedback Type	Model	R^2
Physical Line Background	MT = -13.42 + 216.89 ID	0.96
Physical Line Center	MT = 57.63 + 223.47 ID	0.97
Physical Line Leading Edge	MT = -57.71 + 245.44 ID	0.94
Electrostatic Fill	MT = -72.54 + 256.58 ID	0.96
Electrostatic Line Center	MT = -6.88 + 257.56 ID	0.97
Electrostatic Line Leading Edge	MT = -75.18 + 264.01 ID	0.96
Electrostatic Line Background	MT =-41.74 + 271.18 ID	0.97
No Feedback	MT = -81.93 + 277.82 ID	0.96

Table 1. Fitts' law models for all modality-design pairs.

pared with *No Feedback* (Figure 4). However, post-hoc multiple means comparison tests showed no significant differences between these three feedback types.

Fitts' Models

Although not a true Fitts' Law task, our study can be used to construct an approximate Fitts' model for each of our modality/designs as an additional means of comparison. Indeed, our data results in very good fits ($R^2 > 0.93$ in all cases; Table 1). Lower values of slope indicate that participants' performance deteriorates less rapidly across increasing Indexes of Difficulty (ID). There are two findings of particular note: Foremost, looking at the slope values of the feedback types shows that all haptic designs were superior to *No Feedback* (i.e., lower slope values). Secondly, haptic feedback provided by physical features consistently yielded lower slope values than feedback provided by electrostatics.

Qualitative Ranking

Following the experiment, we asked participants to rank the modality-designs pairs. We assigned the most preferred type with a score of nine, with one being least preferred. The result showed that the *Physical Line Leading Edge* was the most preferable feedback type with an average score of 6.42 (SD=2.09). Conversely, *Electrostatic Line Background* got the lowest average score of 4.26 (SD=2.12). Overall, there was little agreement among the participants, producing large standard deviations. Correlating mean preference rank against slope of the Fitts' regression and against mean movement time yielded no correlations of note (R^2 =0.12 and 0.04). Users had a slightly better sense of their performance with respect to error rate, with an R^2 value of 0.38 for mean preference rank plotted against mean error.

ACKNOWLEDGEMENTS

This research was generously supported by the David and Lucile Packard Foundation, Google and Qualcomm.

REFERENCES

1. Amberg, M., Giraud, F., Semail, B., Olivo, P., Casiez, G. and Roussel, N. STIMTAC: a tactile input device with programmable friction. In *Proc. UIST '11 Adjunct*, 7-8.
2. Bau, O., Poupyrev, I., Israr, A. and Harrison, C. TeslaTouch: Electrovibration for Touch Surfaces. In *Proc. UIST '10*, 283-292.
3. Casiez, G., Roussel, N., Vanbelleghem, R. and Giraud, F. Surfpad: riding towards targets on a squeeze film effect. In *Proc. CHI '11*, 2491-2500.
4. Forlines, C., and Balakrishnan, R., Evaluating tactile feedback and direct vs. indirect stylus input in pointing and crossing selection tasks. In *Proc. CHI '08*, 1563-1572.
5. Giraud, F., Amberg, M., Lemaire-Semail, B., Merging two tactile stimulation principles: electrovibration and squeeze film effect. In *Proc. WHC '13*, 199(203), 14-17.
6. Harrison, C. & Hudson, S. Providing dynamically changeable physical buttons on a visual display. *Proc. CHI '09*, 299-308.
7. Hoggan, E., Brewster, S. and Johnston, J. Investigating the effectiveness of tactile feedback for mobile touchscreens. In *Proc. CHI '08*, 1573-1582.
8. Kane, S.K., Morris, M.R. and Wobbrock, J.O. Touchplates: low-cost tactile overlays for visually impaired touch screen users. In *Proc. ASSETS '13,* 8 pages.
9. Kim, S., Israr, A., and Poupyrev, I. Tactile rendering of 3D features on touch surfaces. In *Proc. UIST '13,* 531-538.
10. Koskinen, E., Kaaresoja, T. and Laitinen, P. Feel-good touch: finding the most pleasant tactile feedback for a mobile touch screen button. In *Proc. ICMI '08,* 297-304.
11. Lee, J., Dietz, P., Leigh, D., Yerazunis, W. and Hudson, S. Haptic Pen: A Tactile feedback stylus for touch screens. In *Proc. UIST '04*. 291-294
12. Lévesque, V., Oram, L., MacLean, K., Cockburn, A., Marchuk, N.D., Johnson, D., Colgate, J.E. and Peshkin, M.A. Enhancing physicality in touch interaction with programmable friction. In *Proc. CHI '11*, 2481-2490.
13. Mallinckrodt, E., Hughes, A. and Sleator, W. Perception by the Skin of Electrically Induced Vibrations. *Science*, 1953. 118(3062), 277-278.
14. Meyer, D.J., Peshkin, M.A. and Colgate, J.E. Fingertip friction modulation due to electrostatic attraction. *World Haptics Conference 2013*, 43(48), 14-17.
15. Meyer, D.J., Wiertlewski, M., Peshkin, M.A., and Colgate, J.E., Dynamics of ultrasonic and electrostatic friction modulation for rendering texture on haptic surfaces, *Haptics Symposium*, 2014. 63(67), 23-26.
16. Mullenbach, J., Shultz, C., Piper, A., Peshkin, M. and Colgate, E. Surface Haptic Interactions with a TPad Tablet. In *Proc. UIST '13 Adjunct*, 7-8.
17. Overholt, D., Pasztor, E., Mazalek, A. A Multipurpose Array of Tactile Rods for Interactive sXpression (Abstracts and Applications), In *Proc. SIGGRAPH '01*.
18. Poupyrev, I., Okabe, M. and Maruyama, S. Haptic feedback for pen computing: directions and strategies. In *CHI EA '04*, 1309-1312.
19. Senseg, Inc. http://senseg.com
20. Weiss, M., Wagner, J., Jansen, Y., Jennings, R., Khoshabeh, R., Hollan, J. and Borchers, J. SLAP widgets: bridging the gap between virtual and physical controls on tabletops. In *Proc. CHI '09*, 481-490.
21. Xu, C., Israr, A., Poupyrev, I., Bau, O., and Harrison, C., Tactile display for the visually impaired using TeslaTouch. *CHI EA '11*, 317-322.
22. Wolfe, J.M., Kluender, K.R., Levi, D. M., Bartoshuk, L. M, Herz, R.S., Klatzky, R.L. and Lederman, S.J. Sensation and Perception. Sinauer Associates, 2006.

Estimating 3D Finger Angle on Commodity Touchscreens

Robert Xiao **Julia Schwarz** **Chris Harrison**
Qeexo, Co.
2483 Old Middlefield Way, Suite 202, Mountain View, California 94043
info@qeexo.com

ABSTRACT
We describe a novel approach for estimating the pitch and yaw of fingers relative to a touchscreen's surface, offering two additional, analog degrees of freedom for interactive functions. Further, we show that our approach can be achieved on off-the-shelf consumer touchscreen devices: a smartphone and smartwatch. We validate our technique though a user study on both devices and conclude with several demo applications that illustrate the value and immediate feasibility of our approach.

Author Keywords
Touchscreen input; mobile devices; rich touch; capacitive sensing; finger orientation.

ACM Classification Keywords
H.5.2. Information interfaces and presentation (e.g., HCI): User Interfaces: Input devices and strategies.

INTRODUCTION
Today's touch interfaces are primarily driven by the 2D location of touch events. As we describe in Related Work, there are many other dimensions of touch that can be captured and utilized interactively. By increasing the richness of touch input, users can do more in the same small space, potentially enabling richer applications. In this work, we describe a new method that estimates a finger's angle relative to the screen. The angular vector is described using two angles – *altitude* and *azimuth* – more colloquially referred to as *pitch* and *yaw*. Our approach works in tandem with conventional multitouch finger tracking, offering two additional analog degrees of freedom for a single touch point.

In this work, we present a new algorithm for simultaneously estimating finger pitch and yaw across a wide range of poses, from flat to perpendicular. Uniquely, it uses only data provided by commodity, off-the-shelf touch devices, requiring no additional hardware or sensors. We prototyped our solution on two platforms – a smartphone and a smartwatch – each fully self-contained and operating in real-time. We quantified the accuracy of our technique through a user study, and explored the feasibility of our approach through example applications and interactions (see Video Figure).

ITS '15, November 15-18, 2015, Funchal, Portugal
© 2015 ACM. ISBN 978-1-4503-3899-8/15/11···$15.00
DOI: http://dx.doi.org/10.1145/2817721.2817737

RELATED WORK
There has been significant research into enhancing interaction on touch devices. One approach is to use conventional touch data in combination with spatial or temporal sequences, for example, tap-and-hold and multi-finger chording gestures [2,11]. More experimental are efforts that capture e.g., pressure [12], shear forces [8], shape of the hands [4], rolling motions of stationary fingers [14], and what part of the finger touched the screen [7].

In addition to X/Y finger tracking, most modern touchscreens fit an ellipse to finger contact areas, obtaining ellipse axes and orientation [1]. The ellipse size is often used as a proxy for "pressure", and can also trigger different interaction functions via thresholds [3]. Ellipse orientation is similar to yaw, though true finger direction is ambiguous (orientation is not directional, thus offering two possible vectors). More importantly, as we will show, the ellipse orientation varies with finger pitch. Thus, prior work using ellipse orientation for yaw (e.g., [16,17]) required fingers to lie nearly flat on the screen surface. We improve upon these results (see Video Figure, where yaw is tracked even when fingers are *perpendicular*), and further add finger pitch tracking, which no touchscreens report today.

It is important to note that, while prior systems have achieved pitch and yaw tracking, all use *special hardware* that is impractical for mobile devices. For example, PointPose [10] used a depth camera mounted obliquely to the touchscreen to capture finger "rotation and tilt". Similarly, KinectTouch [5] also uses a depth camera, but it is mounted above the display. Z-Touch [15] uses a series of multiplexed infrared line lasers to create a shallow-field depth sensing touchscreen, capable of recovering finger angle. Using a commercial-grade fingerprint scanner, Holz and Baudisch [9] were able to estimate pitch and yaw based on the fingerprint patch that was visible, which was used to improve

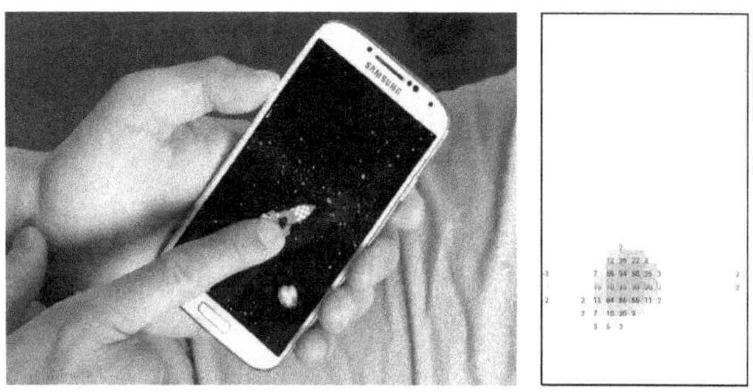

Figure 1. Left: A ship is piloted through 3D space using the finger's vector. Right: 16x28 capacitive image from the smartphone's touchscreen.

targeting accuracy. Zaliva [18] uses neural networks to estimate finger pose, though no hardware or results are described. Finally, and most similar to our work, is Angle-Pose [13], which used a 4x6 grid of capacitance-to-ground sensing electrodes (offering high SNR) and a particle filter to estimate a finger's 3D pose. This setup is used to evaluate how pose information can improve 2D targeting accuracy, but the pitch/yaw estimates themselves were not evaluated.

In addition to being the first approach that can run on commodity devices, we are also the first to consider how pitch/yaw can be valuable at smartwatch scales, and also evaluate our approach's performance. Further, we bring new interactions to light through our example applications.

IMPLEMENTATION

Projected capacitive sensing is the most pervasive touchscreen technology today. It works by sensing disturbances in a projected electric field caused by a proximate capacitive object (e.g., a fleshy finger). Field strength diminishes significantly with increasing distance. However, importantly, the sensitivity is not zero - nearby finger parts will still produce weak signals. This produces a characteristic "comet" artifact for non-perpendicular fingers (Figures 1 and 2).

More specifically, our implementation uses the *capacitive image* (Figures 1 and 2, right) provided by the touchscreen. Put simply, this is the capacitance measured at each point of a touch sensor's capacitive grid; the data is used internally by the touchscreen controller to detect touch events. The capacitive image is also provided as a debugging feature by many touchscreen controllers. We gained access to the capacitive image on our proof-of-concept devices (both of which run Android) by modifying the Linux kernel. Of note, although the capacitive image is not directly accessible in Apple iOS and Windows Phone, the underlying hardware almost certainly supports it.

Proof-of-Concept Platforms

We selected two popular devices to represent smartphone and smartwatch form factors. For the phone, we chose a Samsung Galaxy S4 (Figure 1), which features a 16x28 capacitive touch grid over top of a 5.0" 1080x1920 pixel screen. On this device, we can poll the capacitive image 25 times per second. For the smartwatch, we chose an LG 'G' smartwatch (Figure 2), which has an 8x8 capacitive grid on top of a 1.65" 280x280 pixel screen. Due to the smaller image size, we can poll the capacitive image at 60 FPS.

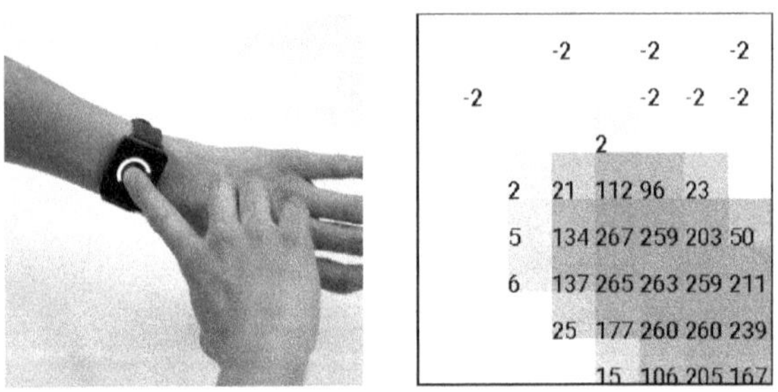

Figure 2. Left: Yaw controlling volume level. Right: 8x8 capacitive image from the smartwatch's touchscreen.

Feature Extraction

We use the direction and magnitude of the "comet" shape to estimate the pitch and yaw of a finger. Starting from each identified touch point, we flood-fill within the capacitive image to find the set of non-zero pixels sensing the finger B (the touch blob). We discard all grid points that have a capacitance delta (compared with background) below a noise threshold (3 pF in our implementation).

For each remaining point in the touch blob, let x and y denote its position and let z denote the capacitance deviation at that point. We derive seven datasets:

- The power-transformed datasets $S_i = \{(x, y, z^i) | x, y, z \in B\}$ for $i = 0, 1, 2$
- The thresholded power-transformed datasets $T_i = \{(x, y, z^i) | x, y, z \in B, z \geq 30\}$ for $i = 0, 1, 2$
- The log-transformed dataset $U = \{(x, y, \ln z) | x, y, z \in B\}$

Note that $S_1 = B$. We then fit an ellipsoid to each dataset by computing the centroid $(\bar{x}, \bar{y})$ where:

$$\bar{x} = \frac{\sum_{x,y,z} xz}{\sum_{x,y,z} z}, \bar{y} = \frac{\sum_{x,y,z} yz}{\sum_{x,y,z} z}$$

and the central image moments $\mu_{02}, \mu_{20}, \mu_{11}$ where:

$$\mu_{ij} = \sum_{x,y,z} (x\text{-}\bar{x})^i (y\text{-}\bar{y})^j z$$

From these moments, we compute the ellipsoid orientation:

$$\theta = \frac{1}{2} \tan^{-1} \frac{2\mu_{11}}{\mu_{20} - \mu_{02}}$$

and the eigenvalues: $$\lambda_{\pm} = \frac{\mu_{20} + \mu_{02} \pm \sqrt{4\mu_{11} + (\mu_{20} - \mu_{02})^2}}{2}$$

and finally the ellipsoid's eccentricity: $$\varepsilon = \sqrt{1 - \lambda_- / \lambda_+}$$

We combine these parameters with the distance and angle between the touch point and the ellipsoid centroid to obtain a set of 6 features for each of our 7 datasets. We use these 42 features to compute the pitch and yaw.

Pitch Estimation

The electric field strength decreases as the square of the distance, reducing the measured capacitance. Due to the differing dielectric constants of glass and air, the decrease does not perfectly fit an inverse-square law. Thus, to produce reliable estimates of finger pitch, we used Weka [6] to train a Gaussian process regression that takes our 42 features as input and produces an estimate of the pitch angle.

Yaw Estimation

When a user's finger is low to the screen, we see the characteristic "comet" shape, in which the major axis of the ellipsoid of the sensed touch pixels extends *parallel* to the finger's yaw angle (Figure 3, left two panels). However, when the user's finger is sufficiently vertical (pitches near 90°), the fingertip's contact area with the screen forms a small, flattened ellipsoid, with a major axis *perpendicular* to the finger's yaw angle (Figure 3, far right). In between, for angles between 45° and 60°, the ellipsoid is nearly a perfect circle (Figure 3, center right), allowing for accurate pitch,

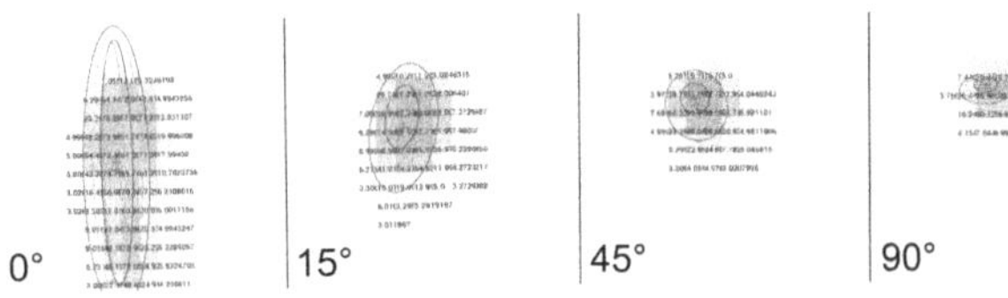

Figure 3. A finger at varying pitches, but constant yaw (0°). Note how the S_i ellipsoids vary; in particular, how they are vertically elongated below 45°, near circular at 45°, and horizontally elongated above 45°.

but poor yaw estimation. To account for these differences, we implemented a simple heuristic: the yaw angle is simply the orientation of the S_I ellipsoid, with a 90° correction applied if the pitch exceeds 50°.

USER STUDY

Prior to running our study, the three authors used the procedure described below to collect data, which was used to train the pitch regression model. Thus, the study (purposely) contains *no* per-user training or calibration. Also, pitch and yaw estimates were computed *live*, for a real time result (i.e., no post hoc corrections or algorithm tweaks).

We recruited 10 participants (2 female, mean age 35.2) to participate in a 20-minute user study. Participants were asked to replicate a series of pitch and yaw positions. Specifically, we tested 7 finger pitches from 0° (flat on the screen) to 90° (perpendicular) in 15° increments, and tested 9 finger yaw from -60° to +60° in 15° increments (a range we found comfortable to replicate in piloting). Each of these 63 combinations was tested on both our phone and watch prototypes. For each combination of device and pitch angle (randomized), users performed all yaw angles in sequence from -60 to 60 to streamline collection.

In each trial, users placed their fingertip in the center of the display. The requested yaw was displayed on screen using an arrow. However, we found no reliable way to illustrate a requested pitch. In response, we laser-cut plastic wedges for all of our tested angles. Participants placed the appropriate wedge under their finger to establish the correct finger pitch. Once satisfied, the participant removed the wedge (to avoid capacitive interference) and then the experimenter triggered the data collection function.

Two participants had long nails, which precluded the touchscreen from detecting their input at 90° pitches. This inability to sense is not related to our method, but rather the touchscreen hardware and sensitivity settings. Minus these two participants' 90° pitch blocks, we obtained 1224 pitch/yaw trials in total. There were no significant performance differences between users.

RESULTS

As seen by the relatively flat lines in Figure 4 left, the angular accuracy of both pitch and yaw across the full range of yaws we tested varies little. This is also true of pitch when analyzed across the full range of pitches (Figure 4, right, solid lines). However, yaw accuracy varies significantly with changing pitch, as seen by the "hump" in the dashed lines in Figure 4 right. This is due to the appearance of fingers at intermediate pitches (around 45°) as circular patches on the capacitive image (Figure 3). This circular shape is useful in inferring that the finger is at an intermediate pitch, leading to high pitch accuracies. However, it provides little data for inferring yaw, and as such, error is high (Figure 4, right, dashed lines).

The smartphone generally had superior accuracy to the smartwatch. We believe this was chiefly due to the larger touchscreen better capturing the full extent of fingers' capacitive signal (i.e., useful data simply extends off the smartwatch screen, as seen in Figure 2, right), The phone had a mean angular pitch error of 9.7° (SD=8.9°), while the watch had 14.5° (SD=12.6°). Mean angular yaw error was 26.8° for the phone and 31.7° for the watch. However, as noted previously, estimating yaw when pitches are around 50° is near impossible, leading to misleading averages, so the latter averages can be misleading. If we look only at mean angular yaw error for pitches 30° or less, the phone and watch achieve 10.6° (SD=18.9°) and 13.1° (SD=20.1°) mean angular yaw error respectively. Similar results are found when the finger is mostly perpendicular.

EXAMPLE APPLICATIONS

Holz and Baudisch [9] found that finger pitch systematically affected targeting accuracy, and note that if pitch was known, targeting accuracy could be significantly increased. Our pitch estimation approach could be readily deployed onto today's devices (e.g., a software update) to enable such accuracy gains. We also believe pitch and yaw are also exciting first-class input dimensions, used to trigger interactive functionality directly. This is especially true on smartwatches, where small screens make spatial gestures (e.g., pigtails) and multi-finger chording cumbersome. To more concretely demonstrate these interactive possibilities, we created several demo applications (see also Video Figure).

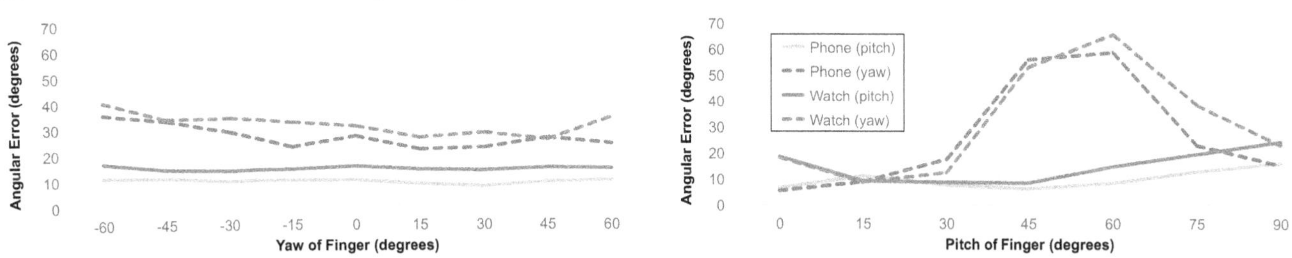

Figure 4. Accuracy of pitch (solid lines) and yaw (dashed lines) for smartphone (blue lines) and smartwatch (orange lines) prototypes. Summarized here is angular accuracy with respect to the range of yaws (left) and pitches (right) evaluated.

Figure 5. Left: map panning and zooming. Center: pan and rotate images. Right: 3D Object manipulation

Twist to Set Value

Setting analog values on contemporary touch interfaces generally means manipulating (through finger translation) a small slider or "spinner" widget. By tracking yaw, "twist" sensitive controls (demonstrated in [16,17] using orientation) can be created, which provide relative or absolute, in-place, analog input. As a demo, we created a volume control for our smartwatch (Figure 2). This interaction could also be used to set a kitchen timer, modify screen brightness, aid in color selection, and other analog manipulation tasks.

Pan and Zoom

Today's smartwatch interfaces generally lack mapping applications that can pan *and* zoom. With such limited screen space, two-finger pinch to zoom is cumbersome; for example, the Apple Watch instead moves zooming functionality to a mechanical thumb wheel. With pitch and yaw tracking, users can translate the map with one finger panning and zoom with one-finger twists (Figure 5, left).

Pan and Rotate

We also created a photo album viewer for our smartwatch prototype. Photos can be navigated with left and right swipes, while relative pitch movement controls the image crop. In a direct manipulation manner, users can twist the image with a single finger to rotate it (Figure 5, center).

3D Manipulation

Pitch and yaw lends itself well to 3D object manipulation. We created a demo where users can rotate an object *on all three* rotational axes without translating the finger (Figure 5, right). Relative pitch motions along the horizontal and vertical axes control rotation about the Y- and X-axis respectively. Yaw naturally controls rotation about the Z-axis.

Vector into 3D space

In contemporary touch interfaces, a fingertip pressed against a screen is thought of as a point on a 2D plane. However, thinking more holistically about the *entire* finger, it is also a vector pointing into 3D space. As a demonstration of this, we created a simple game: a spaceship is rendered on the tip of the finger and tracks with the finger's 3D pointing direction; the goal is to shoot and avoid asteroids (Figure 1).

CONCLUSIONS AND FUTURE WORK

In this work, we described and evaluated a new method of tracking finger angle using unmodified off-the-shelf touchscreens. We provided a number of example applications to demonstrate interactions made possible using finger angle information. In the future, hover-sensing touchscreens could be used to further extend sensing above the display plane, enabling improved accuracy across a wider range of pitch angles, while future improvements in touchscreen accuracy and sensor density could improve angle estimations and enable more fine-grained interactions.

REFERENCES

1. Android API. http://developer.android.com/reference/android/view/MotionEvent.html#AXIS_ORIENTATION
2. Apple, Inc. Multi-touch gesture dictionary (2008). US Patent 20070177803.
3. Boring, S., Ledo, D., Chen, X., Marquardt, N., Tang, A. and Greenberg, S. The fat thumb: using the thumb's contact size for single-handed mobile interaction. In *Proc. MobileHCI '12*. 207-208.
4. Cao, X., A. Wilson, R. Balakrishnan, K. Hinckley, S. Hudson. ShapeTouch: Leveraging contact shape on interactive surfaces. In *Proc. ITS '08*. 129–136.
5. Dippon, A and Klinker, G. KinectTouch: accuracy test for a very low-cost 2.5D multitouch tracking system. In *Proc. ITS '11*. 49-52.
6. Hall, M., Frank, E., Holmes, G., Pfahringer, B., Reutemann, P., Witten, I. H. The WEKA Data Mining Software: An Update. *SIGKDD Explorations*, 11(1), 2009.
7. Harrison, C., Schwarz, J. and Hudson S. E. TapSense: Enhancing Finger Interaction on Touch Surfaces. In *Proc. UIST '11*. 627-636.
8. Heo, S. and Lee, G. Force gestures: augmented touch screen gestures using normal and tangential force. In *Proc. UIST'11*. 621-626.
9. Holz, C. and Baudisch, P. The generalized perceived input point model and how to double touch accuracy by extracting fingerprints. In *Proc. CHI '10*. 581-590.
10. Kratz, S., Chiu, P and Back, M. PointPose: finger pose estimation for touch input on mobile devices using a depth sensor. In *Proc. ITS '13*. 223-230.
11. Lepinski, J.G., Grossman, T., and Fitzmaurice, G. The design and evaluation of multitouch marking menus. In *Proc. CHI '10*. 2233-2242.
12. Ramos, G., Boulos, M., and Balakrishnan, R. Pressure widgets. In *Proc. CHI '04*. 487-494.
13. Rogers, S., Williamson, J., Stewart, C., and Murray-Smith, R. AnglePose: robust, precise capacitive touch tracking via 3d orientation estimation. In *Proc. CHI '11*. 2575-2584
14. Roudaut, A., Lecolinet, E. and Guiard, Y. MicroRolls: expanding touch-screen input vocabulary by distinguishing rolls vs. slides of the thumb. In *Proc. CHI '09*. 927-936.
15. Takeoka, Y., Miyaki, T., and Rekimoto, J. Z-touch: an infrastructure for 3d gesture interaction in the proximity of tabletop surfaces. In *Proc. ITS '10*. 91-94.
16. Wang, F. and Ren, X. Empirical evaluation for finger input properties in multi-touch interaction. In *Proc. CHI '09*. 1063-1072.
17. Wang, F., Cao, X., Ren, X. and Irani, P. Detecting and leveraging finger orientation for interaction with direct-touch surfaces. In *Proc. UIST '09*. 23-32.
18. Zaliva, V. 3D finger posture detection and gesture recognition on touch surfaces. In *Proc. ICARCV '12*. 359-364.

One-Touch Pose Detection on Touchscreen Smartphones

Karsten Seipp
Goldsmiths, University of London, UK
k.seipp@gold.ac.uk

Kate Devlin
Goldsmiths, University of London, UK
k.devlin@gold.ac.uk

ABSTRACT

We present a technique that allows distinguishing between index finger and thumb input on touchscreen phones, achieving an average accuracy of 82.6% in a real-life application with only a single touch. We divide the screen into a virtual grid of 9mm^2 units and use a dedicated set of training data and algorithms for classifying new touches in each screen location. Further, we present correlations between physical and digital touch properties to extend previous work.

ACM Classification Keywords

H.5.2 User Interfaces:: Graphical user interfaces

Author Keywords

Finger detection; Input detection; Touch; Mobile

INTRODUCTION AND PREVIOUS WORK

To maximise the usability of a GUI for one-handed interaction, researchers have devised a set of approaches comprising enlarged buttons or curved interfaces. However, these often need manual activation or even lock the user to a static GUI once they have configured the application, making it hard to switch between single-handed and bimanual use. Thus, a flexible system for input mode detection is required that allows input pose detection and ultimately interface adaptation on the fly – ideally using a single tap when starting an app.

Some researchers have attempted to detect interaction context using contact-sensitive hardware attached to a device [3, 7, 14] or changes in resonance when vibrating an object [9]. Others have used computer vision [1, 5] to process the shape of a touch, or measured differences in impedance to distinguish between users [4]. However, such approaches do not work on commodity smartphones without additional hardware. Therefore, some researchers have explored the potential of motion and touch sensors intrinsic to modern devices. Wang and Ren [12] provide a detailed description of the finger's physical properties, and how these may be used to enrich the digital dialogue, and use a finger's landing process on the screen of a tabletop to differentiate between left and right hand [11]. On smartphones, researchers use a device's motion sensors to infer where on screen a touch may have occurred [15, 8] and thereby illustrate how different screen regions possess a distinctive motion profile. Combining changes in device motion and touch size is GripSense [2], which uses the spatiotemporal differences of touch and motion properties to distinguish between different hand postures in an average of four to five interaction steps [p.551]. Yet, as a premise for dynamic input mode detection this may be inadequate in cases where users only interact with a small area of the screen. What is needed is an approach that allows the detection of mode of operation within a single interaction step – ideally by performing only a simple touch of the screen. To address this, we examine whether the limited data provided by screen and motion sensors can be used to infer whether the phone is operated one-handedly via the thumb or with two hands, using the index finger of the one hand while holding it in the other.

ITS '15, November 15-18, 2015, Funchal, Portugal.

DOI: http://dx.doi.org/10.1145/2817721.2817739

INITIAL DATA COLLECTION

To map out the characteristics of a human touch in all areas of a 4.7" smartphone screen, we collected data from 27 participants (8 F, mean age 22.3, SD 2.94, 1 left-handed, 1 ambidextrous). For this we divided the screen of a HTC Sensation XE phone running Android 4.03 into a grid of 6x10 units, each unit with a physical dimension of about 9x9mm, derived from the ideal target size suggested by Parhi et al. [10]. To facilitate data collection, each grid unit was populated by a button. Buttons were highlighted at random to signify the screen area users had to touch (Fig. 1). Users had to complete a total of eight rounds, operating the device with one hand using the left and right thumb, and holding it in either hand, operating it with the index finger of the other, while walking and sitting. Each round started with a full grid of targets which vanished from the display when touched (Fig. 1). After touching the target grid unit, the next one was highlighted with a delay of one second. Errors, such as pressing the wrong button, had no effect, as only the highlighted grid unit was "active" and responded to touch events. The sitting condition was performed in an office, the walking condition on the pavement of a quiet street at about 2.5 km/h, measured via an app.

As a human touch has properties such as duration, location and size, we decided to record the following properties to describe the digital touch: *Grid ID, Touch Size Mean, Number of Touches, Touch Time*, *Offset* on the X/Y axis, the difference between first and last touch point of a touch event on the X/Y axis (*Diff X/Y*) as well as the rotation of the device over three axes during the touch (*Gyro X, Y, Z*) and before and during the touch (*Gyro All X, Gyro All Y, Gyro All Z*). Compared to previous work classifying input pose and hand, we introduce touch duration, number of touch points, and differentiation of device movement *during* and *before and during* a touch. Following [12] and [2], the accelerometer was not recorded.

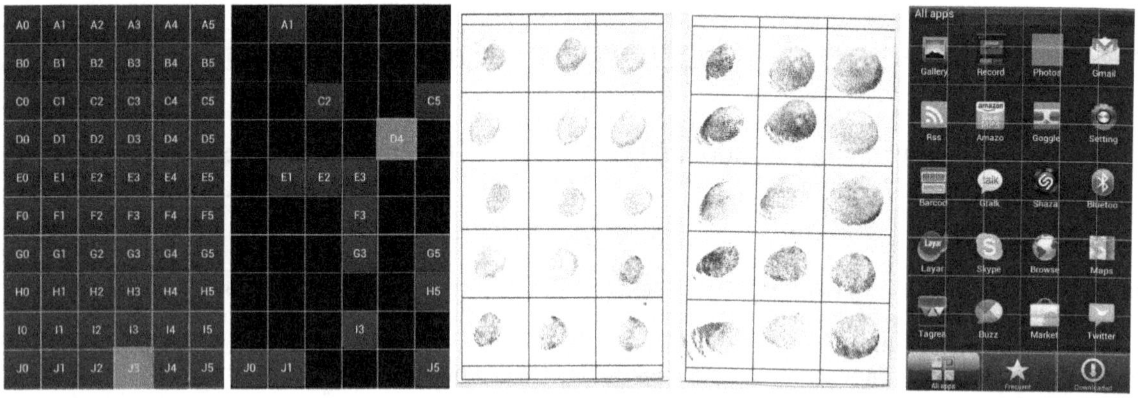

1 2 3 4 5

Figure 1. ***1:*** **Screen of the initial data collection with an overlaid grid. The button/screen area to be tapped is red.** ***2:*** **Once a screen area had been tapped and touch data collected, the target was removed.** ***3+4:*** **Tap shapes of the left index finger and left thumb on the device, recorded on paper using ink.** ***5:*** **Application: Users have to launch an application by tapping the red icon. The grid, in which touch data has been collected in** ***1*** **and** ***2*****, is overlaid to illustrate the principle of attributing a new touch on the screen to a unit of the grid.**

Physical Data

In addition to the digital properties, we recorded the length of index finger and thumb of both hands by measuring the distance from each finger's base (the bottom of the proximal phalanx) to its tip (the end of the distal phalanx). To ascertain the physical size of the area of the fingertip that might be used for a full-contact touch, we measured width and height of the participants' fingerprints. We asked them to press the top of their finger, ranging from the bottom of the distal phalanx right up to the nail bed, onto an ink pad and roll their finger to cover all parts of the skin that could potentially come into contact with the display. We then asked them to position their finger on a parallel line to the tabletop and lower it onto a sheet of paper on the table, without rolling it to either side. Width and height of the print on paper were measured in cm. To examine the shape of the physical touch area in different parts of the screen, a sheet of paper was attached to the phone's display. The sheet replicated the layout of the button grid, but buttons were combined into groups of four, creating 15 zones (Fig. 1). This procedure is similar to Katre's [6] for measuring the thumb's shape in different parts of the screen.

INITIAL EVALUATION

A set of ANOVAs together with a visualisation in the *Weka Explorer* showed *Touch Size Mean* and *X, Y,* and *Z* gyroscope amplitudes as suitable for pose classification. *Number of Touches*, *Touch Time*, *X* and *Y* gyroscope amplitudes and *Offset X* were shown as suitable for hand classification.

The mean values of the digital touch properties for the thumb often exceeded those of the index finger by several orders of magnitude. The thumb's physical touch ellipse was an average of 26.2% wider and 17.5% higher than that of the index finger, which resulted in the thumb's *Touch Size Mean* property being an average of 39.8% larger. Further, touches of the left hand seemed to be slightly larger in size than those of the right. This suggests that touches with the non-dominant hand are less precise and dexterous than those performed with the dominant hand, resulting in a "sloppier" touch with increased *Touch Size Mean*, *Touch Time*, and gyroscope movement.

The strongest physical factor impacting the digital touch properties seemed to be the limited dexterity and reach of the thumb, mainly caused by the thumb's total length, which was 16.6% shorter than that of the index finger. This may be the cause of a prolonged contact time with the display when touching (*Touch Time* +26.1% in comparison to the index finger), and found its strongest manifestation in the greatly increased gyroscope amplitudes, caused by the comparatively strong device movement when reaching for a target outside the thumb's natural movement arc, supporting the findings of Goel et al. [2]. This held true for all three gyroscope axes, but was especially visible for the rotation around the Z-axis before and during the touch, where the amplitude was an average of 235.1% higher for the thumb. The data of the walking condition showed the same trends but amplified, possibly due to higher device movement or reduced dexterity, likely to be caused by a higher cognitive load while walking [13]. Table 1 shows the degree of correlation between the average values of physical and digital properties in the sitting condition.

Digital property	Physical property	Sp. *rho*	*p*
No. of Touches	Touch shape width (index f.)	.423	.028
Gyro Y Ampl.	Limb length (thumb)	.464	.015
Gyro Z Ampl.		.533	.004
Gyro X All Ampl.		.576	.002
Gyro Y All Ampl.		.644	< .001
Gyro Z All Ampl.		.632	< .001
Gyro X All Ampl.	Touch shape width (thumb)	.479	.012

Table 1. Correlations of digital and physical properties, measured in Spearman's *rho* (Sp. *rho*). Degree of significance given as *p*.

Table 1 suggests that the ergonomic characteristics *limb length* and *touch shape width* of the thumb are related to the change in the digital touch values. The thumb's fixation to the hand holding the device and the resulting limited area of movement may cause a greater degree of device motion together with a flatter connection angle of thumb and screen, as also found by Goel et al.[2] and Katre [6]. The shortage of statistically significant correlations between physical and digital properties for the index finger indicates that distinctions between finger and thumb input (based solely on correlations between their average physical and digital properties) may

Mode	App. A	App. B
P (S)	84.1	82.1
P (W)	78.7	80.8
H (S)	61.8	64.5
H (W)	60.9	63.7

Table 2. Mean classification accuracy in % derived from the cross-validation for input pose (P) and hand (H) when using *App. A* and *App. B*, sitting (S) and walking (W).

Mode	App. A	App. B
P (S)	82.2	82.5
P (W)	73.8	73.9
H (S)	58.6	62.5
H (W)	60.8	62.9

Table 3. Mean classification accuracy for input pose (P) and hand (H) in% when using *App. A* and *App. B* on the verification data set of the second study, sitting (S) and walking (W).

Mode	App. A	App. B
P (S)	83.1	82.3
P (W)	77.3	75.2
H (S)	61.6	62.2
H (W)	62.3	61.9

Table 4. Mean accuracy for *App. A* and *App. B* in % for classifying input pose and hand, while sitting (S) and walking (W), derived from the cross-validation and the verification.

Config.	S	W
App. A	82.6	71.1
App. B	81.9	72.3

Table 5. The average pose classification accuracy of *App. A* and *App. B* in % when embedded into the example application, while sitting (S) and walking (W).

not be made sweepingly for the whole screen, but rather require a subdivision of the screen to detect differences in the values of each with reference to a spatial location.

Analysis Using Machine Learning

The initial data collection created a set of reference values for each of the 60 grid positions for each of the poses in the two conditions. For further examination, we applied various machine learning algorithms to the data set of each grid point individually to examine their effectiveness for classifying input pose and hand in this region: Three *K Nearest Neighbour* algorithms with a configuration of *K*=1, *K*=3 and *K*=5; one *Random Forest* algorithm using 12 attributes of the touch event (all but the *Diff X/Y* properties, which were unsuitable) and *Weka's J48* classifier in standard configuration:

- ***KX:*** weka.classifiers.lazy.IBk -K X -W 0 -A weka.core.neighboursearch. LinearNN Search -A weka.core.EuclideanDistance -R first-last
- ***J48:*** weka.classifiers.trees.J48 -C 0.25 -M 2
- ***RF12:*** weka.classifiers.trees.RandomForest -I 10 -K 12 -S 1 -num-slots 1

The algorithms were chosen in order to explore whether pose and hand can be determined based on a degree of similarity of their overall characteristics (*KNN*) or based on the values of certain key properties in relation to others (*J48, Random Forest*). To avoid overfitting, we validated each model for each target position with a stratified tenfold cross-validation. Using this approach we defined the classification performance of each algorithm in each of the 60 grid units while sitting and walking. From this, we created a classification accuracy map of the screen for both input pose and hand, while sitting and while walking. For a detailed breakdown of grid position and algorithm performance, please see the additional material. All data was evaluated using *Weka*.

As shown by previous work [2, 15], touch properties may vary greatly between different screen areas. Therefore, using a single algorithm to evaluate all grid points may not be adequate. Although the *RF12* algorithm provided the best overall accuracy (82.7%), its performance was sometimes shadowed by the various *NN* algorithms, depending on screen position. To address this, we developed two approaches:
Approach A uses the highest-ranking algorithm in each of the 60 grid units determined by the cross-validation to classify new data.
Approach B uses the three highest-ranking algorithms (determined by the cross-validation) in each of the 60 grid units in a majority voting process to classify new data. In the case of equal performance, preference was given to higher *K* over lower ones, and to decision trees (*J48, RF12*) over *NN*. Applying these approaches to our classification accuracy map suggests a potential average classification accuracy of input pose and hand as defined in Table 2. **While one-tap input pose classification (index finger/thumb input) seems possible, hand classification (left/right) does not.**

Model Verification

To verify the cross-validated model performance for each screen location, we conducted a second study with 10 new users (5 F, mean age: 33.8, SD: 3.97, 2 left-handed, 1 ambid.) using the same design as the first study. The new data points for each grid unit were then evaluated in *Weka* using the cross-validated models (Tab. 3). Using the verification data set, the average accuracy for input pose and hand classification differs slightly from the accuracy predicted by the cross-validation (Tab. 2), but, as differences are rather small, the results suggest the models may be considered stable under the study conditions. Therefore we suggest the classification accuracy to be derived from the mean performance of cross-validation and verification (Tab. 4).

REAL-LIFE APPLICATION

In order to adapt the interface or interpretation of input events to the input pose of the user, it ought to be determined using only a single touch – ideally at the start of the application, so as not to surprise the user with a sudden change. To assess our technique's performance for this purpose, we mimicked the layout of a typical application grid on a HTC Sensation XE using Android 4.03, showing a total of 23 icons, including three action buttons at the bottom of the screen. At random, one of the elements was highlighted in red (Fig. 1), indicating to the user to tap it. Once an icon had been tapped, it vanished. After a delay of one second the next item was highlighted. Only "active" icons responded to a user's touch and errors could not be made. Fourteen new users (8 F, mean age: 35.1, SD: 4.98, 1 left-handed, 2 ambid.) performed eight rounds, operating the device with one hand using the left and right thumb, and holding it in either hand, operating it with the index finger of the other. The tasks were performed in two conditions: While sitting in an office and while walking on a busy street at approximately 2.5 km/h. The study was counterbalanced by input pose and mobility (sitting/walking).

The classification of incoming touches works as follows: The screen is divided into a virtual grid of 9mm^2 sized squares, corresponding to the grid of the initial data collection. Each square presents a screen area for which the best algorithm (*Approach A*) or the best three algorithms (*Approach B*) for pose classification have been determined earlier in the cross-validation. When a new touch occurs on the screen, its XY coordinate is matched to a position in the grid into which dimensions and coordinates it fits. Once the corresponding grid unit has been determined, the new touch data is evaluated against the previously collected reference data for this grid unit and screen area using the *Weka* library implemented into the application. It is important to understand that grid units do not have to be actual buttons. Rather, they are invisible, laid over the interface to serve as points of reference from which to draw comparison data and algorithm configuration (Fig. 1). Hitting a unit off-centre is of little relevance, as the offset property is not important for pose classification.

Results

The performance of *Approach A* and *Approach B* for classifying the user's input pose using a single touch on the screen in our example application are as described in Table 5. The accuracy rates are close to the ones given by the cross-validation and verification, showing that one-tap input pose classification is possible with a promising degree of accuracy in a real-life application, but reduced by about 10% when walking, due to greater device movement. However, hand detection is not reliable with a single touch and was therefore not evaluated.

COMPARISON TO PREVIOUS WORK

Wang et al. [11] use the angle between first and last touch point to classify a user's hand on tabletops. We applied their approach to our data and achieved an average of 68.8% accuracy. This is likely due to the unfulfillable prerequisite of expecting users to perform an "oblique" touch for the algorithm to work best. Still, this is preferable to our approach (62.3%) when aiming to classify the user's hand. A comparison to GripSense [2] is twofold: For differentiating between index finger and thumb input, *Approach A* provided an average accuracy of 82.6% compared to GripSense's 84.3%, but with the advantage of using up to only a fifth of the interactions and without spatial and procedural constraints. For distinguishing between input via the left and right hand, GripSense has 85.4% accuracy (when the device is used with the thumb) and is 23% more accurate than our technique, but still needs multiple touches. Yet, it has to be considered that GripSense's accuracy was evaluated using a different set of applications and that its power consumption may be lower due to its simpler algorithm, complicating a direct comparison.

CONTRIBUTION

We have shown how physical and digital finger and touch properties relate to each other (Tab. 1) and thus extended the work of [12] and [2]. Further, we have presented an approach that allows a device to differentiate between index finger and thumb input with an average accuracy of up to 82.6% using only a *single touch*. This is possible by recording touch and movement data for 60 screen regions on a 4.7" smartphone and evaluating new touches by attributing these to a given reference unit in the grid with a specified algorithm. This is an advance over previous work, which uses spatiotemporal differences in touch and movement data from *multiple touches* [2], yielding a similar degree of accuracy. Yet, accuracy is susceptible to device movement (walking) and hand detection is not possible with a single tap. We therefore suggest to pair our technique with a hardware-based approach, such as HandSense [14], for maximum effectiveness. While this paper has shown the potential of the technique, future work will examine the scalability of the approach, whether it can be used to differentiate between other poses and fingers, and aim to limit the effect of walking on accuracy.

REFERENCES

1. Cao, X., Wilson, A. D., Balakrishnan, R., Hinckley, K., and Hudson, S. E. Shapetouch: Leveraging contact shape on interactive surfaces. In *Proc.TABLETOP'08*, 129–136.
2. Goel, M., Wobbrock, J., and Patel, S. Gripsense: using built-in sensors to detect hand posture and pressure on commodity mobile phones. In *Proc.UIST'12*, 545–554.
3. Harrison, B. L., Fishkin, K. P., Gujar, A., Mochon, C., and Want, R. Squeeze me, hold me, tilt me! an exploration of manipulative user interfaces. In *Proc.CHI'98*, 17–24.
4. Harrison, C., Sato, M., and Poupyrev, I. Capacitive fingerprinting: Exploring user differentiation by sensing electrical properties of the human body. In *Proc. UIST'12*, 537–544.
5. Holz., C., and Baudisch, P. Fiberio: A touchscreen that senses fingerprints. In *Proc.UIST'13*, 41–50.
6. Katre, D. One-handed thumb use on smart phones by semi-literate and illiterate users in india. vol. 316 of *IFIP Advances in Information and Communication Technology*. Springer, 189–208.
7. Kim, K.-E., Chang, W., Cho, S.-J., Shim, J., Lee, H., Park, J., Lee, Y., and Kim, S. Hand grip pattern recognition for mobile user interfaces. In *Proc.IAAI'06*, 1789–1794.
8. Miluzzo, E., Varshavsky, A., Balakrishnan, S., and Choudhury, R. R. Tapprints: Your finger taps have fingerprints. In *Proc.MoSys'12*, 323–336.
9. Ono, M., Shizuki, B., and Tanaka, J. Touch&activate: Adding interactivity to existing objects using active acoustic sensing. In *Proc.UIST'13*, 31–40.
10. Parhi, P., Karlson, A. K., and Bederson, B. B. Target size study for one-handed thumb use on small touchscreen devices. In *Proc.MHCI'06*, 203–210.
11. Wang, F., Cao, X., Ren, X., and Irani, P. Detecting and leveraging finger orientation for interaction with direct-touch surfaces. In *Proc.UIST'09*, 23–32.
12. Wang, F., and Ren, X. Empirical evaluation for finger input properties in multi-touch interaction. In *Proc.CHI'09*, 1063–1072.
13. Wilson, G., Brewster, S. A., Halvey, M., Crossan, A., and Stewart, C. The effects of walking, feedback and control method on pressure-based interaction. In *Proc.MHCI'11*, 147–156.
14. Wimmer, R., and Boring, S. HandSense: discriminating different ways of grasping and holding a tangible user interface. In *Proc.TEI'09*, 359–362.
15. Xu, Z., Bai, K., and Zhu, S. TapLogger: inferring user inputs on smartphone touchscreens using on-board motion sensors. In *Proc.WISEC'12*, 113–124.

Dynamir : Optical Manipulations using Dynamic Mirror Brushes

Florent Berthaut
University of Bristol
florent@hitmuri.net

Deepak Ranjan Sahoo
University of Bristol
deepakranjan@gmail.com

Jess McIntosh
University of Bristol
jm0152@my.bristol.ac.uk

Diptesh Das
University of Bristol
diptesh.das09@gmail.com

Sriram Subramanian
University of Bristol
sriram@sussex.ac.uk

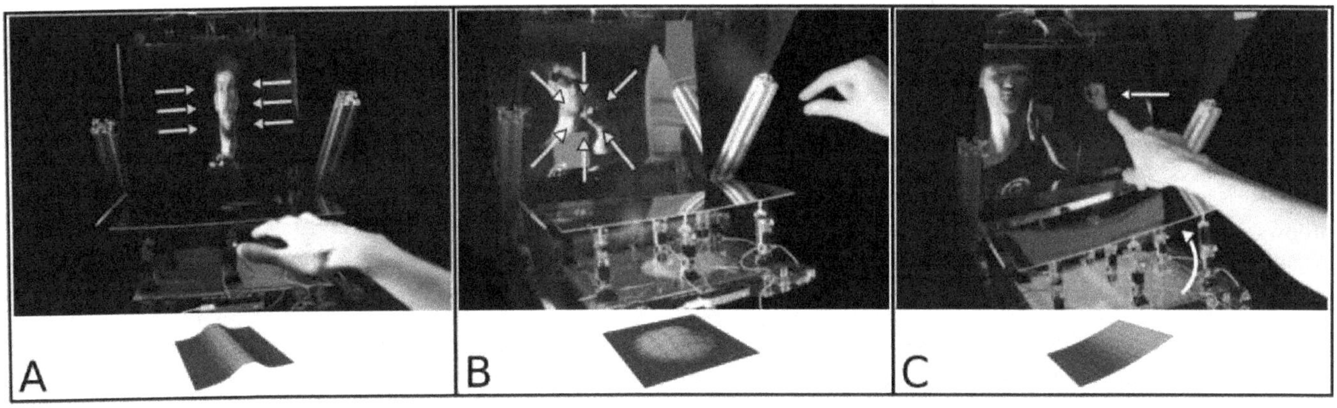

Figure 1. Dynamic mirror brushes allow for optical manipulations by deforming the mirror surface (displayed below). A) Applying a controlled stretching effect using a vertical brush with a 1D curvature. B) Contracting the user's hand for the selection of a small sphere on a stereoscopic screen by changing the curvature and position of a small brush interactively. C) Moving the reflection of physical objects with a finger by changing the orientation of a large brush.

ABSTRACT
Mirror surfaces are part of our everyday life. Among them, curved mirrors are used to enhance our perception of the physical space, e.g., convex mirrors are used to increase our field of view in the street, and concave mirrors are used to zoom in on parts our face in the bathroom. In this paper, we investigate the opportunities opened when these mirrors are made dynamic, so that their effects can be modulated to adapt to the environment or to a user's actions. We introduce the concept of dynamic mirror brushes that can be moved around a mirror surface. We describe how these brushes can be used for various optical manipulations of the physical space. We also present an implementation using a flexible mirror sheet and three scenarios that demonstrate some of the interaction opportunities.

Author Keywords
Dynamir; Shape Changing Mirrors; Mixed Reality;

ITS '15, November 15 - 18, 2015, Funchal, Portugal

ACM 978-1-4503-3899-8/15/11\$15.00
*DOI : http : //dx.doi.org/*10.1145/2817721.2817744

ACM Classification Keywords
H.5.m. Information Interfaces and Presentation (e.g. HCI): Miscellaneous

INTRODUCTION
Curved mirrors are extensively used in everyday life, from theme parks to street signs. These surfaces create a reflection of the physical space that can be altered while preserving some of its physical qualities. For example, convex traffic mirrors are often used at road intersections so on-coming vehicles can see around corners. Large field of view convex mirrors are also embedded in side-view mirrors of vehicles to minimise blind spots. It is common to find concave mirrors in hotel bathrooms that provide a magnified image of the face for shaving. Curved mirrors have also been used in the context of imaging and displays. For instance, in [5], the authors increase the field-of-view (FOV) of a head mounted projected display using a hyperbolic half-silvered mirror. Continuous deformable mirrors are commonly used to correct optical aberration in telescopes, microscopes and laser optical systems. Discrete deforming mirror array are used in projectors [7], as well as solar cells, camera and interactive art. Planar mirrors have been used extensively in mixed-reality displays, however these mirrors remain static. For example, a semi-transparent flat-mirror enables the reflection of a virtual screen to be projected in a physical space allowing

augmentation of an interactive surface [3]. Another use is in [6], where the authors show how the shared space created by semi-transparent mirrors can be used for bidirectional augmentations, e.g., of physical objects on both sides. However, the mirrors remain flat and static, and manipulations of the physical space are done through the virtual augmentations.

Dynamir is a shape changing mirror system that enables a novel approach to optical manipulations based on dynamic mirror brushes. These brushes allow for controlling local deformation of the surface of a flexible mirror with the purpose of enabling manipulations of the physical space, resulting in novel interaction possibilities. Dynamic street mirrors could adapt to the traffic, giving a wider field of view when more and/or faster vehicles are detected. Bathroom mirrors could allow for different levels of zoom when shaving. Individual mirrors could emerge from a collective one when practicing sports or arts and provide private views on movements of users. Users could also be augmented with physical content in novel ways. For example their reflection could be adjusted so that it fits specific clothes or accessories in shopping windows, or they could be made smaller with a convex mirror and integrated in miniature scenes during storytelling performances. On the contrary to augmented mirrors based on cameras and displays, which might limit resolution and contrast of the mirrored scene, Dynamir preserves the optical scene, including the visual cues. Finally, Dynamir can also be used for 3D user interfaces similar to the HoloCubtile [1], adding the possibility of optically manipulating the physical part of interaction techniques, e.g. hands and props, in addition to the virtual part.

Our contribution is three-fold: 1) We propose dynamic mirror brushes that allow for optical manipulations with shape-changing mirrors; 2) We propose an implementation of the brushes with a flexible mirror sheet that also allows for augmented reality scenarios; 3) We demonstrate three novel interactive scenarios.

DYNAMIC MIRROR BRUSHES

Mirrors produce specular reflection of light, i.e., the angle of incidence θ_i at a point P on the mirror equals the angle of reflection θ_r. When an object is placed in front of the mirror, the reflections of the rays coming from the object produce a reflected image of this object. The perception of this reflected image by an observer will depend on the positions of both the observer and the object relative to the mirror. It will also depend on the normals on the mirror surface at all intersections with the light rays coming from the object. Manipulating the reflections therefore amounts to controlling the normals at all points of the surface of the mirror. In this paper, we propose to simplify this manipulation in the context of interactive applications by introducing the concept of dynamic mirror brushes. These brushes are local deformations of the mirror surface which: 1) are aimed at a group of observers, 2) affect a certain region of interest (ROI), and 3) have several attributes that define the effect that they create. The ROI can be the observers themselves or any group of objects in the physical space. As depicted on Figure 2, several brushes can be created and manipulated on a single mirror surface, allowing for different optical effects for different groups of users. Next, we describe the attributes of the optical brushes, i.e., how various optical effects can be specified using them, and how they can be translated into the description of the curvature of the mirror.

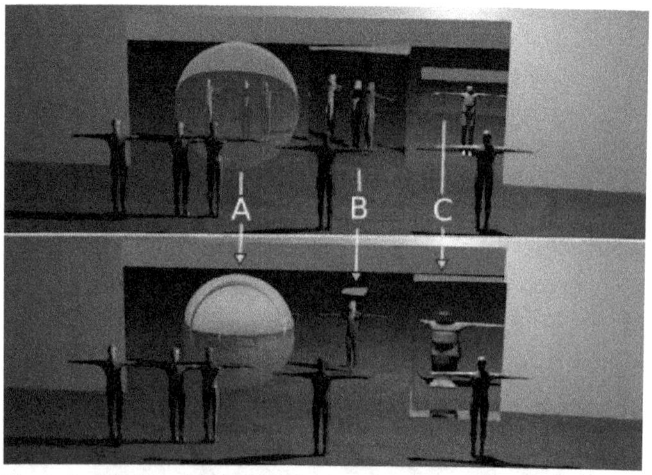

Figure 2. Mockup of three brushes controlled on a large mirror: Left) a group of observers changes the curvature of the Brush A to perceive more of the physical space, Center) the blue character controls the orientation, size and position of the Brush B to select the head of the green character, Right) the yellow character scales his body by controlling the curvature of Brush C.

Size and shape attributes

The first group of attributes, *size and shape*, allow for controlling both the number of observers and the size of the ROI. Changing the size allows, for example, to control how much of a group of people an observer can watch. By varying the shape of the brush, a particular selection of physical objects can be defined from the observer's point of view with any contour, as shown on Figure 2.B. Given the extremities of a ROI, we can calculate the brush size from the lines forming the frustum which define the view of the observer. Finding the intersection points between these lines and the mirror plane give us the coordinates for the corners of the brush.

Position and orientation attributes

The second group of attributes correspond to the *position and orientation* of the brushes relative to the mirror surface. They can be seen as allowing for three different effects. The first is the selection of a region of interest from the observer's point of view. In this case, a brush with a fixed position is rotated according to the observer and ROI positions. The second effect is the manipulation of the position of the reflected image of the ROI. The brush can be moved and rotated in order to move the reflection relative to the observer. Finally, these attributes can be used to inspect the ROI from different angles.

Curvature attribute

The *curvature* attribute enables two main effects, contraction and expansion (i.e., zoom in and zoom out) of the ROI. These effects can be applied either horizontally or vertically as 1D effects, or by combining both as 2D effects. A possible use is the modification of the field of view so that observers can perceive more of a scene while preserving the size of the brush, as demonstrated in Figure 2 Left. It can also be used as a way of enriching 3D interaction done through the observer's reflection, by manipulation the observer himself. The contraction/expansion and hence, zooming out/in of the ROI is achieved by decreasing/increasing the radius of curvature, making the brush respectively convex or concave.

IMPLEMENTATION

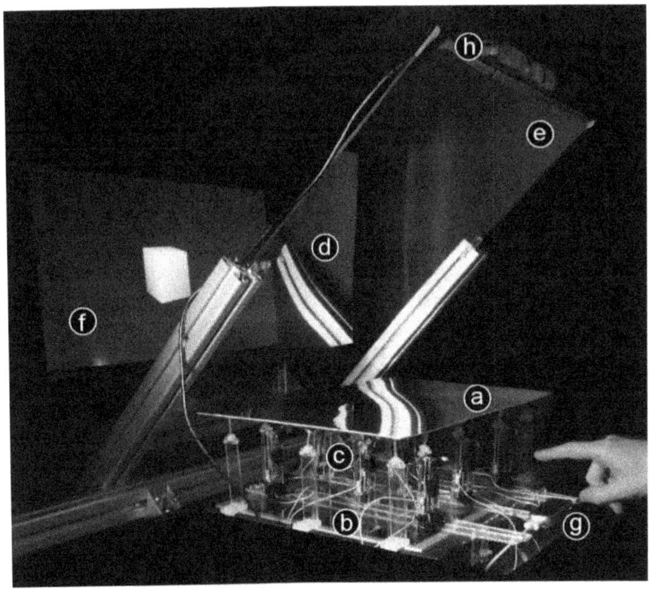

Figure 3. Implementation of dynamic mirror brushes: The shape of a horizontal HIPS mirror sheet (a) is controlled using a LCD monitor (b) displaying a depth-map of the mirror surface and the Shapeclips (c). The reflection image of the mirror is formed as a vertical surface (d) using a half-silvered semi-transparent mirror (e) and is overlapped with a stereoscopic screen (f). A Leap Motion (g) and an Asus Xtion depth camera (h) are used for tracking the positions of the user's head and hands to interact with the mirror.

Hardware

We used a silvered high impact polystyrene (HIPS) sheet with area 420 mm $\times$ 297 mm (A3 size) and thickness $t = 1$ mm as the shape changing mirror surface in our implementation. The HIPS mirror is highly flexible with flexural modulus $E \approx 2.4 \times 10^5$ psi, and highly stress resistant with flexural strength $\sigma_m \approx 4.21 \times 10^3$ psi. This corresponds to yield strain $\epsilon_m = \sigma_m/E = 1.75 \times 10^{-2}$, which means that a sharp edge can be approximated with a round edge with minimum radius of curvature $\rho_m \approx t/2\epsilon_m = 2.85$ cm. Using the HIPS sheet with $t = 0.1$ mm, very sharp edges with $\rho_m = 2.85$ mm can be achieved. Large HIPS mirror with size 2500 mm $\times$ 1250 mm are available off-the-shelf. HIPS is a copolymer of polybutadiene rubber, which has high Poisson ratio $\nu \approx 0.5$. In other words, the HIPS mirror shows good flatness for undistorted reflection, and at the same time good bending, stretching and twisting performance for local shape control.

To change the shape of the mirror, we used a new linear actuator, ShapeClips [4], which has a footprint W^2 of 2 cm $\times$ 2 cm and travel range $R = 6$ cm. The ShapeClips were mounted vertically to support the weight of the mirror for simplicity; i.e., we kept the actuated mirror surface horizontal. A spring mechanism was used to attach the HIPS sheet that allowed the desired deformation of the mirror. In our implementation, the maximum magnitude of shapes is 6 cm, and the maximum angle of sharp edge is $\tan^{-1}(R/W) = 71.56°$. Due to the inherent solid mechanics of the HIPS sheet, the shapes generated comprise of hyperbolic functions; the radius of curvature can be calculated from the solid mechanics analysis [9]. The maximum speed of the ShapeClips is 8 cm/s, which dictates the speed of our implementation. We used nine ShapeClips in our implementation. The ShapeClips are compact and modular, and more of them can be incorporated in our implementation seamlessly to create shapes with higher complexity [2], and to alleviate the trade-off between achieving flat surface and sharp edges. For example, more ShapeClips and thinner HIPS mirror are required to effectively demonstrate the application described in Figure 2.B that uses both flat surfaces and sharp edges. Our implementation with nine ShapeClips and a thicker HIPS mirror allows for curved brushes, either two dimensional (bumps), or one dimensional vertical or horizontal curved ridges, as well as flat brushes when rotating the the entire mirror sheet. As depicted on Figure 3, we placed a half-silvered mirror at $45°$ angle above the shape changing mirror. The space in front of this half-silvered mirror is therefore reflected on to the shape changing mirror, and back to the front space towards the user. In addition, a polarized stereoscopic screen is placed behind the half-silvered mirror at the virtual image of the shape changing mirror, making it possible to overlap virtual content with the manipulated/deformed reflection space.

Software

The software part of our implementation is mostly written in Javascript and runs in a browser. 3D shapes are rendered with Three.js, Leap Motion data is gathered with the leap Javascript sdk and position of the head computed from the depth camera is sent from a C++ application to the browser via a node.js bridge and OpenSoundControl messages. We want to be able to manipulate the optical brushes by simply generating and controlling corresponding virtual brushes in the form of meshes. Because ShapeClips translate the light field below them to a vertical displacement, we render the virtual brushes in a 3D scene below them. The frustum is defined so that near and far clipping planes match the minimum and maximum physical heights, and its dimensions match the dimensions of the screen. We then use a GLSL fragment shader that renders the depth of the meshes instead of their color. In order to compensate for variations in the ShapeClips heights, we also integrate a calibration texture in our fragment shader, which offsets the rendered depth separately for each ShapeClip. The virtual brushes themselves can be created in different ways depending on which attributes need to be controlled. For example, spheres with changes in position and scale can serve as brushes with a controllable 2D curvature, cylinders as brushes with a controllable 1D curvature, simple planes for flat brushes with changes in orientation. A more generic method consists in building the brush mesh from a Non-Uniform Rational B-spline surface, allowing for changes in size, shape and curvature on both axes, following the guidelines on shape-changing displays given in [8].

SCENARIOS

We propose three interactive scenarios enabled by Dynamir which demonstrate the effectiveness of our implementation.

The first scenario, depicted on Figure 1.A, and demonstrates the use of the position and curvature attributes. It allows an observer to apply a vertical contraction effect to himself, which remain applied to him as he moves, contrary to what would be possible with a static mirror. The magnitude of the contraction, is increased and decreased by moving the hand respectively away from and towards the mirror. With a larger scale implementation, several brushes could be created and applied to different regions of interest of the scene reflected in the mirror. Being defined relative to the user, these brushes would move with him as the single brush does in our scenario, keeping the region of interest of each brush constant. Each of their attributes could be set independently. In effect, this scenario corresponds to an optical version of an image manipulation application.

The second scenario, depicted on Figure 1.B, demonstrates how the curvature attribute can be controlled to expand and contract a region of interest in two dimensions. It draws inspiration from augmented mirrors such as the ones presented in [6], which allow users to manipulate virtual content through their reflection. Using our dynamic mirror brushes, their reflection can be altered to enrich the interaction techniques. In our case, a small sphere and a large cube are displayed on the stereoscopic screen placed behind the half-silvered mirror. By closing / opening their hand, the user controls the curvature of the brush, which in turns makes their hand smaller or larger, allowing them to select and manipulate the object of corresponding size at an appropriate scale. Other 3D manipulation and navigation techniques could be enriched by manipulating the user's image, for example to optically modify the control-display ratio.

With our third scenario, depicted on Figure 1.C, we demonstrate the use of the orientation attribute to manipulate the physical world. The user is able to move the reflection of a pre-defined physical object, here a mug. From the point of view of the user, the mug remains at the tip of his finger. The optical brush, which covers the whole mirror, changes orientation in order to align the virtual image of the object with the finger. With multiple brushes, multiple objects from the physical space could be manipulated at the same time.

CONCLUSION

In this paper, we proposed a novel approach for optical manipulations using shape changing mirrors. We described dynamic mirror brushes that allow for describing these manipulations with controllable attributes. We described an implementation of a shape-changing mirror and three interactive scenarios demonstrating the use of the brushes. We believe that our approach opens opportunities for research in public displays, augmented reality and 3D interaction. It could also benefit many everyday life applications. Finally, it leads to more interesting research questions. A large scale implementation will for example require studying materials with different stretchability and actuation mechanisms, in order to enable large changes in position and size attributes and sharp changes of orientation anywhere on the surface.

ACKNOWLEDGEMENTS

This project was funded by the EC FP7 through the Marie Curie Fellowship (PIEF-GA-2012-330770), ERC Starting Grant (278576) and FET Open Scheme (309191).

REFERENCES

1. De la Rivière, J. B., Dittlo, N., Orvain, E., Kervégant, C., and Courtois, M. Holocubtile: 3d multitouch brings the virtual world into the user's hands. In *ACM International Conference on Interactive Tabletops and Surfaces*, ITS '10, ACM (New York, NY, USA, 2010), 311–311.
2. Follmer, S., Leithinger, D., Olwal, A., Hogge, A., and Ishii, H. inform: Dynamic physical affordances and constraints through shape and object actuation. In *Proceedings of the 26th Annual ACM Symposium on User Interface Software and Technology*, UIST '13, ACM (New York, NY, USA, 2013), 417–426.
3. Hachet, M., Bossavit, B., Cohé, A., and de la Rivière, J.-B. Toucheo: Multitouch and stereo combined in a seamless workspace. In *Proceedings of the 24th Annual ACM Symposium on User Interface Software and Technology*, UIST '11, ACM (New York, NY, USA, 2011), 587–592.
4. Hardy, J., Weichel, C., Taher, F., Vidler, J., and Alexander, J. Shapeclip: Towards rapid prototyping with shape- changing displays for designers. In *Proceedings of the SIGCHI Conference on Human Factors in Computing Systems*, CHI '15, ACM (New York, NY, USA, 2015), xxx–xxx.
5. Kiyokawa, K. A wide field-of-view head mounted projective display using hyperbolic half-silvered mirrors. In *Proceedings of the 2007 6th IEEE and ACM International Symposium on Mixed and Augmented Reality*, ISMAR '07, IEEE Computer Society (Washington, DC, USA, 2007), 1–4.
6. Martinez Plasencia, D., Berthaut, F., Karnik, A., and Subramanian, S. Through the combining glass. In *Proceedings of the 27th Annual ACM Symposium on User Interface Software and Technology*, UIST '14, ACM (New York, NY, USA, 2014), 341–350.
7. Nayar, S. K., Branzoi, V., and Boult, T. E. Programmable imaging: Towards a flexible camera. *Int. J. Comput. Vision 70*, 1 (Oct. 2006), 7–22.
8. Roudaut, A., Karnik, A., Löchtefeld, M., and Subramanian, S. Morphees: Toward high "shape resolution" in self-actuated flexible mobile devices. In *Proceedings of the SIGCHI Conference on Human Factors in Computing Systems*, CHI '13, ACM (New York, NY, USA, 2013), 593–602.
9. Ventsel, E., and Krauthammer, T. *Thin Plates and Shells: Theory: Analysis, and Applications*. CRC Press, 2001.

CapAuth: Identifying and Differentiating User Handprints on Commodity Capacitive Touchscreens

Anhong Guo **Robert Xiao** **Chris Harrison**
Human-Computer Interaction Institute
Carnegie Mellon University, 5000 Forbes Avenue, Pittsburgh, PA 15213
{anhongg,brx,chris.harrison}@cs.cmu.edu

ABSTRACT

User identification and differentiation have implications in many application domains, including security, personalization, and co-located multiuser systems. In response, dozens of approaches have been developed, from fingerprint and retinal scans, to hand gestures and RFID tags. In this work, we propose CapAuth, a technique that uses existing, low-level touchscreen data, combined with machine learning classifiers, to provide real-time authentication and even identification of users. As a proof-of-concept, we ran our software on an off-the-shelf Nexus 5 smartphone. Our user study demonstrates twenty-participant authentication accuracies of 99.6%. For twenty-user identification, our software achieved 94.0% accuracy and 98.2% on groups of four, simulating family use.

Author Keywords

Touchscreen input; mobile devices; capacitive sensing; user identification; user differentiation; groupware.

ACM Classification Keywords

H.5.2. Information interfaces and presentation (*e.g.*, HCI): User Interfaces: Input devices and strategies.

INTRODUCTION

Understanding *who* is interacting with a computing device has many implications and applications. It is most often used for authentication [1,5,10], where only certain users are permitted to use the system or privileged functionality. It can also be used for personalization [9,12], where different users can have custom settings, browser bookmarks, email accounts, favorite applications and so on. Furthermore, knowing who is performing what action is also tremendously valuable in co-located computer supported collaborative work [2,13] and games [4], for example, on large interactive tabletops.

Recently, Bodyprint [6] demonstrated how unmodified, commodity touchscreens can be used to identify and authenticate users. This is done by capturing a capacitive "image" of various body parts when they are pressed to the touchscreen, for example the ear. We extend this paradigm with a new "hands-flat" pose, which reveals more distinguishing user features, enabling higher recognition accuracies. During evaluation, Bodyprint used a single round of data collected in one sitting, and ran a post hoc cross-fold analysis. We extend this feasibility study to additionally validate stability over time, where users attempt to authenticate at a later time. We also extend the study to account for real world issues, such as hand moisture level and accuracies amongst small groups of users.

ITS '15, November 15-18, 2015, Funchal, Portugal
© 2015 ACM. ISBN 978-1-4503-3899-8/15/11···$15.00
DOI: http://dx.doi.org/10.1145/2817721.2817722

IMPLEMENTATION

Modern projected capacitive touchscreens work by detecting changes in a projected electric field caused by a proximate finger. The touch controller collects capacitance measurements across the touch-sensing grid (Figure 1), which are taken together to form a *capacitive image*. This image is generally used inside the touch controller to resolve the pixel position of touch contacts, which are subsequently reported to the operating system.

We developed our proof-of-concept CapAuth implementation on a Nexus 5 smartphone running Android 5.0.1, with a Linux kernel specially modified to provide access to the Synaptics ClearPad 3350 touchscreen controller's debugging interface. We use this interface to obtain the 16-bit 15×27 capacitive image at 25 FPS. Each pixel of the image corresponds to a 4.1mm×4.1mm square on the screen. The pixel values are the picofarad (pF) differences between the baseline measurement and current measurement. CapAuth uses the capacitive image to derive a series of features designed to capture material (*e.g.*, varying dielectric effects from skin thickness) and geometric (*e.g.*, heights of fingers) variations between the hands of different users.

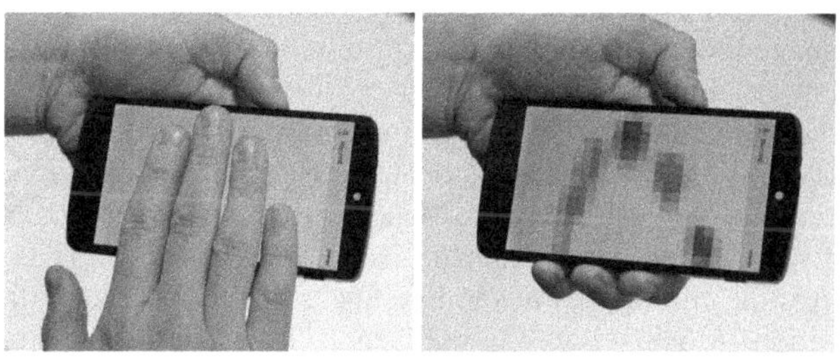

Figure 1. Capacitive image on Nexus 5. Left: hand position on the screen. Right: resulting capacitive image.

Features

We compute the following set of 550 features from the capacitive image: each raw data point as an independent feature, mean values of the capacitive image / each row / each column, length of each finger, number of pixels with a value of over 15pF for each finger, sum of value of each finger, coordinates of the 9 points (overall centroid / four fingertips / centroids of each finger), and the distances and angles of each of the two points among the 9 points. Using feature selection, we found that a subset of 150 features was sufficient for reasonably accurate classification.

Classification Algorithm

The full feature set is used to train quadratic-kernel support vector machine (SVM) classifiers using the Weka machine-learning toolkit [3]. For authentication, we use a binary classifier specific to each user, which distinguishes between that user and all other users. For identification, we train a multi-class, one-to-one classifier, which uses binary classifiers trained to distinguish each pair of users. Each binary classifier output is treated as a vote for that user, and the votes are tallied to form the final classifier output.

Correct Hand Placement

We use a separate process for ensuring that users place their hands on the screen in a standard fashion; consistency is important for reliable user differentiation. A separate binary SVM classifier is trained to distinguish between correct and incorrect hand placements. This classifier uses the same feature set described in the previous section.

This classifier is exposed to users through a basic visualization. Our application starts with a grey screen with a suggestive handprint rendered on screen (Figure 2). Improper placements cause the screen to turn red, indicating the user should reposition their hand. The screen turns green when an acceptable handprint is detected.

Classifier Confidence

In our real-time classifier running on the phone, we use the binary classifier vote tallies to compute a confidence score for each class, outputting the class corresponding to the highest confidence score. In the event of a tie, the classifier outputs a null result meaning "not confident", after which the user interface will prompt the user to "try again".

RELATED WORK

Many systems in the literature aim to extract biometric data from touchscreens; see *e.g.*, Blažica *et al.* [1] for a survey. However, most such systems use camera-based setups to image the user's hand at high resolution, in contrast to our low-resolution capacitive image. Fiberio [5] uses a high-resolution camera to capture fingerprints. HandsDown [12] uses a diffuse-illumination interactive tabletop and hand contours for user identification (see *e.g.*, [7,11] for more discussion on hand geometry-based approaches). MTi [1] uses the coordinates of the five finger tips for user identification. Mock *et al.* [8] used an FTIR screen and blob-geometry analysis for user identification from typing.

Figure 2. CapAuth classification. Left: initial state. Middle: unauthorized user (red). Right: authorized user (green).

Carpus [9] used a high-resolution overhead camera and the back of users' hands as identifiers. Capacitive Fingerprinting [4] used a special sensor attached to an infrared touch panel to measure the swept-frequency impedance of a user. Vu *et al.* [14] authenticated users on a capacitive touchscreen by using a finger-worn ring device to inject a pattern of false events onto the screen. Finally, "Biometric-Rich Gestures" [10] used five-finger touch gestures and movement of palm and fingertips for authentication. In contrast to these methods, our approach uses low-resolution commodity touchscreens found in nearly every "smart" device today, without needing user or device augmentation.

As discussed previously, we extend work presented in Bodyprint [6], which authenticated users via various body parts (*e.g.*, ear, fist, and hand grips) pressed against a conventional capacitive touchscreen. Compared with Bodyprint, we demonstrate improved accuracy (99.6% authentication precision with 5.5% false rejection rate), live classification, accuracy persistence and moisture robustness, all with more users (20 participants).

EVALUATION

We recruited 20 participants, gender balanced, with a mean age of 26.0. Our primary study consisted of five sessions of handprint data collection, each separated by a short break to avoid over-fitting to transient physical properties of the hand and repetitive (and thus similar) placement of the hand by the user. In total, the study took approximately 30 minutes and participants received $10 for their time.

Following a brief demonstration of proper hand placement on our Nexus 5 prototype, participants proceeded to record one session of data. Participants placed their right hand down onto the screen in a natural fashion and pressed the physical volume button (located on the side of the device) to record one handprint trial. Participants were asked to lift their hands from the screen between trials before replacing them, adding variety to the collected data. Fifty handprints were collected in each session. In total, four sessions were collected in the manner, producing 4000 handprint instances (20 participants × 4 sessions × 50 trials).

One additional and special session collected *improper* hand placements, which we use to train our "correct hand placement classifier". In this session only, users were instructed to put their hands on the screen in a way that did not match the onscreen guide. This produced 1000 improper handprints (20 participants × 1 session × 50 trials).

Thus in total, there was five data collection sessions. In the breaks between these sessions, participants were asked to perform an activity. After round one, they completed a survey. After round two, they traced an outline of their hand on paper. After round three, they completed another survey, and in the last break, they washed and dried their hands. We included this hand-washing step to see if altering the moisture level (and likely the capacitance) of the hands would affect classification.

We also asked 10 of our participants to return for a follow-up study several days later (3 female, mean age 25.2, mean gap of 8.0 days). Using *all* handprint data collected from procedure above (20 participants), our Nexus 5 was initialized with participant-specific authentication and identification classifiers. Each participant then collected handprints following the same procedure as before. However, this time, classification was performed in *real-time* on the phone for a "live" experimental result. Of note, the interface was the same as the first study, which lacked graphical feedback (thus preventing participants from adjusting their hand pose to match classification results).

RESULTS

Beyond immediate authentication and identification accuracies, we also designed our study to provide insights into a variety of peripheral questions relevant to our method.

Authentication

To assess authentication accuracy, we ran a simulation consisting of 1000 handprint-events for each of our 20 participants (*i.e.*, 20,000 rounds). In each round of the simulation, we randomly combined 3 (out of 4) sessions of data from each participant and used this to train an "authorized" class. At the same time, we used 3 randomly selected sessions of data from each of the remaining 19 participants for an "unauthorized" class. We then trained a binary classifier on this data. The unused session from each of the twenty participants was used for testing. Thus, the classifier was trained on 2850 negative and 150 positive instances, and tested on 950 negative and 50 positive instances.

Overall, our technique achieved twenty-participant authentication accuracies of 99.6% (SD=0.76%). More specifically, 94.5% of the time, the "authorized" participant was correctly logged into the system. And 5.5% of the time, the system falsely rejected that participant, which would prompt the user to "try again" in real world applications. On the other hand, an unauthorized user was falsely accepted only 0.1% of the time. See Table 1 for the confusion matrix.

Identification

To assess identification accuracy, we ran another 1000 round classification simulation. In each round, we randomly combined 3 (out of 4) sessions of data from each participant and used this as a training set. Each participant was labeled as a separate class (*i.e.*, a twenty-class classifier). The single unused session of data from all twenty participants was used for testing. We forced our classifier to make a best guess, even when it was "not confident". Overall, our technique achieved a mean twenty-participant identification accuracy of 94.0% (SD=2.7%); see Table 2.

Not Authenticated	Authenticated	←Classified as
99.9%	0.1%	Not Authenticated
5.5%	94.5%	Authenticated

Table 1. Confusion matrix for authentication simulations.

Small Groups

We also conducted a post hoc experiment simulating family units of size four. In each of the 1000 simulation rounds, we randomly picked 4 (out of 20) participants to form a "family", and constructed an identification classifier for that family. We randomly combined 3 (out of 4) sessions of data from each of the four family members and used this for training. The unused session of data for each member was used for testing the classifier.

Overall, our technique achieved four-participant identification accuracies of 98.2% (SD=3.95%). The histogram in Figure 3 shows the family member identification accuracy result as percentages of rounds (*i.e.*, simulated families). More than 40% of the families achieved 100% accuracy, and 90% of families achieved exceeded 95% accuracy.

Correct Hand Placement

To assess the accuracy of our hand placement classifier, we ran 1000 simulation rounds. In each round of the simulation, we chose a stratified sample consisting of 70% of correct and improper hand placements to use as training data. We then trained a binary classifier (*i.e.*, the classifier returned "correct" or "incorrect" hand placement as its output). The remaining (30%) data was used for testing the classifier. Overall accuracy was 99.7% (SD=0.15%), demonstrating robust rejection of incorrect hand placements, which is an important pre-check before attempting authentication or identification.

Hand Washing

In our user study, we asked participants to wash and dry their hands in the restroom before the last session. This was

	P1	P2	P3	P4	P5	P6	P7	P8	P9	P10	P11	P12	P13	P14	P15	P16	P17	P18	P19	P20
P1	99.5	0.0	0.0	0.0	0.4	0.0	0.0	0.0	0.0	0.0	0.0	0.1	0.0	0.0	0.0	0.0	0.0	0.0	0.0	0.0
P2	1.0	98.6	0.0	0.0	0.0	0.0	0.0	0.0	0.0	0.0	0.0	0.0	0.0	0.0	0.0	0.5	0.0	0.0	0.0	0.0
P3	1.0	0.0	98.9	0.0	0.0	0.0	0.0	0.0	0.1	0.0	0.0	0.0	0.0	0.0	0.0	0.0	0.0	0.0	0.0	0.0
P4	1.0	0.0	0.0	98.5	0.0	0.5	0.0	0.0	0.0	0.0	0.0	0.0	0.0	0.0	0.0	0.0	0.0	0.0	0.0	0.0
P5	2.9	0.0	0.0	0.0	96.8	0.0	0.0	0.0	0.0	0.0	0.0	0.0	0.0	0.0	0.0	0.2	0.0	0.0	0.1	0.0
P6	11.5	0.0	0.0	0.0	0.0	87.6	0.0	0.0	0.2	0.0	0.0	0.0	0.1	0.0	0.0	0.0	0.1	0.0	0.5	0.0
P7	0.5	0.0	0.0	0.0	0.0	0.4	98.5	0.0	0.0	0.0	0.0	0.0	0.0	0.0	0.2	0.4	0.0	0.0	0.0	0.0
P8	2.6	0.0	0.0	0.0	0.0	0.0	0.0	97.3	0.0	0.0	0.0	0.0	0.0	0.0	0.0	0.0	0.0	0.0	0.0	0.0
P9	16.5	0.0	0.4	0.0	0.0	0.4	0.0	0.0	82.2	0.4	0.0	0.0	0.1	0.0	0.0	0.0	0.0	0.0	0.0	0.0
P10	1.7	0.0	0.0	0.0	0.0	0.8	0.0	0.0	0.0	97.4	0.0	0.0	0.0	0.0	0.0	0.0	0.0	0.0	0.0	0.0
P11	1.9	0.0	0.0	0.0	0.0	0.0	0.0	0.0	0.0	0.0	97.8	0.0	0.0	0.3	0.0	0.0	0.0	0.0	0.0	0.0
P12	3.0	0.0	0.0	0.0	0.0	0.0	0.0	0.0	0.0	0.0	0.0	97.0	0.0	0.0	0.0	0.0	0.0	0.0	0.0	0.0
P13	1.0	0.0	0.0	0.0	0.0	0.0	0.0	0.0	0.0	0.0	0.0	0.0	99.0	0.0	0.0	0.0	0.0	0.0	0.0	0.0
P14	1.0	0.3	12.1	0.0	0.1	0.0	0.0	0.2	0.1	0.0	0.5	0.0	0.1	85.7	0.0	0.0	0.0	0.0	0.0	0.0
P15	30.8	4.0	0.0	0.8	0.0	0.1	0.1	0.0	0.1	0.4	0.0	0.3	0.0	0.0	61.9	0.0	0.2	1.4	0.0	0.0
P16	5.7	0.0	0.0	0.0	0.0	0.0	0.0	0.0	0.0	0.0	0.0	0.0	0.0	0.0	0.1	93.4	0.4	0.3	0.0	0.0
P17	3.9	0.0	0.0	0.0	0.0	0.0	0.0	0.0	0.0	0.0	0.0	0.2	0.0	0.0	0.0	0.0	95.9	0.0	0.0	0.0
P18	1.3	0.0	0.0	0.0	0.0	0.0	0.0	0.0	0.0	0.0	0.0	0.5	0.0	0.0	1.2	0.0	0.0	97.0	0.0	0.0
P19	2.0	0.0	0.0	0.0	0.0	0.0	0.0	0.0	0.0	0.0	0.0	0.0	0.0	0.0	0.0	0.0	0.0	0.0	97.8	0.0
P20	0.2	0.0	0.0	0.4	0.0	0.0	0.0	0.3	0.0	0.0	0.0	0.0	0.0	0.0	0.0	0.0	0.0	0.0	0.0	99.1

Table 2. Confusion matrix for identification simulations.

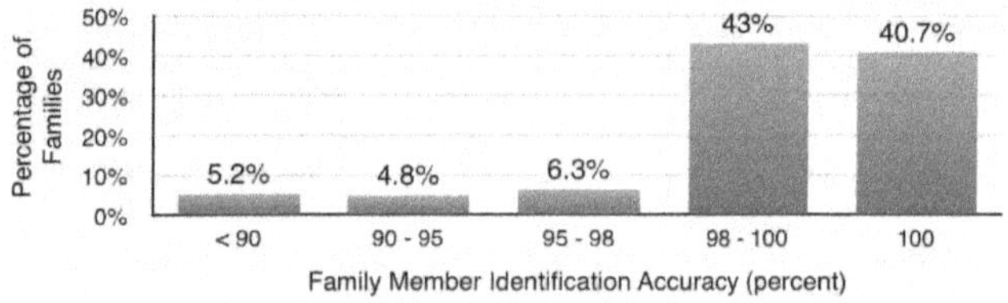

Figure 3. Histogram of family member identification accuracy.

included to see if altering the moisture of the hands would affect classification accuracy. Like our other experiments, we randomly combined 3 (out of 4) sessions of data from each participant, and used this as a training set. The unused sessions were used for testing.

For authentication, the accuracy for the session after hand washing (99.5%, SD=1.06%) had no significant difference in accuracy from the other three (pre-wash) sessions (99.7%, SD=0.52%). For identification, the accuracy for the session after hand washing is slightly worse: 91.7% (SD=20.9%) compared to 95.4% (SD=9.38%) for the pre-wash sessions, though this is not statistically significant.

Stability Over Time & Live Accuracy

As described previously, to study the robustness of classification over time, we invited ten of our participants to return after several days (mean gap of 8.0 days). We then evaluated authentication and identification accuracies "live" (trained using the data collected days earlier).

The new authentication accuracy was 98.0% (SD=2.62%), slightly down from 99.6%. However, identification accuracy was up: 96.5% (SD=4.70%) vs. 94.0% previously. Neither result was statically significant, suggesting that CapAuth may be stable overtime.

Questionnaire Data

We collected various demographic and qualitative information, including age, height, weight, and thirstiness to see if there was any affect on classification accuracy. We also computed a BMI estimate using this data. However, we found no significant correlations, though we warn that our participant pool is too small to draw any strong conclusions.

DISCUSSION AND CONCLUSION

Our results indicate that CapAuth is not well suited for high-security applications, nor use cases desiring user differentiation among large groups of users (*e.g.*, ten or more people). However, CapAuth can accurately identify users within smaller groups at 98.2% accuracy, such as families, suggesting its use as a simple user differentiation mechanism for shared devices where security is not paramount. This could be used to *e.g.*, provide parental control on a family tablet, or to enable tracking of individual users on a shared workspace touch table.

Similarly, authentication accuracies, even in large groups (20 or fewer people), is reasonably high (99.6% and 98.0% from our two studies). While acceptable for *e.g.*, family use, this result is still not sufficiently secure for security applications (which typically require accuracies in excess of 99.9%). However, even in high-security settings, CapAuth could prove useful as a two-factor authentication method.

Finally, one limitation of this technique is its potential susceptibility to environmental effects. Similar to the difficulty of detecting faces under varying illumination conditions, our system may not function as well under varying electrical conditions (*e.g.*, grounding to a charger, proximity to high-power electrical devices) as these could affect the capacitive image. Similarly, liquid on the screen (*e.g.*, raindrops) and certainly gloves, rings, watches and other accessories could affect accuracies.

ACKNOWLEDGEMENTS

This research was generously supported by Qualcomm, Google and the David and Lucile Packard Foundation.

REFERENCES

1. Blažica, B., Vladušič, D. and Mladenić, D. (2013). MTi: A method for user identification for multitouch displays. *Int. J. of Human-Computer Studies, 71*(6), 691-702.
2. Gutwin, C., Greenberg, S., Blum, R., Dyck, J., Tee, K. and McEwan, G. Supporting Informal Collaboration in Shared-Workspace Groupware. *J. UCS, 14*(9), 2008, 1411-1434.
3. Hall, M. *et al.* The WEKA Data Mining Software: An Update. *SIGKDD Explor.*, 11,1. 2009.
4. Harrison, C., Sato, M. and Poupyrev, I. Capacitive fingerprinting: exploring user differentiation by sensing electrical properties of the human body. In *Proc. UIST '12.* 537-544.
5. Holz, C. and Baudisch, P. Fiberio: A touchscreen that senses fingerprints. In *Proc. UIST '13.* 41-50.
6. Holz, C., Buthpitiya, S. and Knaust, M. Bodyprint: Biometric User Identification on Mobile Devices Using the Capacitive Touchscreen to Scan Body Parts. In *Proc. CHI '15.* 3011-3014.
7. Jain, A., Ross, A. and Pankanti, S. A prototype hand geometry-based verification system. In *Proc. AVBPA '99.* 166-171.
8. Mock, P., Edelmann, J., Schilling, A. and Rosenstiel, W. User identification using raw sensor data from typing on interactive displays. In *Proc. IUI '14.* 67-72.
9. Ramakers, R., *et al.* Carpus: a non-intrusive user identification technique for interactive surfaces. In *Proc. UIST '12.* 35-44.
10. Sae-Bae, N., Ahmed, K., Isbister, K. and Memon, N. Biometric-rich gestures: a novel approach to authentication on multi-touch devices. In *Proc. CHI '12.* 977-986.
11. Sanchez-Reillo, R., Sanchez-Avila, C., & Gonzalez-Marcos, A. (2000). Biometric identification through hand geometry measurements. *IEEE Trans. Pattern Anal. Mach. Intell.* 22(10), 1168-1171.
12. Schmidt, D., Chong, M. K. and Gellersen, H. HandsDown: hand-contour-based user identification for interactive surfaces. In *Proc. NordiCHI '10.* 432-441.
13. Stewart, J., Bederson, B. B. and Druin, A. Single display groupware: a model for co-present collaboration. In *Proc. CHI '99.* 286-293.
14. Vu, T., *et al.* Distinguishing users with capacitive touch communication. In *Proc. Mobicom '12.* 197-208.
15. Zheng, N., Bai, K., Huang, H. and Wang, H. You are how you touch: User verification on smartphones via tapping behaviors. In *Proc. IEEE ICNP '14.* 221-232.

TalkingTiles: Supporting Personalization and Customization in an AAC App for Individuals with Aphasia

Thomas Huijbregts
Department of Knowledge Integration
University of Waterloo, Canada
thomashuijbregts@hotmail.com

James R. Wallace
School of Public Health and Health Systems
University of Waterloo, Canada
james.wallace@uwaterloo.ca

ABSTRACT
The development of 'Post-PC' interactive surfaces, such as smartphones and tablets, and specialized support software informed by HCI research has created new opportunities for Augmentative and Alternative Communication (AAC) technologies. However, it is unclear to what degree these opportunities have been realized in practice. We conducted a field study to explore the use of one such application, TalkingTiles, by individuals with aphasia. Following a training session and one week of use, we conducted interviews with participants, their partners, and their caregivers at a local support facility. We found that TalkingTiles can be effective in supporting communication when used in concert with other communication methods, and when time can be invested in customizing the app. We discuss our findings, and implications for design with respect to customizability, simplicity, and the limitations of interactive surfaces in supporting communication.

ACM Classification Keywords
H.5.2. Information Interfaces and Presentation (e.g. HCI): User-Centred Design

Author Keywords
aphasia; augmentative and alternative communication

INTRODUCTION
The development of Augmentative and Alternative Communication (AAC) technologies has long been a promise of Human-Computer Interaction (HCI) research. These technologies enable individuals who may otherwise be unable to communicate to participate and engage with those around them. For example, prototype systems have been developed to support communication for individuals living with Alzheimer's disease [6, 14], memory impairments [27], and disorders such as aphasia [5, 7, 26]. However, the emergence of 'Post-PC' interactive surfaces, such as smartphones and tablets, has created new opportunities to develop more personal and more powerful AAC tools. These devices provide unprecedented access to advanced graphics and processing capabilities, a simple multi-touch interface, cameras, GPS, and built-in motion sensors, as well as wireless internet access – all in a light-weight, mobile form factor.

ITS '15, November 15 - 18, 2015, Funchal, Portugal
Copyright is held by the owner/author(s). Publication rights licensed to ACM.
ACM 978-1-4503-3899-8/15/11...$15.00
DOI: http://dx.doi.org/10.1145/2817721.2817723

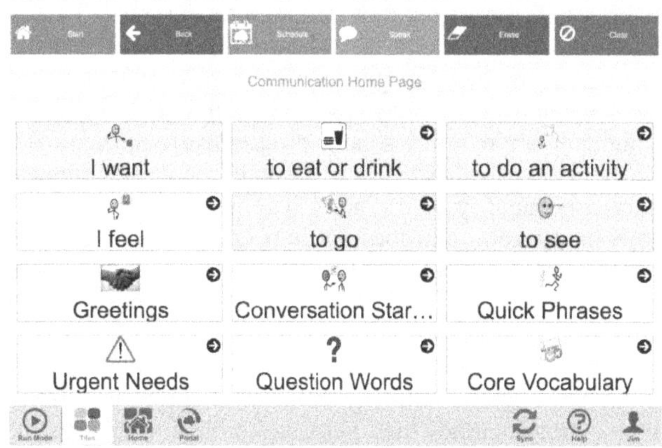

Figure 1. TalkingTiles is an Augmented and Alternative Communication app that enables users to construct sentences by tapping on tiles associated with words or short phrases.

Where HCI research has already explored the design of AAC devices, this work predates the emergence of interactive surfaces as pervasive, rich, and developed ecosystems [3, 5, 6, 7]. Interactive surfaces provide an opportunity for novel, accessible interaction appropriate for AAC applications, and are displacing existing, and often less accessible computer infrastructure such as desktop PCs. In embracing these opportunities for surface interaction, commercially available apps are implementing research outcomes from the HCI literature [3, 26]. Given the knowledge translation that has taken place, we wanted to explore how lessons learned through research conducted on early mobile devices carries over to modern applications and devices, and to understand the new roles that they are are playing in facilitating AAC.

We conducted a field study with a new commercial AAC app for iPad, called TalkingTiles[1] (Figure 1). We chose to focus on individuals with aphasia, a communication disorder caused by damage to areas of the brain controlling language, because of the established related research and availability of design considerations in the literature [3, 5, 7, 18, 26]. After training participants in the use of the software, we asked them to use the app over a one week period to understand how it

[1]http://www.mozzaz.com/index.php/products/talkingtiles

fulfilled their daily communication needs. Following the trial period, we conducted an in-depth interview that explored how participants, their caregivers, and family members had used the app to support their daily communication. We found that TalkingTiles can be effective when used in concert with other communication methods, and when time can be invested in customizing the app. We discuss our findings, and design implications with respect to customizability, simplicity, and the limitations of post-PC devices in supporting communication.

APHASIA: MASKING INTELLIGENCE

Aphasia is a communication disorder caused by damage to areas of the brain controlling language, resulting in the complete loss or impairment of language function [4]. This damage is most often the result of a stroke [25], with aphasia being one of the most frequent symptoms in acute and chronic stroke patients [21], but can also be caused by brain tumours, traumatic brain injuries, and progressive neurological disorders [19]. Aphasia has a particularly drastic impact on survivors' quality of life since it inhibit's a person's ability to communicate, but does not impact their cognitive ability. That is, while individuals know what they want to say, they are unable to form the words, often leaving them feeling isolated and frustrated. These symptoms are particularly pronounced immediately following the onset of aphasia, as individuals struggle to adjust to their new abilities, and the communication methods they must now utilize to express themselves. Aphasia is therefore said to 'mask intelligence'.

The severity and symptoms associated with aphasia can vary dramatically between individuals, depending on the type and extent of brain damage [21]. For some individuals, aphasia may be very mild and impact only one aspect of communication, such as the ability to recall the names of objects. However, more typically, aphasia affects multiple aspects of communication to varying degrees; for example an individual may have the ability to comprehend images and speech, but not recognize text. In the extreme, severe forms of aphasia can inhibit any form of communication. We base our investigations on three working classifications of the disorder: *receptive, expressive, and global aphasia.* Wernicke's Aphasia, otherwise known as *receptive* aphasia, impacts comprehension abilities. Broca's Aphasia, which is one of the most common forms of aphasia, and is often referred to as *expressive* aphasia, reduces the ability of individuals to produce speech output, and also affects typing and writing abilities. These individuals are often unable to form complete sentences, and can have difficulty understanding complete sentences. Finally, *global* aphasia hinders both the expression and comprehension of language.

As a result of the limitations aphasia places on language comprehension and expression, and its negative impact on an individuals' quality of life, treatment methods have been developed to reduce impairments [15, 22]. However these treatments are not always effective, and individuals who show significant symptoms one year after onset are likely to have some form of aphasia for the rest of their lives. In these instances, there is a need for communication methods and assistive devices to remove language barriers to living with aphasia and give hope to individuals and their families [10]. Many organizations that work with individuals on a long term basis embrace this philosophy. Included in this group of organizations is the Aphasia Institute (AI) in Toronto, Ontario, Canada where we conducted our field study.

Figure 2. A communication board allows individuals to point to symbols for basic needs and wants such as food. The board shown here enables individuals to specify several different types of food and drink.

Revealing Competence with AAC

Since individuals with aphasia typically have full cognitive abilities, promoted communication methods focus on acknowledging and revealing competence. One such method called Supported Conversation for Adults with Aphasia (SCA) [9, 10, 16] promotes the use of trained communication partners to acknowledge and reveal the competence of individuals with aphasia and has been found to be extremely effective [10]; however it also has shortcomings. For example, the focus on the communication partner allows for the facilitation of conversation, but also means that an individual relies very heavily on their partner. If the partner is not able to reveal what the individual is thinking, they cannot express what they would like to communicate. It is also extremely difficult for an individual with aphasia to guide the conversation, since they are relying on their communication partner to enable them to do so. Finally, there is little awareness of aphasia within the general public [8, 23], making it difficult for individuals to engage with the community through SCA. These limitations have motivated research into assistive technologies that can enable individuals with aphasia to engage in conversation more independently [3, 5, 7, 18, 26].

Early advances in technology allowed for the digitization of communication boards, physical boards with a grid of symbols that individuals can point at to aid communication (Figure 2), with the goal of building complex sentences in software [24]. In designing C-VIC, Steele et al. created an interactive, card-based communication system that still influences the design of AAC tools today. Steele et al. report that creating a digital system was particularly beneficial in enabling individuals with poor expressivity, and that digitizing the system addressed key practical considerations such as removing physical barriers to use such as the sorting of card decks between communication tasks, which improved communication outcomes. Koul et al. [13] confirm these findings for individuals with chronic severe Broca's aphasia and Global aphasia.

Building on these initial PC-based prototypes, AAC software was developed for early portable and mobile devices such as PDAs [3, 5]. These devices provided a number of advantages for individuals with aphasia, such as their small and lightweight form factor, low cost, and built-in cameras that could be used to personalize communication. For example, Allen et al. [3] developed PhotoTalk, an application that allows individuals with aphasia to capture and manage photos, which could then be used to facilitate communication related to the day's events, their family, and hobbies. Daemen et al. [7], Camelendar [26], and CoCreation [18] take a similar approach for sharing and story-telling tasks. While initial feedback for these prototypes has been positive, researchers have noted trade-offs between customization and usability that often vary significantly among participants, since individuals' capabilities vary according to their severity of aphasia.

Designing for Individuals with Aphasia

The use of interactive pictures and icons as building blocks for larger sentences has been well established in the literature [3, 12, 18]. Through the development of these systems, researchers have proposed guidelines targeted at maximizing their utility and usability for individuals with aphasia:

1. **Customization of Settings** The abilities and needs of individuals can vary significantly along the receptive and expressive dimensions [1, 17]. Applications should support communication of basic needs as well as more in-depth conversational topics, and labels and navigation should be structured to suit an individual's abilities.

2. **Adding Personalized Content** An app's content should reflect an individual's personal interests [3, 5]. Applications should allow individuals to add personal content to communicate about the topics they care about.

3. **Use of Mobile Devices** The lightweight form and built-in camera have been identified as beneficial features in supporting individuals with aphasia [3, 5]. However, a need to calibrate touch interaction for those with motor impairments has also been identified [7].

4. **Simplicity** Individuals with aphasia have difficulty understanding text and other visual GUI elements. Designers should therefore avoid abstraction, complex structures, and minimize the number of steps required to perform a task [1, 7]. Al Mahmud [1] suggests that categorization and visual support pervade the interface.

5. **One-Handed Use** Aphasia is often accompanied by impairments to a user's right hand, due to injury on the left side of their brain [7]. Applications should therefore not require two hands to use.

In this work, we investigate how these guidelines have been applied in practice, and aim to understand how modern tablets can serve as platforms for AAC. To focus our exploration, we studied the use of one application, TalkingTiles.

TALKINGTILES

TalkingTiles (Figure 1) is a commercial AAC app designed for individuals with a variety of verbal communication difficulties, including autism, amyotrophic lateral sclerosis (ALS), memory impairments, and aphasia. The TalkingTiles name is derived from the interaction metaphor of building sentences from representative images, or tiles. As a user taps on individual tiles featuring pictographic and textual labels, corresponding text is immediately vocalized and added to a constructed sentence which can later be spoken via the iPad's Text-to-Speech functionality. By supporting communication in this manner, TalkingTiles is designed to enable individuals to engage in a variety of communication activities, ranging from therapy sessions, to basic daily needs, to storytelling and in-depth conversation.

The app commercializes customization features developed in research systems, such as PhotoTalk [3], allowing users to create personal tile sets (called 'Pages') and link those tiles to captured photos or online content. In addition to those features, the combined use of the cloud and extensive editing functionality to support deployment, customization, and daily use of the app is a key differentiating feature between TalkingTiles and other commercially available AAC apps. The use of the cloud to store user data enables caregivers to remotely upload content to a user's account, which can then be downloaded onto a user's device without taking it away from them. Usage data is also tracked using the cloud, enabling caregivers to track which components of the app are used, and how often. The ability to launch observation/question forms from tiles also provides an opportunity to receive more detailed and explicit feedback from users. In providing this functionality, the app addresses the above guidelines:

- Simple Interface – The app provides a simple, touch-based interface that enables users to create sentences of various complexity levels by tapping on tiles associated with words or phrases. While one-handed use was not a specific design consideration, the interaction metaphor enables interaction for a broad group, including those with aphasia.

- Customizable – Users can edit aspects of the app's interface to suit their individual needs, including: language, gender and speed of text to speech output, image and text size, colours, number of rows and columns of tiles featured on pages, and their size, representative text or image, and functionality.

- Personalizable – Users can create custom pages (and tiles) from text, captured photos, or online content to meet their personal communication needs, and link tiles on these pages to webpages, videos, and pictures.

- Cloud Storage – TalkingTiles provides access to pre-made pages though their customer portal. This feature eases setup and reduces required storage space on the device, and allows for content to be updated remotely by users' family, friends, and caregivers.

Users interact with TalkingTiles through two modes: run and edit. In run mode (Figure 3) users construct sentences, and pages are separated into tiles that have associated words or

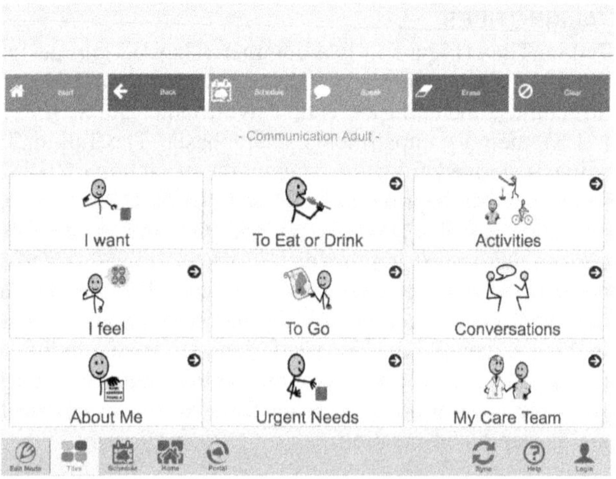

Figure 3. In run mode, participants tap on tiles corresponding to words or short phrases to create sentences. As tiles are selected they are verbalized by the app and combined into a sentence, displayed at the top of the screen, that can be replayed as a whole using the 'speak' tile.

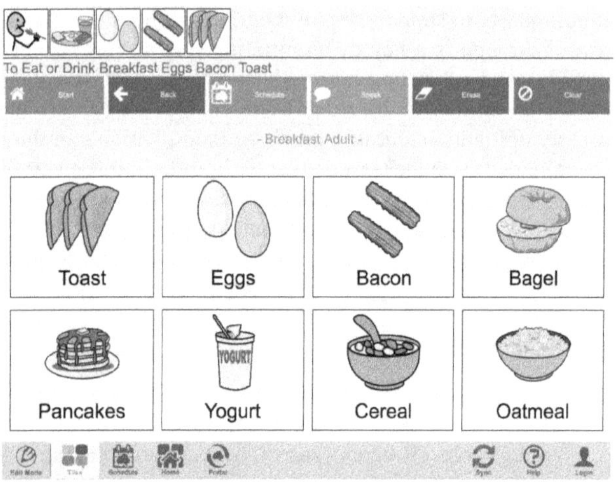

Figure 4. An example sentence is constructed and displayed symbolically at the top of the display. 'I want', 'to eat or drink', 'breakfast', and 'eggs','toast', 'bacon'. The sentence can be edited on the fly using the 'Back space' and 'Erase all' tiles.

phrases. When the user taps on a tile its associated text is vocalized using Text-to-Speech (TTS), and added to an in-construction sentence in the speech bar (top). Tiles can also have actions associated with them when they are tapped, for example tapping on the 'Breakfast' tile would navigate the user to a new page containing common breakfast items (Figure 4). Other actions can include linking to web pages, the start page, visual schedules of upcoming dates or events, or loading an image or video file for display.

Once a sentence is created, it can be vocalized by tapping the 'Speak' button, the most recent item erased using the 'Erase' tile, or deleted using the 'Clear' tile. The menu bars are customizable, and may be different for participants in this study. If users do not wish to create full sentences by selecting multiple tiles, they can disable the speech bar, which removes the tiles associated with editing from the menu bar. Finally, at the top of each page there are 'Back Page', 'Home Page', and 'Select Page' navigation tiles, enabling users navigate through the app without vocalizing text.

In edit mode users make customizations to the app, including: images and text visible on tiles, the size, colour, and number of tiles displayed on each page, and global accessibility settings such as the rate of speech and gender of the TTS agent. TalkingTiles allows for these customizations to be uploaded and downloaded from the cloud, allowing for caregivers and family members to edit pages remotely.

FIELD STUDY

We conducted a field study to understand how TalkingTiles could help remove language barriers to living with aphasia. We chose a one-week duration to allow sufficient time for participants to configure and familiarize themselves with the application, use it in a variety of settings, and identify strengths and weaknesses. As TalkingTiles is a commercial application that implements features developed in research, we were interested in how its features were used in practice, and in identifying barriers to acceptance and areas for improvement.

Participants

Participants were recruited from an iPad working group at the Aphasia Institute. Focusing on this working group ensured that all participants were familiar with tablet use. We relied on AI staff to provide information on the severity of aphasia for all individuals interested in participating in the study, and limited involvement to individuals who could understand pictures/symbols or written text. This requirement meant that individuals with more severe forms of aphasia could not be included in the study, but ensured that we were able to confidently assess their interactions with the TalkingTiles app.

In total, we recruited four participants with different severities of aphasia who we identify using the following pseudonyms:

Emmett is a 70 year old male who has had moderate aphasia for 18 years. He has excellent comprehension skills, and is physically able, but has limited verbal expression and writing capabilities. Although he has impaired use of his right arm, he is able to drive. Emmett is technologically savvy, and uses apps such as TalkRocket and Proloquo2Go. Emmett's wife also participated in the sessions.

Nina is a 68 year old female who has lived with more severe aphasia for 14 years. While she has reasonable comprehension abilities, she has limited verbal expression abilities, and extremely little writing ability. Nina is able to formulate basic sounds such as 'uh-hmm', 'nono', and 'ohohoh' but cannot formulate any words.

Victor is a 60 year old male who has lived with mild aphasia for 2 years. He has excellent comprehension and expression skills and is often able to write the first few letters or verbalize words. Although he has little control over his right arm, he is otherwise physically capable and drives himself to sessions. Victor primarily attends the Aphasia Institute for the iPad working group but had not previously used AAC apps.

Sonya is a 74 year old female who has lived with severe aphasia for 7 years. She is only able to verbalise basic words such as 'yes' and 'no', but has strong comprehension skills. Sonya has severe physical limitations as a result of her stroke and requires the use of a wheelchair. She had previously downloaded Proloquo2Go, but only used it infrequently. Sonya completed all sessions with a caregiver.

Procedure

This study consisted of two sessions per participant, with each session lasting between 1-2 hours in length. Investigators were trained by the Aphasia Institute in SCA to facilitate effective communication with the participants. Participants were encouraged to bring a spouse, family member, or friend to the sessions as they were likely to play an important role in customizing the app for participants.

During the first session, participants learned how to use the TalkingTiles app and cooperatively created customized communication page sets with the investigators. Following this session, participants were given the app to take home to continue to use over a one week period. During the second session, scheduled at least one week later, participants were asked to complete a variety of communication tasks they engage in on a daily basis such as requesting to watch TV shows, reading the news, or telling stories about themselves and their families. Finally, they engaged in a semi-structured interview to assess the app's support for less structured situations, and to reveal additional use cases or usability issues.

Data Collection & Analysis

Video was recorded throughout all interviews, and was accompanied by the investigator's field notes. We performed a grounded theory analysis of all collected data, and examined how the app supported basic tasks such as requesting something to eat, to do an activity, or to go somewhere. We also gathered and analyzed data regarding how participants used the app to support daily activities, and what improvements could be made to support those use cases. Although interaction data can be logged by the app, this feature was not completed in time for the study, and thus our analysis does not include quantitative aspects of use.

RESULTS

We present key themes that arose during our analysis of study sessions. We present these themes as a series of vignettes, with each theme illustrated through a particular use case with a specific user. However, our data suggests that each identified issue was experienced by *all* participants, and we later discuss broader implications for the design of AAC. In presenting these themes, we pay particular attention to the experiences of our participants in relation to configuring the TalkingTiles application, how it supported their daily activities and storytelling, and what deficiencies they may have identified during their week of use.

Emmett: Creating Personal Content

Emmett, one of our technically savvy participants, was quickly able to understand the TalkingTiles interface and use the app effectively. We therefore placed a stronger emphasis

Figure 5. Emmett created pages with content associated with his recent vacation, such as images for Epcot Centre in Disney World.

on teaching Emmett and his spouse how to edit TalkingTiles during the training session. By the end of the training session, Emmett and his wife understood and could use most of TalkingTiles' editing functions, but at a slow pace. In the following week, Emmett spent considerable time customizing the app to suit his needs, and used the app regularly. During the interview Emmett and his wife noted a need for enhanced editing functions, and to be able to do so more efficiently. One of their main concerns was the ability to manipulate text and image sizes, especially for the purpose of storytelling. For example, they found that images were not big enough to show other people, even when it was the only image on the screen, and that the user interface should be more flexible in minimizing space for UI elements when users would like to share a single image. However, they offered the caveat that these features were most appropriate for users with high expressiveness, and that others with severe aphasia may find the app useful without customization.

One way in which Emmett personalized the app was to add options for common items that he would want to communicate about, such as family and friends and places to go such as shopping malls, parks, and restaurants. These options served to establish subject matter for the conversation, after which his wife could determine more precise detail via SCA. For example, Emmett is interested in NHL hockey, and added an extensive page to help him communicate that his favourite team is the Toronto Maple Leafs, and that they are not playing well. He could indicate that he wanted to talk about the recent game played between Toronto and Ottawa by selecting the two teams in succession. Between the study sessions Emmett had been on vacation and uploaded pictures he took with his iPad to the TalkingTiles app. With the help of his wife, he was able to add sentences describing the vacation; such as which attractions and restaurants at Disney World they had visited, and with whom they had vacationed (Figure 5).

Emmett also configured the app for use outside of the home. For example, due to Emmett's aphasia, he cannot use bank machines, and thus needs to talk directly with a bank teller. These interactions are very stressful and difficult, if not impossible, unless the teller is aware of aphasia and trained in communication methods such as SCA. Emmett and his wife therefore edited this bank page to include common phrases, such as his name and communicating that he has aphasia, and common bank transactions such as making a deposit or withdrawal. These phrases were simple enough that Emmett could understand them without the help of pictures, allowing him to select the phrase he desired from the Talking Tiles app. Emmett and his wife stated that this functionality was promising, and could be used for other circumstances such as placing an order at a coffee shop.

Nina: Customization Improves Navigation

Nina was not accompanied by another individual to her sessions, and has more severe aphasia than Emmett. Communication was therefore more difficult, and it took her longer to become proficient with the app. In particular, Nina struggled with navigating the app's tiered menus, and consistently confused menu buttons such as 'Erase', 'Back', 'Start', and 'Speak' (Figure 1). After 40 minutes of training Nina was better able to navigate the app, but still struggled with the 'Clear', 'Earse', and 'Speak' buttons. Due to these difficulties, and Nina not having someone to help her with customization, she did not receive full training in TalkingTile's editing functionality.

Overall, Nina found TalkingTiles hard to navigate during the first session, but after a week of infrequent practice it was less difficult. When Nina returned for her second session she was much better able to use the app, and could use each of the menu buttons and access some pages such as 'activities', 'food and drinks', and 'about me'. Nina still struggled with accessing other pages such as 'urgent needs', 'to go' (places), and 'I feel'. When Nina struggled to complete a task, she would sometimes become very frustrated, and would click many buttons, start gasping, and place her hands on her head. When this occurred, we reminded Nina to go back to the beginning, and she was consistently able to tap the home page button, after which she was almost always able to navigate correctly.

During the session it became apparent that some of Nina's confusion arose from the phrasing used in text labels. The communication page had been constructed to enable users to string together icons to create sentences, and therefore labels were created using language that would fit into sentences. For example, the feelings page was entitled 'I feel' and could be combined with other tiles to create a sentence, such as 'I feel happy'. During Nina's second session we edited these labels to be more direct, and not to fit into sentences. We noticed an immediate difference in Nina's ability to select the desired page, but she still struggled with completing tasks that required her to navigate to the 'urgent needs' page, such as requesting to go to the washroom, or saying that she was in pain. When Nina was asked to request to go to the washroom, she consistently went to the 'places page', which made it seem as if the 'urgent needs' label did not carry meaning for her. It was also much easier for Nina to navigate the app when the homepage was changed to the communication page, reducing the steps required to indicate a need or desire.

Nina was unable to further edit the app or change it to suit her needs since she was not able to have a caregiver attend

Figure 6. During Nina's sessions, we worked extensively to edit the TalkingTiles interface to provide clear navigation. In particular, Nina had difficulty with labels representing parts of sentences such as 'To go', which we renamed 'Places'.

the sessions. This lack of customization was less of an issue since Nina's priority was to express basic needs and desires. At the end of her second session, Nina reported that the TalkingTiles app better supported basic wants than SCA. However, the inability to edit the app was raised again in this session, and we made some additional customizations. Due to time constraints and a lack of personal knowledge about Nina, the level of personalization was limited, but we were able to create a page entitled 'about me' that held information about Nina's spouse, children, and her home address.

Victor: Unsupported Editing

Although Victor attended the sessions by himself, he quickly understood how to use TalkingTiles and was able to reliably use the app to communicate. He initially struggled with the 'Activities' label, but was able to use it more reliably after we showed him the content on the Activities page. With all other tasks such as requesting something to eat or drink, requesting to see or talk to someone, or requesting to go somewhere, Victor was quickly and accurately able to use the app to express his desires.

His training session therefore focused on editing the app, and training him to complete the editing independently. By the end of the two hour training session Victor had completed a considerable amount of editing with the investigator's assistance, but found editing himself very confusing and could not remember which buttons to press. In order to ensure that the app was sufficiently customized to suit Victor's preferences, two additional editing sessions took place over the following weeks. By the end of the second two hour session Victor was consistently able to use the editing functionality to complete tasks such as creating new pages and editing tiles. However, he would occasionally require assistance in remembering where certain buttons were located.

Victor wanted to use the app to engage with others, rather than communicating basic needs. He planned to use the app for needs such as requesting to see or talk to someone, but less so for requesting food and drinks. He therefore placed most of his focus on creating pages that would help him tell stories, and creating ways to begin conversations and share his interests. For example, he had detailed 'Hobbies', 'Family', and 'Friends' pages that allowed him to quickly establish subjects. Much like Emmett, Victor was an avid sports fan who wanted to use the app to guide conversations around topics such as the FIFA Women's World Cup. To do so, he created a schedule for his favourite team that enabled him to start conversations about upcoming games.

Sonya: Managing Complexity

Sonya quickly understood how to use the app, and could accurately use the menu buttons for their intended purposes. She, like Nina who also had severe aphasia, wanted to use the app for basic communication needs. Her caregiver felt it best to simplify the content of the app as much as possible, and therefore reduced the number of tiles on the Start page to six, all of which linked to other pages. These linked pages were also customized to focus on more limited and practical communication tasks. For example, Sonya's 'About Me' page listed her phone number, home address, medical condition, and allergies instead of providing more personal details such as the names of relatives, as had been created by Emmett and Victor.

Since Sonya's severity of aphasia inhibited her from editing the app herself, the majority of the training session was spent teaching her caregiver to edit the app. Her caregiver found the editing interface confusing at first, and even after some practice would need reminders of where buttons were located. Sonya's caregiver advocated increased simplicity, and thereby fewer editing options. She found the various editing features to be overwhelming, and she did not plan to use most of them. In her opinion it could make the edit mode much less confusing if some of these features were removed.

One set of editing features she found difficult to use were those related to Text-to-Speech. The app has been developed to require a number of steps to change all Text-to-Speech related fields, including the text that the app reads aloud for each tile. Sonya noted that this process is unintuitive and, in combination with a bug that required the user to select an additional option when changing the TTS engine, created significant confusion. Finally, she reported a need for the pre-made pages to better reflect the needs of individuals with aphasia, as she spent considerable time editing the default templates to suit Sonya's needs.

OPPORTUNITIES FOR DESIGN

Although TalkingTiles was used differently by each of our participants, it was ultimately effective in supporting many of their communication needs. Emmett customized the TalkingTiles interface to meet his needs, both at home and while running errands. Nina initially struggled with the application, but customization with the investigators enabled her to effectively use the 'places', 'about me', and 'food/drinks' pages, supporting her most critical communication needs. While Victor struggled with customizing the app himself, he was able to effectively communicate interests such as the FIFA Women's World Cup. Sonya's caregiver was careful to focus customizations around only Sonya's most critical activities. However, our field study also revealed areas for improvement, not only for the TalkingTiles app, but general opportunities to understand how modern, interactive surfaces can be used

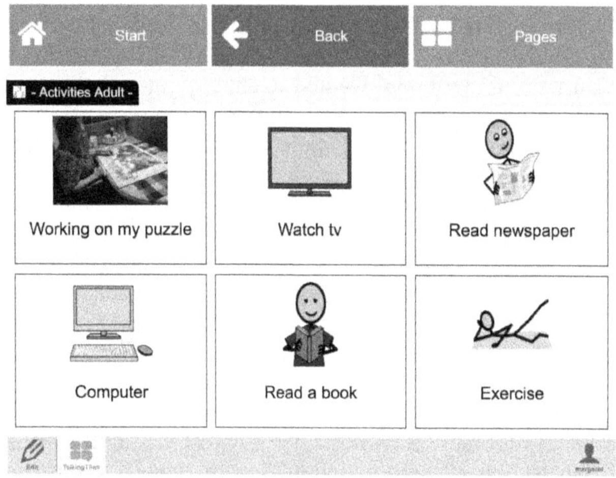

Figure 7. Sonya's caregiver limited pages to six options to reduce complexity. Her activities page comprised 'working on my puzzle', 'watch tv', 'read newspaper', 'computer', 'read a book', and 'exercise'.

to remove language barriers to living with aphasia. We now discuss these opportunities and challenges, and in particular, the advantages and disadvantages of customization, balancing customization with navigation, the role devices play in supporting communication, and new opportunities for supporting communication with interactive surfaces.

Editing is an Ongoing Responsibility

Customization and personalization of AAC software is often recommended [1, 17]. Our interviews confirm the need and utility of these features; our participants universally supported the need for an app that they could tailor to suit their own communication needs. For example, Emmett and Victor were very positive about their ability to add information about hobbies and sports, favourite restaurants, and even recent vacations. However, the work required to customize or personalize an app creates overhead that is often difficult for individuals with aphasia to manage on their own, and is typically carried out by a caregiver, therapist, or family member [5]. This reliance on others for personalization and customization may ultimately impact the utility of the AAC software, and should itself be considered in its design.

All of our participants noted that the current customization and personalization interface was too complex for individuals with aphasia. Difficulty in performing personalization or customization are significant barriers to adoption, and occurred both initially and on an ongoing basis. For example, during the first session we changed labels such as 'to go' and 'I feel' to 'places' and 'feelings', respectively, to better enable all our participants to navigate the app's interface. Such customizations should be expected to ensure that generic application presets match an individual's needs, and incur a one-time cost in data entry and may be manageable through caregivers and loved ones. During this initial setup, participants also unanimously wanted to personalize their app by including details surrounding their family, friends, hobbies, interests, and nearby places. However, even these tasks may be prohibitive for individuals such as Nina who do not have support from caregivers.

Other personalization and customization tasks take place on an ongoing basis. For example, when Emmett went on vacation with his wife and wanted to share photos, he needed to add words or sentences for each photograph. Victor wanted access to an up-to-date schedule for upcoming FIFA matches. This type of editing can be expected to take place on a regular basis, as individuals hope to expand the topics available for conversation to reflect changes in their lives. Emmett and his Wife suggested that training volunteers at the Aphasia Institute would be a good way to support this customization, but it is unclear if this solution would be practical based on the time demands placed on support staff. It is also more difficult for individuals who do not know the user well to edit the app, as editing requires a deep knowledge of the user's personal preferences, hobbies, and tastes. We suggest that an opportunity exists to better enable individuals with aphasia to customize the app, and that automated support for the creation of new materials could play a significant role in these developments.

Balancing Personalization, Customization, and Simplicity

Personalization was critical to the adoption of TalkingTiles, but also incurred a cost in the simplicity of navigating the app; an important consideration for individuals with aphasia [7]. Many researchers have investigated the use of custom photos in supporting communication, but we are not aware of any research that has provided means for individuals with aphasia to easily manage those photos. This need was reflected in the edits made by Sonya's caregiver, who was concerned with balancing personalized content with ease of navigation and limited most pages to contain only 6 tiles. Sonya's caregiver also felt that the edit mode was more complex than necessary, and that a simplified interface would be sufficient for individuals with severe aphasia. As apps become loaded with personalized content, this burden is shifted to navigation – an identified weak point for individuals with aphasia [1, 7] – and there is a need to understand how simple, multi-touch interfaces can be designed to simultaneously support personalization and customization for these users.

However, not all customization resulted in this trade-off. For example, we found that for all of our participants, the ability to edit the keywords displayed on tiles made navigating the app easier. We also found that modifying TalkingTiles' interface to hide the speech bar tended to improve its usability. Participants found it difficult to navigate the app when they were encouraged to string together sentences, and being able to focus only on which keyword to press next was a welcome simplification. The reduced complexity of the interface also made it easier for participants to interpret and navigate the remaining menu buttons. The ability to perform these customizations in-app, in collaboration with users provided an opportunity for participatory design, and through the course of the study we identified edits that enabled the general-purpose AAC application to be tailored for use by individuals with aphasia.

Augmenting, not Replacing, SCA

We found that participants were not interested in forming complete sentences, contrasting Steele et al.'s [13, 24] findings. Instead, TalkingTiles was typically used to vocalize individual keywords to indicate basic needs or *steer* conversation. For individuals like Nina and Sonya who focused on basic communication, such as indicating a need to eat or go to the washroom, TalkingTiles' default vocalization features enabled individuals to quickly communicate these needs to their caregivers. The creation of personalized content such as details about their family further enabled these individuals to initiate conversations about more personal topics.

For Emmett and Victor, the tiles provide a means of grounding and steering topics during more in-depth conversations. When conversing with his wife without the app, Emmett needed to go through an extended process to steer the conversation. If no pictures were nearby, he would first establish the general subject, such as people or parks, and then answer 'yes' or 'no' questions to narrow down the topic. For example, if Emmett wanted to talk about a person, he would start by saying the word 'people'. His wife would then list 'West', 'East', 'South', and 'North' (in relation to their house), providing Emmett a chance to confirm each option. After confirming one of the options, Emmett's wife would list possibilities, and in response to each one Emmett could say closer, farther, or confirm the choice. Personalizations within the app significantly reduced the need for these questions, and allowed both Emmett and Victor to create shortcuts to topics that they frequently wanted to discuss, such as professional sports and hobbies. However, the degree to which conversations can be steered is limited by what custom content has been added, meaning that even when TalkingTiles is available SCA is vital to having more complex, detailed discussions.

These limitations, in light of our discussion surrounding the difficulty and ongoing nature of customizations, provide guidance for the development of future AAC applications. In particular, they suggest that AAC is likely to continue to play a support role for individuals with aphasia, rather than a wholesale replacement for SCA, and that future development may benefit from a focus on additional support for this role. Our findings also suggest that the types of customization and personalization that are most useful to users may be those oriented around keywords or short phrases. Many of these customizations are candidates for automation, such as contextually-aware suggestions for nearby places [11].

Accessible Surface Ecosystems

Previous work has largely explored the use of older hardware, such as PDAs and desktops, as platforms for assistive technology. However, recent advances in mobile, interactive surfaces provide new opportunities for support, and we found that individuals with aphasia are living with improved access to technology; suggesting there may be a need to revisit opportunities for HCI research to impact these users. For example, Boyd-Graber et al. [5] report that designing software to prevent users from exiting to the Windows desktop was an important consideration in 2006, since the Windows desktop could be particularly difficult to interpret for individuals with aphasia. When preparing to conduct our study, we found that many individuals with aphasia were already engaged with technology on a regular basis, and we were able to recruit participants directly from an iPad working group.

The touch interface of modern personal devices, with large icons and a touch interface, provides a welcoming platform for individuals with aphasia. In interviewing our participants, we found that many already used smartphones and tablets regularly. Our participants reported using a variety of applications on their iPads, suggesting an opportunity for an ecosystem of applications that support the communication needs of individuals with aphasia. For example, research has explored the development of dedicated email clients [2] and social networking sites [20] for individuals with aphasia. TalkingTiles is currently only available on tablets, and thus is only appropriate for one-handed use when a surface upon which the tablet can be rested is nearby. However, we believe that support for smartphones, which can be used in a greater number of settings with one hand, will increase the app's utility in mobile contexts. We envision that additional applications could be developed to take advantage of these usage contexts, and to support activities such as web browsing, navigation (maps), and instant messaging.

LIMITATIONS

As is common in studies of AAC for aphasia [3, 5, 7, 26, 18], we conducted interviews with a small number of individuals that excluded those who were unfamiliar with iPads due to the amount of training and practice required to become proficient with TalkingTiles. Individuals with more severe forms of aphasia were excluded from this study since communication with these individuals is difficult, even for experts in SCA [3]. These choices were made for practical reasons, and allowed us to identify needs within the one-week field study, but may not reflect the needs of individuals with aphasia as a whole who have a very wide variety of communication issues [1, 17]. A broader sampling would have likely identified additional usability issues, and we expect to continue to refine our understanding through additional field work.

CONCLUSION

We conducted a field study that investigates the use of an AAC app, called TalkingTiles, over a one week trial period by individuals with aphasia. Our results demonstrate that these apps, which build on years of scientific research from the HCI community, have significant potential in enabling individuals to communicate with others. However, to fully realize this potential a careful balance must be struck between the support an application provides or customization and its simplicity. The combination of lightweight, portable, powerful computing devices with a simple touch interface and access to high-resolution cameras enables individuals with aphasia to address a variety of topics that are often infeasible with traditional communication methods, such as Supported Conversation for Adults with Aphasia. Our participants were overwhelmingly positive about the potential for TalkingTiles to enhance their lives and remove barriers to communication.

While effective, we found that time and effort must be invested in training individuals and customizing the app to suit their needs, personalities, and preferences. Enabling this customizability is often cited as an important design criterion in the literature, but its ongoing nature is not. Thus, we found that modern AAC apps must often be used in conjunction with, not instead of, other communication methods. Our field study also identified practical areas for improvement in these apps, particularly related to often-cited design goals in the literature, such as personalization [3, 5] and simplicity. We found that support for such editing often required support from caregivers or loved ones, and may not be feasible on a long-term basis. Finally, we reflected on the potential for Post-PC devices for long-term support, and that improved access to these technologies provides new, unexplored opportunities to support communication for individuals with aphasia.

ACKNOWLEDGMENTS

We thank our participants and staff at the Aphasia Institute in Toronto for their extensive support, especially Caryl Pereira, Rochelle Cohen-Schneider, and Melodie Chan. We also thank the Natural Sciences and Engineering Research Council of Canada for funding this research.

REFERENCES

1. Abdullah Al Mahmud. 2014. Considerations for Designing Technology with and for Persons with Aphasia. In *Proceedings of the 26th Australian Computer-Human Interaction Conference on Designing Futures: The Future of Design (OzCHI '14)*. ACM, New York, NY, USA, 535–538. DOI: http://dx.doi.org/10.1145/2686612.2686698

2. Abdullah Al Mahmud and Jean-Bernard Martens. 2013. Amail: Design and evaluation of an accessible email tool for persons with aphasia. *Interacting with Computers* 25, 5 (2013), 351–374.

3. Meghan Allen, Joanna McGrenere, and Barbara Purves. 2008. The Field Evaluation of a Mobile Digital Image Communication Application Designed for People with Aphasia. *ACM Trans. Access. Comput.* 1, 1, Article 5 (May 2008), 26 pages. DOI: http://dx.doi.org/10.1145/1361203.1361208

4. David Frank Benson and Alfredo Ardila. 1996. *Aphasia: A clinical perspective*. Oxford University Press.

5. Jordan L. Boyd-Graber, Sonya S. Nikolova, Karyn A. Moffatt, Kenrick C. Kin, Joshua Y. Lee, Lester W. Mackey, Marilyn M. Tremaine, and Maria M. Klawe. 2006. Participatory Design with Proxies: Developing a desktop-PDA System to Support People with Aphasia. In *Proceedings of the SIGCHI Conference on Human Factors in Computing Systems (CHI '06)*. ACM, New York, NY, USA, 151–160. DOI: http://dx.doi.org/10.1145/1124772.1124797

6. Tira Cohene, Ron Baecker, and Elsa Marziali. 2005. Designing Interactive Life Story Multimedia for a Family Affected by Alzheimer's Disease: A Case Study. In *CHI '05 Extended Abstracts on Human Factors in Computing Systems (CHI EA '05)*. ACM, New York, NY, USA, 1300–1303. DOI: http://dx.doi.org/10.1145/1056808.1056901

7. Elke Daemen, Pavan Dadlani, Jia Du, Ying Li, Pinar Erik-Paker, Jean-Bernard Martens, and Boris De Ruyter.

2007. Designing a Free Style, Indirect, and Interactive Storytelling Application for People with Aphasia. In *Proceedings of the 11th IFIP TC 13 International Conference on Human-computer Interaction (INTERACT'07)*. Springer-Verlag, Berlin, Heidelberg, 221–234. http://dl.acm.org/citation.cfm?id=1776994.1777022

8. Laura Flynn, Ashlyn Cumberland, and Jane Marshall. 2009. Public knowledge about aphasia: A survey with comparative data. *Aphasiology* 23, 3 (2009), 393–401.

9. Audrey L Holland. 1998. Why can't clinicians talk to aphasic adults? Comments on supported conversation for adults with aphasia: Methods and resources for training conversational partners. *Aphasiology* 12, 9 (1998), 844–847.

10. Aura Kagan. 1998. Supported conversation for adults with aphasia: Methods and resources for training conversation partners. *Aphasiology* 12, 9 (1998), 816–830.

11. Shaun K. Kane, Barbara Linam-Church, Kyle Althoff, and Denise McCall. 2012. What We Talk About: Designing a Context-aware Communication Tool for People with Aphasia. In *Proceedings of the 14th International ACM SIGACCESS Conference on Computers and Accessibility (ASSETS '12)*. ACM, New York, NY, USA, 49–56. DOI: http://dx.doi.org/10.1145/2384916.2384926

12. Tom Koppenol, Abdullah Al Mahmud, and Jean-Bernard Martens. 2010. When words fall short: helping people with aphasia to express. In *Computers Helping People with Special Needs*. Springer, 45–48.

13. Rajinder Koul, Melinda Corwin, and Summer Hayes. 2005. Production of graphic symbol sentences by individuals with aphasia: Efficacy of a computer-based augmentative and alternative communication intervention. *Brain and language* 92, 1 (2005), 58–77.

14. Stephen Lindsay, Katie Brittain, Daniel Jackson, Cassim Ladha, Karim Ladha, and Patrick Olivier. 2012. Empathy, Participatory Design and People with Dementia. In *Proceedings of the SIGCHI Conference on Human Factors in Computing Systems (CHI '12)*. ACM, New York, NY, USA, 521–530. DOI: http://dx.doi.org/10.1145/2207676.2207749

15. Felice L Loverso, Marilyn Selinger, and Thomas E Prescott. 1979. Application of verbing strategies to aphasia treatment. (1979).

16. JG Lyon, D Cariski, L Keisler, J Rosenbek, R Levine, J Kumpula, C Ryff, S Coyne, and M Blanc. 1997. Communication partners: Enhancing participation in life and communication for adults with aphasia in natural settings. *Aphasiology* 11, 7 (1997), 693–708.

17. Xiaojuan Ma, Jordan Boyd-Graber, Sonya Nikolova, and Perry R. Cook. 2009. Speaking Through Pictures: Images vs. Icons. In *Proceedings of the 11th International ACM SIGACCESS Conference on Computers and Accessibility (Assets '09)*. ACM, New York, NY, USA, 163–170. DOI: http://dx.doi.org/10.1145/1639642.1639672

18. Abdullah Al Mahmud, Yvonne Limpens, and Jean-Bernard Martens. 2013. Expressing Through Digital Photographs: An Assistive Tool for Persons with Aphasia. *Univers. Access Inf. Soc.* 12, 3 (Aug. 2013), 309–326. DOI: http://dx.doi.org/10.1007/s10209-012-0286-8

19. Skye E McDonald, Chris Code, and Leanne Togher. 2000. *Communication disorders following traumatic brain injury*. Psychology press.

20. Hannah Miller, Heather Buhr, Chris Johnson, and Jerry Hoepner. 2013. AphasiaWeb: A Social Network for Individuals with Aphasia. In *Proceedings of the 15th International ACM SIGACCESS Conference on Computers and Accessibility (ASSETS '13)*. ACM, New York, NY, USA, Article 4, 8 pages. DOI: http://dx.doi.org/10.1145/2513383.2513439

21. Palle Møller Pedersen, Kirsten Vinter, and Tom Skyhøj Olsen. 2004. Aphasia after stroke: type, severity and prognosis. The Copenhagen aphasia study. *Cerebrovascular Diseases* 17 (2004), 35–43.

22. Hildred Schuell, James J Jenkins, and Edward Jimenez-Pabon. 1964. *Aphasia in adults*. Harper & Row.

23. Nina Simmons-Mackie, Chris Code, Elizabeth Armstrong, Lillian Stiegler, and Roberta J Elman. 2002. What is aphasia? Results of an international survey. *Aphasiology* 16, 8 (2002), 837–848.

24. Richard D Steele, Michael Weinrich, Robert T Wertz, Maria K Kleczewska, and Gloria S Carlson. 1989. Computer-based visual communication in aphasia. *Neuropsychologia* 27, 4 (1989), 409–426.

25. Iosif Moiseevich Tonkonogiĭ. 1986. *Vascular aphasia*. The MIT Press.

26. Maarten Woudstra, Abdullah Al Mahmud, and Jean-Bernard Martens. 2011. A Snapshot Diary to Support Conversational Storytelling for Persons with Aphasia. In *Proceedings of the 13th International Conference on Human Computer Interaction with Mobile Devices and Services (MobileHCI '11)*. ACM, New York, NY, USA, 641–646. DOI: http://dx.doi.org/10.1145/2037373.2037474

27. Mike Wu, Jeremy Birnholtz, Brian Richards, Ronald Baecker, and Mike Massimi. 2008. Collaborating to Remember: A Distributed Cognition Account of Families Coping with Memory Impairments. In *Proceedings of the SIGCHI Conference on Human Factors in Computing Systems (CHI '08)*. ACM, New York, NY, USA, 825–834. DOI: http://dx.doi.org/10.1145/1357054.1357186

“Callout Bubble Saved My Life”: Workspace Awareness Support in BYOD Classrooms

Y.-L. Betty Chang[1,3,4], Cresencia Fong[4], Edward Tse[4], Mark Hancock[2,3], Stacey D. Scott[1,3]

[1]Systems Design Engineering, [2]Management Sciences,
[3]Games Institute
University of Waterloo, Waterloo, Ontario, Canada
{betty.chang|mark.hancock|stacey.scott}@uwaterloo.ca

[4]SMART Technologies
Calgary, Alberta, Canada
{cresenciafong|edwardtse}@smarttech.com

ABSTRACT

Co-located students working in a bring-your-own-device (BYOD) classroom have limited awareness of their peers' work. We investigated the design of an awareness cue for students aged 6 to 17, in a large web-based canvas shared among tablets and laptops. By incorporating teacher and student feedback in an iterative design process, the project's goal was to support workspace awareness needs on touch devices, as well as to ensure age-appropriateness and technical feasibility. Specifically, we aimed to balance awareness, distraction, and clutter. We designed an awareness cue for students, a Callout Bubble, which is displayed near the object being manipulated by a peer, and fades away over time. A study of 71 students and 4 teachers revealed that, with our awareness cue design, students' awareness of their peers' actions in the shared canvas was significantly correlated with increased task focus and decreased frustration levels when peer conflicts arose. We also found that students understood the awareness information conveyed and were able to self-monitor and coordinate within the group.

Author Keywords

Workspace awareness; shared canvas; BYOD classrooms; education

ACM Classification Keywords

H.5.3. Information interfaces and presentation (e.g., HCI): Group and Organization Interfaces;

INTRODUCTION

The proliferation of the Internet and wirelessly connected devices is driving greater demand for equal participation in classrooms, particularly among young learners. In 2011, 28% of children 0 to 8 years of age had used a smartphone or tablet. In 2013, that number had risen to 72% [23]. With

ITS '15, November 15 - 18, 2015, Funchal, Portugal

ACM 978-1-4503-3899-8/15/11...$15.00
DOI: http://dx.doi.org/10.1145/2817721.2817733

Figure 1: Posters to remind students of good behaviours in the shared canvas. The highlighted text says “Don't shout out to the whole class” and “Practice patience with peers and technology”.

the goal of providing equity among students and leveraging their experience with computational devices, individual devices were introduced into classrooms with shared online digital workspaces to provide more engaging learning experiences. The system we studied, SMART amp™ [1], provided a large web-based canvas shared across tablets and laptops for BYOD classrooms. We observed that without workspace awareness of their peers' actions, the collaborative workspace became chaotic, as students were frustrated and confused by other students' actions, even in the co-located environment. Teachers had to focus on behavioural issues, such as posting signs about workspace etiquette, verbally reminding students not to shout out to the class, and asking students to be patient with peers and technology while working together (see Figure 1). Given that children, even during adolescence, are still developing their ability to control their attention and focus [21], high levels of frustration and confusion among learners occurred. A chaotic workspace distracts students and teachers from their top priorities: learning and teaching, respectively.

In this project, we aimed to provide students with awareness of their peers' actions to address two aspects of student-reported frustrations when working in the shared canvas environment. First, students were frustrated when objects were mysteriously moved or changed by an unknown

[1] https://www.smartamp.com/about

peer "ghost" in the same workspace. Second, students found themselves in conflict when multiple students tried to act on the same object, resulting in a final object state that may not have matched students' expectations.

The main contributions of our paper include:

- *Callout Bubble,* an awareness cue optimized for touch devices for learners in a shared canvas,
- empirical results from a study with 4 teachers and 71 students of the Callout Bubble design, and
- lessons of real-world BYOD classroom problems, and design tips for BYOD awareness cues.

RELATED WORK

While different types of awareness have been studied [e.g., 3,4,16], we aimed to support workspace awareness [9] to reduce student frustration while working on a shared digital canvas, with care to balance awareness and distraction.

Workspace awareness refers to people's "up-to-the-moment understanding of another person's interaction with the shared workspace" [11:417] through observing collaborators and artifacts. Lack of workspace awareness support can contribute to frustration during group work [10]. Previous research has shown that supporting workspace awareness for remote work can improve coordination and rate of conflict resolution [25] as well as task completion times, communication, and user preference [10].

This section introduces relevant commercial and research work to survey the existing alternatives for supporting awareness of student collaboration on touch-devices in BYOD classrooms.

Awareness Techniques for Remote Work

There are many commercial online collaboration tools that support group brainstorming and creative processes, such as Google Docs[2], Mural.ly[3], and Padlet[4]. However, only a few of them provide awareness of the collaborators' actions. In most cases, users only see the updated state without information regarding who did what.

Insertion cursor: Google Docs previously showed the location of collaborators using insertion cursors with users' first initials, and last names. It now shows the users' full names. Although the insertion cursor is a widely recognized approach, students cannot always be associated with a specific insertion location in a free-form virtual canvas that supports different media types in addition to text.

Mouse cursor: Telepointers [24] can be used to show the collaborators' mouse pointers to allow coordination based on the whereabouts of others. Mural.ly shows the collaborators' mouse cursors with the users' full names. Since most touch-based devices do not support hover, our design could not leverage telepointers. However, we valued its benefit of conveying users' current attention, and our design also sought to provide hints of user attention.

Mini map: Many multi-player games provide a mini map partially centered on the user [6, 11]. However, inferring students' locations may be difficult or inaccurate since students' workspaces may be too zoomed out on the canvas.

Awareness Techniques for Student Collaboration

Research on supporting workspace awareness has recently gained popularity within the domain of computer-supported collaborative learning (CSCL). Janssen and Bodemar [14] conceived of collaborative spaces as consisting of ***content space*** (e.g., cognitive activities, the subject-matter content) overlapping with a ***relational space*** (e.g., collaborator social interaction). These two spaces often focus on aspects of student work that is difficult to observe.

Concept map: Providing students with their group mates' self-created concept maps have been shown to be an effective way for students to share and compare their learning [8, 19], which increases discussion and co-manipulation of items in the concept map.

Group evaluation: Providing team members' participation levels and peer assessments has shown benefits manifesting in higher levels of active contribution [16], group performance [15], and group satisfaction [22].

This CSCL literature offers insights into providing feedback about student collaborators' learning progress. On the other hand, our work investigated how student workspace awareness may be supported by providing the interaction information in the relational space.

Awareness Techniques for Large or Multiple Surfaces

The research in multi-surface environments for co-located work has explored ways to share information and manage information across devices [12, 18, 26]. Supporting workspace awareness is mostly done via the shared workspace rather than on the individual devices [18, 26].

Large interactive whiteboards and tabletops present a similar challenge where collaborators are co-located but many awareness cues for collaborators' interactions are hard to gather due to the size of the workspace [5]. Thus, we surveyed related work to inform our design.

Replay animation: In the context of large whiteboards for individual use, Bezerianos et al. [1] animate changes that happened at previously unattended areas when users pay attend to them. Although this approach may address change blindness, detecting and inferring students' attention on touch devices reliably without additional equipment is technically challenging and infeasible for our project.

Collaborator action indicator: Cambria [13] is a digital tabletop visual analytics application. It provides indicators for documents and search terms used by the co-located peers. Notifications of relevant actions are displayed near

[2] https://www.google.ca/docs/about/
[3] https://mural.ly/
[4] https://padlet.com/

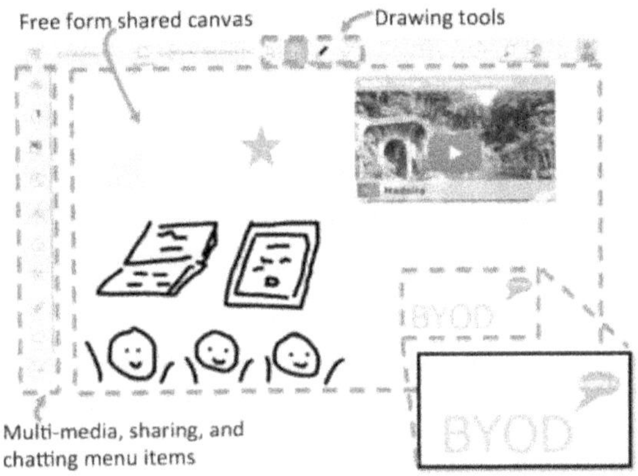

Figure 2: The commercial shared canvas application. Sophia K. is interacting with the "BYOD" text (also see Figure 7).

users' personal space. Our work took a similar approach, and we displayed a cue near the objects being manipulated in the user's workspace.

Historical timeline: Chang et al. [5] use an event timeline to provide a historical view of actions carried out in the workspace. However, students usually have a set amount of time for the lesson and collaborative activities, and they may not have time to browse through historical event logs.

APPLICATION AND BYOD LEARNING ENVIRONMENT

Our awareness cues were design for the commercial web application, SMART amp™, offered by some of the co-authors' company, SMART Technologies (see Figure 2). It is a collaborative learning environment designed for BYOD classrooms, targeting students aged 6 to 17. Students each had a laptop or tablet, and SMART amp™ connected them to a shared flexible canvas. The canvas allowed students to add text, drawings, and pictures in a free-form manner. Students can freely zoom and pan with gestures, add shapes, and move and resize any content. Students can also link websites, online images, and embed YouTube videos.

While the application is primarily used for co-located students in a classroom, remote students can, individually or as a group, participate with equal access. Small groups can work in the same or different canvases. A chat system is provided for student discussion within the workspace.

The shared canvas is implemented using the Google Realtime API[5]. Any manipulation in the canvas is broadcast immediately. When a student drags an object across the workspace, all students in the workspace see the object moving across the canvas rather than jumping to the final destination. The API provides a limited amount of space for storing variables so data communicated between devices must be kept to a minimum.

[5] https://developers.google.com/drive/realtime/

Issues Identified in BYOD Classrooms

Since students are very focused on their specific virtual area in the workspace, gathering awareness of others to understand and coordinate changes can be difficult. From our interviews and observations with teachers and students, we learned that they experienced frustration due to problems related to *ghosting* and *action conflicts*:

Ghosting: Students were frustrated that their objects may be moved, changed, or deleted by peers in the same workspace, without their awareness or permission. Since the shared canvas showed real-time updates of object manipulations without identifying information, the experience was described as "ghosts" sabotaging students' work.

Action conflicts: Students' actions may collide with each other, such as when multiple students simultaneously tried to move the same object, or when one student tried to move an object while another was editing it.

While students did not intend to disrupt each other's work, the lack of awareness meant that students did not know if someone else was working on that content until it was too late. The result was conflict resolution through a busy chat system or yelling out to peers in the classroom. This resulted in significantly more frustration and coordinating efforts.

DESIGN REQUIREMENTS

We hypothesized that workspace awareness would mitigate the frustration caused by ghosting and action conflicts to allow them to focus on their learning activity. Teachers preferred to allow students to learn respectful behaviour in the digital environment rather than automatically enforce particular behaviours. Thus, we felt that workspace awareness of peers would encourage positive behaviours and we used the design requirements below to guide our design process.

Balancing awareness and distraction: Students need to focus on the learning content and not be distracted by the awareness cue. Since the workspace may already be cluttered, the visual design of the awareness cue should be salient enough to be noticed, but subtle enough to avoid distraction and clutter. The literature in awareness and distraction point toward creating a minimalist awareness cue [7, 20]. Students also need to be able to visually associate the cue to the correct object.

Appropriate for classrooms: The cue design must be understandable and easily interpreted by our target student age group (6 to 17 years old). Moreover, the design needs to take into consideration that students are easily distracted and tend to alternate between working and socializing with other students. The awareness cue needs to suit different subjects (e.g., language, science, and math), and activity formats (e.g., individual work, small group work, and large group brainstorm). Teachers may transition between different activities in a lesson and may split and combine student groups several times. The cue should not discourage students from contributing to the workspace.

Figure 3: Conceptual design of student awareness cue. A) Student John is interacting with a star on his tablet. B) Another student sees the star begin to move. C) With the awareness feature, she finds out that John moved it. D) The awareness cue fades out and disappears after some time.

Applicable to a wide variety of devices: Schools use a wide variety of mobile devices with different processor speeds and display resolutions. Our design cannot assume a certain resolution, the presence of mouse pointers, or the existence of a hover state. The performance of the cue needs to be efficient enough for slower low-cost devices.

CONCEPTUAL DESIGN

To address the ghosting and action conflicts, we wanted a transient awareness cue to show the current state of the objects being manipulated. For example, in Figure 3, when John manipulates an object in the canvas (e.g. text, video, shape), all other students see a visual cue showing John's name by the object, if the object is in their viewport (see Figure 3C). The visual cue then fades away over time (see Figure 3D). Identifying the student acting on the object is intended to address the ghosting issue. As John's cue appears on the object, it signals to other students that he is working with it. This also allows others to decide if they should refrain from interacting. Providing this actor-object visual association is intended to address the action conflict problem.

Since the awareness cue is displayed upon active selection of an object, it conveys the actor's identity, real-time actions, and workspace location. Requiring active selection (as opposed to hovering) thus works for devices that do not have mouse cursors. Moreover, if an area already has many awareness cues, students can coordinate their actions by working in a less busy area and teachers can get a sense of where in the workspace students' attention is, to inform their subsequent teaching activities.

METHODOLOGY: DESIGN ITERATION OVERVIEW

This section provides an overview (see Figure 4) of the procedure used in our design iterations, from low- to high-fidelity and the final redesign. The next two sections present our design rationale and how we incorporated findings from the teacher and student evaluations, we then provide an analysis and discussion of the final classroom evaluation.

Low-Fidelity Iterations: Sketches

We first explored the design space through sketches. In several design feedback sessions, stakeholders preferred the Dots design (see Figure 4A) based on our design requirements. Next, we created higher fidelity digital prototypes in PowerPoint and consulted with three teachers. They preferred the Balloon design (see Figure 4B) to minimize distractions. See our design rationale in *Use of Findings in Evolution of Designs* section.

High-Fidelity Iterations: Balloon

We implemented the Balloon design (see Figure 4C) which displayed a collaborator's initials and faded out in a fixed amount of time.

Student Evaluation

After improving the design through an informal testing session with 13 company employees, we conducted an evaluation with a teacher and ten grade 5 students (ages roughly 10-11), who had previously used the SMART amp™ system (with no awareness cues), to understand the noticeability of the cue, and how it would be used. We created two 10-minute lesson plans on one workspace. A post-condition questionnaire contained Likert-scale and free-form questions, and asked about students' usage and experience with the cue, such as awareness of their peers, task focus, frustration level when conflicts arose, and whether they noticed the cue. Since the student participants were in Grade 5, the Likert scale questions also had emoticons below the rankings (inspired by [3]) to prevent misinterpretation.

During the school visit, the teacher led two exercises based on material developed by the researchers. Students used laptops and did the first exercise on "What is your favourite food?" without the new awareness cue, as our baseline. Then, they did the second exercise on "What are your favourite hobbies?" with the Balloon awareness cue. After each condition, students completed a post-condition questionnaire. The study was video- and audio-recorded.

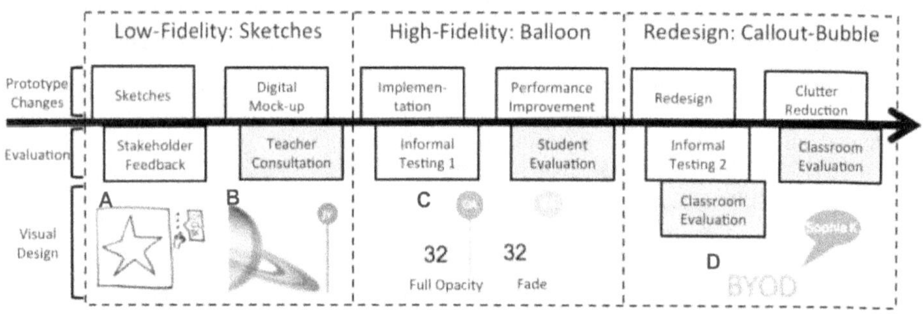

Figure 4: Our design iterations. Boxes above the arrow depict steps taken, and boxes below the arrow are the evaluations. Orange boxes denote evaluations with teachers and/or students. Pictures at the bottom show the selected visual designs that were being iterated upon. (A) Dots; (B) Balloon – PowerPoint mockup; (C) Balloon – Implemented; (D) Callout Bubble

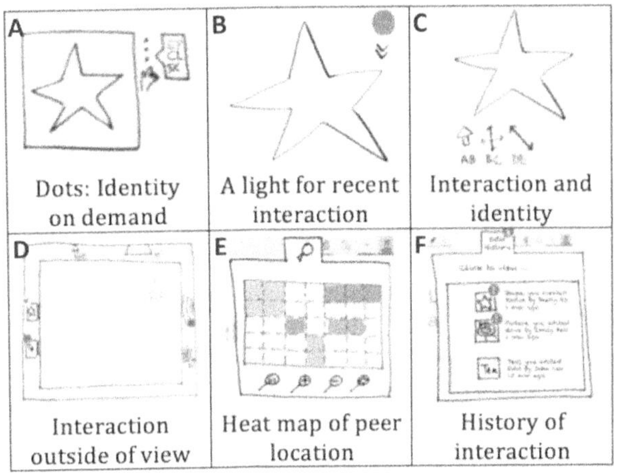

Figure 5: Some of the initial sketches showing varying amounts of identity, interaction, and history information as well as different locations for awareness information.

Although students did notice the cue, they were confused about who the initials belonged to.

Redesign: Callout Bubble

We redesigned the cue to incorporate students' first names, and the visual design resembled a Callout Bubble pointing towards its associated object (see Figure 4D). After two rounds of informal testing with brainstorming and small-group collaboration tasks, we shortened the cue's persistency to reduce distraction. As soon a student with a visible cue started interacting with an object, the student's previous cue on other students' workspaces disappeared automatically to better convey attention. We conducted a final evaluation in 4 classrooms, which included two versions of the Callout Bubble revised based on the informal testing (see *Impact of Callout Bubble* section).

USE OF FINDINGS IN DESIGN EVOLUTION

We incorporated the findings from the student and teacher evaluations in the design evolution. We examined the location of the awareness information, the amount of information (e.g., actor's identity, number of actors, and actions being performed), amount of historical information, persistency of visualization, and interactivity of the awareness visualization (see the variety of initial designs in Figure 5). This section presents the iterations on our design.

Cue Visual Design

The visual design of awareness cues has two main components: actors' identity information and a tether to specify the object being acted upon. We explored different shapes, styles, colours, and locations of the tether (see Figure 6).

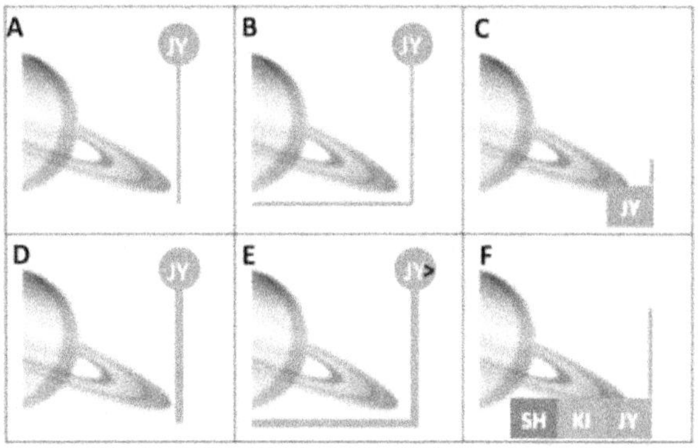

Figure 6: Some of the digital mock-ups showing different designs of awareness cue. (A) Balloon; (B) Elbow; (C) Line; (D), (E), and (F) depict when more than one user has interacted with the object recently for A, B, and C, respectively.

We narrowed down to the Balloon design with a gray tether (see Figure 6A) as it satisfies the teachers' preference on minimizing clutter while balancing noticeability, distraction, and clutter. In our student evaluation, all 10 students noticed the Balloon. The student survey showed a small but positive trend in average ratings of awareness of collaborators ($M_{control}$=3.78, $M_{Balloon}$=4.45) and ease of focus on task at hand ($M_{control}$=3.11, $M_{Balloon}$=3.78). Student ratings of action conflict frequency and frustration level during these conflicts showed a negative trend (frequency: $M_{control}$=3.44, $M_{Balloon}$=3.22; frustration: $M_{control}$=4.00, $M_{Balloon}$=3.75).

Although these are positive signs for the visual design, we had to redesign the cue to incorporate students' first names (see *Identity Information* section below). To accommodate for the longer identifiers, we decided to adopt a Callout Bubble metaphor (see Figure 7), and attach the cue to the object as if it were "speaking", rather than using the more abstract grey tether line in the Balloon design. This simplified actor identification for rotated objects, since the cue remained upright and is pointing at the object even when the object was rotated.

Identity Information

The Balloon design (see Figure 6A) used the students' first and last initials to indicate who was interacting with the object. This identity representation required minimal space and was consistent with how identity was displayed in SMART amp™. (Identity of creator and editor of an object was shown in a square box at the top right corner of an object). Moreover, we used the students' colours, uniquely generated based on their system logins, to provide additional cues of identity.

In the student evaluation, 7/10 students reported looking at the awareness cue when others got in their way. From the video recordings, we observed that, rather than being confused about who moved an object, students noticed the cue and asked who it represented (e.g. "Who is JP?"). Although this showed a positive impact, it became apparent to us that initials were not sufficient for students' awareness.

Figure 7: Callout Bubble design. (A) Sophia K. is interacting with the "BYOD" text; (B) cue fades out; (C) cue re-adjusts its position when there is no sufficient space at the top.

Our redesigned cue became a Callout Bubble with a student's full first name and last initial (see Figure 7). The last name was abbreviated as our study showed that students did not remember the last names of their peers.

Interactivity & Interaction Information

We iterated on whether the awareness cue should be interactive and how much interaction information to show. We considered the spectrum from using abstract representation (e.g., Figure 5A & Figure 5B) to showing the exact type of manipulation being done (e.g., Figure 5C). However, an abstract representation might not be noticeable enough. Considering the additional difficulty in selecting small targets, we chose a visualization that has no interactivity.

In the high-fidelity phase, we initially increased the thickness of the Balloon tether as more people acted on an object (see Figure 6A vs. 6D & Figure 6C vs. 6F). In our testing we found that few participants noticed this change in tether thickness so we removed this cue to simplify the design and reduce clutter.

In the Balloon and Callout Bubble designs, the cue automatically appeared when a peer interacted with an object within the user's view. Actions that modified the objects' visual properties (e.g., move and edit text) would trigger the cue. A selection also triggered the cue since it hinted at a person's potential intent to start manipulating an object.

Persistency of Cue

The awareness cue information becomes quickly outdated so we designed it to disappear after some time. We iterated on a cue that persists for a while and then automatically fades out quickly. This resolved the issue of students' connections dropping due to unstable networks in some schools so that a cue would indicate a recent interaction. It also resolved the issue of a student selecting an object but then not actively working on it.

In our first informal testing (see Figure 4, middle), the Balloon faded away gradually in 10 seconds, and the participants reported that the initials were barely readable by the time they noticed the Balloons. Thus, we made the Balloon opaque for 8 seconds before fading out for 2 seconds.

Our second informal testing (see Figure 4, right) with the Callout Bubble revealed that multiple Callout Bubble cues by the same student cluttered the shared workspace. A mischievous student could overwhelm the workspace with Callout Bubbles by selecting many objects. Based on this feedback we changed the timing of the awareness cue (opaque for 5 seconds, then fade out in 2 seconds) and allowed only one Callout Bubble per student.

To ensure the Callout Bubble stayed close to the object being acted upon, we automatically moved the cue to a different corner of the object if it became too close to the edge or partially off-screen (see Figure 7C).

CLASSROOM EVALUATION OF CALLOUT BUBBLE

This section describes our classroom evaluation on the final Callout Bubble design and its impact on students' behaviour, and teachers' classroom management.

We conducted the evaluation in 4 classrooms (4 teachers and 71 students) to test the balance between awareness and distraction and the cue's impact on students' behaviours. Due to the timing of the software release, all groups used SMART amp™ but with two different versions of the Callout Bubble: two groups (38 students) used the first version (Callout Bubble persists for 10 seconds and multiple cues per student) and two groups (33 students) used the modified version (Callout Bubble persists for 7 seconds and one cue per student). Students were in Grades 3, 4, 5, and 12. The group sizes ranged from 2, 3, and 6 students, to the whole class. Students used iPads, iPad Minis, and laptops.

All participants had used our system prior to the study. The teachers conducted their daily lesson as usual, but used the version with Callout Bubbles. The students and teachers filled out an online survey at the end of their lessons. Teachers were invited to participate in a phone interview session; and 1 teacher participated in the call.

Questionnaire

The student survey contained the same Likert-scale questions described in the *Student Evaluation* section above, without the emoticons (since the online survey tool did not allow images for Likert scales). It also contained questions pertaining to students' workspace behaviour, such as whether they changed their behaviour when using the Callout Bubble (vs. no Callout Bubble), whether they noticed the cues, and how they handled workspace conflicts with their peers. The teacher survey asked teachers about the lesson conducted, group size, and their feedback on the Callout Bubble.

Data Analysis

For the Likert-scale questions, we formed hypotheses and tested them with Pearson Correlations. For the question probing frustration level when others got in their way, we allowed students to skip the question if they did not encounter a conflict. Thus, only 58 data points were used for correlation analysis related to student frustration level.

For free-form answers on whether students' behaviour changed with the new feature, we coded them using Gutwin and Greenberg's Workspace Awareness Framework [9]. We coded for the awareness elements (*who*, *what*, and *when* for present information) and awareness activity (*coupling*, *communication*, *coordination*, *anticipation*, and *assistance*). Two researchers coded the student answers and reached full agreement on the final coding.

Awareness, Conflicts, Distraction, and Frustration

First, we wanted to confirm that student conflicts in our system and higher levels of frustration are related. Our results confirmed this and showed that frequency of conflict is correlated with higher frustration (r_{58}=.395, p=.002).

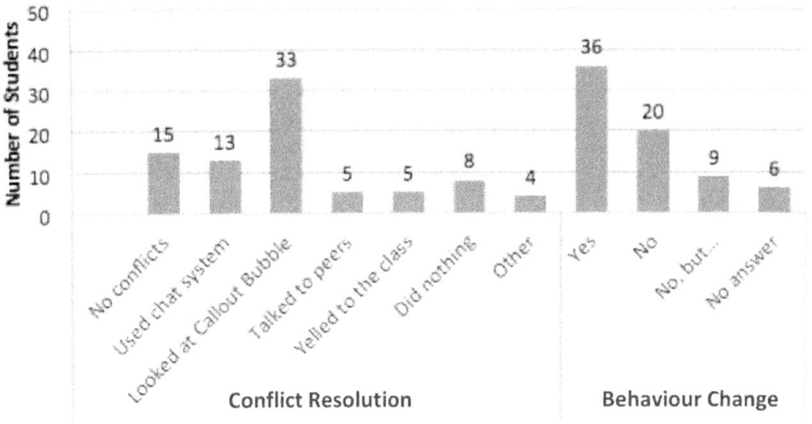

Figure 8: (Left) Self-reported actions taken by students when conflicts arose. This was a multiple selection question. (Right) Break down of students' answers to whether Callout Bubble changed how they work with other student. "No, but..." indicate students that responded no but then commented on how their behaviours changed.

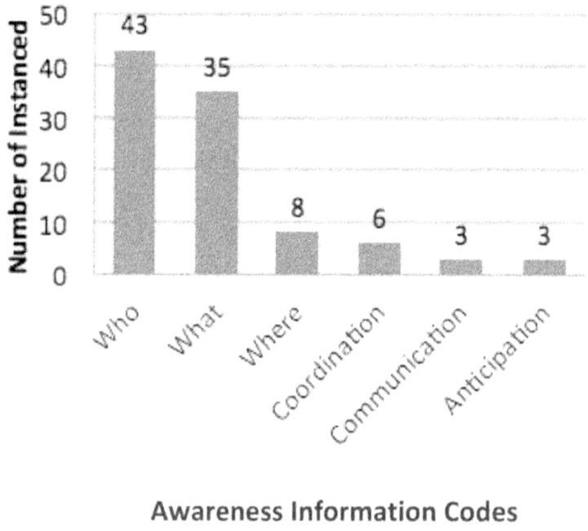

Figure 9: Count of awareness element and activity coded. See Gutwin & Greenberg [9] for code definition.

As we aimed to provide Callout Bubbles to address student frustration from ghosting and action conflicts, we sought to confirm that we had made improvements in students' awareness of peers' actions, their concentration at tasks, and their frustration levels. We first asked if students noticed and/or used the Callout Bubble. Almost all students (66/71) noticed the Callout Bubbles. Nearly half of the students (33/71) reported looking at the awareness cues when conflicts arose, while 15 students reported that nobody "got in their way" as indicated in Figure 8, left.

A potential disadvantage of providing awareness cues is that they may distract students while they were working. We hypothesized that higher levels of awareness of peers' actions would be linked to more difficulties concentrating on tasks at hand. Surprisingly, we found that the students' ranking of awareness of peers and ease of focus were positively correlated (r_{71}=.336, p=.004). One teacher (T4) commented on the fact that students were more focused on their work after the Callout Bubbles were added, since they did not need to spend time or cognitive effort to figure out their peer collaborators' actions: "*It kept them moving on the project and not focusing on who was moving what.*" This result suggested that awareness cues may be beneficial in helping students to focus in a shared workspace.

The teachers reported that students' initial "wow" moments spurred by seeing the Callout Bubbles appearing for the first time were distracting to the lesson. However, that quickly subsided and the Callout Bubbles provided a good balance between awareness and distraction after students got used to working in the environment with this new feature.

We also hypothesized that higher levels of peer awareness would correlate with less frustration when conflicts arose. This was supported by the results, which showed a negative correlation between awareness of peers' actions and frustration when conflicts arose (r_{58}=-.322, p=.014). Students' comments further indicated that having more awareness of peers might have minimized frustration when others were in their way.

> S21: "*It is easy cause now we know if someone is just messing around cause [of] the bubble.*"

> S58: "*This Callout Bubble has saved my life because this can tell me who has been touching my stuff and been doing stuff.*"

S58's dramatic comment suggests the level of frustration he/she experienced without the awareness cue and the perceived value of the Callout Bubbles.

Comprehensibility and Behaviour Change

Our results showed that students were able to associate the identity information with the interactions. First, students understood the cue and acted upon it. For example, showing the identity of students helped the class to subsequently resolve issues that arose.

> S34: "*... we now know who the source of the problem is so we can fix it easily.*"

In total, 43 students' comments indicated awareness of their peers, and 35 students' comments specifically showed the ability to link identity with interactions that happened in the workspace. For example:

> S17: "*Yes because if someone was making a picture the size of the workspace I could see who it was.*"

More than half of the students (45/71) reported the Callout Bubble changed how they worked with others, while 20 students reported it did not change how they worked and 6 students did not answer or responded with irrelevant comments (see Figure 8, right). Moreover, students commented on the type of awareness information they have gained.

More than half of the students (43/71) reported knowing the identity of peers (who), 35 students reported knowing the types of actions being carried out (what), and 8 students commented on knowing where other peers were working in the shared canvas (see Figure 9). The reported behaviour change and awareness information gain revealed that students understood the meaning of the Callout Bubbles.

Student Coordination & Self-Monitoring

The Callout Bubble also conveyed a sense of peers' locations and their current focus of attention. The results showed that some students were able to act upon this information. A total of 9 students commented that they could anticipate peers' actions, as well as coordinate their actions accordingly (see Figure 9).

> S2: "... *I knew where other people were working so I knew where to do my things so I wouldn't get in the way of others.*"

> S40: "*now it's easier to work so you know who's working on something so you don't get in their way.*"

Although the awareness cue was designed to help students coordinate the virtual workspace, one student (S3) commented on the ability to coordinate their learning activities. This showed the potential of the Callout Bubble to facilitate learning in addition to just coordinating space.

> S3: "*If I seen someone working on that part [of the project] I would go to a different problem.*"

We did not expect students to use the awareness cue as a way to monitor each other's progress. Surprisingly, the teacher feedback also indicated that the Callout Bubble allowed for students to self-monitor and kept each other accountable during the collaboration.

> T3: "*It kept them more on task and they kept each other more accountable for what was happening in the work space ... [keeping each other accountable] helped improve efficiency of work and helping students identify where to work in the workspace...*"

Teacher Monitoring

In addition to students' behaviour changes, teachers noted that they were able to monitor activities from individual screens, which made determining student problems easier.

> T4: "*It helped me for having to look and see who was doing what if a student had a problem because I could see it right on their screen.*"

Having the awareness cue automatically appear as the students were interacting with objects on the shared canvas also reduced the cognitive and physical workload required to monitor student activities.

> T2: "*I could keep tabs easier on who was doing what without having to check attribution [a feature in our system], and it was real-time.*"

Concern with Showing Identity Information and Clutter

Despite the positive comments on improved student and teacher work, one teacher (T1) wondered whether shy students would be reluctant to collaborate with others now that all students could see who is doing what in the shared canvas. However, the teacher also mentioned that the benefits outweigh this potential concern.

> T1: "*My only concern is that some reluctant collaborators will not be free with their responses if they know all others will see it? But really this shouldn't matter. The pros outweigh the cons for sure.*"

We designed the awareness cues to be transient with this exact concern in mind. Since the Callout Bubble faded away automatically, we believe the impact should be minimal.

In terms of clutter, while the Callout Bubble worked fine for the group sizes tested, a few teachers felt that being able to turn off the awareness cues for much larger groups would be a nice-to-have feature since the workspace would already be cluttered. As we also found in our informal testing, the awareness cue may not be useful in this scenario where students cannot avoid bumping into each other in the virtual space due to a large number of collaborators and content.

Summary of Results

Overall, the design of the Callout Bubble satisfied the design requirements and our goal to provide awareness while balancing distraction as indicated by our data analysis and teacher's qualitative feedback. The results showed that the cue was noticed, used, and understood by students. Subsequently, students were able to coordinate their actions and self-monitor.

DISCUSSION OF REAL-WORLD LESSONS

The highly iterative design process drove substantial design modifications (see Figure 4). In this section, we discuss the lessons learned from this process.

Design Lessons

Visual Design and Amount of Information

We aimed to balance awareness, distraction, and clutter through the iterative design process. We found that our visual design became more precise and minimalist over iterations. For example, we switched from the vertical tether to a directional triangle in Callout Bubble to more precisely and effectively convey the association. We dropped the changing thickness of the tether, as it was too subtle. We also found that our use of initials to convey identity information in the earlier versions was not effective for the students. Designers should consider the suitability of identity representation for a particular domain, e.g., initials vs. full names, or roles vs. names.

Interactivity and Persistency

We explored using interactive visualization to further reduce clutter and distraction. Although Dabbish and Kraut [7] suggested using abstract representation to reduce distraction, a small indicator might be too subtle to be noticed in a crowded canvas, and students might not be able to use their peripheral attention to maintain awareness of their peers. Moreover, since the awareness cue moves with the object, a small moving target would be hard to select on touch devices. The use of interactive abstract symbols would need to consider if the symbols were easily distinguishable from the content in a free-form canvas and how easy it was to interact with on mobile touch devices.

Determining how long the cue should be persistent required several iterations to balance awareness and clutter. We found that the cue had to stay visible for several seconds for students to notice and gain the intended awareness information before the cue faded away. An awareness cue's precise timing of visibility may need adjustment in different contexts, depending on the size of the canvas and amount of contextual visual clutter.

Conveying Attention on Touch Devices

We chose to use the awareness cue to indicate a student's active selection and interaction to accommodate the fact that there is no mouse pointer available on the touch tablets used in schools. By allowing for one Callout Bubble per student, the design better conveyed the object of student's current attentional focus.

Moreover, teachers sometimes design a lesson such that multiple applications are used in addition to the shared canvas. Students may be actively researching and exploring information in other applications while appearing to be idling in the shared canvas. Visualizing a persistent object that may be idling for a long time (e.g., mouse pointers) could add clutter and distract students rather than providing awareness. Thus, conveying active student actions in a transient way allows us to provide only the necessary information. If designers prefer to visualize a persistent object in this context, they should consider ways to detect and communicate the in-app idling situation and activities outside of the collaborative workspace.

Awareness for Collaborators and Moderators

Although we designed the awareness cue mainly for students, the teacher feedback revealed that students' self-monitoring behaviour also helped teachers. It is typically difficult for teachers to monitor student activities while students are using their own devices. Applications with moderators should also consider how the awareness of the moderator is hindered or supported by the physical setup and the built-in awareness mechanisms.

Pedagogical Concerns

As we were designing for students, we took the approach of providing awareness cues that allowed for social mitigation of potential conflicts, rather than system-enforced coordination of virtual resources to address teachers' concerns on *encouraging learning*. By incorporating transient cues into our design, our system supported *student work patterns*. Showing the identity of actors may discourage shy students' contributions, yet the transient nature of the awareness cue may mitigate this concern. Teachers were concerned with permanently showing the creator and editors of objects in the shared canvas. This can be particularly troubling for low-performing students who may be discouraged, while the high-performing students may be embarrassed about being called out. Transient awareness cues help to minimize these concerns, and our results showed that it made a positive impact in real classroom situations. We sought teacher input throughout our iterative design process and their feedback kept us mindful of the unique needs of students.

Practical Concerns

As a real-world application, there were several practical constraints we had to overcome. The awareness cues represented interaction events rather than states due to potential network issues and underlying software architecture. In order to convey attention, we automatically made the students' previous cues disappear. We also had to decide on when the awareness cue location will be updated to provide close to real-time update experience while taking the slower network and devices into consideration.

CONCLUSION, LIMITATIONS, & FUTURE WORK

This project aimed to support students' awareness in a shared digital canvas by providing identity and location information of collaborators' active interaction with objects. This paper contributed a minimalist and practical design of a student awareness cue, Callout Bubble, for a shared virtual canvas being used across individual devices in a co-located environment. Our real-world, in-class evaluation, showed that Callout Bubbles effectively balanced awareness, distraction, and clutter. It also allowed for self-monitoring and more effective coordination among students. Our design was optimized for use across touch tablets, mouse-based laptops, and interactive whiteboards. We also contributed lessons learned through an iterative approach that effectively provoked refinement and redesign.

This project focused on synchronous collaboration within one class. Further investigation is needed to understand the effectiveness of the cue for multi-class lessons and asynchronous usage. Our results showed that there is also a need to provide teachers with in-class situation awareness, to better inform their coordination of student activities in the shared canvas. Further research is needed to investigate teachers' information need, the types of medium to facilitate their situation awareness, and ways to leverage existing classroom technologies, such as interactive whiteboards. Considering the vastness of virtual workspaces, a relevancy model and an appropriate algorithm for notifying students of relevant actions while minimizing distractions warrant further investigations.

ACKNOWLEDGMENTS

We thank SSHRC IMMERSe (the Interactive and Multi-Modal Experience Research Syndicate), NSERC (Natural Sciences and Engineering Research Council of Canada),

Mitacs, and SMART Technologies in supporting this project. We thank our participants for their valuable feedback.

REFERENCES

1. Bezerianos, A., Dragicevic, P. and Balakrishnan, R. 2006. Mnemonic rendering : an image-based approach for exposing hidden changes in dynamic displays. *UIST*, 159–168.
2. Bodemer, D. and Dehler, J. 2011. Group awareness in CSCL environments. *Computers in Human Behavior*. 27, 3, 1043–1045.
3. Bradley, M.M. and Lang, P.J. 1994. Measuring emotion : the self-assessment manikin and the semantic differential. *J. Behavior Theraphy & Experimental Psychiatry*. 25, 1, 49–59.
4. Carroll, J.M., Rosson, M.B., Convertino, G. and Ganoe, C.H. 2006. Awareness and teamwork in computer-supported collaborations. *Interacting with Computers*. 18, 1, 21–46.
5. Chang, Y.-L.B., Scott, S.D. and Hancock, M. 2014. Supporting situation awareness in collaborative tabletop systems with automation. *ITS*, 185–194.
6. Cheung, V., Chang, Y.-L.B. and Scott, S.D. 2012. Communication channels and awareness cues in collocated collaborative time-critical gaming. *CSCW*, 569–578.
7. Dabbish, L. and Kraut, R.E. 2004. Controlling interruptions : awareness displays and social motivation for coordination. *CSCW*, 182–191.
8. Engelmann (née Keller), T., Tergan, S.-O. and Hesse, F.W. 2009. Evoking knowledge and information awareness for enhancing computer-supported collaborative problem solving. *Experimental Education*. 78, 2, 268–290.
9. Gutwin, C. and Greenberg, S. 2002. A descriptive framework of workspace awareness for real-time groupware. *Computer Supported Cooperative Work*. 11, 411–446.
10. Gutwin, C. and Greenberg, S. 2000. The Effects of Workspace Awareness Support on the Usability of Real-Time Distributed Groupware. *TOCHI*. 6, 3, 243–281.
11. Gutwin, C., Greenberg, S. and Roseman, M. 1996. Workspace awareness support with radar views. *CHI*, 210–211.
12. Houben, S., Tell, P. and Bardram, J.E. 2014. ActivitySpace: managing device ecologies in an activity-centric configuration space. *ITS*, 119–128.
13. Isenberg, P. and Carpendale, S. 2007. Interactive tree comparison for co-located collaborative information visualization. *IEEE Trans. on Visualization and Computer Graphics*. 13, 6, 1232–1239.
14. Janssen, J. and Bodemer, D. 2013. Coordinated computer-supported collaborative learning: awareness and awareness tools. *Educational Psychologist*. 48, 1, 40–55.
15. Jongsawat, N. and Premchaiswadi, W. 2009. An empirical study of group awareness information in web-based group decision support system in a field test setting. *ICT and Knowledge Engineering*, 15–23.
16. Kimmerle, J., Cress, U. and Hesse, F.W. 2007. An interactional perspective on group awareness: alleviating the information-exchange dilemma (for everybody?). *Int. J. Human Computer Studies*. 65, 11, 899–910.
17. Markopoulos, P., Ruyter, B. de and Mackay, W. eds. 2009. *Awareness systems: advances in theory, methodology and design*. Springer-Verlag London.
18. Marquardt, N., Ballendat, T., Boring, S., Greenberg, S. and Hinckley, K. 2012. Gradual engagement : facilitating information exchange between digital devices as a function of proximity. *ITS*, 31–40.
19. Molinari, G., Sangin, M., Nüssli, M.-A. and Dillenbourg, P. 2008. Effects of knowledge interdependence with the partner on visual and action transactivity in collaborative concept mapping. *Proc. of Int. Conf. for Learning Sciences*, 91–98.
20. Obermayer, R.W. and Nugent, W.A. 2000. Human-computer interaction for alert warning and attention allocation systems of the multimodal watchstation. *SPIE 4126. Integrated Command Environment, 14.*
21. Petersen, S.E. and Posner, M.I. 2012. The attention system of the human brain: 20 Years After. *Annual Review of Neuroscience*. 35, 73–89.
22. Phielix, C., Prins, F.J. and Kirschner, P. a. 2010. Awareness of group performance in a CSCL-environment: effects of peer feedback and reflection. *Computers in Human Behavior*. 26, 2, 151–161.
23. Rideout, V. 2013. *Zero to eight: children's media use in America 2013.*
24. Roseman, M. and Greenberg, S. 1996. Building real-time groupware with GroupKit, a groupware toolkit. *TOCHI*. 3, 1, 66–106.
25. Sarma, A., Redmiles, D. and van der Hoek, A. 2008. Empirical evidence of the benefits of workspace awareness in software configuration management. *Int. Symposium on Foundations of software engineering*, 113–123.
26. Scott, S.D., Besacier, G., Tournet, J., Goyal, N. and Haller, M. 2014. Surface ghosts: promoting awareness of transferred objects during pick-and-drop transfer in multi-surface environments. *ITS*, 99–108.

Smart Makerspace:
An Immersive Instructional Space for Physical Tasks

Jarrod Knibbe[1,2], Tovi Grossman[1], George Fitzmaurice[1]

[1]Autodesk Research, Toronto, Canada
{firstname.lastname}@autodesk.com

[2]University of Bristol, UK
Jarrod.Knibbe@bristol.ac.uk

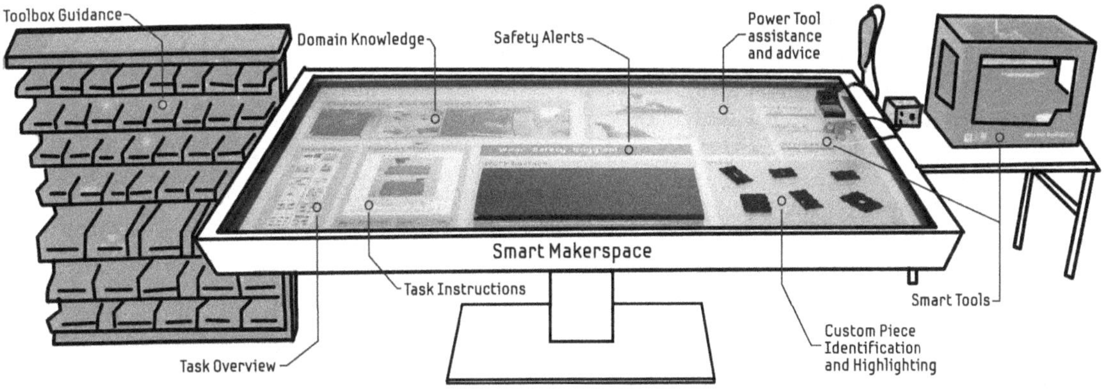

Figure 1. The *Smart Makerspace*. Focused around a smart workbench, toolbox and power-tools, the *Smart Makerspace* provides an immersive, integrated instructional experience for novice makers.

ABSTRACT
We present the *Smart Makerspace*; a context-rich, immersive instructional workspace for novice and intermediate makers. The Smart Makerspace guides makers through the completion of a DIY task, while providing detailed contextually-relevant assistance, domain knowledge, tool location, usage cues, and safety advice. Through an initial exploratory study, we investigate the challenges faced in completing maker tasks. Our observations allow us to define design goals and a design space for a connected workshop. We describe our implementation, including a digital workbench, augmented toolbox, instrumented power-tools and environmentally aware audio. We present a qualitative user study that produced encouraging results; providing features that users unanimously found useful.

INTRODUCTION
Do-it-Yourself tasks (DIY) and 'maker' activities are supported by a wealth of instructional resources online. Websites such as Instructables[1], Make[2], and IkeaHackers[3] provide guidance across a broad range of topics, through illustrated walkthroughs similar in style to traditional paper manuals. However, research on tutorial systems for complex software highlights the benefits of a more integrated and multimedia-based instructional experience [3, 5, 6, 9, 11].

We suggest that there are similarities between the difficulties faced in using complex software systems and completing DIY tasks. These include: uncertainty over tool location, correct tool usage, and steps required to achieve a goal. In a DIY 'maker' task, these concerns are further emphasized as actions are often irreversible and procedures may be dangerous. Based on these similarities, we draw on software tutorial research to develop an instruction-delivery and training system for DIY maker tasks. [123]

In this paper, we present the *Smart Makerspace*; a context-rich, immersive instructional workspace for novice and intermediate makers. The Smart Makerspace is designed to provide an informed and safe environment in existing machine shops and maker spaces where initial maker skills can be learned and refined. Although the maker community emphasizes peer learning, this occurs not only in-situ, but through a 'build and blog' spirit and active online community [20, 23]. Our work seeks to bring this online material 'to-life' within the physical environment of making. Through augmented tools and surfaces, the Smart Makerspace can monitor, record and respond to makers' physical actions in real time. This 'smart' approach provides opportunities for workflow monitoring and the delivery of interactive tutorials. The environment also presents an opportunity for automated recording [2]. However in this paper we focus on the *delivery* of a

ITS '15, November 15-18, 2015, Funchal, Portugal
© 2015 ACM. ISBN 978-1-4503-3899-8/15/11...$15.00
DOI: http://dx.doi.org/10.1145/2817721.2817741

[1] www.instructables.com
[2] www.makezine.com
[3] www.ikeahackers.net

context-rich, multi-faceted instructional experience for a single novice or intermediate level maker.

In the first step of our research, we performed an observational study of the difficulties faced within makerspace practice and the differences between novice and expert makers. Based on these observations we define the design goals of our system and present a hardware design space. We then present the *Smart Makerspace* (Figure 1). Our makerspace delivers detailed task instructions through a manual, a workflow overview and task- and skill- based videos. Tracked power tools enable tool status monitoring, in turn providing tool readiness, usage information and time-relevant safety advice. An augmented 47-bin toolbox gives tool location cues and environmentally aware audio feedback provides task progress and safety warnings. Finally, we report on an observational study in which participants responded positively to the features of our makerspace.

RELATED WORK

Current Instructional Practices for Physical Tasks

Previous research has explored the resources used for physical tasks [26–28, 30]. The online maker/DIY communities are by far the most popular source of instructions and guidelines [27]. While instruction sets are available on a wide range of topics, individual instructions typically focus on: introducing a specific skill; or providing a guide to building a specific item [26, 30]. Within this, some instructions provide detailed background and debugging information, where others focus on the fewest steps to complete the task [28]. These different styles necessitate continuous research and content switching in order to complete a task, distancing the user from the original task itself [27, 30]. Wakkary et al. suggest the creation of instruction sets based on the principles of interaction design [30] and our work could be considered one such example.

Research has also highlighted the importance of task feedback [29]. While feedback is available online, through forums and comments, this adds a further time-cost overhead to the learning process [29]. With the *Smart Makerspace* we bring the differing types of instruction sets together, such as skill-based instructions, task-specific guidance, and variations in possible approaches.

Delivering Software Tutorials

Similarly to physical task instructions, software tutorials are abundant online. However, instructions and tutorials can also be integrated within the software itself [3, 6, 9]. This can allow for a more relevant and immersive learning experience. For example, with ToolClips [5] users are provided with tool-relevant videos during system use. Pause-and-Play [17] provides time-relevant information by synchronizing video assistance with a user's task progress.

Beyond providing relevant cues, software tutorials can also provide system guidance and facilitate learning from experts. In Sketch Sketch Revolution [3] and Stencils-based Tutorials [9] the user is guided through a task, whilst the system highlights the correct tools and configurations to use, and reduces opportunities for error. Grabler et al. [4] and MixT [1] both demonstrate systems that automatically produce tutorials and guides from expert user demonstrations. In Chronicle [6] and Community Enhanced Tutorials [13], users can explore a system based on the execution of experts, viewing how tools were used, how processes were combined and how end goals were achieved.

We leverage and adapt these principles within our Smart Makerspace to provide a learning environment that seamlessly combines digital and physical environments.

Immersive Physical-Task Environments

Previous work has explored the use of in-situ and contextual cues for performing tasks in physical environments (e.g. [16, 25]). A popular approach within this work is the use of projection for augmented walls and surfaces [10, 16] and overlaid graphics [14, 29]. Beyond projection, real-time systems have attempted to place a remote expert in the scene [7, 21, 25]. In this, the requirement for constant expert presence makes this unsuitable for an amateur or personal makerspace.

Augmented reality systems have been developed to assist with physical tasks. Henderson et al. [8] built a head-mounted display providing detailed overlaid graphics to assist complex airplane engine mechanical tasks. Similar techniques have been used in other settings, including automotive manufacture [18] and Lego building tasks [24].

The work of Henderson et al. is close to ours, yet we believe that our approach is the first of its kind. While Henderson's work focuses on the psychomotor phase of a procedural task, our work looks at high-level tasks in which multiple steps must be performed, and a variety of new skills and tools must be learned.

ELabBench [22] provides a digital benchtop for biological experimentation, bringing a wide range of desktop computing capabilities into the sterile laboratory environment. ELabBench supports the annotation of test tube racks, note taking, web browsing and document editing. Our work is complementary to this and builds on its core principles. ELabBench focuses on personal recording during a physical task, where our system is instructional, actively monitors and feeds-back on the status of tools and materials in the wider environment and focuses on content delivery. We draw inspiration from a range of 'smart' tools previously presented by the HCI community (such as [31–33]) to augment existing tools and facilities across an entire space, thereby seeking to better support a maker throughout the entirety of their practice.

OBSERVATIONAL STUDY

To better understand the intricacies of practice within maker and DIY tasks and to derive requirements for our system we conducted an exploratory think-aloud study with both novice and expert makers. We explored the online maker communities and referenced the Makerspace Playbook [15] (an educational guidebook) to gain an understanding of the types of tasks performed by makers. From this, we designed a 'hello world' style maker project which consisted of a box with lights that blinked when an object approaches (Figure 2). Our intention was to incorporate a range of tools and skills popular within this domain (including electronics, drilling, soldering and 3D printing), to provide a broad base from which to explore the challenges of making and motivate our work. Although an ethnographic observation may have highlighted further nuances of practice, our generalized task served to provide generalized observations to drive our prototype's design. The box consists of 6 side pieces, housing a proximity sensor, 2 LEDs and a Phidget. We authored a 13 step *Instructable* entitled "Proximity Box", which can be viewed on the *Instructables* website[4]. While websites such as *Instructables* support videos within their instructions, the majority of sets (~95% on *Instructables*) consist solely of text and images. As such we did not include video, to allow us to understand the challenges users encounter with the most typical style of instruction sets.

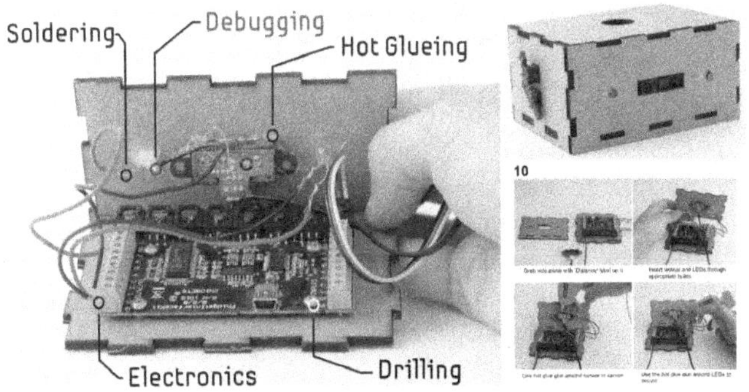

Figure 2. The 'Proximity Box.' Clockwise from left - breakdown of different skills, finished box, example of step.

Participants

We invited 8 participants (3 female, age: M=28, SD=5.5 years) to build our proximity box. The participants rated their skill and experience levels (3 beginners, 2 intermediate, 3 experienced) and provided examples of projects completed, including: building IKEA furniture, home improvement DIY and personal robotics. Three participants described themselves as tinkerers or makers. Five participants had done educational courses (primarily during college) or online research to improve their maker skills (primarily through online forums and Youtube). While five participants suggested they used online tutorials for new tasks, only 3 participants said they like to read a manual when conducting a DIY task.

We invited both novice and expert makers to take part in this study in order to highlight the differences in their practice. Furthermore, our intention was to design a system that could be integrated into existing maker spaces, thus the system would need to support expert and novice use alike.

Apparatus

The study took place at a workbench. The bench was equipped with a 3D printer, glue gun, soldering iron, rotary tool and protective surface for drilling. A laptop was provided for viewing the *Instructable*. Behind the participants was a 47-bin toolbox that contained all other components needed for the task. Of the 47 bins, 17 had parts necessary for the task. The participants were recorded with 2 video cameras, one focused on the workbench and the other focused on the toolbox.

Procedure and Design

The participants completed a questionnaire prior to beginning the task, including questions relating to their skill, experience and confidence with different tools. The users were then instructed to build the box, following the *Instructable* as closely as they wished, while vocalizing their thoughts. The participants were allowed to look for additional resources online. The building-tasks took approximately 1 hour to complete. An experimenter was present to take notes on their spoken thoughts, the details of their actions and to carefully monitor the situation for any safety issues. The users were instructed to complete all steps to the best of their abilities. Help was only provided to participants who had previously attempted a step and then asked for help or when safety concerns arose. Upon finishing, users completed another questionnaire regarding their strengths and weaknesses with the building task.

Observations were analyzed to highlight recurrent themes across the participants relating to making.

Challenges Encountered

Here we will focus on four principal issues which arose during our study: an overview of the task, domain knowledge, tool selection and tool usage details.

An Overview of the Task

Inexperienced makers followed the instructions precisely, often on a per sub-step basis, without any understanding of (or interest in) the wider task. This reluctance to explore the task further made it difficult to resolve issues that arose. As an example, at one stage the maker prepared two lengths of wire, though the required lengths were not given. Those with more experience knew to look further ahead into the instructions to determine the wire's purpose and thus calculate its length, whereas those focused only on the precise step guessed.

In general, the experienced participants were keen to see an overview of the build so they could proceed with a more personally-driven execution.

'I think if I saw the overview of the whole project, rather than step-by-step [instructions], I would have completely ignored the instructions and just tried to 'Macgyver' it together. At least with the physical box, the electronics, which I am less comfortable

[4] http://www.instructables.com/id/Depth-sensing-Box/

with, I probably would have gone back to figure out what was going on there.' (P2)

This understanding of the wider task also allows expert makers to know where they can 'cut corners.' For example, when referring to a step which required securing bolts to be fitted, P7 said: *'Now I'm only using 2 because I hate putting bolts on.'* Similarly, in order to save time, P2 chose to glue the circuit board into their box as opposed to using the suggested drill.

Domain Knowledge

Another clear divide between participants in our study was over domain knowledge. The more experienced makers continuously referenced prior experience *'I would normally put [the Dremel] in reverse to make sure it's tight'* (P5) or *'I do know you are supposed to sort of curl the end of the wire around the end that you are soldering to'* (P6). In another example, those with more experience soldering would look for support tools (e.g. a 3rd hand) or additional components (e.g. heat shrink) to help them complete the task. In this instance, domain knowledge could also be used to confirm whether the soldering was 'good enough.' However, this required additional background knowledge that the novices did not share, affecting their confidence throughout the build.

Tool Selection

An important function of a 'makerspace' is the variety of different tools that are available and the uncertainty surrounding correct tool selection. Our makerspace has a 47 bin toolbox, holding a variety of different components including: different sized screws, transistors, LEDs, screwdrivers, wires, drill bits etc. A toolbox of this size is not unusual and, regardless of experience, all participants spent a significant amount of the total task time looking for tools. While expert makers could confidently select an appropriate tool once located, novice makers also struggled with the selection process as many tools appear similar.

Tool Usage

During the task participants used three power tools: a rotary tool (Dremel), a soldering iron and a glue gun. Each of these tools presents its own set of challenges, for example a drill can slip and toxic fumes are produced when soldering. While more expert users are accustomed to these hazards (e.g. P1 knew to exhale when soldering), they are an important concern for novices. P3, P6 and P8 were all concerned with whether they were using the Dremel tool correctly and whether their technique posed any danger. Upon starting drilling, P8 asked: *'Am I being safe?'*

The participants demonstrated varying levels of awareness of the tools around them. For example, some participants would meticulously tidy after every stage, ensuring tools were turned off and their workspace was clear, where others would neglect tools once they were done with them – leaving soldering irons and glue guns turned on. While perhaps not an immediate risk during a short build, these risks can become more serious when partaking in a longer or multi-participant build.

Discussion

Our observational study has highlighted some clear differences between novice and expert makers that our system can aim to address.

Firstly, an important aspect of making is understanding an overall aim and then attempting it personally based on prior knowledge. It is through this individuality that makers express their creativity and derive their enjoyment. This, in turn, is what sets making apart from standard, result-oriented DIY tasks. Secondly, prior knowledge helps problem solving and provides the confidence to multi-task, use different tools, add personalization to a build or divert from the instructions. Novice makers do not have this corpus of knowledge to draw upon and are thus more constrained by the bounds of the instructions.

Novice makers display more risk aversion and uncertainty over tool usage and tool selection. Both through past experience and a greater understanding of different tools, expert makers are more confident, adaptable and safer in their practice.

Additionally, the usage of the laptop within the study provides an important insight for the design of our makerspace. As a laptop affords similar freedom of movement as a paper manual, we had expected to see a similar attitude to its use, such as repositioning for the most un-obstructed view and carrying to the toolbox for direct tool reference. Instead, participants clearly oriented themselves around the laptop, bringing work surfaces and tools towards it, making the laptop, and by extension the digital manual, the key anchor within the space. Whilst this orientation may have been for a number of reasons, including damage limitation, it highlights an important consideration when designing 'expensive' technology into a workshop environment. Any novel technology should be positioned to encourage maker participation.

DESIGN GOALS

In this section, we outline the design goals for our Smart Makerspace. These goals are derived from the observations from our study and the lessons learned from research on software tutorial systems.

D1. *Provide an Overview.* Our study highlighted the potential benefits of providing a task overview. This encourages a wider exploration of the build, assists in problem solving and supports personalized approaches.

D2. *Provide domain knowledge.* We have shown that prior knowledge plays a significant role in the successful completion and enjoyment of a maker task. Our system should showcase different methods and practices for completing the given task as a proxy for missing domain knowledge. This helps to teach and inspire [11, 13], while generating community spirit [23].

D3. *Limit the opportunity for error.* Our study demonstrated the importance of confidence in tool selection and usage. Building upon research in software tutorials, which guides the user towards intended tools and locations [3, 9], our system should inspire maker confidence through clear information on tool locations, usage and practice.

D4. *Provide clear spatially- and contextually- relevant instructions.* Our study showed that during the execution of specific skills, our participants focus changed between task-based and skill-based. Similarly to Chronicle [6], our system should support both of these focuses, allowing a maker to progress, knowing that relevant help will always be provided.

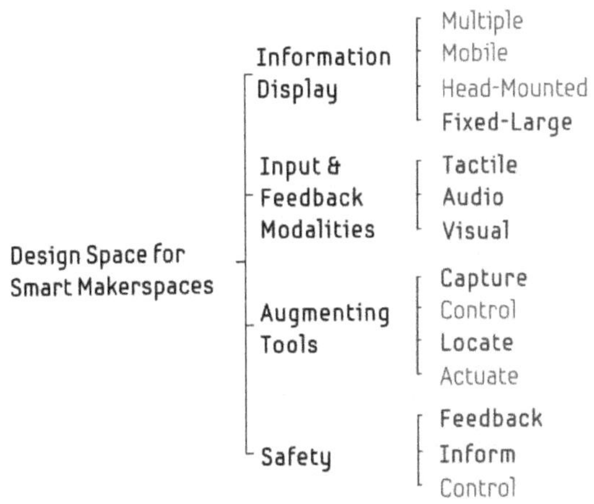

Figure 3. Design Space for Smart Makerspaces. (Emboldening highlights features used in our Smart Makerspace).

DESIGN SPACE FOR SMART MAKERSPACES

Here we explore the hardware design space that can enable our design goals (Figure 3); presenting a variety of the opportunities and motivating the decisions that we made. This is not intended as a full taxonomy, rather a subset of the possibilities most relevant to our work.

Information Display

As we move towards a connected, smart makerspace, we encounter opportunities to display varied information. We define four scopes of display: *multiple*, *mobile*, *head-mounted* and *fixed-large*.

Maker tasks frequently take place across a range of different locations within a space, for example separate woodwork, metalwork and electronics spaces. As such *multiple displays* could be used to provide area-relevant information. *Mobile displays* could provide similar functionality, while replicating the affordances of traditional paper manuals. Makers could 'dock' their device at different stations within a makerspace, thus triggering appropriate resources. *Head-mounted displays* could be used to provide view-specific overlays or peripheral information [8]. These devices provide the greatest opportunity for continuous or 'always on' instruction.

From our experience, makerspaces are typically based around a central 'construction' zone. This fixed central location supports the use of a *fixed large display*, which encourages a maker to research a task or skill before proceeding to practice what they have learned in the different zones. A *fixed large display* could be positioned as a smart workbench [22] or be located on a wall. The display could be projected or make use of a large screen. As a result of the usage style of the laptop in our observational study and the benefits of a clearer co-location of workspace and information display [12, 19], we adopt a fixed large display as a workbench in our makerspace. We chose to use a tabletop screen to mitigate the risk of occlusion from participants leaning over the work surface (as we observed in our observational study). Although large screens may seem a less feasible technology than projection today due to damage risks, there is good reason to believe such displays will be ubiquitous and damage resistant in the future[5]. That said, a projector based system could be similarly implemented without impacting the overall design principles and spirit of our work.

Input and Feedback Modalities

As making is a manual activity already including significant *tactile* action and feedback. We suggest the use of *audio* feedback, alongside *visual* display, to enrich the feedback experience. This could encode spoken feedback or simply provide a prompt to retrieve information from a display. Similarly, *audio* and *visual* input could be used alongside tactile action to drive the system.

Augmenting Tools

Across smart tools there are opportunities to *capture*, *locate*, *control* and *actuate*. Tool information can be *captured* to know when and how a tool is being used. Tools can be *located* such that the system can guide a maker towards them. The system could *control* the tools use, for example automatically disabling or setting its speed where appropriate, or *actuate* tools, automatically performing tasks with them.

Safety

Safety information can be provided to *feedback* to or *inform* the maker or to *control* the situation. Given system knowledge of a tool's current state, *feedback* could alert the user to wear safety goggles and the user could be *informed* of relevant safety information. Should the safety glasses not be worn, the system could disable the tool (*control*).

THE SMART MAKERSPACE

We developed a prototype Smart Makerspace, delivering an integrated instructional experience for a single maker in existing public or private machine shops and maker spaces (Figure 1). The system can be divided into 3 main components: an augmented workbench, instrumented power-tools and an instrumented tool-box. As we describe

---

[5] www.corning.com/ADayMadeofGlass

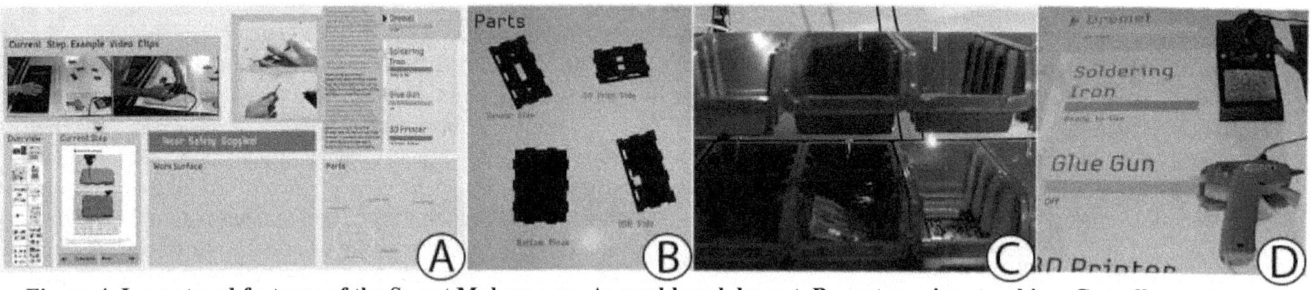

Figure 4. Layout and features of the Smart Makerspace. A: workbench layout, B: custom piece tracking, C: toolbox guidance, D: augmented power tools.

our system's features, we indicate in parentheses the relevant design goals they address.

Augmented workbench

We use an 84-inch, 4K digital whiteboard on a horizontal stand. We chose a display of this size as there is adequate space to provide a wealth of information alongside a traditional workspace.

We placed a 3mm sheet of transparent acrylic over the display to prevent scratches. An additional wooden block marked the intended workspace and added further protection for drilling and soldering. We mounted a depth-sensing camera above the display to enable object tracking and touch interaction. Any sensors used were interfaced to the central desktop computer using Phidgets USB interfaces.

The Dremel (precision rotary tool), soldering-iron and glue gun are positioned on the workbench. Due to its weight, the 3D printer was placed on a side-table.

Manual

The augmented workbench experience is based around an illustrated manual - providing the exact same information as the *Instructable* used in the pilot study. Below the manual there are soft-buttons to enable navigation between steps (Figure 4a, bottom left).

Overview

Beside the manual is an overview of the task, containing a thumbnail of every step (Figure 4a). The overview provides a quick reference for the sequence of subsequent steps and is designed as a cue to encourage the exploration of the entire manual (*D1*).

Previous user's videos

Above the manual are videos of other users performing the current task (Figure 4a)(*D4*). These videos provide additional cues to the images in the manual, assisting with trouble-shooting and demonstrating the variation in approaches to completing the manual tasks. The videos are intended to provide novice makers with broader knowledge of a current task. As our instruction set was manually configured, the user videos were captured from the side. However, in the future these videos could be captured from above, to provide first-person view. Additional information is also available in the ToolClips (explained below).

On-table Tool Prompts

The power-tools required to complete each step are highlighted on the table (*D3*) (Figure 4a). The table prompts users to turn on/off relevant tools either before they are needed or once they have been used. Additional information about the current status of tools is also provided, for example the status of the 3D printer (i.e. 'printing') or the soldering iron ('hot, ready to use') (*D4*).

ToolClips

When a tool is to be used, relevant ToolClips are displayed (*D4*), including both text and video. For example, if a soldering iron is to be used, an explanation of its use is displayed, including best practices, safety tips and troubleshooting advice (Figure 4a). These tips are purposefully positioned near the workspace, such that they are easy to follow or refer to when using the tool.

Custom Piece Highlighting

Beside the work surface, our system tracks, highlights and identifies custom pieces required for a build (Figure 4b) (*D3*). From our exploratory study, we found that the custom pieces caused the most difficulty amongst participants as they are unique to the build and thus no prior knowledge can be referenced. Using visual highlighting, the pieces required for each step are uniquely identified and annotated.

Environmentally Aware Audio Feedback

The system provides *positive* and *warning* audio feedback based on a number of different events (*D3*). The system provides a *positive* audio tone for correct tool usage (i.e. once the 3D printer has been turned on), when a process is complete (i.e. printing finished) or a tool is ready for use (i.e. glue gun heated). The system provides a warning tone and corresponding visual cues should safety glasses be needed or if a tool is used incorrectly (i.e. the drill being used faster than a given speed). The volume of the audio alerts is dynamically adapted to account for any tools that are being used. For example, the tone alerting that the drill is being used too fast is significantly louder (to account for the sound of the drill) than the tone reminding the maker to wear safety glasses when removing the soldering iron from the holster.

Augmented Power-tools

We have equipped our makerspace with four 'power tools/devices': a 3D printer, a precision rotary tool (Dremel), a soldering iron and a glue gun (Figure 5). These tools were chosen as representative of those routinely used in maker and DIY procedures. Each of these tools is instrumented such that the system knows its current state and location, can provide feedback on its use and can remind users to turn tools on/off according to task instructions (*D3, D4*). Here we detail the instrumentation of the tools as examples of possible instrumentation techniques, not necessarily as best case sensor scenarios.

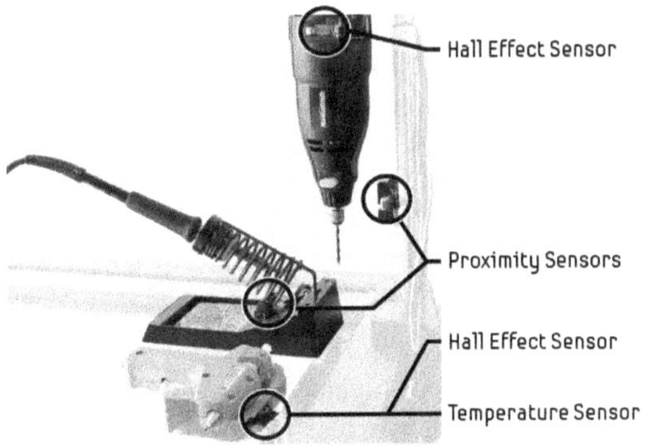

Figure 5. We augmented power-tools with sensors to monitor their state and usage.

Soldering Iron - The soldering iron has a precision light sensor placed over its power light. As the light can be off (indicating tool off), constant (heating) or flickering (ready), the system can infer its state. A proximity sensor is placed beneath the iron's holster, such that the system can determine whether the iron is present or has been removed.

3D printer - The 3D printer has a voltage monitor attached to its power cable. The system can identify when the printer is on (low-constant voltage), heating (medium, fluctuating voltage), printing (high, fluctuating voltage), and finished (low constant voltage).

Precision Rotary Tool - The Dremel has a hall-effect sensor and a magnet attached to the variable power switch (Figure 5). This allows the system to know the state and speed of the Dremel and thus enables feedback regarding required, suggested, or safe, speeds. The Dremel stand houses a proximity sensor so that the system knows when the tool is present or has been removed, allowing for additional relevant safety prompts.

Glue Gun - The glue gun has a custom 3D-printed holster that includes a temperature sensor, which enables the system to know the state of the device (Figure 5). A hall-effect sensor and magnet lets the system know when the device is present in the holster.

Instrumented Toolbox

We instrumented the 47 bin toolbox such that each bin is equipped with an LED (Figure 4c). The system triggers these LEDs to guide the maker towards the correct toolbox bins needed for each step of the manual. By clearly indicating the correct tool locations, the system can significantly reduce the uncertainty of novice makers when selecting tools for a task (*D3*).

EVALUATION

We conducted a qualitative think-aloud user study to evaluate the initial design and features of the Smart Makerspace.

Participants

We recruited 8 new participants to conduct a maker task using our system. The participants (2 female, age: M=35, SD=9 years) rated their skill and experience levels (3 beginners, 3 intermediate and 2 experienced). We chose to include a range of experience such that we could assess differences in practice and explore our makerspace's ability to scale between users. Similarly to our observational study, previous experience involved tasks such as home renovation, personal robotics and musical instrument making. One participant described themselves as a maker and 6 participants suggested they enjoyed 'making' tasks. 3 participants stated that they like to read manuals when building something and 5 participants said they used online tutorials. Five participants had previously used the *Instructables* website.

Apparatus

The participants used our Smart Makerspace. The system was manually configured to provide instructions for the same box as used in our previous study. The participants' were recorded on a video camera that encompassed the workbench, the 3D printer and the toolbox. An experimenter was present to take notes on the participant's thoughts and actions.

Procedure and Design

Before beginning the build, the participants completed a questionnaire about their previous maker and DIY experience. They were then given a 3 minute introduction to the makerspace and its features. After the introduction, the participants were asked to use the system to build the proximity box.

Upon completing the build, the participants filled out another questionnaire. For each individual feature of our system, the questionnaire asked them to rate, on a 5-point Likert scale, the statement 'I found it useful' (1 = strongly disagree, 5 = strongly agree).

Quantitative Results

Overall, participants genuinely enjoyed using the Smart Makerspace, giving an average enjoyment score of 4.75 out of 5 and were keen to conduct other similar tasks in the future. Participants gave our table on average 4.38 for usefulness. Based on user responses, the most useful features of our table were: the toolbox highlighting, as it enabled quick tool locating; the safety goggles warnings, as a timely reminder; and ToolClip Text, as a tool walkthrough, helping those unsure about specific tool usage (Figure 6). The lowest average rating was for the rotary tool speed alerts. We believe this is because the alert interrupted the ongoing action (as makers attended to it), but provided no further information as to 'why' the speed was too fast or ‘what’ problems this may cause. There was no correlation between participant’s skill level and feature ratings.

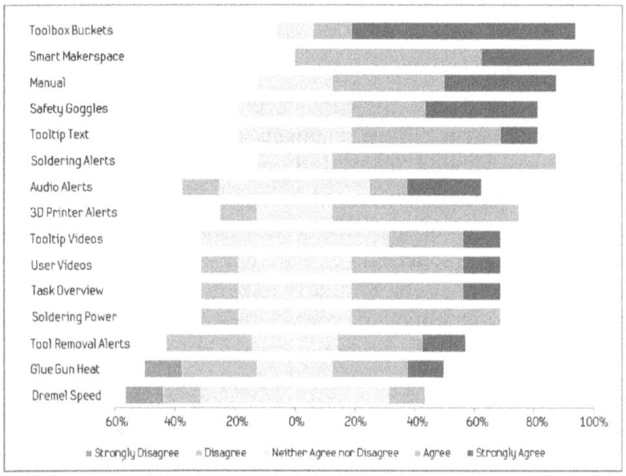

Figure 6. Chart showing Likert usefulness ratings of the Smart Makerspace features (ordered by average usefulness).

Analysis

We focus our analysis on the four issues identified in the observational study and our design goals (referenced in parentheses).

An Overview of the Task (D1)

The system displayed an overview of the task, in the form of a thumbnail of every manual page. P5 briefly examined the overview initially, exploring the steps involved in the build. P6, P7 and P8 used the overview to gauge how far through the build they were. P5 and P7 commented that it provided hints for them to explore the manual more widely, thus pre-emptively finding solutions to problems that would have later arisen. P7 was the only participant to step through the entire manual before beginning the task. Alongside the overview, the participants could also use the user videos for problem solving, without the need for a better understanding of the task as a whole.

Upon starting the task P5 said:

> *‘If I was doing this normally, my first thing would be to pick up these pieces and look at them before I looked at any tutorial, just to get a feel for what I am dealing with here.’*

It is during this initial exploration that makers formulate a sense of what a task may involve and how component features will fit together. This comment demonstrates an interest in exploring a task through physical materials and tools in additional to through the manual, in turn supporting a more natural skill-based exploration.

Domain Knowledge and Tool Usage Details

All of the participants used the additional information beyond the manual (*D2*). The participants typically began by looking at the manual, before exploring the previous user videos (the next closest information) and finally the ToolClips. Six participants used tools not called for in the manual as a direct result of the additional videos, for example using a ‘3rd hand’ device to assist with soldering. This both encouraged novice makers to learn about a new tool and prompted more experienced makers about the existence of additional tools. The more experienced participants used the ToolClips to clarify details of tools they were not familiar with, such as the preparation of the rotary tool. The less experienced participants used both the additional user videos and the ToolClip information (*D3*).

All participants commented on the audio alerts in the system. Upon hearing the positive audio tone as a result of correctly initializing the 3D printing, P2 said: *‘Did it know I just did that? That’s cool!’* Similarly, 6/8 participants responded quickly to the alert tones concerning the power tool usage, with 5 heeding the rotary tool speed warnings and 6 stopping to look for safety goggles (*D3*).

Tool Selection

The toolbox lights were universally liked by the participants (*D4*). Upon noticing the lights, P5 commented: ‘*Oh that’s great.’* This was one of the most noticeable differences between the two studies. It was clear from our observations that the toolbox lights reduced the time spent looking for tools and increased confidence in correct tool selection.

DISCUSSION

We are encouraged by the positive response to our system; the perceived usefulness of our features (13/15 rated useful on average) and that both novice and expert makers alike enjoyed using our system and made use of the wider information provided.

When using the *Smart Makerspace*, our novice participants made use of tools and techniques more akin to ‘experienced makers’ (D2). In our initial observation study, novice makers struggled to maintain contact between wires when soldering. As a result of the *Tooltips* and *User Videos* in our Smart Makerspace, participants used both the 3rd hand tool (to hold wires in place) and twisting techniques for creating temporary wire joints – as you would expect to see in more experienced maker practice. Furthermore, in our original study 5 participants had to be reminded to wear safety goggles for soldering, though the instruction material specifically prompted for their use (a rarity in existing *Instructables*). In our *Smart Makerspace,* only 2 participants had to be explicitly prompted (with 1 wearing prescription glasses, affording a level of safety that the more experienced participant was comfortable with) as a result of our table’s visual and auditory prompts (D4). These more nuanced approaches to maker tasks, and demonstrations of safer practice, serve to highlight the benefits of our system.

Finally, we were keen to explore the concerns surrounding technology adoption in makerspace-style environments. As we used a large and expensive display as a workbench, we were encouraged to see participants freely adopting the surface. P4 repeatedly swept and blew the dust and off-cuts onto the wider screen (which was protected by an acrylic sheet). P5 and P7 stripped wires and prepared for soldering on the screen itself beside the protective wooden surface. So, whilst damage is still a constraint for large tabletop screen adoption today, given the increased ubiquity of screens in varied environments and the adoption of the surface we witnessed in our study, we believe that this style of screen usage is promising for the future.

The Smart Makerspace was motivated and evaluated based upon our authored maker task. This task was intentionally designed to span the common skills and tools required in making and thus included a more varied skillset than typically required for any one task. This provided a broad platform from which to motivate our work and observe a wide range of maker practice. That said, no one task can capture the full spectrum of maker intricacies, which further exploration may come to highlight. With this in mind, this work sought to highlight the wider similarities in the challenges faced by novice hardware and software users and demonstrate the suitability of software-tutorial techniques in hardware practices, such as with ToolClips [5] and tool guidance [3, 9]. Our observations demonstrate increased occurrences of 'expert' and safe practice, alongside widespread adoption and appreciation of the additional information, supporting this approach.

FURTHER SYSTEM REFINEMENTS

Based on the analysis and feedback of our Smart Makerspace study, we implemented 3 additional features.

First, as a result of the overview observations regarding exploration through materials and tools, we have since included a 'query-by-material' and 'query-by-tool' function to the beginning of a task (*D2, D4*). Thus, when a maker picks up a material piece or specific tool, the manual automatically jumps to the first step in which that piece/tool is used; highlighting other related pieces and tools and displaying related videos (*D4*). This functionality is similar to the UI and Data probes used in Chronicle [6] and begins to facilitate a less-prescriptive task ordering.

Secondly, we originally configured our system such that the ToolClips and other user's videos were displayed automatically for every stage (*D2*). Our rationale was to make the build as easy as possible for novice makers. However, some participants suggested they would prefer to choose when and if the additional supporting information would be available. Thus, we now include a mode where this additional information is only displayed if the users explicitly request it by pressing a button. In this way, makers can better challenge themselves before seeking further help. Furthermore, this information opt-in reduces the amount of structure that the Smart Makerspace adds to maker tasks – an inherently unstructured activity. Finally, while participants appreciated the safety goggle warnings, they were surprised that our tone played when a tool was removed from its base, regardless of whether they were wearing the glasses or not. To address this limitation, we created a pair of smart safety glasses (Figure 7). Using conductive tape on the nose rest and a wireless transmitter, the system can sense if the glasses are being worn, thus further increasing the relevance of any safety information.

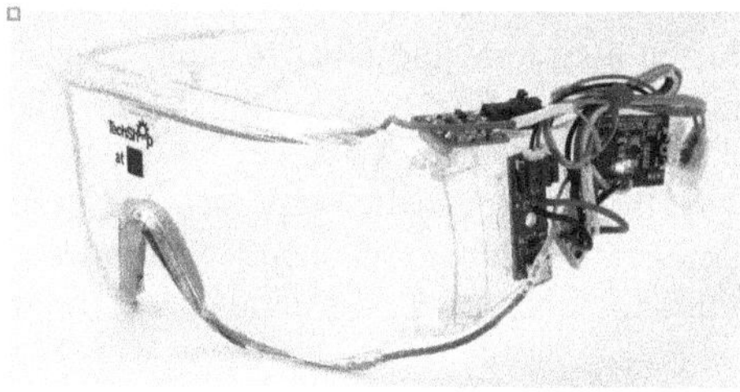

Figure 7. Custom smart safety glasses

FUTURE WORK

To enable our exploration of the *Smart Makerspace*, we manually authored the current example task. Dynamic instruction generation, however, remains an interesting and promising avenue for future work. Many of the sensing techniques that we deployed (tool sensors, toolbox highlighting, overhead camera tracking) could also be used for capture, with little or no additional augmentation. Furthermore, editing of instructional videos and automated tutorial preparation has been explored at length in the domain of software tutorials (e.g. [1, 4, 5, 13]), and we would be keen to combine these techniques with the physicality of our content delivery technique. Such efforts would build upon the DemoCut work [2] which has already tackled some of the issues with generating instructional content for physical tasks.

The Smart Makerspace has wider implications for existing makerspaces. While a fully-implemented smart space, may not be feasible, the standalone implementation of smart tools for safety alerts could provide significant benefits within group makerspaces. Not only would the alerts serve as a timely reminder for safe practice, but also alert other makers to potential dangers around them. While our smart makerspace goes some way towards reducing the need for constant supervision, we do not attempt to completely remove the need for an expert. It is hard to foresee a future where tools are so 'smart' that they can mitigate all risk without constraining freedom of use, however this remains an exciting avenue for further work.

In the future, we would like to perform a formal quantitative study of the Smart Makerspace. Our observational studies were not designed to elucidate quantitative A/B comparative results, rather to provide informed design rationale and initial feedback for our work. From here, we aim to inform and motivate future work in this area, while providing feedback on our design criteria.

CONCLUSION

We have presented a Smart Makerspace; providing a rich instructional experience for physical tasks. We conducted an initial exploration of maker tasks that highlighted 4 target areas for augmentation: an *overview of the task*, *domain knowledge*, *tool selection* and *tool usage details*.

We detailed the features of our Smart Makerspace, utilizing varied media types and tool-based sensing to provide additional context-relevant information. Our design drew upon lessons learned from research on software tutorials. We conducted a system study that resulted in positive user feedback, with 13 / 15 features of our Smart Makerspace considered useful. Overall, we have shown that increased connectivity through a 'smart' approach (as promised by the *Internet of Things* concept) provides exciting opportunities for immersive instructional environments for makers.

REFERENCES

1. Chi, P.-Y., Ahn, S., Ren, A., et al. MixT: Automatic Generation of Step-by-step Mixed Media Tutorials. *UIST '12*, 93–102.
2. Chi, P.-Y., Liu, J., Linder, J., et al. DemoCut: Generating Concise Instructional Videos for Physical Demonstrations. *UIST '13*, 141–150.
3. Fernquist, J., Grossman, T. and Fitzmaurice, G. Sketch-sketch Revolution: An Engaging Tutorial System for Guided Sketching and Application Learning. *UIST '11*, 373–382.
4. Grabler, F., Agrawala, M., Li, W., Dontcheva, M. and Igarashi, T. Generating Photo Manipulation Tutorials by Demonstration. *SIGGRAPH '09*, 66:1–66:9.
5. Grossman, T. and Fitzmaurice, G. ToolClips: An Investigation of Contextual Video Assistance for Functionality Understanding. *CHI '10*, 1515–1524.
6. Grossman, T., Matejka, J. and Fitzmaurice, G. Chronicle: Capture, Exploration, and Playback of Document Workflow Histories. *UIST '10*, 143–152.
7. Gurevich, P., Lanir, J., Cohen, B. and Stone, R. TeleAdvisor: A Versatile Augmented Reality Tool for Remote Assistance. *CHI '12*, 619–622.
8. Henderson, S.J. and Feiner, S.K. Augmented Reality in the Psychomotor Phase of a Procedural Task. *ISMAR '11*, 191–200.
9. Kelleher, C. and Pausch, R. Stencils-based Tutorials: Design and Evaluation. *CHI '05*, 541–550.
10. Kim, J., Seo, J. and Han, T.-D. AR Lamp: Interactions on Projection-based Augmented Reality for Interactive Learning. *IUI '14*, 353–358.
11. Kong, N., Grossman, T., Hartmann, B., Agrawala, M. and Fitzmaurice, G. Delta: A Tool for Representing and Comparing Workflows. *CHI '12*, 1027–1036.
12. Korn, O., Schmidt, A. and Hörz, T. The Potentials of In-situ-projection for Augmented Workplaces in Production: A Study with Impaired Persons. *CHI EA '13*, 979–984.
13. Lafreniere, B., Grossman, T. and Fitzmaurice, G. Community Enhanced Tutorials: Improving Tutorials with Multiple Demonstrations. *CHI '13*, 1779–1788.
14. Löchtefeld, M., Gehring, S., Jung, R. and Krüger, A. guitAR: Supporting Guitar Learning Through Mobile Projection. *CHI EA '11*, 1447–1452.
15. Makerspace Team ed. Makerspace Playbook. Makerspace.
16. Olivier, P., Xu, G., Monk, A. and Hoey, J. Ambient Kitchen: Designing Situated Services Using a High Fidelity Prototyping Environment. *PETRA '09*, 47:1–47:7.
17. Pongnumkul, S., Dontcheva, M., Li, W., et al. Pause-and-play: Automatically Linking Screencast Video Tutorials with Applications. *UIST '11*, 135–144.
18. Reiners, D., Stricker, D., Klinker, G. and Müller, S. Augmented Reality for Construction Tasks: Doorlock Assembly. 31–46.
19. Rosenthal, S., Kane, S.K., Wobbrock, J.O. and Avrahami, D. Augmenting On-screen Instructions with Micro-projected Guides: When It Works, and when It Fails. *UbiComp '10*, 203–212.
20. Rosner, D. and Bean, J. Learning from IKEA Hacking: I'M Not One to Decoupage a Tabletop and Call It a Day. *CHI '09*, 419–422.
21. Sodhi, R.S., Jones, B.R., Forsyth, D., Bailey, B.P. and Maciocci, G. BeThere: 3D Mobile Collaboration with Spatial Input. *CHI '13*, 179–188.
22. Tabard, A., Hincapié Ramos, J.D. and Bardram, J. The eLabBench in the Wild: Supporting Exploration in a Molecular Biology Lab. *CHI '12*, 3051–3060.
23. Tanenbaum, J.G., Williams, A.M., Desjardins, A. and Tanenbaum, K. Democratizing Technology: Pleasure, Utility and Expressiveness in DIY and Maker Practice. *CHI '13*, 2603–2612.
24. Tang, A., Owen, C., Biocca, F. and Mou, W. Comparative Effectiveness of Augmented Reality in Object Assembly. *CHI '03*, 73–80.
25. Tecchia, F., Alem, L. and Huang, W. 3D Helping Hands: A Gesture Based MR System for Remote Collaboration. *VRCAI '12*, 323–328.
26. Torrey, C., Churchill, E.F. and McDonald, D.W. Learning How: The Search for Craft Knowledge on the Internet. *CHI '09*, 1371–1380.
27. Torrey, C., McDonald, D.W., Schilit, B.N. and Bly, S. How-To pages: Informal systems of expertise sharing. *ECSCW 2007*. L.J. Bannon, I. Wagner, C. Gutwin, R.H.R. Harper, and K. Schmidt, eds. Springer London. 391–410.
28. Tseng, T. and Resnick, M. Product Versus Process: Representing and Appropriating DIY Projects Online. *DIS '14*, 425–428.
29. Uriu, D., Namai, M., Tokuhisa, S., et al. Panavi: Recipe Medium with a Sensors-embedded Pan for Domestic Users to Master Professional Culinary Arts. *CHI '12*, 129–138.
30. Wakkary, R., Schilling, M.L., Dalton, M., et al. Tutorial Authorship and Hybrid Designers: The Joy (and Frustration) of DIY Tutorials. *CHI '15*, 609–618.
31. Weichel, C., Alexander, J., Karnik, A. and Gellersen, H. SPATA: Spatio-Tangible Tools for Fabrication-Aware Design. *TEI '15*, 189–196.
32. Yamashita, M.M., Yamaoka, J. and Kakehi, Y. Enchanted Scissors: A Scissor Interface for Support in Cutting and Interactive Fabrication. *SIGGRAPH '13*, 33:1–33:1.
33. Zoran, A. and Paradiso, J.A. FreeD: A Freehand Digital Sculpting Tool. *CHI '13*, 2613–2616.

Studying Attraction Power in Proxemics-Based Visual Concepts for Large Public Interactive Displays

Victor Cheung, Stacey D. Scott
Systems Design Engineering, University of Waterloo, Waterloo, Ontario, Canada
{victor.cheung|stacey.scott}@uwaterloo.ca

ABSTRACT
A key challenge in designing interfaces for large interactive displays deployed in public settings is to draw (and keep) a passerby's attention. *Proxemic interactions*—a design approach that applies human spatial behavior to guide system behavior in response to a user's proximity to a display—has been proposed for attracting and engaging potential users. Yet, the effectiveness of this approach has not been evaluated. Moreover, little research exists in the broader literature on the relative efficacy of possible visual design strategies to attract and engage large display users. We conducted a study to the effectiveness of promising visual concepts applied in a proxemic interactions framework: content motion and user shadows. While both visual concepts were more effective than a control condition at capturing attention, the inclusion of user's shadow was found to have stronger attraction power than content motion alone. In contrast, they were found to be ineffective for communicating possible user interactions in the display, limiting their potential to facilitate further system use.

Author Keywords
Large public interactive displays; attention; proxemic interactions; shadow; interaction design; laboratory study

ACM Classification Keywords
H.5.m. Information interfaces and presentation (e.g., HCI): Miscellaneous.

INTRODUCTION
Large interactive displays are increasingly appearing in public settings such as airports, museums, and retail locations for a range of purposes, such as providing information or entertainment. However, evidence from observational studies of deployed systems indicates that such systems are largely underutilized. Findings indicate many passersby fail to notice the display [5, 29] or, if they notice it, they often do not understand whether or how it is interactive [16, 27].

Two main approaches to attract and engage potential users include using external aids and designing the system interface, primarily its visual interface. External aids include, exploiting the "honey-pot effect" (displays with existing users draw in more users), incorporating a human helper, or providing external signage [5, 22]. Though anecdotally reported as effective, these techniques are not always easily controlled (e.g., the "honey-pot" cannot be artificially created), and hence, are non-trivial to implement and evaluate.

Design strategies to attract passersby typically focus on exploiting the visual channel to draw passersby's attention, since other channels, such as audio, may already be saturated in many public settings. Several visual techniques have been proposed to increase the noticeability of the interface, such as animating or applying other visual effects to interface content [13, 24], and displaying a real-time shadow or silhouette representation of the user in the display [25, 26].

In recent work, Wang et al. [35] combined the use of such visual techniques with the *proxemic interactions* design approach [21], which applies the concept from *proxemics* social science theory [11] that humans engage in certain types of interactions with others at specific, universally understood distances. The proxemics interaction design approach extends distances to other dimensions such as orientation and movement, to which systems are designed to response in an appropriate, meaningful way, thus better facilitate user intention and system use [14, 21, 30, 34].

However, effectively applying this design approach—and gaining the promised benefit of establishing meaningful system engagement with potential users—relies on providing "appropriate" system responses at different proximity levels. In our case, we wish to provide "appropriate" visual cues that will attract and engage potential users. Yet, little empirical evidence exists on the relative "attraction power" [4]—the ability to grab the attention of a passerby—of visual techniques used in systems employing proxemic interactions, or the ability of these techniques to entice subsequent interaction.

To address this gap, we conducted an empirical evaluation of two promising visual techniques previously used to attract and engage potential users: content animation and displaying the user's shadow. Following the proxemic interactions design approach, the degree of visual effect applied to the interface varied based on the person's proximity to the display. Within this context, animating content alone and animating content while also displaying the user's shadow both attracted participant's attention, with the latter com-

ITS '15, November 15 - 18, 2015, Funchal, Portugal

ACM 978-1-4503-3899-8/15/11...$15.00
DOI: http://dx.doi.org/10.1145/2817721.2817749

ACKNOWLEDGMENTS

This work is funded in part by the Natural Science and Engineering Research Council of Canada (NSERC) and the NSERC Digital Surface Software Application Network (SurfNet). We would also like to thank our colleagues at the EngHCI group at University of Waterloo for their invaluable insights on this work.

REFERENCES

[1] Alt, F., Schneegass, S., et al. How to evaluate public displays. *Proc. PerDis '12*, 1–6.

[2] Beyer, G., Alt, F., et al. Audience behavior around large interactive cylindrical screens. *Proc. CHI '11*, 1021–1030.

[3] Bodenhausen, G. V and Hugenberg, K. Attention, perception, and social cognition. *Social Cognition: The Basis of Human Interaction*. F. Strack and J. Förste, eds. Psychology Press. 1–22.

[4] Boisvert, D.L. and Slez, B.J. The relationship between exhibit characteristics and learni ng-associated behaviors in a science museum discovery space. *Sci. Educ.* 79, 5 (1995), 503–518.

[5] Brignull, H. and Rogers, Y. Enticing people to interact with large public displays in public spaces. *Proc. INTERACT '03*, 17–24.

[6] Cheung, V., Watson, D., et al. Overcoming Interaction Barriers in Large Public Displays Using Personal Devices. *Proc. ITS '14*, 375–380.

[7] Christensen, L. Deception in psychological research: when is its use justified? *Personal. Soc. Psychol. Bull.* 14, 4 (1988), 664–675.

[8] Convertino, G., Neale, D.C., et al. A Laboratory Method for Studying Activity Awareness. *Proc. NordiCHI '04*, 313–322.

[9] Dalton, N.S., Collins, E., et al. Display blindness? Looking again at the visibility of situated displays using eye tracking. *Proc. CHI '09*, 3889–3898.

[10] Franconeri, S.L. and Simons, D.J. Moving and looming stimuli capture attention. *Percept. Psychophys.* 65, 7 (2003), 999–1010.

[11] Hall, E.T. *The Hidden Dimension*. Anchor.

[12] Hinrichs, U., Schmidt, H., et al. EMDialog: bringing information visualization into the museum. *IEEE Trans. Vis. Comput. Graph.* 14, 6 (2008), 1181–1188.

[13] Huang, E.M., Koster, A., et al. Overcoming assumptions and uncovering practices: When does the public really look at public displays?. *Proc. Pervasive '08*, 228–243.

[14] Ju, W., Lee, B.A., et al. Range: exploring implicit interaction through electronic whiteboard design. *Proc. CSCW '08*, 17–26.

[15] Krueger, M.W., Gionfriddo, T., et al. VIDEOPLACE -- an artificial reality. *Proc. CHI '85*, 35–40.

[16] Kukka, H., Oja, H., et al. What makes you click: exploring visual signals to entice interaction on public displays. *Proc. CHI '13*, 1699–1708.

[17] Kules, B., Kang, H., et al. Immediate usability: a case study of public access design for a community photo library. *Interact. Comput.* 16, 6 (2004), 1171–1193.

[18] Loftus, G.R. and Mackworth, N.H. Cognitive determinants of fixation location during picture viewing. *J. Exp. Psychol. Hum. Percept. Perform.* 4, 4 (1978), 565–572.

[19] Marquardt, N. The proximity toolkit: prototyping proxemic interactions in ubiquitous computing ecologies. *Proc. UIST '11*, 315–326.

[20] Marquardt, N., Ballendat, T., et al. Gradual engagement: facilitating information exchange between digital devices as a function of proximity. *Proc. ITS '12*, 31–40.

[21] Marquardt, N. and Greenberg, S. Informing the Design of proxemic interactions. *IEEE Pervasive Comput.* 11, 2 (2012), 14–23.

[22] Marshall, P., Morris, R., et al. Rethinking "multi-user": an in-the-wild study of how groups approach a walk-up-and-use tabletop interface. *Proc. CHI '11*, 3033–3042.

[23] Michelis, D. and Müller, J. The Audience Funnel: Observations of Gesture Based Interaction With Multiple Large Displays in a City Center. *Int. J. Hum. Comput. Interact.* 27, 6 (2011), 562–579.

[24] Müller, J., Alt, F., et al. Requirements and design space for interactive public displays. *Proc. Int. Conf. Multimed. '10*, 1285–1294.

[25] Müller, J., Eberle, D., et al. Communiplay: a field study of a public display mediaspace. *Proc. CHI '14*, 1415–1424.

[26] Müller, J., Walter, R., et al. Looking glass: a field study on noticing interactivity of a shop window. *Proc. CHI '12*, 297–306.

[27] Müller, J., Wilmsmann, D., et al. Display blindness: the effect of expectations on attention towards digital signage. *Proc. Pervasive '09*, 1–8.

[28] Norman, G. Likert scales, levels of measurement and the "laws" of statistics. *Adv. Heal. Sci. Educ.* 15, (2010), 625–632.

[29] Ojala, T., Kostakos, V., et al. Multipurpose interactive public displays in the wild: three years later. *Computer.* 45, 5 (2012), 42–49.

[30] Schmidt, C., Müller, J., et al. Screenfinity: extending the perception area of content on very large public displays. *Proc. CHI '13*, 1719–1728.

[31] Shoemaker, G., Tang, A., et al. Shadow reaching: A new perspective on interaction for large wall displays. *Proc. UIST* 53–56.

[32] Snibbe, S.S. and Rafle, H.S. Social Immersive Media. *Proc. CHI '09*, 1447–1456.

[33] Streitz, N., Röcker, C., et al. Situated interaction with ambient information: facilitating awareness and communication in ubiquitous work environments. *Proc. Int. Conf. Human-Computer Interact. '03.*

[34] Vogel, D. and Balakrishnan, R. Interactive public ambient displays: transitioning from implicit to explicit, public to personal, interaction with multiple users. *Proc. UIST '04*, 137–146.

[35] Wang, M., Boring, S., et al. Proxemic peddler: a public advertising display that captures and preserves the attention of a passerby. *Proc. PerDis '12*, 1–6.

[36] Wigdor, D. and Wixon, D. *Brave NUI World: Designing Natural User Interfaces for Touch and Gesture*. Morgan Kaufmann Publishers Inc.

[37] Yantis, S. How visual salience wins the battle for awareness. *Nat. Neurosci.* 8, 8 (2005), 975–977.

bined technique providing higher attraction power. The study also revealed that both visual concepts had limited ability to communicate the interactivity of the display, which is crucial to transition a passerby to a system user.

ATTENTION AND INTERACTIVITY

Previous research on large public interactive displays has highlighted a number of unique design requirements [13, 24], particularly the need to make the existence of the display known to passersby, and convey its interactivity. These requirements are challenging because interaction with such displays is often serendipitous and the process is ephemeral.

The main obstacle in getting people to notice a display arises from "display blindness", a phenomenon observed in many field studies (e.g., train stations and inside a store [13], various city locations [27]), where passersby overlooked the displays. In many occasions this was due to their attention being elsewhere, and only very quickly glanced over the displays. Huang et al. [13] suggested that such glances are rare and typically brief (less than 800ms), which is later confirmed by Dalton et al. [9] using eye-tracking. To combat against display blindness, the display has to "stand out" at the right moment from other distractions.

With the attention drawn, the display then needs to quickly communicate its interactivity, which is not trivial. From interviews and diary studies of display deployments, researchers have discovered most people did not interact with the displays because they simply did not know they could [29]. A stronger and familiar means to suggest that the displays are responsive to people's action has to be provided.

Hence, when designing interfaces for large public interactive displays, it is important to evaluate the design's effectiveness for drawing people's attention and communicating interactivity. It is also important to see these two aspects as related, but separate, stages of interaction. Thus, a design suitable for one may not be suitable for the other.

RELATED WORK

To set the context of this research, we provide an overview of both the relevant research on the use of visual concepts for drawing attention and communicating interactivity, and on the proxemic interactions design approach.

Drawing Attention

Literature in psychology and cognitive science describe attention as an internal state of the perceiver, which can be initiated simultaneously by top-down (high-level stimuli such as goals) and bottom-up (low-level stimuli such as motion) perception processes [3]. These stimuli can be generated externally and can therefore be incorporated into interface designs for drawing attention. We describe the use of these two forms of stimuli in the context of large public interactive displays, with a focus on the visual concepts.

High-level Visual Stimuli

High-level stimuli refer to cognitive expectancies and goals that modulate selective attention, which can be driven by an active search of related object (e.g., entomologist finding a favorite insect [3]), or surprised by "oddballs" (e.g., viewer spotting an octopus in a farm [18]). In the context of public displays, Müller et al. [24] described this as "motivation" giving passersby incentive for using the displays, and used this as the building blocks for their Magical Mirror system [23]. This system used an augmented mirror image of passersby to raise their curiosity. Later research compared the visual representation of the user in the display (realistic image of the user vs. silhouette-style user shadow) and found both to be effective at drawing passersby's attention [25, 26]. Other examples of high-level visual stimuli can be found in installations at places such as museums (artist's catalog [12]) and tourist information centres (e.g., tourist planner [22]). Contextual oddballs are less common but were suggested in interviews and situated studies in various city locations [27], revealing passersby's desire to see content that were very different from what they expected.

Apart from the content design, an extension of this type of stimuli is to consider the spatial and social context of the displays, that is, how and where they are placed, as these factors also affect the perception and hence expectations from the passersby. For example, Brignull and Rogers suggested placing the display near traffic flow to increase the likelihood of it being noticed and facilitate "honey-pot effect" [5]. A similar suggestion was also made by Huang et al. in placing the display based on direction of people's movement, and enhancing the surrounding area [13].

High-level stimuli involve managing people's goals and expectations, and hence are typically context specific. This requires a good understanding of the environment to provide consistency (or completely unexpected as "oddballs") with the intents of the potential users.

Low-level Visual Stimuli

Low-level stimuli, on the other hand, are less context dependent as they rely on instinctive responses from passersby (e.g. motion and scale [10], saliency [37]). Many of these visual features are directly transferrable to designs for public interactive displays. These features include use of colors, animation, text and icons [16]. In their interviews Müller et al. [27] identified "colorfulness" as the most important factor influencing whether people thought they would look at the displays. A recent study by Kukka et al. [16] revealed a difference in effectiveness in features such as colors and icons, and the role of gender.

Researchers have also explored associating proximity to the displays with degree of visual effect (e.g., [34, 35]) to entice interaction and provide a more engaging experience. However, such association poses a higher technological requirement on the display's capability (e.g., detecting proximity requires a system to track its users).

Communicating Interactivity

Another important aspect in interface designs for large public interactive displays is the ability to communicate their interactivity, as being intrigued does not necessarily result in realizing interactivity (interaction blindness [29]).

Simple techniques such as calls-to-action and attract loops have been proposed [17], but are typically language and culture dependent, or might mistakenly be associated with arcade games. Müller et al. [26] evaluated the use of mirrored user images or silhouettes in communicating interactivity, and showed that they were superior over traditional call-to-action approaches. Ojala et al. [29] evaluated the use of "Touch me!" animations but did not find any noticeable increase in user interaction. These results suggest more work is needed to understand how to convey interactivity.

Proxemic Interactions Design Approach

Advances in sensing technologies have enabled interactive systems to be more aware of the environment, and thus, enables more refined responses to their uses. For example, depth sensors (e.g., Microsoft Kinect) can track the body movements of one or more users and respond in real-time to those movements (e.g., [25, 26]). With a more elaborate tracking setup, one can obtain rich information about the user and their movements, such as distance, orientation, movement, identity, and location [19], and consequently, produce finer responses tailored to the current situation.

Marquardt and Greenberg [21] proposed associating this rich information with *proxemics*, a social theory modeling the use of personal space in everyday social interactions [11], in order to create an interaction dialog between displays and users that resembles common proxemics social norms. Under this *proxemic interactions* design approach, contents of an interactive system adapt to changes in the sensed information (e.g., showing more details when the user gets closer). This approach has received growing interest from the interactive display community looking to increase a system's power to capture and maintain attention (e.g., Proxemic Peddler [35]), or to facilitate more sophisticated and nuanced interaction forms that build on familiar social behaviour (e.g., cross-device information transfer [20] and notification management [34]). A defining feature of this design approach is to provide different feedback, typically visual, depending on the user's proximity to the system, using either discrete distance "zones" [5, 33, 34] or continuous distances [35] to drive feedback changes.

As aforementioned, the Proxemic Peddler [35] utilized this design approach to capture the attention of passersby and then further engage them into system interaction. To attract user attention, the system used two types of low-level content motion visual effects. Rapid content movement across

Figure 1. Different levels of contrast in relation to user's proximity to the display: low when far, high when near.

the screen was used to draw a passersby's initial attention. Then, at a closer distance, in-place content animation causing a "jiggling" effect was used to regain a user's attention back to a specific object in the interface. To engage the user as they looked at and approached the display, the system applied a low-level effect, reducing the content speed. Then at a closer distance, the system applied a high-level effect where the system began revealing more details about the displayed content. Although the effectiveness of the low- and high-level visual stimuli used in their system was not evaluated, this combined approach seems promising to address the attraction and engagement goals of a public system. Yet, the specific high-level visual concept of personalizing the content view may not be appropriate for all public display applications. Therefore, we applied a more general high-level visual concept, user shadows, in our study.

VISUAL CONCEPTS TO ATTRACT AND ENGAGE

To facilitate our investigation of attraction and engagement power of visual concepts within the context of proxemic interactions, we implemented a large display prototype that provided different types of low- and high-level feedback.

Based on the above literature review, we selected two promising visual elements: content motion (low-level) and user shadows (high-level). In addition, to balance between ease of setup and adaptiveness of the content, we chose to implement proximity tracking using the Kinect depth sensor rather than a more elaborate user-tracking such as a Vicon system. We used the depth information to determine the degree of visual effects applied to the visual elements.

Changes in Content Motion and Use of User Shadow

Similar to Proxemic Peddler [35], we included both low- and high-level visual concepts in our study. This is consistent with the recommendation made by Müller et al. [27] where designs from both levels should be used together.

The low-level visual element we focused on were the changes in motion of the displayed content, for their applicability towards most contexts, and freedom from language and cultural differences. The motion change includes varying the speed of content moving in the display, and controlling its trajectory (direction of movement).

The high-level visual element we focused on was the use of user shadow, which is a virtual representation of the user on the display, and was used in prior work to successfully augment media interaction [15, 32]. The shadow is a silhouette filled with a solid color and scaled to be of a similar size to the user. Its appearance is similar to a projection of the user from a spotlight situated across from the display.

Another high-level visual element we included, and held consistent across all conditions, was to use application content relevant to our study participants (university students). The application content included images of the local university and campus life. The low-level content motion effects were applied to these images. The content originally comprised text-based inspirational quotes on virtual coloured Post-It-Notes, yet results from the pilot study indicated that this content was not sufficiently relevant or interesting to the study demographics.

Applying the Proxemic Interactions Design Approach

We aimed at appropriating the above concepts during the application of the proxemic interactions design approach. This was achieved by associating the degree of visual effects with the participant's proximity towards the display. The original proxemic theory by Hall [11] correlates four proxemics zones (*Public, Social, Personal, Intimate*) to decreasing levels proximity. Here we only used the first three for their relevance to the early stages of interaction.

Specifically, we designed two types of motion changes of content, namely, *adaptive speed* and *adaptive trajectory*. In adaptive speed, speed of the content (images and quotes) decreased in a stepwise fashion as the user walked closer to the display and crossed between zones. In adaptive trajectory, content gravitated towards the closing-in user, regardless of its original direction of movement, and changed rapidness as the user crossed between zones. The slowing down, and change in trajectory of images at a zone closer to the display was based on the rationale of providing users with enough time to look at and interact with content when they were within touching distance of the display, similar to the Proxemic Peddler system [35].

Regarding the user shadow, we designed the *adaptive shadow*, where the contrast of the shadow to the background was inversely related to the distance of the user to the display along a continuous scale, as shown in Figure 1. We incorporated this change in contrast to provide a sense of distance and display responsiveness to the user.

The way both motion and shadow adapted to proximity is illustrated in Figure 2. We divided the experimental room into three zones (Zones 1, 2, and 3) corresponding to the first three proxemic zones using the distances from the display. Participant entering a specific zone would trigger a change in the level of visual effect according to our design. In addition, this change is bound within one of the three horizontally divided grids on the display so only the content closest to the participant will be affected.

EXPERIMENTAL DESIGN

As we were interested in evaluating the ability of visual elements to draw people's attention and to communicate interactivity, we adopted the lab-study methodology which allowed us to isolate only the first parts of the interaction process. This section describes our selection criteria of the visual elements, and the steps we took to evaluate them.

Use of Deception

Contrary to most of the lab studies where participants were briefed ahead with the purpose of the study (e.g., [26, 30, 34]), this study relied on the assumption that the participants were unaware of the display's interface and its attempt to draw their attention (and later communicate interactivity). To ensure this assumption, we used a deception task to mask the real study, and recruited participants with it. Our deception task involved participants walking around while using their mobile device. Participants were never directed to the display until the last part of the study, where the real purpose of the study was revealed and a questionnaire with more relevant questions being provided.

Deception has been used in various research areas including psychology [7] and Human-Computer Interaction [2, 8]. It typically involves withholding the true purpose of (or part of) the study from participants, in attempt to not bias their responses. It most cases, participants will be debriefed with all the relevant information about the true nature of the study when it is sensible to do so, which in our case was the last part of the study, as we wanted to elicit their perception towards the display's attraction power and interactivity.

Pilot Study

Before running the main study we conducted a pilot study to help us settle on which visual techniques were the most promising, and gauge the practicality and appropriateness in conducting the study using deception. Proximity sensing

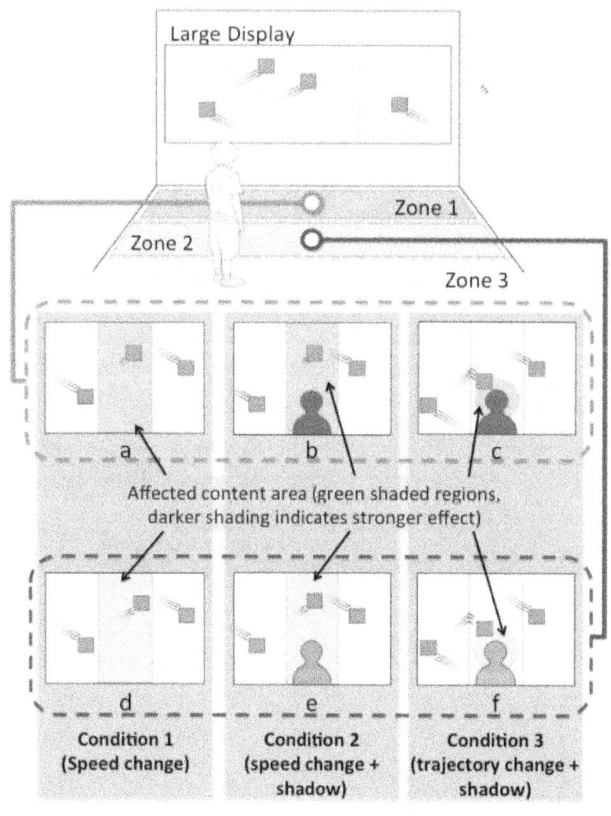

Figure 2. Proximity-based feedback relative to the large display. Zone 1 (dark green) applies the strongest visual effect. Zone 3 (white) applies no effect. Effects are only applied to the grid section on the large display closest to the user. Figures a, b and c represent the effects in Zone 1. In Conditions 1 & 2, images within the grid section move much slower than elsewhere (a & b). In Conditions 2 & 3, a shadow with high contrast is shown (b & c). In Condition 3, images change trajectory towards the shadow instead of slowing down (c & f). Figures d, e, f show the more moderate effects applied in Zone 2.

was done in a Wizard-of-Oz manner where an experimenter changed the speed and contrast of the displayed content based on a pre-defined proximity mapping of the experimental room (similar to the mapping used in the main study as shown in Figure 3).

Pilot study results indicated that changes in speed and contrast of content (images and inspirational quotes) based on a person's proximity towards the display was too subtle to be noticed. This led to its ineffectiveness in drawing attention, and thus inability to evoke any perception of interactivity. The use of deception (to walk around while using mobile apps), on the other hand, appeared to be practical and appropriate, as we were able to quickly recruit enough participants (16). Moreover, all participants completed the deception task without hesitation, and did not express any discomfort after they were explained to about the deception. The participants were also able to recall what happened and elaborated their answers concerning their perception towards the display's attraction power and interactivity.

Main Study

Based on results from our pilot study, we decided to use images of the university where the study took place as the sole content for a higher level of relevance. The images moved constantly at random directions within the display (and bounced off edges upon contact).

The main purpose of this study was to compare change in speed of the content (images) movement with the additional use of user shadows, in terms of drawing attention and communicating interactivity of the display. We hypothesized that the inclusion of user's shadow was more effective due to its appearance. We were also interested in the impression on interactivity the participants had towards the display with the visual elements as part of the design.

Table 1 shows the study design and conditions experienced by the participants. The study (actual study) had three conditions: *adaptive speed* – images slow down upon proximity, *adaptive speed & shadow* – images slow down upon proximity & user's shadow appears with increasing contrast upon proximity, and *adaptive trajectory & shadow* – images actively follow the user upon proximity & user's shadow appears with increasing contrast upon proximity.

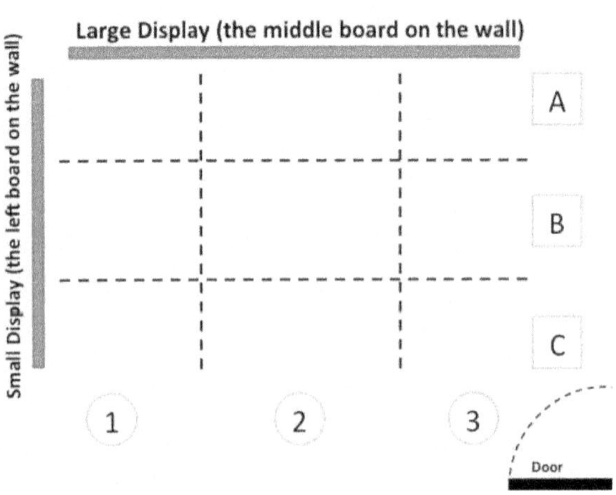

Figure 3. Navigation points in the experiment room. Participants were asked to walk between different grid cells using visual on-device instructions or verbal instructions issued by the researcher. Each row (A, B, C) corresponds to a different level of proximity-based visual effect (Zones 1, 2, and 3).

		Navigation Study (Deception study)	
		Visual (Condition A)	*Verbal (Condition B)*
Study on effectiveness of animating saliency (Actual study)	*Adaptive speed*	Condition 1A	Condition 1B
	Adaptive speed & shadow	Condition 2A	Condition 2B
	Adaptive trajectory & shadow	Condition 3A	Condition 3B

Table 1. Main study design, with the deception task being walking with the navigation instructions provided visually or verbally. The small display was used as a control in all conditions, thus reducing a condition in the actual study.

Figure 4 shows the setup of the experimental room. Proximity sensing in the main study was provided by a Microsoft Kinect positioned at the back of the experimental room, and was relayed to an application written in Processing[1] running on a Windows 7 machine. The large display (display 'b') comprised a 124-inch diagonal display of 2560x800 pixel resolution provided by two tiled Hitachi CP-AW251N ultra short-throw projectors. A control display (display 'a') was positioned on an adjacent wall, perpendicular to the large display. Due to limitations of the environment and available equipment, this display was smaller than the large display, yet was adequately large enough (70-inch diagonal with 1280x800 pixel resolution) to be considered a relevant "large" display. It comprised a single Hitachi CP-AW251N ultra short-throw projector. It showed the same content but did not respond to any actions of the participant. A camcorder was setup during the study to capture the entire walking sequence.

Deception Phase

The study was advertised as to "*observe how different forms of navigating instructions affect the way a person arrives at a destination*". Each participant was first greeted

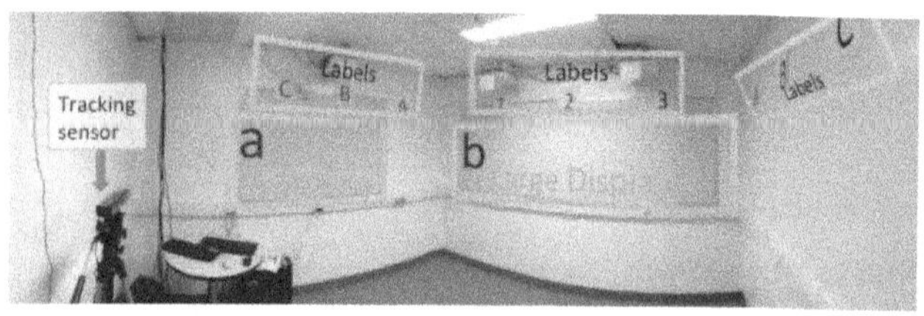

Figure 4. Setup for the main study. Labels were attached to the walls to simulate signage, with a grid layout for a less straight-forward navigation.

[1] https://processing.org

and asked to read the information letter (of the deception task). The participant then underwent two counter-balanced navigation tasks within the experimental room: one was to receive navigating instructions visually through the display of a mobile device; the other was to receive the same navigating instructions verbally from the researcher. The navigating instructions were either one-step routes (e.g., from A1 to A3), or two-step routes (e.g., from C1 to C3, then C3 to A3), both of which were designed to cover all the possible directions a passerby could take in relation to the large display (i.e., away, towards, across), and the corresponding directions in relation to the small display (which was perpendicular to the large display). Figure 3 shows the destination points in the experimental room.

Once the task was finished, the participant was led out of the experimental room and asked to complete a post-session questionnaire, which began with questions closely related to the deception task, and then steered to probing questions about their impressions of the surroundings (e.g., whether they noticed the content on the displays, and what they thought they could do with the displays).

Reveal Phase

After the post-session questionnaire was completed, the participant was asked further probing questions about the display. The researcher then revealed the real purpose of the study and explained why the deception task was needed. The participant was provided with a choice to withdraw from, or to proceed with the study, along with contact information of the counseling services.

Finally, a second post-session questionnaire with more elaborate questions about the display, and a condition-specific questionnaire were provided. The participant was then thanked, paid, and asked to not share the experience, or disclose the real purpose of the study to anyone.

DATA COLLECTION AND ANALYSIS

We recruited 30 participants (21 males, 9 females) from our local university for this two-week main study. Our study methodology allowed us to both evaluate the ability of each visual concept (i.e., individual or combined use of the visual elements) to draw attention against the control, as well as against each other. The data was collected from the questionnaires, researcher's notes, and video recordings. We analyzed the data for attention drawing by keeping the two deception conditions (visual and verbal) separated, so as to provide a clearer picture of the results and illustrate two possible usage scenarios: a passerby heavily focused on a separate object (the mobile device for navigation instructions), and a passerby loosely focused on the surrounding environment (while listening for navigation instructions).

To analyze the effectiveness of visual concepts against the control condition (the small display), we conducted repeated measures Analysis of Variance (ANOVA)[2] tests on the collected Likert-scale responses within participants. To compare the visual concepts against each other, we conducted one-way ANOVA test on the Likert-scale responses across participants. The open-ended questionnaire responses and video data were reviewed for emergent themes.

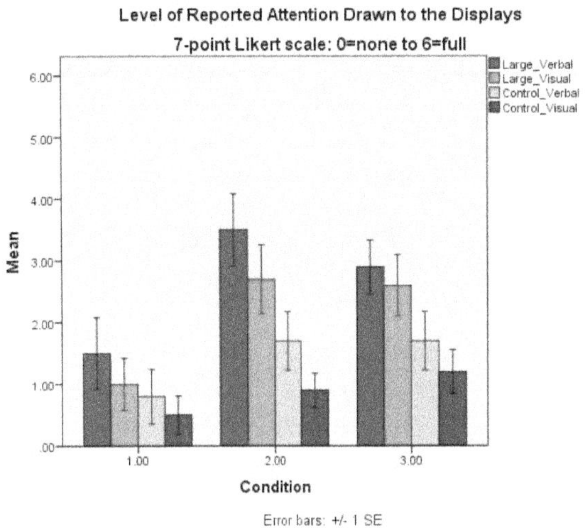

Figure 5. Reported attention drawn for each condition: 1) speed change, 2) speed change & shadow, 3) trajectory change & shadow. Verbal and visual correspond to the navigation conditions used in the deception task.

RESULTS AND DISCUSSION

The data analysis revealed that proximity-based content movement and user shadow was effective in drawing unknowing participants' attention to the display. Yet, as shown in Figure 5, the effect of changing content's movement speed (Condition 1) was much smaller than that of the combined content speed changes and user's shadow (Condition 2 and 3), when compared to the control. We expand on these along with our observation below.

Effectiveness of Visual Concepts over the Control

To determine how much attention was being drawn to the displays, we asked the questions "*Please indicate how much each of the displays [small/large] drew your attention when the instructions were provided [vocally/visually]*", in the form of a 7-point Likert scale from no attention to full attention. When only relating proximity to the display with content's speed, there was a main effect in the verbal case: $F_{verbal}(1, 9)=10.76$, MSE=.23, p=.01, but not in the visual case: $F_{visual}(1, 9)=2.65$, MSE=.47, p=.138, *n.s.* However, in both cases the difference in means was very small between the condition ($M_{verbal}=1.50$, $M_{visual}=1.00$) and the control ($M_{verbal}=0.80$, $M_{visual}=0.50$). Adding the user's shadow to the display resulted in a larger difference in means between the condition ($M_{verbal}=3.50$, $M_{visual}=2.70$) and the control

[2] The validity of using ANOVA tests on Likert-scale data has been shown by Norman [28].

(M_{verbal}=1.7, M_{visual}=0.90). It also led to a main effect in both the verbal case: $F_{verbal}(1, 9)=16.57$, MSE=.98, p<.01, and the visual case: $F_{visual}(1, 9)=18.69$, MSE=.87, p<.01. Replacing change in speed with a more elaborate change in content's trajectory, while keeping the user's shadow, also resulted in a larger difference in means between the condition (M_{verbal}=2.90, M_{visual}=2.60) and the control (M_{verbal}=1.7, M_{visual}=1.20), as well as a main effect in both the verbal case: $F_{verbal}(1, 9)=6.00$, MSE=1.20, p=.037, and the visual case: $F_{visual}(1, 9)=10.76$, MSE=.91, p=.01.

The small differences in means between varying speed of content movement (Condition 1) and no variation at all (control) were consistent with our findings in the pilot study. The significant effect found in the case where verbal navigation instructions were given indicates a consistent higher ranking of attention drawn, and may be explained by a higher chance of the display in the participants' view. Yet, we still believe such small differences in means suggest that varying speed of content movement alone would not be an effective mechanism in drawing passersby's attention.

On the other hand, the larger differences in means between adding user's shadow (Conditions 2 and 3) and the control, together with the statistical significance, strongly suggests that such mechanism was effective in drawing attention. In fact, some of the participants were able to recall that the shadow, in relation to their movement, "*followed [my] movements*", "*mirror [my] motions*", and "*got bigger when [I] got close to [the display] and was gone totally when [I] moved away from [the display]*". Interestingly, attention towards the small display was also increased. Though participant feedback offered no explanation, we hypothesize this was a consequence of the large display being noticed.

Attraction Power of Content Motion and User Shadow

As mentioned above, and also from the pilot study, change in content speed in relation to display proximity alone did not appear to have strong attraction power, especially when the deception task was in play. Therefore, we were also interested in comparing the effectiveness of combining it with the user's shadow. The ANOVA revealed a main effect of the Conditions (1, 2 and 3) on reported attention drawn for both verbal and visual cases: $F_{verbal}(2, 27)=3.65$, MSE=2.89, p=.04, $F_{visual}(2, 27)=3.70$, MSE=2.463, p=.038. A linear contrast was then conducted to test the a-prior prediction that the conditions with shadow (2 and 3) would have a stronger effect than the condition without (1). It was found to be significant for both the verbal and visual cases, $t_{verbal}(27)=2.58$, MSE=1.32, p=.015; $t_{visual}(27)=2.72$, MSE=1.22, p=.011. The use of the contrast test was also supported by the answers from the participants, which indicated the majority of them were predominantly attracted by their own shadow but not the changes in content's motion.

The fact that the majority of the participants in Conditions 2 and 3 reported noticing their own shadow (19 out of 20), in contrast to only a few noticed the changes in content motion (5 out of 20), indicates that reflecting participants' shadow was more compelling at drawing their attention than the more subtle visual effect caused by changes in content motion. We believe this was mainly because reflecting one's own live-sized shadow was unexpected and novel (an "oddball"), and provided a compelling psychological sense of ownership, while floating content had been commonly used as screen-savers or decorative ambient displays.

Ability to Communicate Interactivity of the Display

To understand the display's potential interactivity, one first needs to notice that display. Thus, in Condition 1 where the majority of the participants failed to notice the display, most were not able to assess its potential interactivity. Only one participant in this condition rated the display as "somewhat interactive". The remaining participants rated the display as having low interactivity or stated that they did not notice. In contrast, 17 of the 20 participants in Conditions 2 and 3 rated the display as "somewhat interactive" or higher. Yet, when asked what they thought they could do with the display, only three of these 20 participants mentioned they could touch/move/interact with content. This suggests that while the user's shadow may help indicate the interactivity of the display, further cues may be needed to communicate possible *types* of interactions (e.g., touch).

Overall, our results suggest that including user shadows was able to increase the attraction power and communicate *some* interactivity. But other forms of interface designs are required to further bring the users through the interaction process with the interactive display.

This finding corroborates Müller et al's [26] previous work that revealed that *representing* the user in the display (via shadows or user images) was more effective at engaging passersby than simply changing content in *response to* user actions, similar to our changes in content motion.

Ownership of and Playing with One's Shadow

Displaying the user's shadow appeared to have another positive consequence to the interaction process. Our video analysis revealed that some participants, upon noticing the shadow, played with the shadow by moving their own body in experimental ways (Figure 6). The fact that the tracking and output were done in near real-time allowed the virtual shadow to respond with similar behaviour to a person's real-world shadow. Analysis of questionnaire responses also revealed a similar "sense of self" theme in participant's open-ended responses about the displays. Eighteen of the 20 participants who experienced the user shadows used personal pronouns, adjectives, or possessives to refer to the shadows, indicating that most participants perceived the

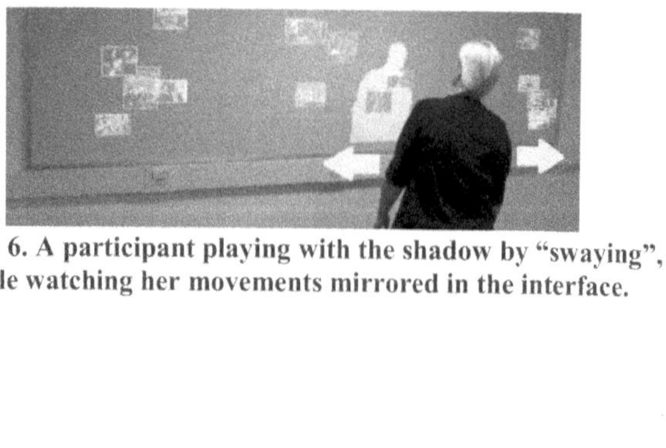

Figure 6. A participant playing with the shadow by "swaying", while watching her movements mirrored in the interface.

shadow as a representation of themselves in the interface. This observation suggests the shadow being displayed in the interface has the potential to quickly invoke a sense of "self" and its ownership.

This sense of playfulness, familiarity, and ownership of the user shadows suggest that user shadows may also provide a means to help minimize people's social inhibitions of using a display in public, which has previously been recognized as a common barrier for use of public display use [6].

Disney recently exploited the playful aspect of user shadows in a marketing campaign[3] utilizing shadows to draw passersby's attention and invite them to interact with a large display. In a Wizard-of-Oz style approach, back-lit actors (dressed as famous Disney characters) mirrored passersby's movements from behind the display, and casted their shadows onto it. After capturing the passerby's attention, the actors started to deviate from strictly mirroring the user actions, thereby creating an engaging experience to the passersby. Intentional deviation from true representations of "self" to actively engage the user is discussed below.

LESSONS LEARNED AND DESIGN EXTENSIONS

Based on our study findings and anecdotal observations, we reflect on some of the lessons learned through our study, and discuss some possible design improvements and extensions that may increase the attraction and engagement power of visual design of large public interactive displays.

Provide Continuous Proximity-Based Feedback

While most existing systems employing proxemic interactions apply interface changes based on discrete distance "zones" [5, 33, 34] (emulating to some degree, Hall's [11] original proxemics zones), this discrete feedback approach may have contributed to the limited attraction power of the content speed changes condition included in our study. While the psychological literature has found this approach to be highly effective for capturing attention, these findings assume that people have adequate opportunity to *observe* the speed changes. Given our discrete application of the proximity-based feedback, changes in content speed were only applied at the proximity zone boundaries. It is likely that this limited amount of feedback changes, combined with the intentionally distractive deception task provided even fewer opportunities for participants to notice the speed changes when they occurred.

In contrast, the proximity-based feedback changes for the user shadows were applied continuously. The transparency level of the user shadow decreased, along a linear scale, as the user approached the display, making it more visible as the user was closer to the display. This continuous feedback was observable at any position in the environment, not just at the zone boundaries, as long as the person was moving perpendicularly to the display. Thus, in a public setting, where the display may have limited time and opportunity to capture a user's attention, providing continuous proximity-based feedback is likely to be more effective at attracting their attention simply due to the fact that feedback changes are applied throughout the environment, not just at the proximity zone boundaries.

User Shadow Placement

Although the study found that user shadows are visually compelling, the video data and our observations revealed issues with their current implementation. We utilized the mirror metaphor to be consistent with Müller et al.'s use of shadows [26], where the shadow appeared as if a person was standing in front of a mirror. Thus, when someone walked parallel to the display the shadow appeared directly beside them. This often placed the shadow outside their peripheral view, limiting its potential to be noticed. Moreover, delays in user tracking or shadow update sometimes positioned the shadow slightly behind the user, further decreasing its potential visibility (see Figure 7). To address this limitation, the shadow could be shifted slightly ahead of the user's movement so it would appear within the visual perception field of a passerby. Ideally this approach would be used when user orientation information is available (e.g. [35]), and only applied when the user is turned parallel to the display to ensure appropriate feedback.

This alternative shadow placement may help to address the "landing effect" observed by Müller et al. [26], where passersby noticed (or understood) the interactivity of a display after passing it, and had to back-up to interact with it.

Improving the Engagement Power of User Shadows

While our study found that adding user shadows increased the attraction power of the display, the results also showed they were less effective at communicating interactivity. The simple mirroring of the user's body movements did not appear to communicate how one might interact with the application content itself, only with one's virtual shadow. On the surface, this finding is inconsistent with Muller el al.'s [26] finding that user shadows effectively communicated interactivity (though not as effectively as video-based representations of the user). However, in their system, interacting with the application content (virtual balls) simply required body movement and controlling one's shadow (which most of our participants quickly figured out how to

Figure 7. The user shadow appeared beside someone walking by the display. Slight tracking or display update delays caused the shadow to lag behind the user, placing the shadow outside of the user's peripheral view.

[3] https://www.youtube.com/watch?v=Hd_2Y29_FLU, video of Disney's use of shadows in a shopping mall.

do). Yet in systems such as the Proxemic Peddler [35], and implied in ours, interacting with application content requires touching content directly on the display surface. User shadows do not appear to offer an inherent knowledge about transitioning to this type of behaviour.

It may be possible to leverage people's sense of playfulness, familiarity, and ownership of user shadows to improve its ability to engage the user. For example, by dropping the strict "mirroring" nature of the user shadow, it could provide a fun means of guiding user action or providing new methods of interacting with the display (e.g., shadow-based interactions for interacting with graphic objects [15], reaching distant content on a large display [31], and interactive graphics to suggest full-body input [32]).

We have identified several attributes of the user shadows that warrant further exploration for their effectiveness in assisting various stages interaction with a large display employing proxemics interactions:

Contrast: the degree of difference the shadow's visual appearance has from the application background. Following the proxemic interactions design approach, we altered the visual contrast of the user shadows based on the user's relative distance to the display. As the user approached the display, the level of transparency of the user shadow decreased (increasing its contrast against the background), along a linear scale. This contrast change appeared to be noticed and appreciated by our participants. It may be possible to further exploit such contrast change to guide desired user behaviour, such as using different levels of contrast to highlight different body parts (e.g. the user's hands) the user could use for system interaction.

Autonomy: the degree of control a user has over the shadow's behaviour. In our study, we used a strict mirror metaphor, where the shadow was completely driven by (i.e., mirrored) user action. In the aforementioned Disney marketing campaign, the "mocked-up" shadows used a hybrid approach, where initially the shadow mirrored the passerby's behaviour, and then behaved more autonomously once the person's attention was captured, for instance, to start a mimed conversation. While this "autonomy" was faked by actors in a Wizard-of-Oz approach and would require a significant amount of artificial intelligence to actually implement, a more subtle form of shadow autonomy could also be employed using proxemic interactions. For instance, at far distances, a mirror-type shadow could be used. When a person has approached the display, an autonomous arm could appear out of the user shadow and point towards, or poke, a nearby piece of interactive content, to suggest user behaviour (e.g., touch). This "shadow-guided" concept is similar to the concept of "self-revealing gestures" [36], where context-based visual hints are displayed to help guide user interaction within gestural interfaces.

Realism: the degree of fidelity of the user shadow (e.g., how closely it resembles the actual user). In our study, the user shadow was displayed as semi-transparent, monochromatic, filled silhouette. Müller et al. [26] previously found that higher-fidelity, video-based representations were more effective at engaging passersby than were silhouette-based shadows. Yet, they also found that some users prefer the anonymity of shadows over more realistic representations, especially in a public setting. It may be possible to mitigate this concern using proxemic interactions, and potentially combining this attribute with others: closer users could be shown higher-fidelity user representations with a lower-contrast to be compelling for themselves, but be more difficult to see at a distance.

LIMITATIONS

To gain precision and control, we used a laboratory-based study methodology. However, this approach involves a cost of lower ecological validity compared to the more commonly used "in-the-wild" field study for evaluating public displays, as pointed out by Convertino et al. [8] and Alt et al. [1]. To help mitigate this issue, we employed a deception task to emulate key aspects of public settings, such as participants being initially unaware of the existence or purpose of the display, and providing a compelling distraction to compete with the display for their attention. Also, the presence of the researcher and camcorder might affect the way participants responded to the displays. Thus, to truly achieve a high ecological validity, a follow-up field study, with unobtrusive data capture methods, is needed to validate the results in specific public contexts.

Another limitation is the sample group of participants included in the study, who were recruited through our university mailing lists, and thus, were limited to a particular user demographic, including certain age range, background, and more importantly, relatedness to the content and experience in using interactive displays. However, the fact that the studied visual concepts were based on previous psychological findings suggests that our results would likely to apply across a broader user demographic than we recruited.

CONCLUSION

In this paper, we empirically evaluated different types of visual concepts in a large display employing proxemic interactions, namely changes in content motion and additional use of user shadow. The study examined the effectiveness of these visual concepts to draw attention and communicate interactivity to passersby. Our results indicated that while both were able to attract participant's attention, inclusion of user shadow was found to be more visually compelling than changes in content motion alone. However, neither of them was able to effectively communicate the purpose or potential interaction mechanisms within the display application.

We have also discussed potential design strategies to improve the engagement power of the user shadows. For instance, the autonomy, contrast, and realism of user shadows could be altered within the context of proxemic interactions to improve its ability to guide user behaviour toward effective system interaction.

What People Really Remember – Understanding Cognitive Effects When Interacting with Large Displays

Philipp Panhey[1], Tanja Döring[1], Stefan Schneegass[2], Dirk Wenig[1], Florian Alt[3]

[1]University of Bremen
Research Group Digital Media
first.last@uni-bremen.de

[2]University of Stuttgart
Human-Computer Interaction Group
stefan.schneegass@vis.uni-stuttgart.de

[3]University of Munich
Media Informatics Group
florian.alt@ifi.lmu.de

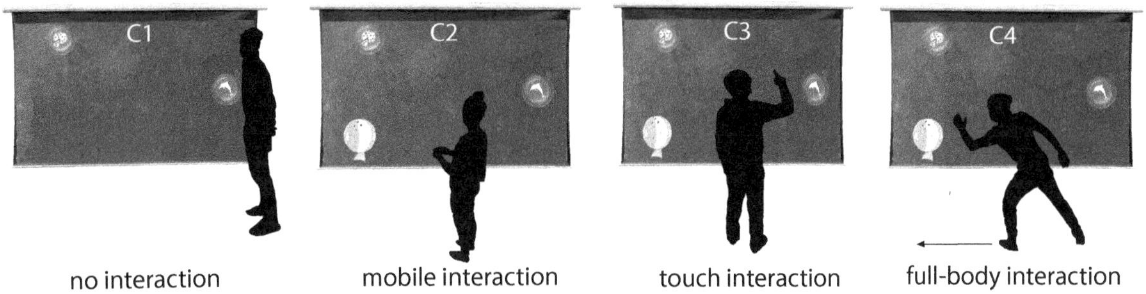

Figure 1. We investigate how different types of interaction (mobile interaction, touch interaction, and full-body interaction) impact on how well people can remember content of large screen displays. In contrast to prior work on interactive TV and the WWW, our findings reveal that more movement can negatively influence recall, hence leading to a trade-off for designers between user experience and memorable content.

ABSTRACT

This paper investigates how common interaction techniques for large displays impact on recall in learning tasks. Our work is motivated by results of prior research in different areas that attribute a positive effect of interactivity to cognition. We present findings from a controlled lab experiment with 32 participants comparing mobile phone-based interaction, touch interaction, and full-body interaction to a non-interactive baseline. In contrast to prior findings, our results reveal that more movement can negatively influence recall. In particular we show that designers are facing an immanent trade-off between designing engaging interaction through extensive movement and creating memorable content.

Author Keywords

Pervasive displays; interactivity; cognition; recall.

ACM Classification Keywords

H.5.1. Multimedia Information Systems: Evaluation / Methodology; H.5.2. User interfaces: Interaction styles

INTRODUCTION

The past years have witnessed a proliferation of our daily life with digital displays due to falling hardware prices. Particularly museums but also municipalities employ interactive displays to convey information. Though such displays have the potential to increase the experience as people can interact with the content, it is unclear as of today, whether there are benefits from a learning perspective – i.e., can we assume that users remember content shown on a screen better as they interact with it? In particular, do performative techniques, requiring a lot of movement, have a positive effect?

Prior research found interaction to positively influence cognition, particularly in the context of interactive TV [8] and on the WWW [9]. At the same time it is unclear, whether these findings hold for large interactive screens. Early work suggests a general effect on recall [1]. However, it focuses on gesture as the sole interaction technique. Our work provides the first detailed comparison of different interaction techniques, focusing on mobile phone, touch, and full-body interaction as the most popular interaction techniques for large displays. This paper contributes a detailed investigation of how these different types of interaction impact on users' ability to learn content shown on a large interactive display.

We hypothesize that, similar to prior findings, interaction leads to an increase in recall, particularly if users are required to move extensively and if interaction provokes positive emotions. To investigate our hypotheses, we built an interactive game that allows for interaction by means of mobile phones, touch, and full-body gestures and compared it to a learning task without any interaction. Results show that, in contrast to our hypothesis, recall may be negatively affected by interaction, particularly if physically demanding. Hence, designers need to decide whether to optimize for user experience through extensive movement or for cognition.

ITS '15, November 15 - 18, 2015, Funchal, Portugal

ACM 978-1-4503-3899-8/15/11 $15.00
http://dx.doi.org/10.1145/2817721.2817732

APPROACH AND HYPOTHESES

This work explores how different interaction techniques with varying degrees of *movement* and the ability to invoke *positive emotions* impact on cognition. We designed a controlled lab experiment, that allowed us to account for any external influence that may impact on cognition. We created an interactive game where users had to destroy bubbles containing different symbols on the screen. Users controlled the game using one of three input modalities – the mobile phone, touch, and full-body gestures – thus allowing techniques that require different degrees of movement to be compared (Figure 1). After the game, we tested for recall of the symbols and assessed the different techniques through questionnaires.

Hypothesis 1. More movement results in higher recall. Prior work found positive effects on recall rates and acute cognitive performance based on motion and motor processes [1, 3, 4]. We hypothesize that similar effects occur for interaction with large displays. To address H1, we designed different interaction techniques with varying degrees of movement.

Hypothesis 2. More positive emotions while interacting result in higher recall. According to results from prior work on positive emotions (in form of positive valence) and recall [11] and on emotional arousal and memory [7], we hypothesize positive emotions (which combine positive affect with arousal, cf., [10]) during interaction with large displays to increase recall. Thus, we assess positive affect after interacting.

USER STUDY

Apparatus and Setup

We implemented an interactive display game where a blowfish on the lower border of the screen had to be moved horizontally to destroy falling bubbles. The bubbles contained different symbols that we used later to assess recall. The game design (same drop distance and speed of bubbles, bubbles bursting at the bottom of the screen) ensured that all bubbles were shown for the same amount of time (3 s), no matter if destroyed by the blowfish or not. In each game, all symbols were shown 3 times. The symbols appeared at random horizontal positions, hence minimizing any spatial memory effects. The game was deployed on a 3,5 m $\times$ 2 m screen (Figure 2).

Bubbles contained particular symbols. Each symbol belonged to one of four categories we assigned to the interaction techniques. The categories were animals (S_1), food (S_2), transport (S_3), and household (S_4) each consisting of 15 items.

Interaction Techniques

The techniques for controlling the blowfish varied in their extent of body movement necessary to perform the interaction.

- For *mobile interaction* (C_2), players stood in front of the screen and held a mobile phone horizontally in one of their hands. Tilting the phone more than 30 degrees sideways moved the blowfish while a smaller angle stopped it. The data was send to the computer connected to the display.
- For *touch interaction* (C_3), players had to directly touch the screen and, thus, move with both their arms and body. The blowfish then moved to the touched location on the screen. We used diffused illumination for finger tracking.

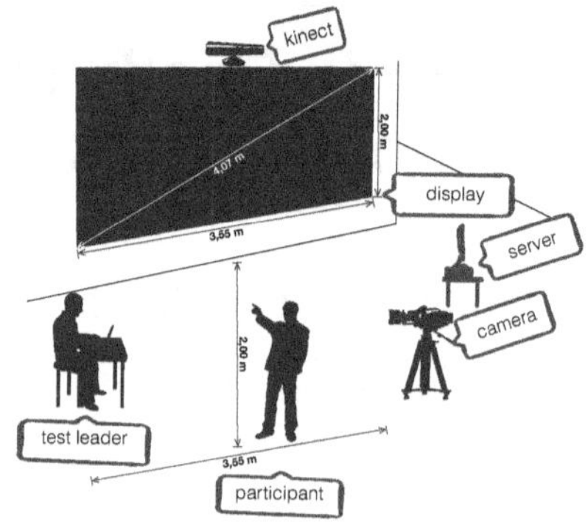

Figure 2. Study Setup. Participants interacted from a distance of 2 m with the 3.55 m $\times$ 2 m screen. The experimenter and a camera observed the players during the game.

- For *full-body interaction* (C_4), players positioned themselves in front of the screen. To control the blowfish, players simply moved horizontally in front of the screen. We used a Microsoft Kinect sensor for tracking the player's position and directly map it to the location of the fish.

A *non-interactive* baseline condition (C_1) was implemented, in which users had to stand in front of the screen, solely watching the contentpresented in the same manner as in the other conditions (e.g., falling bubbles with 15 symbols, 3 s per fall). As the participants did not interact and thus could focus completely on memorizing the symbols, the experiment is biased in favor of this condition. C_1 to C_4 are ordered by the degree of movement from least to most. In all conditions except touch, participants were to position themselves at 2 m in front of the screen with the game being shown in full-screen mode. To compensate for the closer distance during the touch interaction (0.5 m) we reduced the game size on the screen proportionally (width: 0.88 m; height: 0.5 m). Thus we ensured that bubbles appeared in constant size in all conditions.

Data Collection

During the game we logged all symbols shown on the screen as well as whether and when a bubble was destroyed by the user. All data was time-stamped. Furthermore, all blowfish destination coordinates were logged. During the study, all sessions were videotaped for post-hoc analysis.

Study Design and Metrics

The study was designed as a repeated-measures experiment where each participant played the game in each condition. The order of the four conditions and the symbol sets were counterbalanced. Participants played the game for 135 s in each condition (15 symbols were shown 3 times for 3 s each). We chose such a short time to minimize any influence of fatigue and to reproduce a typical, usually short, public display interaction [2]. Before the game we asked participants to try and remember as many items as possible. All participants were naive to the hypotheses. During the study we provided the participants different questionnaires. At the outset of the study, participants had to fill out a *demografic questionnaire*. After each condition, participants then had to complete a *recall test*; the participants had to write down the items they remembered from the previous interaction stage. In addition, we asked them to fill in a *game experience questionnaire*

(GEQ) [5] and a *user experience questionnaire* (UEQ) [6]. The GEQ quantifies tension, positive and negative affect, immersion, flow, competence, and challenge. The UEQ assesses attractiveness, design quality, and use quality. At the end, we conducted semi-structured interviews with the participants.

Procedure

We recruited participants by approaching people on campus. All participants were students or university employees but came from a wide range of subjects. As participants arrived at the lab we had them fill in the initial questionnaire and then introduced the game, the different interaction techniques, and the task. We allowed participants to practice each condition so that they could familiarize with it. Then they started to play the game in the first condition for 135 s. After that, they had to complete the recall test and the questionnaires. This procedure was repeated for all conditions.

RESULTS

We invited 32 people (16 female) with an average age of 27.5 years (SD=6.8). All participants had an academic background (25 students, 7 employees). All participants owned at least one touch device, 7 had prior experience with Kinect and 22 with Nintendo Wii. When asked about how easily they could remember things, answers were mainly neutral (5-Point Likert scale, 1=don't agree at all, 5=completely agree; M=3.09, SD=0.89). For all follow up analyses we applied a Holm-Bonferroni correction.

Game Performance

Among the three interactive conditions, participants performed best in the mobile condition, on average destroying 91.53% of the bubbles (M=41.19, SD=2.68), followed by full-body interaction with 89.51% (M=40.28, SD=2.4). In the touch condition participants on average destroyed 87.58% of the bubbles (M=39.41, SD=2.92).

Recall and Interaction Techniques

Figure 3 shows the mean recall scores per technique. Ordered by recall rate, the ranking is as follows: no interaction (76.5%), mobile interaction (69.2%), full body interaction (66.7%), and touch interaction (62.9%). A one-way repeated measured analysis of variance (ANOVA) reveals a significant effect of the interaction modality on recall, $F(3, 29)$=7.799, p<.001. Follow-up comparisons show that people could recall significantly more symbols in the non-interactive baseline condition than mobile phone (p=.009), touch (p<.001), and gestures (p=.005). Furthermore, people could recall significantly more symbols when interacting with the phone, compared to touch (p=.014). All comparisons were not statistically significant. Thus, we reject H1.

Game Experience and User Experience

Using the GEQ we investigated the impact of "positive affect". An ANOVA reveals a statistically significant effect of the interaction technique on "positive affect", $F(3, 29)$=6.142, p<.001. Mobile interaction significantly evokes more positive affect than touch (p=.008) and static interaction (p<.001). Full-body interaction significantly engenders more positive affect than static interaction (p=.004).

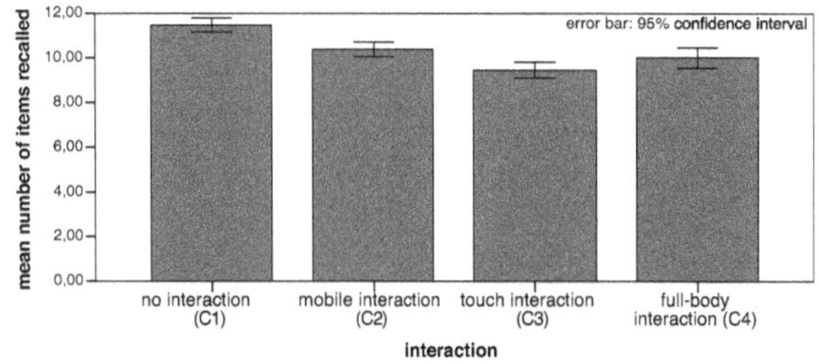

Figure 3. Mean number of items recalled for interaction techniques (out of 15 items in total). In the non-interactive baseline (C_1), participants could recall most items. The mobile phone-based interaction technique (C_2) performed significantly better than touch interaction (C_3).

Analyzing the results from the UEQ reveals a significant effect regarding attractiveness, $F(3, 29)$=16.367, p<.001. Posthoc analysis shows that mobile interaction is significantly more attractive than touch interaction (p=.001) and the baseline (p<.001). The static condition is significantly less attractive than touch (p=.003) and full-body interaction (p<.001). Positive affect and attractiveness do not significantly correlate with recall. Therefore H2 has to be rejected in this context.

Qualitative Results

Semi-structured interviews revealed that most participants liked *mobile interaction* best (53.1%). They described it as accurate and liked the haptic element in their hand. Furthermore, they felt that it closely resembles other controller-based techniques. P5 pointed out that he liked the 'low mental effort'. With regard to *full-body interaction* participants who favored this technique (37.5%) reported to like not having to hold something in their hands. Others, however, felt that too much movement was required to accurately recall all items. They reported this technique to 'disturb' the recall process and that the task shifted into the background. Still the technique was considered to be innovative and exhilarating. *Touch interaction* (9.4%) required some familiarizing, but was in general perceived positively. Yet, participants felt to be too close to the screen to properly recall items. The fact that people could best recall items in the *static condition* is reflected in answers during the interviews. People stated that it was easier to recall items since they did not have to focus on the interaction.

DISCUSSION

There is strong evidence from prior work that interaction supports cognition. At the same time, earlier studies were conducted in situations, where (1) people are highly familiar with interaction modality and technique and (2) interaction only requires a limited amount of motion. This situation changes in front of large screens. Interaction can be designed in a way that it is physically demanding and, particularly if encountered in public space, users often need to learn the interaction.

The results of our study reveal that when designing interaction with large screens for supporting recall attention needs to be payed to the details of the interaction techniques beyond movement. The interaction technique should be highly usable, easy to learn, keep the cognitive load low, fit to the interactive content, and be engaging (e.g., through movement, but not too much of it) while letting the user keep the eyes on the content.

This is, of course, in practice not an easy task, but from our study we can derive a number of recommendations.

First of all, although our baseline condition with "no interaction" gave the best recall results, it is not an option for real settings as prior research has shown that people pay much less attention to non-interactive content [1]. In line with this, our interviews revealed that most participants found it boring.

Second, our results indicate that touch interaction may not be appropriate for recalling content on large displays due to the close distance to the screen. Although we compensated for potential effects by adjusting the screen size to the field of view and by using only the x coordinate for interaction (i.e., the users could touch at an arbitrary height on the screen), we still found the lowest recall performance, and participants gave feedback that the distance to the screen was perceived as too short. Thus, we do not recommend direct touch interaction for large screens when optimizing for recall.

Third, comparing mobile and full-body interaction, we obtained better results for mobile interaction in recall, in the subjective rankings as well as regarding mean scores for attractiveness (UEQ) and positive affect (GEQ). This shows that it was designed in a way that seemed to fit the task better. Participants pointed out that they liked its unobtrusiveness, and that they could fully concentrate on the screen. In comparison, full-body interaction was perceived as containing too much movement, which caused disturbance, especially because of moving the head changed the field of vision. Nevertheless, the participants found full-body interaction very stimulating and original. The results show that too much movement can negatively influence recall. Designers need to carefully consider whether they want to design for engaging interaction through extensive movement or to convey knowledge to the user. In our study, the mobile phone provided a good compromise that many users liked and that led to good recall rates.

LIMITATIONS & FUTURE WORK

Our study has some limitations. Participants may have had different degrees of experience with the interaction techniques. Hence, we allowed them to practice the interaction in all conditions. Also the ecologic validity of our findings is limited, since we did not conduct it in a public setting. Yet, the focus of the study was on internal validity and hence on the comparability of our study conditions. Hence, we deliberately designed the game and the interaction techniques as well as the study procedure in a way to ensure that the users kept their focus on the content and were as little as possible distracted by performing the interaction.

First of all, we did this by designing very simple interaction techniques that did not require much learning. By observing each participant we made sure that we did not start the study until his or her focus was completely on the content. In none of the conditions, the users had to look at their hands, other body parts, or at any devices to perform the interaction.

Furthermore, we focused on playful content. While we believe games to be among the most important applications for interactive displays, we cannot make any assumptions with regard to other content. This should be subject to future work.

Finally, we did not explicitly measure arousal, which was shown to impact on cognition (e.g., [7]). Future work could investigate this relationship in more detail.

CONCLUSION

In this work we investigated the effect of movement and positive emotions on recall during interaction with large displays using different modalities. In contrast to our hypotheses, neither movement nor positive emotions led to an increase. Too much movement can even negatively affect cognition. From this we learn that when deploying for interactive displays, designers need to carefully consider whether they want to design for engaging interaction through extensive movement or to convey knowledge to the user. Our findings yield that mobile phone-based interaction may be a good compromise.

ACKNOWLEDGMENTS

We thank Rainer Malaka for his valuable feedback. The research received funding from the EU Seventh Framework Programme ([FP7/2007-2013]) – grant agreement no. 612933.

REFERENCES

1. Alt, F., Schneegaß, S., Girgis, M., and Schmidt, A. Cognitive effects of interactive public display applications. In *Proc. of PerDis'13*, ACM (2013).
2. Alt, F., Schneegaß, S., Schmidt, A., Müller, J., and Memarovic, N. How to evaluate public displays. In *Proc. of PerDis'12*, ACM (2012).
3. Gao, Y., and Mandryk, R. The acute cognitive benefits of casual exergame play. In *Proc. of CHI'2012*, CHI '12, ACM (2012), 1863–1872.
4. Hannaford, C. *Smart moves. Why learning is not all in your head.* Great Ocean Publishers, 2007.
5. Ijsselsteijn, W., De Kort, Y., and Poels, K. The game experience questionnaire: Development of a self-report measure to assess the psychological impact of digital games. Manuscript in Preparation, 2013.
6. Laugwitz, B., Held, T., and Schrepp, M. Construction and evaluation of a ux questionnaire. In *Proc. of USAB'08*, Springer (2008).
7. Libkuman, T. M., Nichols-Whitehead, P., Griffith, J., and Thomas, R. Source of arousal and memory for detail. *Memory & Cognition 27*, 1 (1999).
8. Risden, K., Czerwinski, M., Worley, S., Hamilton, L., Kubiniec, J., Hoffman, H., Mickel, N., and Loftus, E. Interactive advertising: patterns of use and effectiveness. In *Proc. of CHI'98*, ACM (1998).
9. Rodgers, S., and Thorson, E. The interactive advertising model: How users perceive and process online ads. *Journal of Interactive Advertising 1*, 1 (2000).
10. Russell, J. A. A circumplex model of affect. *Journal of Personality and Social Psychology 39* (1980), 1161–1178.
11. Talarico, J. M., Berntsen, D., and Rubin, D. C. Positive emotions enhance recall of peripheral details. *Cognition and Emotion 23*, 2 (2009).

Understanding Researchers' Use of a Large, High-Resolution Display Across Disciplines

Fateme Rajabiyazdi[1], **Jagoda Walny**[1], **Carrie Mah**[1], **John Brosz**[2], **Sheelagh Carpendale**[1]
[1] Department of Computer Science, [2] Libraries and Cultural Resources
University of Calgary
{frajabiy, jkwalny, cmah, jdlbrosz, sheelagh}@ucalgary.ca

ABSTRACT

A driving force behind the design of increasingly large and high resolution displays (LHRDs) has been the need to support the explosion of data in the natural sciences such as physics, chemistry, and biology. However, our experience with an LHRD accessible to researchers across multiple disciplines has shown that they are useful for a wide range of research activities involving large images and data. We conducted in-context, semi-structured interviews with researchers from a variety of disciplines about their experiences using the LHRD with their own data. Notably, it became apparent that the size and resolution of the LHRD supported a multitude of activities related to observation, for which zooming or other enlargement methods on standard resolution screens were not sufficient. The interview findings lead to implications for further research into supporting a broader range of disciplines in using large, high-resolution displays.

Author Keywords

large, high-resolution displays; multi-disciplinary; research support; observation; education; qualitative study.

ACM Classification Keywords

H.5.m. Information Interfaces and Presentation: Miscellaneous

INTRODUCTION

Over the last few years, large, high-resolution displays (LHRD) have become less costly and easier to construct [17] and therefore accessible to a wider population. The resulting displays with pixel counts in the tens of millions allow for more, larger, and higher resolution digital objects, such as images, visualizations, and other types of files, to be viewed at a larger scale and in more detail than on standard displays. LHRDs have been shown to have various benefits, such as supporting team work and analysis of large or complex data [2, 10, 19, 20], where increased performance and satisfaction has been compared to working on typical desktop displays. Most of these benefits have been investigated from the perspective of natural scientists and data analysts working with large, complex datasets [7], and many, though not all, of these studies have relied on examining performance or satisfaction with pre-defined tasks [2, 10, 19, 24, 29].

However, once a new technology becomes available for more widespread use, it often gets used in ways that were not initially expected or intended. To gain a broader understanding of how LHRDs are actually used, we investigate the naturally arising usage of an LHRD "in the wild" that is available to researchers on a university campus. We conducted a qualitative study using in-context semi-structured interviews of researchers working in a variety of disciplines. We found that researchers from many fields of study other than the natural sciences are making considerable use of this display, in particular for observation-based research. Moreover, they are making important, publishable discoveries on the LHRD that they were not able to make with the use of standard resolution displays or projectors.

Our participants' perspective on how the LHRD can support their own research and related activities centered around the themes of immersive observation, observation strategies, collaboration, and education. They also shared with us discoveries they made on the LHRD: verified, publishable discoveries; some fledgling discoveries; and opportunities for design improvements. We discuss how observation was key to the discoveries made, how the size and resolution of the display affected the tasks performed, and the ways in which participants wanted to use the display. These findings lead to implications for further research into supporting this broader range of disciplines in using large, high-resolution displays.

RELATED WORK

There has been a consistent desire to use displays that are bigger and have ever higher pixel counts.This has taken various forms ranging from the development of IMAX and OMNIVAX [22] theatres, to the development of CAVEs [11], and to large, high resolution display walls made up of tiled displays [1]. Within the past two years, NVIDIA and ATI have released commercial graphics hardware capable of creating a composite display that allows 16 individual displays to behave as a single display. This makes it possible to run an LHRD from a single machine, rather than as previously when it was necessary to resort to using clusters of comput-

ITS 2015, November 15–18, 2015, Funchal/Madeira, Portugal.

ACM 978-1-4503-3899-8/15/11$15.00.
Include the DOI: http://dx.doi.org/10.1145/2817721.2817735

ers. Using clusters of computers needs parallelization that makes running "normal" applications challenging.

Task Experiences on LHRDs

Bezerianos and Isenberg [8] studied the perception of angle, length, and area when close to, and far away from, the LHRD, finding that people are more accurately able to compare these variables when further away from the screen than when close or even when moving to and fro. Additionally, lower placed screens seem to feature more perceived distortion than screens at chest height and above. Yost et al. [29] note that LHRDs with pixels in excess of visual acuity require physical navigation to fully explore displayed information. Their study found that even with the extra time required for the physical navigation task, performance was more efficient and in some cases more accurate.

Czerwinski et al. [13] found that the wide field-of-view provided by large displays improves task performance of both men and women and, additionally, narrows the gender gap in performance on the spatial task of navigating a virtual world.

A concern is that the move to LHRDs will enact changes in perception in comparison to visualizations presented in smaller areas on desktop displays. Endert et al. [15] examined how the use of different visual variables (colour, length, slope, and position) causes differences in physical navigation and task performance in front of large displays. They found colour to be a preferred encoding, likely due to its position-independence as well as the ease with which the visual system aggregates colour as one moves further away.

Utilizing LHRD Space

Studies [5, 9] have compared everyday usage of LHRDs to that of standard desktop scenarios for usual applications such as word processing, reading papers, and data analysis. LHRDs were preferred by participants in both sets of studies, noting their strengths in task switching, peripheral awareness, collaborative work [5], rich-information tasks, and enhancement of focus due to the ability to physically separate focal (working) and peripheral (supporting) information [9].

Knudsen et al. [20] performed an exploratory study of large display interaction through groups of two or three using whiteboards. They noted persistent use of space, data comparisons performed both side-by-side (in space) and sequentially through interaction, temporary use of large spaces to select/modify data, use of space to leave a history of analysis, and physical movement to achieve overview (and vice versa to achieve focus).

Andrews et al. [2] completed two observational studies; one comparing the use of space on a standard desktop display to that of an LHRD and the other observing professional analysts' usage of space with an LHRD. From these observations the authors noted the participants' use of space as external memory where full documents were accessed by location and physical navigation of the screen, rather than virtual navigation of the computer's file system. Participants also made use of operations such as ordering, proximity, stacking, and alignment as a flexible semantic layer of information. Andrews and North built upon these findings to develop an application [4] that uses the space in LHRDs to support sensemaking analysis.

Collaborative Work on LHRDs

By increasing resolution and size, LHRDs provide room to lay out, organize, and structure applications or information in general for both individuals and collaborating groups. Guimbretière et al. [16] note that LHRDs are suited for collaboration, bringing a digital interface to the utility of a whiteboard.

Bradel et al. [10] studied pairs of participants engaged in visualization or text analysis tasks. With independent mice and keyboards, participants had the opportunity to work independently or collaboratively. Pairs that collaborated closely shared the display space and produced higher quality results, whereas pairs that worked independently separated the workspace into individual and shared territories. Jakobsen and Hornbæk [19] studied a pair task on a multitouch LHRD. With the close proximity to the screen, participants were able to switch fluidly between parallel and joint work but seemed to share the display without territoriality.

Andrews et al. [3] also raised the question of whether LHRDs with more than 4.35 million pixels are wasting resources. They noted that physical navigation to concentrate on important areas, as well as group collaboration, both provide scenarios where even higher pixel counts remain useful.

Beaudouin-Lafon et al. [7] wrote about the use of their LHRD by experts in a variety of science fields including astrophysics, particle physics, chemistry, molecular biology, neuroscience, mechanical engineering, and applied math. In providing an overview, the authors noted the following common applications of their display wall: navigating a single, very large object (such as a complicated 3D molecule or an extremely large image), comparison of a large number of related visuals (such as photographs or information visualizations), and juxtaposition of data from different sources (e.g., mixes of applications, articles, data tables, notes, and so forth). For our purpose, we conducted a study to investigate how people from various disciplines — including humanities, design, and social sciences — found the LHRD useful in their work. To create a natural and close to real life environment, we allowed our participants to perform self-directed tasks with their own data.

Summary

Investigators [6, 12, 21, 25] have studied how LHRDs are useful in many respects, such as changes in performance of perception, collaboration, and analysis tasks. However, most of these studies follow a predefined procedure, asking participants to perform series of directed tasks, answering the specified questions about interaction performance [23, 6] and the tasks and applications studied [2, 19, 24, 29]. In contrast, our work focuses on naturally arising usage and application of LHRDs in an open, academic setting. In this work, we asked participants to bring their own data, show us their use of LHRDs in a self-directed procedure, and describe their previous experiences using the LHRD.

Figure 1. The 34.5 million pixel display wall used in the study.

STUDY DESIGN

To gain a rich picture of real-world usage and potential of LHRDs, we conducted semi-structured interviews with researchers in context of a mega-pixel display while displaying the researchers own large or high-resolution data. We analyzed these interviews using qualitative methods. Our study goal was to better understand whether there are advantages in the sheer scale of displays: do size (physical dimensions) and resolution (pixel count) hold advantages for people in a variety of disciplines? Since much of the driving force for the creation of these displays has come from the natural sciences, we were particularly interested in investigating whether any possible advantages extend into other disciplines.

Participants

We recruited the 14 participants, who work with high resolution data (large datasets or images bigger than 2 mega-pixels), through word-of mouth and email across the university. Participants were asked to bring large datasets or images that they had explored previously on their typical office displays.

From these 14 participants, there were five females and nine males whose ages ranged between 26 to 66+ years. All participants were university researchers who regularly worked with large digital data. More than half of the participants were professors. We obtained a good interdisciplinary mix with people from a variety of research areas including: Medieval & Renaissance Literature and Art, Multi-resolution Data Vis, Environmental Psychology, Digital Humanities, Ecology Maps GIS, Landscape Visualization, Bio-inspired Design, Medieval Manuscripts, Photography Design, Sociology, Radiology/Psychology, Virtual Reality & 3D Imaging Architecture Planning, Computer Graphics, and Environmental Design.

The LHRD at our academic institution is open to all faculty and graduate students. Some participants had already used the LHRD in their research and were familiar with the general set up and with how their data appeared on the screen, while others were using it for the first time.

Set up

The LHRD is 4.95m X 1.85m and made with 15 rear projection screens. Each projector has a 1920 X 1200 resolution for a total of 34.56 million pixels (9600 X 3600 pixels at 50 DPI). The wall is operated by a single PC with dual Xeon E5505 processors, 96 GB RAM, and four NVIDIA Quadro K5000 GPUs running a Windows 7 operating system. The room was configured as shown in Figure 1, with a wireless keyboard and mouse on a desk. The room offered a quiet working space similar to an office or research space where researchers would ordinarily explore their data. The front of the desk was positioned roughly one meter away from the display. Participants were free to get up and walk around as needed. A variety of applications (e.g., Photoshop, GIMP, Mathematica, Excel, InDesign, Illustrator, ArcGIS, MeshLab, Unity) were installed on the system to allow participants to easily access files with familiar software. This familiar interface and software environment on the LHRD provides an extremely easy transition from standard desktop environments.

Procedure

After showing participants that the LHRD operates like a Windows desktop, we asked participants to put their own data on the screen and to work with and explore it at their own pace (for up to half an hour). Then we started the semi-structured interview portion, asking questions prepared in advance as well as questions based on the participant's data, actions, and responses. Initial questions were structured around three main categories: participants data and how it was used, envisioning tasks on LHRDs, and specific activities participants would undertake when working with their data. Follow-up inquiries explored how participants conducted research, processes they used when working with their data, and any insights and discoveries they had made. We also discussed the participants' experience of looking at their own data on the LHRD, possible tasks they can perform on the display, and any future possibilities with the display. Intentionally, in our study, we did not start by asking our participants to perform any particular tasks; instead, we asked them to describe different "actual" usage of the LHRD for their work and the tasks for which they found the LHRD useful.

Data Collection and Analysis

Two experimenters were present in the interviews at all times and took field notes. We video and audio recorded the interviews. The data was transcribed and then analyzed as follows. First, we identified the main categories together based on the interviews. Second, we used open coding and coded the video transcripts line by line. One researcher independently coded the transcripts and two other researchers coded a subset of the transcripts. After this phase, we cross checked our codes to reach an agreement. From this step, we gathered approximately 500 codes. Working with this extensive list of codes, we used iterative affinity diagramming and group discussions to identify a total of twelve different participant activities. We grouped these activities into four activity classes: immersive observation, observation strategies, collaboration, and education (see Table 2).

RESULTS

Our interviews have shed light on the usage of LHRDs by people in disciplines generally not targeted by LHRD designers and creators: disciplines including the humanities, social sciences, art, and environmental design. None of our participants thought of their data as "big data", which has been imagined to be the most frequent use case for LHRDs [27]. Our participants' data was usually highly detailed image data (10 of 14 participants). We also had a wide range of usage experience with the LHRD ranging from people who had made publishable discoveries; to people for whom the LHRD had become part of their research processes; to people who had little experience with the LHRD, and including people who were bringing their data to the LHRD for the first time. We have speculative comments from all participants, provided in-context of the display while examining their own data, about ways they envisioned using the LHRD. In addition, we have a strong set of experience-based comments from the participants who had used the display in their own work, providing a reliable picture of the benefits they had already experienced from using the display.

We first note the range of disciplines and range of types of data studied because we think that usage across disciplines is an important part of our results. We then show the results of our coding, and list the data insights and discoveries that participants told us about.

Multiple Disciplines and Data Types

Table 1 shows the wide disciplinary spread amongst our participants. Most of our participants work in disciplines outside of the natural sciences. All of our participants had previously used their data on typical office displays (with less than 5 million pixels) or using projectors that had, at best, HD resolution.

Discipline	Data discussed
GIS Librarian	Historical maps
Literature	Old manuscripts
Urban Design	3D city neighborhood models
Computer Graphics	Satellite city photo
Medieval and Renaissance Literature and Art	Paintings & engravings
Urban Design	3D city models and layered city maps
Art	Panoramic photos
Computer Graphics	Large photographs & satellite imagery
Environmental Design	3D models
Art, Design, & Education	Online magazine
Environmental Design	3D modeling
Radiology/Psychology	2D & 3D brain images
Sociology	Network graphs & spreadsheet data analysis
Literature	Old manuscripts

Table 1. Participants' research area and the data type discussed.

	Activities	P1	P2	P3	P4	P5	P6	P7	P8	P9	P10	P11	P12	P13	P14
Immersive Observation	Spatially immersive observation			2		2		1	1	3	2	1			4
	Temporally immersive observation	1	1			1	1							1	
	Double immersion or internalizing data	1	2	1				4		4		2			
Observation strategies	Find common source		2			2									2
	Examine traces	2	4			2									3
	Compare details	3	6	4	6	1	3	3	3	3	1	4	4	4	4
	Assemble & organize	2	2	2		2	3	1	1	2	2			3	3
Collab-oration	Share with groups		3	1				1	2	1				2	1
	Verification among experts		1											3	
Education	Understand patterns & unfamiliar data	1	1			1	1			1					
	Explain work processes	1	1			1	1	2		1		1		6	1
	Make experiences accessible	1	1			1						1			1

Speculated Both Experienced

Table 2. Coding results: Numbers shown are the count of times each participant mentioned the activity. Colours indicate whether mentions discuss activities experienced, speculated upon, or both situations.

Activities on the LHRD

During our interviews, we asked our participants to describe the range and types of tasks they used on the LHRD, noting which they found useful in their work. Since we are interested in both how the LHRD is currently being used and whether new or different interactions might be of interest, we coded both for the interaction they had experience using and those that they speculated about: the ones they were interested in being able to use. Table 2 shows these results. The left column holds the resulting categories for which we coded.

LHRD Aided Discoveries and Insights

Seven of our fourteen participants had either previously, as part of their own research, or during the study made discoveries with the LHRD. For several of these people the discoveries were publishable. They attributed these discoveries to their use of the LHRD because they had previously explored

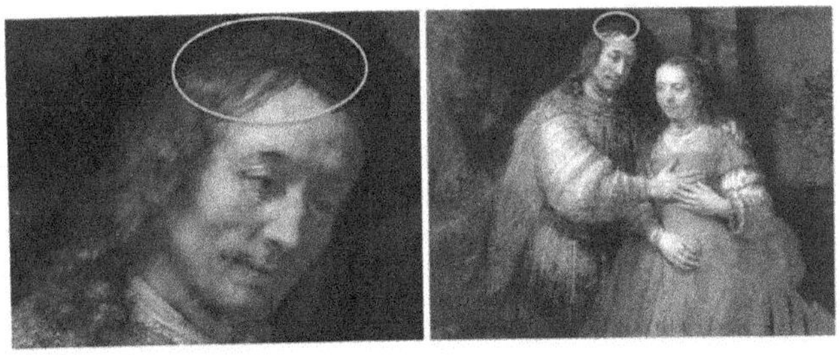

Figure 2. P5 discovered a yarmulke under a hat in *The Jewish Bride* [26].

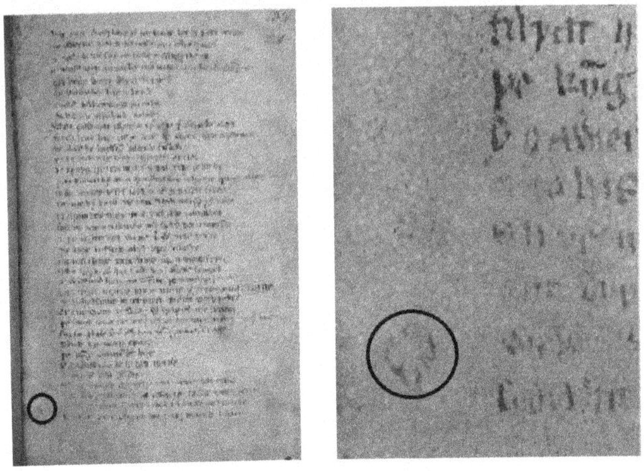

Figure 3. P14 discovered an asterisk in the form of a rose petal on a page of a manuscript. © The British Library Board, Cotton Nero A.x. (art. 3) f. 104/108.

this same data on standard-sized screens in their regular office environments without this success.

The discoveries mentioned to us include:

- Medieval literature and art: A yarmulke hidden under a hat was noticed in one painting, and traces of a mustache on a model across several paintings. This credibly added to the body of evidence that the same model had been used for multiple paintings; the yarmulke (Figure 2) also gave further clues as to the model's identity.
- Medieval literature: On examining old manuscripts, several annotations made on a manuscript were discovered: a manicule, a half-finished manicule that s/he had originally thought was an insignificant scribble, and an asterisk in the form of a rose petal (Figure 3).
- Medieval literature: Another related to the variations in the "aspect" of a manuscript's pages (the particular characteristics of the handwriting across a page), which were qualified as not enough for a separate publication, but said *"it will definitely form a paragraph in our introduction to the online facsimile and therefore constitutes knowledge."*

Besides these publishable discoveries, many participants noticed new aspects of their data, which were intriguing and sometimes useful for their research. These included:

- Digital humanities: A manicule (an annotation in the shape of a hand) was noticed on a manuscript page when s/he was using the LHRD to translate the page from middle to modern English.
- Urban design: Various imperfections in a 3D neighbourhood model s/he had created were noticed and subsequently corrected.
- Computer graphics: New details were noticed in satellite imagery that s/he was using as a reference for 3D models, such as the start point of a sharp slope, a depot in the back yard of a building, and building textures.
- Art: Imperfections in his/her panoramic photographs were noticed.
- Environmental design: The participant felt that s/he developed a better sense of how shade affects pedestrians in a 3D model of a neighbourhood.

DISCUSSION

Our qualitative, interview-based approach uncovers a multifaceted picture of several researchers' actual usage of an LHRD, which, in addition to the purely technical aspects of the display itself, includes aspects of time, environment, and data. We discuss how participants viewed the LHRD's role in supporting multiple aspects of their work: its immersive environment, its support of particular observation strategies, its support of collaboration, and its unique benefits for education.

Immersive Observations

One of the more striking results of our interviews was that two participants had made three publishable discoveries while using the LHRD. These discoveries all involved *seeing things that no one had seen before* in high-resolution photographs of old manuscripts or paintings. There were also many other explicitly mentioned personal discoveries and discoveries that might yet be verified as significant. To better understand the role of the LHRD in these discoveries, we describe how our participants talked to us about observation. Observation was a key concept addressed in every interview. This is not surprising because observation has long been known to be a deeply important process to discovery. Since Aristotle, and perhaps before, scientific discovery has been based on observation. Also, as we have seen in this study, observation is also important to discovery in other disciplines. In their comments there are two levels at which observation is mentioned. In terms of the LHRD, all-encompassing observations, or immersive-observations, are composed of spatial and temporal factors. More specific, detailed observations result from smaller more focused observation strategies.

Spatially Immersive Observations

One potential factor was the *immersive experience* of being in the room with the LHRD. For instance, P5 cited the darkness and isolation of the room as allowing for a different feeling than even being in a museum with a painting: *"in this room we can be very intimate with the great work of art."* He also spoke to the quality of the image: *"...whereas this room can be very dark and we can appreciate pixels."* P14 found the flexibility of spatial arrangement allowed him to better understand differences in *aspect*, which refers to the overall characteristics of handwriting on a line or page. Aspect can differ from scribe to scribe and even based on the tools the scribe is using. Previously, the best way to see differences in aspect was to flip through the pages of the physical manuscript; the LHRD allowed him a more beneficial view of the data: *"Because in the British Library, they are strangely resistant to you pulling the pages out of the manuscript and putting them side by side [laughs]. So we can only do that with imaging. And only when you can look at the whole page can you really get some of these things about aspect, so that's another thing that we've been using this [LHRD] for."*

Temporally Immersive Observations

Another factor may have been that researchers can use the room for a long stretches of time. Although we do not have specific data about how long it took to make these discoveries on the LHRD, we do have some indication of the amount of time tasks such as these take. P5 cited one observation task that involved him spending eight hours looking at one object depicted in a painting before finally seeing relevant details. This is consistent with Bi and Balakrishnan's [9] report that LHRD immersion assisted their study participants in focusing on attentive tasks. This recalls an anecdote about the work of the artist David Hockney, who along with physicist Charles Falco proposed the theory that the sudden transition in realism in paintings in the 1400s was due to the use of optical aids such as the *camera obscura* [18]. Hockney used this technique of long-term observation as part of his discovery process. He arranged print-outs of 400 years of paintings in chronological order on a large wall in his studio, which he called his "Great Wall". In the documentary [28] about his work, he notes, *"the wall was necessary because I could then sit back and scan centuries of Western painting"*. In some ways the LHRD is similar to Hockney's Great Wall, an environment conducive to long periods of detailed observation.

Double Immersion or Internalizing Data

Participants talked about the combined effect of spatial and temporal immersion as internalizing the data. Seeing digital artifacts on the LHRDs was a different experience from seeing them on standard displays. Participants variously described it as "feeling like you are there in the data"(P11), "you can get right up to it"(P9), and being "immersed"(P07). This experience allows participants to internalize patterns and forms inherent to their digital artifacts. For example, while learning to translate medieval manuscripts, P2 displayed them in order to familiarize herself with the way language looked on the page. She said: *"I am not familiar with old English the way that specialists might be, so for someone like me, it was very helpful to have this resource. Because I was so unsure and I had to basically learn the language and what it looks like. And that was impossible for me on my own laptop ... the letters were [so small] you know, and I just couldn't do it. For this, I actually got to the point where to begin with, it was painstaking and took me forever, where in here [the LHRD] I was able to do it a lot quicker and to learn a lot more about the letters, I think, seeing them in a larger format. So it was great that way."*

Observation Strategies

In addition to the high level immersion experienced by participants, they also utilized low level observation strategies to examine and explore their data.

Find Common Source

One task common among the historians we interviewed was to search for commonalities across distinct artifacts. For instance, P5 was searching for evidence that a collection of paintings depicted the same model. He displayed photographs of two paintings and two etchings, magnified the man's face in each one, then pointed out details common to both, such as a faintly visible scar on the man's face, mustache, and shape of nose and chin. These details, particularly the scar and mustache, were difficult to spot at lower magnifications. Similarly, P14 closely examined the details of the lettering across many pages of a manuscript, searching for evidence that the entire text had been written by the same scribe. *"You can take pieces of each of those [pages] and have a word for each that it is the same and see, ok, this is clearly the same writing so it is the same scribe, which is a very interesting finding in medieval literature."*

Examine Traces

Old artifacts frequently have faded, lost ink, or brightness due to the effects of time, dust, and human contact. However, reading and understanding the original traces is valuable for further investigation. Four participants in our study found the LHRD useful for deciphering these traces in their own work. P1 was able to closely follow traces of pencil sketches on an old city map to determine previous planning on the map that could help her in the process of gathering data for urban designers. P2 and P5 adjusted contrast, brightness, and hue (activities that they had previously used on standard displays) to reveal faded, difficult to see details such as identifying Middle English letters (P2) and specific facial characteristics (P5).

In addition, P14 was investigating old manuscripts to find how and by whom they have been annotated. He put up the manuscript on the screen to magnify the details and examine several faded manicules in the manuscripts; meanwhile he found several unexpected manicules he had not seen before. It should be noted that size and high resolution of the screen was the main reason for this finding.

Compare Details

Having access to LHRDs allowed participants to compare multiple items with viewable detail. Although this simple task was common to many participants, there are variations in the way it was actually performed: laying out multiple pages of manuscripts at once, comparing different versions of translations, and zooming in on paintings and searching for details.

The high resolution and large size of the LHRD supported these detailed tasks that involved spotting small differences. For instance, participant P2, was interested in distinguishing "minims", which are similar-looking blackletter-style letters such as *i, m,* or *n*, in a word or sentence. This task was only possible when s/he could see details of the letters set in the detailed context of the word or sentence. She achieved this by magnifying the whole page and changing colour tone to increase the contrast. This task was useful in for translation purposes. De la Flor et al. [14] have studied this type of task of transcribing ancient texts in detail, supporting this task with an overview+plus detail system presented on a standard resolution projector screen. However, they noted issues with the quality of the projection image as well as lack of space to compare images and juxtapose text and notes. Spotting a small difference between artifacts is also a common procedure with scientific data, especially for finding relationships or patterns. For example, the psychology participant, who compared multiple MRI brain images to find relationships between regions of the brain network, says she *"needs to see the context of the brain to see whole region it is in"* which was possible with the large high resolution display.

There also is a reliance on "foot-powered" zooming [2, 20, 21] where details are examined through physical rather than virtual navigation. P13 noted the utility of this zooming mechanism in a collaborative setting *"If I was illustrating to someone I could say look at [the network graph's node] number 19 and I could walk over there .. here is number 19. It's supposed to have three connections, does it? Let's check them."*

Assemble and Organize

Assembling heterogeneous data sources, such as the juxtaposed text and notes mentioned by de la Flor et al. [14], was another common activity noted by other LHRD researchers [2, 7]. Participants mentioned several examples of using the space of the wall to layout and interpret data, creating a single, contiguous presentation from many sources. As stated by P3, *"We are also working on dash boarding and trending information and trying to pull all different components together from four different databases into a single reporting structure. Being able to see the different components and relate the data, I think this would be pretty useful for that."*

Collaboration

Another theme of participants' comments was in making use of the LHRD space and resolution to collaborate with groups for different purposes, including collaboratively solving problems, collaboratively comparing activities during translation and referring to additional materials while translating, and collaboratively viewing data with colleagues for analysis and verification.

Share With Group

Many participants used the LHRD to share artifacts with others in scenarios that require space and high resolution to be able to see details. P14 stated this directly, *"It would be nice if we could bring everyone in here to show them how does it look like on this big screen because sometimes in the points of comparison are not so obvious when you are looking at that little square."* P9 noted that ten years ago for big projects he printed everything out, covering an entire wall. Now, with slide presentations, people lose track once the slides pass, whereas on the LHRD you can display all this information at once.

Another participant, P2, who had come with her colleagues previously, mentioned how their collaboration process changed once they started to use the LHRD. They had been trying to solve problems on their laptops. However, they suddenly realized they could use the LHRD to share the problems' data with everyone and collaboratively solve the problem. This collaborative use may point towards the future potential of LHRD usage once these displays have been more widely spread and the potential usages have been better identified and supported.

Verification Among Experts

Verification among colleagues is also noted as important and this process needs multiple people, sometimes with different backgrounds gathering and comparing various items of data. The LHRD was helpful in these situations for displaying material in a manner that lets everyone to refer to it, P13: *"And also what we really want to do with that is have multiple people on it so to be able to have three people in here and literally to go through every single record and confirm, all three of us confirm, I think that is the same author."*

Education

Education is rarely mentioned in the HCI literature on LHRDs, but our participants in general were enthusiastic about the utility of the display for educational purposes, volunteering many ideas about how they have used or would like to use it for education. While this is not entirely unexpected considering that most of our participants were educators or students, their enthusiasm revealed a desire to share digital artifacts in higher fidelity and at a larger scale than they are currently able in conventional classrooms. Some had already used the screen for educational purposes, both for learning by themselves, for teaching students to analyze paintings, for student presentations, and for sharing research processes and results with graduate students. Others described to us how they intended to use the screen for education or what they thought it would be useful for.

Understand Patterns and Unfamiliar Data

Several participants mentioned that it was their experience that students have a hard time understanding patterns in unfamiliar data, and that being able to show them the entire view of the data while explaining smaller parts was very useful. This was common across design-, process-, and observation-oriented education. One design-oriented researcher, P9, told us that he would like to be able to show students full-scale maps of various city infrastructures: *"I have been working with these sorts of images for 17 years, so for me I can do the zooming in and out on my computer. I have done it so many times that I'm used to it. I paint a mental picture of the whole city but even then it is still hard if you are unfamiliar with the place. But for students it is really hard. So to be able to see the whole screen and show them patterns, that could be a really good teaching tool to be able to do that on the screen."* The usefulness of this sort of situation was confirmed by P2, who you may recall used the LHRD as a student to *"learn how [Old English] looks"* - in other words, to internalize the forms of the "data" - the language - that s/he needed to work with.

Explain Work Processes

There were several comments about the screen being useful for explaining processes to students. P14 used it to explain to a team of graduate students how he had found the manicules in the manuscripts. P13 wanted to bring new researchers in her lab to the room to explain the analysis process they would be using for the data; this would allow all of them to learn the process consistently and simultaneously. P13: *"When we did that project with grad students that was so useful to be able to all look at the data together, it is so much better ... to be able to say does it match does it right over here? We were combining variables, all that stuff, it was really useful."* P7, with the photography background, stated that to find the perfect combination of lenses and sizes, it is important for his students to be able to see the process and compare the results of different combinations, which was possible on the LHRD due to the amount of space.

The resolution of the LHRD allows many people to simultaneously see the details of what is happening on-screen. This can be helpful in the classroom, as noted by P11, who compared the LHRD to the projectors typically used in classrooms: *"Yes, I think if you are doing any sort of demoing, especially with GIS, one of the big failures of ordinary projection is that they can't read anything. Even if you zoom in, they can't read it, it is just blurry."*

Make Experiences Accessible

The screen could also be useful for allowing students to have experiences they otherwise could not have. For instance, it can provide access to paintings or items from a museum in a different city, which students who did not have access to as noted by P5: "*... the impact here is overwhelming because it captures the structure ... [and] the size of the painting on the wall is important, here it is quite good and students can actually relive it.*"

LESSONS LEARNED

In this section, we present the most important lessons we learned about the naturally arising use of LHRDs across multiple disciplines. This includes pointers to as of yet under explored avenues for further research related to LHRDs and the types of interaction that might lead to richer support of research processes in multiple disciplines.

Size Plus Resolution

The size and resolution of the display helped the participants identify details and/or flaws in their data or in general gain more insight about their data. Many of our participants said that there were other options, projectors and LCD panels, for simply viewing their data on large format displays, but that simply the larger format was not sufficient. They needed the size plus resolution. It is important to emphasize that all the data belonged to and had previously been worked with by the participants on standard displays. Consequently the LHRD was an instrumental element of the new discoveries.

Participants also mentioned that it is natural to take advantage of the size of the display to collaborate in a group. For instance, P2 stated: *"I think people don't necessarily know and even when they hear about it, it is like OK you can make the images bigger, it is great, and you don't really think about it in a way of collaborative until you are in here."*

Use of LHRDs in multiple disciplines

Our initial questions centred on whether LHRDs were of interest or in use in disciplines outside of the natural sciences. The answer is a resounding *yes*. Every single one of our participants discussed multiple usage scenarios and saw existing benefits and potential for new benefits to accessing their data on the LHRD. They were able to use the LHRD as a tool to aid in discovery in their research and design processes. Moments of insight occurred multiple times during the interviews suggesting that this technology may be game-changing for work across many disciplines that involve large scale information.

The Process of Observation

A particularly fascinating aspect of this study is that our participants spoke in detail about how the use of the LHRD helped their process of observation. There were two important parts to their observation process: factors that helped to immerse them in their data; and the more specific lower-level observation strategies that they used during observation. The immersive factors were explicitly connected to:

- Size: Factors included seeing data at normal scale, and magnified.
- Local and global detail: Every single participant talked about the importance of being able to see the details; both globally in terms of details in an entire image and locally when zooming to specific areas.
- Time: This interesting factor is not a factor of the display but of the policy around its use: it was relatively simple for researchers to arrange for prolonged access.

In combination these factors produced what some of the participants referred to as a data-immersive experience. The lower level observation strategies included:

- Finding a common source: Several participants find evidence of a common origin some data aspects that might be repeated, perhaps with variations.
- Examining traces: This involved looking for particular details but also often about looking for details of previous human interaction with the data.
- Assembling and organizing: The ability to arrange and rearrange their data played an important role.
- Compare details: The observation strategy was discussed by all participants and included many variations.

Through using these lower-level strategies our participants made many discoveries in their data, some of which have already led to publications. The LHRD provided people with a fresh, immersive experience that helped them to identify details or flaws in their digital artifacts.

Future directions for LHRD Interaction Research

The researchers we spoke to had used and/or planned to continue to use the LHRD as a tool for discovery. Even those using the display for the first time noticed various details in their own digital artifacts that they had not seen before. The impact of the LHRD on expanding knowledge could be comparable to that of magnifying lenses, which, when introduced, allowed people to see their objects of study in a completely different way than previously.

It is particularly interesting that the researchers we spoke to had used — and planned to continue using — the LHRD as a tool for discovery despite the fact that its interaction was essentially that which is available on desktop-sized displays. This limitation of the LHRD to mouse and keyboard was not ideal, as often participants wanted to touch the board to point something out, but the physical transition between the table with the keyboard and the screen was cumbersome. Using regular software such as Adobe Illustrator, which was not designed for such a large screen, was difficult due to exceedingly small interface elements. We acknowledge that there is richer interaction design available than we had access to for our LHRD, such as touch-based interaction [2, 3, 4], gesture-based interaction and multi-device interaction [7].

There are also positives to this set up. It allows people with limited technical backgrounds to easily use familiar desktop software and related interaction mechanisms. The keyboard and mouse on the table as shown in Figure 1 encouraged participants to look at the overview of the screen. This likely led to some of the observed interaction patterns noted previously, such as the foot-powered zooming. Importantly, these limitations did not prevent our participants from finding uses for the display and making discoveries.

Based on these observations, we would like to encourage more interaction design for LHRDs, specifically for the observational practices described by our participants. There is a strong need for better observational tools that support the noted observation strategies. In particular the comparing details activity included many more scenarios than the commonly discussed need for detail-in-context. In comparison to a large-sized display with low resolution or a high resolution, small-sized display, the LHRD provides readily visible access to both detail and context simultaneously. For instance, participants talked about:

- Having access to local details inside a *detailed* context.
- Comparing full details of two or more distinct data images.
- Comparing small parts at full zoom.

Lastly, we do not want to imply that the activities we observed were the only uses of the LHRD, merely that these are additional, underexplored, but real uses.

LHRDs' potential to create rich educational experiences

While some of the researchers we talked to felt they could cope with some of their large data on their own laptops, as they had the experience to develop useful mental models of their data, they were very keen to use the LHRD to aid in sharing their knowledge with others. This potential of the LHRD for educational purposes also opens up new questions for future research. That size and resolution together make it possible to share richer and more detailed digital artifacts with students, enriching the educational experience.

Systems conducive to observation for discovery

We would like to encourage the design and building of systems conducive to observation. We recognize that these are difficult to study because they require long-term use. However, it was clear from our interviews that observation is extremely important to making discoveries across a variety of disciplines, and that this is worth supporting. For our participants, the new perspective provided by the combination of size, resolution, time, and basic tools (image manipulation, zooming, and spatial arrangement) helped make their observation-based discoveries possible. There are bound to be additional, less apparent observation processes at work that could be better supported by LHRD systems.

CONCLUSION

We have presented an exploratory study of the use of large, high resolution displays (LHRDs) across multiple disciplines. We discovered that these LHRDs are successfully being used for research across many disciplines outside the natural sciences. Perhaps most importantly, from our participants we learned that — while they had access to large or high-resolution displays in their labs and offices — it was the combination of a very large display with high resolution that made it worth going out of their way to use the LHRD.

We also learned interesting details about observation strategies, which we hope will motivate new interaction research. These strategies include: looking for common factors, examining traces, flexible assembly and organization, and the importance of comparing details. In particular, our participants valued local details set in global details, comparisons done at full scale, and comparisons done at high zoom. The wide range of people taking advantage of the capabilities of the LHRDs suggests that designing for these displays needs to go beyond considering how scientists and data analysts would use them to include the particular needs of other diverse disciplines.

Our participants gained various types of insights from using the display, including publishable discoveries. They shared their experiences regarding immersion, observation strategies, collaboration, and education. We hope that the clear significance of LHRDs in promoting observation and discovery will encourage more interaction research in this area. We reiterate that it was neither the size nor the resolution on their own that promoted the types of insights and experiences we saw in the use of the LHRD; it was size plus resolution that made the difference.

ACKNOWLEDGMENTS

This research was supported in part by AITF, NSERC, GRAND, SurfNet, and SMART Technologies. We would like to thank our participants and reviewers for the expert knowledge they brought to this project.

REFERENCES

1. Alphonse, G. A., and Lubin, J. Psychophysical requirements for tiled large-screen displays. In *Proc. SPIE*, vol. 1664 (1992), 230–240.
2. Andrews, C., Endert, A., and North, C. Space to think: Large high-resolution displays for sensemaking. In *Proc. CHI*, ACM (2010), 55–64.
3. Andrews, C., Endert, A., Yost, B., and North, C. Information visualization on large, high-resolution displays: Issues, challenges, and opportunities. *Information Visualization 10*, 4 (2011), 341–355.
4. Andrews, C., and North, C. Analyst's workspace: An embodied sensemaking environment for large, high-resolution displays. In *Proc. IEEE VAST* (2012), 123–131.
5. Ball, R., and North, C. Analysis of user behavior on high-resolution tiled displays. In *Proc. INTERACT*, Springer (2005), 350–363.
6. Ball, R., North, C., and Bowman, D. A. Move to improve: Promoting physical navigation to increase user performance with large displays. In *Proc. CHI*, ACM (2007), 191–200.
7. Beaudouin-Lafon, M., Huot, S., Nancel, M., Mackay, W., Pietriga, E., Primet, R., Wagner, J., Chapuis, O., Pillias, C., Eagan, J., Gjerlufsen, T., and Klokmose, C. Multisurface interaction in the wild room. *Computer 45*, 4 (2012), 48–56.
8. Bezerianos, A., and Isenberg, P. Perception of visual variables on tiled wall-sized displays for information visualization applications. *IEEE Trans Vis Comput Graph 18*, 12 (2012), 2516–2525.
9. Bi, X., and Balakrishnan, R. Comparing usage of a large high-resolution display to single or dual desktop displays for daily work. In *Proc. CHI*, ACM (2009), 1005–1014.
10. Bradel, L., Endert, A., Koch, K., Andrews, C., and North, C. Large high resolution displays for co-located collaborative sensemaking: Display usage and territoriality. *Int J Hum-Comput St 71*, 11 (2013), 1078 – 1088.
11. Cruz-Neira, C., Sandin, D. J., and DeFanti, T. A. Surround-screen projection-based virtual reality: The design and implementation of the cave. In *Proc. SIGGRAPH*, ACM (1993), 135–142.
12. Czerwinski, M., Smith, G., Regan, T., Meyers, B., Robertson, G., and Starkweather, G. Toward characterizing the productivity benefits of very large displays. In *Proc. INTERACT*, IOS Press (2003).
13. Czerwinski, M., Tan, D. S., and Robertson, G. G. Women take a wider view. In *Proc. CHI*, ACM (2002), 195–202.
14. de la Flor, G., Luff, P., Jirotka, M., Pybus, J., Kirkham, R., and Carusi, A. The case of the disappearing ox: Seeing through digital images to an analysis of ancient texts. In *Proc. CHI*, ACM (2010), 473–482.
15. Endert, A., Andrews, C., Lee, Y. H., and North, C. Visual encodings that support physical navigation on large displays. In *Proc. GI*, CHCCS (2011), 103–110.
16. Guimbretière, F., Stone, M., and Winograd, T. Fluid interaction with high-resolution wall-size displays. In *Proc. UIST*, ACM (2001), 21–30.
17. Hereld, M., Judson, I., and Stevens, R. Introduction to building projection-based tiled display systems. *IEEE Computer Graphics and Applications 20*, 4 (July 2000), 22–28.
18. Hockney, D. *Secret Knowledge (New and Expanded Edition): Rediscovering the Lost Techniques of the Old Masters*. Viking Studio, 2006.
19. Jakobsen, M. R., and Hornbæk, K. Up close and personal: Collaborative work on a high-resolution multitouch wall display. *ACM Trans. Comput.-Hum. Interact. 21*, 2 (2014), 11:1–11:34.
20. Knudsen, S., Jakobsen, M. R., and Hornbæk, K. An exploratory study of how abundant display space may support data analysis. In *Proc. NordiCHI*, ACM (2012), 558–567.
21. Liu, C., Chapuis, O., Beaudouin-Lafon, M., Lecolinet, E., and Mackay, W. E. Effects of display size and navigation type on a classification task. In *Proc. CHI*, ACM (2014), 4147–4156.
22. Max, N. L. Computer graphics distortion for IMAX and OMNIMAX projections. In *Proc. Nicograph* (1983), 137–159.
23. Robertson, G., Czerwinski, M., Baudisch, P., Meyers, B., Robbins, D., Smith, G., and Tan, D. The large-display user experience. *IEEE Computer Graphics and Applications 25*, 4 (July 2005), 44–51.
24. Shupp, L., Andrews, C., Dickey-Kurdziolek, M., Yost, B., and North, C. Shaping the display of the future: The effects of display size and curvature on user performance and insights. *Human-Comp Interaction 24*, 1-2 (2009), 230–272.
25. Tan, D. S., Gergle, D., Scupelli, P., and Pausch, R. Physically large displays improve performance on spatial tasks. *ACM Trans. Comput.-Hum. Interact. 13*, 1 (Mar. 2006), 71–99.
26. van Rijn, R. H. Isaac and Rebecca, known as 'The Jewish Bride'. Painting, oil on canvas, c. 1665 - c. 1669.
27. Vogt, K., Bradel, L., Andrews, C., North, C., Endert, A., and Hutchings, D. Co-located collaborative sensemaking on a large high-resolution display with multiple input devices. In *Proc. INTERACT*, Springer (2011), 589–604.
28. Wright, R. *David Hockney's Secret Knowledge*. British Broadcasting Corporation [TV Movie], 2003.
29. Yost, B., and North, C. The perceptual scalability of visualization. *IEEE Trans Vis Comput Graph 12*, 5 (2006), 837–844.

BodyLenses – Embodied Magic Lenses and Personal Territories for Wall Displays

Ulrike Kister, Patrick Reipschläger, Fabrice Matulic, Raimund Dachselt
Interactive Media Lab Dresden
Technische Universität Dresden, Germany
{firstname}.{lastname}@tu-dresden.de

Figure 1. ***BodyLenses*** **are body-controlled magic lenses that support parallel work in multi-user scenarios through territoriality (a), can be of various shapes, e.g. body-centric shapes being modified by arm gestures (b), and provide personal tools and clipboards for local interaction on the display (c).**

ABSTRACT

Magic lenses are popular tools to provide locally altered views of visual data. In this paper, we introduce the concept of *BodyLenses*, special kinds of magic lenses for wall displays that are mainly controlled by body interactions. After motivating the rationale for body-centric lenses, we present a comprehensive design space of BodyLenses, where we analyse fundamental aspects such as appearance, function, interaction and use in multi-user contexts. Within that space, we investigated and implemented a number of design alternatives and propose solutions for lens positioning, dynamic shape modification, distance-based parameter mappings and the use of BodyLenses as portable tool belts. We demonstrate the practicality of our novel concepts with four realised application scenarios. With this work, we hope to lay the foundation for future research and systems based on body-driven lenses.

ACM Classification Keywords

H.5.2. Information Interfaces and Presentation: User Interfaces – Interaction styles

Author Keywords

Body-centric interaction; embodied interaction; territoriality; magic lenses; proxemic interaction; co-located collaboration.

ITS'15, November 15 - 18, 2015, Funchal, Portugal.

ACM 978-1-4503-3899-8/15/11...$15.00
DOI: http://dx.doi.org/10.1145/2817721.2817726

INTRODUCTION

Magic lenses [4] are a convenient focus and context technique that present another view onto the data within a local area of interest. They have been used for very diverse tasks in visualisation [36] but are also applicable to many other domains [4].

Large displays are increasingly available and support both the visualisation of large information spaces as well as multi-user scenarios. However, while most magic lens applications in research rely on mouse and keyboard interaction, this is obviously not convenient for display walls and multi-user scenarios. They rather call for more natural user interface techniques. In addition to multi-touch, researchers have analysed mid-air gestures, body movement and body-controlled manipulations [17, 31]. It has been shown that physical navigation, i.e. the actual physical movement of the user in front of a display, improves user performance when navigating information spaces [3]. For collaboration, Tang et al. [34] found that territories on tabletops [29] are transient, a result that Jakobsen and Hornbæk confirmed for interactive high resolution wall displays [18]. Therefore, we believe that a new version of flexible, dynamic territories should be considered.

By creating interactive body-enhanced magic lenses we combine these diverse research topics: We apply the knowledge of body-centric interactions [17, 31], proxemic interactions [14] and the advantages of magic lenses [4, 36] to create *BodyLenses*, flexible work territories with various functions and tools. *BodyLenses* are body-controlled magic lenses that appear when users move in front of a display wall and which follow the users' movements, adapting their properties to the user's motion (see Figure 1b). They can additionally be adjusted through other interaction modalities, e.g. using touch on the display when in close proximity (see Figure 1c).

It is possible to apply our proposed *BodyLenses* in various application scenarios, e.g. for the analysis of bio-medical images, for information visualisation tools, for graph exploration and mind-map creation. In these cases, lens functions can be helpful, e.g. to reduce edge congestion in graphs [35], to apply colour filters to images [12], or to identify and show users' annotations [28]. However, *BodyLenses* are more than magic lenses as users can seamlessly navigate the information space and focus on the data while the tool automatically follows. Moreover, the user can navigate not only along the display, but also towards and back from the wall display. This can be used to transition between different parametrisations of the lens function, e.g. to switch between different levels of contrast when looking for possible tumours in an MRI image. Further, in multi-user scenarios, users are made aware where and what collaborators are currently working on, thanks to their *BodyLenses* (see Figure 1a). Also, the personal properties of the lens allow access to personalised tools or items from individual collections. In collaborative mind-map or brainstorming activities, for example, users can add previously prepared sketches from their lenses.

In this paper, we contribute the concept of *BodyLenses* unifying aspects of magic lenses [4, 36] with territoriality [29], personal tools and proxemics [14]. We introduce the characteristics of *BodyLenses* and define the concept in the next section. This is followed by a thorough analysis of the design space based on prior work as well as our own contributions. We suggest several novel concepts derived from the design space that have not been covered in the literature and present our own practical investigations of the field: We examine different possible *BodyLens* shapes and manipulations of the lens as well as the modification of its parameters using the distance between users and the wall display. We further extend the concept of body-controlled magic lenses by including a tool belt for all kinds of manipulations within the lens and personal clipboard areas. We implemented these novel concepts in four prototype applications that incorporate the discussed scenarios. Finally, we explore various challenges and research question that arise when working with *BodyLenses*.

BODYLENS CONCEPT

We first describe the basics of the *BodyLens* concept by discussing its background in magic lenses and body-controlled interaction. Then, we introduce and define the term *BodyLens* and characterise these body-enhanced lenses.

Background

The concept of magic lenses, as introduced for user interfaces by Bier et al. [4], describes an arbitrarily shaped area where filters can be applied to present another view onto the data of that region of interest. These filters can be any selection or alteration of the data or its view, e.g. a distortion of all or parts of the selection (e.g. [1, 5]) or a revelation or reduction of information (e.g. [22, 35]). This principle has been used for various application contexts, tasks and data types. They have recently been summarised for information visualisation in a comprehensive survey by Tominski et al. [36]. The interactive quality of the lens that allows selecting different parts of the data set, while typically leaving the context visualisation

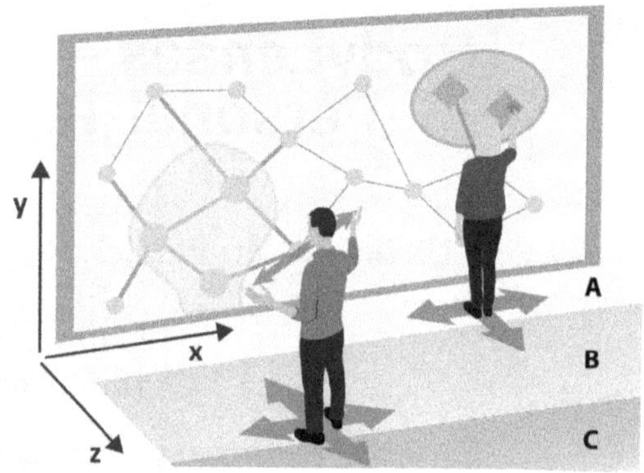

Figure 2. Conceptual depiction of the *BodyLens* interaction space. In a seamless way, users can move in front of the display, perform mid-air gestures and interact directly on the screen to control the lenses.

unchanged, makes it a very convenient tool for exploration for very diverse application cases.

So far, lenses have been mainly controlled in desktop environments using mouse interaction (e.g. [1, 35]), but they have also been implemented for touch-enabled tabletops (e.g. [19, 21]) or made tangible and spatially-aware [32]. In this paper, we use the *body* as the main input device to control the lens, which is what characterises our *BodyLens* concept. Similar to magic lenses, body-centric interaction has been extensively studied in the literature. Embodied interaction for wall displays is the focus of design space analyses conducted by Shoemaker et al. [31] and Müller et al. [24], but those research efforts do not address the specific case of lenses. Using the body's shadow as a magic lens has been proposed very shortly by Shoemaker et al. in their work on shadow reaching [30]. However, we call this idea into being, considerably extend it and generalise the concept. We combine principles of territoriality [29] and magic lenses [4, 36] to form a new concept using both (mid-air) movement of individual body parts as well as proxemic dimensions [14], such as distance and movement. Additional interaction modalities, e.g. touch and pen, are used to manipulate the lens' parameters. While these individual components are known, we unify them and, with *BodyLenses*, provide a coherent local tool for the flexible exploration and manipulation of information spaces, thereby also creating adaptable personal territories for users.

Definition and Characteristics

We define the term *BodyLens* as any type of personal, body-controlled magic lens used on a vertical display. Thus, the *magic lens* can apply any function to a user-centred region of interest, including selection, zooming, focus+context, advanced visual modifications, or semantic changes to the data. "*Body-controlled*" refers to a) any type of body movement with regard to the fixed display as well as b) gestures of any body part – most prominently arms and hands, but also head, legs and feet – and any combinations thereof. Furthermore, provided the display is an interactive surface, c) direct interaction *on* the display is also possible, e.g. by means of multi-touch, pen or tangible input. While horizontal movements along the wall display typically influence the position of the lens, distal movements, body gestures and direct interactions may influence any other parameter associated with the lens.

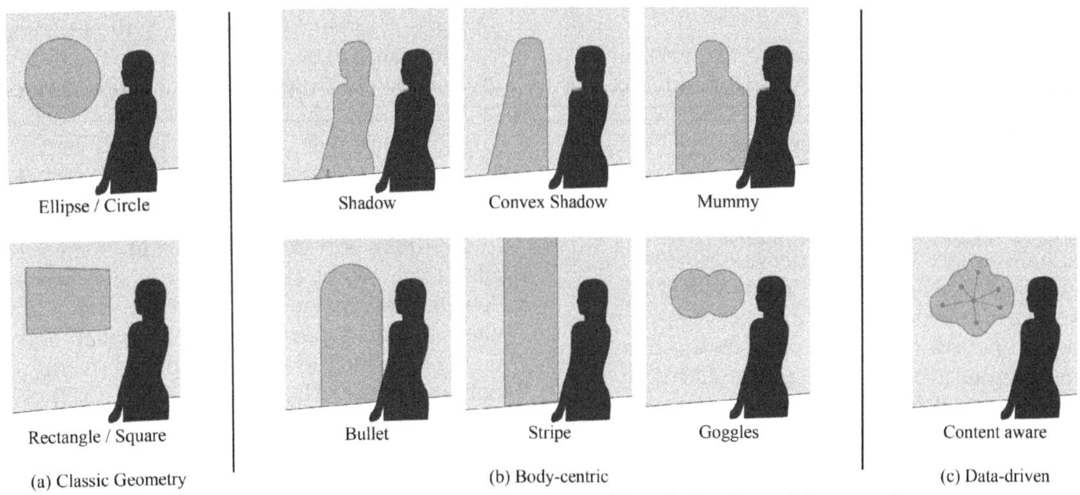

Figure 3. Three categories of *BodyLens* shapes with typical and promising examples.

We believe that the combination of the human body and a magic lens is more than a simple mapping of novel means of interaction to well-known functions. A *BodyLens* is indeed not just a filter, but also a personal tool and a work territory. *BodyLenses* support effortless, *implicit* navigation within an information space as they automatically move with the user. They can also be adjusted *explicitly* using either direct manipulation, e.g. touch on the display, or mid-air gestures. In multi-user contexts, the lens function alters a local view into the data space, not disturbing other users. Additionally, the lens presents a personal territory that supports mutual awareness and fosters collaboration. Through personalisation we also support individual tools along the lens, private annotations and ownership of associated elements.

BODYLENS – DESIGN DIMENSIONS

Both magic lenses and body-centric interaction have been extensively studied in the literature. The design space we propose here extends that prior work and establishes a general frame of reference for body-centric interactive lenses in a variety of contexts. We divide our exploration of the space into four main dimensions: *appearance, function, interaction* and *multi-user contexts*. They are described with their properties in the following sections using examples from prior work when relevant aspects are covered.

Appearance

The appearance of a *BodyLens* refers to its characteristic visual features, specifically position on the display, shape and rendering effects. The most common representations of magic lenses are detailed in [36].

Position

The choice of the position of the lens on the display with respect to the user's body, i.e. the anchor point of the lens, is an important design aspect. Perhaps the most obvious materialisation of a *BodyLens* is a circle or a rectangle roughly centred at eye-level of the user (Figure 3a). If such a lens is mapped to the user's physical movement in front of the screen, it can only move horizontally, since the user's head remains at the same height. Therefore, additional means have to be devised to also allow the lens to move vertically and to enable 2D positioning in the whole screen space. This problem can be avoided at the cost of additional space monopolised by the lens, if the latter is made to span the entire height of the display, e.g. by using vertical stripes (Figure 1a). Such kind of lenses might be particularly appropriate in multi-user scenarios, where each person working on the display occupies a dedicated personal territory delimited by such a band.

Shape

The shape of magic lenses is typically round or rectangular, but they can also have arbitrary silhouettes either explicitly determined by the user (e.g. with a sketch) [5, 20] or by the underlying data [16, 26]. Those types of shapes are of course also applicable to *BodyLenses*, where the contours can be dynamically modified using body gestures (see *Interaction*).

Beyond the classic examples, other forms more specific to body-centric lenses are conceivable. A *BodyLens* can be considered as a kind of augmented shadow, with the lens contour more or less matching that of a virtual shadow cast by the body on the display (e.g. [30]). "True shadow" *BodyLenses*, i.e. lenses, whose outline exactly mirrors the contour of the user's body, presumably find more relevance in artistic installations or games such as [6, 9]. *BodyLenses* as virtual user embodiments might also be useful for collaborative telepresence [40] and to represent personal spaces [11]. For co-located computing tasks, however, in particular information visualisation applications, the projected shape of the human body may not constitute an adequate view space for magnified or filtered data. Thus, for those contexts, body-based lens shapes are likely to take more organic or geometric forms, e.g. vertical stripes or bands, whose width roughly corresponds to that of the body (as in [8]), to vertically elongated ellipses or other oblong shapes.

In Figure 3, we propose a number of typical *BodyLens* shapes that designers may choose to use in their applications, ranging from conventional formats such as ellipses and rectangles (a) to more body-centric silhouettes such as convex shadows, mummies, stripes etc. (b), without forgetting data-driven, content-aware shapes (c). We elaborate on practical aspects of some of those proposed shapes further below.

Rendering Effects

Various rendering effects can be applied to the inner area as well as to the borders of lenses. Borders, for instance, can be fully rendered (thus mimicking real lenses) or they can be implicit, i.e. the lens area is determined and visualised only by the filtered content within or outside its bounds. Smooth transitions between focus and context can also be introduced, similar to soft vs hard shadows and Sigma Lenses [25], which use time and translucence to smooth transitions between the filtered content and the surrounding non-modified context. Similarly, the area within the lens can exhibit various degrees of opacity and filling patterns, e.g. a translucent image of the user, depending on whether the lens should strictly display processed content or also fulfil other purposes (such as providing visual feedback for awareness).

3D BodyLenses

While this paper mainly focuses on *BodyLenses* in 2D spaces, the concept can readily be extended to 3D. In virtual 3D worlds and augmented reality scenarios, the user's body can conceivably act as a 3D *BodyLens* that selectively filters volumetric information in the target space. In such contexts, the standard shapes of 2D lenses, i.e., ellipses and rectangles, respectively become ovoids and cuboids that "cut through" chunks of volume data (3D magic lenses [37]). Similar to vertical stripes that stretch from the bottom to the top of the display, 3D stripes or cuboids mapped to the user's physical position can extend completely across one or more dimensions (that is, not only height, but also depth) to cover infinite 3D slices, and hence reduce the need for physical movement or additional interactions to reach distant areas within the 3D space. Closer to embodied representations still, one can also conceive of a 3D avatar-lens of the user (the 3D version of a shadow) that performs truly body-based 3D-filtering operations through the volumetric information space.

Function

The function of the *BodyLens* is the operation that is performed on the selected data. Most lenses are used for visualisation purposes [36], the most prominent example being magnification (with a variety of scaling styles) emulating a physical lens. Zooming lenses allow finer details of objects within the magnified region to be observed, but they can also allow more precise interaction with the content within that zone [1, 19, 27]. Such kinds of scenarios are well suited for *BodyLenses*, since the body naturally provides an interaction area within which the user can perform fine-grained (multi-)touch and/or pen operations on the screen. In case the *BodyLens* is entirely controlled by body (torso) or head movements, the user's hands and fingers can fully devote themselves to the main task, as they are not required for (re-)positioning the lens. An immediate extension of that concept for lenses, whose source data and visualisation view are decoupled, is reaching assistance, that is local lenses used as proxies to interact with physically distant or unreachable elements [13].

Further popular uses of visualisation lenses are to provide different views of the underlying data, i.e. filters [33], and to isolate desired items inside the lens (e.g. node links in graphs [21]). Most lenses modify the elements inside them, but they can also be used as samplers to modify the surrounding content [12]. Again, *BodyLenses* can be directly utilised in those cases, e.g. as "magic shadows" that offer alternative visualisations of data within their body-based bounds [30] or to uncover portions of a hidden image overlapping with the user's body passing in front of the display [8, 9].

Lenses often provide tools to modify their functional parameters (e.g. zoom factor) or to manipulate their associated content. In this sense, interactive lenses also function as convenient tool palettes. The individual tools can be placed on the lens itself as semi-transparent overlays (as in the initial toolglass interface [4] and in [11, 31]) or attached to its edges [21]. Thus, a *BodyLens* can have a tool belt that hugs its contour, so that the tools remain constantly at the user's fingertips as they follow him/her around when s/he moves to different areas of the workspace (Figure 6).

Interaction

Interaction here deals with manipulation of *BodyLenses* themselves and their generic properties and not with the underlying data, which is task-specific. The design space of the former is however obviously influenced by the gestural vocabulary of the latter, as the two have to form a coherent and conflict-free whole in the final application. In principle, we can differentiate between fine-grained, finger-based interaction *on* the screen (such as multitouch or pen input) and coarse input through whole-body movements and arm or hand gestures *in front* of the display, with possible transitions between both types of input.

Position control

As introduced above, the standard mapping of body motion to a lens is to couple the user's physical position in front of the display to the location of the lens on the screen. In such a configuration, the *BodyLens* follows the user like a shadow as s/he moves in front of the screen. There are several ways in which that mapping can be realised. Depending on the shape of the lens and the application requirements, a simple unidimensional mapping along the x-axis (Figure 2) suffices [8, 9, 38]. If the lens needs to be steerable over the entire 2D coordinate space of the screen, movement along the y-axis also needs to be supported. One way to achieve this that we propose is to map the user's distance from the display to vertical movements (Figure 4a). Other approaches include using gaze direction [2], head tilt or arm gestures (see below), depending on the availability of those interactions for lens operation. Further, the moving element might not be the lens, but the content underneath, e.g. a "cockpit view" with a fixed lens where the background changes according to user movement. In further applications, both the location of the lens and of the data on the display might be simultaneously modifiable, for instance, when the lens view is decoupled from its source data.

Shape control

While position is likely the most obvious parameter of a *BodyLens* that the user's body can control, embodied interactions may also govern other attributes of the lens, including and especially its shape. In Figure 3, we presented a number of examples of typical *BodyLens* shapes. Some of those shapes, such as the shadows, continuously change by nature. The other more geometric forms can also be modified by appropriate body gestures. For example, one of the interactions that we propose for stripe-shaped lenses is to allow their width to be increased by stretching the arms sideways, thereby expanding the area covered by their function. For more organic shapes, the arms can be used to punch bulges in the lens contour to stretch it in desired directions, similar to sculpting gestures used in BodyAvatar to grow virtual limbs [39]. To ensure that the lens size does not constantly change with any arm movement, an explicit hand pose can be required for shape-modifying interactions. Our contribution includes implementations of several dynamic shape-modifying techniques, which we describe further below.

Distance mapping and proxemics

The ability of users to move freely in the physical space in front of the wall display to control a *BodyLens* is at the heart of its interaction paradigm. We have seen that such control can be based on a simple unidimensional mapping along the x-axis to allow the lens to follow the user like a shadow, or that it can also involve user movement towards and away from the display, i.e. along the z-axis (see Figure 2), to allow it to move vertically on the screen. Depth movement can also be used to modify other lens parameters, especially that of the filter function via which the target data is viewed. While not explicitly making use of magic lenses, there are examples in the literature, in which user-to-display distance has been used to modify zoom [15], detail [10] and abstraction [22] levels of visual data. Depending on the function and the parameter to modulate, the distance-to-variable mapping can be continuous or discrete. While the former associates a variable with continuous values to the distance between the user and the screen (e.g. zoom factor), the latter often implies the partition of the physical space in front of the display into several zones corresponding to different discrete states of the variable (e.g. layer type). We discuss novel distance-based functional mappings for *BodyLenses* in more detail in the next section.

Distance-based *BodyLens* interactions can also be designed to mirror interpersonal engagement, based on familiar spatial relationships governing social interactions, a principle known as proxemics [14]. Thus, following the observation that approaching a person or a device signifies an increasing interest in interacting with that entity, *BodyLenses* can be made to progressively react to users nearing the display following a gradual engagement design pattern [23]. Perhaps the most straightforward realisation of that pattern is a progressive fade-in of the lens as the user comes closer to the screen. When the lens is completely materialised, further distance-based interactions controlling a functional parameter can be performed, as described above. If the display detects contact input as well, a further "at-the-wall" stage might exist, where users can directly operate lenses and content on the screen using touch, pen or tangible interactions.

Multi-User Contexts

Another important dimension to consider is the number of lenses and users interacting simultaneously. We can differentiate between single-user and multi-user scenarios which include parallel individual and collaborative work. For instance, with multiple active lenses, users have the possibility to overlap them to combine their effects. Examples using classic lenses include operation composition in collaborative visual queries [20] and, in the case of personal lenses with user-specific IDs, sharing of private spaces [28, 31]. Adapted to *BodyLenses*, those applications could rely on multi-user embodied interactions to collaboratively create compound lens functions and grouped spaces. Thus, *BodyLenses* that completely or partially merge through concerted user actions can form common embodied territories with shared properties and elements, e.g. a coalesced convex shadow lens within which users work together on a common task. Thanks to the very dynamic nature of *BodyLenses*, ad hoc groups with temporarily joint territories can be quickly formed and split as users move towards and away from each other. This scenario can be viewed as an application of F-formations [23] and more generally of proxemics [14].

Multiple non-overlapping lenses (and therefore presumably also *BodyLenses*) have notable benefits in InfoVis situations where visual datasets need to be viewed side by side and compared, with the help of dynamically varying filter functions. An example of such parallel body-based data view control (albeit not through lenses per se) is presented in [10]. Extended to flexible and versatile *BodyLenses*, this paradigm allows groups of people to collaboratively examine multiple arbitrary facets of a common dataset through vignettes that can be freely moved, scaled and adapted using natural proxemic and body-driven interactions (Figure 4).

A further advantage of *BodyLenses* in multi-user contexts is their ability to provide mutual awareness. Much like digital shadows, which are known to possess that property [30], *BodyLenses* that follow the user continuously indicate his/her current locus of attention (i.e. "I am currently working on the content in that lens"). Those moving lenses are noticed by the other collaborators, who can then adapt their behaviour accordingly. As with shadows and visual feedback reflecting users' motions and postures, we imagine that the awareness benefits of *BodyLenses* particularly manifest themselves in co-located situations, in which users interact in a contactless manner with the display. This is likely true to an even greater extent in remote collaboration conditions, where the lack of physical co-presence of other participants needs to be further compensated (similar to what virtual embodiments achieve for remote collaborative whiteboard applications [40]). In such settings, the lens would therefore function both as a tool to interact with the data as well as a mechanism to maintain mutual awareness between workers (co-located or remote).

Finally, we mention a particular category of multi-user scenarios in which the user's body plays a role not only as input to control a *BodyLens*, but also as a physical obstacle in front of the display. Those cases occur particularly in situations, when privacy needs to be safeguarded in (semi-)public environments. Specifically, the body blocks access to other people in the vicinity, while the lens creates a confined view of the private content that can only be visualised by the owner [7].

NOVEL CONCEPTS AND PRACTICAL INVESTIGATIONS

Based on our design space already including several suggestions that advance prior work, we implemented a number of application prototypes. They serve as examples for the feasibility of our concepts and demonstrate the potential of *BodyLenses*. Several HCI experts regularly provided feedback during our iterative development process, leading to a number of novel concepts which, to the best of our knowledge, have not been reported before. Those concepts are introduced below along with a more in-depth exploration of the dimensions of *BodyLenses* and solutions for some of the practical challenges that we faced.

We address adjustment of dynamic shapes to the user's position and pose as well as the mapping of their distance to the wall to various properties and parameters of the lens, as we see these aspects as the main differentiators between magic lenses and *BodyLenses*. We also explore the role of the lens as a personal territory and tool belt with menus and clipboards. We end this section by discussing open research questions.

Applications and Implementation

We implemented four applications derived from the scenarios presented in the introduction, which we then use for our practical investigations. As magic lenses have been proved valuable tools for information visualisation, we implemented 1) a graph explorer with various lens functions derived from this background, e.g. *Local Edge*, *Bring Neighbours* and *Fisheye* [35]. For multi-user brainstorming, we further developed 2) a mind mapping tool that allows creation and manipulation of items using personal lens territories. Further, 3) an image analysis tool allowed us to investigate the application of body-enhanced lenses with different colour filters and optical zoom lenses. Finally, we also implemented 4) a small artistic application that explores the casual exploration of proxemic dimensions and gestural interaction to create a dynamic piece of art. Our prototypes show the variety of possible usage scenarios for *BodyLenses* and feature various shapes from our proposed design space. We will further elaborate the important aspects and challenges in the next sections.

Similar to previous work [22, 23, 24], we divide the area in front of the wall into multiple zones (Figure 2). In our particular setting, we label the area closer than 0.5 m to the wall as "touch-interaction zone" (A). The area from 0.5 m to roughly 2.5 m is the main zone for body-centric interaction ("body-interaction zone", B). Beyond 2.5 m the user is considered outside of the interaction zone (C) and no *BodyLens* is created or the existing lens fades out.

The prototypes were developed in Python using libavg[1] framework for visualisation. Our setup consists of an interactive display wall of 4.86 m in width and 2.06 m in height (frame at 2.3 m), with a resolution of 7680×3240 pixels. The movements and body of each individual user is tracked using a Kinect One[2] fixed to the ceiling at the back, i.e. behind the users facing the wall.

[1] http://www.libavg.de
[2] http://www.kinect.com

Dynamic Shapes

In our design space, we identified several different shapes for the lenses (Figure 3), divided into three categories. We implemented a selection of them for our prototypes which enables us to investigate multiple levels of embodiment (for some results, see Figure 4). Specifically, we created the elliptical and rectangular shapes (classic geometries), content aware shapes (data-driven), as well as the stripe, bullet, convex shadow and mummy shapes (body-centric). These lenses were used to various degrees in the prototypes. All shapes were tested with the graph explorer while the artistic application was designed for the stripe shape.

Body-driven lens movement

When users step in front of the wall, a new *BodyLens* is created in correlation to the user's position, which follows whenever users move. As previously discussed, our proposed default mapping positions the lens to encompass the area in front of the user at eye level. The lens movement is closely coupled to the central body motion of the user (i.e. the torso) on all axes. For geometric and content-aware shapes, the lens is centred at the user's shoulder position, while the body-centric shapes present a widened shadow in front of the user. When in the "touch-interaction zone", users can drag the lens on the screen, which creates an offset relative to their current position. This offset is maintained when users move, thus allowing them to easily reach top or bottom areas of the display across its entire length. When the distance to the wall is too large for touch interaction, one of the solutions we propose to control the vertical position of the lens is to use up-and-down hand movements. When users are within the "touch-interaction zone", the lens is frozen and its position no longer coupled with their movement. This enables working on details of the data and avoids jitter. Users may still drag the lens while it is frozen.

Body-driven shape adjustments

Depending on the type of shape that is used and the current goal of the user, there are several ways in which the shape of the lens may react to the user's movements. The shape of the lens can be adjusted **implicitly** by using the user's current pose. If, for example, the user raises a hand to access some data, the shape may bulge outward at that location, mimicking the user's movement. The lens may also react in a more subtle way as the relation between body parts changes during movement. However, in most scenarios the user focuses on the underlying data, not on the lens itself. Therefore, the closely coupled shapes might not be suitable. We strongly reduced lens shape movements in our prototypes by not considering the very active body parts, e.g. hands or fingers, but the more body-centric movements (the torso). This further supports the active movement of hands for touch interaction.

Users can also **explicitly** change and adapt the lens shape to include or exclude data. For this, we propose a grabbing gesture, which consists of raising the arms and closing the hands in mid-air. To provide feedback, the shape becomes highlighted and can then be modified as the shape's border is "attached" to the user's fist. For the stripe shape, only horizontal movement is possible, which widens or shrinks the stripe.

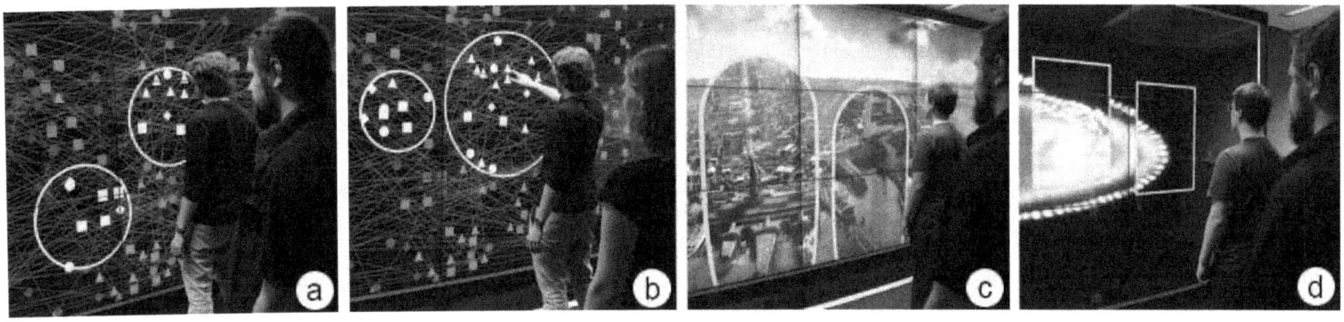

Figure 4. User's *distance* to the display changes a) vertical position of the lens, b) size of the lens, c) function parameter (here: zoom), or d) visualisation parameters (here: selected time steps).

All implemented classic geometric shapes allow adjustment in both horizontal and vertical directions. Embodied shapes can similarly be altered by bulging the contour when grabbing their border and moving the hands. Clutching is possible when the user re-opens, moves and re-forms the fist.

One of the main challenges while implementing this functionality was the placement of the Kinect to guarantee robust tracking of all users. As the recognition is best when the Kinect is placed in front of the user, integrating it directly into the wall (as in [9]) would give the best results. This, however, was not possible in our setup. Placing the Kinect above or below the wall results in unreliable recognition because of the steep angle. Thus, we decided to place the device behind the users, who face the wall. This results in reliable tracking, but makes the detection of certain gestures such as closed fists more difficult.

Mappings of User-to-Wall Distance and Movement

While movement along the wall is tightly coupled with the horizontal position of the lens, the distance can be mapped more freely and in interesting ways. In the following, we propose a number of promising mappings, that we investigated and implemented within our application scenarios.

Mapping distance to lens features

From the design space, we derived four categories of lens control based on distance-mapping: mapping to a) lens position, b) lens properties, c) lens function parameters, and d) visualisation parameters. The suitability of those mappings depends on the application context and task as well as user preferences.

The user's distance to the display can be used to change the **vertical position** of the lens, moving it up and down by stepping forward or backward (see Figure 4a). This way, all areas of the display can contain data and can still be explored by the user through the lens. However, the mapping should always ensure that the lens is at eye-level when moving at arm-distance to the wall, so that manipulations using touch are still possible. In our implementation, the user can move the lens up and down when far from the wall. When stepping closer to the wall, the *BodyLens* returns to eye-level.

Different **lens properties** can be controlled by changing the distance to the wall. We define a lens property as any parameter of the lens that is independent from its currently selected function or content. One example is the mapping of the distance to the *size* of the lens, i.e. the width and height of a geometric shape, the width of a stripe, or a factor to enlarge a body's mapped shadow. However, different mappings and factors to manipulate size are possible: 1) When stepping back from the wall, the lens becomes larger, thus increasing the spatial coverage of the lens function. This type of mapping coincides with the notion of considering the lens as a shadow with the light source behind the user [31]. 2) Alternatively, we can consider the lens as a tool for the data in front of the user. Here, users standing in front occlude, and thereby occupy, more data than users in the back. Hence, when stepping back, the lens area becomes smaller (Figure 4b). This also coincides with the fact that by stepping back we assume that the user's intention is to get an overview of the data, focusing more on the context, not the lens and its focus area. As with the mapping type, however, its direction may be very dependent on task, context and user preferences.

The lens function itself may also have certain parameters, which can be adjusted, e.g. the zoom level of a lens (Figure 4c). It is possible to map these **parameters of the lens function** to the distance from the wall. A useful application for this are for example lenses for graph visualisations as mentioned above, or a semantic zooming lens: By stepping closer to the wall, nodes expand and the user can see more details. In our small artistic installation, we use lenses to paint and manipulate colour stripes on the screen. Here, the distance changes the colour of the user's stripe. Based on our implementation, we suggest that when the lens is used not only for exploring but also to manipulate content, it is essential to choose a distance at which the user can simply look at the result without changing it. For the art installation, we additionally use a dwell time before any stripes are painted onto the display.

Finally, general **visualisation parameters** of the data can be influenced by the user's distance to the wall. One example is the mapping of the third dimension of the information space to the distance, so that movement from and towards the display actually maps to depth movement in the *3D virtual space*. This way, we propose the local exploration of arbitrary slices of volumetric or spatial data by using *BodyLenses*. Another important dimension in today's big datasets is the special property of *time*. Data such as the measurements of traffic behaviour or the development of a tumour are often analysed with respect to time. Comparing different time steps with each other and slicing through these time-dependent data sets are essential tasks during analysis. In our image analysis prototype, we map the user's distance from the wall to the time dimension. To the best of our knowledge, we are the first to propose this mapping of body movement to time. It allows the user to individually select a desired time frame, which can often be changed only globally. This further supports parallel work on the whole data set (Figure 4d).

Selecting the direction of the mapping

In our observations, we found that even for the simple case of zooming, some users prefer having the detailed view close to the wall and the less detailed view from afar, supporting the assumption that stepping back equals focusing on the context, while others preferred seeing the details from afar, helping them to better compare them to the context data. Hence, it is not only the application designer's selection that should be considered, but also the personal embodiment character of the lens and therefore users' individual preferences. This can be specifically supported when including user identification, e.g. by using the Kinect, or other biometric approaches, such as the hand contour [28].

Comparing different slices of the visualisation

To compare different slices of the data, a user will generally move back and forth within the visualisation dimension. For example, when time is mapped to the distance to the wall, the user can compare different time cuts by moving towards the display. To see multiple slices of the data at the same time, users can work cooperatively, with each user selecting a value of the dataset to be compared, as implemented in our prototypes. Conceptually, users can also freeze their lens and create a second one to compare two different slices of the visualisation.

Compensating visual shrinking at larger distances

Previously, we discussed using the distance to the wall to change the function, e.g. to create other views onto the data, and imply the user's intentions, e.g. to see details when stepping closer. However, when stepping back, e.g. slicing through time, elements seem smaller from further away. To be able to still properly compare these layers, it is important that users see the same amount of detail and content that they saw before from close by. Hence, we contribute the concept of automatically enlarging the *BodyLens* and the elements within to compensate for the user's movement. Thus the user *perceives* the content to be always the same size (see Figure 5) regardless of the distance, which is used to control another parameter like time.

Reachability of all areas of the wall

A problem that arises when working with body-controlled lenses on and in front of a display wall is the reachability of certain areas of the wall. This especially concerns the upper areas, which might not be reachable because of the user's size, and the lower areas, as kneeling down might be uncomfortable or inappropriate. For example, the top of our wall display is at roughly 2.3 m, which can be unreachable even for people of average height. This reachability problem arises for any shape that does not cover the complete height of the wall, i.e. all but the stripe shape in our selection. We implemented four alternatives in our prototypes, that we found promising

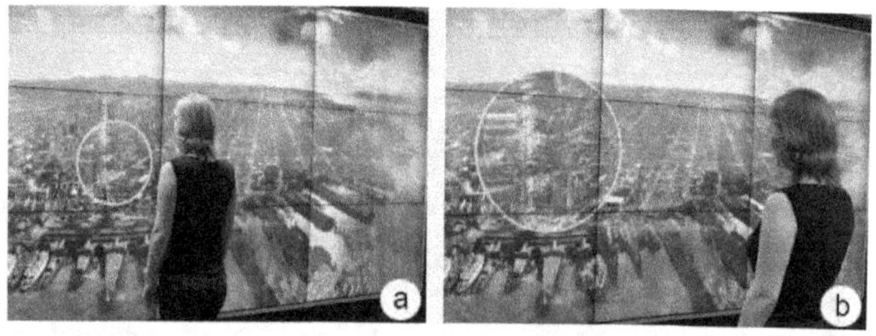

Figure 5. The lens is compensating the distance of the user by enlarging its content so that it appears to be the same size.

in addressing this problem: It is possible to 1) use the hand motion to move the lens up and down. The user can also 2) resize the lens to reach the upper or lower part of the display. Alternatively, it is possible to 3) set an offset by dragging the lens using touch, which is maintained upon moving in front of the display. Finally, the height can be influenced by 4) the user's distance from the wall. We believe the whole subject of reachability for wall displays is an interesting question for future research.

BodyLens as a Personal Tool Belt and Clipboard

The *BodyLens* is not only a tool in itself, it can also provide additional tools depending on the current task and context. For network manipulation, tools for node or edge creation might be necessary. Similarly, our mind-map application requires tools for creating and manipulating items (see Figure 1c). We suggest **personal tool belts** as a means to arrange and access these menus and tools attached to a lens. Thereby the lens becomes a user's personal territory for work on the mind-map. In accordance to the *BodyLens* concept, tool belts will move implicitly with the user. In previous work menu icons or applications were placed within a user's shadow [11, 31]. As we apply this concept to *BodyLenses*, the content within that shadow is very important. Hence, in our implementation, we found placing menus and tools at the border to be beneficial as it enables the content of the lens to be entirely visible (Figure 6a). The selection of required tools is dependent on the role, current task or general preference of the user. If the system supports user identification, content created within a lens can be associated with a specific user. This means not only the tools but also the content can be personalised and highlighted per user, which we also investigated in our prototype. This offers further possibilities, such as users locking their content to prevent changes from other users or removing all their personal content from the display if they decide to no longer participate in the collaboration.

BodyLenses can also function as individual **storage containers** with access to personal data, which can be accessed on the tool belt of the personal lens. Within our mind-map application, images or previously prepared sketches can be added to the mind-map through the lens. To categorise, sort and manage these items, a part of the lens can function as a clipboard to which items can be attached (Figure 6b). When multiple people want to work together and exchange items, individual clipboards can be shared.

Since the shape of a *BodyLens* can be very dynamic, the placement of elements like menus and clipboards is not easy. We therefore suggest that for each shape certain parts of the

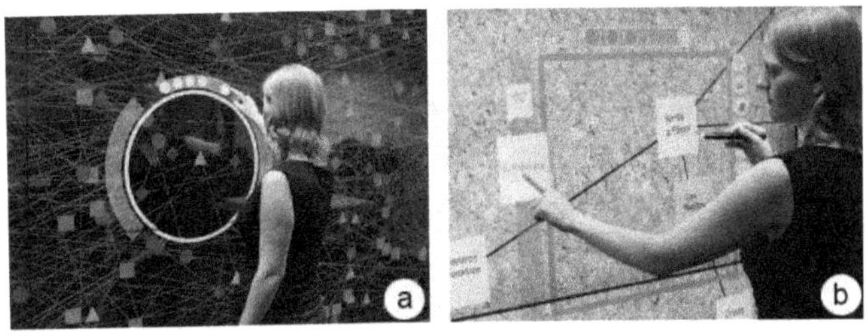

Figure 6. a) The lens' tool belt is placed along the border, so that the result of the LocalEdge function [35] is visible; b) The user can add post-its from the mind-map to the clipboard.

border need to be defined as paths where the tools may be placed. In our prototype, the circular lens defines a circular path for the clipboard and menu, while the rectangular lens defines straight paths (Figure 6). However, the design has to take into account the probable position of the user's arms. When positioning the menu at the top, the user might occlude the data within the lens when switching functions. It is our goal to conduct further research regarding this placement along dynamic body-centric lenses, since early experiments within our prototypes have revealed this to be a challenging topic.

Open Research Questions

With the presentation of the design space, concepts and initial prototypical implementations of *BodyLenses*, we have laid the foundations of a research framework for embodied magic lenses. From this foundational work a number of research questions emerge that require further investigation. Perhaps most fundamental to the validation of the concepts underlying *BodyLenses* are the application contexts within which those lenses should be applied to efficiently support the tasks at hand. A particular challenge is to design efficient and intuitive lens interactions that work as intended by the user by a) avoiding always-on problems and involuntarily activating functions, b) allowing to explicitly trigger desired lens changes (e.g. by raising the arm or performing mid-air gestures) and most importantly c) that do not interfere with the primary data exploration and manipulation tasks.

There is considerable freedom within the design space and it remains to be investigated what lens shapes, attributes, interaction techniques and embodied tools are most suitable for each considered scenario. Specific solutions have to be investigated for the placement of elements along body-centric lenses, to conveniently reach all areas of the display (particular top and bottom areas) and for the freezing functionality which allows to temporarily fix lenses, their properties and their parameters. In terms of experimental validation, appropriate evaluations will have to confirm the advantages of *BodyLenses* compared to traditional magic lenses. The intricate case of multi-user environments, with issues such as territoriality, awareness, group dynamics, privacy and further social factors within both co-located and remote collaborative work, will also have to be tackled specifically. Related to that, technical solutions have to be developed for reliably tracking occluded users in crowded situations and for user identification to allow true personalisation.

CONCLUSION

We presented *BodyLenses*, a novel concept combining the principles of magic lenses with the advantages of body-centric and gestural interaction. Our body-enhanced lenses support implicit movement together with the user in front of the display. They apply the rich set of existing functions of magic lenses in very diverse application scenarios. Thanks to their embodiment capabilities, *BodyLenses* incorporate transient personal work territories that provide awareness of the user's position and work content.

In this paper, we contributed a thorough analysis of the design space dimensions of *BodyLenses* including related work and our novel concepts. We focused on new concepts for lens positioning, dynamic shape adjustment and possible mappings of the user's distance to various lens properties as well as personalisation aspects. We presented multiple prototypes that strengthen and confirm the potential of *BodyLenses* including a graph explorer, an image analysis tool, a mind-map creator, and an artistic application. Further, we discussed challenges and important issues to address when designing for body-enhanced lenses on interactive wall displays.

ACKNOWLEDGMENTS

This project was in part funded by the DFG (DA 1319/3-1) and the Excellence Initiative of the German Federal and State Governments (Institutional Strategy, measure "support the best").

REFERENCES

1. C. Appert, O. Chapuis, and E. Pietriga. 2010. High-precision Magnification Lenses. In *Proc. CHI '10*. ACM, 273–282.
2. M. Ashmore, A. T. Duchowski, and G. Shoemaker. 2005. Efficient Eye Pointing with a Fisheye Lens. In *Proc. GI '05*. 203–210.
3. R. Ball, C. North, and D. A. Bowman. 2007. Move to Improve: Promoting Physical Navigation to Increase User Performance with Large Displays. In *Proc. CHI '07*. ACM, 191–200.
4. E. A. Bier, M. C. Stone, K. Pier, W. Buxton, and T. D. DeRose. 1993. Toolglass and magic lenses: the see-through interface. In *Proc. SIGGRAPH '93*. ACM, 73–80.
5. J. Brosz, M. A. Nacenta, R. Pusch, S. Carpendale, and C. Hurter. 2013. Transmogrification: Causal Manipulation of Visualizations. In *Proc. UIST '13*. ACM, 97–106.
6. Brother System. 2013. Vitrine Interactive "Les Rives de l'Orne". https://youtu.be/KLOB-T1mgdY. (2013).
7. F. Brudy, D. Ledo, S. Greenberg, and A. Butz. 2014. Is Anyone Looking? Mitigating Shoulder Surfing on Public Displays Through Awareness and Protection. In *Proc. PerDis '14*. ACM, 1:1–1:6.
8. BUT Dubai and Firmavision. 2011. Interactive Video Wall. https://youtu.be/b2kqRv1WdEM. (2011).
9. B. Chung and O. Li. 2013. Domain Mall Interactive Wall Display in Hong Kong. https://youtu.be/NRhDpDxTsLA. (2013).

10. J. Dostal, U. Hinrichs, P. O. Kristensson, and A. Quigley. 2014. SpiderEyes: Designing Attention- and Proximity-aware Collaborative Interfaces for Wall-sized Displays. In *Proc. IUI '14*. ACM, 143–152.
11. I. Elhart, F. Scacchi, E. Niforatos, and M. Langheinrich. 2015. ShadowTouch: A Multi-user Application Selection Interface for Interactive Public Displays. In *Proc. PerDis '15*. ACM, 209–216.
12. N. Elmqvist, P. Dragicevic, and J.-D. Fekete. 2011. Color Lens: Adaptive Color Scale Optimization for Visual Exploration. *IEEE Trans. on Vis. and Comp. Graphics* 17, 6 (June 2011), 795–807.
13. J. Gilliot, G. Casiez, and N. Roussel. 2014. Direct and Indirect Multi-touch Interaction on a Wall Display. In *Proceedings of the 26th Conference on L'Interaction Homme-Machine IHM '14*. ACM, 147–152.
14. S. Greenberg, N. Marquardt, T. Ballendat, R. Diaz-Marino, and M. Wang. 2011. Proxemic Interactions: The New Ubicomp? *interactions* 18, 1 (Jan. 2011), 42–50.
15. C. Harrison and A. K. Dey. 2008. Lean and Zoom: Proximity-aware User Interface and Content Magnification. In *Proc. CHI '08*. ACM, 507–510.
16. A. Ion, Y.-L. B. Chang, M. Haller, M. Hancock, and S. D. Scott. 2013. Canyon: Providing Location Awareness of Multiple Moving Objects in a Detail View on Large Displays. In *Proc. CHI '13*. ACM, 3149–3158.
17. M. R. Jakobsen, Y. S. Haile, S. Knudsen, and K. Hornbaek. 2013. Information Visualization and Proxemics: Design Opportunities and Empirical Findings. *IEEE Trans. on Vis. and Comp. Graphics* 19, 12 (2013), 2386–2395.
18. M. R. Jakobsen and K. Hornbæk. 2014. Up Close and Personal: Collaborative Work on a High-resolution Multitouch Wall Display. *ACM Trans. Comput.-Hum. Interact.* 21, 2 (Feb. 2014), 11:1–11:34.
19. D. P. Käser, M. Agrawala, and M. Pauly. 2011. FingerGlass: efficient multiscale interaction on multitouch screens. In *Proc. CHI '11*. ACM, 1601–1610.
20. K. Kim and N. Elmqvist. 2012. Embodied Lenses for Collaborative Visual Queries on Tabletop Displays. *Information Visualization* 11, 4 (Oct. 2012), 319–338.
21. U. Kister, P. Reipschläger, and R. Dachselt. 2014. Multi-Touch Manipulation of Magic Lenses for Information Visualization. In *Proc. ITS '14*. ACM, 431–434.
22. A. Lehmann, H. Schumann, O. Staadt, and C. Tominski. 2011. Physical Navigation to Support Graph Exploration on a Large High-Resolution Display. In *Advances in Visual Computing*. Lecture Notes in Computer Science, Vol. 6938. Springer Berlin Heidelberg, 496–507.
23. N. Marquardt, T. Ballendat, S. Boring, S. Greenberg, and K. Hinckley. 2012. Gradual Engagement: Facilitating Information Exchange Between Digital Devices As a Function of Proximity. In *Proc. ITS '12*. ACM, 31–40.
24. J. Müller, F. Alt, D. Michelis, and A. Schmidt. 2010. Requirements and Design Space for Interactive Public Displays. In *Proc. MM '10*. ACM, 1285–1294.
25. E. Pietriga and C. Appert. 2008. Sigma lenses: focus-context transitions combining space, time and translucence. In *Proc. CHI '08*. ACM, 1343–1352.
26. C. Pindat, E. Pietriga, O. Chapuis, and C. Puech. 2012. JellyLens: content-aware adaptive lenses. In *Proc. UIST '12*. ACM, 261–270.
27. G. Ramos, A. Cockburn, R. Balakrishnan, and M. Beaudouin-Lafon. 2007. Pointing Lenses: Facilitating Stylus Input Through Visual-and Motor-space Magnification. In *Proc. CHI '07*. ACM, 757–766.
28. D. Schmidt, M. K. Chong, and H. Gellersen. 2010. IdLenses: Dynamic Personal Areas on Shared Surfaces. In *Proc. ITS '10*. ACM, 131–134.
29. S. D. Scott, M. S. T. Carpendale, and K. M. Inkpen. 2004. Territoriality in Collaborative Tabletop Workspaces. In *Proc. CSCW '04*. ACM, 294–303.
30. G. Shoemaker, A. Tang, and K. S. Booth. 2007. Shadow Reaching: A New Perspective on Interaction for Large Displays. In *Proc. UIST '07*. ACM, 53–56.
31. G. Shoemaker, T. Tsukitani, Y. Kitamura, and K. S. Booth. 2010. Body-centric Interaction Techniques for Very Large Wall Displays. In *Proc. NordiCHI '10*. ACM, 463–472.
32. M. Spindler, C. Tominski, H. Schumann, and R. Dachselt. 2010. Tangible Views for Information Visualization. In *Proc. ITS '10*. ACM, 157–166.
33. M. C. Stone, K. Fishkin, and E. A. Bier. 1994. The movable filter as a user interface tool. In *Proc. CHI '94*. ACM, 306–312.
34. A. Tang, M. Tory, B. Po, P. Neumann, and S. Carpendale. 2006. Collaborative Coupling over Tabletop Displays. In *Proc. CHI '06*. ACM, 1181–1190.
35. C. Tominski, J. Abello, F. van Ham, and H. Schumann. 2006. Fisheye Tree Views and Lenses for Graph Visualization. In *Proc. IV '06*. IEEE Computer Society, 17–24.
36. C. Tominski, S. Gladisch, U. Kister, R. Dachselt, and H. Schumann. 2014. A Survey on Interactive Lenses in Visualization. In *EuroVis - STARs*. The Eurographics Association.
37. J. Viega, M. J. Conway, G. Williams, and R. Pausch. 1996. 3D Magic Lenses. In *Proc. UIST '96*. ACM, 51–58.
38. D. Vogel and R. Balakrishnan. 2004. Interactive Public Ambient Displays: Transitioning from Implicit to Explicit, Public to Personal, Interaction with Multiple Users. In *Proc. UIST '04*. ACM, 137–146.
39. Y. Zhang, T. Han, Z. Ren, N. Umetani, X. Tong, Y. Liu, T. Shiratori, and X. Cao. 2013. BodyAvatar: Creating Freeform 3D Avatars Using First-person Body Gestures. In *Proc. UIST '13*. ACM, 387–396.
40. J. Zillner, C. Rhemann, S. Izadi, and M. Haller. 2014. 3D-board: A Whole-body Remote Collaborative Whiteboard. In *Proc. UIST '14*. ACM, 471–479.

BricoSketch: Mixing Paper and Computer Drawing Tools in Professional Illustration

Theophanis Tsandilas
Inria; Univ Paris-Sud
Orsay, France
theophanis.tsandilas@inria.fr

Magdalini Grammatikou
Inria; Univ Paris-Sud
Orsay, France

Stéphane Huot
Inria
Lille, France
stephane.huot@inria.fr

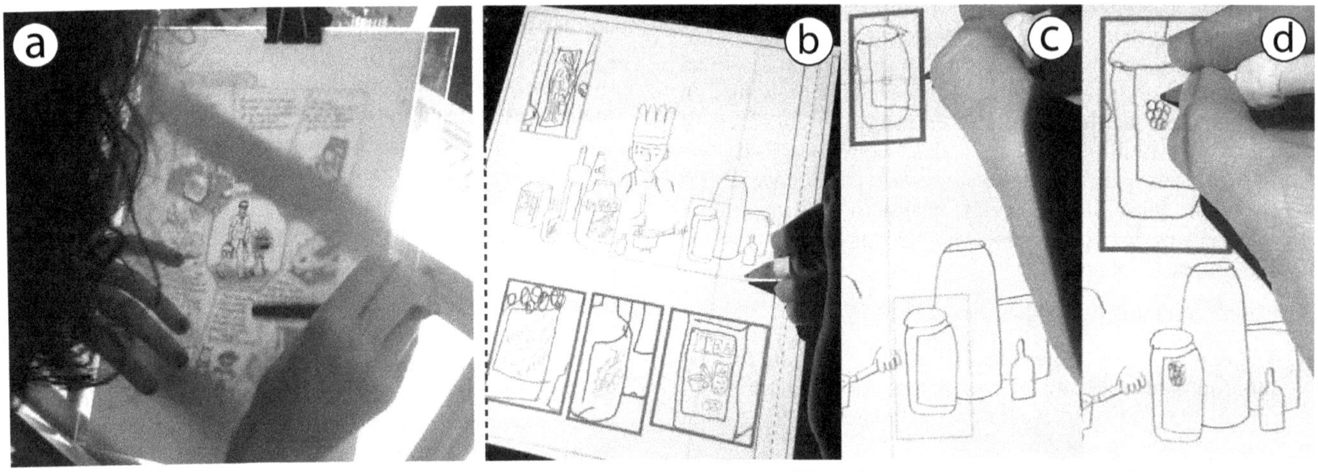

Figure 1. (a) An artist works on layers of physical paper with a home-made light table. The artist draws the panels of a page for a graphic novel by using earlier sketches as guides. (b-d) The same artist uses our system to add details to different parts of her illustration through partial scaled views.

ABSTRACT
Illustrators are advanced users of both traditional and computer-assisted drawing tools, and therefore, observing their strategies is very valuable for research on drawing interfaces. We interviewed four professional illustrators in their work environment. We also followed the work of an artist for a two-year period. We observed that artists mix a variety of techniques that involve specialized computer software and hardware such as Adobe Photoshop, a graphics tablet and a scanner, and traditional physical tools such as pencils, paper, and customized light tables. Our findings inspired BricoSketch, an augmented paper interface that enables illustrators to zoom into parts of their drawings and work at different levels of detail on paper. Our early results demonstrate that BricoSketch supports real tasks, improving productivity on paper while enhancing illustrators' creative ways of working.

Author Keywords
Illustration; drawing interfaces; sketching; augmented paper

ACM Classification Keywords
H.5.2. Information Interfaces and Presentation: User Interfaces - Graphical User Interfaces

ITS '15, November 15-18, 2015, Funchal, Portugal
©2015 ACM. ISBN 978-1-4503-3899-8/15/11...$15.00
DOI: http://dx.doi.org/10.1145/2817721.2817729

INTRODUCTION
Interactive technologies have radically changed the way visual artists work, and a large portion of the artistic production has now moved from paper to the computer. Powerful drawing and image-processing software such as Adobe Photoshop, InDesign, Illustrator and Corel Painter as well as pen displays such as the Wacom Cintiq series[1] have played an important role in this change. However, many artists still work on paper and keep using traditional painting and drawing tools. This is not only due to resistance to progress or due to the well-known usability properties of physical tools [7]: despite the progress of artistic stroke-rendering techniques [11], existing computer tools fail to fully capture the richness and variety of artistic styles supported by physical media [21]. Therefore, artists still rely heavily on paper for styles and techniques that software tools currently do not offer.

We interview four professional illustrators to understand how they mix physical and electronic media in their creative process. We also follow the work of one of these illustrators for a period of two years. We observe that professional illustrators do not have a unique process of work but adapt their style and tools depending on the requirements of their different projects. All of them use both physical and computer drawings tools at different phases of a project, from early sketches to final illustrations. We also learn that productivity has a major role in the selection of their tools as they often deal with pressing deadlines. Unfortunately, although commercial drawing software can increase productivity, much of

[1]`http://www.wacom.com/products/pen-displays`

its power does not apply when creative work takes place on paper. In particular, we observe that switching from traditional tools to software and vice-versa often involves significant manual effort. Previous work [8, 18, 23, 24] has introduced augmented-paper technologies and projection-based systems to enhance traditional drawing and painting techniques. Yet, these systems either target novices [8, 18] or non-artistic tasks [23, 24].

Our goal is to fill in this gap with smoother transitions that could help artists take advantage of the power of computer tools earlier in their creative process. We designed *BricoSketch*, an augmented-paper system that enables professional illustrators to define alternative views of their drawings on paper and then use these views to draw at different levels of detail through multiple drawing scales (see Figure 1b-d). We show how users can combine such views to explore variations and produce final illustrations. Our system gets inspiration from a real work scenario and was designed in interaction with a professional artist.

Our contribution is twofold:

1. We explore how professional illustrators use traditional and computer tools in their work and look at their motivations. Our results reveal new challenges for the design of novel drawing systems.
2. We introduce a novel system that helps illustrators work on paper while taking advantage of computer functionality. We show how artists can divide their workspace into layers and work at different scales through *transposed views* of their paper drawings.

RELATED WORK

Interactive Drawing Assistance

Previous HCI work has examined a range of interactive tools for drawing and animation. Several of these tools target professional artists such as illustrators, animators, and designers. For example, Vignette [17] facilitates the creation of textures in pen-and-ink illustrations. ILoveSketch [2] assists professional designers in sketching 3D models. Draco [15] allows artists (but also casual users) to add animation to drawings.

Other systems target novices, offering assistance through tutorials and guides. For example, PortraitSketch [14] assists novices by adjusting the quality of their strokes as they draw portraits from image models. Sketch-Sketch Revolution [6] offers step-by-step tutorials for drawing. ShadowDraw [19] helps users with shadows of blended images taken from a large database. ICanDraw [5] provides instructions and corrective feedback to assist the drawing of human faces. Iarussi et al. [12] use construction lines and corrective feedback to guide the drawing of generic objects and postures. Tsang et al. [27] guide 3D sketching by integrating suggestive 2D images into 3D models. Finally, other approaches guide painting by projecting images and color on a physical canvas [8] or assist drawing by projecting interactive 3D scenes [18].

Here, we focus on professionals users, and therefore, providing drawing guidance is out of our system's scope. We find, however, that professional illustrators use a range of personal *scaffolding* techniques to guide their drawing. Our system gets inspiration from these work practices.

Physical vs. Virtual Tools and Materials

We identify three categories of drawing and painting systems with respect to how they mix traditional and computer-based techniques and tools.

Simulate the Physical World. The first category draws inspiration from how artists manipulate physical materials and applies their observed practices to the digital world. For example, SandCanvas [16] is a tabletop system that gets inspiration from sand-animation performances. By simulating sand-manipulation gestures with a virtual environment, the system enhances animation with new operations, e.g., video recording and playback, that are not available in the physical world. However, the approach deprives artists of the richness of tangible manipulation provided by physical materials and tools.

Model the Footprint of Traditional Tools. The second category combines interactive surfaces and physical tools. As an example, FluidPaint [28] captures the footprint of real wet brushes and simulates it with a virtual brush. Vogel and Casiez [29] follow a similar approach and study how artists manipulate a real Conté crayon to inform the design of a new multimodal device for drawing on tabletops. Otsuki et al. [22] push this approach further by allowing users to paint on arbitrary physical objects through a mixed reality system. Such systems preserve the physical properties of the drawing or painting tools, but the artistic result is still less natural, as rendering is based on an imperfect model rather than a precise image of their physical footprint.

Change the Traditional Workflow by Mixing the Two Worlds. The third category keeps intact both the use of traditional tools and their natural footprint. In this case, the goal of the interactive system is to change the traditional workflow of the artist and improve artistic production. The work by Nakajima et al. [21] is a representative example of this direction. Their system provides a computer interface for creating animation sequences through sketches. The artist prints the sketches and paints them with physical tools such as pencils or oil paints. The system then creates the final animation sequences by compiling the scanned paintings.

Our system belongs to the last category. We preserve the footprint of physical drawing tools by creating a new workflow that enhances traditional illustration techniques.

Augmented Surfaces and Paper Interaction

Early work on interactive paper dates almost 25 years back [30], and Video Mosaic [20] was seminal in supporting creative tasks with augmented paper. More recent work has studied the use of interactive paper in domains such as architectural design [1, 23, 24], music composition [9], and collaborative design [10]. Much of this work is based on front-projection setups [30, 20, 1, 23, 24, 10], while others [25] use portable devices as displays. In some of these systems [23, 9], users only interact with a pen. Others [3, 24, 25] examine bi-manual interaction techniques, e.g., Pen+Touch.

Our work gets ideas from these systems but is especially influenced by PenLight [23] and MouseLight [24]. For example, we also support above-the-surface interaction for command use, overlaid layers of physical and virtual ink, and copy-and-paste actions over physical content. However, our interaction design is adapted to professional illustration rather than architectural design and focuses on a more specific drawing approach and task. We also introduce a more lightweight approach and allow for more personal drawing tools, e.g., pencils, that previous work did not support.

INTERVIEWS

We wanted to better understand the process of illustration and, particularly, learn how professional artists use technology and traditional tools in their workflow. Books and online videos provide rich information about drawing and illustration techniques, and a lot of previous work [5, 12, 16, 17] has used them as main sources of reference for their solutions. Other approaches [9, 13] were based on a direct contact with professional artists. This allowed the researchers to investigate very specific scenarios and tasks but also get valuable information about the environment in which these people work as well as their problems and constraints.

We chose to follow the second approach for our design. In this section, we present our interviews with four professional illustrators and discuss our results and insights.

Participants

We interviewed two men and two women, 31 to 36 years old. We refer to them with the initials of their first name (M, C, S, and E). They were all freelancers with 4 to 11 years experience as professional illustrators. They shared the same studio but each worked independently on their own projects. Their projects included illustrations for books, magazines, and newspapers. Three of them (C, S, and E) also worked as writers of graphic novels.

Method

The interviews took place in June 2013 on two different days in the artists' studio. Participants first answered a pre-questionnaire about their profile and experience. We then invited them to speak about their current or their recent projects. We asked them to go through the whole creative process for each of their project, focusing on the materials and tools that they use, both traditional and digital, hardware or software. We also encouraged them to show their drawings on either paper or the computer and demonstrate the techniques that they used through concrete examples from their work. Each session lasted 30 to 50 minutes. All sessions were videotaped.

Results

The Lifecycle of an Illustration Project

A regular illustration project consists of the following stages:

Task Assignment. An editor or art director contacts the artist and provides the details of the project. The illustrator can then negotiate the price and the time constraints proposed by the client. The art director usually provides precise instructions about the size and placement of the illustrations on a page. However, the level of detail can vary significantly among different projects. For example, C talked about her experience with a book. She mentioned that she found this project hard, as she was not given enough information at the beginning, and she then spent a lot of time iterating with the editor.

Sketches. The illustrator starts by exploring and sketching ideas, which finally take the form of rough concept sketches. For smaller projects, the artist usually produces more than one idea for each illustration. Sketches are communicated to the art director. The art director selects one of the proposed ideas, makes suggestions and sometimes asks for changes.

Detailed Drawings. The artist works on the detailed drawing by using the selected sketch as a reference. This is the most time-consuming phase as the artist pays attention on the details and the artistic quality of the result.

Colors and Refinements. Colors and textures are usually added at the very end of the process. Again, the illustrator iterates with the art director, who can again ask for small changes or refinements.

A project can consist of a single or a small number of illustrations, e.g., for a newspaper article. The artist is often asked to complete the task in very limited time, sometimes within the same or the following day. Thus, being able to produce results fast is important for illustrators. Larger projects can take several weeks or several months, where the artist may have to illustrate an entire book.

Looking for Sources of Inspiration

Before starting a project, all our participants search for documentation related to the subject. If the project is a book, a graphic novel or an article, they first read the text that is provided by the publisher so as to extract important information about the context of the project. They regularly search images and videos on the Web. For large projects, they often buy and read related books or create folders with all the material they gather. C explained that she even visits specific places for her projects and takes photos and draws the scenery and related objects. She then sticks this material around her desk to recreate the atmosphere needed to get inspired while working. E often looks for inspiration in films of specific directors.

Drawing on Paper vs. Drawing on the Computer

Over the years, illustrators have developed their personal artistic styles that differentiate them from other artists. An editor or art director contacts an illustrator knowing his or her previous work and expecting a good match between the proposed project and a specific work style of the artist. Yet, our participants explained that their styles evolve from one project to the next. For example, E mentioned that he likes *"changing techniques for every new project"* and added: *"If I see something that I like, I want to try it"*. The medium plays an important role in the development of an artistic style, and interestingly, we observed very diverse working practices, where traditional (e.g., paper, pencils, ink-drawing pens) and digital tools (e.g., graphics tablet, scanner, printer, Adobe Photoshop) are often intermixed.

Figure 2. The head of the girl has been redrawn on a different page with a light table. The drawings are later merged with Photoshop.

Figure 3. Drawing technique used by E for a comic book. Sketches created on the computer (left) are printed in blue. The artist then draws the detailed contours with a pen ink on top of the printed sketches (right).

Keeping the Real Original. M completes all his drawings on paper and moves to a graphics tablet and Photoshop only to add colors. He explained that he wants to keep the *"real original"* and *"preserve the paper and manual aspect"* of his work so he usually goes back to paper to make corrections by erasing and "retouching" the drawing with his pencils. According to the artist, this process is more time consuming than making changes directly in Photoshop as it requires additional scanning. However, he prefers it as it ensures that there is a *"true correspondence"* between the original drawing on paper and its digital version.

Mixing Sketches on Paper. S exhibited a number of different working styles but explained that she usually starts by sketching on paper. Her sketches often evolve in multiple steps. Rough sketches help her develop and think about ideas while more developed sketches communicate detailed ideas. They also serve as scaffolds for drawing the final picture. She gave an interesting example from her ongoing work for a book for children that demonstrates this evolution of sketches. She starts with a rough ideation sketch and then moves to a more detailed but small-scale sketch. She then scans this sketch and prints it in a larger scale corresponding to the target illustration size. She creates a more detailed sketch on top of that, which then serves as the model for drawing the final picture. She uses pencil for her sketches and an ink pen for the final polished drawing. As a final step, she scans the final drawing and adds colors in Photoshop with the graphics tablet. She also uses the tablet to make small corrections.

S also explained that she also frequently uses extra pieces of paper to draw specific parts of a picture, e.g., the face of a character (Figure 2), in more detail and then merge them with the rest of the scene on separate layers on the computer. We see that in contrast to M, S is only concerned about the final digital version sent to the editor, not the original on paper, which in some cases consists of several different pieces. The *light table* has a prominent role in this process, as it allows the artist to incrementally move from lower to higher-fidelity drawings. Light tables are viewing devices that evenly illuminate a subject, e.g., an early sketch, from below by emitting fluorescent light. Artists use light tables to trace their final images on new pages. Figure 1a shows S drawing the final panels of a graphic novel on a home-made light table.

Sketching on Paper vs. Detailed Drawing on the Computer. In addition to the above method, S often uses the graphics tablet to work on the final version of a drawing, where the scanned sketches appear in a separate Photoshop layer in transparency. This is a common approach that simulates physical drawing over sketches with a light table. S explained that each method produces a different artistic style. She liked more her illustrations produced with a pencil or an ink pen on paper. However, some clients contacted her for her illustrations created with the graphics tablet.

Sketching with the Graphics Tablet. In contrast, C always uses a graphics tablet for sketching. She explained that she can sketch very fast with the tablet as the digital tool allows her to erase easily, copy-paste and quickly explore ideas. In her usual workflow, she exclusively uses the tablet for the whole creative process, from sketching to the very final step. Nevertheless, she expressed the desire to return more often to the traditional drawing method on paper and presented an example from her previous work for a book where she mixed both digital and physical drawing. For this project, she completed all her sketches in Photoshop. She then printed them on paper and used a light table to draw the detailed illustrations with an ink pen. She then scanned the final drawing and added colors in Photoshop. C explained that the ink pen allowed her to draw fast without paying too much attention on the details. The graphics tablet imposes a different working style, where the artist has to frequently erase and zoom in to refine the drawing or draw additional details.

Working with Masses on Photoshop. Our fourth participant, E, usually creates his sketches on the computer. However, he demonstrated a variety of different styles. He showed his project for a book cover, where he used *"masses"* (i.e., black volumes) rather than contours to draw in Photoshop. The technique allowed him to define detailed forms incrementally by drawing volumes and then sculpturing them with the eraser tool. E was very effective with this technique and reused it in several projects both for quick sketches and final illustrations.

Printing Sketches in Blue. For another comic-book project, the artist started by creating his sketches on the computer with the "masses" technique. He then printed the sketches on paper in a light blue color and used them as templates to draw the detailed contours with the ink pen. The scanner filtered out the blue ink of the printed sketches but preserved the black ink of the pen. This technique replaces the light table: *"I cannot support the lamp on my eyes".* As a final step, E used Photoshop to add volume and color.

Summary

All our four participants have experience with both traditional and digital drawing tools. However, we identified a variety of different ways in which they use these tools in their projects. Sometimes, almost all the work is done on paper. For other projects, paper is never used. In other scenarios, artists switch from paper to software but also from software to paper (see Figure 4) in different variations. Which strategy to choose each time depends on the artistic style that the artist wants to achieve, the quality of the expected result, as well as the drawing speed that each approach affords. These observations are in support of previous approaches [21] that enhance artists' workflow without affecting their artistic styles.

We also found that projects evolve at multiple stages where early sketches and drawings serve as reference and templates for higher-fidelity ones. Artists use either physical layers on top of a light table or virtual ones in computer software to make copies of their images and draw on top of them new versions. Finally, we discovered that although artists develop very personal artistic styles during the years, most of them are still very open to novel technologies and continuously look for new tools and techniques.

LONGER-TERM OBSERVATIONS AND CONCEPT

We continued working with S and have observed the evolution of her work practices during the last two years. We can identify two major milestones in her personal work during this period, very related to the focus of our research.

Six months after our initial interview, the illustrator acquired a 13HD Wacom Cintiq, which replaced her graphics tablet and became her primary computer drawing device. In addition, she started adopting the same strategy as C and E, producing most of her early sketches on the computer. According to the artist, this approach helped her to significantly improve her productivity. Yet, she kept drawing on paper for most of her projects.

Her major project during this time was the illustration of an 175 page graphic novel in collaboration with a writer. The project was funded by a large publisher and was subject to two major constraints:

1. The artist had eight months to complete all the sequences in the book. As she worked on other projects in parallel, this deadline was not easy to meet.
2. The artist was required to draw all the images with a pencil and rarely use color on selected images. Unfortunately, producing high-quality images with this style was very time consuming for her.

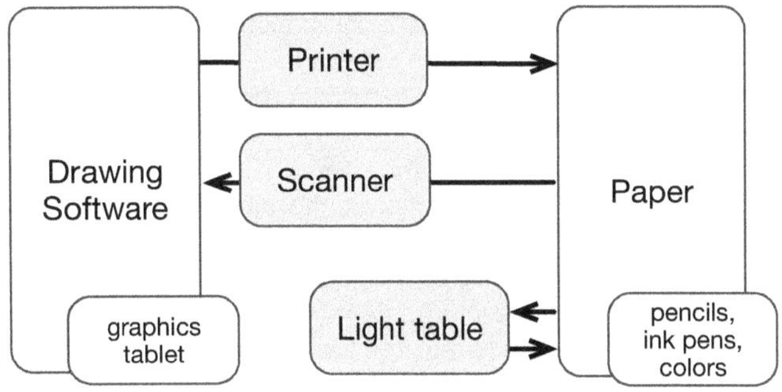

Figure 4. Devices and drawing tools used by our participants as they shift from paper to the computer and vice-versa.

She experimented with various solutions to accelerate production while struggling to preserve the quality of her final images. She ended up developing an interesting workflow, which eventually became the basis of our system design.

Workflow

Comic-book artists often draw their panels in a scale larger than the size of the printed pages. This gives them more precision in drawing details. However, drawing larger images takes more time. S tried to balance between drawing precision and speed by splitting the image on multiple layers where drawing takes place at different scales. For example, she drew the global scene at a smaller scale and completed details such as faces of people at a larger scale. This approach is similar to the one shown in Figure 2 but involves additional steps:

Step 1: The artist scans the initial drawing, adjusts its size on the computer, and prints it at larger scale.

Step 2: She draws details on a different page. She works on the light table by using the printed page as reference.

Step 3: She scans the new page and blends the partial drawings together with Adobe Photoshop.

Although efficient according to the given time and style constraints, this process required significant manual effort as the artist had to scan and print her drawings several times in order to switch between paper and electronic versions of her work.

The above drawing technique forms the basis of our design concept whose goal is to enable the artist to work seamlessly at different scales on paper through multiple physical layers. To achieve this goal, we had to leverage the best of the two worlds, traditional and digital, and to augment paper with functionalities, e.g., copy, paste, scale, and superimpose, that are only available in computer drawing software. The next section introduces *BricoSketch*, which realizes this approach.

BRICO*SKETCH*

The name of the system (*bricolage* + sketch) is inspired by the observation that professional illustration is not a straightforward process. Artists often invent new techniques for their projects. Such techniques involve not only sketching and drawing but, sometimes, a lot of *engineering*, scaffolding, and remixing. BricoSketch extends traditional light tables by combining interactive paper technology with a front-projection augmented-reality system.

Overview

Figure 1b-d shows a scenario of use of the system that captures the workflow presented in the previous section. The artist's workspace contains the main illustration, drawn on paper with a pencil, and a number of rectangular areas around it. These areas represent partial virtual views of the original drawing. The user creates and transposes the views interactively by moving the pencil over the drawing surface. In this specific example, the artist has created transposed views to decorate the labels of ingredient boxes. The scale of these views is larger so that the artist can draw small parts of the image with finer control and higher detail.

As shown in Figure 1, the physical ink of the pencil within a given view is blended with projected copies of ink drawn in other views. In order to produce the final illustration, we need to blend the partial images of the physical ink together. We discuss how blending can be performed manually, but we also provide computer tools to automate this process.

Hardware and Software Platform

We implemented our first prototype with Anoto paper technology[2], but we fast start looking for a different solution. Anoto is a mature technology, allowing for the detection of the position of a pen on paper with high precision. Nevertheless, it requires the use of a very limited set of digital pens, and unfortunately, these pens have not been designed with professional illustration in mind. Wacom's Inkling[3] is better adapted to design and sketching tasks, but again, it does not let users draw with their own pens or pencils.

We opted for the new iSketchnote[4] pen tracking technology. iSketchnote uses a 7.1×9.7 inch magnetic surface (the *slate*) that captures the 3D position and 3D orientation of small magnetic rings with a latency of about 50 ms. A ring can be fixed on any physical object, and thus, it can serve to detect the position of a pen's or pencil's tip on a piece of paper placed on the slate's surface. iSketchnote has recently released an SDK (April 2015) that provides low level events about the 3D position of a pen moving on or over the slate within a limited distance range of about 10 cm. However, the iSketchnote SDK is still in progress and presents several problems. According to our own tests, the space of detected events is deformed, which makes calibration highly problematic. We tried to reduce deformation by applying bi-polynomial interpolation functions, but results were not satisfying. We finally tackled the problem by exhaustive 2D sampling on a 15×22 grid on the slate's surface, resulting in cells with a size of $9.4 \times 9.4\ mm^2$ each. We find the position of the pen within this grid and then estimate its coordinates with respect to the coordinates of the four closest samples. This solution minimizes the problem of deformation at a global scale. On the other hand, it does not deal with local deformations within individual cells of the grid.

[2] http://www.anoto.com

[3] http://inkling.wacom.com

[4] http://www.isketchnote.com

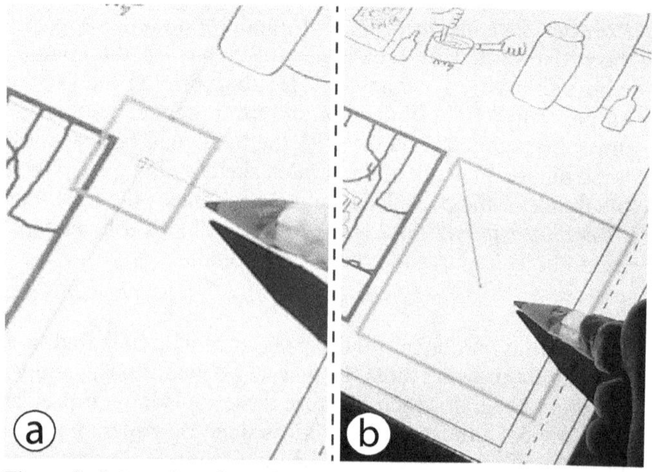

Figure 5. Interacting above the surface. (a) Transposition: The user moves the pencil to transpose a selected rectangular area to a new position. The pointer appears left to the tip of the pencil to avoid occlusion. (b) Rescaling: The user moves the pencil to rescale the selected transposed view. Moving away from (or closer to) its top-left corner increases (or decreases) the view size.

The slate is connected with a 13 inch MacBook Pro through USB. Our application is written in Java 2D 1.8 and we use Open Sound Control[5] to receive pen events from the native iSketchnote SDK. To reduce the noise of detected pen events, we use OpenCV's implementation of a Kalman filter. An ACER K11 mini projector mounted 50 cm above the table displays the virtual space on paper. We apply a perspective transformation to calibrate the virtual with the physical space.

Illustrations and Transposed Views

Illustrations take a single A5 page that corresponds to the active surface of a slate. Each illustration I can consist of multiple views $V_i = T_i(I)$, where a view can be created anywhere on the page. We define T_i as a transposition function:

$$T_i(I) = (s_i \circ t_i)(c_i(l_i(I))) \tag{1}$$

where l_i contains a subset of the illustration's strokes as a distinct layer, c_i crops an area (rectangular in our implementation) of the illustration surface, while s_i and t_i are scale and translate transformations performed in any order.

Users can split their work between views. Partial views are then blended together to compose the full illustration:

$$I = \bigcup_i (s_i \circ t_i)^{-1}(V_i) \tag{2}$$

According to the above equation, we apply an inverse scale and translate transformation to each view before blending all the views together. Views are synchronized, which means that when the user draws within the space of a view, the other views are updated by rendering the virtual image of new strokes. Users can deactivate, reactivate or delete a view.

[5] http://www.opensoundcontrol.com

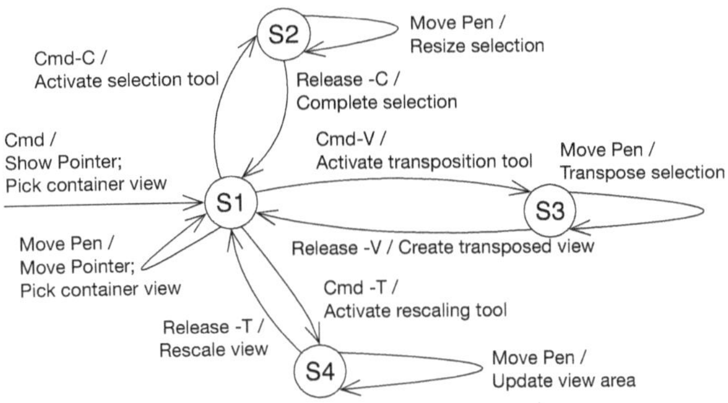

Figure 6. State diagram describing the main functionality of the system, i.e., how to create and transform views, through quasi-modes.

They can also nest views by creating new ones over existing ones. These functionalities allow for great flexibility as they let users create alternative versions of different parts of an illustration by working at multiple scales.

Interaction Design

Drawing vs. Command Layer of Interaction

Traditional pens and pencils leave a permanent trace on paper, which constraints interaction design. For example, moving the pen on paper to make a selection and create a new view is not desirable. Our initial Anoto version of BricoSketch avoided this problem by making use of additional inkless pens dedicated to interaction. Other approaches deal with the problem by introducing tiny command gestures that leave minimal trace on paper [26] or using a transparent ink-resistant piece of plastic underneath the pen to avoid writing on paper [25].

Our final design follows PenLight's [23] approach. More specifically, we distinguish between a command and a physical layer of interaction, where the command layer takes place above the drawing surface. The artist uses the same pen both for drawing, when the pen touches the page, and for carrying out complementary tasks, e.g., creating a transposed view, by interacting over the page (see Figure 5). PenLight uses Anoto technology to detect the 2D position of the pen on paper but also enhances Anoto pens with a Polhemus magnetic tracker that captures their 3D position. In contrast, we take advantage of iSketchnote's ability to capture 3D pen events above the slate's surface.

Note that the iSketchnote slate has been designed for indirect only input. Deber et al. [4] showed recently that humans perceive lower latencies with direct input that are considerably lower than the minimum latency (50 ms) of the slate. This could be considered as an obstacle to high-quality drawing. In our case, however, the latency problem does not affect the quality of the drawing as artists draw directly on paper with traditional zero-latency tools. Latency is only an issue for virtual copies of the ink shown in views other than the current view and for user actions taking place above the slate.

Handling Interaction Modes

Related work supports interaction on paper by means of contextual toolglass palettes and menus [23, 24] or touch sensitive devices used in combination with the pen [25]. Although our approach does not exclude such solutions, we decided to concentrate on expert use of the system and base our interaction design on the use of command shortcuts. We have observed that illustrators make heavy use of both hands as they work on the computer, where the non-dominant hand controls command shortcuts and drawing modes. Graphics tablets and pen displays like Wacom Cintiq are equipped with hard buttons to be used as control keys. However, several artists still prefer using the shortcuts of the keyboard. As S explained, the number of the hard buttons in these devices is very limited and cannot cover the diverse range of functionality required by common illustration tasks. In line with such practices, we rely on key shortcuts to support interaction.

We avoid persistent modes by making use of *quasi-modes*. The state diagram in Figure 6 describes our interaction design. To enter the command mode ($S1$), the user presses and holds the *Command* (Cmd) key. This action displays a pointer. The user can move the pen or pencil above the page to control the position of the pointer and select a view. As shown in Figure 5, the pointer appears left to the tip of the pencil to avoid occlusion. The user can then hold an additional key to activate specialized tools: $Cmd\text{-}C$ to activate a selection tool ($S2$) and select a rectangular area in the current view to transpose, $Cmd\text{-}V$ to activate a transposition tool ($S3$) and create a new view by copying the selected area to a new position, and $Cmd\text{-}V$ to activate a scaling tool ($S4$) to change the size of the view.

Figure 5 illustrates the use of the transposition and the scaling tool. In addition to the above functions, users can deactivate or re-activate selected views ($Cmd\text{-}A$), delete them ($Cmd\text{-}D$), and save their drawing sessions ($Cmd\text{-}S$).

Blending Transposed Views Together

The final illustration can be created from its partial views by first scanning the page and then aligning the drawn images with specialized image-processing software. For example, the user can perform this task in Adobe Photoshop by following three main steps: (1) select an area of interest, (2) copy and then paste it on a new layer by using the *multiply* blend mode, and (3) use the transformation tool to align it with the image of other layers.

We built a Java 1.8 Swing tool (see Figure 7b-c) to automate the above process. As shown in Figures 1b and 7a, pages contain a red rectangular frame. This printed frame must be aligned with a virtual frame projected on paper. This allows our tool to automatically calculate the exact correspondence between the virtual workspace and the scanned illustration. We use the OpenCV library to detect the red frame of the page and, then based on its boundaries, apply a perspective correction to the image. Users import their saved session containing the detailed description of all the view transpositions. The tool uses this description to automatically crop the image into separate images, where each represents a user-defined view of the illustration. The images are then blended together according to Equation 2. Our tool currently preserves the strokes of all blended views. As we discuss later, future implementations should consider additional blending techniques.

Figure 7. Results from our user session. (a) The artist has created three transposed views for: (1) the head of the diver, (2) a fish, and (3) an urchin. (b) The final scanned page on our Java application. The application automatically removes the red frame of the page and corrects perspective deformations due to the scanning process. (c) Automatic blending of the first view with the main scene after loading the saved session description. (d) Manual blending using the tools of Adobe Photoshop. Please, zoom in to view results in more detail.

EARLY USER FEEDBACK

We ran two drawing sessions with S to test the system and get early feedback about our design.

Procedure

The sessions took place in two consecutive days. The first session lasted approximately 40 minutes. We introduced the system and asked the artist to explore its functionality. We discussed and updated our command shortcuts with her and selected a pen and a pencil to use in the second session.

The second session was approximately 1-hour long. We asked the artist to draw whatever she liked without giving further instructions. We also asked her to explain her strategies and report on any problems she found or ideas about features that she would like to see in future versions of the system.

Figure 8. The artist explores different uses of the user interface. Here, she creates multiple copies of the starfish and places them in different positions in the scene. According to our participant, these copies could be integrated into the final scene or, alternatively, they could serve as templates for drawing new variations of the starfish.

Results

The artist worked on two pages, each for a different illustration. She used a black pen for the first page and a pencil for the second one. Figure 7 shows her first page that illustrates a woman diving under water. It consists of a main view with the global scene and several transposed views that zoom into smaller parts of the scene: the head of the woman, a fish, an urchin, a starfish, and the eyes of the woman. The artist created the views to draw the above elements with finer detail. Figure 1b-d shows the artist interacting and working on the second illustration by using a pencil. The illustration shows a cook preparing a meal. Here, the artist has created views to zoom into labels of ingredient boxes.

The artist learnt quickly how to use the system's functionality and shortcuts with minimal practice. She was very enthusiastic about mixing physical ink with projection-based assistance. She also found that the user interface was very well adapted to her needs and was exactly the kind of system that she wanted. However, she also found problems. In particular, she complaint that the calibration between the physical and the virtual space was not always accurate (see our earlier discussion). The problem became more apparent when she started working between different views as their different scales helped her better perceive calibration errors.

Figure 7c shows how our Java tool automatically blends the detailed head of the diver with the global scene. The result is certainly not optimal. The reason is that our current implementation only deals with situations in which the artist creates a view to add new strokes. In other words, it blends the pixels of the views to preserve the full set of their strokes. In the above example, however, the artist has drawn a completely new version. Figure 7d shows a better result achieved by manually blending the views using Photoshop.

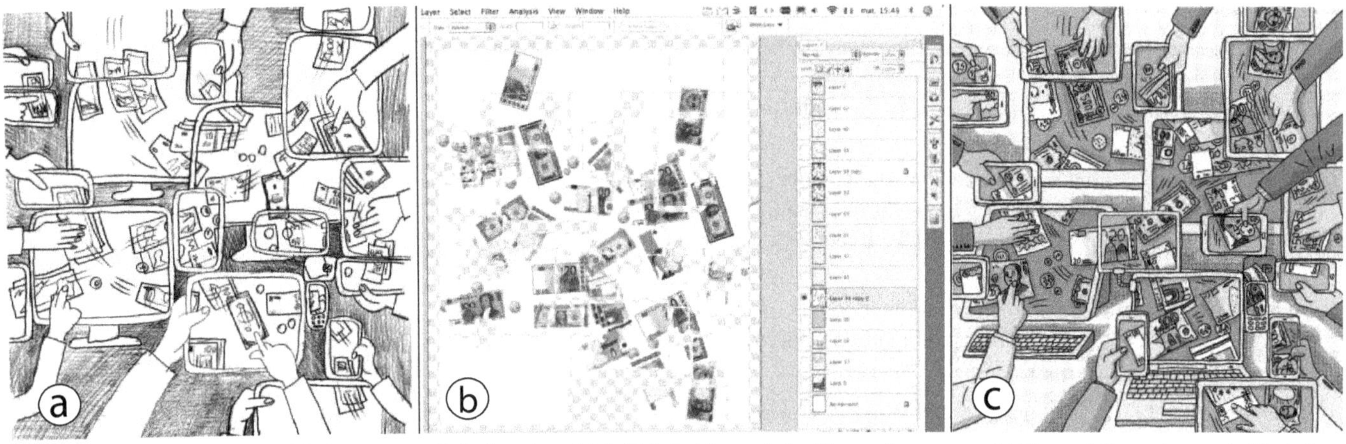

Figure 9. Use of images as models for more realistic drawing: (a) Initial sketch created with pencil on paper. (b) The artist's workspace in Photoshop containing several overlapping layers. The active layer shows cropped images of banknotes that serve as models for drawing the final illustration on the computer. (c) Final illustration realized with a graphics tablet. Artwork by ©Sandrine Martin.

Finally, the artist found that the system is an excellent tool for exploring ideas and trying out alternative versions of drawings. She also proposed some new scenarios. Figure 8 shows her using the tool to create multiple copies of a starfish. She explained that such copies can be used to quickly test ideas by reusing parts of her drawings directly on paper. Alternatively, as she proposed, copies can serve as templates for drawing new variations. For example, in a sequence of panels for a comic strip, the artist could copy the face of a character and use it as model to draw its variations in other panels.

DISCUSSION AND FUTURE DIRECTIONS

We showed how BricoSketch can support real tasks and needs of a professional artist. We acknowledge that this is a preliminary study and that we need a larger group of experts to validate our approach. Our future goal is to evaluate BricoSketch with additional artists and longer projects. We are especially interested in capturing additional illustration tasks such as coloring, adding handwritten captions, and creating animated sequences [15, 21].

According to our current implementation, an illustration can be created from its partial pieces by using either our custom desktop tool or image-editing software like Photoshop. Our blending mechanisms are still primitive and lack the breadth of image-blending and image-processing algorithms of commercial software. Our plan is to replace it by a Photoshop plugin that automates the merging of the views and, at the same time, allows users to take advantage of the software's powerful functionality. Another idea is to move some of this functionality directly on paper. As an example scenario, an artist could test the result of alternative blend modes while she draws. The artist could also add filters and effects or experiment with colors, which, as our interviews suggest, are often added with software. We believe that this approach can help the artist preview the outcome of her work earlier in the process and make faster decisions about alternatives.

We learnt from our interviews that illustrators often make use of photographs, films or even sceneries and physical objects not only for ideas and inspiration but also as direct support for their drawings. Famous illustrators like Norman Rockwell are well known to make extensive use of model photographs in their work. Software tools allow artists to reuse material like photographs in new creative ways. Figure 9 shows a representative example from the previous work of our participant (S). The artists here has created several layers in her workspace to mix sketches with photographs that serve as models. More specifically, she has created a collage of banknotes such that she can depict them with more realistic details. We are interested in letting users develop similar strategies when they draw on paper. The current version of BricoSketch does allow for such functionality, so we plan to provide support for virtual layers that accept photographs and videos in addition to sketches.

CONCLUSION

We conducted interviews with four professional illustrators and investigated how they use technology and paper in their creative process. We also studied the evolution of the work of one of these illustrators for a period of two years. In interaction with her, we designed BricoSketch, an augmented-reality system for creating illustrations on paper by working at different scales. BricoSketch enables illustrators to interactively create partial views of their drawings. Such views can be transposed and rescaled. Artists can then use them to create variations of their illustrations or add details with higher drawing precision. Our implementation is based on interactive paper technology that allows for above-the-surface interaction and supports traditional drawing tools such as common pens and pencils. We discussed how BricoSketch supports a more effective transition between paper and computer tools. Early feedback from an artist suggests that our approach can support real user needs in new creative ways.

ACKNOWLEDGEMENTS

We thank the four illustrators who participated in our studies. We are especially grateful to Sandrine Martin and Erwann Surcouf for giving their permission to publish extracts from their artwork. This project was partly funded by ANR (ANR-12-JS02-003-01 DRAO).

REFERENCES

1. Aliakseyeu, D., Martens, J.-B., and Rauterberg, M. A computer support tool for the early stages of architectural design. *Interact. Comput. 18*, 4 (July 2006), 528–555.
2. Bae, S.-H., Balakrishnan, R., and Singh, K. Ilovesketch: as-natural-as-possible sketching system for creating 3d curve models. *UIST '08*, ACM (2008), 151–160.
3. Brandl, P., Forlines, C., Wigdor, D., Haller, M., and Shen, C. Combining and measuring the benefits of bimanual pen and direct-touch interaction on horizontal interfaces. *AVI '08*, ACM (2008), 154–161.
4. Deber, J., Jota, R., Forlines, C., and Wigdor, D. How much faster is fast enough?: User perception of latency & latency improvements in direct and indirect touch. *CHI '15*, ACM (2015), 1827–1836.
5. Dixon, D., Prasad, M., and Hammond, T. iCanDraw: Using sketch recognition and corrective feedback to assist a user in drawing human faces. *CHI '10)*, ACM (2010), 897–906.
6. Fernquist, J., Grossman, T., and Fitzmaurice, G. Sketch-sketch revolution: an engaging tutorial system for guided sketching and application learning. *UIST '11)*, ACM (2011), 373–382.
7. Fitzmaurice, G. W., Ishii, H., and Buxton, W. A. S. Bricks: Laying the foundations for graspable user interfaces. *CHI '95*, ACM (1995), 442–449.
8. Flagg, M., and Rehg, J. Projector-guided painting. *UIST '06*, ACM (2006), 235–244.
9. Garcia, J., Tsandilas, T., Agon, C., and Mackay, W. Interactive paper substrates to support musical creation. *CHI '12*, ACM (2012), 1825–1828.
10. Hartmann, B., Morris, M. R., Benko, H., and Wilson, A. D. Pictionaire: Supporting collaborative design work by integrating physical and digital artifacts. *CSCW '10*, ACM (2010), 421–424.
11. Hertzmann, A. Tutorial: A survey of stroke-based rendering. *IEEE Comput. Graph. Appl. 23*, 4 (July 2003), 70–81.
12. Iarussi, E., Bousseau, A., and Tsandilas, T. The drawing assistant: Automated drawing guidance and feedback from photographs. *UIST '13*, ACM (2013), 183–192.
13. Jalal, G., Maudet, N., and Mackay, W. E. Color portraits: From color picking to interacting with color. *CHI '15*, ACM (2015), 4207–4216.
14. Jun, X., Aaron, H., Wilmot, L., and Holger, W. PortraitSketch: Face sketching assistance for novices. *UIST '14*, ACM (2014), 407–417.
15. Kazi, R. H., Chevalier, F., Grossman, T., Zhao, S., and Fitzmaurice, G. Draco: Bringing life to illustrations with kinetic textures. *CHI '14*, ACM (2014), 351–360.
16. Kazi, R. H., Chua, K. C., Zhao, S., Davis, R., and Low, K.-L. Sandcanvas: A multi-touch art medium inspired by sand animation. *CHI '11*, ACM (2011), 1283–1292.
17. Kazi, R. H., Igarashi, T., Zhao, S., and Davis, R. Vignette: Interactive texture design and manipulation with freeform gestures for pen-and-ink illustration. *CHI '12*, ACM (2012), 1727–1736.
18. Laviole, J., and Hachet, M. Papart: interactive 3d graphics and multi-touch augmented paper for artistic creaton. *3DUI '12*, IEEE (2012), 3–6.
19. Lee, Y., Zitnick, C., and Cohen, M. Shadowdraw: real-time user guidance for freehand drawing. *ACM Trans. on Graphics (Proc. SIGGRAPH) 30*, 4 (2011), 27.
20. Mackay, W., and Pagani, D. Video mosaic: Laying out time in a physical space. *MULTIMEDIA '94*, ACM (1994), 165–172.
21. Nakajima, M., Sakamoto, D., and Igarashi, T. Offline painted media for digital animation authoring. *CHI '14*, ACM (2014), 321–330.
22. Otsuki, M., Sugihara, K., Kimura, A., Shibata, F., and Tamura, H. Mai painting brush: An interactive device that realizes the feeling of real painting. *UIST '10*, ACM (2010), 97–100.
23. Song, H., Grossman, T., Fitzmaurice, G., Guimbretiere, F., Khan, A., Attar, R., and Kurtenbach, G. Penlight: Combining a mobile projector and a digital pen for dynamic visual overlay. *CHI '09*, ACM (2009), 143–152.
24. Song, H., Guimbretiere, F., Grossman, T., and Fitzmaurice, G. Mouselight: Bimanual interactions on digital paper using a pen and a spatially-aware mobile projector. *CHI '10*, ACM (2010), 2451–2460.
25. Tsandilas, T. Interpreting strokes on paper with a mobile assistant. *UIST '12*, ACM (2012), 299–308.
26. Tsandilas, T., and Mackay, W. E. Knotty gestures: Subtle traces to support interactive use of paper. *AVI '10*, ACM (2010), 147–154.
27. Tsang, S., Balakrishnan, R., Singh, K., and Ranjan, A. A suggestive interface for image guided 3d sketching. *CHI '04*, ACM (2004), 591–598.
28. Vandoren, P., Claesen, L., Van Laerhoven, T., Taelman, J., Raymaekers, C., Flerackers, E., and Van Reeth, F. Fluidpaint: An interactive digital painting system using real wet brushes. *ITS '09*, ACM (2009), 53–56.
29. Vogel, D., and Casiez, G. Conté: Multimodal input inspired by an artist's crayon. *UIST '11*, ACM (2011), 357–366.
30. Wellner, P. Interacting with paper on the digitaldesk. *Commun. ACM 36*, 7 (July 1993), 87–96.

Ghost Touch: Turning Surfaces into Interactive Tangible Canvases with Focused Ultrasound

Asier Marzo[1,2,3], Ricky McGeeham[2], Jess McIntosh[2], Sue Ann Seah[2], Sriram Subramanian[3]
[1]Computer Science, Public University of Navarre, Spain. [2]Computer Science, Bristol University, UK.
[3]Informatics, University of Sussex, UK.
amarzo@hotmail.com, {rm1381, jm0152, s.a.seah}@bristol.ac.uk, sriram@sussex.ac.uk

Figure 1. a) Ghost Touch can remotely draw traces and detect the user's input turning a normal surface into an interactive canvas. b) Simultaneous traces of different thicknesses can be created with a novel algorithm that controls an ultrasound phased array. c) Other media such as milk and ink can also be manipulated with Ghost Touch.

ABSTRACT
Digital art technologies take advantage of the input, output and processing capabilities of modern computers. However, full digital systems lack the tangibility and expressiveness of their traditional counterparts. We present Ghost Touch, a system that remotely actuate the artistic medium with an ultrasound phased array. Ghost Touch transforms a normal surface into an interactive tangible canvas in which the users and the system collaborate in real-time to produce an artistic piece. Ghost Touch is able to detect traces and reproduce them, therefore enabling common digital operations such as copy, paste, save or load whilst maintaining the tangibility of the traditional medium. Ghost Touch has enhanced expressivity since it uses a novel algorithm to generate multiple ultrasound focal points with specific intensity levels. Different artistic effects can be performed on sand, milk&ink or liquid soap.

ITS '15, November 15-18, 2015, Funchal, Portugal
© 2015 ACM. ISBN 978-1-4503-3899-8/15/11…$15.00
DOI: http://dx.doi.org/10.1145/2817721.2817727

Author Keywords
Tangible Canvas; Focused Ultrasound; Pressure Levels.

ACM Classification Keywords
H.5.2 Information Interfaces and Presentation: User Interfaces

INTRODUCTION
Since the appearance of the early computer systems, digital counterparts of traditional arts have taken advantage of their processing power as well as input and output capabilities. For instance, Sand Canvas [3] is a system composed of a tabletop that emulates the art of sand painting. With digital art technologies, the skill and time required to create various effects can be reduced compared to the traditional medium. Also, the artists are able to perform remotely, record and reproduce their creations.

However, there is still a preference in offering tangibility to the world of digital art. Full digital systems sometimes lack the physicality and expressiveness of the traditional arts. Here, we present Ghost Touch (Figure 1.a), a system that can transform a surface into an interactive tangible canvas. Ghost Touch uses an ultrasound phased array to remotely draw in the artistic media (Figure 1.bc), and a camera to detect the user traces. Differently from full digital artistic systems, Ghost Touch does not replace the traditional medium but augments it.

The effects of focused ultrasound range from displacing light objects [7] or deforming bubbles [8], to burning biological tissue when high intensities are applied [4]. Yet, to our knowledge, only one work has used focused ultrasound for artistic creations. Namely, Graffiti Fur [9] utilizes a focal point to raise or flatten fur and thus change the amount of light that it reflects. However, the system lacked interactivity and only one point with a constant level of intensity was used, thus limiting the artistic expressivity.

The pressure that we employ while performing different types of art is of paramount importance. For example, in music there are specific symbols for defining the notes intensity (e.g. piano, forte or crescendo). Also, in the ancient art of Chinese calligraphy, the level of pressure is essential for the correct formation of lines and strokes [6].

Algorithms for generating several focal points have been developed [2]. However, to date, they only maximize the total level of pressure. Consequently, the effects of different ultrasound levels on artistic media have never been explored. In order to provide more output expressiveness to Ghost Touch, we developed an algorithm that can create simultaneous focal points with specific levels of pressure.

The contributions of this paper are:

- A system to transform a surface into an interactive tangible canvas.
- An algorithm to create several focal points with specific levels of pressure.
- A list of artistic effects that can be created on different media depending on the pressure level of focused ultrasound.

THE GHOST TOUCH SYSTEM

Hardware

Ghost Touch is composed of an ultrasound phased array, a camera and a projector. The phased array is employed to generate several focal points into the artistic media and thus manipulate it. The camera is used to detect the user traces or gestures. Finally, the projector can be employed as an auxiliary output to indicate where the traces are going to be drawn or the current status of the system.

The phased array is composed of a flat 16x16 grid of transducers driven at 40KHz and 16Vpp. A phased array is a grid of transducers all emitting with the same frequency and amplitude. By adjusting their phase delay, the waves act constructively at the desired locations thus creating focalized pressure points without the necessity of mechanically translating the array.

Apart from the camera, other input devices such as mice and multi-touch tablets can be used. Furthermore, we created a fabric input device (similar to [1]) composed of an elastic fabric, a depth camera and a projector (Figure 2). This is so that we can capture multiple points with different intensities depending on the depth of the fingers. This is important in our application, since we want to enable the user to easily create multiple focal points of different intensities into the canvas. The fabric input was used for several creations presented in this paper.

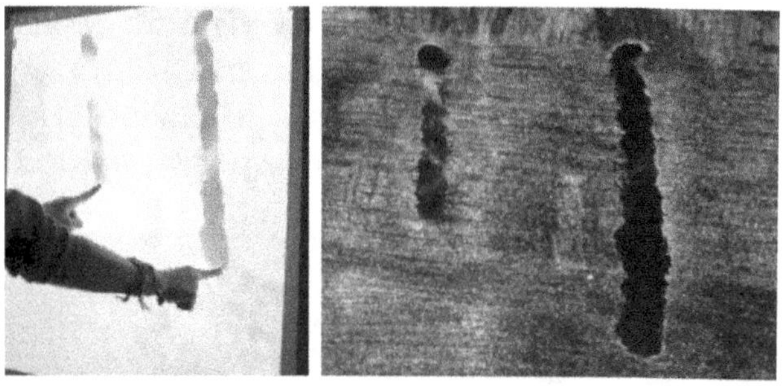

Figure 2. The fabric input (left) detects the levels of pressure and Ghost Touch applies them in the artistic medium (right).

Software

The phased array is controlled by an algorithm that sets the phase delays of each transducer in order to generate the target focal points with the desired intensity. Additionally, an image processing algorithm is applied on the video feed of the camera to detect the user's input. External input devices can send commands to Ghost Touch since an UDP server awaits for commands. These commands can come from multiple devices and be merged enabling collaborative interactions.

To detect the user's traces, the video stream from the camera undergoes a perspective transformation to rectify the distortion, then a Gaussian blur is applied followed by a threshold segmentation. Finally, a skeletonization is utilized to extract the trace.

Ultrasound Focal Points Algorithm

Our algorithm is based on defining a function that gives the amplitude at one point as a function of the phase delays of the transducers. With this function at several points, we compose a new target function that gives the deviation of the amplitude levels at the desired points from the specified amplitudes. Finally, we use a BFGS optimizer [5] to get the phase delays that will minimize the target function.

A monofrequential acoustic field can be defined with a complex value at each position, the pressure. The modulus of the pressure is the amplitude (the intensity per se) and its argument is the phase. The acoustic field that the jth transducer creates at a point a can be expressed as $p_{j,a} = e^{i\varphi_j} M_{j,a}$ where φ_j is the phase delay of the transducer and $M_{j,a}$ is a complex number that is constant for a given transducer and point in space. We have used the Piston model to calculate the $M_{j,a}$ values:

$$M_{j,a} = amp\ dir(\alpha) \frac{1}{d} e^{ikd}$$

where amp is the power of the transducer, k is the wavenumber $k = 2\pi f / c_m$, d is the distance from the transducer to the point and α is the angle between the transducer and the point. $dir(\alpha)$ is the directivity function that can be obtained from the manufacturer specification.

The total pressure at point a is the addition of the pressures generated by the transducers at that point: $p_a = \sum_{j=1}^{N} p_{j,a}$. The target function to generate specific amplitude values A, B… at points a, b … is:

$$f(\varphi_1, \dots, \varphi_N) = (|p_a| - A)^2 + (|p_b| - B)^2 + \dots$$

The deviation of the algorithm for five focal points (located above 30 cm. of the array) with random target intensities (ranging from 100 to 2500 Pa) was nearly zero with continuous phase resolution, 0.17 Pa for 1000 phase values, 1.65 Pa for 100 and 10.34 Pa for 20.

EFFECTS OF FOCUSED ULTRASOUND ON MEDIA

The unique feature of Ghost Touch is that simultaneous point of focused ultrasound with specific intensities can be produced with the phased array. This allows us to create multiple effects on the artistic medium based on the use of different intensities. In this section, we present the different artistic effects that can be achieved with focused ultrasound on different media depending on the level of pressure.

Sand

Fine sawdust offered the best results due to its low weight and high absorbance of sound. Other powders such as sand, flour or cornstarch can be used. Depending on the level of pressure applied, the amount of displaced dust varies and thus creates lines of different thicknesses (Figure 3).

Milk and Ink

Milk represents a white canvas in which ink of different colors can be dropped. Due to the differences in viscosity, the blobs will be contained but allow deformation at the same time. Depending on the pressure level, ink can be dragged, pulled or generate torrents that create interesting patterns due to the dynamics of the fluid (Figure 4).

Soap solutions

In a solution of a liquid and soap it is possible to either create bubbles or pop them depending on the intensity (Figure 5). Therefore, the creation can be done by generating bubbles as traces or by popping a canvas fully covered with bubbles. This medium allows one to completely erase the creation and start from scratch. Additionally, with low intensity it is possible to move blobs of bubbles around.

Objects

Objects made of expanded polystyrene could be pushed around with a focal point. Similarly, objects floating in liquids can be controlled accurately adjusting the intensity. Ultra Tangibles [7] used a similar principle but objects had to be enclosure by transducers from all sides. In our case, a single array above the objects is enough, making this approach more suitable for exhibitions and public displays.

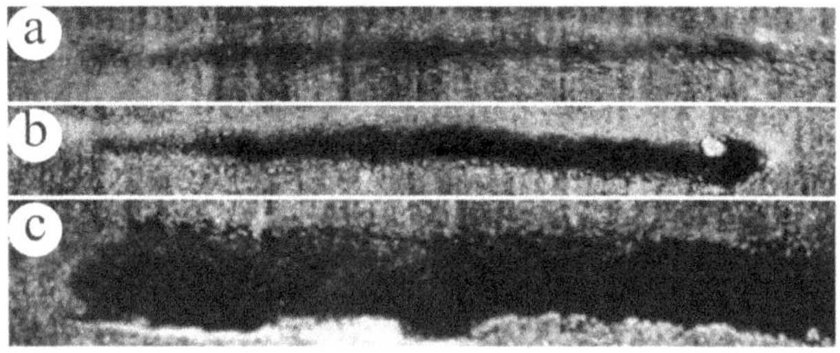

Figure 3. Effects of pressure on sawdust: low intensity for thin traces (a), medium for normal (b) and strong for thick (c).

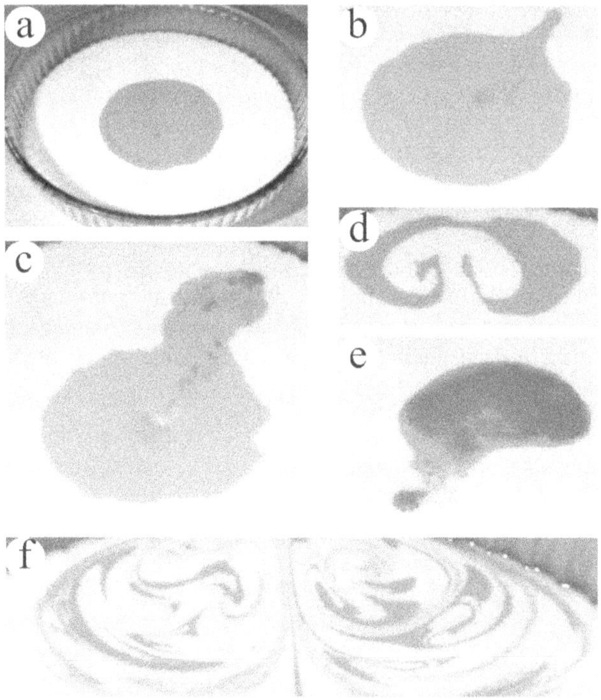

Figure 4. Effects of pressure on ink over milk. a) the original blob. b) weak pressure drags thin strokes of ink. c) medium intensity drags thicker traces. d) medium-strong can drag milk inside ink. (e) strong focal points collapse the blob when applied on it or (f) induce flow patterns if applied near it.

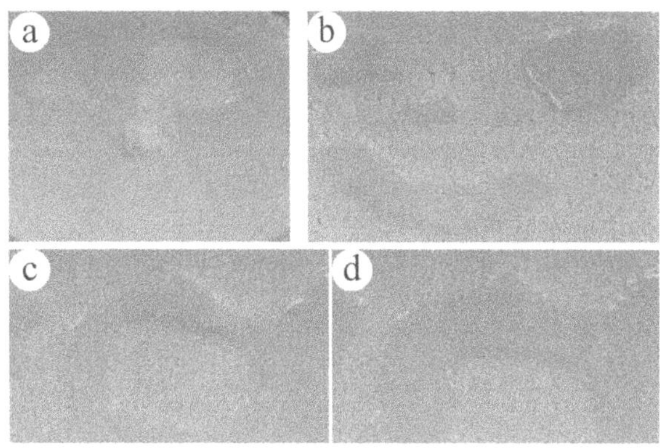

Figure 5. Effects of pressure on a soap solution. a) strong focal points generate bubbles. b,c) medium intensity pop bubbles. d) weak focal points can be used to move bubbles.

INTERACTION TECHNIQUES

The ultrasonic phased array can modify the artistic medium at multiple points simultaneously and apply different effects. Also, the user's traces can be detected with the camera. Both the user and Ghost Touch share the same artistic medium. Finally, other external input devices such as the fabric input, mice or tablets can be used and a projector is employed as an auxiliary output when it is not desirable to physically modify the medium. This combination enables Ghost Touch to support some common digital operations:

Copy & paste (Figure 6.a): The user performs a gesture to indicate Ghost Touch to copy the last trace. Then, the user can paste that trace at any position. The projector can be used to temporally show how the final trace will appear. Traces can be copied from a template library, also during the paste operations transformations such as scale or rotation can be applied to the copy.

Beautifying (Figure 6.b): When the user inputs is performed on an external device and not directly in the canvas, the computer system can preprocess the trace before outputting it in the artistic medium. For instance, straightening lines, making circles perfect or snapping to the grid.

Mirroring (Figure 6.c): Once that some symmetry axes have been established, the user can draw on one region and Ghost touch will duplicate the trace on the symmetry regions in real-time.

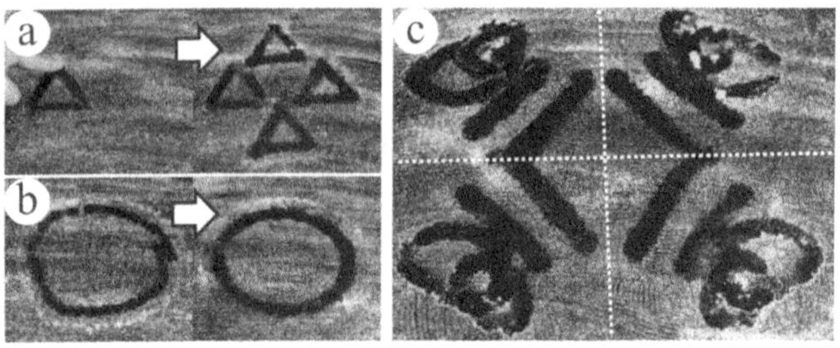

Figure 6. Some interaction techniques supported by Ghost Touch. a) Copy and paste. b) Beautification of circles or straight lines. c) Mirror painting, only the top left corner was drawn by the user.

APPLICATIONS

The input and output capabilities of Ghost Touch will enable multiple applications to take advantage of the combination of traditional artistic media with digital operations. For instance, a collaborative system composed of two interconnected Ghost Touch permits remote users to draw in a shared canvas.

Ghost Touch could enable other applications such as tutoring systems and art exhibitions. The users can draw from any distance to the canvas using external devices or their own Ghost Touch, this allows more artists to work simultaneously without having problems of interfering with each other. Also, audiences can see the performances without occlusion from the artists and at multiple remote locations.

CONCLUSION

We have presented a system that can remotely produce different artistic effects on sand, milk&ink or soap by means of focused ultrasound. Ghost Touch have been used to transform a surface into an interactive tangible canvas in which the user as well as the system can draw. Thereby, the advantages of digital technologies are brought to the tangibility of the traditional medium.

Nonetheless, the system presented some limitations. The interaction space was restrained to 60x50cm; however, it can be increased by placing Ghost Touch higher or by using several phased arrays. Gestures, projected images and output traces should be further explored.

Being able to generate specific levels of pressure with a phased array have additional applications. While delivering haptic feedback, it is possible to adjust the intensity to add an extra dimension of information to each haptic point. For instance, to convey the proximity of obstacles in navigation systems for blind people.

ACKNOWLEDGMENTS

Work supported by the European Research Council, 7th framework programme (Starting Grant Agreement 278576).

REFERENCES

1. Dand, D., and Hemsley, R. 2013. Obake: interactions on a 2.5 D elastic display. Adjunct UIST, 109-110.
2. Gavrilov, L. R. 2008. The possibility of generating focal regions of complex configurations in application to the problems of stimulation of human receptor structures by focused ultrasound. Acoustical Physics, 54(2), 269-278.
3. Kazi, R. H., Chua, K. C., Zhao, S., Davis, R., and Low, K. L. 2011. SandCanvas: A multi-touch art medium inspired by sand animation. SIGCHI, 1283-1292.
4. Kennedy, J. E., Ter Haar, G. R. and Cranston, D. 2014. High intensity focused ultrasound: surgery of the future? Br J Radiol, 76, 590-599.
5. Liu, D. C. and Nocedal, J. 1989. On the limited memory BFGS method for large scale optimization. Mathematical programming, 45(1-3), 503-528.
6. Long, J. 2001. The art of Chinese calligraphy. Courier Corporation.
7. Marshall, M., Carter, T., Alexander, J. and Subramanian, S. 2012. Ultra-tangibles: creating movable tangible objects on interactive tables. SIGCHI, 2185-2188.
8. Ochiai, Y., Hoshi, T., Oyama, A. and Rekimoto, J. 2013. Poppable display: A display that enables popping, breaking, and tearing interactions with people. Consumer Electronics (pp. 124-128). IEEE.
9. Sugiura, Y., Toda, K., Hoshi, T., Kamiyama, Y., Igarashi, T. and Inami, M. 2014. Graffiti fur: turning your carpet into a computer display. UIST 149-156.

Eyes-Free Touch Command Support for Pen-Based Digital Whiteboards via Handheld Devices

Fabrice Matulic
Interactive Media Lab,
Technische Universität Dresden
fabrice.matulic@tu-dresden.de

Maria Husmann **Seraiah Walter** **Moira C. Norrie**
Department of Computer Science,
ETH Zurich
husmann@inf.ethz.ch, walteser@student.ethz.ch, norrie@inf.ethz.ch

ABSTRACT
Digital whiteboards that only sense pen input are limited in their interactive capabilities. One way to artificially add touch support is through personal mobile devices, which people carry with them. This work investigates how smartphones can be used as portable quick-access toolboxes held by the non-dominant hand to provide assistive touch commands for pen-driven whiteboard tasks. We developed two interface designs, one based on a classic remote with standard GUI controls and another optimised for eyes-free operation to eliminate gaze shifts between the two devices. In a controlled evaluation based on an established mode-switching study protocol, we compare the two phone interfaces and a baseline technique consisting of a pen-triggered popup menu on the whiteboard. Our results show a superior efficiency of the phone UIs over the popup. The eyes-free UI only partially performed better than the classic interface at the subtask level after subtracting the costs of errors.

Author Keywords
Interactive whiteboards; mode switching; eyes-free interface; bimanual pen and touch coordination.

ACM Classification Keywords
H.5.2 [User Interfaces]: Input devices and strategies, Interaction styles.

INTRODUCTION
Whiteboards are popular tools for a wide range of activities including brainstorming, collaborative sketching, classroom work and personal note-taking. Interactive whiteboards offer the affordances and convenience of regular whiteboards and augment them with tools from the digital world to enhance their capabilities. Depending on the underlying hardware and software technologies, those capacities can vary tremendously. Modern products such as the SMART Board support touch in addition to pen input. This allows the non-dominant hand (NDH) to fulfil assistive tasks, such

ITS '15, November 15 - 18, 2015, Funchal, Portugal

ACM 978-1-4503-3899-8/15/11...$15.00
DOI: http://dx.doi.org/10.1145/2817721.2817728

Figure 1. A user drawing with her dominant hand on a digital whiteboard, while operating controls on a smartphone with her non-dominant hand.

as manipulating the workspace, operating widgets or performing complementary actions. If the system is able to differentiate the two modalities, they can be assigned distinct roles, typically inking for the pen and command input for touch [10]. However, not all whiteboards have that capability. In many cases, either touch is indistinguishable from pen input or the device only supports pen interaction, e.g. whiteboard systems based on external IR digitisers or on Anoto technology [6]. With such setups, interaction mechanisms have to be devised to enable command triggering while preserving the natural experience of direct inking with the pen. The two most common solutions for tackling that problem are widgets, i.e. specific areas of the interface within which the pen behaves as a different tool (e.g. a menu or a toolbar), and gestures, i.e. pre-defined strokes that the system recognises as commands instead of regular ink. A gesture can also be used to summon a widget, from which operations can then be selected and executed (e.g. marking menus). Both of these methods have drawbacks, as either valuable UI space is consumed or users have to learn special strokes and potentially cope with misinterpretation errors. Some pens are equipped with barrel buttons that enable different mode activations but these also come with their own issues [5, 14].

Beyond the surface of the whiteboard, practitioners have sought to explore extended interactive spaces created by the introduction of other devices, especially personal mobile devices such as tablets and smartphones. Examples include the use of handhelds to transfer content to and from the whiteboard [6, 20], to remotely point at or control objects on the display [2, 17] and even as physical objects used for tangible input [8, 21]. In most of the cases studied so far, the mobile device is also an active centre of (visual) attention, even if temporary, and users have to shift their focus between the board and their devices to manipulate content, locate a control or perform a gesture. This is generally not a problem in scenarios with little cross-device interaction, but for more intense whiteboard activities, smoother flows with lighter context switches might be desirable.

In this paper, we study the use of personal smartphones as low-attention touch-based assistive devices to efficiently support fluid pen-driven whiteboard tasks. We created two phone interfaces integrating a core set of whiteboard tools activated by the thumb of the user's NDH holding the device. One design resembles a classic remote or palette with standard GUI controls, while the other is optimised for eyes-free use and includes large buttons as well as a gesture pad. The latter is aimed at reducing the demands on visual attention by eliminating the to-and-fro gaze shifts between the mobile device and the whiteboard. In a set of controlled experiments involving various patterns of alternating atomic inking and command subtasks, we compare the efficiency, accuracy and qualitative merits of those interfaces as well as a baseline pen-only technique with a pen-triggered popup menu on the whiteboard.

RELATED WORK

There is a sizeable body of work related to interactive whiteboards in the literature. From the first Liveboard prototypes developed at Xerox PARC in the early 90's [5] to modern displays incorporating multiple sensing capabilities, a broad range of systems and dedicated applications have been created and studied. As motivated in the introduction, our main scope of interest concerns the integration of personal mobile devices into the interactive space of basic pen-based digital whiteboards, not as independent working and content-sharing devices, but mainly as controls facilitating the operation of the whiteboard. This concept falls under the category of multimachine user interfaces (MMUIs), a term coined by Myers et al., who extensively explored the interoperation of handhelds with desktop computers within the Pebbles project [17]. Around the same period, Rekimoto investigated the combination of mobile devices with whiteboards both for content-sharing and UI control [20]. While the first version of his system involved weighty tablets that required the DH to interact with both the whiteboard and the handheld, a second version based on PDAs made activations by the NDH possible via the PDA's physical buttons.

Tool palettes held in the NDH in a painter-like fashion need not be computing devices. For their NiCE discussion room, Haller et al. utilise acrylic and magnet palettes with Anoto patterns to provide a mobile and more direct tool-selection alternative to their digital pie menus triggered by pen long presses on the whiteboard [6]. Those physical palettes have the advantages and disadvantages of inert tangibles: they are convenient and always "on", but they only allow one fixed design and do not provide dynamic feedback.

Pushing further the spatial cross-device relationship are techniques in which phones are used as tangibles that physically contact the display surface to trigger particular actions [8, 21]. Interaction with the whiteboard via mobile devices can of course also be done in a contactless fashion, not only by the main whiteboard operator, but also by other participants in the background. For instance, Code Space is a system in which members of the audience can remotely point at and drag objects on a display as well as execute gestural commands [2]. A similar effort for TV sets proposes a set of gestures to remotely control the screen [7]. Those gestures range from easy flicking motions for navigation to more complex shape interactions to trigger commands.

As mentioned above, with the exception of when it is used as a pointer, the handheld engaged in a cross-device interaction with the whiteboard or large display necessitates the user's visual focus. The user, therefore, has to divide their attention between the multiple devices involved, which can have a notable performance and cognitive cost, if context switches are frequent [19]. In their third experiment on bimanual pen and touch coordination, Matulic and Norrie show that blind pen mode switching using NDH postures can reduce that cost, provided mode errors are few [15]. Eyes-free interfaces have been considered by other authors as well, but more as alternatives to operate the devices themselves in the absence of visibility rather than as a means to reduce attention shifting. Thus, most prototypes developed so far rely on I/O techniques that require the user's full attention such as audio feedback [4, 13, 25] and compound gestures [22]. Other methods based on simpler gestural motions such as jerks and tilts [1, 11] have also been proposed and while such device gestures could potentially be applied in bimanual MMUI contexts, we think they are less common than regular touch-based manipulations and so do not consider them at this stage of our work.

Looking at prior experimental evaluations that are relevant to our approach, Li et al. compared techniques to switch from pen inking to gesture mode on tablets and found that a physical button pressed by the NDH performs best [14]. In [9], Hinckley et al. propose and test various spring-loaded techniques allowing function selections to remain enabled for repeated actions. They report that such quasimodal activations are both effective and also preferred by people over status quo alternatives. While they reveal relevant results, those two studies utilised only single actuators to trigger or maintain one mode switch and were conducted on tablets. These conditions do not apply in our case as we focus on a combination of multiple modes and commands in a multi-device environment. However, the methodology used in those experiments could be suitably adapted for our purpose, especially [9], hence we based our protocol on it, as described in the Experiment section. Finally, in [3],

Bragdon et al. experimentally determine that gestures are superior to soft buttons under conditions of high environmental distraction. Based on eye-gaze data, they also note that gestures are much more suited to eyes-free usage compared to soft buttons, which users have to look at to properly operate. However, their UI comprising 12 buttons laid out at the top of the phone screen was not designed with eyes-free use in mind and so that result is not generalisable. Wang et al., for instance, show that for a 3×4 grid of touch areas covering the whole screen, people achieve an eyes-free targeting accuracy of about 90% [23]. For lower densities, such as 3×2 or 2×2 layouts, the reported accuracy is even close to 99% and 100%. Those findings suggest that soft buttons can also be effective eyes-free controls.

APPROACH

We first explain the rationale that motivated our approach and formulate our hypotheses before describing the techniques used in our experiment.

Rationale

Our starting point is a digital whiteboard based on Anoto technology and front-projection, similar to that of the NiCE room [6]. Such a setup allows high-precision pen sensing and wide interactive surfaces, but on the other hand, it does not support touch input, which limits its interactive capabilities. Hence, one of our goals is, to some extent, to compensate for the lack of touch input on such whiteboard systems through the agency of smartphones that people always carry with them. However, we also think that personal handheld devices can make sense for pen and touch displays as well, for instance, as personalised or private palettes or to reduce occlusions caused by widgets on the board.

A second aspect concerns the efficiency of pen tasks on the whiteboard. As we have seen, there are many examples showing how new functionality is created to manipulate and exchange content in novel ways, but performance aspects are often not considered, both in terms of task productivity and cognitive demand.

A further factor that differs from performance studies made on tablets and tabletops (such as mode-switching) is the arm fatigue caused by protracted in-air interaction with a vertical display. The active use of a device held up in the NDH while writing with the pen might even amplify that adverse effect. These considerations motivated us to explore the potential of smartphones essentially as quick-access and low-attention assistive toolboxes that can be held in a casual and relaxed manner rather than as other primary devices that also tax the user's attention and stamina. This requirement suggests the need for the device to also be usable without having to look at it, that is, it should be operable in an eyes-free manner.

In order to frame our target scope more precisely, we enumerate the practical and theoretical benefits of smartphone-aided pen interaction on whiteboards using visible and eyes-free interfaces, as we see them:

General advantages of handheld-based controls:

1. Provides separate touch support for whiteboards that only support pen input
2. Allows menus and widgets to be relocated to the handheld, thereby reducing clutter on the whiteboard
3. Enables personalised controls
4. Presumably reduces mode-switching and command activation time

Additional advantages of eyes-free controls:

5. In meeting situations, the presenter's gaze is always on the board or the audience, not on their personal device
6. Enables private controls (if UI is hidden)
7. Presumably reduces mode-switching and command activation time even more
8. Presumably reduces cognitive and physical effort (but probably only minimally and after much training)

Analysing the items in the above list and relating the identified theoretical advantages of eyes-free interfaces to Yi et al.'s taxonomy of motivations for eyes-free interaction [24], we notice that: 1 is system-specific. 2, 3 and 6 depend on the target application (with 6 falling in the M5 category of Yi et al.'s classification). 5 (an M4 case) is conditioned by the type of whiteboard activity considered. This leaves 4, 7 and 8, the "presumable" performance aspects, (with 7 and 8 falling in the M10 category) that we are interested in and that we seek to validate or invalidate experimentally.

To summarise: within our considered usage scope of eyes-free interfaces, we contextually cover but do not study some of the social benefits identified by Yi et al. (M4 and M5) and we closely examine perceived improvements to personal efficiency (M10). In that respect, our focus is similar to that of Matulic and Norrie's third experiment [15] but with different environments: a vertical display and separate surfaces/devices for the two hands, where the NDH also holds a device instead of a single tabletop with which both hands freely interact (and are able to rest on the surface). We further do not want to restrict ourselves to purely quasimodal pen mode switching, as we would like to also include simple modal activations as well as general independent commands that do not involve the pen.

Another important aspect that Matulic and Norrie emphasise in their report is the importance of visual feedback to maintain correct awareness of the currently active mode or selected properties. While our study does not involve multiple users interacting at the same time, whiteboards are often used collaboratively and so we should not ignore those situations when designing awareness mechanisms. Therefore, large visuals such as surface-wide coloured borders are likely not appropriate in our case.

With regard to the operations to support, we select a set of core whiteboard functions commonly used for note-taking and brainstorming activities: pen colours, a stroke style change (thickness), delete and undo/redo. This choice reflects our main driving concern to find a satisfactory balance between simplicity (to keep eyes-free manipulations tractable) and integration of standard tools typically available in whiteboard applications. Furthermore, it covers properties that are activated and modified in different ways and thus, we believe, form an ecologically valid mix of tools in our context: in a reduced palette, such as the one we are considering, colour and style options are assigned discrete values that remain active once selected (normal mode), because we assume that in most cases those changes are meant to be permanent, until explicitly changed again. Delete can also be implemented as a system-maintained mode, but it is usually only needed on a temporary basis, so it is a good candidate for quasimodal activation in an eyes-free interface, i.e. the user would have to continuously maintain a pose, such as a finger pressed, to keep the mode active (as in [16]). Finally, undo/redo are independent and instantaneous commands that do not affect the pen status.

We now describe the designs of our phone interfaces based on that set of requirements.

Phone UI Designs

Eyes-Free Interface

The main challenge of designing an efficient eyes-free interface is to create controls that can be quickly located and triggered with a minimal number of mistakes. In the case of a mobile device held and operated by the NDH, the controls have to be easily accessible by the user's thumb. Furthermore, in our particular case, the user's attention is also consumed by the pen-holding DH, not to mention by the main whiteboard activity and potentially other users. We therefore aim for simple controls that can be easily and quickly triggered rather than more sophisticated interactions such as path-based gestures, which are reportedly difficult to execute with one hand [3].

Our functions to be mapped can be divided into three categories: functions with a directional or ordinal quality, i.e. that convey a sense of movement (undo/redo) or corresponding to a value that can be increased or decreased (stroke thickness), a function associated with a categorical value (pen colour) and a mode (delete). The first group can be conceptually mapped to the two screen axes, which suggests as suitable UI component a virtual D-pad or directional gestures such as flicks. The delete mode can be assigned to an isolated modifier button (which needs to be kept pressed to maintain the non-default mode active) and the colours to regular soft buttons activated by single taps.

Following these considerations, we created the design shown in Figure 2 comprising two separate areas. At the top is a gesture pad on which flicking gestures mapped to undo/redo (horizontal flicks) and stroke thickness changes can be executed (vertical flicks). The pad also functions as the modifier button for the quasimodal activation of the delete mode (thumb pressed down). When the delete mode is engaged, users can strike out strokes with the pen to remove them from the screen.

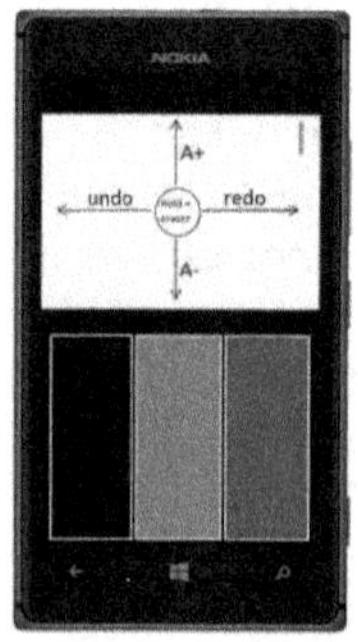

Physical dimensions on Nokia Lumia 925	
Gesture pad	5.8 × 4 cm
Colour button	1.7 × 4.2 cm

Figure 2. The Eyes-Free phone UI with the physical dimensions of its components

In the lower part of the UI are a group of three mutually exclusive buttons corresponding to the three colours that we (arbitrarily) select: black, red and blue. We chose this number of divisions and layout with components filling the entire screen space based on the most efficient tile arrangements for eyes-free use reported by Wang et al. in [23]. Their analysis shows that there is a higher decrease in eyes-free targeting accuracy in the vertical direction than in the horizontal one. According to their experimental data, a division into two parts along the Y-axis and into two or three sections along the X-axis yields accuracies of, or very close to, 100%. We further note that the physical dimensions of the UI components when rendered on the screen of a Nokia Lumia 925 (see table in Figure 2) exceed by far Parhi et al.'s recommended size of 9.6mm for eyes-free targets [18].

With regard to user awareness of selected properties and active mode, we integrated visual feedback both on the phone screen and on the whiteboard. On the phone, it is located in the top right corner (Figure 2). On the whiteboard, we have to deal with the problem touched upon earlier of providing user-specific feedback on a large surface potentially used by several people. Our solution consists of an icon placed near the last drawn stroke (see Figure 1). This method is satisfactory as long as the user's strokes remain relatively close to each other, but is obviously less helpful if they move to other areas of the board between two strokes. We did not include any tracking that would allow icons to "follow" the user's movements but this feature could easily be added to our system.

The feedback icons give a representation of the currently selected stroke width and colour in inking mode and show an eraser in delete mode. A brief notification is also shown when an undo or a redo is triggered. Users can therefore remain aware of their actions and the selected stroke style only by monitoring the whiteboard. For the colours in particular, the buttons are such that they are triggered as soon as a dragged touch contact enters its active area. Thus, users can blindly slide their thumb across the lower area of the screen while checking the visual feedback on the board to keep track of changes. For delete mode toggling, haptic feedback is also integrated in addition to the visual aid: the phone shortly vibrates when the thumb is pressed down on the pad to indicate that the mode has been engaged.

Classic "Visible" Interface

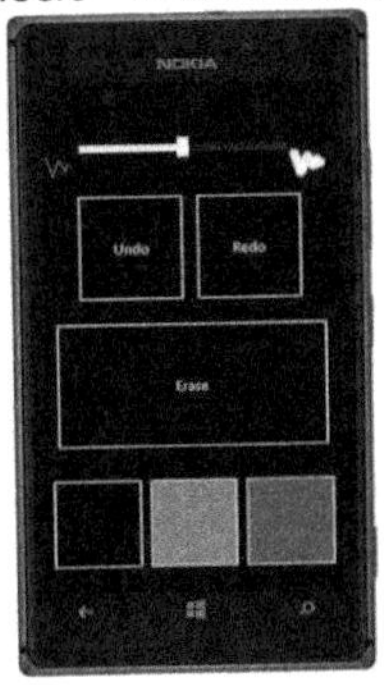

Physical dimensions on Nokia Lumia 925	
Slider (interactive area)	4 × 0.4 cm
Undo/Redo buttons	2 × 2 cm
Erase button	5.3 × 2.4 cm
Colour button	1.7 × 1.7 cm

Figure 3. The classic "visible" phone UI with the physical dimensions of its components

While there is naturally nothing precluding non-blind usage of this first design, we decided to create another interface without the eyes-free concern in mind following classic UI patterns and controls. The reasons for this choice are threefold: first, we wanted to compare design strategies based on different usage intents. If the experimental analysis revealed no significant differences, then we could make a stronger statement on the equivalence of two different UI designs rather than only of operational or contextual factors. Secondly, a condition where users would forcibly be required to look at an interface using an artificial mechanism would be unrealistic and therefore have little ecological validity. The third reason is to counteract possible learning effects that would likely skew the results of our within-subjects study, which also includes a whiteboard-only technique (see next section). We however also had to take into account the opposite, i.e. possible adverse learning effects caused by a totally different UI layout with different button arrangements, which would likely have confused participants when testing the other phone technique.

Our classic "visible" interface, shown in Figure 3, is our attempt at satisfying the aforementioned concerns while still following standard design practices for such kinds of UIs. Since, in effect, we were creating a simple toolbar or palette, we assigned one widget in a dedicated screen space to a given function. Thus, our classic design has four vertical layers of components with individual soft buttons for colour, erase and undo/redo, and a slider for stroke thickness. Compared to the eyes-free design, there are more widgets with slightly larger gaps between them so that blind usage is more difficult and therefore less of an option for users. Their arrangement and position are however similar to the eyes-free interface in order not to confuse users and their sizes are still sufficiently large to allow precise targeting. All buttons follow a standard tap-once-to-trigger behaviour. Hence, the erase button needs to be tapped to engage and disengage the delete mode and the colour buttons do not activate when dragging in from an external position.

Whiteboard Menu

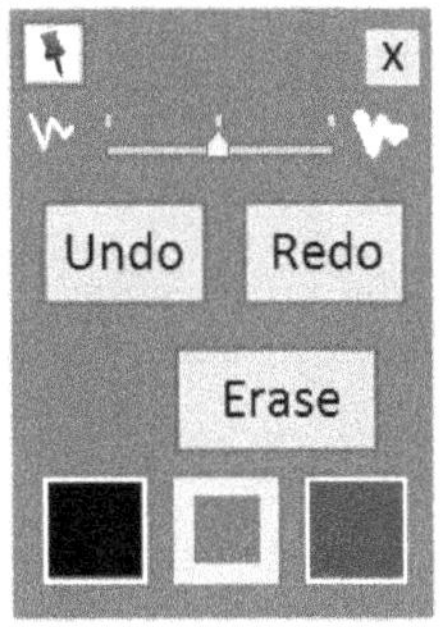

Physical dimensions on whiteboard	
Pin button	2.2 × 2.2 cm
Slider (interact. area)	7.7 × 1.3 cm
Undo/Redo buttons	5.6 × 3.4 cm
Erase button	7 × 3.4 cm
Colour button	3.4 × 3.4 cm

Figure 4. The whiteboard popup menu with the physical dimensions of its components

The whiteboard menu is our baseline "phoneless" technique. It consists of a popup menu with a component layout resembling that of the classic phone UI (Figure 4). It is summoned by a pen long-press on the whiteboard, which is a standard technique to trigger an action differing from the default pointer function (here inking). As hold timeout we used the system value of 1000 ms, which is slightly more conservative than the delay used in [12]. The menu appears so that its centre is located at the tip of the pen to minimise subsequent arm movements to select items.

To reduce UI clutter and possible hindrances, by default, the menu disappears as soon as the pen taps outside it. This behaviour is however clearly not suitable in the case of frequent menu calls and so to avoid repetitious pen dwelling, we endowed the menu with a pin feature allowing it to remain visible. The menu can be moved to other locations by dragging its background or by calling it again with a long press, regardless of its pinned status.

Enabling hardware and software

As stated above, our interactive whiteboard is based on an apparatus similar to that used in the NiCE discussion room [6]. It features a large front-projected vertical surface with an Anoto pattern for the detection of the optical pen. The dimensions and resolution of our display are respectively 360 × 112.5 cm and 2560 × 800 pixels. Our smartphone is a Nokia Lumia 925 with a 4.5" screen measuring 5.9 cm × 9.7 cm and with a resolution of 768 × 1280 pixels.

The software was implemented in C# on Windows 8 and Windows Phone 8.0. As communication protocol between the phone and the server we used TCP over Wi-Fi.

EXPERIMENT

To compare the usability, performance and subjective value of our phone techniques, we conducted a controlled within-subjects study in our lab. We used the popup menu introduced above as baseline condition. While there are, of course, several other valid pen-only techniques that we could have included in the comparison, e.g. marking menus or path gestures [12], we selected only this one pen technique to keep the experiment tractable in terms of time and effort. Pilot studies indeed revealed that arm fatigue was an issue that had to be taken into account and so we decided to

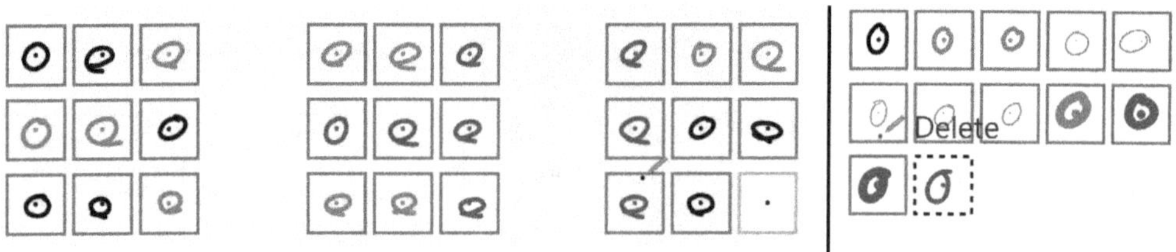

Physical dimensions of the stimuli on the whiteboard	
Box edge length	16.8 cm
Gaps adjacent boxes, X and Y axes	X=1.6 cm Y=3.2 cm
Gap between blocks	29 cm

a) *Distributed* Scene 1 b) *Local* Scene 4

Figure 5. Examples of the two types of scenes used in the experiment

compare only three techniques to keep the physical demand at acceptable levels.

For the experiment, the screen of the eyes-free UI was made completely black, in order to ensure that participants operated the device in the intended manner.

Design

Our study design was modelled after the paradigm developed by Hinckley et al. for their evaluation of spring-loaded controls [9]. It consists of a series of dot-circling tasks (imitating the act of writing) with different patterns of pen modes that users have to match. The costs of those mode switches are then calculated by subtracting the mean completion times of baseline tasks from that of the switched tasks. Our experiment followed a similar methodology but with notable differences that we point out in the following description.

Tasks

As in the Springboard study, our tasks were composed of blocks of atomic actions (subtasks) to be executed from left to right (but in our case also from top to bottom, since we use multiple rows), with basic inking subtasks involving circling a dot stimulus contained in a box using a single stroke. The colour and thickness of the dot indicated the style that had to be matched by the input ink. Participants used the tested technique to select the correct stroke colour and thickness before marking the box. To remain in manageable territory and facilitate equality checks in the analysis, we limited the range of the stroke thickness to three discrete values: small, medium and large.

Where we departed from the Springboard study is that we also included command stimuli to be acted upon. Hence, in between circling subtasks participants were required to delete strokes and issue undo/redo operations, where the latter concerned both inking and deleting actions. Another important difference is that our commands actually performed their actions on the UI instead of just leaving a trail representing the selected tool without doing anything. When a command subtask, say delete, was correctly executed, both the stroke and the box were erased so that the next subtask stimulus appeared at the same location as the one that was just removed. This mimicked a real correcting action, in which one stroke is replaced by another. Commands were enabled at all times, even when not prompted by the stimulus. This means that participants could make mistakes and also correct them using the tools at their disposal. If, for instance, a participant inadvertently triggered two stroke undos instead of one, they were required to re-input the mistakenly removed circle before they could move on. For that, they had the possibility to either redo the action or redraw the stroke. We believe that this kind of task model, where commands and errors have actual consequences, as in a real whiteboard activity, increases the ecological validity of our study design. Furthermore, by factoring those corrective manipulations into the completion times, we can determine realistic costs of making mistakes compared to simply playing a sound and registering an error.

A further condition that differs from tablet environments and whose influence we wanted to investigate is display real estate. When writing or sketching on whiteboards people often make use of the large space available to them, for example, if they want to spatially group different categories of notes. We attempted to model that aspect through tasks with several subtask blocks separated by wide gaps (Figure 5a). We hypothesised that this task type would be particularly unfavourable to the popup menu, as participants would either have to move it along or reach far away for it.

Protocol

We created a protocol composed of five series of subtask blocks which we called scenes. These included scenes of the two types described above: *Distributed* scenes containing three separated 3×3 blocks (Figure 5a) and *Local* scenes containing one compact 3×5 block (Figure 5b). *Distributed* scenes focused on the whiteboard width aspect and therefore only consisted of circle subtasks, where the stroke style had to be changed once for every segment of three subtasks. *Local* scenes concentrated on switching and command input and therefore required the user to change stroke styles and execute commands with increasing frequency.

The five scenes with their respective numbers and types of subtasks were the following:

1. *Distributed*: 27 circles with 9 colour changes
2. *Distributed*: 27 circles with 9 thickness changes
3. *Local*: 19 circles with 3 thickness changes, 1 delete, 6 undos and 3 redos
4. *Local*: 18 circles with 3 thickness and 3 colour changes, 6 deletes and 3 undos
5. *Local*: 21 circles with 5 thickness and 7 colour changes, 9 deletes, 6 undos and 3 redos

This yields a total of 112 circles with 20 thickness and 19 colour changes, 16 deletes, 15 undos and 6 redos per technique. Thus, with 3 techniques and 12 participants, a grand total of 4032 circles with 720 thickness and 684 colours changes, 576 deletes, 216 undos and 108 redos were performed for the main tasks (i.e. not counting training).

To counteract learning effects, we created three protocols following the above pattern with subtasks appearing at different indexes in the sequences but with the same type order, i.e. if a delete subtask followed a redo subtask in protocol A, that order was maintained in protocols B and C. These protocols were then used for each technique to be tested, where the order of techniques was permuted between participants.

Each scene started and ended with a circle subtask in the default style, which was medium stroke width and black colour. The completion times for those subtasks were not included in the analysis. Before each scene, a dialog specifying the type of task that the participant was about to carry out was shown. The dialog was to be tapped with the pen to start the scene. At the start of the first training task, a window picturing a mock 3×5 block of subtasks was displayed on the whiteboard. Participants were then given the opportunity to adjust the position and particularly the height of the window to their liking so that they could comfortably reach the three rows.

Participants were instructed to execute the tasks in a natural way, in particular, the circles were to be drawn in a pace and manner matching that of their handwriting.

Participants

We recruited 12 volunteers, 9 males and 3 females with a mean age of 29.7 years old (SD=5.38) for our study. One of the participants was left-handed. In the pre-study questionnaire, all participants indicated that they owned a smartphone. Four people stated that they had some experience with digital pens, whereas all others had none at all.

A session with a participant consisted of the following steps: introduction, filling-in the pre-study questionnaire, height adjustment on the whiteboard, training and main task execution using the 3 techniques, post-study questionnaire and interview. Participants were given the possibility to take breaks between technique trials and between scenes.

Training phases, in which participants familiarised themselves with each technique included example scenes of both types. For the eyes-free UI, participants trained with the visible controls first and then with the black screen, as used during the main tasks.

RESULTS

A full session with a participant took about one hour.

Repeated measures ANOVA and post-hoc pairwise comparisons were performed on scene completion times, subtask completions times, mode switching times and number of extra actions. The latter represent actions, which participants performed in addition to the minimum operations required to complete the given subtask, in other words, actions due to hesitations, errors and their corrections.

Scene Completion Times

Figure 6 shows the mean scene completion times. We conducted a 3×5 repeated measures ANOVA on Technique (*Eyes-Free*, *Classic*, *Popup*) by Scene (1 to 5). We obtained main effects for Technique ($F(2, 22) = 53.975$ $p < 0.001$) as well as for Scene (which is obvious since the five scenes are different). Post-hoc comparisons revealed that both *Eyes-Free* (mean time 59.0 s) and *Classic* (59.7 s) were significantly faster than *Popup* (77.5 s) with $p<0.001$. In particular, the phone UIs were more efficient than *Popup* not only in *Distributed* scenes but also in *Local* scenes. To rule out that the *Popup* technique was disadvantaged by the time spent dwelling or dragging to bring up or relocate the menu, we subtracted the time used for those operations from the total time. This resulted in a mean scene completion time of 72.8 s, which is still significantly higher than the times of both phone UIs ($p < 0.001$). Thus, the differences cannot be attributed only to the mechanical effort of having to move or re-call the menu. Other possible factors are increased cognitive effort to locate and position the popup menu or more time spent physically moving to reach the menu instead of repositioning it. We had expected *Eyes-Free* to perform better than *Classic* at least in Scene 5 where switches and commands were frequent, but this was not borne out by the data ($p=1.0$). Thus, it seems that the two types of phone UIs were not significantly different overall in terms of performance. We now deepen our analysis by examining the individual subtasks more closely.

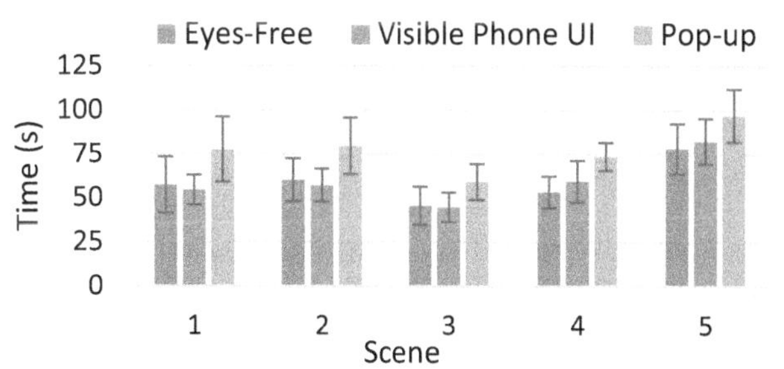

Figure 6. Mean scene completion times.

Subtask Completion Times

We considered our four types of subtasks: Circle, Delete, Undo and Redo. For each type, we discarded the two (three for Circle) best and worst observations from the dataset, in order to minimise outlier effects. This resulted in 3816 observations for Circle, 432 for Delete, 440 for Undo and 172 for Redo. We then calculated the mean task completion time for each task type with the remaining data points.

Repeated measures ANOVA on Technique by Task revealed a significant effect of Task ($F(2, 22)=162.007$, $p<0.001$), Technique ($F(2, 22)=43.431$, $p<0.001$), and Technique*Task ($F(2.069, 22.756)=6.087$, $p=0.0214$) on mean task completion time. A further ANOVA performed on each task type revealed that for all three subtasks, *Eyes-Free* and *Classic* were both faster than *Popup* (p≤.013), but there was no significant difference between the two phone UIs (p≈1 in all cases). Therefore, we were also not able to detect any significant differences at the subtask level. We continued breaking down the individual actions and next looked at switching costs between subtasks.

Cost of Switching

We first considered circle tasks and calculated the cost of changing the colour and the stroke thickness by subtracting the mean task completion times of consecutive circle tasks requiring no style modification from those requiring one. After finding significant main effects for Technique, Style Change (Colour, Thickness) and Technique*Style Change interaction, we found no significant difference between *Eyes-Free* and *Classic* both for Colour (p=0.584) and for Thickness (p=1.0). When comparing the two types of style switches for *Eyes-Free*, we found that changing Colour (735ms) was significantly faster than Thickness (979 ms) (p=0.004), which is a result that we did not expect. Some of the stroke thickness switches involved changing from small to large and vice versa, which required two flicks on the gesture pad instead of one. To analyse the effect of that factor, we removed those instances from the dataset (leaving 305 data points out of 440 originally) and performed the test again. The result is an increased p value of 0.044, but which is still under the cut-off threshold, albeit only slightly. Hence, it appears that soft buttons were more efficient than flicking gestures as a trigger method.

We then compared the cost of switching from a delete to a circle subtask. An ANOVA on Technique revealed a significant effect (F(2, 22)=32.843, p<.001) on that cost. Post-hoc comparisons showed that *Eyes-Free* (mean cost 790 ms) was significantly faster than both *Classic* (1507 ms) (p=0.001) and *Popup* (1875 ms) (p<0.001). *Classic* was however not significantly faster than *Popup* (p=0.082). The most likely explanation for the significant difference between the two phone UIs is that reverting to inking mode with *Eyes-Free* only requires releasing the thumb, whereas in the other two conditions the button needs to be located and pressed again. While the delete action itself does not benefit from the quasimode when it is engaged, its disengagement enables rapidly segueing to the subsequent inking action.

Extra Actions

The number of extra actions was calculated by subtracting the minimum number of operations required to fulfil the different subtasks from the number of actions actually performed by participants, i.e. with inclusion of errors and their corrections. The types of errors that we observed were:

- Stroke errors: circle not containing the dot stimulus, not entirely inside the box or drawn with multiple strokes
- Dwelling errors: pen moved while holding to summon the popup, thereby accidentally inking the canvas
- Style errors: circle drawn in an incorrect colour or with the wrong stroke thickness
- Command errors: wrong command executed, e.g. doing an undo instead of changing the stroke size or colour
- Mode errors: pen used in the incorrect mode (erasing instead of inking and vice versa)

Repeated measures ANOVA on Technique revealed a significant effect (F(1.385, 15.233)=20.568, p<0.001) on the number of extra actions. Post-hoc comparisons confirmed that *Eyes-Free* (Mean=9.7 extra actions per scene) resulted in significantly more extra actions than *Classic* (4.8 extra actions) (p=0.002) and *Popup* (3.6 extra actions) (p=0.008). *Popup* and *Classic* did not exhibit a significant difference (p=0.377). This shows that despite training, participants had not completely mastered the controls of the Eyes-Free UI that they had to operate blindly. Further analysis of the data of *Eyes-Free* revealed that switching thickness in Scene 2 resulted in 54% more extra actions compared to switching colour in Scene 1, indicating that soft buttons could be easier to use than vertical swipe gestures. However, ANOVAs revealed no significant differences (F(1, 11)=4.121, p=0.067). A comparison of the same two scenes showed roughly the same number of undos and redos, thus, participants appeared to have no problems distinguishing horizontal swipes for undo/redo from vertical swipes for thickness.

Error-Corrected Analysis

Seeing that participants made significantly more mistakes with *Eyes-Free*, we wanted to investigate the possibility that those errors and the extra actions performed to correct them might be the cause of the two phone UIs not exhibiting any significant performance differences. We therefore compared the techniques in ideal theoretical conditions with no errors. For that, we filtered out subtasks with extra actions and repeated the analysis of their completion times using the remaining error-corrected data (3276 circles, 401 deletes, 345 undos and 172 redos). The results were somewhat surprising, as only circle subtasks exhibited a significant difference between the two phone UIs. Specifically, *Eyes-Free* was faster than *Classic* for Circle (p=0.005), but not for Delete (p=0.690), Undo (p=0.149) or Redo (p=0.909). We surmised that this might be due again to the quasimodal delete switch in *Eyes-Free* favouring quick transitions back to inking for the next circle subtask so we performed a new analysis without unmodified circle subtasks occurring immediately after a delete (4 instances per technique) and the difference remained statistically significant, albeit with a higher p-value (p=0.029). We are therefore left to conjecture that this divergence might be due to the different number of data points for each subtask and that possibly Delete, Undo and Redo might also become significantly faster with more data.

We also repeated the procedure for the cost of switching. In comparison to the analysis including errors, the switching costs were reduced on average by 24% for colour (SD=14%), 24% for thickness (SD=19%) and 24% for switching from delete to a circle task for *Eyes-Free* (SD=19%). For *Classic*, the respective reductions were 6% (SD=13%), 14% (SD=11%), and 4% (SD=17%). As *Popup* had the smallest number of extra actions, it naturally had the smallest reduction in the error-corrected case with all values below 5% (SD=13%, 8%, 8% respectively). Despite the larger reductions for *Eyes-Free*, we did not find any new significant effects compared to the previous analysis.

Subjective Preferences

We asked participants to rank each technique on a 5-point Likert scale in terms of perceived efficiency and concentration and effort (from 1="not at all", to 5="very much") for each type of task, *Distributed* and *Local*. A Friedman test showed a statistically significant difference in efficiency for Technique with the *Distributed* tasks ($\chi2(2)$=9.282, p=0.010). Median values were 4.5 for *Eyes-Free*, 4 for *Classic*, and 3 for *Popup*. A Wilcoxon signed-rank test showed a significant effect of higher perceived efficiency of *Eyes-Free* over *Classic* (Z=-2.496, p=0.013) as well as *Popup* (Z=-2.448, p=0.014). *Classic* and *Popup* did not exhibit any statistically significant difference (Z=-2.456, p=0.145). While the higher rating of *Eyes-Free* over *Popup* is justified, it is interesting to notice that participants felt more productive with *Eyes-Free* than with *Classic*, even though the data do not vindicate that impression. For the *Local* tasks, participants seemed to prefer the phone UIs over the Popup as well, with median values of 4.5 for *Eyes-Free*, 4 for *Classic* and 3 for *Popup*, however the differences were not significant ($\chi2(2)$=4.343, p=0.114). In the *Local* condition, the mobility of the UI was likely not as big a factor. The variation in the data was quite large for *Popup*, however. In particular, one participant rated all UIs with a 5. Excluding him from the analysis yielded a significant preference of *Eyes-Free* over *Popup* (p=0.035).

With regard to perceived concentration and effort, the obtained median values of 2.5 for *Eyes-Free*, 3 for *Classic*, and 3 for *Popup* for the *Distributed* tasks and 3 for all techniques for the *Local* tasks were not statistically significant. One user commented that *Eyes-Free* required higher concentration, but that the physical effort was lower. Conversely, three participants noted that *Popup* required less concentration but more physical effort. One person said that they would prefer a phone interface in a classroom setting, as it would provide them with more freedom to move about. Another participant stated that "it is better when the attention can be focused on the screen". Yet another remarked that "the pop-up is always in the way".

Participants rated the suitability of each technique for regular whiteboard activities (e.g. brainstorming, in meetings) on a 5-point Likert scale. Their answers are shown in Figure 7. All of the techniques had a median value of 4. All but one participant rated *Eyes-Free* with a 4 or a 5 and did not rate any other technique higher. The one participant who rated it with a 2, said that he preferred *Classic* because he "felt more in control". Three participants orally expressed a preference for *Eyes-Free* over *Classic*, but gave them equal ratings on the questionnaire. Despite being clearly the slowest interface, nine participants gave *Popup* a 4 or a 5. One participant mentioned that it could make sense to use the popup menu in combination with a phone UI and depending on the task, use one or the other.

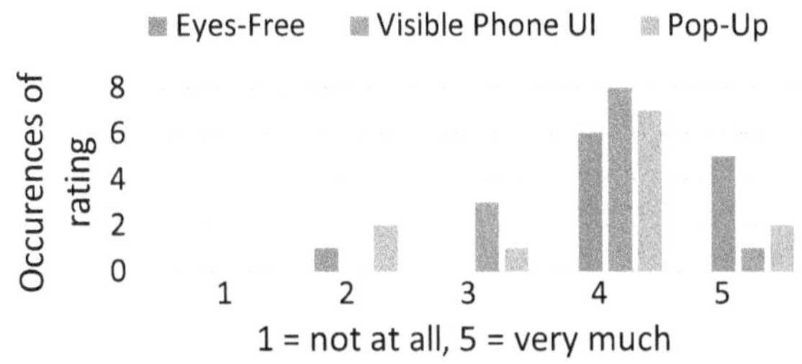

Figure 7. Suitability for general whiteboard usage.

DISCUSSION

The results of the experiment show a clear performance superiority of the phone UIs over the whiteboard-only popup menu in both types of task, which validates the first presumption from our list (item n°4). On the other hand, comparisons of the two phone UIs yielded mixed results. In general, participants made more errors with *Eyes-Free* than with the two other techniques. The error-corrected data suggest those errors are mainly responsible for *Eyes-Free* not performing significantly better than its *Classic* counterpart. Thus, if people are able to master the eyes-free UI they can likely surpass the other techniques, which tend to have lower improvement potential. Consequently, our second hypothesis (item n°7) is only valid in this ideal case.

Our participants did not cope with the eyes-free UI in the same way, as evidenced by the large variance in the data. The gains obtained from blindly manipulating the phone therefore highly depend on the user's skill and experience with the UI. A further observation that we made is that, despite its slightly more crowded design, some participants also occasionally used the classic phone UI in an eyes-free manner. We did not use any eye-tracking monitoring and so are not able to quantify to what extent that behaviour might have had an influence on the results and potentially reduced the performance gap between the two phone interfaces.

At the lower subtask and switching levels, our main findings concern the ability of quasimodes to speed up the transition back to the default mode upon release and the superior effectiveness of soft buttons over vertical flicking gestures to trigger an action. While the first result is logical, we find it more difficult to explain the second. A possible reason might be that the gesture pad was located at the top of the phone screen and the colour buttons at the bottom. It would be interesting to see if switching the positions of those two items has an impact.

With regard to the subjective feedback and ratings given by participants, in particular those concerning cognitive and physical effort, we did not obtain statistically significant results that allow us to make any conclusions. Hence, we cannot validate our last hypothesis (n°8), although we suspected that any possible difference might have been too small to elicit in our conditions.

CONCLUSION AND FUTURE WORK

In this paper, we presented a set of phone-based techniques to assist tasks performed on pen-enabled whiteboards. We introduced two phone interfaces with a set of standard controls, one optimised for eyes-free use and another following a classic remote design. In a controlled experiment, we compared the real and perceived performance of the two phone interfaces and that of a baseline whiteboard-only technique consisting of a pen-triggered popup menu. We established the superior efficiency of the phone UIs over the popup and the theoretical benefits of the eyes-free UI in ideal conditions when no errors are made. We further confirmed the performance benefit of quasimodes for temporary switching and showed that it manifests itself at the moment when the transitory mode is released to return to default mode. Finally, we demonstrated the suitability of soft buttons as eyes-free controls, which even performed better than simple flicking gestures.

Finally, even though our study was less about testing the chosen whiteboard tools themselves than the way they were activated via their controls, our results were obtained using specific UI layouts with a fixed number of functions. The natural next step of this work would therefore be to investigate how those results scale with different designs and with various kinds of whiteboard functions and compare those interfaces in visible and eyes-free conditions.

REFERENCES

1. Baglioni, M., Lecolinet, E. and Guiard, Y. JerkTilts: using accelerometers for eight-choice selection on mobile devices. In *Proc. ICMI 2011*.
2. Bragdon, A., DeLine, R., Hinckley, K. and Morris, M. R. Code space: touch + air gesture hybrid interactions for supporting developer meetings. In *Proc. ITS 2011*.
3. Bragdon, A., Nelson, E., Li, Y. and Hinckley, K. Experimental analysis of touch-screen gesture designs in mobile environments. In *Proc. CHI 2011*.
4. Dicke, C., Wolf, K. and Tal, Y. Foogue: eyes-free interaction for smartphones. In *Proc. MobileHCI 2010*.
5. Elrod, S., Bruce, R., Gold, R., Goldberg, D., Halasz, F., Janssen, W., Lee, D., McCall, K., Pedersen, E., Pier, K., Tang, J. and Welch, B. Liveboard: a large interactive display supporting group meetings, presentations, and remote collaboration. In *Proc. CHI 1992*.
6. Haller, M., Leitner, J., Seifried, T., Wallace, J. R., Scott, S. D., Richter, C., Brandl, P., Gokcezade, A. and Hunter, S. The NiCE Discussion Room: Integrating Paper and Digital Media to Support Co-Located Group Meetings. In *Proc. CHI 2010*.
7. Hao, L., Matei, N. and Yang, L. Gesturemote: interacting with remote displays through touch gestures. In *Proc. AVI 2014*.
8. Hardy, R. and Rukzio, E. Touch & interact: touch-based interaction of mobile phones with displays. In *Proc. MobileHCI 2008*.
9. Hinckley, K., Guimbretiere, F., Baudisch, P., Sarin, R., Agrawala, M. and Cutrell, E. The springboard: multiple modes in one spring-loaded control. In *Proc. CHI 2006*.
10. Hinckley, K., Yatani, K., Pahud, M., Coddington, N., Rodenhouse, J., Wilson, A., Benko, H. and Buxton, B. Pen + touch = new tools. In *Proc. UIST 2010*.
11. Kajastila, R. A. and Lokki, T. A gesture-based and eyes-free control method for mobile devices. In *Proc. CHI EA 2009*.
12. Leitner, J. F., Perteneder, F., Liu, C., Rendl, C. and Haller, M. Kolibri: tiny and fast gestures for large pen-based surfaces. In *Proc. CHI 2013*.
13. Li, K. A., Baudisch, P. and Hinckley, K. Blindsight: eyes-free access to mobile phones. In *Proc. CHI 2008*.
14. Li, Y., Hinckley, K., Guan, Z. and Landay, J. A. Experimental analysis of mode switching techniques in pen-based user interfaces. In *Proc. CHI 2005*.
15. Matulic, F. and Norrie, M. Empirical evaluation of uni- and bimodal pen and touch interaction properties on digital tabletops. In *Proc. ITS 2012*.
16. Matulic, F. and Norrie, M. Pen and Touch Gestural Environment for Document Editing on Interactive Tabletops. In *Proc. ITS 2013*.
17. Myers, B. A. Using handhelds and PCs together. *CACM, 44*, 11 (2001).
18. Parhi, P., Karlson, A. K. and Bederson, B. B. Target size study for one-handed thumb use on small touchscreen devices. In *Proc. MobileHCI 2006*.
19. Rashid, U., Nacenta, M. A. and Quigley, A. The cost of display switching: a comparison of mobile, large display and hybrid UI configurations. In *Proc. AVI 2012*.
20. Rekimoto, J. A multiple device approach for supporting whiteboard-based interactions. In *Proc. CHI 1998*.
21. Schmidt, D., Seifert, J., Rukzio, E. and Gellersen, H. A cross-device interaction style for mobiles and surfaces. In *Proc. DIS 2012*.
22. Serrano, M., Lecolinet, E. and Guiard, Y. Bezel-Tap gestures: quick activation of commands from sleep mode on tablets. In *Proc. CHI 2013*.
23. Wang, Y., Yu, C., Liu, J. and Shi, Y. Understanding performance of eyes-free, absolute position control on touchable mobile phones. In *Proc. MobileHCI 2013*.
24. Yi, B., Cao, X., Fjeld, M. and Zhao, S. Exploring user motivations for eyes-free interaction on mobile devices. In *Proc. CHI 2012*.
25. Zhao, S., Dragicevic, P., Chignell, M., Balakrishnan, R. and Baudisch, P. Earpod: eyes-free menu selection using touch input and reactive audio feedback. In *Proc. CHI 2007*.

Gesture Bike: Examining Projection Surfaces and Turn Signal Systems for Urban Cycling

Alexandru Dancu[1], Velko Vechev[2], Adviye Ayça Ünlüer[3,1], Simon Nilson[2], Oscar Nygren[2], Simon Eliasson[2], Jean-Elie Barjonet[2], Joe Marshall[4], Morten Fjeld[1]

[1]t2i Lab, Chalmers, Sweden alexandru.dancu@gmail.com [2]Interaction Design, Chalmers, Sweden
[3]Yıldız TU, Turkey ayca.unluer@gmail.com [4]University of Nottingham, UK joe.marshall@nottingham.ac.uk

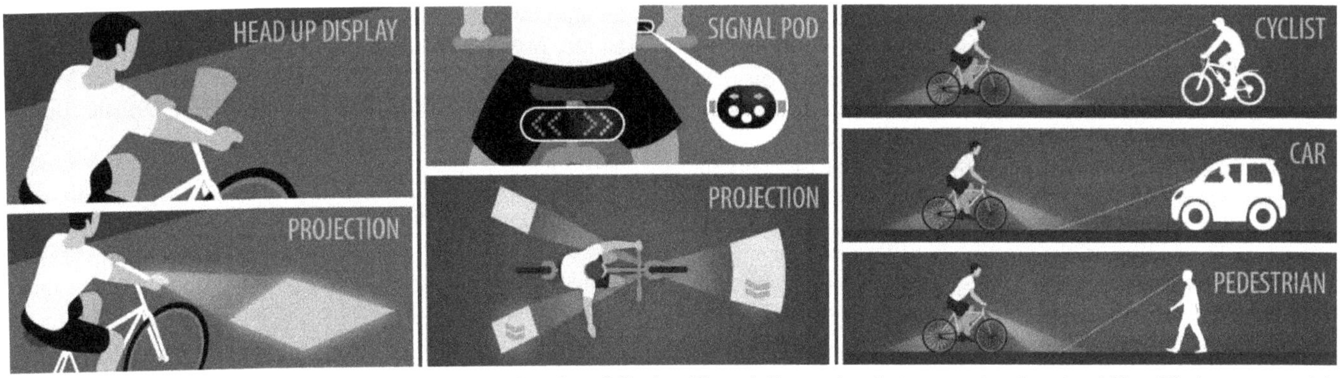

Figure 1. (Left) Comparison between head-up display and projected display (Center) Comparison between gesture input and Signal Pod, a commercial-turn signalling system, (Right) Evaluation using videos recorded from the perspective of participants in traffic

ABSTRACT

Interactive surfaces could be employed in urban environments to make people more aware of moving vehicles, showing drivers' intention and the subsequent position of vehicles. To explore the usage of projections while cycling, we created a system that displays a map for navigation and signals cyclist intention. The first experiment compared the task of map navigation on a display projected on a road surface in front of the bicycle with a head-up display (HUD) consisting of a projection on a windshield. The HUD system was considered safer and easier to use. In our second experiment, we used projected surfaces to implement concepts inspired by Gibson's perception theory of driving that were combined with detection of conventional cycling gestures to signal and visualize turning intention. The comparison of our system with an off-the-shelf turn signal system showed that gesture input was easier to use. A web-based follow-up study based on the recording of the two signalling systems from the perspective of participants in traffic showed that with the gesture-projector system it was easier to understand and predict the cyclist intention.

Author Keywords

Bicycle; Cycling; Turn Signal; Head-up-display; Gibson; Map Navigation; Projector;

ITS '15, November 15-18, 2015, Funchal, Portugal.
Copyright ©2015 ACM. ISBN 978-1-4503-3899-8/15/11$15.00
DOI: http://dx.doi.org/10.1145/2817721.281774

ACM Classification Keywords

H.5.m. Information Interfaces and Presentation (e.g. HCI): Miscellaneous

INTRODUCTION

Bicycles enable efficient [37] and sustainable personal transport with more than one billion bicycles produced worldwide in the last fifteen years [1]. Technological systems for use when cycling are a recent growth area. However, a fundamental challenge for these interactive systems is the unsuitability of traditional user interfaces for use while cycling, which can cause safety problems as systems constrain and capture attention [12]. One potential solution to this challenge is to use the environment in the vicinity of the bike as a display and user interface. Relevant and contextual information can be displayed where it is needed, and interaction can harness already known tasks and expectations. In this paper, we study interfaces which combine support for nighttime map navigation with cycling safety aids. We note that projectors are getting more powerful and accessible, potentially allowing for daytime use. The three contributions of this paper are:

(a) Comparing road projection with a head-up display (HUD) for the task of map navigation while cycling (Figure 1, left);

(b) Proposing the concept of displaying information such as minimum stopping distance and rider "safety envelope" through projections on the road (Figure 7)

(c) Comparing a gesture-enabled projection system with an off-the-shelf turn signalling system (Figure 1, center & right)

RELATED WORK

Below we review bicycle conventions and devices for signalling, traffic safety issues, displays and navigation systems implemented for bicycles, as well as a driving perception theory meant for improving safety.

Signalling Systems for Bicycles

A main factor affecting bicycle safety is motorized traffic [26]. Workshops organized with other road users showed the need for improving cyclist visibility [9]. Nighttime cycling was found to be up to five times more dangerous than during the day [16, 19]. A review summarizes the effectiveness of visibility aids at day and night time [19]. A case study showed that only 25% of night cyclists had front lights, 50% had a rear reflector, and 12% had a reflective vest [15]. There is a growing trend towards designing lighting systems for bikes to display information. For example a research project with a helmet based display [35] has been used to study social exertion activities, and to explore "cyclists' safety, skateboarders' self-expression and riders' communication of heart rate" [34]. Several commercial projects also exist, for example, Zackees Turn Signal Gloves employ LED lights displaying an arrow on the back of the glove [32] that are combined with gestures typically used to express turning intention while cycling. Blaze is an LED and laser light system that projects a bike symbol in front of the bicycle [4]. Xfire uses laser light to project two "lanes" at the sides of the bike, helping drivers in keeping a safe distance to the bike [38]. Inspired by Blaze and Xfire, Gesture Bike combines projections in the front and to the sides of the bike.

Bicycle Gestures

The Vienna Convention on Road Traffic mentions that a driver shall signal the intention of moving laterally by means of either a direction-indicator of the vehicle or using arm gestures [2]. For cyclists, the arms are normally used to indicate the intention of turning. We chose to employ existing gestures for bike ride signalling as most cyclists know their meaning, context of use, and are familiar with them. We detect these gestures using a depth sensor, repurposing and signalling them using corresponding symbols projected on the road. Since the user does not have to learn extra controls, this contributes to ease of use and ease of learning. In gesture controlled interfaces, the simpler the controls, the better [30]. These deictic gestures that involve showing the direction the user will turn by hand, align with Norman's physical analogy [23] and to an average user's mental model [7]. From the perspective of traffic participants, gestures can independently signify the user's intention, while interaction with the system amplifies their effectiveness by making this public interface highly visible to others [28].

Bicycle Proxemics

Research in civil traffic shows that motorized vehicles pass bicycles at a distance of minimum 0.85m, while at 30mph the distance is normally 1.05m [8, 24]. The cycle lane width determines the proximity between the bicycle and the passing vehicle [24]. Passing distances were investigated and correlated with factors related to vehicle type, road (markings, lane width), and bicycle (physical appearance, change in wheel angle, speed) [10]. A longitudinal study suggested that wearing fluorescent colors may increase a cyclist's safety [31]. However, a study on the influence of a cyclist's outfit and the proximity of cars during overtakes concluded that the rider appearance does not contribute to increasing the distance of the vehicles [33]. On the other hand, employing the ground surfaces near the bicycle to signal intention and alert the participants in traffic might contribute to safety. The concept of augmenting the physical space in front of a vehicle with information suggesting optimum driving resembles Gibson and Crooks' perception theory for driving proposed in 1938 which provides a set of concepts "applicable to any type of locomotion", such as minimum stopping zone, terrain, destination, obstacle, collision, path, and the assumption that the driver aims to drive in the middle of a "field of safe travel" [14]. These concepts and the field of safe travel could be computed and visualized, thus increasing safety for vehicles in traffic.

Head-up Displays for Cars

Research on aviation interfaces has shown that important information should be displayed closer to the "normal line of sight (NLOS), which is a line about 20° below the horizon extending from the eyes" [36]. Human Machine Interface principles recommend having visual displays for in-vehicle interfaces positioned "as close as practicable to the driver's normal line of sight" and the driver should be able to assimilate relevant information with a few glances [13]. Head-up-displays have been researched in cockpits, but have recently been introduced by many car manufacturers such as Audi, BMW, and Mercedes which developed a head-up display[1] showing speed, navigation, and lane guidance information, "keeping the eyes where they should be, focused on the road ahead". Consumer HUDs for cars have been released by Garmin[2] that project directly onto the windshield information about navigation, speed, and traffic. Jaguar revealed a virtual windscreen concept that shows virtual cones for driver training, virtual cars for racing, and virtual racing lines for optimum track route and braking [17]. As HUDs gain wider adoption in related industries, various aspects of their performance, safety and applicability should be evaluated.

Displays and Navigation Systems for Bicycles

Findings from exploratory bike trips using handlebar-mounted smartphones offered map navigation while cycling [25]. It was reported that by not offering turn-by-turn navigation, the bike rider could be more aware of the environment, but most cyclists had to stop to read the map anyway, "since they found it too small" [25]. The Copenhagen City Bike is a bicycle equipped with a touch screen tablet computer mounted below the handlebar, offering GPS map navigation and real-time departure times of trains, buses and the metro [6]. Hammerhead is a T-shaped handlebar-mounted device connected to the smartphone, helping with turn-by-turn bike navigation using LED lights [22]. Previous work by Rowland et al. on designing interactive experiences for cyclists employed mobile phones mounted on the bicycle's handlebars or worn on the cyclist's lower arm [29]. Audio instructions were employed to support a "heads-up approach", however

[1] Mercedes HUD: `https://youtu.be/Wkf_WEek8bc`

[2] Garmin HUD: `https://youtu.be/_B7GIDyN32Y`

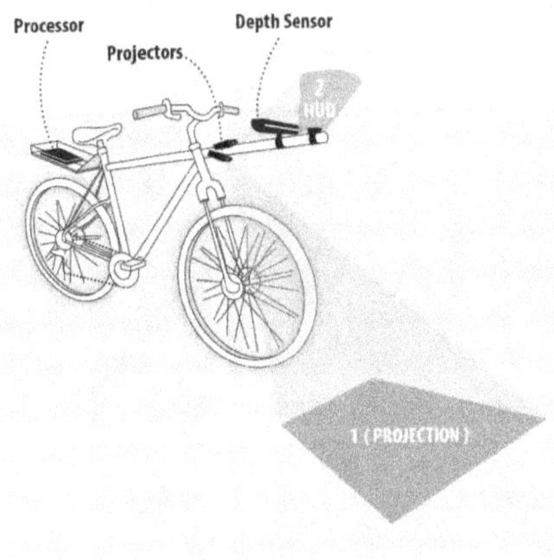

Figure 2. Head-up-display and projected display mounted on the bike. Only one of the two displays were used during the experiment. Both are shown for illustration purpose.

Figure 3. Map navigation using a bike-mounted head-up display. The navigated route is shown in pink. Landmarks are highlighted.

one user was very distracted and in danger of a collision. They found that for map navigation, adapting digital media to the cycling activity was essential. Another way to improve the safety while cycling is considering the routes and informing cyclists about their characteristics [27]. GPS map navigation is considered a skilled activity where users should support their navigation with the system and not follow instructions blindly [5]. Design choices are drawn from recent GPS navigation guidelines suggesting active drivers are "interpreting, ignoring, and re-using instructions while also combining them with related information from the environment and their own route knowledge" [5].

In our previous work, Smart Flashlight, we proposed replacing bicycle headlights with information projected on the road [11]. We showed that map navigation was possible by projecting a map in front of the bike and compared it with map navigation on a bike-mounted smartphone, finding out that with projection cyclists could be more attentive to the route and that it was perceived easier and safer to use. In this follow-up study, we first investigated whether a head-up display would be preferred over a projected display (Experiment 1). Additionally, we were interested in employing the projection surfaces in making the bike and cyclist intention more visible on the road (Experiment 2).

EXPERIMENT 1: HUD VS. ROAD PROJECTION

The goal of the experiment was to compare map navigation on a bike-mounted head-up display (HUD) with a projected display in front of the bike (Figure 2). The experiment was a within-subjects comparative study evaluating the two conditions over two different routes using a balanced distribution of route-display combinations. Each subject received either an HUD or projector equipped bike, and was tasked with following a highlighted route on a map with the assistance of a GPS location marker. (Figure 3 shows the route colored in pink). After each condition, subjects completed a NASA Task Load Index (TLX) and a System Usability Scale (SUS) questionnaire. After completing both conditions, the subjects filled out a questionnaire comparing the two devices and were interviewed about their ratings.

Apparatus and Interfaces

The hardware of our prototype consisted of a mountain bike equipped with two Brookstone pocket projectors mounted on an aluminum reinforced styrofoam extension of the frame (Figure 2). The projected graphical interface consisted of an OpenGL application displaying a high contrast map with the route thickened, colored in pink, and the current position displayed as a blue dot. two different HUD materials were tested: $2mm$ thick half-transparent low density polyethylene (LDPE) and transparent plexiglass sheets mounted at a distance of $52cm$ from the handlebar (see Figure 2). We cut the sheet as $28cm$ high trapezoids with the small base of $20cm$ and the large base of $28cm$. The sheet was then slightly bent in the form of a windshield and mounted at a $24°$ angle from the vertical (see Figure 2). The projector was at a distance of $32cm$ from the HUD, placed on a $16cm$ high styrofoam block glued on top of the aluminum reinforced extension of the frame in front of the handlebar, resulting in an image of $23 \times 16cm$ (see Figure 3) with a projection area of $365cm^2$. The ground projection system used a single projector mounted in front of the handlebar and under the aluminum frame. The front projection area was at a distance of $104cm$ from the end of the front wheel, and measured $13776cm^2$. We asked two pilot study participants to cycle two routes, one with an HUD, the other with the display projected on the road. Map visibility was better with LPDE, but one could not see through it as in the case of a head-up display of a car, so we replaced it with the plexiglass. The HUD was also made removable so that it would not affect the view of the projected road display.

Experiment Results

We recruited 12 participants (5 females); university students and interaction design professionals aged between 21 and 50 (mean 28.0, s.d. 7.9) with an average cycling proficiency of 3.3 (s.d. 0.8) on a scale ranging from 1 (no experience) to 4 (advanced). The within-subjects comparative study evaluated the two display conditions over two different routes.

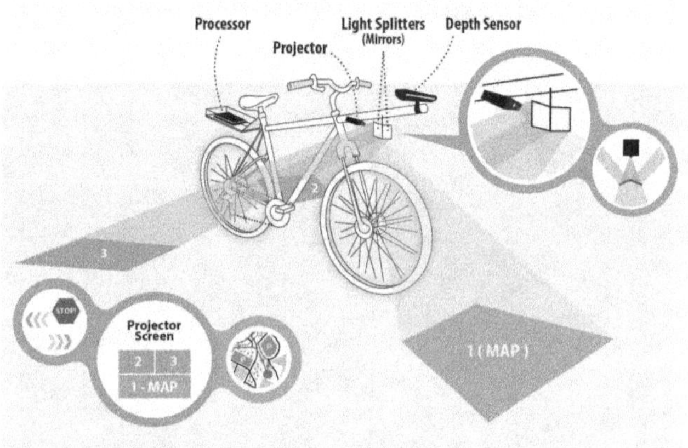

Figure 4. Illustration of how the projection was split using mirrors

Subjective Measures

Paired t-tests for each of the NASA TLX questions revealed a significant effect of device type on performance (t = -1.8, df = 11, p <0.04) with the projector ranking lower than the HUD (3.0 points difference in means). The other task load questions showed no significant effect. Regarding the sources of workload, mental demand was ranked the highest (mean 3.3, s.d. 0.9), followed by performance (mean 3.1, s.d. 1.1), effort (mean 2.75, s.d. 1.0), frustration (mean 2.5, s.d. 2.1), and temporal demand (mean 1.9, s.d. 1.7). The average SUS score for the HUD was 68.3 (s.d. 7.8) and for the projector was 69.5 (s.d. 7.6). When asked to compare the two displays, the participants considered that with the head-up display they could be more attentive to the route (58.3%), have better road and traffic visibility (HUD 50%, same 8%), have better aid in navigation (HUD 58.3%, same 8%), it was safer to use (66.7%), and it was easier to use (66.7%). On the other hand, when asked which system was more fun to use, 66.7% opted for the road display.

Participant Comments

From a cyclist's perspective, participants noted that the HUD was more visible since it was less susceptible to surface variations than the projector: "The image changed when you went over different surfaces." However, one user observed that the the light reflected in the windshield affected the visibility of the HUD. "Sometimes there was a reflection of traffic lights on the screen." The angle of the line of sight to each display was an important factor when participants rated their attention to the route. Several users noted that with the projector, they had to shift focus between the projector and the road, while one taller (196cm) participant noted:"[The projector] is better because you are not looking down so much." Participants also took issue with the brightness of the projector, noting that it was distracting: "The projector would distract me more. It was very bright and caught my attention more". Users requested a turn-by-turn navigation feature that alerts participants before a turn is coming up. As one user suggested, this could be implemented via augmented reality displayed on the HUD. Another participant proposed a system which considers selective attention: "If new information is coming, it beeps to me. It's good to have the map on all the time, but I want to know when to look at it."

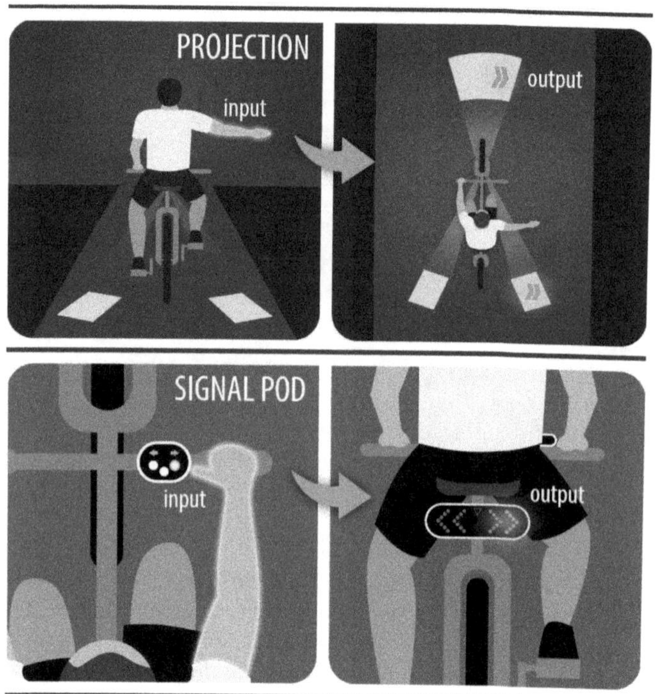

Figure 5. Turn signalling through gestures and projection (top) and Signal Pod, an off-the-shelf system which uses buttons and LEDs (bottom)

EXPERIMENT 2: BIKE PROJECTOR SIGNALLING

We built a system for a bicycle that recognizes a cyclist's turning gestures and projects the cyclist's intention on the road (Figure 5). This prototype was evaluated in two ways:

(a) using cyclist participants who compared this system with an off-the-shelf turn signalling system, and

(b) using an online survey containing video recordings from the perspective of participants in traffic (pedestrians, car drivers, cyclists) presenting a cyclist using the gesture-projector and the commercial system.

The task was to navigate two routes displayed on the road and to signal turning intention; one route using gestures, the other one using a commercial off-the-shelf signal turning system called Signal Pod (see Figure 5). The latter system was composed of two devices; one mounted on the handlebars that had three buttons, out of which only the left and right button were required in the task, while the other device was a group of LED lights arranged as left and right arrows (Figure 5, bottom right image). Pressing the buttons would send a wireless signal triggering the arrows to blink and an audio signal (one beep for left, two beeps for right). Pressing them again would stop the blinking and beeping. The arrows projected around the bike had the same color and style as Signal Pod's arrows.

Apparatus and Interfaces

Standard hand signalling used with bicycles was employed as an input to our system that detected this gesture and projected the cyclist's intention on the road in the direction of

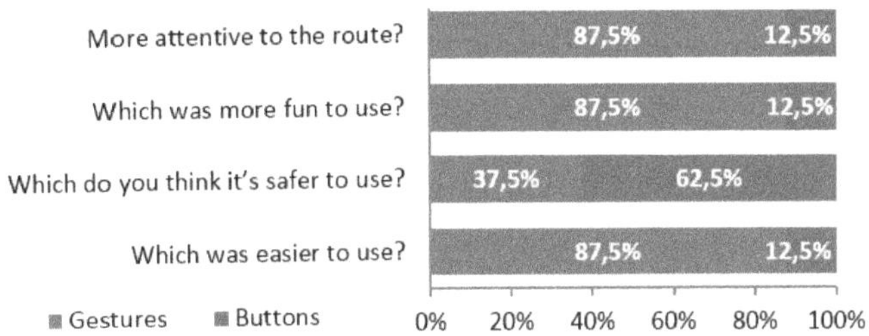

Figure 6. Experiment results (n=8) ranking gestures and buttons as input while navigating routes on a map projected in front of the bicycle

turning. This concept was implemented by splitting the projection space as shown in Figure 4. The bottom of the illustration shows how we split the projection into three parts – the two at the top (2 and 3) are reflected using two mirrors oriented at an angle so that they are displayed on the sides of the rear bike wheel. The remaining larger image (1) projects a map directly in front of the bike and is used for navigation. The front projected area remained the same area and location as in the first experiment, while each side projection measured $3072cm^2$ to create a total projection area of $1.6848m^2$. The detected gestures would trigger the display of symbols shown on the two displays at the rear but also in front on the sides of the map.

The gesture recognition hardware consisted of an Xtion depth sensor mounted in front of the bike, connected to a MacBook laptop fixed to the back of the bike (see Figure 4). The software was based on the OpenNI library[3]. We created a framework that supports adding multiple gestures. In our experiments we focused on the left and right gestures. The projector was a Brookstone HDMI projector. We iteratively improved the prototype and conducted two experiments with this system. For the pilot study, the static map displayed in front of the bike was improved in contrast, and did not rotate or show the current position. The route required for navigation was shown in red 4. For the experiment, the map showed the current position on the map using a blue dot. Based on a set of unique gesture inputs, the system was able to recognize and trigger the display of left and right turning arrows, stop signs, pass-me arrows, awareness markers, and hazard signs. Symbols were projected both in the front on the sides of the map, and also on each side of the rear of the bike. Only the turn signals were evaluated for the experiment. The majority of the visuals have been implemented as animations (blinking or scrolling) to improve visibility and attention of participants in traffic.

Pilot Study

We conducted a pilot study to confirm the prototype was usable for navigation, to get early feedback, improve the system, and design the final experiment. We recruited 5 university students (1 female) aged between 19 and 28 (mean 23.8, s.d. 4.0) to evaluate the gesture signalling system. The task was to perform map navigation and signal turning intention. After initial training, the route was completed, and a SUS questionnaire was filled out. An average SUS score of 77 (s.d. 5.4) was obtained. Pilot study participants thought it felt both safe and natural to use the system, since they used these kinds of gestures regularly whilst cycling. However, they considered using the bike made them look down on the ground more than normal and that they sometimes had to "hold" the gestures for too long to make the system recognize them. An experienced cyclist considered that most gestures did feel natural to use in spite of it not being part of his regular biking routine. Another subject commented that this kind of system may be useful in teaching people to use gestures when biking. However, he did not feel that all gestures felt equally natural to use, in particular the stop gesture struck him as less comfortable.

[3]`https://github.com/OpenNI/OpenNI`

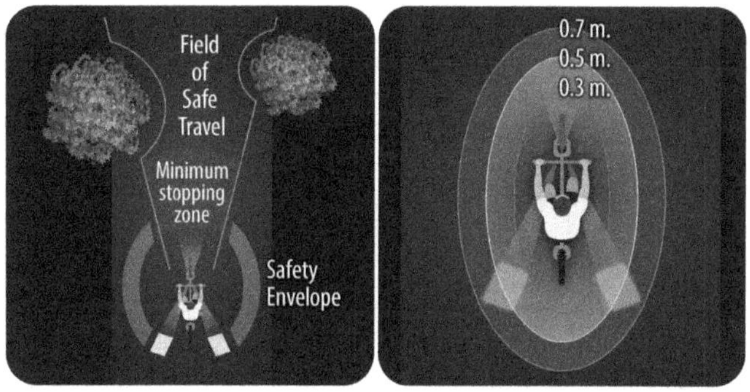

Figure 7. Field of safe travel, minimum stopping zone [14], and safety envelope illustrated in the context of our Gesture Bike design

Following the pilot study, we improved the system with the following features for the final experiment: i) we added the current position of the cyclist on the map (added a GPS module) ii) moved the position of the sensor higher and further from the handlebar in order to improve the user skeleton tracking iii) tested and improved reliability of Signal Pod by measuring the voltage and replacing batteries with higher amperage iv) improved robustness of the system and slightly increased the projection size v) replaced the routes with more similar ones that had the same number of turns vi) added visualizations, such as the "safety envelope" based on Gibson's driving perception theory [14].

Safety Envelope

Projections around vehicles could be used to improve visibility and safety of participants in traffic. The following visualizations are inspired by Gibson's driving perception theory [14]. The minimum stopping zone is displayed in front of the vehicle showing the distance needed to bring the vehicle to a halt. This depends on the speed of the vehicle. The visualization for the minimum stopping zone was implemented by placing two bars inside the front road projection (to the sides of the map) that would increase in height depending on the speed of travel (Figure 7 left). The other visualization is the "safety envelope" projected on the ground near the sides of the vehicle that becomes larger according to the speed of the vehicle. Figure 7, right shows the ideal safety envelope surrounding the whole bike and the position of the rear projections from our implementation. Safe distances between bicycles and motorized traffic during overtaking should be larger than 0.85m [8]. The two rear displays were used to show the "safety envelope" that was visualized as bars scrolling from front to back, growing outwards depending on speed. Both visualizations were increasing outwards in front and to the sides of the bike, proportionally to speed. The minimum stopping zone is visible to the cyclist and participants in traffic, while the safety envelope is intended to be seen by others.

Experiment Results

The experiment was a within-subjects comparative study evaluating the two input conditions over two different routes. After each condition, a NASA TLX and a SUS questionnaire were completed. Finally, a questionnaire for comparing the two input methods was completed, followed by an interview. The participants were 8 university students and interaction designers (2 females) aged between 25 and 33 (mean 28.7, s.d. 3.0) with an average cycling proficiency of 2.8 (s.d. 0.5) on a scale ranging from 1 (no experience) to 4 (advanced).

Subjective Measures

Paired t-tests for each of the NASA TLX questions revealed a significant effect of device type on performance ($t = 1.8$, $df = 7$, $p < 0.01$) with buttons ranking lower than gestures (3.1 points difference in medians). The other task load questions showed no significant effect. The sources of workload were mental demand (mean 3.1, s.d. 1.1), effort (mean 2.8, s.d. 1.4), followed by performance (mean 2.7, s.d. 1.4), physical demand (mean 2.2, s.d. 1.9), frustration (mean 2.1, s.d. 2.0), and temporal demand (mean 1.7, s.d. 1.8). The average SUS score for gesture input was 73.7 (s.d 6.4) and for the Signal Pod buttons input was 67.8 (s.d. 6.1). The average perceived percentage of recognized input was 92% for gestures and 75% for the buttons of Signal Pod. When asked to compare the two inputs, the participants considered that with gesture input they found they could be more attentive to the route (87.5%), have better road and traffic visibility (75%), and was easier to use (87.5%) (Figure 6). Regarding safety, participants were in favour of the buttons input (62%) .

Participant Comments

We noticed that the safety depends on several factors: *keeping balance*, *visibility*, and *attention*. The gesture system requires users to take their hand off the handlebar to signal intention, causing concern about their ability to balance: "I think buttons are safer because you don't need to take your hand off the handlebar. With gestures, you can lose your balance." The button system also caused similar complaints about balance, with one user suggesting that the buttons should be in reach without letting go of the handlebar and placed close to the fingers like with motorcycles.

Participants commented on traffic visibility noting that gestures can be easily distinguished from a distance, while one participant had the opposite opinion, noting that "buttons are safer because drivers can see the lights better than the indicators on the road." Another safety concern was raised by a participant regarding false positives. He reported waving to onlookers and triggering the turn signal gesture. He suggested having the option of enabling and disabling gesture recognition. Although triggering gestures is an analog action, users preferred its visual feedback, which they trusted to reflect the

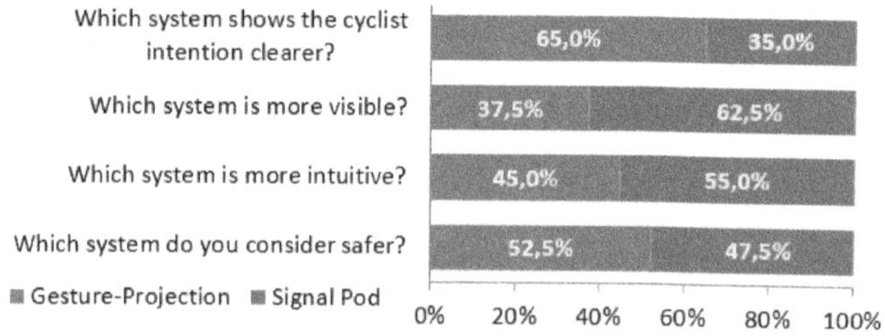

Figure 8. Online survey rankings (n=40) comparing preference between gesture-projection and commercial off-the-shelf turn signals. Gesture-projection is ranked higher than Signal Pod when it comes to showing biker intention. However, Signal Pod is more visible.

current state of the system: "For gestures, I really know that it went on. So it's safer that way."

Participants complained about the button signalling system, mentioning that they had to turn their attention away from the road and look at the handlebar when pressing buttons. Many agreed that for button signalling the location should be on the left and right handlebars. They were disturbed by the fact that the left and right buttons were so close to each other and too small. The two-step activation and deactivation procedure of the button system took more time to control and thus reduced route attention. The feedback provided by both systems had a strong effect across all ratings. Multiple participants noted that traffic noise reduced the effectiveness of button beeps as a feedback system. Most users found gestures intuitive and natural, which contributed to the high ratings: "You don't have to do anything special, it comes naturally and it augments the reality." Lower button ratings could also be attributed to additional effort required, as one user noted: "With gestures, because you do it normally, it's fine, but with buttons I need to put in more effort to push it."

Online Survey

We created a survey to help us compare the two signalling systems using videos recorded from the perspective of participants in traffic (cyclists, car drivers, and pedestrians). Two videos were recorded from all three perspectives: one presenting a cyclist using the gesture-projector system, the other with a cyclist using Signal Pod. Each video contained the following scenes:

Cyclist perspective: seeing cyclist from the back (turning left, turning right, and stopping), seeing cyclist coming from the front and turning right

Car driver perspective: seeing cyclist from the back (turning right, left, and stopping), seeing cyclist coming from the front and turning left

Pedestrian perspective: cyclist passing by and turning left, cyclist coming from the front and turning right.

The survey was created using the LimeSurvey platform and shared with online cyclist and student groups from Europe and North America. Forty persons (seven females) aged between 21 and 60 (mean 32.8, s.d 9.8) completed our survey. We balanced the order of watching the videos, so that half watched the gesture-projector video first, and the other half watched the Signal Pod video first. After watching the first video, participants answered questions regarding their ability to identify visual cues, understand, and predict the cyclist's intention and actions, followed by rating the corresponding mental effort required, both having a 4-point scale (very easy, fairly easy, somewhat difficult, very difficult). These questions were derived from the Mission Awareness Rating Scale (MARS) [21], which assesses subjective measures that are "suitable for soliciting self-reports of a driver's confidence in their situation awareness abilities" [3]. The final questions compared the two systems in regard to safety, ease of use, and visibility.

Participants rated the following on a scale of "very easy", "fairly easy", "somewhat difficult", and "very difficult". The corresponding ratings are listed in this respective order. In comparing their **ability** to identify visual cues (Projector: 37.5%, 45%, 17.5%; Signal Pod: 15%, 30%, 42.5%, 12.5%), to understand (Projector: 57.5%, 40%, 2.5%; Signal Pod: 35%, 40%, 20%, 5%), to predict future actions (Projector: 57.5%, 35%, 7.5%; Signal Pod: 15%, 42.5%, 30%, 12.5%), and awareness of the cyclist's intention (Projector: 65%, 32.5%, 2.5%; Signal Pod: 42.5%, 37.5%, 15%, 5%). When comparing the **mental effort** required, the participants rated the projector as being somewhat difficult for the following abilities: ability to identify visual cues (17.5%), ability to understand the cyclist's intention (7.5%), ability to predict the cyclist's actions (15%). For the mental effort required for these capabilities, the Signal Pod was rated "very easy" and "fairly easy". However, regarding situation awareness ("How difficult - in terms of mental effort required – was it for you to be aware of the situations presented in the video?"), there was a significant difference between the projector (17.5% rated "somewhat difficult") and Signal Pod (37.5%).

Figure 9 depicts the final survey questions showing that 65% of participants considered that the gesture-projector system showed the intention of the cyclist clearer and 52.5% rated it safer. However, the survey participants rated Signal Pod more visible (62.5%) and more intuitive (55%). Overall 37.5% preferred Signal Pod, 25% the gesture-projector system, and 37.5% chose "other" which allowed them to suggest another system, such as "project on the cyclist's back", "reflective neon gear and hand signals", "combination", more advanced Signal Pod ("LED placed further apart", "lights on both sides"), hand signs with LED and reflective details on gloves.

DISCUSSION

This paper presented a mobile system, Gesture Bike, designed to evaluate bicycle map navigation and turn signalling using a projector. The projector display could serve as both flashlight and map during the night. The road acts both as a transportation medium and an information carrier. It does not constrain and capture attention, imposing limitations on behavior and separating us from the physical environment. Instead, relevant and contextual information is displayed where it is needed and harnesses already known tasks and expectations.

Figure 9. Cyclist navigates a map and signals the intention to turn right. The map is in the front, while arrows are shown in front and at the back.

Bicycle Displays

Electric bicycles are becoming more popular with over 100 million vehicles purchased in China only [18]. Having an electrical power source on bicycles would allow electronic devices like sensors and display systems to improve the cyclist's safety and experience. Many city authorities offer bikes for rent and are now beginning to be equipped with displays. In Copenhagen, for example, a tablet computer is mounted under the handlebars allowing for map navigation [6]. Our findings can inform such bicycle designs in improving safety and ease of use.

In this paper, for the task of map navigation, the head-up display was considered safer, easier to use, and more helpful in navigation than a projected display in front of the bike. This is in line with research that suggests that information should be as close as possible to the normal line of sight [36]. However, our previous work comparing mobile phones mounted on handlebars with road projection showed the more distant road display was considered safer and easier to use [11]. This could be explained by the fact that the position of the phone display was lower than the projection, requiring looking down. So a larger head movement angle required during locomotion might be perceived as more distracting and more difficult than having information further away on the road. The HUD's placement of information is comparable with the road projection from the perspective of the normal line of sight, but is positioned closer. This could explain why the HUD was considered safer and easier to use.

Regarding size and placement of the HUD, the cyclist height should be taken into account, so it should be adjustable, as noticed by one participant. The transparency, contrast, and colors used in the HUD could be the agenda of future research, as well as the visualization of information relevant to support situation awareness in traffic [3]. The normal line of sight and the angle to information are important aspects which should be considered when designing interfaces and displays for bicycles.

Improving vehicle safety using projected surfaces

Many battery-powered locomotion devices are coming to market, such as electric skateboards, uni-cycles, self balancing scooters and dual wheels. As projectors are getting cheaper and widely available, augmenting the physical space around vehicles has the potential of improving safety and the interaction between participants in traffic.

The experiment results comparing our gesture-projector system with the button-LED system showed that gesturing was easier to use. From the perspective of participants in traffic (pedestrians, drivers, and cyclists), our online survey presenting videos of the two systems suggests that the projector system showed the cyclist's intention clearer, but the LED system is more visible. However, the visibility of the mobile projector could be improved in the future. The context of traffic demands high awareness of the situation for which our study shows that the gesture-projector system yields better results than Signal Pod in the ability to identify visual cues, understand, predict, and be aware of the cyclist's intention. On the other hand, mental effort was rated higher for the gesture-projector for all abilities except situation awareness. In regard to safety, the experiment participants were equally divided, while the survey participants were slightly in favour of the projector. One advantage of the projector system is the potential of transforming the physical environment around the vehicle and creating a safety envelope (see Figure 7) that could make the participants in traffic more aware of the presence of the vehicle on the road. The visualization of the minimum stopping zone could take into account physical factors such as tire type, braking strength, road surface, and weather conditions. Furthermore, Gibson and Crooks' concepts of field of safe travel could be visualized and improve the safety of drivers and cyclists. The field of safe travel could be displayed on a head-up display, while the minimum stopping zone which depends on the vehicle speed could be communicated to other drivers through a projected surface in front of the vehicle.

Designing to repurpose and support familiar tasks

Creating systems which allow direct interaction while moving is a difficult challenge [20], and can add extra attentional load and reduce safety [12]. By repurposing bicycle headlights through projecting information and employing this familiar context of cyclists, the flashlight is thus transformed into a display, a digital output system that could be used to inform and improve safety. Similary, employing conventional gestures for controlling projected signals allows cyclists to interact with the system without extra mental load. There is a need to design displays that present information on the go, non-intrusively, and hands-free. Currently, we use small computing devices that we call mobile and that we carry in our pockets at all times, but which isolate us from our surroundings. Instead of just placing computing devices on and around our bodies, we could integrate information into our environment and take advantage of familiar tasks and our context.

CONCLUSION AND FUTURE WORK

Our first experiment showed that a bike-mounted head-up display was considered easier and safer to use than a projection in front of the bicycle. Our second experiment proposed the implementation of the minimum stopping distance and safety envelope through projections on the road and compared a gesture-enabled projection system with an off-the-shelf turn signalling system. The gesture-projection system was considered easier to use and allowed the users to be more attentive to the route. Future work could include a system that combines a head-up display with a safety envelope. We hope that this work will give rise to a new class of headlights for vehicles that would support people in their tasks by projecting information where they need it. Our findings will be useful for designing future vehicles and could help participants in traffic to be more attentive to their environment while navigating, providing useful information while moving.

ACKNOWLEDGMENTS

We thank Fabius Steinberger, Yanke Tan, Karthik Ramani, Haimo Zhang, James Wen, Stig Anton Nielsen, Gabrielė Kasparavičiūtė, and Philippa Beckman. This work was supported by Leverhulme Trust (ECF/2012/677) and the EU FP7 People Programme (Marie Curie Actions) under REA Grant Agreement 290227.

REFERENCES

1. Roney, J. M., Earth Policy Institue. Bicycle production. `http://www.earth-policy.org/indicators/C48` (2008).

2. United Nations Economic Commission for Europe (UNECE) . Vienna convention on road traffic (with amendment 1), article 14, paragraph 3 (1968).

3. Bolstad, C. A., Cuevas, H. M., Wang-Costello, J., Endsley, M. R., and Angell, L. S. Measurement of situation awareness for automobile technologies of the future.

4. Brooke, E. Blaze bike light. `www.kickstarter.com/projects/embrooke/blaze-bike-light` (2011).

5. Brown, B., and Laurier, E. The normal natural troubles of driving with gps. In *Proceedings of the 2012 ACM annual conference on Human Factors in Computing Systems*, ACM (2012), 1621–1630.

6. Bycyklen. Copenhagen city bike. `http://bycyklen.dk/en/` (2014).

7. Carey, S. Cognitive science and science education. *American Psychologist 41*, 10 (1986), 1123.

8. Centre for Research and Contract Standardisation in Civil and Traffic Engineering, Netherlands. Design manual for bicycle traffic.

9. Christmas, S., Helman, S., Buttress, S., Newman, C., and Hutchins, R. *Cycling, safety and sharing the road: Qualitative research with cyclists and other road users.* Department for Transport: London, 2010.

10. Chuang, K.-H., Hsu, C.-C., Lai, C.-H., Doong, J.-L., and Jeng, M.-C. The use of a quasi-naturalistic riding method to investigate bicyclists behaviors when motorists pass. *Accident Analysis & Prevention 56* (2013), 32–41.
11. Dancu, A., Franjcic, Z., and Fjeld, M. Smart flashlight: map navigation using a bike-mounted projector. In *Proceedings of the SIGCHI Conference on Human Factors in Computing Systems*, ACM (2014), 3627–3630.
12. de Waard, D., Schepers, P., Ormel, W., and Brookhuis, K. Mobile phone use while cycling: Incidence and effects on behaviour and safety. *Ergonomics 53*, 1 (2010), 30–42.
13. European Commission. Updated european statement of principles on human machine interface for in-vehicle information and communication systems. In *Official Journal of the European Union. - Brussel* (2006).
14. Gibson, J. J., and Crooks, L. E. A theoretical field-analysis of automobile-driving. *The American journal of psychology* (1938), 453–471.
15. Hagel, B. E., Lamy, A., Rizkallah, J. W., Belton, K. L., Jhangri, G. S., Cherry, N., and Rowe, B. H. The prevalence and reliability of visibility aid and other risk factor data for uninjured cyclists and pedestrians in edmonton, alberta, canada. *Accident Analysis & Prevention 39*, 2 (2007), 284–289.
16. Jaermark, S., Gregersen, N., and Linderoth, B. The use of bicycle lights. *Stockholm: Transportfroskningsberedningen* (1991).
17. Jaguar. Virtual windscreen concept. `https://youtu.be/FeK9IkSD_nI` (2014).
18. Ji, S., Cherry, C. R., J. Bechle, M., Wu, Y., and Marshall, J. D. Electric vehicles in china: emissions and health impacts. *Environmental science & technology 46*, 4 (2012), 2018–2024.
19. Kwan, I., and Mapstone, J. Visibility aids for pedestrians and cyclists: a systematic review of randomised controlled trials. *Accident Analysis & Prevention 36*, 3 (2004), 305–312.
20. Marshall, J., and Tennent, P. Mobile interaction does not exist. In *CHI '13 Extended Abstracts on Human Factors in Computing Systems*, CHI EA '13, ACM (New York, NY, USA, 2013), 2069–2078.
21. Matthews, M. D., and Beal, S. A. Assessing situation awareness in field training exercises. Tech. rep., DTIC Document, 2002.
22. Morgan, P., Wattrus, L., and Beemsingh, R. Hammerhead bike navigation. `www.dragoninnovation.com/projects/23-hammerhead` (2014).
23. Norman, D. A. *The design of everyday things*. Basic books, 2013.
24. Parkin, J., and Meyers, C. The effect of cycle lanes on the proximity between motor traffic and cycle traffic. *Accident Analysis & Prevention 42*, 1 (2010), 159–165.
25. Pielot, M., Poppinga, B., Heuten, W., and Boll, S. Tacticycle: Supporting exploratory bicycle trips. In *Proceedings of the 14th international conference on Human-computer interaction with mobile devices and services*, ACM (2012), 369–378.
26. Pucher, J., and Buehler, R. *City cycling*. MIT Press, 2012.
27. Reddy, S., Shilton, K., Denisov, G., Cenizal, C., Estrin, D., and Srivastava, M. Biketastic: sensing and mapping for better biking. In *Proceedings of the SIGCHI Conference on Human Factors in Computing Systems*, ACM (2010), 1817–1820.
28. Reeves, S., Benford, S., O'Malley, C., and Fraser, M. Designing the spectator experience. In *Proceedings of the SIGCHI conference on Human factors in computing systems*, ACM (2005), 741–750.
29. Rowland, D., Flintham, M., Oppermann, L., Marshall, J., Chamberlain, A., Koleva, B., Benford, S., and Perez, C. Ubikequitous computing: designing interactive experiences for cyclists. In *Proceedings of the 11th International Conference on Human-Computer Interaction with Mobile Devices and Services*, ACM (2009), 21.
30. Saffer, D. *Designing gestural interfaces: Touchscreens and interactive devices*. " O'Reilly Media, Inc.", 2008.
31. Thornley, S., Woodward, A., Langley, J. D., Ameratunga, S. N., and Rodgers, A. Conspicuity and bicycle crashes: preliminary findings of the taupo bicycle study. *Injury Prevention 14*, 1 (2008), 11–18.
32. Vorhies, Z. Zackees turn signal gloves. `www.kickstarter.com/projects/zackees/zackees-turn-signal-gloves` (2014).
33. Walker, I., Garrard, I., and Jowitt, F. The influence of a bicycle commuter's appearance on drivers overtaking proximities: an on-road test of bicyclist stereotypes, high-visibility clothing and safety aids in the united kingdom. *Accident Analysis & Prevention 64* (2014), 69–77.
34. Walmink, W., Chatham, A., and Mueller, F. Interaction opportunities around helmet design. In *CHI '14 Extended Abstracts on Human Factors in Computing Systems*, CHI EA '14, ACM (New York, NY, USA, 2014), 367–370.
35. Walmink, W., Wilde, D., and Mueller, F. F. Displaying heart rate data on a bicycle helmet to support social exertion experiences. In *Proceedings of the 8th International Conference on Tangible, Embedded and Embodied Interaction*, TEI '14, ACM (New York, NY, USA, 2013), 97–104.
36. Wickens, C. D. Oxford handbooks online. attention.
37. Wilson, S. Bicycle technology. *Scientific American 228*, 3 (1973).
38. Xfire. Bike lane safety light. `http://thexfire.com/products-page/lighting-system/bike-lane-safety-light` (2011).

The dBoard: a Digital Scrum Board for Distributed Software Development

Morten Esbensen, Paolo Tell, Jacob B. Cholewa, Mathias K. Pedersen & Jakob Bardram
The Pervasive Interaction Technology Laboratory
IT University of Copenhagen, Rued Langgaards Vej 7, 2300 Copenhagen S, DK
{mortenq,pate,jbec,mkin,bardram}@itu.dk

ABSTRACT
In this paper we present the dBoard—a digital Scrum Board for distributed Agile software development teams. The dBoard is designed as a 'virtual window' between two Scrum team spaces. It connects two locations with live video and audio, which is overlaid with a synchronized and interactive digital Scrum board, and it adapts the fidelity of the video/audio to the presence of people in front of it. The dBoard is designed to work (i) as a passive information radiator from which it is easy to get an overview of the status of work, (ii) as a media space providing awareness about the presence of remote co-workers, and (iii) as an active meeting support tool. The paper presents a case study of distributed Scrum in a large software company that motivates the design of the dBoard, and details the design and technical implementation of the dBoard. The paper also reports on an initial user study, which shows that users found the dBoard both useful and easy to use. Based on this work, we suggest that superimposing collaborative applications onto live video is a useful way of designing collaborative meeting and awareness systems.

Author Keywords
dBoard; Scrum Board; Videoconferencing; Scrum; Task Board

ACM Classification Keywords
H.5.2 Information Interfaces and Presentation: User Interfaces

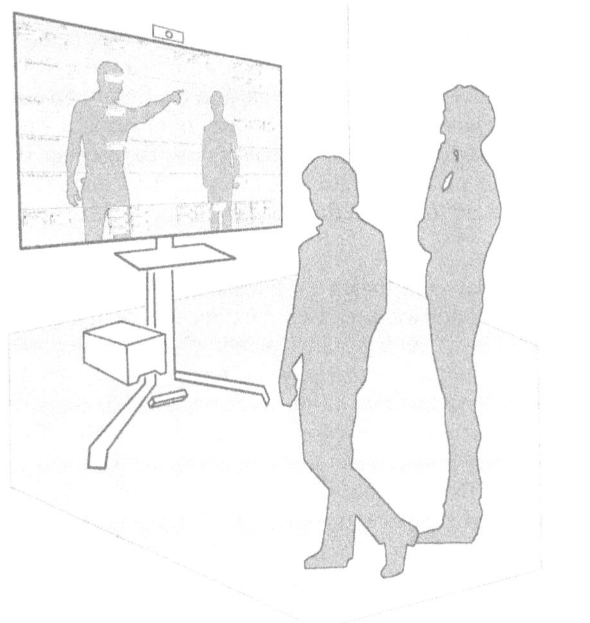

Figure 1. The dBoard is an interactive scrum board and videoconferencing tool designed for distributed teams.

INTRODUCTION
Videoconferencing technologies play a core role in today's globalized business world, and many types of videosystems are used from low-cost and easily available technologies like Skype and Google Hangout, to high-cost dedicated videoconferencing rooms like the Cisco Immersive TelePrecense system. However, when people meet using video it is often with a specific task at hand. Studies have shown that videoconferencing is often conducted as part of a shared experience [4], and that there is a need for integrating videoconferencing with other systems that are used in such arrangements [25]. Moreover, most videoconferencing systems are often only designed for planned meetings in dedicated meeting rooms or spaces, and therefore do not support ongoing awareness information that comes from seeing and informally interacting with co-workers in a shared office space [1].

One important application area for videoconferencing is distributed software development. In particular, in Agile development methods, like Scrum, which puts an emphasis on close collaboration and frequent meetings, videoconferencing has become essential in coordinating work across remote sites [18]. Core to Agile software processes is the use of a Scrum board, which is a large physical task board situated in the software development team's office [19]. The board works as a boundary object, helping to reduce the amount of articulation work [20] and serves two main functions: during the daily meetings it is used to guide the discussion on task progression, and during ordinary work it is used as a passive information radiator showing the status of work as team members update the information on the board. However, the benefit of the Scrum boards relies on the fact that the team is collocated with the board, and a (physical) Scrum board is

ITS 2015, November 15–18, 2015, Funchal/Madeira, Portugal.

ACM 978-1-4503-3899-8/15/11 ...$15.00.
DOI: http://dx.doi.org/10.1145/2817721.2817746

less useful for distributed software development. While concerns have been raised with respect to replacing physical task boards with digital counterparts [23], recent studies suggests that companies will adopt and use technological solutions as their Scrum board [2, 11].

In this paper, we present the design, implementation and evaluation of the dBoard —a digital Scrum board designed specifically for distributed Scrum teams. The dBoard as conceptualized in Figure 1 is designed to support three main functions: (i) as a regular Scrum board revealing task information; (ii) as a media space providing awareness about the presence of remote co-workers, and (iii) as an active meeting support tool during daily Scrum meetings. Instead of separating support for videoconferencing and Scrum board, the dBoard integrates these two by superimposing the Scrum board onto a full screen video-channel. The design of dBoard was based on insights from an observational study of a distributed Scrum team. Once the dBoard was designed and implemented, it was subject to a scenario-based evaluation with Scrum practitioners.

This paper contributes to a detailed understanding of the hardware, software, and user interaction design and implementation of 'collaborative window' technology, which is comprised of a full screen video feed overlaid with domain-specific information—in this case designed to support a distributed Scrum team. Moreover, the study of the dBoard revealed that practitioners found it useful and easy to use, arguing that dBoard would reduce the setup cost of engaging into collaborative ad-hoc meetings, while also pointing to areas for improvements to increase its efficiency in work.

RELATED WORK

dBoard builds on and extends prior research on immersive teleconferencing, media spaces and Scrum boards.

Immersive Teleconferencing

The idea of superimposing a shared user interface on top of videoconferencing has been researched in a number of projects. ClearBoard [16] was designed based on a metaphor of looking through and drawing on a transparent window into another office. This line of research have since been extended to include systems that capture the image of a user through half-silvered screens to provide parallax free videoconferencing systems that convey eye contact [17, 24]. Recently, 3D sensors have been used in conjunction with cameras to capture people and provided interfaces in which 3D realistic representations of participants are presented blended with user interface elements [13, 26]. Despite such focus on gaze and gesture, these systems demonstrate an idea in which videoconferencing and task specific user interfaces can be combined into one technology instead of keeping each tool in its own window or on separate screens. This research has mostly focused on techniques for preserving eye-contact and conveying gestures to provide more immersive teleconferencing, and less on how to make the content shown on top of the video interactive.

Media Spaces

Traditional videoconferencing setups have mostly been designed for meetings. However, in collocated environments, much information is conveyed outside meetings by being aware of the presence of nearby colleagues or during informal talks outside scheduled meetings. This fact has been recognized by system designers who have proposed videoconferencing systems capable of providing awareness information. Portholes [7] demonstrated an early version of such systems in which still images were broadcasted throughout an office space to provide co-workers sitting in different offices with awareness of each other. The PARC media space [1] and VideoWindow [9] connect different offices using live video. More recently, systems such as MirrorSpaces [21] and Pêle-Mêle [12] further explored the concept of media spaces by offering always-on video systems that take into account the proximity of people to the system screen as a means of altering the video.

Scrum Board Technologies

While the Scrum board as an artifact has been subjected to different studies (e.g. [11, 23]), less focus has been on developing new tools. Rubart has proposed using an interactive tabletop-based Scrum board as a tool for collocated Scrum [22], and Boden et. al. demonstrated how an implementation of articulation spaces was appropriated as a Scrum board for a collocated software development team [2]. Along similar lines, Agile planning on tabletops has been demonstrated with the APDT system [10]. However, in general research on collaborative digital Scrum boards is scarce and little is known about how to design Scrum boards for distributed teams.

In comparison to prior research, the dBoard contributes an immersive teleconferencing system that supports displaying a highly dense information overlay with detailed Scrum information, while also supporting direct touch-based interaction with this content. The dBoard is designed to work as both as a video meeting tool as well as a media space for remote awareness, and it utilizes a proxemics-based interaction model to seamlessly move between these two modes of operation.

DESIGN

The dBoard is designed as part of a larger project studying the work of distributed software developers[1]. The motivation of designing the dBoard came partly from the related work we described and partly from an ethnographic field study of distributed software developers [8]. The design was done in a user-centered iterative design process involving two different companies in the studies and design process.

Field Study of Distributed Software Development

To understand the challenges of distributed Scrum we conducted a field study of such a collaboration. The collaboration we observed involved a group of developers distributed across India and Denmark. The group was one coherent

[1]The *NexGSD* project is a research project dedicated to studying global software developement.

Figure 2. The user interface of the dBoard with menu (1), privacy menu (2), user filters (3), story filters (4), and tasks (5)

Scrum team of ten people working on a financial product for the Scandinavian market. Two researchers—one located in Denmark, one located in India—observed the collaboration concurrently. The study applied participant observations in which we observed daily work and meetings of the developers and onsite interviews with team members.

Our observations identified a set of recurring challenges in running an Agile distributed software development process. First, the Agile methodology encourages team members to do a short and efficient daily stand-up meeting for easy and low-level coordination. Such meeting should take place in the shared workspace of the team in front of the Scrum board and should not exceed more than 15 minutes. However, because the team was distributed, setting up and running daily stand-up meetings was cumbersome. The problems often were related to the lack of proper tool support in the right location—both for video meetings and for handling tasks on a Scrum board. For example, the team distributed between Denmark and India would try to meet at the same time each day (9:45 CET in Denmark and 1:15 PM in India). For this to happen, the team first had to go to dedicated videoconferencing rooms at each site. Then, they had to set up the videoconference call and all the software development tools needed. The meetings were usually initiated by an Indian developer setting up all the required systems and then calling the Danish side. The team used a traditional videoconferencing setup in conjunction with the HP Application Lifecycle Manager (ALM) system to manage and update their tasks. As this application was not designed for collaborative use, the Scrum master—located in Denmark—controlled the ALM application while the team in India used VPN and Remote Desktop Connection to connect to the Scrum master's computer and project the application onto a screen next to the videoconferencing screen. As such, the amount of work needed to set up and conduct a stand-up meeting was extremely demanding, and, when the experienced developer was not around to start the meeting, we observed how the others struggled to get the video conferencing, ALM, VPN and Remote Desktop Connection up and running. Hence, these meetings were far from the ideal Agile stand-up meeting taking place in the developers' workspace and only lasting 15 minutes.

A second recurring challenge we observed in the distributed teams was the lack of mutual awareness, especially outside the daily stand-up meetings. In one instance for example, two Indian developers were working on the same bug. When using a traditional Scrum board in a collocated team workspace, such a situation would seldom happen, since a developer would physically go to the board and move the 'bug ticket' from one column to another, thereby signaling a status change. However, in the distributed setup there was no way for a developer to notice such a change if not explicitly communicated. To account for this lack of awareness between the developers, the lead developer located in Denmark contacted the Indian developers on a daily basis using instant messaging. This process allowed him to get an overview of the status of work, but this information then only resided with him and no mutual awareness among team members was maintained.

SYSTEM OVERVIEW

The dBoard is an augmented version of the traditional physical Scrum board that integrates video and Scrum board features into one single tool designed to run on a large multi-touch surface. Based on the field study we formulated the following set of core design features that was used to design the dBoard:

- *Virtual Window*—The dBoard should provide a 'virtual window' between two remote sites thereby enabling seamless communication between two distributed teams.
- *Scrum Board*—The dBoard should support task management (i.e., user stories) in a Scrum fashion by supporting direct manipulation of 'virtual post-it notes' on a grid-like task board.
- *Proximity-based Interaction*—The dBoard should adapt to the environment in which it is situated; in particular, it should adapt to whether people are in front of it or not and to how they are using it.
- *Minimal Setup Costs*—The dBoard should allow people to easily establish meetings with minimal setup costs.
- *Tool Integration*—The dBoard should integrate to relevant digital software engineering tools like issue tracking and Agile project management used in the Scrum practices.

We designed and implemented a prototype based on these design guideliens and presented this prototype in a workshop with a company that works with distributed Scrum. Based on the feedback from this workshop we finalized design and implementation of the dBoard. In the following we describe the features of the dBoard in detail.

Video Window

The dBoard applies a 'window' metaphor to its video conferencing features. The whole background of the dBoard user interface is a large video stream from a connected dBoard designed to give the same feeling that can be experienced when looking through a window into another office. All other user interface elements such as the Scrum board and the menus are placed on top of this video. Similar to a media space [1], the dBoard video is always on and is started automatically when the system is started. The dBoard also captures and streams audio from a connected microphone. This always-on feature makes initiating a meeting as simple as walking up to a board. To get the attention of people at the location of another dBoard, we implemented a 'knock knock' feature. When a user performs a knocking gesture on the board, a knocking sound is played at the other board signaling that someone requests attention.

Scrum Board

The Scrum board elements of the dBoard are superimposed onto the full screen video stream from the other dBoard (see Figure 2). The Scrum board is organized as a traditional physical board: tasks are represented as small digital post-it notes that are arranged into columns indicating their state and rows representing the user story they belong to. Tasks not belonging to a user story are placed in an *Unassociated* row. The tasks display information about their name, type, the user story they belong to, description and the person assigned to it as seen in Figure 3. Tasks can be repositioned using touch, and dragging a task from one column to another changes its state. Tasks can be placed anywhere on the board and do not 'snap' into position when dropped allowing users to arrange the tasks on the board in a similar way that post-it notes can be arranged on a physical board. To assign a task to a developer, users can tap the task's name or user icon to access a dropdown list of people to whom the task can be assigned (see Figure 3).

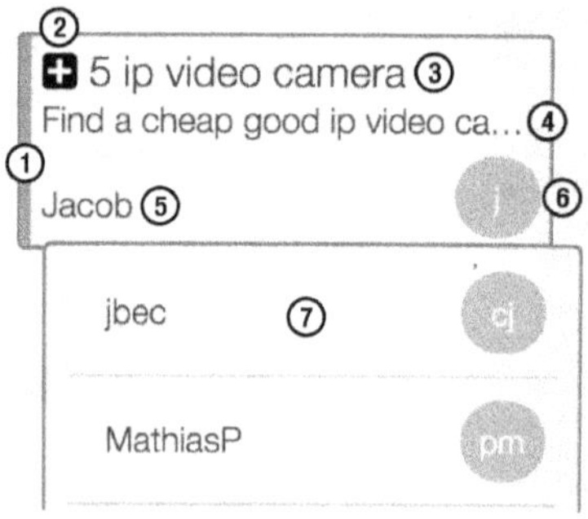

Figure 3. A closeup of a task on the dBoard with task color (1), task type (2), title (3), description (4), assigned user (5), assign button + user initial (6), and assign dropdown (7)

The state of the dBoard is kept synchronized across the two connected boards and all task movements on one board are immediately updated on the other. As in traditional video-conferencing setups, the camera on the dBoard is mounted on top of the stand, which makes it impossible to point to specific tasks due to the parallax. To address this issue we implemented interaction awareness on the screen. When a user drags a task, the task is highlighted in red on both boards. When a user touches anywhere else on the board, a small red pointer is shown on both boards.

We also implemented a number of options to filter and sort the tasks on the board. Two filter menus (Figure 2(3 and 4)) can be used to highlight specific tasks based on two parameters: user and user story. When a user selects a user or user story filter, the dBoard opacifies all tasks that do not match the given filter. As tasks can positioned anywhere on the board we also implemented two ways to sort the board. When sorting, tasks are automatically positioned in the row and column that correspond to their state and user story. To sort the entire board, a user can tap the sorting button in the menu. To sort only a specific tile (i.e. row/column intersection), a user can tap and hold that tile. As the state of the board is kept synchronized across the two connected sites, sorting in one end results in tasks on the other board being sorted as well. Lastly, the rows on the dBoard can be switched to show users rather than user stories. This means that all tasks are re-positioned to be located in the row representing the user they belong to.

Tasks on the dBoard are deliberately designed to be small post-it notes-like elements (Figure 3). These notes contain the very basic information about the task however, to access detailed information users can bring up a side panel. The panel (Figure 4) slides in from the right side of the board when a use performs a tap-and-hold gesture on a task or a user story and it contains much more detailed information about the task. The side panel contains task name, full description, state information and legal states, time estimate and change history list. From the side panel, a user can change the time estimate by performing a dragging gesture on the progress bar or change the state by tapping one of the state buttons. The side panel can be hidden again by performing a swipe gesture on it.

Proxemic Interaction

To provide a seamless transition between awareness tool and meeting tool, the video of the dBoard is automatically blurred and de-blurred and the audio turned on and off by sensing the proximity of people. If no people are in front of the dBoards at both ends, the video is blurred and the audio is turned off. If people are present at only one of the dBoards, the video is blurred less in both ends while the audio is kept turned off. If people are present in both ends, the video is completely un-blurred and the audio is turned on. The blur is used to enhance visibility of the Scrum board – when blurred, the contours in the video are washed out and the colors are faded thus bringing forward the non-blurred user interface elements of the scrum board. Furthermore, the audio is only turned on if people are present at both ends to ensure that the dBoard does not become too much of a distraction if placed in a busy working environment. While blur has been shown to be able to provide the balance between awareness and privacy [3], we also implemented a privacy button that instead of blurring the video removes it altogether until people are present at both boards. Figure 5 shows a example these three modes.

To provide transparency to users with respect to what the dBoard senses, the proximity button in the menu changes color based on the state of the sensing (Figure 2(1)). When green, the button signals that the dBoard has sensed one or more people in front of the board, yellow signals that the sensing is running but no people are seen, while flashing red signals a disconnection to the sensing application. This information is also available when tapping the button in which case a dropdown appears in which the colors are explained in more detail and the current state is highlighted.

Minimal Setup Costs

We built a prototype of the dBoard mounted on a wheeled stand that can easily be moved anywhere. Alternatively, the screen of the dBoard can be setup using a wall display. We thus want to stress that the hardware of the dBoard system can be setup in many configurations as it doesn't require any specially engineered hardware or large physical space. This allows the dBoard to be deployed in the place that best fits its needs or that would be chosen for placing a physical board—for example among the developers. When the system is started, the dBoard application is automatically launched and the video and audio connection established.

Tool Integration

All sprints, user stories, tasks, bugs and users are synchronized with a Microsoft Team Foundation Server (TFS) installation. The synchronization makes sure that all information on the dBoard is taken from a TFS instance and that all changes made either on the dBoard or on another system are

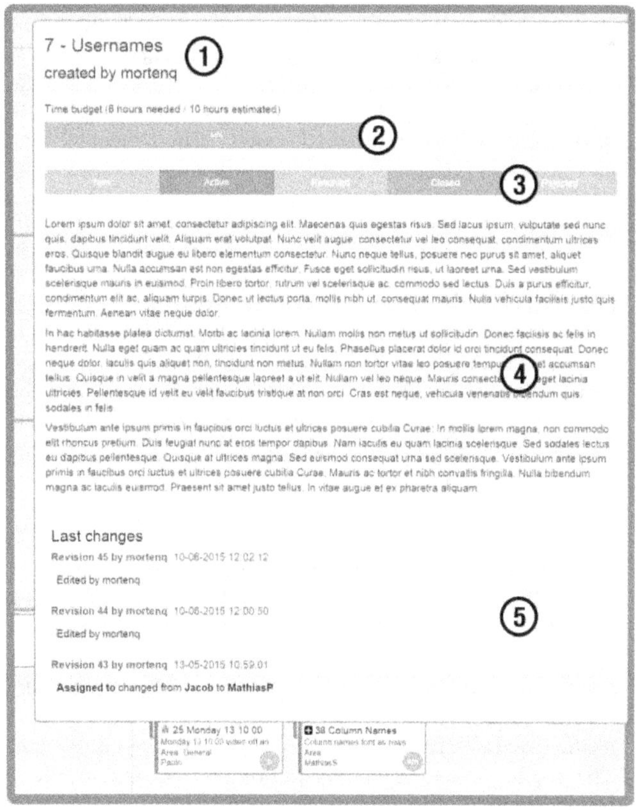

Figure 4. The side panel of dBoard can be used to see detailed information about tasks and user stories. The panel contains title (1), time estimate (2), state (3), rich text description (4), and change history (5)

kept synchronized across the dBoards and TFS. In case of inconsistency between the dBoard and TFS due to network problems, TFS is considered the master.

IMPLEMENTATION

The dBoard system consists of two main parts: the *dBoard*, which is the board itself; and the *backend* which handles communication between dBoards and integration with external tools. This section presents the implementation details of these parts.

dBoard

The dBoard hardware consists of a large 65" display with a 3840 x 2160 resolution and PQ Labs multitouch overlay. A connected high-definition camera and a quality microphone

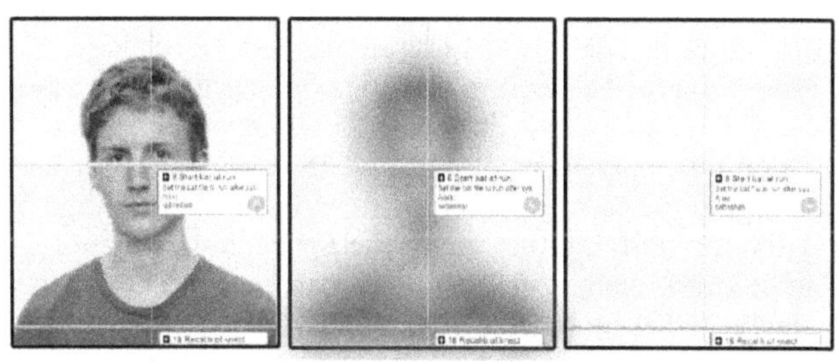

Figure 5. The dBoard in its normal mode (left), with blurred video (middle, and with privacy enabled (right).

captures video and audio. All the hardware is mounted on a movable stand and all components are connected to a fan-less computer strapped to the stand. The setup ensures that setting up and starting the dBoard is as simple as moving it to the desired location and plugging in power. The Kinect v2 sensor used to sense proximity to the board is mounted between the wheels of the stand. Alternatively, the screen can be hanged on a wall.

On startup, the dBoard launches the dBoard frontend application in fullscreen. The dBoard frontend is an HTML5 and JavaScript application built with AngularJS and designed for Google Chrome. Two connected dBoards send and receive video and audio using WebRTC, which is a peer-to-peer based JavaScript framework while all other information (such as tasks, user stories and state information) is communicated through the server using websockets.

Proximity Sensing

The dBoard senses proximity with a Microsoft Kinect v2 attached between the wheels of the system. The Kinect is accessed through the official .NET SDK in a C# application, which analyzes skeletal information and depth frames to infer human presence. Depth frames are used in addition to skeletal tracking as it is possible for people to stand too close to the dBoard for the Kinect to pick up skeletal information. The depth frames are analyzed in two ways: large frame-by-frame pixel changes suggest movement in front of the sensor and a large summed difference between the current frame and a calibration frame suggests proximity. In case presence information is sensed for an extended period of time without any movements happening, the application assumes that a non-human artifact (such as a chair) has been placed in view of the camera and the application recalibrates automatically. A menu button also allows to manually request a recalibration of the proximity sensing application. All presence information is sent to the dBoard web application over a websocket.

Backend

As shown in Figure 6, the dBoard backend consists of three main components: (i) a Node.js web server, (ii) a Microsoft Team Foundation Server (TFS), and (iii) the activity-centered infrastructure NooSphere [15] with a plugin to communicate with the TFS instance.

The Node.js server is responsible for serving the AngularJS web application to the dBoards along with facilitating websocket connections for task and interface synchronization between the boards and the backend. Any change made on the dBoard or in TFS is synchronized through NooSphere. NooSphere exposes all Scrum activities (i.e. sprints, user stories, tasks, bugs and users) through a RESTful web interface. We added this extra layer on top of TFS as it allows for easily changing the task tracking software from TFS to, e.g., Jira without modifying the rest of the application. Changing or adding task management systems can be done by writing a plugin. Other tools would then in turn also be able to access the same data in NooSphere making it an infrastructure able to support other collaborative tools.

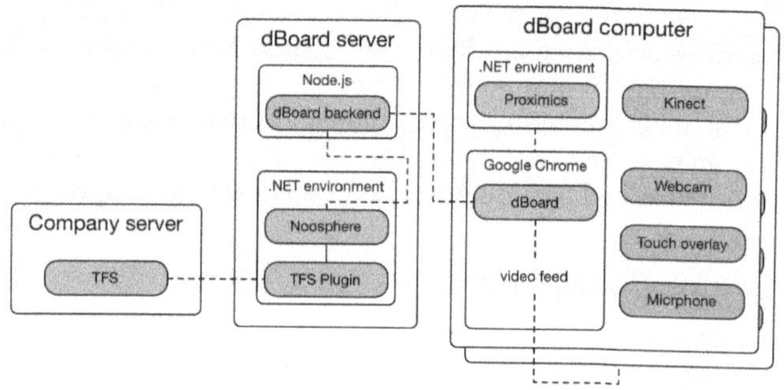

Figure 6. An overview of the architecture of dBoard with its three main components; the TFS server, the dBoard server and the dBoards.

STUDY

To evaluate the design of the dBoard, a scenario-based user evaluation [5] was done. The goal was to (i) study perceived usefulness and ease of use, (ii) observe how participants would use dBoard for performing standup and ad-hoc meetings, and (iii) gather feedback on the features of dBoard.

Participants

The study was conducted by inviting local software development companies using Scrum to participate in an evaluation workshop. Seven software engineers from three different companies participated in the study (age μ = 30,5; σ = 4,53). Participants reported to be experienced Agile and Scrum practitioners, their seniority ranging from 6 months to 10 years (μ = 4,3; σ = 3,98). wo participants were Scrum masters, two product owners, and the rest were developers or testers.

Method

Figure 7 shows the evaluation setup. One board was placed on the stand shown in Figure 1 while the other board was deployed on a large wall display. This setup enabled us to evaluate different hardware form factors of the dBoard system.

The workshop was divided into four parts: (i) an introduction to the dBoard in which the participants were welcomed to the study, signed an informed consent form, filled out a demographic questionnaire, and were given a detailed presentation of the dBoard features; (ii) a hands-on session in which the participants were invited to experiment with the two different dBoards; (iii) a session in which we asked participants to act in two different scenarios; and, (iv) a closing group discussion in which participants, after completing a short survey, were asked to reflect on the dBoard and elaborate on their survey answers.

The two scenarios were chosen from common activities in traditional distributed Scrum teams. Scenario I required the participants to first perform a simple design task (i.e., select a template for a website design based on inspirations from existing websites); update the status of the task on the dBoard; and, contact the remote team (enacted by confederates [5]) to communicate that the design task was completed as well as seek information about the progress on the remote site. Scenario II simulated a standup meeting; participants were given

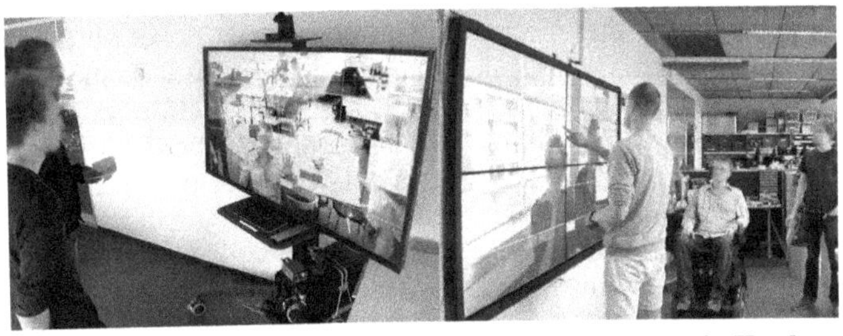

Figure 7. Snapshot of the evaluation taken during Scenario II—the 'standup meeting' using the dBoard on a mount (left) and on a wall-sized display (right).

a script describing the role of the enacted character (one of which was the Scrum master dictating the pace of the meeting), the work done on the previous day, the one planned for the coming day, and whether there were some impediments or clarifications required from the remote site.

The survey applied the technology acceptance model (TAM) [6] to which four questions were added to assess the usefulness of specific dBoard features (i.e., videoconferencing, Scrum board, privacy through proxemic, and 'knock knock'). Each question was measured with a seven-point Likert scale.

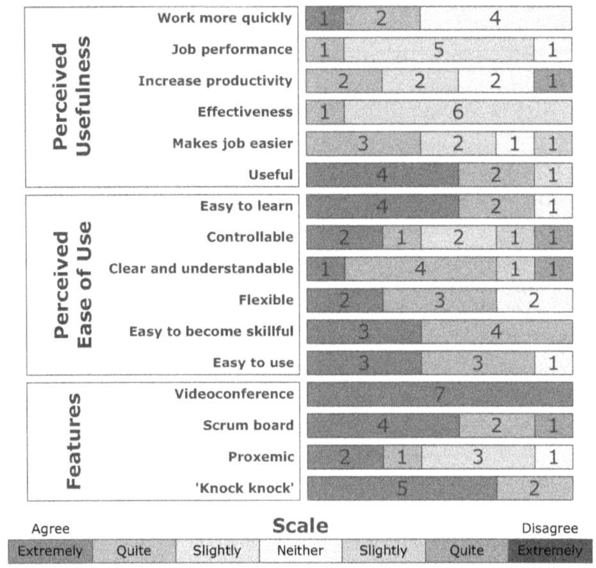

Figure 8. The results of the 7-point Likert scale questionnaire on perceived usefulness, perceived ease of use, and usefulness of the different dBoard features. The figures in each cell shows the number of answers for a given score.

Results

Figure 8 depicts an overview of the results of the questionnaire on the perceived usefulness, perceived ease of use, and usefulness of the different features of the dBoard.

Perceived Usefulness

Even though overall participants scored positively the usefulness of the dBoard, on average they remained quite neutral with answers that varied across participants. In particular, they reported to be uncertain about the ability of the dBoard to enable them to accomplish tasks more quickly ($\tilde{x} = 4$, iqr = 2); a pattern that is repeated across the next four questions related to the ability of the system to: improve performance ($\tilde{x} = 3$, iqr = 0); improve productivity ($\tilde{x} = 3$, iqr = 1,5); enhance effectiveness on the job ($\tilde{x} = 3$, iqr = 0); and, make it easy to do the job ($\tilde{x} = 3$, iqr = 1,5). Nonetheless, on a more direct question about the usefulness of the dBoard in their job, the participants scored the dBoard very positively ($\tilde{x} = 1$, iqr = 1). When asked about the usefulness of the appication in the post-evaluation interview, several participants mentioned that the dBoard should support sprint planning through access to features of creating new tasks at the board and access to the backlig.

Perceived Ease of Use

All participate managed to appropriate the system with more or less confidence in a very brief period of time and reported that it was easy to become skillful in using the dBoard ($\tilde{x} = 2$, iqr = 1); they reported the dBoard to be very easy to learn ($\tilde{x} = 1$, iqr = 1) and to use ($\tilde{x} = 2$, iqr = 1). The analogy with the post-it notes often used in physical Scrum boards was well received; participants appreciated the flexibility provided by the dBoard in terms of freely arranging tasks at arbitrary locations ($\tilde{x} = 2$, iqr = 1,5). The question related to how clear and understandable the dBoard was however, received some negative scores ($\tilde{x} = 2$, iqr = 1,5); a trend visible also in the question related how easy it was to control the dBoard ($\tilde{x} = 3$, iqr = 2,5). The ease of use was also apparent from our observations of the participants during the evaluation sessions. Even with the limited training and experience of interacting with the dBoard from the evaluation introductions, all participants confidently interacted with the boards to complete the evaluation scenarios.

Feature Usefulness

When confronted with more specific questions about the usefulness of the different features provided by the dBoard, participants provided very positive scores. Especially with regards to the videoconferencing capabilities, all participants considered this feature extremely useful (Videoconference: $\tilde{x} = 1$, iqr = 0) and provided comments like:

– *"The entire video is really cool – really helpful."* – P3 – *"You are actually interacting with your colleagues that you do not normally see."* – P5

The Scrum board features were also received very well (Scrum board: $\tilde{x} = 1$, iqr = 1); participants found the integration with TFS to be an essential feature for a digital version of a Scrum board as it represents the main shortcoming of the physical counterpart, and they saw a significant value in the affordances provided by the dedicated setup mimicking physical Scrum boards. One participant stated:

– *"One of the things I like of a Scrum board like this is that you have not the digital but the post-its like interactions, and you can walk up there, take a task up here, and put it over here. I know you can do it on your computer—it might be easier—but I just like that feeling, I like to be able to do that."* – P5

Moreover, the simplicity of the scrum board representation was also appreciated; as one of the participants ironically pointed out:

– *"[speaking about a feature] it is definitely also there [in Jira], but it would take a couple of days to find out where." – P7*

In relation to the proxemic interaction that supports gradual engagement and privacy, participants found it less useful (Proxemic: $\tilde{x} = 3$, iqr = 1,5). On the one hand, some participants valued the ability of mitigating the disturbance of a constant video feed from a large display:

– *"Without the blur, it would be like [being] in a sport bar during a soccer match where everyones' attention is capture by the game..." – P2,*

– *"I like the idea that when one team is working, they can see when a person is at the board." – P4*

On the other hand, the quick and automatic de-blurring of the video feed due to the detection of presence on the remote site was considered by some as potentially distracting. Participants also mentioned that it would be useful for the content to change based on proximity of people. One participant for example, mentioned that the Scrum board could change to a burndown chart.

Finally, the 'knock knock' feature was also found very useful ('Knock knock': $\tilde{x} = 1$, iqr = 1). One participant stated:

– *"[...] we use Slack for things like 'do you have time for a Skype call?'. And that is basically the 'knock knock' right, so I think you got it pretty good there." – P3*

Some participants also suggested using the knock-knock gesture to initiate de-blurring so this would happen via an explicit gesture rather then through the implicit proxemics-based interaction.

– *"[...] it should only activate [the video] when you knock " – P4*

DISCUSSION

This paper contributes to a detailed understanding of the hardware, software, and user interaction design of 'collaborative window' technology, which is comprised of a full screen video feed overlaid with domain-specific information—in this case designed to support a distributed Scrum team. This section presents a discussion of this design space, the lessons learned from the evaluation study, and the more general concept of a 'collaborative window'.

Hardware, Software, and Interaction Design of dBoard

The design of dBoard shows how an ad-hoc video conferencing tool can be integrated with a Scrum-based task management board. While prior research have shown such system design (e.g. [16, 24, 26]), these systems apply advanced and special-designed hardware setups to remove camera parallax and to correctly convey eye-contact, gaze and gestures. This has not been the focus of dBoard, which instead uses off-the-shelf top-mounted cameras and displays. This does introduce camera parallaxes, but in our evaluation participants did not consider this a problem. Moreover, in contrast to prior work, dBoard does not flip the remote image horizontally. This means that if a participant points to a ticket on the left of the Scrum board, the remote video image will show him pointing to the right and hence not on the right ticket. If the design was to accommodate this problem, the display could be flipped horizontally in two ways: either the video or the content. In the design of dBoard, neither of the two were flipped. The content (i.e., the Scrum board) was not flipped, since tickets flow from the left column ('backlog') to the right column ('done') hence, horizontal orientation carries a semantic meaning. Moreover, if the content was flipped, then all text on the Scrum board (including each task ticket) would be mirrored and hence unreadable. The video was not flipped either, since this would distort the view from the remote site into the local office, and would—we argue—contradict the 'window' design metaphor that allows users to directly look into the remote office however, one participant mentioned in the scenario that the video could be flipped. In addition, participants were able to see from the remote pointer what task was being pointed at and moved around.

The overall interaction design of dBoard incorporates two core design principles, which could be of general use for collaborative technologies; 'reducing startup costs' and 'beyond being there'.

The design principle of *Reducing Startup Costs* addresses the need for making it extremely easy and effortless to engage in collaboration. Rather than having to book and setup a video meeting, dBoard was designed as an 'always-on' video window to the other site. It would always show the current status of the Scrum board and all task information is easily accessible through a very straightforward gesture-based touch interface. As such, there is a very limited cost in terms of time, effort, and cognitive load associated with engaging in a distributed ad-hoc Scrum meeting – the dBoard is literally a 'walk-up-and-use' technology. This was also recognized by the study participants, who argued that this was a core benefit of the system (as e.g. reflected in the high score on the 'videoconference' feature evaluation).

The design principles of *Beyond Being There*[2] addresses how technology can go beyond collocated interaction. As said, Scrum is inherently based on collocated practices where the Scrum team meets, works, discusses, and demos in a team room with a Scrum board. This collocated practice allow for high-bandwidth informal communication but it also carries with it the problems of open-space offices in terms of noise, disturbances, (lack of) privacy, and stress. The dBoard allows a team to reduce (blur) noise and disturbances from the remote team and to preserve local privacy. As noted by P2 during the evaluation; blurring the video made it less disturbing. It must, however, be underlined that the current study of dBoard did not compare collocated with distributed Scrum practices; this is the subject for a future study.

Perceived Usefulness and Usability

In general, the study of dBoard showed that practitioners found it useful and easy to use, arguing that it would reduce the setup cost of engaging into collaborative ad-hoc meetings,

[2]This principle paraphrases Hollan & Stornetta's CHI'92 paper [14].

while also pointing to areas for improvements to increase its efficiency in work.

The evaluation of the usefulness of the dBoard showed some mixed results. On one hand, the *overall* usefulness and the usefulness of the four specific features (videoconferencing, Scrum board, Proxemic, and 'Knock-knock') were rated high. On the other hand, specific usefulness parameters on *performance*, *productivity*, and *effectiveness* received moderate scores. When interviewing participants, they argued that they did not see dBoard as a productivity-enhancing tool, but rather as a convenient way to conduct remote ad-hoc Scrum meetings and to maintain an awareness on the status of work. As such, dBoard would not 'enhance' or 'improve' on anything they did not do already. Moreover, the participants also pointed out that the dBoard had to incorporate support for sprint planning, if it was to be used throughout the entire Scrum process.

In general, the evaluation showed that participants found dBoard easy to use. There are, however, still some performance issues that affect ease of use, which was also reflected in the evaluation scores of the TAM (Controllable and Clear and understandable). During the evaluations, some gestures such as swiping or dragging multiple tickets suffered from 'lagging'. Despite the computational power of today, we experienced that implementing such a complex collaborative application as a web application could cause some performance bottlenecks. Multi-touch and gesture-based interaction on web application is still in its initial stage and needs to be improved before dBoard can get widespread adoption.

The evaluation showed that the specific dBoard features were all found very useful, with the videoconferencing as a significant high score. During the interviews, several issues and suggestions for improvements were raised by the participants. A recurrent question was related to 'information overload', i.e. what happens if too much Scrum information is shown on the dBoard display? Is there a risk of covering most of the video? Another line of comments was related to the usage of proxemics. Several participants mentioned that they would prefer to have the de-blurring of video triggered by the knock-knock feature rather than the proxemic interaction. This later issue relates to whether blurring – or any other feature – should be based on implicit (proxemics) or explicit interaction. This limited study shows that users tend to prefer explicit gestures for initiating (de-blurring) a video meeting, whereas automatic blurring the video once users is no longer in front of dBoard seems to be feasible. However, studying the pros and cons of implicit interaction in dBoard would require a longer deployment study.

Collaborative Windows

Based on our work of designing, implementing and evaluating dBoard, we argue that combining video with collaborative user interfaces using a 'collaborative window' metaphor is a promising design guideline for collaborative applications. A collaborative window is designed as a window into a distant location upon which interactive collaborative content is superimposed. Despite not solving camera parallax or providing support for gaze and gestures, we demonstrated how a collaborative window application such as dBoard was perceived very well by users with respect to usefulness and ease of use. In particular, such applications allow for a richer collaborative experience as they do not require users to constantly switch attention from the video to the tasks at hand and the combination of video and content furthermore reduces startup costs.

CONCLUSION

In this paper we presented the design, implementation and evaluation of the dBoard—a digital distributed Scrum board that blends together videoconferencing and Scrum task management. This is achieved by bringing them together in a setup where the Scrum board specific elements are superimposed onto the video. The dBoard was designed to provide support both as a passive information radiator from which the state of work can be collected, as a media space proving awareness about the presence of remote co-workers, and as an active meeting support tool. By sensing the proximity of people the dBoard provides a way to seamlessly switch between these three modes of operations.

We designed the dBoard based on observations of distributed Scrum practices and implemented the system as a web application that runs on large multitouch enabled screens. The dBoard was evaluated in a scenario based setting with experienced Scrum practitioners. The evaluation revealed that users found the dBoard both useful and easy to use. In particular, the combination of video and Scrum board was very well received. Based on this work, we argue that adopting the metaphor of a 'collaborative window' as a means of designing collaborative videoconferencing systems can lead to new and interesting applications supporting distributed collaboration.

ACKNOWLEDGMENTS

This research has been funded by the Danish Agency for Science, Technology and Innovation under the project "Next Generation Technology for Global Software Development", #10-092313.

REFERENCES

1. Sara A. Bly, Steve R. Harrison, and Susan Irwin. 1993. Media Spaces: Bringing People Together in a Video, Audio, and Computing Environment. *Commun. ACM* 36, 1 (Jan. 1993), 28–46.

2. Alexander Boden, Frank Rosswog, Gunnar Stevens, and Volker Wulf. 2014. Articulation Spaces: Bridging the Gap Between Formal and Informal Coordination. In *Proceedings of the 17th ACM Conference on Computer Supported Cooperative Work & Social Computing (CSCW '14)*. ACM, New York, NY, USA, 1120–1130.

3. Michael Boyle, Christopher Edwards, and Saul Greenberg. 2000. The Effects of Filtered Video on Awareness and Privacy. In *Proceedings of the 2000 ACM Conference on Computer Supported Cooperative Work (CSCW '00)*. ACM, New York, NY, USA, 1–10.

4. Jed R. Brubaker, Gina Venolia, and John C. Tang. 2012. Focusing on Shared Experiences: Moving Beyond the

Camera in Video Communication. In *Proceedings of the Designing Interactive Systems Conference (DIS '12)*. ACM, New York, NY, USA, 96–105.

5. Gregorio Convertino, Dennis C. Neale, Laurian Hobby, John M. Carroll, and Mary Beth Rosson. 2004. A Laboratory Method for Studying Activity Awareness. In *Proceedings of the Third Nordic Conference on Human-computer Interaction (NordiCHI '04)*. ACM, New York, NY, USA, 313–322.
6. Fred D. Davis. 1989. Perceived usefulness, perceived ease of use, and user acceptance of information technology. *MIS Q.* 13, 3 (1989), 319–340.
7. Paul Dourish and Sara Bly. 1992. Portholes: supporting awareness in a distributed work group. In *Proceedings of the SIGCHI Conference on Human Factors in Computing Systems (CHI '92)*. ACM, New York, NY, USA, 541–547.
8. Morten Esbensen and Pernille Bjørn. 2014. Routine and Standardization in Global Software Development. In *Proceedings of the 18th International Conference on Supporting Group Work (GROUP '14)*. ACM, New York, NY, USA, 12–23.
9. Robert S. Fish, Robert E. Kraut, and Barbara L. Chalfonte. 1990. The VideoWindow system in informal communications. ACM Press, 1–11.
10. Y. Ghanam, Xin Wang, and F. Maurer. 2008. Utilizing Digital Tabletops in Collocated Agile Planning Meetings. In *Agile, 2008. AGILE '08. Conference.* 51–62.
11. Stevenon Gossage, Judith M. Brown, and Robert Biddle. 2015. *Understanding Digital Cardwall Usage*. Technical report tr-15-01. Carleton University - School of Computer Science.
12. Sofiane Gueddana and Nicolas Roussel. 2006. Pêle-Mêle, a Video Communication System Supporting a Variable Degree of Engagement. In *Proceedings of the 2006 20th Anniversary Conference on Computer Supported Cooperative Work (CSCW '06)*. ACM, New York, NY, USA, 423–426.
13. Keita Higuchi, Yinpeng Chen, Philip A. Chou, Zhengyou Zhang, and Zicheng Liu. 2015. ImmerseBoard: Immersive Telepresence Experience Using a Digital Whiteboard. In *Proceedings of the 33rd Annual ACM Conference on Human Factors in Computing Systems (CHI '15)*. ACM, New York, NY, USA, 2383–2392.
14. Jim Hollan and Scott Stornetta. 1992. Beyond Being There. In *Proceedings of the SIGCHI Conference on Human Factors in Computing Systems (CHI '92)*. ACM, New York, NY, USA, 119–125.
15. Steven Houben, Søren Nielsen, Morten Esbensen, and Jakob E. Bardram. 2013. NooSphere: An Activity-centric Infrastructure for Distributed Interaction. In *Proceedings of the 12th International Conference on Mobile and Ubiquitous Multimedia (MUM '13)*. ACM, New York, NY, USA, Article 13, 10 pages.
16. Hiroshi Ishii and Minoru Kobayashi. 1992. ClearBoard: A Seamless Medium for Shared Drawing and Conversation with Eye Contact. In *Proceedings of the SIGCHI Conference on Human Factors in Computing Systems (CHI '92)*. ACM, New York, NY, USA, 525–532.
17. M. Kuechler and A. Kunz. 2006. HoloPort - A Device for Simultaneous Video and Data Conferencing Featuring Gaze Awareness. In *Virtual Reality Conference, 2006.* 81–88.
18. M. Paasivaara, S. Durasiewicz, and C. Lassenius. 2008. Distributed Agile Development: Using Scrum in a Large Project. In *Global Software Engineering, 2008. ICGSE 2008. IEEE International Conference on.* 87 –95.
19. J. Paredes, C. Anslow, and F. Maurer. 2014. Information Visualization for Agile Software Development. In *Software Visualization (VISSOFT), 2014 Second IEEE Working Conference on.* 157–166.
20. Lene Pries-Heje and Jan Pries-Heje. 2011. Why Scrum Works: A Case Study from an Agile Distributed Project in Denmark and India. In *Agile Conference (AGILE), 2011.* 20 –28.
21. N. Roussel, H. Evans, and H. Hansen. 2004. Proximity as an interface for video communication. *MultiMedia, IEEE* 11, 3 (July 2004), 12–16.
22. Jessica Rubart. 2014. A Cooperative Multitouch Scrum Task Board for Synchronous Face-to-Face Collaboration. In *Proceedings of the Ninth ACM International Conference on Interactive Tabletops and Surfaces (ITS '14)*. ACM, New York, NY, USA, 387–392.
23. H. Sharp, H. Robinson, J. Segal, and D. Furniss. 2006. The role of story cards and the wall in XP teams: a distributed cognition perspective. In *Agile Conference, 2006.* 75–86.
24. Kar-Han Tan, I. Robinson, R. Samadani, Bowon Lee, D. Gelb, A. Vorbau, B. Culbertson, and J. Apostolopoulos. 2009. ConnectBoard: A remote collaboration system that supports gaze-aware interaction and sharing. In *Multimedia Signal Processing, 2009. MMSP '09. IEEE International Workshop on.* 1–6.
25. John C. Tang, Chen Zhao, Xiang Cao, and Kori Inkpen. 2011. Your Time Zone or Mine?: A Study of Globally Time Zone-shifted Collaboration. In *Proceedings of the ACM 2011 Conference on Computer Supported Cooperative Work (CSCW '11)*. ACM, New York, NY, USA, 235–244.
26. Jakob Zillner, Christoph Rhemann, Shahram Izadi, and Michael Haller. 2014. 3D-board: A Whole-body Remote Collaborative Whiteboard. In *Proceedings of the 27th Annual ACM Symposium on User Interface Software and Technology (UIST '14)*. ACM, New York, NY, USA, 471–479.

SoD-Toolkit: A Toolkit for Interactively Prototyping and Developing Multi-Sensor, Multi-Device Environments

Teddy Seyed, Alaa Azazi, Edwin Chan, Yuxi Wang, Frank Maurer
University of Calgary, Department of Computer Science
2500 University Drive NW, Calgary, Alberta, T2N 1N4
{teddy.seyed, alaa.azazi, edwin.chan, yuxwang, frank.maurer}@ucalgary.ca

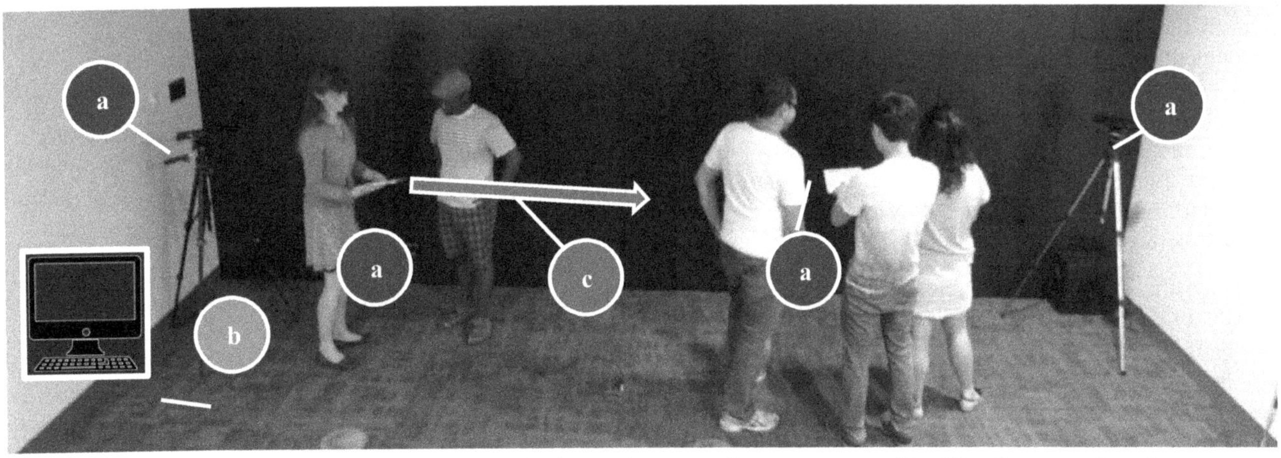

Figure 1. The *SoD-Toolkit* consists of (a) numerous devices and sensors that are supported by (b) software tools and components providing information that facilitates (c) spatial interactions between devices and the environment.

ABSTRACT
As ubiquitous environments become increasingly commonplace with newer sensors and forms of computing devices (e.g. wearables, digital tabletops), researchers have continued to design and implement novel interaction possibilities. However, as the number of sensors and devices continues to rise, researchers still face numerous instrumentation, implementation and cost barriers before being able to take advantage of the additional capabilities. In this paper, we present the *SoD-Toolkit* – a toolkit that facilitates the exploration and development of multi-device interactions, applications and ubiquitous environments by using combinations of low-cost sensors to provide spatial-awareness. The toolkit offers three main features. (1) A "plug and play" architecture for seamless multi-sensor integration, allowing for novel explorations and ad-hoc setups of ubiquitous environments. (2) Client libraries that integrate natively with several major device and UI platforms. (3) Unique tools that allow designers to prototype interactions and ubiquitous environments without a need for people, sensors, rooms or devices. We demonstrate and reflect on real-world case-studies from industry-based collaborations that influenced the design of our toolkit, as well as discuss advantages and limitations of our toolkit.

ITS 2015, November 15–18, 2015, Funchal/Madeira, Portugal.

http://dx.doi.org/10.1145/2817721.2817750

Author Keywords
Sensors; Toolkit; Kinect; Cross-device interactions; Gestural Interaction; Multi-Surface; Prototyping.

ACM Classification Keywords
H.5.2. Information Interfaces. User Interfaces – input devices and strategies, prototyping.

INTRODUCTION
The consumer space of computing technologies is experiencing a dramatic explosion of different size and form factors for devices (e.g. wearables, multi-touch wall displays). The capabilities of these devices can be expanded significantly when used collectively with other devices and sensors, effectively creating multi-device ubiquitous environments. Ubiquitous environments provide people with access to their information across many of their devices, with some devices being spatially aware of other devices in the environment. Spatial awareness in ubiquitous environments is directly linked to the sensors (either dedicated or device-based) and further magnifies existing challenges as to how information and tasks can be performed effectively across

different types of devices, within varying degrees of spatial awareness [32].

Research in ubiquitous environments primarily focuses on novel interaction forms between people and a set of devices [41] (e.g. digital tabletops, mobile devices, smart watches), with proxemics being a common method of conceptualizing the interaction space [1, 8]. As different form factors for devices becomes commonplace and the capabilities of sensors increase, novel forms of explorations between different devices (e.g. a Google Glass and a Smart Watch) is still fairly limited in the context of spatially-aware ubiquitous environments. Furthermore, exploration into real-world scenarios also faces limitations, much of which arises from the difficulty in building multi-device, spatially-aware environments, as many existing development kits are limited in support for different multi-sensor configurations, multi-device platforms and cross-connectivity and typically require complex software and hardware setups [13].

To bridge the gap and allow for richer explorations into spatially-aware ubiquitous environments, we introduce the Society of Devices (SoD) Toolkit (or *SoD-Toolkit)*, a toolkit that facilitates exploring and developing multi-device applications and interactions in spatially-aware ubiquitous environments (Figure 1). Overall, our primary research goal was *to allow for novel explorations of different types of multi-device, spatially-aware (through multi-sensor fusion) ubiquitous environments that can be augmented with a multitude of newer sensors and device platforms*. To address this goal, our toolkit abstracts sensor information from a multitude of sensors into a "plug and play" architecture, allowing researchers and developers to seamlessly fuse sensor information and utilize commercially available off-the-shelf tracking technologies to provide spatial awareness in ubiquitous environments. Researchers and developers can also create additional modules for future sensors through the modular architecture of the toolkit. The toolkit also provides a number of client libraries that are built upon existing operating systems and platforms which include iOS, Android, Windows, as well as web-based technologies such as HTML5, Node.js and Javascript. This allows for a wide range of skill sets and experience, letting researchers and developers implement and design interactions and ubiquitous environments in languages they are comfortable with, reducing many common platform, language, technology and device barriers [28]. In addition, the toolkit offers tools for researchers and developers to visualize and prototype interactions within varying levels of spatially-aware ubiquitous environments (due to limited hardware availability) or without the need of specialized hardware entirely. This reduces a significant hardware and cost barrier for researchers and developers, and can assist in more widespread research and application development for ubiquitous environments in both the research and consumer space.

The remainder of this paper, is organized as follows. We first review related work and then introduce the design of the *SoD-Toolkit*, including its key features, architecture and components.

Next, we describe two real-world domain-specific case studies that demonstrate the flexibility of the toolkit, how they influenced the design rationale of the toolkit and lessons we learned. This is followed by a discussion and reflection on the design and features of the toolkit compared to other approaches. Finally, we conclude this paper describing limitations and future work.

RELATED WORK

SoD-Toolkit is inspired by Weiser's vision of ubiquitous computing [41] and built upon prior work in three areas of research: (1) Proxemics and Ambient Interactions, (2) Multi-Surface Interactions and (3) Application Programming Interfaces (APIs) and Toolkit designs.

Proxemics and Ambient Interactions

The research space of proxemic interactions is extremely rich and well explored. Greenberg et al. conceptualized proxemics in the context of ubiquitous environments with a number of investigations that focused on spatial relationships between users and objects, specifically applying five proxemic dimensions: orientation, distance, motion, identity and location [8]. The intention of much of the research in this space is to "leverage people's natural understanding of their proxemic relationships to manage the entities that surround them" [23]. Applying these proxemic theories to sensors in ubiquitous environments was further explored by Ballendat et al, who used sensors to detect people and their devices, and better understand different types of interactions (i.e. implicit and explicit) [1]. Follow-up work by Marquardt et al. examined the relationships between people in closer spaces through F-formations and micro-mobility and sociological constructs [25].

Marquardt and Greenberg also identified major challenges for proxemics, which included providing meaningful feedback, managing privacy and security and establishing connections between different types of devices [22]. Establishing connections with different types of devices was the focus of early work in proxemics by Vogel and Balakrishnan, who explored proxemics in relation to public ambient displays [38]. They defined four discrete areas in front of devices, similar to Edward Hall's proxemic zones surrounding a person [7]. In more recent years, research focused on devices such as whiteboards [15, 31] and other forms of displays [35].

While a majority of proxemics research has been heavily device-centric in relatively small or enclosed spaces, proxemics in larger more ambient spaces (and not around smaller displays) has been less researched. Active Badge by Want et al., is an early example of exploring larger scale proxemics [40]. Their system uses a beacon sensor to track position of users in a work environment. UbER Badge by

Laibowitz et al is another example, whose system uses proxemic badges [19]. The badges are used to facilitate social interaction in various large meetings. In the context of a ubiquitous home, the EasyLiving project explored multi-room proxemics by combining a number of technologies to track people and their devices on a larger scale [2]. Research into proxemic interactions in larger and more ubiquitous spaces is directly tied to different types of tracking technologies, a large research area within ubiquitous environments itself. *SoD-Toolkit* builds upon many of the concepts in proxemics and ambient spaces with a goal of providing lightweight tools and libraries for developing and exploring interactions and applications in larger scale ubiquitous environments and domains, without researchers and developers being restricted in room size or choice of sensors.

Multi-Device Interactions

Multi-device interactions with a number of different device configurations is a rapidly growing research area, particularly with newer form factors of devices increasing in the consumer market (e.g. wearables). A major task in multi-device interactions involves the movement of information or content from one device to another [32]. Much of the early work in multi-device interactions is based upon Rekimoto's Pick and Drop, where pen input is synchronized across multiple computers, allowing a user direction manipulation of content between screens [30]. Hinckley explored the notion of bumping tablets and stitching tablets together (via pen stroke across displays) as multi-device interactions for transferring content [11, 2]. Lucero et al followed a similar approach, but instead used a pinching gesture across multiple mobile devices [21]. In these types of multi-device interactions, input is typically *synchronized* to facilitate smooth interaction and information transfer [3].

Multi-device interactions can also be impacted by *spatial awareness* and proxemic relationships [3]. Numerous sensors are employed to provide positioning and tracking of devices (and users) to take advantage of spatial relationships. Kortuem et al. used this approach when creating novel spatial widgets for user interfaces [17]. Kray et al., used a digital tabletop as a center of mediation for proxemic relationships between mobile devices [18]. More general work in these types of interactions were explored by Marquardt et al with the gradual engagement pattern, that maps device-to-device proximity as a function of different levels of information exchange [22]. LightSpace by Wilson and Benko [42], uses spatial awareness for interactions between and on physical surfaces.

Dividing information and interfaces across multiple devices results in interactions that are *distributed* [3]. The iLand system by Streitz et al [37] is an early example of interactions distributed in a ubiquitous environment. Roomware is another example that inter-connects smart artifacts in a room, to augment both individual and collaborative tasks [36]. More recently, interactions between newer forms of devices such as wearables has begun to appear in the research literature. Chen et al., explored interaction techniques and gestures for distributed interactions between a watch and smartphone [3]. In a similar fashion, Mayer et al. [26] explored head-mounted display to interact with objects within view of a user. Overall however, distributed interaction techniques for wearables and newer forms of devices is still extremely underexplored [3, 13, 39, 44].

Much of this work indicates the potential interaction techniques for ubiquitous environments, however a significant amount of implementation work is repeated for interactions that are *synchronized*, *spatially-aware* or *distributed*. *SoD-Toolkit* easily allows for the exploration of these types of interactions (or combinations thereof) and can facilitate researchers in exploring unconventional and yet-to-be explored multi-device spatially-aware interactions (e.g. between a head-mounted display and a smart watch).

Application Programming Interfaces and Toolkits

A significant amount of recent research has explored creating multi-device toolkits, primarily designed to overcome different aspects of the engineering challenges that come with building ubiquitous environments. Toolkits, such as Conductor [9] and Panelrama [43] and others [4, 16, 33], focus specifically on multi-device application development through web-based interfaces. XDStudio also supports cross-device application development, through the use of a GUI builder [27].

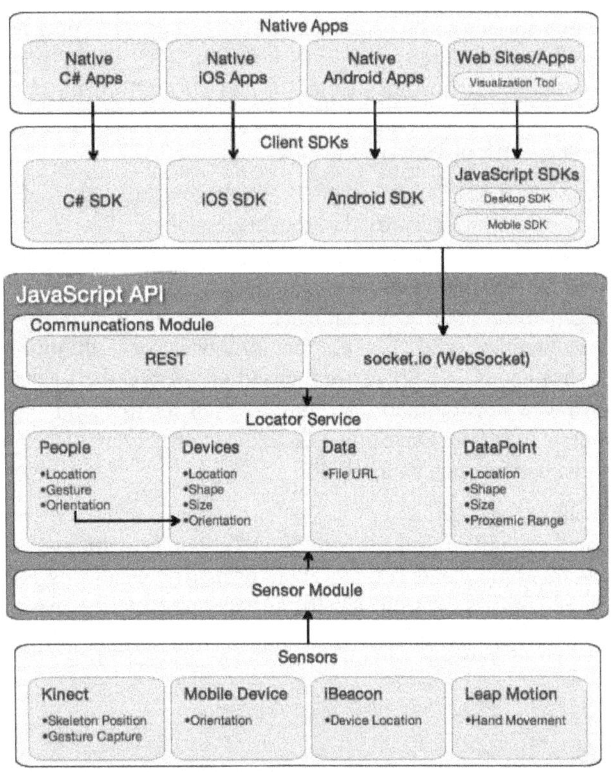

Figure 2. An overview of the architecture of the *SoD-Toolkit*

The Proximity Toolkit is the canonical example of a toolkit focused on larger ubiquitous spaces [23]. The toolkit gathers data from various tracking sensors to allow for sensor fusion, and provides an easily accessible API. It also allows for interactions to be observed via a visual tool. A major challenge with the toolkit however, is its reliance on high-end tracking systems [27] that are ideal for prototyping but not feasible in real-world deployments [28] and its limited support for additional sensors. This inspired further work, such as XDKinect [28] which uses a single Kinect sensor to mediate interaction between different devices and also allows proxemic interaction and multi-modal input. In toolkits such as these, enabling multi-device interactions in ubiquitous environment requires knowledge about presence and position of devices, typically provided by a variety of sensors. Numerous approaches have been taken in the research literature, such as magnet based tracking [14], radio tracking [21] and sensor fusion approaches [23]. Much of the work in prototyping ubiquitous environments also faces issues of cost (for sensors and devices) and room size, making it difficult for researchers to properly explore novel types of ubiquitous environments and multi-device interactions.

Implementing ubiquitous environments that are deployable in real-world environments still requires substantial engineering efforts for researchers and developers. It is still possible to build applications for different devices, with different sensors in ubiquitous environments, but the effort required prevents richer explorations [29]. In contrast, *SoD-Toolkit* provides support for exploring multi-sensor, multi-device ubiquitous environments by providing (1) a "plug and play" architecture multi-sensor fusion, (2) native client libraries for major device, sensor and UI platforms and (3) tools that allow rapid prototyping without the need for people, sensors, rooms or devices.

SOD-TOOLKIT

In this section, we provide an overview of the *SoD-Toolkit* architectural components, its visualization and prototyping tool, as well as its multi-sensor fusion approach to create larger ubiquitous environments. To facilitate real-world deployments and novel explorations of ubiquitous environments, we primarily focused on off-the-shelf sensor hardware and common devices, as well as free and open source software. Our source code is also freely available to download as open source[1].

Architecture

The software architecture of *SoD-Toolkit* is composed of several components (Figure 2) but primarily, we discuss: (1) client libraries, (2) the locator service, and (3) the central server and communications module.

Client SDK Libraries

The client SDK libraries have two primary functions: (1) they provide necessary information for spatial awareness in the environment, depending on the sensor or device and (2) provide a platform to be built upon for native application development. Within each client library, a sensor module captures and sends data to the locator service frequently (discussed in the next section) and the data captured varies, depending on device or sensor type. The libraries support:

1. **Various form factors of devices** such as digital tabletops, wall displays, smart watches, head mounted displays and mobile devices (regardless of implementation platform). If a device has built in sensors (e.g. accelerometers, gyroscopes), this information is sent over the network to the locator service, which is discussed in the next section. Due to the modular nature of the architecture, spatial information from a device is easily fused with other supported sensors in the environment. For example, we allow for the position and orientation of a device to be determined by fusing skeletal information of a user (from a Microsoft Kinect) with orientation of a device (from gyroscopes and accelerometers). For devices that are stationary (e.g. a wall display), we allow researchers and developers to set the physical location in space, through the visualization tools we provide, as we discuss later.
2. **JS web client** that is both platform and browser agnostic, deriving information from a device if it has sensors available. This client is similar to the platform specific device clients, however, this allows for support of web-based multi-sensor, multi-device ubiquitous environments, which is not common in many toolkits.
3. **The Microsoft Kinect** provides skeletal, position, identity and gestural information through its available skeletal stream. The Kinect client library supports a single Microsoft Kinect (version 1 or 2) and sends information over the network to the locator service at a rate of 30 skeleton frames per second. A single Kinect sensor has a tracking range from 1.2 to 4.5 meters, which creates difficulties when trying to create larger ubiquitous environments. We address this by allowing multiple Kinects to track users and use sensor fusion to expand the tracking area, create novel tracking areas, as well as improve tracking accuracy. We discuss this sensor fusion in the Sensor Fusion approach section. Additionally, our Kinect client currently supports the "grab" and "release" gestures.
4. **The Leap Motion** provides detailed finger tracking of a user. Overall the sensor provides a more fine grained level of tracking that typically needs to be paired with a sensor that covers a larger area (e.g. Microsoft Kinect) to provide meaningful interactions. For example, if a user is further away from a Kinect and close to a wall display that isn't touch enabled, but is connected to a Leap motion, the locator service interprets the position of the user and

[1] *SoD Toolkit* - http://sodtoolkit.com/

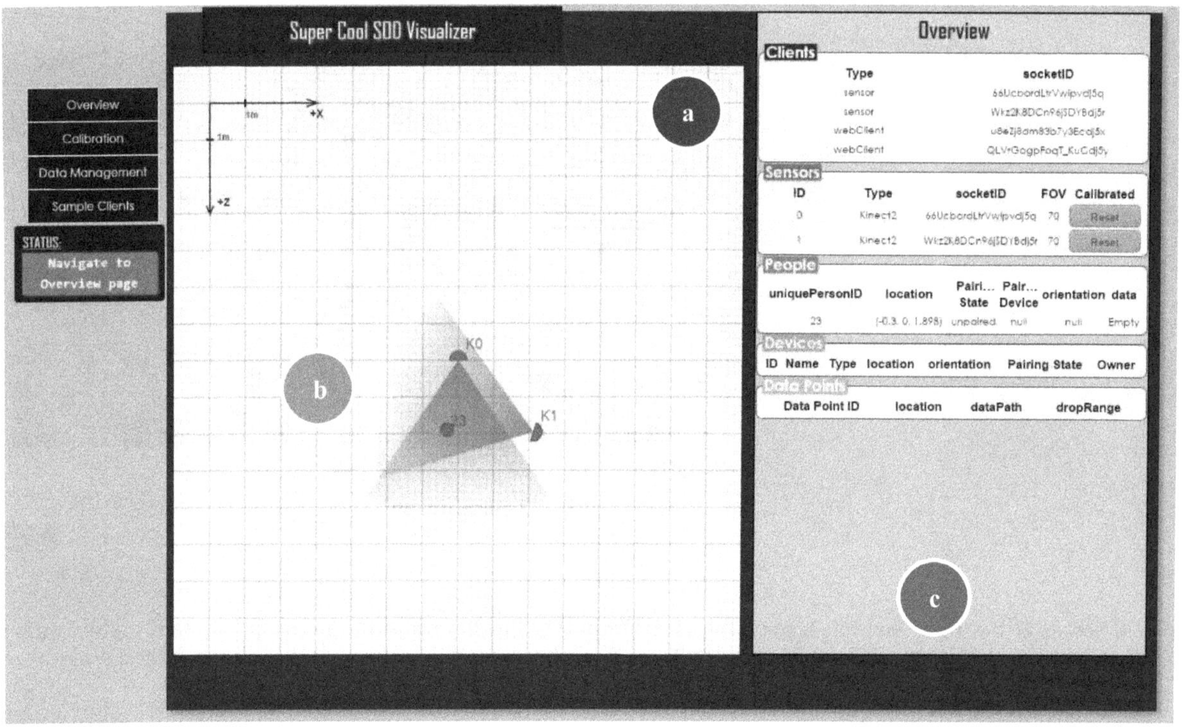

Figure 3. The visualization and prototyping tool for the *SoD-Toolkit.* (a) The tracked environment, (b) Entities tracked in the environment, (c) List of available entities and their current state, as well as clients currently connected in the environment.

prioritizes sensor information from the Leap motion over potentially inconsistent Kinect skeletal data, particularly for skeleton and joint data.

5. **Apple's iBeacon** which provide coarse grained positional information. The sensor provides position information of a device (either Android or iOS) or person (a person must have an iBeacon tag) in the form of close, near or far. While the sensor doesn't provide as accurate tracking as a Kinect sensor, it can facilitate a larger ubiquitous space and server as a mediator, transitioning between high and low spatially-aware regions.

All clients for sensors and devices support native development platforms which include Windows (C#), iOS (Objective-C and Swift), Android (Java) and HTML5/JS, as well as support for popular IDEs (Microsoft's Visual Studio, Android Studio and Apple's Xcode), significantly reducing start-up effort for researchers and developers. For other programming languages, environments, developers are able to write wrappers over the libraries and APIs we provide. We also provide a set of example applications using different sensors and devices to illustrate code required to implement novel spatially-aware multi-device interactions (e.g. "flick" to device) or multi-sensor ubiquitous environment.

Locator Service

The Locator service is the hub that amalgamates spatial information from different sensors and devices, allowing the *SoD-Toolkit* to build multi-sensor spatially-aware ubiquitous environments. Information that is tracked includes different types of entities, such as sensors, devices (as well as their orientation) as well as users in the room. The locator service processes raw positional data from device and sensor clients that are distributed over the network, and transforms the data from a device-specific coordinate space into a locator service coordinate space, while also building higher level information about the state of the environment and the relationships between entities. Additionally, all entities that are tracked and processed by the locator service are in 3D.

As the locator service maintains position and distance between all entities, proxemic functions are readily available for researchers and developers to build upon. These functions include querying and filtering entities based on distance or within a certain distance range, and whether an entity is in the field of view of another entity, similar to [23]. We also allow researchers and developers to dynamically change proxemic properties of entities (e.g. location and orientation) through our visualization tool that we discuss in the next section.

The locator service uses an event-driven design, where clients subscribe to events that occur in the locator service, such as the proxemics previously discussed. For example, a wall display client can subscribe to an event that allows it to be aware of when a user approaches a certain range (similar to [23]) or when other entities are pointing in its direction. Lastly, the locator service also maintains information about data points, an entity unique to the *SoD-Toolkit.* The data point allows data to be assigned to specific physical locations in the room (through code or the visualization tool) and also supports proxemic properties already available to other entities. For example, a user can create virtual information spaces with different types of data in regions of a room or

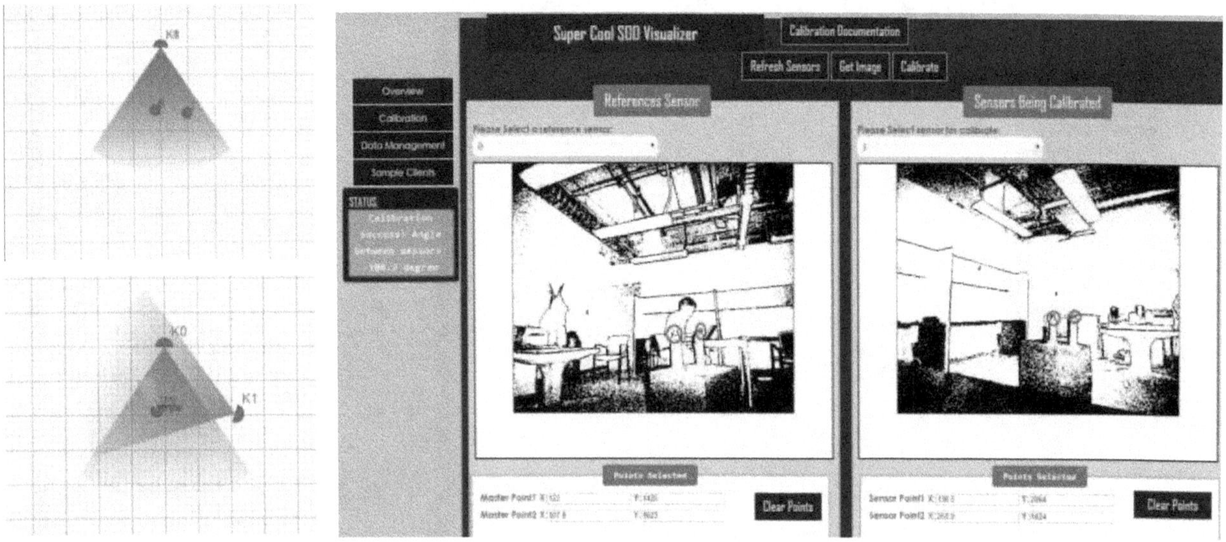

Figure 4. Sensor Fusion using multiple Kinect sensors. (a) 2 uncalibrated Kinect sensors (overlapping) showing skeletons tracked in the environment. (b) Interface for calibration. (c) Properly calibrated environment with overlapping Kinect areas.

assign data to physical objects (e.g. a table) that can be interacted with via gestures or a device-based interactions.

Central Server and Networking

The central server is built into the locator service, and follows a client-server architecture. The server is implemented using the highly scalable and efficient Node.js platform and the underlying communication between the server and client libraries (on all platforms) use the Socket.IO networking module. These components are based upon the WebSocket protocol, which uses duplex bidirectional communication with significantly less overhead than other traditional methods based on HTTP. All information and data exchanged between the server and clients uses the standard JSON format.

Through the modular design of the networking and client library components, the *SoD-Toolkit* allows researchers and developers to easily extend support for future devices and sensors with minimal development effort. As we discuss in the upcoming case studies section, this was a direct result of collaboration with industry partners building real-world deployable ubiquitous environments.

Visualization Tool

The visualization tool for the *SoD-Toolkit* (Figure 4) has three primary functions, (1) to allow researchers and developers to monitor and understand entities – sensors, users, data points and devices – that are being tracked in the environment, as well as provide the state of fused sensors, (2) to allow for quickly prototyping ubiquitous environments without the need for hardware, people or room space and (3) maintain calibration data for multiple sensors (discussed in the next section).

In the visualizer tool, an overview list is provided, detailing the connected clients in the system, a list of available sensors in the environment, people and details on their location information, pairing state and if they currently hold any data, a list of devices and according details, and finally the location of data points and what data is contained in the data point. All entities that are visible in the tool, are user moveable components and easily configurable, allowing researchers and developers to physically remap sensors in the environment and dynamically change the layout of the environment with no additional code-required.

The tool also allows for quickly prototyping environments by allowing sample sensor and device clients to be created and connected into the system. This allows researchers and developers to conceptually build applications, environments and multi-device interactions independent of hardware and sensors and physical space. However, should they later decide to add in real-world sensors and hardware into their virtual environment, their built application or environment will already support the hardware. Furthermore, researchers and developers can also prototype mixed fidelity ubiquitous environments, allowing for a mixture of real and virtual sensors and devices (e.g. a virtual leap motion and a real-world Kinect sensor, with a fixed virtual wall display). Overall, the visualization tool is meant to be used throughout the development process – from development to deployment.

Sensor-Fusion Approach

As discussed earlier, one of our research goals was the novel exploration of ubiquitous environments with an expanded tracking space and multiple newer sensors. This goal requires sensor fusion techniques that are seamless in nature, as well as modular. The *SoD-Toolkit*, primarily relies on the Kinect (version 1 or 2) as the means for providing room-based tracking, as opposed to more expensive and harder to setup motion-tracking systems [25]. Given the limitations of a single Kinect tracking system, we use a method of image comparison between multiple Kinect sensors to expand tracking area and improve accuracy.

Generally, the sensor fusion method for multiple Kinect sensors in *SoD-Toolkit* works as follows: (1) A common object (e.g. a water bottle) is placed in the common viewing and tracking area of two Kinects, (2) Two points from each sensor's view are selected (based on the common object) in the Calibration interface in the Visualization tool and (3) One Kinect sensor's vector (the user selected reference sensor) is translated to another Kinect sensor's vector through a custom algorithm and saved. Figure 4 illustrates this specific process from the perspective of the Visualizer tool. The translation of the Kinect data is also reflected in the skeletal tracking, as the Location service compares skeleton data with the list of people being tracked in the environment. The location service then ensures that a person being tracked by multiple Kinect sensors is presented only once by comparing its position with the relative position of tracked users. This process is for two sensors at a time, and for larger spaces with multiple Kinect sensors, the process is repeated for each additional Kinect sensor and the reference sensor.

Information from Kinect sensors and individual device orientations is also fused by the Location service to provide position and orientation of a device. This type of fusion, which we call a paired state – where a device and user are paired – then allows for multi-device interactions such as "flicking" and "pouring" [32] that require more accurate spatial-awareness. We also allow for sensor data from other sensors such as the iBeacon and Leap motion to augment existing information that can be inconsistently provided by Kinect sensors in certain situations (e.g. a user is too far away from the sensor for fine grained finger tracking or is out of consistent tracking range to determine distance). In code, a researcher or developer can simply choose which sensor to use, either based on confidence levels or preference.

REAL-WORLD CASE STUDIES

To demonstrate the functionality and test the feasibility and applicability of the toolkit for real-world deployments of spatially-aware ubiquitous environments, we present two real-world industry case studies. The implementations we discuss were built in parallel with the toolkit itself, and shaped many of the decisions that led to the features and design of the toolkit. Both of the systems described in this section were built with different teams of developers and industry partners with whom we collaborated closely with. For each case study, we briefly describe the system and reflect on lessons learned from the domain that influenced the design of the toolkit.

Oil and Gas Exploration

The very first ubiquitous environment built in parallel with the *SoD-Toolkit* was [34]. We worked closely with SkyHunter Exploration Ltd. who are located in Canada, and specialize in oil and gas exploration, and have proprietary technology that collects a variety of geo-spatial data. The data they collect is multidisciplinary, and ultimately increases the chances of discovering oil and gas significantly. Prior to building the ubiquitous environment, much of their collaboration with the stakeholders in the exploration and decision-making processes (i.e. geophysicists, geologists) was paper-based and ineffective due to large volumes of geo-spatial data, as well as the reliance on single user non-collaborative tools. Upon building the environment with spatial-awareness and various multi-device interactions, we received positive feedback in areas such as collaboration and interaction with geospatial data [34].

Emergency Response

Following the first industry case study for the toolkit and the adjustments made based on developer and industry feedback, we then continued to the emergency response domain. We collaborated with C4i Consultants, also located in Canada, who specialize in training software for military operations and emergency response. They provide a software tool ePlan, which is designed to simulate large scale emergencies, and train civic operators on how to respond with different types and scales of emergencies. Given the collaborative nature of emergency response planning environments and the number of individuals and devices that can be involved in the decision-making process, this was an ideal candidate for building a ubiquitous environment. We built a ubiquitous emergency response environment that built upon ePlan to drive simulations [4]. It allowed for larger groups of different stakeholders (e.g. fire, police, hazmat) to collaborate and communicate within a spatially-aware environment that contained a large wall display, tablets and a digital tabletop. Spatial interactions such as "flick" and "pour" allowed transfer of vital emergency information amongst the different stakeholders and their devices.

Lessons Learned

As we began to develop the toolkit in collaboration with our first industry partner, we relied exclusively on the Microsoft Kinect sensors for spatial-awareness and tracking in the environment. However, when developers deployed the system built with the toolkit and received feedback from system users about the general uncomfortableness of multiple highly visible tracking sensors in an environment (particularly in an office or meeting context), this facilitated our change in the toolkit from *single sensor rigidity* to *multi-sensor flexibility*. We also provided a set of common gestures from multi-device interactions (flick, pour, bump from [32]) for the developers to use for information transfer tasks, but our feedback from them indicated *the need for accessing raw information* to customize/ explore more detailed interactions, particularly as the skill on the development team was varied.

After the subsequent changes made in the toolkit based on feedback from developers in the first industry project, we then worked closely with a second industry partner in a different domain, emergency response. A primary challenge for developers of ubiquitous environments in this domain, is information is distributed across the room, usually in highly concentrated regions around specific personnel. At the time, the toolkit wasn't optimized enough to handle regions of coarse and fine grained tracking. This lead to the change of allowing for *sensor transition*, depending on the sensors available in the environment. The developers and industry partner also expressed interest in applying of *proxemic interactions to region specific data*, which led to the development of data points in the toolkit. Lastly, the developers and industry collaborators faced challenges in developing their ubiquitous environment due to limited access to highly confidential and private emergency response environments. To help facilitate developers, we found it important to enable them to *develop unencumbered by room access, devices or sensors*. This created features in the toolkit for easy prototyping, allowing developers to mock ubiquitous environments and multi-device interactions.

DISCUSSION

Implementing and designing larger ubiquitous environments, applications and multi-device interaction techniques is an extremely complicated task. We introduced the *SoD-Toolkit* that provides researchers and developers with a number of tools that support the design, prototyping and implementation of deployable multi-device, multi-sensor ubiquitous environments, applications and interactions. We allow researchers and developers to choose their own sensors and devices to build ubiquitous configurations (regardless of owning hardware) and use the tools provided to explore their ubiquitous designs. In this section, we compare *SoD-Toolkit* to other approaches using Olsen's thematic framework approach [6], similar to [13].

Problem not previously solved

A number of toolkits such as XDStudio [27], Conductor [9] and Panelrama [43] reduced the barrier of entry for researchers and developers in creating and exploring ubiquitous environments, applications and interactions. *SoD-Toolkit* builds upon many of the concepts in these toolkits, and further extends the work with greater support for a diverse set of devices and sensor platforms, multi-sensor mappings, and the ability to explore novel multi-device interaction combinations. We also focused on providing a toolkit that is easily configurable and deployable in real-world contexts, a common criticism of toolkits for ubiquitous environments [28, 29]. The toolkit also draws upon previous work in proxemic interactions and applications (such as Proximity Toolkit [23] and Grouptogether [24]), generalizing ubiquitous approaches, and spatial awareness, allowing for the exploration and development of different facets of research in ubiquitous environments, such as multi-device interaction techniques and sensor fusion approaches.

Another limitation of several existing toolkits lies in the physical reliance on sensor and device hardware for prototyping and developing ubiquitous environments and multi-device interactions. We allow researchers and developers to explore multi-device, multi-sensor ubiquitous environments without the need for all hardware or sensor components, which becomes increasingly important and relevant as the underlying technology moves rapidly both in terms of cost and capability. Reducing this limitation allows for an expansion of research into ubiquitous environments.

Generality

To demonstrate the expressivity of the building block components of the *SoD toolkit* [6], we discussed two industry case-studies that included interaction techniques and scenarios considered state of the art [4, 34]. We also highlighted the versatility and generality with these industry case studies, but through them recognized the limitations and strengths of the toolkit. A number of limitations of the toolkit, particularly in its focus for providing larger ubiquitous environments stem from the usage of the Kinect hardware. The Kinect does not provide the same level of extremely accurate tracking by large scale systems (e.g. Vicon) even with multiple Kinect sensors. This is further enhanced when coarser grained sensors (e.g. iBeacons) are used entirely. However, based on our collaborations with industry partners, we believe that for more real-world deployments of ubiquitous environments, this is a necessary trade-off. This provides an advantage, as hardware and sensor limitations are nullified by simply using existing hardware and sensor setups to develop novel and more futuristic multi-sensor, multi-device ubiquitous environments, applications and interactions. Furthermore, the toolkit can easily be extended to support newer sensor and hardware platforms as they emerge.

Reducing Solution Viscosity

Compared to other methods to develop real-world deployable multi-sensor, multi-device ubiquitous environments, applications and interactions, the *SoD-Toolkit* dramatically lowers the development viscosity [34] by providing a flexible architecture that allows for "expressive leverage" [13]. The design of the architecture also allows for the potential to transform several existing multi-device toolkits (e.g. XDStudio [27]) into multi-sensor and spatially-aware toolkits. Furthermore, as the toolkit abstracted and simplified many challenges in creating complex ubiquitous environments (as discussed previously), novice researchers and developers can focus on creating novel systems and interactions with minimal overhead, while those with more experience can freely modify different aspects of the toolkit, such as sensor-fusion approaches and sensor support.

Empowering new design participants

The lack of real-world deployable examples of larger multi-device ubiquitous environments (prototypes or otherwise) despite widely available sensors and devices, indicates a need for adequate toolkit support for researchers and developers. In the research literature, a number of elicitation studies have been performed to study interactions in ubiquitous environments, but very little follow-up work is typically performed, particularly from an implementation perspective. Additionally, multi-device explorations with newer forms of devices in ubiquitous environments (e.g. wearables) is still very minimal in the research literature, particularly in multi-sensor spatially-aware ubiquitous environments [13]. *SoD-Toolkit* focuses on lowering the threshold for non-expert programmers, researchers and interaction designers and empower them to explore with new and existing sensor and device technologies for real-world deployments and contexts. To date, we have not performed an in-depth study with developers for the toolkit, but we have worked closely with developers and industry from the onset of implementation and design of the toolkit. This remains as future work, but we believe the toolkit is an important step in exploring novel larger scale ubiquitous environments with multiple sensors and multiple devices, as well as necessary for exploring novel multi-sensor, multi-device interactions.

Power in combination

Similar to prior toolkits, *SoD-Toolkit* combines hardware and sensor management, sensor fusion techniques, networking, disributed interfaces and prototyping into a single toolkit. As mentioned earlier, the architecture design allows for these components to be extremely decoupled, allowing for the addition or subtraction of different approaches. Additionally, as the *SoD-Toolkit* supports multiple platforms, it already integrates with several major UI frameworks (e.g. Objective C and Xcode), meaning developers can both prototype and build upon commercially available hardware.

Can it scale up?

In building multi-sensor, multi-device spatially-aware ubiquitous environments, particularly ones designed for deployment, the scalability of the sensors that provide spatial awareness for multi-device interactions becomes an issue. For toolkits such as Panelrama [43] and Conductr [9], the solutions are scalable as they do not rely on sensors and use scalable web-based technologies (e.g. HTML5). Alternatively, toolkits such as Proximity Toolkit [23] and XDKinect [28], are either scalable but face challenges for real-world deployment due to complex setups or are limited in functionality due to limited sensor support. Undoubtedly, balancing spatial awareness and scalable solutions is difficult, especially when not using motion-tracking systems that aren't feasible for deployment [28, 29]. The design of *SoD-Toolkit* supports multiple low-cost off the shelf sensors that can be used in concert, for a larger spatially-aware ubiquitous environment. Additionally, as *SoD-Toolkit* allows researchers to choose their sensors and devices, researchers and developers can choose their granularity of spatial-awareness in a ubiquitous environment.

CONCLUSION

The *SoD-Toolkit* offers a rich set of tools and software libraries for researchers and developers to prototype and develop deployable multi-device, multi-sensor interactions, applications and environments. We allow researchers and developers to easily "plug-and-play" popular off-the-shelf hardware (sensors and devices) to build their ubiquitous environments, while removing network and device management, sensor fusion and complex algorithmic challenges. The toolkit abstracts these challenges into an easily accessible API and events, integrating with several existing UI development software tools. As a result, the toolkit reduces complexity and lowers the barrier of entry for researchers and developers to design larger and more intricate multi-device ubiquitous environments. The toolkit also allows for future explorations of novel multi-device interaction techniques, multi-sensor designs and other unique ubiquitous environments that can be deployed in new and unexplored contexts and domains. Future work for the *SoD-Toolkit* includes integrating powerful device-centric sensors like the Google Tango, and gesture detection for different types of interactions in ubiquitous environments.

ACKNOWLEDGEMENTS

We would like to thank our many colleagues from the Agile Surface Engineering (ASE) Lab and our industry partners for their useful discussions and advice as we developed the toolkit. We also thank the anonymous reviewers for their careful and valuable comments and suggestions. This research was supported in by the NSERC SurfNet Research Network, NSERC and Alberta Innovates Technology Futures (AITF).

REFERENCES

1. Ballendat, T., Marquardt, N. and Greenberg, S. Proxemic interaction: designing for a proximity and orientation-aware environment. In *Proc of ITS 2010*, 121-130.
2. Brumitt, B., Meyers, B., Krumm, J., Kern, A. and Shafer, S. A. EasyLiving: Technologies for Intelligent Environments. In *Proc of UbiComp 2000*, 12-29.
3. Chen, X. A., Grossman, T., Wigdor, D. J. and Fitzmaurice, G. Duet: exploring joint interactions on a smart phone and a smart watch. In *Proc of CHI 2014*, 159-168.
4. Chi, P. and Li, Y. Weave: Scripting Cross-Device Wearable Interaction. In *Proc of CHI 2015*, 3923-3932.
5. Chokshi, A., Seyed, T., Rodrigues, F. M. and Maurer, F. ePlan Multi-Surface: A Multi-Surface Environment for Emergency Response Planning Exercises. In *Proc of ITS 2014*, 219-228.
6. Dan R. Olsen, J. Evaluating user interface systems research. In *Proc of UIST 2007*, 251-258.
7. Edward, T. *Hall, The Hidden Dimension*. Garden City, NY: Doubleday, City, 1966.
8. Greenberg, S., Marquardt, N., Ballendat, T., Diaz-Marino, R. and Wang, M. Proxemic interactions: the new ubicomp? *interactions*, *18*, 1 (2011), 42-50.
9. Hamilton, P. and Wigdor, D. J. Conductor: enabling and understanding cross-device interaction. In *Proc of CHI 2014*, 2773-2782.
10. Hartmann, B., Beaudouin-Lafon, M., and Mackay, W. HydraScope: creating multi-surface meta-applications through view synchronization and input multiplexing. In *Proc of PerDis 2013*, 23-28.
11. Hinckley, K. Synchronous gestures for multiple persons and computers. In *Proc of UIST 2003*, 149-158.

12. Hinckley, K., Ramos, G., Guimbretiere, F., Baudisch, P. and Smith, M. Stitching: pen gestures that span multiple displays. In *Proc of AVI 2004*, 23-31.

13. Houben, S. and Marquardt, N. WatchConnect: A Toolkit for Prototyping Smartwatch-Centric Cross-Device Applications. In *Proc of CHI 2015*, 1247-1256.

14. Huang, D.-Y., Lin, C.-P., Hung, Y.-P., Chang, T.-W., Yu, N.-H., Tsai, M.-L. and Chen, M. Y. MagMobile: enhancing social interactions with rapid view-stitching games of mobile devices. In *Proc of MAM 2012*, 1-4.

15. Jakobsen, M., Haile, Y., Knudsen, S. and Hornbæk, K. Information Visualization and Proxemics: Design Opportunities and Empirical Findings. *IEEE Transactions on Visualization and Computer Graphics, 19, 12* (2013), 2386-2395.

16. König, A., Rädle, R. and Reiterer, H. Squidy: a zoomable design environment for natural user interfaces. In *Proc of CHI'EA 2009*, 4561-4566.

17. Kortuem, G., Kray, C. and Gellersen, H. Sensing and visualizing spatial relations of mobile devices. In *Proc UIST 2005*, 93-102.

18. Kray, C., Rohs, M., Hook, J. and Kratz, S. Group coordination and negotiation through spatial proximity regions around mobile devices on augmented tabletops. In *Proc. Horizontal Interactive Human Computer Systems, 2008. TABLETOP 2008. 3rd IEEE International Workshop on*, IEEE (2008), 1-8.

19. Laibowitz, M. and Paradiso, J.A. The UbER-Badge, a versatile platform at the juncture between wearable and social computing. In: *Fersha A, Hortner H, Kostis G (eds) Advances in Pervasive Computing*. Oesterreichische Computer Gesellschaft, Wien, pp 363-368.

20. Lucero, A., Holopainen, J. and Jokela, T. Pass-them-around: collaborative use of mobile phones for photo sharing. In *Proc of CHI 2011*, 1787-1796.

21. Lucero, A., Keränen, J. and Korhonen, H. Collaborative use of mobile phones for brainstorming. In *Proc of MobileHCI 2010*, 337-340.

22. Marquardt, N., Ballendat, T., Boring, S., Greenberg, S. and Hinckley, K. Gradual engagement: facilitating information exchange between digital devices as a function of proximity. In *Proc of ITS 2012*, 31-40.

23. Marquardt, N., Diaz-Marino, R., Boring, S. and Greenberg, S. The proximity toolkit: prototyping proxemic interactions in ubiquitous computing ecologies. In *Proc of UIST 2011*, 315-326.

24. Marquardt, N. and Greenberg, S. Informing the Design of Proxemic Interactions. *IEEE Pervasive Computing*, *11*, 2 (2012), 14-23.

25. Marquardt, N., Hinckley, K. and Greenberg, S. Cross-device interaction via micro-mobility and f-formations. In *Proc. of UIST 2012*, 13-22.

26. Mayer, S. and Sörös, G. User Interface Beaming -- Seamless Interaction with Smart Things Using Personal Wearable Computers. In *Proc. Proceedings of the 2014 11th International Conference on Wearable and Implantable Body Sensor Networks Workshops*, IEEE Computer Society (2014), 46-49.

27. Nebeling, M., Mintsi, T., Husmann, M. and Norrie, M. Interactive development of cross-device user interfaces. In *Proc of CHI 2014*, 2793-2802.

28. Nebeling, M., Teunissen, E., Husmann, M. and Norrie, M. C. XDKinect: development framework for cross-device interaction using kinect. In *Proc of EICS 2014*, 65-74.

29. Rädle, R., Jetter, H.-C., Marquardt, N., Reiterer, H. and Rogers, Y. HuddleLamp: Spatially-Aware Mobile Displays for Ad-hoc Around-the-Table Collaboration. In *Proc Proceedings of ITS 2014*, 45-54.

30. Rekimoto, J. Pick-and-drop: a direct manipulation technique for multiple computer environments. In *Proc of UIST* 1997, 31-39.

31. Schmidt, D., Seifert, J., Rukzio, E. and Gellersen, H. A cross-device interaction style for mobiles and surfaces. In *Proc of DIS 2012*, 318-327.

32. Seyed, T., Burns, C., Sousa, M. C., Maurer, F. and Tang, A. Eliciting usable gestures for multi-display environments. In *Proc of ITS 2012*, 41-50.

33. Schreiner, M., Rädle, R., Hans-Christian, J. and Reiterer, H. A Framework for Cross-Device Web Applications. In *Proc of CHI'EA 2015*, 2163-2168.

34. Seyed, T., Sousa, M. C., Maurer, F. and Tang, A. SkyHunter: a multi-surface environment for supporting oil and gas exploration. In *Proc of ITS 2013*, 15-22.

35. Snibbe, S. S. and Raffle, H. S. Social immersive media: pursuing best practices for multi-user interactive camera/projector exhibits. In *Proc of CHI 2009*, 1447-1456.

36. Streitz, N., Prante, T., M, C., ller-Tomfelde, A., Tandler, P. and Magerkurth, C. Roomware: the second generation. In *Proc of CHI EA 2002,* 506-507.

37. Streitz, N. A., Holmer, T., Konomi, S. i., M, C., ller-Tomfelde, Reischl, W., Rexroth, P., Seitz, P. and Steinmetz, R. i-LAND: an interactive landscape for creativity and innovation. In *Proc of CHI 1999*, 120-127.

38. Vogel, D. and Balakrishnan, R. Interactive public ambient displays: transitioning from implicit to explicit, public to personal, interaction with multiple users. In *Proc of UIST 2004*, 137-146.

39. Wagner, J., Nancel, M., Gustafson, G., Huot, S. and Mackay, W. Body-centric design space for multi-surface interaction. In *Proc of CHI 2013*, 1299-1308.

40. Want, R., Hopper, A., Falc, V., #227 and Gibbons, J. The active badge location system. *ACM Trans. Inf. Syst.*, *10*, 1 (1992), 91-102.

41. Weiser, M. The computer for the 21st century. *SIGMOBILE Mob. Comput. Commun. Rev.*, *3*, 3 (1999), 3-11.

42. Wilson, A. D. and Benko, H. Combining multiple depth cameras and projectors for interactions on, above and between surfaces. In *Proc of UIST 2010*, 273-282.

43. Yang, J. and Wigdor, D. Panelrama: enabling easy specification of cross-device web applications. In *Proc of CHI 2014*, 2783-2792.

44. Zadow, U., Büschel, W., Langner, R. and Dachselt, R. SleeD: Using a Sleeve Display to Interact with Touch-sensitive Display Walls. In *Proc of ITS 2014*, 129-138.

Coordinating Collaborative Interactions in Web-based Mobile Applications

Kennedy Kambona, Lode Hoste, Elisa Gonzalez Boix & Wolfgang De Meuter
Software Languages Lab
Vrije Universiteit Brussel
Brussels, Belgium
{kkambona, lhoste, egonzale, wdmeuter} @vub.ac.be

ABSTRACT

Mobile applications for interactive surfaces that utilize the web as a platform now have the ability to provide richer interactions hitherto unrealized by running them on isolated devices. These modern applications can now support proximal and remote collaborative interactions for multiple clients simultaneously connected to each other. Most technologies however currently lack programming language abstractions for coordinating complex interactions, such as to define, detect and combine complex events coming from multiple clients or other software entities. Furthermore, they lack the expressiveness required to support non-trivial levels of collaborative interactions for connected clients.

In this paper we identify two software mechanisms that web-based mobile applications should provide to support the development of collaborative interactions: distributed event composition and group coordination. We present the Mingo framework, which provides dedicated coordination programmer constructs for these two mechanisms by blending techniques common in complex event processing and group communication. Consequently, we validate our framework by implementing a mobile drawing application with support for collaborative interactions and evaluate it by comparing it with a related implementation.

Author Keywords

Collaborative mobile applications; coordination; complex event processing; interactive applications

ACM Classification Keywords

H.5.3 [Group and Organization Interfaces]: Collaborative Computing, Computer-supported cooperative work, Web-based interaction

INTRODUCTION

Traditional software applications have recently started experiencing a fundamental shift due to cheaper broadband internet connections. Many applications are increasingly residing on the web and their services provided to clients (e.g. mobile phones) using a multitenant cloud-based architecture. These applications can now run in vastly improved resources compared to those available a decade ago, and have the ability to provide richer functional interactions.

In this paper we investigate how to provide software support for collaborative surface interactions using such contemporary infrastructures. Coordination of interactions is vital in applications running on the because it is involves managing multiple users, tasks and devices. This is becoming increasingly important as evidenced by the popularity of ubiquitous devices with internet access. Recent advancements in standardized web-based technologies such as HTML5 have increased the support required for coordinating various types of collaborative applications, such as document editing software, instant messaging and online multiplayer games.

The common technique employed by existing applications, however, is to impose restrictions on software entities in order to deal with the complexities of simultaneous collaborative interactions of participants within the same session. An example of such restrictions is to enforce exclusive access, where interactions on an object is allowed for only one participant at any one time. In a collaborative drawing application, for instance, this means that a participant is said to exclusively 'own' shape (e.g. by selecting and editing it), and it can only be modified by that user until the ownership is relinquished (e.g. by deselecting it). Another type of limitation is sequential access, where interactions on an object by several participants are performed in succession – in the order that they were detected. Rather than imposing such software restrictions, we envision a programming model where events coming from a group of different participants in interactive devices can be composed and integrated. This will result in a mechanism in which advanced collaborative interactions can be orchestrated, a significant advantage in mixed interactive surface applications.

We propose the Mingo framework, which provides programming abstractions for coordinating collaborative interactions in mobile applications running over the web. Mingo combines techniques from complex event processing and group coordination to assist developers implement applications supporting collaborative interactions such as collaborative drag-

ITS 2015, November 15–18, 2015, Funchal/Madeira, Portugal.

ACM 978-1-4503-3899-8/15/11... $15.00.
DOI: http://dx.doi.org/10.1145/2817721.2817742

ging on a surface. Mingo has been implemented as an extension to JavaScript, the dominant language on the web. Interactions are modelled in the asynchronous message-passing style which aligns with JavaScript's event-driven programming model. Mingo constructs thus allow developers to specify collaborative interactions involving several participants in a declarative and reusable way. Mingo is targeted for devices that are co-located or in low-latency environments to provide immediate feedback for the interactions.

We present our model in the subsequent sections. We first motivate the need for coordinating mobile applications on the web and present some related concepts. We then present our coordination model, the Mingo framework and its coordination constructs. Using Mingo, we proceed to implement a collaborative drawing editor and compare it with a similar implementation using the current state-of-the-art. We conclude by discussing possible future improvements to the framework.

THE NEED FOR COORDINATING COMPLEX COLLABORATIVE INTERACTIONS

A number of research has identified the need for collaborative interactions – user actions spanning a distributed system that occur together – such as synchronous gestures [9] and co-browsing [2]. This allows users in proximity to combine multiple devices heterogeneously to exploit pooling input capabilities, content and resources such as displays.

In this paper, we motivate the need for providing programming support for such advanced coordination mechanisms for complex interactions. We introduce a running example of a sample application requiring these mechanisms: an illustrative collaborative drawing editor.

Motivating Example: Online Collaborative Drawing Editor

Consider a traditional collaborative drawing application similar to Cacoo[1] where several distributed participants on mobile phones are connected via the web using a server. The participants share the same canvas on multiple mobile devices. The users are participating in the same session and can therefore interact at the same time. The shared canvas can be used by the several participants connected via the web to draw and interact with (or manipulate) shapes already drawn on the canvas.

In addition to the normal functionality provided by a traditional drawing application (as described thus far), we envision that the collaborative web-based drawing application further allows users on mobile devices to perform advanced collaborative interactions to users[2]. We illustrate two examples of these collaborative interactions that can be applied:

(a) **Collaborative resize interaction.** Consider when one participant on a mobile device starts to drag a drawn shape to the right, while at the same time a different participant in the same session drags the same shape to the left (Figure 1a). Typically an application recognizes two separate

[1]Cacoo - Create diagrams online, `https://www.cacoo.com`

[2]The users should already be aware of this e.g. from a description of the application features

Figure 1. Collaborative interactions for a drawing application: (a) collaborative resize (b) collaborative bind

sequential interactions (e.g. drag-right and drag-left respectively), and proceeds to enforce techniques to determine ownership and which action to apply. In contrast, our sample application recognizes this as a single collaborative resize interaction. As a result, the application then reacts by causing the shape to resize according to the input of the participants.

(b) **Collaborative bind interaction.** Consider when one participant drags onto an empty canvas to the right, while another one drags on the canvas to the left. When both participants reach the canvas borders as shown in Figure 1(b)[3], an application could then virtually bind the canvases in the two devices to give the impression of an extended shared canvas. Participants can then for instance share objects by 'throwing' them to other devices using a sliding gesture.

Similar features can be applied to other applications in need of collaborative interactions: for instance in a virtual dancing game, where two or more users are required to press a sequence of button combinations or other actions at the same time to successfully perform a cooperatively-synchronized dance move in a group.

Requirements

We now identify two requirements that support coordination of complex interactions for collaborative web-based mobile applications.

i) Processing and Composition of Events:

Interactions in most mobile web applications are primarily internally represented as events. A basic programming challenge in this setting is that it is arduous to detect and distinguish between simple events that the application receives e.g. a local drag operation, from the composed collaborative events e.g. the collaborative resize from two or more participants in a session. A simple event involves one participant and is usually local. The collaborative events can possibly involve several distinct participants. Our vision is that developers of such collaborative applications need to be able capture to both types of events.

Detecting simple (or *local*) events from different areas of the application and subsequently creating a composed collaborative event is known as *event composition*. Programmers face great difficulties (denoted as accidental complexity in [17]) when specifying and orchestrating such interactions or events. Interactive applications developed using various

[3]The right border for the first participant and the left border for the second.

frameworks should be able to define and detect when such composed events occur.

ii) Group Coordination:
In traditional mobile and desktop applications, software entities (like shapes objects in a drawing editor, or dancing avatars in a dancing game) were designed to be implemented and used autonomously in a local device. In contrast, distributed applications using the web have the potential to run multiple instances of software entities distributed over several mobile clients, while at the same time exposing the more advanced functionality. These replicas or groups of software entities require a group coordination mechanism in order to address them as one unit and to manage their respective objects with the aim of making their operations resilient. For instance, in a collaborative drawing application, a drag event performed on a shape by a participant should be transparently propagated to all the different mobile clients of the same session that have this shape; in a dancing game a dancing avatar's local movements should be updated in all other participants' screens. The coordination abstraction should provide a means to manage the group behaviour of these replicas.

Summary
This paper envisions a programming framework that integrates these two requirements to coordinate collaborative web-based mobile applications. Developers can utilize abstractions that allow several participants in a session to interact simultaneously and collaboratively, utilizing more advanced combined distributed interactions.

RELATED WORK

Coordination Models

Most coordination models and languages for concurrent and distributed systems are based on the *tuple space* model of Linda [6]. A tuple space is a globally shared virtual data structure which allows processes to communicate by posting and reading data objects known as *tuples*. Some tuple space implementations have targeted the web such as WWWinda[7]. This approach employs a separate browser architecture with tuple spaces shared across web applications. Conceptually, a tuple represents local interactions or events. As such, developers using tuples for coordination still need to manually apply additional logic in applications in order to manage complex collaborative interactions from individual tuples.

Multi-device Interaction

Groupware frameworks such as GroupKit [15] and Sync [11] expose extensible high-level architecture or interfaces that applications are required to adhere to in order to receive support for collaboration. Sync embeds generic collaboration capabilities into several base classes that need to be extended by the application. Groupkit requires an application to extend a registration client to create conferences that act as a mediator between the application and the framework. Our vision is to have no such restrictions on applications or objects in need of coordination support.

PointRight [10] provides mechanisms for redirecting pointer input across screens in an interactive workspace. For coordination, it uses a custom blackboard architecture derived from tuple spaces which only allows a user to control a single display at a time. ARIS [3] is an interactive window space manager that uses Gaia middleware. Gaia supports management of distributed devices and services through an information repository for entities. It however provides little or no support for managing filtering and historical data context processing, which is useful for coordinating more complex interactions. Work in [9] allows support for multi-person or multi-display interaction. The driving technique behind this approach is a predetermined algorithm that uses various inputs to recognize synchronous spikes in data. However, the approach is rigid and does not support dynamic addition of gesture definitions at runtime.

Web-based Collaboration

The web was primarily intended for single-person use in its conception: the original architecture did not support real-time synchronous interaction. Nowadays, however, support of real-time interaction is increasingly popular with the advent of web technologies supporting real-time collaboration. Etherpad[4] and GoogleDocs[5] allow users to collaborate on text documents simultaneously. Schmid et al. [16] coordinate simultaneous collaborative web browsing by using specialized proxy servers that intercept web page requests and inject JavaScript code into the pages, providing functionality for simultaneous access into web pages. However, their simplified approach of interaction of multiple pointers on the screen is limited to single-pointer interaction per object. Furthermore the use of a proxy increases the *a priori* knowledge and configuration needed.

Complex Event Processing

Complex event processing (CEP) is a technique that provides support for detecting, analysing and composing multiple simple interactions or events into more meaningful or higher-level (complex) events. *Computation-oriented* CEP engines focus on aggregating data from a number of incoming events (e.g. Borealis [1]), while *Detection-oriented* CEP engines focus on finding patterns within multiple event instances rather than the aggregation of these instances (e.g. Drools [13] and Midas [17]). Computation-oriented engines are unable to detect and compose events through specific, fine-grained coordination interaction patterns, making detection-oriented engines is better suited for composing collaborative interactions. One of the most representative of detection-oriented CEP engines is Drools [13]. However, Drools lacks constructs for spatial and temporal operators that can enable us to easily express interaction patterns, significant when performing composition of interactions. Nools[6] is a rule engine for the web written in JavaScript. Both implementations are based on the Rete algorithm [5], which employs an efficient implementation for pattern-matching complex events.

MINGO

We now present our framework for coordination of complex interactions in collaborative mobile applications running on

[4] `http://etherpad.org`
[5] `http://google.com/docs/about`
[6] `http://github.com/C2FO/nools`

the web. Mingo is an object-oriented framework employing web-based infrastructure to coordinate collaborative interactions found in interactive surfaces. JavaScript has emerged as the de-facto language for web development due to the native support of all modern web environments. The framework therefore extends the language with blended constructs for group coordination and complex event processing.

In particular, Mingo employs the CEP Midas engine [17] at the heart of its execution model. Midas is a detection-oriented rule-based CEP framework for the recognition of complex interactions that allows developers to easily express advanced interaction patterns. Consequently, Midas provides ample support for modelling multi-user interactions as events. A benefit of using the Midas engine is therefore that there is no difference in reasoning over simple events (represented as facts) vis-a-vis composite or complex events. This provides significant support for advanced software engineering abstractions [17]. The engine however lacks native support for distribution on the web. We therefore extended the engine to support this, required for such collaborative interactions. The Mingo framework is mainly targeted for co-located devices and similar low-latency environments for the prompt feedback of the possible activated rules and interactions.

In addition, the abstractions supporting coordination of collaborative interactions in Mingo are designed along the principles of *separation of concerns* [12]. The main benefit that this separation provides is that it enables developers to concentrate on an application's functionality separate from the coordination mechanisms that it may require. Papadopoulos et al. [12] already identified this as a significant design principle that helps in alleviating issues related to compositionality and extensibility in the development of distributed applications.

Mingo Execution Model

The execution model of Mingo utilizes a number of technologies to achieve its coordination functionality, as illustrated in Figure 2. The server manages the coordination mechanism of the framework. It consists of the Mingo server later and the Midas CEP engine, with the Mingo bridge acting as an interface between them. The bridge translates Mingo constructs received from the clients into rules and facts to be consumed by Midas (and vice-versa).

A number of interactive client devices can be connected to the server. The clients run JavaScript code augmented with Mingo constructs necessary for coordination. When the constructs are applied in the application the Mingo runtime takes care of packaging and sending this information to the server. The Mingo layer on the server side will take care of transforming and injecting the necessary rules in the Midas engine, as represented in the constructs. Whenever a simple event that has been denoted to comprise a complex interaction is performed, Mingo intercepts its invocation and sends the event information to the server. If a complex interaction has been realised, Mingo propagates this new information to all clients in the session.

To clarify Mingo's coordination orchestration, we illustrate how a collaborative interaction is realized.

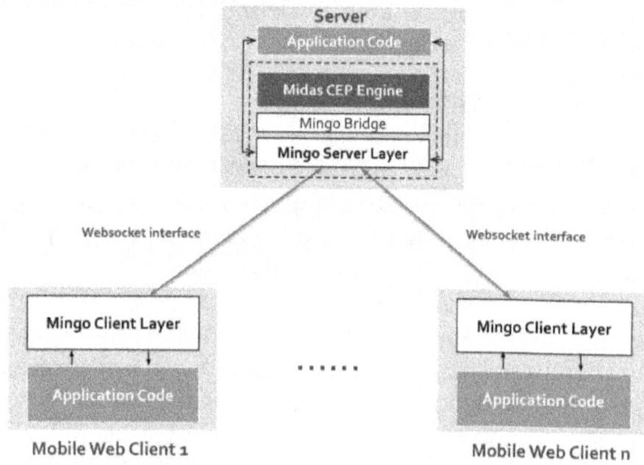

Figure 2. Mingo Execution Model

1. A developer writes the application in JavaScript and employs Mingo Client constructs to coordinate the application's distributed interactions (described in the next section).
2. The Mingo runtime sends the interactions and their relevant information to the server by means of websockets.
3. The Mingo layer on the server assembles the local interactions from client devices with their respective information and sends them to the Midas CEP engine by mapping invocations and their definitions into facts and rules that Midas can consume. Thus in Mingo a fact is an internal representation of a simple interaction in the application.
4. Midas then asserts the interactions. If the interactions trigger a pre-defined rule created from constructs previously defined by the developer, it can combine the simple interactions into one composed event.
5. The composed event is then pushed back to the runtime which in turn delivers it to the awaiting client devices that defined a handler for the composed event.

Programming Support for Coordinating Complex Interactions

In this section we describe the programming language constructs that Mingo avails for complex event composition and group coordination. Although we employ our running example in explaining these abstractions, they can also be applied to other application scenarios requiring these coordination mechanisms.

Group Coordination Abstraction.
Mingo provides the ability to coordinate the behaviour of distributed software entities by means of the `groupObject` construct. When `groupObject` is applied to a new object, Mingo proceeds to assign a group identifier to the object, and transparently assigns the same group identifier to the replicas in every client mobile device (Figure 3). The effect of this is Mingo will subsequently replicate any specified actions performed on that object to each replica of the object in the other client devices through assertions to the CEP engine. Therefore the group object can be visualized as a virtual object that

Figure 3. Two distributed object groups

links all replicated objects to it and will distribute interactions or events to the all objects with the same identifier in the same session. In our running example, we have employed the `groupObject` construct to model the shapes drawn in the shared canvas as shown in Listing 1.

Listing 1. Defining a Group Shape in Mingo

```
1 var shape = new Shape({
2   touchMove: function(e){
3     //update shape position
4   }
5   //...
6 });
7 var groupShape = Mingo.groupObject(shape, {
8   collabResize: Mingo.rule(/*rule definition here*/)
9 });
```

As shown in line 1, a developer defines a shape with basic operations e.g. `touchMove` for a mobile client (equivalent to a `mouseMove` operation on a desktop device). Additionally, in line 7 we define that shape as a Mingo group object using the `groupObject` construct. The construct takes as the first argument the shape, and the second argument an object containing the behaviour which will be part of collaborative interactions in form of a rule (explained in the next section). As shown in Listing 1, when the end user draws a shape, the Mingo creates a `groupShape` object, and the canvases of the rest of the participants in the drawing session will be populated with a replica of this shape.

The `groupShape` object conceptually represents the replicas of a shape which all belong to one group. The developer can then replicate operations through the Mingo `replicateAction` construct available on a `groupObject`. For instance, when the `touchMove` operation (line 2) is performed on any member of `groupShape`, this action will be replicated on all the other shape replicas in the mobile application in the same session.

Listing 2. Replicating Actions on an Object Group

```
1 groupShape.replicateAction('touchMove');
```

Thus Mingo group coordination constructs address a number of distributed object *replicas* as a single unit. Given a set of group objects, when a client changes a copy of the object Mingo transparently propagates updates to all the replicas in the application. An invocation on `touchMove` sends the information to the server and which is then asserted in Midas. The assertion of an replicated action triggers Mingo to systematically send the action to the rest of the users in the same session. Each replicated action is internally represented in Mingo as a rule that triggers upon the assertion related facts.

In the next section we explain how a developer can perform distributed actions such as the collaborative resize operation in line 8 of Listing 1.

Distributed Event Composition.

In web-based interactive applications, simple events are usually detected by registering a handler to a named event. In order to detect collaborative events however, Mingo contains rule composition operators similar to the ones found in rule-based languages. A Mingo rule consists of a name, the left-hand side (LHS) which contains *conditions* for the detection of a complex event, a $\rightarrow$, and a right-hand side (RHS) for *reactions* after the complex event is detected. We introduce the rule for the collaborative resize from our running example in Listing 3. The rule is defined in the application in an object literal using Mingo's `rule` construct which packages the rule. The construct which exposes syntax that developers to write custom complex interactions declaratively.

Listing 3. A Collaborative Resize Rule in Mingo

```
1 rule('collabResizeRule',
2   '(Invoked (function "touchMove") (dev ?d1) (args ?a1) (time ?time1))
3   (Invoked (function "touchMove") (dev ?d2) (args ?a2) (time ?time2))
4   (test (time:within ?time1 ?time2 1000))
5   →
6   (assert (collabResize (args ?a1 ?a2) (dev ?d1 ?d2))')
```

The `rule` construct expects two arguments: the name of the rule (which denotes the name of the collaborative interaction) and the rule definition – a set of LHS statements followed by a set of RHS statements.

The LHS of the definition (lines 2-4) captures the invocation of simple events from the different entities of the mobile application. This rule captures two `touchMove` invocations and their arguments from two different devices (lines 2-3) that occur within a certain amount of time (line 4).

When all the conditions specified in the LHS are satisfied, then the actions defined in the RHS are activated. Here, we store a new fact `collabResize`(line 6), which is the composition of the two invocations and their arguments. With this assertion Mingo triggers a collaborative event and propagates it to the devices as a collaborative action. In the LHS and RHS of a rule, the ? operator denotes a variable binding (e.g. `?dev1` in line 2).

The collaborative application can react to a collaborative action by registering a listener. Recall from the previous section that Mingo creates a group object to replicate actions on a shape (thereby updating its changes) to all participants. On this group object we register a listener to the group object by using the Mingo `on` construct, as in Listing 4. The first argument to the `on` construct is a string denoting the collaborative interaction, and the second is a callback that will be invoked once the interaction is achieved.

Listing 4. Reacting to a Collaborative Resize

```
1 groupShape.on('collabResize', function(args){
2   //perform resizing of shape
3   collaborativeResize(this, args);
4 });
```

The shape and its replicas can now receive coordination support. If there is *only* one client device interacting then a normal, single action (e.g. a move) will be invoked. When Mingo detects two actions (e.g. 2 touch downs) from different devices, it will treat this as a collaborative interaction provided it meets the conditions in the LHS part of the respective rules of the shape. On a shared tabletop, if the device can distinguish inputs from different hands [4] we can create a rule condition take this into account: for instance a test that checks the `handIds` are different.

Managing States in Mingo

Composing complex events such as collaborative interactions is simple when done as single-state events e.g. detecting when two participants both perform a touch down interaction. Most collaborative interactions, however, work in a *multi-state* pattern e.g. recognizing a complete gesture done between touchDown and touchUp interactions. We observed that writing single-state rules for a these kinds of higher-level events leads to an inherent complexity in their rule definitions and additional orchestration logic is needed in the application code. This is especially because when composing events into complex events using rules, some inaccuracies that cause arbitrary behaviour when a series of events are detected might delude the developer.

Mingo solves this problem by providing a structured way to define such *multi-state rules* to detect a series of complex events in addition to single ones. Each collaborative operation in Mingo can be represented as a *state machine* that will compose invocation of multi-state events. A *state* in this case is a phase in the detection of a complete composite event. Each of these phases can be of interest to a developer to react to in an application. Mingo rules provide the necessary support to compose the state machine relating to such a composite event. In order to exemplify the problem, consider again the collaborative resize from Listing 3. Whenever a collaborative drag is performed on a shape, a developer has to first check if a collaborative touch down has been performed by the two of the participants before proceeding to listen for a collaborative resize. To implement the detection of the interaction in stages, we redefine the collaborative resize interaction in terms of the following states:

1. **Resize start** – When the two participants perform a `touchdown` at almost the same time; the collaborative interaction has begun.
2. **Resize body** – After resize start, when one or both participants start (and continue) performing a `touchmove` in opposite directions.
3. **End** – When one or both participants perform a `touchup`, the collaborative interaction comes to an end.

The states can be encoded in Mingo as shown in Listing 5. The `collabResize` composite event now consists of the three aforementioned states (denoted in the code as `start`, `body` and `end` states). `collabResize` is actually an object that simply contains a start, body and an end state defined as Mingo rules. A developer can thus detect any number of multi state operations separately – such as the *start*, *body* and *end* of the collaborative resize operation – and execute code in their respective handlers.

Listing 5. Collaborative Resize in Mingo - With States

```
1 collabResize = {
2    start: rule('collabResizeStart', /* rule definition here */),
3    body: rule('...'), /* rule indicating the body */
4    end: rule('...') /* rule indicating the end */
5 };
6 groupShape.on(collabResize.start, function(args){
7    //handle resize start operation
8 });
```

Note that the developer can react to any of these states of the collaborative resize separately with a handler on each one. For example, lines 7-9 show the reaction to a collaborative resize event for the `collabResize.start` rule on the shape object of our running example.

In the next section we illustrate how a developer defines a multi-state rule.

Defining a Multi-State Collaborative Rule

Mingo provides an extended version of the `rule` construct which allows developers to define a rule that is only triggered when the application detects a concrete state of an extended interaction. Listing 6 shows such a rule for the `start` state of the collaborative resize seen in the previous listing Listing 5.

Listing 6. Structure of a Multi-state Rule

```
1  //SP
2  ?currstate ← (State (name "end") (operation "collabresize"))
3  //IP
4  (Invoked (function "touchDown") (dev ?d1) (args ?a1) (time ?t1))
5  (Invoked (function "touchDown") (dev ?d2) (args ?a2) (time ?t2))
6  (test (time:within ?t1 ?t2 1000))
7  →
8  //SS
9  (retract ?currstate)
10 (assert (State (name "start") (operation "collabresize") (args ?a1 ?a2)))
11 //CB
12 (assert (collabResizeStart (args ?a1 ?a2)))
```

The `collabResizeStart` rule has the LHS and RHS as defined earlier. Every multi-state rule is further defined in a four-part structure, each of which have specific purposes.

On the left-hand side (LHS) of the multistate rule we have:

State predicates (SP) – The conditions about the state of the operation needed to detect the composed event. This is the first part where we can detect any states that are needed prior to the execution of this rule. For instance, in line 2 we avoid multiple activation of a state by making sure that any previous state must currently be in the `end` (or idle) state before transitioning to the `start` state. Mingo provides the '←' symbol binds the `end` state to the `?currstate` variable, which can be used to modify the current state within the rule, as shown in the third part.

Invocation predicates (IP) – Conditions about the invocations required to compose the event. This describes the invocations that need to be detected in order to realize the composed event. In lines 4-5 we detect that two touch down operations are performed as the invocation conditions for the `collabResize` start operation, which we defined in Listing 5.

And on the right hand side (RHS) we have:

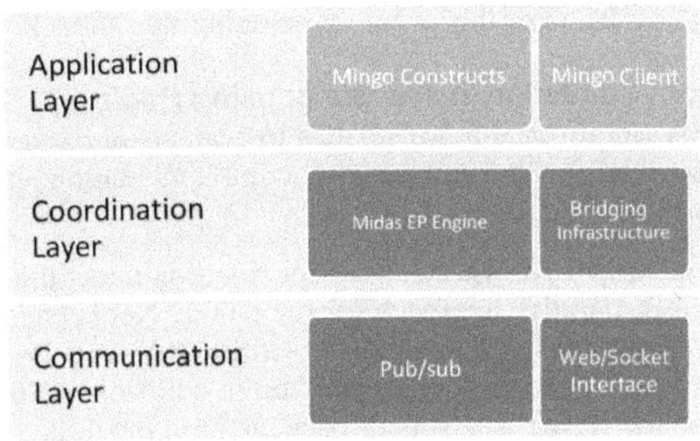

Figure 4. Mingo's layered architecture

State switching (SS) – Change in states of the operations (e.g. `start`, `body` and `end`) based on the current state. Here we provide the logic that will transform the state of the composed complex event represented in this rule from one state to another. This is often done simply by the *retraction* or deletion of the current state (in line 9, using the bound variable `?currstate` from line 2 representing the `end` state); and the addition or *assertion* of a new state (`collabresize` start state in line 10).

Callback (CB) - The callback part consists of one or more *asserts* that produce the collaborative event. Here we can deliver all the arguments that the callback may need for handling the event. In this case, Mingo adds the `collabResizeStart` fact, and triggers the associated callback of this event in the application (line 12). Note that this is different from the change of state, since this assert actually triggers the collaborative interaction to all clients.

It is important to note that the multistate rules allow developers to coordinate collaborative multistate interactions while avoiding the complexity introduced by composing rules with multiple states. Without support for multistate rules, the developer will be forced to manually maintain state logic within the handler whenever a collaborative event is realized.

IMPLEMENTATION

We now have a look at the general Mingo architecture. The structure is realized as a layered architecture, depicted in Figure 4. This is largely due to the target implementation technology that is the web, which imposes a layered architectural style. We briefly discuss each of the layers of the stack in detail in the rest of this section.

Communication Layer

The Communication Layer in Mingo is tasked with handling the transportation of any possible event information from the Application Layer to the Coordination Layer. For the introductory example, this layer would handle the multicasting of all drawing interaction information to the event processing engine, as well as to other participants in the session. Mingo utilizes techniques from the publish/subscribe paradigm in order to broadcast this event information to the rest of the participants and to the Midas engine. This multicasting is propagated using a Node.js server, through the use of HTML5 websockets. When an object is tagged as a `groupObject` in Mingo, the actions that relate to a collaborative interaction on the object will be replicated to the rest of mobile devices in the session.

Coordination Layer

The coordination layer handles the actual internal distributed coordination mechanism of Mingo. It contains the event processing engine Midas, the Node.js server and the bridging infrastructure needed for internal event subscription and detection. The Mingo runtime employs an extension of Midas to provide this kind of bridging interface to register and listen to activations of complex events as well as to replicate actions on object groups, thus utilizing the engine for coordinating collaborative interactions.

To coordinate collaborative events, every action on a `groupObject` that may contribute to a collaborative interaction is sent to the server as an event. Mingo transparently translates all simple interactions or events are into temporal facts in the Midas engine. When a fact is asserted it can trigger a collaborative event if all the conditions of the rule hold. In this case Mingo will then invoke the respective collaborative interaction in all the mobile clients in the session – through the callback provided as the second argument of the `on` construct.

Application Layer

For the previous two layers to be helpful to the developer for creating a collaborative application, there needs to be a suitable way to expose their functionality. The Application Layer in Mingo provides the necessary abstractions for developers of web-based mobile applications that make it simple to introduce collaborative mechanisms to their applications using the `on` and `groupObject` constructs. The Mingo client intercepts calls to operations on objects and sends them to be stored in the CEP engine.

When an object is tagged as a `groupObject`, Mingo assigns a unique identifier to the object and proceeds to create replicas in the other mobile devices connected to the session. Additionally, Mingo detects the rule defined and sends it to the server to be stored in the event processing engine Midas. The engine stores pre-defined rules with the aim of detecting a possible distributed collaborative event in the mobile application through the actions of the participants in the current session. Subsequently, using the `on` construct on such a replicated object will cause the callback assigned to be invoked whenever the engine triggers a collaborative event as defined by its respective rule. The application layer thus exposes these mechanisms to the developer of a collaborative mobile application.

EVALUATION

In this section we demonstrate how Mingo's language support eases the development of complex cloud-based applications

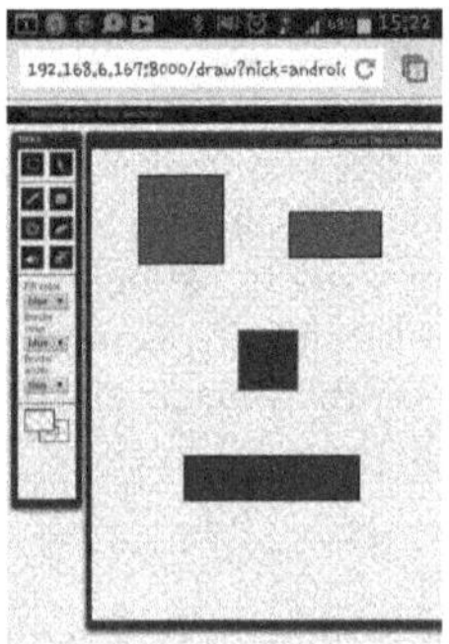

Figure 5. mDraw mobile application

by implementing a collaborative drawing mobile application. We then implement a similar application supported by a rule based approach for the web. We subsequently compare the two approaches and their support for implementing collaborative interactions.

i) Collaborative Drawing Application: mDraw

mDraw is the concrete implementation of the collaborative drawing application introduced in the motivating example. It runs on mobile browsers supporting JavaScript and HTML5. To join a session, clients simply connect to the application using a url. The application code of the web app can be cloned from Github[7].

Having explained the collaborative resize operation used in mDraw, we now explain the implementation of the *collaborative bind* operation from the second motivating example of collaborative interactions and illustrated in Figure 1 (b). This interaction consists of a `start` state when two participants touch the canvas, a `body` state where they continue dragging in opposite directions and `end` state where the canvas borders have been touched by both participants. Since the start and body states are similar to the collaborative resize interaction, we illustrate the implementation of the completed `end` state in Listing 7.

Listing 7. mDraw: Collab Bind Start Rule

```
1  rule('bindEndRule',
2      '?bodystate ← (State (name "body") (operation "bind") )
3      (Invoked (function "touchMove") (args ?x1 ?y1) (time ?t1)))
4      (Invoked (function "touchMove") (args ?x2 ?y2) (time ?t2)))
5      (Canvasbounds (right ?right))
6      (test (and (>= ?x1 ?right) (<= ?x2 0)))
7      (test (and (<= (abs (− ?y1 ?y2)) 10) (time:within ?t1 ?t2 1000)
8      →
9      (retract ?bodystate)
10     (assert (State (name "end") (operation "bind")))
11     (assert (bindEnd (args ?x1 ?y1 ?x2 ?y2)))')
```

To detect when the bind action has been completed we need to first check if a bind was already detected (line 2) and that it is currently in the body state. Next we check if there are two `touchMove` operations (line 3-4) that have reached the opposite sides of the border of the canvases in the two devices (lines 6-7). We change the state to a bind end state (line 9-10), and finally assert that a completed collaborative bind interaction has been realized (line 11). The application can then react to the assertion of this event by invoking its callback.

[7] **http://bit.ly/mingomdraw**

ii) Implementation in JavaScript using Nools

In this section we employ mDraw to evaluate our approach by comparing it with a similar ad-hoc implementation written in JavaScript.

We identified Nools, a JavaScript rule engine as the closest to our declarative approach for the cloud. Nools enables developers to specify complex interactions as logic rules in their applications and trigger events though callbacks. Nools can run in the server as a Node.js package or in the desktop client as a library.

In order to provide functionality for collaborative interactions using Nools, we were forced to provide static rule definitions on the server. In Listing 8 we show the relevant sections when defining collaborative bind interaction programmatically in Nools.

Listing 8. Nools: Reacting to a Collaborative Bind

```
1  var collabBind = flow.rule("bindEnd", [
2      [Invoked, "inv1", "inv1.function == 'touchMove'", {x: "x1", y: "y1", time:
           "t1"}],
3      [Invoked, "inv2", "inv2.function == 'touchMove' && (Math.abs(y1 − y2)
           <= 10) && (Math.abs(t1 − t2) <= 1000)", { x: "x2", y: "y2", time
           : "t2"}],
4      [Canvasbounds, "b", "(b.right <= x1) && (x2 <= b.left)", {right: "?right",
           left: "left"}],
5      [State, "state", "state.name == 'body' && state.operation == 'bind'"]
6      ],
7      function(facts){
8          var inv1 = facts.inv1, inv2 = facts.inv2;
9          var args = [facts.args1, facts.args2];
10         this.assert(new State('end', 'bind', inv2.time));
11         this.assert(new bindEnd(args, inv2.time);
12         clientManager.sendCollabEvent('collabBind', [inv1.dev1, inv2.dev2],
               args);
13     }
14  );
```

Because nools is a rule-based language, the rule structure is similar to that of Mingo rules. Line 1 defines the collaborative bind detection operation using Nools' `flow.rule` construct. The construct takes an array that contains rule definitions as the first argument. In lines 2,3 we detect if the touchMove operation has occurred from the client browsers within a time range of 1000 milliseconds. Line 4 detects if the operations have both touched the canvas borders and line 5 is an additional check to see if the bind operation already begun in its previous body state.

The third argument to `flow.rule` is a callback (line 7), which is invoked whenever the rule fires. The callback is invoked with the facts that triggered the rule as arguments. We use the arguments to assert the new state of the collaborative interaction (line 10-11), similar to the states in the multistate rules. We then call the code that will eventually send to the participants that the collaborative interaction has been detected, sending all the arguments in an array (line 12).

Discussion

We proceed to compare the approaches provided by the Mingo framework and the Nools engine. We begin by a lines of code (LOC) quantitative comparison illustrated in

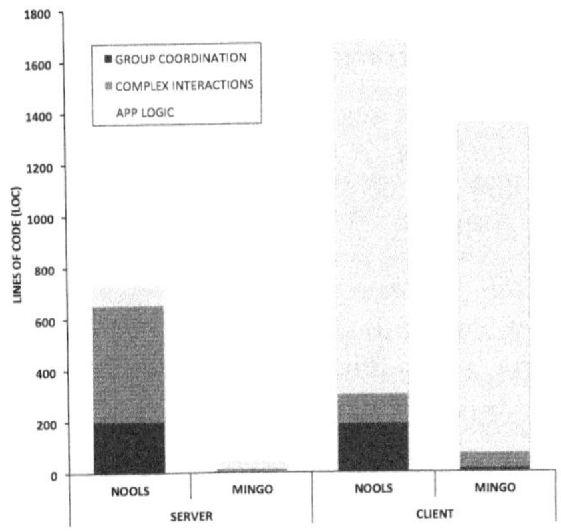

Figure 6. LOC Comparison of Sample Application

Support for	Mingo	Nools
Group coordination	✓	×
Declarative interactions	✓	✓
Dynamic definitions	✓	×
Temporal abstractions	✓	×
Distribution	✓	×
DSL	×	✓
SOC for coordination	✓	×
Mobility	✓	×

Figure 7. Feature Support Comparison

Figure 6. We measured the code on the server and client sides in terms of group coordination (replication, communication, session management), complex interactions (collaborative events definitions, detection and activations) aside from the rest of the application logic. We find that the Mingo framework reduces the code a developer writes to enforce collaborative interactions – particularly on the server side where the orchestration of events is implemented.

Next we qualitatively compare each of the two approaches in terms of support of various coordination features (illustrated in Table 7). For *group coordination*, Mingo maintains consistency by transparently replicating specified actions to all connected mobile clients within the same session while Nools provides no mechanism for this. Both approaches are rule-based, they therefore support definition of complex interactions *declaratively*.

In Nools, the rules need to be statically defined in order to be utilized in an application. This limits the *dynamism* of rule definitions. Dynamically adding rules enables developers to add separate rules for different groups of replicated objects thereby providing specialized types of interaction on different shapes (e.g. we can dynamically define separate collaborative interactions for rectangles and circles). Through Midas, Mingo natively supports temporal abstractions such as the `time:within` construct while in the Nools approach we had to specify time calculations and assert the facts with temporal annotations.

Mingo rules can be defined by a developer on the mobile client side and registered to be processed on the server by the runtime. Nools natively has no support for this *distribution*; when one defines rules on the browser they work only in the browser, and if on the server then only the server code can utilize the rules.

In our sample application for Nools, we observed that most coordination code was interspersed with the application logic for the drawing editor and the server code, making debugging difficult and modification prone to unexpected errors. This goes against the principle of *separation of coordination concerns*. Mingo code isolates the coordination logic, making development less vulnerable to such limitations.

Nools does provide a *DSL* (Domain-Specific Language) for 'cleaner' rule definition syntax, while Mingo does not. However, the Nools rules defined with the DSL need to be compiled before beforehand. A final point is that Nools lacks support for *mobile* devices.

LIMITATIONS & FUTURE WORK

Mingo utilizes HTML5 websockets for communication, identified as one of the best performing web technologies for collaborative groupware [8]. Furthermore the performance of the Midas CEP engine in processing real-time event streams has been previously documented in [14]. In the prototypes we developed and tested the applications were quite responsive. Nevertheless, Mingo is currently restricted to low-latency environments since it is constrained to the inherent limitations of the distributed web architecture. For instance, when several simultaneous interactions from different clients are asserted to the server, their effects may cause the replicas to diverge. In future we intend to investigate how enforcing techniques such as eventual consistency with operational transformation [18] will ensure that the operations *eventually* converge on all the clients, thereby relaxing this restriction.

We would also like to investigate how Mingo can estimate and handle small delays in communication between clients and server with respect to the defined rules, which affects detection of delayed events. Finally, we intend to create a DSL for more intuitive definitions of Mingo's collaborative rules both on the server and in the mobile clients.

CONCLUSION

We have focused on programming support for interactive web-based mobile applications in which a number of clients participate in performing collaborative surface interactions. We identified requirements that a suitable programming model for coordinating these kinds of interactions should adhere to: event composition and group coordination.

We propose Mingo, an object-oriented framework that extends JavaScript with coordination abstractions that blend complex event processing and group coordination. Mingo allows developers to cohesively compose events coming from distributed client devices by defining rules and to coordinate behaviour of distributed objects by defining group constructs. Furthermore, the framework enables developers to program their coordination concerns separate from their application logic. The major contribution of Mingo is to merge techniques found in declarative complex event processing and distributed group coordination into a coherent object-oriented framework for collaborating interactions in mobile applications running on web architecture.

REFERENCES

1. Daniel J Abadi, Yanif Ahmad, Magdalena Balazinska, Ugur Cetintemel, and Mitch Cherniack. 2005. The Design of the Borealis Stream Processing Engine. In *Proceedings of the Second Biennial Conference on Innovative Data Systems Research. (CIDR'05)*. Asilomar, CA.
2. Sriram Karthik Badam and Niklas Elmqvist. 2014. PolyChrome: A Cross-Device Framework for Collaborative Web Visualization. In *Proceedings of the Ninth ACM International Conference on Interactive Tabletops and Surfaces (ITS '14)*. ACM, New York, NY, USA, 109–118. DOI: http://dx.doi.org/10.1145/2669485.2669518
3. Jacob T. Biehl and Brian P. Bailey. 2004. ARIS: An Interface for Application Relocation in an Interactive Space. In *Proceedings of Graphics Interface 2004 (GI '04)*. Canadian Human-Computer Communications Society, 107–116. http://dl.acm.org/citation.cfm?id=1006058.1006072
4. Florian Echtler, Manuel Huber, and Gudrun Klinker. 2008. Shadow Tracking on Multi-touch Tables. In *Proceedings of the Working Conference on Advanced Visual Interfaces (AVI '08)*. ACM, New York, NY, USA, 388–391. DOI: http://dx.doi.org/10.1145/1385569.1385640
5. Charles Forgy. 1982. Rete: A Fast Algorithm for the Many Pattern/Many Object Pattern Match Problem. *Artificial Intelligences* 19, 1 (1982), 17–37. http://dx.doi.org/10.1016/0004-3702(82)90020-0
6. D. Gelernter. 1985. Generative communication in Linda. *ACM Transactions on Programming Languages and Systems* 7, 1 (Jan 1985), 80–112.
7. Yechezkal-Shimon Gutfreund and John R Nicol. 1997. WWWinda Orchestrator: a mechanism for coordinating distributed flocks of Java Applets. In *Society of Photo-Optical Instrumentation Engineers (SPIE) Conference Series (Electronic Imaging'97)*, M. Freeman, P. Jardetzky, and H. M Vin (Eds.). 295–302.
8. Carl A. Gutwin, Michael Lippold, and T. C. Nicholas Graham. 2011. Real-time Groupware in the Browser: Testing the Performance of Web-based Networking. In *Proceedings of the ACM 2011 Conference on Computer Supported Cooperative Work (CSCW '11)*. ACM, New York, NY, USA, 167–176. DOI: http://dx.doi.org/10.1145/1958824.1958850
9. Ken Hinckley. 2003. Synchronous Gestures for Multiple Persons and Computers. In *Proceedings of the 16th Annual ACM Symposium on User Interface Software and Technology (UIST '03)*. ACM, New York, NY, USA, 149–158. DOI: http://dx.doi.org/10.1145/964696.964713
10. Brad Johanson, Greg Hutchins, and Terry Winograd. 2000. *PointRight: A System for Pointer/Keyboard Redirection among Multiple Displays and Machines*. Technical Report.
11. Jonathan P. Munson and Prasun Dewan. 1997. Sync: A Java Framework for Mobile Collaborative Applications. *Computer* 30, 6 (June 1997), 59–66. DOI: http://dx.doi.org/10.1109/2.587549
12. George A. Papadopoulos and Farhad Arbab. 1998. Coordination Models and Languages. In *Advances in Computers. (The Engineering of Large Systems)*. Academic Press, New York, NY, USA, 329–400.
13. Mark Proctor. 2012. Drools: A Rule Engine for Complex Event Processing. In *Applications of Graph Transformations with Industrial Relevance*, Andy Schürr, Daniel Varrò, and Gergely Varrò (Eds.). Lecture Notes in Computer Science, Vol. 7233. Springer Berlin Heidelberg. DOI: http://dx.doi.org/10.1007/978-3-642-34176-2_2
14. Thierry Renaux, Lode Hoste, Stefan Marr, and Wolfgang De Meuter. 2012. Parallel Gesture Recognition with Soft Real-time Guarantees. In *Proceedings of the 2Nd Edition on Programming Systems, Languages and Applications Based on Actors, Agents, and Decentralized Control Abstractions (AGERE! 2012)*. ACM, New York, NY, USA, 35–46. DOI: http://dx.doi.org/10.1145/2414639.2414646
15. Mark Roseman and Saul Greenberg. 1992. GROUPKIT: A Groupware Toolkit for Building Real-time Conferencing Applications. In *Proceedings of the 1992 ACM Conference on Computer-supported Cooperative Work (CSCW '92)*. ACM, New York, NY, USA, 43–50. DOI: http://dx.doi.org/10.1145/143457.143460
16. Oliver Schmid, Agnes Lisowska Masson, and Béat Hirsbrunner. 2012. Collaborative Web Browsing: Multiple Users, Multiple Pages, Concurrent Access, One Display. In *Proceedings of the 4th ACM SIGCHI Symposium on Engineering Interactive Computing Systems (EICS '12)*. ACM, New York, NY, USA, 141–150. DOI: http://dx.doi.org/10.1145/2305484.2305508
17. C. Scholliers, L. Hoste, B. Signer, and W. De Meuter. 2011. Midas: A Declarative Multi-Touch Interaction Framework. In *Proceedings of 5th International Conference on Tangible, Embedded, and Embodied Interaction. (TEI'11)*. Funchal, Portugal.
18. Chengzheng Sun and Clarence Ellis. 1998. Operational Transformation in Real-time Group Editors: Issues, Algorithms, and Achievements. In *Proceedings of the 1998 ACM Conference on Computer Supported Cooperative Work (CSCW '98)*. ACM, New York, NY, USA, 59–68. DOI: http://dx.doi.org/10.1145/289444.289469

Pins 'n' Touches: An Interface for Tagging and Editing Complex Groups

Sven Strothoff*, **Wolfgang Stuerzlinger**†, **Klaus Hinrichs***
*Visualization and Computer Graphics Research Group, University of Münster, Germany
†School of Interactive Arts + Technology, Simon Fraser University, Vancouver, Canada

ABSTRACT
Influenced by mouse/pen-based user interfaces, most touch-based object tagging techniques rely mostly on a single interaction point. Once objects are tagged, typically only individual object inclusions/exclusions are possible. Yet, for tagging larger groups with complex spatial layouts, more refinement may be necessary to achieve the desired result. We apply visual tag markers to objects to visualize their group association. Through a new multi-touch pin gesture that "pins" one or more objects "down" while tagging, our new interface is capable of efficiently grouping objects, as identified in our user studies.

ACM Classification Keywords
H.5.2. Information Interfaces and Presentation (e.g. HCI): Input devices and strategies; Interaction styles.

Author Keywords
Multi-touch; Pin gesture; Complex group selection; Selection editing; Tagging.

INTRODUCTION
Selection of one or more objects is a fundamental operation in user interfaces, and usually done with the mouse or pen. Such interfaces rely on a single interaction point (cursor). Touch interfaces have (largely) adopted the single-touch convention, especially for tagging. Yet, this design does not leverage the unique capabilities of multi-touch, such as multiple simultaneous touches, which enable the user to effectively control multiple cursors. Here we explore the idea that using multiple touches enables more efficient tag editing by adding or removing *multiple* objects to/from existing groups. We first examine existing selection techniques, discuss the relationship between tagging and grouping, and present use cases for tagging of complex groups. Then we introduce our new multi-touch tagging technique and how it edits tags of complex groups. To evaluate our interaction technique we present two user studies comparing different aspects of our method to identify its performance characteristics.

Motivation
While examining existing multi-touch input methods, we noticed a lack of techniques that enable the user to tag complex groups. Looking at the design space for such a technique, we developed the following questions:

- How can we support tagging of more than a single object at a time, which resembles a grouping task?
- For tagging with multiple concurrent tags, how is overlap, *i.e.*, objects belonging to more than one group, handled?
- How do we show that an object belongs to multiple groups?
- How can we use multiple touches to support efficient editing of multiple concurrent tags?

ITS 2015, November 15–18, 2015, Funchal/Madeira, Portugal.

ACM 978-1-4503-3899-8/15/11 ...$15.00.
DOI: http://dx.doi.org/10.1145/2817721.2817731

Related Work
We first compiled a list of references [2–5, 7, 10, 12, 14, 16, 17, 19, 21–23, 26] to survey existing work for group selection. Then, we categorized them by assigning classifiers based on input hardware, mode of operation and capabilities. For brevity, we list the classifiers directly with the references at the end. We used the following criteria:

MOUSE, PEN, TOUCH For which input method was the selection technique designed?

MULTI-TOUCH This classifier is only assigned if more than one simultaneous touch is used.

HOLD A hold gesture, *i.e.*, a stationary touch for a prolonged period of time, is used in addition to the normal tap gesture.

PIN A hold gesture, that is used in combination with other user actions.

RECTANGLE, LASSO If a rectangular region can be specified RECTANGLE was assigned. LASSO was assigned if an arbitrary region can be selected by lassoing around it.

IN/OUT Is there a difference between interaction that is performed/started inside or outside of an existing selection?

REGION, OBJECTS Is the selection technique used to select objects or a region of interest, such as a region in an image?

AUTO MODE Is there an automatic switch between selection and de-selection, *i.e.*, does the system support more than tapping objects to toggle selection.

ON/OFF OBJECTS Is there a differentiation between interactions/gestures that are performed/started on objects or in the surrounding space?

DIRECT, INDIRECT Are objects selected directly, *i.e.*, by tapping on them, or indirectly, *e.g.*, by surrounding them?

SURROUND, CROSSING Is the selection performed by surrounding the desired objects or by crossing them?

PATH Is the selection performed along a path? Or are only selection areas supported?

The overview of all pair-wise combinations of classifiers is shown in Figure 1. The numbers at the intersections indicate

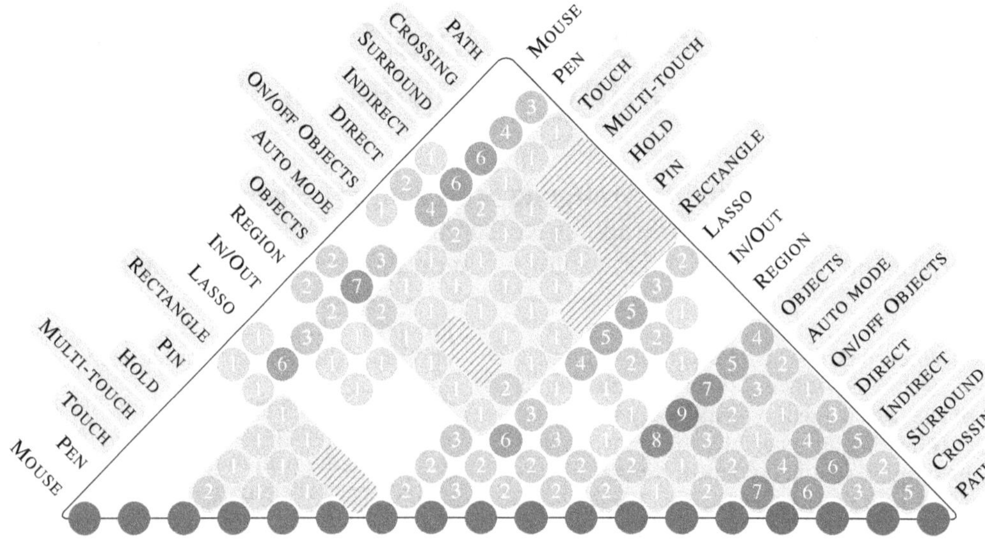

Figure 1. All pair-wise combinations of classifiers with their number of occurrences provide an overview of the examined body of previous work on group selection. The classification of our novel tagging interface (shaded in green) and the new contributions (hatched area) are also shown.

how often the corresponding combination is present in previous work. The classification of our novel tagging interface is shaded in green. Hatched areas represent new contributions.

Multi-touch interaction is often constrained to a single touch. There are two reasons for that. Most multi-touch systems are small hand-held devices. When one hand holds the device, only a single hand is available for interaction. Second, most user interface development was influenced by mouse- or pen-based interfaces, which implies a single cursor/touch. The only multi-touch interaction that is truly "multi" is common gestures, such as two finger scrolling or pinching. As large tablets and notebooks and desktop computers with multi-touch capable displays become available, true multi-touch input becomes more important. Moscovich et al. [18] argued that controlling two independent points of interaction using a single hand is difficult and have shown that two hands perform better than one for these tasks. Furthermore, a single moving touch can be augmented by additional stationary ones. These additional touches can be used to define contextual information for the action performed by the primary one. Strothoff et al. [23] used this idea to select rectangular regions.

Looking at the gaps in Figure 1 one can identify that true *multi*-touch interaction together with common group selection techniques like path or rectangular region has not been explored. The results of previous works suggest that there is a potential benefit in combining existing elements to close the gap with a multi-touch group selection technique. The combination of pin and hold gestures with other selection techniques yields new possibilities for editing of tags or selections. Wobbrock et al. [25] identified a gesture similar to our *pin* gesture, but did not explore further.

Contribution

We propose a novel combination of interaction techniques based on pinning touches that facilitates the definition of complex groups through tagging. With the classifiers used for structuring related work we classify our technique as: TOUCH, MULTI-TOUCH, HOLD, PIN, RECTANGLE, OBJECTS, AUTO MODE, ON/OFF OBJECTS, DIRECT, INDIRECT, SURROUND, CROSSING, PATH and introduce the following contributions:

- A classification and visual summary of previous work on group selection;
- a multi-touch user interface technique for tagging of complex groups;
- support for multiple concurrent and overlapping groups;
- pin gestures for efficient editing of existing groups;
- an evaluation of our new techniques in two user studies.

Pinning Touches

In contrast to a tap, a hold gesture is a stationary touch for a prolonged period of time. We call our extension of the touch input vocabulary *pinning touches*, *i.e.*, stationary touches that are held during *other* touch actions. These pinning touches *pin down* objects or user interface elements. Through pinning touches we can associate additional contextual information with standard touch actions, such as tapping, swiping, tracing paths, flicking and two finger swipe or pinch gestures. Thus, operations that typically require a mode switch can be performed directly with pinning touches.

Use Cases for Pinning

Currently, deleting images in a photo application usually requires a temporary switch to a delete mode and then tapping on individual images. With pinning touches the explicit mode switch is unnecessary. Images can be pinned down to specify them as context for the delete action: The user can touch and hold, *i.e.*, pin, several images and then tap a button to delete them. Alternatively, the delete button can be pinned to implicitly activate a delete mode. All images that are then selected, by tapping or some other method, will be deleted. As two simultaneous touches (one of them on the delete button) are required, accidental deletion is unlikely. Similarly, text attributes can be applied by pinning down an attribute in text processing, for instance to *paint* a bold font attribute over a passage. Multiple pinning touches can even apply multiple attributes concurrently. Also, pinning touches can copy styles. Then, pinning a word and painting over text changes the style to match that of the pinned word. Pinning touches also extend multi-touch gestures. Thus a scaling gesture (pinch) can be constrained to horizontal, vertical or uniform scaling by pinning down respective modifier buttons.

Moreover, pinning touches can also enable functionality similar to a context menu. When a context menu is invoked, the properties of the object at the cursor determine what actions to display in the menu. Similarly, pinning touches can also supply context to actions performed with the primary touch. Gutwin et al. [6] presented a command selection technique that combined a pinning touch for menu access with taps to select commands from this menu. Yet, no context was derived from the pinning touch.

Li et al. [13] identified that pressing a button with the non-dominant hand is effective for switching between modes in pen-based interfaces. But this is limited to a single pair of modes. Hinckley et al. [8] also used a button as a mode switch. They extended the number of accessible modes through a pop-up menu. With multi-touch, the menu itself can act as a collection of switches that can be held down (*pinned*) to select the desired mode. This combines the semantics of holding a button to temporarily switch modes with the choices a menu offers. Hinckley et al. [9] presented a combination of touch and pen-based input. They used touches similar to our pinning touches to augment pen-based actions.

Using Pinning and Tags to Define Groups

Combining objects into groups is a common user interface operation in graphic design or layout software. Usually objects are first selected and then a widget or a shortcut is used to group these objects. Through pinning touches, groups can be defined without a menu or shortcut. For this, a single object is first pinned down and then other objects to be grouped are selected. If the pinned object is already part of a group, the additional objects are added to its group. Note that a pinning touch *implicitly* selects the target group as part of the interaction. In photo management software grouping is also frequently used to structure and sort photos, into events or by subject. For example, a user wants to group all photos taken while visiting Madeira, while all photos of the user's dog are collected in another group. When the user brought his dog along to a trip to Madeira, these photos belong to more than one group. To represent such group associations, tags can be added to the objects. Then, all photos from Madeira share one tag and those of the user's dog another one.

In this paper we present an interaction technique that combines pinning touches and tags to enable the definition and editing of complex group associations.

Use Cases for Tag-based Groups

In recent versions of OS X multiple tags can be assigned to files to assist with categorization. As touch-sensitive laptops are becoming more common, there will be an increased need to select, tag and group files using touch gestures. Modern photo applications permit users to assign tags based on faces in a picture or the location the photo was taken at, supported by (semi-)automatic classification. Many e-mail clients support tagging of messages with different colors, and Gmail permits multiple tags per e-mail. All these cases represent multiple overlapping tag groups, such as an e-mail that is both *work related* and *important* or a photo of *my dog* taken on *Madeira*.

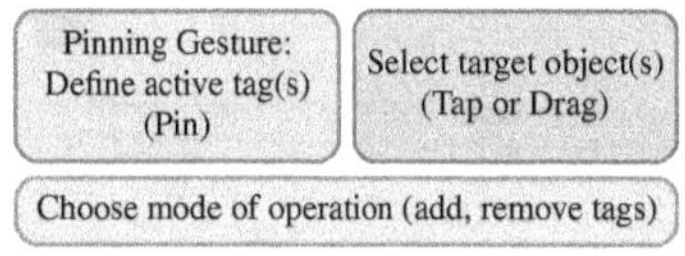

Figure 2. The three components of our interface: One technique to define a set of active tags and one to select target objects. We require another technique to choose the mode of operation, *i.e.*, adding or removing objects to the group.

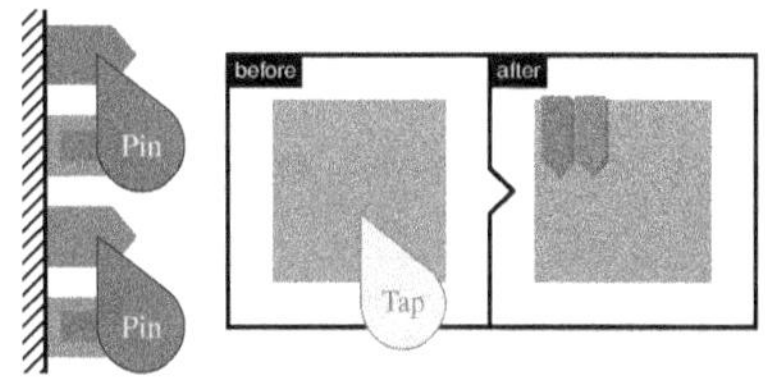

Figure 3. A set of tag widgets is displayed at the screen border. Pinning down widgets defines a set of tags for selection operations. Alternatively, the user can pin existing objects with desired tags, see Figure 4.

OUR PIN-BASED INTERFACE FOR TAGGING

We propose a new interaction technique, which enables tagging of objects. With it multiple tags can be assigned concurrently to each object, permitting objects to belong to multiple groups at the same time. The association is visualized through different colored tags. Once tags have been assigned, our technique enables easy modification of these tags. Three main components are necessary in our interface: A way to define a set of active tags, a technique for selecting target objects, and a way to specify the mode of operation: active tags can either be added to or removed from target objects (see Figure 2).

Defining a Set of Tags

Our tagging technique uses *pinning* touches. If the user touches and holds tagging widgets or already tagged objects while performing other actions, we call those *pinned* down. Pinned widgets/objects are used in our technique to define the set of active tags for subsequent operations.

Tag Widgets. We show a set of widgets, one for each available tag, at the border of the screen. Pinned widgets activate the corresponding tags, which are applied on selection. Through pinning multiple widgets the user can compose any combination of tags, as illustrated in Figure 3.

Pinning Already Tagged Objects. When the user pins down an object, this adds the tags assigned to this object to the set of active tags (cf. Figure 4). Pinning down multiple objects simultaneously activates the union of the objects' individual tags (cf. Figure 5). The tag widgets provide visual feedback of the active set. Assuming that similar objects are in close proximity, such as sequences of photos in a camera roll, applying the same set of tags to similar objects is then a *local* operation:

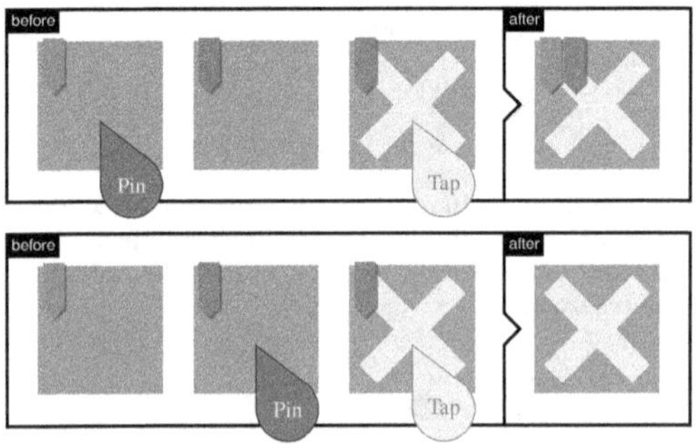

Figure 4. Pinning down a single tag: tapping an object toggles the tag on that object.

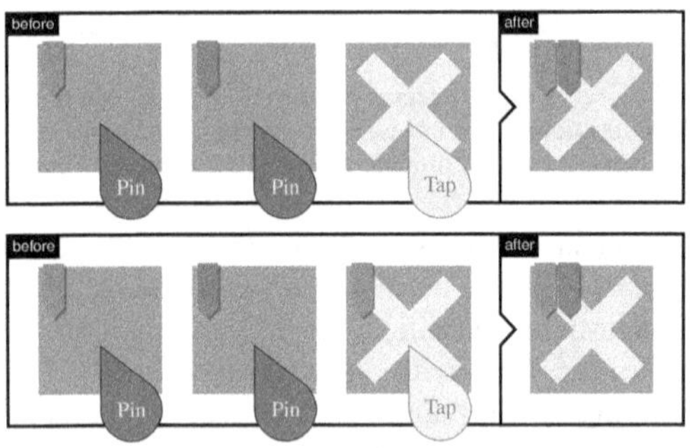

(a) If multiple objects are pinned down, the union of their tags is applied when tapping.

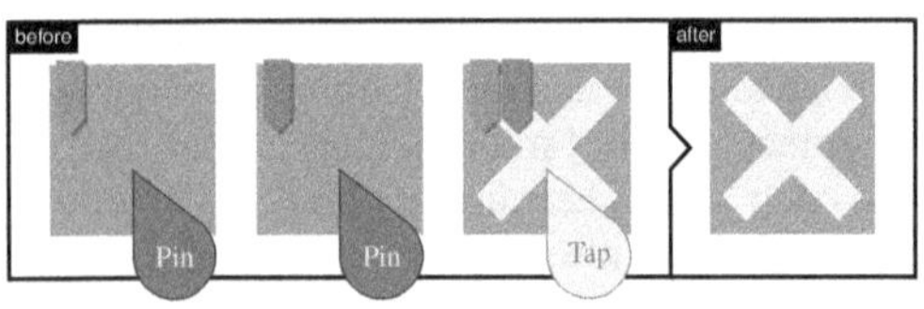

(b) Tags are removed if the tapped object already has all pinned tags.

Figure 5. Semantics for multiple pinned tags.

First, pin an already tagged object down and then select the other (close by) objects. For example, the user can then easily specify that *this* is *also* a photo of my dog taken on Madeira.

Selecting Target Objects

With a set of active tags, one or more target objects have to be chosen. Our tagging technique supports tapping for single and path-based operations for multiple objects.

Selecting Single Objects Through Tapping. Selecting single objects via tapping is common in touch interfaces, *e.g.*, [12, 26]. If a single tag is pinned down with our technique, this tag is toggled on any (other) tapped object. In the top sequence in Figure 4, the yellow tag is pinned down. As the tapped target object does not yet have the yellow tag, it is added to it. In the bottom sequence the pinned blue tag is already assigned to the target object, so it is removed. When multiple tags are pinned, the result depends on the current tags of the tapped object. Figure 5(a) shows two sequences with a pinned set of yellow and blue tags. In both cases the tapped object has not been assigned both tags, so the pinned tags are added. If, on the other hand, the target object has already all active tags, as shown in Figure 5(b), the pinned tags are removed.

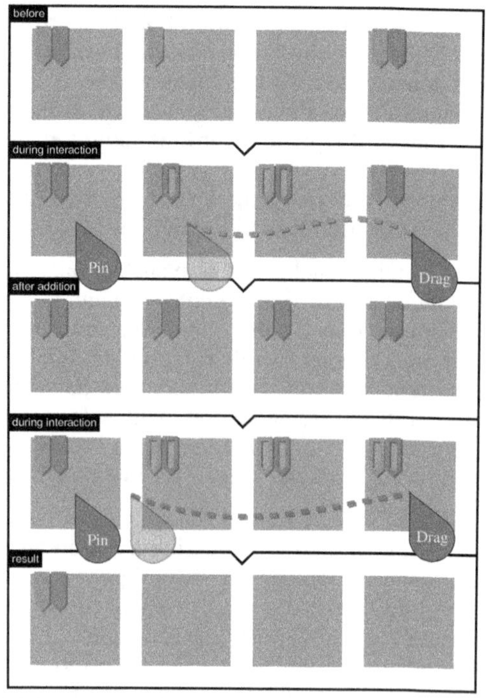

Figure 6. The starting point of the path decides the operation for the intersected objects. If the path begins inside an object tags are added (green path). If the path begins in the *void* (*i.e.*, on the background, outside of all objects) tags are removed (red path). Outlined markers preview the changes that will be applied.

Pinning the void, *i.e.*, the background area between objects, and tapping on an object removes all tags from said object.

Tagging Multiple Objects. The user can trace a path to operate on, *i.e.*, tag, multiple targets. While interacting with single objects the user's intent to add or remove a tag can be deduced automatically, using the approach outlined above. Yet, for multiple objects it is in general necessary to explicitly define the operation as either adding or removing tags. The operation is then applied to all objects intersecting the path. In our technique, the position of the first touch starting the path determines the mode. If the touch is inside an object, the current set of pinned tags will be added. Else, if the first touch is in the *void*, *i.e.*, on the background, the pinned set of tags will be removed from the objects. See Figure 6 for illustrations. This extends previous work [23], which only supported selection of a single rectangular region.

Visual Feedback and Order of Operations

The color of the traced path shows the mode of operation: green for adding tags, red for removing them. While the path is traced, the system shows a preview of the resulting tag changes. Solid tags remain unchanged by the operation, while outlined tags illustrate changes. See Figure 6. The order of the three interaction components, shown in Figure 2, is not predefined and our technique supports all combinations. For instance, if the preview does not show the desired result, it is possible to change the set of pinned tags while tracing a path and see an updated preview. Even tagging target objects by first tracing a path and afterwards pinning tags down is possible, as long as the finger defining the path is not lifted.

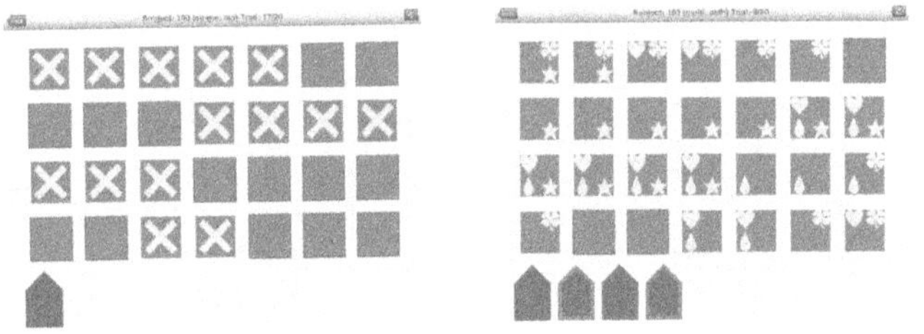

Figure 7. Screenshots of the two phases of the first study. (left) In the first phase all objects marked with an X had to be tagged. (right) In the second phase four different tags had to be assigned: heart → red, clover → green, drop → blue, star → yellow.

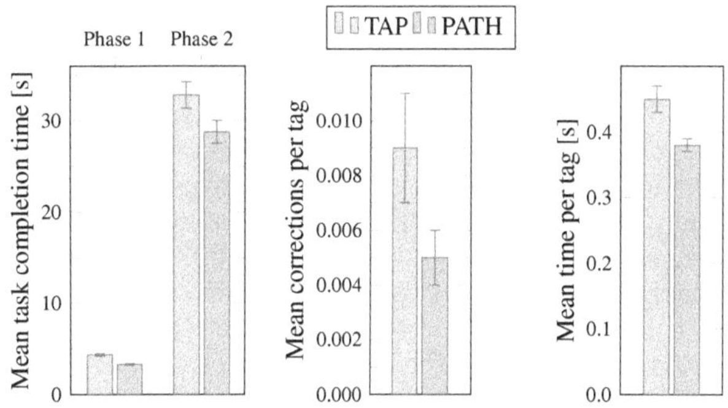

Figure 8. Comparison of TAP and PATH for: (left) mean task completion time in both phases of the first study, (center) mean number of corrections for each placed tag, (right) mean time for each placed tag.

As long as pinning touches exist, they continue to define the set of active tags, which can be used for future operations.

USER STUDY 1: INITIALLY ASSIGNING TAGS

Initially, we contemplated an evaluation of pinning in isolation. Yet, the results of directly related work in pen-based interfaces [8, 9] convinced us that the outcome of such an experiment would be predictable. Therefore we decided to validate and evaluate our new multi-touch tagging technique directly in two user studies. In the first one we compared a variant of our technique that permits path gestures to tag multiple objects (PATH) with a more traditional single-touch tapping approach (TAP), where objects are tagged by tapping them one by one, as the control condition. We presented participants with a task similar to tagging photos in a photo application.

Participants and Setup. 21 participants (20 male, 1 female), ages 20 to 34 (median 28), participated in the study. All but two were students from the local university. All participants reported to have at least some experience with multi-touch devices. Most of them use smartphones or tablets regularly. The experiment, including instructions, training and debriefing, took about 45 minutes per participant. Breaks were permitted at any time. One participant had to be dropped due to a series of interruptions. The experiment was performed using an Apple iPad attached to a desk in front of the sitting participant.

Procedure. With each technique participants were asked to assign tags to split the presented objects into groups, based on their content. The order of techniques was counterbalanced using a 2 × 2 Latin square. After the experiment participants completed a short questionnaire.

Experimental Task. The study was divided into two phases. The first one used a single tag and participants were asked to tag all objects marked by an X (see Figure 7, left). The second phase used four tag categories: red, green, blue and yellow. Objects were marked with zero to four symbols representing the target tag set to be applied to each object, see Figure 7 (right). Tags had to be assigned as follows: heart → red, clover → green, drop → blue, star → yellow.

Initially, we contemplated using photos. However, the lack of a suitable photo set in the public domain led us to choose a different approach. Moreover, we did not want to deal with issues of users not being able to differentiate between similar images. Thus, we chose to simplify the task to a symbol recognition task, also because we are only interested in analyzing pinning and tagging performance. We first randomized the symbol positions on the objects to more closely resemble features in a photo. However, a pilot study revealed that the cognitive load for this was too high and resulted in both very high selection variability and overall slow performance. As we are looking for reliable measurements of selection task performance we needed to eliminate the potential confound of image recognition. Therefore, we simplified the task and assigned symbols to fixed locations on the objects.

In both phases no tags were assigned initially. When all tags were correctly assigned, the trial was automatically completed. After a notification, the experiment automatically advanced to the next trial. A colored border was added to objects that had all tags correctly assigned. This helped participants identify single missing tags towards the end of each trial.

Experiment Design. In each trial a sequence of 28 objects (7 × 4) was displayed. For each phase 10 object sequences were generated and shown twice to the participants, resulting in a total of 80 trials per participant (2 phases, 2 techniques, 10 sequences, 2 repetitions). The order of sequences was randomized for each user and technique. To minimize the effect of switching selection techniques, four training trials were added before each trial set, but discarded from analysis.

Photo organization applications usually display photos in the order they were taken, *e.g.*, in a camera roll. This results in sequences of similar photos that would require similar tags. Therefore, we generated symbol sequences using an exponential distribution with an expected sequence length of 3 ($\lambda = 1/3$) for the trials in our study. For the second phase, sequences of each symbol were generated independently of each other, resulting in zero to four symbols per object.

Results

To analyze the data of the experiment we performed a 2 × 2 within-subjects, repeated measures ANOVA ($\alpha = .05$) for the used selection technique and the presented sequence. The dependent measure was the task completion time, measured from the first touch in each trial until all tags were correctly assigned. The results are summarized in Figure 8.

Task Completion Time. For the first phase (single tag) a significant main effect of technique, $F(1, 19) = 100.79, p < .001$, was found, with mean times of 4.35 s (SE = 0.12) for TAP and 3.28 s for PATH (SE = 0.10). A significant main effect of the presented sequence, $F(9, 171) = 70.56, p < .001$, was found, with mean times ranging from 2.25 s to 5.12 s. There was a significant interaction of technique and sequence, $F(4.53, 86.24) = 3.62, p = .007$. For the second phase (up to four tags) a significant main effect of technique, $F(1, 19) = 6.93, p = .016$, was found, with mean times of 32.84 s (SE = 1.44) for TAP and 28.77 s for PATH (SE = 1.25). A significant main effect of the presented sequence, $F(9, 171) = 20.42, p < .001$, was found, with mean times ranging from 24.40 s to 36.17 s. There was no interaction of technique and sequence, $F(4.57, 86.78) < 1$. Post-hoc analysis for both phases showed that the differences in completion time were caused by the sequences that required the least/most tags to be completed. We observed a linear trend between the number of target tags and the completion time: task completion time = -3.41 + (0.59 × number of target tags), $R^2 = 0.8$.

Error Rate. To measure the error rate, we looked at the number of corrections a user performed in relation to the total number of tags to be placed. There are two types of such *errors*: Assigning a wrong tag to an object and removing a tag that was correctly assigned. We combined the error rates for both phases and performed a 2 × 2 within-subjects, repeated measures ANOVA with experiment phase and technique as factors. A significant main effect of phase, $F(1, 19) = 48.33, p < .001$ was found, with mean error rates of 0.002 (SE = 0.001) for the first and 0.012 (SE = 0.002) for the second phase. Overall, a significant main effect of selection technique, $F(1, 19) = 5.97, p = .024$ was found, with mean error rates of 0.009 (SE = 0.002) for TAP and 0.005 (SE = 0.001) for PATH. There was no interaction of phase and technique, $F(1, 19) = 1.74, p = .203$.

Time per Tag. To further investigate how the two techniques compare to each other and to illuminate the difference between the two phases, we looked at the mean time to place a tag. We calculated the time per tag for each trial by dividing the task completion time by the number of tags that had to be assigned to complete the sequence. Any wrong tags that had to be removed again were not counted, thus yielding the mean time it took to correctly place a tag. To analyze the time per tag we performed an ANOVA of the combined values of both phases. A significant main effect of phase, $F(1, 19) = 261.77, p < .001$, was found, with mean times of 0.29 s (SE = 0.01) for the first phase and 0.55 s (SE = 0.02) for the second phase. A significant main effect of selection technique, $F(1, 19) = 22.41, p < .001$, was found, with mean times of 0.45 s (SE = 0.02) for TAP and 0.38 s (SE = 0.01) for PATH. There was no interaction of phase and technique, $F(1, 19) < 1$.

Observations. Overall, users had no problems understanding and using the pinning touches in the tagging interface. While it was possible to assign multiple tags at the same time and participants were shown how to do so, we noticed that after the first few operations during the training virtually all tags were placed one after another. We also observed a change in the usage of the path gesture between the two phases of the experiment. Thus we took a closer look at the recorded paths. Figure 9 shows the distribution of path lengths, measured as the number of affected objects. In the first phase a length of five was most frequent, but considerably longer paths occurred as well. For the second phase the peak shifted towards a path length of 2, followed by a steep fall-off. An overlay of all recorded paths for a representative sequence of each phase is shown in Figure 10. In the first phase, many long winding paths were used, in most cases to tag each connected component of marked objects via a single path gesture. During the second phase, most tags were applied in a *scanline* pattern. Rows of objects were considered one after another, resulting in predominantly horizontal linear paths, as in Figure 10 (right). Users selecting a whole row caused the secondary peak for paths of length 7 in phase two.

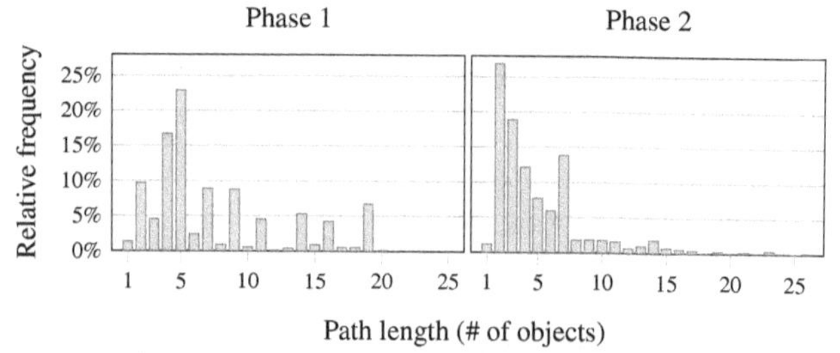

Figure 9. Histogram of path lengths, *i.e.*, the number of affected objects, for both phases of the experiment. A clear shift towards shorter paths is visible for the second, more complex, phase.

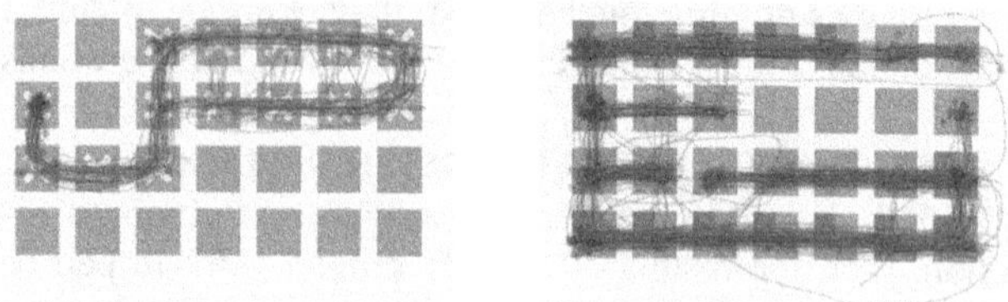

Figure 10. Illustrations overlaying paths of representative tag operations for each phase of the experiment. (left) In the first phase longer, curved paths were used. (right) The paths of the second phase were shorter and show a distinct *scanline* pattern.

Subjective Ratings. After the experiment participants were asked which tagging technique they perceived as faster. All but two thought they were faster with the path technique. The remaining rated both techniques as equal. Additionally, participants were asked for their preferred technique. All but one preferred the path technique to tapping. Most participants found individually tapping objects one by one to be tedious. One participant preferred tapping and stated that path had a higher risk of selecting more objects than intended. However, that participant also stated that the path technique would still be faster overall. Some participants that started the study with tapping inquired if there was a way to affect multiple objects at once—some even proposing tracing a path through them.

USER STUDY 2: MODIFYING TAGS

The first user study showed that the path-based selection technique is well suited for assigning tags to an untagged set of objects. Although the participants were introduced to the mechanism for addition or removal of tags, they rarely used it, likely because it was only needed for the removal of individual accidentally placed tags. Thus, the first study yielded no insight on how users respond to the mechanism for adding or removing tags. Our second study forced participants to use both add and removal operations.

Participants and Setup. 16 participants (15 male, 1 female), ages 26 to 38 (median 29), participated in the study. All but one were students recruited from the local university department. All participants reported to have at least some experience with multi-touch devices. Most of them use smartphones or tablets on a regular basis. Participants took about 20 minutes to complete the study and were permitted breaks. The setup was identical to the first user study.

Procedure. Sequences of objects with already assigned tags were presented to the users. With each technique participants were asked to correct the tag assignment, so that only the marked objects were tagged—adding and removing tags as necessary. The order of techniques was counterbalanced using a 2 × 2 Latin square. After the experiment participants were asked to complete a short questionnaire to provide their subjective ratings and preference of both techniques.

Experimental Task. The experimental task was similar to phase one of the first study. However, this time there were already some tags assigned. Only a single tag category was available. Participants were asked to edit the presented tags, so that only the objects marked by an X were tagged. In contrast to the first study, users not only had to add but also to remove wrongly assigned tags. When all tags were correct, the trial was automatically completed and the experiment advanced to the next trial. To help locating the final missing or misplaced tags a colored border was added to correctly tagged objects.

Experiment Design. In each trial a sequence of 28 objects (7 × 4) was displayed. Ten object sequences were generated and shown twice to each participant, for a total of 40 trials (2 techniques, 10 sequences, 2 repetitions). The order of sequences was randomized for each user. Four training trials were added before the trials and discarded from analysis. The sequences were generated as in the first study. For each object sequence a sequence of tags was independently generated using the same distribution. Layering the tag and object sequences resulted in groups of correct and wrong tag assignments. In a first pilot for this experiment tags were assigned completely randomly. While randomly distributed errors may occur, we aimed to simulate a pre-tagged data set with some kind of systematic issue. For instance, if a face detection algorithm fails for one image, it is likely that it will also fail for very similar images in a sequence.

Results

The collected data was analyzed using a within-subjects, repeated measures ANOVA ($\alpha = .05$) using technique and the presented sequence as factors. If the assumption of sphericity was violated degrees of freedom were adjusted via Greenhouse-Geisser. The results are summarized in Figure 11.

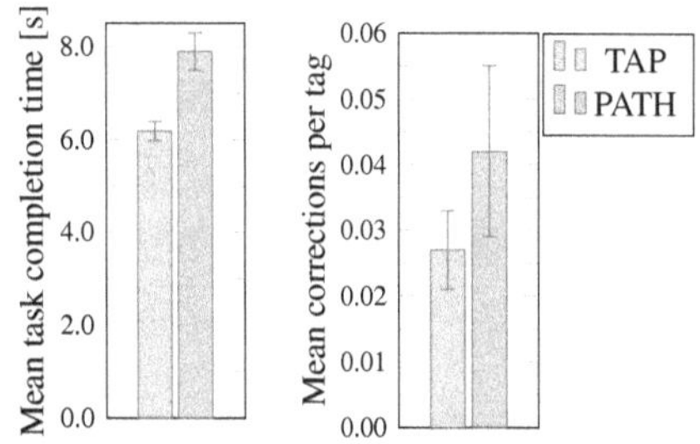

Figure 11. Comparison of TAP and PATH for: (left) mean task completion time, (right) mean number of corrections for each changed tag.

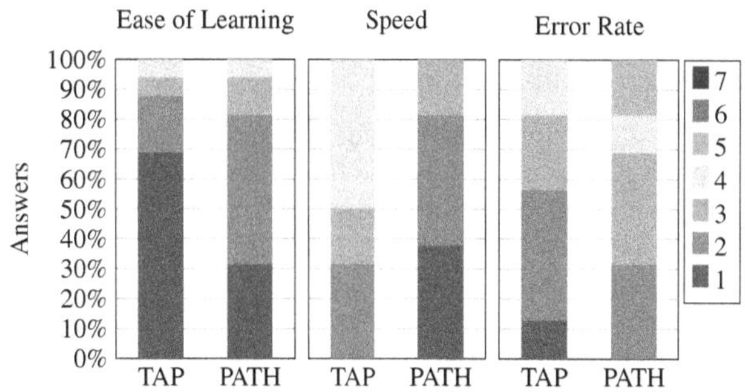

Figure 12. Ratings on ease of learning, speed and error rate based on a 7-point Likert scale (1 = very good).

Task Completion Time. The task completion time for each trial was measured from the first touch until the trial was completed successfully. We were able to find significant main effects for technique, $F(1, 15) = 40.19, p < .001$, and presented sequence, $F(9, 135) = 29.41, p < .001$. The mean times were 6.18 s (SE = 0.21) for TAP and 7.89 s (SE = 0.40) for PATH. As in the first study, post-hoc analysis showed that the significant differences in completion time were caused by the sequences that required the least/most tags to be changed. There was a significant interaction of technique and sequence $F(9, 135) = 6.59, p < .001$.

Number of Corrections per Tag. We analyzed the number of superfluous tag changes a user performed in relation to the minimum number of tag changes required to complete a trial, *i.e.*, the sum of tags that had to be added and removed. There was no effect for technique, $F(1, 15) = 1.334, p = .266$, nor for sequence, $F(3.76, 56.35) = 1.64, p = .180$ and no interaction of technique and sequence $F(3.29, 48.72) = 1.40, p = .252$.

Subjective Ratings. After each set of trials participants were asked to rate each technique concerning ease of learning, speed and error rate. Each category was rated using a 7-point Likert scale (1 = very good to 7 = poor). The results are summarized in Figure 12. After the trials, participants were asked which technique they preferred for each category and their overall preference. The results are shown in Figure 13. The collected data suggests that the participants' overall preference was influenced mostly by the perceived speed. All participants that preferred PATH for its speed also preferred it overall.

DISCUSSION

While the technique was not universally rated as *very* easy to learn, users had no problems understanding and using pinning

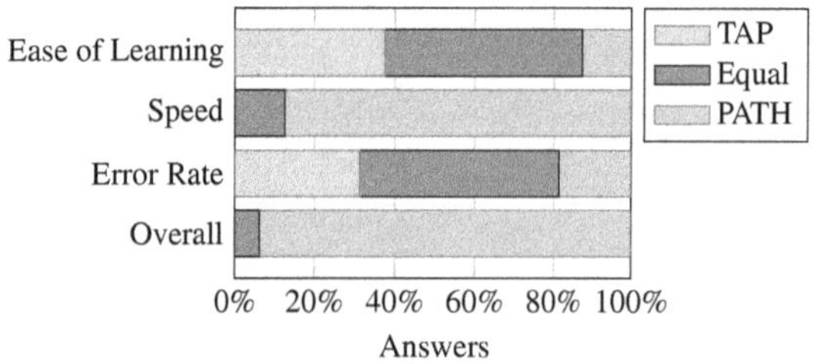

Figure 13. After completing the experiment participants were asked to state their preferred techniques regarding ease of learning, speed, error rate and their overall preference.

touches in the experiments, which matched our expectations and previous work [8, 9]. This supports the utility of pinning touches in multi-touch interfaces.

The results of the first study demonstrate that tracing a path through groups of objects was faster than tapping each object individually. This is not unexpected [1, 15], but current tagging techniques rarely support this. While the second phase of the first study required four times more tags on average, users took nearly ten times longer due to the increased task complexity. Although there is a significant difference in completion times between both techniques, the time is also dependent on the number of tags that needed to be assigned to complete a trial. To understand this interaction, we analyzed the time and corrections required for each correctly placed tag in both phases. PATH was significantly faster than TAP, by about 15%. Using a path gesture to tag multiple objects is more complex than tapping each single object individually, as multiple objects have to be considered while planning the gesture. Our results show that the benefit of affecting multiple objects outweighs the seemingly higher complexity of the path gesture. This is very promising as it opens the way for more efficient touch interaction compared to tapping.

In the second phase of the first study it took users nearly twice as long to correctly assign a tag. The mean error rate was six times higher than in the first one, which is expected due to the higher task difficulty. Still, the error rate remained surprisingly low for the large amount of fast tagging operations: one error per 83 modifications. Although the time for tagging and the error rate increased when dealing with multiple tags, we believe that the results show that our interface still works well. Some users modified multiple tags in final corrections at the end of a trial. We believe that this is due to the nature of our experimental task, which started with an *empty* object sequence. Consequently, it was somewhat easier to pin one category and finish setting all tags before moving to another tag, compared to constantly switching the set of active tags. The increased complexity of the second phase likely caused users to consider one row after another, which was easier than identifying larger connected components. The resulting *scan-line* pattern is illustrated in Figure 10 and also explains the shorter paths observed during the second phase (cf. Figure 9).

The first study provided little insight into our method for changing the mode of operation, *i.e.*, if tags are to be added or removed, which motivated our second study. After a short explanation of the principle and a bit of experimentation during training, participants quickly grasped the concept and were able to complete the task successfully. Yet, we were surprised to find that, in contrast to the first study, individual tapping was faster. After a closer look at the sequences generated for the experiment, these results were not unexpected. Baudisch [1] identified that several objects need to be manipulated in one mouse drag to see a speed-up over single mouse clicks. The same insight holds true here. In our task, the sequences of consecutive objects with missing or misplaced tags were often no longer than three objects. For such short paths there is no speed benefit for path selection. Even though the quantitative measurements show that tapping was significantly faster, all but two users *rated* the path technique as faster. Users reported that they perceived tapping objects individually as tedious. Thus tapping many objects may seem to take longer than a few path gestures. The qualitative results further show that tapping was rated as both easier to learn and less error-prone. Yet, the perceived speed appears to dominate the overall rating.

The measured number of corrections should not be interpreted as an error rate. It is a combination of accidental errors and deliberately superfluous actions. With the path technique a few users added more tags than necessary and later removed them again. During debriefing three participants highlighted that they did this to chain smaller actions together, by cleverly combining add and remove operations. This behavior was not observed during the first study.

Kin et al. [11] have shown that experienced users can perform better by using more than one finger and tapping multiple objects at once. While our implementation supported this, during the experiment all users performed taps and pins with a single finger. Some users discovered the option to tap multiple objects at once, but reverted back to single tapping for the study. Although we only tested our interface on objects in a regular grid layout, previous work [3] suggests that path-based selection should also work for node networks with non-rectangular layouts. In our studies, users relied primarily on the tagging widgets to complete the task. Although pinning down (multiple) objects was always enabled, it was not used much. We plan to evaluate the object pinning aspect and the rectangle selection variant in more detail in the future.

DESIGN CONSIDERATIONS

Here we mention several design considerations for integrating our new technique into applications. It is not possible to present a single best variation of our technique, which fits all scenarios and devices. Thus, we present variations for different components of our interaction technique. However, all variants use the same underlying principle. The two main components, *i.e.*, defining a set of tags and selecting target objects, are independent of each other. This provides the flexibility to pick the best match to the target application and device combination. Moreover, object layout, *e.g.*, grid vs. random, also influences the choice of the "best" method to select multiple objects as well. We also discuss the need to adapt to different devices: not only for different screen sizes but also uni- vs. bi-manual input.

Necessity of Tagging Widgets

Pinning objects that already have the desired set of tags works best if related objects are close to each other. However, if there is no object nearby that can be used to *gather* the desired tags by pinning, an appropriately tagged object has to be found first. Assuming such an object exists, such a search could take time. But, if a tag has not been used yet, finding said tag among the objects is impossible. Another example is the removal of a single specific tag. The user would have to find and pin first an object that has only the desired tag(s). Thus another mechanism is necessary and the user can always use the tagging widgets at the side of the screen. when there is no object with the desired set of tags available (or it would simply take too long to find it).

Copying vs. Toggling vs. Combining Tags

There are several possibilities for applying a set of tags to one or more target objects. The simplest possibility is to copy the tags to all target objects, overwriting any previous tags—effectively *painting* the tags on the objects. However, for complex tag assignments this may require more steps than ideal. Adding another tag to differently tagged objects could become tedious, as existing tags would have to be re-selected, to avoid overwriting. We decided to permit a more expressive combination of tags, as presented. During early development we played with toggling all selected tags on target objects. Yet, toggling all tags simultaneously results in hard to predict changes. Thus we decided that the explicit choice of either adding or removing tags is a better alternative.

Adaptation to Smaller Devices

Depending on the used device, the presented tagging widgets might not be the best possible interface for accessing single tags. The two main factors are display size and if the device is operated using a single or both hands. While pinning objects and performing selections is possible with a single hand, it is much more limiting than bi-manual input. Yet, the behavior of the tagging widgets at the display border can be adjusted for uni-manual input by making them *also* toggle-able. On larger devices, such as tabletop displays, there is enough space for tag widgets at the border of the screen. This way any desired combination of tags can be activated at all times, independent of the tags currently assigned to the visible objects. Pinning tagged objects that are close to the objects being modified also remains useful. Large screens benefit from this *local* operation, as attention then does not need to be divided between the target area and the tagging widgets. For smaller multi-touch devices, such as smartphones or tablets, most often a single hand is used to interact, while the other hand is holding the device. Wagner et al. [24] provided an interesting related discussion. On small devices, a pop-up menu with selectable tags, activated with a single hold gesture, is likely a good alternative—it can be operated using a single hand and does not consume screen real estate, unless it is invoked. To resolve the ambiguity with a pin gesture, we cancel the menu if a second touch is registered.

Selecting Rectangular Groups of Objects

In addition to selecting objects crossed by a path, our technique can also support the selection of objects inside rectangular regions. Naturally, this depends on the usage scenario, object layout and application. To select a rectangular group of objects an area can be defined by dragging the diagonal of the rectangle. All objects intersecting or completely inside the

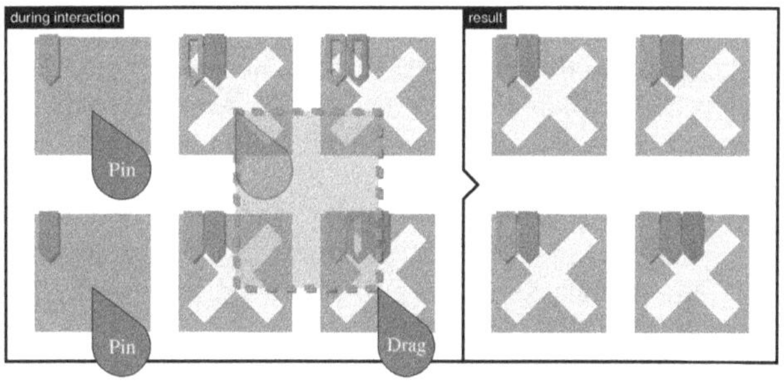

Figure 14. Dragging a rectangle selects all objects that are contained or intersecting it. As with the path technique the initial touch position of the dragging operation defines if the pinned tags are added (as shown here) or removed. Outlined tags preview impending changes.

rectangle are then selected. Figure 14 illustrates this idea. The mechanism for choosing the mode of operation, *i.e.*, if tags are to be added or removed from the selected objects, remains the same, *i.e.*, is based on the position of the first touch. Depending on the spatial layout and application context, rectangular or path selection is more useful. For cases when both are required, Saund et al.'s overloaded version of lasso and rectangle selection [21] is compatible with our work.

Simplification to a Single Group

Many existing applications support only selection of a single group. These can still benefit from the selection *editing* capabilities of our interface. In this scenario the interaction technique of pinning a selected object is still very useful for adding *additional* objects to an existing selection with a rectangle or path gesture. Yet, highlighting is likely more appropriate than a tag interface. This idea effectively enhances existing multi-touch group selection approaches, which typically do not support editing of a selection.

Selecting Overlapping Objects

If objects overlap each other it might not be possible to select the desired objects using a single selection operation. One of the benefits of our technique is its capability to easily extend and modify selections. The user can compose the desired set of objects through multiple selection steps. Harpoon [12] already demonstrated that *partially* overlapping objects can often still be selected using path-based techniques. For objects that completely overlap, a technique such as *Tumble! Splat!* [20] could be added to access occluded objects. Intelligent selection assistance systems such as *Suggero* [14] might also be helpful. If the background is completely covered by an object, *e.g.*, while the view is zoomed in, it is impossible to signal a subtraction by starting a path gesture on the background. In this case the editing gesture could be started on the bezel.

CONCLUSION AND FUTURE WORK

We introduced our new multi-touch tagging interface. It employs tag widgets to define multiple overlapping tag groups. One of its key features is the ability to easily edit existing tags by adding and removing items, even just for a single group. Our interface relies heavily on pin gestures, *i.e.*, holding touches, to provide a context for other actions performed at the same time. We validated our design in user studies and demonstrated that our tagging interface performs faster than alternative interfaces that rely on tapping of individual objects.

The work of Dehmeshki et al. [3] suggests that our path-based technique directly generalizes to other, non-rectangular layouts and we will explore this. We also plan to investigate what other interaction tasks could benefit from pinning.

REFERENCES WITH CLASSIFIER TAGS

1. Baudisch, P. Don't Click, Paint! Using Toggle Maps to Manipulate Sets of Toggle Switches. In *Proc. UIST '98*, ACM (1998), 65–66.
2. Dehmeshki, H. and Stuerzlinger, W. Design and Evaluation of a Perceptual-based Object Group Selection Technique. In *Proc. BCS '10*, (2010), 365–373. INDIRECT, CROSSING, ON/OFF OBJECTS, PATH, AUTO MODE.
3. Dehmeshki, H. and Stuerzlinger, W. GPSel: A Gestural Perceptual-Based Path Selection Technique. In *Proc. SG '09*, (2009), 243–252. PEN, PATH, CROSSING, SURROUND, INDIRECT, OBJECTS, LASSO, AUTO MODE.
4. Dehmeshki, H. and Stuerzlinger, W. ICE-Lasso: An enhanced form of Lasso selection. In *Proc. TIC-STH '09*, IEEE, (2009), 630–635. PEN, LASSO, OBJECTS, IN/OUT, INDIRECT, SURROUND.
5. Dehmeshki, H. and Stuerzlinger, W. Intelligent Mouse-Based Object Group Selection. In *Proc. SG '08*, Springer (2008), 33–44. MOUSE, OBJECTS, DIRECT, INDIRECT.
6. Gutwin, C., Cockburn, A., Scarr, J., Malacria, S., and Olson, S. C. Faster Command Selection on Tablets with FastTap. In *Proc. CHI '14*, ACM (2014), 2617–2626.
7. Hinckley, K., Guimbretiere, F., Agrawala, M., Apitz, G., and Chen, N. Phrasing Techniques for Multi-stroke Selection Gestures. In *Proc. GI '06*, CIPS (2006), 147–154. PEN, CROSSING, LASSO, SURROUND, INDIRECT, DIRECT, OBJECTS, IN/OUT, AUTO MODE.
8. Hinckley, K., Guimbretiere, F., Baudisch, P., Sarin, R., Agrawala, M., and Cutrell, E. The Springboard: Multiple Modes in One Spring-loaded Control. In *Proc. CHI '06*, ACM (2006), 181–190.
9. Hinckley, K., Yatani, K., Pahud, M., Coddington, N., Rodenhouse, J., Wilson, A., Benko, H., and Buxton, B. Pen + Touch = New Tools. In *Proc. UIST '10*, ACM (2010), 27–36.
10. Kawasaki, Y. and Igarashi, T. Regional undo for spreadsheets. In *Adjunct Proceedings of UIST '04*, ACM (2004), 2 pages. MOUSE, REGION.
11. Kin, K., Agrawala, M., and DeRose, T. Determining the Benefits of Direct-touch, Bimanual, and Multifinger Input on a Multitouch Workstation. In *Proc. GI '09*, CIPS (2009), 119–124.
12. Leitner, J. and Haller, M. Harpoon Selection: Efficient Selections for Ungrouped Content on Large Pen-based Surfaces. In *Proc. UIST '11*, ACM (2011), 593–602. PEN, CROSSING, SURROUND, INDIRECT, DIRECT, LASSO, OBJECTS, PATH.
13. Li, Y., Hinckley, K., Guan, Z., and Landay, J. A. Experimental Analysis of Mode Switching Techniques in Pen-based User Interfaces. In *Proc. CHI '05*, ACM (2005), 461–470.
14. Lindlbauer, D., Haller, M., Hancock, M., Scott, S. D., and Stuerzlinger, W. Perceptual Grouping: Selection Assistance for Digital Sketching. In *Proc. ITS '13*, ACM (2013), 51–60. PEN, CROSSING, INDIRECT, DIRECT, OBJECTS, PATH.
15. Luo, Y. and Vogel, D. Crossing-based Selection with Direct Touch Input. In *Proc. CHI '14*, ACM (2014), 2627–2636.
16. Mizobuchi, S. and Yasumura, M. Tapping vs. Circling Selections on Pen-based Devices: Evidence for Different Performance-shaping Factors. In *Proc. CHI '04*, ACM (2004), 607–614. PEN, OBJECTS, LASSO, DIRECT, INDIRECT, SURROUND.
17. Moran, T. P., Chiu, P., and Melle, W. van. Pen-based Interaction Techniques for Organizing Material on an Electronic Whiteboard. In *Proc. UIST '97*, ACM (1997), 45–54. PEN, IN/OUT, LASSO, RECTANGLE, REGION, AUTO MODE.
18. Moscovich, T. and Hughes, J. F. Indirect Mappings of Multi-touch Input Using One and Two Hands. In *Proc. CHI 2008*, ACM (2008), 1275–1284.
19. North, C., Dwyer, T., Lee, B., Fisher, D., Isenberg, P., Robertson, G., and Inkpen, K. "Understanding Multi-touch Manipulation for Surface Computing". In *Human-Computer Interaction INTERACT 2009*, vol. 5727. LNCS. Springer Berlin Heidelberg (2009), 236–249. TOUCH, OBJECTS, DIRECT, INDIRECT, SURROUND, ON/OFF OBJECTS, HOLD, PIN, MULTI-TOUCH.
20. Ramos, G., Robertson, G., Czerwinski, M., Tan, D., Baudisch, P., Hinckley, K., and Agrawala, M. Tumble! Splat! Helping Users Access and Manipulate Occluded Content in 2D Drawings. In *Proc. AVI '06*, ACM (2006), 428–435.
21. Saund, E., Fleet, D., Larner, D., and Mahoney, J. Perceptually-supported Image Editing of Text and Graphics. In *Proc. UIST '03*, ACM (2003), 183–192. MOUSE, RECTANGLE, LASSO, ON/OFF OBJECTS, REGION, OBJECTS, DIRECT.
22. Seifried, T., Rendl, C., Haller, M., and Scott, S. Regional Undo/Redo Techniques for Large Interactive Surfaces. In *Proc. CHI '12*, ACM (2012), 2855–2864. PEN, SURROUND, OBJECTS, REGION.
23. Strothoff, S. and Hinrichs, K. Adding Context to Multi-touch Region Selections. In *Proc. MUM '13*, ACM (2013), 15:1–15:8. TOUCH, IN/OUT, RECTANGLE, REGION, MULTI-TOUCH, AUTO MODE.
24. Wagner, J., Huot, S., and Mackay, W. BiTouch and BiPad: Designing Bimanual Interaction for Hand-held Tablets. In *Proc. CHI '12*, ACM (2012), 2317–2326.
25. Wobbrock, J. O., Morris, M. R., and Wilson, A. D. User-defined Gestures for Surface Computing. In *Proc. CHI '09*, ACM (2009), 1083–1092.
26. Xu, P., Fu, H., Au, O. K.-C., and Tai, C.-L. Lazy Selection: A Scribble-based Tool for Smart Shape Elements Selection. *ACM Trans. Graph. 31*, 6 (Nov. 2012), 142:1–142:9. TOUCH, CROSSING, OBJECTS, CROSSING, DIRECT, INDIRECT, PATH.

Personal Device as a Controller for Interactive Surfaces – Usability and Utility of Different Connection Methods

Jouni Vepsäläinen[†], **Antonella Di Rienzo**[‡], **Matti Nelimarkka**[¬], **Jouni A. Ojala**[¬], **Petri Savolainen**[¬], **Kai Kuikkaniemi**[¬], **Sasu Tarkoma**[†], **Giulio Jacucci**[†]
†University of Helsinki, Finland, firstname.lastname@helsinki.fi
‡Politecnico di Milano, Italy, antonella.dirienzo@polimi.it
¬ HIIT / Aalto University / University of Helsinki, Finland, firstname.lastname@hiit.fi

ABSTRACT

The popularity of touch-screen-equipped smart phones has made them an attractive choice for interacting with large display surfaces, especially in public spaces. The challenge in using a personal mobile device for interaction in such a setting lies in the usability of methods to initiate the interaction, as the users may give up if the interaction is not immediately successful. For this reason, a few commercial systems have already opted to use web-based interaction instead of dedicated mobile applications. However, the usability of different methods of initiating the web-based interaction has not been extensively studied. In this paper we present the results of a laboratory usability study with 20 participants, in which we studied how the users experienced four different methods of initiating web-based interaction between a smart phone and a large display surface. The compared initiation methods were NFC, QR code, typing an URL and connecting to a WiFi access point. Additionally, in order to study how the users experienced the quality of the connection, the first three methods were used over 3G. Our results indicate typing an URL to be the most usable method for initiating the connection between the smart phone and the large display surface. The difference in quality between the 3G and WiFi connections was deemed hardly noticeable by the subjects. We acknowledge that our results are only preliminary, and the subject needs to be studied in a more realistic setting to get a more comprehensive picture.

Author Keywords

connection method; public display; game;

ACM Classification Keywords

H.5.2 User Interfaces: Evaluation/methodology

INTRODUCTION

Using personal mobile devices for controlling large display surfaces has become an viable option, as smart phones with touch screens and various connectivity options have become commonplace. Using a personal mobile device provides an opportunity to use personal content [14], and allows several users to use the same display at the same time without breaking social boundaries [13, 10]. Furthermore, using personal devices as remote control makes it posible to use ordinary displays as interactive screens, without the need of additional hardware such as movement sensors.

Researches have previously examined how dedicated mobile applications could be used for controlling interactive screens [2, 8, 16]. The downside of this approach is that installing an app can be too time-consuming and cumbersome to attract users to interact with a public screen. A faster approach is to redirect the web browser of the mobile device to a web page that acts as the screen controller. Commercial systems that have chosen this approach include NoviSign[1], CAYIN[2] and Scala[3], all of which use QR codes as their primary method for redirecting the mobile browser to the controller web page. However, little research about the usability and utility of different connection methods has been conducted.

In this paper we present a laboratory usability study with 20 subjects, where we compare the usability of four methods of initiating web-based interaction between a smart phone and a large display surface. We compare using NFC, QR code, typing an URL, and connecting to a WiFi access point as methods for redirecting the mobile browser to the screen controller web page. Additionally, in order to study how the users experience the connection quality in latency-sensitive applications such as games, we chose 3G as the data connection to be used in the NFC, QR code, and URL methods. We chose 3G instead of 4G as the mobile data connection to be compared against the WiFi in order to find out how users perceive the connection quality when there is a clear difference in the measured latency. We excluded using Bluetooth as a data connection in this study because Bluetooth web APIs are not widely available on current mobile web browsers.

Our results show typing an URL to be the most usable method for initiating the connection between the smart phone and the large display surface. The difference in quality between the 3G and WiFi connections was deemed hardly noticeable by the subjects, even though the measured round-trip times of 3G were 1.5 times longer on the average.

ITS '15, November 15-18, 2015, Funchal, Portugal
Copyright © 2015 ACM. ISBN 978-1-4503-3899-8/15/11$15.00
DOI: http://dx.doi.org/10.1145/2817721.2817745

[1] `http://www.novisign.com/signage-widgets/games/`
[2] `http://www.cayintech.com/digital_signage_solutions/QR_code_digital_signage.html`
[3] `http://scala.com/explore/mobile-social/`

RELATED WORK

In recent years, the emerging field of pervasive display systems [11, 9] and developments in interaction techniques enabling the use of mobile devices with large screens [12, 3, 14] have attracted attention in the research community. While several arguments indicate that mobile phones are well suited as mediator device for mobile mediated interaction, the question arises what interaction techniques and communication technologies are practical.

In the Spaceify smart space system [15], Savolainen et al. used connecting to a WiFi access point as the primary method of initiating interaction with space resources such as big screens. Hardy and Rukzio implemented the Touch & Interact technique based on NFC [7], which allowed basic interaction with grids of NFC tags augmented displays using an NFC phone and an application running on it. Alt et al. presented Digifieds [1], a platform for creating digital classified ads on public displays and elaborated on mobile phone-based interaction techniques to exchange content with the display using QR codes.

Several dedicated mobile applications for achieving interaction with public displays have been developed, with different connectivity options such as Bluetooth, WiFi, SMS and MMS [5, 17]. MAGIC Broker [6] allowed interaction using SMS, the WWW and speech. Anzures et al. [2] exploited mobile devices as game pads for controlling multi-user applications on public screens - an SWFLoader application installed on the mobile devices enabled WiFi communication to the screen. Jin et al. [8] explored how to initialize file transfer between an interactive surface and a mobile device, and notably, compared using QR codes and WiFi as the connection method.

We see these approaches interesting, but want to further understand how people perceive these different approaches to control an interactive surface. We highlight that to allow in situ use, installing a separate application should not be required, but instead, applications commonly available on the mobile devices, such as web browsers and QR code readers should suffice. Thus, we focus on examining methods that can be used for initializing web-based interaction.

EMPIRICAL APPROACH

The goal of our study was to compare the usability and utility of different methods of connecting mobile devices to a public screen without requiring the user to install any dedicated mobile applications.

We conducted the study with four different connection methods to access the service: a) opening a web browser and typing the controller URL (`spaceify.net`), b) starting a barcode reader application to read a QR code to open a browser to the controller URL, c) turning on the NFC functionality of the phone and reading an NFC tag to open a web browser to the controller URL, d) joining a WLAN, opening a web browser and typing *any* URL, after which the access point would automatically redirect the browser to the controller web page. We examined the differences of usability between these connection methods, as well as the perceived connection quality between the 3G and WiFi connections.

To entice participants to our study we had as an incentive a reward for everyone (approximately 15 USD) and provided additional reward three times higher to person who scored best in the game. To study the connection methods, we had a total of 20 participants, all of which tested using all of the methods. The participants consisted of 7 females and 13 males and their ages ranged from 21 to 62 years ($\bar{x}$ = 35.95, SD = 11.218). To ensure technical system compatibility, all participants used an Android device provided by the research team. The big-screen service used in this study was a shooting gallery game, presented in detail in the following subsection.

In order to ensure all the participants would have the minimum skill level to complete the tasks, so that our experiment could measure actual usability intead the skill level of the individual participants, the participants were first trained to use each connection method. The training was conducted by verbally instructing each participant on how to use each connection method to open a regular web page (`hiit.fi`). The training was considered completed after the participant had opened the web page using all four connection methods.

After the training, the participants were tasked to play a round of the game on the big-screen using each connection method in succession. Each task was given written on a piece of paper that the participants may keep during completing the task. This ensured that the participants would not forget the URL or the name of the WiFi network. After each round, they were asked to evaluate the experience of the specific connection method using the System Usability Scale (SUS) [4]. Finally, the participants were asked to play a fifth round of the game in which they could freely choose the connection method.

To reduce potential learning effect, fatigue and other error factors, we randomized the order the connection methods were trained in, and the order in which the tasks were given.

Interactive surface application used in the study

The application used in the study was a shooting gallery game called "Ducks and Pirates". In the game, players control a crosshair on the big-screen with a mobile device, and try to collect points by shooting ducks and other objects moving on the big-screen. The big-screen runs a web browser and displays the game graphics using WebGL. The big-screen browser is connected to the game server on the Internet over a WebSocket connection. The players are also connected to the game server over WebSocket connections, using a HTML5 page that emulates an analog gamepad for controlling the game on the big-screen. Figure 1 shows a player playing the game using a mobile device, and a screenshot of the emulated gamepad.

Measurements and methods

The System Usability Scale (SUS) includes ten standardized questions that evaluate the usability on a Likert-scale. We specifically asked the participants to consider the usability of the connection method only, not the game experience. We analyzed these using standard statistical methods of ANOVA to compare the SUS score between each of the four connection methods. Furthermore, we tested for ordering effect by SUS score for each connection method by comparing the different

Figure 1. The system setup for the study and the emulated gamepad used for controlling the game.

Table 1. Descriptive statistics on the usability scores

	NFC	QR	URL	WiFi
min	50.00	57.50	42.50	32.50
1st Q	60.62	71.25	77.50	56.88
median	71.25	77.50	82.50	73.75
mean	72.64	79.61	81.88	70.75
3rd Q	81.88	92.50	90.00	82.50
max	100.00	100.00	100.00	95.00

rounds it was used. During these surveys, we also collected standard background data on participants' use and knowledge regarding smart phones.

The round trip time (RTT) was measured every time the player fired a shot in the game using a small (size under 100 bytes) JSON-formatted message. We compared connection methods that used the 3G connection (QR-code, NFC and typing an URL) to the WiFi connection method. For the comparison, we applied Wilcox's test between these groups, as we expected the RTTs to be clearly non-normally distributed.

Finally, we asked the participants for a final summative evaluation on the connection methods and gaming experience, especially in terms of different connection methods and their impact on the gaming experience.

RESULTS

Usability of connection methods

Participants evaluated each method using the System Usability Score (SUS), ranging from 0 to 100 points. We observe that overall all connection methods were evaluated high on overall usability (see Fig. 2). We further provide descriptive statistics on Table 1. Users experienced the URL connection method the best, also with lowest variance. We also observe that the score of the WiFi connection method had the highest variance and especially its minimum scores were lower than other connection methods.

We statistically confirmed that the difference on the methods was significant under the 10%-margin for error (F-value 2.354, df = 3, p = 0.079). Thus, we continued to pair-wise analysis using the Wilcox's test between different methods.

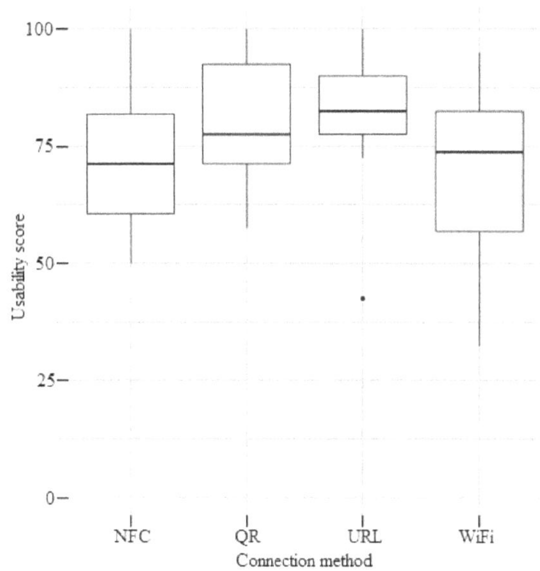

Figure 2. Usability score per connection method

Through this data analysis, we conclude that the statistical significance is lead by the URL method outperforming both NFC and WiFi on statistically significant levels ($p_{\mathrm{URL,NFC}} = 0.073$, $W_{\mathrm{URL,NFC}} = 241.5$, $p_{\mathrm{URL,WiFi}} = 0.053$, $W_{\mathrm{URL,WiFi}} = 271.5$). Other pair-wise comparisons were not significant at 10%-level.

Lastly, we examined for potential ordering effects in this study, but can not statistically observe any effects, the highest F-value was 1.554 (df = 3, p = 0.239), well above the 10%-margin. Thus we conclude that the differences stated above were not caused e.g. on fatigue on the test settings.

The quality of the connection

We measured the connection quality using round trip time (RTT) as our metric. Not surprisingly, the WiFi had a significantly lower RTT than the 3G (W = 4755700, $p < 0.001$). In practice, WiFi connections were on median twice as responsive as the 3G connections, and on average 1.5 times more responsive.

Summative experience

The summative evaluations after the gaming showed that most of the participants did not experience differences in playability between the connection methods. Rather, 16 participants said that they observed no difference based on the method they used to connect. Although WiFi had the lowest latency, only one subject was able to notice this definitely. The other three made vague observations of changes in responsiveness or of nonspecific differences. In general, the rationale related to WiFi being fastest did not apply in our study. The 3G connection was fast enough not to make any noticeable difference.

DISCUSSION AND FUTURE WORK

The connection method that acheived the highest SUS score in our study was typing an URL, with high medium and high minimum values. We suggest that this might be related to familiarity of the browser as an environment compared to tag-based environments or configuring the WiFi settings.

We acknowledge that this is only an indicatory study, and more work is needed before final verdicts can be passed on choosing the connection method between the mobile device and public screen. As our future work, we plan to install Ducks and Pirates in various public locations, and observe in the real life, which connection methods people prefer outside the laboratory setting.

REFERENCES

1. Florian Alt, Alireza Sahami Shirazi, Thomas Kubitza, and Albrecht Schmidt. 2013. Interaction Techniques for Creating and Exchanging Content with Public Displays. In *Proceedings of the SIGCHI Conference on Human Factors in Computing Systems (CHI '13)*. ACM, New York, NY, USA, 1709–1718. DOI: http://dx.doi.org/10.1145/2470654.2466226
2. Herón Anzures and Sonia Mendoza. 2011. Multi-user interaction with public screens using mobile devices. In *Electrical Engineering Computing Science and Automatic Control (CCE), 2011 8th International Conference on*. IEEE, 1–5.
3. Till Ballendat, Nicolai Marquardt, and Saul Greenberg. 2010. Proxemic Interaction: Designing for a Proximity and Orientation-aware Environment. In *ACM International Conference on Interactive Tabletops and Surfaces (ITS '10)*. ACM, New York, NY, USA, 121–130. DOI: http://dx.doi.org/10.1145/1936652.1936676
4. John Brooke. 1996. SUS-A quick and dirty usability scale. *Usability evaluation in industry* 189, 194 (June 1996), 4–7.
5. Nigel Davies, Adrian Friday, Peter Newman, Sarah Rutlidge, and Oliver Storz. 2009. Using bluetooth device names to support interaction in smart environments. In *Proceedings of the 7th international conference on Mobile systems, applications, and services*. ACM, 151–164.
6. Aiman Erbad, Michael Blackstock, Adrian Friday, Rodger Lea, and Jalal Al-Muhtadi. 2008. Magic broker: A middleware toolkit for interactive public displays. In *Pervasive Computing and Communications, 2008. PerCom 2008. Sixth Annual IEEE International Conference on*. IEEE, 509–514.
7. Robert Hardy and Enrico Rukzio. 2008. Touch & Interact: Touch-based Interaction of Mobile Phones with Displays. In *Proceedings of the 10th International Conference on Human Computer Interaction with Mobile Devices and Services (MobileHCI '08)*. ACM, New York, NY, USA, 245–254. DOI: http://dx.doi.org/10.1145/1409240.1409267
8. Huiliang Jin, Tao Xu, B. David, and R. Chalon. 2014. Direct migrator: Eliminating borders between personal mobile devices and pervasive displays. In *Pervasive Computing and Communications Workshops (PERCOM Workshops), 2014 IEEE International Conference on*. 557–562. DOI: http://dx.doi.org/10.1109/PerComW.2014.6815267
9. Kai Kuikkaniemi, Giulio Jacucci, Marko Turpeinen, Eve Hoggan, and Jörg Müller. 2011. From space to stage: How interactive screens will change urban life. *Computer* 6 (2011), 40–47.
10. Kai Kuikkaniemi, Vilma Lehtinen, Matti Nelimarkka, Max Vilkki, Jouni Ojala, and Giulio Jacucci. 2014. Designing for presenters at public walk-up-and-use displays. In *Proceedings of the 8th International Conference on Tangible, Embedded and Embodied Interaction - TEI '14*. ACM Press, 225–232. DOI: http://dx.doi.org/10.1145/2540930.2540949
11. Jörg Müller, Florian Alt, and Daniel Michelis. 2011. *Pervasive advertising*. Springer.
12. Nick Pears, Daniel G. Jackson, and Patrick Olivier. 2009. Smart Phone Interaction with Registered Displays. *IEEE Pervasive Computing* 8, 2 (April 2009), 14–21. DOI: http://dx.doi.org/10.1109/MPRV.2009.35
13. Peter Peltonen, Esko Kurvinen, Antti Salovaara, Giulio Jacucci, Tommi Ilmonen, John Evans, Antti Oulasvirta, and Petri Saarikko. 2008. It's Mine, Don't Touch!: interactions at a large multi-touch display in a city centre. In *Proceedings of the SIGCHI Conference on Human Factors in Computing Systems*. ACM, 1285–1294.
14. Markus Rittenbruch. 2015. Supporting Collaboration on Very Large-Scale Interactive Wall Surfaces. *Computer Supported Cooperative Work (CSCW)* 24, 2-3 (2015), 121–147. DOI: http://dx.doi.org/10.1007/s10606-015-9221-x
15. Petri Savolainen, Sumi Helal, Jukka Reitmaa, Kai Kuikkaniemi, Giulio Jacucci, Mikko Rinne, Marko Turpeinen, and Sasu Tarkoma. 2013. Spaceify: A client-edge-server ecosystem for mobile computing in smart spaces. In *Proceedings of the 19th annual international conference on Mobile computing & networking*. ACM, 211–214.
16. James She, Jon Crowcroft, Hao Fu, and Pin-Han Ho. 2014. Smart Signage: A Draggable Cyber-Physical Broadcast/Multicast Media System. *IEEE Transactions on Emerging Topics in Computing* 1, 2 (21 January 2014), 232–243.
17. Anthony Tang, Mattias Finke, Michael Blackstock, Rock Leung, Meghan Deutscher, and Rodger Lea. 2008. Designing for bystanders: reflections on building a public digital forum. In *Proceedings of the SIGCHI Conference on Human Factors in Computing Systems*. ACM, 879–882.

Reducing Latency with a Continuous Prediction: Effects on Users' Performance in Direct-Touch Target Acquisitions

Elie Cattan[1], Amélie Rochet-Capellan[2], Pascal Perrier[2], François Bérard[1]

LIG, University of Grenoble[1]
Grenoble, France
{first.last}@imag.fr

GIPSA-lab, University of Grenoble[2]
Grenoble, France
{first.last}@gipsa-lab.grenoble-inp.fr

ABSTRACT

Latency in direct-touch systems creates a spatial gap between the finger and the digital object when dragging. This breaks the illusion of presence, and has a negative effect on users' performances in common tasks such as target acquisitions. Latency can be reduced with faster hardware, but reaching imperceptible levels of latency with a hardware-only approach is a difficult challenge and an energy inefficient solution.

We studied the use of a continuous prediction of the touch location as an alternative to the hardware only approach to reduce the latency gap. We implemented a low latency touch surface and experimented with a constant speed linear prediction with various system latencies in the range [25ms-75ms]. We ran a user experiment to objectively assess the benefits of the prediction on users' performances in target acquisition tasks. Our study reveals that the prediction length is strongly constrained by the nature of target acquisition tasks, but that the approach can be successfully applied to counteract a large part of the negative effect of latency on users' performances.

ACM Classification Keywords

H.5.2 User Interfaces: Input devices and strategies (e.g., mouse, touchscreen)

Author Keywords

latency; direct-touch; dragging task; continuous prediction; target-acquisition; user performances

INTRODUCTION

Direct touch is a key element of the success of touch-sensitive devices, giving the sensation of moving digital objects with a direct contact of a finger. However, the immediacy of direct touch interaction and its "naturalness" comes up against a technical limit: the latency of the system, defined as the delay between a user action and the feedback of this action. With direct touch, latency materializes as a spatial gap between the finger and the virtual object under control. Latency in direct touch systems can be perceived at levels as low as 2ms [15], and it was shown to deteriorate users' target acquisition performances at levels as low as 10ms [7]. However, current commercial touch-sensitive devices still suffer from latencies in the range [50ms-200ms] [15], providing a sub-optimal experience to the users and a decrease in performances. The spatial gap induced by latency increases when the finger is moving faster to cover larger distances. This amplifies the negative effect of latency on large interactive surfaces compared to smaller devices such as tablet computers or smartphones. The omnipresent hindrance induced by latency may conceal the benefits of novel forms of direct touch interactions. The compensation of hardware latency is thus a core challenge for interaction designers on large interactive surfaces.

A radical way to eliminate the negative effects of latency is to develop a touch system that has a small enough latency that it is not perceived by users. Ng et al. built such a system and reached 1ms of latency by using custom developed sensor, processing and display hardware [15]. This *pure hardware* approach was successful in providing an experimental device that allowed detailed studies on the perception and on the effect of latency. However, achieving 1ms of latency came at the cost of strong limitations: the system could not display color, it had a width of only 24cm, and the software had to run on an embedded real-time OS, hence it could not rely on common OSes and their graphics libraries. The display part of the system also appears as a bottleneck: going from the vast majority of current 60Hz display refresh rate to the 1kHz refresh rate of Ng et al. [15] requires a 17x improvement which is a major technical challenge. Besides, augmenting the display refresh rate for the sole purpose of reducing the latency gap appears as a very inefficient use of computing and energy resources. As such, the approach does not appear as a practicable solution to the latency problem in general purpose direct touch systems.

Here, we study the benefits of using a *software prediction*. With prediction, the virtual object under control is not displayed at the most recently sensed location of the finger, but rather at a location predicted based on the finger's past trajectory. Compensating latency with prediction has been well studied in various domains such as robotics and virtual reality. In the HCI literature, prediction has been used to anticipate which target a user is aiming at. A *single* prediction was made well before the end of the acquisition in order to guess the *end-point* of a user controlled trajectory [2, 4, 8, 16]. These

ITS 2015, November 15–18, 2015, Funchal/Madeira, Portugal.

ACM 978-1-4503-3899-8/15/11 ...$15.00.
DOI: http://dx.doi.org/10.1145/2817721.2817736

efforts dealt with "large" prediction errors by requiring final user adjustments. The single prediction approach was also successfully used in direct touch in order to achieve "zero-latency tapping" [20]. In this paper, we tackle a different problem as we use the prediction to *continuously* reduce the gap between the finger and the digital object while dragging. This poses the challenge of predicting a "no-latency" position at every sample. However, predicting the future always come with uncertainty, which is a source of tracking mismatch on its own. A predictive approach is only useful if the benefits of reducing the latency gap surpass the negative effects of the prediction mismatch. While device makers have started to use continuous predictions to reduce touch latency on mobile devices [18], the prediction is limited in length (16ms) and only attempts to partially compensate the device's latency. There is no published work that informs about the amount of latency that can be compensated through a continuous prediction and, more fundamentally, that provides an objective evaluation of the benefits of the prediction on users' performances.

In this work, we studied the total compensation of a device's latency through continuous prediction. We selected users' performances in target acquisitions as an objective measure of the benefits of the prediction. The target acquisitions were performed by sliding a digital object onto a target location, which we chose as the most common direct touch dragging interaction. In order to experiment with low levels of system latency, we created an experimental device with a baseline latency of 25ms. By artificially adding delays to this baseline, we could experiment with higher system latencies at 42ms, 58ms and 75ms. Our main objective is to inform about the levels of latency where a continuous prediction is a viable approach to users' performance improvements.

In the remainder of the paper, we review previous work related to the effect of latency on HCI and to the use of users' motion predictions. We then describe our experimental apparatus, and our software prediction approach. We next report on the user study that evaluates the benefits of this prediction on user's performances. We also provide an indication of user's preferences when comparing the system with and without prediction in target acquisitions and free-movement tasks. We finally discuss the results of the study in regard to the effect of latency on touch interaction and the feasibility of prediction in current systems.

RELATED WORK

Effects of latency

The detrimental effect of latency on HCI has been investigated from different viewpoints: from the subjective annoyance felt by users to the more objective measurement of degradations in users' performance. Studying visual immersion, Meehan et al. compared users' self reported sense of presence and measured the change of heart rate when moving from a calm to a stressful virtual environment, under two conditions of latency: 50ms and 90ms [13]. They found that participants in the low latency condition had a higher sense of presence and a higher change in heart rate. More recently, Ng et al. used the just noticeable difference (JND) protocol to objectively explore users' ability to perceive latencies on touch screens [15]. With an experimental device having only 1ms of latency, they showed that participants were able to perceive latencies only 6ms above the baseline on average, with some participants reaching 2ms. In another study, the ability to perceive latency was found to be strongly dependent on the task [14]. Using a stylus, the perceivable latency was found to be smaller when dragging a small square (2ms) compared to a big square (6ms) and to scribbling (40ms). This higher perceptual threshold for more demanding tasks was confirmed by Annett et al.: the threshold was found around 53ms for writing or drawing [1]. Recent work from Deber et al. [5] confirms that the latency is more perceivable with direct interaction compared to indirect, and they show that small improvements of latency (e.g. 8ms) are noticeable from a wide range of baseline latencies, particularly when dragging. These studies indicate that even though very small level of latencies are perceivable, it may or may not be considered an annoyance by users depending on their expectations from the system and the task being performed.

Rather than *explicitly* asking participants about their perception of latency, an *implicit* effect of latency can be observed by measuring users' performances in the execution of a common task such as target acquisition. This was studied by MacKenzie and Ware for regular mouse interaction [12]. By testing 8ms, 25ms, 75ms and 225ms of latency, they showed its strong negative effect on user's performance, with the movement time increasing by 63% and error rate jumping from 9% to 21% when latency increased from 8ms to 225ms. Users' performance also degraded between 25ms and 75ms of latency, but *not* between 8ms and 25ms. Ivkovic et al. ran a similar experiment with mouse pointing but for a central reticule-aiming task [6]. They observed performance degradation when varying latency from 164ms down to 41ms, but not between 41ms and 11ms. Although not studying exactly the same pointing tasks, these two studies considered together indicate that a threshold of the influence of latency on (indirect) mouse interaction is in the range [41ms-75ms]. Ivkovic et al. also demonstrated that latency could be efficiently counteracted by the use of a target-aware "sticky target" technique. With the widespread diffusion of direct-touch interaction through smart-phones and tablet computers, the influence of latency on users' performance came back as a major concern. Using the same 1ms latency hardware as Ng et al [15], Jota et al. studied users' performances for a dragging task [7]. Contrary to mouse interaction, the detrimental influence of latency was found at levels lower than 41ms. By doing a linear regression on their experimental data, the authors suggest that there may not be a floor effect and that users' performance may increase as long as latency decreases, at least down to 1ms. However, due to the constrained size of the experimental device, only "easy" dragging tasks were tested with the highest Fitts' Index of Difficulty (ID) at 2.58bit. Thanks to the availability of a larger touch device, our work extends these results to a more common range of IDs including "difficult" targets up to ID=6.3bit.

Predicting trajectories in HCI

Prediction has been used in several research efforts in an attempt to speed up target acquisition in pointing tasks. Asano et al. made a target prediction based on the peak velocity of the pointer [2]. Subsequent efforts studied more complex models of prediction: motion kinematics [8], neural networks and Kalman filters [4], and kinematic template matching [16]. In all these efforts, complex models are used to address the challenge of a long prediction: there are typically several hundreds of milliseconds between the date of the prediction, at the beginning of the pointing gesture, and the final target acquisition. The prediction is never accurate enough to automatically select the target, and final adjustments from the user are expected. The most recent efforts involve the learning of the model's parameters from example trajectories [4, 16]. Our work focuses on similar target acquisition tasks, although the approach is quite different: rather than guessing which target the user is pointing at, we improve the coupling between the user's finger and the virtual object, aiming at the ideal zero latency condition that would allow users to perform the task with optimal performances.

Xia et al. recently studied the use of a prediction as a means to reduce latency in direct touch systems, however they focused on tapping tasks, i.e. when the finger makes the first contact on the surface [20]. Using the hovering trajectory of the finger before it touches the surface, they predicted both the endpoint of the movement and the touch time by fitting a parabola on the current trajectory and using a linear extrapolation on the last phase of the gesture. The system was able to provide an immediate feedback when the user was tapping, virtually removing the latency of the system. Our work shares the same objective, but we focus on dragging instead of tapping.

Our approach finds its inspiration in the efforts to create visual immersion in Virtual Reality systems. Latency has long been acknowledged as a bottleneck for visual immersion: it is a source of simulator sickness [9] and may completely break the illusion of presence [19]. Continuous predictions of the user's head position and orientation have been used in various attempts to compensate latency. Lengthy predictions were used to deal with large latencies, typically in the range of 300ms [19]. However, as improvements in sensing and display have reduced systems' latency, more simple prediction models were used. LaViola showed that a prediction based on simple linear regressions performed as well as extended Kalman filters when predicting head pose for 50ms and 100ms [10]. More recently, LaValle et al. discussed the predictive methods used in the popular Oculus rift HMD [9]. The method predicts head orientation for 20ms and 40ms using only "a few milliseconds of data" from 1kHz sampling of angular velocity, and a simple constant acceleration model. The authors emphasize the requirements for a successful prediction: dense, accurate sensor data, and a limited length of the prediction. Our work follows the same path of using only the most recently sensed data, a simple prediction model, and a short prediction. We aim at discovering if and how the same convergence of fast hardware and accurate enough prediction can be successful. Compared to visual immersion, direct touch faces the challenge of touch sensors reporting positions rather than speed, and usually at a much lower sample rate. In addition, direct-touch interaction has different requirements and may be even more sensitive to latency, as hinted by the results from Jota et al. [7].

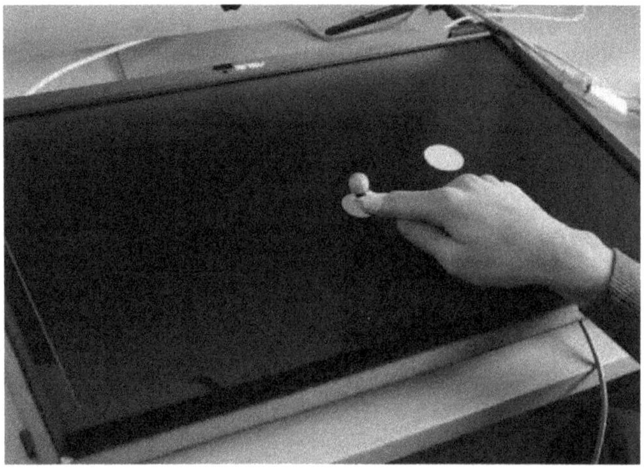

Figure 1. The experimental system in use during the experiment. The finger is localized by optical tracking using a marker. Users touch the red disc to bring it into the white target.

The soon to be released iOS 9 mobile operating system offers touch prediction services in order to reduce direct touch latency [18]. While the details of the predictive algorithm are not published, the system uses the 120Hz touch sampling of the iPad Air 2 to provide positions predicted 16.7ms in the future (i.e. one 60Hz display period). With the iOS rendering pipeline, the prediction theoretically reduces the latency to 1.5 display period (25ms). We follow the same continuous prediction approach to reduce latency, but we experiment with a larger interactive surface that is subjected to more visible lag due to faster dragging. We also experiment with longer predictions in an attempt to entirely compensate the system's latency. We finally provide an objective assessment of the prediction efficiency by measuring its effect on users' performance.

EXPERIMENTAL SYSTEM

A low latency direct-touch surface

Previous efforts indicate that users' performances in target acquisition are very sensitive to tracking errors: even a small gap created by 10ms of latency has a detrimental effect on performances [7]. We thus anticipated that the continuous prediction approach might not work for long predictions meant to compensate the high latencies of currently available commercial devices: for any prediction model, the longer the prediction, and the larger the predicted error. We thus built a specific touch device that allowed us to test various levels of latency starting at 25ms. However, contrary to the system used by Ng. et al [15], our system only relied on off-the-shelves hardware that did not deviate too far from the capabilities of standard direct touch hardware. In particular, our system used a standard monitor that offers a width of 52cm and a color display, and the software used a standard rendering pipeline on a common OS.

A 24inch Asus VG248E 1920x1080 LCD display without its foot and horizontally set on a desk was used as the direct-touch surface. The display was set in a "game mode" which disabled any processing on the video signal to provide fast response time. The display was driven at a refresh rate of 120Hz (period of 8.33ms). To get fast touch sensing on the display, we used two Natural Point Optitrack Flex-13 cameras for optical tracking. The tracking system reported the 3 degrees of freedom of reflexive markers at 120Hz. We calibrated the parameters of the display's plane in the cameras' 3D space by sliding a marker on the surface of the display. A spherical marker was attached to the participants' index finger, as illustrated on Figure 1. The 3D position of the marker is used to inform the system about the contact of the finger on the display and is then projected onto the display plane to get the position of the finger's projection on the display. By recording the sensed position of a stable marker put on the monitor, and repeating the operation in various locations on the monitor, we measured the precision of the sensing at less than 0.1mm (sub-pixel). The tracking software ran on a dedicated PC that sent marker positions to the main PC via the UDP protocol on a 1Gbit/s wired network. The round-trip time was measured below 0.5ms with low variability. The main PC was running Mac OS X 10.9.5 on a quad-core 3.4GHz processor and was equipped with an NVIDIA GeForce GTX 680MX graphic card. The system's software was custom written in C++ and used the OpenGL library for graphical rendering.

We assessed the end-to-end latency of our system by using the "high accuracy" approach introduced by Berard and Blanch [3]. Doing several measurements during the course of the experiments, we verified that the average latency was stable. In each measurement, latency averaged at 25ms and varied in the range [17ms-33ms]. From this variability, 8.33ms can be explained by the display refresh period. The remaining variability can be attributed to variable delays introduced by the system's components: computation of the 3D position of the marker on the tracking PC, communication between the tracking and main PCs, rendering of the scene and its communication to the display. We implemented artificial latencies by queuing finger motion events and releasing them only after a number of display cycles. We used 3 levels of latency in addition to the baseline: 42ms (+2 cycles), 58ms(+4 cycles) and 75ms(+6 cycles). The artificial latencies were controlled using the same procedure as for the baseline, and showed the same stability of the averages and the same variability around the averages.

Predicting finger trajectories

Jota et al. decomposed target acquisition trajectories in 3 phases: initial reaction, large ballistic motion, and "feedback-adjusted final adjustments" where the finger is inside the target area [7]. They found that the last phase was the most affected by latency. This could be explained by the fact that, with direct touch, the physical finger has no latency and allows users to control their gesture during the large initial motion. The lagging digital object is only required at the end of the gesture for its precise positioning within the target. To get a better understanding of this phenomenon, we studied twenty finger trajectories of different participants aiming at small distant targets (amplitude = 33.2cm, width = 0.42cm). We hand labeled the duration of the small final adjustments by looking at the speed profiles. We found that correction lasting less than 70ms were frequent and were often separated by even shorter motionless phases. We also observed that these corrections were quite erratic and thus appeared as unpredictable. This uncovers the challenge of a continuous prediction for target acquisition: compensating latency is most needed on the last phase of the acquisition gesture, which is irregular and rapidly evolving. It results that the amount of latency that can be compensated is bounded by the duration of these small adjustment motions: a system with 70ms of latency is only informed about the beginning of such short motion when the motion has already finished in the physical world; the system has no way to predict it.

These observations point to a highly reactive prediction model using only the most recent sensor data, similar to the most recent approach in visual immersion [9]. We considered using a constant acceleration parabolic model by fitting two parabolas (x and y) on the 3 most recent samples. To get a sense of the prediction's accuracy, we plotted a predicted trajectory alongside a no-latency "physical" trajectory that we simulated by removing a constant latency on each sample, i.e. translating a recorded trajectory on the time axis by the simulated latency. We used a simulated latency of 75ms to magnify the effect of the prediction. As illustrated on Figure 2(A), we observed that the instability of the parabolic fit interacted badly with the sensor noise and produced unstable predictions. To deal with sensor noise, we added more samples to the fit. However, any added sample is 8.33ms older than the previous one. The more sample added, and the less reactive the model becomes as it represents outdated evolutions of the trajectory. The phenomenon is revealed on Figure 2(B) with a 10 samples least-square optimized fit of the parabolic model: the prediction is much smoother, but at the cost of inertia that does not prevent strong under- and overshoots. We also experimented with a simpler constant speed linear prediction. The benefit of using a first order polynomial is that it only requires the two most recent samples for its estimation; hence it is very reactive. In addition, it only requires only one level of time integration for the position prediction, which results in lesser amplification of sensor noise. The result is illustrated on Figure 2(C, D) for a 75ms and a 25ms prediction.

We thus focused the scope of our study on the simple linear prediction model and with prediction lengths at or lower than 75ms. We attempted to entirely counteract the system's latency: we made a prediction of Xms for a system that has an average latency of Xms. In our model, we approximated the latency of the system as a constant l, measured with the "high accuracy" method of Berard and Blanch [3]. Although we observed some variability (±8ms) around the average, we had no way to estimate the exact latency at each sample. This situation is representative of most current direct touch system running on standard time-sharing OSes. We observed that the Optitrack sampling rate was very stable and thus we approximated the sample period as a constant $\Delta t = 1000/120 = 8.33ms$.

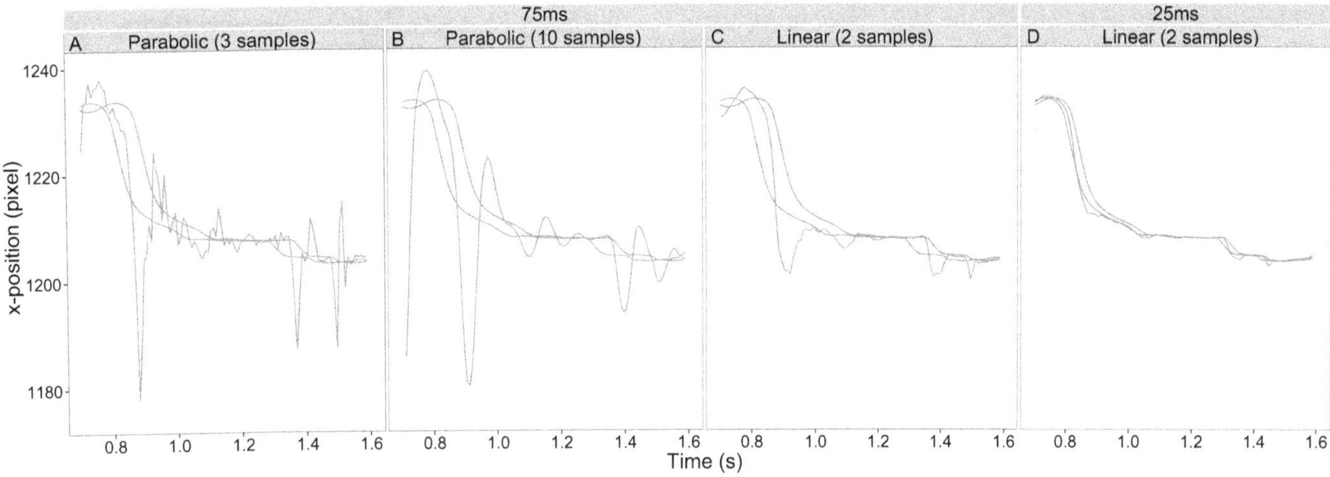

Figure 2. Final phase of a target acquisition. Simulated physical trajectory (red line), raw trajectory with lag (blue line) and predicted trajectory (green line). Prediction at 75ms of latency with a constant acceleration parabolic model fit on 3 samples (A) and on 10 samples (B), and with a constant speed linear model fit on 2 samples (C). Prediction with the linear model at 25ms of latency (D). Only the x-position is shown for a mostly horizontal trajectory.

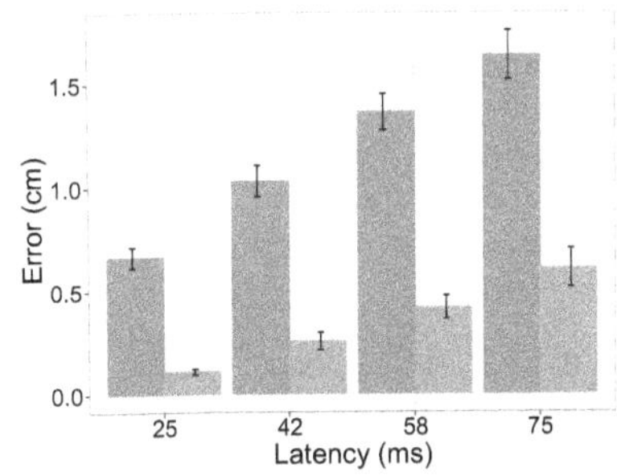

Figure 3. Average error per sample between simulated no-latency trajectories and lagging trajectories (in red) or predicted trajectory (in blue).

Finally, the *predicted* 2D position of the finger $\hat{\mathbf{x}}_\mathbf{i}$ at display cycle number *i* was computed as:

$$\hat{\mathbf{x}}_\mathbf{i} = \mathbf{x}_\mathbf{i} + l * \hat{\mathbf{s}}_\mathbf{i} \qquad \hat{\mathbf{s}}_\mathbf{i} = \frac{\mathbf{x}_\mathbf{i} - \mathbf{x}_\mathbf{i-1}}{\Delta t} \qquad (1)$$

where the $\mathbf{x}$ are the *observed* finger positions, $\hat{\mathbf{s}}$ is the speed estimation, l is the measured system's latency and $\Delta t = 8.33ms$. One of the benefits of this simple model is its user- and target- agnostic nature; hence it can be implemented with minimal effort in most direct-touch systems.

To get a sense of the accuracy of the prediction, we computed the average position error per sample for raw and for predicted trajectories. The error was computed by comparison to no-latency "physical" trajectories simulated as described above. These errors were averaged on 7428 trajectories recorded during our experiments. The results are illustrated on Figure 3. At 25ms of system latency, the average error is lowered from 0.66cm down to 0.11cm, an 84% improvement. At 75ms, it is lowered from 1.6cm down to 0.61cm, a 63% improvement. Although this gives a very positive picture of the global prediction's accuracy, looking at trajectories in details gives another picture (i.e. Figure 2(C)): the prediction introduces undershoots in accelerating phases of a motion, and overshoot in decelerations. This is particularly visible at 75ms of system latency, and in the final adjustments of a target acquisition. In this particular case, the challenge of predicting rapidly evolving corrections from late data appears distinctly, with the prediction introducing more perturbation than the lagging trajectory.

A user study was thus required to get an objective picture of the benefits of the predictive approach on users' performance.

USER EXPERIMENTS

The main objective of this user experiment was to evaluate if the predictive approach could effectively counteract the negative effect of latency on target acquisition tasks in term of users' *performance*, but also in terms of users' *preferences*. Doing so, we wanted to find which levels of latencies were tractable with the predictive approach. A secondary objective was to reproduce Jota et al.'s results [7] assessing the *detrimental effect of latency* on users' performance in direct-touch target acquisitions, and extending it to higher Fitts' ID.

The participants were 24 volunteers from our academic environment (average age=27.4, range 22 to 39, 8 women). After a short training session (10-15min), the participants performed the first experiment involving target acquisitions with varying Fitts' IDs for about 25min. They were then invited to perform the second experiment in order to express their preferences when dragging a virtual object with or without prediction.

EXPERIMENT 1: EFFECT OF LATENCY AND PREDICTION ON TARGET ACQUISITION PERFORMANCES

Task

Participants' task was to land their finger on a red disc *object* (1.38cm radius) and drag it on top of a white disc *target*. The acquisition of the target was successful only when the object was totally inside the target. Therefore, in the remainder of the paper, we refer to the width of the targets in terms of Fitts Index of Difficulty (ID): the target width is the difference in diameter between the object and target discs. The graphical display is illustrated on Figure 1. Participants validated the acquisition by releasing their control on the object, i.e. by lifting their finger from the surface. On finger release, the target turned green or red depending on the success or failure of the acquisition. After a random delay in the range [0.2s-1.2s] to prevent participants' anticipation, the target of the next trial appeared. Between two successive trials, the object remained at the location where the user released it. We asked participants to be as fast as possible while trying to limit their error rate at "around one mistake between each pause", which corresponds to 5%. All targets were located on a horizontal line vertically aligned with the middle of the screen to avoid the occlusion of targets by the hand. Every 20 trials, the message "you can take a break" was displayed. When they were ready, participant resumed the experiment by grabbing the object again. We recorded the trajectory of the object.

Design, measurement and analyses

Our design involved three main factors:

- PREDICTION. Two levels: *false* (no prediction) or *true* (with prediction). When *true*, the prediction attempted to entirely counteract the latency of the system: we did not study partial compensations in order to limit the number of experimental conditions;
- LATENCY. Four levels: 25ms, 42ms, 58ms and 75ms. The smallest latency was defined by the best performance of our system. For the upper bound, 75ms was a typical value of the duration of the shortest corrective motions at the end of target acquisitions.
- ID. Four levels: Fitts IDs are provided in bits and distances in cm.: 2.32 (d=11, w=2.77), 3.64 (d=22.14, w=1.94), 5.04 (d=22.14, w=0.69), 6.34 (d=33.2, w=0.42). These cover big and small targets at large and short distances.

Overall, the experiment included 32 conditions (2 PREDICTION x 4 LATENCY x 4 ID) and 20 repetitions for each condition, which amounted to 15360 trials (24 participants x 32 conditions x 20 trials). The order of presentation of PREDICTION and LATENCY was balanced across participants as a means to equilibrate a potential order effect. Within each block of PREDICTION x LATENCY, the presentation of the 80 targets (4 IDs x 20 repetitions) was randomized, but the same order was used in all blocks and all participants. Presentation of conditions was ordered by PREDICTION first, then LATENCY.

In our approach, touch detection was achieved by thresholding the altitude of the finger above the surface, with a hysteresis to avoid instabilities. However, the finger 3D pose varies depending on the touch location: the further away the user is touching, the more horizontal the finger. This introduced variability in the altitude of the marker, and required that the threshold be defined for the pose that yielded the highest altitude. The consequence was that our touch detection was not as sensitive as on a typical capacitive or FTIR touch surfaces. As a result, the virtual object often remained under control of the finger for a very short moment after the finger was lifted from the surface, and this frequently generated unintended object's motions. Parasitic motion on release exists with any kind of touch technology; however, our experimental optical tracking approach clearly inflated the problem and increased the acquisitions' failure rate. As this may have biased our participants to slow down, we verified that this was not the case by looking at the evolution of the velocity profiles during the experiment. They showed no sign of a slow down, but rather a tendency of increasing speeds that we attributed to the participants' training to the task.

We then removed, for each subject and condition, trials with duration at more than 1.5 interquartile above the upper quartile or below the lower quartile. These outliers amounted to 3.125% of all trials.

Based on these pre-processing, we then computed, for each subjects and experimental condition:

- *mean_time* as the mean target-acquisition time defined as the time span between the touch and release of the finger;
- *err_rate* as the ratio of failed trials over the number of analyzed trials. The acquisition was considered as failed when the object was not entirely within the target on release;
- the throughput TP as defined in Soukoreff and MacKenzie [17], expressed in bits per second.

The effects of PREDICTION, LATENCY and ID and their interaction were evaluated with within-subjects ANOVAs. Paired Student's t-tests were computed to test for the effects of planned comparisons related to our hypotheses: (1) a negative effect of latency on users' performance and (2) a positive effect of prediction for lower latencies.

Results

Effect of latency on users' performances

In order to compare our study with previous work [12] and to test the effect of latency on a larger range of ID than in Jota at al. [7], we analyzed the effect of LATENCY and ID on *mean_time*, *err_rate* and TP. This analysis concerns only the subset of data in the PREDICTION=*false* condition. As previous work didn't include a condition with prediction in their design, we first added the presentation order of PREDICTION levels (*true* first vs. *true* second) as a between subject factor to the ANOVAs. The effect of order on *mean_time*, *err_rate* and TP was not significant and didn't significantly interact with the effect of LATENCY and ID. We thus merged the two groups for further analyses. We refer to this subset of the experimental data as the "no prediction" dataset. The effects of ID was always highly significant, the following analyses focus on the effect of latency and its interaction with IDs.

mean_time significantly increases with LATENCY ($F_{3,69} = 13.6, p < .0001$, Figure 4) between 25ms and 42ms (+61ms, $t(23) = 2.9, p = .017$) and between 58ms and 75ms (+80ms, $t(23) = 3.1, p = 0.005$), the change between 42ms and 58ms was not significant (+4ms, $t(23) = 1.3, p > .2$). The effect of LATENCY on *mean_time* was also larger for higher IDs

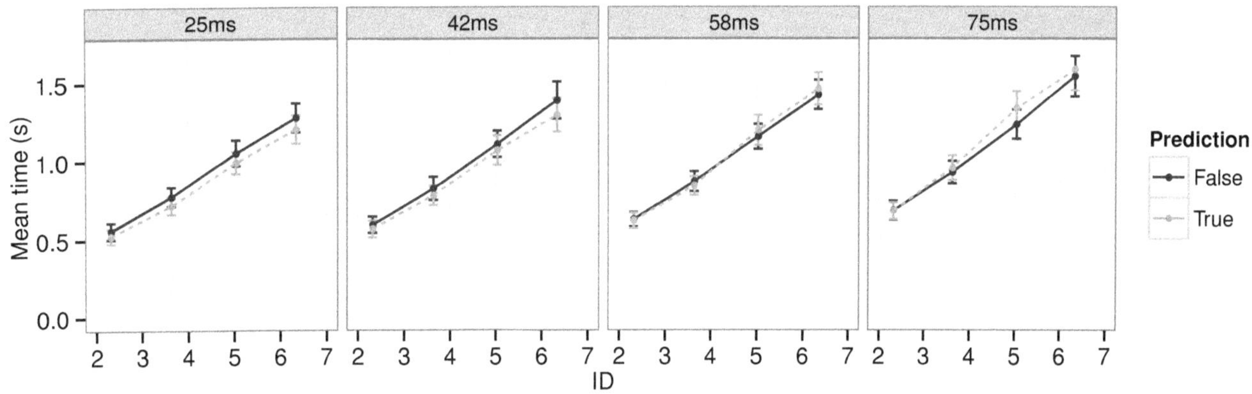

Figure 5. Mean target-acquisition time depending on target ID, latency, and prediction. Error bars give the 95% confidence intervals of the mean across participants.

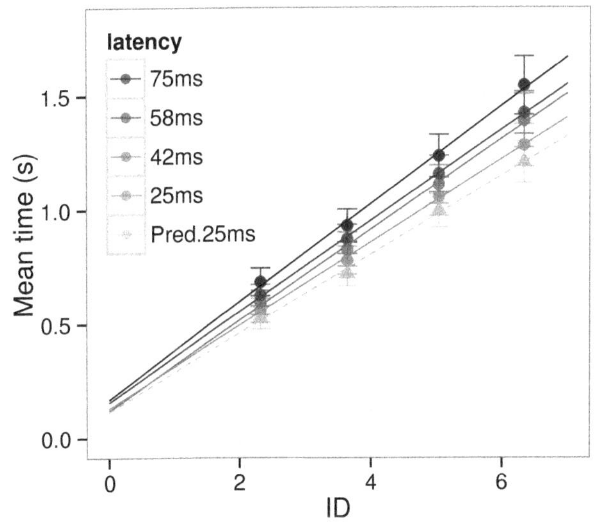

Figure 4. Effect of system latencies on the mean target-acquisition time when no prediction is used. The condition with prediction at 25ms of latency is added on the figure for comparison. The points are the mean values across 24 participants and error bars give the 95% confidence intervals of the means. The lines are linear fits of the data in each condition.

than smaller ones ($F_{9,207} = 4.7, p < .0001$): the slopes of a linear regression of *mean_time* according to ID increased with LATENCY ($F_{3,69} = 7.3, p < .001$) between 25ms and 42ms (+0.016, $t(23) = 2.4, p = .023$) and between 58ms and 75ms (+0.015, $t(23) = 2.6, p = 0.015$), the slope change between 42ms and 58ms was not significant ($t(23) = 0.1, p > .9$). TP decreased with increasing LATENCY ($F_{3,69} = 21.0, p < .0001$), changes were significant between 25ms and 42ms (-0.22bit/sec, $t(23) = 2.1, p < .05$), between 42ms and 58ms (-0.34bit/sec, $t(23) = 3.0, p < .006$) and between 58ms and 75ms (-0.28bit/sec, $t(23) = 3.2, p < .005$). There was no global effect of LATENCY on *err_rate* ($F_{3,69} = 0.99, p > .4$), and no interaction between LATENCY and ID ($F_{9,207} = 1.7, p > .1$).

Effect of the prediction on users' performance

The effect of the prediction on users' performances was analyzed using the full dataset. The individual effects of ID and LATENCY were comparable to the ones observed in the "no prediction" dataset. We thus only focus on the effects related to PREDICTION.

The global effect of PREDICTION on *mean_time* was not significant ($F_{1,23} = 0.4, p > .5$), due to different effects of PREDICTION according to LATENCY and ID ($F_{9,207} = 4.0, p < 0.0001$, Figure 5). PREDICTION appears to have a negative effect at 75ms, a neutral effect at 58ms and a positive effect at 25ms and 42ms. Independent within subjects ANOVAs with PREDICTION and ID as factors were ran for each of the LATENCY conditions to better understand these interactions. At 25ms of latency, the average *mean_time* across IDs and participants was significantly reduced by 6.2% with the use of the prediction (-57ms, $F_{1,23} = 6.4, p = .02$). A non-significant tendency was observed at 42ms ($F_{1,23} = 3.9, p = .06$) but no effect of PREDICTION was found at 58ms and 75ms ($F_{1,23} < 1.1, p > .3$ in both cases). The effect of PREDICTION didn't clearly depend on ID at 25ms ($F_{3,69} = 1.8, p = .16$), while it tended to increase with higher IDs for the three higher levels of LATENCY ($F_{3,69} > 3.2, p < 0.03$).

err_rate was significantly affected by PREDICTION ($F_{1,23} = 41.6, p < .0001$, Figure 6). However, PREDICTION had different effects on *err_rate* according to ID ($F_{3,69} = 29.9, p < .0001$) and LATENCY ($F_{3,69} = 12.7, p < .0001$). Independent ANOVAs for each levels of LATENCY showed that, at 25ms, *err_rate* was globally not significantly affected by PREDICTION ($F_{1,23} > 3.3, p > .0.08$). PREDICTIONS effects on *err_rate* were significant for 42ms, 58ms and 75ms ($F_{1,23} > 18.5, p < .001$).

The effect of LATENCY on TP was significantly different according to PREDICTION ($F(3, 69) = 9.3, p < .001$). The prediction increased throughput at 25ms (+0.15) but not significantly ($t(23) = 1.4, p > .17$), at 42ms, the throughput remains stable. The prediction decreased throughput at 58ms and 75ms ($t(23) > 2.5, p < .03$).

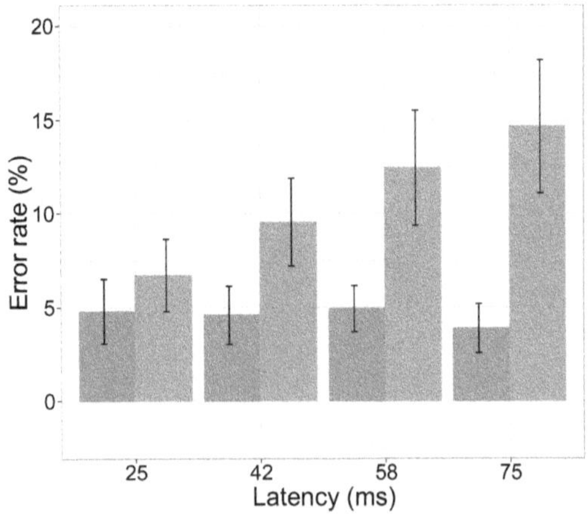

Figure 6. Mean error rates across participants averaged across IDs, and 95% confidence intervals of the mean. Left side red bars represent the "no prediction" condition, right side blue bars the "with prediction" condition.

EXPERIMENT 2: EFFECT OF LATENCY AND PREDICTION ON USER'S PREFERENCES

Task and design

Performance is not the only criteria to design a good user-interaction: users' comfort is another important aspect. We evaluated users' preference for the interaction with or without prediction. We asked participants to interact with a draggable virtual disc in two conditions A and B. Both conditions had the same amount of latency, one was using the prediction and the other was not. As in experiment 1, the prediction was set to entirely compensate the systems' latency. Participants were not told which of A or B was using the prediction and the assignment of prediction to A or B was randomized across trials. Participants could switch between A and B by pressing the space key on a keyboard as many times as they wanted. They ended each trial at their convenience, by expressing which of A or B they found "the most comfortable". They were asked to always provide an answer, even when the difference between the 2 conditions was difficult to perceive (mostly at low latencies).

As the preference may depend on the type of task performed, we split the sessions in two parts. In the four first trials, the 4 latencies were tested with no specific task: participants could explore freely the dragging interaction with the disc. In the next 16 trials, participants were asked to do target acquisition tasks for the 4 IDs and 4 latencies. The order of presentation of the latencies was balanced across participants. For a given latency, IDs were presented in the following order: 2.32, 5.04, 3.64, and 6.34.

Results

Figure 7 illustrates the results of the preference experiment. We tested each preference score with a chi-square to check if the null hypothesis of a random choice could be rejected. When asked to perform target acquisitions, participants preferred the "no prediction" condition in the three highest latencies ($\chi_2(1,96) > 13, p < 0.001$), but the random choice hypothesis could not be rejected at 25ms ($\chi_2(1,96) = 0.67, p > 0.41$). When freely interacting, 17 out of 24 participants (70.8%) preferred the condition with prediction at 25ms latency ($\chi_2(1,24) = 4.17, p < 0.05$), while a random choice could not be rejected for the three highest latencies ($\chi_2(1,24) < 1.50, p > 0.22$).

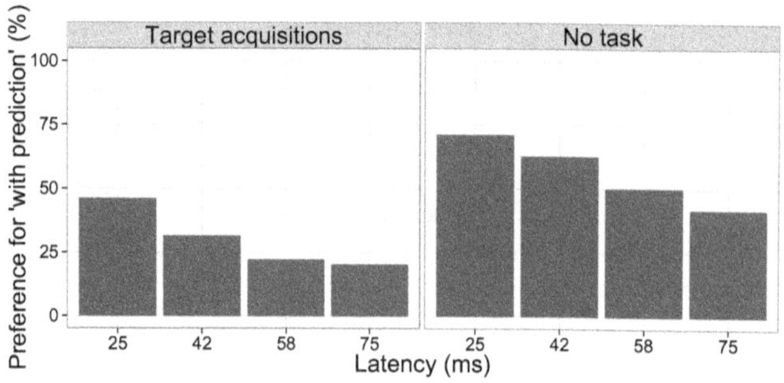

Figure 7. Proportion of participant preferring the "with prediction" condition during the subjective experiment.

DISCUSSION

Effect of latency on users' performances

The analysis of the "no prediction" dataset replicates and confirms previous work, which showed the strong detrimental effect of latency on users' performance in target acquisition tasks [7, 12]. Latency acts as a multiplicative factor of the index of difficulty: as latency increases, the throughput decreases and the slopes of the performance curves in Figure 4 increase. Performance continued to improve as latency was reduced to our lowest achievable value of 25ms. This is coherent with the results from Jota et al. [7], which we extended to the acquisition of targets IDs greater than 2.6bit up to 6.3bit. The first outcome of this replication of previous work was to validate our system and our experimental design. It also provided an indication of the expected users' performance depending on latency, which we discuss later in the paper.

Counteracting latency with a continuous prediction

Using prediction with latencies *above 42ms* did not yield better users' performances overall. Performances with prediction were the lowest for the two targets with the highest IDs. The small sizes of these targets (0.7cm and 0.4cm) required precise control and thus several adjustments in the final phase of the acquisition. Our results corroborate previous studies that indicate that latency has its strongest negative influence on the final adjustment phase of target acquisitions [7]. In addition, the study reveals that the continuous prediction approach has a rather low upper bound on the amount of latency that it can compensate, at least when used to perform tasks that require precise positioning. 42ms may appear as a small prediction length compared to typical prediction lengths used in endpoint prediction, which often exceed 100ms. However, endpoint prediction is essentially based on the initial motion of a target acquisition, which is much more regular (and thus predictable) than the final adjustment motions. In addition, endpoint prediction is generally used for target identification, which has a lower accuracy requirement compared to latency compensation.

By including target acquisitions of high IDs in our experiments, we probably have selected tasks that are amongst the most sensitive to prediction errors. Other direct-touch tasks, such as scrolling in lists or navigating in maps typically don't require sub-centimeter precision. As a consequence, our results should be considered as a worst-case scenario of the use of a continuous prediction in direct-touch interaction. In addition, the subpar touch-release detection of our experimental device should also be taken into consideration when considering the measured error rates: larger than average final parasitic motions probably increased the number of errors. Better touch release detection on common capacitive or FTIR surfaces would provide lower error rates in all the conditions represented on Figure 6. However, as the prediction amplifies the parasitic motions on release, the error rates with prediction should see greater improvements, hence the gap in error rates with and without prediction is expected to decrease.

Even with high precision target acquisitions, the prediction did improve users' performance when the latency of the system was at 25ms. To get a sense of the scale of the improvement we used the "no-prediction" dataset: in Figure 4, the improvement from 41ms to 25ms is similar to the improvement provided by the use of prediction at 25ms. As in Jota et al. [7], we computed a linear regression of the average task accomplishment time across IDs and participants, depending on latency. We found a good fit ($R^2 = 0.984$), and used it as an indicator of the performance that could be expected depending on the latency of the system. We identified the latency of a hypothetical device that would yield an average task accomplishment time of 0.795s, which corresponds to the performances of participants using prediction at 25ms. The linear regression indicates that the prediction allowed users to perform as well as with a 9ms of latency system, a 64% improvement over 25ms. In summary, assuming that the baseline latency of the system is low enough, the experiment demonstrated that the continuous prediction approach can bring the apparent system latency much closer to the ideal no latency, and this allows users to improve their performances.

Users' preferences

The results of the users' preferences experiment bring another light on a similar picture: participants favored the prediction only for the lowest levels of latencies, and only when we did not ask them to perform a task that required notable accuracy. When free to interact as they wanted, participants tended to make slow and smooth movements. This favored the prediction since there was no sudden speed variation and the amplitude of the prediction error remained small. In this context, the preference of participants was largely in favor of the prediction at 25ms of latency as illustrated in Figure 7 (right).

When asked to perform target acquisitions, participant preferred the "no-prediction" condition overall, as illustrated in Figure 7 (left). To justify their choice, participants commented that they felt "instability" and "absence of control" of the dragged object. In addition, the parasitic motion generated by our system may have played as a negative bias against the preference for the prediction. At 25ms of latency, some participants expressed difficulties in perceiving a difference between the two conditions. This is coherent with the non-rejection of the null hypothesis in this condition: a random choice is expected from undistinguishable conditions. Considered in regard to the performance increase shown in the first experiment, this result indicates that even though users may not perceive the difference, reducing the virtual object's lag allows them to be more efficient in precision tasks.

Applicability to current hardware

Current commercial and experimental devices usually have baseline latencies well above 25ms. However, reaching 25ms of latency does not seem out of reach or to require significant hardware improvements. 120Hz displays are widely available thanks to the push for stereo 3D. The iPad Air 2 already senses touch at 120Hz, and recent research work demonstrated touch sensors running at 4000Hz and with 0.04ms of latency [11]. USB3 cameras offer high spatial and temporal sensing for the implementation of large FTIR interactive surfaces (e.g. 2048x1088pixels at 170fps). A 120Hz display has 0ms of latency just after refresh, 8.33ms just before the next refresh, hence it introduces 4.17ms of average latency to the system. This leaves more than 20ms of additional average latency that may come for the other sources such as the sensing, the graphical rendering, and the synchronization overheads. The time needed to render the graphical feedback can vary greatly depending on the complexity of the scene, but for simple 2D user interfaces, this is typically done in a few milliseconds by current graphic cards[1]. With a 60Hz display refresh rate, 17ms of average latency are still available once the 8.33ms of average display latency are removed.

Our study should thus provide a strong incentive for touch system and application designers to maintain the non-display sources of latency in the range of 20ms. When this is the case, the continuous prediction offers a low effort instrument to provide users with a close to ideal system. Contrariwise, reaching 9ms of system latency using a pure hardware approach appears to be more difficult and energy inefficient.

However, the relevance of the predictive approach could be more general than the single case of 25ms latency systems. This points to further studies, as detailed below.

Future work

Deber et al. recently demonstrated that small improvements of latency, such as 16ms, were easily perceived by users in a direct touch dragging task on systems with various baseline latencies ([8.3ms-167ms]) [5]. Combined with our study, this creates strong expectations for a follow up study on the use of a continuous prediction for a *partial* compensation of latency on high latency systems.

In addition, ways to improve the continuous prediction and allow longer prediction lengths should be investigated. We observed that adding touch samples to average sensor noise had the negative effect of adding inertia to the prediction. Increasing the *sample rate*, however, allows increasing the number of samples without looking further in the past. Using high touch sampling rate, such as 4kHz demonstrated by

[1]The very simple scene of our system was rendered in less than 2ms, which we attributed mostly to OpenGL synchronisation overheads.

Leigh et al. [11], should be a promising approach to allow the use of higher degrees of freedom prediction models that remain reactive. A more ambitious path of improvement will be to study if some regularity can be found in the final adjustment motions of target acquisition. If it is the case, this could used to inform a specific prediction model.

CONCLUSION

In this paper, we have provided the first objective evaluation of the benefits of a continuous prediction to reduce latency and improve users' performances in direct touch systems. We showed that the length of the prediction is strongly constrained by the fast adjustments that make the end of target acquisition gestures. However, the experiment revealed that the continuous prediction approach could compensate a large part of latency's negative effect on target acquisition performances when running on a 25ms latency system. These results contribute to the quest of zero-latency direct touch.

ACKNOWLEDGEMENT

This work has been partially supported by the LabEx PERSYVAL-Lab (ANR-11-LABX-0025-01).

REFERENCES

1. Michelle Annett, Albert Ng, Paul Dietz, Walter F. Bischof, and Anoop Gupta. 2014. How Low Should We Go?: Understanding the Perception of Latency While Inking. In *Proceedings of Graphics Interface (GI)*.
2. Takeshi Asano, Ehud Sharlin, Yoshifumi Kitamura, Kazuki Takashima, and Fumio Kishino. 2005. Predictive interaction using the delphian desktop. In *Proceedings of ACM UIST*. 133–141.
3. François Bérard and Renaud Blanch. 2013. Two Touch System Latency Estimators: High Accuracy and Low Overhead. In *ACM ITS*. ACM, 241–250.
4. Pradipta Biswas, Gokcen Aslan Aydemir, Pat Langdon, and Simon Godsill. 2013. Intent recognition using neural networks and Kalman filters. In *Human-Computer Interaction and Knowledge Discovery in Complex, Unstructured, Big Data*. Springer, 112–123.
5. Jonathan Deber, Ricardo Jota, Clifton Forlines, and Daniel Wigdor. 2015. How Much Faster is Fast Enough?: User Perception of Latency & Latency Improvements in Direct and Indirect Touch. In *Proceedings of ACM CHI*.
6. Zenja Ivkovic, Ian Stavness, Carl Gutwin, and Steven Sutcliffe. 2015. Quantifying and Mitigating the Negative Effects of Local Latencies on Aiming in 3D Shooter Games. In *Proceedings of ACM CHI*.
7. Ricardo Jota, Albert Ng Ng, Paul Dietz, and Daniel Wigdor. 2013. How Fast is Fast Enough? A Study of the Effects of Latency in Direct-Touch Pointing Tasks. In *ACM CHI*. ACM.
8. Edward Lank, Yi-Chun Nikko Cheng, and Jaime Ruiz. 2007. Endpoint prediction using motion kinematics. In *Proceedings of ACM CHI*. ACM, 637–646.
9. Steven M LaValle, Anna Yershova, Max Katsev, and Michael Antonov. 2014. Head tracking for the Oculus Rift. In *IEEE International Conference on Robotics and Automation (ICRA)*. IEEE, 187–194.
10. Joseph J. LaViola. 2003. Double Exponential Smoothing: An Alternative to Kalman Filter-based Predictive Tracking. In *Proceedings of the Workshop on Virtual Environments 2003 (EGVE '03)*. ACM, New York, NY, USA, 199–206.
11. Darren Leigh, Clifton Forlines, Ricardo Jota, Steven Sanders, and Daniel Wigdor. 2014. High rate, low-latency multi-touch sensing with simultaneous orthogonal multiplexing. In *Proceedings of ACM UIST*. ACM, 355–364.
12. I Scott MacKenzie and Colin Ware. 1993. Lag as a determinant of human performance in interactive systems. In *Proceedings of ACM CHI*. 488–493.
13. Michael Meehan, Sharif Razzaque, Mary C Whitton, and Frederick P Brooks Jr. 2003. Effect of latency on presence in stressful virtual environments. In *Virtual Reality, 2003. Proceedings. IEEE*. IEEE, 141–148.
14. Albert Ng, Michelle Annett, Paul Dietz, Anoop Gupta, and Walter F. Bischof. 2014. In the Blink of an Eye: Investigating Latency Perception During Stylus Interaction. In *ACM CHI*. ACM, 1103–1112.
15. Albert Ng, Julian Lepinski, Daniel Wigdor, Steven Sanders, and Paul Dietz. 2012. Designing for low-latency direct-touch input. In *Proceedings of ACM UIST*. ACM, 453–464.
16. Phillip T Pasqual and Jacob O Wobbrock. 2014. Mouse pointing endpoint prediction using kinematic template matching. In *Proceedings of ACM CHI*. ACM, 743–752.
17. R. William Soukoreff and I. Scott MacKenzie. 2004. Towards a standard for pointing device evaluation, perspectives on 27 years of Fitts' law research in HCI. *International Journal of Human-Computer Studies* 61, 6 (2004), 751 – 789.
18. Peter Tsoi and Jacob Xiao. 2015. *Advanced Touch Input on iOS*. Technical Report. Apple Inc.
19. Jiann-Rong Wu and Ming Ouhyoung. 2000. On latency compensation and its effects on head-motion trajectories in virtual environments. *The visual computer* 16, 2 (2000), 79–90.
20. Haijun Xia, Ricardo Jota, Benjamin McCanny, Zhe Yu, Clifton Forlines, Karan Singh, and Daniel Wigdor. 2014. Zero-latency tapping: using hover information to predict touch locations and eliminate touchdown latency. In *Proceedings of ACM UIST*. ACM, 205–214.

A Predictive Approach for an End-to-End Touch-Latency Measurement

Elie Cattan
University of Grenoble
LIG, UJF
Grenoble, France
elie.cattan@imag.fr

Amélie Rochet-Capellan
University of Grenoble
Gipsa-lab, CNRS
Grenoble, France
amelie.rochet-capellan@gipsa-lab.grenoble-inp.fr

François Bérard
University of Grenoble
LIG, Grenoble-INP
Grenoble, France
francois.berard@imag.fr

ABSTRACT

With direct-touch interaction, users are sensitive to very low levels of latency, in the order of a few milliseconds [3, 6]. Assessing the end-to-end latency of a system is thus becoming an important part of touch-devices evaluation, and this must be precise and accurate. However, current latency estimation techniques are either imprecise, or they require complex setups involving external devices such as high-speed cameras.

In this paper, we introduce and evaluate a novel method that does not require any external equipment and can be implemented with minimal efforts. The method is based on short-term prediction of the finger movement. The latency estimation is obtained on the basis of user calibration of the prediction to fully compensate the lag. In a user study, we show that the technique is more *precise* than a similar "low overhead" approach that was recently presented [1].

ACM Classification Keywords

H.5.2 User Interfaces: Input devices and strategies (e.g., mouse, touchscreen)

Author Keywords

latency; measure; direct-touch; prediction

INTRODUCTION

Recent expansion of direct touch systems has prompted several research efforts on the effect and measurement of systems' end-to-end latency (or lag). The lag is defined as the time between a user's action and the display of the system's corresponding feedback. Lag was shown to reduce users' performances and the sense of presence in direct touch interaction. Users are able to perceive latencies down to 6ms [6] and their pointing performances are still affected at 10ms [3]. Most of current commercial touch surfaces exhibit levels of latency higher than 50ms [3], i.e. levels that are far from optimal. Researchers and designers of direct-touch systems should thus control the latency of their systems, which, as a first step, requires measuring it.

Measuring the end-to-end latency of touch system, however, is not an easy task. Several measuring instruments have been proposed in the literature. These instruments often require important efforts to set-up and operate, and they often require additional hardware such as cameras, pendulums or oscilloscopes. Berard and Blanch recently introduced a novel approach that requires the assistance of a human operator, but it is easy to implement and does not require any external hardware [1]. The approach is based on users' ability to accurately trace a circular path at constant speed. This is actually a difficult task that requires significant training to obtain good results.

In this paper, we introduce a new method that follows a similar approach of using the help of a human operator. The method requires the operators to slide a finger in straight lines at a constant speed of their choice, which is arguably an easier task that tracing circles at a constant rotational speed imposed by the system. This approach is based on the finger's motion prediction and the operator ability to perceive a mismatch between the finger and the lagging feedback. The technique only requires minimal efforts to implement and does not require any external device, or specific skills. We compared our predictive method to the low overhead (LO) method of Berard and Blanch [1] in a user study and showed that our new method is more *precise* than the LO method and generally preferred by participants.

ITS 2015, November 15–18, 2015, Funchal/Madeira, Portugal.

ACM 978-1-4503-3899-8/15/11 ...$15.00.
DOI: http://dx.doi.org/10.1145/2817721.2817747

RELATED WORK

Estimating latency requires that, at a particular instant, the positions of the finger and the feedback are known. The feedback position is computed by the system and is thus easily reported. By contrast, it is more difficult to measure the physical position of the finger at the moment the feedback was displayed. A common approach to solve this problem is to use an external video camera that takes pictures of both the finger and the feedback [6]. However, this approach requires the time consuming hand labeling of many images to account for the variability of the latency. In addition, the precision of the approach is limited by the thickness of the finger, which makes difficult the estimation of the position of contact and the speed of the finger.

Berard and Blanch recently introduced an automated method of touch latency measurement [1]. It is based on the extraction of the finger position as well as the display frame number by computer vision processing of the images captured by the camera. The approach provides an accurate estimation of the physical position of the finger. In addition, it allows the automated computation of latency on many samples, which results in an accurate estimation of the average latency, but also provides the spread of the latency. However, the approach requires an external camera, several calibration steps, and complex software, which make it unsuitable for quick latency estimations.

Rather than using an external camera to measure the physical position of the finger, the system may require an operator to follow a predefined trajectory with the finger. Hence, the system does not have to actually measure the position of the finger, it simply assumes that the finger is where it should be. The idea was introduced and implemented by Berard and Blanch [1] in their low overhead approach (or "LO approach"). This approach saves the requirement for external equipment and complex calibrations, and it can be implemented with minimal efforts. However, Berard and Blanch used the tracing of a circle at constant speed as the predefined trajectory. They report that the task was difficult to perform by the operators, which resulted in a range of latency estimations across participants having a width of 8ms. They also report that the average estimation was offset by 2ms compared to the ground truth, which gives an indication of its accuracy. Our approach builds on the idea of benefitting from the help of operators to save the complexity of external equipment, but we chose a task that is simpler to perform in order to improve the precision of the measure.

A predictive approach to measure the latency of the system was introduced by Knibbe et al. [4]. Using a projector-camera system, a trajectory prediction improved the accuracy of the real-time projection on juggling balls. With no assumption on its own latency, the system is able to calibrate itself: starting from 0ms, the prediction length is incremented (by 33ms and then by 5ms for refinement) and the projection error is measured at each step until a local minimum is found. The prediction length when the error is minimal is then considered as the end-to-end latency of the system. We follow a similar approach, but we adapt it to touch surfaces, and we ask human operators to match the object and the feedback, which saves the requirement for external cameras and calibration.

A NEW MEASUREMENT OF TOUCH LATENCY

Predicting the finger trajectory can reduce the perception of latency and improve user performances [2]. With prediction, the feedback is not displayed at its last known position but at a predicted position so as to compensate the system lag. A perfect prediction can theoretically compensate the latency totally. Reasoning backwards, if the prediction length is adjusted until the feedback exactly matches the physical finger, then the prediction length is equal to the system's latency. We use this as a means to measure the latency of the system.

Our approach consists in showing a simple vertical line to users that follows the index finger on the touch surface. Users can tune the prediction length until they observe the best match between the position of their finger and the position of the feedback. The prediction length is used as the latency estimation. Compared to the "LO approach" [1], users' motion is less constrained by the system. Users must perform straight line trajectories at the (constant) speed of their choice, which is arguably easier than tracing circles at a constant speed imposed by the system.

Ng et al. have showed that users are more likely to notice difference of latency when dragging small objects compared to bigger ones [5]. Therefore, we minimize the size of the dragged object, to improve users' perception accuracy: we display a 1-pixel line (0.28mm). To ease the matching between the line and the finger, a line is also drawn (with a pen) on users' index finger, and the positions are matched on a static finger.

This predictive approach provides accurate latency estimation only if the prediction model is correct. However, predicting the future is a difficult task prone to errors. We use a simple constant speed linear model for the prediction [2]. At each display cycle i, a predicted position $\hat{\mathbf{x}}_\mathbf{i}$ is computed as

$$\hat{\mathbf{x}}_\mathbf{i} = \mathbf{x}_\mathbf{i} + L * \hat{\mathbf{s}}_\mathbf{i} \qquad \hat{\mathbf{s}}_\mathbf{i} = \frac{\mathbf{x}_\mathbf{i} - \mathbf{x}_\mathbf{i-1}}{\Delta t} \tag{1}$$

where the $\mathbf{x}$ are the observed finger positions, $\hat{\mathbf{s}}_\mathbf{i}$ is the speed estimation and Δt is the display cycle time. The prediction length L is tunable and is used to measure the latency.

By design, this model perfectly predicts the finger position only when the finger is moving at constant speed in straight lines. But actual user trajectories are neither perfectly straight nor performed at perfectly constant speed. We remove the *straight line* problem by working in 1D: we ask users to make mostly horizontal translations on the surface, and display a vertical line at the x-position of the prediction. The *constant speed* constraint is more problematic: every user trajectory has an acceleration and a deceleration phase, which respectively induce undershoots and overshoots of the prediction model. We thus ask users to focus on the finger-feedback alignment in the middle of their motion, and ask them to stabilize their finger's speed as much as possible. Even so, the speed is never perfectly constant. However, a user choses the best finger-feedback alignment after several translation gestures in both directions. We assume that the prediction error averages across these gestures and allows for an accurate latency estimation. The accuracy is assessed in the user experiment presented in the next section.

In addition, large system latencies require large prediction lengths, which result in larger prediction instabilities. We thus envision that the precision of our approach will decrease with increasing latency of the system. In the user experiment, we evaluate two different levels of latency to study this phenomenon.

VALIDATION: USER EXPERIMENT

We designed a user experiment to assess the precision and accuracy of our approach. We also compared our approach to

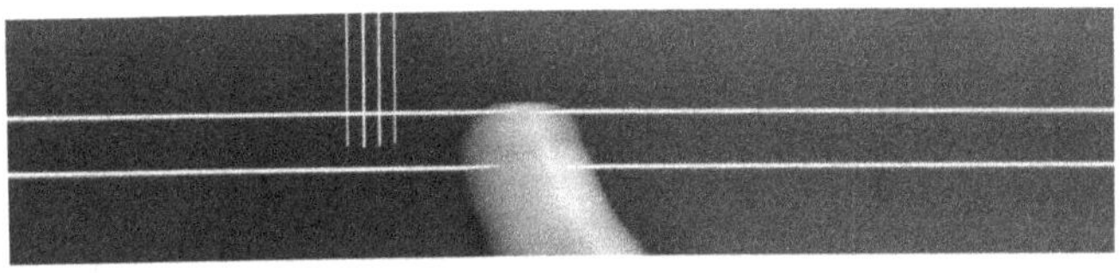

Figure 1. A user executing the predictive approach measurement: the finger, equipped with an optical marker, moves between the two guidelines. Users have to tune the prediction length to make the feedback match their finger when moving. Several vertical lines appear because of the exposure time of the camera.

the "LO approach", considered as the state of the art in quick latency measurements that require no external equipment.

8 participants took part in the experiment, with mean age = 26.75 [21-33], and including 3 women. All the participants came from our lab and had previous knowledge in computer science but no experience with neither the LO approach nor the predictive approach.

Our experiment was performed on a custom device that allowed us to control its latency with precision, and to test a low level of latency (30ms). However, it should be clear that the approach is not bound to this specific hardware and can be easily implemented on any commercial tablet for example. We used the same high performance touch system as in [2]. The system uses 120Hz optical tracking and requires that an optical marker be taped to the user's fingernail. The precision of the sensing was measured at less than 0.1mm (subpixel). We used the "high accuracy" approach [1] to measure the ground truth latency of our system at the various studied levels.

Task

In the LO task, we used a wheel similar to the one used by Berard and Blanch [1]: we displayed a circle of radius 8.8cm with a spinning radius at constant speed $s = 3rads^{-1}$. Participants were requested to follow the intersection of the radius and the circle. Pressing the space bar of a keyboard began and ended the recording. We asked participants to perform at least one and a half of a circle before ending the measurement.

In the predictive task, a white 1 pixel vertical line was displayed at the x-position of the finger. While the finger was static on the surface, we asked participants to draw a line on their fingernail that matched the feedback line on the screen. As illustrated in Figure 1, two white horizontal lines were displayed, and we asked participants to try to keep their finger within these lines when moving. Participants could tune the prediction length with the keyboard: two keys were used for $\pm$1ms increments, two others for $\pm$0.1ms increments. Participants were asked to tune the prediction length until the line on the finger and the feedback line matched when executing horizontal movements on the screen at a speed as constant as possible.

Protocol

The experimental design includes two factors: METHOD was either *LO* (following the LO approach) or *PRED* (following our prediction approach); LATENCY was either 30ms or 80ms.

Participants were asked to execute 5 measurements in each of the 4 conditions (2 METHOD x 2 LATENCY). We thus recorded 160 latency measurements (8 participants x 4 conditions x 5 repetitions). Presentation of conditions was ordered by METHOD first, then LATENCY. The order of presentation of METHOD and LATENCY was balanced across participants as a means to equilibrate a potential order effect. Post study ANOVA tests confirm no significant effect of ordering. At the beginning of the experiment, we explained both methods to participants and gave them a demonstration.

When executing the LO method, participants were first given 1min to train to following the wheel. Then, they executed five measurements in the first latency condition and five measurements in the second one. To encourage participants to improve their performances, standard error was displayed at the end of each measurement.

When executing the predictive method, participants were asked to move at the most constant speed as possible from one side of the screen to the other and to focus on the middle of their motion when the speed is the most constant. The prediction length, hidden to participants, was set to 0ms at the beginning of the run. They were given as much time as they wanted to tune the prediction length. The task was more easily performed using the *key repeat* feature of the keyboard, which is hardly reproducible, and ensured that participants did not simply repeat the same keyboard actions at each measurements. When they were satisfied with the feedback matching their finger, the final prediction length was recorded and reset to start another evaluation.

Results and discussion

Finger's speed during prediction measurements was variable amongst participants. We observed a trend of increasing speed during a single measurement. When the finger moves faster, it is easier to perceive a gap due to uncompensated lag; yet, speed also increases prediction error (as it is difficult to maintain a constant high speed) and creates a blurry effect on the feedback that makes difficult to match the lines. Globally, speeds peaked around 1.1m/s, where participants found a tradeoff between precision and blur.

On the 160 latency measurements, we removed 10 within-subject outliers that were 1.5 interquartile either above the upper quartile, or below the lower quartile. Measurements of participant 2 at 80ms with the LO method were around 35ms and very variable. This whole condition was considered as an outlier compared to the other results and was discarded from the study, given 145 measurements left for analysis.

The within subject variability of the estimation was greater with the LO method compared to the prediction method, as illustrated on Figure 2. The standard deviation of the five measurement repetitions, averaged across participants and the two latencies was significantly smaller with the predictive method (1.6ms) than with the LO method (8.4ms) ($F_{1,7} = 21.9, p <$ .005).

Estimating the latency with the prediction method takes more time (between 30s to 1min depending on participants) compared to a *single run* of the LO method (less than 10s). This

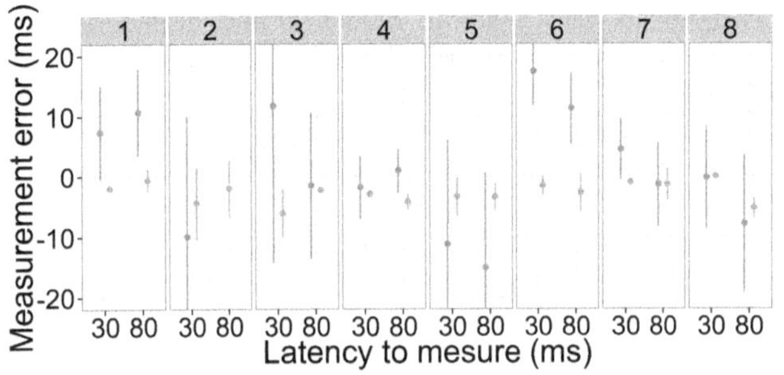

Figure 2. Averaged measurement error for each participant at 30ms and 80ms latency with the LO method (red, left) or the predictive method (blue, right). 95% confidence intervals indicate the within subject variability.

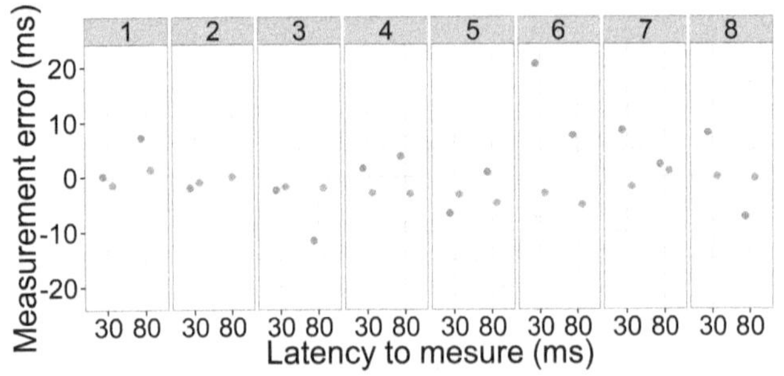

Figure 3. Error of the most stable LO run (red, left) compared to the error of the first predictive measurement (blue, right) for each participant at 30ms and 80ms latency.

is due to the multiple adjust and observe steps needed in the predictive approach. However, Berard et Blanch recommend that multiple runs of the LO method are performed by an operator in order to select the best run, defined as the one with lowest standard error. We thus compare a single run of the prediction method (the first run) to the best of five runs of the LO method, so that the operator time was similar. The LO method was found to be surprisingly accurate when averaged across participants: the best measurement average was 33.5ms at 30ms and 80.4ms at 80ms. The predictive approach gives a similar accuracy of 28.1ms at 30ms and 78.4ms at 80ms. However, the confidence interval for the mean of the measurement error (taking both 30ms and 80ms values) is narrower with the predictive approach (2.0ms) than with the LO approach (8.7ms). This indicates that a quick 2min latency measurement will be as *accurate* and more *precise* with the predictive method compared to the LO method.

With the LO method, the results uncover a high variability within and between participants. This could be explained by the limited training that the participants performed. The task certainly required more training to be mastered. The LO method provides good accuracy when averaged over several users. However, our results indicate that using the estimation of a single user could lead to large errors. On the contrary, the predictive method provides better accuracy and more precise results when considering the measurement of a single user.

The predictive measurements appear to suffer form a negative offset, compared to the ground truth. It can be due to the prediction length zeroed at the beginning of the measurement. A convergence of the prediction length from lower value could have lead to under-estimation. In further studies, we will set different prediction values at the beginning of each evaluation.

Contrary to our hypothesis, the predictive method did not yield less precision at 80ms than at 30ms. One explanation is that the human eye seems to be good at averaging the blurred feedback caused by the prediction instabilities.

When asked, "Which approach was the easier to perform?", 6 participants answered that they preferred the predictive approach. They argued that the wheel was hard to follow as they were constrained by the system. By contrast, the predictive approach allowed them to adopt their own rhythm.

Further evaluation will be needed to validate our approach at lower sensing rate. Even if 120Hz sensing is already available in commercial devices (for example, on the iPad Air 2), most current commercial devices have lower sensing frequencies in the range [60Hz-85Hz]. This could lead to more unstable predictions. However, the similar results of our experiment at 30ms and 80ms of latency indicate that users are good at coping with blurry feedback due to unstable prediction.

In conclusion, we introduced a new latency measurement approach using prediction. It is easy to implement and does not need any external device. A user study indicates that our approach is as *accurate*, more *precise*, and easier performed by users compared to previous work.

ACKNOWLEDGEMENT

This work has been partially supported by the LabEx PERSYVAL-Lab (ANR-11-LABX-0025-01).

REFERENCES

1. François Bérard and Renaud Blanch. 2013. Two Touch System Latency Estimators: High Accuracy and Low Overhead. In *ACM ITS*. ACM, 241–250.
2. Élie Cattan and François Bérard. 2015. Reducing Latency with a Continuous Prediction: Effects on Users' Performance in Direct-Touch Target Acquisitions. In *ACM ITS*. ACM.
3. Ricardo Jota, Albert Ng, Paul Dietz, and Daniel Wigdor. 2013. How Fast is Fast Enough? A Study of the Effects of Latency in Direct-Touch Pointing Tasks. In *ACM CHI*. ACM.
4. Jarrod Knibbe, Hrvoje Benko, and Andrew D Wilson. 2015. Juggling the Effects of Latency: Motion Prediction Approaches to Reducing Latency in Dynamic Projector-Camera Systems. *Microsoft Research Technical Report MSR-TR-2015-35* (2015).
5. Albert Ng, Michelle Annett, Paul Dietz, Anoop Gupta, and Walter F. Bischof. 2014. In the Blink of an Eye: Investigating Latency Perception During Stylus Interaction. In *ACM CHI*. ACM, 1103–1112.
6. Albert Ng, Julian Lepinski, Daniel Wigdor, Steven Sanders, and Paul Dietz. 2012. Designing for low-latency direct-touch input. In *Proceedings of ACM UIST*. ACM, 453–464.

A Public Ideation of Shape-Changing Applications

Miriam Sturdee, John Hardy, Nick Dunn, and Jason Alexander
Lancaster University, United Kingdom
{m.sturdee, j.hardy, nick.dunn, j.alexander}@lancaster.ac.uk

ABSTRACT

The shape-changing concept—where objects reconfigure their physical geometry—has the potential to transform our interactions with computing devices, displays and everyday artifacts. Their dynamic physicality capitalizes on our inherent tactile sense and facilitates object re-appropriation. Research both within and outside HCI continues to develop a diverse range of technological solutions and materials to enable shape-change. However, as an early-stage enabling technology, the community has yet to identify important applications and use-cases to fully exploit its value. To expose and document a range of applications for shape-change, we employed unstructured brainstorming within a public engagement study. A 74-participant brainstorming exercise with members of the public produced 336 individual ideas that were coded into 11 major themes: entertainment, augmented living, medical, tools & utensils, research, architecture, infrastructure, industry, wearables, and education & training. This work documents the methodology and resultant application ideas along with reflections on the approach for gathering application ideas to enable shape-changing interactive surfaces and objects.

Author Keywords

Shape-change; Shape-changing Interfaces; Shape-changing Applications; Brainstorming;

ACM Classification Keywords

H.5.2. Information Interfaces and Presentation (e.g. HCI): User Interfaces

INTRODUCTION

The study of shape-changing interfaces, displays, and objects is an emerging area of research. Shape-change allows objects to physically re-configure their external geometry to convey information [1], exploit perceived affordances in physical form [20], enhance output by exploiting the users' rich tactile sense [6], influence social behaviours [13], and re-appropriate objects through dynamic affordances [10].

Currently, shape-change research is driven by technology explorations or prototypes with a specific application focus—diverse user-led or applications-driven research has not yet occurred. Instead, we see a trend in the literature of documenting (for example): *cartography* [1, 28], *wearable technology* [3, 23], and *mobile phone notifications* [8, 12, 15]. However, to explore the full-potential and range of shape-change, and to focus technical development work, there is a need to better understand potential use-cases and applications [30] that drive future adoption.

Figure 1. (Top left) Study location; (Top right) ShapeClip display components (minimum/maximum heights); (Bottom) Public demonstration using 16 ShapeClips [14].

This paper proposes a complementary way to address this knowledge gap through the analysis of 336 ideas generated by 74 members of the general public during a creative thinking experiment. We hypothesize that large public groups can ideate novel research directions and indicate requirements for shape change that are grounded in a diverse range of individual needs and demographics. Our findings include themes that expand and diversify the academic design space, and characteristics that help researchers reflect on producing appropriate solutions for the needs of a public user base. Specifically, over half of the generated ideas were categories such as *Augmented Living*, *Entertainment*, or *Medical*.

This paper aims to assist in generating future uses and research directions for shape-changing technology and subsequently contributes: (1) An unstructured brainstorming methodology involving non-expert individuals, carried out

ITS '15, November 15-18, 2015, Funchal, Portugal.
 ISBN 978-1-4503-3899-8/15/11...$15.00.
DOI: http://dx.doi.org/10.1145/2817721.2817734

over *seven days* with *74 participants* generating a total of *336 unique ideas*; (2) Analysis of the generated ideas using Grounded Theory, identification of common theme categories, characteristics, and descriptive statistics; (3) Discussion around associated emergent themes, ideation output, and ideas relating to existing research (4) Reflection on the methodological approach—discussing generalisability, limitations, and considerations for future practitioners and; (5) A database of the generated ideas made available online at http://www.shape-change.org/brainstorm/.

RELATED WORK

Existing Shape-changing Prototypes

Shape-changing prototypes encompass a diverse range of materials, hardware, and usage scenarios. Many of these prototypes focus on a single application output (such as physically dynamic bar charts [36]) or interaction focus (displays that emulate reading a book [40]), or on material-based technological advancement of the field (Shape Memory Alloys [26] or partical jamming [32]), although there are cases where subsequent iterations of the same prototype have explored new application directions (e.g. inForm [10], deForm [9] and TRANSFORM [22]).

A large body of research in this area also looks at developing shape-changing versions of pre-existing technologies such as mobile phones [12, 15], tablets [35, 33] and desktops [37], although there are also more novel approaches considering artistic output [21] or emotive social-touch surfaces [24]. Another way in which research into these technologies progresses is to build upon previous prototypes incrementally, or to re-purpose components or ideas from existing work for development in other contexts. By following the citations within any given paper, justification for the prototype could be seen to come from the research community at large, rather than via ideation means.

User-studies & Prototype Evaluation

Taking a user-centered approach for evaluation of a prototype is commonly seen in a commercial context although the details surrounding this methodology are not always given [18]. In academic research institutions it is common to ask colleagues/student participants to evaluate prototypes, or for studies to use low numbers of participants. Methodologies utilise observational studies either from product placement [13], or artistic installation [25]. Other issues surrounding participant selection due to local availability can stem from gender bias or incentivisation [41], and research familiarity [27]. This is not to say that researchers employing such methods of participant selection are not making valid contributions to the field, but that there is space for an expanded viewpoint around such studies.

Brainstorming and Ideation

Brainstorming is a methodology commonly employed within groups for freely generating ideas to solve a particular problem or to generally come up with new ideas. As a non-experimental method, it is uncommon to see this kind of free-associative thinking in scientific research. In contrast to the

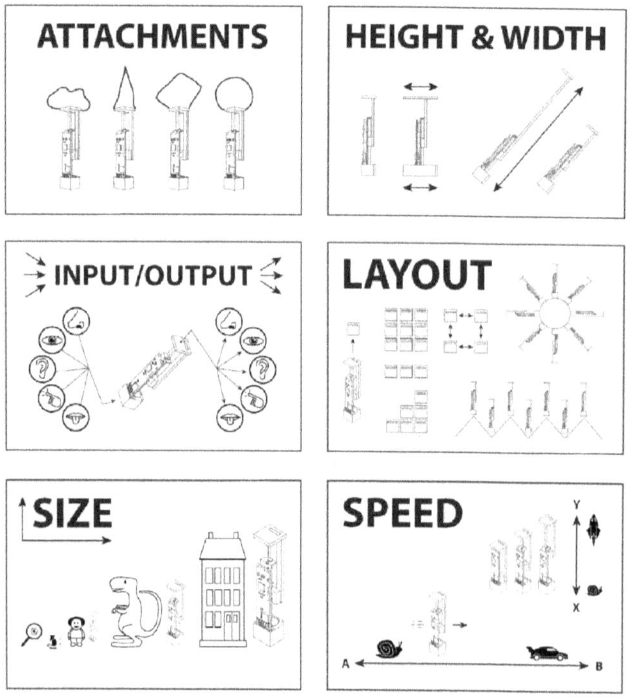

Figure 2. Indicative parameter posters

norm, Hardy et al's [14] experimental set-up utilised brainstorming to generate new research directions using designers and expanded upon these with rapid prototyping of viable ideas for shape-change. Notably, Jung et al. [17] also held sessions within their process (albeit with fewer participants). Utilising the general public in evaluation is unusual within the sphere of shape-changing interface research, although as previously mentioned both Gronvall et al. [13] and Nakajima et al. [25] successfully integrate a prototype within a public space. This allows both observation of diverse public interaction with shape-changing artefacts, and user testing in a non-pressurised setting. Follmer et al. hosted an *open-house* during which deFORM was showcased [9] but little information is provided as to demographic and experimental organisation. What is missing from research methodology in this area is purposeful and transparent recruitment of a participant pool from the general public. This paper hopes to elaborate upon participant selection and the use of non-institutional spaces in shape-changing research, following the success of such public-focused studies in co-design scenarios [31] and using brainstorming techniques such as De Bono's system outlined in *Serious Creativity* [7].

METHODOLOGY

The study goal was to generate shape-changing application ideas from a non-expert public group during an unstructured brainstorming session. These ideas were captured following demonstration of, and interaction with, an existing shape-changing display prototype. Analysis of the ideas isolated themes and characteristics of interest. By sampling a 'general public' user-base we hoped to: (1) obtain grounded application ideas that go beyond those currently documented; (2) examine the effectiveness of public involvement; (3) compare and contrast ideas onto existing research literature.

Experimental Setup and Location

The study took place in a vacant retail unit with high footfall in a UK town-centre (Figure 1, top left). Banners invited the public to "Take part in a creative thinking experiment". No financial incentive/reward was offered. Participants self-selected, with minors required to be accompanied by an adult. Due to the random nature of such participation, data was collected individually, and without using published ideation techniques. This was to ensure consistency as no group facilitation or other structure could be planned for. The study ran over seven consecutive days including one weekend during school holidays. Alongside writing/drawing space, the unit contained a demonstration of ShapeClip prototyping units [14] and posters that facilitated the brainstorming/creative thinking task by communicating the theme of shape-change as a technology to the participants [11, 34]. These are detailed below and in Figures 1 & 2.

Shape-changing Display: In the study space was an example of a z-actuating shape-changing display using ShapeClip units [14] (Figure 1, top right). ShapeClips are modular prototyping tools containing individually programmable Arduino units. The grid demonstrated how vertical movement can be combined with visual output in a magic-lens style configuration [4]. Participants manipulated the ShapeClip lens by moving it across a Samsung SUR40 touch table over a variety of graphical outputs: checkerboard, stripes, sunburst gradient (Figure 1). Each individual shape-pixel actuated vertically between black/darkest output (0% actuation) to white/lightest output (100% actuation) over a travel range of 60mm.

Parameter Posters: Six posters depicted possible shape-change parameters to consider: different attachments, height & width changes, different input/outputs, layouts, sizes, & speeds. The posters served to broaden the range of divergent thinking by suggesting how the prototype might be altered (i.e. room-scale transformation) without overtly implying specific ideas, and regulated explanation of such parameters as part of the experimental design (Figure 2).

Process

The experimental process consisted of four stages: (1) *Introduction & Consent*: The aims of the study were explained and appropriate consent forms completed. (2) *Demonstration & Interaction*: The prototype was demonstrated, participants were encouraged to interact with the technology, and were shown parameter posters. (3) *Ideation*: Participants were asked—without time constraints, and on an individual basis—to generate as many uses for shape-changing technology as possible (previously generated ideas were not made available). Responses were paper-based rather than verbal, so as to capture ideas, and provide participants with a familiar medium with which they could express themselves without interference. Participants indicated when they had run out of ideas. (4) *Exit Questionnaire*: Participants were asked to provide demographic and other relevant written data as pertaining to the study.

	Characteristic	Value
1	Gender	Male (58%), Female (42%)
2	Age (years)	$\mu : 30.07, \sigma : 14.10, range : 5 - 71$
3	Education	School (12%), GCSE (3%), A-Level/Vocational (17%), Undergraduate (34%), Postgraduate (31%), Ph.D (3%)
4	Sector	SciTech (31%), Management & Law (10%), Healthcare & Medicine (4%), Arts & Social Sciences (27%), Unspecified (28%)
5	Creativity (1-5)	$\mu : 3.75, \sigma : 0.87$
6	Tech Comfort (1-5)	$\mu : 3.82, \sigma : 1.06$
7	Ownership	Smartphone (85%), Tablet (64%), Laptop (84%), Desktop (55%), Wearables (9%), Games Console (62%)
8	Ideas Produced	$\mu : 4.51, \sigma : 3.34, range : 1 - 21, q1 : 2, q3 : 6$

Table 1. Descriptive characteristics of participants

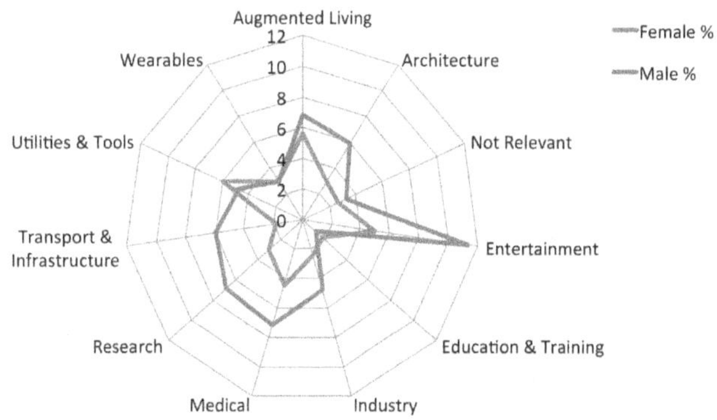

Figure 4. Percentage of ideas, per theme, by gender

Data Analysis

The demographic responses and raw ideas were collated and cross-referenced. All of the ideas were then coded according to the basic principles of Grounded Theory in three iterations. This resulted in clusters of idea themes, sub-themes, and characteristics (i.e. three independent 'idea feasibility' estimates), and a 3-point measure of elaboration. Ideas were also annotated with (approximate) scale, interactivity, and use of parameter posters. Our choice was informed by Rasmussen et al's classifications [30]. The data set was then queried by aspects of the questionnaire to identify any interactions between demography and participant output levels, i.e. age, gender, technological comfort, and also discover further variables that might improve the methodology.

DATASET ANALYSIS

Participant Demographic

Table 1 presents descriptive characteristics of the 74 sampled participants. The age ranged between 5–71 years ($\mu : 30.07$, $\sigma : 14.10$, line 2). The majority held a university qualification (67%, line 3). On 5-point Lickert responses, people typically agreed with the statement that they were 'creative' ($\mu : 3.75$, line 5) and 'comfortable with technology' ($\mu : 3.82$, line 6). The majority were technology consumers (line 7). Participants typically generated ($\mu : 4.51$, $\sigma : 3.34$, line 8) ideas.

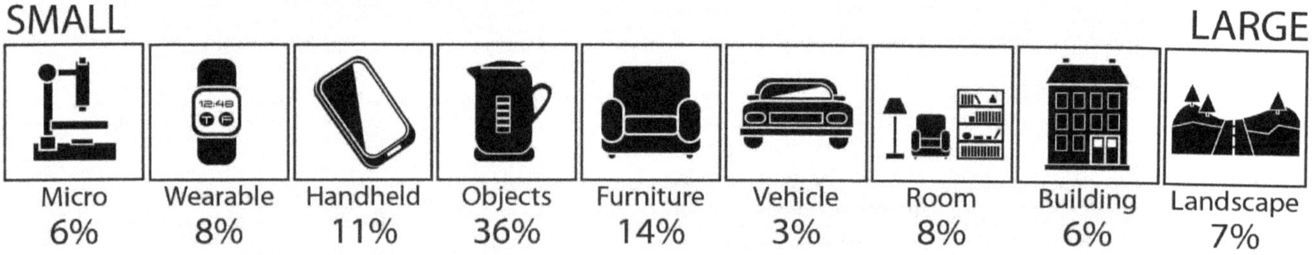

Figure 3. Ideas classified by approximate level of scale and type (Note: there is potential overlap between wearables/objects/hand-held but these were felt to be better represented as distinct entities for the purpose of scaling).

Systematic Chi-squared and correlation tests found no significant relationship between any of the demography characteristics and the number of ideas produced.

Gender Differences

An independent samples t-test was applied to the data to determine if there were significant gender differences between number of ideas generated. There was no significant difference in the number of ideas for men (M=4.767, SD=2.843) and women (M=4.226, SD=3.955); t(0.686)=72, p = 0.495 (there were no participants who identified with other gender identities). However, plotting the thematic data by gender does suggest that there may be evidence of bias toward particular themes (see Figure 4). A larger sample would be required for generalisation, but it does indicate the importance of mixed groups.

Idea Themes

A total of 336 ideas were generated. These ideas were presented using drawings (6%), writing (46%), and a mixture of both (48%). Grounded coding sessions produced 11 major themes. The themes identified for using shape-change were (with examples for each) *Entertainment* (physical 3D television, drawings which come to life); *Augmented Living* (responsive fake plants, furniture that responds to the body); *Medical* (beds to reduce pressure on injuries, responsive prosthetic limbs); *Utensils and Tools* (re-sizable joinery tools, reactive camera tripod); *Research* (responsive sculpting materials, "Holodeck"); *Architecture* (earthquake-responsive building foundations, reconfigurable rooms); *Infrastructure* (flood-resistant bridges, roads which respond to accidents); *Industry* (remote engineering in space, moulds for slip-casting); *Wearables* (re-sizable bags, anti-mugging wallet); and *Education & Training* (3D white-boards, shape-changing museum exhibits), with 6.2% of ideas counting as 'not relevant' (headphones that play music when they sense your ear, voice controlled ovens).

Each theme also contained associated sub-categories and cross-over: i.e. a medical bed for coma patients might have a primary theme of *Medical* but a secondary theme of *Augmented Living* with a minor catergory of *Furniture*. The ideas with associated major, minor and secondary themes can be seen at http://www.shape-change.org/brainstorm/.

Table 2 summarises the total idea database, the associated categories, and lists these according to most frequent to least frequent. The most ideas were generated in the *Entertainment* category, with *Education & Training* the least populated idea category. A category for ideas that did not map onto the theme of shape change, or were insufficiently explained was included here as this category comprises a portion of the data set on a par with *Industry, or Wearables*. It is not clear whether participants generating unrelated ideas were simply carried away by the brainstorming task, or misunderstood the parameters of the study.

Themes are described in more detail in the discussion, alongside sample ideas in Table 2. This also presents small graphs that indicate idea feasibility and elaboration within each theme, as well as showing idea frequency per theme.

Feasibility: Each idea was coded according to how viable it was to produce this item using current levels of technology, with a high value (5) indicating that it could be built almost immediately, and a low value (1) indicating only a slight probability that the item could be built, even in long time-frame. Average idea feasibility across the entire data set on a 5-point scale was (μ : 2.72, σ : 0.77) (scored from *unfeasible* at the lower end, to *very feasible* at the higher end). Coding was carried out independently by three researchers in the shape-change field using the same method, after which an average feasibility level was generated. Feasibility by theme can be seen in column 4 (Table 2), darker blue indicates higher feasibility, e.g. ideas within the *Augmented Living* and *Entertainment* themes appear to be more feasible given current technological advances than *Infrastructure* or *Architecture* – possibly because shape-change in the home/office is already in place, albeit at a lower level of technology (adjustable office chairs), but also at the research stage (shape-changing bench [13], or computer game controller [42]).

In comparison, architectural and landscape/infrastructure level shape-change would require not only a large amount of resource/space, but also significant changes in highly regulated building practices. Although there are real life examples (automatically raising road barriers, meeting-room dividers) in daily use, these are at a much smaller scale of what would be necessary to realise the generated ideas in these themes. Comparatively, the *Wearables* category shows a lower feasibility, possibly because the ideas generated rely on microscopic shape change (high shape-resolution) that is not currently in evidence in day to day

Theme	Description	Freq.	Feasibility	Elaboration
Entertainment	Relating to devices, toys, games and other recreational activities such as sports or events. *E.g. Skate park ramps; 3D chess; Sensory feedback for video-games; Physical 3D TV.*	16.36%	$\mu3.24$ $\sigma0.86$	$\mu0.74$ $\sigma0.75$
Augmented Living	Improving general life via home improvements and/or smaller aspects of interior architecture. *E.g. Form sensing furniture; Ventilation controls; Reactive aesthetics.*	12.79%	$\mu3.33$ $\sigma0.89$	$\mu0.79$ $\sigma0.74$
Medical	Based within the medical or inclusive living field, for the benefit of both staff and patients. *E.g. Wheelchair ramps; Surgical staff training; Braille displays/announcements.*	11.60%	$\mu3.21$ $\sigma0.65$	$\mu0.74$ $\sigma0.63$
Utensils & Tools	Activity or task orientated hand-held, tabletop or other movable objects which fulfill a set purpose. *E.g. Multi-use screwdriver head; Intuitive weapons; Reactive pizza pan.*	10.71%	$\mu2.94$ $\sigma0.82$	$\mu0.88$ $\sigma0.66$
Research	Loose themes or research based projects with no immediate product value, or that require significant development and further iterations to become practical. *E.g. Shape changing alloys; Environmentally reactive fabrics.*	9.82%	$\mu2.76$ $\sigma0.96$	$\mu0.48$ $\sigma0.56$
Architecture	Large scale building forms and major interior alterations. *E.g. Seismic-reactive buildings; Architectural visualization tools; Re-configurable rooms.*	8.92%	$\mu2.63$ $\sigma0.89$	$\mu0.70$ $\sigma0.59$
Infrastructure	Concerned with roads and pathways, vehicles, or town/city level adaptations. *E.g. Dynamic speed-bumps; Weather-responsive vehicles; Intuitive livestock fencing.*	7.73%	$\mu2.08$ $\sigma0.68$	$\mu1.07$ $\sigma0.48$
Industry	Based primarily in manufacturing, farming or at a business level. *E.g. Remote manipulation for engineering in a vacuum; Slip-casting mould; Bomb disposal tool.*	6.84%	$\mu2.76$ $\sigma1.02$	$\mu0.65$ $\sigma0.48$
Wearables	Technology carried, worn on the body, or incorporated into fabrics. *E.g. Reactive radiation suit; Clothes that adjust to body shape; Traction-adjusting shoes.*	5.95%	$\mu2.35$, $\sigma0.48$	$\mu0.75$, $\sigma0.71$
Education & Training	Educational context, specific training tools, and imagery. *E.g. Physically interactive white boards; Data communication in museums; 3D instructions.*	2.97%	$\mu3.10$, $\sigma0.73$	$\mu1.00$, $\sigma0.81$
Not Relevant	Did not fit into shape changing parameters, possibly due to misunderstanding the concept, or generated as adjunct to shape change.	6.25%	$\mu1.48$, $\sigma0.81$	$\mu0.52$, $\sigma0.60$

Table 2. Idea themes, descriptions, and examples. Theme frequency, breakdowns of feasibility and elaboration are shown for each theme. *Feasibility (5-point, red=unfeasible/blue=very feasible). Elaboration (3-point, red=minimal/blue=specific).*

living or cutting edge research. The overall feasibility for all themes (excluding those not relevant) is high, showing that participants were able to generate ideas within the realms of practicality, whilst also thinking speculatively.

Elaboration: Participant responses ranged from single words (e.g. *games*) to long essays or highly detailed images with accompanying texts. Text responses made use of bullet points, as well as descriptive prose, and whilst the variety of explanation is interesting, there do not appear to be any indicators for type of response in comparison to demographic data. *Elaboration* was coded in the same way as feasibility, on a three point scale indicating how much information about each idea was available, after initial analysis indicated the range of such information. Highly elaborate (and relevant) ideas suggest a greater understanding of the prototypical technology on display, as well as an analytic mindset.

Idea Properties

Beginning with the poster parameters, 23% of ideas involved attachments to the actuators (such as soft coverings or building foundations, 14% required different heights / widths, 72% used inputs/outputs that integrated the shape-change with other systems or senses i.e. light, sound, 21% required non-rectangular or grid layouts of multiple actuators, 92% differed in size from the prototype shown, and 19% required significantly different actuation speeds. These differences are worth noting as the chosen prototype has comparable technical specifications to works in recent literature (closed length: 80 mm, fully actuated length: 120 mm, maximum actuation speed: 80 mm/s), particularly in terms of size and actuation travel. This makes the resulting ideas even more interesting (1) because participants were able to generalise beyond the object we showed them; and (2) because the literature might be missing categories of actuation/ideas.

To explore the differences in scale and use between our idea-set and the literature, ideas were classified according to dominant scale; ranging from microscopic to landscapes. The percentage of the total ideas for each scale are shown in Figure 3. The largest number of responses at any one scale was 'object' (36%), followed by furniture (15%) and hand-held (11%). This indicates people are willing to see shape-changing devices as 'human sized'. The number of furniture-based shape-change ideas indicates the integration of re-purposability/customisation into what surrounds us rather than stand-alone monolithic devices will be an important design consideration in the future.

To analyse interactivity, ideas were mapped onto Rasmussen's modes of interaction [30]. The majority of the generated ideas reacted automatically to conditions or input (indirect, 44%) or were hypothesized as needing to have direct input to produce actuation (direct, 37%). No human interaction (16%) and remote interaction (3%) made up the remainder. After our interpretation and categorisation of the ideas, we were surprised by the number of ideas that suggest operation without human interaction.

DISCUSSION

In addition to statistical and descriptive analysis, other themes and comparisons emerged from the data and are discussed below. These range from dimensionality, display/device com-

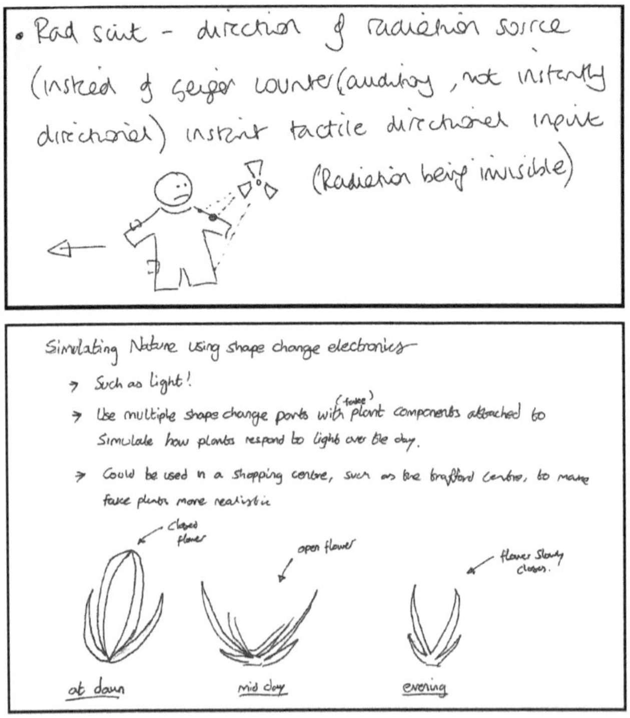

Figure 5. (Top) Reactive clothing; (Bottom) Shape-changing plants.

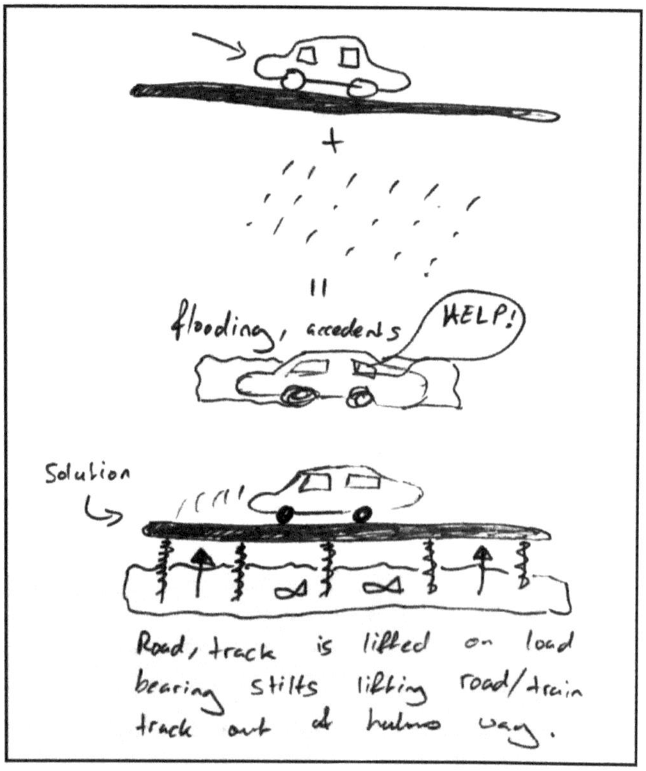

Figure 6. Narrative imagery describing shape-change

parison, validation of existing research from a public perspective, sustainable design, gaming, technology vs simplicity, and interdisciplinary thoughts around narrative imagery and temporality.

Most ideas do not exceed a single dimension of shape-change: Despite diverse applications and actuation scales within the idea-set, most ideas actuated to achieve a single purpose (e.g. unlocking a door) or transformation (e.g. moving 3D Braille paper) as opposed to multi-purpose shape-change. From our procedure it is difficult to know if there is no desire for 'generic objects', or if people could not ideate beyond simple actuation.

A dichotomy exists between displays and devices: The majority of ideas were devices (78%) rather than displays (22%). This differs from the focus of much technical research that looks at communication through dynamic visual display affordances. This indicates that initial shape-change applications may be welcome in day-to-day mundane scenarios. The main types of displays suggested were 3D televisions used for entertainment, or tangible browsers for online shopping.

Sense-making in shape-changing ideas: Participants were found to generate data that maps onto existing categories of shape-change and also makes sense to the world around them, such as realistic product predictions or feasible items. They tended not to ideate about things that could be enabled as the wider technological ecosystem evolves (for example, ideas which do not already link to existing items or structures). Ideas appear to be largely driven by desire (e.g. entertainment applications) or actual need (e.g. wheelchair adaptations) rather than technological speculation.

Familiar, mundane, self-actuated shape-change (e.g. convertible cars, automatic doors) did not play a major role in the idea-set. However, several ideas can be mapped onto existing prototypes, e.g. shape-changing vacuum cleaner head [39], shape changing coffee mugs [17], data visualisation [36], responsive plants [5] or air-quality reactive clothing [19].

This serves as validation for this method of consultation in two ways: (1) Current research projects are validated from a user-led perspective; and (2) Other ideas generated from the public data are thus likely to be viable directions for shape-changing application research.

The influence of nature: Rasmussen's review describes shape change being rooted in nature (the behaviour of the Southern White-faced Owl) [30]. This link was seen during the study duration whereupon participants either foresaw shape changing technology as attempting to purely emulate nature (*responsive fake plants*), using examples from nature to describe the movements they wished to outline (*millipede walking platform*) or create animal/technology forms with which to interact (*interactive worm*).

Use of narrative imagery to elucidate shape-change: The transitional nature of shape-changing technology lends itself to highly descriptive methods such as lengthy explanations or movements drawn in stages. This parallels comic strips in which advancement of time is shown over several drawings.

Several participants chose to explore their ideas using this methodology (see Figure 5), although there was a greater tendency for participants to draw one image and use text to explain the intricacies of their idea. This usage of narrative imagery is already finding a place in shape change, be it in describing Ishii's futuristic *Perfect Red* [16] or Poupyrev et al's *Lumen* prototype [29]. Using narrative imagery to explore the nature of shape change is yet to be examined in research, yet appears to be vital in communicating complex iterations of these novel prototypes in research papers.

"Phygital" gaming: Entertainment was one of the most populated categories of idea, with gaming as a minor theme. Participants either suggested the notion of *gaming* in general, or leaned toward imagining highly specific versions of existing software such as *Minecraft* in 3D. Physical, non-console based gaming was also suggested - ideas in this sub-category ranged from chess pieces that reacted to illegal moves or cheating behaviours, to drawn imagery that fed into 3D playmats onto which toy cars could be placed, to *Legos* that maintained only a transient physical presence. This duality of ideas supports the *phygital* (physical/digital) presence of tangible user interfaces - occupying a space somewhere between the traditional table-top board game and richly detailed visual simulations or displays.

Overly technical solutions to simple problems: One potential issue in looking for applications for a novel technology, is that we may end up generating ideas that do not require actuated technology or a shape-changing display. This does not negate the ideas that were generated to specifically satisfy a *desire* rather than a *need* however (e.g. entertainment).

Such examples could be: a chair that adjusts to the shape of the bottom – already evident in memory foam; skinny jeans that adjust to the leg – achieved by stretchy materials such as lycra; or automatic ventilation systems – in use as air-conditioners. Despite the existence of these products that do not relying on shape-changing gadgetry, this does not prevent novel technologies from eventually replacing their low-tech forerunners, such as micro-level shape-changing materials in clothing, which may then not only fit the form of the wearer, but also offer customisation opportunities.

Novelty of ideas between subjects: Despite the individual nature of the brainstorming methodology, in some cases, unrelated participants were seen to generate similar ideas over several categories. This duplication of ideas could be seen to indicate a collective desire for these technologies, or simply that these ideas are more obvious given the prompting of the prototype, posters and/or study environment. However, novelty within the dataset in some cases could also indicate ideas that are less feasible, or do not meet a practical need. To elaborate, below are some examples of duplication and novelty that were uncovered during analysis.

Examples of duplicated ideas: window blinds, re-sizable rooms, adjustable beds, prosthetic limbs, object detection for blind people, braille displays, real 3D TV, aerodynamic vehicle bodywork, re-sizable bags, flooding reactive bridges.

Examples of novel ideas: sun-shelters which grow when there is a high UV index, extendable target-sensing swords, shape-changing electric guitar, the perfect pizza-pan, Elizabethan suffocation collar, 3D police identi-fit, reactive shoe grips, interactive animal enclosures.

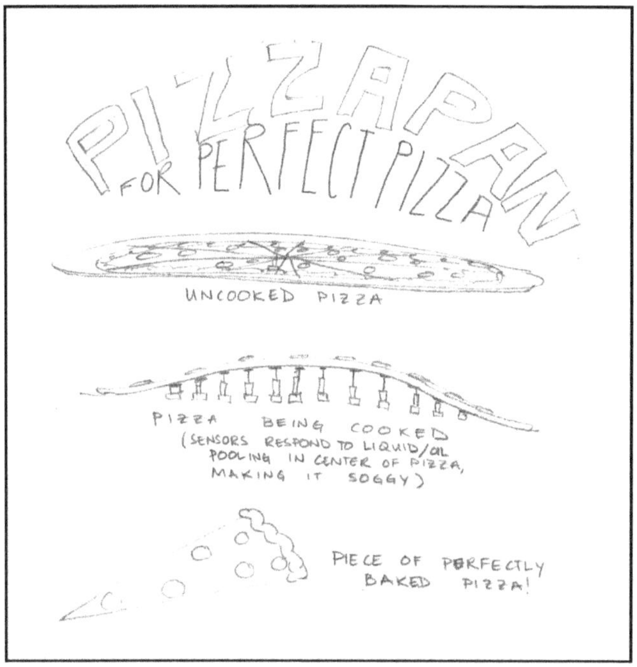

Figure 7. Novelty in idea generation – pizza-pan

Shape-change for sustainability: Themes surrounding sustainability are largely evident within the idea set, with several participants mentioning the housing crisis, or multiple/variable use objects (re-sizable pots, kettles (Figure 9), houses and aeroplanes). Successful commercialisation and implementation of shape-changing technology at levels from the micro to the macro could reduce drain on resources, over-population and lower waste production. Current prototypes which embrace both shape change and sustainability largely focus on design for behaviour change [38] rather than reducing the need for consumption in the first instance. An interdisciplinary approach working with designers in this field, might enable a valuable step forward in making these products a tangible reality.

The discussion above picks out the most interesting observations from the collected data but is by no means exhaustive. There may also be even more of interest from both the ideas themselves, and the qualitative data gathered post-ideation. What can also be taken away from this is that there is a wealth of information that can be gleaned from public engagement that is not only relevant to existing research, but can further inform shape-change, and other research.

METHODOLOGICAL REFLECTION

The experiment method was successful in collecting data on a volunteer basis from a general population without incentivising participation. The diversity of shape-changing applications generated is impressive, and, as we hoped, grounded in the needs and backgrounds of the sampled public. Having analysed the individual ideas, we are left with the impression that not only is there a demand for shape-changing technologies in mundane, day-to-day settings, but also that these technologies will be actively embraced.

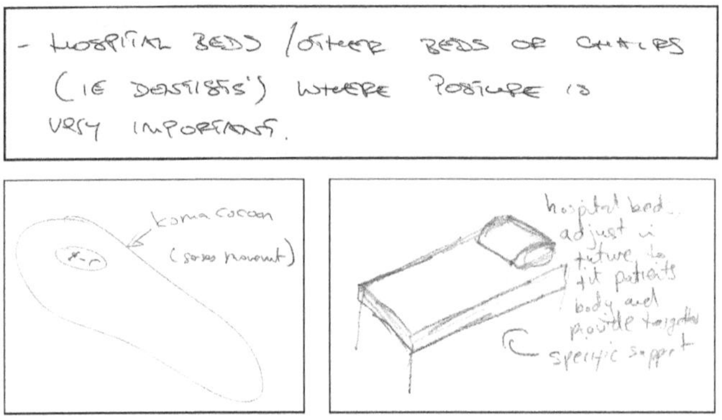

Figure 8. Duplication in idea generation

Figure 9. Adjustable, responsive kettle

Interpersonal factors

For the researcher(s) running the experiment, interpersonal factors were an important component of the delivery. Therefore any public-facing researcher must be able to engage on multiple levels, whilst delivering consistent communication and design in order to reduce the risk of bias. We specifically did not pressure any participants to engage, and felt this helped create a fruitful result. In some instances individuals entered the shop unit and asked to see the technology, but felt that they were not able to take part. This non-participatory interaction nevertheless suggests that there is a interest amongst the general public for engagement in new technologies.

Prototype effects

In terms of experimental limitations, the large number of object-level ideas is arguably linked to the object-level prototype. Although we took steps to expand this with the parameter posters, we suspect that if the study had been conducted with a material-level or room-sized prototype the results would have been different (although it is also possible that the ideas generated may have been more or less diverse) Shape-change is a very broad domain, and we hope that the characteristics of our idea-set will provide researchers with interesting reflections.

Using public spaces for research

Research using neutral non-laboratory spaces fulfills boundary principles [11] when used to run public facing studies, offers a possible solution to the skew that may be found when using an academia-specific participant pool/setting [2], and can produce a viable data set. Further work might investigate location-based differences as an adjunct.

Outside of the laboratory setting however, controlling all variables can present a difficulty. Despite this, the study is designed to be repeatable, and it can be seen that the specificity of the prototype used does not hinder the final data-set as participants were easily able to think outside of the study setting, and across themes/properties. Further work might focus on not only on varying location however, but also the study population, as identified subsets (such as *designers* or *engineers*) in the demographic could be isolated and then examined in more detail.

Qualitative data

Feedback questionnaires recorded demographic data and responses to the study design, demographic data did not contain any predictors relating to idea variation however. Comments relating to the prototype focused on seeing shape-change occur at a micro (i.e. material level), and wishing to experience variable actuation output in order to facilitate ideation.

Other types of qualitative data were also gathered which related to personal experience but did not offer an analytic viewpoint at this stage. Investigation of these types of responses may be beneficial however, as it could serve to enhance the human factor that can occasionally be missed from HCI research [2].

Some qualitative responses detailed the positive experience gained from being part of the research project, i.e. P34 *"It is good to know that the public have had the opportunity to contribute ideas"*, P46 *"Thanks for including me"* and P40 *"Interested to see where this tech goes"*. The overall response from the participant pool was overwhelmingly positive, supporting the possibility of applying this type of user study to other HCI research areas (e.g. wearables or mobile phones).

Related methodologies

Although this study is novel in its approach, it does bear some small similarity to Jung's SKIN methodology [17], in that brainstorming sessions were used, although Jung et al. used only 2 participants with art/design backgrounds to explore and draw concepts. What can be taken from this study's structure however, is the process with which ideas were developed and prototyped *after* the initial ideation process (see also [14]). The other study in which there is a parallel is Follmer et al's deFORM [9]) whose *open-house* style session invited a mixture of adults and children into the research setting to interact with the prototype, and informal feedback was given. In this case, however, no detail as to the background of the participants is given, and the focus of the *open-house* is not specific (i.e. were other prototypes on display?). This makes it difficult for other researchers to repeat the process.

The ShapeClip brainstorming experiment [14] utilised the same base demonstration prototype as our study, but chose participants with a design-based background to generate ideas, and focused on developing these ideas in situ as part of a rapid prototyping experiment. There were also less ideas generated (86 compared to 336), via fewer participants, and across fewer themes, although more ideas were generated per participant. There were similarities within the themes however, such as *Augumented Living* and *Wearables*, although ideas mapped specifically onto the ShapeClip prototype, rather than shape-change in general. The difference in format (full day workshop as opposed to drop in session of self-selecting length) might have led to pressure to generate more ideas than the public study. Additionally, by using experienced designers, there is a tendency for individuals to have familiarity with such processes. With regards to these preceding research scenarios, our ideation study can be seen as not only responding to Banon's call [2], but also building on portions existing research.

Reflection Summary

This work shows that institutional public relations can be enhanced, a larger participant pool accessed, and useful product and theory-level ideas gathered for which there is a user-demand by utilising accessible public spaces in shape-changing research. This builds upon previous studies, and offers a viable alternative for research participant selection.

FUTURE WORK

Following the success of eliciting ideas in a non-research environment, it will be possible to further develop the methodology used here in an extended and revised fashion. Possible avenues of development might investigate whether using structured ideation techniques such as co-design might generate more cohesive results. Additionally, given that there are also differences for demographic factors (although non-significant at the current sample size), running specialised sessions for under 16s or, for example, those with a background in the arts, might produce even more exciting data. There is also the possibility of using different shape-changing prototypes in the ideation sessions to explore differences in boundary objects/technology.

Work on the existing data set can also be taken a step further by developing several of the feasible ideas into working prototypes (as in Hardy 2015 [14]), or focusing existing research into areas that are desirable in a commercial setting [18]. Given that several of the ideas generated are already part of exciting research projects, it stands to reason that other ideas within the data set would produce meaningful results in the research setting and beyond.

CONCLUSION

In summary, 74 people generated 336 ideas that, after coding, split into 11 themes. These themes define directions for shape-change and insights into how and where people see it being used to solve problems in their day-to-day life. The responses of the public to the experiment were positive, and sufficient data was gathered to perform analysis and generate feasible ideas for future research directions.

The relative ease in which data was gathered suggests that an over-reliance on readily available participant pools is unnecessary, as an enthusiastic and diverse public can be surveyed if given the opportunity. Thus, the methodology implies that the current range of users for shape changing prototypes may be unnecessarily reliant on university-based data, which may produce bias. That is not to say that this data should be disregarded, but that it should be used comparatively with data collected from a wider pool.

Using an appropriate qualitative methodological approach it is possible to create a space in which a public participant pool can ideate around the theme of shape-change. The resulting data suggests that the public are not only able to generate ideas directly relating to current shape-changing research prototypes, but additionally, novel problem/desire-based directions for research. This reinforces previous calls for a more human-focused HCI [2] and shape-changing applications research perspective [30].

ACKNOWLEDGEMENTS

This research was supported by HighWire, a post-disciplinary Doctoral Training Centre at Lancaster University funded by the RCUK Digital Economy Programme through the EPSRC (Grant Reference EP/G037582/1), and partially-supported by GHOST, a project funded by the European Commission's 7th Framework Programme, FET-Open scheme (Grant #309191).

REFERENCES

1. Alexander, J., Lucero, A., and Subramanian, S. Tilt Displays: Designing Display Surfaces with Multi-axis Tilting and Actuation. MobileHCI '12, ACM (2012), 161–170.
2. Bannon, L. J. Reimagining HCI: Toward a More Human-centered Perspective. *Interactions 18*, 4 (2011), 50–57.
3. Berzowska, J., and Coelho, M. Kukkia and Vilkas: Kinetic Electronic Garments. ISWC '05 (2005), 82–85.
4. Bier, E. A., Stone, M. C., Pier, K., Buxton, W., and DeRose, T. D. Toolglass and Magic Lenses: The See-through Interface. In *SIGGRAPH '93*, ACM (1993), 73–80.
5. Cheng, B., Gomes, A., Strohmeier, P., and Vertegaal, R. Mood fern: exploring shape transformations in reactive environments. ACE '14, ACM (2014), 60.
6. Cholewiak, R. W., and Collins, A. A. Sensory and Physiological Bases of Touch. *The Psychology of Touch* (1991), 23–60.
7. De Bono, E. Serious creativity. *Journal for Quality and Participation* (1995), 12–12.
8. Dimitriadis, P., and Alexander, J. Evaluating the Effectiveness of Physical Shape-change for In-pocket Mobile Device Notifications. CHI '14, ACM (2014), 2589–2592.
9. Follmer, S., Johnson, M., Adelson, E., and Ishii, H. deform: an interactive malleable surface for capturing 2.5 d arbitrary objects, tools and touch. UIST '11, ACM (2011), 527–536.

10. Follmer, S., Leithinger, D., Olwal, A., Hogge, A., and Ishii, H. inFORM: Dynamic Physical Affordances and Constraints Through Shape and Object Actuation. UIST '13, ACM (2013), 417–426.
11. Fox, N. J. Boundary Objects, Social Meanings and the Success of New Technologies. *Sociology 45*, 1 (2011), 70–85.
12. Gomes, A., Nesbitt, A., and Vertegaal, R. MorePhone: A Study of Actuated Shape Deformations for Flexible Thin-film Smartphone Notifications. CHI '13, ACM (2013), 583–592.
13. Grönvall, E., Kinch, S., Petersen, M. G., and Rasmussen, M. K. Causing Commotion with a Shape-changing Bench: Experiencing Shape-changing Interfaces in Use. CHI '14, ACM (2014), 2559–2568.
14. Hardy, J., Weichel, C., Taher, F., Vidler, J., and Alexander, J. Shapeclip: towards rapid prototyping with shape-changing displays for designers. CHI '15, ACM (2015), 19–28.
15. Hemmert, F., Hamann, S., Löwe, M., Zeipelt, J., and Joost, G. Shape-changing Mobiles: Tapering in Two-dimensional Deformational Displays in Mobile Phones. CHI Extended Abstracts '10, ACM (2010), 3075–3080.
16. Ishii, H., Lakatos, D., Bonanni, L., and Labrune, J.-B. Radical atoms: beyond tangible bits, toward transformable materials. *interactions 19*, 1 (2012), 38–51.
17. Jung, H., Altieri, Y. L., and Bardzell, J. Skin: designing aesthetic interactive surfaces. TEI '10, ACM (2010), 85–92.
18. Kildal, J., Paasovaara, S., and Aaltonen, V. Kinetic device: designing interactions with a deformable mobile interface. CHI' 12 Extended Abstracts, ACM (2012), 1871–1876.
19. Kim, S., Paulos, E., and Gross, M. D. Wearair: expressive t-shirts for air quality sensing. TEI '10, ACM (2010), 295–296.
20. Klemmer, S. R., Hartmann, B., and Takayama, L. How Bodies Matter: Five Themes for Interaction Design. DIS '06, ACM (2006), 140–149.
21. Kodama, S. Dynamic ferrofluid sculpture: organic shape-changing art forms. *Communications of the ACM 51*, 6 (2008), 79–81.
22. Leithinger, D., Follmer, S., Olwal, A., and Ishii, H. Physical telepresence: shape capture and display for embodied, computer-mediated remote collaboration. UIST '14, ACM (2014), 461–470.
23. Moere, A. V., and Hoinkis, M. A Wearable Folding Display for Self-expression. OZCHI '06, ACM (2006), 301–304.
24. Nakajima, K., Itoh, Y., Hayashi, Y., Ikeda, K., Fujita, K., and Onoye, T. Emoballoon. In *Advances in Computer Entertainment*. Springer, 2013, 182–197.
25. Nakajima, K., Itoh, Y., Yoshida, A., Takashima, K., Kitamura, Y., and Kishino, F. Fusa 2 touch display. SIGGRAPH '10, ACM (2010), 11.
26. Nojima, T., Ooide, Y., and Kawaguchi, H. Hairlytop interface: an interactive surface display comprised of hair-like soft actuators. WHC '13, IEEE (2013), 431–435.
27. Parkes, A., and Ishii, H. Bosu: a physical programmable design tool for transformability with soft mechanics. DIS '10, ACM (2010), 189–198.
28. Piper, B., Ratti, C., and Ishii, H. Illuminating Clay: A 3-D Tangible Interface for Landscape Analysis. CHI '02, ACM (2002), 355–362.
29. Poupyrev, I., Nashida, T., Maruyama, S., Rekimoto, J., and Yamaji, Y. Lumen: interactive visual and shape display for calm computing. SIGGRAPH '04 Emerging technologies, ACM (2004), 17.
30. Rasmussen, M. K., Pedersen, E. W., Petersen, M. G., and Hornbæk, K. Shape-changing Interfaces: A Review of the Design Space and Open Research Questions. CHI '12, ACM (2012), 735–744.
31. Sanders, E. B.-N., and Stappers, P. J. Co-creation and the new landscapes of design. *Co-design 4*, 1 (2008), 5–18.
32. Sato, T., Pardomuan, J., Matoba, Y., and Koike, H. Claytricsurface: An interactive deformable display with dynamic stiffness control. *Computer Graphics and Applications, IEEE 34*, 3 (2014), 59–67.
33. Schwesig, C., Poupyrev, I., and Mori, E. Gummi: a bendable computer. In *CHI '04*, ACM (2004), 263–270.
34. Star, S. L., and Griesemer, J. R. Institutional Ecology, Translations' and Boundary Objects: Amateurs and Professionals in Berkeley's Museum of Vertebrate Zoology, 1907-39. *Social Studies of Science 19*, 3 (1989), 387–420.
35. Steimle, J., Jordt, A., and Maes, P. Flexpad: highly flexible bending interactions for projected handheld displays. CHI '13, ACM (2013), 237–246.
36. Taher, F., Hardy, J., Karnik, A., Weichel, C., Jansen, Y., Hornbæk, K., and Alexander, J. Exploring interactions with physically dynamic bar charts. CHI '15, ACM (2015), 3237–3246.
37. Takashima, K., Aida, N., Yokoyama, H., and Kitamura, Y. Transformtable: a self-actuated shape-changing digital table. ITS '13, ACM (2013), 179–188.
38. Togler, J., Hemmert, F., and Wettach, R. Living interfaces: the thrifty faucet. TEI '09, ACM (2009), 43–44.
39. Vyas, D., Poelman, W., Nijholt, A., and De Bruijn, A. Smart material interfaces: a new form of physical interaction. CHI' 12, ACM (2012), 1721–1726.
40. Watanabe, J.-i., Mochizuki, A., and Horry, Y. Bookisheet: bendable device for browsing content using the metaphor of leafing through the pages. UbiComp '08, ACM (2008), 360–369.
41. Weiss, M., Voelker, S., and Borchers, J. The benddesk demo: multi-touch on a curved display. ITS '10, ACM (2010), 317–317.
42. Ye, Z., and Khalid, H. Cobra: flexible displays for mobile gaming scenarios. CHI '10 Extended Abstracts, ACM (2010), 4363–4368.

ART-Chess: A Tangible Augmented Reality Chess on Tabletop

Frédéric Rayar
Laboratoire Informatique
Université François Rabelais
Tours, France
frederic.rayar@univ-tours.fr

David Boas
Polytech Tours
Université François Rabelais
Tours, France
boas.dav@gmail.com

Rémi Patrizio
Polytech Tours
Université François Rabelais
Tours, France
remi.patrizio@etu.univ-tours.fr

ITS '15, November 15-18, 2015, Funchal, Portugal
ACM 978-1-4503-3899-8/15/11.
http://dx.doi.org/10.1145/2817721.2823485

Abstract
Chess is a traditional board game that is still popular. Several works have been done to make its gaming experience richer using augmented reality technology. But the proposed user interactions to move the chess pieces are still unfamiliar and not appealing to chess players. To answer this issue, we propose ART-Chess, a tangible augmented reality chess on tabletop. Using a camera-aware tabletop, the recognition of markers is made easier, which allows a human player to use real chess pieces. The game is augmented, thanks to an AR headset, with 3D virtual chess pieces.

Author Keywords
Augmented Reality; Tangible User Interface; Tabletop; Chess

ACM Classification Keywords
H.5.2 [Information interfaces and presentation (e.g., HCI)]: User interfaces.

Introduction
Virtual reality (VR) technology is becoming mainstream. After being a non-stater innovation in the last century, it will become available to general public in a few years. Indeed, major companies are or will propose soon products to the consumer market. Notable VR headsets are Oculus

Rift (Facebook), Project Morpheus (Sony), Gear VR (Samsung) or Vive (HTC). The game industry will not miss the boat, and is already focusing its attention towards the use of VR in computer games. Nevertheless, traditional games, such as chess, checkers, card games and board games are still popular and appealing for the general public [14].

The field of *pervasive games* has emerged a few years ago. It aims at "bridging computer entertainment game back to the real world" [15]. Among others, augmented reality (AR) is a popular approach: it allows the player to keep in touch with the real world while enhancing the reality and the gaming experience with virtual content.

One of the limitation of augmented reality games may be the interaction of the user with the virtual content. Tangible (graspable) [13] paradigm allows to overcome such limitation. It specifies that the user may be able to physically grasp or manipulate the virtual content.

In this paper, we present ART-Chess, an augmented reality and tangible tabletop chess game. This platform allows a human to play against an artificial intelligence (AI). The player will use real chess pieces while the AI chess pieces will be virtually created and displayed to a headset system. For this purpose, we leverage an existing camera-aware tabletop and a AR headset camera to propose a simple gaming environment without external camera or projector.

Related works

There are few works that propose AR based chess. Most of them are projects that leverage the well-known AR library ARToolkit [2].

The major limitation of these prototypes is the user interaction, especially how the player move his chess pieces. Several ways have been proposed to address such interaction. In [4], simple printed markers are used, and the player has to move them with his hand. [6] used the same approach, but icons of the chess pieces are printed on the tags allowing the player to know which chess piece he is manipulating. Nevertheless, moving plain piece of paper may not be appealing. In [3] and [1], they propose to use a tag-based paper stick to move the markers on the board. [5] leverages the infrared sensor capability of a Wiimote to select positions of a move. The two latter interaction are not natural for chess players. In [11], a smartphone is used to move the chess pieces: the player select a chess piece and the destination case on the screen of his device. As the player uses the tactile screen, one may wonder why not directly play on a chess smartphone application with a 2.5D view.

Using physical pieces seems to be a relevant alternative. As stated in [12], even if neither iconic nor symbolic pieces affect the understanding of the game or the gaming experience, iconic play pieces are preferred. Thus, real chess pieces seems to be the straightforward solution to please a chess player. Henceforth, it boils down to the recognition of the chess pieces. In [16], the authors propose to avoid the use of markers. Computer vision techniques is used to recognize simple pawns in a board game, and they are augmented with visual effects. But players can occlude pawns with parts of their arms during interaction.

Another limitation is the complexity of the gaming environment setup: external camera or projector are often used to process markers detection or project virtual content on gaming surface [14].

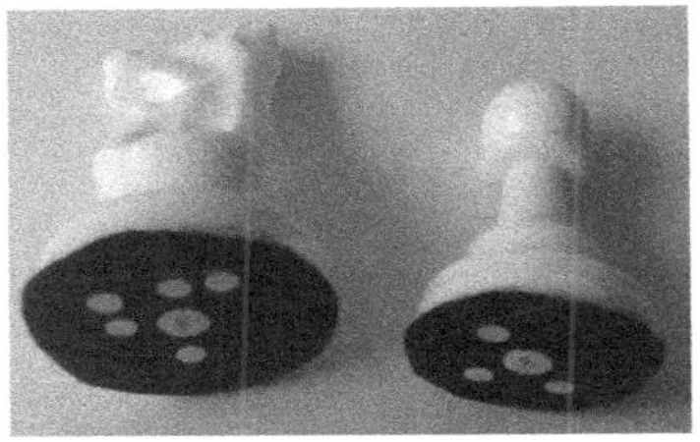

Figure 1: Markers attached underneath a knight and a pawn chess pieces.

Figure 2: Virtual chess pieces are placed upon detection of at least one of the target QRCode.

Prototype

ART-Chess consists in two components:

- a main application for a camera-aware tabletop
- an application for an Android device (tablet, smartphone or AR headset)

The communication between these two application is managed using Bluetooth.

For the tabletop, a Samsung SUR40 has been used. The choice of this tabletop was motivated by the fact that it runs with Microsoft PixelSense [7]. Using a layer the PixelSense technology allows to detect various contact types such as fingers, blobs and tags. Consequently, it is easy to detect and recognize chess pieces with markers attached underneath (see Figure 1). Each chess pieces have an unique marker that allow the tabletop to detect and recognize the exact position of the chess pieces on the surface.

Regarding the Android application, two platforms have been chosen. First, the Unity3D [10] has been used to create the virual reality. Chess piece, light, device camera and piece animation can easily be handled using Unity3D. Second the Qualcomm Vuforia [8] platform is leveraged for the AR functionalities. Vuforia is a "vision-based augmented reality software platform". It has an object recognition feature that allow to target, among others, images or user-defined markers. The current prototype uses four QRCode as targets to place the virtual chess pieces on the chessboard (see Figure 2). VR headset such as Google Cardboard or Espon Moverio BT-200 can be used along with the Vuforia platform.

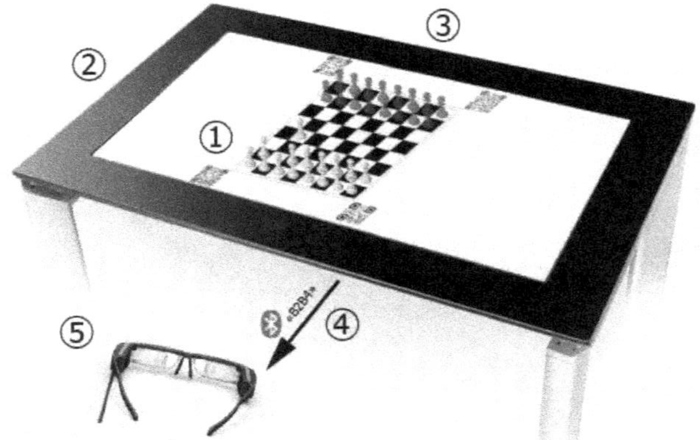

Figure 3: Game play of ART-Chess.

A game of chess using ART-Chess is as follows. First the player starts a new game. A communication channel between the tabletop and the Android device is opened using Bluetooth. Then, the player places the physical white chess pieces on the chessboard. The tabletop application checks if the pieces are correctly positioned. When the 16 chess pieces are set, a "start" message is sent to the android device. Figure 3 illustrates the main steps of a game:

1. The player makes his move.
2. The tabletop detects the new position of the chess piece, and deduces the move. It checks the validity of the move to continue.
3. The AI [9] decides its own move.
4. A message with the selected move is sent to the Android device via Blutooth.
5. The Android device analyses the received message, and adapts the virtual scene consequently (piece movement or removal) .

Figure 4: Interface of ART-Chess tabletop application. The human player white chess pieces are real (bottom side of the chessboard) while the AI black ones are virtual (top side of the chessboard). A textual feedback is displayed to the player at the left of the screen for the chess pieces initialisation and the moves during the game. An audio feedback is also given.

The game ends when a checkmate or a draw is detected. Figure 4 illustrates the view of the tabletop application through the Android device.

Conclusion and Future work

We have presented ART-Chess, a tangible augmented reality chess on tabletop. Using a camera-aware tabletop, the recognition of markers is made easier, which allows a human player to use real chess pieces. The game is augmented, thanks to an AR headset, with 3D virtual chess pieces. Overall, ART-Chess is perceived well, and the gaming experience is appealing.

Several ideas to improve the prototype can be considered. First, the possibility for others human to join the game as spectator, even after the start of the game. Second, the possibility of a remote human vs. human game. This will allow distant players to enjoy augmented chess. Finally, one can easily think about a richer experience in terms of chess piece custom models and animations (such as in the Harry Potter or the Star Wars movies).

Acknowledgements

The authors wish to thank Yann Suteau and Steven Poupeau for their work on the first tactile chess prototype. This work would not have been possible without the hardware provided by Polytech'Tours

References

[1] AR Chess. https://www.youtube.com/watch?v=GOzPtKTbHsU.

[2] ARToolKit. http://www.hitl.washington.edu/artoolkit/.

[3] Augmented Reality Chess. https://www.youtube.com/watch?v=W94CEyVGrm0.

[4] Augmented Reality Chess Game. https://www.youtube.com/watch?v=__LbAr2DJOs.

[5] Augmented Reality Chess with WiiMote. https://www.youtube.com/watch?v=Zz5CD_99H8g.

[6] Contra Labs Augmented Reality Chess Game. https://www.youtube.com/watch?v=MiBeYslAmv4.

[7] Microsoft PixelSense. https://www.microsoft.com/en-us/pixelsense/.

[8] Qualcomm Vuforia. https://www.qualcomm.com/products/vuforia.

[9] SolidChess. http://studentguru.gr/b/solidus/archive/2010/06/04/solidchess-a-chess-program-for-my-thesis.

[10] Unity3d Game Engine. https://unity3d.com/.

[11] Virtual Chess - Augmented Reality Chess for Android. https://www.youtube.com/watch?v=T7-7Ebod7bc.

[12] Bakker, S., Vorstenbosch, D., van den Hoven, E., Hollemans, G., and Bergman, T. Tangible interaction in tabletop games: Studying iconic and symbolic play pieces. In *Proc. International Conference on Advances in Computer Entertainment Technology* (2007), 163–170.

[13] Ishii, H. The tangible user interface and its evolution. *ACM. Organic user interfaces 51*, 6 (2008), 32–36.

[14] Iwata, T., Yamabe, T., Polojärvi, M., and Nakajima, T. Traditional games meet ict: A case study on go game augmentation. In *Proc. Fourth International Conference on Tangible, Embedded, and Embodied Interaction*, TEI '10 (2010), 237–240.

[15] Magerkurth, C., Cheok, A. D., Mandryk, R. L., and Nilsen, T. Pervasive games: Bringing computer entertainment back to the real world. *ACM Computers in Entertainment 3*, 3 (2005), 4–4.

[16] Molla, E., and Lepetit, V. Augmented reality for board games. In *ISMAR*, IEEE Computer Society (2010), 253–254.

Augmenting Remote Presence For Interactive Dashboard Collaborations

Rodrigo Pizarro
EVENT Lab
Universitat de Barcelona
Barcelona 08035, Spain
rodrigo.pizarro@ub.edu

Mark Hall
Airbus Group Innovations
Newport NP10 8FZ, UK
mark.hall@eads.com

Pablo Bermell-Garcia
Airbus Group Innovations
Newport NP10 8FZ, UK
pablo.bermell-garcia@airbus.com

Mar Gonzalez-Franco
Airbus Group Innovations
Newport NP10 8FZ, UK
mar.gonzalez@airbus.com

ITS '15, November 15-18, 2015, Funchal, Portugal
ACM 978-1-4503-3899-8/15/11.
http://dx.doi.org/10.1145/2817721.2823486

Abstract
We implement the use of silhouette representation for collaboration using interactive dashboards. In order to test its effectiveness against other modalities of interaction we ran a guided data exploration task in a Visual Analytics tool using a tactile dashboard in three modes: face-to-face, teleconference, and enhanced teleconference with silhouette representation. Even though no performance differences were found across the conditions, results show increased coordination abilities of the participants when the remote person is represented by a silhouette, furthermore important behavioral changes related to the presence illusion are also found only in the silhouette condition.

Author Keywords
Dashboard collaboration; Presence; CSCW; Silhouette shadowing

ACM Classification Keywords
H.5. Information interfaces and presentation; H.4.3: Computer conferencing, teleconferencing, and videoconferencing; I.3.7. Color, shading, shadowing and texture

Introduction
Computer Supported Co-operative Working (CSCW) systems enable distributed individuals to work together on tasks which improves their level of productivity [1] and enhances collaboration [4]. This collaboration may be broadly divided into three categories, namely (i)

communication (ii) information sharing, and (iii) co-ordination [9]. Inevitably, face-to-face encounters will provide a richer form of collaboration due to eye contact, body gestures and proxemics, and there is a benefit to achieving similar experiences during remote collaboration [6,7,11]. In that line, Mixed Presence Groupware aims to support remote participants working over a shared workspaces [8] by combining video conferencing with synchronized devices [10]. These systems include: distributed tabletops [15], large interactive displays [3], immersive telepresence [11], robots [12] and tangible interfaces [2].

To provide richer presence on an interactive dashboard we implement a real-time silhouette shadow (Figure 1) that can provide body gestures and offer an improved means of collaboration [5]. Although presence is sometimes understood as the illusion of being transported to a remote location [13,14], in this research we focus on the contrary effect of feeling somebody present in the local destination. We tested our silhouette approach following a user study that further evaluates the effectiveness of the CSCW system in providing communication, information sharing and co-ordination. Participants undertake a guided task using the interactive dashboard in three conditions of interaction, including both face-to-face and remote situations, with and without silhouette.

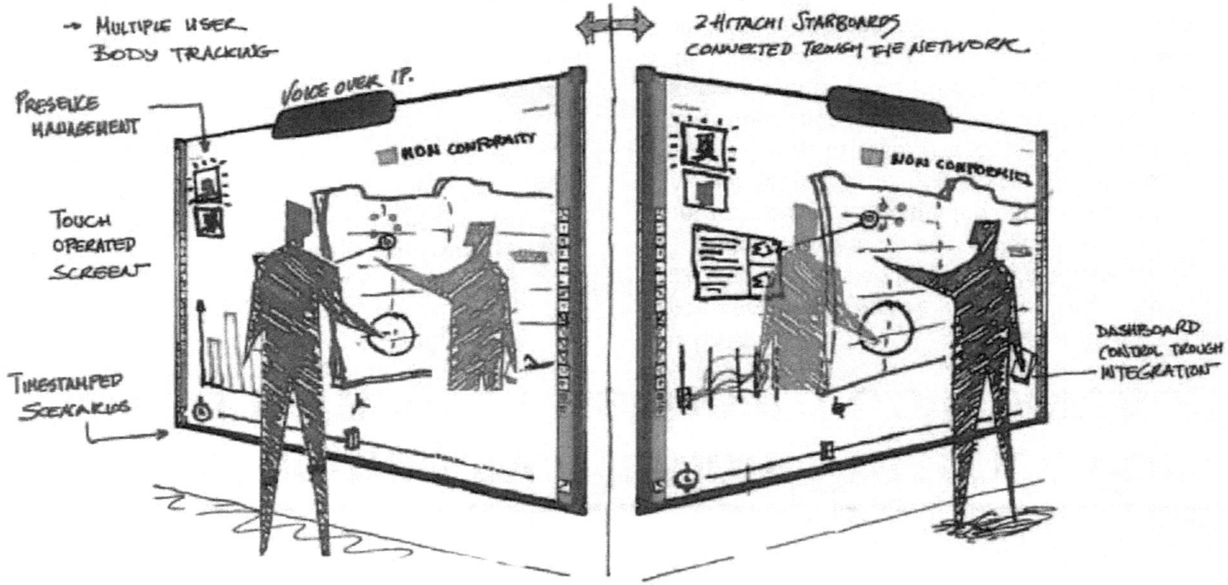

Figure 1: Concept with two tactile whiteboards with silhouettes to augment remote presence during interactive collaborations.

Figure 2: Top: Face-to-face interaction. Bottom: remote silhouette interaction.

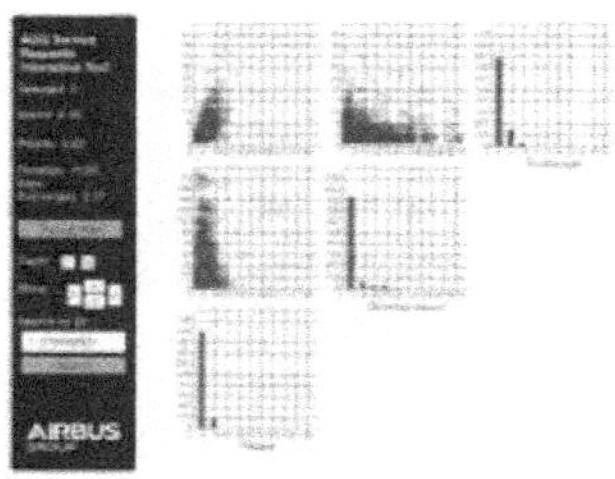

Figure 3: Dashboard containing a multidimensional data Scatterplot Matrix (SPLOM) with histograms. On the left side of the screen we show statistical information of the selected points.

Materials and Methods

We carried out an experiment to test different means of interactions with touch whiteboards. In particular we wanted to explore the use of this technology for Visual Analytics dashboards in remote collaboration (Figure 1). In order to do so we ran three different experimental conditions: real face-to-face interaction, teleconference interaction, and teleconference interaction with silhouette representation (Figure 2).

Participant recruitment

18 participants aged 32 ± 10.5 years old (1 female) volunteered for the experiment. Following the Declaration of Helsinki all participants were given an information sheet, signed informed consent and agreed to participate in the study. Participants were distributed across conditions balancing technological expertise using scatterplots, videoconferencing and tactile systems.

Apparatus

During the experiment, participants stood in front of an infrared based multi-touch whiteboard (Hitachi Starboard FX-DUO-77) combined with board pens, which emulate mouse movements and clicks. The display was presented through a ceiling-hung NEC VT695 projector at a 1024x768 resolution. The whiteboard was 1.57 x 1.18 meters and driven by an HP ZBook 17 laptop running the client application in Windows 7. In the multi-touch screen we implemented a dashboard with over 4,000 data points (Figure 3). The interaction with the data can be performed by clicking and dragging the board pen. The area contained in the selection while performing it is marked in a transparent gray rectangular shape. All selected points are highlighted in green (See Supplementary Video).

We used Photon Networking[1] engine to deal with the communication between computers and application. Additionally, with that engine, all the interaction with the data was synchronized, i.e. selection areas and selected points.

Silhouette

Using a Logitec C310 camera mounted to the ceiling projector we monitored the activity at the whiteboard. The video footage was used to calculate and later overlay the silhouette of the participants in a remote location. The images were streamed to the remote location at 5 fps, 160x120 resolution and PNG compression. In order to calculate the silhouette we capture an initial image of the whiteboard without the participant and then all subsequent frames calculate the pixel-by-pixel difference with respect to the original one using GPU fragment shading. The silhouette is then overlaid as semi-transparent. Choosing the right threshold we were able to filter the noise produced by echo, small changes in ambient lighting and sensor errors, thus distinguish the human silhouette.

To crop the camera capture to the area of the whiteboard we perform a four-point calibration where the experimenter manually selects the four edges of the board. With that information, we can calculate the distortion produced by the angle in which the camera is looking at the screen, and counter the linear distortion to generate an output image that looks aligned with the renders.

[1] http://www.photonengine.com

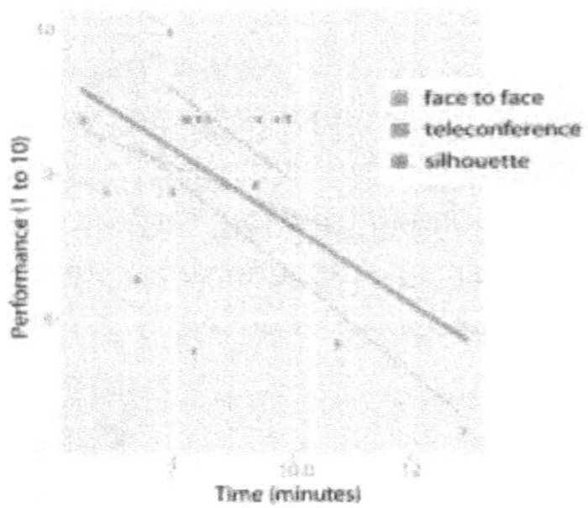

Figure 4: Correlation between time and performance (from 1 to 10) in solid blue.

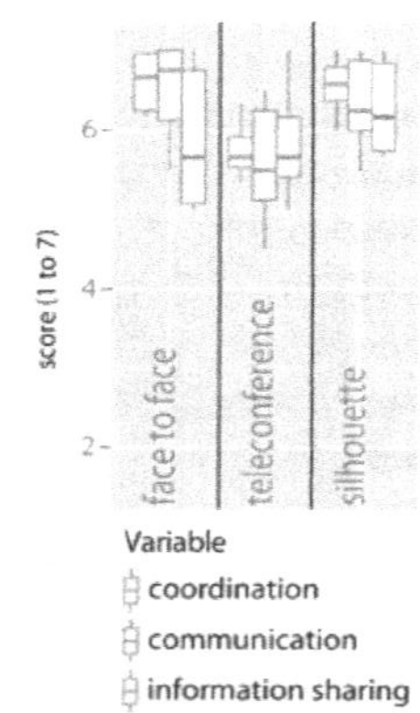

Figure 5: Collaborative Work scores (from 1 to 7).

Experiment procedure
We ran a between-groups study, i.e. each participant underwent only one of the three conditions. Participants were guided through a task that was identical in all conditions so we could measure performance effects. Participants completed a demographics questionnaire and familiarized themselves with the touchboard and the pen for a brief period before starting the actual experiment to ensure they knew how to operate the hardware. When they felt comfortable with it, the experiment was ready to begin.

In the face-to-face condition, the experimenter stood in front of participants, while in the teleconference and silhouette conditions, the experimenter was in a remote location and communicated remotely with participants through a phone call and through the dashboard, as both the experimenter and the participants could draw selections. The only difference between the two remote conditions is that in the Silhouette one we overlaid the shadow of each user in the remote location.

At the beginning of the guided task, the experimenter gave some context to the data, explaining its origin and meaning. Subsequently, we asked participants to perform some operations that involved selecting particular cases or sets of cases that followed specific criteria stated by the experimenter. A second experimenter silently monitored the actions of the participant and evaluated if they were performed correctly and kept track of the time spent.

Finally, participants filled a CSCW post-questionnaire to assess their Information Sharing, Communication and Coordination experience during the task. Those who were assigned to the remote conditions filled an additional questionnaire related to their feeling of presence [13] that included questions such as: "*While I was interacting I tried to avoid occupying the same side as the experimenter's shadow*", "*I felt as if the experimenter was just by my side, I could feel her presence*", "*I felt the experimenter was being transported to my location*". The last two questions were combined to create a presence score.

Results and Discussion

Performance
No Significant differences were found on the correctness of the task performance score (Kruskal-Wallis, $\chi^2(2)=1.2$, $p=0.5$) nor in the time spent to complete the task ($\chi^2(2)=0.33$, $p=0.8$). This is probably due to a ceiling effect, as we find all the participants completed the task notably well. However, a significant correlation between time and performance score was found (Pearson correlation, $r(16)=0.52$, $p=0.024$) (Figure 4). In general, participants that performed better also did it faster. Although this might seem contradictory, the reality is that the participants that had to interact more with the experimenter in order to understand the question or were not sure about their answers and took more time to finalize the task.

Collaborative Work
When looking at the collaborative work related questions the scores are also high for all conditions (Figure 5). However, a significant difference was found in the coordination capabilities of the different methods ($\chi^2(2)=9.1$, $p=0.01$). Furthermore, the multiple comparison post-hoc test shows significant differences between the face-to-face condition and the teleconference conditions ($p<0.05$) as well as between the teleconference and the silhouette conditions

($p<0.05$), but not between the face-to-face and the silhouette conditions ($p>0.5$). This result could be interpreted as if the silhouette condition was able to provide similar levels of coordination to the real face-to-face situation, which was not always possible using only teleconference.

The other two main variables related to collaborative work (communication and information sharing) did not show significant differences among the three conditions. This lack of difference in the communication score could be due to the high expertise of the participants in the use of videoconferences, as at least 66% of the participants reported using videoconferences at least on a monthly basis. Regarding the information sharing, the technology and methods for information and dashboards remained consistent across all conditions, all participants used the same tactile board to display and interact with the data, and therefore it is within our expectations to find no differences.

Presence

The presence questionnaire was provided only to the participants in the remote conditions (teleconference and silhouette). We find a significant differences ($\chi^2(1)=8.4$, $p=0.003$): participants in the shadow condition felt more as if they were in the same location as the experimenter (Figure 6). Furthermore, in the shadow condition, we found that most of the participants significantly preferred to look at the shadow than to actually follow only the audio instructions ($\chi^2(1)=8.3$, $p=0.004$).

Interestingly we also found a great amount of participants that would avoid occupying the space of the experimenter shadow (score 5.7, std=1.6 out of 7), which is in line with the stronger feeling of having the experimenter located by their side ($\chi^2(1)=3.6$, $p=0.05$).

Conclusions

In recent years, teams and companies have adopted workflows that involve working remotely. The current findings could prove useful for many situations in which those groups require remote collaborative work.

The present results indicate that when people see the remote person's shadow, they feel as if that person had been transported to their location to a greater extent that when there is no shadow. Even though participants were consciously aware that the other person was interacting with them remotely, they developed behaviors associated with face-to-face encounters, such as keeping an interpersonal space distance or paying attention to the body language and gestures rather than only focusing on the auditory clues. This presence illusion may explain the differences found in collaboration capabilities among the two remote conditions. Evidence suggests that those who experienced the silhouette condition were able to work collaboratively as they would do in a face-to-face encounter, while that was not achieved in the only teleconference condition. In traditional remote CSCW non-verbal communication is lost; our approach seems to provide at least a subset of that information that could enhance collaboration, being thus a Mixed Presence Groupware.

Additionally, unlike many screen sharing setups, e.g. Webex, our approach allowed bidirectional interaction and that might be also key to understanding the performance ceiling effect.

References

[1] Baecker, R.M., Grudin, J., Buxton, W. a S., and Greenberg, S.Readings in Human Computer Interaction: Toward the Year 2000. (1995), 950.

[2] Brave, S., Ishii, H., and Dahley, A.Tangible interfaces for remote collaboration and communication. *CSCW*, ACM Press (1998), 169–178.

[3] Elrod, S., Pier, K., Tang, J., et al.Liveboard: a large interactive display supporting group meetings, presentations, and remote collaboration. *CHI*, ACM Press (1992), 599–607.

[4] Eseryel, D. and Edmonds, G.S.Review of Computer-Supported Collaborative Work Systems. *Educational Technology & Society 5*, 2 (2002), 130–136.

[5] Everitt, K.M., Klemmer, S.R., Lee, R., and Landay, J. a.Two worlds apart: bridging the gap between physical and virtual media for distributed design collaboration. *CHI*, ACM Press (2003), 553–560.

[6] Gonzalez-Franco, M. and Chou, P.A.Non-linear modeling of eye gaze perception as a function of gaze and head direction. *QoMEX*, IEEE (2014).

[7] Gonzalez-Franco, M., Hall, M., Hansen, D., Jones, K., Hannah, P., and Bermell-Garcia, P.Framework for remote collaborative interaction in virtual environments based on proximity. *3DUI*, IEEE (2015), 153–154.

[8] Greenberg, S., Greenberg, S., Boyle, M., Boyle, M., Tang, A., and Tang, A.Display and presence disparity in Mixed Presence Groupware. *28*, 2003 (2004), 73–82.

[9] Grudin, J Poltrock, S.Computer Supported Cooperative Work. In *The Encyclopedia of Human-Computer Interaction, 2nd Ed.* Aarhus, Denmark: The Interaction Design Foundation., 2014.

[10] Gumienny, R., Meinel, C., Gericke, L., Quasthoff, M., LoBue, P., and Willems, C.Tele-Board: Enabling Efficient Collaboration In Digital Design Spaces Across Time and Distance. In *Design Thinking*. Springer Berlin Heidelberg, Berlin, Heidelberg, 2011, 147–164.

[11] Higuchi, K., Chen, Y., Chou, P.A., Zhang, Z., and Liu, Z.ImmerseBoard: Immersive Telepresence Experience using a Digital Whiteboard. *CHI*, ACM Press (2015), 2383–2392.

[12] Kishore, S., González-Franco, M., Hintermuller, C., et al.Comparison of SSVEP BCI and Eye Tracking for Controlling a Humanoid Robot in a Social Environment. *Presence: Teleoerators and Virtual Environments 23*, 3 (2014), 242–252.

[13] Slater, M., Usoh, M., and Steed, A.Depth of presence in virtual environments. *Presence 3*, 2 (1994), 1–33.

[14] Spanlang, B., Normand, J.-M., Borland, D., et al.How to Build an Embodiment Lab: Achieving Body Representation Illusions in Virtual Reality. *Frontiers in Robotics and AI 1*, November (2014), 1–22.

[15] Tuddenham, P. and Robinson, P.Distributed tabletops: Supporting remote and mixed-presence tabletop collaboration. *Tabletop*, IEEE (2007), 19–26.

Walls Have Ears: Using Conductive Surfaces of Furniture and Everyday Objects for Room-Wide Power Usage and Crowd Activity Sensing

Adiyan Mujibiya
Junji Torii
Rakuten Institute of Technology,
Rakuten, Inc.
1-14-1 Tamagawa, Setagaya-Ku,
Tokyo. Japan
adiyan@acm.org
ts-junji.torii@rakuten.com

ITS '15, November 15-18, 2015, Funchal, Portugal
ACM 978-1-4503-3899-8/15/11.
http://dx.doi.org/10.1145/2817721.2823487

Abstract
We propose a design of self-powering room-wide power usage and crowd activity sensing that uses a single point of contact on a conductive surface of furniture or everyday objects such as metal frame of table or window, desktop PC case, rack, cabinet, and so on. We utilize these surfaces for energy scavenging from capacitive reactance and electromagnetic inductance, which are typically, occur in indoor house and office where there are many electrical appliances. We incorporate energy store and release strategy, and treat the charge accumulation time as a function of electrical appliance usage and human activity within a certain location. In this paper, we highlight principle of operation and prototype implementation result showing sensing log of an office room for 7 days timespan.

Author Keywords
Infrastructure-mediated sensing; localized crowd activity sensing; energy harvesting.

ACM Classification Keywords
H.5.m. Information interfaces and presentation (e.g., HCI): Miscellaneous

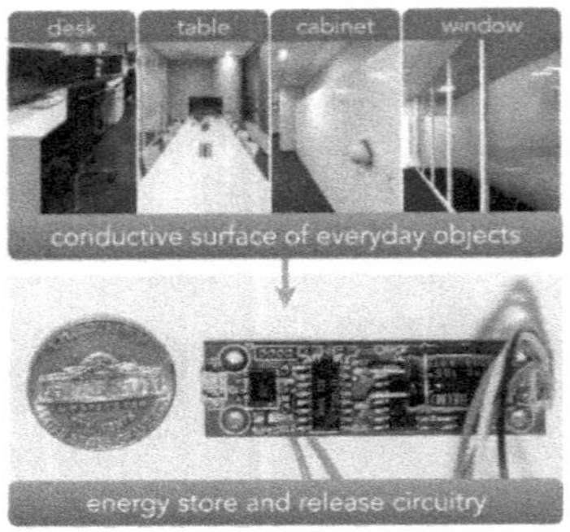

Figure 1: Scenario of our approach in leveraging the surface of everyday objects such as desk, table, cabinet, or window frame to perform room-wide power usage and activity sensing.

Introduction

Activity recognition is one of the main subjects in UbiComp and HCI field that can deliver great value and service for the users. Although personal activity recognition has been actively researched and commercially widespread (see [6] for a review), crowd activity recognition has been facing many challenges in providing effective and privacy aware solution. In separate work [6], we have shown that by measuring temporal characteristics of the ambient electric field we could infer a user's motion, gesture, and a short period of activity. However, we still need to source the power external from the sensor. Additionally, extended signal logging contains low signal-to-noise ratio (SNR).

In this paper, we present the design and feasibility evaluation of a self-powering room-wide power usage and crowd activity sensing that uses a single point of contact on a conductive surface of a furniture or everyday objects. We show that a table's metal frame paired with a reasonably good grounding from a desktop PC case can be utilized for energy scavenging, which leverages capacitive reactance and electromagnetic inductance typically occur in indoor house and office where there are many electrical appliances. We incorporate energy store and release energy scavenging strategy, and treat the capacitor's charge accumulation time as a function of electrical appliance usage and activity within a location. Figure 1 depicts overall scenario of our approach.

In contrast to other solutions such as utilizing optical sensors combined with computer vision techniques, or more conventional methods by analyzing data of an electricity meter; our approach offers the following advantages: 1) novel and effective utilization of a furniture's conductive surface towards infrastructure-mediated sensing; 2) completely self-powering, without any need for external power supply; 3) most houses and offices have sufficient amount of electrical appliances emitting considerable amount of electric fields for power scavenging; 4) preserves user privacy by not collecting camera frames or user specific inertial data; 5) low-cost both in bill-of-material and data storage/analysis; 6) completely localized single-point deployment. Therefore, directly wiring or clamping power line are unnecessary. Our contributions are therefore, summarized as follows:

- We propose a circuit model to explain the theory of operation, implemented our sensor design, and present details on its characteristics.
- We demonstrate power charge and delivery using our prototype hardware, and present a weeklong power usage and activity sensing experiment.

Related Work

Crowd activity sensing solutions often require massive deployment of sensors within an environment [4,9]. Add-on sensor installation cost for an existing office or house is not currently a feasible economy. Additionally, massive amount of sensors outputting large data will pose a challenge to process. Realizing this challenge, a hybrid approach that combines sensing from user individual smartphone and central computation server has been proposed [13]. In this scenario, user intention and a confirmation of participation are required.

Non-invasive sensing solutions to infer individual user's state have also been actively researched [1,6]. In this work, we aim to leverage similar non-invasive approach to infer activity within a certain location (e.g. room in typical house or office). Infrastructure-mediated

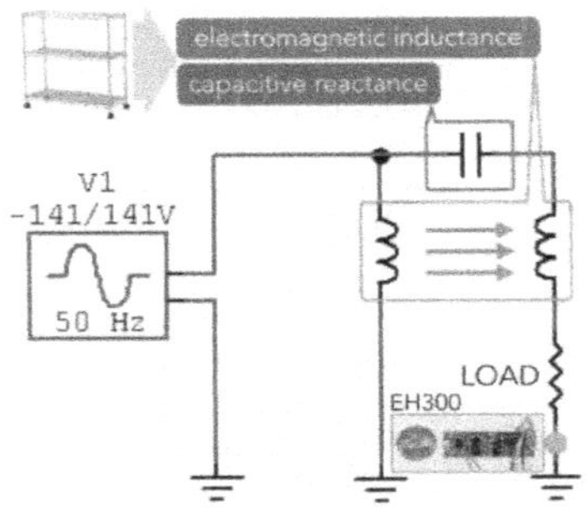

Figure 2: Circuit model and illustration of the hardware setup used for experiments to evaluate our proposed method.

sensing has been an active field of research due to its promising affordance in real-world deployment [2,3,11,12]. We share similar interest and aim to extend research in the domain of infrastructure mediated sensing. In this work, we extend [6,7] and propose self-powering solution that leverages readily available surfaces of the furniture and other surrounding everyday objects, which treats the charge accumulation time as a function of electrical appliance usage and human activity within a certain location.

Harvesting energy from an ambient wave, especially from radio waves have been actively researched. Previous research have proposed power harvesting from Radio Frequency (RF) [8,10,14], broadcasting TV towers [15], and from electromagnetic compatibility of leakage from a microwave oven's radio wave [5]. In this work, we explore the feasibility to use everyday objects, which are configured from conductive materials to harvest, store, and log charge accumulation to infer room-wide power usage and users activity.

Theory of Operation

Within our indoor living space, we often surrounded by various types of electrical appliances such as PCs, monitors, printers, HVAC system, and power lines that are continuously emitting electric fields. In this work, we use the resulting capacitive reactance and electromagnetic inductance (Figure 2) to provide electrical power to our sensing solution, and as a signal to infer the power usage and temporal activity.

In this work, we incorporate EH300[1] energy harvesting modules produced by Advanced Linear devices, which enable collection of energy from generators that produce low current. The charging input is specified above 4V at 200nA. Output of EH300 is enabled as soon as the capacitor reaches 3.5V and the output is kept active until the capacitor discharges to 1.9V.

Application: Activity Log in an Office Room

In this section, we explore the usability of our technique when deployed on a typical office work desk, located in an approximately 90m^2 wide non-partitioned office room. The room has many electrical appliances, such as PCs, LCD monitors, printers, etc. The actual setting of the study is depicted in Figure 3, which resembles the circuitry model depicted in Figure 2.

The desk we used was measured at 160×60cm. It had metal supporting frame that was exposed in the underside of the table's surface. The metal frame was coated by paint; therefore to ensure stable connection we located and connected the table's frame securing screw to EH300's J1+ terminal. In this experiment, we utilized an exposed screw of a PC's graphic card display connector as ground. The PC was always turned off during the entire period of this experiment.

Output Characteristics

Using the aforementioned setup, we took 10 measurement samples that were in average of 25 seconds. With this result we estimate the charging parameters. EH300 is equipped with 1000μF capacitor. The V_p terminal will be activated once the capacitor's charge achieved V_H=3.5V, and deactivated when discharged until V_L=1.9V. Therefore, electric charge for one charging period Q is:

[1] Advanced Linear Devices. Datashet - EH300/301: EPAD energy harvesting modules. http://www.aldinc.com/pdf/EH300.pdf

Figure 3: We deployed our approach on a work desk in an office room. The EH300's J1+ terminal was connected to the desk's metal frame, while the J1– terminal was connected to a display connector screw on a PC that was turned off during the experiments. We used a separate PC with a TWE-Lite USB-C receiver to log the capacitor charging time.

$$\mathrm{Q} = \mathrm{CV} \tag{1}$$
$$\mathrm{Q} = 1000 \cdot 10^{-6} \cdot (3.5 - 1.9)$$
$$\mathrm{Q} = 1600\mu\mathrm{C}$$

Hence, the charging current I_C for the aforementioned experiment environment was:

$$I_C = \frac{Q}{T} \tag{2}$$
$$I_C = \frac{1600\times10^{-6}}{25}$$
$$I_C = 57.16\mu\mathrm{A}$$

We estimate usable energy from EH300's capacitor:

$$\mathrm{E} = \frac{CV^2}{2} \tag{3}$$
$$E_{total} = \frac{1000\times10^{-6}\times3.5^2}{2} = 6.125mJ$$
$$E_{remain} = \frac{1000\times10^{-6}\times1.9^2}{2} = 1.805m$$

$$\mathrm{E} = E_{total} - E_{remain} = 4.32mJ$$

We conducted a weeklong experiment using our proposed strategy. Our experiment setup was configured as Figure 3. This experiment spanned from Monday February 23rd to Monday March 2nd, 2015.

Data Logging Configuration
We utilized a IEEE802.15.4 wireless module to send three consecutive packets to a receiver (TWE-Lite USB-C), which was located separately (d ≅ 5m). Within each packet, we send a sender device ID and a timestamp in milliseconds. Device ID was useful to avoid confusion between our experiment setup and other general communications. The timestamp was used to record the elapsed time between the beacon packets.

We designed our wireless module's firmware to send three consecutive packets when the module is powered using the accumulated energy from the environment. We verify the arrival of the three packets to filter bad transmission. We subtracted first packets of the consecutive period of operation to obtain capacitor's charging time.

Statistics of the Obtained Data
The statistics of the collected data are as follows:

- We collected 71,587 beacon packets during the one-week experiment.
- We filtered the collected data based on elapsed time, where we omit data with elapsed time less than 300 milliseconds, or greater than 60,000 milliseconds. This threshold values were decided by taking account of average elapsed time data (upper boundary), as well as to omit second and third beacon packets within the same period of operation (lower boundary).
- As the result of our filtering approach, we kept 24,654 data points.

Experiment Result
Our extended activity logging experiment results is shown in Figure 4. For easier interpretation, we show dateline, as well as both office working hours and non-working hours. We also show hourly moving average of the capacitor charging time by averaging consecutive 148 data points. This value was decided from the overall average charging time, which was 24.25 seconds. From the results, we can easily observe the temporal fluctuations, which are the capacitor charging time, ranged between 21 to 26 seconds. From the energy harvesting point-of-view, this result was encouraging when we consider the simplicity and affordability of our strategy.

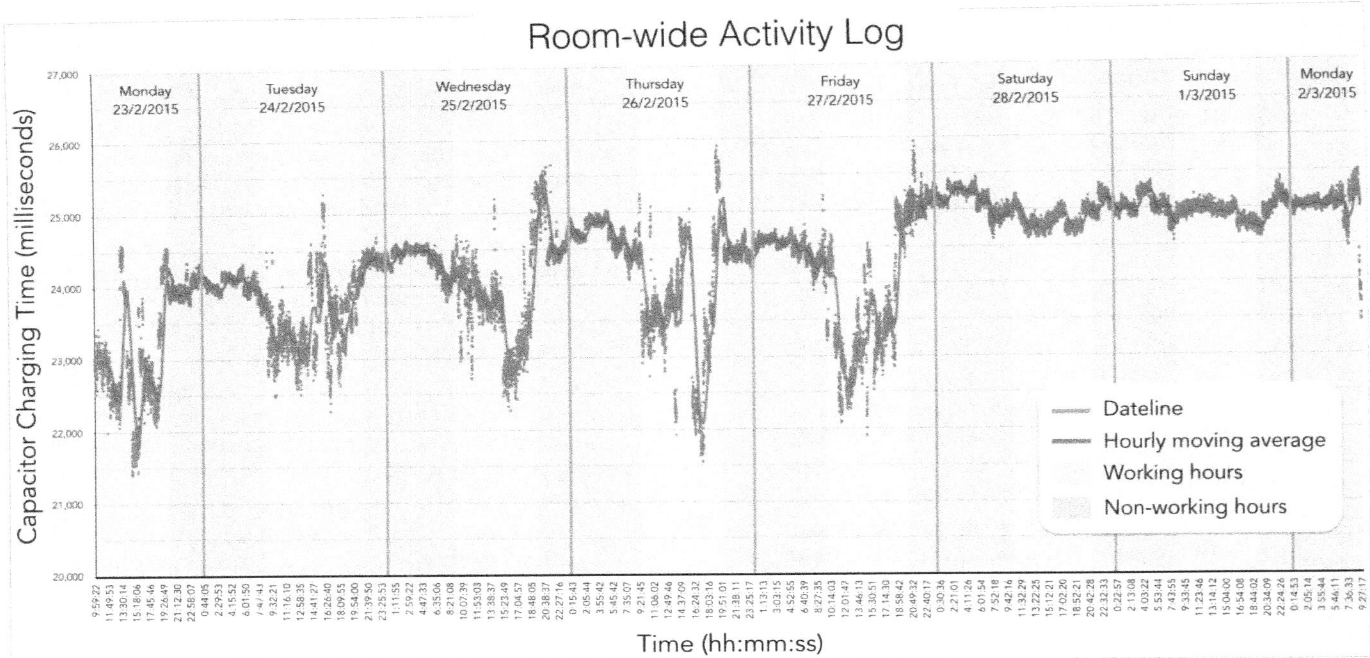

Figure 4: A weeklong room-wide activity log result using our proposed method.

Moreover, the temporal fluctuations in the capacitor charging time are intriguing. We highlighted office working hours and non-working hours in yellow and blue shade, accordingly. From Figure 4 we can easily observe that during the office working hours, the capacitor charging time were generally lower. Therefore we can conclude that there were larger magnitudes of ambient electric fields thus enable faster capacitor charging. This was mainly caused by the increasing amount of electric field emitted by electrical appliances such as PCs, monitors, etc., that were turned on during these hours. In contrast, non-working hours and weekends (Saturday and Sunday) depict less temporal fluctuations but longer capacitor charging time.

Conclusion and Future Work

We presented the design and feasibility evaluation of a self-powering room-wide power usage and crowd activity sensing that uses a single point of contact on a conductive surface of a furniture or everyday objects. We demonstrated that a table's metal frame paired with a reasonably good grounding from a desktop PC case can be utilized for energy scavenging from capacitive reactance and electromagnetic inductance, which are typically occur in indoor house and office where there are many electrical appliances emitting electrical field. We incorporated energy store and release energy scavenging strategy, and treated the capacitor's charge accumulation time as a function of electrical appliance usage and people's activity within a room. By conducting one weeklong office room logging experiment, we identified limitations to further refine our design and implementation.

References

1. Adib, F., Mao, H., Kabelac, Z., Katabi, D., Miller, R.C. Smart homes that monitor breathing and heart rate. In Proc. of CHI '15, pp. 837-846.
2. Cohn, G., Stuntebeck, E., Pandey, J., Otis, B., Abowd, G.D., Patel, S.N. SNUPI: sensor nodes utilizing powerline infrastructure. In Proc. of UbiComp '10, pp. 159-168.
3. Gupta, S., Reynolds, M.S., Patel, S.N. ElectriSense: single-point sensing using EMI for electrical event detection and classification in the home. In Proc. of UbiComp '10, pp. 139-148.
4. Intille, S.S., Larson, K., Tapia, E.M., Beaudin, J.S., Kaushik, P., Nawyn, J., Rockinson, R. Using a live-in laboratory for ubiquitous computing research, Proceedings of the 4th international conference on Pervasive Computing, pp. 349-365, 2006.
5. Kawahara, Y., Bian, X., Shigeta, R., Vyas, R., Tentzeris, M.M., Asami, T. Power harvesting from microwave oven electromagnetic leakage. In *Proc. of* UbiComp '13, pp. 373-382.
6. Mujibiya, A. and Rekimoto, J. Mirage: exploring interaction modalities using off-body static electric field sensing. In *Proc. of* UIST '13, pp. 211-220.
7. Mujibiya, A., and Torii, J. Demo: Energy Harvesting Using Everyday Objects. In *Proc. of* MobiSys '15, pp. 457-457.
8. Nishimoto, H., Kawahara, Y., Asami, T. Prototype implementation of ambient RF energy harvesting wireless sensor networks. In *Proceedings of the IEEE Sensors,* pp. 1282-1287, 2010.
9. Noguchi, H., Mori, T., Sato, T. Attentive information support with massive embedded sensors in room. In *Proc. of* HCI'07, pp. 883-892.
10. Parks, A.N., Sample, A.P., Zhao, Y., Smith, J.R. A wireless sensing platform utilizing ambient RF energy. In *Proceedings of the 2013 IEEE Topical Conference on Wireless Sensors and Sensor Networks (WiSNet)*, pp. 127-129, 2013.
11. Patel, S.N., Reynolds, M.S., Abowd, G.D. Detecting human movement by differential air pressure sensing in HVAC system ductwork: an exploration in infrastructure mediated sensing. In Proc. of Pervasive '08, pp. 1-18.
12. Patel, S.N., Robertson, T., Kientz, J.A., Reynolds, M.S., Abowd, G.D. At the flick of a switch: detecting and classifying unique electrical events on the residential power line. In Proc. of UbiComp '07, pp. 271-288.
13. Rachuri, K.K., Efstratiou, C., Leontiadis, I., Mascolo, C., Rentfrow, P.J. Smartphone sensing offloading for efficiently supporting social sensing applications. Pervasive Mob. Comput. 10 (February 2014), pp. 3-21, 2014.
14. Sample, A., Smith, J.R. Experimental results with two wireless power transfer systems. In *Proceedings of the IEEE Radio and Wireless Symposium, 2009 (RWS '09)*, pp. 6-18, 2009.
15. Vyas, R.J., Cook, B.B., Kawahara, Y., Tentzeris, M.M. E-WEHP: a batteryless embedded sensor-platform wirelessly powered from ambient digital-TV signals. In *Proceedings of the IEEE Transactions on Microwave Theory and Techniques*, vol.61, no.6, pp. 2491-2505, June 2013.

MoBat: Sound-Based Localization of Multiple Mobile Devices on Everyday Surfaces

Adrian Kreskowski
Jakob Wagner
Jannis Bossert
Florian Echtler

Bauhaus-Universität Weimar
Weimar, Germany
firstname.lastname
@uni-weimar.de

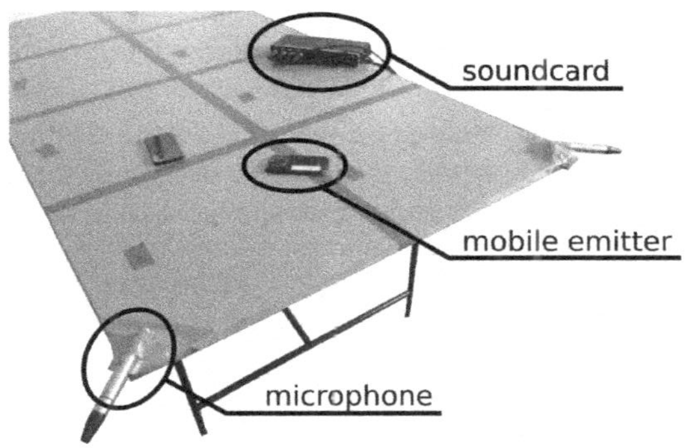

Figure 1: An overview of the used hardware. Shown is the USB sound device in the back, two mobile phones on the table and two microphones in front.

ITS '15, November 15-18, 2015, Funchal, Portugal.
ACM 978-1-4503-3899-8/15/11.
http://dx.doi.org/10.1145/2817721.2823488

Abstract

We present MoBat, a combined hard- and software system designed to locate and track multiple unmodified mobile devices on any regular table using passive acoustic sensing. Barely audible sound pulses are emitted from mobile devices, picked up by four microphones located in the corners of the surface and processed in a low-latency pipeline to extract position data. We demonstrate an average positional accuracy and precision of about 3 cm on a table of 1 m x 2 m size, and discuss possible usage scenarios regarding proxemics and tangible interaction.

Author Keywords

Sound-based Localization; Tangible Interfaces; Multitouch Surfaces; Mobile Devices; Time Difference of Arrival

ACM Classification Keywords

H.5.2 [User Interfaces]: Input devices and strategies

Introduction and Related Work

Personal mobile devices are quickly turning into a central element of users' information behaviour. Various types of data are collected and shared using these devices, and novel interaction metaphors like proxemics need to take this aspect of personal information management into account. Multiple approaches exist to locate mobile devices with respect to each other and to the environment. However, such

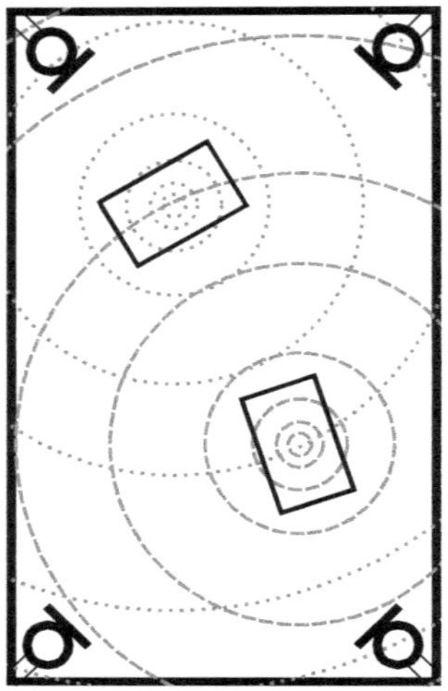

Figure 2: A sketch of the tabletop hardware setup: The rectangle indicates a tabletop area of arbitrary 2D dimensions. The black circles near the corner indicate the four microphones, which are used to record the audio sources. We furthermore sketched two audio sources emitting sound on different frequencies as illustrated by the color coding and different stroke style of the concentric circles. The center of each circle represents the position of the audio sources.

methods usually require prior setup in the form of attaching fiducial markers or other tracking aids.

In this paper, we present *MoBat*, a hard- and software system designed to locate mobile devices on a surface using passive acoustic sensing of barely audible sound pulses. We distinguish between two core parts, the emitter and the tracking side. On the emitter side, only the capability to play an audio stream is required. For the tracking, the surface merely needs to be augmented using four cardioid microphones in the corners.

The usage of passive acoustic sensing to turn a flat surface into an input device was first realized by *Ishii et al.* [2], detecting the impact points of a ball on a Ping Pong table. This system was extended by *Paradiso et al.* [3] to detect and discern both taps with knuckles and a metal object on a glass surface. *Urashima et al.* [4] developed another system to identify letters from pen movements. However, all of these systems focus on detecting discrete sound events like taps rather than continuous signals.

There are two approaches for locating sound sources. The first one is the "Location Pattern Matching", which utilizes a collection of recorded signals and was used in [1] [2]. By comparing the recorded signal with the signals in the database, a position is determined. This pattern matching approach allows application on arbitrary surfaces with few microphones but requires a learning phase for each new setup. The second approach, "Time Difference of Arrival" (hereafter TDOA) was used in [3] [4] [5]. It is based on measuring the time difference of the sound's arrival at the different microphones. Knowing the position of the microphones and the speed of sound, the sound source can be located. This approach requires no learning phase but a homogeneous transfer medium and at least three microphones. For reasons of portability, we decided to base our system on TDOA.

Hardware Architecture

Due to the TDOA technique we apply for our sound localization, we rely on synchronously transmitted audio buffers. Therefore, the core part of our hardware setup is an external sound card with four connected microphones at known positions. It streams an audio buffer containing four channels via USB to our localization pipeline. Initially, we experimented with piezoelectric elements to sense the vibration within a chipboard table. However, the signal-to-noise ratio was insufficient for our transformation pipeline. By utilizing low-budget directional microphones, it was possible to clearly identify the signal. In addition to the soundcard and the microphones a standard PC was used for the signal processing. Figure 2 sketches a possible setup with four mounted microphones, and two audio sources; Figure 1 shows a photo of the used hardware.

Software Architecture

The first part of our software architecture is a sound emitting application. Running on a mobile device, it emits periods of a sine wave alternating with a pause. The sine signals can have a frequency of up to 20 kHz, depending on the individual devices' audio properties. The sine signal and the pause each have a fixed length. This alternation allows for continuous tracking of the devices by identifying peaks in the frequency domain after a pause (see Figure 4). Our system is able to parallel track multiple emitters with each of them producing different sine frequencies.

The pipeline is built to record an audio signal and locate the individually configured sound sources. The three main stages of the pipeline can be classified as the **Recorder**, **Analyzer** and the **Locator Stage** and are shown in Figure 3. In the following paragraphs, we will describe these in

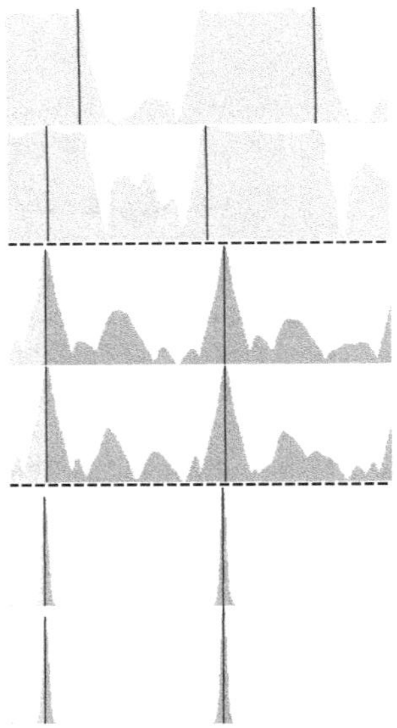

Figure 4: The image above visualizes three different types of accumulated amplitudes of a 19 kHz signal, for 2 channels each. The top third shows the results for 2 audio channels when the emitter is configured to use a longer sine than pause signal. A lot of consecutively executed STFTs will contain a similar frequency sum amplitude and therefore finding a peak is error prone. The center third shows the characteristic for a pause that is five times longer than the sine. The peaks, indicated by the black vertical bars, are detected within a valid range. The last third shows a post-processed signal.

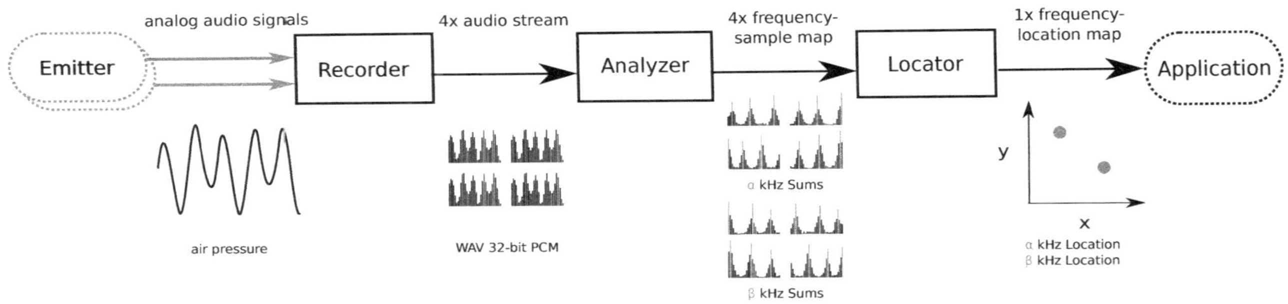

Figure 3: A simplified version of the MoBat Pipeline: Several emitters produce signals of different trackable frequencies, which are fed into the pipeline. They are then processed in three stages indicated by the boxes. These perform the recording of the audio signal, determination of frequency peaks per channel and the localization based on determined TDOAs per frequency. The output of the pipeline is a position for each located emitter.

detail.

RECORDER STAGE In this stage the analogue signal of the ambient sound is recorded and converted to digital 32-bit PCM by the sound card. The communication with the audio device is done using the *ALSA* sound library. For each of the four microphones, the audio signal is recorded within a time interval of 130 ms (contingent on the sound card) to natively ensure a high update rate for the entire localization.

ANALYZER STAGE The analyzer is responsible for determining a time-delta of the recorded channels for each of the frequencies registered in the pipeline. Similarly to the implementation in the Toffee pipeline of Xiao et al. [5], this is done by considering amplitudes per sample of each audio channel. However, since we aim to detect not only a single audio signal but multiple frequencies over time, it is not sufficient to sample the amplitude of the buffer of the recorded signal. In order to retrieve information about the different frequencies over time, we apply a series of short-time Fourier transformations (STFT) for each of the chunks per channel. For our pipeline, we consider a Fourier window size of 256 samples. Furthermore, a sliding window offset of one sample is used to work efficiently and with a sufficient temporal resolution for our purpose. Since the signal-to-noise ratio of the Fourier transformation of just one window per time-step is too low for a reasonable peak detection, we sum up the results of several consecutive Fourier windows. The latter can be applied with negligible costs by caching all but one result for the next frequency-amplitude sum. In order to reduce the memory footprint of our application, only the amplitudes of the registered frequencies are stored and further analyzed.

The frequency sums tend to take the shape of banks and therefore contain several local maxima as shown in Figure 4. The first step to distinguish the peaks from noise is a

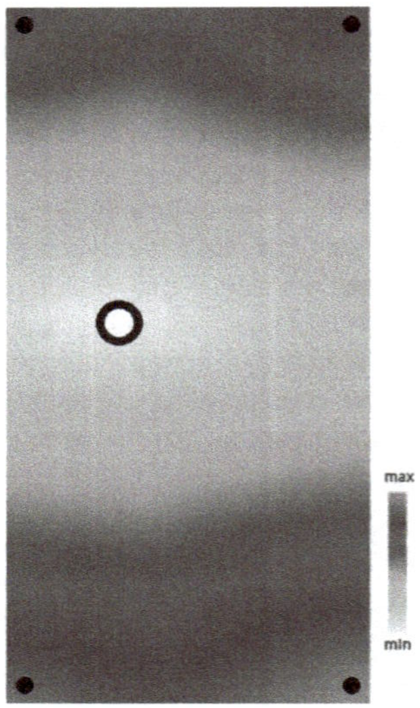

Figure 5: The error distribution of the TDOA method: The color coding of this heatmap visualizes the TDOA error for each of the uniform grid cells. The emitter (white circle) is assumed to be on the cell with the lowest error.

normalization of the frequency sums per chunk. The lowest and highest sums act as normalization limits. Hereby, the peaks below a certain threshold are filtered out. Yet, it is still not possible to accurately distinguish frequency peaks from intermediately high values by simple thresholding. This is due to different amounts of noise in recorded chunks, which can result in peaks of different height or different sharpness. In order to obtain a small number of distinct peaks, we exponentiate the sums at each sample. This operation results in a set of easily distinguishable peak candidates per chunk and channel.

When all channels contain a peak and the time distance between them is not larger than an adjustable threshold, closest peaks are matched. This is done under the assumption that the corresponding frequency peaks in different channels have a relatively small sample distance in a real environment. Based on this method, we achieve satisfactory results for our application as seen in the following section. Naturally, further filtering steps can be applied to the raw position data depending on the application context.

As a final remark on the analyzer stage, it should be noted that the STFT will create a power spectrum containing all frequencies. This transformation is by far more time consuming than the peak detection for a transformed signal. Therefore, the peak detection for additional frequencies does not severely affect the overall runtime.

LOCATOR STAGE The final stage of the MoBat pipeline receives the four determined signal starting times for each registered frequency. The area between the microphones is then uniformly divided into a 2D grid and the error is computed for each of the vertex positions in a TDOA manner using the same error formula as *Xiao et al.* Figure 5 shows the error distribution of the grid cells. Note that we concentrated on the analyzer stage for recognizing multiple sound sources; therefore, the locator stage does not employ a gradient-based optimization step. The processing overhead introduced by this naïve error-sampling approach can be considered as negligible for our system since the most expensive part of the pipeline remain the Fourier transformations.

Performance and Accuracy

SYSTEM SPECIFICATION The test set-up consisted of 4 *t.bone EM700* microphones, one *Behringer U-PHORIA UMC404* sound-card and a notebook with an *Intel Core i7-2630QM 2Ghz* CPU. As sound emitters, several *Nexus 4* devices were used. In each test we measured the position error and calculated the distance to the actual position, standard deviation and the 90-percentile.

The following list shows the most important parameters used in the tests described below:

- sine length: 5 ms
- pause length: 25 ms
- recording duration per smartphone position: 1 min
- table size: 2m x 1m
- sampling grid cell size: 1cm
- Fourier window size: 256 samples

The parameters above were established empirically and led to the best test results.

TEST SERIES

Test 1 One smartphone playing a 19 kHz frequency was placed at 12 different test positions on the table. Figure 6 visualizes the results. The test results show a standard deviation of 1.55 cm, while the mean distance to the actual

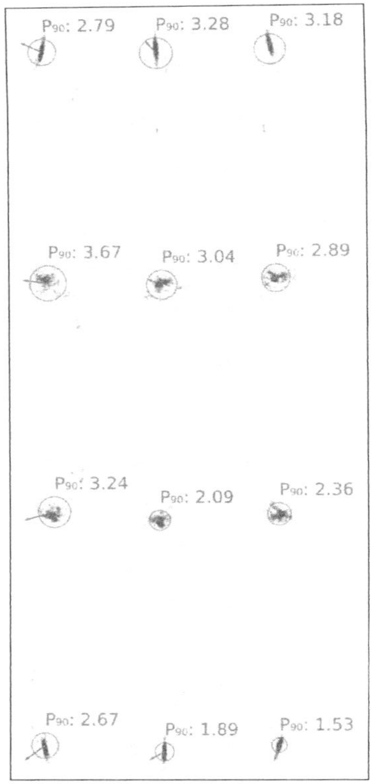

Figure 6: Position distribution for Test 1: One 19 kHz smartphone was placed sequentially on different positions on the table. The located points are shown in blue. The darker the blue, the higher the amount of positions that fell on this very location. The red arrow indicates the shift of the mean position to the original position of the smartphone. The red circle indicates the 90 percentile.

smartphone position was 3.16 cm. The average 90 percentile was 2.72 cm.

Test 2 In this test, the influence between two emitters with frequencies of 18 and 19 kHz was evaluated. We ascertained a similar standard deviation of 1.44 cm and a 90 percentile of 2.94 cm. The average distance to the actual position was 1.77 cm.

Test 3 In this test, the influence between three emitters with frequencies of 16, 18 and 20 kHz was evaluated. The results can be seen in Figure 7. The average standard deviation of the three emitters amounted to 2.18 cm. The average 90 percentile was 3.7 cm. The distance to the actual position was 4.56 cm.

As indicated by the test results, the usage of multiple smartphones leads to a decreased accuracy and precision. This behaviour is likely caused by the limited frequency resolution for the chosen pipeline parameters. Throughout all tests, the system had an average position update-rate of 20.26 positions per second. Even after using the system for several months, we could not observe an impairment of the speaker caused by the permanently emitted signals. Furthermore, the devices' batteries lasted for more than 12 hours of continuous use.

It is worth mentioning that the performance of the system is dependent on the speaker quality and placement of the smartphone. On some devices (e.g. Nexus 4) the speakers are located on the back, which causes noticeable damping of the signal when the device is lying flat on the surface. We also observed a slight directional component for phones with side-mounted speakers (e.g. Nexus 5).

Discussion and Outlook

In this paper, we showed that continuous sound-based tracking of multiple devices is possible using a normal desk, four microphones and a semi-professional sound card. In the following paragraphs, we discuss the performance and applicability of our system.

In contrast to the reference systems, which focus on impulse detection of one sound source, MoBat is designed to continuously locate multiple sources simultaneously. Despite these differences, the applied localisation techniques are similar enough to allow a performance comparison.

Compared to existing systems such as Toffee [5], our hardware setup is similarly simple. Furthermore, our system does not require specialized devices except a four-channel sound card.

The accuracy of our system is on par with other sound based tracking systems. PingPongPlus [2] has an accuracy of a few inches, just as Toffee [5]. Our system determines the position of the emitters several times per second and has a maximum standard deviation of 2.2 cm. With the continuous tracking approach the position variance becomes noticeable. The variance decreases as the table size increases. This is due to the audio signal's increased time of flight, which allows for greater TDOA differences. Consequently, the peak detection becomes more resistant to inaccuracies on larger tables.

The latency of our system is not only caused by the processing time but also the inclusion of recently determined positions to stabilize the results. As with all post-processing methods, there is a trade-off between latency and precision.

MoBat is especially well suited for applications in which the emitters are not moved frequently. In more dynamic use

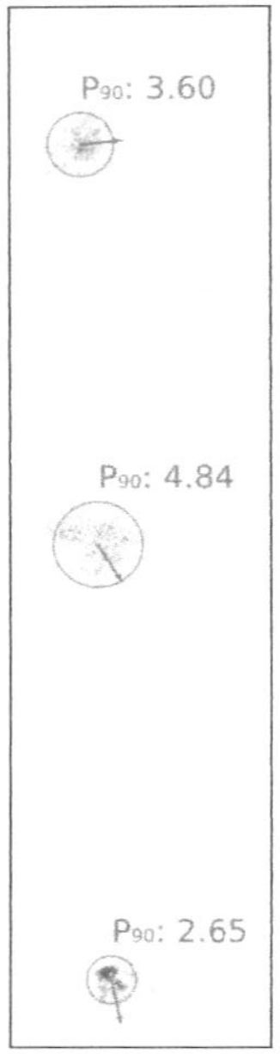

Figure 7: Position distribution for Test 3: Each of the circles indicates one smartphone with one of the frequencies 16, 18 or 20 kHz. The smartphones were simultaneously positioned on one line on the table with a distance of 50 cm from one to the next. The interpretation of the color and shape coding is the same as in Figure 6

cases where movement is a crucial part, our system may not be preferable over conventional input methods because the stabilization of the position causes a higher latency. As a test application, we developed an air-hockey game, using mobile phones as paddles. To get first impressions of the system, we let several persons play the game and observed them. We gained the impression that after a small amount of time, people could adapt to the paddles movements. A side effect of rapidly alternating between sine and silence is a clicking noise produced by the emitters. This may be distracting if a user focuses on it. However, the clicking noise can be easily concealed by other sounds such as music or talking. The accuracy will not be affected as long as the background sounds do not contain frequencies that are produced by the emitters.

In contrast with visual tracking approaches, we do not need to modify the appearance of the tracked devices using markers. As another notable advantage, sound-based tracking is not affected by visual occlusions. As a result the tracking is not interrupted when the emitters are held and moved. However, a disadvantage is the influence of acoustic occlusion caused by obstacles located between emitter and microphones.

For further research, we would like to remove the need for specialized software on the smartphones. For instance, it should be possible to establish a data-link between the emitters and a server that assigns a unique frequency to each smartphone. The server could then stream the corresponding signal to each mobile device via a website. It is also possible to implement proxemics techniques based on the relative distance of the emitters. This implies again an interaction between the mobile devices and a server. For integrating further degrees of freedom into our system, it would be possible to use information provided by the smartphones' sensors (gyroscope, accelerometer, magnetometer) to also incorporate the orientation in the result of the pipeline. This allows for more complex input metaphors. Another interesting approach would be to integrate speakers and a simple circuit into small objects to create low-cost sound-based tangibles. These could provide similar interaction possibilities for users not willing to use their smartphones as input device for this system. At the moment, the tracking capabilities of our system are restricted to two dimensions. To allow for three-dimensional tracking, the system could be extended to work with more microphones. Our system is open-source and is available for download from https://github.com/mmbuw/mobat.

REFERENCES

1. C. Harrison and S. E. Hudson. 2008. Scratch Input: Creating Large, Inexpensive, Unpowered and Mobile Finger Input Surfaces, In Proc. UIST '08. 205–208.
2. H. Ishii, C. Wisneski, J. Orbanes, B. Chun, and J. A. Paradiso. PingPongPlus: Design of an Athletic-Tangible Interface for Computer-Supported Cooperative Play. Marian G. Williams and Mark W. Altom (Eds.). ACM, 394–401.
3. J. A. Paradiso, C. K. Leo, N. Checka, and K. Hsiao. 2002. Passive Acoustic Sensing for Tracking Knocks Atop Large Interactive Displays. 11–14.
4. A. Urashima and T. Toriyama. 2010. Ubiquitous Character Input Device Using Multiple Acoustic Sensors on a Flat Surface.
5. R. Xiao, G. Lew, J. Marsanico, D. Hariharan, S. E. Hudson, and C. Harrison. 2014. Toffee: enabling ad hoc, around-device interaction with acoustic time-of-arrival correlation, In Proc. MobileHCI '14. 67–76.

Connected Paper, EKKO and Analytic Futures: News and Paper Data

John Mills
Media Innovation Studio
University of Central Lancashire
Preston, UK
jmills@uclan.ac.uk

Tom Metcalfe
Thomas Buchanan Ltd
Pervasive Media Studio, 1 Canon's Road, Bristol, UK
tom@tommetcalfe,com

Mark Lochrie
Media Innovation Studio
University of Central Lancashire
Preston, UK
mlochrie@uclan.ac.uk

Professor Paul Egglestone
Media Innovation Studio
University of Central Lancashire
Preston, UK
pegglestone@uclan.ac.uk

Andy Dickinson
Media Innovation Studio
University of Central Lancashire
Preston, UK
asdickinson@uclan.ac.uk

ITS '15, November 15-18, 2015, Funchal, Portugal
ACM 978-1-4503-3899-8/15/11.
http://dx.doi.org/10.1145/2817721.2823489

Abstract
Advances in conductive inks and increasingly accessible and flexible platforms, such as Arduino and Raspberry Pi, are allowing researchers to transform a range of surfaces, including paper and additive layer objects, into capacitive surfaces. When imbued with Internet connectivity, and placed within the 'Internet of things', opportunities to create interactive surfaces that respond to touch and offer audio playback or other data transfer via additional connected peripherals emerge. This poster explores the potential for web-connected paper interfaces with the media and publishing sector and an accompanying content management and system-analytics package to present a range of content, design, interaction and revenue-based opportunities for related industries. It also hints at how paper could be a viable interactive surface and posits potential related work on a wider and cross-industry spectrum.

Author Keywords
Interactive, Internet of Things, mobile, print, paper, conductive ink interfaces

ACM Classification Keywords
H.5.m. Information interfaces and presentation

Introduction
Over the last year, our work has sought to explore the intersection between the physical and digital in the context of the increasingly expansive field of the 'Internet

But why newspapers?

The news industry is one that is founded on paper. Its working practices, business models and identity have been closely aligned to print materials for hundreds of years. However, paper is increasingly becoming sidelined as a delivery platform of choice for audiences and for publishers, which is a trend that is decades old [11].

It is also less attractive for advertisers, who are instead captivated by the lure of the infinite reach of the web, and its personalisation. As such, our research explores both paper's novel properties and its potential for new digital connections both for news and media consumers and for publishers in the monitoring of that data. We frame this not in opposition to a web-based consumption but as an alternative method that combines digital media with the unique properties and opportunities of IoT paper.

of Things'. Our 'physical' incorporates conductive inks and capacitive touch paper and the digital takes the form of 'Interface': an 'Internet of Things' (IoT) publishing platform capable of transferring media and data to and from web-connected print. This poster presentation and extended abstract describes a prototype IoT printed 'supplement' co-created by the Liverpool Echo newspaper, the research team and design agency Uniform.

During the course of the project, our IoT supplement was created to utilise conductive inks connected and powered via a clip, named EKKO. This device recognises touch interactions and connects to Interface as a web-based Content Management System (CMS) and analytics suite. Here we will explore some of the development opportunities presented by a 'CMS for IoT' via a news-industry themed paper prototype and examine some of the unique facets and challenges of capturing analytic data from print, populating print with refreshed content, and reflect on what this could mean for users and content producers. Insights will be offered into how the news industry, a sector that retains print as a cornerstone of its operations, could re-articulate and repurpose print as a digital and dynamic platform within IoT.

Background

Paper has existed as a communications 'platform' for thousands of years. When production became scalable via the Gutenberg press, unprecedented social and political change followed. Parallels can be made between the 'adoption' of paper, and the rise of the Internet. Attempts to create a paper-digital product spanned a range of user-scenarios. Interactive Paper notebooks [8], replication of screen-based interfaces [3], maps [10], images [2, 13] and newsprint have all sought to re-imagine print as digital interface. A range of work has been carried out recently in exploring a range of opportunities conductive inks offer in terms of sensors, craft (www.bareconductive.com) and music posters (www.novalia.com). Within this work, the uniqueness and emotional connection that printed circuits on paper can offer, that perhaps sits aside user experiences of screen-based digital media, has also been articulated [10]. Exploring systems to manage paper-based digital or media content has also been explored in related contexts, for example Singer [1] examined paper-encompassing CMS opportunities ten years ago. Although this work will focus mainly on conductive inks and affordable processing and peripherals, printed electronics have been manufactured and used for several years in the printing of conductive traces in flexible conductors [3]. Since the late 1990s functional devices such as batteries, displays and transistors have been printed via ink-jet, screen-printing or spray coating.

News Content Management Systems and analytics
Although the print is at the head of the user experience, the potential advantages for publishers also resides in the digital management and monitoring of that content. The scale and reach of the web has meant that creating content for news websites has moved quickly from hand- tooled HTML to complex CMS that automate the process of publishing online. A key concept of CMS is the separation of content from the code needed to display that content, an abstraction that has become more important and challenging with the rise of mobile technologies.

Discussion Traditional measure of print
Newspapers function on a dual-product model [12] creating content to build an audience that they can, in turn, measure and package to sell to advertisers. The most common measure in this context is circulation. In the UK circulation figures are self-reported to the Audit Bureau of Circulation (ABC) who independently audit and certify the figures. Whilst circulation figures are often cited as an indicator of popularity, they contain no qualitative data. The National Readership Survey (NRS) uses continuous large-scale surveys, to gather a more detailed view of readership and offers more socio-

Figure 1: EKKO connecting to Super 8

economic detail about the reader and their engagement with the print brands. The ABC and NRS have substantial industry support and provide the benchmark for setting advertising rates in print. However both offer little or no data that relates to interaction with content. Gathering insights into how a reader might engage with content is commonly done through focus groups. But researchers and designers have looked for more concrete measured by experimenting with eye tracking technology [9]. By using hardware that track a reader's 'gaze' on the page, researchers have sort to test design decisions more effectively [7].

Measuring content in the digital world
As the publishing industry moves into a digital marketplace, the dual-product model remains. The primary role of data is still to quantify audience for advertisers. Site metrics echo print's circulation and readership data with broad measures such as page views and unique visitors. However, tracking software and cookies (small files that store browsing data), allow publishers and advertisers to build a real-time picture of individual browsers far beyond the level of detail available to print. Publishers are turning their attention to metrics for engagement, with some moving away from advertising rates based on clicks or visitors to measures of 'time-spent' on a page.

The increasing consumption of multimedia online has created a similar focus on engagement. Traditional measures of audience for TV and radio (BARB, RAJAR) mirror print, with broad estimates of viewers and listeners. Digital platforms enable producers not only to measure how many people view a video but also the time each viewer spent watching and when they stopped.

Ink, IoT and bridging the gap of the physical/digital
The research presented here develops work from previous position papers [6] around using conductive ink to enable users to interact with print and connect it to the Internet. This work has been carried out over the last year. This research investigates the questions around bridging the gap between the physical and digital, what types of analytic data can be derived from print, but more importantly what analytic data publishers require; what lessons are learnt from web analytics; are they transferable to print? This is a potentially unique moment in understanding paper interactions and digital data outlining user-behaviour can be captured and analysed by publishers and content creators within the news industry. There are also intriguing opportunities around taking standard online practices, often informed by the deep cultural and design understanding of print interaction - such as design for scanning personalisation, and reinterpreting them for a print experience. Equally, there are key challenges that span user interaction, scalability, robustness and design limitations around the conductive inks.

Case Study EKKO and Echo
The 'Super 8' prototype is a collaboration between Uniform, the University of Central Lancashire and publisher Trinity Mirror and was designed for regional newspaper the Liverpool Echo. The print takes eight of the most memorable moments from the career of Liverpool Football Club's former captain Steven Gerrard. By connecting a clip to the one page supplement, users can listen to audio, via a smartphone, from eight individual goals that are considered momentous. EKKO is connected to the edge of the print like a bookmark, pressing the printed buttons trigger online interactions through the use of conductive ink. This is dynamic so that the content can change over time whilst the print is static. Connected paper offers a radical expansion on a traditional platform. Through augmenting the print experience its readers move into an alternative space to the one offered by augmented reality platforms and QR codes. Paul Gallagher, Digital Innovations Editor at MEN Media said: "[The project allows us to] see if an internet-

connected product could drive new audiences, and ultimately lead to a new revenue model."

EKKO and Experiences
The work so far has explored the design and implementation of the EKKO clip and the experiences of two interactions; newsprint and games [6]. EKKO consists of three components; the clip, companion app and publishing platform. By designing EKKO to run independently of the publication, third party publishers can develop content and release it onto the platform. The platform has been designed to work for any publication. It is as simple as reconnecting EKKO to a different print artefact. EKKO comprises off the shelf technologies; an Electric Imp combined with a capacitance sensor to measure the ink button presses, a small rechargeable Li-Po battery and an LED for user feedback. It is situated at the edge of a piece of print and clip pressure enables a circuit connection (Fig. 1). The Electric Imp was adopted due to its ability to easily scale, open community and security.

The companion app is a second screen to print, currently developed for iOS. It connects the user with the rich content from the print. Each user first pairs the two devices by specifying the friendly name or MAC Address of the clip with the mobile application; this allows multiple users to connect. When ready, users specify the print they are reading, this then downloads the media for that publication to a user's device to allow for seamless playback. The media is removed when the user selects a different publication. EKKO enables publishers to create novel and exciting experiences in addition to print such as playing audio, video and revealing information via feedback mechanisms.

The publishing platform is the glue to the project; it allows publishers to curate the rich content and monitor interactions through an analytics dashboard. The platform allows publishers to gain unique, rich insights into how users are interacting with their print products in much the same way that readers' interactions with web-based content can be recorded through analytics platforms.

Collecting Data from Print
As discussed above, audience measures and engagement with print have centred around distribution figures and focus group responses. Digitally generated figures for Internet traffic present publishers with specific datasets to which they can respond on a broad range of levels, many of which are now considered to be industry standard approaches. These include tailoring content, tracking data and user behaviour, monitoring advertising campaigns and targeting specific demographics. Our research suggests a range of factors that could emerge from conductive ink and IoT paper. These generally span two forms: updatable content consumed from static print, and monitoring users' usage of a paper-based platform. The latter could include listen time, page navigation, location and personalisation. We've have termed this process 'Paper Data'. The interactive functionality also allows users to engage with print in new direct ways, so to complete voting tasks or rating.

Interface: Analytics and CMS platform
'Interface' provides real-time updatable audio content to internet-connected print and displays analytics associated with the print, its touch-points and user engagement with content, and therefore generate record and visualise 'Paper Data'. Additionally, Interface is being developed to work with other internet-connected objects.

It is designed to be only accessible by the publishers of the audio and print content and therefore the design choices for how it works are influenced by ease of use for publisher, their workflow and how they would choose to experience the platform. There are three principal areas to consider for the user-experience of Interface. 1) The initial, one-off setup to configure the print and its connection to the database and therefore the physical print within the publisher's account on the Interface website, 2) The CMS that enables the publisher to relate audio content to the physical print in real-time, and subsequently update it, and 3) analytics that provide real-time figures and charts of user interaction and data that is associated to the print, i.e. location and print id.

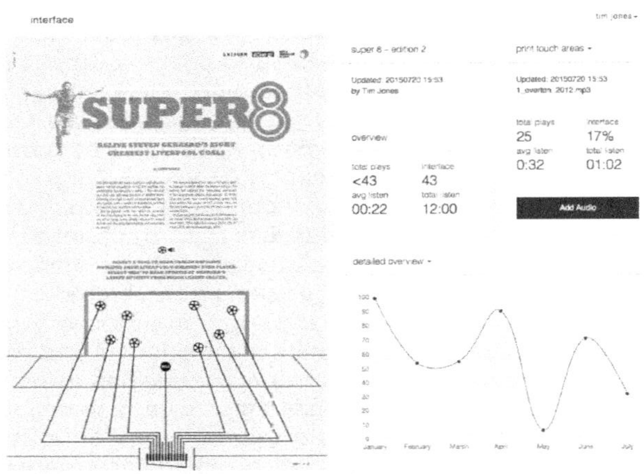

Figure 2: A screenshot from Interface analytics

Interface is designed to be simple and add little work to the publisher's workflow. Once a print version file is finalised, it is uploaded to the Interface platform. This file will then appear on the publisher's Interface CMS platform. The next step is to configure the location of the touch-points so each can become connected to the Interface database and to the corresponding touch-points on the physical prints (Fig. 2).

Once setup, the physical print touch-points correspond to clickable buttons that appear on the website. Interface treats this in two ways; it allows each touch-point on the print to be associated with audio content and analytics. To add content or see analytics the publisher simply clicks the button associated to the physical touch-point. A tool-tip type menu will appear and display a choice of 'analytics' or 'add audio'. Click 'analytics' and the hovering tooltip expands and the publisher is presented with analytics that currently include: the publication; reader; location; dwell time on content; the duration between interaction; number of clicks; average duration of listen; and percentage of engagement based on a predefined time threshold of the audio content. To add audio, the publisher can either drag and drop audio content to the button, or click and a Finder window will appear and the publisher selects an appropriate file, this all happens in real-time and every print that the publisher has in the world will instantly be updated.

Further work and conclusions

Following the development of Interface and EKKO, the research team feel there is a broad range of future work to be pursued within the news industry, but also beyond it. The ubiquity of paper and its role in our everyday lives heralds a range of opportunities. For example, rather than conceptualising paper-based news as newspaper, publishers could reimagine 'news paper' and find opportunities for audio publication that is activated by non-newsprint paper products that can be updated and monitored via a CMS/Analytics platform. These could be, for example, connected coffee cups, travel tickets or posters.

There are also key opportunities to explore advertising models via conductive inks. It is well documented that newspapers reliance on print advertising revenue has been challenged online by social media, search engines and web only news startups. Digitally-connected paper, and related Paper Data analytics, could leverage the industry's long and deep experience of print to offer advertisers opportunities that have only previously been possible through internet-connected and screen-based interaction. Equally, packaging and other paper goods could offer a range of functionalities if located within IoT, and a degree of 'smartness' i.e. an awareness of location and monitoring user interactions could create valuable data for users and the organisations that produce, ship, sell or recover/recycle paper-based products. Interface and EKKO could offer intriguing opportunities within these fields and others.

Nevertheless, there are key challenges that the research team have begun to identify. These include further developing the robustness of conductive ink platforms within a real-world environment, to explore additional analytic data sets generated by Interface that are derived firmly from within the context of print interactions, and are uniquely encapsulated within an IoT use-scenario rather than one curated via a standard PC, laptop or smart-device. For example, how do users navigate augmented paper content? Other work would be required to establish what infrastructure would need to be created within industry standard desktop publishing workflows to allow publishers, such as Trinity Mirror, to seamlessly integrate existing enterprise level CMS systems with the IoT counterpart Interface. Additional work could be undertaken to understanding and analyse analytics from a publisher's perspective, explore what this data might 'mean' or indicate.

References

1. Beat Signer. Fundamental concepts for interactive paper and cross-media information spaces. Diss. Swiss Federal Institute of Technology Zurich, 2005
2. David Frohlich, Guy Adams, Ella Tallyn. Augmenting photographs with audio."Personal and ubiquitous computing 4, no. 4 (2000): 205-208.
3. David A. Roberson, et al. Microstructural and process characterization of conductive traces printed from Ag particulate inks. Materials 2011
4. David Holman, et al. Paper windows: interaction techniques for digital paper. Proceedings of the SIGCHI conference on Human factors in computing systems. ACM, 2005.
5. Edison C. Tandoc Jr. & Ryan J. Thomas. The Ethics of Web Analytics, Digital Journalism
6. John Mills, Mark Lochrie and Paul Egglestone. Paper-based web connected objects and the Internet of Things through EKKO. British HCI 2015
7. Kenneth Holmqvist and Constanze Wartenberg. The role of local design factors for newspaper reading behaviour-an eye-tracking perspective. Lund University Cognitive Studies 127 (2005): 1-21
8. Lisa J. Stifelman. Augmenting real-world objects: A paper-based audio notebook. Conference companion on Human factors in computing systems. ACM,1996.
9. Mario R. Garcia, Margaret Mary Stark, and Ed Miller. Eyes on the News. Poynter Institute, 1991
10. Michael Shorter, Jon Rogers, and John McGhee. Enhancing everyday paper interactions with paper circuits. Proceedings of the 2014 conference on Designing interactive systems, pp. 39-42.
11. Philip Meyer, The vanishing newspaper: Saving journalism in the information age. University of Missouri Press, 2009.
12. Robert G. Picard. Media economics: Concepts and issues. Vol. 22. Sage Publications, Inc, 1989
13. Tim Kindberg, Ella Tallyn, Rakhi Rajani, Mirjana Spasojevic. Active photos. In Proceedings of the 5th conference on Designing interactive systems: processes, practices, methods, and techniques, pp. 337-340. ACM, 2004.
14. Volker Paelke and Monika Sester. Augmented paper maps: Exploring the design space of a mixed reality system. ISPRS Journal of Photogrammetry and Remote Sensing 65.3 (2010): 256-26

Collaborative Position Patterns for Pairs Working with Shared Tiled-Wall Display using Mobile Devices

Ragaad AlTarawneh, Razan N. Jaber, Shah Rukh Humayoun, Achim Ebert
Computer Graphics and HCI Group
University of Kaiserslautern
67663 Kaiserslautern, Germany
{tarawneh, humayoun, ebert}@cs.uni-kl.de
razan.jabir@gmail.com

ITS '15, November 15-18, 2015, Funchal, Portugal
ACM 978-1-4503-3899-8/15/11.
http://dx.doi.org/10.1145/2817721.2823490

Abstract
Recent advances in smart mobile devices (e.g., smartphones and tablets) encourage researchers to utilize them in collaborative environments as a medium of interaction with large shared interactive wall displays. Such collaborative setups have additional advantages over the previous ones, e.g., users' freedom to move around the environment, full view of the whole screen, etc. In this work, we focus on finding different possible collaborative position patterns for pairs of users working in a collaborative setup, equipped with a shared interactive tiled-wall display and multiple mobile devices. For this, we observed users in a controlled study with 36 participants, who performed the collaborative test in 18 pairs.

Author Keywords
Computer-Supported Cooperative Work (CSCW); Interactive Tiled-Wall Collaborative Environment; User Study; Collaborative Position Patterns.

ACM Classification Keywords
H.5.2 User Interfaces: Input devices and strategies; H.5.3 Group and Organization Interfaces: Computer-supported collaborative work.

Introduction and Motivation

Establishing and maintaining a proper collaborative relation between users while working in computer supported collaborative environments is important for executing successfully the common interested tasks [6]. However, the underlying collaborative setup, the users' sitting/standing positions, and the freedom to move around play critical roles in building effective collaborative relations between the partners. This is because working in interactive collaborative environments, equipped with multi-user interfaces, users need to align the actions of their partners into their own mental models [5].

To perform some common interested tasks in collaborative manners, two kinds of environments are the most common ones: tabletop collaborative environments (e.g., [5, 8]), where users stand or sit around the tabletop display and perform the targeted tasks; and wall-display collaborative environments (e.g., [3, 7]), where users stand in front of a large shared wall display and perform the targeted tasks. Compared to tabletop collaborative environments, interactive wall-display collaborative environments give users the freedom to move, equal role in collaboration, and a common angle to watch the screen. However, most of the wall-display collaborative set-ups are built either with a multi-touch wall-display (e.g., setup in [7]) or mouse controlled wall-display (e.g., setup in [4]). These setups have their own limitations, e.g., some restriction in freedom of movement, single interaction with an object at one time, hidden of some screen parts when one user touches the screen, etc.

Recently, researchers focused on utilizing smart mobile devices (i.e., smartphones or smart tablets) to interact with large shared screen displays, e.g.: Baldauf et al. [3] used a setup where users utilized smartphones to interact with the wall-display and conducted a user study on a public screen to find out the general acceptance towards such setup; while Zadow et al. [10] developed a prototype where they used an arm-mounted smartphone to interact with multi-touch wall-display. These kinds of setups (which use smart mobile devices for interaction) can be utilized more effectively and efficiently from the collaboration perspective if we know different possible collaborative position patterns and their effect on building a better collaborative relation amongst the partners.

In this work, we focus on finding different possible collaborative position patterns (i.e., the physical arrangements and standing positions) for pairs of users in a collaborative environment setup, which we built using a large shared tiled-wall display and multiple mobile devices for interactions. To find out different possible collaborating position patterns, we conducted a controlled user study in a laboratory environment with 18 pairs, who worked in our built setup to perform a predefined list of tasks that required some closed collaborations amongst the pairs. These findings would help the researchers in concentrating on those collaborative positions that support users in building effective collaborative relations, in order to get maximum benefits from these setups.

The Built Collaborative Setup

We built our collaborative environment setup (same as in [1]) using a large shared tiled-wall display and multiple mobile devices that were able to remotely interact with the tiled-wall display. Figure 1 shows two

Figure 1. The built collaborative environment setup (same as in [1]), where users can interact remotely with the large tiled-wall display using their mobile devices.

users working in our built environment. The tiled-wall in our case was a vertical display containing nine monitors (in a 3x3 matrix with a total resolution of the tiled-wall display was 7680 x 4800) with 78 inches height and 47 inches width. Our setup supported simultaneously multi-user interactions through smart mobile devices, which were Apple iPad in our case, through wireless connections. We used the ESSAVis application [2] on the tiled-wall that supports multiple views (e.g., the 3D model view or the safety abstract representation view) of the underlying system components. This application supports more than one interaction simultaneously with a single provided view or multiple provided views.

The User Study

The goal of our conducted user study was to find out different collaborative position patterns (i.e., their physical arrangements and standing positions) of pairs working in two, supported by a collaborative setup built with tiled-wall display and multiple mobile devices.

Study Design and Procedure
Based on the identified goal, we designed the study as a controlled study under the laboratory conditions with 36 participants. These participants worked in pairs (that means total 18 pairs) to perform the predefined list of tasks in our built collaborative setup with a maximum time frame of one hour per session for each pair.

The participants were chosen randomly amongst the 80 students from a semester HCI course, a mixture of master and bachelor level students with a background in Computer Science, Social Computer Science, or Cognitive Science. Out of 36 participants, 27 were male and 9 were female. Partners in 13 pairs knew each other well, partners in 1 pair knew each other as classmates, while partners in the remaining 4 pairs did not know each other before the experiment. The average age of participants ranged from 20 to 32 years with a median of 24.5 years. They were from six different countries and 26 of them were international students. Most of the participants (i.e., 68%) commented that they can do simple interaction while working on mobile devices (i.e., replying a person or communicating with a person), 11% commented they can not do any kind of interaction while working on mobile devices, while the remaining 16% responded with "may be" answer. All participants had considerable experience using computer interface due to their background; however, 92% did not have any experience of working on some collaborative system. It was told to students that the experiment is not graded. Further, the involved trainer was new to them.

A pre-questionnaires form was used before starting each test to find out participants' background (i.e., age, gender, field of study, their relation, and their experience with collaborative environment). After it, a tutorial session was conducted to introduce the application and the environment settings. Then 10 minutes were given to the participants in the test to try out the whole setup. They were allowed to ask further questions during the training session and during the test session in case of any technical issues. After the training session, participants in pair were briefed about the tasks on a printed document.

Participants were then asked to perform the test and they were given a maximum 20 minutes for completing the tasks. Participants were allowed to freely make any physical arrangement and standing position that suits them, as no instructions were given for some particular arrangements or positions. They were asked to act naturally around the tiled-wall display. The participants were also asked to verbalize their thoughts and to talk freely while performing the given tasks, as well as to comment on any problem they face while using the setup. The same trainer monitored the experiment in order to avoid any difference or biasness. The participants' interaction with the system and with each other during the test was audio and video recorded for the later analysis.

The test scenarios were designed carefully by including parallel and joint fashion, e.g., interacting with different views that do not require deep collaboration or interacting with the same view that required a closed collaboration between the partners. In total, six tasks were designed for the used ESSAVis application in our setup with the help of a domain expert in a way that did not require much prior expertise with the interface. Each task had a number of closely connected steps.

Metrics

The quality of building an effective collaborative relation between two persons working on solving a certain problem can be observed in the way they are standing, their body positions, and their verbal and visual communication [5, 7].

For finding the possible collaborative position patterns, we focus on the standing positions made by participants in pairs as well as their body and head orientation towards each other and towards the wall display. While for finding the quality of building a collaborative relation between partners in a pair, we focus on:

- *Eye Contact (M1):* when one person pays attention to his/her partner in certain situations.
- *Looking (M2):* when one person gives at least 5 second (this time duration was proposed in [7]) long gaze to the partner to indicate some meanings (e.g., to tell that the task has been completed or now it is the partner's turn to work on).
- *Talking (M3):* when one partner or both partners talk for at least 5 seconds (e.g., to collaborate during the task or to talk about the next task).
- *Talking & Looking (M4):* when one partner or both partners talk and give a long gaze for at least 5 seconds.

Collaborative Position patterns

Previously, researchers (e.g., [7]) have described how users' physical arrangements around the display support the collaboration differently. In our case, we were focusing on the physical arrangement of the body position (i.e., the body and the head orientation of participants towards each other and towards the wall display) and their standing position in the environment to find out different collaborative position patterns (CPPs). For this, we conducted a heavy video and audio analysis of the test sessions to calculate interactions between the partners.

In total, we observed six different collaborative position patterns (see Figure 2) that were used by different pairs in different timings. Out of 18 pairs, 5 pairs used CPP1, 4 pairs used CPP2, 1 pair used CPP3, 5 pairs used CPP4, 2 pairs used CPP5, and the remaining one pair used CPP6. Most of the pairs used only one pattern; however, few of them changed slightly their positions but came back to their preferable one.

Therefore, we counted them in their dominated used pattern. From the pairs' selection of collaborative position patterns, we can easily see that the most preferable collaborative positions were where the pairs were facing the tiled-wall display and standing close or far away from each other (i.e., CPP1 and CPP2) or when they were in diagonally standing each other far away from each other (i.e., CPP4). In the case of CPP4, it was easy for the pairs to monitor their partner as well as watching the whole tiled-wall display without turning their necks. Further, we can also see that pairs preferably choose to stand faraway (4 patterns compared to 2 and 12 pairs compared to 6 pairs). This shows that mostly people even in a collaborative environment prefer to maintain their own space. The usage of mobile devices as an interaction medium with the shared interactive wall-display enabled them working in the collaborative environment while keeping their own space.

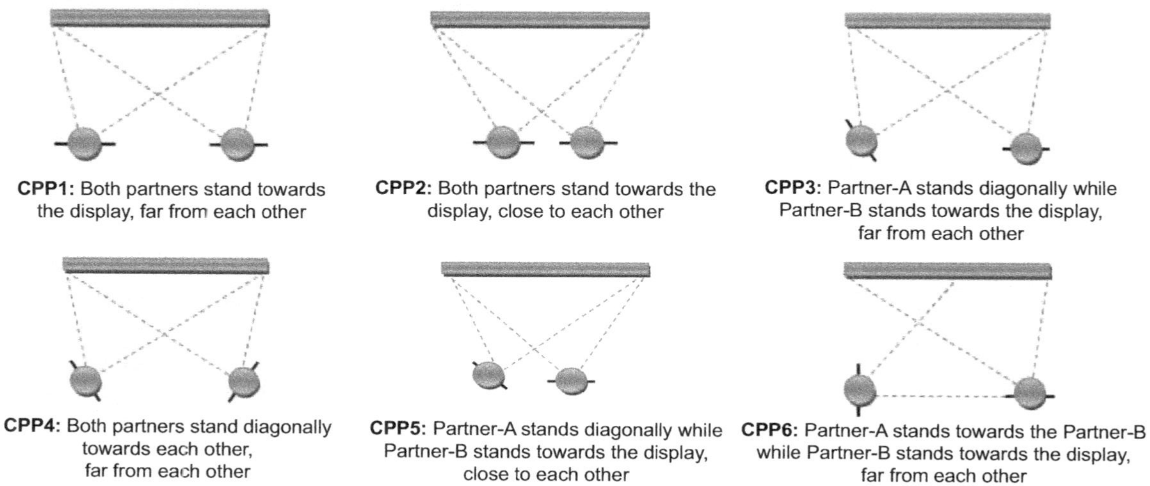

Figure 2. The six collaborating position patterns found out during the experiment

Patterns' Effect on Building Effective Collaborative Relations

Previous research findings (e.g., [5]) have shown that the user's position affects the level of participation when working around a collaborative environment. In Figure 3, we show each interaction frequency for all partners when it lasted for at least 5 seconds, except the eye contact interaction. While in Figure 4, we show the average percentage of all interactions in each pattern done by all pairs who used that pattern.

From these results, we observe that pairs who were standing next to each other communicate more (e.g., CPP2 and CPP5) compared to those who were standing far from each other. Further, standing diagonally, either

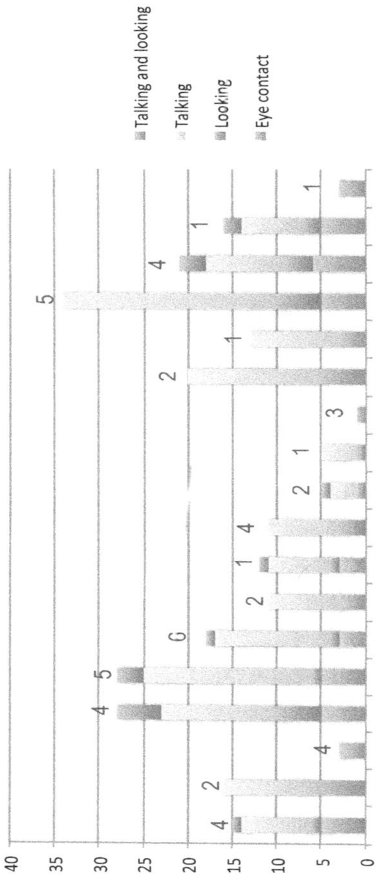

Figure 3. Frequency of interactions inside the pairs. Top of each bar shows the pair's used CPP id.

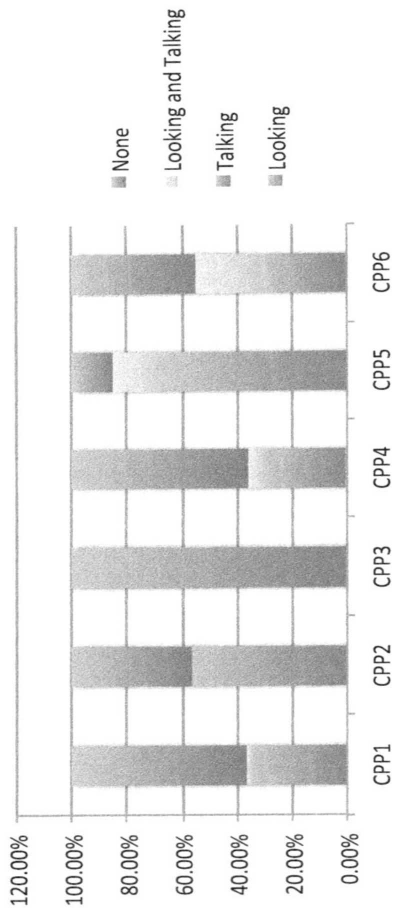

Figure 4. Average percentage of all interactions in each collaborative position pattern.

one or both partners (e.g., CPP4 and CPP5), also increases their communication, even in both cases (i.e., standing closely or far away). It is interested to note that most of the pairs choose those patterns (i.e., CPP1, CPP2, and CPP4) where both partners would have the same physical arrangements and standing positions, which shows a balance role division. However, they preferred CPP2 if their emphasize was on the talking interaction between them (i.e., 56%) compared to CPP1 and CPP4 (34% and 29% respectively). Another interesting finding is that pairs focused on the talking and looking interaction between them only when one or both were standing diagonally (e.g., CPP4 and CPP5), as it helped them to monitor their partner activities as well as the tiled-wall display. Further, in these patterns partners also used more eye contact between them compared to other CPPs.

Concluding Remarks

From our user study, we found six collaborative relation patterns and observed some interesting findings, e.g.: when equipped with mobile devices for interaction with wall-display, partners prefer to have their own personal space except when they need more talking interaction between them; standing far away while diagonally facing their partner and the wall-display provides the most relax position and enables the pairs to build effective collaborative relations through all means of interaction mode between the pair partners.

In the future, we plan to perform enhanced studies with more pairs in order to generalize our findings. Further, we also plan to compare the future findings with the other studies previously done for other types of collaborative setups.

References

[1] AlTarawneh, R., Bauer, J., and Ebert, A. A Visual Interactive Environment for Enhancing Collaboration between Engineers for the Safety Analysis Mechanisms in Embedded Systems. *CSCW Companion '14*, ACM, 125-128, 2014.

[2] AlTarawneh, R., Bauer, J., Humayoun, S. R., Ebert, A., and Liggesmeyer, P. Enhancing Understanding of Safety Aspects in Embedded Systems through an Interactive Visual Tool. *IUI Companion '14*, 9-12, 2014.

[3] Baldauf, M., Lasinger, K., and Fröhlich, P. Private Public Screens: Detached Multi-User Interaction with Large Displays through Mobile Augmented Reality. *MUM '12*, 2012.

[4] Birnholtz, J. P., Grossman, T., Mak, C., and Balakrishnan, R. An Exploratory Study of Input Configuration and Group Process in a Negotiation Task using a Large Display. *CHI '07*, 91-100, ACM, 2007.

[5] Heinrich, P., Kilic, M., Aschoff, F. R, and Schwabe, G. Enabling Relationship Building in Tabletop-Supported Advisory Settings. *CSCW '14*, 171-183, ACM, 2014.

[6] Isenberg, P., Fisher, D., Paul, S. A., Morris, M. R., Inkpen, K., and Czerwinski, M. Co-located Collaborative Visual Analytics around a Tabletop Display. *IEEE Trans. On Vis. and Comp. Graphics*, 18(5): 689-702, 2012.

[7] Jakobsen, M. R. and Hornbæk, K. Up close and personal: Collaborative Work on a High-Resolution Multitouch wall display. *TOCHI*, 21 (2):11, 2014.

[8] Jones, A., Kendira, A., Gidel, T., Moulin, C., Lenne, D., Barthès, J-P., and Guerra, A. Evaluating Collaboration in Table-centric Interactive Spaces. *DCIS '12*, 1-10, 2012.

[9] Scott, S. D., Carpendale, M. S. T., and Inkpen, K. M. Territoriality in Collaborative Tabletop Workspaces. *CSCW '04*, 294-303, ACM, 2004.

[10] Zadow, U., Büschel, W., Langner, R., and Dachselt, R. 2014. SleeD: Using a Sleeve Display to Interact with Touch-sensitive Display Walls. *ITS '14*, ACM, 129-138.

pART bench: a Hybrid Search Tool for Floor Plans in Architecture

Veronika Krauß
Ekaterina Fuchkina
Gabriela C. Molina León
Oana-Iuliana Popescu
Florian Echtler
Sven Bertel

Bauhaus-Universität Weimar
Weimar, Germany
`firstname.lastname`
`@uni-weimar.de`

Figure 1: The set of tangibles for the tabletop prototype.

ITS '15, November 15-18, 2015, Funchal, Portugal.
ACM 978-1-4503-3899-8/15/11.
http://dx.doi.org/10.1145/2817721.2823491

Abstract
Architectural databases often contain thousands of different floor plans which have either been collected from historical designs or, more recently, auto-generated by suitable algorithms. Searching for a floor plan that fits specific requirements in such a database involves setting a large number of parameters, such as lines of sight, lighting levels, room types and many more.

We present *pART bench*, a hybrid tabletop/tablet tool which allows the use of intuitive touch commands and tangible objects to quickly adjust search parameters, view resulting floor plans and iteratively refine the search. We report on a comprehensive requirements analysis with practising architects, on the design process, and describe our prototypical implementation of the system, both on a tablet and on a PixelSense tabletop device.

ACM Classification Keywords
H.5.2 [Information Interfaces and Presentation (e.g. HCI)]: User Interfaces

Author Keywords
tablet; touchscreen; tabletop; tangibles; architecture; search

Introduction

Architectural design processes often make ample use of existing designs, either for inspiration, exploring possible design variants or constraints, or allowing for a reuse of previously found design solutions. Traditionally, such information is accessed through large collections in books. Examples are Neufert's *Architects' Data* [9] or *Raumpilot* [4]. They are complemented by collections held as digital databases, such as *ar:searchbox* [6] or *Detail* [2]. More recently, it is not just information about historical designs that is being used, but also about designs which have been auto-generated by suitable algorithms [8]. Collections are typically very large and include large numbers of design parameters, such as relating to room types and sizes, lighting levels, spatial constraints of occupants' movements, etc.

Whereas learning to productively search in book-bound collections for existing designs fitting one's own design brief has traditionally been a part of architects' education, the usually very large number of designs held in more recent collections in databases requires specific types of interfaces for a productive use. To this end, we have designed *pART bench*, a hybrid tabletop/tablet tool which allows the use of intuitive touch commands and tangible objects to quickly adjust search parameters, view resulting floor plans and iteratively refine the search. The acronym *pART* stands for *parametric Architecture Retrieval Tool* while the *bench* extension is a reference to the concept of a work*bench* and expresses the project's aim to create a retrieval tool that frictionlessly fits into the established workflow of architects during design. In the following, we will report on a comprehensive requirements analysis with practicing architects, on the design process, and describe our prototypical implementation of the system on a PixelSense tabletop device and a tablet.

Related Work

One of the best-known examples of bringing tangible interaction into the architectural domain is *URP* by Underkoffler et al. [15]. URP provides tangible building models which can be repositioned on a tabletop surface to observe changing effects of sunlight and shadows over the course of a day; it is best characterized as a planning tool.

Most other research at the intersection of architecture and human-computer interaction also focuses on tools to support the planning process. Examples include *Urban Sketcher* by Sareika et al. [12], an augmented reality application for urban planning; the *Tangible 3D urban simulation table* by Salim et al. [11], an interactive tabletop system for wind simulation in urban settings; or *Illuminating Clay* by Piper et al. [10], a clay-based tangible landscaping simulation.

A different focus is set by *CubeExplorer* by Song et al. [13], a tangible interface to support the teaching of fundamental concepts of architecture — in this case, the concept of negative space or void.

When going beyond the specific application domain of architecture, the topic of enhancing general search tasks with tangible interfaces should not be overlooked. A recent example is *FacetStreams* by Jetter et al. [3], a hybrid touch/tangible interface which allows users to adjust a wide range of parameters relating to a product search using tangibles and to combine different search constraints through Boolean operations. A similar system, *CubeQuery* by Langner et al. [7], uses active tangibles based on Sifteo cubes to select search terms for a music collection. In a more general context, Ullmer et al. have investigated generic database search tasks with tangible input devices [14].

Figure 2: Setting of the preferred value for the square meter parameter on a Nexus tablet. The filled, green semicircle represents the admissible parameter range for floor plan search, while the black line running inside it represents the preferred parameter value.

Initial Prototype

In this section, we will first outline some basic considerations that drove our design process before describing our investigation of architects' requirements for tools that support their floor plan retrieval from digital databases.

Design Concept

In order to offer a more efficient and interesting search tool for floor plans than atlas or architectural blogs, a proper and figural depiction of the retrieval parameters and the values setting was needed, such that the user would be able to directly understand the underlying metaphors. It was also crucial not to overload the interface with information, while still being sufficiently precise in the parametrization. During the early stages of design, we took the decision to employ pie menus [1] for the parametrisation of queries. This was driven by the observation that they allow a quick interaction and are easy to understand.

A visualization with a high level of abstraction from the floor plan structure, especially from its geometric appearance, was desired. Our selected visualization excludes geometric elements that could resemble room or flat shapes (e.g., squares). This is also why pie menus with their circular shape seemed a good choice. Furthermore, the segments of a pie can directly represent set parameters and their values are represented through segment filling levels. When interviewed, architecture experts stated that they appreciated our approach when compared to querying by sketches: because of the pies' abstraction from a concrete geometry, the architects can focus on topology and other parameters. The concrete geometry would be visible in the retrieved floor plans that result from the search.

To guarantee a structured line of actions during the search and to provide a better overview, we introduced two different parametrisation levels: a flat level, with only one pie for the entire flat or floor plan, and a room level, on which users can create any number of pies, one per room in a flat, with individually set parameters. Existing pies, including their segments, can be copied to speed up the parameter setting. Connections between rooms are visualized by lines, which, again, can be parametrized. This representation was chosen because it resembles a graph and is easily understood.

Formative Evaluation

It was decided to first endeavour on further understanding the work flow and work processes of our target group. This included establishing architects' familiarity with various devices and tools, and their willingness to adapt to new technologies. Available test participants were allocated to one of two groups according to their architectural expertise: (1) students of architecture in Bachelor's and Master's degree programs, who were found to be more likely to query in a creative way, to explore and learn about possible design solutions; (2) professional researchers in architecture (either professors or advanced Ph.D. students, most of whom were also practicing architects, at least part-time), who were found to query more often task-based (i.e., directly for floor plans with specific parameters). The students were treated as non-experts with a higher affinity to new devices and novel ideas, whereas the researchers were treated as specialists and were expected to possibly give deeper insights into work processes.

Different methods such as questionnaires and interviews were used to collect data and review our preliminary assumptions about the design process of the architect and our design. Assumptions included benefits of non-geometry based querying with pies, how the users would interact with the tool and their expectations regarding retrieval tools. 14 architecture students completed the online questionnaire; five experts were invited to semi-structured interviews during

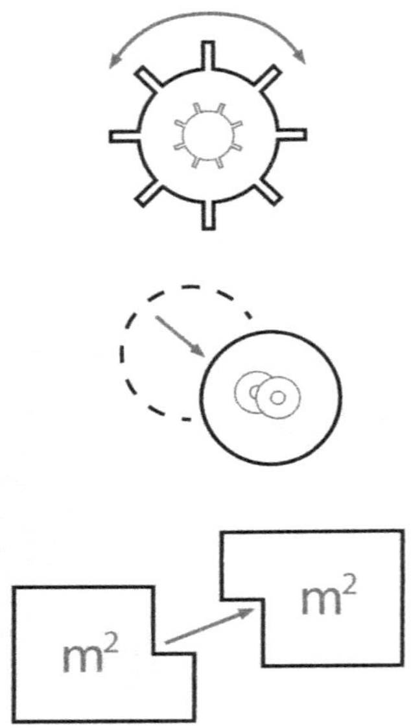

Figure 3: Schematic interactions type with tangibles: Turn the sun to set the solar gain. Use the pie stamp to create new pies. Move apart the area tangible to set the flat size.

which their usual work flow as well as design ideas and first prototypes were discussed more detailed. The main topics were commonly used floor plan sources, frequency of use of touch devices, various ideas of how tangible interfaces might be used during floor plan retrieval, and, of course, details of the architects' work process.

Based on the results, we established that floor plan search is mostly used in the design phase of the work flow. However, such search is not performed very frequently, but rather selectively. The main resources are commonly known floor plan atlases and (more rarely) architectural blogs (because only few digital sources are available). Architects prefer working at desktop computers or on touch devices, as such hardware is already accessible; they were, however, very open to the idea of using tangibles for further interaction if their use would speed up the search or simply improve user experience. The most common expectation of the participants regarding the tangible use was that the tangibles should represent the search parameters (e.g., room size) in a metaphorical way. They also stated that the tangibles should improve the attractiveness and playfulness of the tool.

Based on these results, a paper prototype for touch devices was created, that evolved later on into a prototype implementation supporting touch and tangible interaction. Since the floor plan search is not done very often, it was necessary to create a self explanatory interface that does not require to learn and memorize interaction metaphors. In consequence, the visual scheme of the buttons was developed to signal possible interaction gestures. This design is consistent throughout the interface by associating similar interactions with similar designs. For example, every button that needs to be tapped is black, while every button that needs to be dragged is white. The prototype was, again, tested with groups of varying architectural expertise, from students to experts; we also included a mobile interaction expert as a test person.

During the paper prototype test, the think-aloud technique was used. After the test, participants answered additional questions about their experience while interacting with the prototype. The tests revealed that the visual scheme was largely ignored by users. They applied their preconceived idea of gestures, regardless of the scheme. Nevertheless, the test results achieved by the paper prototype tests were satisfying.

pART bench

In this section, we will link the requirements derived from the formative evaluation with our prototypical implementation of *pART bench* for use with touch and tangibles.

Requirements & Implementation

Supporting a range of touch devices is important for developers and users. Therefore, we take into consideration tablets (starting from 7" screen size) as well as large screen devices, including tabletops. To allow the user to perform actions in zoomed-in mode in case the screen is too small, we introduce different zoom levels of interaction. On the other hand, large devices such as tabletops provide not only a larger workspace, but also the possibility to use tangibles. To support general touch-enabled devices, the interface shown in figure 2 was developed. By means of standard tap and drag commands, users can create new pies, assign values and permissible ranges for one or more parameters (currently including area, solar gain, exterior view, energy and room type) and create connections between room pies.

In order to take advantage of the size and the capacities afforded by a tabletop device, we included a supplementary tangible interaction mode that includes touch with new tangible gestures for a subset of the actions. Although both

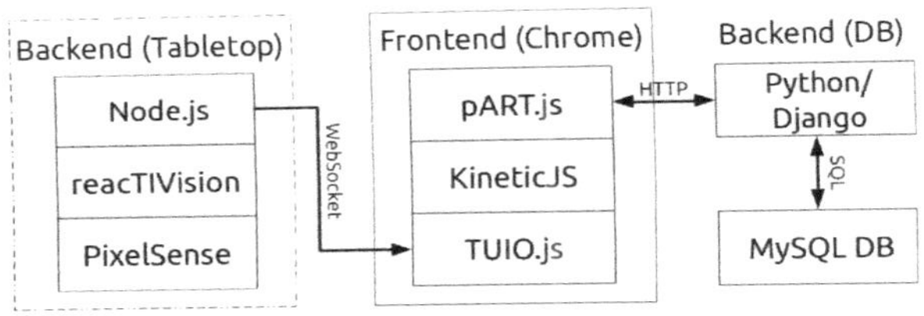

Figure 4: System architecture

versions provide the same functionalities, the main goal of this version is to provide an additional level of comfort, speed, novelty as well as fun during the work process. While the pie menus themselves still provide visual feedback of the parameter values, their creation and adjustment moved to the physical level as figural tangibles. Examples for these tangibles are the "pie stamp" for creating new pie menus, the sun symbol for solar gain and the dual square tangibles for setting the area (see also figure 3 and 1).

On the other hand, interaction should still be as simple and intuitive as possible and introduction or substitution of new methods should indeed provide interaction improvements. As tangibles exist in the real world, we enable architects to transfer their experience of working with physical tools onto the floor plan search process. For example, to set the area parameter, we use two tangibles that can be moved relatively to each other. Their L-shaped form implicitly creates a rectangle whose diagonal length is mapped to the area value. This resembles the real world action of people indicating size or area by moving their hands apart.

System Architecture
pART bench is designed as a web application to allow easy switching between different device classes. The frontend is structured around the Javascript frameworks PrototypeJS and KineticJS and currently runs on the Chrome browser which is available on a multitude of platforms, while the backend is based on the Python framework Django, which connects to a MySQL database containing the actual floor plans (see figure 4).

This section of the overall system architecture is already sufficient for deploying *pART bench* on a wide range of devices such as tablets or laptops. However, to support tangible interaction on the interactive surface, we require a secondary software stack running on the PixelSense device. The raw video from the touch screen surface is processed by reacTIVision [5] to detect the common "Amoeba" fiducial markers. Data about marker IDs and positions is first sent via UDP in the widely used TUIO format, which is then adapted to a WebSocket transport by an intermediate layer based on node.js and finally received and interpreted by the TUIO.js library within the browser frontend. To support transparent handling of different input event types (touch/tangible), minor internal changes in KineticJS were required.

Conclusion & Outlook

We have presented *pART bench*, a hybrid touch/tangible tool to search databases of floor plans for architectural design. While our current setup is still in the prototype stage, we believe it is already capable of being used in a research context for exploratory search.

The pie model enables the user to search for specific floor plans with concrete geometries through an abstract graphical representation. The touch component provides search mobility between devices with varying sizes. The tangible component extends the touch interactions through physical, figural, and analogous representations of the most important query components.

We current plan further prototype evaluation with the group of architects who participated in the initial user study. We also plan to investigate an extension of our setup using active tangibles such as Sifteo cubes, similar to CubeQuery. [7].

Acknowledgments

This work was in part funded by BMBF through grant T_209_M_SB. Thanks to Felicitas Höbelt, Aaron Solbach and Georg Erfurt as members of the original pART project, and to Anna Rack, Marie Bornemann, Adrian Kreskowski, Jannis Bossert, Jakob Wagner and Stefanie Wetzel for support in the lab and helpful discussions.

REFERENCES

1. J. Callahan, D. Hopkins, M. Weiser, and B. Shneiderman. 1988. An Empirical Comparison of Pie vs. Linear Menus, In Proc. CHI '88. ACM, New York, NY, USA, 95–100.
2. Institut für internationale Architektur-Dokumentation. 2015. DETAIL. (2015). `http://www.detail-online.com/`.
3. H.-C. Jetter, J. Gerken, M. Zöllner, H. Reiterer, and N. Milic-Frayling. 2011. Materializing the Query with Facet-streams: A Hybrid Surface for Collaborative Search on Tabletops, In Proc. CHI '11. ACM, New York, NY, USA, 3013–3022.
4. T. Jocher, S. Loch, A. Lederer, B. Pampe, M. Gasser, C. zur Brügge, M. Tvrtkovic, W. Stamm-Teske, K. Fischer, and T. Haag. 2010. *Raumpilot: 4 Bände*. Wüstenrot Stiftung.
5. M. Kaltenbrunner and R. Bencina. 2007. reacTIVision: A Computer-vision Framework for Table-based Tangible Interaction, In Proc. TEI '07. ACM, New York, NY, USA, 69–74.
6. C. Langenhan, A. Seifert, A. Teichert, and F. Petzold. ar:searchbox - Knowledge Management for Architecture Students, In Proc. eCAADe '12. eCAADe, 639–645.
7. R. Langner, A. Augsburg, and R. Dachselt. 2014. CubeQuery: Tangible Interface for Creating and Manipulating Database Queries, In Proc. ITS '14. ACM, New York, NY, USA, 423–426.
8. P. Merrell, E. Schkufza, and V. Koltun. 2010. Computer-generated Residential Building Layouts, In Proc. SIGGRAPH ASIA '10. ACM, New York, NY, USA, Article 181, 12 pages.
9. E. Neufert, P. Neufert, and J. Kister. 2012. *Architects' Data*. John Wiley & Sons.
10. B. Piper, C. Ratti, and H. Ishii. 2002. Illuminating Clay: A 3-D Tangible Interface for Landscape Analysis, In Proc. CHI '02. ACM, New York, NY, USA, 355–362.
11. F. Salim. 2014. Tangible 3D Urban Simulation Table, In Proc. SimAUD '14. Society for Computer Simulation International, San Diego, CA, USA, Article 23, 4 pages.
12. M. Sareika and D. Schmalstieg. 2007. Urban Sketcher: Mixed Reality on Site for Urban Planning and Architecture, In Proc. ISMAR '07. IEEE Computer Society, Washington, DC, USA, 1–4.
13. H. Song, F. Guimbretière, M. A. Ambrose, and C. Lostritto. 2007. Cubeexplorer: An Evaluation of Interaction Techniques in Architectural Education, In Proc. INTERACT'07. Springer-Verlag, Berlin, Heidelberg, 43–56.
14. B. Ullmer, H. Ishii, and R. J. K. Jacob. 2003. Tangible Query Interfaces: Physically Constrained Tokens for Manipulating Database Queries, In Proc. INTERACT '03. IOS Press, 279–286.
15. J. Underkoffler and H. Ishii. 1999. Urp: A Luminous-tangible Workbench for Urban Planning and Design, In Proc. CHI '99. ACM, New York, NY, USA, 386–393.

Hi-AppV: Viewing Tabletop Application Windows on Mobile Devices

Shah Rukh Humayoun[1], Jahanzeb Khan[2], Syed Moiz Hasan[2], Ragaad AlTarawneh[1], Achim Ebert[1]
Computer Graphics and HCI Group
University of Kaiserslautern
67663 Kaiserslautern, Germany
[1]{humayoun, tarawneh, ebert}@cs.uni-kl.de
[2]{jkahn, shasan}rhrk@uni-kl.de

ITS '15, November 15-18, 2015, Funchal, Portugal
ACM 978-1-4503-3899-8/15/11.
http://dx.doi.org/10.1145/2817721.2823492

Abstract
In interactive surface supported collaborative environments, team members may need to look on some important information available on some hidden or minimized application in order to perform the collaborative task on the current active application, which may occupying the whole screen to give a better view to all team members. Targeting this issue, we provide **Hi-AppV** (**Hi**dden **App**lications **V**iewer) framework that enables the team members to see the view-image of any currently opened application on tabletop (either hidden behind the current active application or minimized) to their mobile devices. Further, team members can also switch any opened application as the current active one through their mobile devices. Overall, the framework provides an intuitive interaction in the collaborative environment for performing collaborative tasks.

Author Keywords
Mobile Interaction; Tabletop Surfaces; Collaborative Environment.

ACM Classification Keywords
H.5.2 User Interfaces: Input devices and strategies; H.5.3 Group and Organization Interfaces: Computer-supported collaborative work.

Introduction

The current tabletop surfaces provide an interactive medium useful to perform collaborative tasks amongst the team members. That's why researchers have suggested using of tabletop surfaces for different collaborative environments, e.g., during financial advisory sessions [7], for collaborative concept mapping [9], for supporting group creativity [4], for enhancing face-to-face collaboration [6], etc.

Many times in such collaborative setups, the current active application occupies the whole screen in order to provide a better view to all team members. However, team members may need to look some additional information on the passive opened applications, which are either minimized or behind the current active application, in order to perform the collaborative task in the current active application. Generally, this is done through minimizing or resizing the current active application so that maximizing or viewing the targeted passive application in order to see the required information on it. However, minimizing the current application results in the loss of context while resizing it could affect the viewing of one or more team members.

The current advancements in smart mobile devices (e.g., smart watches, smartphones, tablets, etc.) encouraged the researchers to use them as an interaction medium in different collaborative environments (from tabletop-based to large wall-display based) for achieving different goals [1, 3, 5, 8, 10, 11, 12]. In the context of the above-mentioned problem, we propose using of smart mobile devices (i.e., smartphones and tablets in our case) as a medium to get the required information from the passive applications currently minimized or hidden behind the current active application without disturbing the view of the current active application.

For this, we developed a framework, called **Hi-AppV** (**Hi**dden **App**lication**s** **V**iewer), that provides the facility to view any of the opened application on mobile devices without disturbing the current active application on tabletop. Further, it provides the option to switch any of the passive application to be the active one on the tabletop through the connected mobile devices. The developed framework is consisted of three modules: the tabletop-side server module to handle the viewing and switching of all currently opened applications, an Android-based mobile app to give the facility on mobile devices to see the view of any of the currently opened applications or to make any opened application as the current active one on the tabletop, and the communication channel module to handle the communication through WIFI between the tabletop and the connected mobile devices. Thus the framework supports the team members in performing their collaborative task more efficiently.

Related Work

Recently, researchers have started using smart mobile devices to enhance the interaction with tabletop surfaces. Few recent examples are: Scott et al. in [11] developed a way to improve the awareness of transferred objects while picking and dropping them between tabletop and mobile. MultiTask [5] is a digital tool to plan projects and assign related tasks. It provides a tabletop application for detailed discussions and an Android app with limited interaction possibilities to use it while on the move. Rodrigues et al. in [10] proposed to use tablets as zoomable magic lenses over the overview map displayed on a tabletop or with a wall-display. In [8], Jin et al. proposed a way for wiring home devices on a tabletop display while providing a web-based UI for mobile devices in order to control home devices.

The work is not just limited to tabletop surfaces, but researchers have also started to utilize smart mobile devices with other interactive surfaces like wall-displays. For example: Zadow et al. [12] developed a prototype where they used an arm-mounted smartphone to interact with multi-touch display wall. AlTarawneh et al. [1, 2] used mobile devices to interact with tiled-wall display for analyzing safety aspects of embedded systems. Badam and Elmqvist [3] developed an application that allows users to work on their tablets using brush and link interaction to explore the dataset, while visualizing the brushes on an overview visualization on the wall display. Our approach is based on enhancing the overall interaction with the tabletop (or any other large display) in a collaborative environment rather than an application centric; therefore, it can be used as a general interaction approach.

The Hi-AppV Framework

Figure 1 shows the overall architecture of our developed Hi-AppV framework. The framework mainly consists of three modules: the *Hi-AppV Server* module on the tabletop side, the *Hi-AppV mobile app*, and the *Hi-AppV Communication* module for managing the communication channels between the tabletop and the connected mobile devices. The Hi-AppV Server module was implemented in C# using Microsoft Visual Studio, as the underlying tabletop in our case is Samsung SUR40 Tabletop Surface with Microsoft PixelSense. The client side Hi-Appv mobile app is Android-based and was implemented in Java using Android Studio. The Hi-AppV Communication module for managing the communication channels was implemented through socket programming where the data is passed through the JSON (JavaScript Object Notation) strings using the TCP/IP protocol.

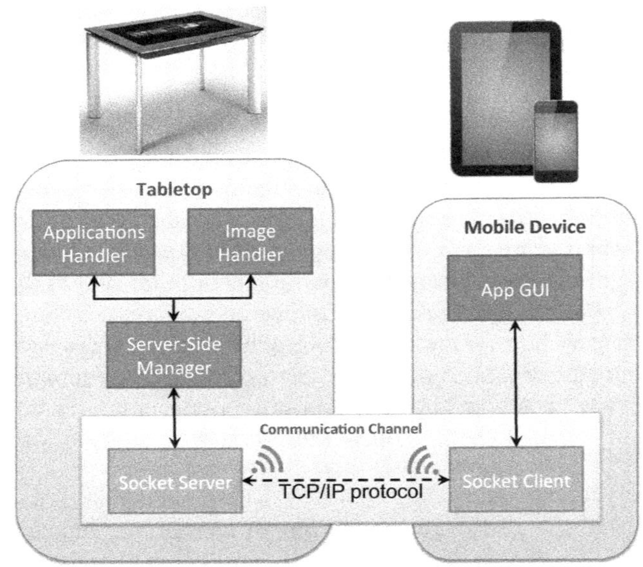

Figure 1: Architectural overview of the Hi-AppV framework

Although, the Hi-AppV framework was developed to keep in mind the tabletop-supported collaborative environment; however, it can be portable to other collaborative environments (e.g., large wall-display supported collaborative) after few modifications.

The Hi-AppV Server Module

The Hi-AppV Server module is responsible for managing the activities on the tabletop side. It is responsible to fetch all the currently opened applications (either active or passives) information and sends the view-image of the requested application or makes it active one whenever it is requested. This module is mainly consisted of three components, i.e.: *Application Handler*, *Image Handler*, and *Server-Side Manager*.

The *Application Handle* component is responsible to get all the relevant information (e.g., applications' IDs, names, etc.) about the currently opened applications on the tabletop that are required to send to the connected mobile devices. Further, it is also responsible to make a requested passive application as active one.

The *Image Handle* component is responsible for two tasks: Whenever a mobile device is connected to the tabletop, it sends the icon images of all the active applications as well as when a new application is opened on the tabletop, it sends the image icon of this new opened application to all connected mobile devices. Secondly, when a mobile device requests to get the view-image of any passive opened application, then it creates the view-image (i.e., the screenshot of the application in its normal active form) of the requested application and passes it to the Server-Side Manager component in order to send it to the requested mobile device. This is done through creating a hidden layer where the targeted application is activated and then taking the screenshot of this application. Before closing this hidden layer, the targeted application is made passive or minimize in the normal desktop layer of tabletop. In order to make the solution more scalable, the Server-Side Manager component keeps the dimension of each connected mobile device. Whenever a request is generated by a mobile device, the Server-Side Manager receives and passes the dimension of the requested mobile device to the Image Handle component in order to resize the image accordingly. Therefore, the sent view-image of the same application would be different for different mobile devices according to their dimensions. The Server-Side Manager component is responsible to interact with the other components and forwards or receives the required information to and from the Hi-AppV Communication module.

The Hi-AppV Communication Module
The communication between the server side (i.e., the tabletop) and the client side (i.e., the connected mobile devices) is done through the Socket Server and Socket Client components on server and clients respectively. These two components in fact transfer all the data to each other in the form of JSON string over the wireless connection using the TCP/IP protocol, where the server side knows the ID of each of the connected mobile device. This makes the solution scalable to use multiple mobile devices simultaneously.

The Hi-AppV Mobile App
The Hi-AppV mobile app is responsible to give an interface to the users to view on mobile device any of the currently opened application on the tabletop or to switch any of the passive application to the active mode on the tabletop. Figure 2 shows team members using the Hi-AppV mobile app on their mobile devices while working on some collaborative task.

Initially, users need to give IP address of the targeted tabletop in order to connect to it and then the app fetches information about all the currently opened applications on the tabletop. The app main view then shows titles of the currently opened applications, their

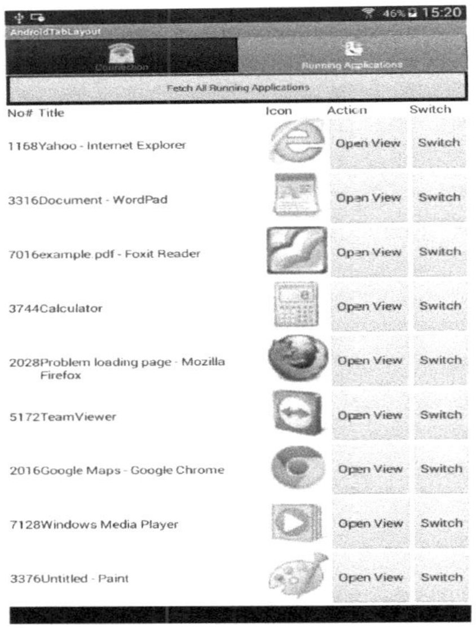

Figure 3. Hi-AppV mobile app view for showing the currently opened application on tabletop. Two opens are shown, to open the view-image or to switch an application in the active mode.

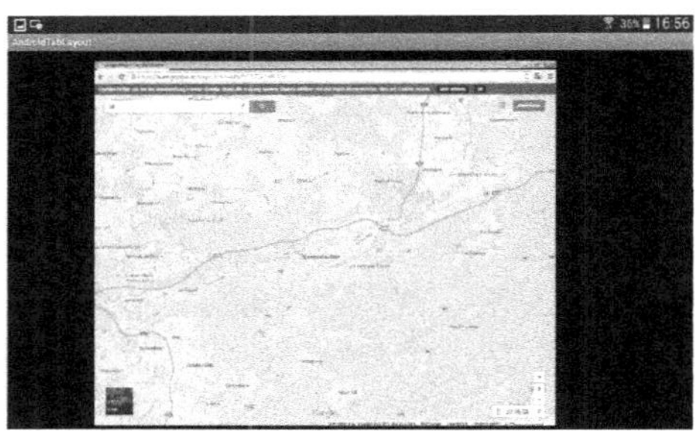

Figure 4. A screenshot of an application view image on mobile tablet device.

icons, and two options for each application (see Figure 3). The first one is to open the view-image of the application on mobile device while the second one is to make the corresponding application as active on the tabletop. When a user requests to open view-image of an application, a new view appears on the mobile device where the view-image of the requested application is shown initially according to the dimension of this device (see Figure 4). User can zoom or rotate this view-image in order to know further details. Currently, we do not provide the option of controlling the scrolling of the selected application, which we intend to do in the future. The list of applications in the main view is automatically updated whenever a new application is opened or an already opened application is closed on the tabletop.

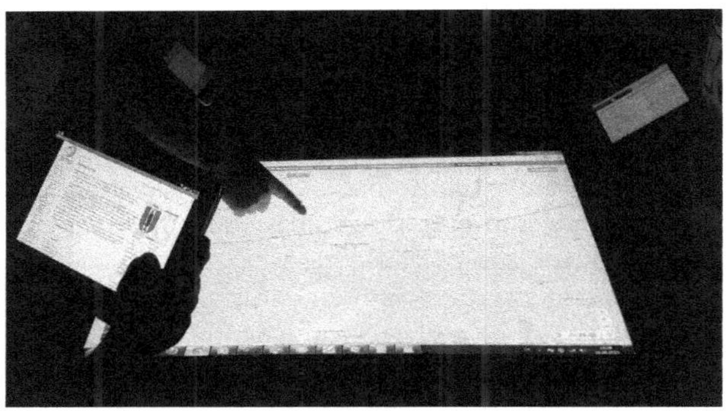

Figure 2: Two team members are connected with tabletop using Hi-AppV mobile app.

Application Scenarios

The presented Hi-AppV framework is an application-independent framework from the perspective of tabletop and provides system-level interaction approach. Therefore, it works perfectly irrespective of the kind of underlying collaborative task or the collaborative application. Team members can use this framework in the different scenarios for better execution of their collaborative tasks. Here we illustrate two exemplary scenarios in order to show the framework usage.

The first scenario is related to the teaching in class. In this case, the main surface (i.e., tabletop or wall-display) could be used for teaching some concepts. However, the teacher may want to show some other information that might be necessary for students in order to understand the concept more properly. This is specially happens in learning programming classes. Resizing or minimizing the current view might not be good solution in this case. However, using the Hi-AppV framework, students would be able to see the necessary information available on the other application simultaneously without losing the main view.

The second scenario is related to situations where two parties discuss some formal issues and the tabletop surface is used to provide a medium to see the information and other interesting things. An example of such a scenario is also illustrated in [7] where a bank manager and a customer sit around the tabletop during the financial advisory session. In such scenarios, the bank manager may need to look some other information that should be hidden from the customer, might be due to some privacy and security issues. In such cases, using the Hi-AppV framework it would be easy for managers to see the required information, available on the hidden/minimized application, just by themselves on their mobile devices.

Concluding Remarks

We performed a brief evaluation studies with 4 teams, each consisted of 2 members, where they performed two collaborative tasks in a given scenario. For each task, it was required to see some information available on some other applications that were either minimized or hidden behind the main task-targeted application window. Two teams were asked to perform first task 1 without the Hi-AppV framework and then task 2 with the framework, while the two other teams were asked to perform first task 1 with Hi-AppV framework and then task 2 without the framework. In the given feedback, collected at the end of both tasks, members of all the teams preferred to work with our Hi-AppV framework, as it helped them to see the required information without losing the main application view. However, they pointed out the lack of scrolling facility that in many cases is necessary.

In the future, we aim to provide the scrolling facility so that users can scroll down the acquired application view on their mobile devices. We also plan to provide the pointer and clicking facility so that users can also interact with the acquired application interface on their mobile devices. Further, we intend to perform detailed evaluation studies in tabletop-supported setups as well large wall-display supported setups in order to show the feasibility and effectiveness of our framework.

References

1. AlTarawneh, R., Bauer, J., and Ebert, A. A Visual Interactive Environment for Enhancing Collaboration between Engineers for the Safety Analysis Mechanisms in Embedded Systems. *CSCW Companion '14*, ACM, 125-128, 2014.
2. AlTarawneh, R., Bauer, J., Humayoun, S. R., Ebert, A., and Liggesmeyer, P. Enhancing Understanding of Safety Aspects in Embedded Systems through an Interactive Visual Tool. *IUI Companion '14*, 9-12, ACM, 2014.
3. Badam, S. K. and Elmqvist, N. 2014. PolyChrome: A Cross-Device Framework for Collaborative Web Visualization. *ITS '14*, ACM, 109-118.
4. Buisine, S., Besacier, G., Najm, M., Aoussat, A., and Vernier, F. Computer-supported creativity: Evaluation of a tabletop mind-map application. *EPCE '07*, 22-31, 2007.
5. Haas B. and Echtler, F. 2014. Task Assignment and Visualization on Tabletops and Smartphones. *ITS '14*, ACM, 311-316.
6. Haller, M., Billinghurst, M, Leithinger, J, Leitner, D., and Seifried, T. Coeno: enhancing face-to-face collaboration. *ICAT '05*, 40-47, ACM, 2005.
7. Heinrich, P., Kilic, M., Aschoff, F. R, and Schwabe, G. 2014. Enabling relationship building in tabletop-supported advisory settings. *CSCW '14*, 171-183.
8. Jin, Y., Dang, C. T., Prehofer, C., and André, E. 2014. A Multi-Display System for Deploying and Controlling Home Automation. ITS '14, 399-402.
9. Maldonado, R. M., Kay, J., and Yacef, K. Collaborative concept mapping at the tabletop. *ITS '10*, 207-210, ACM, 2010.
10. Rodrigues, F. M., Seyed, T., Maurer, F., and Carpendale, S. 2014. Bancada: Using Mobile Zoomable Lenses for Geospatial Exploration. *ITS '14*, ACM, 409-414.
11. Scott, S. D., Besacier, G., Tournet, J., Goyal, N., and Haller, M. 2014. Surface Ghosts: Promoting Awareness of Transferred Objects during Pick-and-Drop Transfer in Multi-Surface Environments. *ITS '14*. 99-108.
12. Zadow, U., Büschel, W., Langner, R., and Dachselt, R. 2014. SleeD: Using a Sleeve Display to Interact with Touch-sensitive Display Walls. *ITS '14*, ACM, 129-138.

Capture The Flag: Engaging In A Multi-Device Augmented Reality Game

Suzanne Mueller
Massachusetts Institute of Technology
Cambridge, MA
suzmue@mit.edu

Andreas Dippon
Technische Universitat München
Boltzmannstr. 3
Garching, 85748 Germany
dippona@in.tum.de

Gudrun Klinker
Technische Universitat München
Boltzmannstr. 3
Garching, 85748 Germany
klinker@in.tum.de

ITS '15, November 15-18, 2015, Funchal, Portugal
ACM 978-1-4503-3899-8/15/11.
http://dx.doi.org/10.1145/2817721.2823493

Abstract
We present a Capture the Flag based game that investigates the possible engagements in a multi-device game. The distinction between a publicly used space and a player's private space is made and utilized to display different information to players. The tablet and the Augmented Reality component are used to see how players can be drawn to a certain physical space, to create a social and engaging game.

Author Keywords
Augmented Reality; Multi-device; tablet;

ACM Classification Keywords
H.5.2. User Interfaces: Input devices and strategies, Interaction styles

Introduction
There are many different devices used in all aspects of everyday life. Many games typically are played using one main device (e.g. a smartphone, computer, television). Multiplayer computer games are often created so that users can play remotely and do not rely on the physical presence of the other players. However, games are also often played in a social setting. Families and friends often play board or card games together to pass the time.

This project challenges the traditional setup of a multi-player game and examines the possibility of engaging a

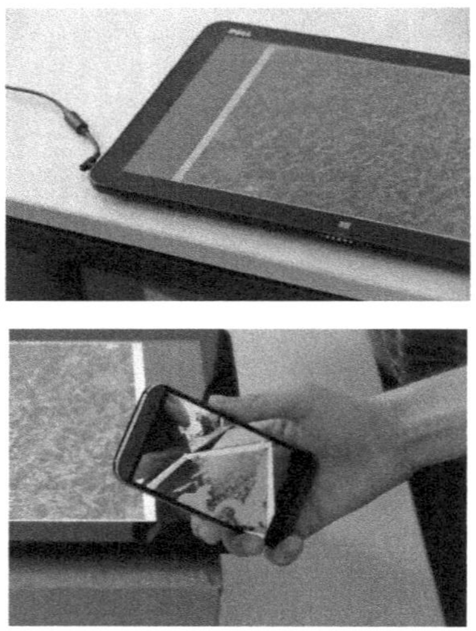

Figure 1. The game was developed to be played on a large multi-touch tablet and multiple smartphones.

group of players in a single game, while still allowing the possibilities that a computer or video game provides. It uses Augmented Reality (AR), an indirect view of the physical world, to provide each player with his or her own information unavailable to other players. Augmented Reality involves "augmenting the real world with computerized information" [2]. In this case, the real world is locked on top of a shared tablet screen that displays certain aspects of the game to users. This project experiments with different information being displayed on different devices to highlight important information.

Related Work

Previous work has been done to investigate the shared and private spaces to allow the multiple users to interact at once with media facades [5]. This project found that one could avoid cluttering up the space on a shared interface, by augmenting a live feed of the video on a smartphone to give the users more information. Interactions using a live video have not always allowed a natural interaction for the user. Object-oriented interactions use tracking to allow the smartphone to be physically oriented in the real world [3]. This gives the user a more natural of sense of how their interactions will affect the video. This is incorporated through the movement interactions of the user.

Through the implementation of a Tower Defense game, the use of a smartphone as more than a controller was investigated [4]. The game involved using a tablet to provide certain input and using motions and touches on the smartphone as a different source of input. This project focused on a game that did not require time sensitive input from the user, allowing the acceleration and position of the smartphone to be used. In the capture the flag game, certain interactions that require more precision, such as moving artificially into a tower, were avoided due to the real time nature of the game.

Game Implementation

In order to investigate the possibilities to engage the user with multiple devices, a Capture the Flag game was implemented. The game was created to be run using a XPS 18 Windows Multi-touch Tablet and 2-4 Android smartphones.

The game was created using Unity and written in C#. The UNET networking system from Unity is used to accommodate the multi-device aspect of the game. In order to include features specific to the Android platform, Java plugins were also incorporated. To incorporate the augmented reality features used in the game play, Vuforia was chosen as a free option that could be easily incorporated into a Unity game.

Game Play

The implemented 2-4 player game is based off of Capture the Flag [1]. There is a public space, the tablet, that hosts the game. On this public space, each player's location and their immediate surroundings are displayed, as well as each of the bases and flags. In addition to the information the players can see on the public tablet, each player receives additional information on the Android smartphone they use to connect to the game. The player's view of the playing field is enhanced using Augmented Reality, to show the objects and obstacles, or lack thereof, at the locations the player has already visited. This private information is only available to a single player at each location, providing that player with additional expertise of the terrain at that location.

Figure 2. Players playing capture the flag on a tablet. The player in the front right is tapping on the table to steal the flag. The players on the left are moving by touching on their smartphones and are blowing into the microphones.

The game begins with each player at their own base. The players can gain the view of the playing field on their devices by pointing the smartphone's camera at the tablet. The Vuforia system can recognize the target, and the objects will appear as a 3D representation over the board. Each player can then move by touching the target location on the game world representation or his or her smartphone. The player can also blow into the microphone on his or her smartphone in order to move faster.

In order to steal a flag from another player, the player must first move into the base of the other player. Then he or she must tap 5 times on the tablet in the base of the player whose flag they are trying to steal. This then sends a vibration notification to the player whose flag is being stolen. Once the player brings the other flag back to his base, the player whose flag was stolen is eliminated from the game. The last player remaining at the end of a round, wins the game.

To defend his or her flag, a player can take a couple of measures. Once their flag is stolen, a player can no longer steal another flag, but must go defend his or her own flag. To do this, the player essentially needs to run down the other player. If he or she hits against the other player who is carrying his or her flag, the flag is immediately returned to the base and the other player is stunned. To aid in catching a player, or escaping a player, each player can set traps using the volume controls on the smartphones. Although there is no limit to how many traps a player can place, there is a time interval after each placed trap before another can be placed. These traps stun the other players if run over, but will not affect the player that placed them.

Design Decisions and Results

Throughout implementation and testing, there were several decisions made about how the game should be played, and how the user can interact with each of the devices.

Real Time vs Turn Based

The game was initially intended to be a turn based game, allowing only one player to move and act at a time. The decision to switch from this initial set up to the real time game that was ultimately implemented was made in order to increase the engagement the players would need to have with the game. With a turn based game, only one player would even need to be near the tablet at a time to play. Since did not facilitate engagement of all users both with their phones and the tablet, this style of play was not chosen.

Movement

Several options were considered for the input method for player movement. Each of the options were considered and evaluated based on their ability to enhance user engagement, ease of use, and feasibility within the context of the game. The options considered were as follows:

1. With the camera focused on the tablet, the user then clicks on a location on the smartphone screen. The player will then move in the direction of the location that the touch is pressing in the game world.

2. Four buttons appear on the user's smartphone screen. Each button corresponds to a direction that the player can move in. These directions are relative to the view that the user sees with the augmented reality, so that the arrow pointing away from the user, will move the player away from the player as well.

3. With the camera focused on the tablet, the user can then focus the center of the camera to a particular location in the game world. The player will then move towards the location that the player is focusing on.

Figure 3. A player trying to move toward the upper left corner of the board using movement method 1.

The merits and drawbacks of each method were considered to ultimately choose the first option. The first and third options forced the user to interact with the game world, providing an inherent draw to the tablet that the second option did not possess. However, since the AR aspect did not always work perfectly, there are times in a game when a player may lose the tracking of the target on the tablet. In these cases, the third movement options is rendered useless, since the user cannot change his view of the screen. In addition, the user may want to move the phone away to interact with the tablet and force the player to move in an unwanted direction. Although the first option does not allow for perfect movement in these cases, some movement was still allowed while the user tried to recapture the target. The second option would continue to allow movement in all directions even if the target was lost. In all three movement options, simply moving the smartphone or changing the view of the game, will affect the direction that the player moves if all other interactions remain the same.

Due to these reasons, the first option was chosen for this implementation of the game. However, further testing may need to be conducted to determine how well the different options test.

Information Overload

While trying to find ways for users to engage with the implemented game, testing revealed the real possibility of overloading the user with too much information. In order to move quickly, the user would have to keep the phone pointed at the tablet, click on the appropriate spot he or she wanted to head towards, and blow into the microphone. User feedback showed that while all of this was manageable, the addition of more features could very well make it too much for a player to handle in such a quick round.

With the issue of information overloading in mind, the trap feature was added. There were two options considered for traps being set during game play. The first option would allow the user to place the trap anywhere he or she had visible on the playing field. This would allow the user to place a trap someplace that no one else could see. The other players are totally unaware of the location of the trap being placed. To indicate where the user wants to place the trap, the user would have to be able to select the appropriate location while continuing to play the game. For this reason, the second option was chosen. The user simply has to press the button to release the trap at their current location. Although placing the trap at the current location allows the other players to see the trap

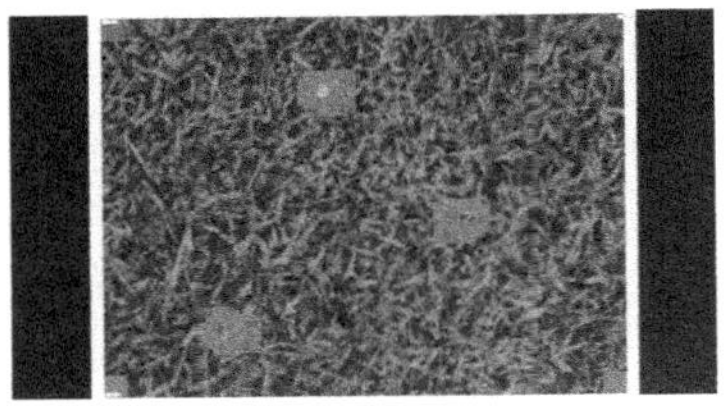

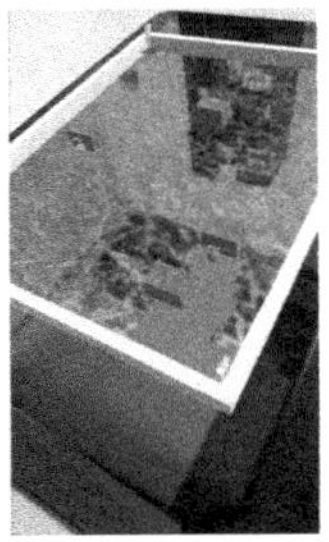

Figure 4. Screenshots from the tablet and the smartphone. The first shows three players on the tablet, where one is carrying the flag. The other shows the the green area and obstacles covered by the red player on the smartphone, information that is invisible on the tablet, as well as the 3D augmentation.

as soon as the player moves from the position, this disadvantage is negligible since players are often focused on other things and will not remember every location where a trap is placed.

AR Component

The AR component was included in an effort to draw the players to the tablet. A problem with the AR in the game scenario was that it was sometimes difficult to see. After initial testing, the tablet was moved closer to the level on which the smartphones were being held. This allowed the users to see the 3D augmentation over the 2D rendering on the tablet. Increasing the size of these objects and ensuring that the tablet is within a short distance of the smartphones would allow the features to be better seen by users, drawing them into the space.

Tablet Interactions

In order to create a game that used multiple devices but also created a feeling of interacting with one another that is often created with board games, interactions were distributed between the smartphones and the tablet. The tablet interactions (eg tapping to steal the flag) are used to draw attention to important events that users should pay attention to. Instead of sending a heads up notification to the players telling them that these important things were happening, the physical movement of players reaching across the table alerts them of this information. On the other hand, using the smartphone for movement allowed all players to move at the same time without confusion and using the volume controls to place traps was a subtle way to allow players to act without bringing attention to it.

Figure 5: A player attempting to steal the flag from the pink base by tapping on the tablet.

Conclusion

Capture the Flag was effective in being able to draw users into a space and force them to interact with each other as a multi-device Augmented Reality game. It uses each user's smartphone and an AR component to reveal a private space with information only available to a single user. However, the AR must be utilized in such a way that it does truly enhance the experience of the user and provide something additional to improve the user's gaming experience. There are still several options that were not implemented for the final Capture the Flag game, that can be tested in further iterations.

References

1. Capture the Flag - wikipedia, the free encyclopedia. http://en.wikipedia.org/wiki/Capture_the_flag, 2015.[Online; last accessed 16-08-2015].
2. Emmanuel Dubois and Laurence Nigay. 2000. Augmented reality: which augmentation for which reality?. In *Proceedings of DARE 2000 on Designing augmented reality environments* (DARE '00). ACM, New York, NY, USA, 165-166.
3. Masayuki Tani, Kimiya Yamaashi, Koichiro Tanikoshi, Masayasu Futakawa, and Shinya Tanifuji. 1992. Object-oriented video: interaction with real-world objects through live video. In *Proceedings of the SIGCHI Conference on Human Factors in Computing Systems* (CHI '92), Penny Bauersfeld, John Bennett, and Gene Lynch (Eds.). ACM, New York, NY, USA, 593-598.
4. Paul Tolstoi and Andreas Dippon. 2015. Towering Defense: An Augmented Reality Multi-Device Game. In *Proceedings of the 33rd Annual ACM Conference Extended Abstracts on Human Factors in Computing Systems* (CHI EA '15). ACM, New York, NY, USA, 89-92.
5. Sebastian Boring, Sven Gehring, Alexander Wiethoff, Anna Magdalena Blöckner, Johannes Schöning, and Andreas Butz. 2011. Multi-user interaction on media facades through live video on mobile devices. In *Proceedings of the SIGCHI Conference on Human Factors in Computing Systems* (CHI '11). ACM, New York, NY, USA, 2721-2724.

Tabletop-Supported Rehabilitation with fun.tast.tisch. – Lessons Learned

Mirjam Augstein
University of Applied Sciences Upper Austria
Hagenberg, Austria
mirjam.augstein@fh-hagenberg.at

Thomas Neumayr
University of Applied Sciences Upper Austria
Hagenberg, Austria
thomas.neumayr@fh-hagenberg.at

Isabel Karlhuber
LIFEtool gemeinnützige GmbH
Linz, Austria
isabel.karlhuber@lifetool.at

Sabine Dielacher
University of Applied Sciences for Health Professions Upper Austria
Linz, Austria
sabine.dielacher@fhgooe.ac.at

Josef Altmann
University of Applied Sciences Upper Austria
Hagenberg, Austria
josef.altmann@fh-hagenberg.at

Sylvia Öhlinger
University of Applied Sciences for Health Professions Upper Austria
Linz, Austria
sylvia.oehlinger@fhgooe.ac.at

ITS'15, November 15–18, 2015, Funchal, Portugal.
ACM 978-1-4503-3899-8/15/11.
http://dx.doi.org/10.1145/2817721.2823494

Abstract
Within the fun.tast.tisch. project, new therapeutic approaches involving an interactive tabletop have been explored. The project did not aim at replacing conventional therapy but at providing optimal support for both therapists and patients. This paper summarizes findings of two years of experience with the system with a focus on patients' and therapists' attitude and system perception. It further outlines implementation challenges and findings on therapeutic efficacy.

Author Keywords
Tabletops; Neuro-Rehabilitation; Therapy Software

ACM Classification Keywords
H.5.2 [Input devices and strategies]: User Interfaces; H.5.2 [Interaction styles]: User Interfaces; H.5.2 [User-centered design]: User Interfaces

Introduction
The success of neuro-rehabilitation crucially relies not only on the adequateness of therapeutic exercises and periodic training with a therapist and in the familiar (domestic) environment, but also on the patient's motivation. Within the fun.tast.tisch. project, a tabletop system providing 16 different modules training different skills (e.g., memory, attention or visuo-constructive skills) for rehabilitation of patients with acquired brain injury has been developed. The aim was

The fun.tast.tisch. system
The system consists of 16 therapeutic exercises organized in so-called modules. It is targeted towards use in a therapy setting involving a therapist and at least one patient. A module requires a therapeutic task to be solved by the patient (e.g., remembering goods to be bought from a (digital) shop or rebuilding a given shape by using physical objects). All tasks can be configured for the patient individually by the therapist (e.g., regarding level of difficulty).

Selection of the technology
The tabletop (we used the Samsung SUR40 with Microsoft PixelSense) was chosen because i) its surface is of sufficient size for common therapy tasks (which often involve a conventional table), ii) the table is a familiar object, and iii) its horizontal surface allows for physical objects to be placed on it which is beneficial for training of e.g., motor skills.

mainly to support conventional therapy by transferring over time-consuming tasks (e.g., computation of statistics or individual configuration of the exercises for the patient) to the system. Additionally, we assumed the tabletop setting to increase patients' motivation due to the novelty of the technology and the numerous possibilities to provide motivating system feedback in addition to the therapist's. The system has been developed with thorough involvement of patients and therapists. This paper is focused on aspects related to system perception by the stakeholders and factors influencing user acceptance that have not been published so far and should be considered when planning (tabletop-based) rehabilitation software. Further it provides the first concise summary of the results of an efficacy study. The system itself is not discussed in detail as it has been described already in our earlier publications (see e.g., [1], [2]).

Interaction Concepts

The interaction concept of a holistic rehabilitation system that can be used to (re-)train motor as well as cognitive abilities should depend on the therapeutic aims. For instance, a therapeutic task aiming at training two-hand coordination, presumes two-handed interaction (which is naturally not possible with single-touch surfaces). The following sections and Table 1 describe our system's interaction methods and the skills for the training of which they are used. Table 2 shows the interaction activities patients need to carry out within our system and patients' perception.

Touch
Touch interaction is the basis of our system's interaction concept and is used for all interaction activities necessary to navigate through the system, select and configure exercises (done by the therapist), and also for patients' tasks in many of the modules. While the therapist's touch-based interaction mostly uses the standard touch activity (the "simple touch"), we introduced two more touch variants for patients: "delayed touch" and "two-handed touch" operations. The delayed touch requires a patient to hold a touch for a pre-defined period of time before the system reacts. This is necessary to prevent a user from trying to solve a task on a trial-and-error basis (e.g., by just randomly tapping the display in order to hit the correct touch position). The two-handed touch (Figure 1) requires a patient to perform two concurrent touches at two different positions on the screen, which is needed to train two-hand coordination. Touch interaction is easy to implement as touch recognition is natively supported by most modern devices. However, not all touch devices also enable multi-touch. Potential challenges include limited number of concurrent touches (in our system some of the modules have been conceptualized to support multi-user settings) or inaccurate localization of touch input.

	Interaction Modality		
Skill Category	*Touch*	*Tangibles*	*Pen*
Motor	+	++	+
Cognitive	++	+	o
Memory	++	++	--
Attention	++	--	--
Visual Exploration	++	+	--
Visuo-Constructive	o	++	-
Spatial Cognition	--	++	--
Spatial Construction	--	++	--
Problem Solving	+	+	+

Table 1: Interaction modalities and how frequent they are used by fun.tast.tisch. for training specific skills (between ++ (very frequent) and -- (not at all)). The assignments are based on therapists' recommendations and can be used as a basic guide for the implementation of computer-based therapeutic exercises.

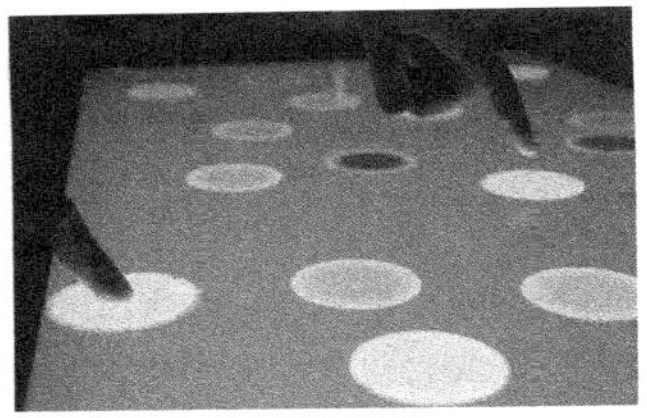

Figure 1: Two-handed touch

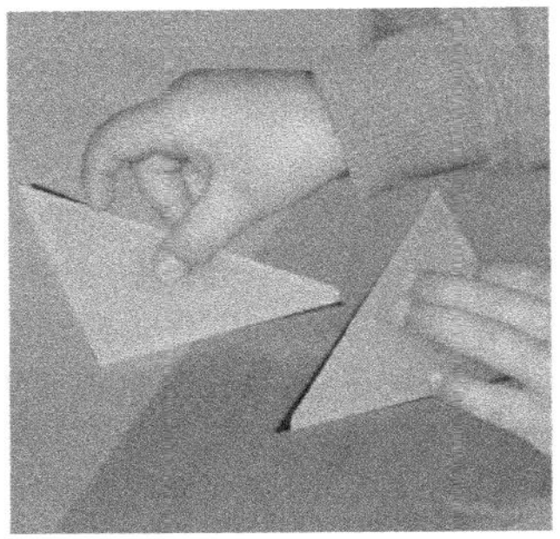

Figure 2: Flat objects

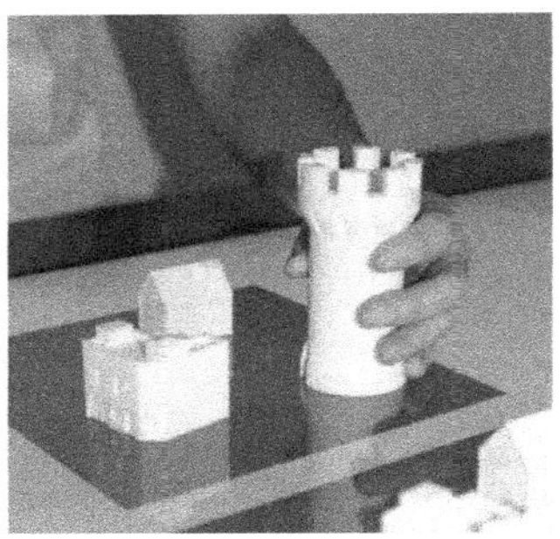

Figure 3: 3D objects

Tangibles
Tangibles are used by many modules as they have been suggested by therapists to be used for the training, e.g., of motor or spatial skills. The system uses different kinds – first, flat, semitransparent objects that have to be arranged on the surface and can be used from both sides (Figure 2).

These objects are not recognized by a tag on their bottom side but by their shape. This kind of object recognition is not natively supported by the technology and thus needed to be implemented by the project team.It was necessary to introduce this kind of object recognition as therapeutic tasks require patients to flip over the object (for reasons of training particular fine motor skills). Also, we wanted to use a special kind of positive feedback with these objects (the area under the object is colored in light green by the table which makes the object appear to shine in light green); This kind of feedback was accepted exceptionally well by the patients. Second, we use three-dimensional objects recognized by tags that can be arranged on the surface (Figure 3). These objects are better graspable and better suitable for training spatial skills. fun.tast.tisch. uses such objects to i) select digital items shown on the screen and ii) train spatial skills by arranging them on the surface. Object recognition is not supported by most touch-based devices as most use capacitive screens. MS PixelSense relies on an optical display and offers native support for tag-based object recognition. Regarding patient interaction, severe impairment of both upper extremities could be an exclusion criterion for tasks where patients have to handle objects.

Pen
We introduced pen interaction for tasks where a patient needs to trace a line (Figure 4). Pen interaction in the rehabilitation process could, however, also be used to retrain handwriting or other fine motor skills. For optical displays based on infrared technology, infrared pens can be used. Recognition is usually not natively supported but can be implemented relatively easily. One major challenge involved with pen interaction is that e.g., writing skills (or in general, handling of a pen) are usually present with one hand only. Thus, patients with hemiplegia might be forced to use the pen with their non-dominant hand which is likely to be problematic. Therefore, the system should provide an alternative interaction way for tasks that rely on the pen. Bilateral paralysis of the upper body as well as severe impairment of upper extremity functionality could be exclusion criteria.

	Perception by Users		
Interaction Activity	*Intuitive*	*Motivating*	*Easy to Handle*
Simple Touch	++	o	++
Delayed Touch	+	o	+
Two-Handed Touch	+	+	++
Selection via Tangibles	-	+	++
Arrangement of Flat Tangibles	++	++	+
Arrangement of 3D Tangibles	++	++	+
Tracing a Line with Pen	++	++	o

Table 2: Users' interaction activities and how they were perceived (agreement between ++ and --).

Figure 4: Pen interaction

Infrared pen selection
We chose an infrared pen based on usability for patients. The pen (irpens Infrared Pen Djewel)triggers radiation by pressing it on the surface, instead having to press a button while using it.

Usability studies
Two usability studies in a rehabilitation clinic have been conducted earlier (see [2]). There, part of the modules was used in real therapy settings for several months. Therapists answered a detailed questionnaire after the test period. For ethical reasons, it was not possible to involve patients in these studies more thoroughly. We however repeatedly gathered additional feedback by patients in a less formal way during development.

Technical and Implementation Challenges

The challenges using MS PixelSense were mainly related to object recognition, infrared pen interaction and the tabletop's dependence on certain lighting conditions. The limitations regarding object recognition concerned a few modules only, but within these they played a decisive role.

When selecting a technology in the beginning, the fact that PixelSense claimed to be able to recognize over 50 concurrent touches was convincing. Thus, our experience with the object recognition capabilities was extremely sobering. We found the reliable recognition of tags at run-time to be limited to about 10 tags, when making use of the standard 256 byte tags. Thus, for the modules using more than 10 objects we had to create new tags with bigger and simpler design and the related image recognition algorithm (based upon AForge.NET [1]). Our tags contain a quadrilateral and a circle placed not exactly in the middle of it (so the orientation of the tag can be identified). Regarding recognition of the infrared pen tip, our algorithm searches for a point of specified size (considering a tolerance range as the brightness of the pen may vary due to battery issues). The table's sensitivity to ambient light with an infrared component and changing lighting conditions are responsible for our most severe technical problems. These issues are meanwhile well reported which was not the case at project start. Changing light was particularly problematic for the recognition of our untagged objects. We were not able to offer a run-time solution but implemented a calibration module where object recognition can be manually recalibrated to better fit the current lighting conditions.

Patients' Attitude

Patients' perception of a rehabilitation system is probably the most decisive factor regarding system acceptance. In this section we identify supporting and limiting factors that should be considered when implementing tabletop-based rehabilitation systems. Our user tests have shown that the system's feedback as a reaction to a patient having solved a therapeutic exercise plays a crucial role. Thus, the system's feedback for the patient should be motivating and unambiguous and it should appeal to different sensory channels (e.g., acoustic feedback combined with visual one – our tests have shown that feedback on one sensory channel only can be easily overseen/overheard). Further, the patients that have been using our system described the combination of different interaction modalities as especially appealing. Interaction should be intuitive, thus it usually pays off to invest time in the interaction design. The same applies for the general design of the user interface – our users named the detailed design elements as well as the different design options we offer for different target groups (e.g., children) as particularly motivating. Factors decreasing acceptance are wrong, missing or tardy feedback and inappropriate (too high or too low) level of difficulty of the exercises. The latter lies partly in the responsibility of the therapist who selects and configures the exercises for the patient. Table 3 summarizes the most relevant supporting and limiting factors related to user acceptance.

Therapists' Attitude

Therapists are an equally important target group as they are responsible for a major part of the interaction with the system (including configuration of modules and navigation through the system) and the decision whether or not to use the system at all. In our tests, therapists attached great importance to the configurability of the exercises according to the individual patients' needs. Further, the automated computation of statistics was particularly important. Also for therapists, intuitive interaction was one of the most decisive aspects (therapists did not only pay attention to the

[1] http://www.aforgenet.com/

Factor	Importance for …	
	Patients	*Therapists*
Motivating Feedback	++	++
Varied Exercises	++	++
Configurability of Exercises	o	++
Adjustable Task Difficulty	o	++
Therapeutically Approved Exercises	o	++
Therapeutic Effect	+	++
Multi-Patient Exercises	++	o
Sophisticated Design	++	o
Unconventional Input Modalities	++	-
Recognizability of Design and Interaction Elements	+	+
Modern Technology	++	o
Screen Size	+	+
Error-free Software	+	++
Reliable Hardware	o	++
Easily Transportable Hardware	--	+
Accessibility for Wheelchair Patients	++	++
Adjustable Table Height	o	++
Surface Constitution (Disinfectable)	--	++
Availability of Statistics	+	++
Availability and Quality of Support	--	++
Availability and Quality of Tutorials	--	+
Low Expenses for Hard- and Software	--	++

Table 3: Importance of factors related to the design and development and overall perception of a tabletop system for rehabilitation for patients and therapists (between ++ and --).

intuitiveness of their interaction with the system but also at patients'). Hardware-related problems like e.g., unexpected shutdown of the whole system or software bugs (e.g., a memory leak that caused slowdown of the system's reaction to user input) led to lowered acceptance of the system as a whole. In the therapy sector, schedules are extremely tight, thus error-free IT systems are presumed. Further, therapists also pay attention to aspects only marginally related to system design like e.g., tutorials and support.

Therapeutic Implications

Different clinical studies have taken place in order to evaluate the therapeutic effect. This section shortly outlines two studies and provides a preview on the results[2]. A single case study (A-B-A design) was conducted with a 25 year old female patient after Subarachnoid Haemorrhage who received repeated training over a period of several weeks with a focus on motor skills. For this patient, touch, tangibles and pen were used and individualized intervention was necessary. According to her therapist, the system offered sufficient possibilities to adapt the program individually but it was necessary that the therapist attended the training, assisted and instructed the patient. Three standardized ways of assessment (e.g., MESUPES scale) were used in addition to non-standardized ones (e.g., a questionnaire concerning activities of daily living). The results show an improvement in mobility and function of the upper limb which were still present in the follow up measurement after 5 weeks. Further, the patient stated to be able to implement the improved abilities in everyday life and that she exceptionally liked the training and wanted to continue with it.

An efficacy study (mainly regarding attention skills) organized as randomized controlled group study was con-

[2]The results are prepared and analyzed in more detail at the moment and will be published in the neuro-rehabilitation community.

ducted together with occupational therapists and neuropsychologists over several months in a rehabilitation clinic. We aimed at finding out whether therapy with our system would achieve at least equivalent results, compared to conventional one. TAP [3] was used to measure the effect. The study involved 26 patients with limited cognitive functions (average age 58.17) who received 8 training sessions with our system or 8 sessions of conventional training. In both groups, a significant improvement in attention performance was measured. Further, both showed significant improvements in specific attention-related skills (e.g., selective attention). Regarding the clinical aspect, the results suggested that the system is a valuable supplement to conventional therapy, as different effects appeared in various categories of skills (results were better in some categories but worse in others). Regarding motivation, the training with the systems mostly outperformed conventional one.

Hardware considerations
For the therapy setting it is not easy to find an alternative hardware as it must meet many requirements. It must offer native object recognition support, be of comparable size for training of motor skills, it must be robust enough not to get damaged after uncontrolled handling of objects on the surface and the surface must be disinfectable. Further, it must be flat enough so a patient in a wheelchair can get close to it and it mustn't be too heavy so it can be transported relatively easily. Also, the table must be cheap enough (with approx. 7000 €as upper limit) so it can be afforded by smaller therapy institutions. These requirements unfortunately exclude common tablets, touch screens and most commercially available tabletops. Within fun.tast.tisch.. , alternative tabletops are still evaluated at the moment.

Conclusions

This paper is a concise summary of findings and recommendations related to tabletops in (neuro-)rehabilitation. In general, our user studies suggest that tabletops can be applied well for rehabilitation purposes, regarding motivational as well as clinical aspects. Especially for patients, the new technology seems to be a welcomed change to the therapy process which is often perceived as monotonous. Also, therapists' attitude towards our system was a positive one in general. However, for both target groups the lasting acceptance of the system strongly depends on the quality of the software and its UI. A thoughtful design and interaction concept as well as error-free software are prerequisites for the success (turned out to be even more important than e.g., the variety of exercises). As patients and their individual abilities are highly diverse, it is necessary to offer high configurability. For therapists it is of crucial importance to provide not only a modern representation of conventional therapeutic exercises but a significant addition to it. In our case this addition involved e.g., a statistics feature which took over time-consuming work that therapists otherwise need to do manually. It is also highly recommended to rely on therapeutically approved exercises only and to repeatedly involve all target groups. Regarding hardware, we used PixelSense because it promised to meet our requirements. Although most needs were in general met, there were severe problems with ambient light because certain conditions interfere with the table's touch and object recognition. We thus cannot recommend the selected hardware for the development of a professional rehabilitation system.

Acknowledgments

fun.tast.tisch. acknowledges the financial support within the COIN program, managed by the Austrian Research Promotion Agency and funded by the Federal Ministry for Transport, Innovation and Technology and the Federal Ministry of Economy, Family and Youth. Project partners: LIFEtool, ARTGROUP, UAS for Health Professions Upper Austria, UAS Upper Austria, Irene Schacherl-Hofer, softaware gmbh and TRANSPARENT DESIGN.

References

Augstein, M., Neumayr, T., Ruckser-Scherb, R., Karlhuber, I., and Altmann, J. The fun.tast.tisch. project – a novel approach to neuro-rehabilitation using an interactive multiuser multitouch tabletop. In *Proc. of the ACM Conf. on Interactive Tabletops and Surfaces* (St. Andrews, 2013).

Augstein, M., Neumayr, T., and Schacherl-Hofer, I. The usability of a tabletop application for neuro-rehabilitation from therapists' point of view. In *Proce. of the 9th ACM Int. Conf.on Interactive Tabletops and Surfaces* (Dresden, Germany, 2014).

Zimmermann, P., and Fimm, B. *TAP – Testbatterie zur Aufmerksamkeitsprüfung*. Psytest, Herzogenrath, 2002.

PhySig: Incorporating Physical Products with Digital Signage in Shopping Environments

Masafumi Muta
Soh Masuko
Adiyan Mujibiya
Rakuten Institute of Technology,
Rakuten Inc.
1-14-1 Tamagawa, Setagaya,
Tokyo, JAPAN
masafumi.muta@rakuten.com
so.masuko@rakuten.com
adiyan.mujibiya@rakuten.com

ITS'15, November 15–18, 2015, Funchal, Portugal.
ACM 978-1-4503-3899-8/15/11.
http://dx.doi.org/10.1145/2817721.2823495

Abstract
In this paper, we propose the concepts, design guidelines, and implementation details of *PhySig*, a novel interactive in-store shopping experience that annotates information about products, which are physically located in the store, by a projector and enables shared content between the products and mobile devices. Multiple users access the system from their own mobile devices to move a cursor projected on the wall or floor of the store to select an item and obtain additional information associated with the item in the projected space. They can also download the information to their mobile devices or upload their related content, including comments, reviews, or photos, of the item. In short, PhySig is an example of how to extend and combine digital signage with the surrounding physical environment.

Author Keywords
Interactive advertising; projection mapping; digital signage; e-commerce; content sharing.

ACM Classification Keywords
H.5.2 [Information Interfaces and Presentation]: Input devices and strategies, Interaction styles

Figure 1: Illustrating the concept behind PhySig.

Introduction

The spread of personal mobile devices, such as smartphones and tablets, provides us with more convenient and easier shopping experiences. We can search for product details, read reviews from others who have purchased the item, and find the cheapest price – even if we are standing in front of the item in the store. Thus, brick and mortar retailers selling products at physical retail stores are suffering from a *showrooming* phenomenon where customers visit real stores to examine a product but finally purchase the product from online retailers, often because of lower prices [3].

To minimize the impact of showrooming on retailers, user experiences need to be enhanced in the actual stores by bridging the gap between the online and actual stores [5, 3]. One approach here is to place terminals, e.g., interactive kiosks or digital signage, directly in the stores. As an example, Tesco installed transactional kiosks in their retail stores, enabling users to browse and purchase items, including products they may not find in the actual store [1].

Utilization of personal devices is also an effective approach. Using this approach, stores can offer suitable information based on customer information, including user location or purchase history; moreover, they can offer discounts to specific users based on this information. For example, Walmart recently released the *Savings Catcher* service as part of their mobile application [10]. With this service, a customer can scan the barcode shown on his or her receipt after a purchase at the retailer and obtain coupons for the balance if other retailers are advertising one or more items at cheaper prices.

One of the biggest advantages of stores such as brick and mortar retailers is their ability to show the actual products; however, in prior approaches, user interactions have been separate from physically located products, i.e., users do not see or touch the products during their interaction with the devices. We hypothesize that we can enhance the user experience by seamless connection of the online and the real world with combining personal devices and projector.

In this paper, therefore, we propose PhySig, a method for bridging physical products in retail stores with online information by providing interconnectivity between the projected annotations and personal mobile devices. Using this system, a user can continuously control a personalized cursor in the projected area, assumed to be a store's wall or floor. When the user points his or her cursor at a product located physically in the store, additional content, such as the details of the item, is projected near the item. In addition, users can download the content to their devices and purchase the corresponding product in the retailer's online store. While we previously proposed the *WallSHOP* [4], a private-and-public content sharing system for digital signage, we now extend this concept beyond digital displays to use real products as signage. An example of PhySig usage is shown in Figure 1.

In this current research, we contribute to the human-computer interface (HCI) research community by presenting the details of PhySig's concept and design guidelines for using physical objects as digital signage. Furthermore, we describe the implementation details of our prototype PhySig and report the insights acquired from the system.

Related Work

In 2001, Raskar et al. proposed a methodology for interactive projection mapping [7]. Such technologies have since been widely used for various entertainment scenes, such as artistic performances, live music, and commercial promotions. Raskar et al. also presented a conceptual application of projection mapping on the workspace as a *Spatially Augmented Reality (SAR)* [6]. Although numerous studies have attempted to implement this concept to enhance productivity in the working environments, only few studies have applied the concept to shopping environments.

In [9], Sukaviriya et al. applied projection mapping to the retail environment, where the system recognized user gestures, actions, and location. The system provides information, such as product directories, directions, and product details by projectors, which is needed in retail environments. Our study uses a similar concept, except that we use customer mobile devices for interaction instead of gesture recognition, thus enabling simultaneous use and personalization.

Some retail stores already make use of interactive signage with digital displays. Among various studies conducted to increase the effectiveness of such signage, She et al. highlighted the importance of combining public display and customer mobile devices [8]. In [4], we proposed a detailed design and implementation for digital signage connected with mobile devices. In another digital signage study, Colley et al. showed that displaying annotations by "see-through" Augmented Reality drew significantly more attention as compared with static content [2].

PhySig Design and Implementation

In this section, we describe the design and implementation of a proof-of-concept PhySig prototype. PhySig comprises two web applications, i.e., the *renderer* and *controller*. The renderer is an application that generates the display to be output to the projector by composing annotation content and customer cursors. Customers use the controller to connect with the renderer, and then move individually assigned cursors to select items in the projected area. When a cursor hovers on a product, annotations, such as item information, reviews, and recommendations, are shown as balloons. Moreover, users can download additional detailed information to their device and navigate to the retailer's online store to purchase the given product.

Design Guidelines

We designed PhySig based on knowledge regarding the digital signage explored in the HCI community. Below, we discuss our design guidelines from two points of view, i.e., the customers and retailers. For the customer's experience, we considered guidelines based on the *new evolved model* proposed by She et al. [8], which defines three gradual user experience stages for interactive digital signage, i.e., *attention*, *interaction*, and *conation*. Attention represents how to make users become aware of the system, then prepare to interact with it. In this stage, we must consider how to overcome *display blindness*, where passersby do not notice the display, and *interaction blindness*, where passersby do not recognize that the display is interactive. Next, interaction represents how users interact with the system to explore available content. Therefore, providing users with intuitive

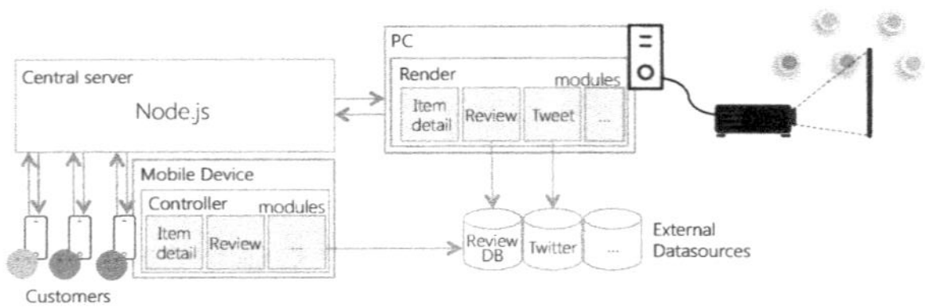

Figure 2: PhySig system configuration. [1]

user interfaces (UIs) and reducing complexity is essential. Accepting interactions from multiple people simultaneously is also important here, because we are trying to use physical objects as the signage; therefore, people forming a queue might cause a crowd in the store. Finally, conation represents the follow-up actions for users who have decided to interact with the system.

From the retailer's point of view, we considered the ease of deployment, sustainability, and extensibility. Ease of deployment is crucial, especially for small retailers with small staffs. We avoided complex calibration procedures and any requirements for special equipment. Sustainability indicates that the system can work for long periods of time and easily adapt to changes in the displayed products. In other words, the system should not be a projection mapping artwork for only a special product or campaign. Extensibility means that retailers can select the content displayed for each item, and developers can customize or add new kinds of content.

System Architecture
We show the PhySig system architecture in Figure 2. The renderer and controllers are connected by a central server, which is implemented using Node.js. They communicate with one another via WebSocket. Both applications are built on standard web technologies to enable users to access the controller application simply by opening a URL.

As the main feature of the renderer is to project additional information for products, the corresponding functions are modularized; therefore, retailers can select what types of information to present (e.g., static text, reviews from the Web, and comments from customers who visited the store). Each module accesses an individual retailer's data sources.

The function of the controller is split into modules. A retailer can select modules to choose what information is shown on customer mobile devices for a product. Note that some modules impact both the renderer and controller. For example, the *comment* module, which allows a customer to post a comment for a given product, provides multiple functions to both the controller and renderer, i.e., one for providing a form to the user and the other for displaying the posted comments.

Interactivity from Controllers
Customers can remotely control their own cursors on the projection area using the controller application. This application is separated into two views with the following features: (1) control the cursor; and (2) view detailed product information. The user can update the cursor's position by swiping their finger on the virtual trackpad of the control view, as shown in Figure 3(a). Furthermore, the user can download the content associated with the "selected" item by moving the cursor over the item, then tapping the trackpad; as a result, the detailed product information view is opened. In this view, the specific modules associated with the item (as set by the retailer) determine what content is to be shown. In a typical situation, the *product info* module will show the specifications of the product or photos of the item in use and provide a link for purchasing it on the

[1] "Computer Tower" icon by Creative Stall, "Projector" icon by Sunny Xuyi Wu from the Noun Project.

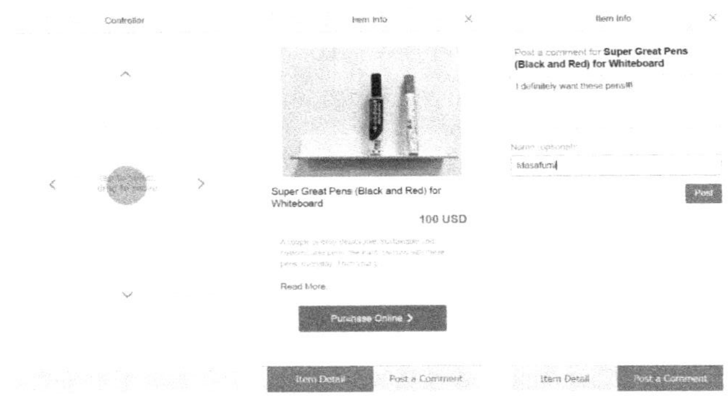

(a) Virtual trackpad. The customer controls their cursor by swiping their finger on the screen. (b) A product is selected by the customer. The details of the item are displayed. (c) The customer can post a comment by the comment module.

Figure 3: Screenshots of the controllers.

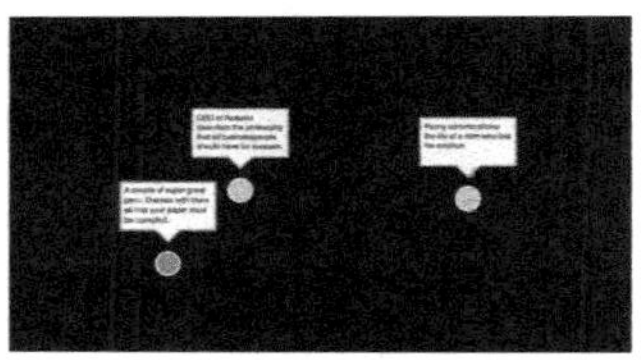

(a) The renderer's output.

(b) The output projected near the real products.

Figure 4: Working scenes of the renderer.

retailer's online store, i.e., the configuration shown in Figure 3(b). The *user review* module may also show reviews of the item posted on the website. Customers may post their comments through the comment module, as shown in Figure 3(c). If multiple modules are defined, the user can view the different information provided by each of the modules by switching tabs presented to the user.

Projection from the Renderer

As shown in Figure 4, the renderer shows annotations for products via projections. The information is shown as a balloon that extrudes from an item. While the modules associated with an item determine the content shown, advertising copy is shown via the *Ad copy* module in a typical use case. In addition, the renderer shows the cursor of each connected customer. The cursors have individual colors that correspond to the colors of the circles shown on the controllers, thus customers can easily distinguish their own cursors.

Content Mapping UI

For retailers, we provide the UI shown in Figure 5(a) to map the content projected in the real world to the physical objects. This UI enables retailers to decide where the associated annotations should be shown while observing the actual projection area. First, the retailer places the projector in front of the desired items, then opens the mapping UI. The UI is projected to the area. The remaining operations are then performed by the retailer as he or she looks at the projection area. The retailer moves the mouse pointer over the item to be annotated, then double-clicks to identify the annotation area. A box appears enabling the retailer to indicate the rectangular area. The retailer can move this rectangle by dragging it or change its size by dragging its corners. Finally, the retailer configures the content by clicking the box to open the configure window, then selects the modules to be associated with the item. Some modules may have extra fields to be filled in as compared with others.

Currently, this mapping is manually set up using our system. It is a straightforward process, but its weakness is the movement of the projector. Particularly for small retailers, the projector might be moved due to cleaning, relocating, or being bumped in tight quarters. Considering these situations, we added a feature to adjust the scale and position of the entire marked area, with features shown in Figure 5(b).

Conclusions and Future Work

In this paper, we proposed PhySig, a method for bridging the gap between the physical products in retail stores and information provided during online shopping by providing interconnectivity between the projected annotations and per-

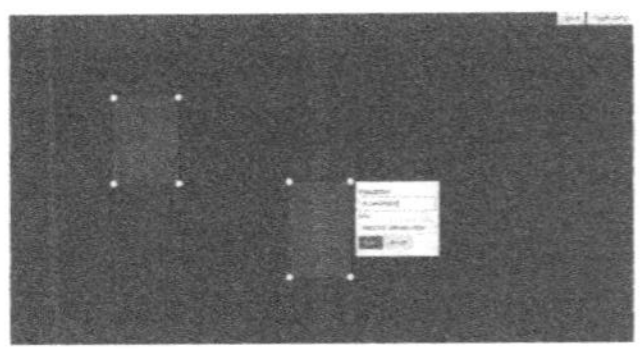

(a) The retailer moves and resizes the markers (i.e., red boxes) to fit to an actual product; a marker has its configuration window opened allowing the retailer to provide information to the module for a product.

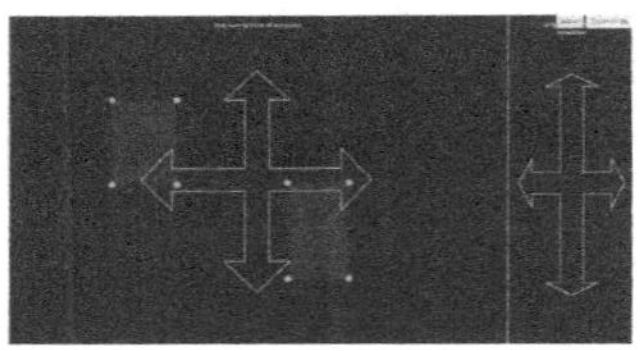

(b) In the adjustment view, the retailer can move all boxes using the left region of the view or scale them via the right region.

Figure 5: Screenshots of the mapping UI.

Figure 6: A failed example in which the balloon from a book overlapped with another book placed above.

sonal mobile devices. We presented details of our system's concept and design guidelines, thereby encompassing a gradual transition of the user experience stage through digital signage. Moreover, we realized an actual deployment for a typical retail store. Finally, we described the implementation details of our prototype system.

In this work, we encountered a problem in which a balloon from a product may overlap with another item (or items), as shown in Figure 6. This problem makes reading the content rather difficult. As future work, we aim to implement an algorithm to avoid such overlaps of the given balloons, perhaps via automatic relocation. To achieve this, we consider the introduction of a *block-marker* in the mapping UI to enable the system to know where the balloon should not be shown (e.g., to avoid a poster on the wall or other obstructions). Furthermore, we aim to investigate methods to show product-related information, for example, by playing a video in the entire area when a user hovers the cursor on a special item. We also can foresee digitally drawing a line from one item to other items to indicate recommendations of "similar" items. Finally, we aim to conduct user studies to measure the effectiveness and ease of use of our system.

REFERENCES

1. Cisco Consulting Services. 2013. Tesco Launches Innovative Pilot To Drive the In-Store Digital Experience. PDF. (2013). Retrieved August 8, 2015 from https://www.cisco.com/web/about/ac79/docs/retail/Tesco.pdf.
2. Ashley Colley *et al.* 2015. Insights from Deploying See-Through Augmented Reality Signage in the Wild. In *Proceedings of PerDis '15*. 179–185. DOI: http://dx.doi.org/10.1145/2757710.2757730
3. IQmetrix. 2014. In-Store Technology: Delivering the Shopping Experience Customers Want. PDF. (2014). Retrieved August 8, 2015 from http://www.iqmetrix.com/files/documents/XQ/Customer-Experience_Whitepaper.pdf.
4. Masafumi Muta *et al.* 2015. Interactive Study of WallSHOP: Multiuser Connectivity between Public Digital Advertising and Private Devices for Personalized Shopping. In *Proceedings of PerDis '15*. 187–193. DOI: http://dx.doi.org/10.1145/2757710.2757732
5. Sydney Pratte *et al.* 2014. Exploring Multi-Surface Interactions in Retail Environments. In *Proceedings of ITS '14*. 393–398. DOI: http://dx.doi.org/10.1145/2669485.2669552
6. Ramesh Raskar *et al.* 1998. The Office of the Future: A Unified Approach to Image-based Modeling and Spatially Immersive Displays. In *Proceedings of SIGGRAPH '98*. 179–188. DOI: http://dx.doi.org/10.1145/280814.280861
7. Ramesh Raskar *et al.* 2001. Shader Lamps: Animating Real Objects with Image-based Illumination. In *Proceedings of EGWR '01*. 89–101. DOI: http://dx.doi.org/10.2312/EGWR/EGWR01/089-101
8. James She *et al.* 2014. Convergence of Interactive Displays with Smart Mobile Devices for Effective Advertising: A Survey. *ACM Trans. Multimedia Comput. Commun. Appl.* 10, 2, Article 17 (Feb. 2014), 16 pages. DOI: http://dx.doi.org/10.1145/2557450
9. Noi Sukaviriya *et al.* 2003. Augmenting a Retail Environment Using Steerable Interactive Displays. In *CHI '03 Extended Abstracts*. 978–979. DOI: http://dx.doi.org/10.1145/765891.766104
10. Walmart. 2015. Your Savings Dashboard. (2015). Retrieved August 8, 2015 from https://savingscatcher.walmart.com/.

Studying User-Defined Gestures Toward Off-the-Screen Interactions

Kohei Matsumura
Ritsumeikan University
1-1-1 Nojihigashi, Kusatsu, Shiga 525-8577, Japan
matsumur@acm.org

ITS '15, November 15-18, 2015, Funchal, Portugal
ACM 978-1-4503-3899-8/15/11.
http://dx.doi.org/10.1145/2817721.2823496

Abstract

This study describes the concept of *off-the-screen interactions*. People often point or gesture not only on the touch-sensitive screen of a device but also around the screen. In this study on off-the-screen interactions, we investigated user-defined gestures on the surrounding area of the screen through a user study using paper prototypes. Through our results, we found that there are different styles of off-the-screen interactions and requirements that are to be considered for realizing our concept.

Author Keywords

off the screen; experiment; mobile surface; finger pointing; gestures;

ACM Classification Keywords

H.5.m. Information interfaces and presentation (e.g., HCI): Miscellaneous;

Introduction

While using a map, people often point to the outside of the map with their finger to indicate the place. There may be several reasons for doing this. Possibly, the place he/she wants to indicate is out of bounds of the map and he/she does not want to change page or expand the map due the time it takes or perhaps because it is too much of a bother.

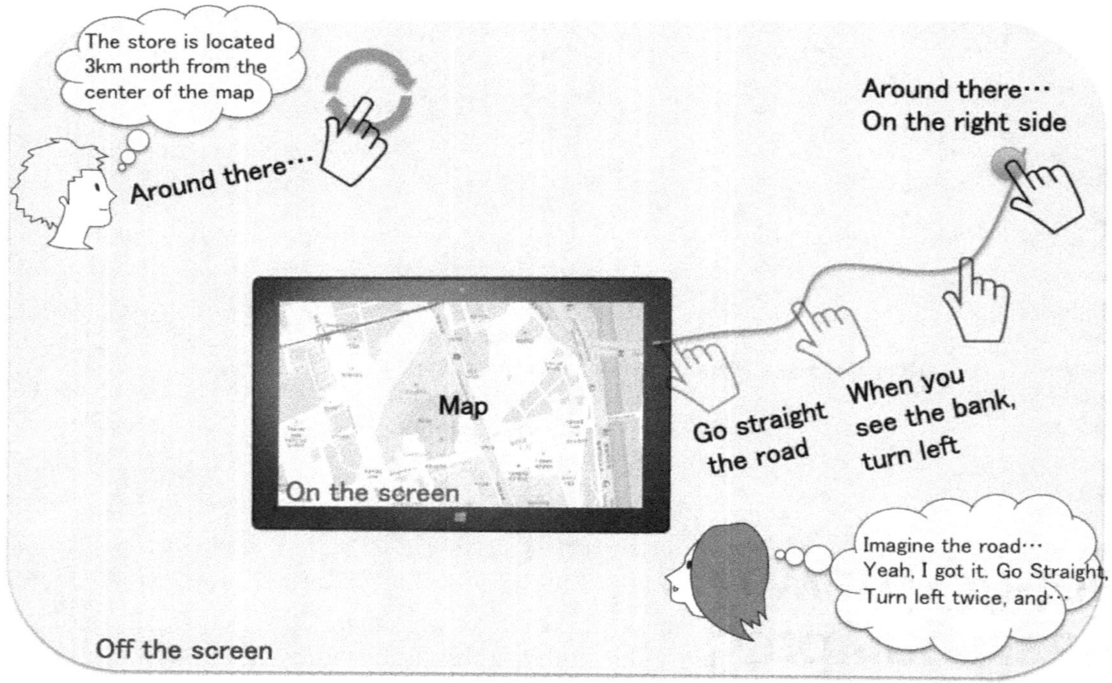

Figure 1: The concept of the *off-the-screen interaction*. A device tracks the position of the finger and recognizes gestures.

This study uses these out-of-screen interactions to enhance user experience on touch-enabled devices such as tablets and smartphones. Figure 1 illustrates the concept of the off-the-screen interactions. In the figure, two examples of off-the-screen gestures are shown. A man imagines a map that is out of the screen bounds and draws a circle to indicate somewhere off the screen. In the other example, a woman imagines a map and draws a line that continues the road shown on the screen.

In this study toward realizing our off the screen concept, we investigate user-defined off-the-screen gestures through a user study performed using paper prototypes.

The contributions of the study are as follows:

- Proposes a novel concept to enhance user experiences on touch-enabled devices.
- Investigates user-defined gestures of off-the-screen interactions and classifies them.
- Finds requirements to realize off the screen interactions.

Related Works

Baudisch et al. proposed a display that combines both a large low-resolution display and a small high-resolution display [1]. Their concept aimed to provide large-sized abstract information using the surrounding area of a small-sized screen. Jones et al. proposed a concept to enhance the viewing experience by augmenting the area surrounding a television with projected visualizations [2]. They used the off-the-screen (of the television screen) area to enhance the expression of

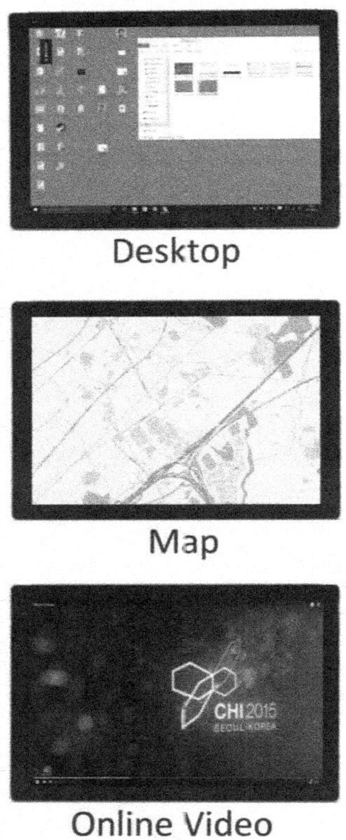

Figure 2: Three displayed contents.

content and the user experience, i.e., they used the off the screen area as output; in contrast to their approach, we aim to use the off the screen area as input.

Vatabu proposed the concept of AROUND-TV [3]. In this concept, the physical area of the TV is extended into the surrounding ambient by employing a projector that displays supplementary content. The idea is similar to the above mentioned studies [1, 2], however, they introduce an interaction technique to the concept. They employ a Wii remote that enables interactions with content shown in the surrounding area by gestural actions since the Wii remote has inertinal sensors as well as physical buttons. In contrast with the AROUND-TV concept that targets a TV that is located away from users, we focus on mobile touch-enabled devices such as tablets and smartphones and use the surrounding area as gestural input space.

User-defined gestures have been studied in the domains of tabletop interactions [4, 5], multi-display environments [6], and distant large displays [7]. Wobbrock et al. investigated user-defined gestures elicited from non-technical users [4]. Kurdyukova et al. studied appropriate gestures for data transfer between two tablets, a tablet and a tabletop, and a tablet and a public display by investigating user-defined gestures [6]. In this study, with respect to these studies, we investigate user-defined gestures for off-the-screen interactions.

Off the Screen Interactions: Investigation

To understand off-the-screen interactions, we investigate user-defined gestures through a user study using paper prototypes. The prototype consists of a large paper and a screen-sized paper. The size of the large paper is 900 mm × 600 mm, which is roughly equivalent to A1 size. We prepare three conditions of displayed content, as shown in Figure 2. One shows a Windows 10 standard desktop screen, another shows a map, the last shows an online video service. We printed them out along with a tablet-form frame on screen-sized paper and placed it on the center of the large paper as shown in Figure 3.

Four healthy people (two males and two females) aged 23 to 32 participated in the user study. We asked them to discuss off-the-screen gestures to make changes to the displayed content and to write them on the large paper using pens. Since we prepared three displayed contents, the user study consisted of three sessions. Each session took 15 minutes and we asked the participants to take a five minutes rest between sessions. So, the user study took about one hour to finish. We started with the desktop content, followed by the map and online video content. For further analysis, we recorded the user study using a video camera.

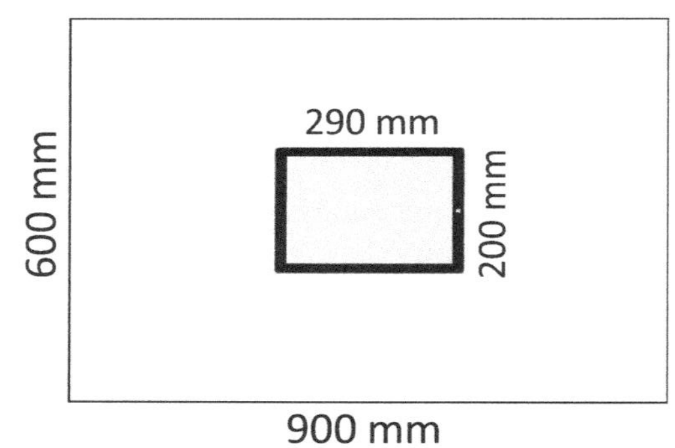

Figure 3: A paper prototype. The screen-sized paper is placed on the center of the large paper.

Figure 4: Participant discussed with gestures in the session.

Results

The participants discussed the topic for one hour in the user study. Figure 4 shows some pictures from each session. We counted gestures annotated on the large papers. They defined eight gestures for the desktop content, 12 gestures for the map content, and 13 gestures for the online video conditions, making it a total of 33 gestures. Figure 5 shows examples of user-defined gestures.

Through the video investigation and analysis of annotated user-defined gestures, we found that the participants defined generic gestures for the desktop content, i.e., most of these gestures did not rely on the content. For example, they defined a gesture to take a screenshot and a gesture to archive a file or download content. These gestures are commonly used and did not rely on content or situations. Contrary to gestures defined for the desktop content, those defined in the session for the map and the online video content depend on the situations. They defined a gesture to control an online video using start/stop, cue, and skip content gestures for the online video content. For the map content, they defined content-dependent gestures such as a creating a route gesture, a gesture to show the detail of the place, and to change the center of the map.

Through the discussion, they also found that determining a starting/ending action is important, because it is otherwise difficult for the device to understand the gesture. After they identified this importance, they started to define the gestures explicitly.

Through the video investigation, we found that the participants used some voice commands along with gestures. The voice commands were used during the gestures in some cases, but in other cases, they used the voice commands to express the end of the gesture.

Concluding Remarks

In this study, we proposed our concept of off-the-screen interactions. The off-the-screen interactions utilize users' off-the-screen gestures to enhance the user experience on touch-enabled devices such as tablets and smartphones.

To realize off-the-screen interactions, we have to understand the relationship (i.e., the user interaction) between the content and the off-the-screen gestures. We thus investigated user-defined gestures through a user study using paper prototypes.

Through the results of the user study, we found that there are two types of off-the-screen gestures. One is a generic type of gesture that may be commonly used for multiple situations, since the gesture does not depend on the content. The other is a content-dependent-type gesture. The gesture may be used to operate the content shown on the screen. We also found that it is important to include an action and/or a voice command to express an explicit period for the gesture. This implies the use of the microphone and voice recognition technology may be required to realize the off-the-screen interactions.

Gesture recognition technology is also required. We plan to use multiple proximity sensors to recognize the position of fingers around the device. We will implement this gesture recognition feature on a device in the future.

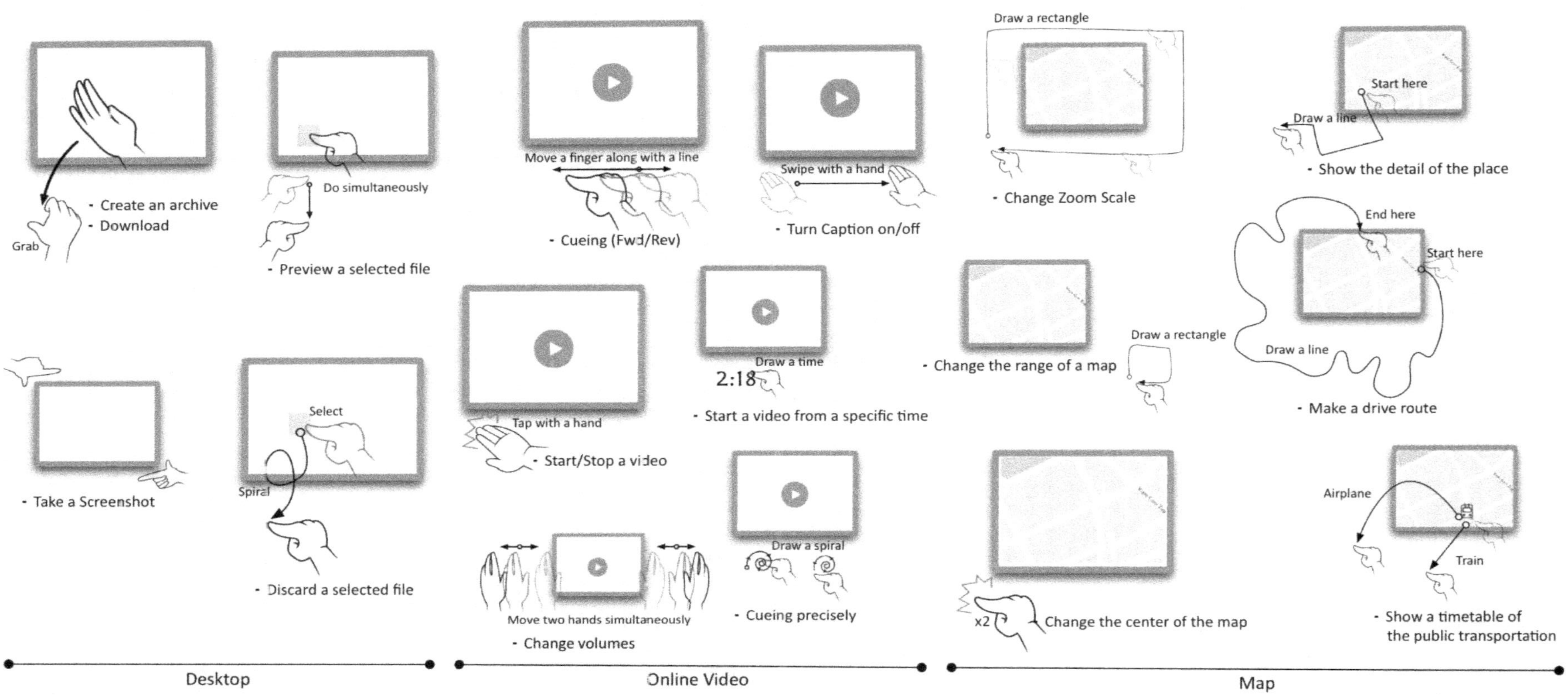

Figure 5: Examples of user-defined gestures for each content.

References

1. Patrick Baudisch, Nathaniel Good, and Paul Stewart. 2001. Focus plus context screens: combining display technology with visualization techniques. In *Proceedings of the 14th annual ACM symposium on User interface software and technology* (UIST '01). ACM, New York, NY, USA, 31-40. DOI=10.1145/502348.502354
2. Brett R. Jones, Hrvoje Benko, Eyal Ofek, and Andrew D. Wilson. 2013. IllumiRoom: peripheral projected illusions for interactive experiences. In *Proceedings of the SIGCHI Conference on Human Factors in Computing Systems* (CHI '13). ACM, New York, NY, USA, 869-878. DOI=10.1145/2470654.2466112
3. Radu-Daniel Vatavu. 2013. There's a world outside your TV: exploring interactions beyond the physical TV screen. In *Proceedings of the 11th european conference on Interactive TV and video*(EuroITV '13). ACM, New York, NY, USA, 143-152. DOI=10.1145/2465958.2465972
4. Jacob O. Wobbrock, Meredith Ringel Morris, and Andrew D. Wilson. 2009. User-defined gestures for surface computing. In *Proceedings of the SIGCHI Conference on Human Factors in Computing Systems* (CHI '09). ACM, New York, NY, USA, 1083-1092. DOI=10.1145/1518701.1518866
5. Jun Rekimoto. 2002. SmartSkin: an infrastructure for freehand manipulation on interactive surfaces. In *Proceedings of the SIGCHI Conference on Human Factors in Computing Systems* (CHI '02). ACM, New York, NY, USA, 113-120. DOI=10.1145/503376.503397
6. Ekaterina Kurdyukova, Matthias Redlin, and Elisabeth André. 2012. Studying user-defined iPad gestures for interaction in multi-display environment. In *Proceedings of the 2012 ACM international conference on Intelligent User Interfaces* (IUI '12). ACM, New York, NY, USA, 93-96. DOI=10.1145/2166966.2166984
7. Shahzad Malik, Abhishek Ranjan, and Ravin Balakrishnan. 2005. Interacting with large displays from a distance with vision-tracked multi-finger gestural input. In *Proceedings of the 18th annual ACM symposium on User interface software and technology* (UIST '05). ACM, New York, NY, USA, 43-52. DOI=10.1145/1095034.1095042

A See-Through Display for Interactive Museum Showcases

Andrea Bellucci
Universidad Carlos III de Madrid
Leganés, 28911, Spain
abellucc@inf.uc3m.es

Paloma Diaz
Universidad Carlos III de Madrid
Leganés, 28911, Spain
pdp@inf.uc3m.es

Ignacio Aedo
Universidad Carlos III de Madrid
Leganés, 28911, Spain
aedo@ia.uc3m.es

ITS '15, November 15-18, 2015, Funchal, Portugal
ACM 978-1-4503-3899-8/15/11.
http://dx.doi.org/10.1145/2817721.2823497

Abstract
We present a prototype of an interactive showcase for museum exhibits that exploits a multi-touch see-through display screen. The transparent display makes it possible to superimpose an overlay of digital information while observing the physical object behind the screen. We developed an application that allows visitors to tell their experience with the object as well as to introduce comments on other visitors contributions. Our goal is to engage users in the creation of digital narratives with cultural heritage artifacts, thus constructing new layers of meaning that are parallel to the official ones provided by curators. Results from a formative study give promising feedbacks on the usefulness, novelty and attractiveness of the prototype.

Author Keywords
See-Through Display; Multi-Touch; Cultural Heritage

ACM Classification Keywords
H.5.m. Information interfaces and presentation (e.g., HCI): Miscellaneous

Introduction
Cultural heritage has been traditionally dominated by an authoritative knowledge transmission, where the producers (the experts or curators) provide adequate

interpretations to the receivers (the visitors). In such a model, the exhibition is conceived as a unidirectional flow, in which curators transmit the meaning to the visitors. Recent approaches [3], however, recognize the active role that visitors might play in the construction of that meaning and the role of technology in fostering higher levels of participation and engagement [5].

Allowing both professional and unprofessional to express their point of view activates a process of value creation that otherwise would remain unuttered and that finds in participatory models the ground for its expression [7]. To this end, we present a prototype of an interactive showcase to engage visitors of an exhibition in the creation of digital narratives around cultural heritage artifacts. The prototype exploits a multi-touch see-through display that makes it possible to interact with digital content while observing the physical object behind the screen. A dedicated application allows visitors to tell their experience with the object as well as to comment on other visitors entries that are displayed on the interactive surface.

Background

Extensive research has been made to introduce technology to create engaging museums exhibits [1]. Some works investigated new kind of interactions in the exhibition context (e.g., tangible and multi-touch) [5], while others enabled curators to overcome the technical difficulties and create interactive collections by their own [8]. In this research we are interested in supporting the final users (the visitors) in the creation of parallel narratives around cultural objects [7].

Indeed, new technologies such as interactive surfaces and smart objects can assist curators in creating more attractive and pleasant visitor experience, thus establishing a stronger relationship with visitors [1]. The caveat is that "emerging technologies can also divert visitors' attention from an authentic experience, undermine any real depth of cultural understanding" [9]. Smart exhibits must be carefully designed in a way that the integration with digital technologies does not tuck away the physical object, which is the real value of the exposition. Recent approaches to smart exhibitions, for instance, are emphasizing on the role of materiality for cultural heritage experience and are exploring new tactics to make innovative use of digital repositories while providing embodied experiences [8]. In this line, see-through interactive displays are an attractive technology for museum showcases: they allow to interact with digital content while maintaining the physical object always present.

A Multi-Touch See-Through Display to Augment Cultural Objects

With our installation we intend to allow visitors, who are usually consumers, to express their perspective and become producers of collaborative narratives around objects in an exposition. We want to empower people to generate different understandings of an artifact or collections that go beyond the "official" meaning transmitted by curators. To this end, we augmented a traditional museum showcase by means of a multi-touch see-through window screen (Figure 1, left) and built an application with a distributed interface that allows users *(a)* to tell their experience with the object by recording a video and *(b)* to watch and interact with other visitors contributions so to generate different threads of discussion. The visitors can view, at same

Figure 1. The interactive showcase to augment cultural objects with user-generated digital content. On the left: the interface is displayed on the multi-touch see-through window screen. On the right: a visitor using her mobile device to tell her experience.

time, the physical object behind the screen and the user interface displayed on the interactive surface. Cultural objects are labeled with Radio Frequency IDentification (RFID) sticker tags. When placed into the showcase, an RFID reader (hidden into a stand behind the screen) can recognize the object and, subsequently, retrieve all the associated content (the user-generated video stories) and display it. People can then start interacting with the digital content by, for instance, viewing and listening to other visitors' contributions. In current implementation, user-generated videos are displayed as thumbnails in a list on the left of the screen (see Figure 1, left), ordered according to the number of views. When selecting (touching) a thumbnail, the video starts in a separate interface element where social functionality is provided. The widget supports standard multi-touch manipulations such as two fingers resize and rotation or swipe gesture to close the video. Visitors can rate the video entry or add their comment to it, both with a textual or a video message. In this way, it is possible to create conversations around specific topics of an object and generate alternative stories, by starting new threads or by contributing to an existing one.

Two modalities are provided to add comments or new video entries: visitors can use directly the interface on the interactive screen (Figure 2) or they can capture a QR-code (Figure 3) and display a mobile version of the interface on their personal device. Figure 1 (right), shows a user recording a new video in which she tells about her encounter with the cultural object in the showcase. Once she finishes, the video is uploaded to

Figure 2. The user interface to add a comment from the interactive surface.

Figure 3. A user capturing the QR-Code to enable the interaction from his mobile device.

the system and displayed on the list of available entries for the object (Figure 1, left).

Implementation details

The system was implemented as a Node.js (https://nodejs.org) web application using the Express framework (http://expressjs.com), which made it easier to develop the functionality of the distributed user interface across the vertical screen and mobile devices. The content (e.g., videos) associated to the RFID tag for each object was stored in a MongoDB database (https://www.mongodb.com). A Representational State Transfer (REST) Application Programming Interface (API) was also implemented with the goal of providing quick access to the user-generated information that developers could use to build new applications. See Table I for a list of available request URLs in the current implementation. As an example, the following call will retrieve all the comments of the video with id *123456* and return results in the JSON format:

GET /videos/123456/comments/list

Formative Evaluation

We installed the interactive showcase in a hallway of the UC3M campus for one day (eight hours from 9 a.m. to 17 p.m.) in order to collect preliminary observations on its perceived usefulness, usability and design. The object behind the screen was a Russian military hat from the First World War that we already used in a previous co-design workshop and for which some user-generated videos were already available [2]. Passersby were free to interact with the showcase by watching existing contributions, adding comments or recording new videos about the military hat. At the end of their experience, participants were asked to fill a questionnaire. We used the AttrackDiff™ [4] questionnaire to rate how attractive the interactive showcase was in terms of usability and appearance.

Table I. List of available request URL for the REST API

HTTP Verb	Request URL
GET	/objects/id
GET	/objects/list
DELETE	/objects/id
POST	/objects/new
GET	/videos/id
GET	/objects/id/videos/list
DELETE	/videos/id
POST	/objects/id/videos/new
GET	/comments/id
GET	/videos/id/comments/list
DELETE	/comments/id
POST	/videos/id/comments/new
PUT	/videos/id/comments/id/add

The questionnaire employs pairs of opposite adjectives through which participants could express their perception of an interactive system. Those pairs are organized in four evaluation dimensions: (1) *Pragmatic Quality (PQ),* indicating how successful were participants in achieving their goals with the system, (2) *Hedonic Quality - Stimulation (HQ-S),* indicating to what extent participants perceived the interactive showcase as novel, appealing and stimulating, (3) *Hedonic Quality – Identity (HQ-I),* indicating to what extent participants identified with the interactive showcase, and (4) *Attractiveness (ATT),* describing the overall perceived quality of the system. Pragmatic and hedonic dimensions are independent and contributed equally to the rating of attractiveness. At the end of the day we collected 24 non compulsory questionnaires (62.5% male, age range 20-40) from master students, Ph.D. students, Postdocs and faculty members of the Polytechnic School at UC3M.

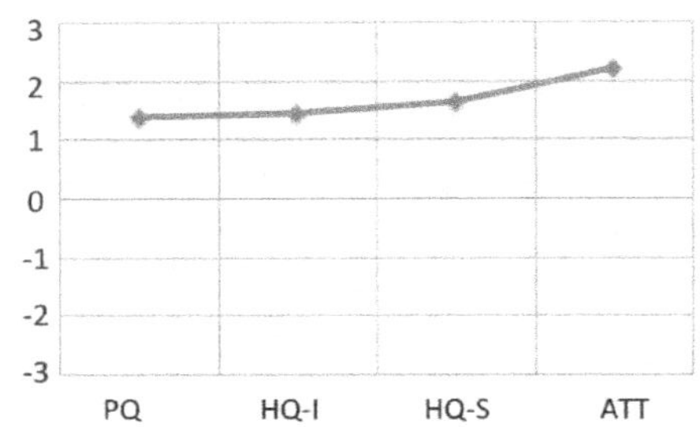

Figure 4. Mean values of the four AttrakDiff™ dimensions.

Figure 4 shows the mean values for the four AttrakDiff™ dimensions. All the values are above the average area: PQ=1.4 95% CI [0.87, 1.91], HQ-I=1.45 95% CI [1.13, 1.76], HQ-S=1.63 95% CI [1.17,2.1], and ATT=2.2 95% CI [2.1,2.3]. This shows that the general acceptance of the interactive showcase is good: the system is clearly attractive and people appraised positively both its usefulness, novelty, playfulness and aesthetic. Nevertheless there is room for improvement as highlighted by the pairwise analysis (Figure 5). Even if the evaluation is always positive, some characteristics are close to the neutral axis, such as the *technical-human* pair. Participants liked to be able to use their mobile devices to interact with the showcase, but they found challenging and not intuitive the use of the QR-code to display the mobile interface.

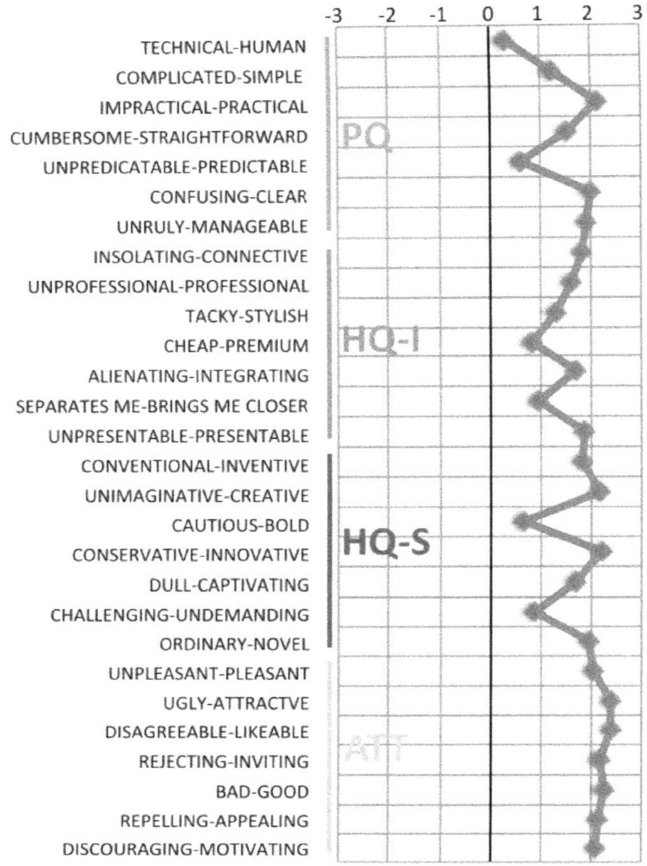

Figure 5.Mean values of the AttrakDiff™ word-pairs

As described in previous studies with public displays [6] we found that the most used social learning technique was *passive observation then attempt*: that is, users first watched others using the interactive showcase and then attempted to imitate their use. Users who started interacting by their own reported lower ratings for the *unpredictable-predictable* and *challenging-undemanding* pairs. This indicates that, even if the system was found overall easy to use, understandable and engaging, further attention need to be paid to enhance the "walk-up-and-use" experience. For instance, we plan to explore how adding gestures that go beyond classic manipulations would entice users to interact with the system.

Conclusion and future work

In this paper we have presented an interactive showcase technology that tries to increase social participation in museums. Though the authoritative stories created by curators have an undeniable value, this hierarchical model does not satisfy the expectations of all visitors and indeed museums have been looking for different ways to attract and, particularly, retain visitors. Results from the preliminary evaluation are encouraging but still very limited to understand the different dimension of interactive exhibitions. Open questions are: *How does the augmented dimension of digital narratives enhance people experience with the object? How can we design for augmented exhibitions without diverting the attention from the real subject (the cultural object)?* We plan to conduct in-situ longitudinal studies involving museums in Madrid to investigate these questions.

Acknowledgment

This work has been funded by the meSch project FP7-ICT-2011-9 under the Grant Agreement 600851.

References

1. Liam Bannon, Steve Benford, John Bowers, and Christian Heath. 2005. Hybrid design creates innovative museum experiences. *Commun. ACM* 48(3), 62-65.
2. Andrea Bellucci, Paloma Diaz, and Ignacio Aedo. 2014. Digitally augmented narratives for physical artifacts. In *Proc. of* AVI '14, 229-232.
3. Monica Calcagno and Claudio Biscaro. 2012. Designing the Interactions in the Museum: Learning from Palazzo Strozzi. Int. Studies of Mgt. & Org. 42(2), 43–56.
4. Marc Hassenzahl, Michael Burmester, and Franz Koller. 2003. AttrakDiff: Ein Fragebogen zur Messung wahrgenommener hedonischer und pragmatischer Qualität. In*Mensch & Computer 2003*, 187-196.
5. Eva Hornecker. 2008. "I don't understand it either, but it is cool"-visitor interactions with a multi-touch table in a museum. In *Proc. of TABLETOP '08,* 113-120.
6. Giulio Jacucci, Ann Morrison, Gabriela T. Richard, Jari Kleimola, Peter Peltonen, Lorenza Parisi, and Toni Laitinen. 2010. Worlds of information: designing for engagement at a public multi-touch display. In *Proc. of CHI '10*, 2267-2276.
7. Paul Mulholland and Trevor Collins. 2002. Using digital narratives to support the collaborative learning and exploration of cultural heritage. In Proc. of *DESA '02*, 527-531.
8. Daniela Petrelli, Luigina Ciolfi, Dick van Dijk, Eva Hornecker, Elena Not, and Albrecht Schmidt. 2013. Integrating material and digital: a new way for cultural heritage. ACM Interactions 20(4), 58-63.
9. Maggie B. Stogner. 2009. The Media-enhanced Museum Experience: Debating the use of Media Technology in Cultural Exhibitions. Curator: The Museum Journal, 52(4), 385–397.

Police Analyst Workstation: Towards A Multi-Surface User Interface

Craig Anslow
Department of Computer Science
Middlesex University
London, UK
c.anslow@mdx.ac.uk

Chris Rooney
Department of Computer Science
Middlesex University
London, UK
c.rooney@mdx.ac.uk

Neesha Kodagoda
Department of Computer Science
Middlesex University
London, UK
n.kodagoda@mdx.ac.uk

William Wong
Department of Computer Science
Middlesex University
London, UK
w.wong@mdx.ac.uk

ITS '15, November 15-18, 2015, Funchal, Portugal
ACM 978-1-4503-3899-8/15/11.
http://dx.doi.org/10.1145/2817721.2823498

Abstract
Developing applications for multi-surface user interfaces is challenging. Sharing and transferring information between these surfaces requires the need for multi-modal interaction methods. In this paper we describe the Police Analyst workstation for supporting multi-surface interaction for criminal intelligence analysis with sense making using multi-touch and mid-air hand gestures for input. We outline our requirements, design, and an initial implementation.

Author Keywords
Criminal Intelligence, Interactive Surfaces, Multi-Touch Gestures, Mid-air Hand Gestures, Visual Analytics.

ACM Classification Keywords
H.5.2 [User Intefaces)]: Interaction styles

Introduction
The VALCRI project is a large European Union Framework Programme (FP7) project that aims to support visual analytics for sense making in criminal intelligence analysis. One of the goals of the project is to design and build novel interfaces that support analysts with sense making using multi-touch and mid-air hand gestures for input. This involves building an interface for police analysts to explore information across multiple surfaces and to collaborate with other analysts.

Early work by Pierre Wellner produced a novel workstation to support general purpose work with the Digital Desk which was a tabletop computer [2], but does not cater for 3D mid-air hand gestures nor specifically analyst work. IBM's i2[1] is a desktop analyst tool that caters for many analyst tasks but does not provide any novel interaction techniques or use of large displays. Guenther et al. [1] propose using multi-touch interfaces to support cyber security analysis but do not describe the physical configuration of their system. In this paper we give a preliminary overview of the *Police Analyst Workstation* we are developing that utilizes large displays, multi-touch interaction, and 3D mid-air hand gestures.

Requirements Analysis

We conducted some requirements from our end-user police analysts. The various concepts were based on a number of requirements, user expectations, and interviews and discussions. The collection of this data was significant for the design of the analyst workstation.

Collaboration. At the beginning, intelligence analysts work independently when carrying out their tasks. Afterwards, they start discussing their initial ideas, or their possible explanations for the facts present in a case or encountered during the analysis. During such discussions, they analyze various alternatives and banter or debate with each other to discover if there are weak links in the presentation of the case or other ideas they did not consider. Afterwards, they proceed to search for more information or to re-assemble the data. Collaboration in intelligence analysis is unlikely to require real-time group collaboration.

Tabletop. A tabletop display is useful for short discussions with several people standing around the table, but not for working on a case or analysis for long periods. Discussions involving several people happen less frequently than long periods of individual work.

Transferring Data. A significant amount of time is currently spent transferring data (e.g. from one spreadsheet to another, between different applications). This often forces the analyst to open and close several applications, thus breaking the flow of their work in several steps, and forcing them to remember which applications were involved, and why. This transfer of data often occurs due to program incompatibility, because the data is located on different computers, and also due to the lack of appropriate screens, which are too small to accommodate several applications at once.

Timeline. Cases or analyses often can extend over long periods of time (e.g. 13–16 weeks) as new information becomes available and the situation changes. During these periods, however, the analyst works on a specific topic in bursts of a few days. Despite this, the analysts need to keep the case within their sphere of attention, even though it may be "on the backburner" when nothing new has happened. Having information about a case or analysis persistently available (which specific type of information is yet to be determined) helps them to think and see other possibilities and associations.

Status Dashboard. Apart from information related specifically to a single case or analysis, there are other kinds of information that would be useful if displayed in a persistent way. For instance, alerts about new information that might be relevant for the current analysis or investigation, or about information that breaches a user-defined threshold, or about the current intelligence situation, or about cases that should be kept in-view. Moreover, if key information is displayed persistently, it may be possible to minimize forgetfulness, to remember and quickly retrieve transient and

[1] http://www-03.ibm.com/software/products/en/analysts-workstation

changing information, and perhaps to address some issues regarding situation awareness.

Public Display. A vertical large screen display where an analyst would stand in front of, and work on a case or carry out an analysis, is not considered a core part of the work methods that an analyst would use. A large screen display in an intelligence analysis room, to provide a "common operational picture" (or its intelligence equivalent) is also not considered a core part of the analysts' work methodologies. This happens primarily because the information is likely to be partially or fully sensitive for the police, and not intended for open distribution. A large screen, however, is most likely to be used mainly for briefings among a larger group of people, and perhaps for the display of largely static pieces of information.

Large Display. Access to a big display "real estate" with high resolution is preferred, as it would allow the analyst to keep applications open with their respective results persistently accessible, and to keep the necessary information constantly visible. This enables the use of spatial memory to support search and location tasks and also problem solving tasks such as the construction of plans and the free-form assembly of data objects into stories that may explain the data acquired during the investigations. Multiple displays can be utilized for space and explore separation of workflow (focus + content) for multiple case analysis. If multiple displays are used we need to maintain a similar pixel density display between displays to make data presentation consistent when moving from one display to another.

Externalization. The availability of display real-estate will enable the analyst to invoke the use of real-world concepts such as places, proximity, and spatial arrangements, to externalize meanings such as we observe in the physical world, and to assign meanings to actions. The analyst would also be able to assign meanings to object and places: By means of these assignments, also the creation of new information is possible (e.g., by manipulating the information objects to assemble them into an explanatory narrative).

Tactile Reasoning. In VALCRI, data objects can be imbued with physical characteristics (e.g. they look like an index card and behave as an index card in that they can be laid out and can overlap and obscure information, but they can also be augmented with computational power). They can be electronically duplicated, automatically grouped by semantic similarity, or organized by differences, and show occurrences of keywords or concepts across a set of cards. Their placement and manipulation, such as when an analyst drags one set of data objects onto another, can be used to initiate computational processes such as Boolean operations. Such interactional affordances will be effective when there is a large persistent display space. We refer to this form of interaction as tactile reasoning, an interaction technique that supports analytical reasoning by the direct manipulation of information objects in a user interface.

Touch and 3D Gestures. Tactile reasoning, together with large display spaces, can change the way we interact with computers. Large display real-estate affords the possibility of new forms of interactions such as multi-touch and 3D mid-air hand gestures that are impractical with smaller screens. Larger screens should not be considered mainly as a larger view port for observing and manipulating complex visualizations.

Personal Displays. Besides the large displays individual smaller displays such as tablets can be used to interact with data or for reading individual case reports and documents.

Minimal Cost. We need to construct the workstation with

readily available hardware components as multiple workstations are required to support many analysts.

These factors collectively form the basis for proposing a non-conventional design configuration for the Analyst Workstation that breaks away from the standard desktop arrangement that only uses a mouse and keyboard. In summary, the envisioned Police Analyst Workstation is based on three key factors: (i) a large enough multi-touch interface to enable direct manipulation of information objects (including data visualizations and information graphics) that an analyst can interact with in free-form manner that changes the approach to query formulation and query specification; (ii) a large enough display surface that enables places that can be used to persistently display information such as alerts, status information, and on-going cases or analyses that are temporarily set aside but need to be kept in view for awareness reasons as the situation changes and new information may become available – directly or indirectly; (iii) for security and confidentiality reasons, the design of the large display working space, should primarily consider the screens largely as private or personal, rather than shared and collaborative.

Police Analyst Workstation

Based on our requirements we are designing and building the Police Analyst Workstation (see Figure 1). The individual workspace (Figure 1(a)) consists of a desk, 2 screens including security filters, keyboard, mouse, phone and tablet. The 1st display (X) is 40 inches and is multi-touch, located on a table in a 30 degree (adjustable) angle. The 2nd display (Y) is 55 inches with technology that allows mid-air hand gesture interaction recognition and multi-touch. The display is located on a stand that allows the height and angle to be adjusted as well as moving the screens together for collaboration purposes. Figure 1(b)

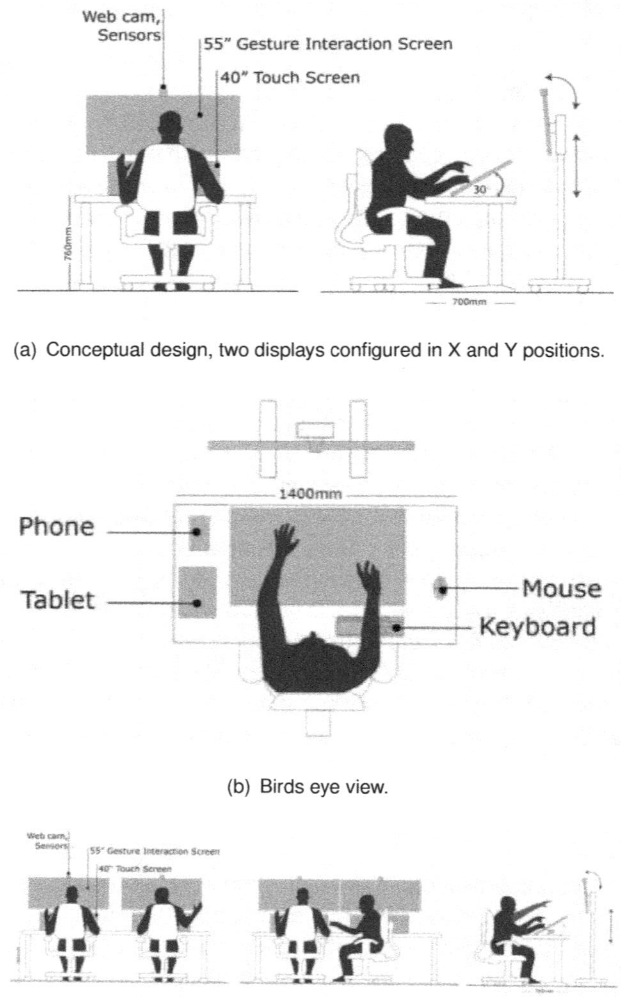

(a) Conceptual design, two displays configured in X and Y positions.

(b) Birds eye view.

(c) Multiple analysts collaborating.

Figure 1: Police Analyst Workstation Design - consisting of two touch screens, phone, tablet, mouse, keyboard, and 3D sensor to support mid-air hand gestures.

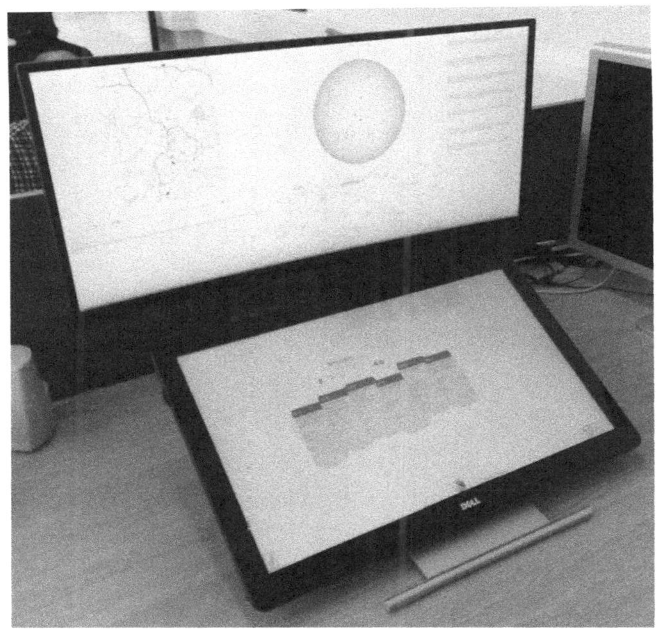

Figure 2: Police Analyst Workstation - preliminary implementation: 27 inch horizontal display (X) and 34 inch vertical display (Y). Content can be transferred between displays using multi-touch and 3D mid-air hand gestures.

shows a birds eye view of the workstation that also supports displaying and sharing information on a mobile phone and tablet. The workspace can be also be used in a collaborative environment by moving the screens together to help support police analysts working together (Figure 1(c)). We are currently in the process of designing the various user interface components and how data would be shared between devices using gestures.

Our first attempt meeting the requirements and design involved exploring the Dell SmartDesk. Figure 2 shows the SmartDesk setup, which utilises a 27 inch 1920 x 1080 pixels monitor with touch-capacitive (X), and a 34 inch curved 5 megapixel display (Y). We adopted an X-Y configuration such that physical interaction tasks can occur on the horizontal (X) display, while data analysis tasks can occur on the vertical (Y) display. The two screens show different data visualizations from the VALCRI application of criminal intelligence activities. We are currently exploring a larger configuration setup where each display is 40 inches and 3840 x 2160 pixels (4K).

In summary we have presented the analyst workstation setup for police analysts to explore data for criminal intelligence. We described our requirements, design and an initial implementation. We are currently exploring a larger physical setup, evaluating what the optimal setup is for analysts, and developing our VALCRI software applications further.

Acknowledgements

The research leading to the results reported here was received in 2013 through Project VALCRI, European Commission Grant Agreement No. FP7-IP-608142, awarded to Middlesex University and partners.

REFERENCES

1. Jeffrey Guenther, Fred Volk, and Mark Shaneck. 2010. Proposing a Multi-touch Interface for Intrusion Detection Environments. In *Proc. of VizSec.* ACM, 13–21. DOI: http://dx.doi.org/10.1145/1850795.1850797

2. Pierre Wellner. 1993. Interacting with Paper on the DigitalDesk. *Commun. ACM* 36, 7 (July 1993), 87–96.

STRIPE – Fluid and Zoomable Lean-back Interface for Navigating Content Landscape on a Large Screen

Jinha Lee
Samsung Electronics
Interaction Group
Suwon, Korea
lee.jinha@samsung.com

Ben Cerveny
TEEM
Los Angeles, USA
Ben@neb.me

Josh Nimoy
TEEM
Los Angeles, USA
josh@jtnimoy.net

Gabriel Dunne
TEEM
Los Angeles, USA
gldunne@gmail.com

Seran Jeon
Samsung Electronics
Interaction Group
Suwon, Korea
seran.jeon@samsung.net

Varun Nigam
Samsung Electronics
Interaction Group
Suwon, Korea
varun.nigam@samsung.net

ITS '15, November 15-18, 2015, Funchal, Portugal
ACM 978-1-4503-3899-8/15/11.
http://dx.doi.org/10.1145/2817721.2823499

Abstract
We present Stripe, a fluid and zoomable interface for navigating content datasets with a remote control on large screens. By bringing multi-level semantic zooming, fixed focus, and fluid user interaction to linear layouts of content, Stripe provides easy, learnable "television-like" interactions to complex online content datasets.

Author Keywords
Multi-scale interface; Fluid interface; Remote-control UI; TV interace;

ACM Classification Keywords
H.5.m. Information interfaces and presentation (e.g., HCI): Miscellaneous;

Figure 1. Stripe combines multi-level semantic zoom and fixed focus UI to enable lean-back yet immersive browsing.

Introduction

Over the past decades, the way we consume video content has gone through a massive shift. Gone are the days of selecting from a handful of TV channels. Now people watch new videos through online media stores, social networks, and subscription services. As our habits change, more and more content is watched on phones and computers and less on larger displays like TVs, despite their ever-increasing resolution and size, which enables an immersive yet social viewing experience. One of the primary factors that contributed to this shift is the lack of legible ways to navigate through complex datasets on distant, large screens like TVs which have long worked with channel-based linear interaction. We believe that creating a comfortable but powerful interaction language to browse vast datasets on distant large screens can bring about a new culture of collaborative navigation and viewing experience.

Researchers have tried computer-like direct manipulation interfaces on a distant screen using remote controls equipped with a motion-based or touchpad-based cursor. This can result in fatigue and precision issues when used for extended periods. Fluid fixed-highlight interfaces [1] have shown alternative ways to effortlessly navigate through linear contents. In shared social browsing, a fixed focus provides an easy reference for all participants, rather than a cursor which can easily be lost by those not in control. Interaction with a large number of faceted contents are shown to be enhanced with multi-scale navigation techniques [2][3][4]. Our project builds on top of this previous research to create interaction patterns suitable for a large distant screen.

STRIPE

In this demo, we present *Stripe*, a fluid and zoomable interface based on the channel metaphor for navigating through a media content database with remote controls. By combining centered highlight UIs and multi-scale interaction techniques, *Stripe* employs semantic zoom to indicate the selection and keep the users focused. In doing so, *Stripe* allows for an experience of playfully flying into and out of a large content landscape by simple motions or touch gestures on a remote control.

Figure 2. Multiple (Semantic) Zoom Levels of *Stripe*

Fovea

The first thing you see when you launch *Stripe* is a series of colored bars that make up the *Stripe*. Each bar represents a video or a channel, whose color is extracted automatically from the thumbnail image so that users can easily recognize the content. User's attention is drawn to the center band which shows more detailed information than the rest of the bars and indicates that the center item is selected. We call this behaviour Fovea. The user can browse through choices quickly and linearly by simply sliding his finger across the touchpad, or tilting the remote control left and right. As the panning moves new content into focus, smooth transitions between selected and unselected view of each object makes overall navigation experience fluid and playful.

Semantic Zoom

Stripe can be visualized in four different levels of details (Figure 2). The users can quickly shift between these levels by sliding his finger up and down the touchpad or tilting the controller forward or back. For example, he can quickly zoom out to the holistic view of the entire content landscape or seamlessly zoom in to play a video in the full screen view at any state of the *Stripe*. At all levels, the content at the center or Fovea, always shows more detailed information (level n+1) than the rest of the *Stripe*. For example, if you are navigating at the bar-level, the object in *Fovea* is represented as a portrait thumbnail image of the content which obviously has more information than a colored bar(Figure 3-II). At the block-level, the object in *Fovea* maintains the state of separate bars revealing what individual contents constitute the block (Figure 3-I).

As you zoom out from the bar view, the bars merge into blocks (Figure 3-II → I). Each block represents a collection of contents of a genre if arranged based on genre; or contents from a year if arranged based on time. If you zoom back in to the bar view, then zoom in further, each bar unfolds into its respective portrait view while the state of the *Fovea* transforms from a

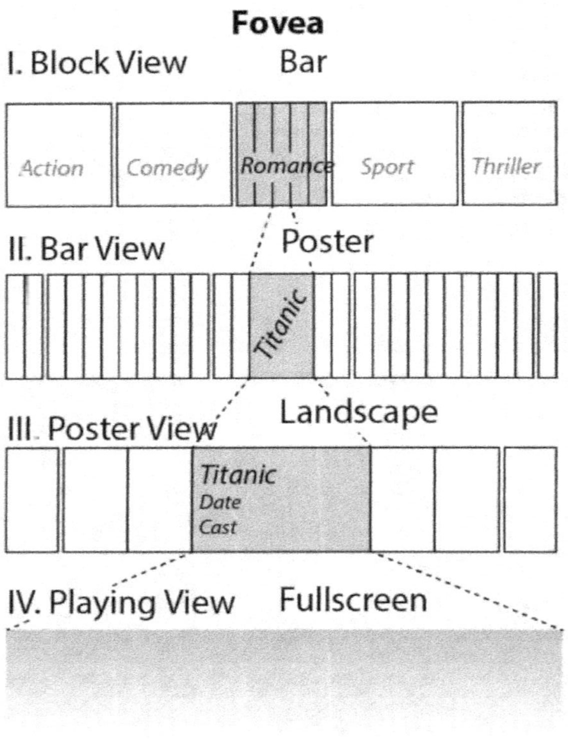

Figure 3. *Fovea* for four different levels of Stripe

portrait to a landscape view. As the user zooms further in from the portrait view, the landscape view of the content at the center grows, maintaining the aspect ratio to occupy the full screen and starts playing the video. Overall, it provides the users with the experience of diving into and out of the content landscape.

Drawing an Arch Path

The user can easily transition between linear scrolling and zooming, or scroll and zoom simultaneously. This allows the user to reach a desired location faster and easier. For example, if Tom is watching a full screen sporting event, he can quickly zoom out to the bar *Stripe* level while simultaneously panning across the channel bars toward a news channel, which he might already have in his motor memory. He can begin to zoom back even before he reaches the destination channel, never losing context through the changing zoom levels thanks to the fixed center *Fovea*, and finally landing in the running full screen video of his destination just as he finishes his translation motion. The fluidity of the combined zoom and pan actions gives Tom instantaneous targeting feedback for his gesture in real time.

Resorting

Although linear interaction models allow for easily navigable constraints for zooming and panning, content datasets are inevitably more complex than one dimension can represent. At any zoom level, the user can 'pivot' on a focused object or category, rearranging the entire *Stripe* around a new sorting axis drawn from the metadata available on the contents. For example, Judy has arranged the *Stripe* UI by broadcaster, so she may easily find and select her favorite channel, HBO.

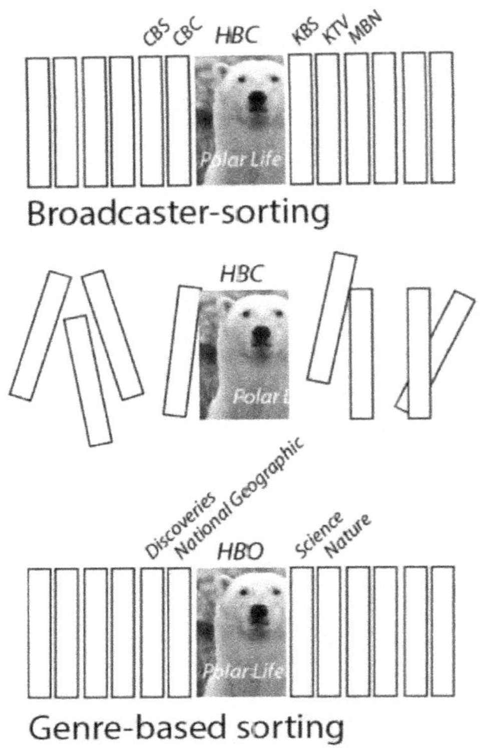

Figure 4. Resorting Interaction

Zooming in to content view, she learns that a nature documentary program is playing. She finds the topic interesting, so she re-sorts the entire *Stripe* based on genre, the contents about nature dynamically arranged around the item she initially found interesting (Figure 4).

Initial Observation

We recruited 12 participants to try out *Stripe*. Even though no guidance was given at the beginning, majority of the users (10/12) were quick to pick up the interaction with pan and zoom. Most of the users (11/12) said that they had a positive experience described as "simple and easy to learn", "natural extension from channel zapping" "flying into a content space". Nine users preferred motion over touch at the beginning, but after using for ten minutes only four preferred the motion, expressing some exhaustion. Seven answered that motor memory was helpful, but only two said color patterns helped identifying content. One user commented that her color pattern can represent herself and it would be interesting to see which color pattern other users might have.

Conclusion and Future Work

We presented *Stripe*, a fluid and zoomable interface concept that allows for a seamless navigation of complex content datasets with a remote control on a large display. We think the power of *Stripe* could be realized to an even greater extent when each user can configure their own *Stripe* that represents their content consumption pattern, and invoke that custom *Stripe* at any big display to share with others. We believe this can bring about a new culture of collaborative navigation and shared viewing experiences, taking advantage of the social and immersive nature of large displays.

References

1. Cover Flow, https://en.wikipedia.org/wiki/Cover_Flow
2. Dachselt, R., Frisch, M., and Weiland, M., FacetZoom: a continuous multi-scale widget for navigating hierarchical metadata. In Proc. CHI '08, 1353-1356.
3. Appert, C., and Fekete, J., OrthoZoom scroller: 1D multi-scale navigation. In Proc. CHI '06, 21-30. Ramos, G., and Balakrishnan, R., Zliding: fluid zooming and sliding for high precision parameter
4. Ramos, G., and Balakrishnan, R., Zliding: fluid zooming and sliding for high precision parameter manipulation. In *Proc.* UIST '05, 143-152.

Tangible Holographic 3D Objects with Virtual Touch

Péter Tamás Kovács
Tibor Balogh
Zsolt Nagy
Attila Barsi
László Bordács
Gáspár Balogh
Holografika
Budapest, 1192, Hungary
p.kovacs@holografika.com
t.balogh@holografika.com
zs.nagy@holografika.com
a.barsi@holografika.com
l.bordacs@holografika.com
g.balogh@holografika.com

ITS '15, November 15-18, 2015, Funchal, Portugal
ACM 978-1-4503-3899-8/15/11.
http://dx.doi.org/10.1145/2817721.2823500

Abstract
This poster describes the design of a display and interaction device that allows a natural mid-air manipulation and feedback of floating, true 3D objects. This so called virtual touch will create a natural feeling of manipulating and touching of the virtual 3D object for the user. The 3D display system allows users to reach into the viewing volume to touch virtual objects, and even feel gradients of haptic feedback as the hands penetrate into virtual objects. True 3D objects are dynamically relit according to the real-world environment captured by cameras, which is reflected on shiny virtual surfaces to reach more realistic user experience. On the other hand, 3D virtual objects can cast real shadows on the real workspace. In case the virtual objects are defined as light-emitting, glows can also be projected onto the desk and the real objects. These techniques together form the basis of an ultra-realistic visualization and interaction system that will find its way into many technical and educational uses.

Author Keywords
Light-field display; mid-air interaction; tactile feedback.

ACM Classification Keywords
H.5.2. User Interfaces: Haptic I/O;
I.3.1. Hardware Architecture: Three-dimensional displays.

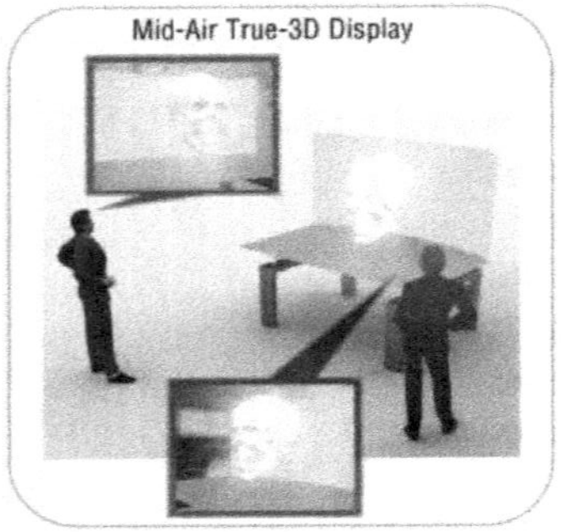

Figure 1: Mid-air 3D display concept: the image is visible without 3D glasses, and appears floating in free space, without an apparent screen plane

Figure 2: Haptic feedback is generated by the use of ultrasound transducers which generate tactile sensation through the air (concept drawing)

Introduction

Users increasingly expect to be able to control and manipulate digital media content, including the ability to dexterously interact with digital content as they do with real world objects, and experience natural touch while doing so. This is already apparent considering the increasing use of gestures for interaction. Leap Motion [1] and Kinect [2] are two examples of novel interactive systems. Such an experience requires advancement in both display and interaction technologies. Current 3D displays are at best stereo-/auto-stereoscopic displays which provide limited viewing experiences. These will give way to novel technologies like 3D light field displays, which are capable of presenting 3D digital objects visualized floating in the air (see Figure 1).

On the display research side, this work advances the state of the art with the design and implementation of a screen-less 3D light-field display prototype, which has it's screen plane in mid-air – as opposed to current light-field displays, which have half of the useful displaying area inside the screen, and only half outside the screen. As the depth range of all autostereoscopic displays is limited, it's important not to lose half of this range when it comes to natural hand-based interaction. While light-field displays have a considerably wide Field Of Depth (FOD, in the range of 15cm .. 1.5m both inside and outside the screen), still doubling the effective interaction space has definite advantages. The prototype will thus allow free-hand manipulation of objects both inside and outside the "screen plane".

This "mid-air" display technology is innovatively combined with a novel tactile system using ultrasound, producing feelable forces and tactile sensations that are projected through the air, directly onto the user (see Figure 2). These can take the form of discrete points of feedback, a varying tactile landscape or three dimensional shapes. A wave-field synthesis algorithm is used to generate an interference pattern that corresponds to the desired feedback or shape. The interference pattern is produced by a phased array of ultrasound transducers.

Tracking of the user's hands will be provided by a tracking system which feeds data into a physics engine that uses the information from the light-field algorithm to generate appropriate forces for the tactile system.

The most innovative aspect of this combined approach is that by combining the light-field synthesis technique with the wave-field synthesis technique we can algorithmically determine salient tactile feedback points for the user without knowing anything about the application context. This means our system is able to provide users with the best interactive experience without having any additional information about the context of its use. The user will have to load the 3D data that they want to explore onto our system and the system will render it in true-3D while allowing them to feel tactile sensations in salient locations in the system.

Several rendering and lighting effects enable bidirectional interaction of the real and virtual world: virtual 3D objects are dynamically relit according to the real-world environment captured by cameras, which is reflected on shiny virtual surfaces to reach more realistic user experience. On the other hand, 3D virtual objects can cast real shadows on the real workspace. In case the virtual objects are defined as light-emitting, glows can also be projected onto the desk.

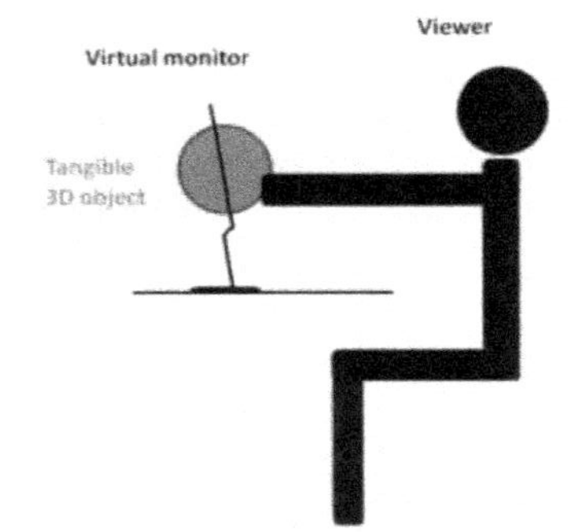

Figure 3: Positioning of the viewer in the workstation

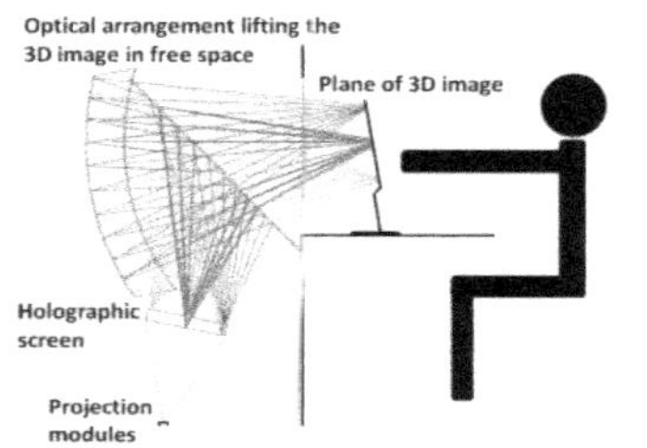

Figure 4: Optical design of the "mid-air" display

Viewer distance	60 cm
Size of virtual screen	320 x 240 mm
Number of optical modules	54

Table 1: Main characteristics of the display

Optical design

As the system is intended to take the shape of a workstation, we first determined the convenient position of a user in such an environment (see Figure 3). Then, taking the intended eye position of the user into account, we can determine the necessary range of the light field to be projected. The display system is decomposed into two parts: a 3D display based on HoloVizio technology [3], and an optical arrangement that lifts the image that normally appears around the holographic screen into free space. This optical arrangement is composed of a large scale spherical mirror of optical grade, and a half mirror, which together project the image into the range of the virtual monitor.

The built-in HoloVizio display uses 54 projection modules in a custom arrangement, all of them projecting light rays onto the holographic screen. The light rays projected outside the holographic screen are recovered using side mirrors. The number and placement of the projection modules has been optimized to generate the necessary light field with minimum amount of lost light rays. The other requirement for the optimization process was to minimize the total volume of the display. Therefore the long light path necessary to create the relatively large image has been folded with mirrors, resulting in a compact projection design (see Figure 4). The results of the optimization process gave the final parameters of the optical setup, the main cahacteristics of which are provided in Table 1.

During the selection of the projection modules, the most important criteria is the physical width of the module. Therefore we have selected a module with VGA resolution, HDMI input, and only 10 mm physical width.

Mechanical design

The mechanical system holds 4 major components of the system together:

- Workbench with panel
- Virtual monitor placed on the workbench
- 3D display based on HoloVizio
- Computer system for rendering light-field images, controlling interaction and haptic feedback devices

Workbench

The workbench is an integral part of the screen-less design. Its appearance mimics a classic wooden table with the necessary support. Behind the workbench, a darkened Plexiglas separates the core of the display system from the working area. The Plexiglas lets the light pass through only in the specific area necessary for image formation.

Virtual monitor

The image projected by the HoloVizio appears in free space. To surround the area in space where the 3D image may appear, it is surrounded by a frame mimicking a classical monitor. The user sitting next to this workbench will perceive the image appearing inside this frame.

3D display

The frame holding the display and the image lifting optics are surrounded by a mechanism created from aluminum profiles, and tinted Plexiglas sheets. The

Figure 5: Preview of the exterior of the integrated system based on the current mechanical design

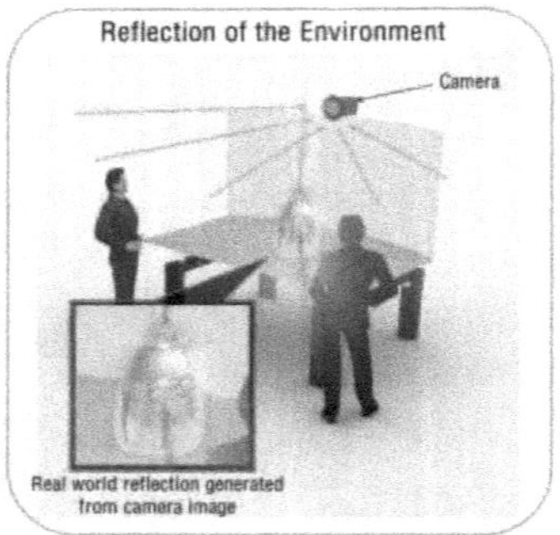

Figure 6: Reflection of the environment is implemented by means of a wide-angle camera and the rendering system

projection array is positioned on the bottom of the mechanism, and light is propagating upwards. As parts of the image are directly projected, while others are indirectly through side mirrors, the side mirrors are mounted using a precision mounting and adjustment system to ensure consistent 3D image formation. The spherical mirror and the half mirror are also mounted on the metal frame.

The biggest challenge of designing the mechanical system lies in the optimization of the length of light paths, light ray directions, and other, partially conflicting parameters, which has been optimized down to millimeter scale to achieve the current design (see Figure 5).

Rendering system

The light field to be visualized on the display needs to be rendered and updated in real time to enable direct interaction with the virtual scene. This requires both an appropriate hardware setup and rendering software system to generate more than 15 million light rays (megapixels) in real time.

Rendering hardware

The rendering hardware needs to drive 54 separate HDMI inputs. The design strives to solve this using the least number of rendering computers. A single mainboard based on the Intel Z97 chipset can accommodate 4 GPUs, while a single GPU (e.g. NVidia GTX750) can drive 4 separate video outputs (in this specific example, 2 DVI and 2 HDMI outputs). Due to cooling considerations, we have chosen to use 3 GPUs per node, and using 4 outputs per GPU. A rendering cluster consisting of such 5 computers can be used for the purpose. These rendering nodes are interconnected via Gigabit Ethernet, and run a customized version of Linux to execute parallel rendering algorithms based on the HoloVizio software system.

Rendering software

The architecture of the software system consists of the following main components:

- Clustered light field synthesis
- Height / depth map generator
- Ultrasound / haptics controller module
- Calibration module

The purpose of the clustered light field synthesis module is to render the virtual scene into the 3D light field format as controlled by the application software, and to maintain frame synchronization between the rendering nodes. Light field synthesis also takes into account data from the sensors capturing the environment (as described in the next section), as well as controls the supplementary projection module that provides lighting effects in the real environment.

The virtual scene is also used to generate a height map of the scene that contains to the distances of scene points from the ultrasound-based haptic system. The ultrasound controller module can in turn drive the ultrasound transducers to generate the force field appropriate to the provided depth map.

The calibration module ensures that the light field is coherent and uniform in terms of light ray positions, directions, intensity and color, as well as matches the 3D space of the display with the 3D space of the haptic subsystem.

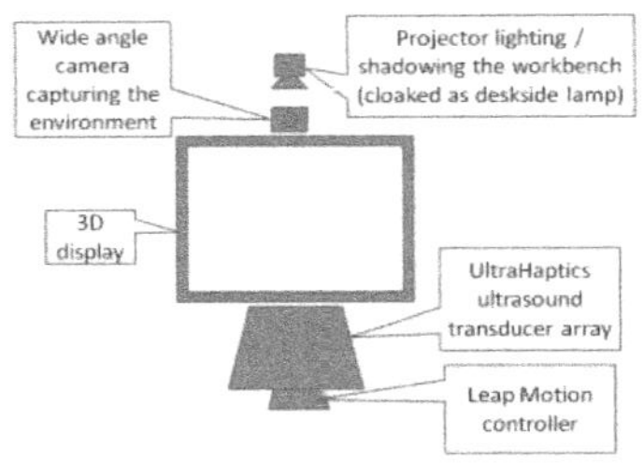

Figure 7: Main components of the interactive system

Figure 8: Real object casting shadow on the workbench

Interactive system

To provide the envisioned level of interactivity with the user and environment, several devices are integrated into the design on top of the 3D display, as seen on Figure 7. These include:

- A wide angle camera captur ng the environment
- A projector to project light / shadows onto the real workspace (hidden in a deskside lamp)
- Ultrasound transducer-based haptic feedback device
- Leap Motion controller

The wide angle camera is facing the user and the environment surrounding the user. The captured environment map is used to dynamically relight the virtual scene, as well as for creating reflections in case of having reflective surfaces in the scene.

The projector cloaked as a deskside lamp projects mid-level grey light onto the workspace by default. The rendering engine uses shadow mapping techniques from the viewpoint of the lamp, determining which virtual objects cast shadows onto the workspace, as well as adding glows around virtual objects defined as light emitting. Shadows are implemented by "removing" light from the mid-level light, while glows add to this level of ambient lighting.

The non-contact tactile feedback system will use wave-field synthesis algorithm to generate an interference pattern that corresponds to the desired feedback or shape. Constructive areas are strong enough to be felt through vibrations in the skin while residual ultrasound is canceled elsewhere ensuring that only the desired feedback can be felt. The interference pattern is produced by a phased array of ultrasound transducers. This technique has been pioneered by Prof. Subramanian and his team at the University of Bristol [4]. The system, called Ultrahaptics is the first system to be able to generate tactile feedback in mid-air at multiple locations simultaneously. This activity is now continued by the spin-off company Ultrahaptics [5], which is the first company that is designing and manufacturing systems to provide non-contact tactile feedback in mid-air. Our design thus incorporates the system from Ultrahaptics to achieve non-contact tactile feedback, necessitating the software system of the display and the haptic system to be tightly integrated.

Use cases

Displays are used in virtually all areas of life, thus widespread markets are foreseen for integrated 3D display systems as well. These can be subdivided into professional, governmental and home use. Specific professional / governmental areas include mechanical and shape design, civil planning, mission and defense planning, GIS, oil & gas exploration, traffic monitoring and control. These usage areas are specifically interaction intensive, thus appreciate the added value of full-volume natural interaction and touch.

Education and research is a major application area for systems which allow students not just to see but feel the spatial relationships of 3D objects, especially medical and dental, geometry and design, meteorology and astrology, physics and mechanics, hydrodynamics.

Entertainment applications like museums, interactive games and edutainment applications are also prevalent, with theme parks being early adopters of novel display / interaction technologies.

Figure 9: Relighting of virtual objects according to real environment

Conclusions and future work

This poster presented the architecture and design of an integrated system that displays "holographic" 3D objects in free space, allows direct hand-based interaction with the visualized objects, while the user feels haptic feedback from the objects. The system will furthermore enable other ways of interaction with the environment, such as environmental light conditions affecting the real environment, as well as the real workspace being lit / shadowed by the virtual objects.

The next phase of the project will involve the implementation of the designed system including optical, electrical and mechanical manufacturing, software development, calibration, as well as its extensive testing by users and improvement of the subsystems based on the feedback received.

Acknowledgements

The research leading to these results has received funding from the Tangible3D Eureka project, funded by the National Research, Development and Innovation Office of Hungary.

References

1. Leap Motion. Retrieved August 28, 2015 from https://www.leapmotion.com/.
2. Kinect for Windows. Retrieved August 28, 2015 from https://dev.windows.com/en-us/kinect
3. Tibor Balogh: The HoloVizio System. SPIE-IS&T SD&A (2006).
4. Tom Carter, Sue Ann Seah, Benjamin Long, Bruce Drinkwater, Sriram Subramanian, Ultrahaptics: Multi-Point Mid-Air Haptic Feedback for Touch Surfaces. UIST'13. October 2013.
5. UltraHaptics. Retrieved August 28, 2015 from http://ultrahaptics.com/.

A Tabletop System to Promote Argumentation in Computer Science Students

Marisol Wong-Villacres
Escuela Superior Politecnica del Litoral
Guayaquil, Ecuador
lvillacr@espol.edu.ec

Katherine Chiluiza
Escuela Superior Politecnica del Litoral
Guayaquil, Ecuador
kchilui@espol.edu.ec

Margarita Ortiz
Information Technology Center, CTI-ESPOL
Guayaquil, Ecuador
margarita.ortiz@cti.espol.edu.ec

Vanessa Echeverria
Information Technology Center, CTI-ESPOL
Guayaquil, Ecuador
vecheverria@cti.espol.edu.ec

ITS '15, November 15-18, 2015, Funchal, Portugal
ACM 978-1-4503-3899-8/15/11.
http://dx.doi.org/10.1145/2817721.2823501

Abstract
This study explores the design of a tabletop system that seeks to bolster the argumentative skills of Computer Science students. A set of four design guidelines - positive interdependence, stages, interference, and awareness - were derived from user research and used for designing and prototyping a multi-display tabletop application. Four students evaluated a video prototype; the overall results showed that the application's features have great potential to support the design guidelines. Moreover, students' impressions about the prototype's enforcement of positive interdependence indicate possibilities for augmenting argumentation opportunities. Steps for future work are presented.

Author Keywords
Software Design; Tabletops; Computer Science Education; User-Centered Design; Argumentation

ACM Classification Keywords
H.5.m [Information interfaces and presentation (e.g., HCI)]: Miscellaneous.

Introduction
Software design is an inherently collaborative and argumentative activity that demands designers to successfully present ideas to peers as well as to

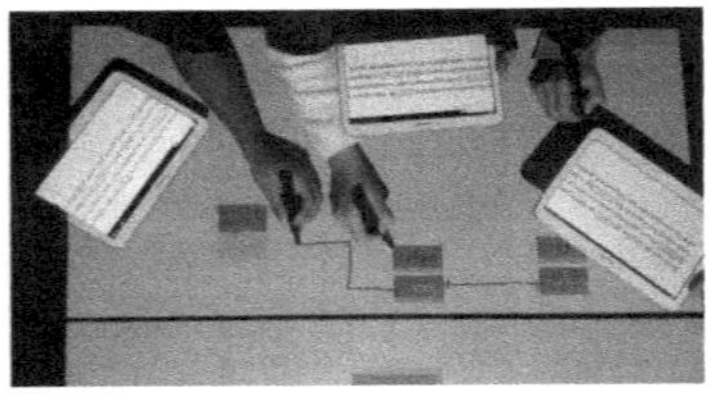

Figure 1: Proposed multi-display tabletop application

collaboratively refine these ideas through discussion [17]. Nonetheless, employers' accounts on the struggles recent graduates face when communicating [15] strongly suggest Computer Science (CS) education requires support in this area. Within this context, multi-touch tabletop displays become a promising technology for supporting the development of argumentative skills. Previous research on tabletops indicates such technology has the potential to enhance collaborative learning (CL) [16, 8, 5] by fostering a more enjoyable, playful environment that promotes exploration [19] and equity of participation [18]. Furthermore, former studies suggest tabletop applications can encourage argumentation [6, 5]. Nevertheless, little research on the area has focused on tasks relevant for college students [14]. Moreover, the existing explorations on collaborative software design (CSD) supported by interactive surfaces [1, 12, 2] have not explored the specific needs of software design learners. In this study, an iterative user-centered design approach was used to develop the prototype of a multi-display tabletop application for collaborative database design learning (Figure 1). The application aims to augment the possibilities for argumentation among participants. In what follows, a set of design principles derived from user research is presented, the prototype of the proposed solution is described, and the results of a first exploratory evaluation are discussed.

Related Work

Several studies have explored the potential of tabletops for CL [16, 8, 5, 14]. Kharrufa et al.[8] found that tabletop applications that support externalization and reflection can encourage higher-level thinking and elicit effective learning. Schneider et al. [16] concluded that engagement can act as mediator for productive collaboration. Additionally, Wallace et al.[18] found that tabletops can support equitable participation in learning situations. On the realm of tabletop support for group argumentation and discussion, previous research concluded that by prompting interference, multi-touch tabletop applications can elicit curiosity, raise awareness of others' actions and encourage verbal negotiation[5] [6]. Some of the different mechanisms explored to afford interference are: allowing lack of territorial constraints [19], enabling participants to intrude at each other's work [6] and supporting high-level physical interactions [5] [14]. Nonetheless, few studies have explored tabletops' support for argumentation in groups of college students, addressing tasks directly related to their interest[14]. Finally, in spite of the existing explorations of CSD supported by interactive surfaces[1, 12, 2, 3, 7], to our knowledge only [11] focused on CSD learning. After studying college students' use of a tablet application for software design [12] over an academic term, [11] reported that the proposed application enabled students to work effectively in teams as well as to quickly develop, refine, and evaluate their designs. In contrast, the present study seeks to explore the design of a tabletop application considering the needs of collaborative software design learners.

User Research

In order to better understand the struggles software design learners experience when engaging in collaborative argumentation, we carried out two user research activities. The activities took place in the Ecuadorian setting of an engineering-oriented university, Escuela Superior Politecnica del Litoral (ESPOL), and involved the participation of twenty-two undergraduate students, enrolled in a Database System course of a CS program. The first activity consisted of two observation sessions; in each session, students were handled a paper-based description of a typical database design problem and

Figure 2: Tabletop system used for user research

Figure 3: Second iteration of the paper-based prototype

asked to solve the problem in groups of 3 to 4 members. To contrast the variety of needs that different types of interaction elicit, half of the groups were observed performing the activity using a tabletop application for CSD [7] (Figure 2) while the other half worked in a paper-based environment, using black markers and a large paper sheet. The second user research activity was a diary study of students' reflections on their immediately previous group work experience.

Design Guidelines

Our user research's findings on the factors that hinder argumentation initiatives in a CSD class are consistent with [9] findings: a) academic unpreparedness, b) group dynamics, c) mix levels of experience, d) shyness, and e) poor listening skills. To address these issues while augmenting opportunities for argumentation during CSD, this research proposes the following design guidelines for a tabletop application:

Positive Interdependence (PI): In a collaborative setting, it refers to group members relying on one another in order to succeed [10]. A tabletop application for CSD learning could prompt PI by ensuring each group member owns a piece of information necessary to complete a problem description. In this way, students with a lower lever of academic preparation are empowered to participate (issue a). Furthermore, this can buttress effective group dynamics (issue b) by augmenting the need for members to verbally interact in order to achieve full understanding of a problem.

Stages: Mix levels of experience (issue c) among group members cause some of them to move faster through a problem while others fall behind. Furthermore, shyness(issue d) can hinder a member's ability to let the group know that he or she is falling behind. To enable equal opportunities for each member to engage in argumentation, a tabletop application for CSD learning should enforce the division of a software design assignment in stages. In such scenario, a group would only be able to advance to a new stage once the previous has been declared as finished.

Interference: Although it can be seen as something negative, interference can prompt discussion [5] [6], forcing members to overcome shyness (issue d) and to listen to others (issue e). A tabletop application for a CSD learning environment could trigger interference by introducing unexpected behaviors, such as misleading design clues.

Awareness of others: Similarly to the impact of interference, a tabletop application that enables each member to know other people's contributions, not only allows individuals to be aware of what is happening in the design process, but creates opportunities for them to argue about others' decisions (issue d, e)[4].

System Design

The proposed prototype evolved through a design process that consisted of three iterations. The goal of the first trial was to explore the potential impact of the design guidelines. For that purpose, the designers engaged in a bodystorming session with a paper-based prototype. The second trial was conducted with two groups of CS students of 3 and 4 members each. Groups where asked to design a database solution using the second iteration of the paper-based prototype (Figure 3). The goal was to analyze the quality of students' argumentation while interacting with the prototype. As a result, the third and final iteration proposes the design of a multi-display

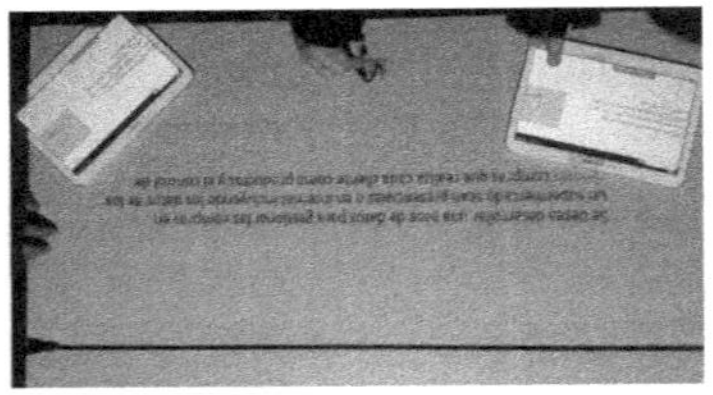

Figure 4: First stage of the design task: shared reading and collaborative gestures

Figure 5: Second stage of the design task: Deck of clues and puzzle-like modeling

approach (tabletop and tablets); its main features can be summarized as follows:

Enforcing structure of the task: Previous iterations showed that students have better opportunities to achieve homogeneous understanding of the description of a design problem if the task is divided into two stages. The first stage is related to reading and understanding the problem description; and, the second focuses on modeling. A cooperative gesture[13] on the tabletop (check marks) defines the end of one phase and the start of the next one (Figure 4).

Clue-based instructions: Contrary to the traditional approach of providing a whole set of instructions from the beginning, the proposed system delivers the instructions in the following manner: during the first stage, a short general instruction is presented on the tabletop as well as on the tablet of each student (Figure 4); during the second stage, specific instructions become clues within a deck of cards on top of the tabletop (Figure 5). Clues can be either useful or misleading. Each student can draw clues from the deck to his/her tablet (Figure 6). Availability of a clue is limited to one student at a time; however, a student can transfer his or her clue to another student's tablet. This new approach promotes interdependence and fosters equal participation in discussion. Additionally, misleading clues introduce interference, triggering further argumentation opportunities.

Shared reading and highlighting: Students are able to highlight keywords of the reviewed text at both stages of the process. Additionally, the application provides students the following opportunities to see others' highlights: during the first stage, the tabletop provides a joint view of all members' highlights (Figure 4); at the second stage, a clue owner can use its tablet to see both his or her highlights and the highlights of all the clue's previous owners (Figure 6). Colors allow to differentiate highlights' owners. These visual cues of others' activities enable awareness of other people's actions, and boost argumentation of key components of the design.

Demonopolizing deck use: In previous iterations, students showed a tendency to assign the task of drawing and reading clues to only one member. This behavior hinders equal participation in the modeling activity. The system addresses this by exhibiting an erratic behavior: when a student attempts to make consecutive excessive use of the clues, the application sends the new clue to the tablet of another randomly selected student.

Puzzle-like modeling: To promote a more flexible modeling process and participation, both entities and attributes within a database conceptual model are represented with cards (Figure 5). The color assigned to each card represents its creator. This level of granularity allows members to more easily interfere in each other's work, enhancing awareness and prompting argumentation.

Implementation

The current application is a horizontal prototype of the solution. It offers limited functionality, emulated by a variety of techniques. It runs under a portable projector camera system that works with two PS3Eye cameras and a mini projector. The interaction with the tabletop is through infrared pens. On the software side, a client-server application supports the user interface. On the side of the server, the application was developed in Python and Kivy Framework and on the side of the client a web application enables student to interact with a tablet.

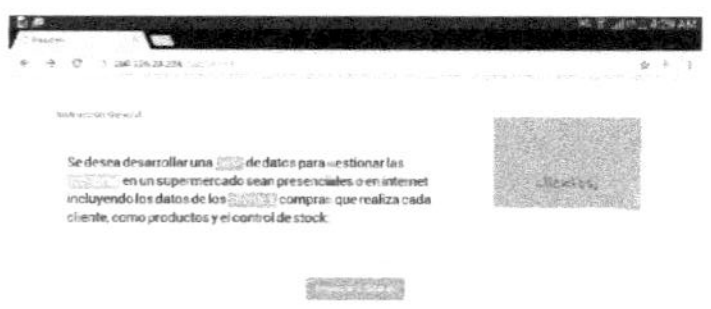

Figure 6: Tablet view of instructions

Evaluation

Before moving to a full implementation, we aimed to evaluate the impressions and reactions of users when observing some key features of the proposed prototype. Moreover, the displacement of users' zone of comfort was sought. For that purpose, a three-minute video prototype of the main features of the system was presented to a group of four students from a CS program who were enrolled in a Database Systems course. These students had previously used a multi-touch tabletop application for database modeling[7]. They were not informed about the ultimate goal of the system, nor were they asked to evaluate the achievement of this goal. Students reacted positively to having the design task divided in stages as well as to features that raise awareness of others' work. For instance, they found that the colored cards were useful to identify the contribution of others and were eager to see their peers' highlights during the shared reading stage. However, their impressions on the interdependence enforced by the clue-based approach were negative. They mentioned they did not like to depend on somebody else and contended they would rather have the whole instructions given to them from the beginning. Additionally, they suggested to have access to the highlights of other users in their tablets, instead of having it only available at the tabletop. Despite the fact that students were not enthusiastic to use pens to write on the tabletop, they welcomed its use when drawing relationships among entities.

Conclusions and Future Work

Overall, our analyses of users' perceptions lead us to conclude that the prototype's features have great potential to accomplish the derived design guidelines. The discomfort caused by the prototype's features that force participants to depend on others suggests possibilities for creating equal opportunities for argumentation. An elaborated version of this prototype will be developed and the effectiveness of the design guidelines' achievement will be evaluated in a real classroom setting. Our work contributes to the research in this area by proposing: 1) Specific design guidelines for collaborative software design learning, drawn from user research sessions; 2) A horizontal prototype of a tabletop application that seeks to augment argumentation among CS students.

References

[1] Basheri, M., Burd, L., and Baghaei, N. A multi-touch interface for enhancing collaborative uml diagramming. In *Proceedings of the 24th Australian Computer-Human Interaction Conference*, OzCHI '12, ACM (2012), 30–33.

[2] Chen, Q., Grundy, J., and Hosking, J. Sumlow: Early design-stage sketching of uml diagrams on an e-whiteboard. *Softw. Pract. Exper. 38*, 9 (July 2008), 961–994.

[3] Dachselt, R., Frisch, M., and Decker, E. Enhancing uml sketch tools with digital pens and paper. In *Proceedings of the 4th ACM Symposium on Software Visualization*, SoftVis '08, ACM (2008), 203–204.

[4] Dourish, P., and Bellotti, V. Awareness and coordination in shared workspaces. In *Proceedings of the 1992 ACM conference on Computer-supported cooperative work*, ACM (1992), 107–114.

[5] Falcão, T. P., and Price, S. Interfering and resolving: How tabletop interaction facilitates co-construction of argumentative knowledge. *International Journal of Computer-Supported Collaborative Learning 6*, 4 (2011), 539–559.

[6] Fleck, R., Rogers, Y., Yuill, N., Marshall, P., Carr, A., Rick, J., and Bonnett, V. Actions speak loudly with words: Unpacking collaboration around the

table. In *Proceedings of the ACM International Conference on Interactive Tabletops and Surfaces*, ITS '09, ACM (2009), 189–196.

[7] Granda, R., Echeverría, V., Chiluiza, K., and Wong-Villacrés, M. Supporting the assessment of collaborative design activities in multi-tabletop classrooms. *Conference Proceedings in the Third Asia-Pacific Conference on Computer Aided System Engineering (APCASE). In Press.* (Jul 2015), 270–275.

[8] Kharrufa, A., Leat, D., and Olivier, P. Digital mysteries: Designing for learning at the tabletop. In *ACM International Conference on Interactive Tabletops and Surfaces*, ITS '10, ACM (2010), 197–206.

[9] Krause, J., Polycarpou, I., and Rader, C. Formal learning groups in an introductory cs course: a qualitative exploration. In *Proceedings of the 17th ACM annual conference on Innovation and technology in computer science education*, ACM (2012), 315–320.

[10] Laal, M. Positive interdependence in collaborative learning. *Procedia-Social and Behavioral Sciences 93* (2013), 1433–1437.

[11] Loksa, D., Mangano, N., LaToza, T. D., and Hoek, A. v. d. Enabling a classroom design studio with a collaborative sketch design tool. In *Proceedings of the 2013 International Conference on Software Engineering*, IEEE Press (2013), 1073–1082.

[12] Mangano, N., LaToza, T. D., Petre, M., and van der Hoek, A. Supporting informal design with interactive whiteboards. In *Proceedings of the SIGCHI Conference on Human Factors in Computing Systems*, CHI '14, ACM (2014), 331–340.

[13] Morris, M. R., Huang, A., Paepcke, A., and Winograd, T. Cooperative gestures: Multi-user gestural interactions for co-located groupware. In *Proceedings of the SIGCHI Conference on Human Factors in Computing Systems*, CHI '06, ACM (2006), 1201–1210.

[14] Piper, A. M., Friedman, W., and Hollan, J. D. Setting the stage for embodied activity: Scientific discussion around a multitouch tabletop display. *Int. J. Learn. Technol. 7*, 1 (May 2012), 58–78.

[15] Radermacher, A., and Walia, G. Gaps between industry expectations and the abilities of graduates. In *Proceeding of the 44th ACM Technical Symposium on Computer Science Education*, SIGCSE '13, ACM (2013), 525–530.

[16] Schneider, B., Strait, M., Muller, L., Elfenbein, S., Shaer, O., and Shen, C. Phylo-genie: Engaging students in collaborative 'tree-thinking' through tabletop techniques. In *Proceedings of the SIGCHI Conference on Human Factors in Computing Systems*, CHI '12, ACM (2012), 3071–3080.

[17] Visser, W. Designing as construction of representations: A dynamic viewpoint in cognitive design research. *Human–Computer Interaction 21*, 1 (2006), 103–152.

[18] Wallace, J. R., Scott, S. D., and MacGregor, C. G. Collaborative sensemaking on a digital tabletop and personal tablets: Prioritization, comparisons, and tableaux. In *Proceedings of the SIGCHI Conference on Human Factors in Computing Systems*, CHI '13, ACM (2013), 3345–3354.

[19] Xambó, A., Hornecker, E., Marshall, P., Jordà, S., Dobbyn, C., and Laney, R. Let's jam the reactable: Peer learning during musical improvisation with a tabletop tangible interface. *ACM Trans. Comput.-Hum. Interact. 20*, 6 (Dec. 2013), 36:1–36:34.

ViZCom: Viewing, Zooming and Commenting through Mobile Devices

Shah Rukh Humayoun[1], Mahmoud Sharf [2], Ragaad AlTarawneh[1], Achim Ebert[1], Tiziana Catarci[2]

[1]Computer Graphics and HCI Group,
University of Kaiserslautern, Germany
{humayoun, tarawneh, ebert}@cs.uni-kl.de

[2]Department of Computer, Control, and
Management Engineering "Antonio Ruberti",
Sapienza University of Rome, Italy
mahmoudsharf3@gmail.com
catarci@dis.uniroma1.it

ITS '15, November 15-18, 2015, Funchal, Portugal
ACM 978-1-4503-3899-8/15/11.
http://dx.doi.org/10.1145/2817721.2823502

Abstract

In tabletop-supported collaborative environments, direct viewing or accessing to all parts of the screen is not possible in many cases. This could affect the performance of team members in executing the common collaborative tasks. Targeting this concern, we developed the **ViZCom** (**Vi**ewing, **Z**ooming and **Com**menting) framework that enables the team members to view the tabletop screen on their mobile devices. It also facilitates them to zoom the screen view on their mobile devices through different zooming options. Further, it provides the facility to write comments or highlight screen parts on their mobile devices, which are then scaled proportionally and shown on the actual tabletop. Overall, the framework extends the collaborative environment by adding these mobile devices in order to provide more spatial flexibility.

Author Keywords

Mobile Interaction; Tabletop Surfaces; Collaborative Environment; Zooming; Focus+Context Zooming.

ACM Classification Keywords

H.5.2 User Interfaces: Input devices and strategies; H.5.3 Group and Organization Interfaces: Computer-supported collaborative work.

Introduction
In tabletop-supported collaborative environments, users stand or sit around the tabletop display and perform the collaborative tasks. Many scenarios of such collaborative tasks can be found in the literature, e.g., for financial advisory sessions [8], to group creativity [4], for safety analysis in embedded systems [1, 2], etc. However, such environments have few limitations (e.g., the interface orientation on the tabletop, inaccessibility to all part of the screen, leading role in users, etc. [11]) that could influence users in better performing the targeted collaborative tasks.

Recently, researcher have started utilizing smart mobile devices (e.g., smart watches, smartphones, tablets, etc) to overcome the limitations of such collaborative environments and to enhance the interaction (e.g.: [7, 9, 10, 12]) amongst the team members as well as between the environment and the team members. In this work, we focus on utilizing smart mobile devices (in our case, we are talking about tablets and smartphones) to overcome the limitation of directly inaccessible view of tabletop screen.

Targeting this, we developed a framework, called **ViZCom** (**Vi**ewing, **Z**ooming, and **Com**menting), that enables the users to view the current tabletop screen on their mobile devices. The framework also allows users to zoom any particular area of the acquired tabletop screen on their mobile device through three different zooming options for a better viewing of the inaccessible area. Further, users can use their mobile devices to write comments or highlight particular parts of the tabletop screen through some drawing options, which are then scaled proportionally and shown on the actual tabletop. The framework uses different colors in order to distinguish the comments and drawing of different users. The idea is to enable users to overcome the limitations of direct interaction with the tabletop surface by extending the workspace on their mobile devices in order to provide a spatial flexibility during interaction and collaborative working.

Related Work
Few recent examples of mobile devices interaction with tabletop-supported environments are: Scott et al. in [12] developed a way to improve the awareness of transferred objects while picking and dropping them between tabletop and mobile. MultiTask [7] is a digital tool to plan projects and assign related tasks. Rodrigues et al. in [10] proposed the usage of tablets as zoomable magic lenses over the overview map displayed on a tabletop or with a wall display. In [9], Jin et al. proposed a way for wiring home devices on a tabletop display while providing a web-based UI for mobile devices in order to control home devices.

Other researchers focused on utilizing mobile devices to interact with wall-display surfaces, for example: Zadow et al. [13] developed a prototype where they used an arm-mounted smartphone to interact with multi-touch display wall. AlTarawneh et al. [1, 2] used mobile devices to interact with tiled-wall display for analyzing safety aspects of embedded systems. Badam and Elmqvist [3] developed an application that allows users to work on their tablets using brush and link interaction to explore the dataset, while visualizing the brushes on an overview visualization on the wall display. While some provided an environment with a combination of mobile devices and different interactive surfaces, e.g., Chokshi et al. [6] developed a prototype for the emergency operation center with the concept of multi-

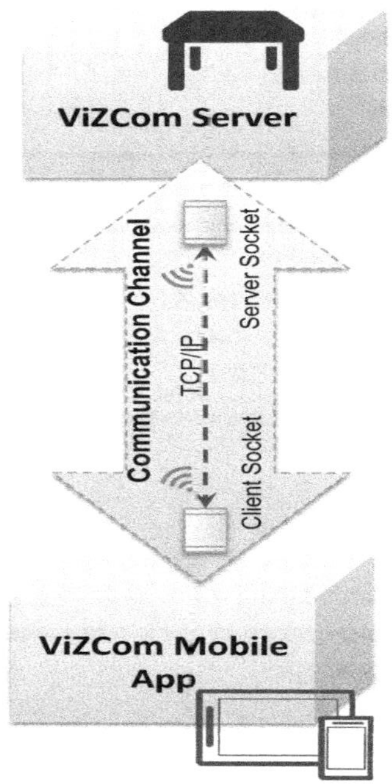

Figure 1. Architectural overview of the ViZCom framework.

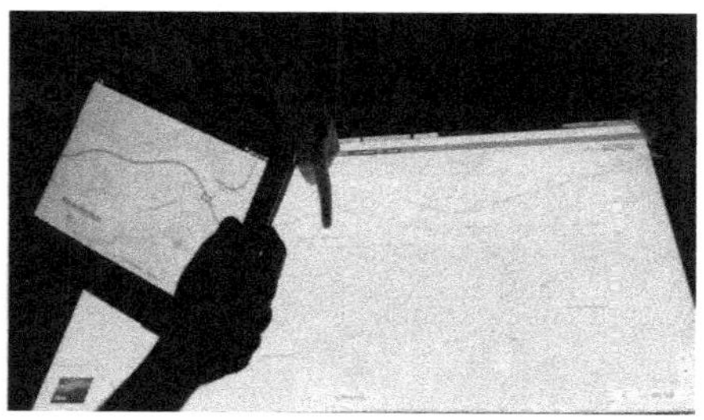

Figure 2. Users interacting with tabletop through the ViZCom framework

surface connected communication environment to enable tablets, tabletops, and large wall-displays to interact with each other. In 2013, a workshop [5] was held in ITS with the concept of "collaboration meets interactive surfaces: walls, tables, tablets, and phones".

The ViZCom Framework Architecture

Our developed **ViZCom** framework enhances the interaction in tabletop-supported collaborative environments, as it enables the users to view any part of the screen, directly inaccessible, on their mobile devices as well as the provision of writing comments useful for the collaborative tasks. Figure 1 shows the overall implemented architectural view of our ViZCom framework. Figure 2 shows team members working on some collaborative task using the ViZCom framework.

The framework is composed of three modules: the *ViZCom Server* that handles the tabletop-side management and interaction, the *ViZCom Mobile App* that works on mobile devices, and the *Communication Channel* that handles the communication between the tabletop and the wireless connected mobile devices. The ViZCom Server module was implemented in C# and Surface SDK using Microsoft Visual Studio, as the underlying tabletop in our case is Samsung SUR40 Tabletop Surface with Microsoft PixelSense. The ViZCom mobile app is Android-based and was implemented in Java using Android Studio. The Communication Channel was implemented through socket programming where the data is passed through the JSON (JavaScript Object Notation) strings using the TCP/IP protocol over WIFI connection. One of the benefits of the ViZCom architecture is that the framework can be transfer to other collaborative environments, such as large wall-display supported one, after just some minor modifications in ViZCom Server module, which makes the overall solution scalable and portable.

ViZCom Mobile App: Viewing, Zooming and Commenting

The ViZCom mobile app enables the users to view the current tabletop window on their mobile devices, which extends the workspace to their mobile devices; hence, they would have more spatial flexibility during the interaction. This enables them to view, zoom, and comment on the parts of the screen that are out of their direct reach.

When a user requests the current screenshot of tabletop, the ViZCom Server module takes it and sends it back to the requested mobile device through the Communication Channel module. For a better viewing and interaction, we recommend usage of tablets; although, this also works perfectly with smartphones. In order to have a closer look on a particular part of the tabletop screenshot, three zooming options are provided: *selection zooming, grid-selection zooming,* and *focus+context* zooming.

The Selection Zooming

In this option, a rectangular box appears on the taken tabletop screenshot on the mobile device (see Figure 3). Users can adjust this rectangular box simply through the dragging gesture on the corner of it in order to select their area of interest. The selected area is then enlarged into another view on the mobile device. By returning back, user can see the whole tabletop screenshot again.

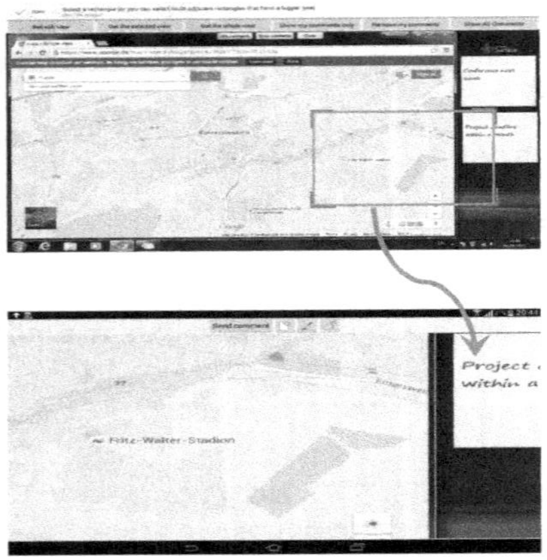

Figure 3. The selection zooming option. The selected area in the upper screenshot is then zoomed and shown into another window on the device.

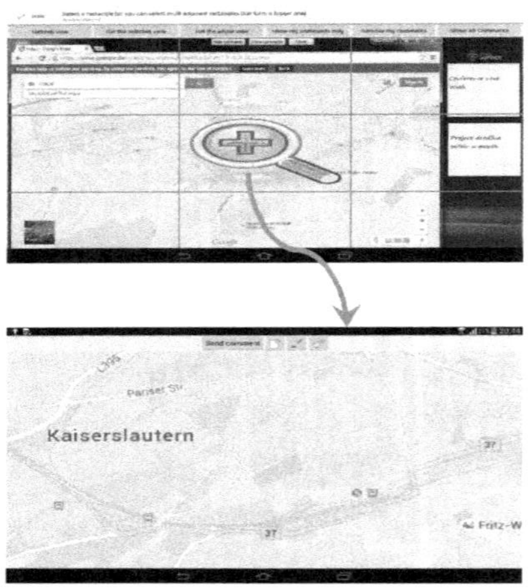

Figure 4. The grid selection zooming option. The selected cell in the upper screenshot is enlarged and shown into another view on the mobile device.

The Grid-Selection Zooming

In this option, a 3X3 grid appears on the acquired tabletop screenshot on the mobile device. Users can select one or more grid cells and then the selected cells are enlarged into another view on the mobile device. However, users are allowed to select only adjacent grid cells. In total, there are seven possible ways to select adjacent grid cells that are supported by the framework (see Figure 5). The resulting zooming (see Figure 4) of the selected grid cells is done with regard to provide the best viewing and orientation. Initially, the acquired tabletop screenshot is shown on the mobile device horizontal direction to reflect the tabletop window by default horizontal direction. Then the zoom is performed according to the selection of adjacent grid cells as follow:

- *Case 1 - Only one grid-cell selection:* The resulting zoom is performed on the selected cell as in the case of the selection zooming.
- *Case 2 - Any two horizontally adjacent cells selection:* The resulting zooming is performed in both directions on the selected cells till it reaches to the maximum of mobile device's vertical height.
- *Case 3 - Any two vertically adjacent cells selection:* The selected cells are rotated 90 degree to the left side and then the zooming is performed in both directions till it reaches to the maximum of mobile device's vertical height.
- *Case 4 - Three vertically adjacent cells selection:* This case is treated same as case 3.
- *Case 5 - Any three horizontally adjacent cells selection:* In this case, the selected cells are not zoomed. However, the remaining cells are taken away from the provided new view on mobile device.
- *Case 6 - Any four squally adjacent cells selection:* The selected grids are zoomed in both directions till it reaches to the maximum of mobile device's vertical height.
- *Case 7 - Any six vertically adjacent cells selection:* This case is treated same as case 3.

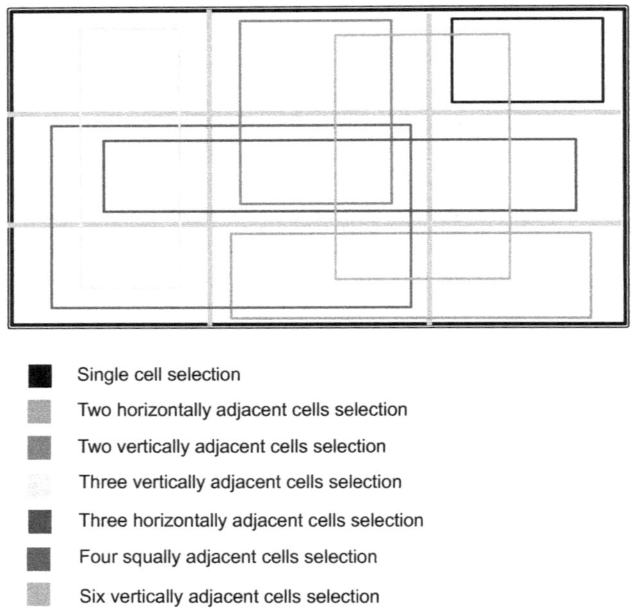

Figure 5: Seven possible ways to select adjacent grid cells.

The Focus+Context Zooming

In this option too, a 3X3 grid appears on the acquired tabletop screenshot on mobile device. However, the zooming is performed in the *focus+context* viewing style, i.e., providing the resulting zooming and overall view using the *Focus+Context* interaction technique. However, in this case the user is allowed to select only one cell at a time. The selected cell is then enlarged to

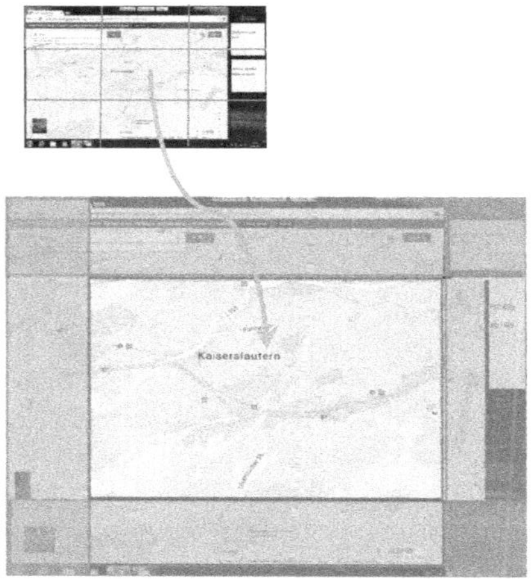

Figure 6. The selectec call is enlarged while the remaining cells are reduced and distorted to the side, in order to provide a *focus+context* style.

provide the required focused view, while the size of the remaining cells are reduced and distorted to keep the context of the global view (see Figure 56). This style can be extended easily to divide the initial grid into another level of details to allow users to change the context to one specific cell and then navigate this cell deeper.

Commenting and Drawing
The ViZCom mobile app also provides the facility to write comments or draw on the acquired tabletop screenshot or any of its zoomed part. The resulting comments or drawings are then shown on the tabletop surface while keeping the ratio and the spatial scaling. For this, the mobile app provides a transparent drawing panel on the top of the current tabletop view on the mobile device, which is used to write comments or drawing different objects. While on the tabletop side, the ViZCom Server module also creates a transparent layer on the top of the screen for each of the connected device (see Figure 7). We use a different color for each user; therefore, it is easy to distinguish between the comments and drawings of different users on the tabletop surface.

On the mobile devices, users can ask to show only their comments and drawings or to show all users' comments and drawings. While on the tabletop side, users can hide all the comments whenever they want to interact with the current view, as the current view becomes inactive when any transparent comments and drawings layer comes on top of it. Currently, the ViZCom mobile app provides only the basic drawing options (i.e., line, circle, and rectangle), which we plan to extend in the future.

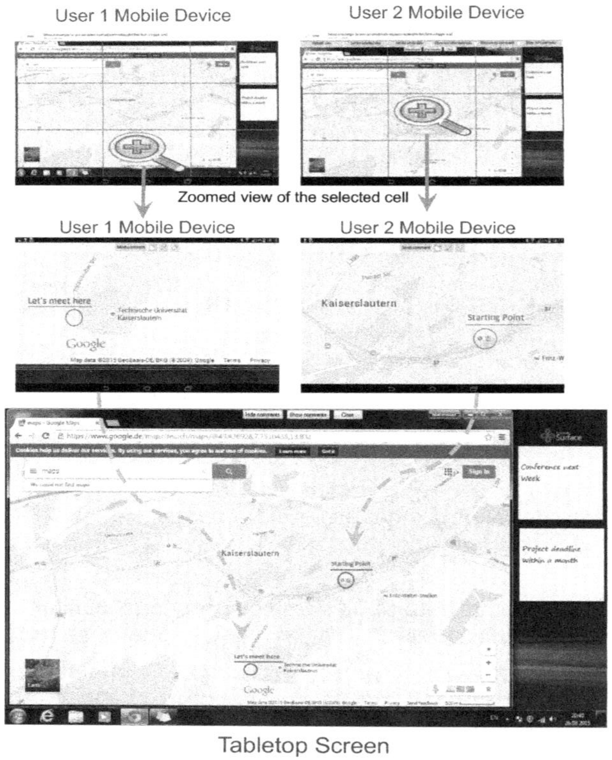

Figure 7: The selected grid cells (see the top two figures) are enlarged on the mobile devices to give both users a better view of the selected cell. Their written comments and drawings (see the middle two figures) are then sent to the tabletop where they are shown on the respective place on the screen through the transparent layers. On the tabletop, color of each user is different in order to distinguish between their comments and drawing.

Concluding Remarks
We presented our ViZCom framework that utilizes mobile devices to overcome the limitations of directly

inaccessible view of the tabletop screen. The goal of such framework is to help the team members in performing their collaborative tasks by extending the workspace to their mobile devices in order to provide a spatial flexibility during the interaction. The advantage of the proposed framework is that it works at system level on the tabletop side; therefore, it works perfectly which so ever application is currently used by team members on the tabletop side. Further, we developed the framework in such a way that it requires minor modifications to be used on any other collaborative environment (e.g., wall-display supported), which makes the overall solution portable and scalable.

In the future, we aim to provide advance drawings and writing facility in order to enhance the interaction. We also plan to provide multi-levels focus+context zooming option, as hinted earlier. Further, we intend to perform detailed user studies to check the feasibility and effectiveness of our approach and framework.

References

1. AlTarawneh, R., Bauer, J., and Ebert, A. A Visual Interactive Environment for Enhancing Collaboration between Engineers for the Safety Analysis Mechanisms in Embedded Systems. *CSCW Companion '14*, ACM, 125-128, 2014.
2. AlTarawneh, R., Bauer, J., Humayoun, S. R., Ebert, A., and Liggesmeyer, P. Enhancing Understanding of Safety Aspects in Embedded Systems through an Interactive Visual Tool. *IUI Companion '14*, 9-12, ACM, 2014.
3. Badam, S. K. and Elmqvist, N. 2014. PolyChrome: A Cross-Device Framework for Collaborative Web Visualization. *ITS '14*, ACM, 109-118.
4. Campos, P., Ferreira, A., and Lucero, A. 2013. Collaboration meets interactive surfaces: walls, tables, tablets, and phones. *ITS '13*, 481-482.
5. Cheung, V., Watson, D., Vermeulen, J., Hancock, M., and Scott, S. 2014. Overcoming Interaction Barriers in Large Public Displays Using Personal Devices. *ITS '14*, ACM, 375-380.
6. Chokshi, A., Seyed, T., Rodrigues, F. M., and Maurer, F. 2014. ePlan Multi-Surface: A Multi-Surface Environment for Emergency Response Planning Exercises. *ITS '14*, ACM, 219-228.
7. Haas B. and Echtler, F. 2014. Task Assignment and Visualization on Tabletops and Smartphones. *ITS '14*, ACM, 311-316.
8. Heinrich, P., Kilic, M., Aschoff, F. R, and Schwabe, G. 2014. Enabling relationship building in tabletop-supported advisory settings. *CSCW '14*, 171-183.
9. Jin, Y., Dang, C. T., Prehofer, C., and André, E. 2014. A Multi-Display System for Deploying and Controlling Home Automation. ITS '14, 399-402.
10. Rodrigues, F. M., Seyed, T., Maurer, F., and Carpendale, S. 2014. Bancada: Using Mobile Zoomable Lenses for Geospatial Exploration. *ITS '14*, ACM, 409-414.
11. Scott, S. D., Carpendale, M. S. T., and Inkpen, K. 2014. M. Territoriality in collaborative tab-letop workspaces. *CSCW '04*, ACM 294-303.
12. Scott, S. D., Besacier, G., Tournet, J., Goyal, N., and Haller, M. 2014. Surface Ghosts: Promoting Awareness of Transferred Objects during Pick-and-Drop Transfer in Multi-Surface Environments. *ITS '14*. 99-108.
13. Zadow, U., Büschel, W., Langner, R., and Dachselt, R. 2014. SleeD: Using a Sleeve Display to Interact with Touch-sensitive Display Walls. *ITS '14*, ACM, 129-138.

Investigating the Potential of a Two-finger Chord Button in Multi-touch Applications

Ioannis Leftheriotis
Ionian University
Tsirigoti sq. 7, Corfu, Greece
and
Norwegian University of Science and Technology
Sem Sælands cei 7-9, 7491
Trondheim, Norway.
iolef@acm.org

Michail N. Giannakos
Norwegian University of Science and Technology
Sem Sælands vei 7-9, 7491
Trondheim, Norway.
michailg@idi.ntnu.no

Konstantinos Chorianopoulos
Ionian University
Tsirigoti sq. 7, Corfu Greece.
choko@ionio.gr

Letizia Jaccheri
Norwegian University of Science and Technology
Sem Sælands vei 7-9, 7491
Trondheim, Norway.
letizia@idi.ntnu.no

ITS '15, November 15-18, 2015, Funchal, Portugal
ACM 978-1-4503-3899-8/15/11.
http://dx.doi.org/10.1145/2817721.2823503

Abstract

With the increasing use of multi-touch (MT) capable devices, MT interaction has become a commodity during the last years. From personal devices to larger multi-user screens, MT functionality is nowadays considered as a standard way of performing rich interactions. However, moving from a single-touch interaction to a dual-touch and consequently to MT is not always without challenges for the average user. Although, the use of single-touch is very common, interaction design have yet to be examined thoroughly by taking into account potential differences of single and multi-touch functionality. In this work, we investigate the potential of a two-finger chord button in comparison to the traditional single touch buttons that we find in touchscreens. Based on the fact that users are familiar with single touch buttons (even before the MT screens) our hypotheses are: the use of a two finger chord button a) decreases users' efficiency, and b) delays users' responses. In order to investigate our hypotheses, we conducted a controlled experiment with 12 users working on an appropriately designed MT application. The empirical results have indicated that the use of two-finger button significantly delays users' response-time while it does not affect users' efficiency on the performed task.

Author Keywords
Multi-touch; chords; two-finger button; buttons; menu; chord interaction

ACM Classification Keywords
H.5.2. Information interfaces and presentation

Introduction

With the advent of multi-touch (MT) surfaces, a large number of onscreen touch manipulations and interaction patterns have been enabled. The way users' working on many onscreen tasks has changed significantly. Instead of moving the mouse and/or typing on the keyboard of a desktop pc, users apply gestures or chords or even work collaboratively on an onscreen task, taking advantages of the new affordances the MT surfaces offer. In addition, programs and their interfaces need to be shifted from the traditional window icon menu pointer (WIMP) environment to a more appropriate one for supporting MT affordances [6].

In this work, we are focused on the most basic interaction of a touch screen, the operation of soft buttons. Most studies investigated the use of touch screen soft buttons in comparison to traditional keyboard buttons (e.g. [4]). It seems that the lack of tactile feedback in soft buttons is associated with lower performance [4]. However, it is widely accepted by the vibrant MT community that MT surfaces have more to offer than simply replicating the traditional way of interacting (e.g. single touch soft buttons). According to studies that investigated the emulation of the mouse in a MT environment (e.g. [7]) tapping with placing *one or two fingers* on the screen is intuitive and often fast. Based on such studies we were motivated to investigate practical differences on a button that could be pressed with a two-finger chord interaction.

Most studies are focused on examining the size or the type of a MT button, or even investigate alternative selection techniques like interactive moving buttons (e.g. [6]) or MT menus. Researchers have also tried to find methods that incorporate the number of the fingers touched on the screen in order to select a function ([5], [1]). However, these "gestures" or chords were not associated with a functionality of a simple button. Besides, according to some studies [3] there is a strong users' preference for using one or two index fingers, even when given the opportunity to use more.

In this ongoing work we examine whether using one or two fingers to touch a button has significant effect on the response time and efficiency of the users. Hence, we conducted a controlled experiment in order to better understand whether the use of a two-finger chord button (experimental condition) has an effect on users' response-time and efficiency compared to a traditional single touch soft button (controlled condition).

Methodology

Research design

In order to be able to investigate our research hypotheses, we have developed a MT application supporting both single and dual finger buttons. In particular, our MT application was developed in Kivy MT framework [9] (next page, Figure 3). With the selection of a small number of plants that are found in our area, we created a taxonomic key with the help of a domain expert. Our MT application allows the user to enlarge and rotate the main picture of the archive, which is positioned in the center (see Figure 3). Users were also

Figure 1. Photo taken during the experimental task: Users interacting with the MT application on the 27″ MT screen.

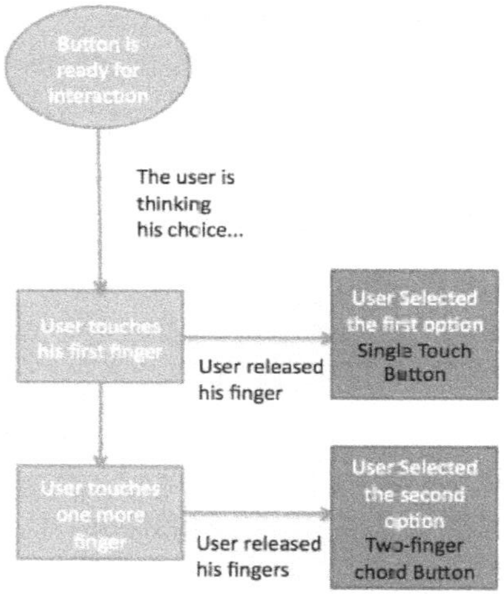

Figure 2. Interaction design of the one/two finger chord button.

able to see specific details of the plant (e.g. its sepals, blossoms). On the left/right side of the screen there is some text and the corresponding images of selection one (left) and two (right). Users have to carefully identify which of the two options corresponds to the plant they have in front of them by touching the button with one finger for the first option or with a two finger chord for the second option (as it is described just below the button). In Figure 2, the interaction design of the two-finger chord button is described. By making all the right selections in a number of steps, users are lead to the family of the plant and some interesting information concerning the plant.

Apparatus

Based on our experience with custom-based MT surfaces, we had to eliminate any factor that would influence the performance, accuracy and robustness of our installation since it would affect our results. Thus, our experimental setup was based on a robust 27″ inch all-in projective capacitive monitor with 1920x1080 video analysis and 5ms response time, which was placed vertically in front of the two users (see Figure 1). The screen was connected via usb to a Windows 7 environment installed on a Mac mini hardware; our system was able to identify only 10 simultaneous touch points, but this number of touches was adequate for the purpose of our application. Users had to sit on their chairs in front of the screen and interact with the application. There was a camera just behind them capturing their interaction strategies and patterns.

Procedure

In the beginning there was an exploratory phase of the application. We wanted the students to understand what they have to do in order to reach the goal of identifying the plant species, and eliminate any potential learning effect from their experience with other applications; hence, we ended up with clear results concerning the interactions. During the warm-up phase they played as a team versus the computer and they had a team score. In order to complete the exploratory task there were 5 plants that were to be identified along with 25 questions.

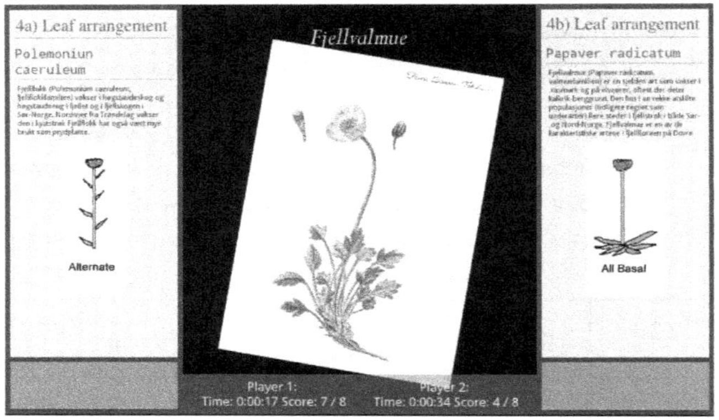

Figure 3. The MT application – a step of the taxonomic key: Users have their own one/two finger chord buttons in the lower part of the screen where they make the appropriate selection (one finger for selecting the left option, two fingers for selecting the right option)

In the phase of the experiment (Figure 1), we explained to the users that there are two different territories/buttons (in dark yellow color) where they should apply one-finger touch in order to select the first alternative (left) or a two-finger touch so as to select the second alternative (right). Users had visual feedback when touching the buttons (a small circle on the touch point) and audio plus visual feedback about their right or wrong selections.

Users were playing against each other and they were competing based on their personal total score along with their personal time that was displayed in the bottom of the screen. Since the procedure of identifying a plant is difficult, users had to carefully examine both options before making the appropriate selection.

Sampling

The sample of participants in this study consisted of 12 students. Of the 12 participants, 2 were boys and 10 girls. All of the students who participated in the experiment were 17-18 years old, enrolled in the third grade of high school, and were following the same syllabus. The experiment took place during an extracurricular activity in a museum/library in Trondheim, Norway.

Research findings

In our experiment we had 322 responses (258 correct); 213 responses (181 correct) of a single touch button and 104 responses (77 correct) of the two-finger chord button.

To examine our research hypotheses regarding the effect of a two-finger chord button (experimental condition) on users' efficiency and response time, compared to a traditional single touch soft button (control condition), we performed a t-test including users' score and response time as dependent variables and chord options as independent variables. All statistical analyses reported were conducted with a significant level of 0.05. As we can see from the outcome data in Table 1, chord selection has indicated a significant difference on users' response time while in users' efficiency we did not find any significant difference between the two alternative buttons.

	Mean (S.D.)		**T**	**p**
	Single touch (N=218)	Two finger chord button (N=104)		
Score (max 1)	0.83 (0.38)	0.74 (0.44)	1.81	0.075
Time (sec)	10.07 (7.58)	12.88 (9.06)	2.74**	0.007

$^*p < 0.05$ $^{**}p < 0.01$

Table 1. This table shows the results of a t-test with users' score and response time as dependent variables and single touch button or two-finger chord button as independent variables.

In Figure 4 (next page), the frequencies of the response time for the single touch button and the two-finger chord button are depicted. The frequency diagram is in accordance to the findings in Table 1; showing that the two-finger chord button demands significantly more time in order for the users to give their answer. In particular, we can see that we don't have any two-finger responses in the first 5 seconds after the question. In addition, in the "less than 10 second" responses, the single touch option dominates. On the contrary, in the "more than 10 second" responses, the two-finger chord button dominates.

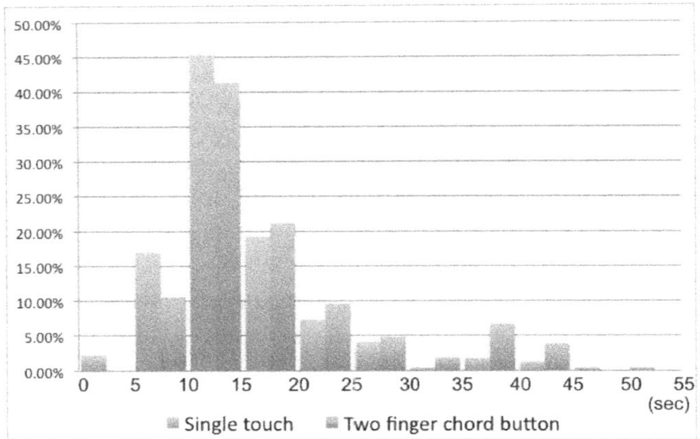

Figure 4. Frequency diagrams for single touch button and the two-finger chord button over the time (starting from questions' appearance).

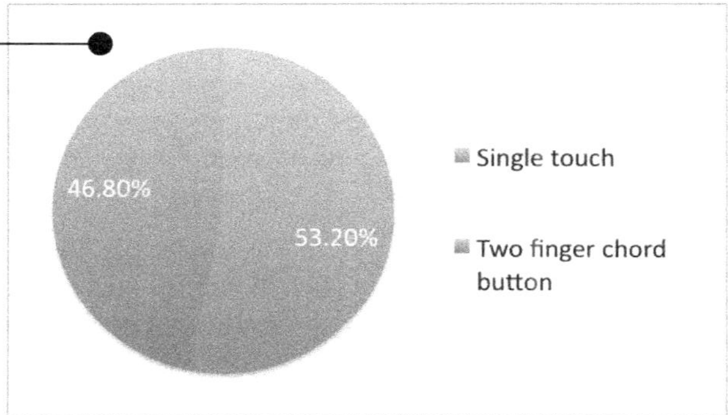

Figure 5. Right answer absolute percentage: This chart demonstrates the absolute percentage of the correct answers for the single touch button condition and the two-finger chord button condition respectively in relation to the total right answers.

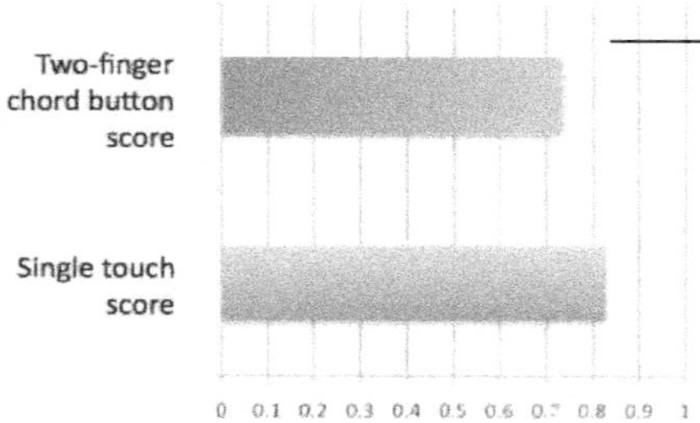

Figure 6. Single finger correct answers were 83% of the total single finger answers and two finger correct answers were 74% of the total two finger chord button answers.

On the other hand, Figure 5 shows that there is a difference in giving the right answer between the single touch button and the two-finger chord button, but this difference is small (Figure 5,6) and insignificant, as indicated from the t-test results (Table 1).

Conclusion

Trying to investigate potential challenges for casual users while moving from the traditional single-touch buttons, we decided to compare a two-finger chord button with the traditional single-touch one. Even though the two-finger chord touch has been commercially used a long time ago [2] and is widely used among users as a gesture for zoom-in or zoom-out (the pinch gesture) or as an emulation technique of the mouse right click (or usually as a context menu), it can be considered as a somewhat more complex interaction due to the slightly higher cognitive and movement load [8] compared to the single touch interaction. Thus, our initial hypothesis was that the use of a two-finger chord button might have a negative effect on users' response time and efficiency (in the case of our application that is the score of students' answers). Our preliminary findings demonstrate a difference in the number of right answers in favor of the single-touch button, however, the difference is not significantly important. The two-finger touch chord might not have been traditionally used as a button, but it is a widely used gesture for rotating or changing the size of objects on a MT surface.

Concerning our second hypothesis regarding the time needed in order to articulate the two finger chord, it seems that our initial hypothesis that the two finger chord button creates a small delay compared to the traditional single touch button was true, since we found that the single touch button demands significantly less time from the users. Our subjects were generally more familiar with the single-touch button, especially compared with the two-finger chord one, however, they had experience with MT devices and by performing a warming-up (training) period we reduced any potential learning effect.

In this study, the subjects were told how the two-finger chord actually worked well and allowed them to have more options in a limited single button area. In our future studies we will examine further the use of a two-finger chord button in MT applications by investigating its ideal size and functionality, while trying to find ways so that the two-finger chord button interaction being intuitive and more effective for users that work on a MT screen. In addition, we will attempt to investigate users' time response and efficiency in more demanding interactions (e.g., more than two-finger buttons). By doing that, we will be able to find the design thresholds and apply them in more complicated chord actions and menus.

Acknowledgements

We would like to thank all the participants of the study. We also thank Aleka Angeletaki for assisting us during the data collection process and Gabriella Papastefanou for the content of our experiment. This work was partially funded by ARK4 project of the National Library of Norway and the NTNU UB.

References

[1] Bailly, G., Müller, J., Lecolinet, E., Design and evaluation of finger-count interaction: Combining multitouch gestures and menus, International Journal of Human-Computer Studies 70, 10 (2012), 673-689.

[2] Furuhata, T., Hirano, T., & Sawada, C. (1999). U.S. Patent No. 5,943,043. Washington, DC: U.S. Patent and Trademark Office.

[3] Kin, K., Agrawala, M., & DeRose, T., Determining the benefits of direct-touch, bimanual, and multifinger input on a multitouch workstation. In *Proceedings of Graphics interface '09,* Canadian Information Processing Society, (2009), 119-124.

[4] Lee, S., & Zhai, S. The performance of touch screen soft buttons. In *Proceedings of the SIGCHI Conference on Human Factors in Computing Systems*, ACM Press (2009), 309-318.

[5] Leftheriotis, I., Chorianopoulos, K., and Jaccheri L. Tool support for developing scalable multiuser applications on multi-touch screens. In Proc. ITS'2012. ACM Press (2012), 371-374.

[6] Leftheriotis, I. and Chorianopoulos, K., User experience quality in Multi-touch tasks. In Porc. EICS'11, ACM Press (2011), 277-282.

[7] Matejka, J., Grossman, T., Lo, J., & Fitzmaurice, G. The design and evaluation of multi-finger mouse emulation techniques. In *Proceedings of the SIGCHI Conference on Human Factors in Computing Systems*, ACM Press (2009), 1073-1082.

[8] D. A. Rosenbaum, F. Marchak, H. J. Barnes, J. Vaughan, J. D. Slotta, and M. J. Jorgensen. Constraints for action selection: Overhand versus underhand grips. Lawrence Erlbaum Associates, Inc, Mahwah, New Jersey, 1990.

[9] Virbel, M., Hansen, T. E., and Lobunets, O. Kivy-A Framework for Rapid Creation of Innovative User Interfaces. In *Mensch & Computer Workshopband,* (2011), 69-73.

Multi-user Multi-device Interaction with Large Displays at the Point of Sale: An Application Case

Figure 1: The system in use.

Ulrich von Zadow
Interactive Media Lab
Technische Universität Dresden
01062 Dresden, Germany
uzadow@acm.org

Andreas Siegel
Interactive Media Lab
Technische Universität Dresden
01062 Dresden, Germany
andreassiegel@acm.org

Raimund Dachselt
Interactive Media Lab
Technische Universität Dresden
01062 Dresden, Germany
dachselt@acm.org

ITS '15, November 15-18, 2015, Funchal, Portugal
ACM 978-1-4503-3899-8/15/11. http://dx.doi.org/10.1145/2817721.2823504

Abstract
The internet raises challenges for retailers, since it provides a competing sales channel that allows effectively unlimited access to arbitrary products. In particular, this enables a phenomenon known as showrooming, where customers inspect products in local stores and subsequently order from arbitrary online shops. By combining large public displays in stores with personal mobile devices, our prototype multi-user shopping system has the potential to alleviate this: Store-specific shopping carts on the mobile bind customers even after they have exited the store. Significantly, the system is optimized to minimize attention switches between the devices by treating the mobile device as eyes-free remote control wherever possible, using the mobile display only for personal data. We report on interaction concepts, our prototypical implementation, and user feedback, contributing an initial iteration for best practices in this domain.

Author Keywords
Multi-display environment; cross-device interaction; large displays; mobile phones; point of sale; attention switches

ACM Classification Keywords
H.5.2 [Information interfaces and presentation (e.g., HCI)]: User Interfaces, Interaction styles

Introduction

Due to hardware advances, large public displays – both output-only and interactive – have become commonplace in retail. However, they are used primarily as additional marketing channel. Although some efforts have been made to establish them as direct sales mechanisms as well, this is still the exception. Also, public displays by themselves are inherently unable to preserve privacy when displaying personal information such as shopping cart contents. At the same time, showrooming (customers inspecting products in local stores and subsequently ordering from an arbitrary online shop) threatens sales in retail [1]. Multi-device interaction with mobile devices allows adequate display of private information. In the context of showrooming, it is also significant that it allows shoppers to take their shopping cart and preferences with them when they leave, thus making it very easy to buy from the retailer's own online shop if and when the decision to buy is made. Furthermore, shopping is often a group experience, and group shopping has the potential to increase the customer base and motivate shoppers [3].

In this work, we therefore present a system that supports two-person shopping in a multi-device environment (Figure 1). Significantly, the concept allows shoppers to preserve their shopping carts on their personal devices for later access and possible purchase. Since attention switches between displays have been shown to be disrupting (e.g., [5, 7]), our interaction design is specifically geared to minimize these. For menu selection in particular, we rely on a pie menu adapted to multi-device operation, where the mobile serves as input device and visual feedback is displayed on the public display.

The rest of the paper is structured as follows: After a short survey of related work, we present requirements. These form the basis of the system design that follows. In further sections, we describe relevant implementation details and informal user feedback we gathered.

Related Work

Research on public displays in general is a very wide and active research field. For space reasons, we therefore refer to Müller et al.'s overview on the subject [4]. In the following, we present a selection of relevant papers that cover multi-device shopping systems, handling of gaze switches and pie menus that separate input and output device.

She et al. have recently published a survey in the area of interactive displays combined with mobiles for advertising [6]. They review methods used at varying stages of interaction and assert that mobile devices "should be integrated" into the process. Yamaguchi et al.'s paper on SWINGNAGE [8] presents a multi-user shopping system that uses a gesture-based mobile interface for interaction. Device pairing is based on matching device accelerometer data with corresponding depth camera data when the user performs a gesture.

Gaze and attention switches as well as change blindness issues have been identified a number of times as obstacles in multi-device interaction. Significantly, Rashid et al. [5] quantify the costs involved and report a time loss of 1.8 seconds per gaze switch on average. von Zadow et al. [7] also find that gaze switches cost time in a multi-device configuration involving an arm-mounted device.

Pie menus have been found to be effective in multi-device contexts several times. In particular, Zhao et al. [9] use an iPod's circular touch pad for a radial menu whose items can be accessed by sliding or taps. The menu provides auditory feedback (reading out menu items + sounds).
A user study shows there is no significant difference between visual and eyes-free menu in terms of selection time

and accuracy. Also, in pieTouch, Ecker et al. [2] present a dwelltime-activated radial touch menu with auditory feedback for in-car information systems control and find faster performance and higher attractivness ratings than a simple touch interface in this particular setting.

Requirements

In an initial step, we gathered requirements based on the one hand on our survey of related work above and on the other hand on experiences with a previous shopping system[1]. We will refer to the requirements throughout the paper as R1-R5:

- (R1) Walk-up-and-use: System usage should be self-explanatory. There should be no need to install additional software on the user's mobile device, as this was found to deter users in the previous system; Yamaguchi et al. have similar findings [8].
- (R2) Minimal hardware requirements: It should be possible to use existing public displays connected to the internet. This precludes using touch functionality on the public display. It also makes it impossible to use bluetooth or NFC for networking.
- (R3) Support collaboration: The system should support more than one user to take advantage of the potential of group shopping [3].
- (R4) Respect privacy: Personal information such as shopping cart and wish-list should not be publicly visible.
- (R5) Minimize attention switches: Attention switches are associated with high time costs and cognitive disruption and should therefore be avoided [5, 7].

[1] ZMOSH by SALT Solutions: http://www.salt-solutions.de/blog/index.php/das-elektronische-einkaufsregal/

Figure 2: User-specific part of standby screen with QR code used to connect to mobile.

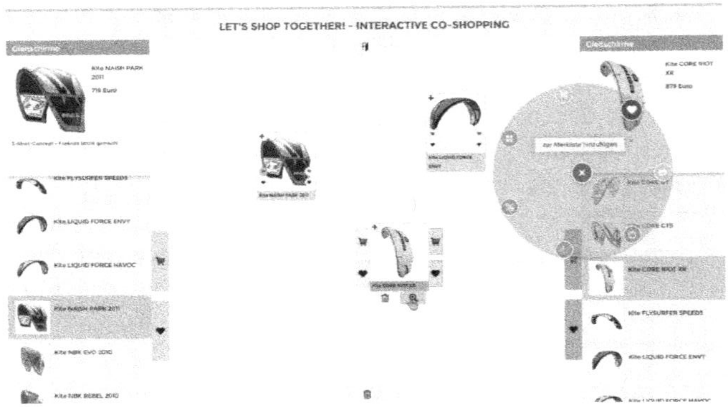

Figure 3: Main application screen: The left user is in item selection mode, the right user has an active menu. Three items are visible in the central discussion area.

System Design

Our system supports browsing through a product list, selecting products and putting them in a personal wish list, a personal shopping cart or a shared discussion area. The large public screen is divided into workspaces for each user on the sides as well as a large central area for shared discussion (Figure 3). As a general principle, visual feedback is delivered on the large screen where possible to avoid an attention switch (R5), while the mobile shows only a minimal interface that can be ignored once usage has been understood (Figure 4). Exceptions are made only for private data such as the user's shopping carts (R4). Mobile device vibration is used as an additional user-specific feedback channel. Furthermore, the mobile device screen orientation is locked to portrait mode to avoid interface rotation while the user is not looking at the mobile.

In idle state, the screen displays QR codes in the user workspaces (Figure 2) that can be used to connect a mo-

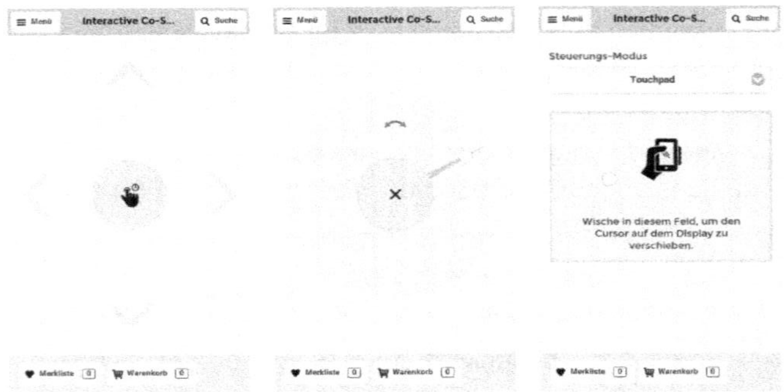

Figure 4: Mobile user interface: List navigation, pie menu control and cursor control. Note buttons that activate wish list and shopping cart views at the bottom border.

bile device (R2). Once a user has connected, the user workspace switches to show a product list. In this mode, the mobile can be used to scroll through the list and select an item using standard gestures (Figure 4, left). Additionally, a long press on the mobile activates a pie menu that enables the user to add the current item to the shared space, her wish list or her shopping cart, switching to a separate discussion mode, or exiting the system.

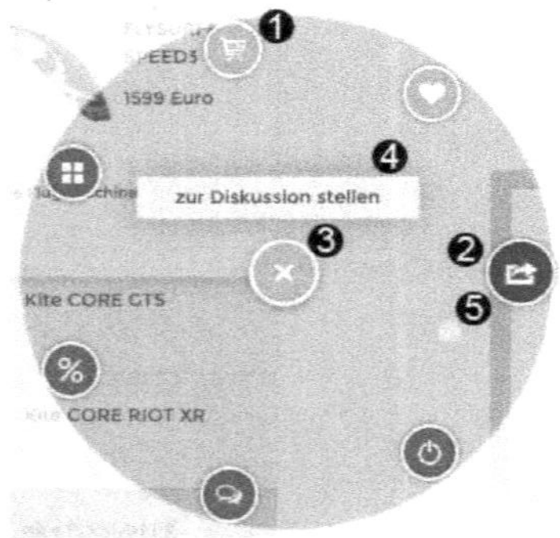

Figure 5: Pie menu interface, showing menu items (1), selection pointer (2), abort button (3), tooltip (4), and finger position indicator (5).

The pie menu is shown on the large display as well (R5). At the same time, an abstract circle is displayed on the mobile for orientation (Figure 4, center). Primarily, the pie menu (Figure 5) displays color-coded menu items (1) as well as a selection pointer in the form of a clock hand (2) that snaps to the item selected. In addition, the menu shows an abort button in the center (3) as well as tooltips (4) that give information about the current menu item. Significantly, we added a finger position indicator (5) after an initial iteration revealed that users otherwise do not know where the center of the menu is on the mobile display and thus have no way of moving the selection in a circle around it.

After opening the menu using a long press, the user simply drags and releases her finger (that is still touching the mobile) to select a menu item - or, if desired, the abort button in the center of the menu. While dragging, the selection pointer, the finger position indicator and the tooltips all give appropriate feedback. In addition, selection changes are accompanied by haptic feedback.

Users can switch to a separate discussion mode using a menu item. In this mode, all interaction takes place in the central area of the large screen; the mobile functions similar to a standard notebook touchpad that moves a cursor in this area. Using the cursor, users can move items in the discussion area, view details, and add them to their wish lists or shopping carts as desired. This is possible using drag-and-drop as well as dedicated tool buttons. If both users switch to discussion mode, they each control a separate cursor. Cursors are color-coded to avoid confusion.

To access the wish list or the shopping cart, users switch their attention to the mobile device and press the appropriate button. These modes have a standard web interface (Figure 6).

Realization

The system described in the preceding section is realized entirely using web technologies. This allows operation on user's smartphones without an additional installation step, allowing immediate use (R1). It consists of a mobile client that is displayed on the smartphone, a public display client for the large display, and an application server. The application server handles connection of user's smartphones to the appropriate side of the large display and handles message forwarding from and to the large display.

The client-side components both use HTML5, CSS3, and JavaScript as base technologies. The mobile client is based

Figure 6: Shopping cart interface.

on jQuery mobile (including fine-grained touch event handling using JQuery touch events), with vibration feedback handled using the HTML5 vibration API. Similarily, the public display client is a jQuery-enhanced web page.

The server is written in JavaScript using node.js as base library. It is not involved in interaction, nor does it track application state. Instead, it just forwards event messages from client to client. This is realized using event-oriented realtime communication via WebSockets using socket.io.

User Feedback

As an initial validation step, we gathered qualitative user feedback from three interaction experts and four regular users. Participants were asked to perform an application walkthrough and select items to buy after an initial description of the application context. Except for one of the interaction experts, participants were not aware of the application concepts before using the system, thus simulating an actual 'walk-up-and-use' situation.

In general, participants were able to use most application features without prompting or hints. There was significant social interaction between participants, with many interaction issues solved by collaboration between the users.

Connection establishment using QR codes was not an issue. Also, gaze switches were not an issue in general, confirming the decision to keep visual feedback on the large display where possible. The use of the smartphone as a remote control was easy once understood by the participants. However, it is unfamiliar; this resulted in a short initial confusion by several participants that expected an interface to be displayed on the smartphone. The pie menu proved to be usable without issues.

Conversely, some participants viewed the mobile as completely passive control pad and were surprised to find the wish list and the shopping cart there. Once this was understood, however, interaction proceeded without issues. We also assume the required attention switch could easily be hinted at when adding items to these lists. Alternatively, a separate application mode for these lists could be activated on the public screen, deactivating the public screen for the current user and displaying an appropriate hint there.

Furthermore, the mode switch to discussion mode proved to be an issue. The function of the corresponding menu item was not obvious to all users, and the change in modes disrupted the flow of interaction. In a future version, we therefore intend to experiment significantly with the discussion mode, possibly replacing the free-form area with a list-based interface.

In summary, while there are issues in details and the discussion mode is subject to redesign, we believe that the study validates the general design, especially concerning attention switches and the pie menu.

Conclusion

In this paper, we presented a prototype multi-user multi-device system for interaction at the point of sale. By using mobile devices, users are able to save their shopping carts and revisit them at a later time, potentially preventing showrooming. The interface of the system is optimized to avoid attention switches between mobile device and large display. To do this, all information is presented on the large display where possible, switching to the mobile display only when personal data needs to be displayed. Significantly, we believe that this principle may be a good basis for interaction involving large displays and mobiles in general, since it avoids gaze switches almost entirely while allowing appropriate interaction with personal data.

Acknowledgements

We thank SALT Solutions GmbH, Dresden, Germany, for their support of this project.

REFERENCES

1. Ruby Roy Dholakia, Miao Zhao, and Nikhilesh Dholakia. 2005. Multichannel retailing: A case study of early experiences. *Journal of Interactive Marketing* 19, 2 (2005), 63–74.
2. R. Ecker, V. Broy, A. Butz, and A. De Luca. pieTouch: A Direct Touch Gesture Interface for Interacting with In-vehicle Information Systems. In *Proceedings of the 11th International Conference on Human-Computer Interaction with Mobile Devices and Services (MobileHCI '09)*. ACM, New York, NY, USA, Article 22, 10 pages.
3. S. Hillman, C. Neustaedter, C. Pang, and E. Oduor. "Shared Joy is Double Joy": The Social Practices of User Networks Within Group Shopping Sites. In *Proceedings of the SIGCHI Conference on Human Factors in Computing Systems (CHI '13)*. ACM, New York, NY, USA, 2417–2426.
4. J. Müller, F. Alt, D. Michelis, and A. Schmidt. 2010. Requirements and Design Space for Interactive Public Displays. In *Proceedings of the International Conference on Multimedia (MM '10)*. ACM, New York, NY, USA, 1285–1294.
5. U. Rashid, M. A. Nacenta, and A. Quigley. The Cost of Display Switching: A Comparison of Mobile, Large Display and Hybrid UI Configurations. In *Proceedings of the International Working Conference on Advanced Visual Interfaces (AVI '12)*. ACM, New York, NY, USA, 99–106.
6. James She, Jon Crowcroft, Hao Fu, and Flora Li. 2014. Convergence of Interactive Displays with Smart Mobile Devices for Effective Advertising: A Survey. *ACM Trans. Multimedia Comput. Commun. Appl.* 10, 2 (Feb. 2014), 17:1–17:16.
7. U. von Zadow, W. Büschel, R. Langner, and R. Dachselt. 2014. SleeD: Using a Sleeve Display to Interact with Touch-sensitive Display Walls. In *Proceedings of the Ninth ACM International Conference on Interactive Tabletops and Surfaces (ITS '14)*. ACM, New York, NY, USA, 129–138.
8. T. Yamaguchi, H. Fukushima, S. Tatsuzawa, M. Nonaka, K. Takashima, and Y. Kitamura. SWINGNAGE: Gesture-based Mobile Interactions on Distant Public Displays. In *Proceedings of the 2013 ACM International Conference on Interactive Tabletops and Surfaces (ITS '13)*. ACM, New York, NY, USA, 329–332.
9. S. Zhao, P. Dragicevic, M. Chignell, R. Balakrishnan, and P. Baudisch. Earpod: Eyes-free Menu Selection Using Touch Input and Reactive Audio Feedback. In *Proceedings of the SIGCHI Conference on Human Factors in Computing Systems (CHI '07)*. ACM, New York, NY, USA, 1395–1404.

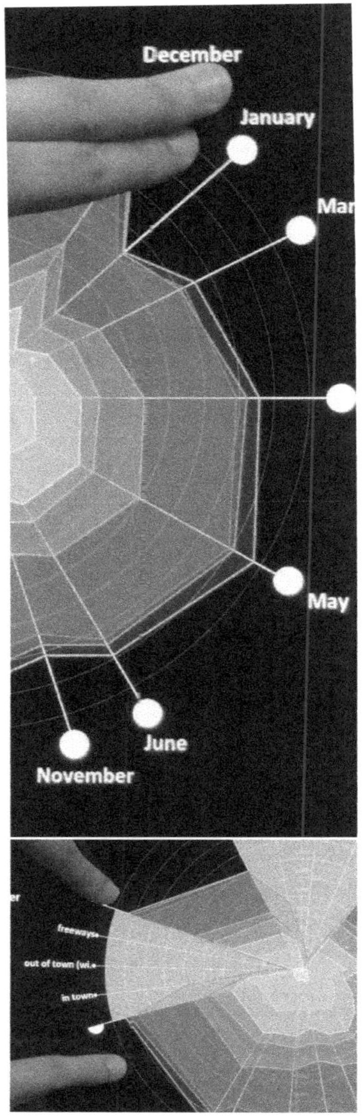

Figure 1: A multi-touch interaction concept for star plots: rearranging axes (↑ top), splitting up an axis to explore a second information layer (↓ bottom)

Towards a Fluid Interaction Concept Bringing Star Plots to Interactive Displays

Ricardo Langner
Interactive Media Lab
Technische Universität Dresden
Dresden, Germany
langner@acm.org

Tom Horak
Interactive Media Lab
Technische Universität Dresden
Dresden, Germany
horakt@acm.org

Ulrike Kister
Interactive Media Lab
Technische Universität Dresden
Dresden, Germany
ukister@acm.org

Raimund Dachselt
Interactive Media Lab
Technische Universität Dresden
Dresden, Germany
dachselt@acm.org

Christin Engel
Interactive Media Lab
Technische Universität Dresden
Dresden, Germany
christin.engel@mailbox.tu-dresden.de

ITS '15, November 15-18, 2015, Funchal, Portugal
ACM 978-1-4503-3899-8/15/11.
http://dx.doi.org/10.1145/2817721.2823505

Abstract
In this paper, we present several concepts towards fluid multi-touch interactions for an interactive star plot visualization. The goal of our research is to improve the usability of visualizations by developing new and natural interaction techniques as well as designing and applying new visualization approaches. To achieve this, we systematically create consistent touch interactions for various tasks typical to information visualizations. Furthermore, we propose a new approach to integrate additional levels of information into a star plot by splitting up axes. Finally, we have successfully implemented many of our concepts in a first prototype, allowing the validation of the usefulness and usability.

Author Keywords
Information visualization; Star plots; Multi-touch; Fluid interaction.

ACM Classification Keywords
H.5.2. [Information Interfaces and Presentation (e.g. HCI)]: User Interfaces

Introduction & Background
Combining the two research fields of *information visualization* and *natural user interfaces* is an upward trend [6]. On the one hand, the use of touch-enabled devices such as

mobile phones, tablets, or interactive tabletops is promising [1, 3, 8], since these devices have become ubiquitous in many places. Direct touch interaction can make the exploration and analysis of data more attractive to users and lower the bar for inexperienced users. On the other hand, dealing with multivariate (i.e., hypervariate) data is an important visualization challenge. Established approaches are coordinate plots such as parallel coordinate plots or star plots.

This is not the first paper addressing multi-touch interfaces for information visualization. Existing work, however, investigated different visualization techniques; a consistent set of natural interactions for star plots has not been developed. Baur et al. developed TouchWave [1] to explore touch interaction for stacked graphs. Drucker et al. [3] investigate interaction bar charts and compare a traditional desktop interface with a new touch interfaces for touch-enabled mobile devices. Sadana and Stasko [8] created an interactive scatterplot visualization for tablet computer and started exploring the design space of multi-touch interactions for visualizations. Rzeszotarski and Kittur [7] use physics-based affordances for data exploration and also compared a touch prototype for tablets with a traditional spreadsheet tool.

In our research, we investigate multi-touch interaction concepts for star plots. Star plots support the understanding of multivariate data objects as visual shapes with diverse properties (Figure 1). These shapes can be used for comparison of data using their glyph characteristics [9]. It is also possible to compare attribute values to the extremes and the distribution of values along the axis [5].

We contribute a consistent touch interface for star plots designed for interactive displays. We investigated specific mappings of touch interactions to visualization tasks, the interplay of different visualization components, and

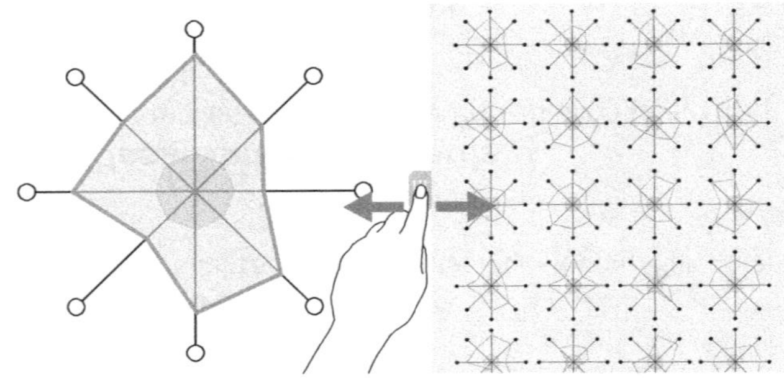

Figure 2: Interface Composition: highly interactive detail view (left), matrix view (right) showing small glyph-like star plots.

the extension of the functionality of star plots. Among others, we designed new interactions for (i) the dynamic rearrangement of one or multiple axes and (ii) the exploration of (semi-)structured data through splitting up axes.

In the following, we will first describe our process and general principles for the design of the multi-touch interface for star plots. We will thereby propose concepts extending the existing star plot technique to visualize (semi-)structured data. Finally, we briefly present our prototype implementation and present first insights.

A Multi-Touch Interface for Star Plots

In the following, we propose specific multi-touch concepts for star plots. We systematically designed solutions for various tasks typical of information visualization. Therefore, our solutions are classified following the categories of interactions identified by Yi et al. [10]: Select, Explore, Reconfigure, Encode, Abstract/Elaborate, Filter, and Connect.

We specifically focus on designing natural interactions and apply phrasing [2] for a seamless interaction style. According to the guidelines of fluid interaction [4] as well as results

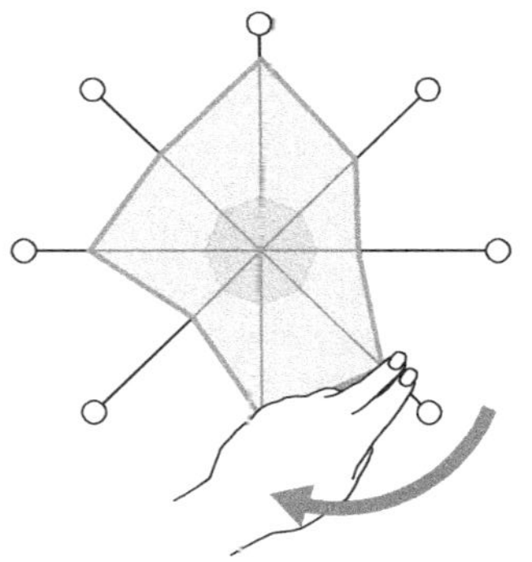

Figure 3: Axes arrangement: axes are pushed in the direction of the movement.

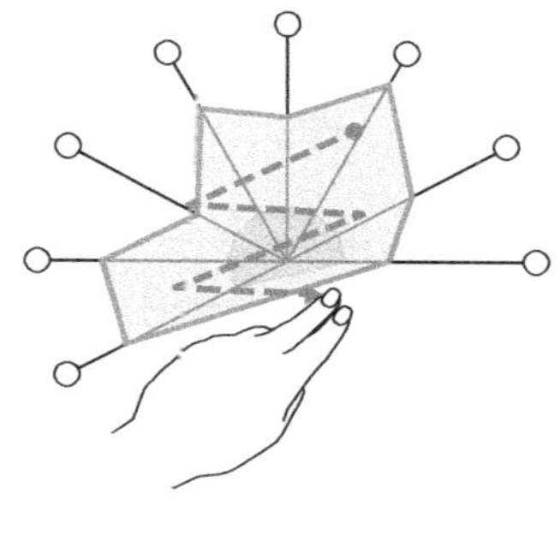

Figure 4: Wipe gesture to reset the distribution of axes.

from Drucker et al. [3], we focus on making the data and visual elements themselves interactive. We use local on-site extensions that allow direct manipulation of the visualization (e.g., interactive axes, data objects, intersections), rather than menus or separated visualization panes.

Interface Composition & General Principles
Typical of star plot visualizations, our interface consists of two major components (Figure 2): a *detail view* and a *matrix view*. The highly interactive detail view allows users to read and compare attribute values by showing one or more selected data objects in a single, large coordinate view. The matrix view is located directly beside the detail view. It shows data objects as separated, small glyph-like star plots arranged in an array. The matrix view provides an overview, gives access to individual data objects, and supports users to reveal patterns or anomalies within the data. Both views are logically linked to each other (interplay). Interacting with one of them can cause changes in the other (e.g., object selection, rearrange axes). Consequently, we expect users to focus more on the detail view than the matrix view. As some devices provide limited display space (e.g., mobile phones, tablets), the matrix view can also be hidden (i.e., by dragging it to the screen border).

Select & Explore
Many interface elements (e.g., text labels, axes, stars and their contours) can be selected by tapping on them. To inspect properties of individual objects, users select them by tapping on a star plot in the matrix view. Selected objects are highlighted in the matrix and shown in the detail view. An object can also be dragged from the matrix to the detail view. In detail view, objects (i.e., the stars) can be highlighted by tapping it or its contour.

Reading of exact attribute values in the detail view can be achieved in various ways. If a star is selected, labels

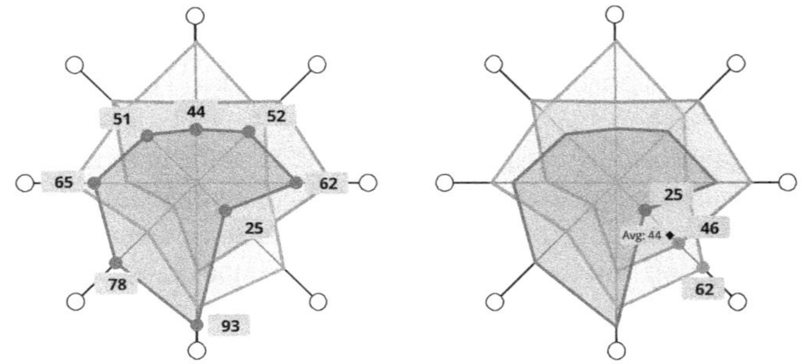

Figure 5: Attribute values of a single object (left), attribute values along a specific axis (right).

show all values of the selected star on shape-axes intersections (Figure 5, left). Tapping on an axis (selection) only shows values along the selected axis (Figure 5, right). In addition, an extra annotation on the selected axis informs about the mean value. Similar to slider and range visualization in DataMeadow [5], this could also be the distribution of objects. To explore objects and read individual values, users can touch and hold the background of the plot and start dragging. While moving the finger across the plot, a selection mark highlights the data point (object-axis intersection) closest to the position of the finger and shows the corresponding value. The selection mark automatically disappears when the finger is released.

Reconfigure
The matrix view allows users to rearrange objects. Users can manually define a specific position in the matrix by touching, holding, and then dragging a star plot. In addition, all objects can be sorted using a pre-defined attribute. If one of the axes in the detail view is selected, users can swipe downwards with two fingers to sort all data objects in a descending order. An upward swipe results in an ascending order.

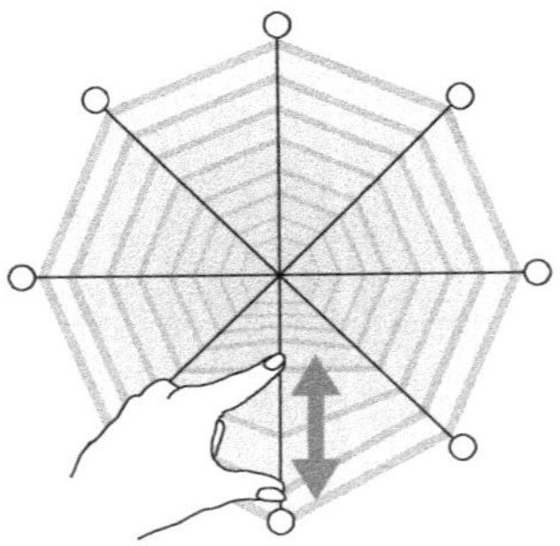

Figure 6: Fisheye distortion applied to an axis.

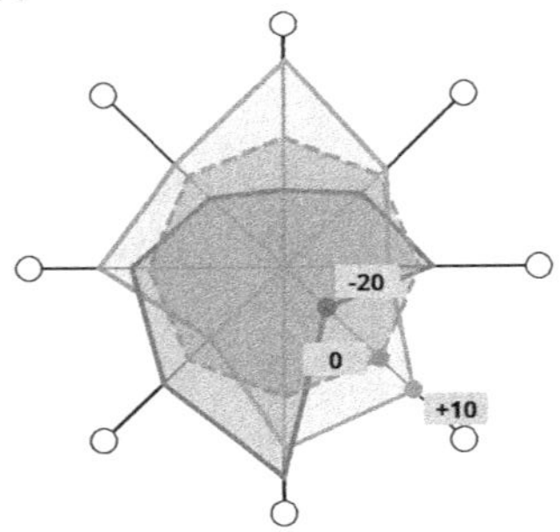

Figure 7: Relative objects presentation.

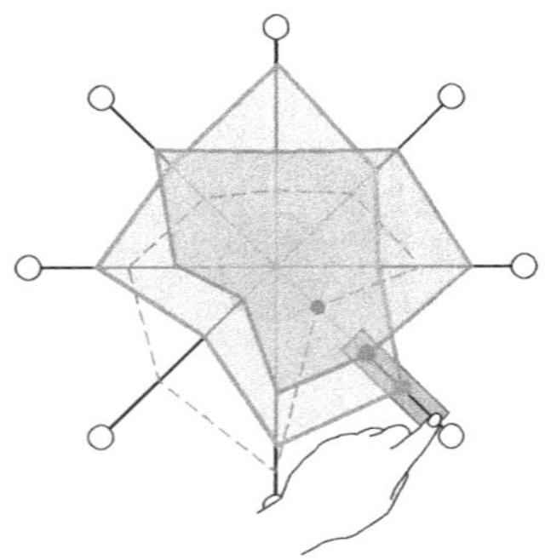

Figure 8: Filter area can be used to define a ranges.

Due to the nature of coordinate plots, the arrangement of axes is critical if users want to reveal, e.g., relations between attributes. Furthermore, the shape of a star depends on this order; and this might help to improve the identification of patterns or anomalies in the matrix view. To move a single axis, users touch and drag an axis (or a handle attached to each axis) in the detail view. Releasing the finger confirms the new position, resulting in a rearrangement and equal distribution of all axes. If two fingers are used (two finger drag), all axes are pushed in the direction of the movement (Figure 3). This creates a gap in the plot and pushes together axes. To prevent one of the axes to rearrange, its position can be locked by touching and holding it for a short time. The state of this lock mode is indicated by the handle of the axis (fill color). Wiping across the plot (Figure 4) restores the equal distribution of axes. All changes regarding the arrangement of axes in the detail view are synchronized with the matrix view. This synchronization, however, can also be deactivated by using an option button in the matrix view.

Encode

To address encoding tasks, we propose two concepts: changing the scaling of an axis and switching between absolute and relative presentation. The scaling of an axis (in the detail view) can be changed by performing a pinch gesture on it. This gesture applies a fisheye distortion to the axis (Figure 6) and allows users to zoom in and out.

Furthermore, the detail view can present objects relatively to a single selected object. Users can specify a reference object by double-tapping it. The reference object appears with a uniform shape; all remaining stars are displayed using the difference regarding the reference object (Figure 7). To switch back to an absolute presentation, users simply tap the reference object twice again (double-tap). The transition between these states makes use of smooth animations and allows users to visually follow the re-encoding.

Abstract/Elaborate

In this part, we propose a new approach for presenting (semi-)structured data with star plots. Our concept allows users to explore data at different levels in a single star plot visualization. If users double-tap the handle of an axis in the detail view, the axis (level 1) splits up and new axes appear in between (e.g., Figure 9). These sub-axes (level 2) represent attributes from another information layer. For instance, if objects represent countries (shape) defined by the number of car accidents per year (attributes, level 1 axes), than level 2 axes could represent data of various causes of accidents for the corresponding year. This approach adds the extra data points to the data objects and therefore changes the shapes of visible stars.

Filter & Connect

We propose different filter and connect interactions performed in the detail view. To modify the shape of objects users can remove axes from the plot by swiping the handle of an axis outwards (i.e., away from the center of the plot). Inspired by brushing from parallel coordinates, users can specify a range (or condition) on a specific axis in order to filter the objects presented in the matrix view. Touching and holding an axis with two fingers for a short time creates a rectangular filter area along the axis (Figure 8). This filter area is not restricted to objects shown in the detail view. It directly filters (e.g., fades out) objects outside of the range. The position of the area can be adjusted afterwards by dragging it along the axis. To change the expanse of the area users simply touch and drag the area's lower or upper border.

In contrast to the 'more permanent' filter area, users can touch and drag along an axis to temporally show objects

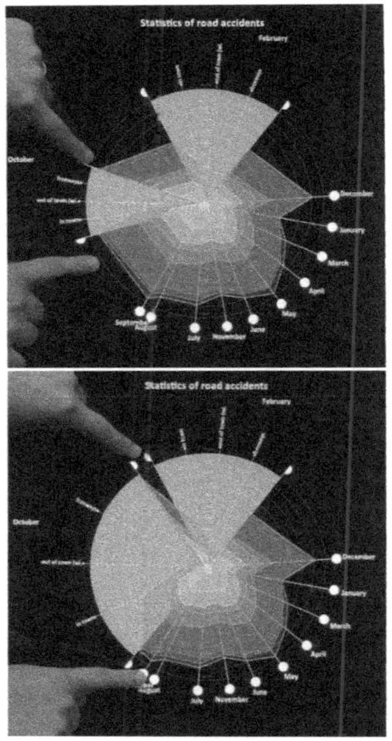

Figure 9: Increasing the area of sub-axes.

that correspond to the specified attribute value. While the detail view shows a flimsy contour of corresponding objects, the matrix clearly highlights them.

Implementation

Our prototype runs on a 27" WQHD display from Perceptive Pixel, supporting both pen and multi-touch input. It is driven by an ordinary desktop computer (i7 3.4 GHz) running Windows. User interface and visualization components are written in Python using the media-centric application framework libavg[1]. Our implementation visualizes four different data sets from Destatis[2] (the Federal Statistical Office of Germany): students, family structures, car accidents, and marriages[3].

At the moment of writing only parts of our concepts have been implemented. Focused on the detail view, our first prototype features many basic functionalities such as selecting one or multiple objects, showing and hiding specific attributes (axes), and showing specific value along axes. Furthermore, users can rearrange axes: drag a single axis as well as push multiple axes (Figure 10). Finally, we implemented our proposed concept of splitting axes (Figure 9) to further explore other levels of information.

Conclusion

We presented a systematic and consistent set of multi-touch interactions for star plot visualizations. We focused on natural and fluid touch interactions addressing several visualization tasks. In addition, we propose a new approach to present and interact with (semi-)structured data within a star plot. Finally, we successfully implemented many of our concepts in a first prototype.

[1] https://www.libavg.de/
[2] https://www.destatis.de/EN/
[3] Data codes: 21311-0006, 12211-0602, 46241-0011, 12611-0005

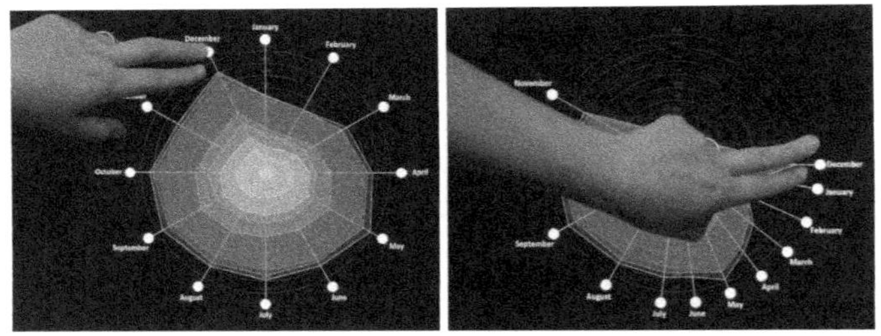

Figure 10: Moving multiple axes using a two-finger drag.

At the current point in time, there has been no formal testing. For future work, we plan to evaluate our concepts by comparing it to a traditional star plot interface and to further investigate new visual extensions for star plots. We want to implement additional concepts and enhance the prototype to better support touch-enabled devices of different size. While our concepts are specifically designed for star plots, we think some of the principles and interactions proposed in our work can be transferred to other visualization techniques.

Acknowledgements

We thank our lab students Tamara Flemisch and Philip Manja for their conceptional as well as programming assistance. We also thank our colleague Wolfgang Büschel for his continuous support. This work has partially been funded by the DFG through the project GEMS (DA 1319/3-1).

REFERENCES

1. Dominikus Baur, Bongshin Lee, and Sheelagh Carpendale. 2012. TouchWave: Kinetic Multi-touch Manipulation for Hierarchical Stacked Graphs. In *Proc. ITS 2012*. ACM, 255–264.
2. William Buxton. 1986. Chunking and Phrasing and the Design of Human-Computer Dialogues. In *Proc. IFIP*

World Computer Congress. 475–480.

3. Steven M. Drucker, Danyel Fisher, Ramik Sadana, Jessica Herron, and m.c. schraefel. 2013. TouchViz: A Case Study Comparing Two Interfaces for Data Analytics on Tablets. In *Proc. CHI 2013*. ACM, 2301–2310.
4. Niklas Elmqvist, Andrew Vande Moere, Hans-Christian Jetter, Daniel Cernea, Harald Reiterer, and T.-J. Jankun-Kelly. 2011. Fluid Interaction for Information Visualization. *Information Visualization* 10, 4 (2011), 327–340.
5. Niklas Elmqvist, John Stasko, and Philippas Tsigas. 2008. DataMeadow: A Visual Canvas for Analysis of Large-Scale Multivariate Data. *Information Visualization* 7, 1 (2008), 18–33.
6. Bongshin Lee, Petra Isenberg, Nathalie Henry Riche, and Sheelagh Carpendale. 2012. Beyond Mouse and Keyboard: Expanding Design Considerations for Information Visualization Interactions. *Visualization and Computer Graphics, IEEE Transactions on* 18, 12 (2012), 2689–2698.
7. Jeffrey M. Rzeszotarski and Aniket Kittur. 2014. Kinetica: Naturalistic Multi-touch Data Visualization. In *Proc. CHI 2014*. ACM, 897–906.
8. Ramik Sadana and John Stasko. 2014. Designing and Implementing an Interactive Scatterplot Visualization for a Tablet Computer. In *Proc. AVI 2014*. ACM, 265–272.
9. Matthew O. Ward. 2008. Multivariate Data Glyphs: Principles and Practice. In *Handbook of Data Visualization*. Springer Berlin Heidelberg, 179–198.
10. Ji Soo Yi, Youn ah Kang, J.T. Stasko, and J.A. Jacko. 2007. Toward a Deeper Understanding of the Role of Interaction in Information Visualization. *Visualization and Computer Graphics, IEEE Transactions on* 13, 6 (Nov 2007), 1224–1231.

Interaction Space of Chords on a Vertical Multi-touch Screen

Ioannis Leftheriotis
Ionian University
Tsirigoti sq. 7, Corfu, Greece
and
Norwegian University of Science and Technology
Sem Sælands cei 7-9, 7491
Trondheim, Norway.
iolef@acm.org

Michail N. Giannakos
Norwegian University of Science and Technology
Sem Sælands vei 7-9, 7491
Trondheim, Norway.
michailg@idi.ntnu.no

Konstantinos Chorianopoulos
Ionian University
Tsirigoti sq. 7, Corfu Greece.
choko@ionio.gr

Letizia Jaccheri
Norwegian University of Science and Technology
Sem Sælands vei 7-9, 7491
Trondheim, Norway.
letizia@idi.ntnu.no

ITS '15, November 15-18, 2015, Funchal, Portugal
ACM 978-1-4503-3899-8/15/11.
http://dx.doi.org/10.1145/2817721.2823506

Abstract

Despite the increasing use of Multi-Touch (MT) capable devices, novel interaction techniques need to be examined in order to swift from a single-touch WIMP interaction paradigm to a MT one.In this work, we focus on chord interaction on vertical MT screens. Chord is the simultaneous touch of more than one finger on the MT screen. Based on a user experiment with 12 users, we explore the positioning - interaction space of the chord technique, by investigating a relation among the type of the chord (number of fingers) and the position on the screen that the chord was applied. The empirical results have indicated an interaction pattern that demonstrates a significant relation between the type of the chord that was applied (number of fingers) and its position on the screen. Our results show that as the number of fingers needed for a chord increases, the nearer from the bottom left of the screen this chord is to be applied. Notably, our results give evidence of the fact that there is a threshold (five-finger-chord) beyond which the above relation is not strong.

Author Keywords

Multi-touch; chords; interaction area; interaction distance; vertical screen; action windows

ACM Classification Keywords

H.5.2. Information interfaces and presentation

INTRODUCTION

In recent years, multi-touch (MT) have become the standard way of interaction in many appliances in our daily lives. From small mobile devices to bigger MT screens using multiple fingers is almost always a key element of the interaction. In this work, we are focused on the simultaneous touch of more than one finger on the MT screen (chord interaction). Previous studies have investigated the use of chords along with the appropriate interface on larger MT surfaces. Most of the studies take advantage of the chord technique in order to help users to select things from a menu. There have been studies such as Bailly et al's [1] who investigated the Finger-Count Shortcuts or marking menus [9] and found that they perform better in menu selection, especially with expert users. Kin et al [6] proposed a finger registration technique and introduced the Palm Menus demonstrating that using finger chords has significant performance advantage. Recently, Ghomi et al. [3] introduced a method in order for the user to learn chord gesture vocabularies. Researchers have studied the mechanical constraints for finger combination and propose appropriate vocabularies. In an alternative context, Leftheriotis [7] propose a multi-touch chord password technique that allows for user authentication on MT screens. Based on the recent research on the field, it seems that chords have gained interest among interaction designers as a novel interaction technique for innovative use of MT screens. Researchers have already proposed a variety of chord interaction strategies such as directional chords [3,9], bimanual chords [6], finger combination chords or simple number-of-finger touch chord systems [4]. However, almost all studies focus on the posture of the hand and its affordances and usually compare the use of chords to other techniques (e.g. menus).

In order to further understand the chord interaction technique and support its use among developers and researchers, we explore its interaction space by trying to find whether there is a relation among the type of the chord and the position on the screen that the chord was conducted. In Nova's literature review [10], the importance of space in collaborative settings is thoroughly discussed. Erickson [2] claims that even when there are spatial constraints, activity might be generated. Since most multi-touch systems are intended for collaborative multi-user environments, the need for exploring the interaction space of chords seems apparent, especially for larger MT surfaces where interacting directly with the entire surface can be difficult for users [5]. In this research, mainly through quantitative analysis of an experimental task on educational context, we investigate whether there is a relation among the type of the chord that was conducted (number of fingers) and its position on the screen.

Our research hypothesis, based on our experience with users working with chords on MT screens, is that chords with fewer fingers will be conducted in different position patterns than the chords that demand more fingers due to complexity difference or due to comfort reasons. The results of this research can be valuable to MT developers and researchers since, if for example the increased complexity of multi-finger chords make them cumbersome for the users, then, other selection techniques should be preferred. On the other hand, if the interaction space of different chords has similarities or patterns that are being followed by the users, then this work helps us to understand them better in order to build more effectively MT interactive applications.

Methodology

Research design

We have developed a MT application supporting multi-user chord interaction in combination with personal action windows. It was developed in Python MT framework, using the chordiaction toolkit [8] and was part of a broader MT educational application dedicated to botanology.

Application Interaction Design

We developed a connect-the-dots drawing application with a focus on MT chords. The idea is simple and intuitive: Users have to apply the appropriate number of fingers in order to select the respective brush and draw inside a new action window. There are four brush types: a) thick black line, b) bold black line, c) thick colored line, d) bold colored line. Each brush has its own chord identifier in order to be selected. Since we have reserved the single touch and two touch interactions for moving action windows and pinch gesture (zoom in and zoom out of action windows), we have matched the three fingers chord to the thick black brush, the four fingers chord to the bold black brush, the five fingers chord to the thick colored brush and the six fingers chord to the bold colored brush respectively. Users used both their hands in the six fingers chord. Since there is lack of research dealing with chords from both hands in the relative literature, we wanted to explore the broader interaction space of chords.

Apparatus

In order to minimize the possibilities of something to go wrong, our experimental setup was based on a robust 27" inch all-in projective capacitive monitor with 5ms response time, which was placed vertically in front of the two seated users. The screen was connected via USB to a Windows 7 environment installed on a Mac mini hardware. There was a camera just behind them capturing their interaction strategies and patterns and the system was logging every touch of the screen.

Sampling

Twelve users participated in our study, of which two were male and ten were females. Users were 17-18 years old. All participants were right-handed so as to all feel comfortable with our interaction technique. The experiment took place during an extracurricular activity for botanology in a museum in Trondheim, Norway.

Procedure

In the exploratory phase of the application there was an educational task with one and two-finger-chord interaction so as the user get acquainted with the MT technology in general. Next, we showed the dot-to-dot - drawing application to the users and explained them how to apply the chords in order to create the action windows inside which they would draw. We let the users to understand how the system works for five to ten minutes until they would feel confident to interact.

The experimental task begins with a number of dots that represent a flower on a white background. We asked from the users to connect the dots and then draw inside the flower with the colors they wanted. There was no limit to their imagination or their time, since we wanted to investigate the interaction space of chord interaction technique. Users had to apply a chord every time they wanted to change their brush or change the color they are painting with.

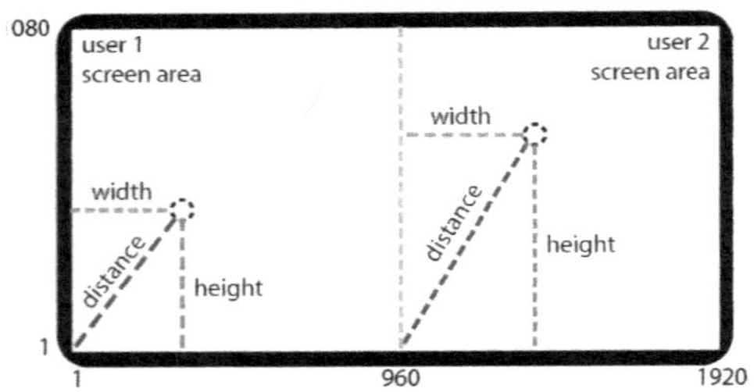

Figure 1. A representation of the MT screen showing how we calculated the Euclidean distance of every position where a chord/window was created. The measures that we used so as to explore the interaction space while two users are working with chords and windows on a 1920 x 1080 MT monitor.

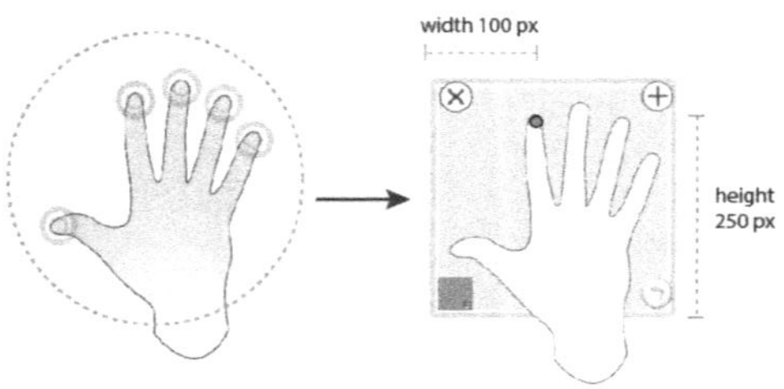

Figure 2. The chord interaction area is enabled in accordance to the pointer finger. This illustration shows the distance from the lower left corner of the (transparent) action window to be created when the appropriate chord has been formed in relation to the positioning of the pointer finger. The action window size could be changed with the pinch gesture (two fingers) and it could be moved all over the screen (one finger).

Measures and Data Analysis
The study was designed to collect both quantitative and qualitative data, including video and observation notes. The majority of the quantitative data used in the statistical tests was obtained by the log-files of the application. After the game play, users completed a paper-based survey. The survey captured users' experience with technology and in particular touch and multi-touch devices.

POSITIONING OF CHORDS/ACTION WINDOWS
The active interaction space of the screen was 1 – 1920 pixels in width and 1 – 1080 pixels in height. We had two users in each session seating side by side in front of the vertical screen. Hence, we make an assumption that chord interactions happened in the left side of the screen (1-960 pixels) belong to user one and chord interactions happened in the right side of the screen (961 - 1920 pixels) belong to user two because: a) personal territories are most often located directly in front of people [11], b) there was no need for storage or group territories [11] in our dot-to-dot drawing application and c) the personal windows that would pop-up after the appropriate chord interaction are free to move all over the screen. That is why users are supposed to articulate the chords to their most convenient spot, which reasonably would be in front of them. Having the spot where the chord was articulated, we then calculated the distance from the bottom of the screen (height) and the distance from the left side of the screen (width) (Figure 1). As such, we ended up with the exact height and width of every chord (actually the positioning of the index finger while articulating the chord). Users had to firstly touch their pointer finger so as to trigger the chord interaction technique and thus we logged the positioning of their first touch. The index finger is the most common hand gesture and it is used in more than 70% of the times a user interacts with touch screen devices. In a drawing application like ours, this percentage reaches 90% of interaction. Users' index finger was mainly used as the basis of the chord. Users were free to also include any other finger they wanted in order to form the chord they wanted. Figure 2 exhibits the positioning of the chord in relation to the action window that pops up when users articulate the chord.

We then calculated the Euclidean distance between each logged spot and the bottom left of the appropriate part screen – the left for user one and the right for user two. In order to identify any potential difference on the spot creation of 3, 5 and 6 chord windows, an independent samples t-test was conducted. Hence, we were able to compare the Euclidean distances of the respective chord type windows.

Research Findings
As it is shown in Table 1, users opened 69 chord windows in total. The mean spot was positioned in (413,544) of the screen (considering its size as 960 x 1080 pixels since it was used by two users and was divided in half). In Figure 3, there is a visualization of the average spot in which a chord was formed in order to open a window. The center of the ellipse is the average point for each chord while the major radius represents the standard deviation in x axis (width) and the minor radius the standard deviation in y axis (height). Based on Figure 3, the distance from the bottom left corner of the screen to the average center of the three-finger-chord seems greater than that of the average center of the five-finger chord or the six-finger-chord. Concerning the four-finger-chord, our

Euclidean Distance			4 finger chord (N=6)	5 finger chord (N=20)	6 finger chord (N=23)
3 finger chord mean = 779.98 SD=172.01	t-test between chords T(p)	3 finger chord (N=20)	0.62 (0.535)	**2.01 (0.049*)**	**2.19 (0.032*)**
4 finger chord mean = 730.77 SD=160.08		4 finger chord (N=6)		0.76 (0.760)	0.84 (0.404)
5 finger chord mean = 670.70 SD=171.44		5 finger chord (N=20)			0.08 (0.935)
6 finger chord mean = 674.55 SD=138.04		6 finger chord (N=23)			

*p < 0.05

Table 1. Results of a t-test between the different finger chords for the Euclidean distance from the lower left point to the point where the chord was conducted.

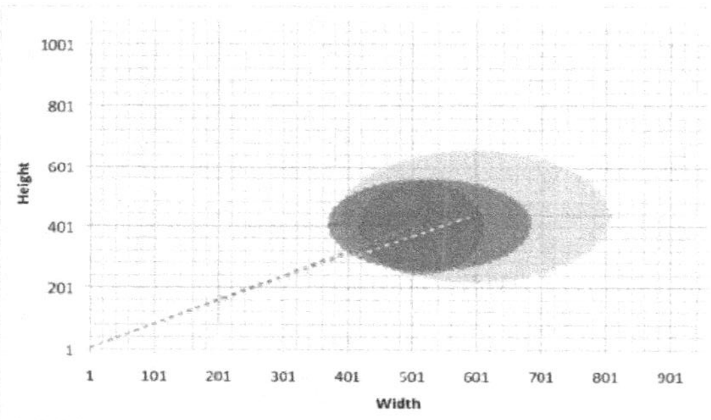

Figure 3. Three (with yellow), five (with green) and six finger chord (with orange) and their average distribution in the MT screen space.

users did not use it extensively and we decided to exclude it from our results despite the fact that it also followed the distribution of five-finger and six-finger-chord having its center in smaller distance than that of the three-finger-chord.

To examine our research hypothesis, we performed a t-test including the Euclidean distance between the bottom left of the appropriate part of the screen - (1,1) for user one and (960,1) for user two - and the position where chord interaction took place as dependent variable and the type of chord as independent. All statistical analyses reported were conducted with a significant level of 0.05. As we can see from the outcome data in Table 1, increasing the fingers of the chord from three to five or from three to six indicated a significant difference on the distance from the lower left bottom of the screen. That said, users preferred to form the three-finger chord in larger distances than when they formed the five and the six finger chord.

Discussion and conclusion

In this study, we explore the interaction space of the chord technique and relations between chord type and its position. Our results indicate that there is a significant difference between the position of the three-finger-chord articulation point and the five-finger-chord and six-finger-chord articulation point respectively (based on the Euclidean distance from the (0, 0) point of the screen). Our four-finger-chord limited interactions cannot support this result, however, it is clear from our data that the more fingers needed for the chord, the nearer from the screen edge the chord was created. In Figure 4 we show the average distances for the three, five and six finger-chord.

Interestingly, the above results contradict our initial expectations that more complex chords (e.g. those with multiple fingers) would be more easily applied in a more comfortable spot for the users – e.g. in the top right position of the screen, where their wrist posture might have been more natural. However, users preferred to interact in more central positions. Extending arm to reach far top right positions might be even more cumbersome (introducing higher level of muscle activations) for the users than articulating the chord in lower positions. As Figure 3 exhibits, users applied the most easy-to-conduct chord of our experiment (the three-finger-chord) within the largest and more centered interaction area. Our observations along with the results of this study show that users feel more comfortable to conduct the chord in larger distances. Figure 4 demonstrates the difference of the mean articulation point, which is an Euclidean distance of more than 100px, that said 10% of our screen interaction area. Considering the largest standard deviation that also occurs in the 3-finger-chords, we conclude that our initial hypothesis that there is a relation among the type of the chord that was conducted (number of fingers) and its position on the screen is valid. Furthermore, the larger deviation denotes higher degree of freedom for the user in order to articulate the chord wherever it feels more convenient for him/her. On the other hand, our results also describe an insignificant difference between the distance of five-finger-chord and six-finger-chord articulation point from the lower left position of the screen. The interaction area of the five-finger-chord seems to be a subset of that of the six-finger-chord

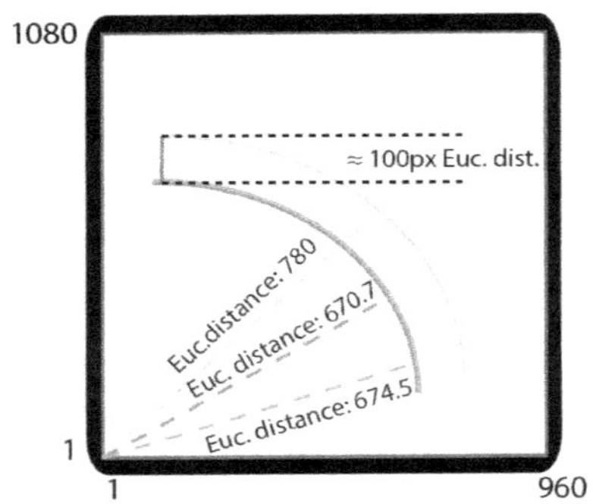

Figure 4. The average distance for three (with yellow), five (with green) and six finger chord (with orange). The difference between the average of three-finger-chord and five or six-finger chord is approximately 100px.

(Figure 3). That is why we propose that there might be a threshold in the number of fingers for a chord beyond which users respond similarly. Both five-finger-chord and six-finger-chord are very close in terms of the distance from the edge (Figure 4). Considering the limited data of the four-finger-chord that would position the four-finger-chord distance in between the three-finger-chord and five/six finger-chord, we can support further this finding.

The initial results of this study build on the potential of using chord interaction in a MT environment. We identify the differences between the diverse finger-chords and shed light on mapping user-centered design requirements for chord interactions. However, there are some limitations such as the fact that we were focused on an in-vitro drawing application with three, four, five and six finger chord options. Further research has to be done in order to make sure that our findings can be extended to apply to chords that demand more fingers. In addition, further research might be also needed in order to investigate the stress that multi-finger chords can cause to users and the connection between this and the positioning of the chords on the interaction surface.

Acknowledgements

We would like to thank Aleka Angeletaki for assisting us during the data collection and Gabriella Papastefanou for the content of our experiment. This work was partially funded by ARK4 project of the National Library of Norway and the NTNU UB.

References

[1] Bailly, G., Lecolinet, E., Guiard Y. (2010). Finger-Count & Radial-Stroke Shortcuts: Two techniques for Augmenting Linear Menus on Multi-Touch Surfaces. In Proc.of CHI '10, ACM Press.

[2] Erickson, T. (1993). From interface to interplace: The spatial environment as a medium for interaction. In Spatial Information Theory A Theoretical Basis for GIS (pp. 391-405). Springer Berlin Heidelberg.

[3] Ghomi, E., Huot, S., Bau, O., Beaudouin-Lafon, M., & Mackay, W. E. (2013). Arpège: learning multitouch chord gestures vocabularies. In Proc. of ITS'13. pp. 209-218. ACM Press.

[4] Haller, M., Brandl, P., Richter, C., Leitner, J., Seifried, T., Gokcezade, A., & Leithinger, D. (2009). Interactive displays and next-generation interfaces. pp. 433-472. Springer Berlin Heidelberg.

[5] Hawkey, K., Kellar, M., Reilly, D., Whalen, T., & Inkpen, K. M. (2005). The proximity factor: impact of distance on co-located collaboration. In Proc. of GROUP '05. (pp. 31-40). ACM Press.

[6] Kin, O., Au, C., Tai, C., (2010). Multitouch Finger Registration and Its Applications, In Proc. of OZCHI'10. ACM New York, NY, USA.

[7] Leftheriotis, I. (2013). User authentication in a multi-touch surface: a chord password system. In Proc of CHI'13 Extended Abstracts. 1725-1730. ACM.

[8] Leftheriotis, I., & Chorianopoulos, K. (2011). Multi-user chorded toolkit for multi-touch screens. In Proceedings of the 3rd ACM SIGCHI symposium on Engineering interactive computing systems. pp. 161-164). ACM.

[9] Lepinski, G. J., Grossman, T., Fitzmaurice, G. (2010). The Design and Evaluation of Multitouch Marking Menus, In Proc. of CHI '10, ACM Press. pp. 2233-2242.

[10] Nova, N. (2004). Socio-cognitive functions of space in collaborative settings: a literature review about Space, Cognition and Collaboration.

[11] Scott, S.D., Carpendale, M.S.T, & Inkpen, K.M. (2004). Territoriality in Collaborative Tabletop Workspaces. In Proc. of CSCW '04. ACM.

aWall – A Socio-Cognitive Tool for Agile Team Collaboration using Large Multi-Touch Wall Systems

Magdalena Mateescu [1]
magdalena.mateescu@fhnw.ch

Martin Kropp [2]
martin.kropp@fhnw.ch

Roger Burkhard [1]
roger.burkhard@fhnw.ch

Carmen Zahn [1]
carmen.zahn@fhnw.ch

Dario Vischi [2]
dario.vischi@fhnw.ch

[1] School of Applied Psychology
University of Applied Sciences and Arts Northwestern Switzerland
FHNW, Olten, Switzerland

[2] School of Engineering
University of Applied Sciences and Arts Northwestern Switzerland
FHNW, Windisch, Switzerland

ITS '15, November 15-18, 2015, Funchal, Portugal
ACM 978-1-4503-3899-8/15/11.
http://dx.doi.org/10.1145/2817721.2835072

Abstract
Agile methods emphasize highly interactive and close collaboration within teams and among stakeholders. Due to still missing adequate digital tools, agile teams use mostly physical artefacts like wallboards and story cards. In this paper, we present *aWall*, an agile team collaboration tool for large multi-touch wall systems. *aWall* was designed based on empirical user research using new interaction and visualization concepts to support and foster the highly collaborative and communicative agile work style. The application is based on web technology and can be used in both co-located and distributed setting. The implemented prototypes were validated with end-users in a user workshop.

Author Keywords
Agile; collaboration; communication; socio-cognitive; team; multi-touch; project management; software development; HCI; surface.

ACM Classification Keywords
H.5.2. Information interfaces and presentation (e.g., HCI): User Interfaces

Figure 1. aWall running on a 2x2 46″ Screen Wall

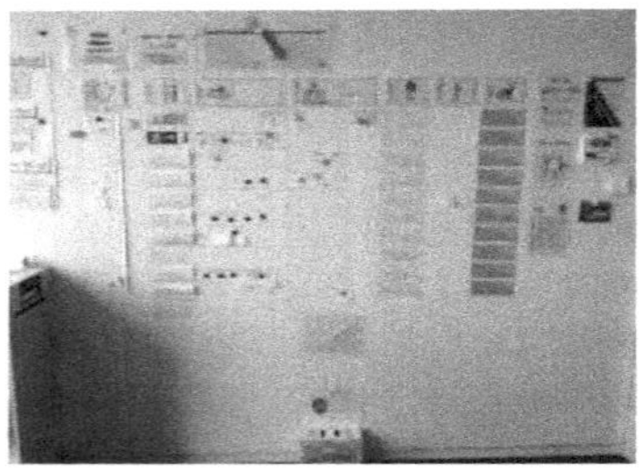

Figure 2. A physical card wall

Introduction

Large multi-user touchscreens have been shown to benefit collaborative work by supporting social interaction and group cognitive activities, are still scarce commodity. In agile software development, which became a predominant method in the IT industry in the last 10 years [8, 10], physical wallboards combined with digital tools like are still used predominantly. Such tools are crucial for agile teams, since the agile process depends on an intensive interaction, collaboration, and constant open communication among all stakeholders between team members [1]. Such intensive collaboration needs very close feedbacks loops in the sense of the Plan-Do-Check-Act (PDCA) management method [6].

Agile management tools like JIRA Agile [3], VersionOne [4] are not sufficient to support the collaborative process in agile teams. Azizyan, Magarian, and Kajko-Matsson [5] found that 31% of the interviewed companies used both project management tools and physical walls. The predominant usage of physical tools reveals their importance for teamwork. Therefore, we consider that it is necessary to deepen our understanding of the requirements for collaborative agile tools and their usage in the agile process.

User Research

We conducted in depth interviews with 44 agile practitioners in 11 companies and observed the collaborative process in four agile teams. Our results show that physical card wall (Figure 2) are valued for their extreme flexibility and light-weight, meanwhile the digital tools employed at the moment (JIRA Agile [3]) are seen as helpful for storing information on long term and being able to provide traceability. The latter are not adequate for the highly interactive agile team collaboration. Neither physical nor digital tools seem to be sufficient to support the collaborative process in agile teams.

Based on the results of this empirical study and by taking advantage of the availability of 4K-technology, we developed a concept for a socio-cognitive tool for agile collaboration for large screen-wall systems. We started implementing the concepts in the *aWall* prototype that supports agile team collaboration and fosters the agile style of work through a large multi-touch wall system (see Figure 1). *aWall* takes advantage of the 4K resolution and web technology and by that surpasses the possibilities of existing desktop tools.

Design Considerations for the Agile Wall

Based on our empirical findings in the study we explored new visualization and interaction concepts for an agile collaboration tool running on an extra-large touch wall to support the whole agile process.

Each agile meeting has specific goals, and different tools are used to achieve them. Different types of artefacts are used and modified during each meeting. During the Daily Stand-Up meeting most teamwork focuses on modifying task cards. However, we observed that during meetings teams usually need additional information (e.g. list of acceptance criteria for a task or "Definition-of-Done", "Impediment-List". They consult this information during meeting and sometimes modify it. On physical card walls this extra information is typically arranged around the main task board as shown in Figure 2. To support these two different types

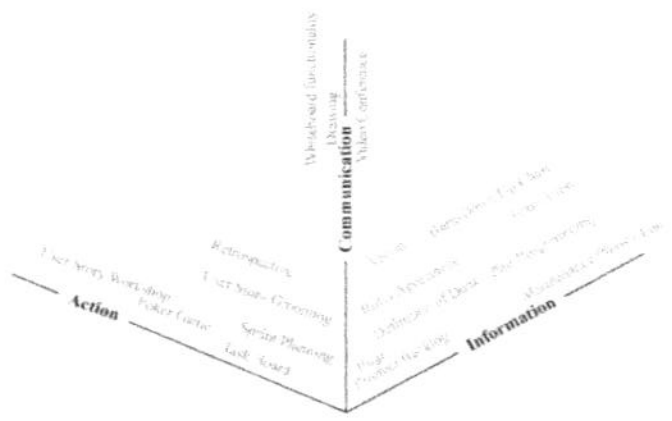

Figure 3. Agile collaboration model

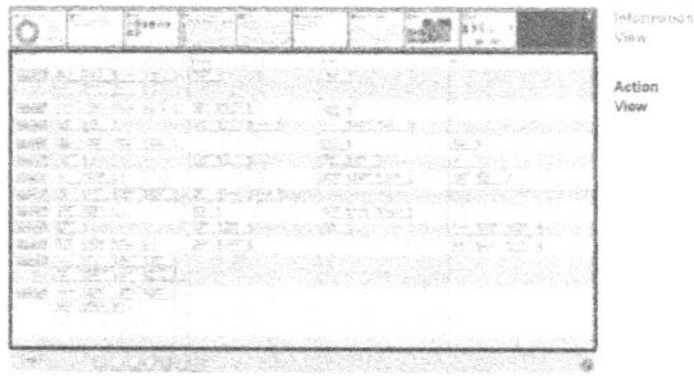

Figure 4. Action and Information View

Figure 5. Information view widgets

of information handling, we differentiate between *action* and *information views*.

We developed a general *agile collaboration model* as shown in Figure 3. The model visualizes three important aspects for agile collaboration tools: the need for tools to sustain the activity of the agile team (action dimension), the communication needs of the agile team, and third their needs to actualize information that might be distributed among team members and artefacts (information dimension). The actions and the information dimensions are represented in dedicated views, that we further call action views and respectively information views.

Agile module	Technology Affordances	Socio-cognitive functions
Action views	Represent information (e.g. create new tasks) Modify the information (e.g. move location of the task card)	Contribute directly to goal achievement. Problem solving process.
Information views	Consult information about project status, agreed norms (e.g. Definition of Done). Modify represented information (e.g. add a new impediment)	Support for team's transactional memory, distributed cognition.

Table 1. Action and Information View for Daily Standup

An *action view* is dedicated to a specific meeting and contributes directly to the main goal. Actions views have been carefully designed to sustain most interactions that need to be performed during a specific meeting. The *information view* provides extra information needed for a meeting, and by that contributes indirectly to goal achievement. Information views represent team's transactional memory. Any memory system needs to allow for change. Therefore, the information represented in these views can be manipulation at any time. Table 1 provides an overview of their technological affordances and socio-cognitive functions.

Design Concepts

Based on the aforementioned requirements and agile collaboration model, we derived the following design guidelines.

Size Matters

Digital walls replacing a physical wall system need to be at least comparable in size with physical walls. They need to provide enough space to display all project relevant information. To embody there design concept built a multi-touch multiuser system consisting of four 46" 4k high-resolution screens with a 12-point multi-touch infrared frame from pqlabs (see Figure 1). The touch wall is 2.05m width and 1.25m height.

Direct Interaction

Manipulation of information on the wall should remain visible to support team awareness. Team members' movement toward the wall increases team awareness. Several interaction technics have been proposed for large displays, like manipulation from afar, direct touch, or visual interaction [9]. However, we consider direct touch to better support the collaborative work.

Support Action and Information View

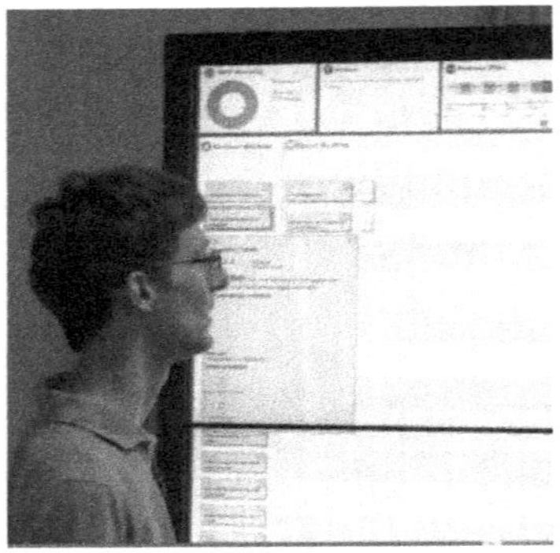

Figure 6. Scaled up User Story

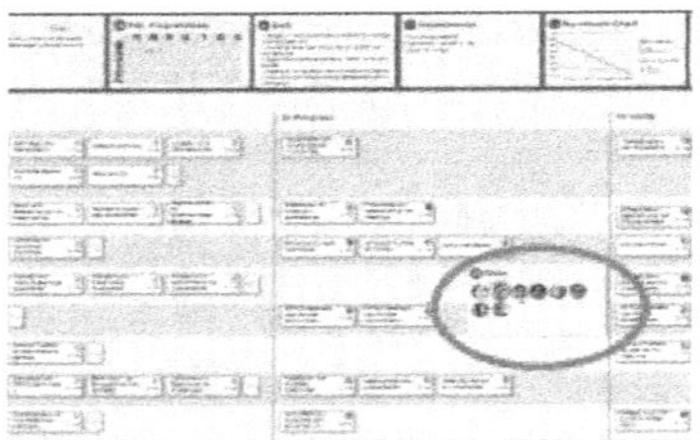

Figure 7. Task board with floating team view

Derived from our agile collaboration model, we divide the layout of the screen into an action-view area and an information-view area. Figure 4 illustrates the basic design for the Daily Stand Up meeting. The **action views** are at the core of the *aWall* application. They provide an optimized view and access to information that is going to be manipulated during meetings. All information can be directly and quickly accessed and edited, new information can be added and existing information can be easily deleted. **Information views** (e.g. Timer, Burn-Down Charts, Team View) represent the teams' transactional memory encoding information about project status, norms and rules - Figure 5. They display the information in small, customized widgets and respond to the transparency and availability of information requirements. These widgets provide context-dependent information during outside team meetings and act as an information radiator.

Scalability of Information
While it usually suffices for the team to see the title of a card to know what it stands for, this does not diminish the importance of being able to easily display more or less information as needed. To enable this the user can modify scale any widget, task card or Use Story to change the amount of shown information by just dragging the frames of the widget as shown in Figure 6 illustrates this principle for the User Story card.

Accessibility with Floating widgets
Widgets can be dragged out of the information view and placed anywhere on the action view. They facilitate easy access to information and enable the team to reposition information near other relevant information and thus creating favorable conditions for team cognition. For example, the team widget can be moved on the action view, to easily drag-and-drop team members onto the task card (Figure 7).

Support the Collaborative Process not only its Result
Most agile management tools sustain remarkably well the product of the agile planning, but fail to sustain the collaborative process. Following our agile collaboration model, the *aWall* provides dedicated views for all typical agile meetings like Daily Stand Up (Task Board), Sprint Planning 1 and 2, User Story Workshop, Poker Game (a cooperative effort estimation method), Retrospective, and User Story Grooming and by that sustains the collaborative process in itself. The user can easily navigate between meetings by choosing a different meeting at the bottom of the *aWall* as shown in Figure 8.

The Digital Realm as Transactional Memory
Through the extra information displayed in the information view, *aWall* acts as a teams' external memory and sustains awareness of information both intra- and inter-team.

Configurability of Functionality
Different meetings require specific information. Therefore, the information view needs to be configurable, so that the user can choose only those widgets they deem necessary. Therefore, the *aWall's* information view can be easily adapted to team needs.

Information at your finger tip
All relevant information should be available instantaneously; therefore we decided to avoid menu trees or lists. The only menu in the system is the bottom level menu used to select the desired meeting

Figure 8. Meeting navigation

Figure 9. The Fun and Avatar widgets

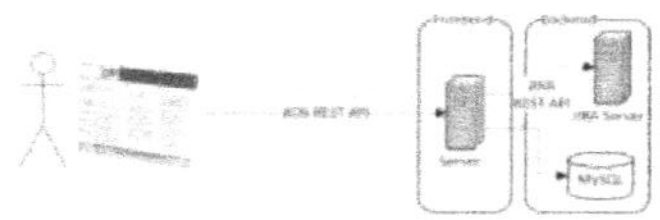

Figure 10. *aWall* System Architecture

as shown in Figure 8. All other information is available through the action views and information views.

Simple and Homogenous layout
It is important that users can easily orient themselves, find information easily and in a constant way especially when it comes to large screens. Thus, throughout the whole system the overall layout of the screen is into three parts, the information view, the action view and the main menu at the bottom as shown in Figure 4.

Foster agile values
Our observations have shown that agile teams often add additional information to the boards that is not necessarily related to the project but contributes to team building and team spirit. For example they often add private information e.g. holiday greeting cards or childbirths. The *aWall* supports this behavior by providing appropriate information widgets as shown Figure 9.

Multi-Device Interaction
While large multi-touch walls perfectly meet team collaboration need to make interaction with information not only possible but also visible to other team members, they are less adequate for data input with keyboards or handwriting, like entering user story descriptions. Therefore, we are striving to implement simultaneous interaction with the information on the board by means of tablets; for example, to enter new task cards in the Sprint Planning 2 meeting.

Prototype System Architecture
The application is developed as a three-tier Web application as shown in Figure 10. Web technology supports very well the collaborative process in distributed teams; no local installation is required; it offers better user interface design capabilities with CSS. An important feature is the connection to third-party issue tracking systems like the JIRA [3]. Many organizations use such tools in their workflow [5] and therefore we can avoid disruption in team process.

Evaluation in User Workshops
We conducted two user workshops with 11 agile practitioners to validate our design. The participants considered it to be very usable and emphasized that such a system may be able to support the collaborative agile workstyle and process very well.

Size Aspects and Display of Information
The participants valued the large size of the wall especially for the fact that it supports real team collaboration as with large wallboards. They mentioned the potential risk that some elements might be out of reach for smaller people. The general concept of larger titles was well accepted. Cards were seen by some participants as being too small. It must be very simple show enlarge the font to be readable from the distance. The participants valued the team view, but requested to have more information integrated into it, like also showing the absence of team members. Offering tags and avatars as well as the fun widget was positively seen as bringing emotions onto the board.

Flexibility and Adaptability
The need for flexibility and customization became evident in the interviews. For example, our time boxing widget which asks for a moderator, allow to run with or without an assigned moderator. The flexibility in the way a meeting is conducted was also positively rated, especially when it comes to the Retrospective Meeting

that sometimes might prove strenuous. Not having to use different media or application was rated positive: e.g. during the Daily Stand-Up meeting the new status of the tasks gets immediately updated in the agile project management tool (JIRA), during the Planning meeting, the user stories can be visualized in the application. The usage of colors for different types of user stories was suggested to increase readability (for example, to distinguish between technical cards, bug reports, user requirement)

Discussion and Future Work

In this paper we presented a user interaction concept for a collaborative agile wall application for agile software development teams. It was designed and evaluated in close collaboration with eleven IT companies. *aWall* is unique in that it is designed for large multi-touch wall systems and to explicitly address fostering the agile work style. We have presented the various underlying concepts and the so far implemented prototype together. Using Web technology for these kind of application is a path. However touch and especially multi-touch support and gesture recognition for the web is very evolving. New frameworks steadily appear, and browser support is still limited. Our future work will focus on developing further concepts to improve and foster collaboration using large wall systems. This includes concepts for interaction with other devices, concepts for recommender and buddy systems, and better support for distributed collaboration. The very promising feedback from the evaluation makes us believe that the large *aWall* system can be the tools to foster agile collaboration in teams by combining the strengths of the physical and digital tools in one system.

References

1. *Agile Manifesto*. Retrieved May 18, 2015 from http://agilemanifesto.org/
2. Apoorve Chokshi, Teddy Seyed, Francisco Marinho Rodrigues, Frank Maurer. ePlan Multi-Surface: A Multi-Surface Environment for Emergency Response Planning Exercises. In *Proceedings of the Ninth ACM International Conference on Interactive Tabletops and Surfaces* (ITS '14). pp 219-228.
3. *Atlassion. JIRA Viewed 24.6.2015. https://www.atlassian.com*
4. *Version One. Viewed 24.6.15. http://www.versionone.com/*
5. Azizyan, G., Magarian, M. K., & Kajko-Matsson, M. (2011). Survey of agile tool usage and needs. IEEE Xplore, 29-38.
6. Deming, W. E. Out of the Crisis. The MIT Press. ISBN-13: 978-0262541152. 2000
7. interact.js Accessed at 25.6.2015. http://interactjs.io/
8. Kropp, M., Meier, A., Swiss Agile Study - Einsatz und Nutzen von Agilen Methoden in der Schweiz (German). Retrieved May 18, 2015 from www.swissagilestudy.ch.
9. Nacenta, M. A., Pinelle, D., Gutwin, C., & Mandryk, R. (2010). Individual and group support in tabletop interaction techniques. In C. Müller-Tomfelde, J. Karat, & J. Vanderdonckt (Eds.), Tabletops - horizontal interactive displays (pp. 303-333). Springer London
10. Version One. State of Agile Development Survey results. Retrieved May 18, 2015 from http://www.versionone.com/state_of_agile_development_survey/11/

Hi Robot: Evaluating RoboTale

Aleksander Krzywinski
Department of Information Science and Media Studies
University of Bergen
Aleksander.krzywinski@infomedia.uib.no

Weiqin Chen
Department of Computer Science
Oslo and Akershus University College of Applied Sciences
Weiqin.chen@hioa.no

Abstract
This paper presents the evaluation of the RoboTale game of interactive storytelling for children. The evaluation assess the usability of tangibles for robot control; their role in the storytelling; and the collaboration among the participating children. In the evaluation 21 children told stories with RoboTale in groups of three. The subsequent evaluation revealed surprisingly creative uses of the tangible markers available to the children, and the collaboration in the telling of stories showed great potential for learning.

ITS '15, November 15-18, 2015, Funchal, Portugal
ACM 978-1-4503-3899-8/15/11.
http://dx.doi.org/10.1145/2817721.2823507

Figure 1 The robot used in RoboTale

Author Keywords
Tangible interfaces; Human Robot Interaction; Table-top computing; Storytelling.

ACM Classification Keywords
H.5.3. Collaborative computing

Introduction
Tangible User Interfaces (TUIs) bridge the gap between the virtual and the physical world by allowing users to grasp, feel and displace real objects to interact with an application [4]. In RoboTale[5] the robot (Figure 1) and the markers used to control it are physical objects, and can thus be picked up and manipulated intuitively by the children. Tabletop computing is an interaction platform for collaboration [2], learning [8] and game playing. The large horizontal surface allows users to interact naturally, share virtual and physical objects and gesture, all while affording face-to-face social activity amongst users.

There has been little research looking at collaborative storytelling on a TUI. It is important to understand how children experience this. In this paper we present an assessment of how children use the game RoboTale to collaboratively create a story revolving around a robot protagonist using a TUI.

Research Question
RoboTale is based on RoboTable [6] and the core game concepts and design is described in [5] allowing for storytelling in accordance to Campbell's monomyth

Objectives
O1: What usability issues concerns the use of tangibles to control a robot on a tabletop?

O2: How are the tangibles used to tell stories about the robot?

O3: How does the children collaborate to create the stories?

structure [3]. The robot in the game is controlled by a set of tangible markers that either push the robot away (Figure 3); pull the robot towards it (Figure 2); or path the robot around it. The assessment of RoboTale has been guided by the following research question:

How do school children collaboratively create a story using tangibles controlling the robot protagonist on a tabletop?

To answer this research question it has been broken down to several specialized research objectives that are addressed individually (see sidebar). To meet these objectives we conducted an evaluation to assess RoboTale as a storytelling platform for school children. The evaluation was designed as a series of sessions where groups of children were invited to tell a story using RoboTale. The evaluation is based on both observations and semi-structured interviews of the children.

Evaluation

The subjects
The subjects were 21 children aged 8-9 from the same class in the same school, and two of their teachers. The children were split into groups of three by the teachers, giving a total of 7 evaluation sessions. The teachers were instructed to include at least one girl and one boy in each group, but were otherwise free to choose the group composition at their own discretion.

Procedure
The sessions were conducted following the same nine steps, and as each session had to fit the time frame of one school class, all the groups were told to tell the story of the robot's first day in a new school.

Introduction and presentation: In this step the facilitators presented themselves to the children and the children were asked for their names and ages.

Quick tutorial of robot control and table: The children were shown the robot, and how the push and pull tangibles worked.

Brainstorming of characters and/or backdrops: The children came up with ideas for other characters or backdrops the story would include.

Distribution of the drawing tasks: As the characters and backdrops were decided, the task of drawing was divided amongst the children in the group.

Drawing the characters and/or backdrops: The children sat at the conference table drawing their allotted characters or backdrops.

Story presentation: The children gathered around the interactive table with the robot and one of the children started to tell the story. The other children joined at their own discretion until the time was up.

Introduction of weather effects: We introduced the weather effects last and observed how the children used these disruptive tangibles towards the end of their story.

Play around with the story elements: We allowed the children to play around with the tangibles and robot to let them unwind and experiment with the technology.

Debriefing and interview: The children were debriefed on their experiences and interview them on their

Step	Time
Introduction and presentation	2 min
Quick turorial	3 min
Brainstorming of characters etc.	3 min
Distribution of drawing tasks	1 min
Drawing the characters etc.	10 min
Story presentation	15 min
Introduction of weather effects	1 min
Play around with story elements	5 min
Debriefing and interview	5 min

Table 1: Evaluation steps

perception of the robot, interface or other aspects of the game.

Methods

In the user study two different methods were employed to assess RoboTale in accordance with the aims of the three objectives. Observation was the primary method for judging how the children used the tangibles; controlled the robot; and to assess collaboration and the tangibles use in story telling. The activity was recorded with two cameras and written notes of situations; remarks; and events that might not be observable in the video recordings were taken. Secondly, the session participants were debriefed together at the conclusion of each session in a semi-structured interview process. The age of the subjects disfavoured a more strict method, and the children were allowed to associate freely from the questions asked by the interviewer. The prepared questions focused on interaction, usability and fun factor.

Analysis and findings

O1: Tangible control

The first objective regards the usability of the tangible-based control of the robot and story elements. The tangibles signified push or pull-commands, backdrop changes or weather effects, and the successful employment of these is imperative to the effectiveness with which the players may tell their stories. The functionality of the push and pull markers were easily comprehended by the children. Generally it took only a few seconds of experimentation before the control scheme was understood.

R5: Aha, it turns with this and comes ahead with that (on push and pull markers respectively)

For some participants it was apparently easier to control the robot by pushing it away, rather than pulling it to the desired spot, as this offered more continuous control and immediate feedback.

R15: (uses push) Ah, yes. It controls the robot (chases the robot with the marker)

Several participants seemingly projected some kind of free will or intelligence on the robot based on how it reacted to the markers – even if it was apparent that the robot simply moved towards or away from the pull/push tangibles. This was most evident in the cases where the participants started to talk to the robot, like they would call a dog or a cat.

R8: (places a pull marker, robot starts moving) Hello, do you want to play? I am [unintelligible]. Come to me (moves the pull marker closer)

In other situations, they would use a push marker and chase the robot away from themselves.

R1: I'm hunting you (moves a push-marker behind the robot)

In both situations the participant related to the robot as if its action granted it with an emergent intelligence – a likely consequence of human's natural inclination to attribute causality to observed events.

From these results it is evident that the simplicity of the control system allowed the participants to quickly grasp the basic strategy for controlling the robot. Most of the problems concerning the manoeuvring of the robot with

Figure 2 Illustration of the push-behaviour. When a pull-marker was placed or moved on the playing surface, the robot started moving toward the position of the marker.

Figure 3 Illustration of the push-behaviour. A push-marker would make the robot move away from it until the robot was a predetermined distance away from the marker.

tangibles were due to the inaccuracy of the robot itself, and not a conceptual problem with the control scheme.

O2: Tangibles in the story
Objective two attempts to explore how the participants used the tangibles to tell their story. The tangibles had three different uses: robot movement control, backdrop swaps and weather effects [5].

When representing story elements, tangibles as characters were by far the most popular choice. Only one item pull marker was created, and even that is questionable as the item was a teddy bear that subsequently were attributed several life-like qualities in the stories.

In the sessions where the tangibles represented story elements the pull and push tangibles were respectively given traits corresponding to positive or negative relationships to the robot. The girlfriend was popular:

R9: That is not the girlfriend (points to the push marker). That is the girlfriend (points to the pull marker).

And the evil/angry teacher was featured as a push marker:

R8: Hey stupid robot! Get out of the way. Go away! (moves evil teacher marker). I am chasing you ha ha ha!

The action was not limited to the robot and the relationship to the characters on the table however, as the characters sometimes had interplay outside of the main scene. Sometimes these acts had significant impact on the story.

R3: [The girlfriend] was stolen.

T1: Was she kidnapped?

R3: By Dumbo (points to marker)

The stories sometimes escalated and became rather brutal, with the characters murdering each other at the conclusion of the narrative. To symbolize death, and thus the inability of that character to influence the robot any more, the tangibles were usually removed from the screen, but one boy had a different idea:

R6: Then comes professor Sneezehill [...] then they fight, and then he dies (flips the marker)

The flipping obviously made the marker symbol invisible to the tracking software, and thus the tangible were effectively not a part of the interaction any more.

In the debriefing this particular function (i.e. tangibles that does not influence the robot or other aspects of the game) was explicitly requested.

R6: Is it possible to have [a marker] that is completely empty, that doesn't mean anything?

Sometimes the robot was moved around using a pull tangible without regard for the relevance of the movement to the story. Seemingly, in those cases, the movement of the robot signified that something was happening, but the pattern of movement was not related to the story or anecdote told.

O3: Story collaboration

Tabletop interaction is claimed to be a suitable vessel for collaboration [1,2,7] and objective 3 seeks to investigate how children participate to tell a story in RoboTale, thus we have focused on inter-player interactions that change or impact the narrative as well as situations where the children help each other to complete a task.

The size of the table (120 cm x 100 cm) required the participant controlling a tangible to sometimes request the aid of other participants better situated to complete a certain action.

R6: Can you take this? (R6 does reach over the entire table, and needs help from R4 to complete the robots trek)

In the previous example the closest player used the requested marker, but it was a more frequent occurrence that the requester wanted to put the marker on the screen – probably due to the effect of placing markers being some of the fun of the game.

R14: But suddenly it started to, ... can you (R15) give me that (points to a weather marker) ... to ... (places rain) ... rain. Lots of rain. (pushes the robot) Then he left. Now he had no one to play with

Naturally, as is expected with a collaborative story, the players did not always have corresponding opinions on the relationships or emotions of the characters.

R3: You! Now he will like it. Look! (places a robotgirl pull marker) Aww, he is in love (laughs)

R1: No, he is not in love! (puts on rain and thunder)

R2: It is beautiful; they are about to kiss in the rain.

As a consequence of the collaborative, undirected and real time creation of the narrative, the final stories were at best disordered and wandering. A common narrative pattern was a patchwork of anecdotes that shared some of the same characters in different situations, and occasionally the game assets were used to tell completely unrelated tales.

R2: (places pull marker) There was a man who went out, he had to pee. He didn't have a toilet. And it flashed (thunder) No Jesus, why did you have to take a picture while I was peeing?

One participant even found the opportunity to reflect on the situation and projected his own task of telling a story on the robot.

R11: First he goes to the blackboard and writes something, because the teacher told him to write a story. [...]

Concluding Remarks

The use of tangibles in the human robot interaction that happens in RoboTale is the core of research objective 1. The tangibles provide a simple and intuitive interface for interacting with the robot. It is important that the different tangibles are easy to distinguish and that the consequences of their use are immediate and obvious. The lack of minute precision with the robot control was surprisingly a problem, as the robot both had an off-centre pivot point and lacked the ability to reverse. Higher precision of manoeuvring and more detailed movement control could alleviate the time spent fine-tuning the positioning and possibly allow for more storytelling and collaboration.

The story is the core product players create when playing RoboTale. It is presented live, and therefore it is imperative that the robot control offers sufficient expressive power to support the narrative the players want to tell. This is the core problem addressed by research objective 2.

As shown in the evaluation, the participants explain the actions of the robot in terms of love, affection, hate, fear and similar emotions. Thus it is observed that the narrative tools necessary to create a compelling story are present. However, the instruments afforded by the game to direct the events of the story were found insufficient. This is most evident by the creative ways the participants broke the constraints of the interface.By flipping makers, balancing tangibles and creating temporary characters for the abstract controllers the players displayed a need to expand the tool set of RoboTale. Especially interesting was the observation that control was easier with the abstract controllers, but there was a desire for having the robot interact directly with characters.

RoboTale is a game for the tabletop and thus well suited for collaboration. The players face each other, can share resources and interact socially with ease. Objective 3 concerns the collaborative storytelling with the robot. The evaluation show that players playing RoboTale interact to a high degree, helping each other with control and passing tangibles, and most of all they tell the story of the robot together. They provide the spectator with an insight into what they imagine are going through the pretended mind of the robot. Often these images are in conflict, forcing the children to agree on a common plot or be forever locked in a struggle over the intentions and desires of the robot.

References

[1] Ananny, M. Supporting children's collaborative authoring: practicing written literacy while composing oral texts. International Society of the Learning Sciences (2002).

[2] Buisine, S., Besacier, G., Aoussat, A., and Vernier, F. How do interactive tabletop systems influence collaboration? *Computers in Human Behavior*, (2012).

[3] Campbell, J. *The Hero with a Thousand Faces*. Pantheon Books, New York, 2008.

[4] Ishii, H. Tangible bits: beyond pixels. *Second International Conference on Tangible and Embedded Interaction*, (2008).

[5] Krzywinski, A. and Chen, W. The Robot's Journey: Designing Robotale - a Table-top Storytelling Game For Children. (2012), 1–7.

[6] Krzywinski, A., Mi, H., Chen, W., and Sugimoto, M. RoboTable: a tabletop framework for tangible interaction with robots in a mixed reality. ACM Request Permissions (2009).

[7] Potvin, B., Swindells, C., and Tory, M. Comparing horizontal and vertical surfaces for a collaborative design task. *Advances in Human-Computer Interaction*, (2012).

[8] Rick, J. and Marshall, P. Beyond one-size-fits-all: How interactive tabletops support collaborative learning. (2011).

Marker-free Object Recognition on Tabletops: An Exploratory Study

Frédéric Rayar
Laboratoire Informatique
Université François Rabelais
Tours, France
frederic.rayar@univ-tours.fr

Armand Renaudeau
Polytech Tours
Université François Rabelais
Tours, France
renaudeau@etu.univ-tours.fr

ITS '15, November 15-18, 2015, Funchal, Portugal
ACM 978-1-4503-3899-8/15/11.
http://dx.doi.org/10.1145/2817721.2823508

Abstract

In the last decade, object recognition placed on tabletop has been advertised as a near future ability on next generation tabletops by several major information technology companies. Markers-based recognition seems the straightforward solution, but one can easily understand that this may not be a lasting solution for real word scenarios. In this paper, we study the marker-free object recognition ability of a commonly used tabletop. This tabletop does not rely on external cameras and thus fits perfectly a future connected house scenario. A proof-of-concept system has been developed and experimented on various objects. Based on this study, we raise some conclusions and perspectives on both software and hardware levels.

ACM Classification Keywords

H.5.2 [Information interfaces and presentation (e.g., HCI)]: User interfaces.

Author Keywords

Tabletop; Object Recognition; Marker-free

Introduction

Since almost ten years, major information technology companies release videos of near future life. The imagine scenario in everyday life [2] and various fields, such as retail, banking, manufacturing, health or productivity. This near future, designed for the next decade, often presents tabletops and surfaces as commons piece of furniture integrated in homes or offices. People will be able to interact with them only by placing various objects on them.

The objects are mostly electronic devices (smatphones, tablets), but also more common objects such as keys, books, food. For the former category, connected objects paradigm solves the communication issue with protocol such as NFC, Bluetooth, or Wifi. For the latter, computer vision techniques can be used. We address the latter category in this study. Two approaches have been proposed: markers-based or marker-free objects recognition. A marker is a two-dimensional pattern that can carry information and label object, *e.g.* barcode used in the industry, QRCodes or fiducial markers. Such markers can be recognized in a camera feed and a system can deduce the related objects.

The marker-free approach is based on computer vision techniques that recognized the objects themselves instead of the markers. We focus the study on this second approach. Indeed, while marker object recognition can be a straightforward solution for usage such as tabletop games, scenarios such as cooking table, or daily life objects recognition call for marker-free object recognition.

In this paper, we propose to perform a study on marker-free object recognition on a commonly used tabletop in the HCI community. State-of-the-art image-based object recognition techniques will be used to evaluate the performance of the tabletop on this specific task.

Related work

To the best of our knowledge, the object recognition on tabletop for non connected objects has not been widely studied.

The first paradigm that can be found in the literature is the use of external cameras pointing at the tabletop. The camera recognize objects placed on the tabletop and communicate the result of the recognition task. It is then up to the tabletop to display digital content. Image-based object recognition [5] is a well studied task in computer vision and machine learning communities. It has application in several field such as robotics or surveillance. This solution may work well, but the idea of external cameras all around the house might be an issue to inhabitants.

The second paradigm is camera-aware tabletops. Here the vision ability is embed within the tabletop itself. Several propositions have been made: first, usage of a camera underneath the table and eventually a projector to display digital content. For instance the Lumisight table [6]. Second, is the use of infrared lights and sensors, as in the Samsung SUR40 [1]. The infrared allows the tabletop to have a raw image of the objects placed on it. With this solution, the table can be open in the bottom (*i.e.* a table top and its legs). This latter approach seems a better fit for the use of several tabletops in homes.

In this paper, we study the recognition performance of the Samsung SUR40, without the usage of any external devices in the tabletop vicinity.

Prototype

Objects description

Each object has to be described by visual descriptors. One can found several types of such descriptor in the

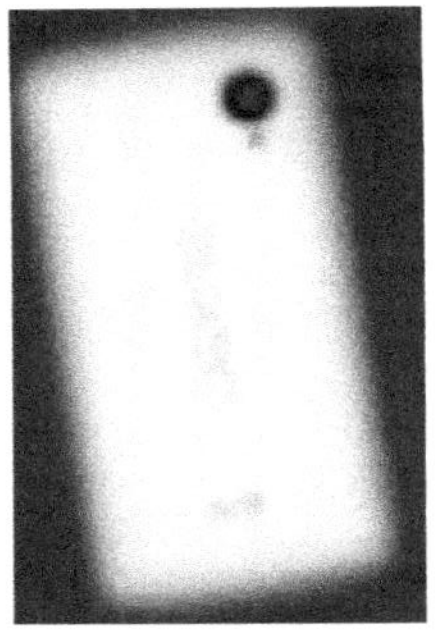

Figure 1: Raw image of a white smartphone obtained with the PixelSense.

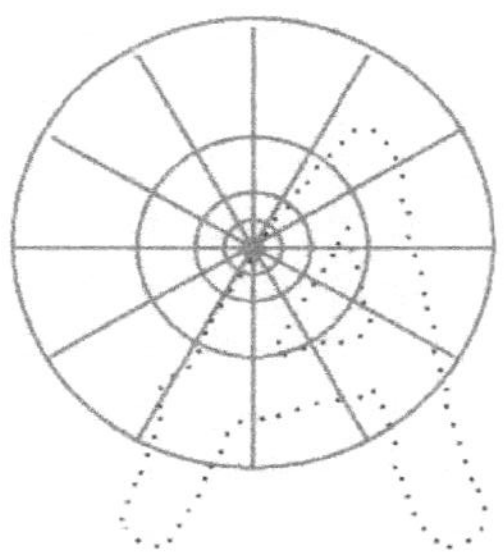

Figure 2: Shape context illustration.

literature, such as colors, textures or shapes. In our first experiments, SURF descriptors [3] have been used, but led to bad recognition rate. This is mainly due to the quality of the images obtained by the PixelSense 1. To fit the type and quality of our images, we have selected a shape based descriptor, namely Shape Context descriptor [4].

Shape context descriptor aims at capturing the relative distribution of points relatively to each point on the shape. It is computed as follows: *(i)* a set of point in the shape is extracted, *(ii)* for each point, a target is centered and the number of points in each cells is computed, *(iii)* the descriptor vector is computed using the previously computed histograms. Figure 2 illustrates the idea behind shape context. The matching between two shape context descriptors is done using a bipartite graph matching problem [4].

Objects recognition
We use here a classic supervised learning workflow (see Figure 3). First, the training phase is performed. A set of labeled objects to be recognized has been selected. These objects have been placed on the tabletop, and the relevant images have been obtained. Then, shape context descriptors have been computed (feature extraction) for each images, and stored in a database.

When a new object is placed on the tabletop (prediction phase), its shape context is computed, and matches against the database one. Using a nearest-neighbour classifier, the system find the most probable class of the new object: the object is recognized. If the matching does not have a good confidence rate, the system can conclude that the object have not been learnt.

As the complexity of finding the nearest match in the database is high (in $O(n^3)$), we have added a simple dimensions based filter to reduce the number of shape context descriptor comparisons. Thus, we can perform real-time recognition of objects.

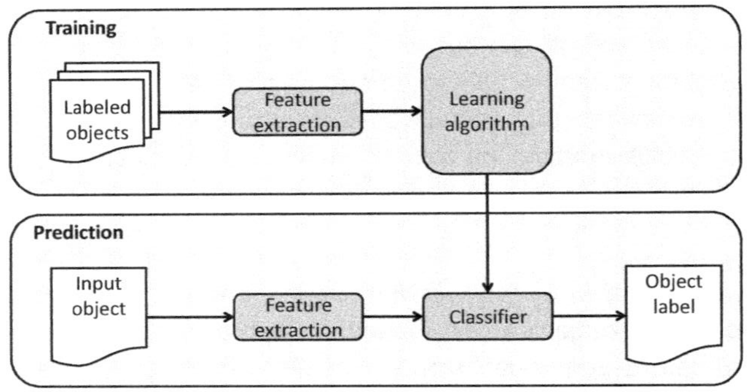

Figure 3: Supervised learning workflow.

Interface
An application has been developed on the PixelSense tabletop using C# language. Figure 4 illustrates the interface of the application, where four objects are recognised. The application can recognise as set of learned objects. When an object is correctly not recognised, the application allows the user to add it in the database. An administrator interface allows to validate or not the proposed new objects.

Experimental study
Seven distinct objects have been selected to assess the recognition capabilities: a 50 cent euro coin, our institute student card, our institute booklet, a business card, a rubber, a ruler and a white smartphone.

We have used the custom administrator interface to make the system learn these objects.

	Coin	Student card	Booklet	Business card	Rubber	Ruler	Smartphone
Recognised	20	20	20	16	18	19	19
Not recognised	0	0	0	0	2	1	1
Wrongly recognised	0	0	0	4	0	0	0
Recognition rate	**100%**	**100%**	**100%**	**80%**	**90%**	**95%**	**95%**

Table 1: Recognition rate of the seven selected objects.

Recognition rate
Each object has been placed 20 times. Table 1 shows the recognition rate obtained for the seven selected objects.

The system gives an average recognition of 94%, which is promising. Nevertheless, we have to put things into perspective: indeed, most of the selected objects have discriminant shapes. When this is not the case, the system may wrongly recognise some objects. For instance, the student card and the business card have more or less the same shape. That is why the business card has been wrongly recognised as a student card four times. This is due to a property of the shape context descriptor: it is invariant to scale and minor deformation. This phenomenon has been verified during a scenario where different coins (1,2,5,10,20,50 cent euro coins) have been used as objects to be recognised. The system failed most of the times by wrongly recognising another coin.

Recognition time
Another aspect that has to be experimented is the time that the system takes to recognise a given object. We have measured the amount of times taken by each of the following steps of our workflow: *(i)* image processing, *(ii)* dimensions based pruning, *(iii)* shape context descriptors matching and *(iv)* interface update. Table 2 presents the results of this experiment. One can see that the recognition could be done is a few seconds in average. This is relevant for proof-of-concept purpose. Nevertheless, even with some pruning based on the dimensions, the shape context matching step is still costly. Thus, the question of the relevance of the shape context descriptor raises with regards to the time computation.

Conclusion
In this paper, we have presented an exploratory study on the object recognition ability of tabletops, that have been sold as a near future ability on next generation tabletops. We focused our study on camera-aware tabletop that do not rely on external cameras, since they fit well a future connected house scenario.

An application has been developed as a proof-of-concept. It obtains relevant recognition rate for medium sized objects that have discriminant shapes. But due to the features selected to describe an object, wring recognition can easily happen. Nevertheless, the recognition times obtained in the experiments is promising for real time recognition.

Based on this study, one can wonder about the possibility to improve such a system with better image processing and machine learning methods. Nevertheless, we also wonder about the possibility to conceive an innovative hardware solutions that will provide a good trade-off

	Coin	Student card	Booklet	Business card	Rubber	Ruler	Smartphone
Image processing	0	0	0	0	1	0	0
Dimensions pruning	0	0	0	0	1	0	0
Shape context matching	0	3	1	2	4	2	1
Interface update	0	0	0	0	1	0	0
Total	**0**	**3**	**1**	**2**	**4**	**2**	**1**

Table 2: Recognition times of the seven selected objects (in second).

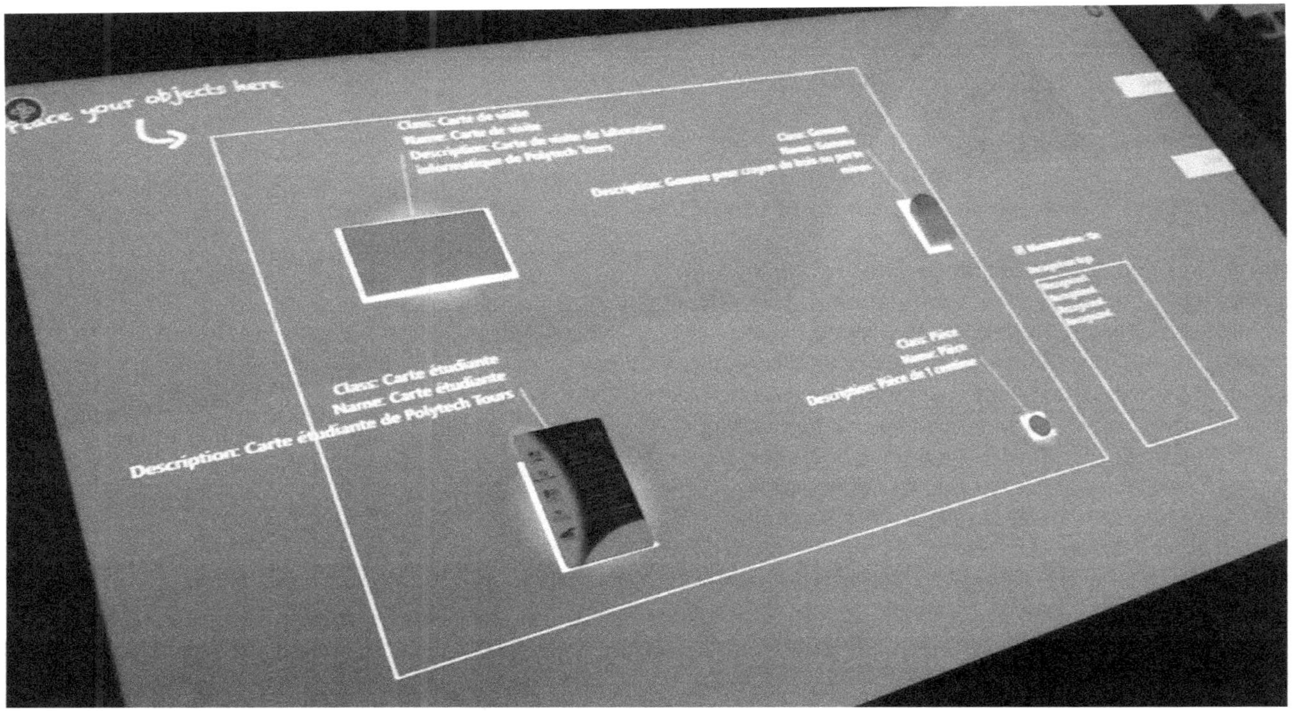

Figure 4: Interface of the tabletop application. Four objects have been placed and correctly recognised.

between the design simplicity, the robustness and the recognition performance.

Future works will try to handle real case scenarios such as the recognition of different coins (helpful for elders) or different student cards (registered collaborative work).

Acknowledgments

The authors wish to thank Ping Xiang for her work on the first prototype, and Pr. Jean-Yves Ramel for his guidance on this work. This work would not have been possible without the hardware provided by Polytech'Tours.

References

[1] Microsoft PixelSense. `https://www.microsoft.com/en-us/pixelsense/pixelsense.aspx`, 2011.

[2] Welcome To The Future. `https://www.youtube.com/watch?v=XyIvSIYOMTM`, 2014.

[3] Bay, H., Tuytelaars, T., and Van Gool, L. Surf: Speeded up robust features. In *Computer Vision ECCV 2006*, vol. 3951 of *Lecture Notes in Computer Science*. Springer Berlin Heidelberg, 2006, 404–417.

[4] Belongie, S., Malik, J., and Puzicha, J. Shape matching and object recognition using shape contexts. *Pattern Analysis and Machine Intelligence, IEEE Transactions on 24*, 4 (Apr 2002), 509–522.

[5] Jain, R., Kasturi, R., and Schunck, B. G. *Machine Vision*. McGraw-Hill, Inc., New York, NY, USA, 1995.

[6] Kakehi, Y., Iida, M., Naemura, T., Shirai, Y., Matsushita, M., and Ohguro, T. Lumisight table: an interactive view-dependent tabletop display. *Computer Graphics and Applications, IEEE 25*, 1 (Jan 2005), 48–53.

Towards Collaborative Modeling of Business Processes on Large Interactive Touch Display Walls

Alexander Nolte
Ruhr-University of Bochum
Bochum, Germany
nolte@iaw.rub.de

Ross Brown
Erik Poppe
Queensland University of Technology
Brisbane, Australia
r.brown@qut.edu.au
erik.poppe@qut.edu.au

Craig Anslow
Middlesex University
London, United Kingdom
c.anslow@mdx.ac.uk

ITS 2015, November 15–18, 2015, Funchal/Madeira, Portugal.
ACM 978-1-4503-3899-8/15/11.
http://dx.doi.org/10.1145/2817721.2823509

Abstract
Analyzing and redesigning business processes is a complex task, which requires the collaboration of multiple actors. Current approaches focus on workshops where process stakeholders together with modeling experts create a graphical visualization of a process in a model. Within these workshops, stakeholders are mostly limited to verbal contributions, which are integrated into a process model by a modeling expert using traditional input devices. This limitation negatively affects the collaboration outcome and also the perception of the collaboration itself. In order to overcome this problem we created *CubeBPM* – a system that allows groups of actors to interact with process models through a touch based interface on a large interactive touch display wall. Using this system for collaborative modeling, we expect to provide a more effective collaboration environment thus improving modeling performance and collaboration.

Author Keywords
Large interactive touch display wall; touch interface; process modeling; collaborative modeling

ACM Classification Keywords
H.5.2. User Interfaces: Interaction Styles

Figure 1. CubeBPM - Example of three actors simultaneously creating business process models.

Introduction

Business process models serve a variety of purposes within organizations. They are used to document processes, analyze them, identify means for improvement or serve as training material for new employees [5]. Analyzing processes in order to visualize them using graphical modeling notations is a complex task especially if the task allocation between several roles has to be represented as well as the usage of technical resources. It is thus reasonable to draft models collaboratively involving process stakeholders and domain experts alike [14,18]. Collaboration between them usually takes place within facilitated workshops in which actors verbally contribute their perspective on a process [7]. Contributions are discussed among the group, translated into a modeling notation and integrated into a process model by a scribe [18] with the discussion being led by a facilitator.

While workshop based approaches are reasonable to allow for actors to exchange perspectives, their effectiveness is often questioned [3]. Approaches like the one described before are time consuming and include long idle times for many actors as only one person may contribute at the same time while the others have to wait for their turn [8]. Furthermore researchers found that limiting actors to verbal contributions results in reduced identification with the outcome of a modeling workshop and also in reduced buy-in when processes are later brought into practice [6,20]. Recent research also revealed the necessity for different modes of collaboration such as break out groups especially when processes have to be redesigned or newly designed [8].

We developed the *CubeBPM* system to allow for actors to directly manipulate process models thus providing direct access to process models and process modeling. CubeBPM allows multiple actors to draft models collaboratively using a large interactive touch display wall (c.f. Figure 1). However while there is a lot of research on interaction techniques on touch surfaces such as smartphones, tablets, or tabletops there is a gap when it comes to analyzing and supporting collaboration on large interactive touch display walls. We attempt to explore how collaborative process modeling can be supported by using CubeBPM on a large interactive touch display wall which provides actors with a gesture based interface that can be used by multiple actors in parallel. We used a set of gestures in order to allow for actors to learn how to use CubeBPM as quickly as possible. These gestures are based upon suggestions by Kolb et al. [10]. By allowing actors to directly interact with process models using a touch based interface we expect to increase the effectiveness of modeling workshops. We also expect the possibility to directly interact with models to influence the way actors collaborate.

The main contribution of this poster thus is to propose a system, which allows multiple actors to collaborate on process models through a touch based interface on a large interactive touch display wall. This means taking established interaction touch techniques to a new real world scenario (collaborative process modeling) as well as expanding on knowledge about how actors collaborate on large interactive touch display walls.

Related work

Modeling (business) processes is a complex activity. The complexity can partly be attributed to the complexity of the process that has to be depicted in a model [5]. Part of the complexity of modeling however also stems from the requirement to use a graphical modeling notation such as BPMN [13]. Modeling notations consist of a number of graphical symbols that represent aspects of a process such as activities that are conducted, actors that carry out those activities and resources that are used. A syntax describes rules on how these graphical symbols or elements can be combined together in order to form a syntactically correct model. Learning how to use a modeling notation to represent a real world process can be considered a challenging task [15].

In collaborative modeling workshops the translation of real world phenomena into constructs of a modeling notation is typically done by modeling experts. Collaboration thus only happens verbally with no direct influence of actors on displayed materials. CubeBPM aims at allowing for stakeholders to take a more active role by enabling them to directly manipulate models with only minimal interference by modeling experts. Recent research provides indications that stakeholders indeed are capable of collaborating on simple process models in a self-directed way [12,19]. CubeBPM builds on this research.

Figure 2. Example image of a menu instantiated at the location of the actor.

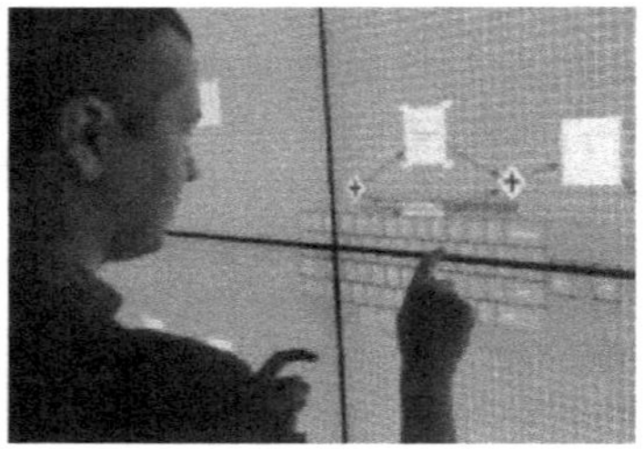

Figure 3. Example of a simulated virtual keyboard interface.

Figure 4. Item connection gesture example (arrow added for emphasis).

Adding to the complexity of model creating, modeling tools are mainly built with the requirements of modeling experts in mind. They are thus hardly usable for lay modelers [14]. Interactive tabletops and walls can provide lay modelers with an easy to use possibility to manipulate process models as they provide a direct means of interacting with the displayed material [4].

Collaboration with tabletops has been explored extensively including territoriality [21], coupling and arrangement strategies [22], and papers that stem from these studies. There has been limited work, however, exploring collaboration with large interactive touch display walls. Rittenbruch [16] explored collaboration on the QUT Cube but did not focus on a specific domain. Some researchers have focused on software development on interactive surfaces including Calico [11] for informal sketches on interactive whiteboards, AugIR [9] for business processes on interactive whiteboards, TouchRam [1] for aspect models on vertical touch displays, and SourceVis [2] for visualizing software artifacts on tabletops. None of these tools, however, have focused on large high-resolution touch walls or business process modeling.

CubeBPM

CubeBPM is a business process modeling tool that supports collaborative modeling on large interactive touch display walls. CubeBPM implements the majority of the control perspective BPMN[1] grammar including: swim lanes to represent actors in processes, gateways to represent decision points, activities, and event types [13]. CubeBPM was developed using C# and OpenGL. To demonstrate CubeBPM we use a large single integrated screen[2]. The tool however is able to run on large segmented displays via the use of synchronized and networked hardware accelerated OpenGL rendering contexts, to produce a highly scalable solution to cover large wall display systems such as those found at the QUT Cube [17].

Utilizing touch event interfaces offered in Windows, gesture recognition and concurrent multi-user interactions were devised and derived from previous research into the use of gestures on tablets for process modeling [10]. As an outcome, we created a system that allows multiple actors to work on the same model at the same time, facilitating group collaboration (c.f. Figure 1). Modifications to single-user tabletop interfaces such as the ones proposed by Kolb [10] were devised in order to support large-scale collaborative modeling. For brevity's sake only key interactions and gestures are listed subsequently. CubeBPM offers location-based flexible menus that provide actors with basic modeling functions at disparate locations. These menus are accessible via double tapping (c.f. Figure 2). In order to create an element actors have to select the elements they want to create and drag the element out of the menu to the screen. After such a drag interaction, the menu remains on screen for a prescribed time interval, within which the menu can be used again, otherwise the menu disappears and has to be reopened again by double tapping. In order to enter element labels, it is possible to use a simulated virtual keyboard on the screen. This keyboard can be accessed by double tapping on an element description (c.f. Figure 3). Like the aforementioned menu it is also possible to open multiple keyboards in parallel thus

1 http://www.bpmn.org/

2 See CubeBPM demo video: https://youtu.be/OuEHsL9vCR8

Figure 5. Example of an item delete crossing gesture (arrows added for emphasis).

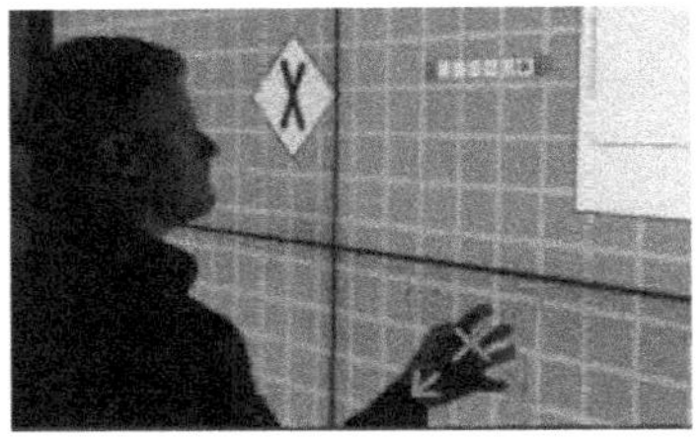

Figure 6. Example of diagram five finger scaling gesture. Fingers are moving outward, enlarging the scale of whole diagram (arrows added for emphasis).

Figure 7. Example of undo/redo circular gesture, showing circular feedback path of gesture.

allowing for multiple actors to alter element labels at the same time. Diagram elements (events, activities and gateways) can be connected with a two-finger drag gesture between two items. In order to create a connection actors have to place one finger on an element and drag another finger to the element that they want to connect the first element with (c.f. Figure 4). Elements can be deleted via a single finger cross over the item to be deleted (c.f. Figure 5). The crossing point of the touch gesture serves as a reference for the element that is to be deleted. We also included a touch gesture that allows actors to scale the diagram via a two finger expanding stretch gesture (c.f. Figure 6). Finally, we included an undo gesture to facilitate reversal of modeling operations. Touching and winding in an anti-clockwise direction performs an undo, a clockwise direction executes a redo (c.f. Figure 7). It should however be noted that undo and redo work on a global rather than an individual level. It could thus be possible to undo actions by others using this gesture. Furthermore it is necessary to state that both zooming and undo potentially interfere with actions of other actors. Implementing control mechanisms that prevent these global interactions from interfering with interactions of others is one of our priorities when it comes to future development.

Summary

We created the CubeBPM system that allows multiple actors to directly interact with a process model on large interactive touch display walls. The goal of this system is to create an environment in which actors can collaborate on process models thus improving modeling performance and collaboration. Currently we are in the process of conducting a study during which groups of four actors collaboratively develop a model of a process they are familiar with. By video recording the subsequent modeling sessions we hope to gain insights into how large interactive touch display walls affect collaboration outcomes (process models) as well as the collaboration itself.

Acknowledgments

This project is partially funded through Project VALCRI, European Commission Grant Agreement No. FP7-IP-608142. We also acknowledge the financial assistance of the Institute for Future Environments (IFE) at QUT.

References

[1] Abed, W. Al, Bonnet, V., Schöttle, M., Yildirim, E., Alam, O., and Kienzle, J. TouchRAM: A multitouch-enabled tool for aspect-oriented software design. In *Software Language Engineering*. Springer, 2013, 275–285.

[2] Anslow, C., Marshall, S., Noble, J., and Biddle, R. Sourcevis: Collaborative software visualization for co-located environments. *Proceedings of VISSOFT*, IEEE (2013), 1–10.

[3] Bostrom, R.P., Anson, R., and Clawson, V.K. Group facilitation and group support systems. In *Group support systems: New perspectives*. Macmillan, 1993, 146–168.

[4] Döweling, S., Tahiri, T., Schmidt, B., Nolte, A., and Khalilbeigi, M. Collaborative Business Process Modeling on Interactive Tabletops. *Proceedings of ECIS*, (2013), 1–7.

[5] Dumas, M., La Rosa, M., Mendling, J., and Reijers, H.A. *Fundamentals of Business Process Management.* Springer, 2013.

[6] Hengst, M. den. Collaborative Modeling of Processes: What Facilitation Support Does a

Group Need? *Proceedings of AMCIS 2005*, (2005), 73–80.

[7] Herrmann, T. Systems Design with the Socio-Technical Walkthrough. In *Handbook of Research on Socio-Technical Design and Social Networking Systems*. Hershey, 2009, 336–351.

[8] Herrmann, T. and Nolte, A. Combining Collaborative Modeling with Collaborative Creativity for Process Design. *In Proceedings of COOP*, Springer International Publishing (2014), 377–392.

[9] Kleffmann, M., Hesenius, M., and Gruhn, V. Connecting UI and business processes in a collaborative sketching environment. *Proceedings of EICS*, ACM (2015), 200–205.

[10] Kolb, J., Rudner, B., and Reichert, M. Gesture-Based Process Modeling Using Multi-Touch Devices. In *International Journal of Information System Modeling and Design 4*, 4 (2013), 48–69.

[11] Mangano, N., LaToza, T.D., Petre, M., and van der Hoek, A. Supporting informal design with interactive whiteboards. *Proceedings of CHI*, ACM (2014), 331–340.

[12] Nolte, A. and Prilla, M. Normal users cooperating on process models: Is it possible at all? *Proceedings of CRIWG 2012,* Springer (2012), 57–72.

[13] OMG. *Business Process Modeling Notation (BPMN) Specification.* Object Management Group, 2006.

[14] Prilla, M., Nolte, A., Herrmann, T., Kolfschoten, G., and Lukosch, S. Collaborative Usage and Development of Models: State of the Art, Challenges and Opportunities. In *International Journal of e-Collaboration. Special issue on "Collaborative usage and development of models" 9*, 4 (2013), 1–16.

[15] Recker, J. Continued use of process modeling grammars: the impact of individual difference factors. In *European Journal of Information Systems 19*, 1 (2010), 76–92.

[16] Rittenbruch, M. Supporting Collaboration on Very Large-Scale Interactive Wall Surfaces. *Computer Supported Cooperative Work (CSCW) 24*, 2-3 (2015), 121–147.

[17] Rittenbruch, M., Sorensen, A., Donovan, J., Polson, D., Docherty, M., and Jones, J. The Cube: A Very Large-scale Interactive Engagement Space. *Proceedings of ITS*, ACM (2013), 1–10.

[18] Rittgen, P. Collaborative Modeling: Roles, Activities and Team Organization. In *International Journal of Information System Modeling and Design (IJISMD) 1*, 3 (2010), 1–19.

[19] Rittgen, P. End-User Involvement and Team Factors in Business Process Modeling. *Proceedings of HICSS*, (2012), 180–189.

[20] Rouwette, E.A.J.A., Vennix, J.A.M., and Mullekom, T. Group model building effectiveness: a review of assessment studies. In *System Dynamics Review 18*, 1 (2002), 5–45.

[21] Scott, S.D., Carpendale, M.S.T., and Inkpen, K.M. Territoriality in collaborative tabletop workspaces. *In Proceedings of CSCW*, ACM (2004), 294–303.

[22] Tang, A., Tory, M., Po, B., Neumann, P., and Carpendale, S. Collaborative coupling over tabletop displays. *Proceedings of CHI*, ACM (2006), 1181–1190.

A TUI Platform for your Desktop

Felix Raymond
Immersion, Bordeaux, France
felix.raymond@immersion.fr

Loic Semelle
Immersion, Bordeaux, France
loic.semelle@immersion.fr

Mathieu Courtois
Immersion, Bordeaux, France
mathieu.courtois@immersion.fr

Cedric Kervegant
Immersion, Bordeaux, France
cedric.kervegant@immersion.fr

Delphine Graeff
Immersion, Bordeaux, France
delphine.graeff@immersion.fr

Julien Castet
Immersion, Bordeaux, France
julien.castet@immersion.fr

JB de la Rivière
Immersion, Bordeaux, France
jb.delariviere@immersion.fr

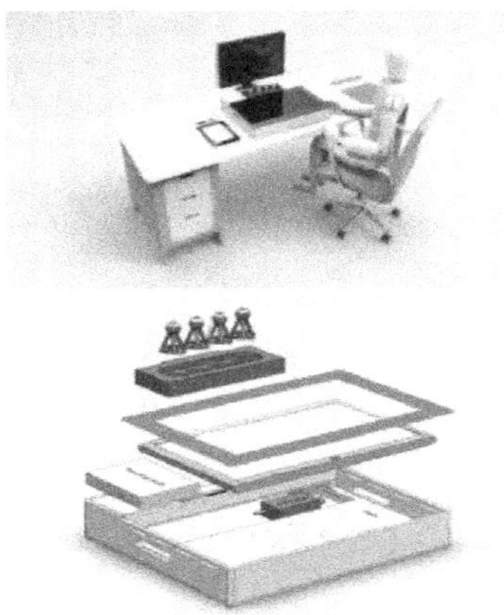

Figure 1: 1st prototype of MAGELLAN platform with their tangible objects designed by Immersion

ITS 2015, November 15–18, 2015, Funchal/Madeira, Portugal.
ACM 978-1-4503-3899-8/15/11.
http://dx.doi.org/10.1145/2817721.28234

Abstract
This sample paper describes the prototype of a TUI platform designed for non-expert that suggests to use tangible stamps as User Interface. This concept offers a process in order to print its own stamps regarding the need.

Author Keywords
Tangible User Interface; Interaction; Design tool.

ACM Classification Keywords
H.5.2 User Interfaces (D.2.2, H.1.2, I.3.6)

Introduction
Authoring complex content is a challenging task in terms of human-computer interaction. Location-based interactive experiences represent one of the most complex forms of interactive content requiring authors to manipulate a large number of complex IT concepts. Tangibles User Interfaces are exploring object-centric ways for people to interact with advanced computing paradigms using familiar gestures. Thus the authoring process should come naturally while novices are interacting with the technology. They represent a promising approach to providing users with intuitive means to author complex content without requiring extensive technical skills or training.

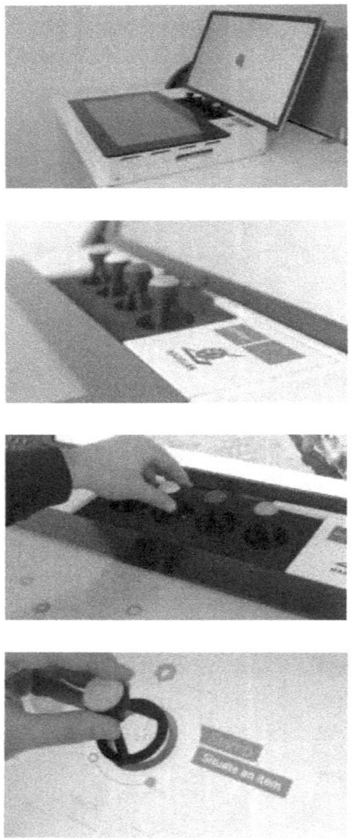

Figure 2: The Tangible User Interface is based on "stamp" metaphor.

The TUI platform

Regarding this objective, Immersion explored since one year tangible solutions to provide this proof of concept (Figure 1). This one will be integrated with an authoring professional software during the second year, but for now, this contribution consists in demonstrating capabilities of such a device in the google map environment.

This all-in-one low-cost prototype is based on projected capacitive multi-touch screen ensuring good touch experience. It can be connected with a second screen in order to enlarge the display area or with tangible devices in order to edit digital content. Indeed, the prototype provides 4 essential features thanks 4 tangible objects allowing users to copy, paste, erase, measure, and navigate on a map. All these objects have been designed regarding a common metaphor: the "stamp" (Figure 1). These objects have been specially though to enhance precision by deleting various occultation issues. Thanks to a 3D printing and coding process, Immersion provides solution allowing users to create their own tangible interfaces to suit specific requirements.

Technical challenge

From technical point of view, most of TUI platforms are either based on video capture either based on capacitive touchscreen. The video tracking solution is really flexible and allows experts to prototype new concepts. For example, a simple camera enables the tracking of QRcode. Unfortunately, this solution is sensitive to light and occlusion. These prototypes are incompatible with working area and hard to manage, from an ergonomic point of view, without going through the camera's range. In contrast, the tracking based on capacitive surfaces is more robust and operational. It is composed of technologies that we are using every day. By using capacitive touchscreen, the solution offers also a combination of high-quality touch and tangible interface. But, one of its limits was to be compatible only with metal objects. This contribution is all-in-one system based on a pending patent using 3D painting in order to produce their own tangible objects for capacitive touchscreen. This contribution is not only a proof of concept for designing geo-localized game, this is mainly the introduction of process allowing to create his own tangible interface.

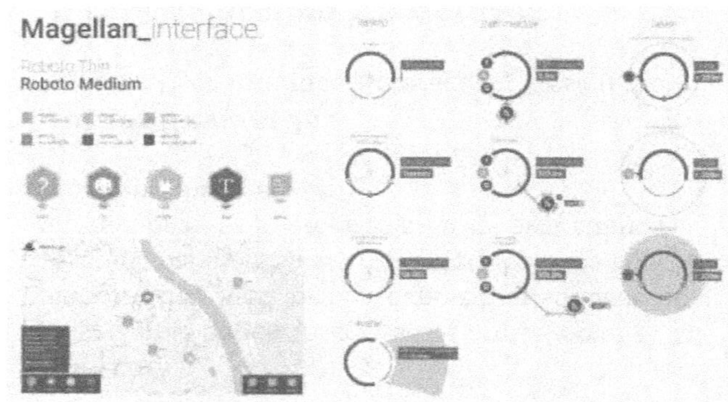

Figure 3: UI details for the MAGELLAN platform designed by Immersion.

Figure 5: Illustration of the process of TUI 3D printing.

The European project Magellan

MAGELLAN's overall vision is to enhance the creativity of people by establishing a web platform for cost-effectively authoring, publishing, executing, and experiencing location based games. This unique integrated web-based infrastructure will be targeted at both skilled professional authors, but also at everyday authors without deep technical skills. MAGELLAN will be underpinned by scientific research into the principles and technologies of creative and location-based experiences in order to ensure that the platform is innovative while also extending our broader scientific understanding of creativity.

Given this vision, the main objectives of MAGELLAN are.

- Creativity for Location-Based Experiences
- Integrated and Collaborative Visual Authoring Environment
- Scalable Web Platform

Acknowledgments

This work is partially supported by the EU FP7 Program under the Magellan project (Agreement number 611526).

Figure 4: tests and experiments with end users.

PERCs Demo: Persistently Trackable Tangibles on Capacitive Multi-Touch Displays

Christian Cherek
RWTH Aachen University
Aachen, Germany
cherek@cs.rwth-aachen.de

Rene Linden
RWTH Aachen University
Aachen, Germany
Rene.Linden1@rwth-aachen.de

Simon Voelker
RWTH Aachen University
Aachen, Germany
voelker@cs.rwth-aachen.de

Florian Busch
RWTH Aachen University
Aachen, Germany
florian.busch@rwth-aachen.de

Jan Thar
RWTH Aachen University
Aachen, Germany
thar@cs.rwth-aachen.de

Jan Borchers
RWTH Aachen University
Aachen, Germany
borchers@cs.rwth-aachen.de

ITS'14, November 15– 18, 2015, Funchal, Portugal
ACM 978-1-4503-3899-8/15/11.
DOI: http://dx.doi.org/10.1145/2817721.2823474

Abstract
Tangible objects on capacitive multi-touch surfaces are usually only detected while the user is touching them. When the user lets go of such a tangible, the system cannot distinguish whether the user just released the tangible, or picked it up and removed it from the surface. In this demo we demonstrate PERCs [2], persistent capacitive tangibles that 'know' whether they are currently on a capacitive touch surface or not. This is achieved by adding a small field sensor to the tangible to detect the touch screen's own, weak electromagnetic touch detection probing signal. In this demo we present two applications that make use of PERC tangibles – An air hockey like game for two players and a single person arcade game.

Author Keywords
Tangible user interfaces; tabletop interaction; capacitive multi-touch

ACM Classification Keywords
H.5.2 [Information Interfaces and Presentation]: User Interfaces Input Devices and Strategies

Introduction
Tangible objects in combination with multi-touch surfaces have been shown to be useful in a large variety of application scenarios. The haptic experience and tactile feedback

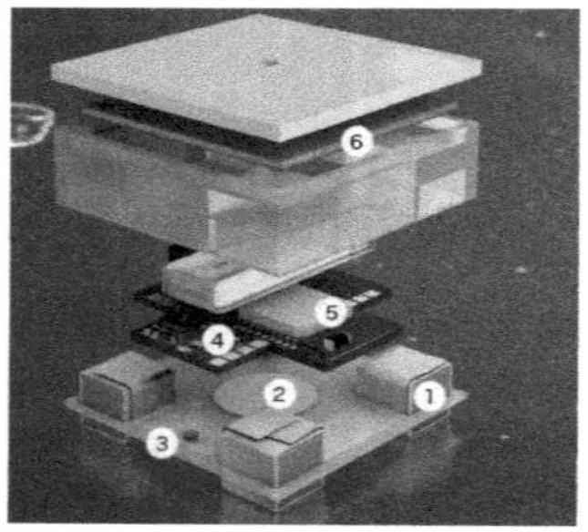

Figure 1: The six main components of a PERC tangible: (1) marker pattern, (2) field sensor, (3) light sensor, (4) micro controller, (5) Bluetooth element, and (6) lead plate.

provided by tangibles guides user input and allows for fast eyes-free interaction [4]. However, using them on modern capacitive touch screens is problematic.

Capacitive touch screens detect touches by creating an electric field above their surface. When an object with high capacitance, such as a human finger, comes close to the surface, this electric field changes. The touch screen measures this change and reports a touch. Tangibles on touch screens, such as Capstones [1] or TUIC [5], normally use electrically conductive material on their bottom and sides, so that a user touching them increases their capacitance enough to register as a touch. However, this means that for the tangible to be detected, the user has to continue touching it. As soon as the user releases the tangible, the capacitance drops, and the system fails to detect the tangible—even if it remains on the surface. This makes it impossible to distinguish whether a tangible has been picked up and removed from the touch screen, or whether the user has just let go of the tangible, leaving it on the touch screen.

PUCs [3] addressed this issue by introducing tangibles that ground themselves through currently inactive sensor electrodes of the capacitive touch screen. However, most touch screens have adaptive filtering mechanisms that remove touches that have been stationary for too long.

PERC tangibles [2] extended the PUCs concept by adding a sensor into the tangibles that detects the signal emitted by the capacitive touch screen's electric probing field. This enables the tangible to determine whether it is currently placed on a capacitive touch surface or not, even when its touches are being filtered out by the touch system. That status is communicated from the PERC tangible to the system via Bluetooth; the communication channel also assigns a unique ID to each tangible independent of its touch pattern, solving the identification problem with PUCs.

In this demo we present two applications that make use of PERCs tangibles [2]. Since PERCs are fast and reliable, users can use tangibles on a capacitive screen just as if they were using their fingers. The additional haptic experience and tactile feedback allow for fast and eyes-free interaction, where typical finger gestures would not suffice.

PERCs

A PERC tangible consists of three main components: A PUCs marker pattern, the field sensor, and a light sensor (Fig. 1). In addition to these main components each PERC also includes a microcontroller, a Bluetooth 4.0 chip, a battery, and a small lead plate on top of the tangible to increase the tangible's weight.

Marker Pattern

The marker pattern consists of three 8x8 mm pads connected via conductive copper foil (Figure 1.1). Each pad creates a touch point that is detected by the capacitive touch screen. For the pads, we use a soft conductive weave that is usually used as EMS shielding[1]. This has the benefit that the pads do not create any scratches on the touch surface and that they remain in good contact with the surface.

Field Sensor

The field sensor is the part of a PERC tangible that actively determines if the tangible is placed on a touch surface at any given time or not. For this purpose, an antenna at the bottom of the tangible picks up the signature of the electric field above the surface, which is created by every capacitive touch screen, shown in Figure 2. The PERC field sensor consists of this antenna, a comparator integrated circuit that

[1] www.we-online.com

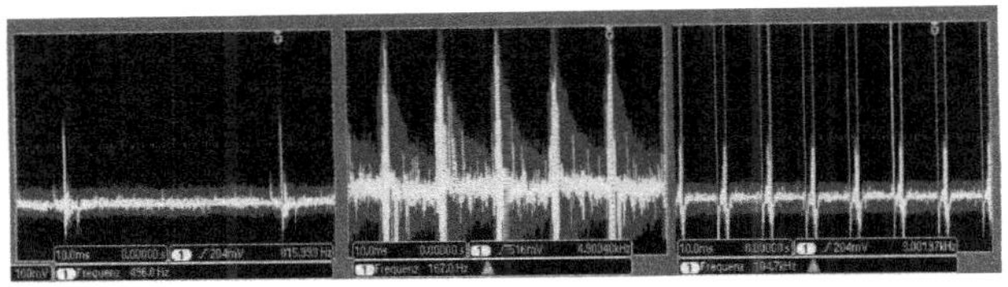

Figure 2: Touch detection signals by (left to right) iPad 4, 3M screen, and Microsoft 55" capacitive screen

detects peaks above a certain voltage threshold, and a microcontroller to trigger a timeout if the next peak was not detected within a specific period of time, determined by the touch screen's pulse frequency. In our current implementation, the threshold of the field sensor is set to detect the capacitive touch screen if the distance between the touch surface and the tangible falls below 1 mm.

Whenever the field sensor detects the presence of a capacitive touch surface, the tangible sends a *set* event via BLE to the system. The system correlates this message temporally to newly appearing touches in order to link the UUID to the tangible's position. Until the tangible recognizes the absence of the electric field and sends a corresponding *lift* event, the system considers it as being on the table even if its touches are filtered out.

Unfortunately, there are still two situations in which the field sensor alone does not suffice to detect a PERC tangible reliably: In situations where two tangibles are placed at the same time and in situations where not all markers are detected by the system.

Light Sensor
To resolve these ambiguities, we added a light sensor underneath the tangible. The light sensor allows to ping stationary tangibles in uncertain situations.

When two tangibles send a *set* event a very short time frame, the system first pings each tangible individually with a bright dot at the position of the light sensor. If a tangible detects this change, it notifies the system via BLE about the change and the ambiguity is resolved.

If the system detects only two touch points and a *set* event is received, the position and orientation of the tangible can only be detected up to a 180° ambiguity. Since the light sensor is placed with an offset from the center, this yields two possible positions of the light sensor. The system now pings these positions as before, and if the light sensor detects the change the orientation is clear.

Other Components and Power Cconsumption
Within each PERC we use a MSP430G2553 microcontroller, a BLE112 Bluetooth module, a TEMD6200FX01 light sensor, and a Renata LIPO battery (3.7 V, 175 mAh).

Since PERCs use active components, we have to deal with battery lifetime. The 175 mAh battery in our PERCs typically yields about 60 hours of continuous use and could be easily recharged via conductive power transfer. If a tangibles battery is low, the system can inform the user via visual feedback on the screen and the user can exchange the tangible with a new one.

Demo experience
In our demo we will present two different usage scenarios for PERCs on a 27" perceptive pixel display.

The first application is an air hockey inspired application where two users play against each other (Fig. 3). The mallets are PERC tangibles, the puck, borders, and goals are displayed on the screen. Each player holds one of the PERC mallets and tries to score a goal against the other player. This scenario demonstrates PERC tangibles in fast abrupt

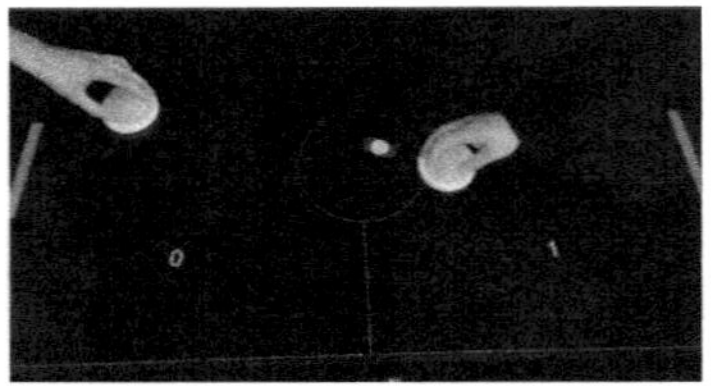

Figure 3: An interactive airhockey game in which PERC tangibles are used as mallets

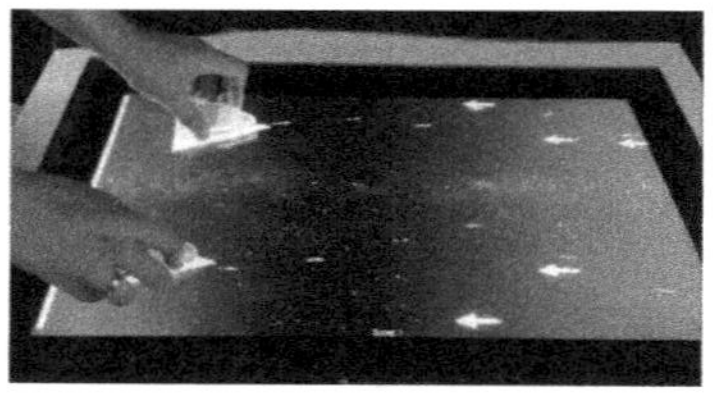

Figure 4: A space-invader game in which PERC tangibles are used as space ships.

movement. Since PERC tangibles make use of the PUCs marker concept, the digital representation of the mallet reacts as fast as the typical touch detection. Most of the time users will touch the mallet, but since PUCs markers are independent of users touching them, pushing the mallet and letting it go at the same time is also possible.

The second application is a space-invader like break out shooter game. As shown in Figure 4, the user gets up to three space ships and has to move them correctly to shoot at incoming enemy space ships. The incoming space ships have different colors and only the correspondingly colored player ship can hit an enemy ship. To force users into moving the space ships even more, space ships mix their colors if they are placed close to each other. There will be enemies who can only be defeated by combining the player ships the correct way.

The players ship will be represented by three tangibles. Since the player ship automatically shoot, one ship can be put aside while the others are operated. This scenario shows a more stationary use of PERC tangibles – the player's space ships constantly shoot at enemy ships as long as they remain on the surface. Even if the touch screen filters out the stationary tangible, the field sensor will inform the system about the tangible still being in place on the surface.

These examples are not the only applications where PERCs can be used. PERC tangibles are not limited in size or shape and since each tangible has a unique Bluetooth UUID, a theoretically unlimited amount of tangibles could be connected to the system. As demonstrated in our applications, PERCs work as fast moving tangibles as well as slow or static tangibles. PERCs also work on a variety of commercially available touch screens. With only very small adjustments we managed to use PERCs on a Microsoft 55" display, on a Perceptive Pixel 27" display, and the iPad.

Acknowledgments

This work was funded in part by the German B-IT Foundation and by the Norwegian Research Council through the MACS project (project number 217788).

REFERENCES

1. Chan, L., Müller, S., Roudaut, A., and Baudisch, P. CapStones and ZebraWidgets: Sensing Stacks of Building Blocks, Dials and Sliders on Capacitive Touch Screens. In *Proc. CHI '12*, ACM (2012), 2189–2192.
2. Voelker, S., Cherek, C., Thar, J., Karrer, T., Thoresen, C., Øvergård, K. I., and Borchers, J. PERCs: Persistently Trackable Tangibles on Capacitive Multi-Touch Displays. In *Proc. UIST '15*, ACM (2015).
3. Voelker, S., Nakajima, K., resen, C. T., Itoh, Y., Øvergård, K. I., and Borchers, J. PUCs: Detecting Transparent, Passive Untouched Capacitive Widgets on Unmodified Multi-touch Displays. In *Proc. ITS '13*, ACM (2013), 101–104.
4. Weiss, M., Wagner, J., Jansen, Y., Jennings, R., Khoshabeh, R., Hollan, J. D., and Borchers, J. Slap widgets: bridging the gap between virtual and physical controls on tabletops. In *Proc. CHI '09*, ACM (2009), 481–490.
5. Yu, N.-H., Chan, L.-W., Lau, S. Y., Tsai, S.-S., Hsiao, I.-C., Tsai, D.-J., Hsiao, F.-I., Cheng, L.-P., Chen, M., Huang, P., and Hung, Y.-P. TUIC: Enabling Tangible Interaction on Capacitive Multi-touch Display. In *Proc. CHI '11*, ACM (2011), 2995–3004.

Capture The Flag Demo: Engaging In A Multi-Device Augmented Reality Game

Suzanne Mueller
Massachusetts Institute of Technology
Cambridge, MA
suzmue@mit.edu

Andreas Dippon
Technische Universitat München
Boltzmannstr. 3
Garching, 85748 Germany
dippona@in.tum.de

Gudrun Klinker
Technische Universitat München
Boltzmannstr. 3
Garching, 85748 Germany
klinker@in.tum.de

ITS '15, November 15-18, 2015, Funchal, Portugal
ACM 978-1-4503-3899-8/15/11.
http://dx.doi.org/10.1145/2817721.2823475

Abstract
We present a Capture the Flag based game that investigates the possible engagements in a multi-device game. The distinction between a publicly used space and a player's private space is made and utilized to display different information to players. The tablet and the Augmented Reality component are used to see how players can be drawn to a certain physical space, to create a social and engaging game. The demo allows the users to experience a different setup for a multi-device game that attempts to engage the users with the space and each other.

Author Keywords
Augmented Reality; Multi-device; tablet;

ACM Classification Keywords
H.5.2. User Interfaces: Input devices and strategies, Interaction styles

Introduction
There are many different devices used in all aspects of everyday life. Many games typically are played using one main device (e.g. a smartphone, computer, television). Multiplayer computer games are often created so that users can play remotely and do not rely on the physical presence of the other players. However, games are also often played in a social setting. Families and friends often play board or card games together to pass the time.

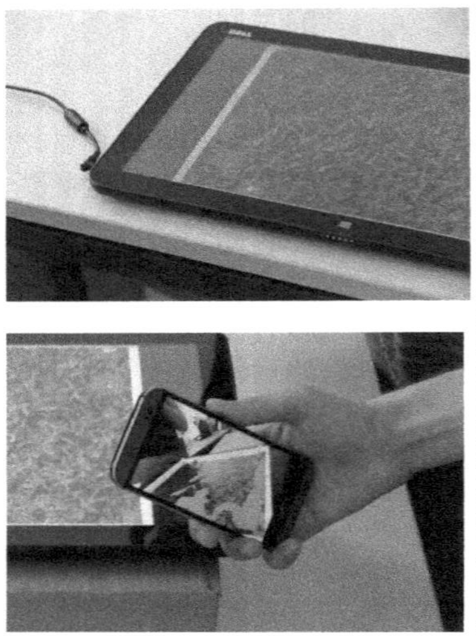

Figure 1. The game was developed to be played on a large multi-touch tablet and multiple smartphones.

This project challenges the traditional setup of a multi-player game and examines the possibility of engaging a group of players in a single game, while still allowing the possibilities that a computer or video game provides. It uses Augmented Reality (AR), an indirect view of the physical world, to provide each player with his or her own information unavailable to other players. Augmented Reality involves "augmenting the real world with computerized information" [2]. In this case, the real world is locked on top of a shared tablet screen that displays certain aspects of the game to users. This project experiments with different information being displayed on different devices to highlight important information.

Related Work

Previous work has been done to investigate the shared and private spaces to allow the multiple users to interact at once with media facades [5]. This project found that one could avoid cluttering up the space on a shared interface, by augmenting a live feed of the video on a smartphone to give the users more information. Interactions using a live video have not always allowed a natural interaction for the user. Object-oriented interactions use tracking to allow the smartphone to be physically oriented in the real world [3]. This gives the user a more natural of sense of how their interactions will affect the video. This is incorporated through the movement interactions of the user.

Through the implementation of a Tower Defense game, the use of a smartphone as more than a controller was investigated [4]. The game involved using a tablet to provide certain input and using motions and touches on the smartphone as a different source of input. This project focused on a game that did not require time sensitive input from the user, allowing the acceleration and position of the smartphone to be used. In the capture the flag game, certain interactions that require more precision, such as moving artificially into a tower, were avoided due to the real time nature of the game.

Game Implementation

In order to investigate the possibilities to engage the user with multiple devices, a Capture the Flag game was implemented. The game was created to be run using a XPS 18 Windows Multi-touch Tablet and 2-4 Android smartphones.

The game was created using Unity and written in C#. The UNET networking system from Unity is used to accommodate the multi-device aspect of the game. In order to include features specific to the Android platform, Java plugins were also incorporated. To incorporate the augmented reality features used in the game play, Vuforia was chosen as a free option that could be easily incorporated into a Unity game.

Game Play

The implemented 2-4 player game is based off of Capture the Flag [1]. There is a public space, the tablet, that hosts the game. On this public space, each player's location and their immediate surroundings are displayed, as well as each of the bases and flags. In addition to the information the players can see on the public tablet, each player receives additional information on the Android smartphone they use to connect to the game. The player's view of the playing field is enhanced using Augmented Reality, to show the objects and obstacles, or lack thereof, at the locations the player has already visited. This private information is only available to a single player at each location,

Figure 2. Players playing capture the flag on a tablet. The player in the front right is tapping on the table to steal the flag. The players on the left are moving by touching on their smartphones and are blowing into the microphones.

providing that player with additional expertise of the terrain at that location.

The game begins with each player at their own base. The players can gain the view of the playing field on their devices by pointing the smartphone's camera at the tablet. The Vuforia system can recognize the target, and the objects will appear as a 3D representation over the board. Each player can then move by touching the target location on the game world representation on his or her smartphone. The player can also blow into the microphone on his or her smartphone in order to move faster.

In order to steal a flag from another player, the player must first move into the base of the other player. Then he or she must tap 5 times on the tablet in the base of the player whose flag they are trying to steal. This then sends a vibration notification to the player whose flag is being stolen. Once the player brings the other flag back to his base, the player whose flag was stolen is eliminated from the game. The last player remaining at the end of a round, wins the game.

To defend his or her flag, a player can take a couple of measures. Once their flag is stolen, a player can no longer steal another flag, but must go defend his or her own flag. To do this, the player essentially needs to run down the other player. If he or she hits against the other player who is carrying his or her flag, the flag is immediately returned to the base and the other player is stunned. To aid in catching a player, or escaping a player, each player can set traps using the volume controls on the smartphones. Although there is no limit to how many traps a player can place, there is a time interval after each placed trap before another can be placed. These traps stun the other players if run over, but will not affect the player that placed them.

Demo

The demo will allow four users each with a smartphone to play Capture the Flag with a large, multi-touch tablet. The tablet will lay flat on an elevated surface, as shown in Figure 2. The players will stand around the tablet, holding a smartphone in hand. The users will have the opportunity to play a round of the game.

The initial screen that is displayed on a users application, asks if they would like to connect as a player or as the host. Once a user connects to the host game he or she is in the lobby. As soon as all connected users in the lobby click that they are ready, the game will start.

Once the game begins, the users will be able to move their players, place traps, and steal flags as described in this paper to try to be the last man standing.

Conclusion

Attendees will be able to interact with a game in a new, nontraditional way. The controls and setup of this Capture the Flag game seek to engage the users in the experience in a way that has not been done. The real time game will provide the users with the challenge of where to focus their attention as they try to move, place/avoid traps, and protect their flags. The method chosen for movement experiments with a possibly natural movement, although it will be up to the user on whether this is actually intuitive. The users will also experience the draw of the 3D augmentation of the 2D tablet, and will get to experience a social, multi-device game played in a common physical space.

References

1. Capture the Flag - wikipedia, the free encyclopedia. http://en.wikipedia.org/wiki/Capture_the_flag, 2015.[Online; last accessed 16-08-2015].
2. Emmanuel Dubois and Laurence Nigay. 2000. Augmented reality: which augmentation for which reality?. In *Proceedings of DARE 2000 on Designing augmented reality environments* (DARE '00). ACM, New York, NY, USA, 165-166.
3. Masayuki Tani, Kimiya Yamaashi, Koichiro Tanikoshi, Masayasu Futakawa, and Shinya Tanifuji. 1992. Object-oriented video: interaction with real-world objects through live video. In *Proceedings of the SIGCHI Conference on Human Factors in Computing Systems* (CHI '92), Penny Bauersfeld, John Bennett, and Gene Lynch (Eds.). ACM, New York, NY, USA, 593-598.
4. Paul Tolstoi and Andreas Dippon. 2015. Towering Defense: An Augmented Reality Multi-Device Game. In *Proceedings of the 33rd Annual ACM Conference Extended Abstracts on Human Factors in Computing Systems* (CHI EA '15). ACM, New York, NY, USA, 89-92.
5. Sebastian Boring, Sven Gehring, Alexander Wiethoff, Anna Magdalena Blöckner, Johannes Schöning, and Andreas Butz. 2011. Multi-user interaction on media facades through live video on mobile devices. In *Proceedings of the SIGCHI Conference on Human Factors in Computing Systems* (CHI '11). ACM, New York, NY, USA, 2721-2724.

EnchanTable: Displaying a Vertically Standing Mid-air Image on a Table Surface using Reflection

Hiroki Yamamoto
The University of Tokyo
yamahiro@nae-lab.org

Hajime Kajita
The University of Tokyo
kajita@nae-lab.org

Naoya Koizumi
The University of Tokyo
koizumi@nae-lab.org

Takeshi Naemura
The University of Tokyo
7-3-1 Hongo, Bunkyo-ku,
Tokyo, Japan
naemura@nae-lab.org

ITS 2015, November 15–18, 2015, Funchal/Madeira, Portugal.
ACM 978-1-4503-3899-8/15/11.
http://dx.doi.org/10.1145/2817721.2823476

Abstract

Figure 1. *EnchanTable* displays upright mid-air image on table. Users can play with virtual character by using cards. Projector casts artificial shadow of mid-air images and visual information of physical object on table surface.

We propose a novel display method, EnchanTable, that can augment a table surface with mid-air images. Users can interact with visual images displayed on the table by using real objects. In our optical design, we place an optical imaging device behind a table so that the light from the device forms a vertically standing mid-air image reflected at the table surface. This design displays the image right on the table. The merit of our method is that the only requirement is for the table to have a reflective surface. Utilizing this, we can place any devices, such as touch sensors, around the table, or display mid-air images on a tablet whose surface is

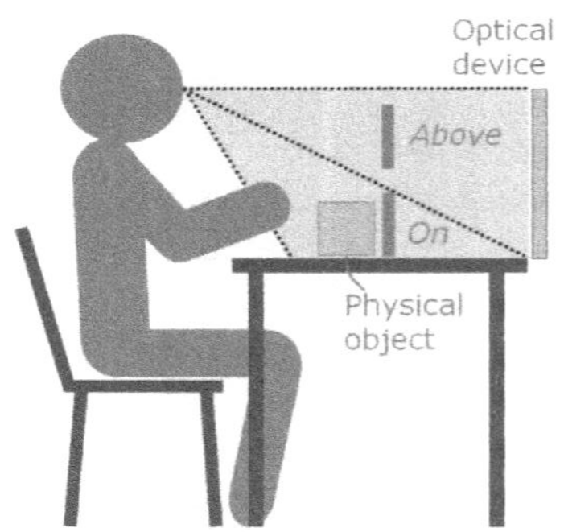

(a) Side view

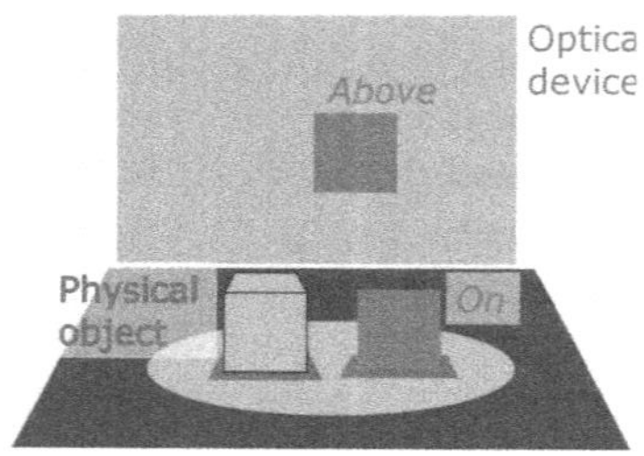

(b) View from user

Figure 2. Problem of mid-air image displaying in tabletop interaction. When optical device is placed behind table, user can view mid-air image only in space *above* table surface (blue triangle). To display information just beside physical objects, vertically standing image should be displayed in space right *on* table (red triangle).

sufficiently reflective. Owing to its compactness, this method can be applied to other tabletop-interaction systems.

Author Keywords

Tabletop Display; Optical Design; Mid-air Image; Augmented Reality; Mixed Reality; Tabletop Interaction

ACM Classification Keywords

H.5.1 [Multimedia Information Systems]: Artificial, augmented, and virtual realities.

Introduction

A table provides a surface on which users can put physical objects. By adding visual images around the objects, a table becomes a useful tool enriched with intuitive manipulation and interaction. To display information directly beside physical objects, vertically standing images are often more useful than images projected directly on the table. This is because projected images appear on the horizontal surface of the table, while vertically standing images can appear next to the physical objects.

The goal of this paper is to display vertically standing mid-air images and allow for interaction with physical objects on a table. A mid-air image is formed by a real imaging optical device which converges incident light by reflection and refraction. Most previous systems cannot display images close to the table because they place optical devices behind the table, whose field of view is in the space above the table. Several other systems can display mid-air images right on the table; however, it is difficult for these to allow for interaction because the space under the table is occupied by the optical devices. The space to install additional devices such as touch sensors is limited.

In this paper, we propose a display method, EnchanTable, that can display a vertically standing mid-air image on a table. Figure 1 shows an image displayed by our method. The proposed system uses the reflection of the table surface as well as the real imaging optical device placed behind the table. Light from a source display pass through the device, is reflected on the surface, and forms a mid-air image on the table. The space over and under the table is free of equipment.

The merit of our method is that the only requirement for the table is that it has a reflective surface. Therefore, a system using this method can use equipment such as touch sensors and cameras. In addition, it can display a mid-air image on plate-shaped objects that have a reflective surface, e.g., a tablet. Owing to its simpleness, this method can be applied to other tabletop-interaction systems. In this paper, we demonstrate the instances of interaction with physical objects by using our method.

Related Work

Figure 2 illustrates the problem of mid-air image displays. Users look down at a table surface while sitting or standing in front of the table. The goal for the display method is that images are displayed not *above* but *on* the table (Figure 2 a). *Above* means that there is a gap between an image and table surface (blue space). *On* means that an image is directly on the table surface (red space). Images *on* the table can display information directly beside objects placed on the table, unlike images *above* the table.

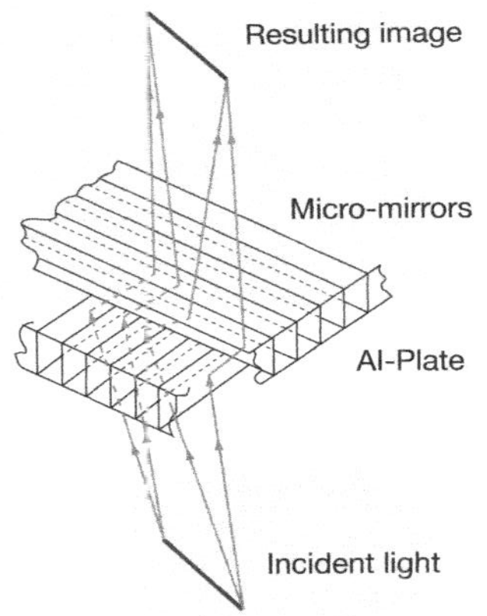

Figure 3. Optical property of Aerial-Imaging Plate (AIP) [1]. Incident light, reflected twice, forms mid-air images at plane-symmetric position.

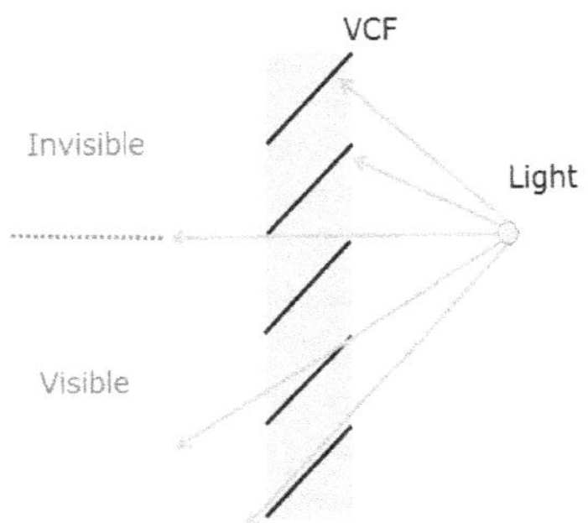

Figure 4. Optical property of View-Control Film (VCF). VCF is louver sheet which blocks upward light and allows downward light to pass for visibility control.

While most previous displays have focused on displaying images *above* the table, some methods have been proposed for displaying mid-air images *on* the table. Chan [2] allows for interaction with a mid-air image of a virtual panel displayed on a table by using a Fresnel lens and polymer dispersed liquid crystal glass. Yoshida proposes fVisiOn [4] that uses a projector array to display 3D images that can be viewed in 360°. HoVerTable [3] uses a real imaging optical device to provide two-layer images in two directions.

Although these systems can display images on a table, additional devices cannot be easily installed since the space under the table is occupied by optical devices or used for the path of light. Additional equipment under the table may block the light. Our system, however, utilizes the reflection of the table surface, which allows for the optical devices to be placed behind the table. The space above and under the surface is free, and thus, we can allow for highly flexible tabletop interaction.

Proposed Optical Design

To display a mid-air image, we introduce a plate-shaped real imaging device called the "Aerial-Imaging Plate" (AIP) [1]. Figure 3 illustrates the optical property. Incident light, reflected two times at a mirror at 90°, converges at a position that is plane-symmetric to the AIP. A part of the light, however, passes through the AIP directly without reflecting. This light reaches users' eyes, causing an unintentional image.

To block this unnecessary light, we introduce a view-control film (VCF). As illustrated in Figure 4, the transmittance of VCF changes in accordance with the incident angle. The transmittance of the film in our system is high for downwardly projecting light and low for upwardly projecting light.

Figure 5 describes the optical design of our method. The design consists of a display (D), an actuator, an Aerial-Imaging Plate (AIP), a view-control film (VCF), and a reflective table surface. The AIP is placed perpendicularly behind the table. When a surface does not reflect the light sufficiently, we can put a half-silvered mirror film on the table to control the reflectance.

D, attached to the actuator, is placed behind the AIP. Light, emitted from D, forms a temporary image D' through the AIP. Reflected by the table surface, it forms a mid-air image (I). By moving D with the actuator, the position of D' and I can be changed. The VCF can block the light to the users directly passing through the AIP (upward), while the light for I (downward) passes through the VCF.

Implementation and Demonstration

Figure 6 shows the optical design implemented in a system. We used a projector and a screen for D, an XY-table for the actuator, and a combining glass to increase the reflectance of the table surface. With this system, we can display a 75-mm image, which can move in space at a depth of 50 to 150 mm.

Figure 7 shows a mid-air image formed by the system. This confirms that the image is standing upright on the table. Figure 8 shows the change of the image in the depth direction. The image moved from the back to the front, and the camera kept the image in focus at each depth.

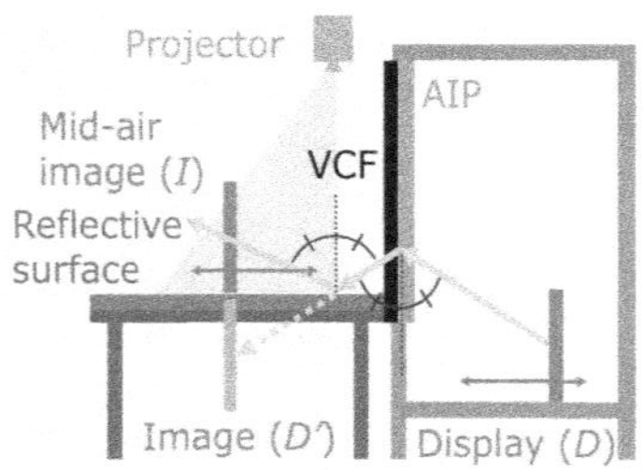

Figure 5. Proposed optical design. AIP forms image *D'*. Light to *D'*, reflected on table surface, forms mid-air image (*I*). VCF blocks light passing through AIP without reflecting.

Figure 6. Implemented system.

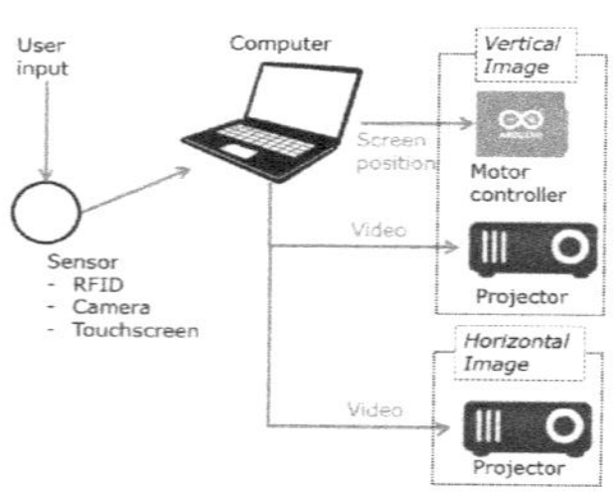

Figure 9. System structure.

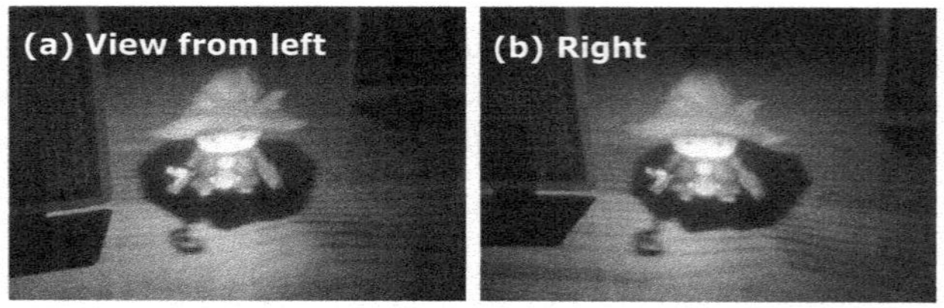

Figure 7. Stereo view of mid-air image. Users can see image beside physical object (card).

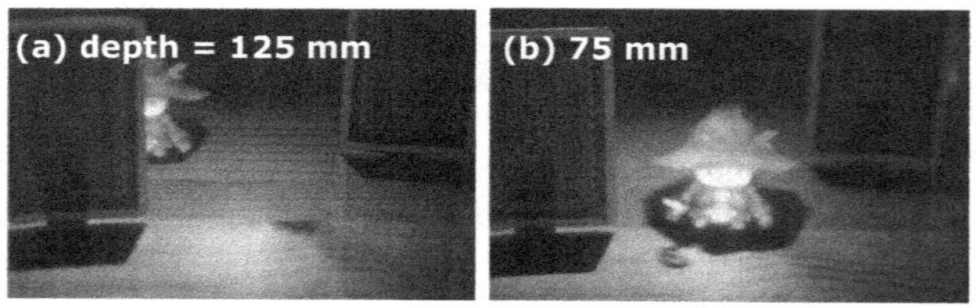

Figure 8. Images at different depths. Camera was focused at two different depths.

We implemented the instances of the demonstration. Figure 9 shows the system structure of our implementation. We use an RFID sensor which receives data from ID tags attached to the objects. The system can display characters depending on the objects. The displayed character moves around on the surface. We can also use a tablet. It has not only a sufficient reflective surface to form mid-air images but is also a touch sensing device for interaction. This sensor enables the system to measure both the position of a user's finger and the position/rotation of physical objects with an electro-conductive marker. Users can interact with a character, which moves toward the point being touched.

Conclusion

We proposed a display method, EnchanTable, that can augment a table surface with mid-air images. We placed an optical imaging device behind a table. The light from the device, reflected by the surface, forms a vertically standing mid-air image. This method requires only a reflective surface, allowing the table to be highly flexible for interaction. We used a sensor and a tablet that enable users to interact with objects in the demonstrations. In the future, our plan is to provide a higher connection between physical objects and represented information. For instance, by displaying annotations just beside design models or exhibit items, users can view spatially consistent information.

Acknowledgement

This project is supported by JST-CREST project "Harmonized Inter-Personal Display Based on Position and Direction Control"

References

1. Asukanet. 2013. Aerial imaging plate. Japanese patent P5437436.
2. Chan, L., et al. 2008. On top of tabletop: A virtual touch panel display. In *Horizontal Interactive Human Computer Systems, 2008.TABLETOP 2008. 3rd IEEE International Workshop on*, 169-176
3. Kim, H., et al. 2015. HoVerTable: Dual-sided Vertical Mid-air Images on Horizontal Tabletop Display. In *Proceedings of the 33rd Annual ACM Conference Extended Abstracts on Human Factors in Computing Systems* (CHI '15), 1115-1120
4. Yoshida, S. 2012. fVisiOn: glasses-free tabletop 3D display to provide virtual 3D media naturally alongside real media. In *SPIE Defense, Security, and Sensing,* International Society for Optics and Photonics, 838411-838411-9

Fall of Humans: Interactive Tabletop Games and Transmedia Storytelling

Figure 1. Top: the *legs* card for the zombie type *Bad Ass*. Bottom: the back of the same card, which can be used as input in *Uprising*, the interactive tabletop version of FoH.

Mara Dionísio
Aditya Gujaran
Madeira Interactive Technologies Institute
Funchal, Portugal
msgdionisio@gmail.com
aditya.gujaran@gmail.com

Miguel Pinto
Novabase
Experience Design
Lisboa, Portugal
luismiguelmaiapinto@gmail.com

Augusto Esteves
Edinburgh Napier University
Edinburgh, UK
augustoeae@gmail.com

ITS '15, November 15-18, 2015, Funchal, Portugal
ACM 978-1-4503-3899-8/15/11.
http://dx.doi.org/10.1145/2817721.2823477.

Abstract
This paper illustrates how transmedia storytelling can help introduce players to interactive tabletop games. To do so, we developed Fall of Humans (FoH), an experience that takes place over two games: Meat factory, a physical card game where players compete to create different zombies; and Uprising, a interactive tabletop game where players can get to see the zombies they have created come to life.

Author Keywords
Transmedia storytelling; game design; tabletop games.

ACM Classification Keywords
H.5.m. Information interfaces and presentation (e.g., HCI): Miscellaneous.

Introduction
Transmedia stories are stories told across multiple platforms such as movies, video games or comic books [3]. There are many industries that make use of this in their Storytelling universes. The Movie industry often elaborates the universe of a movie across different medias in an effort to make it more engaging for the viewer. An example of this are the Star Wars [4] and Star Trek [5] franchises, where often the universe expands in form of books, comics, videogames and card games, which serve as a tie-in to full feature film

Figure 2. Top: the physical token representing a human soldier. Each of these tokens includes a fiducial maker on the bottom so as to be recognized by bespoke interactive tabletops. Bottom: one of Uprising's playtests.

stories or spin-offs for new characters. Pokemon [6] or Yo-kai watch [7], are examples where the universe is born in video games and expands across media such as cartoon, arcade games and comics. In specific markets, such as the Japanese, these franchises use physical artifacts that connect the card and arcade games to make the experience even more attractive to the players (e.g., cards in the Pokémon arcade machine, tokens in the Yokai-watch). These are just a few examples of the commonly used strategies of various media corporations, as transmedia storytelling expands the potential market of an intellectual property by creating multiple points of entry that are suitable to different audience segments [2].

In this paper we rely on this strategy to explore how transmedia storytelling can be used to introduce interactive tabletop games to a wider audience. To do so, we created the Fall of Humans Universe, a transmedia story that takes place over two games: a physical card game and an interactive tabletop game.

Fall of Humans

"Year 2XXX – Earth. A global catastrophe wipes out most of the human race, leaving just pockets of healthy humans and millions of Zombies. Soon the humans take advantage of the zombies and started to enslave and mass-produce them to do menial labor work. Eventually, over a period of a couple years, the Zombies start to get smarter, stronger and in the end, in the shadows, a rebellion begins brewing…"

This is the starting point of Fall of Humans (FoH) a transmedia story that occurs over two games: *Meat Factory* and *Uprising*.

Meat Factory

In Meat Factory the players start their journey in the world of FoH. This is a fast paced game where each card represents a body part of four different types of zombies (*Fresh*, *Puker*, *Bad Ass* and *Scout* – see Figure 1), and the goal of the game is to be the first to create one of the four zombies. Players achieve this by discarding cards to the player to their right as fast as possible, until they have gathered the four body parts. The first player to achieve this can grab a head token that sits at the center of the game, prompting the other players to do the same (there is one less head token than the total number of players). Finally, once the game is over, players can place the cards of any of the zombies they have created during the game on an interactive tabletop game named *Uprising*. Doing so unlocks these zombies as characters in the latter game.

Uprising

Set ten years after the events of Meat Factory, Uprising is an interactive tabletop game where zombies try to break free from human oppression. Inspired by Tower Defense games [e.g. 1], Uprising pits three players controlling two zombies each, against a solo player controlling four humans characters (two *soldiers* and two *builders* – see Figure 2). Each zombie and human character is represented by a physical token that can be placed at strategic positions on a digital map. Once positioned, zombie tokens continuously spawn digital zombies that move in one direction, destroying everything in their path and ultimately capturing all the meat factories across the map. Human tokens, on the other hand, delay the progress of digital zombies by firing in multiple directions (soldier) or building walls that delay their progress (builder). The zombie and human team play alternatively, and each turn is over when the player moves one of his characters to a new location. At the end of 10 minutes, if the zombie team has not succeeded in capturing all of the meat factories in the map, the game is over and they lose the game.

Implementation

Uprising was implemented using conventional technologies: the Processing language; the reacTIVision tracking software; and the TUIO messaging protocol. Furthermore, the game runs on an interactive tabletop of 120x70 cm based on the Diffused Surface Illumination (DSI) method (see Figure 2).

Preliminary User Testing

Both games were developed over three game testing sessions with selected test players. A final fourth session was conducted with members from the general public during a public presentation. The first three tests were an integral part of the development process, and contributed several changes to the original gameplay so as to improve user satisfaction during play. One example of this was how the head tokens would support the connection between the two games. Originally, there was no relationship between player performance in Meat Factory and Uprising. As a result, when a card game was over, players would tally their scores and return the head tokens back. After observing how some participants displayed a strong sense of ownership over these, a new gameplay rule was defined that would allow these tokens to be kept in the player's possession so as allow to carry on their zombies to the interactive tabletop game.

Preliminary Results

During the public game test session, players were invited to first play Meat Factory, followed by an Uprising gaming session on the interactive table.

The first observation was that participants indeed demonstrated a sense of ownership over the won head tokens from the card game. The second was that participants understood the implications of creating a specific zombie for the follow up interactive game. As a result, many would extend gameplay with Meat Factory until they had unlocked their favorite zombie character.

During play on Uprising, players were observed slowly developing group tactics to defeat the human team. Furthermore, the spin presented by the FoH universe (humans are the villains; zombies are the heroes) did not seem to affect gameplay or player enjoyment.

Conclusion & Next Steps

Our test sessions have gathered very positive feedback about the potential of gameplay links across different media. This seems to facilitate a game's story telling, and to better support user enjoyment and engagement.

For the next steps, we envision exploring different gameplay options to improve the connection between media. For example, how to support bidirectional links by having the interactive tabletop empower certain cards that can be then transferred back to Meat Factory. Another example would be to support card gameplay directly in the interactive tabletop, supporting quicker and effortless transitions between the two games by supporting digital animations based on events in the card game on the tabletop.

References

1. Huynh, D. N. T., Raveendran, K., Xu, Y., Spreen, K., & MacIntyre, B. 2009. Art of defense: a collaborative handheld augmented reality board game. In *Proceedings of the 2009 ACM SIGGRAPH symposium on video games*, 135-142.
2. Jenkis, H. 2007. Transmedia Storytelling 101. Retrieved August 26, 2015, from http://henryjenkins.org/2007/03/transmedia_storytelling_101.html
3. Jenkins, H. 2009. *Confronting the challenges of participatory culture: Media education for the 21st century*. Mit Press.
4. StarWars.com | Star Wars: The Force Awakens, Star Wars Rebels & Games. (n.d.). Retrieved September 25, 2015.
5. Star Trek.com (n.d.). Retrieved September 25, 2015.
6. Pokemon.com (n.d.). Retrieved September 25, 2015.
7. http://www.youkai-watch.jp/yw/ 妖怪ウォッチ（ニンテンドー3DSソフト）. (n.d.). Retrieved September 25, 2015.

aWall – A Socio-Cognitive Tool for Agile Team Collaboration using Large Multi-Touch Wall Systems

Magdalena Mateescu [1]
magdalena.mateescu@fhnw.ch

Martin Kropp [2]
martin.kropp@fhnw.ch

Roger Burkhard [1]
roger.burkhard@fhnw.ch

Carmen Zahn [1]
carmen.zahn@fhnw.ch

Dario Vischi [2]
dario.vischi@fhnw.ch

[1] School of Applied Psychology
University of Applied Sciences and Arts Northwestern Switzerland
FHNW, Olten, Switzerland

[2] School of Engineering
University of Applied Sciences and Arts Northwestern Switzerland
FHNW, Windisch, Switzerland

ITS '15, November 15-18, 2015, Funchal, Portugal
ACM 978-1-4503-3899-8/15/11.
http://dx.doi.org/10.1145/2817721.2823478

Abstract

Agile methods emphasize highly interactive and close collaboration within teams and among stakeholders. Due to still missing adequate digital tools, agile teams use mostly physical artefacts like wallboards and story cards. In this paper, we present *aWall*, an agile team collaboration tool for large multi-touch wall systems. *aWall* was designed based on empirical user research using new interaction and visualization concepts to support and foster the highly collaborative and communicative agile work style. The application is based on web technology and can be used in both co-located and distributed setting. The implemented prototypes were validated with end-users in a user workshop. In the demo, users can experience the interaction and visualization concepts hands-on.

Author Keywords

Agile; collaboration; communication; socio-cognitive; team; multi-touch; project management; software development; HCI; surface.

ACM Classification Keywords

H.5.2. Information interfaces and presentation (e.g., HCI): User Interfaces

Figure 1. aWall running on a 2x2 46″ Screen Wall

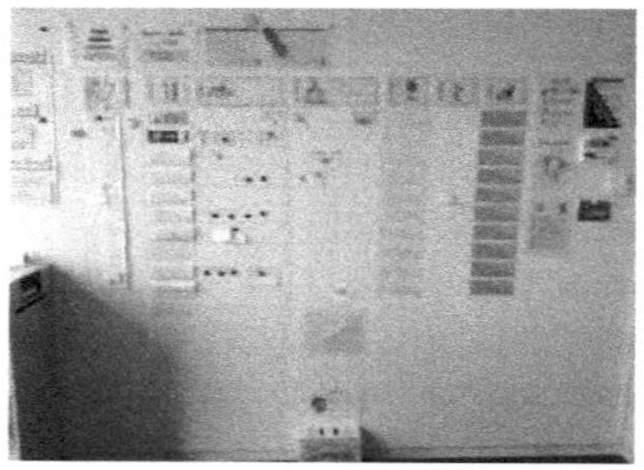

Figure 2. A physical card wall

Introduction

Large multi-user touchscreens have been shown to benefit collaborative work by supporting social interaction and group cognitive activities, are still scarce commodity. In agile software development, which became a predominant method in the IT industry in the last 10 years [6, 7], physical wallboards combined with digital tools like are still used predominantly. Such tools are crucial for agile teams, since the agile process depends on an intensive interaction, collaboration, and constant open communication among all stakeholders between team members [1]. Such intensive collaboration needs very close feedbacks loops in the sense of the Plan-Do-Check-Act (PDCA) management method [5].

Agile management tools like JIRA Agile [2], VersionOne [3] are not sufficient to support the collaborative process in agile teams. Azizyan, Magarian, and Kajko-Matsson [4] found that 31% of the interviewed companies used both project management tools and physical walls. The predominant usage of physical tools reveals their importance for teamwork. Therefore, we consider that it is necessary to deepen our understanding of the requirements for collaborative agile tools and their usage in the agile process.

Design Considerations for the Agile Wall

Based on the results of an empirical study, we developed a concept for a socio-cognitive tool for agile collaboration that supports the whole agile process (aWall).

The *aWall* prototype supports agile team collaboration and fosters the agile style of work through an extra-large multi-touch wall system (see Figure 1). *aWall* takes advantage of the 4K resolution and web technology and by that surpasses the possibilities of existing desktop tools. We explored new visualization and interaction concepts to foster the agile collaboration style.

We observed that each agile meeting has its main specific task and goal, but also needs various supporting information and artefacts. On physical card walls this extra information is typically arranged around the main task board as shown in Figure 2. To support these two different types of information handling, we developed a general *agile collaboration model* as shown in Figure 3. The model differentiates three important aspects for agile collaboration tools: the need for tools to sustain the core activity of the agile team (*action view*), the communication needs of the agile team, and third their needs to actualize information that might be distributed among team members and artefacts (*information view*). The actions and the information dimensions are represented in dedicated views as shown in Figure 4.

An *action view* is dedicated to a specific meeting and contributes directly to the main goal. Actions views have been carefully designed to sustain most interactions that need to be performed during a specific meeting. The *information view* provides extra information needed for a meeting, and by that contributes indirectly to goal achievement. Information views represent team's transactional memory. Any memory system needs to allow for change. Therefore, the information represented in these views can be manipulation at any time.

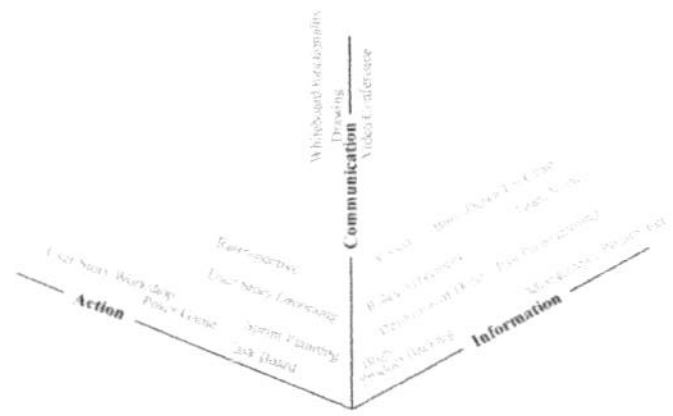

Figure 3. Agile collaboration model

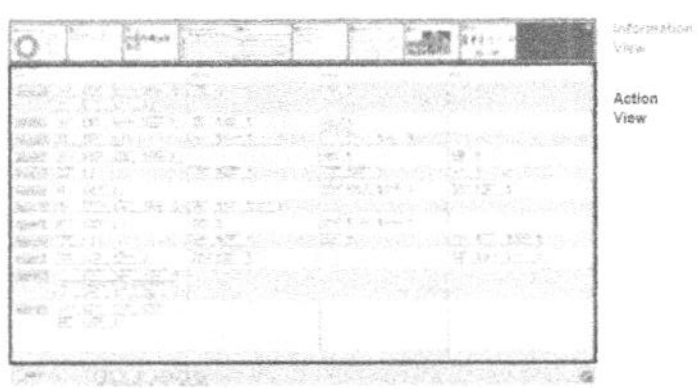

Figure 4. Action and Information View

Figure 5. Information view widgets

Design Concepts

Based on the aforementioned requirements and agile collaboration model, we derived the following design guidelines, which can be experienced in the demo.

Size Matters
Digital walls replacing a physical wall system need to be at least comparable in size with physical walls. We designed a multi-touch multiuser system consisting of four 46″ 4k high-resolution screens with a 12-point multi-touch infrared frame from pqlabs (see Figure 1). The touch wall is 2.05m width and 1.25m height.

Direct Interaction
Manipulation of information on the wall should remain visible to support team awareness. Team members' movement toward the wall increases team awareness. We consider that direct touch effectively supports the highly collaborative work in agile teams.

Support of Agile Collaboration Model
aWall supports the action-view and information-view concept as illustrated in Figure 4. The action view provides an optimized access to the core information needed for the meeting. The information view represents the teams' transactional memory encoding information about the project status (see Figure 5).

Scalability of Information
While it usually suffices to see only the title of a card to know what it stands for, this does not diminish the need of being able to easily display more information. To enable this the user can modify scale any widget, task card or Use Story to change the amount of shown information by just dragging the frames of the widget as shown in Figure 6 illustrates this principle for the User Story card.

Accessibility with Floating widgets
Widgets can be dragged out of the information view and placed anywhere on the action view. They facilitate easy access to information and enable the team to reposition information near other relevant information and thus creating favorable conditions for team cognition as illustrated in Figure 7.

Support the Collaborative Process
aWall provides dedicated views for all typical agile meetings like Daily Stand Up, Sprint Planning 1 and 2, and User Story Workshop, for example. The user can easily navigate between meetings through the meeting menu at the bottom of the *aWall* as shown in Figure 8.

The Digital Realm as Transactional Memory
Through the extra information displayed in the information view, *aWall* acts as a teams' external memory and sustains awareness of information both intra- and inter-team.

Configurability of Functionality
Different meetings require specific information. Therefore the *aWall*'s information view can be easily configured to the team needs.

Information at your finger tip
All relevant information must be available instantaneously. Therefore, we avoided menu lists in the *aWall* design. The only menu in the system is the bottom level menu used to select the desired meeting as shown in Figure 8. All other information is directly available through the action and information views.

Figure 6. Scaled up User Story

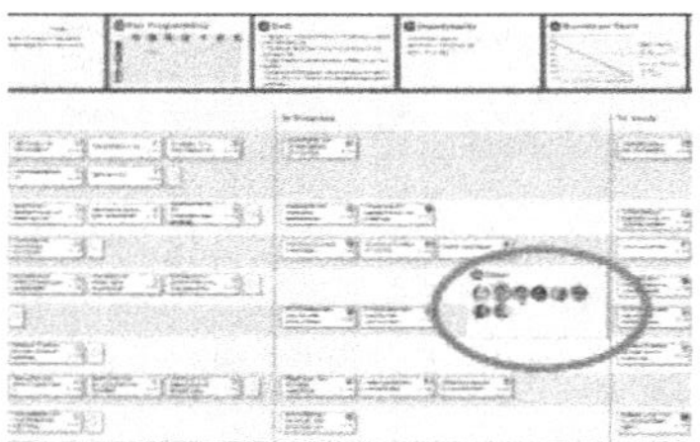

Figure 7. Task board with floating team view

Figure 8. Meeting navigation

Figure 9. The Fun and Avatar widgets

Simple and Homogenous layout
It is important that users can easily orient themselves and effortlessly find information. Thus, simplicity was one of the main requirements. The *aWall* follows a overall layout with the information view, the action view and the main menu at the bottom as shown in Figure 4.

Foster agile values
We observed that agile teams often add additional information to their boards. Such information is not necessarily related to the project, but contributes to team building and team spirit. The *aWall* supports this behavior by providing appropriate information widgets (*e.g.* fun, avatar widgets) as shown Figure 9.

Multi-Device Interaction
While large multi-touch walls perfectly meet team collaboration needs, they are less adequate for data input with keyboards or handwriting. Therefore, we strive to implement simultaneous interaction by means of tablets. Such devices could for example be used to enter new task cards in the Sprint Planning 2 meeting.

Prototype System Architecture
The application is developed as a three-tier Web application as shown in **Error! Reference source not found.**. Web technology supports very well the collaborative process in distributed teams; no local installation is required; it offers better user interface design capabilities with CSS. An important feature is the connection to third-party issue tracking systems like the JIRA [2]. Many organizations use such tools in their workflow [4] and therefore we can avoid disruption in team process.

Summary and Future Work
aWall is a unique agile collaboration platform in that it is designed for extra-large multi-touch wall systems and to explicitly support the agile work style. The demo illustrates the various underlying concepts of the so far implemented prototype. Our future work will focus on developing further concepts to improve and foster collaboration using large wall systems. This includes concepts for interaction with other devices, concepts for recommender and buddy systems, and better support for distributed collaboration. The very promising feedback from first prototype evaluations show that the *aWall* system fosters agile collaboration in teams by combining the strengths of the physical and digital tools in one system.

References

1. *Agile Manifesto*. Retrieved May 18, 2015 from http://agilemanifesto.org/
2. *Atlassion. JIRA Viewed 24.6.2015. https://www.atlassian.com*
3. *Version One. Viewed 24.6.15. http://www.versionone.com/*
4. Azizyan, G., Magarian, M. K., & Kajko-Matsson, M. (2011). Survey of agile tool usage and needs. IEEE Xplore, 29-38.
5. Deming, W. E. Out of the Crisis. The MIT Press. ISBN-13: 978-0262541152. 2000
6. Kropp, M., Meier, A., Swiss Agile Study - Einsatz und Nutzen von Agilen Methoden in der Schweiz (German). Retrieved May 18, 2015 from www.swissagilestudy.ch.
7. Version One. State of Agile Development Survey results. Retrieved May 18, 2015 from http://www.versionone.com/state_of_agile_development_survey/11/

MAPS: A Multi-Dimensional Password Scheme for Mobile Authentication

Jonathan Gurary
Cleveland State University
j.gurary@vikes.csuohio.edu

Jared Oluoch
Oakland University
jooluoch@oakland.edu

Ye Zhu
Cleveland State University
y.zhu61@csuohio.edu

Nahed Alnahash
Oakland University
nalnahas@oakland.edu

George Corser
Oakland University
gpcorser@oakland.edu

Huirong Fu
Oakland University
fu@oakland.edu

ITS 2015, November 15–18, 2015, Funchal/Madeira, Portugal.
ACM 978-1-4503-3899-8/15/11.
http://dx.doi.org/10.1145/2817721.2823479

Abstract
It has been long recognized that no silver bullet exists to achieve both *security* and *memorability*. With the addition of *usability requirements*, the task of designing authentication schemes for mobile devices becomes more challenging. We propose a Multi-dimensionAl Password Scheme (MAPS) for mobile authentication. MAPS fuses information from multiple dimensions to form a password. This fusion enlarges the password space, improves memorability, and enhances usability by reducing the number of gestures needed for authentication. Based on the idea of MAPS, we implement a Chess-based MAPS (CMAPS) for Android systems. Our user studies show that CMAPS can achieve high recall rates while exceeding the security strength of current mobile authentication schemes and exceeding the requirements of banking.

Author Keywords
Shoulder-Surfing, Challenge-Response, Graphical Password, Mobile Security, Multidimensional Password

Introduction
We propose a Multi-DimensionAl Password Scheme (MAPS) for mobile authentication. Because MAPS combines information from multiple dimensions, i.e. different types of information, to generate passwords, MAPS can generate a huge number of passwords with

Figure 1: An Example CMAPS Password

Figure 2: User Interface

just a small number of gestures. Passwords generated by MAPS are easy to remember because (1) MAPS is a type of graphical authentication scheme, which have been proven easier to remember than alphanumeric passwords [8], (2) MAPS fuses information from multiple dimensions through a single gesture on a touch screen, and (3) MAPS can reduce memory interference since the information is from different dimensions. MAPS is also easy to use on mobile devices with touch screens since passwords generated by MAPS can be input with significantly fewer gestures.

In this paper, we present Chess-based MAPS (CMAPS), a mobile authentication based on the board game Chess. With a single gesture, a user can choose the color, type, and location of a piece on the board. We show how this generates a large password space at low gesture counts while still maintaining high memorability and usability.

Related Work

The original proposal for the *graphical password* is the patent filed by Blonder [1] in 1996. The graphical approach is based on the concept that the human brain is relatively weak at remembering sequences of numbers or letters, but excellent at processing visual data [1, 3]. This phenomenon is called the *picture superiority effect*, the notion that humans have a much greater capacity for processing and remembering visual data than numbers and letters [7, 5].

There are three types of graphical schemes, based on human memory *tasks* as outlined in [6]. In recognition based schemes, such as Deja Vu [2], the user is prompted to dentify previously selected images. Recall based schemes, such as Draw-A-Secret [3], ask users to reproduce a secret drawing or gesture. Cued recall schemes, such as Passpoints [9], require users to perform actions on specific locations of an image or screen.

Mainstream mobile operating systems offer a few graphical schemes for authenication. The PIN based scheme, popularized by Apple, allows users to enter a 4-digit PIN on a number pad displaying the digits 0-9. Android's pattern unlock scheme presents a user with a 3×3 grid of dots[1]. Similar to Draw-A-Secret, a user creates a password by drawing lines connecting the dots in a certain way. Windows devices use a cued recall scheme similar to Passpoints [9]. The scheme allows users to upload an image and create a password by drawing a series of three gestures (a gesture is considered a tap, line, or circle) on the image. There are also several schemes based on biometrics, such as the fingerprint scanner, but we will not address those schemes in this work.

According to our knowledge, this is the first attempt to formally define the concept of multi-dimension passwords and analyze their benefits in terms of memory interference, security, and usability. We filed a patent on MAPS [4].

Multi-Dimensional Password Scheme

The key idea of a MAPS is to form a password by fusing information from multiple dimensions. To better explain the design of a MAPS, we present an example MAPS based on the classic game of Chess.

Figures 1 and 2 shows two screen-shots of our implementation of the Chess-based MAPS (CMAPS) developed for Android systems. Users set a password by placing chess game pieces onto a board with 8×8 tiles. The resulting chess formation is a CMAPS password. An

[1] A larger gird is possible on some devices. We focus on the default size of the grid in this paper.

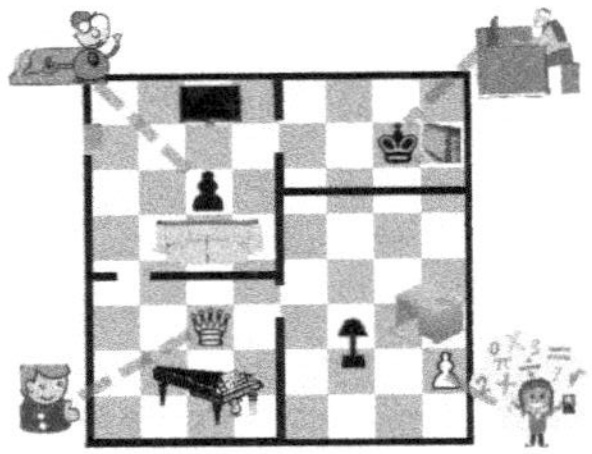

Figure 3: A sample graphical hint we generated to show to some of our participants.

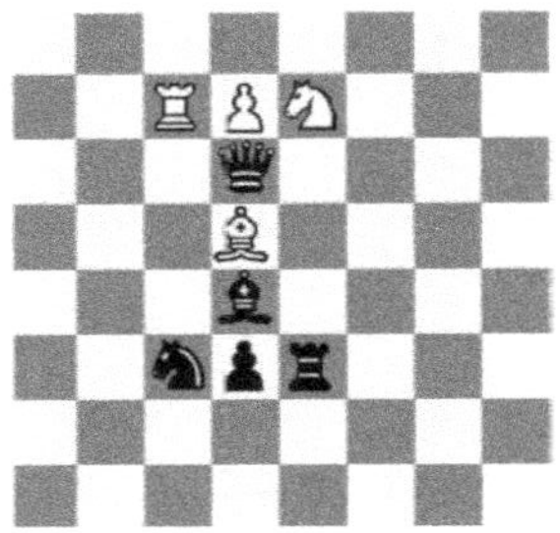

Figure 4: A CMAPS password generated by a user in our user study. The password is a cricket field, with different pieces denoting different players around the two wickets. The queen is the user's favorite player.

example password of CMAPS is shown in Figure 1. When the user wants to unlock the mobile device later, CMAPS will display a blank chess board and the chess game pieces as shown in Figure 2. The user can unlock the system by placing game pieces onto the game board. If the chess formation input by the user is exactly the same as the formation set in the password setting phase, the mobile device will be unlocked. The "Edit" button allows a user to empty a tile.

A user can put a game piece onto the board with one line gesture connecting a selected game piece to a desired tile in the board, or two taps by touching the desired piece and then its desired location. No knowledge of chess is required to use CMAPS; the pieces can be placed anywhere on the board. We hypothesize that chess skills may help to memorize passwords because a user may use a formation with some game pieces related by attacking or defending.

As an example of MAPS, CMAPS fuses information from multiple dimensions. The dimensions used in CMAPS include the color of the game piece, the type of the game piece, and the row and column of the desired tile. CMAPS fuses the information from these dimensions with one gesture on a touch screen that puts a game piece onto the board.

Graphical Hints
We hypothesize that graphical hints can reduce the popularity of hotspots and increase memorability. These graphical hints are kept in the user's memory only. We show graphical hints as shown in Figure 3 to participants and ask them to generate their own. Figure 4 shows an example hint that one of the participants in our user study generated.

Usability Analysis

We can evaluate the usability of mobile schemes with two metrics: number of gestures required to finish one authentication and time needed to finish authentication. CMAPS users can place a game piece onto the board by a drawing a line between a selected game piece and a tile on the board. A CMAPS password having l game pieces can require l gestures to input. Since each gesture allows the user to choose color, piece type, and location, the password space is $2^l 6^l \binom{64}{l}$.

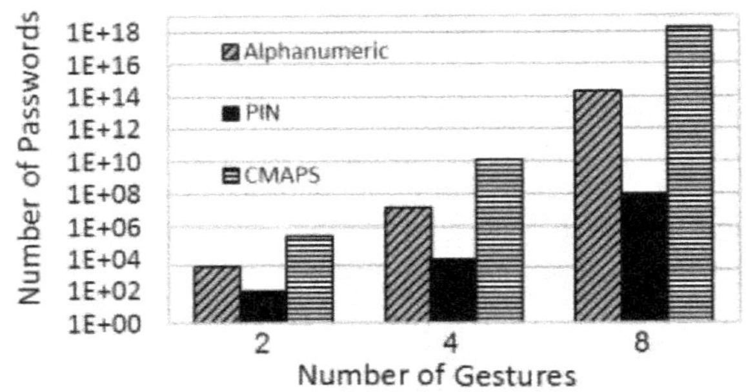

Figure 5: Number of Passwords supported by 2, 4, and 8 gestures

Figure 5 shows the number of passwords supported at low gesture counts using CMAPS, 4-digit PINs, and case-insensitive alphanumeric passwords. A password with 6 CMAPS gestures is stronger than an 8 character alphanumeric password used for secure applications like banking. We will discuss timing data collected from our user study in the next section.

User Study

We conducted a user study with 54 participants, 28 male and 26 female. Participants were asked to generate CMAPS passwords using 2, 8, or "8 or more" pieces. One group was also asked to generate "8 or more" piece passwords with graphical hints. We call these groups 2g, 8g, 8+g, and 8+gh respectively.

Table 1: Recall Rates of CMAPS Passwords.

Condition	Participants	Recall	Recall Rate
2g	8	8	100%
8g	18	18	100%
$8+g$	13	13	100%
$8+gh$	15	13	87%

Table 1 shows the recall rates of CMAPS passwords in the four categories after one week. Our application also studied timing data during the experiment. Although they were not instructed to move quickly, participants required an average of 10, 16, 16, and 20 seconds to authenticate themselves in the 2g, 8g, 8+g, and 8+gh conditions respectively.

Discussion and Future Work

We plan to expand on the idea of MAPS by adding other games, e.g. Monopoly or Checkers. By giving users the ability to use different games, we hope to reduce memory interference between different MAPS passwords.

Acknowledgement

This work was supported in part by the US National Science Foundation under Grants CNS-1338105 and CNS-1343141.

References

[1] Blonder, G. Graphical password, sep 1996. Patent 5,559,961.

[2] Dhamija, R., and Perrig, A. Deja vu: A user study using images for authentication. In *Proceedings of the 9th Conference on USENIX Security Symposium - Volume 9*, SSYM'00, USENIX Association (Berkeley, CA, USA, 2000), 4–4.

[3] Jermyn, I., Mayer, A., Monrose, F., Reiter, M. K., and Rubin, A. D. The design and analysis of graphical passwords. In *Proceedings of the 8th Conference on USENIX Security Symposium - Volume 8*, SSYM'99, USENIX Association (Berkeley, CA, USA, 1999), 1–1.

[4] Manning, P., McLennan, C. T., and Zhu, Y. Authentication method for a computing device using interactive game board and game piece images, 2013. Patent 61782062.

[5] Nickerson, R. *Short-term Memory for Complex Meaningful Visual Configurations: a Demonstration of Capacity*. Defense Technical Information Center, 1964.

[6] Raaijmakers, J. G., and Shiffrin, R. M. Models for recall and recognition. *Annual review of psychology 43* (1992), 205–234.

[7] Shepard, R. Recognition memory for words, sentences, and pictures. *Journal of Verbal Learning and Verbal Behavior 6*, 1 (1967), 156 – 163.

[8] Stobert, E., and Biddle, R. Memory retrieval and graphical passwords. In *Proceedings of the Ninth Symposium on Usable Privacy and Security*, SOUPS '13, ACM (New York, NY, USA, 2013), 15:1–15:14.

[9] Wiedenbeck, S., Waters, J., Birget, J.-C., Brodskiy, A., and Memon, N. Passpoints: Design and longitudinal evaluation of a graphical password system. *Int. J. Hum.-Comput. Stud. 63*, 1-2 (July 2005), 102–127.

Airsteroids: Re-designing the Arcade Game Using MarkAirs

Fernando Garcia-Sanjuan
ISSI/DSIC, Universitat Politècnica de València, Valencia, Spain
fegarcia@dsic.upv.es

Javier Jaen
ISSI/DSIC, Universitat Politècnica de València, Valencia, Spain
fjaen@upv.es

Alejandro Catala
LoUISE/I3A, University of Castilla-La Mancha (UCLM), Albacete, Spain
alejandro.catala@uclm.es

Geraldine Fitzpatrick
HCI Group, University of Technology (TU Wien), Vienna, Austria
geraldine.fitzpatrick@tuwien.ac.at

ITS '15, November 15-18, 2015, Funchal, Portugal
ACM 978-1-4503-3899-8/15/11.
http://dx.doi.org/10.1145/2817721.2823480

Abstract
This paper presents Airsteroids, a multi-player re-design of the classic arcade game Asteroids. The re-design makes use of handheld devices such as tablets and Smartphones and of MarkAirs, an around-device interaction (ADI) with fiducial markers that reduces occlusion on the screens and interference between users' interactions.

Author Keywords
Around-Device Interactions (ADI); fiducial markers; tablets.

ACM Classification Keywords
H.5.2. Information interfaces and presentation (e.g., HCI): User Interfaces – Input Devices and Strategies, Interaction Styles.

Introduction
Handheld devices are becoming very widespread and offer several advantages with respect to tabletops in terms of cost, scalability, and mobility to build collaboration spaces [8]. Despite these advantages, in these devices interaction is usually carried out via touch contacts, which, in multi-user co-located scenarios, can be the source of multiple problems. These include interference if several users try to simultaneously touch the same display, no identification of the source of a

given action, and occlusion of digital content by the participants' hands and arms, among others.

To overcome these problems, Around-Device Interactions (ADIs) could be used in these environments to enable interactions in the available 3D space above the surfaces. However, when ADIs have been implemented in the past they have either required pre-installed specialized hardware that limited the choice of where these interactions could take place, or have not been accurate enough to perform high precision manipulations of objects on the devices.

In this work, we present a re-implementation of the classic arcade game Asteroids called Airsteroids, which enables a multi-user co-located game experience. Each user brings his/her own tablet to the environment and can interact with all devices by means of ADIs using MarkAirs. MarkAirs is an interaction technique that makes use of fiducial markers tracked by the built-in front camera of these handheld devices. The user can perform several aerial gestures with the markers, which entail different behaviors to the game elements.

Related Work

Previous works have explored ADIs with tabletops. These exploit the space above the surface either to explore 3D virtual spaces (e.g., [9]) or to reach and manipulate distant elements (e.g., [1]). These high-precision tasks, however, often rely on complex hardware settings composed of several external cameras, projectors, or gloves with reflective markers like the ones used in motion capture (e.g., [7]).

Other approaches rely on embedded cameras that are installed within tabletops to recognize aerial interactions. Hilliges et al. [3], for example, use an "enhanced" tabletop and make use of hands to perform gestures in the air to manipulate 3D digital objects rendered on a tabletop. However, one of the drawbacks of their approach is that, even though hands enable natural interactions, it is not possible to identify the user who makes a given aerial interaction. To solve this problem, Gallardo and Jordà [2] propose the use of fiducial markers for such interactions. However, their approach requires expensive specially designed hardware to control the degree of transparency of the surface, so that image projection and gesture detection are interleaved. Moreover, their markers cannot be occluded for the system to work properly.

Several works have explored ADIs for handheld devices using external cameras or depth sensors with the purpose of performing 3D rotations using hand gestures around the handheld (e.g., [6]), or reducing the occlusion produced by touch contacts on the screen (e.g., [4]). These approaches allow manipulations to be performed with a certain precision but, again, require careful installation of external hardware. Others reduce the hardware complexity by making use of the built-in sensors in the tablets. Ketabdar et al. [5], for instance, exploit the magnetic (compass) sensor of the device and enable in-air interactions using magnets. Unlike optical approaches, this solution is more robust to occlusion, but it is less precise and the system is not capable of differentiating between different magnets since they do not have an encoded ID.

Interaction with MarkAirs

MarkAirs is an interaction technique performed above a tablet or smartphone conducted by handling a fiducial marker which, when in the field of view of the tablet's built-in front camera, allows a computer vision software to detect the marker and track its 6-DOF pose (position and orientation) in real-time. Markers may be attached

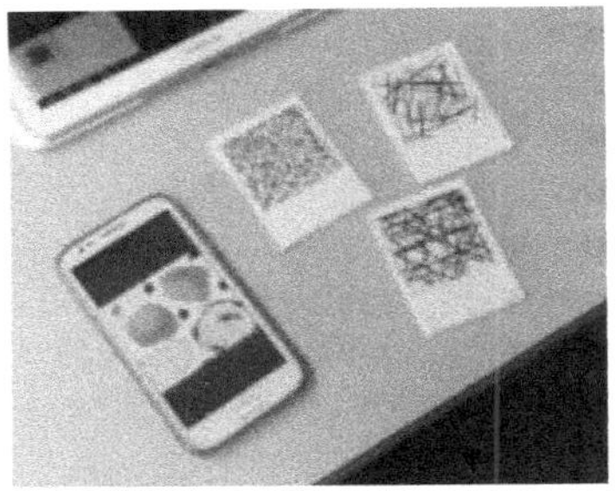

Figure 1. Markers used to perform interactions in the Airsteroids game.

to physical cards or displayed on other digital devices allowing for multi-display ecosystems (see Figure 1). Unlike other works [2], our markers consist of arbitrary drawings which are tracked by Vuforia™'s natural feature tracking algorithms. We adopted these particular markers for several reasons: First, because they can be tracked even if they are partially occluded. Second, because this system allows for a virtually infinite number of markers, since creating a new one can be achieved simply by drawing some arbitrary lines. Finally, because a marker can also be a meaningful photograph, which can be related to the digital information content that is associated with the card (e.g., if we want a card to contain a game element, the marker can be a picture of the element itself).

Airsteroids

Airsteroids consists of a re-design of the classic arcade game, where a ship must destroy some asteroids coming at it before they crash. In our version, several players arrange some tablets on a surface (see Figure 2) and they use different markers with the MarkAirs infrastructure to handle the different game elements. There is no need to touch the screen nor pop up any contextual menus that could occlude the interface. In the proposed demo game there are three types of markers:

- *Ship controllers*: Each one of these markers represent a ship of a specific color for a given player. The marker's XY position and yaw rotation are mapped to the ship allowing it to move around the digital world and cross between surfaces. When the marker is brought down (closer to the tablet), it causes the ship to shoot.
- *Asteroids factory*: These markers allow the user to place some asteroids on any tablet by means of an up/down gesture. Once an asteroid is placed, it starts moving with a given speed and a random trajectory.
- *Property modifiers*: Modifier markers control specific properties of some game elements. For example, to modify the speed at which the asteroids move (bringing the marker up speeds up the asteroids, whereas bringing it closer to the device slows them down); others can make a spaceship undestructible during a given time span; etc.

Figure 2. Several users playing Airsteroids

Conclusion

In this paper we presented Airsteroids, a re-implementation of the Asteroids game using MarkAirs, an ADI technique using fiducial markers. Airsteroids is an example of a multi-player multi-device game that can enable social/collaborative behaviors. We illustrate the ways in which using aerial interactions can reduce occlusion and interference among several users' actions, which is a problem that can occur in similar scenarios where only touch interactions are available.

As future work, we intend to conduct an experiment with real players during the ITS'15 demos session in order to obtain information about the social interactions and collaborative behaviors that emerge during the course of the game. In this evaluation up to 6 co-located tablets will be used and the game will be available for download to enable ITS attendees to participate in a massive multi-player Airsteroids experience.

Acknowledgements

This work received financial support from Spanish Ministry of Economy and Competitiveness under the National Strategic Program of Research with Projects TIN2010-20488 and TIN2014-60077-R, and from Universitat Politècnica de València under Project UPV-FE-2014-24. It is also supported by fellowship ACIF/2014/214 within the VALi+d program from Conselleria d'Educació, Cultura i Esport (Generalitat Valenciana).

References

1. Amartya Banerjee, Jesse Burstyn, Audrey Girouard, and Roel Vertegaal. 2011. Pointable: An in-air pointing technique to manipulate out-of-reach targets on tabletops. *Proc. of ITS'11*, 11–20. http://doi.org/10.1145/2076354.2076357
2. Daniel Gallardo and Sergi Jordà. 2013. SLFiducials: 6DoF markers for tabletop interaction. *Proc. of ITS'13*, 401–404. http://doi.org/10.1145/2512349.2514914
3. Otmar Hilliges, Shahram Izadi, Andrew D. Wilson, Steve Hodges, Armando Garcia-Mendoza, and Andreas Butz. 2009. Interactions in the air: adding further depth to interactive tabletops. *Proc. of UIST'09*, 139–148. http://doi.org/10.1145/1622176.1622203
4. Brett Jones, Rajinder Sodhi, David Forsyth, Brian Bailey, and Giuliano Maciocci. 2012. Around device interaction for multiscale navigation. *Proc. of MobileHCI'12*, 83–92. http://doi.org/10.1145/2371574.2371589
5. Hamed Ketabdar, Kamer Ali Yüksel, and Mehran Roshandel. 2010. MagiTact: Interaction with mobile devices based on compass (magnetic) sensor. *Proc. of IUI'10*, 413–414. http://doi.org/10.1145/1719970.1720048
6. Sven Kratz, Michael Rohs, Dennis Guse, Jörg Müller, Gilles Bailly, and Michael Nischt. 2012. PalmSpace: Continuous around-device gestures vs. multitouch for 3D rotation tasks on mobile devices. *Proc. of AVI'12*, 181–188. http://doi.org/10.1145/2254556.2254590
7. Nicolai Marquardt, Ricardo Jota, Saul Greenberg, and Joaquim A. Jorge. 2011. The continuous interaction space: Interaction techniques unifying touch and gesture on and above a digital surface. *Proc. of INTERACT'11*, 461–476. http://doi.org/10.1007/978-3-642-23765-2_32
8. Roman Rädle, Hans-Christian Jetter, Nicolai Marquardt, Harald Reiterer, and Yvonne Rogers. 2014. HuddleLamp: Spatially-aware mobile displays for ad-hoc around-the-table collaboration. *Proc. of ITS'14*, 45–54. http://doi.org/10.1145/2669485.2669500
9. Martin Spindler, Sophie Stellmach, and Raimund Dachselt. 2009. PaperLens: Advanced magic lens interaction above the tabletop. *Proc. of ITS'09*, 69–76. http://doi.org/10.1145/1731903.1731920

DreamScope Catcher: a Touch Sensitive Interface to Catch Dreams

Mara Dionisio
Madeira - ITI,
University of Madeira,
Campus da Penteada, 9000-150
Funchal, Portugal
msgdionisio@gmail.com

Paulo Bala
Madeira - ITI,
University of Madeira,
Campus da Penteada, 9000-160
Funchal, Portugal
paulo.bala@gmail.com

Rui Trindade
Madeira - ITI,
University of Madeira,
Campus da Penteada, 9000-160
Funchal, Portugal
rui.antero.trindade@gmail.com

Valentina Nisi
Madeira - ITI,
University of Madeira,
Campus da Penteada, 9000-160
Funchal, Portugal
Valentina.Nisi@gmail.com

Nuno Nunes
Madeira - ITI,
University of Madeira,
Campus da Penteada, 9000-160
Funchal, Portugal
Njn@uma.pt

Time's Up
Industriezeile, 33b
4020 Linz, Austria
info@timesup.org

ITS '15, November 15-18, 2015, Funchal, Portugal ACM 978-1-4503-3899-8/15/11.
http://dx.doi.org/10.1145/2817721.2823481

Abstract
Dream Scope is the interactive, stand alone, self-contained portion of a bigger Art installation named Lucid Peninsula. The goal of the installation is to offer a way for people to experience the future through a physical interactive installation. To achieve this aim we designed and developed the interactive DreamScope device, while the Time's Up collective designed and built the physical installation. On one side with the DreamViewer binoculars enable participants to see the Lucid Peninsula fictional world and absorb data relating to factors such as air quality, presence of plant and other life forms, etc. On the other side of the installation, the audience will be able to borrow mobile devices (DreamCatchers) and 'catch' the dreams of the inhabitants of the peninsula, which are mixed with memories of the world before it was transformed.

Author Keywords
Mobile Touch surface, interactive art installation, interaction design, experience design

ACM Classification Keywords
H.5.m. Information interfaces and presentation (e.g., HCI): Miscellaneous;

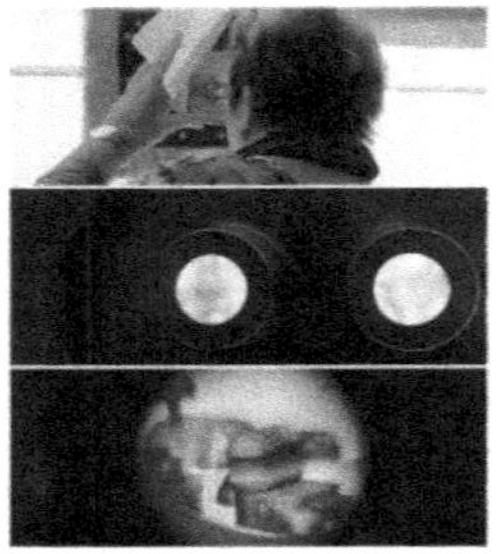

Figure 1: In this image, a participants is looking through the DreamScope viewer in the top slice of the image. In the middle slice and bottom slice, a view of what can be seen from the binoculars interface of the DreamViewer is shown.

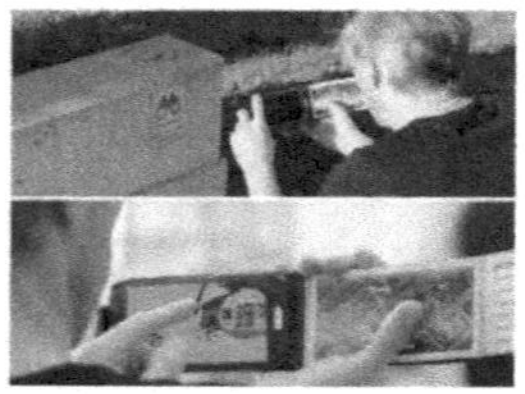

Figure 2: In this image, a participant is using the DreamViewer device outdoors capturing a dream. In the bottom part of the image a participant is exploring the dream by means of touch interaction.

Introduction
Lucid Peninsula is an interactive installation designed to immerse participants in a dreamlike, post-apocalyptic storyworld where changes to the Earth's atmosphere have led to the emergence of new species, conditions, and ways of life. Fragments of memories and dreams belonging to the inhabitants of the previous era still linger in this new world, hovering over certain locations. The Lucid Peninsula storyworld where the lucid dreaming takes place emerged from a future scenario planning activity undertaken by artists and designers from the FoAM and Time's Up collectives in June 2014. We worked closely with these artists to create the Lucid Peninsula interactive physical installation. Lucid Peninsula is a part of Future Fabulators, an EU-funded project that aims to explore and prototype possible futures within a cultural framework. [1]

The goal of the installation is to offer a means for people to experience the future by bringing to life a storyworld the audience can interact with, reflect on, and interrogate with questions such as: Could I live in this world? Could this really happen? How would I adapt?

Lucid Peninsula storyworld
The Lucid Peninsula is a futuristic world that feels familiar, yet strange: an eternal twilight of dreamlike metaphors and shape-shifting beings. Environmental living conditions have radically changed and the search for green plants has become crucial for survival. The outside air is toxic: not immediately lethal, but requiring special gear and treatment after exposure.

Dreamscope Mobile Application
To give the public a chance to experience the Lucid Peninsula firsthand, we designed a physical installation and an interactive environment. A special device called a DreamScope, comprised of Dreamviewer binoculars and a mobile Dreamcatcher, will guide people in the discovery of this world. Ideally, the equipment will be located in a special room, dedicated to the detoxification and recovery of air force pilots who sweep the peninsula in search of rare green plants and need to undergo a special purification treatment before they can fly the next mission. For the scope of the ITS demonstration we will not recreate the pilot room, but set up the dream scope viewer and catcher in a corner of the room where the audience can easily interact with both devices and switch from sweeping the Peninsula landscape and catching the dreams and memories of its inhabitants.

Lucid DreamScope Viewer
The DreamViewer enables the audience to glimpse life in the Lucid Peninsula. The device is used by pilots in the recovery room to check outside conditions (temperature, humidity, visibility), make sure it is safe to exit the room, and find locations with heightened dream activity.

With the DreamViewer, visitors can enjoy a 180-degree panoramic view of the outside world, as if they are looking through a window of the room. The 3D world depicts a desert-like landscape with orange sky and large red sun. The 3D landscape simulates the landscape outside the recovery room, highlighting buildings that the user can explore in the city. Users can zoom in on buildings in the landscape to apprehend more details of the structure. This is possible through the use of a Google cardboard virtual reality kit. [2] The software was built using the Unity game engine and receives input from the compass and the accelerometer in order to show the virtual environment of the Lucid Peninsula.

Figure 3: the DreamViewer device, allowing participants to see the Lucid Peninsula Landscapes

Lucid DreamScope Catcher
With the Dream Catcher visitors will discover the dreams and memories of the Lucid Peninsula inhabitants. The Dream Catcher runs on a mobile device through an Android application built using the Unity game engine. It uses image recognition software to trigger the virtual environments where the characters' dreams are narrated as voice overs. By tapping the mobile device screen, users create circular viewing portals, that show what the Lucid Peninsula world looked like at a different time. An audio narration recounts the dream mixed with memories from the dreamers. The dreams themselves focus on the past and how the world once was (which is a reference to our current world) and the nostalgia the present inhabitants feel about such distant times. Such memories are mixed with dreamlike narrations of their present lives.

In the ITS demo space we envisage setting up a large panoramic image of the Lucid Peninsula (printed from the Dream Viewer 3D landscape). Ideally the large poster will be positioned on a wall near the Dream Viewer device. On this big poster, the audience will find a special icons placed near the depicted buildings where dream activity has been detected (through the previous scanning of the landcape with the Dream Viewer). Upon capturing such icons (or markers) the mobile device will load the 3D environment of such location and where the dream is kept. Upon touch of the screen of he Dream Catcher device the dream will play. Each touch of the screen will reveal a fragment of the dream, and a fragment of the past of the Lucid Peninsula, how this world used to be when the memories were made. Such a juxtaposition of past and present and dream and memories creates an atmosphere of nostalgia but at the same of awareness that our world might not always keep as it is, and that we ought to care for it, cherish and respect its richness and natural beauty.

Figure 4: the DreamCatcher device, closed. See Fig.2 for how it looks once opened.

Conclusions

The Lucid Peninsula full installation was successfully exhibited in Austria and Romania, in the context of the exhibition Intime Raume 2014 by IMA [3] and Future Fabulators exhibition by AltArt [4]. The diverse audience found the Dreamscope entertaining and thought-provoking.

Akcnowledgments

We wish to acknowledge Future Fabulators, EU Culture and Media Project Funds (2013-1659/001-001 CU7 COOP7) for sponsoring our investigation, our fellow researchers at all partner institutions, M-ITI, Time's Up, and FoAM for their help and contributions, and the LARSyS (PEst-OE/EEI/LA0009/2013) research group for support and funding.

References

[1]http://futurefabulators.m-iti.org; http://www.timesup.org/FutureFabulatorsEU

[2] http://www.google.com/get/cardboard/

[3] http://ima.or.at/lucid-peninsula/?lang=de

[4] http://www.altart.org/?p=1322

BlackBlocks: Tangible Interactive System for Children to Learn 3-Letter Words and Basic Math

Wafa Almukadi[1,2]
[1] Florida Institute of Technology
Melbourne, FL 32901, USA
[2] King Abdulaziz University
Jeddah, Saudi Arabia
walmukadi2013@my.fit.edu

A. Lucas Stephane[1]
[1] Florida Institute of Technology
Melbourne, FL 32901, USA
lstephane@fit.edu

ITS '15, November 15-18, 2015, Funchal, Portugal
ACM 978-1-4503-3899-8/15/11.
http://dx.doi.org/10.1145/2817721.2823482

Abstract
We demonstrate *BlackBlocks*, a low-cost portable prototype work as a tangible user interface for children aged 4 to 8 to support language and math learning. This prototype is used as a research instrument to compare learning between toy blocks and a tangible system. A comparative experiment was performed with 18 children for evaluating the effects of learning method.

Author Keywords
Toy blocks, Tangible User Interface, Comparison, Evaluation, Education, Human-Centered design

ACM Classification Keywords
H.5.2 [Information Interfaces and Presentation]: User Interfaces.

K.3.1 [Computers and Education]: Computer Use in Education.

Introduction
Children are able to naturally learn, explore and discover through object manipulation that supports their cognitive development, and facilitates the development of mental models [7]. Toy blocks (TBs) are an example of object manipulation that found their way into most schools and home playrooms longtime

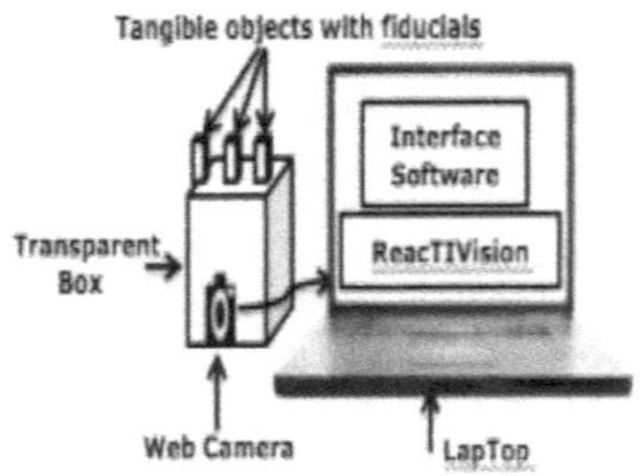

Figure 1: BBs system schema

Figure 3: Black and white tangible block (↑top). A bottom view of tangible blocks shows the fiducial marker (↓bottom)

ago. It helps children to explore the world around them while gaining physical, social, intellectual, and creative benefits [11]. Learning occurs by interacting with physical objects that provide concrete representations of abstract concepts [4]. Several researches [6,9,10] investigated the affordance of 3D blocks as gesture based interaction input devices showing improvements in flexibility, reliability, sensitivity and control. Some other projects [3] developed for children to enhance TBs as a spelling tool. The proposed system BlackBlocks (BBs) provides the following features:

1. TBs augmented with audio-visual feedback facilitating children engagement
2. Includes three applications that support 3-letter words, and practice of basic addition and subtraction up to 10
3. Human-Centered design approach: moving from single-agent models of cognition to multi-agent models [2]
4. Includes children designing properties [1]
5. The system was tested and refined iteratively in several studies for ensuring physical robustness, and usability

BBs System Components

The BBs consists of (Figure1 and Figure2) a transparent box providing a surface where children can play with the blocks. A black foam frame was added on the top surface for defining the playing area. A web camera (Logitech HD webcam C615) is placed at the bottom of the box to ensure optical marker recognition. BBs has 25 tangible "blocks" as follows: 12 letters: " A, B, C, E, F, G, H, N, O, T, U, X", 10 numbers: " 0, 1, 2, 3, 4, 5, 6, 7, 8, 9" and 3 symbols: "+, -, =". All blocks are black and white with unique fiducial markers on their bottom (see Figure 3). Since the colors on regular wooden blocks are not systematic, black and white blocks are used instead for ensuring consistency across all letters, numbers and symbols, avoiding unwanted associations between colors and letters, numbers or symbols. A laptop is used for running the software applications and the reacTIVision[1] framework. All The applications were coded by Processing.

Figure 2: BBs system components with a running example of 3-letter words "BAT"

Applications

BBs offers three different applications. The goal of the first application is to build 3-letter words to support spelling and vocabulary learning. Children have to align three blocks to get a meaningful 3-letter word. When obtaining a meaningful word such as "BAT", a message "You got the word BAT" is displayed with an image corresponding to the word and clapping sounds. The system supports so far 23 different words: cat, fat, hat,

[1] http://reactivision.sourceforge.net/

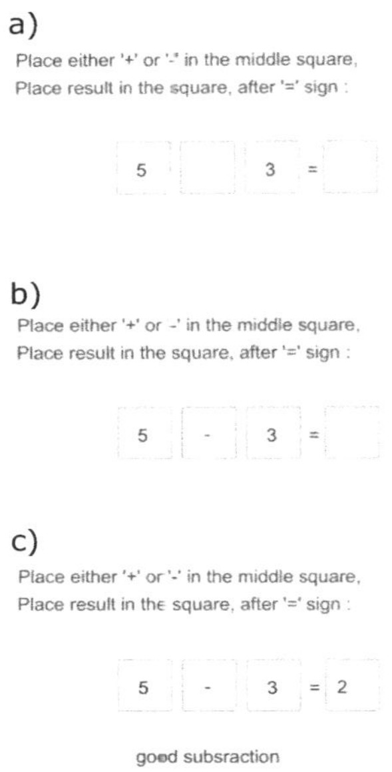

Figure 4: Forward Exercise, a) displaying 2 random numbers b) placing the minus block d) placing number 2 block to solve problem

bat, act, hug, hut, hot, cut, tab, fun, hen, fan, can, tub, bag, bug, hog, bog, cot, fox, fog, box.

The second application is called "Forward Exercise" and its goal is to build and discover mathematical problems, allowing them to go from components to results. At first, two random numbers between 1 and 5 are displayed on the screen. Children have to: 1) place the operator block either "+" or "-" on the surface; 2) place the number block corresponding to the result. If children solve the problem, a "good job sound" is played together with a visual message showing "good addition/subtraction" accordingly (see Figure 4)

The third application is called "Backward Exercise" and its goal is to help children build and discover mathematical problems, allowing them to go from results to components. At first, one random number between 1 and 10 is displayed on the screen after the equal sign. Children have to: 1) place the operator block either "+" or "-" on the surface; 2) place two number blocks that, through the operator, should lead to the result number appearing on the screen. If children solve the problem, a "good job sound" is played together with a visual message showing "good addition/subtraction" accordingly (see Figure 5).

Comparative Evaluation

The comparative evaluation was carried out to determine whether BBs could be successfully used in language and math topics for children classroom. This evaluation compared learning effectiveness and user acceptance of BBs versus the TBs. The study took place in the Crawford building at the Florida Institute of Technology (FIT) with 18 children (8 boys and 10 girls) aged between 5 and 7. The experiment was approved by the FIT, and children were selected in cooperation with personnel from the University Park Elementary School (Melbourne, FL). The effect of the learning method (BBs or TBs) on the dependent variables (i.e. satisfaction, motivation, learning, perceived usability, and system preferences) was measured in an AB design experiment (Figure 6). Children were divided into two groups of equal size, and worked individually in parallel with BBs and TBs, in two separate rooms. The dependent variables were assessed using questionnaire and Smileyometer scale [8].

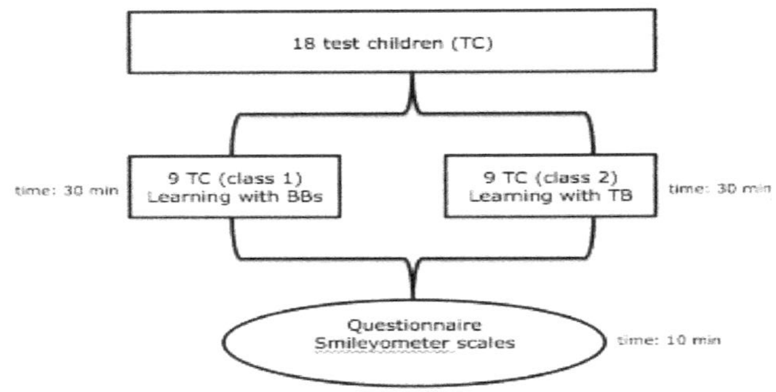

Figure 6: AB experiment design to measure the Effect of learning method (BBs or TBs) on dependent variables

Results

Results showed that children who used the BBs solved the problems more effectively than those using TBs. However, there was no significant difference in the number of solved problems (Table 1), but mostly in the usability, system preference, enjoyability, and acceptance (Figure 7).

Application	Time	Using BBs	Using TBs
3-letter words	12 min.	18 words	12 words
Forward math	9 min.	17 problems	15 problems
Backward math	9 min.	22 problems	22 problems

Table 1: Number of solved problems in TBS vs. BBS groups

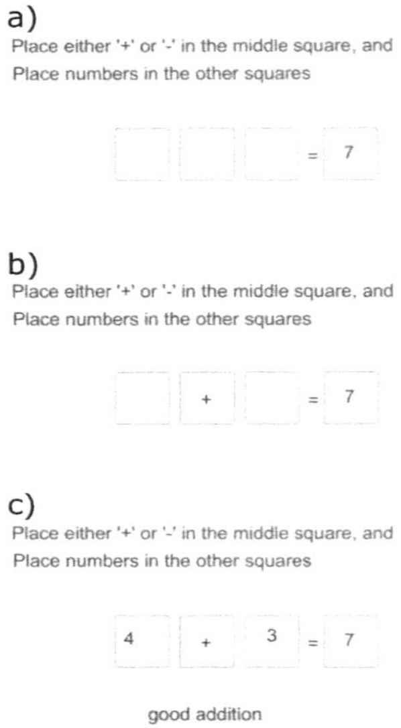

Figure 5: Backward Exercise, a) displaying 1 random numbers b) placing the addition block d) placing 2 number blocks to solve problem

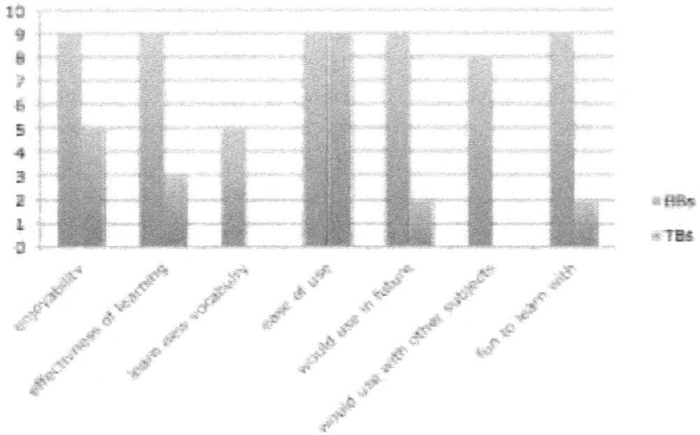

Figure 7: BBs vs. TBs preference by seven criteria.

Conclusion and Perspectives

In this paper we present the BBs system as an interactive system for children to support learning of language and math. Results obtained so far show that tangible interfaces can promote learning through embodied experience and positive mood. It seems so far that BBs helps to stimulate children motivation and engagement. Motivation clearly appeared when children started to think about 4-letter words they could achieve while these were not required. Our results are quite limited regarding to the small sample size, however, it is planned to perform AB-BA experiments [5] with BBs and TBs in order to consolidate the BBs benefits as a hybrid tangible-digital system.

References

1. Antle, A. N. (2007, February). The CTI framework: informing the design of tangible systems for children. In Proc. of the 1st international conference on Tangible
2. Boy, G. A. (2014). From automation to tangible interactive objects. *Annual Reviews in Control, 38*(1), 1-11.
3. Dekel, A., Yavne, G., Ben-Tov, E., & Roschak, Y. (2007, June). The spelling bee: an augmented physical block system that knows how to spell. In Proc. of the international conference on Advances
4. Edgeworth, M., & Edgeworth, R. L. (1835). Practical education. Harper & Brothers.
5. Fjeld, M., Fredriksson, J., Ejdestig, M., Duca, F., Bötschi, K., Voegtli, B., & Juchli, P. (2007, April). Tangible user interface for chemistry education: comparative evaluation and re-design. In *Proc. of the SIGCHI conference on Human factors in computing systems* (pp. 805-808). ACM.
6. Goh, Wooi Boon, et al. "The i-Cube: design considerations for block-based digital manipulatives and their applications." Proc. of the Designing Interactive Systems Conference. ACM, 2012.
7. Inhelder, B., Piaget, J., Iverson, J. M., & Goldin-Meadow, S. (1964). The early growth of logic in the child; gesture paves the way for language development.
8. Read, J. C. (2008). Validating the Fun Toolkit: an instrument for measuring children's opinions of technology. Cognition, Technology & Work, 10(2), 119-128.
9. Sharlin, E., Itoh, Y., Watson, B., Kitamura, Y., Sutphen, S., & Liu, L. (2002, April). Cognitive cubes: a tangible user interface for cognitive assessment. In *Proc. of the SIGCHI conference on Human factors in computing systems*(pp. 347-354). ACM.
10. Sheridan J, Short Ben W, Van Laerhoven K, Villar N, Kortuem G (2003) Exploring cube affordances: towards a classification of non-verbal dynamics of physical interfaces for wearable computing. Eurowearable
11. "Toy block." Wikipedia: The Free Encyclopedia. Wikimedia Foundation, Inc., 18 July 2015. Web. 30 Aug 2015. https://en.wikipedia.org/wiki/Toy_block#History

The MiTable Multi-Touch Gestures Engine

Mauricio Cirelli
Escola Politécnica da
Universidade de São Paulo
INTERLAB
mauricio.cirelli@usp.br

Lucia Filgueiras
Escola Politécnica da
Universidade de São Paulo
lucia.filgueiras@poli.usp.br

Ricardo Nakamura
Escola Politécnica da
Universidade de São Paulo
INTERLAB
ricardo.nakamura@poli.usp.br

ITS '15, November 15-18, 2015, Funchal, Portugal
Copyright © 2014 ACM 978-1-4503-3899-8/15/11.
http://dx.doi.org/10.1145/2817721.2823483

Abstract
From smartphones to large multi-touch surfaces, different devices and applications need a technique to match the input from each user to a known action. The multi-touch gestures recognition problem has been studied for a long time and has obtained its most expressive results in the past decade. However, the multi-user scenario for large multi-touch tables imposes several challenges to existing gestures recognizers. In this paper, we propose a new multi-touch gesture engine which is capable of adding multi-user capabilities to existing state-of-art gesture recognizers.

Author Keywords
Multi-touch; gesture; recognition; frameworks; multi-touch surface; interactive table

ACM Classification Keywords
H.1.2. [User/Machine Systems]: Human factors; H.5.2. [User Interfaces]: Input devices and strategies (e.g., mouse, touchscreen); H.5.2. [User Interfaces]: Interaction styles (e.g., commands, menus, forms, direct manipulation)

Introduction
Smartphones, tablets and large multi-touch tables are examples of touch-capable devices. Users interact with such devices using gestures, which are the movements executed by their fingers while in *contact* with the surface. The *con-*

tact is, in this case, any input that can be detected by the surface sensors and translated into touch events. While in smartphones and tablets, users directly touch the screen, in large multi-touch tables, contact is usually captured by cameras and computer vision algorithms [3].

Despite the technology used to detect users input, the movements they perform with their fingers must be identified and translated into an action in the application context. This problem is known as the *gestures recognition problem* and one of the first researches on this topic was published by Rubine in 1991 [6].

Previous work summarized different gestures characteristics according to: Degrees of Freedom (2D or 3D), Spatiality (on or above the surface), Semantics (symbolic or direct manipulation), Trajectory Complexity, Number of Users, Number of Fingers and Timing (atomic or sequential) [2].

Depending on the size of the touch surface and the interaction context, we may categorize tabletop applications in four groups, considering the number of users and fingers used to interact with the device: Single-Touch and Single-User Applications (STSU), Single-Touch and Multi-User Applications (STMU), Multi-Touch and Single-User Applications (MTSU) and Multi-Touch and Multi-User Applications (MTMU). In this research, we focus on the 2D gestures recognition problem in MTMU scenarios.

Related Work

Modern operating systems support a set of common multi-touch gestures natively. If an application needs custom gestures, developers need to intercept and manipulate low-level touch input in order to identify which gesture has been performed. This is not only a challenging technical task, but also one that requires continual maintenance to deal with updates and changes to underlying systems [5, 8].

This problem has motivated several researches in the past years. Some of them are used herein as examples to support our discussion. For further information, please see [2].

A gesture recognizer is a piece of software responsible for interpreting the touch input and translating it to a meaningful action in the top-level application [6].

Back to 1991, Rubine introduced this concept and proposed a solution for the single-touch gesture recognition problem based on the *Linear Discriminant* functions technique from the Machine Learning field.

The $-family of gesture recognizers started with the simplest scenario (STSU) [8] and evolved until being able to recognize multi-touch gestures (MTSU) [1]. These recognizers are based on the k-Nearest Neighbours algorithm with a specialized distance function for comparing multi-touch gestures.

Other approaches are based on a *formal model*, which consists in defining a set of rules and characteristics for each gesture and in letting a *stream processor* extract the relevant information from the raw input data according to the parameters defined in the model. Examples of this approach are Midas [7] and Proton++ [4].

Although these techniques obtained good results for the gesture recognition problem, it is a developer's task to build an unknown gesture structure from the raw input data before it can be interpreted by the recognizer. These approaches do not have a solution for MTMU environments, where several touch inputs are captured from several users at the same time. There are two questions that must be answered: *How to segregate touch inputs from each user?* and *How to combine previous gestures into sequential or collaborative gestures?*.

We understand that some tabletops are capable of tracking users while tracking their touch inputs, but this is not the case for several devices, which imposes a very challenging problem to solve. Even with such hardware capabilities, the combination of different gestures from different users into collaborative or sequential gestures is still not solved by those recognizers.

In this work we propose a new multi-touch gestures engine that is flexible enough to support any of the aforementioned multi-touch gestures recognizers while adapting them to support MTMU environments, without the need of specialized hardware[1].

The MiTable Engine

The MiTable Engine splits the multi-touch gestures recognition problem into three main steps. First, it decides which touch inputs belong to each unknown gesture object. Then, it feeds a state-of-art recognition algorithm with the unknown gesture to obtain its classification. Finally, the engine combines the classified gesture with previously executed gestures in order to identify if that gesture is atomic or if it is part of a sequential or collaborative gesture (Figure 1).

Figure 1: The MiTable Recognition Process

The *Segmentation* process is responsible for receiving raw touch input from the underlying hardware and for preparing an unknown gesture object for classification. It filters out noisy data and accidental touch inputs, similarly to [9]. Then, depending on the hardware capabilities, it groups each touch trajectory into gestures according to users information. If users identification is provided by the underlying hardware, it is directly obtained. For other cases, users information is inferred based on the location of the touch trajectories (configurable users territories) and/or distance between fingers.

[1] If users information is available with their touch input, the MiTable Engine can make use of it for better performance and accuracy.

The *Classification* process uses a state-of-art recognizer in order to obtain the gestures classification. Finally, the *Combination* process implements a finite state machine to combine previously captured gestures into sequential or collaborative gestures.

The proposed engine is entirely abstracted by interfaces, allowing easy customization of its internal processes. Developers can create their own *Segmentation*, *Classification* and *Combination* algorithms and use them within the engine. The engine comes with two graphical tools: one for recording multi-touch gestures and another to compare the performance and accuracy of different recognizers on a set of common gestures. These tools allow developers to easy build instances of state-of-art classification algorithms properly tuned to their application and use them within the engine.

Conclusion

In this paper we presented the MiTable Engine for gesture recognition. Although we focused in MTMU scenarios, the engine works for other scenarios as well, as they are subsets of MTMU. The architecture proposed is flexible for customization and adapts existing state-of-art recognition algorithms to multi-user scenarios without the need of rewriting the algorithms themselves. The Benchmark tool facilitates the configuration of complex recognizers and allows the comparison between them for any set of captured gestures.

In future works, we plan to study how to combine the results from different classification techniques in order to improve accuracy. Finally, a more general approach for the *Combination* algorithm might be obtained with more powerful algorithms, such as Hidden Markov Models.

REFERENCES

1. Lisa Anthony and Jacob O. Wobbrock. 2012. $N-protractor: a fast and accurate multistroke recognizer. In *Proceedings of Graphics Interface 2012 (GI '12)*. Canadian Information Processing Society, Toronto, Ont., Canada, Canada, 117–120. http://dl.acm.org/citation.cfm?id=2305276.2305296
2. Mauricio Cirelli and Ricardo Nakamura. 2014. A Survey on Multi-touch Gesture Recognition and Multi-touch Frameworks. In *Proceedings of the Ninth ACM International Conference on Interactive Tabletops and Surfaces (ITS '14)*. ACM, New York, NY, USA, 35–44. DOI: http://dx.doi.org/10.1145/2669485.2669509
3. Sergi Jorda, GÃijnter Geiger, Marcos Alonso, and Martin Kaltenbrunner. 2007. The reacTable: exploring the synergy between live music performance and tabletop tangible interfaces. In *Proceedings of the 1st international conference on Tangible and embedded interaction (TEI '07)*. ACM, New York, NY, USA, 139–146. DOI: http://dx.doi.org/10.1145/1226969.1226998
4. Kenrick Kin, BjÃűrn Hartmann, Tony DeRose, and Maneesh Agrawala. 2012a. Proton++: a customizable declarative multitouch framework. In *Proceedings of the 25th annual ACM symposium on User interface software and technology (UIST '12)*. ACM, New York, NY, USA, 477–486. DOI: http://dx.doi.org/10.1145/2380116.2380176
5. Kenrick Kin, BjÃűrn Hartmann, Tony DeRose, and Maneesh Agrawala. 2012b. Proton: multitouch gestures as regular expressions. In *Proceedings of the 2012 ACM annual conference on Human Factors in Computing Systems (CHI '12)*. ACM, New York, NY, USA, 2885–2894. DOI: http://dx.doi.org/10.1145/2208636.2208694
6. Dean Rubine. 1991. Specifying gestures by example. *SIGGRAPH Comput. Graph.* 25, 4 (July 1991), 329–337. DOI: http://dx.doi.org/10.1145/127719.122753
7. Christophe Scholliers, Lode Hoste, Beat Signer, and Wolfgang De Meuter. 2011. Midas: a declarative multi-touch interaction framework. In *Proceedings of the fifth international conference on Tangible, embedded, and embodied interaction (TEI '11)*. ACM, New York, NY, USA, 49–56. DOI: http://dx.doi.org/10.1145/1935701.1935712
8. Jacob O. Wobbrock, Andrew D. Wilson, and Yang Li. 2007. Gestures without libraries, toolkits or training: a $1 recognizer for user interface prototypes. In *Proceedings of the 20th annual ACM symposium on User interface software and technology (UIST '07)*. ACM, New York, NY, USA, 159–168. DOI: http://dx.doi.org/10.1145/1294211.1294238
9. Jiahui Wu, Gang Pan, Daqing Zhang, Guande Qi, and Shijian Li. 2009. Gesture Recognition with a 3-D Accelerometer. In *Ubiquitous Intelligence and Computing*, Daqing Zhang, Marius Portmann, Ah-Hwee Tan, and Jadwiga Indulska (Eds.). Number 5585 in Lecture Notes in Computer Science. Springer Berlin Heidelberg, 25–38. http://link.springer.com/chapter/10.1007/978-3-642-02830-4_4

Making Fashion more Trendy through Touchless Interactive Displays integrated with Mobile Devices

Franca Garzotto
Politecnico di Milano, DEIB
via Ponzio 34, Milan
franca.garzotto@polimi.it

Antonella Di Rienzo
Politecnico di Milano, DEIB
via C. Golgi 42, Milan
antonella.dirienzo@polimi.it

Ayse Naciye Celebi Yilmaz
Luigi Oliveto
Politecnico di Milano, DEIB
Via C. Golgi 39, Milan
aysenaciye.celebi@polimi.it
luigi.oliveto@polimi.it

Paolo Cremonesi
Politecnico di Milano, DEIB
via Ponzio 34, Milan
paolo.cremonesi@polimi.it

Cristina Frà
Telecom Italia S.p.A.,
Open Innovation
via C. Golgi 42, Milan
cristina.fra@telecomitalia.it

Massimo Valla
Telecom Italia S.p.A.,
Open Innovation
via C. Golgi 42, Milan
massimo.valla@telecomitalia.it

ITS '15, November 15-18, 2015, Funchal, Portugal
ACM 978-1-4503-3899-8/15/11.
http://dx.doi.org/10.1145/2817721.2823484

Abstract
Our research focuses on innovative interactive technologies for the retail domain, in particular fashion. We integrate "touchless" large interactive displays, enabling full-body interaction at the distance, and personal mobile devices, to create engaging UXs that have a strong potential for advertisement and branding purposes in the fashion sector.

Author Keywords
Motion-based touchless interaction; large screens; mobile devices; mobile interaction.

ACM Classification Keywords
H.5.m. Information interfaces and presentation: Miscellaneous.

Introduction
The fashion domain is looking for innovative exploitations of interactive technologies to attract customers inside a shop, to make the experience inside the physical store richer and more memorable, and to help traditional retailers to face the growing competition with online sales. Large Interactive Displays (LIDs) are progressively being deployed in many public spaces [Ardito 2015][Cremonesi 2014],

Interaction space
Users located more than 4 meters far from the display will see a loop of videos or images presenting products and models wearing them.

Ambient zone: If users move closer and enter this area (4-3.5 meters) the system will sense their presence and display some extra contents to attract them.

Attraction Zone: When users are within 1.5 and 3.5 meters (interpreted as an intention to interact), a message appears on the display, explicitly showing that the system is aware of their presence, and inviting them to move closer.

Proximity Zone: If users are in this area (<1.5 meters) the system calculates their gender, age and ethnicity by processing their images and biometric data. This information is used to provide personalized (group) recommendations.

and make dynamic interactive digital media a relatively common feature in everyday social settings [Kuikkaniemi 2011]. Still, they have not been so popular in the fashion domain, where we believe they can have an enormous potential for promotion and advertising purposes.

The focus of our current research is a specific category of LIDs hereinafter referred to as "touchless" LIDs. These systems are characterized by the possibility for the user to control multimedia contents and dynamics at the distance, using body orientation, movements, and mid-air gestures.

Our work integrates touchless LIDs and personal mobile devices to offer new engaging user experiences in fashion shops and show rooms (see video https://youtu.be/tbH8x3WMAWU). The research has been performed in the context of a large ongoing international project that started in 2013 and has involved large IT companies, universities, and big and small stakeholders in the retail domain.

UX design: Info Architecture and Interaction
The information architecture of the multimedia contents on display has a hypertextual structure: items are hierarchically organized by categories (see Figure 2.a/c/e). The user can select a category and an item in this category; (s)he can go from the selected item to the next or previous one in the same category, return to the list of items or to the list of categories, or move to any of the "related items" (e.g., from a shirt to a piece of jewelry that can be worn on it).

Interaction has been designed accordingly to account a multiple-phases model that is partially inspired by [Muller 2010]. We distinguish different interaction phases: people "pass by" with no intent to interact (Phase 1); they notice the system and react, e.g., moving closer to the screen (Phase 2); they try a subtle interaction (Phase 3); they explore the multimedia content (Phase 4); they take more complex actions beyond content exploration (Phase 5); they perform multiple sessions with the system (Phase 6). We mapped different phases within areas in the physical space (see Fig. 1 and side bar).

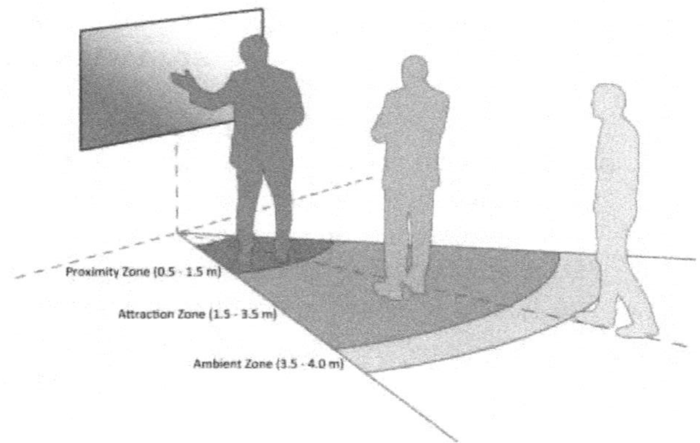

Figure 1: Interactions Zones.

The main area of interaction is the Proximity zone, where the users can explore the proposed products and the entire catalogue, or perform more complex task (e.g., gamification tasks, described in the next section) through the body language described in Fig. 3: *Swipe* (a) to browse items in the left or right, *Push* (b) for the selection of a specific item and *HandsOnHead* (c) to return to the previous category of items.

Figure 2: Ux design and interaction.

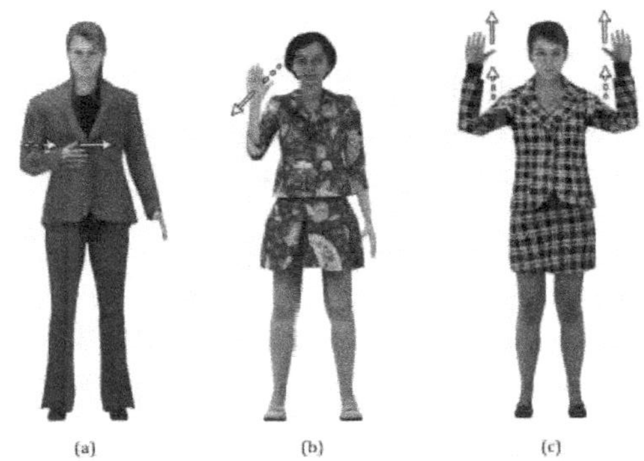

Figure 3: Body language.

Interaction control is performed by a single user only. When multiple users are in the Proximity Zone, the control is issued by the user who is closer to the screen. Different users can take the control simply by exchanging position.

UX design: Gamification features

Gamification features are intended to make the experience with the LDIs more engaging and fun. The "Selfie" game (Fig.2.d/f) allows users in the Proximity zone to take pictures of themselves, immersing their body images in a virtual world of their choice. User can select one of the available backgrounds (e.g., different show rooms, fashion event spaces, the interior of a VIP limousine), playact in front of the screen, and confirm the shooting. Selfies taken in front of the screen are automatically stored in the photogallery, can be downloaded on users' personal devices (see next section) and posted in the retailer's social space (Facebook) if users decide to share and make their images public.

UX design: blending touchless and touch interaction

Users who are interested on a specific product on display can scan the product QR-Code in order to download the shown item on their personal device. In addition, users can install a mobile app to have the entire catalogue and the dynamically created photogallery at their fingerprints. Furthermore, they can share the pictures taken by their mobile device with the LDI application, and make them appear in the photogallery of the large display. (Fig. 2f)

Technology

The general software architecture of the system is depicted in Figure 4. The Screen Application (Sapp) component includes the Core Module and the Sensing Module. Microsoft Kinect is used to detect and collect data about users' presence, movements and actions. During game activities, the Sapp is responsible for images composition, removing background information from the image of the users in front of the display and placing user's body images on the selected background. To estimate users' gender, approximate age and ethnicity, the Image Analysis Web Service exploits an external web service (http://www.betaface.com/).The Recommender System (RS) exploits two recommendation algorithms of different nature: collaborative filtering and content-based. The Content Delivery Platform stores and manages the multimedia content. The Central Controller ensures the control and coordination of the different modules.

Preliminary Evaluation

Our application has been launched and used for the first time in a public setting during the "New Collection Vernissage" of a small fashion brand (see Fig. 2), an

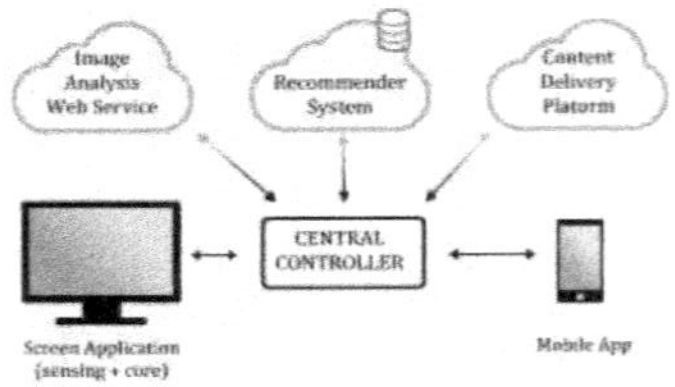

Figure 4: General software architecture.

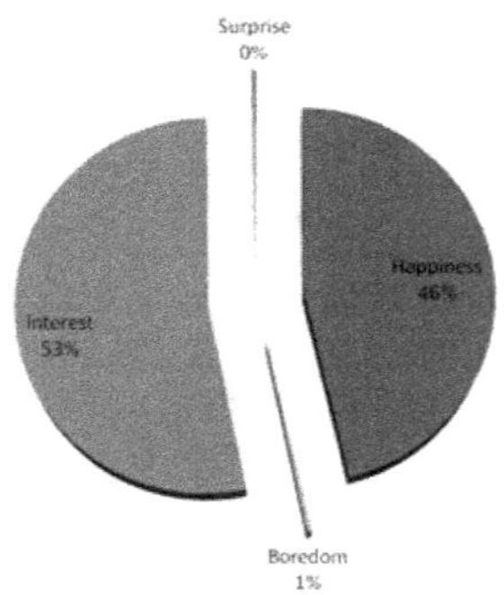

Figure 5: Duration Percentages of Emotions.

event devoted to present the retailer's Autumn-Winter new collection. Two LIDs were installed in the showroom and two cameras per display were placed to capture the users' body movements and actions from two different angles (perspectives): the frontal view recorded users' behavior while they interacted with the display, whereas the back view captured the user perspective, i.e., the on-screen content along with the corresponding user's actions. We recorded 6 hours of video with 52 users interacting with the system.

The video analysis of this material has focused on the emotions that users manifested during the UX. The emotional aspects of interaction have received increased interest not only in HCI but also in marketing. The term "emotional branding" has been coined to express the new dynamic that exists now between brands and people, pinpointing how effective consumer interaction needs to be about senses and feelings, emotions and sentiments. In particular, this paradigm is crucial in fashion branding, which is largely about emotional, hedonic, non-functional dimensions of products. In our study, we considered the emotions manifested by means of *facial expressions*, which are acknowledged as being one of the most universal means for emotions externalization. Specifically, we considered happiness, interest, boredom, and surprise. According to some emotional branding theories [Gobe 2010], these are the emotions that have the strongest impact on the "brand image" (the set of mental constructs that a person associate to a brand).

Figure 5 presents a snapshot of our study results, showing (in percentage) the duration occurrence of *emotion* signals detected during the whole event. It pinpoints the predominance of signals of *interest* (53.10%) and *happiness* (46.27%) compared to *boredom* (0.39%) and *surprise* (0.24%), regardless users' age, gender and technological knowledge. Still, users who had more than one session were significantly happier than users who had one session. We can interpret these data, which certainly require validation in further studies (ongoing), as indicators of the potential of our system to create engagement and positive feelings, which is even stronger if the user has a prolonged interaction.

Acknowledgements
This work is supported by the EC Commission - EIT Digital Program, "HII Street Smart Retail" Activity and by Telecom Italia S.p.A., Open Innovation Department, Joint Open Lab S-Cube, Milan.

References
1. Ardito, C., Buono, P., Costabile, M. F., & Desolda, G. (2015). Interaction with Large Displays: A Survey. ACM Comp. Surveys (CSUR), 47(3), 46.
2. Cremonesi, P., Di Rienzo, A., Frà, C., Garzotto, F., Oliveto, L., & Valla, M. (2014, May). Personalized interaction on large displays: the StreetSmart project approach. In Proc. ACM AVI 2014 (353-354). ACM.
3. Gobe, M. (2010). Emotional Branding, Revised Edition: The New Paradigm for Connecting Brands to People. Skyhorse Publishing, Inc., 2010.
4. Kuikkaniemi, K., Jacucci, G., Turpeinen, M., Hoggan, E., and Muandller, J. (2011) From space to stage: How interactive screens will change urban life. Computer 44, 6 (2011), 40 –47.
5. Müller, J., Alt, F., Michelis, D., & Schmidt, A. (2010,). Requirements and design space for interactive public displays. Proc. ACM Multimedia (1285-1294). ACM.

Usability Guidelines for Co-Located Multi-User Interaction on Wall Displays

Andrea Nutsi
Cooperation Systems Center Munich
Bundeswehr University Munich
Neubiberg, Germany
andrea.nutsi@unibw.de

ITS '15, November 15–18, 2015, Funchal, Portugal
ACM 978-1-4503-3899-8/15/11.
http://dx.doi.org/10.1145/2817721.2820983

Abstract
Today interactive wall displays can be widely seen in industry and research. Due to their size, these displays offer the opportunity for several users to interact co-located and simultaneously. An application supporting multi-user interaction has to be designed differently than traditional single-user interfaces, for example supporting several parallel workspaces or considering by-standers. The overall goal of this thesis is the development of usability guidelines for multi-user applications running on interactive wall displays. These guidelines should aid developers of future applications in ensuring a high multi-user usability. The research approach combines literature analysis with usability studies and controlled laboratory studies. The literature analysis and the usability study will identify aspects specific to multi-user usability. The laboratory studies will deepen the understanding of two selected usability aspects, with readability in a multi-user scenario being one of them.

Author Keywords
multi-user; interactive wall display; usability; guidelines.

ACM Classification Keywords
H.5.2. [Information Interfaces and Presentation (e.g. HCI)]: Ergonomics, Style guides

Introduction

Due to technological progress [19] and falling costs [7] interactive wall displays are readily available today. The displays have become pervasive [25] and can be found in research as well as in industry, in public, semi-public and private places. Due to their size these kind of displays offer the opportunity for several users to interact simultaneously and co-located [6, 25]. Multi-user interaction has several advantages: it fosters social interaction [6] and enables social learning as well as social experience [9]. Despite these advantages research focused on multi-user interaction, especially on the design of such applications, is still rare. Which design factors need to be considered when designing multi-user applications? There is no established set of guidelines for the design of public displays [2], nor can established design guidelines from the desktop be directly applied to multi-touch interfaces [8]. Designing for a great user experience (UX) of public display applications is important, as it might increase the usage motivation as well as extend the interaction duration [2]. In order to create a rich UX it is necessary to consider the specific display characteristics (e.g. size, orientation) [8]. In this context, this work aims at developing design guidelines for multi-user applications running on interactive wall displays, focusing on usability aspects. Usability is by definition part of the UX [1], improving the usability will also result in a better UX.

Related Work

Several design or usability guidelines for desktop applications exist, for example "The Research-Based Web Design & Usability Guidelines" [23] or ISO 9241. Together with Nielsen's usability heuristics [14] and Shneiderman's 8 golden rules [20] these principles or heuristics describe basic usability aspects and require interpretation when applied [5]. These general and device-independent guidelines offer orientation but do not consider specific characteristics of the targeted interface which is a necessary requirement for achieving an acceptable UX [8].

The guidelines for developing applications for Microsoft's Perceptive Pixel display [12] focus on wall displays. But in general industrial guidelines are optimized and targeted for their specific product and cannot be easily applied to other systems and devices [8]. Furthermore, industrial guidelines are usually based on experience rather than empirical evidence and the development process is not transparent.

Alt et al. [2] developed guidelines for the evaluation of public displays. The usability heuristics for large screen information exhibits [22] also support the evaluation of such applications. This work aims at supporting developers early, namely in the design phase. Furthermore, the specific characteristics of multi-user interaction were just marginally considered. Yuill & Rogers [25] developed a design and evaluation framework for collaborative multi-user applications. While collaboration is certainly important for multi-user interaction, it is just one aspect for the usability of such applications.

Research Questions

This thesis aims at answering the following questions:

- Which factors are influencing the usability of multi-user applications running on interactive wall displays?
- How to ensure high readability in a co-located multi-user scenario?

The first question aims at elaborating the specific characteristics of co-located and simultaneous multi-user interaction at wall displays, focusing on usability aspects. Which aspects have to be considered when designing such an application? Answering the first question will result in a set of guidelines for the design of multi-user applications. As the developed guidelines will remain on an abstract level, two identified usability aspects will be selected in the course of the thesis and further investigated.

One already identified aspect is the need for ensuring good readability for by-standers as well as users directly interacting with the screen [17]. As can be seen in Figure 1, two users are interacting with the display while five by-standers are watching in different distances, respective in different interaction zones (see Figure 2) Users in the interaction zone are likely to be interested in details on one or more information particle(s) whereas by-standers in the communication or notification zone are more likely to be interested in getting an overview on the presented information. An application has to conform to the different needs of users in the various interaction zones. According to Vinot & Athenes [24] readability forms a relevant part of interface design. Furthermore, there is still a lack of research on dynamic text on (indoor) LED displays [21]. Therefore, the second question aims at deepening the understanding of one usability factor, namely readability. Answering the second question will provide detailed recommendations on how to ensure multi-user readability on wall displays. This will include (among others) information on font-sizes, text-moving direction, text moving speed and information density. Depending on the answer to the first question, a second key aspect will be chosen.

Methodology

In this section the research approach for developing usability guidelines for multi-user applications is described. Although heuristics and guidelines have a different aim, they do have similar content (design recommendations), with heuristics being more abstract and guidelines being more concrete, including examples and the context [3]. Based on these similarities I follow the research approach of Paddison & Englefield [18] who suggest two methods for developing usability heuristics:

Figure 1: Multi-user interaction with the MeetingMirror

1. Research-based: analysing literature and deriving heuristics based on this analysis
2. Evaluation-based: summing up evaluation results in order to derive heuristics

Although I do not aim at developing heuristics, I combine these two approaches in order to develop guidelines. First, I analyse existing research, and second I conduct usability studies as well as controlled laboratory experiments focusing on aspects unique to multiple users interacting simultaneously with the display. Identification of the aspects unique to multi-user interaction will be done in a literature study complemented by a multi-user usability study of our existing MeetingMirror application [10] (see Figures 1, 3). The

Figure 2: Interaction zone model [16]

Figure 3: Usability-study of the MeetingMirror

MeetingMirror is a suitable application for my evaluation, as it supports the simultaneous touch interaction of several persons. Users may explore the information space for themselves or collaboratively.

In several successive controlled laboratory experiments I aim to identify specific requirements regarding readability for users in different interaction zones, taking into account whether users are standing in front of the screen or walking past the screen.

Preliminary Results

At the moment, the literature study for design recommendations on multi-user applications on wall displays is almost finished. First results have been published in [15] and include e.g. "avoid the use of audio [22]" or "consider bystanders and offer supplementary value to them [13]".

Furthermore, a usability study of the afore mentioned MeetingMirror application was conducted, comparing single- and multi-user usage in a between-group design. We used think-aloud during a free exploration phase, tasks (time measurement) and a questionnaire (comprising amongst others of System Usability Scale (SUS) [4] and User Experience Questionnaire (UEQ) [11]) in order to get quantitative and qualitative results. We observed different group behavior during the multi-user interaction: no communication at all, just watching the second user (see Figure 3) or solving the tasks collaboratively. We found that the application does support multi-user interaction, but it has low usability (SUS score of 48 in both scenarios). The evaluation of this study is still work-in-progress. The same applies to controlled laboratory studies evaluating the influence of the text flow direction on readability in different interaction zones, again comparing single- and multi-user usage scenarios. With this study design I aim at extracting factors specific to multi-user usage.

Future Work

Future work includes evaluating and publishing the results of the already conducted user studies. Furthermore several controlled laboratory studies are in the planning phase.

Regarding readability the text moving speed will be evaluated next, focusing on a multi-user setting with participants standing in different interaction zones. Another study will focus on adapting font sizes to users in different interaction zones. In order to verify the results of the readability studies, the MeetingMirror application will be designed accordingly and evaluated (comparison current version with improved version). Furthermore the decision on the second usability aspect and its elaboration is also future work.

Expected Contributions

The contribution of this research is an overview on usability aspects relevant to multi-user interaction on wall display applications. This will support developers of future applications in avoiding typical usability problems. It will also contribute to the research on multi-user readability on wall displays, naming relevant factors and providing concrete design examples. Furthermore this thesis will deepen the understanding on characteristics specific to co-located and simultaneous multi-user interaction.

References

[1] ISO 9241-210:2010. 2011. Ergonomie der Mensch-System-Interaktion - Teil 210: Prozess zur Gestaltung gebrauchstauglicher interaktiver Systeme. (2011).

[2] Florian Alt, Stefan Schneegaß, Albrecht Schmidt, Jörg Müller, and Nemanja Memarovic. 2012. How to evaluate public displays. In *Proc. PerDis '12*. ACM, New York, NY, USA, 1–6. http://dx.doi.org/10.1145/2307798.2307815

[3] Patricia Böhm, Christian Wolff, and Tim Schneidermeier. 2014. Heuristiken für Information Appliances. In *Mensch und Computer 2014 - Tagungsband*. De Gruyter Oldenbourg, Berlin, 275–284.

[4] John Brooke. 1996. SUS - A quick and dirty usability scale. In *Usability evaluation in industry*, Patrick W. Jordan, B. Thomas, Ian Lyall McClelland, and Bernard Weerdmeester (Eds.). Taylor & Francis, London and Bristol, Pa., 189–194.

[5] M. Burmester and J. Machate. 2003. Creative Design of Interactive Products and Use of Usability Guidelines - a Contradiction? In *Human-Computer Interaction: Theory and Practice*, J. Jacko and C. Stephanidis (Eds.). Lawrence Erlbaum Associates Inc., Mahwah, New Jersey, USA, 43–46.

[6] Céline Coutrix, Kai Kuikkaniemi, Esko Kurvinen, Giulio Jacucci, Ivan Avdouevski, and Riikka Mäkelä. 2011. FizzyVis: designing for playful information browsing on a multitouch public display. In *Proc. DPPI '11*. ACM, New York, NY, USA, 27:1–27:8. http://dx.doi.org/10.1145/2347504.2347534

[7] Sven Gehring and Alexander Wiethoff. 2014. Interaction with Media Façades. *Informatik-Spektrum* 37, 5 (2014), 474–482. http://dx.doi.org/10.1007/s00287-014-0818-0

[8] Tobias Hesselmann, Susanne Boll, and Wilko Heuten. 2011. SCIVA: designing applications for surface computers. In *Proc. EICS '11*. ACM, New York, NY, USA, 191–196. http://dx.doi.org/10.1145/1996461.1996519

[9] Giulio Jacucci, Ann Morrison, Gabriela T. Richard, Jari Kleimola, Peter Peltonen, Lorenza Parisi, and Toni Laitinen. 2010. Worlds of information: designing for engagement at a public multi-touch display. In *Proc. CHI '10*. ACM, New York, NY, USA, 2267–2276. http://dx.doi.org/10.1145/1753326.1753669

[10] Michael Koch, Florian Ott, Peter Lachenmaier, Eva Lösch, Andrea Nutsi, and Martin Burkhard. 2014. MeetingMirror – Interaktives Fenster in Tagungsinformationssysteme. In *Mensch und Computer 2014 Workshopband*. De Gruyter Oldenbourg, Berlin, 33–39.

[11] Bettina Laugwitz, Theo Held, and Martin Schrepp. 2008. Construction and Evaluation of a User Experience Questionnaire. In *HCI and Usability for Education and Work*, Andreas Holzinger (Ed.). Lecture Notes in Computer Science, Vol. 5298. Springer Berlin Heidelberg, Berlin, Heidelberg, 63–76. http://dx.doi.org/10.1007/978-3-540-89350-9_6

[12] Microsoft. February 2014. Designing Windows Store apps for Perceptive Pixel displays. (February 2014). http://download.microsoft.com/download/9/B/F/9BF51507-F82A-4F1F-9D17-54BCA1414D0A/Designing_apps_for_PPI_displays.docx

[13] Jörg Müller, Robert Walter, Gilles Bailly, Michael Nischt, and Florian Alt. 2012. Looking glass: a field study on noticing interactivity of a shop window. In *Proc. CHI '12*. ACM, New York, NY, USA, 297–306. http://dx.doi.org/10.1145/2207676.2207718

[14] Jakob Nielsen. 1994. *Usability engineering*. Morgan Kaufmann Publishers, San Francisco, Calif.

[15] Andrea Nutsi and Michael Koch. 2015. Multi-User Usability Guidelines for Interactive Wall Display Applications. In *Proc. PerDis '15*. ACM Press, New York, NY, USA. http://dx.doi.org/10.1145/2757710.2776798

[16] Florian Ott and Michael Koch. 2012. Social Software Beyond the Desktop — Ambient Awareness and Ubiquitous Activity Streaming. *it - Information Technology* 54, 5 (2012), 243–252. http://dx.doi.org/10.1524/itit.2012.0687

[17] Florian Ott, Andrea Nutsi, and Peter Lachenmaier. 2014. Information Ergonomics Guidelines for Multi-User Readability on Semi-Public Large Interactive Screens. In *Proc. of the Workshop on Information Ergonomics: Leveraging Productivity by Aligning Human-Information Ecologies, i-KNOW '14*.

[18] Claire Paddison and Paul Englefield. 2003. Applying heuristics to perform a rigorous accessibility inspection in a commercial context. In *Proc. CUU '03*, Mary Zajicek and Alistair Edwards (Eds.). ACM, New York, NY, USA, 126–133. http://dx.doi.org/10.1145/957205.957228

[19] Markus Rittenbruch. 2014. Evaluating the Use of a Very Large-scale Presentation and Collaboration Framework. In *Proc. PerDis '14*, Aaron Quigley, Sebastian Boring, and Sven Gehring (Eds.). ACM Press, New York, NY, USA, 124–129. http://dx.doi.org/10.1145/2611009.2611023

[20] Ben Shneiderman and Catherine Plaisant. 2004. *Designing the user interface: Strategies for effective human-computer interaction* (4th ed ed.). Pearson/Addison Wesley, Boston.

[21] So, Joey C. Y. and Chan, Alan H. S. 2008. Design Factors on Dynamic Text Display. *Engineering Letters* 16, 3 (2008), 368–371. http://www.engineeringletters.com/issues_v16/issue_3/EL_16_3_15.pdf

[22] Jacob Somervell, Shahtab Wahid, and D. Scott McCrickard. 2003. Usability heuristics for large screen information exhibits. In *Proc. INTERACT '03*. IOS Press, Amsterdam, 904–907.

[23] U.S. Dept. of Health and Human Services. 2006. *The Research-Based Web Design & Usability Guidelines* (version 2 ed.). U.S. Government Printing Office, Washington, D.C.

[24] Jean-Luc Vinot and Sylvie Athenes. 2012. Legible, are you sure? An Experimentation-based Typographical Design in Safety-Critical Context. In *Proc. CHI '12*. ACM, New York, NY, USA, 2287–2296. http://dx.doi.org/10.1145/2207676.2208387

[25] Nicola Yuill and Yvonne Rogers. 2012. Mechanisms for collaboration: A design and evaluation framework for multi-user interfaces. *ACM Transactions on Computer-Human Interaction* 19, 1 (2012), 1–25. http://dx.doi.org/10.1145/2147783.2147784

Designing Ad-Hoc Cross Device Collaborations For Small Groups

Figure 1: Ad hoc federations of people's personal mobile devices to provide cross-device interactions supporting small group-collaboration when curating digital and non-digital historic documents.

Frederik Brudy
UCL Interaction Centre, University College London
66 - 72 Gower Street, London WC1E 6EA, UK
f.brudy@cs.ucl.ac.uk

Abstract

The curation of historic documents is a difficult task as it requires to combine information and raw material from many different sources. Digital tools can support such a sensemaking task and group collaboration can help the discovery of knowledge. While most of people's personal devices (such as phones, tablets and laptops) are connected to the internet, they are not aware of each other's presence or relationship when in close proximity. Leveraging people's personal devices and other devices in their surroundings provides an opportunity to support the curation of historic documents in ad hoc small group scenarios.

I describe my motivation and a selection of related work, leading to requirements for such a system. I then state how I am planning to address these challenges and my current state of research, following two parallel tracks: building and testing technology as well as conducting observational studies and interviews to inform my designs.

ITS '15, November 15-18, 2015, Funchal, Portugal
ACM 978-1-4503-3899-8/15/11.
http://dx.doi.org/10.1145/2817721.2820984

Author Keywords

Cross device interaction; ad-hoc collaboration; small group collaboration; curation of historic documents and artefacts

ACM Classification Keywords

H.5.3. Group and Organization Interfaces. Computer-supported cooperative work; H.5.2. User Interfaces. Input devices and strategies

Introduction

Analyzing and curating historic documents in order to prepare them for further use (for example in print or online) requires to gather, review and combine large collections of documents and artefacts, making this a demanding task [9]. With growing number of items in such collections and various different document types and formats, digital technology is needed in order to support this. Furthermore, collaboratively curating these collections in a small group can make it easier to reveal interesting facts and find new connections between them (Figure 1). Previous research explored how a single person can do this, e.g. on large screens [1], tabletops [3] or using multiple devices [4]. However most of our devices do not well support such a collaborative task: although we are surrounded with smart devices, such as smartwatches, smartphones, tablets, laptops, and large wall and tabletop displays, we are primarily using them for individual tasks to collect, study and analyze information. Even though these devices can communicate with other devices, they are not aware of their immediate presence, nor of their spatial or semantic relationship. They do not support ad hoc collaborations, e.g., through sharing of content across devices (such as photos, historic maps, video and text) and display space.

I believe that there is a potential for small groups to use their existing devices when analyzing a pool of documents. Therefore I have begun my work with a group of volunteer historians, learning from their curation activities in order to support them with digital technology.

Related work

Sensemaking, as used in Human Computer Interaction (HCI), is the process of analyzing collections of information in order to find common activities, make an understanding and process the data for further use [10]. When compared to analyzing documents on a computer, paper's physical affordance makes for three unique properties, supporting this task [7]:

- **Annotation.** Paper documents can be easily annotated, which is integrated into reading.
- **Movement within and between documents.** Moving quickly through large amounts of documents, while skimming over content is easier with paper.
- **Spatial layouts.** Documents can be arranged in space and laid out representing a structure that supports the knowledge discovery, e.g. grouping documents by topic or arranging them in a timeline.

With an increasing amount of data, doing this with paper documents becomes more tedious (or even impossible) and not all information can be acquired in a printed format (e.g., as in case of video or audio this is simply not possible without further processing). With other formats, richness of information or the context of it will be lost (e.g., location data embedded in a photo). Computer systems can support this, e.g. through search tools, visualization and isolation of content and connection, and finding related content. However it is left to the human to fully understand the meaning and draw connections.

Using large tabletops or wall displays to curate such collections has been proposed and cross-device interactions have been in the focus of HCI research since a few years. Andrews et al. explored how large, high-resolution displays support sensemaking tasks [1]. An example for a system that allows to distribute resources and services across multiple devices is ActivitySpace [5]. Conductor [4] is a single-user multi-device system enabling a person to use up to 10 personal devices in a sensemaking task. A group's appropriation of the space on and around a tabletop display has been described [14], Ryall et al. reported about how a group's strategies and speed are affected by group and table size [11] and MultiSpace [3] explores how a tabletop and wall-display supports ad hoc collaboration in a multi-device environment. However these devices and systems are expensive to buy, need a long setup process, require a permanent place where they are set up or do not support sensemaking with multiple people. They are not suitable for ad hoc curation of documents in small groups.

On the contrary we carry more and more mobile but computationally powerful devices with us. Previous research explored the spatial relationships of devices (e.g. [2,8,15]), cross device interactions which support changing numbers of devices (e.g. [4,8]), the use of personal devices to bring in information (e.g. [12]), as well as body worn devices in concert with wall displays (e.g. [16]). More recently with HuddleLamp [8] a multi-user multi-device framework has been proposed, allowing for spatial tracking of tablets and phones on a table and for cross device interactions.

In summary, a system for sensemaking and curation of documents should support the following features:

- **Portability.** A system should be easy to setup, without the requirement for a permanent place. This would allow for usage in various spaces.
- **Ad hoc.** Supporting a walk-up-an-go collaboration, without a tedious setup and long preparation works.
- **Low cost**. In order to be easily deployable a system should be either available to work with existing devices or only require low initial costs.
- **Multi-user.** In order to support small-group sensemaking and curation of documents, a system should support collaborative multi-user scenarios.
- **Heterogeneous data and environments.** To account for the rich nature of documents in data collections, a system should account for both, digital and non-digital content and allow to work in environments with cluttered work areas and noisy data.

Research objectives

My research addresses the question how we can support the curation of historic documents in small group scenarios with digital technology, using people's personal devices and the devices in their surroundings. I divide my work into three sections.

1. **Study people's current practices.** This will build a framework for group collaborations for ad hoc small group scenarios. Some of the questions I am trying to answer include the following: How do people make use of devices and utilities (paper, pens, tablets, screens, etc.)? How is material and content shared when a group meets to discuss or work on a topic? How are devices being held during particular tasks, e.g. a collaborative research task about a historic event, during office works or when preparing for a class presentation at school?
2. **Develop technology.** In order to support the aforementioned small group collaborations I am building a tool, allowing small groups to curate documents in ad hoc scenarios, leveraging people's personal and publicly available devices. I have started with individual prototypes, which try to solve a single requirement, e.g. digitizing of physical artifacts or temporary sharing of content in small groups.
3. **Deploy and evaluate more collaborative technology.** In a third step I will broaden up the area to which I am applying my technologies and open it up to more use cases (rather than only curation of historic documents). This will broaden up and support the framework of objective 1.

Each of these sections should not be seen as a single unit, nor will they be in a sequential order. Rather each unit will influence and inform the others throughout my work in an iterative design process. For example the lessons learned from unit 1 will help me to understand current collaboration techniques and thus to build the right tools

Figure 2: The Tangible Scanner allows to digitize physical documents, in order to support working with physical and digital objects.

Figure 3: Content can be distributed across multiple devices (here: content can be flicked between two tablets and two phones). Device's position and orientation is tracked using HuddleLamp, allowing for a shared canvas and cross-device interactions.

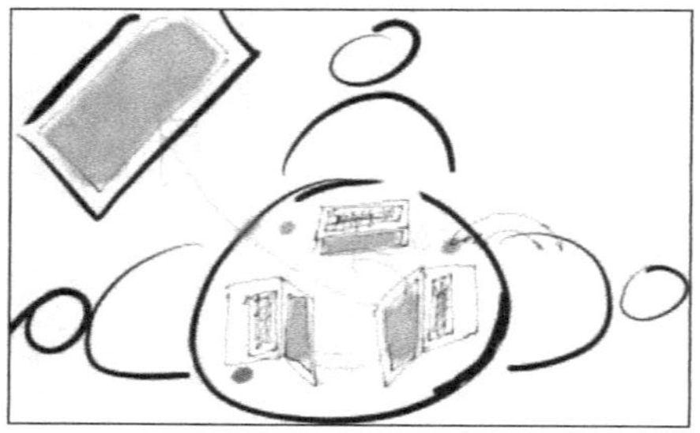

Figure 4: The meeting presenter allows to share content in a meeting with the push of a button.

to support these. I will test these either by deploying them to my target audience or in lab studies.

I have started to follow two tracks in parallel. On one side I am exploring the technological aspects and the potential of cross-device interactions, which will allow me to explore the potential of using everyday devices in ad hoc small group collaborations, leveraging cross-device sharing of, e.g., photos, text, videos and more. For this I am using technology probes prototypes [6] to present ideas and test them with collaborators. **My vision for these tools is that they should be easy to setup, work with existing or low-cost devices and allow to blend physical and digital in order to support heterogeneous data.** For example a Tangible Scanner (Figure 2) allows to easily digitize physical artefact on a table: a paper map is placed in a physical frame and the system takes a pictures of the map, making it immediately available on one of the devices on the table, e.g., a person's tablet. The digital version can then be reviewed on that tablet, copied to another tablet or presented to others (Figure 4).

Distributing content across multiple devices will allow to leverage the spatial properties of them. E.g., laying multiple devices next to each other to build a timeline or stacking multiple devices to group items together, much as it is already done with paper [7] and when using large digital displays [1]. Using different form factors of devices, such as tablets, phones, large screens, laptops and even wearable devices different document formats can be accounted for. Each device will not be assigned a certain content type per-se, rather people using it can appropriate the system in a way that supports their work: a video might be viewed better on a tablet, while a phone displays a list of bookmark which, when clicked, opens a document on a large display (Figure 3).

On the other side I am conducting observational studies and interviews in order to inform my designs. I have begun a collaboration with the Mill Road History Project in Cambridge[1] (MRHP), where volunteers record, learn, curate and present the rich history of this particular street of the city. This work is performed by members of the community (most are volunteers) and accessible by everyone. Depending on the historic data, many different document types are used: historic maps and photos, audio recordings of oral histories, paper documents, location data, books, personal memories and many more. Most of the participants in this project own and use a smartphone on the go, many of them also a tablet and laptop. They meet in various spaces, without a permanent room where they could set up such a system. **The goal of my research is to foster sharing and exploring of digital content across multiple devices when they are in close proximity to one another to support group sensemaking tasks.** These interactions do not have to be limited to phones and wall displays. Extending this interaction space to a user's body through wearable devices could allow for a whole new set of interaction and would give new opportunities to exchange information between users, devices and their surroundings.

Current state of research

I have conducted semi structured interviews with members of the MRHP, where I have learned about their current practices of gathering documents from various sources, how they keep track of their sensemaking status and how information is shared between members of the group. They have divided up

[1] http://www.capturingcambridge.org/

their work on Mill Road into individual building reports, where one or more members of the group research the history of a particular building on the street. They prefer working with digital documents, as opposed to physical ones, allowing them to easily share them with other members of the group without having to worry about archiving after the project has ended or handing them over when someone drops out of the group. However this makes reviewing of documents more difficult as they cannot be grouped and annotated as easily as paper documents. Some members of the group have trouble with existing tools for editing, sharing and collaboratively working on documents and they end up as a group sitting in front of one laptop in order to edit a document, as the co-presence allows for immediate sharing of knowledge and helps when merging multiple sets of information.
When a new person joins a team, information is still handed over in personal meetings, as this allows them to go through the documents together and explain any connections. However, the actual sensemaking in a group rarely happens. This might be because of a lack of tools which could support their current practices, although this will need further exploration.
I have also built technology that supports sharing of content across devices; capturing of physical artefacts, blending them with digital content (Figure 2); separating content across multiple devices (Figure 3); and sharing content in a meeting with the push of a button (Figure 4). Throughout I am deploying the built technologies to my collaborators in order to gather early feedback, to learn how small tools are appropriated and how they could feed into a bigger system.

Further research

I will extend my observations to small group meetings in everyday work life. This will help me understand how people share material deliberate and implicit, what kind of props are being used (such as paper, laptops, tablets, screens, etc.) and how devices are being held and used. I will build upon previous research [13] to deepen the understanding of how meetings are being held so far and to learn what a digital system has to provide in order to support them.
I will deploy a system to members of the MRHP. This tool allows them to explore the digital collections of objects, using various input mechanisms, e.g., gesture recognition, touch based interactions, and spatial arrangements of devices (e.g., their position and orientation to each other on the table). Using this system, objects can be moved across device boundaries (copy, move and flick content between e.g. tablets, phone and displays). Through quantitative measurements and observations on how they appropriate the tool I will inform my further research.

Summary

Growing collections of historic documents makes their curation almost impossible to be done with paper documents only, leading for this to happen on digital devices. Using multiple devices, the physical properties can be used in a similar way as it is with paper: they can be laid out to build a timeline, stacked to group or set aside to offload documents not currently needed. Although most of our digital devices are connected to the internet, they do not communicate to each other when in close proximity, nor are they aware of each other's presence. The overall goal of my research is to enable sharing and exploring of digital content across multiple devices to support collocated group sensemaking tasks. For this I have begun my work with a group of volunteers, curating the history of a street in Cambridge, learning from their current practices and understanding their requirements for their work. I am iteratively building and testing prototype systems. This allows me to explore the technical aspects and will inform the design of a system supporting the curation of documents across devices in ad hoc small-group collaborations.

Acknowledgements

I wish to thank my supervisors Nicolai Marquardt and Yvonne Rogers (University College London) as well as Abigail Sellen and Kenton O'Hara (Microsoft Research Cambridge).

This work is supported by Microsoft Research through its PhD Scholarship Programme.

References

[1] Andrews, C., Endert, A., and North, C. Space to think: large high-resolution displays for sensemaking. *Proc. CHI*, ACM (2010), 55–64.

[2] Ballendat, T., Marquardt, N., and Greenberg, S. Proxemic interaction: designing for a proximity and orientation-aware environment. *Proc. ITS*, ACM (2010), 121–130.

[3] Everitt, K., Shen, C., Ryall, K., and Forlines, C. MultiSpace: Enabling electronic document micro-mobility in table-centric, multi-device environments. *TableTop 2006*, IEEE (2006), 8–pp.

[4] Hamilton, P. and Wigdor, D.J. Conductor: enabling and understanding cross-device interaction. *Proc. CHI*, ACM (2014), 2773–2782.

[5] Houben, S., Tell, P., and Bardram, J.E. ActivitySpace: Managing Device Ecologies in an Activity-Centric Configuration Space. *Proc. ITS (2014)*, 119–128.

[6] Hutchinson, H., Bederson, B.B., Druin, A., et al. Technology Probes: Inspiring Design for and with Families. *Proc. CHI*, ACM (2003), 17-24.

[7] O'Hara, K. and Sellen, A. A comparison of reading paper and on-line documents. *Proc. CHI*, ACM (1997), 335–342.

[8] Rädle, R., Jetter, H.-C., Marquardt, N., Reiterer, H., and Rogers, Y. HuddleLamp: Spatially-Aware Mobile Displays for Ad-hoc Around-the-Table Collaboration. *Proc. ITS*, ACM (2014), 45–54.

[9] Rotman, D., Procita, K., et al. Supporting content curation communities: The case of the Encyclopedia of Life. *JASIST 63*, 6 (2012), 1092–1107.

[10] Russell, D.M., Stefik, M.J., Pirolli, P., and Card, S.K. The cost structure of sensemaking. *Proc. InterCHI*, ACM (1993), 269–276.

[11] Ryall, K., Forlines, C., Shen, C., and Morris, M.R. Exploring the effects of group size and table size on interactions with tabletop shared-display groupware. *Proc. CSCW*, ACM (2004), 284–293.

[12] Schmidt, D., Seifert, J., Rukzio, E., and Gellersen, H. A cross-device interaction style for mobiles and surfaces. *Proc. DIS*, ACM (2012), 318–327.

[13] Scott, S.D., Carpendale, M.S.T., and Inkpen, K.M. Territoriality in collaborative tabletop workspaces. *Proc. CSCW*, ACM (2004), 294–303.

[14] Tang, A., Tory, M., Po, B., Neumann, P., and Carpendale, S. Collaborative coupling over tabletop displays. *Proc. CHI*, ACM (2006), 1181–1190.

[15] Vogel, D. and Balakrishnan, R. Interactive public ambient displays: transitioning from implicit to explicit, public to personal, interaction with multiple users. *Proc. UIST*, ACM (2004), 137–146.

[16] von Zadow, U., Büschel, W., Langner, R., and Dachselt, R.I.M.L. SleeD: Using a Sleeve Display to Interact with Touch-sensitive Display Walls. *Proc. ITS*, ACM (2014), 129–138.

Toward Motor-Intuitive Interaction Primitives for Touchless Interfaces

Debaleena Chattopadhyay
Human-Centered Computing Department
School of Informatics and Computing
Indiana University
535 W. Michigan Street
Indianapolis, IN 46202, USA
debchatt@iupui.edu

ITS '15, November 15-18, 2015, Funchal, Portugal
ACM 978-1-4503-3899-8/15/11.
http://dx.doi.org/10.1145/2817721.2820985

Abstract
To design intuitive, interactive systems in various domains, such as health, entertainment, or smart cities, researchers are exploring touchless interaction. Touchless systems allow individuals to interact without any input device—using freehand gestures in midair. Gesture-elicitation studies focus on generating user-defined interface controls to design touchless systems. Interface controls, however, are composed of primary units called interaction primitives—which remain little explored. For example, what touchless primitives are motor-intuitive and can unconsciously use our pre-existing sensorimotor knowledge (such as visual perception or motor skills)? Drawing on the disciplines of cognitive science and motor behavior, my research aims to understand the perceptual and motor factors in touchless interaction with 2D user interfaces (2D UIs). I then aim to apply this knowledge to design a set of touchless interface controls for large displays.

Author Keywords
Gesture-based interfaces; novel interaction techniques; touchless interaction; motor-intuitive interaction.

ACM Classification Keywords
H.5.2 [User Interfaces]: Interaction Styles; Theory and Methods

Introduction

Touchless interfaces allow individuals to interact with systems using freehand gestures in midair. Because touchless controls can draw on gestures that are commonly used in everyday life, touchless interactions are deemed 'natural' and characterized as Natural User Interfaces (NUI) [16]. NUIs promise to employ users' prior knowledge and to relieve them from orienting toward an input device for an interaction. This potential has prompted the emergence of touchless systems in various domains that involve sporadic and coarse-grained interactions—such as entertainment [12], health [13], visualization [6], or collaboration [1].

To fulfill the promise of naturalness, touchless system design—still in its early stages—is either exploring user-focused gesture-elicitation studies [12] or system-focused interaction techniques [8]. Both of these approaches seek intuitive touchless controls, but user studies found that certain interactions—that were earlier described as suitable or were effectively supported by the system—were difficult to perform during evaluation or perceived less effective [8, 12]. I argue that to explain these limitations, we need to investigate touchless interaction *primitives*, the basic units that constitute an interface control [16]. Thus, instead of assuming that our familiarity with everyday gestures in the physical world directly translates into our ability to perform those exact gestures in touchless interfaces, we need to examine what makes a touchless primitive motor-intuitive. Or which primitives allow unconscious application of our pre-existing sensorimotor knowledge (e.g., visual perception or motor skills) during touchless interactions?

Toward designing easy-to-use touchless interfaces, the goal of my research is to understand motor-intuitiveness of touchless primitives [5]. In interaction design, primitives sit right in the middle of system-recognized actions and interface controls [16]; a proper subset of what is actually recognized by a system makes up a set of primitives, which is then expanded into a larger set of controls (Figure 1, right). Thus, my research complements the ongoing pursuit of user-defined touchless interface controls and system-focused recognizable gestures. Specifically, (a) I investigate perceptual and motor factors in touchless interaction with 2D UIs while drawing on the disciplines of cognitive science and motor behavior. With this knowledge, (b) I then aim to design a set of interface controls for touchless interaction with large displays.

Background

Touchless Interaction

To design intuitive touchless systems, elicitation studies seek to identify interface controls that are based on everyday metaphors, such as preference for a 'wiping' hand movement over a static hand sign to trigger a 'delete' action [7]. On the other hand, system-focused studies design interface controls drawing on mouse, pen, or touch interfaces [8], or based on sensor capabilities [1]. However, when interaction controls—designed by either of these approaches—are evaluated, some are found to be less effective. While such findings are common [8, 12], these interaction limitations are little understood. Exploring touchless interaction primitives, the building blocks of interface controls, may explain the sensorimotor factors that affect user performance in touchless systems.

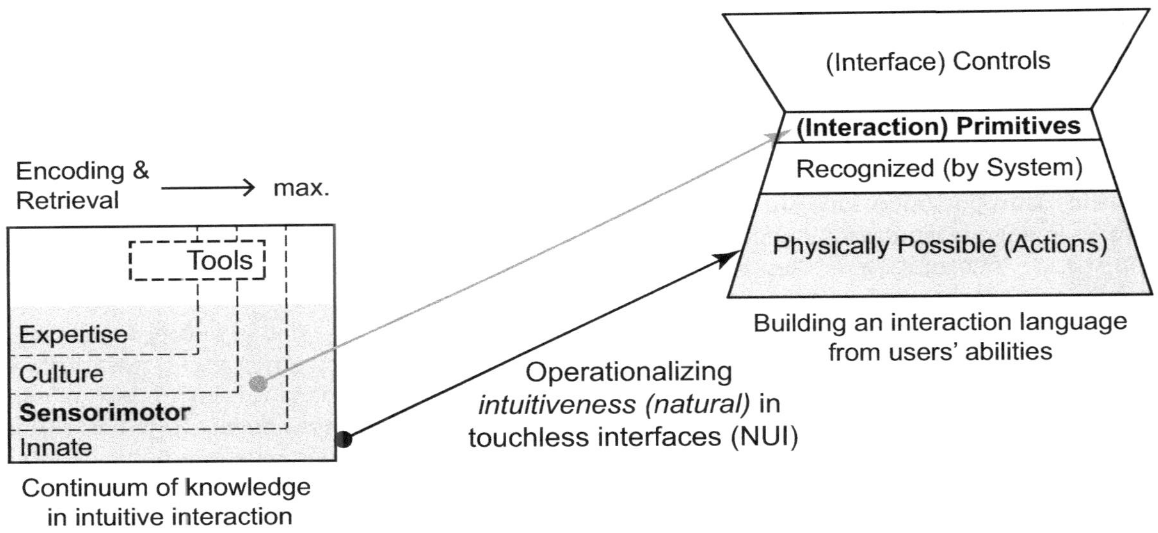

Figure 1: Interface controls often constitute of basic units called interaction primitives (right, [16]). We argue that the intuitiveness of touchless interaction primitives (and thus of a touchless interface) can be classified using the continuum of knowledge in intuitive interaction (left, [9]). For example, gestural controls building upon sensorimotor knowledge would be more intuitive than those drawing upon expertise. To illustrate this, we designed and evaluated a touchless interaction primitive (mid-air, directional strokes) that draws on our sensorimotor level of knowledge (image schemas, more specifically the up-down and the left-right space schemas) [5] (© 2015 Oxford University Press, reprinted with permission).

Role of Perceptual Factors in Touchless Interaction

Touchless gestures lack haptic feedback, thus solely depending upon visual feedback and proprioception. Although auditory feedback for mid-air gestures have been explored, their role in providing guidance also remains unclear. Because of this lack of guidance, touchless gestures are less efficient and more fatiguing than device-based gestures (e.g., touch or gyro mouse). Specifically, in touchless interaction with distant 2D displays, the 3D input space and the 2D display space are decoupled. Because of this decoupling, users need to mentally couple their actions and the feedback on the display—thus making the stimulus-response compatibility difficult. Thus, although touchless gestures can—in theory—draw on our daily-life gestures, interacting with a 2D interface generates a perceptual situation unlike how seeing and acting is related in our familiar 3D world. Because, in daily life, actions and feedback both occur in 3D space and are tightly coupled. I argue that because of this mismatch between visual perception (a 2D UI) and motor action (3D input), psychological principles affecting visual perception will affect touchless interactions [4].

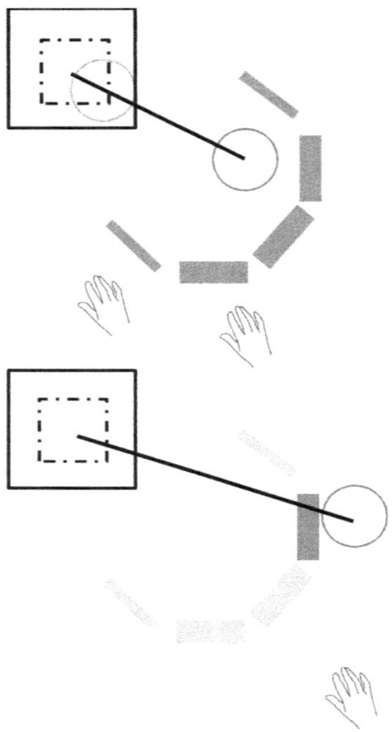

Figure 2: To illustrate motor-intuitive touchless interaction primitives, we designed Touchless Circular Menus (TCM). With TCM, users do not need to comply strictly with system-defined postures, such as a pinch or a fist, but could select commands by making directional strokes in mid-air. Compared with contextual linear menus with grab gestures, TCM were more than two times faster in selecting commands and caused overall lower workload. However, TCMs were less accurate than the static gesture grab [2].

Role of Motor Factors in Touchless Interaction
Apart from the effect of visual feedback in motor control and motor learning, other psychological factors such as grouping or holism may also affect touchless interactions with 2D interfaces. For example, recent research has shown that four fundamental Gestalt principles [15] in perception also apply to the control of motor action—holism, constancy, mutual exclusivity, and grouping in apparent motion [10]. Indeed, gestures following the Law of Pragnanz [15] were found to be more efficient than gestures without meaningful chunking [10]. Furthermore, exploring the user performance of touchless interactions in preferred and non-preferred hands could inform the design of bimanual touchless interfaces [8].

In summary, interacting with a 2D surface (that lacks a 3D worldview) using 3D freehand gestures is unlike gesturing in a 3D world. Thus, to effectively design touchless interfaces, it is crucial to understand the perceptual and motor factors at play.

Understanding Perceptual and Motor Factors in Touchless Interactions

My preliminary studies on touchless interfaces spun off the Wall Display Experience Research—which explores novel interaction techniques and technologies for collocated collaboration around large displays. Specifically, for the last three years, I have explored ways in which we can draw on our motor and cognitive abilities to effectively design touchless interfaces. For example, grounded in prior findings of how visual cues affect motor learning and motor control, I studied visual feedback in touchless interactions; by drawing upon our sensorimotor level of knowledge, such as image schemas, I proposed motor-intuitive interaction primitives [5]. Then, building upon these prior works, I designed a command selection technique (Touchless Circular Menus, [2]) and a feedback language for touchless interfaces (fusing pseudo-haptic and visual feedback [3]). Moving forward, in the spirit of use-inspired basic research—in my dissertation—I am assimilating (1) the broader implications of cognitive theories in touchless interactions (e.g., Gestalt theories [4]) and (2) understanding how these findings can be applied toward designing touchless interaction with 2D UIs (e.g., large displays).

Theoretical explorations of my research is largely complete, and currently I am focusing on using the perceptual and motor factors—that were uncovered during my preliminary research—to design interaction techniques and UI components for large-display touchless interfaces. By participating in this doctoral symposium, I aim to garner feedback from senior researchers and peers about how can I translate these basic research findings effectively into touchless interface design. In what follows, I briefly describe some of the key perceptual and motor factors that I explored in my prior work, and where applicable, the interaction techniques designed based on them.

Image Schemas. In pursuit of intuitive touchless gestures, we proposed motor-intuitive interactions: interactions that unconsciously draw on our pre-existing sensorimotor knowledge, such as basic movements like pulling, pushing, moving up or down. Such movements are based on image schemas like up-down or near-far [5]. Instead of using system-defined postures as interface controls, we then proposed using

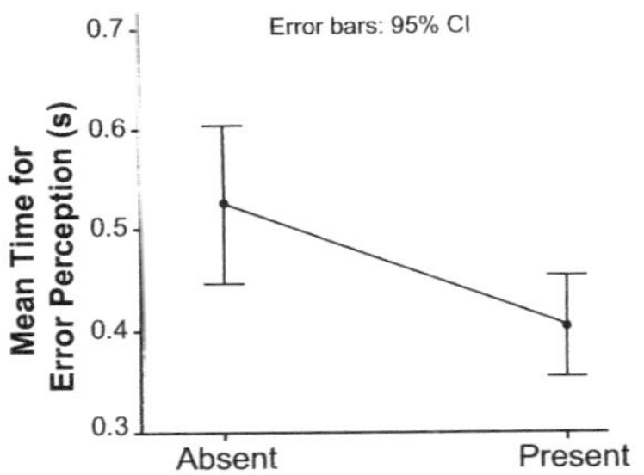

Figure 3: When users' gestures went out of the display range, persistent visual feedback improved users' recovery efficiency, because lack of visual feedback was often perceived as a system error.

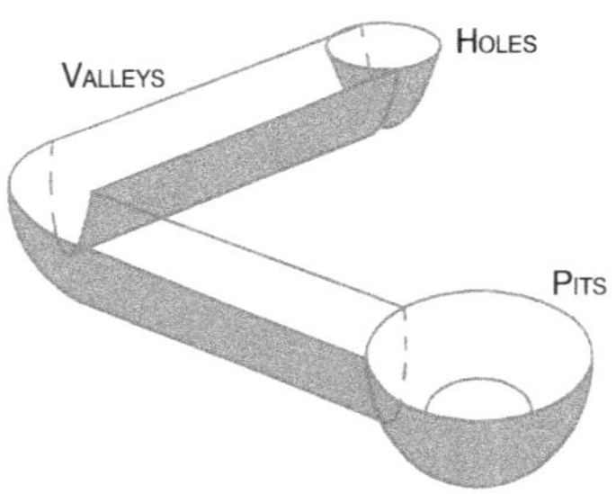

Figure 4: Topography primitives (e.g., holes, valleys, or pits) operate as virtual surfaces that overlay on an interface and modify cursor movements to improve the precision of touchless interactions.

motor-intuitive interaction primitives to build UI components, like Touchless Circular Menus (TCM, [2], Figure 2). We found that users were more efficient with TCM compared with the grab-based linear menus and perceived less workload, but TCM lacked interaction precision.

Perceptual and Motor Gestalt. While exploring touchless interaction precision, we observed that UI elements demonstrating Gestalt principles of perceptual grouping, such as similarity of orientation decreased efficiency, but continuity of UI elements that formed a perceptual whole increased accuracy[4]. Also, following the motor gestalt [10], users often made holistic gestures that minimized energy expenditure [4, 5].

User Feedback. Continuous visual feedback played a crucial role: We found that users perceive lack of visual cues as system errors and slow down. Similar to findings in motor literature, persistent visual feedback (Figure 3) and terminal visual feedback improved user performance. To further improve touchless accuracy, we modified the control-display gain, generated a virtual topography (e.g., holes, valleys, and pits), and provided pseudo-haptic feedback [3] (Figure 4). Results found that interface topographies increased accuracy in difficult steering tasks.

An advantage of the non-dominant hand. Prior research exploring lateral asymmetries in input devices found support for the theory that dominant and non-dominant hands primarily differ in their use of sensory feedback control [10]: Right-handed individuals possess a right-hand superiority for sequential processing of feedback and a left-hand superiority for open-loop, parallel processing. Echoing previous work, our preliminary results suggest that the lack of haptic feedback in touchless interactions facilitates open-loop processing (or pre-planned motor plans). For example, users were far more accurate with longer directional strokes than shorter strokes as longer mid-air strokes require preplanning but shorter strokes primarily depend on sequential processing of feedback (Figure 5, [5]). Similarly, right-handed users were more accurate in touchless steering with left hand than right hand (in a difficult, circular steering-targeting task, Figure 6).

The Next Steps

A central premise of my research is that interface controls are made up of interaction primitives and designing intuitive touchless interfaces would thus require intuitive touchless primitives. This largely assumes that as touchless interface design matures, it will mirror the compositional nature of GUIs. However, an alternative to an additive approach would be to design semantic interactions that are task-oriented, such as gesture sets suggested for touch interfaces [14]. Nevertheless, my research findings could still inform such use-centric design of touchless interfaces.

As a possible user scenario, I am interested in applying my findings into designing touchless interfaces for large display interaction—specifically during collocated collaboration [1] and information visualization [6]. However, interacting with large displays is not a monolithic experience—users may simply brainstorm and use coarse-grained gestures sporadically, or engage in fine-grained, frequent actions, such as collaborative text-editing. While the former kind of interactions would benefit from touchless gestures that relieve users from tethering to devices and allow more

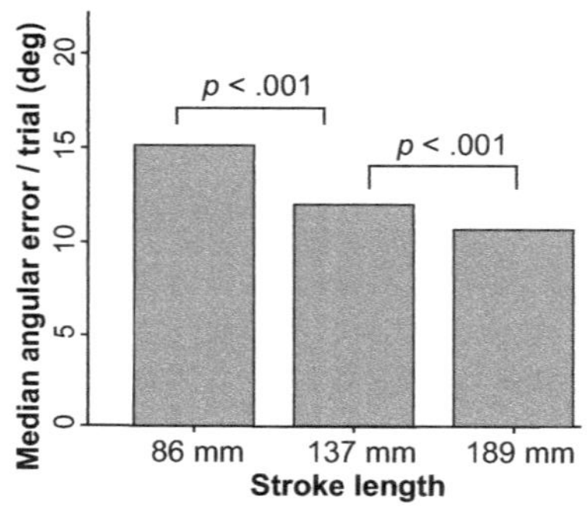

Figure 5: Stroke length significantly affected the angular error of mid-air strokes, $p < 0.001$. Interestingly, participants made significantly less angular error with increase in stroke length, $p < 0.001$.

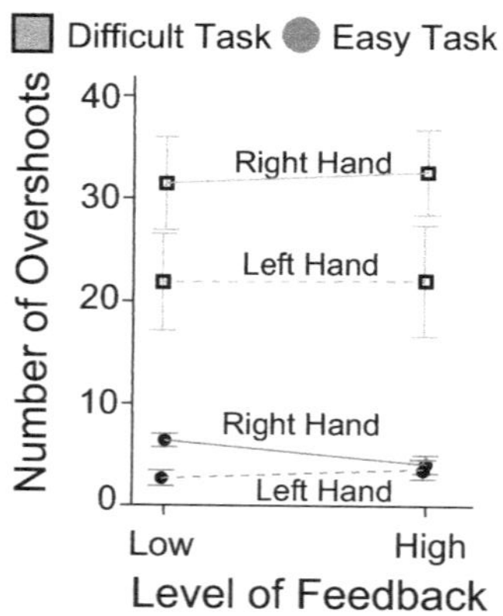

Figure 6: In a difficult circular steering task, right-handed users were more accurate with left than right hand.

spatial mobility, the fine-grained interactions would be more befitting for other interaction modalities (e.g., tablets, tangible controllers, etc.). So, I would like to understand the use-cases in large-display interaction to explore how some of these scenarios can be supported with touchless interaction techniques and what are some of the major interaction challenges in doing so.

Acknowledgements

I would like to thank my advisor Davide Bolchini for his guidance and UITS AVL for the use of their facilities. This research was partially funded by an IUPUI RSFG.

References

1. Bragdon, A., et al. (2011). Code space: touch+ air gesture hybrid interactions for supporting developer meetings. *Proc. ITS*, 212–221, ACM.
2. Chattopadhyay, D., et al. (2014). Touchless circular menus: Toward an intuitive UI for touchless interactions with large displays. *Proc. AVI*, 33–40, ACM.
3. Chattopadhyay, D., Achmiz, S., et al. (2014). Holes, pits, and valleys: Guiding large-display touchless interactions with data-morphed topographies. *Adjunct Proc. UbiComp*, 19–22, ACM.
4. Chattopadhyay, D. (2015). Exploring Perceptual and Motor Gestalt in Touchless Interactions with Distant Displays. *Proc. TEI*, 433–436.
5. Chattopadhyay, D., et al. (2015). Motor-intuitive interactions based on image schemas: Aligning touchless interaction primitives with human sensorimotor abilities. *IWC, 27*(3), 327–343.
6. Dostal, J., et al. (2014). SpiderEyes: Designing attention-and proximity-aware collaborative interfaces for wall-sized displays. *Proc. IUI*, 143–152, ACM.
7. Grandhi, S. A., Joue, G. and Mittelberg, I. (2011) Understanding naturalness and intuitiveness in gesture production: insights for touchless gestural interfaces. *Proc. CHI*, 821–824, ACM.
8. Guimbretière, F., et al. (2012). Bimanual marking menu for near surface interactions. *Proc. CHI*, 825–828, ACM.
9. Hurtienne, J., & Israel, J. H. (2007). Image schemas and their metaphorical extensions: intuitive patterns for tangible interaction. *Proc. TEI*, 127–134, ACM.
10. Kabbash, P., et al. (1993). Human performance using computer input devices in the preferred and non-preferred hands. *Proc. CHI*, 474–481, ACM.
11. Klapp, S. T., & Jagacinski, R. J. (2011). Gestalt principles in the control of motor action. *Psychological bulletin, 137*(3), 443.
12. Nebeling, M., et al. (2014). Web on the Wall Reloaded: Implementation, Replication and Refinement of User-Defined Interaction Sets. *Proc. ITS*, 15–24, ACM.
13. O'hara, K., et al. (2013). On the naturalness of touchless: putting the "interaction" back into NUI. *TOCHI, 20*(1), 5.
14. Schmidt, S., Nacenta, M. A., Dachselt, R., & Carpendale, S. (2010). A set of multi-touch graph interaction techniques. *Proc. ITS*, 113–116, ACM.
15. Wagemans, J., Elder, J. H., et al. (2012). A century of Gestalt psychology in visual perception: I. Perceptual grouping and figure–ground organization. *Psychological bulletin, 138*(6), 1172.
16. Wigdor, D. and Wixon, D. (2011). *Brave NUI World: Designing Natural User Interfaces for Touch and Gesture.* Morgan Kauffman, Burlington, MA.

Interactive Spaces: Models and Algorithms for Reality-Based Music Applications

Marcella Mandanici
CSC - Sound and Music Computing Group
Department of Information Engeneering
University of Padova, ITALY
mandanici@dei.unipd.it

ITS '15, November 15-18, 2015, Funchal, Portugal
ACM 978-1-4503-3899-8/15/11. http://dx.doi.org/10.1145/2817721.2820986

Abstract
Reality-based interfaces have the property of linking the user's physical space with the computer digital content, bringing in intuition, plasticity and expressiveness. Moreover, applications designed upon motion and gesture tracking technologies involve a lot of psychological features, like space cognition and implicit knowledge. All these elements are the background of three presented music applications, employing the characteristics of three different interactive spaces: a user centered three dimensional space, a floor bi-dimensional camera space, and a small sensor centered three dimensional space. The basic idea is to deploy the application's spatial properties in order to convey some musical knowledge, allowing the users to act inside the designed space and to learn through it in an enactive way.

Author Keywords
Blended interaction; Sound augmented reality; Learning environments.

ACM Classification Keywords
H.5.1 [Artificial, augmented, and virtual realities]; H.5.2 [User Interfaces]; H.5.5 [Sound and Music Computing]

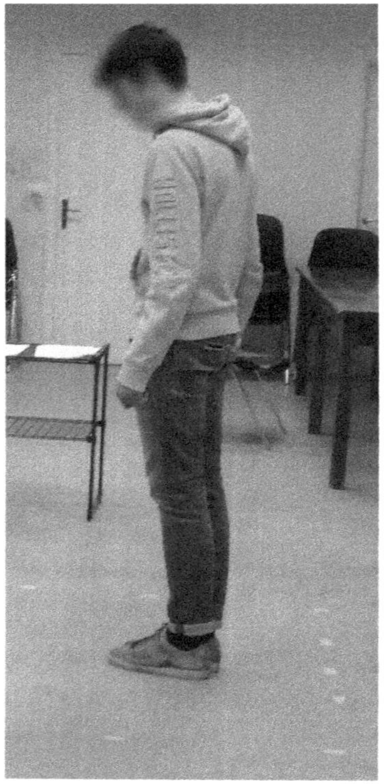

Figure 1: The floor interface of the "Harmonic Walk" application while being tested by a high school student

Motivation and Research Approach

The widespread utilization of cameras, camera software systems and motion tracking devices like Kinect (https://www.microsoft.com/en-us/kinectforwindows/) and the Leap Motion Sensor (https://www.leapmotion.com/), has brought to the attention of a continously growing audience of researchers, designers and practitioners the great potentialities of newborn interaction styles. Physical environments lying in the range of these sensors, allow the users to move freely in everyday spaces, without anything to wear or to hold in their hands, and to produce some audio or/and visual feedback from a computer system, connecting in this way the digital contents to their movements or actions. My research focuses on these kinds of spatial interaction, and on how interfaces belonging to the real world can be arranged to deploy the uniqueness of these interaction styles. In particular, my design experiences concern music expressive interaction, music learning environments (see Fig.1) and music production (see Fig.2). Many musical features, like harmony or melodic movements, have been historically depicted by meaningful spatial representations, e.g. the *Euler's Tonnetz* (see Fig.3, literally "web of tones", a spatial schema showing the triadic relationships upon which tonal harmony is based), or the Gregorian Chant *Neumatic Notation* and *Chironomy*, a gestural system expressing melodic contour variations. The very action of musical instrument involves precise spatial rules and element displacement, whose study has produced a large body of research about new music production interfaces in the field of the Sound and Music Computing. Another interesting example of music spatial interaction is the conductor model, where expressive performance informations are transmitted to performers through free-hands open-space gestures. This led me to consider the possibility of employing physical two dimensional surfaces or 3D spaces to project geometrical representations of musical concepts, thus enabling users to enter and to navigate conceptual maps representing some musical knowledge. The experimental hypothesis upon which my work is based, is that in this situation implicit and tacit knowledge may emerge and drive the users to also accomplish very complex tasks, like melody harmonization, without delivering them any previous information. Implicit knowledge refers to our brain's ability to acquire an abstract representation of any environmental stimulus (like for instance an unknown language), learning its rules in an unconscious way. Implicit learning is linked to the idea of enactivism, that is the ability of learning by doing. These important cognitive and psychological concepts are both involved in reality-based learning environments, which can deploy such powerful tools to convey information in a faster and more direct way. The aim of my work is also to study the cognitive content of musical knowledge and to try to expand the same learning methodology towards other domains, like the STEM disciplines (Science, Technology, Engineering and Mathematics), which very often benefit from being introduced through creativity and arts-based learning.

Research Outlook

In 2010 while attending the 7th Sound and Music Computing Conference and Summer School in Barcelona I was introduced to the *Stanza Logomotoria* [18], a motion tracking, camera-based application where children are asked to match a story tale with sounds positioned on the mapped surface (see Fig.5). Further, the application was presented in some experimental sessions with music didactics students in Conservatories and elementary schools. Nevertheless, my actual research begun in 2012, when I graduated in Electronic Music with a master thesis on *Disembodied voices*, the first of the three case studies described below. This experience disclosed to me the great potentialities of reality based, full body and free handed interaction, especially when coupled with a well established human-to-human communication model, like the one of the music conductor. During my first year of PhD at the Department of Information Engineering of the University of Padova with the Sound and Music Computing Group (2013), I examined in depth various theories about the representation of music harmony spaces and music image schemas. In 2014 I realized my first camera space music application, the *Harmonic Walk*, the second of the three case studies reported below. By the end of 2015 I will conclude my PhD studies, after having developed several applications for entertainment, learning and creative and expressive music interaction. Presently, together with other members of the CSC research group, I am working to a spatial collaborative game to enhance music listening (*Good or Bad*) and to a spatial display for an interactive image sonification installation.

Figure 2: A child playing a Disklavier through gestural input detected by a Leap Motion Sensor

Related Work

My work is based on two different kinds of background. Firstly the analysis of the origins ([4] and [3]) and of the state of art of interactive spaces like

- *Google's Interactive Spaces and Liquid Galaxy* (http://www.interactive-spaces.org/),
- *Aarhus University Research Centre* (http://www.interactivespaces.net/,
- *Blended Interactions Design Studio, Rochester (NY)* (http://blendedinteractions.com/)
- *UCLA REMAP University of California* (http://openptrack.org/)

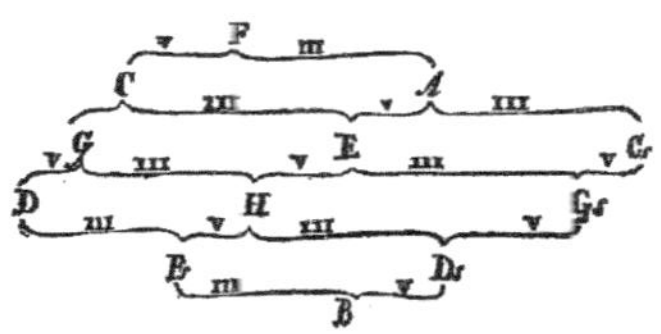

Figure 3: Euler's Tonnetz, 1739.

and blended interaction theory [5], providing also a short survey of interactive spaces definitions, typologies, available platforms and themes. I pay also particular attention to existing learning environments like

- *WizeFloor* (https://www.wizefloor.com/)
- *Smallab* (http://smallablearning.com/)
- *STEP* (http://remap.ucla.edu/research/cultural-civic-computing/791-science-through-technology-enhanced-play-step)

research centres, arts and culture installations and music production environments. Secondly, all the theoretical studies concerning space cognition ([11] and [17]), implicit knowledge ([14] and [16]), enactivism [2] and image schemas ([6] and [1]), which form an interconnected interdisciplinary field, very useful to understand how reality-based applications work. In Fig.4 a tentative conceptual map of the relationships existing among reality-based applications, implicit knowledge and space cognition is proposed, outlining reciprocal interplay and dependencies.

Three Case Studies

In this Section three case studies of music applications are presented. The three cases employ different motion tracking devices and convey musical concepts through geometrical interpretation and spatial representation. Also the projections refer to different spatial models, as the first employs the 3D spherical-polar coordinate system, the second 2D Cartesian coordinates on a flat floor surface and the third 3D space with x, y Cartesian coordinates plus z plane for depth data.

Disembodied Voices

[9] is an interactive environment designed for an expressive, gesture-based musical performance. The motion sensor Kinect, placed in front of the user, provides the computer with the 3D polar coordinates of the two

Figure 5: The "Stanza Logomotoria" basic configuration, with computer, audio monitors and ceiling mounted camera.

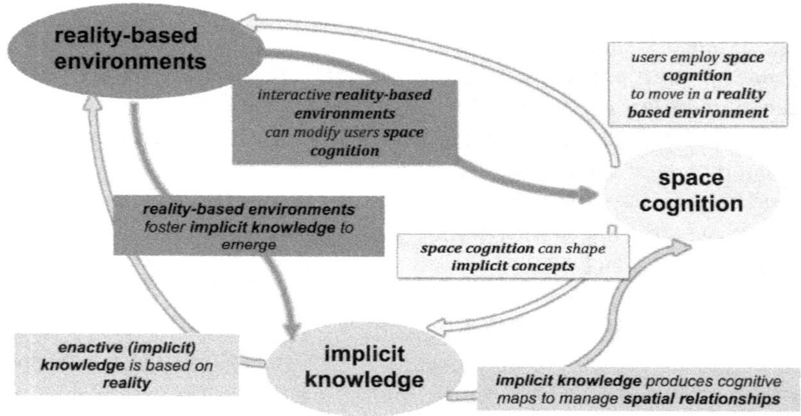

Figure 4: A conceptual map of the main relationships existing among reality-based environments (blue connections), space cognition (green connections) and implicit knowledge (brown connections).

Figure 6: The hemispherical regions for user hands interaction in "Disembodied Voices". For the left hand there is an inner region and two outer regions, one in front and the other at the side of the user.

hands. The application is designed according to the interaction model of the music conductor: the user, through gestures, is able to run a score and to produce a real-time expressive interpretation. The conductor moves her/his arms and hands in the space around her/his torso and in the direction of the performers. Movement analysis ([10] and [12]) as well as the teaching practice[15] subdivide the role of the two hands; in general, the right executes musical cues while the left is devoted to iconics, metaphorics and dynamics. As can be seen from Fig.6, the geometrical interpretation of the conductor's interaction space is a hemisphere with the center at the level of the breastbone of the conductor and the diameter corresponding approximately to the two stretched arms length. Following the conductor's interaction model, the hemisphere is subdivided in two parts, one for the right and the other one for the left hand. For the left hand three different regions are shaped, triggering various digital sound processing effects. (video available at `https://www.youtube.com/watch?v=oyf7GrMMrL8`)

The Harmonic Walk

[8] is an interactive physical environment designed for experiencing a novel spatial approach to musical creation. In particular, the system allows the user to get in touch with some fundamental tonal music features in a very simple and readily available way. The application's interface consists of a camera placed on the ceiling which can trace the presence of a user who walks on a flat surface within the camera's view. The *Harmonic Walk*, through the body movement in space, can provide a live experience of tonal melody structure, chord progressions, melody accompaniment and improvisation. Enactive knowledge and embodied cognition allow the user to build

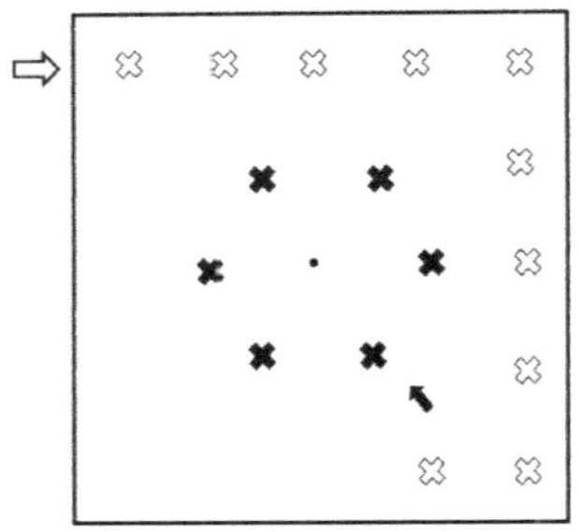

Figure 7: Visual tags of the straight and circular path of the "Harmonic Walk's" interface.

an inner map of these musical features, which can be acted by moving on the mapped surface with a simple step. Listeners interpret a tonal melody grouping the perceived sequence of events after a metrical and harmonic frame [13]. This produces a segmentation of the composition into different harmonic regions which, with the underlying harmonic structure, are the leading features of a tonal composition. The time proceeding of the various musical units is led by the melody, whose metaphoric scheme is expressed by the so-called "source-path-goal" schema [6]. Following this metaphor and employing the simplest motion in space a human can do - the walk - it is possible to represent a tonal composition as a sequence of spatial blocks, where each step corresponds to the next musical unit (white crosses in Fig.7), while the harmonic space is represented by a six parts sliced circular ring containing the six roots of the tonality harmonic space (black crosses). (video available at https://www.youtube.com/watch?v=0jwXfzq_CkU&index=1&list=UU1E9xCq8TWqlzessRIzUGxw)

Hand Composer
[7] is a gesture-driven composition system, based on the analysis of the existing relationships between music generative models and musical composition in the context of the XX century music history background. The system framework is based on a number of interactive machines performing various patterns of music composition and producing a stream of MIDI data to be compatible with a Disklavier performance. Hand gestural input, captured by the Leap Motion sensor (see Fig.8), can control some parameters of the music composing machines, changing interactively their musical output. (video available at https://www.youtube.com/watch?v=mdsn9_5Ig_A&list=UU1E9xCq8TWqlzessRIzUGxw)

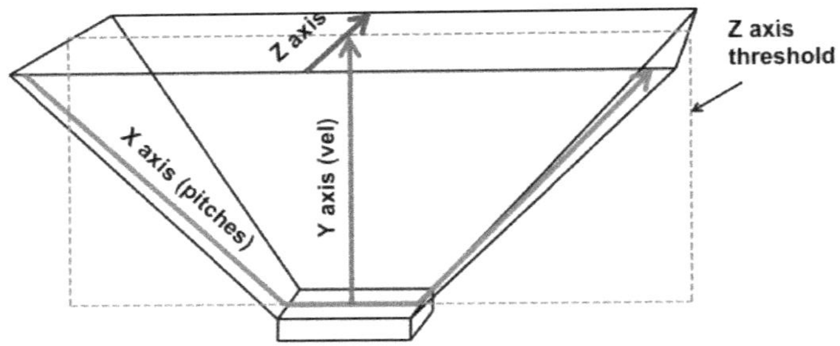

Figure 8: The 3D interaction space of the *Hand Composer* application. x, y Cartesian coordinates are employed to map the two-dimensional vertical plane, while z coordinates map the depth data.

Thesis Scope and Expected Contributions

The experimental hypothesis upon which all my research is based, is that abstract knowledge like musical harmony or tonal music composition structure can be conveyed to the users through the enactive learning induced by interactive space environments. Thus, my thesis will focus on the relationship between space and cognition, and on the ways knowledge can be spatially represented. As I have worked with various kinds of interactive spaces (bi-dimensional floors as well as three-dimensional volumes), I will try to work out a comprehensive, unifying framework for all of them and to highlight their respective properties and differences. If my experimental hypothesis is verified, reality-based learning environments design could benefit of very powerful cognitive tools, which could be extended beyond music also to other knowledge fields, like science, mathematics and technology.

Acknowledgements

I am grateful to my supervisor Sergio Canazza for his precious support and help. I also want to express my gratitude to Antonio Rodà who followed step by step the development of my work and to Davide Rocchesso for his advices and presence.

References

[1] Brower, C. A cognitive theory of musical meaning. *Journal of Music Theory* (2000), 323–379.

[2] Bruner, J. S. The act of discovery. *Harvard educational review* (1961).

[3] Engelbart, D. C. Augmenting human intellect: a conceptual framework (1962). *PACKER, Randall and JORDAN, Ken. Multimedia. From Wagner to Virtual Reality. New York: WW Norton & Company* (2001), 64–90.

[4] Harrison, S., and Dourish, P. Re-place-ing space: the roles of place and space in collaborative systems. In *Proc. ACM conference on Computer supported cooperative work*, ACM (1996), 67–76.

[5] Jetter, H.-C., Reiterer, H., and Geyer, F. Blended interaction: understanding natural human–computer interaction in post-wimp interactive spaces. *Personal and Ubiquitous Computing 18*, 5 (2014), 1139–1158.

[6] Lakoff, G., and Johnson, M. *Metaphors we live by.* University of Chicago press, 2008.

[7] Mandanici, M., and Canazza, S. The "hand composer": gesture-driven music composition machines. In *Proc. 13th Conf. on Intelligent Autonomous Systems* (2014), 553–560.

[8] Mandanici, M., Rodà, A., and Canazza, S. The harmonic walk: an interactive educational environment to discover musical chords. In *Proc. ICMC-SMC Conference* (2014).

[9] Mandanici, M., and Sapir, S. Disembodied voices: a kinect virtual choir conductor. In *Proc. 9th Sound and Music Computing Conference* (2012), 271–276.

[10] Marrin, T., and Picard, R. The 'conductor's jacket': A device for recording expressive musical gestures. In *Proc. International Computer Music Conference* (1998), 215–219.

[11] Montello, D. R. *International Encyclopedia of the Social and Behavioral Sciences.* Oxford, Pergamon Press, 2001, ch. Spatial Cognition, 14771 – 14775.

[12] Murphy, D., Andersen, T. H., and Jensen, K. Conducting audio files via computer vision. In *Gesture-based communication in human-computer interaction.* Springer, 2004, 529–540.

[13] Povel, D.-J., and Jansen, E. Harmonic factors in the perception of tonal melodies. *Music Perception 20*, 1 (2002), 51–85.

[14] Reber, A. S. Implicit learning and tacit knowledge. *Journal of experimental psychology: General 118*, 3 (1989), 219.

[15] Rudolf, M., and Stern, M. *The grammar of conducting: A comprehensive guide to baton technique and interpretation.* Schirmer Books, New York, 1994.

[16] Tillmann, B., Bharucha, J. J., and Bigand, E. Implicit learning of tonality: a self-organizing approach. *Psychological review 107*, 4 (2000), 885.

[17] Tversky, B. Functional Significance of Visuospatial Representations. *Handbook of higher-level visuospatial thinking Handbook of* (2005), 1–34.

[18] Zanolla, S., Canazza, S., Rodà, A., Camurri, A., and Volpe, G. Entertaining listening by means of the Stanza Logo-Motoria: an Interactive Multimodal Environment. *Entertainment Computing 2013*, 4 (2013), 213–220.

Collaborative Learning In An Artifact Ecology: A Distributed Cognition Perception

Christina Vasiliou
Cyprus Interaction Lab
Cyprus University of Technology
30 Archbishop Kyprianou Str. 3036
Limassol, Cyprus
c.vasiliou@cut.ac.cy

ITS '15, November 15-18, 2015, Funchal, Portugal
ACM 978-1-4503-3899-8/15/11.
http://dx.doi.org/10.1145/2817721.2820987

Abstract
This work aims to extend our understanding of how groups of learners collaborate in a learning environment rich in technologies, namely an artifact ecology. For the purpose of this investigation we enriched a postgraduate HCI course with four identical technology rich settings that aimed to support student collaborative activities around a design problem. Following an ethnographic approach, we collected qualitative data from an HCI course over three years resulting in a rich dataset for analysis. Initial studies helped us understand the domain knowledge, context, and learners' needs and experiences. Then, using Distributed Cognition (DC) framework we worked toward understanding the interdependencies of learners, tasks, and technologies in the environment and highlighting aspects of redesign. The findings of these individual studies were then combined in order to provide a holistic understanding of the collaborative activities in an artifact ecology.

Author Keywords
Collaborative learning; distributed cognition; artifact ecology; HCI education.

ACM Classification Keywords
H.5.3. Information interfaces and presentation (e.g., HCI): Group and Organization Interfaces;

Introduction
Technology's evolving nature has brought new possibilities to the design of technology-rich learning environments for collaborative activities. Tablets and smartphones together with personal computers become part of an artifact ecology in which each device acts as a specialized portal into users' personal or shared information space [3]. In a collaborative learning environment these devices may be used for a variety of tasks while each individual may perform a task differently. Therefore, learners, tasks and use of technology in a learning environment cannot be studied independently or in isolation. To design effective technology-rich collaborative learning environments we need to acquire a deep understanding of the complex relations and interactions between collaborators and information technologies. Researchers have identified DC as a powerful tool for understanding the interdependencies of learners, tasks, and technologies in collaborative environments and for highlighting aspects for redesign [5].

Our work focuses on exactly this, using Distributed Cognition (DC) and more specifically Distributed Cognition for Teamwork (DiCoT) as a methodological framework to guide data collection, analysis and interpretation of findings. Through this investigation we aim to understand collaborative learning activities around an artifact ecology, apply and expand DiCoT framework to map them.

Theoretical Framework
As a theoretical framework DC analyses cognition in a distributed manner [4], while it considers an activity taking place across individuals, tools and representations as one cognitive system, instead within an individual's mind.

Researchers in HCI (Human-Computer Interaction) and CSCW (Computer Supported Cooperative Work) communities have identified DC as a valid framework for understanding the interdependencies between users, tools and tasks [2]. In order to design effective artifact ecologies, each tool must allow the distribution of an individual's cognition to the wider cognitive system, e.g. the classroom [7]. Furthermore, DC can provide a detailed identification of issues with existing work practices and mediating artefacts [6], allowing researchers to identify aspects of re-design of the environment.

However, there is no established methodology towards applying DC in the case of collaborative learning environments. In this work, we adopted the DiCoT methodological framework introduced by Blandford and Furniss [1] for collaborative work to extend our understanding of how groups of learners collaborate in a learning environment rich in technologies. This methodology was extensively used in workspace environments and draws together ideas from DC and conceptual design, including 22 principles classified loosely in five models; physical layout, information flow, artefacts, evolutionary and social structures.

Artifact Ecology
We sought to create an artifact ecology, by enriching the classroom environment with various technologies

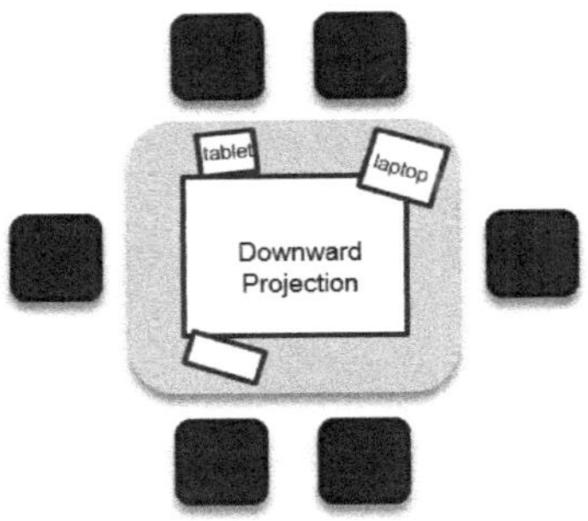

Figure 1: Physical Layout of the artifact ecology where each group of learners' would work.

aimed to support student collaborative activity, particularly brainstorming, researching, reporting or reflecting, both in-class and in distance (in-between the face-to-face meetings). Furthermore, this physical space, together with the problem based learning (PBL) approach aimed to promote openness and flexibility. Students were encouraged to use the technologies as they perceived appropriate for each activity and task. Each group worked in a physical, technological set-up exhibiting three main attributes that we considered important for collaborative learning activity:

- A downward pointing projection was provided as a central focus point to support students' fertile discussions and activities (see Figure 1). This setup would cultivate the blend of physical and digitally projected artifacts, mixing paper and technology, on the same workspace.
- The multitasking nature of the group was invigorated with mobile devices such as tablets, iPods and laptops for concurrent research and record-keeping (see Figure 2). The students were also allowed to enrich the artifact ecology with their own devices.
- A social networking platform (Facebook) was used to strengthen information sharing, coordination and collaboration, both between group members and devices.

Proposed Research Approach

Through the lens of DC, this work aims to extend our understanding of how groups of learners collaborate on design problems in a learning environment rich in physical and digital technologies and blending face-to-face content-and-activity with digital content-and-activity. Furthermore, through this investigation DiCoT methodological framework will be transferred from workspace settings and applied to collaborative learning environments. Further, we aim to highlighting what is salient in the existing collaborative learning environment design and practices and indicate aspects of redesign of the learning environment.

For the purpose of this work, we enriched a postgraduate HCI course with four identical technology rich settings that aimed to support student collaborative activities around a design problem. Following an ethnographic approach, we collected data from a variety of sources (e.g. field notes, focus groups, interviews, video data) from an HCI course over three consecutive years resulting in a rich corpus of data. Each ethnographic study was extended for a period of three months, waving the novelty effect off the participants, increasing the level of the trustworthiness of the study.

In the sections that follow the progress achieved so far as well as the future plans for the current dissertation are outlined.

Work to Date

Study 1 - Exploratory: "Understanding the domain knowledge and exploring learners' expectations in an artifact ecology"

First study acted as a pilot study with the overall aim to understand the domain knowledge of the dissertation (HCI education, problem based and collaborative learning) as well as explore learners' expectations and attitudes in an artifact ecology [8]. More specifically we aimed at finding answers to the following sub-questions:

Figure 2. Mobile technologies and downward projection as used in-class.

- What are the current directions and technologies used that already exist in the literature of technology enhanced problem based learning?
- What are the current goals and directions of HCI education?
- What are learners' expectations, attitudes and technology use in an artifact ecology?

Study 2: "Understanding learners' experiences and applying the DiCoT framework for collaborative learning activities in an artifact ecology"

The second study focused on two main research pillars; first on understanding learners' collaborative experiences in the artifact ecology [9] and second to apply DiCoT in a collaborative learning setting. In this context, we showcase learner-learner and learner-artifacts interactions evident in the workspace that support collaboration and coordination during collaborative learning activities. We describe the cognitive system from three different perspectives - physical layout, information flow and artifacts involved - which allows an in-depth understanding of the interactions and interdependencies among learners and artifacts during collaborative activities. Further, the study also focused on illustrating and validating the utility of DC and DiCoT as a tool for modelling interactions and interdependencies during collaborative learning activities in an artifact ecology [10]. More specifically, this study focused on the following sub-questions:

- What are learners' collaborative learning experience and user experience in the artifact ecology?
- How can DiCoT be applied as a modelling tool for collaborative learning activities in an artifact ecology?
- How learner-learner and learner-artifact interactions evident in the artifact ecology support collaboration and coordination during design activities?

Study 3: "Expanding DiCoT methodological framework for collaborative learning activities in an artifact ecology and extracting design guidelines"

Finally, the third study will focus on expanding the DiCoT methodological framework for collaborative learning settings. Through this study we will highlight the affordances of digital and physical tools in the ecology of artifacts that support collaboration and coordination during collaborative learning activities and how they vary across different groups. Further by providing insights on how the affordances of the artifact ecology supported collaboration and coordination, we wish to provide practical guidelines to designers of collaborative spaces and new research directions to researchers. This understanding will allow us to expand the DiCoT framework to explain learning contexts as well as workspaces. More specifically, this study will focus on the answering the following sub-questions:

- What are the affordances of physical and digital tools in an artifact ecology as tools for distributing cognition?
- What are the group characteristics that underpin the use of physical and digital tools in an artifact ecology as tools for distributing cognition?
- How can DiCoT framework be expanded for collaborative learning activities?

- What design implications emerge as guidelines for interaction designers and practitioners for collaborative learning activities in artifact ecologies?

Significance

Our study aims to illustrate the utility of DiCoT methodological framework as a valuable tool for explaining interactions and interdependencies during collaborative learning activities in an artifact ecology. As claimed in the literature, DC is a well suited conceptual framework when dealing with technology-rich collaborative environments. However, DiCoT framework was explicitly used in the workspace, with no known extend to a collaborative learning setting. Therefore, one important contribution of this work is to transfer and apply the DiCoT framework from workspace to classroom environments, and further verifying its validity in a collaborative learning environment.

Looking at both learners' experiences, needs and expectations and understanding the computational ideas and paradigms through distributed cognition, we perceive that our study has a significant contribution in the use of such technologies across HCI, CSCW and CSCL. If we understand how these technologies can distribute an individual's' cognition towards the group, we can also find out how to design effective artifact ecologies that can support them. The added benefit of examining a complex system through the lens of DC is that it allows researchers to take a step backwards and see the "big picture", focusing on interactions and actions central to the coordination of work activities. Such an understanding will allow researchers and practitioners to pin-point where changes should occur or should not occur in the cognitive system as a whole.

Expected Outcomes

The completion of this project is expected to supply researchers a better understanding of how groups of learners collaborate in a learning environment rich in technologies. Furthermore, we aim to enrich and guide technology designers and practitioners on constructing effective artifact ecologies for collaborative learning activities by crafting a set of design guidelines.

References

[1] Ann Blandford, A. and Furniss, F. DiCoT: A methodology for applying distributed cognition to the design of team working systems. In Proc. DSV-IS 2005. Springer (2006) LNCS, vol. 3941, 26–38.

[2] Halverson, C.A. Activity theory and distributed cognition: Or what does CSCW need to Do with theories? Computer Supported Cooperative Work 11 (2002), 243–267.

[3] Houben, S., Tell, S. and Bardram, J. E. ActivitySpace: Managing Device Ecologies in an Activity-Centric Configuration Space. In Proc ACM International Conference on Interactive Tabletops and Surfaces, ACM Press (2014) 119-128.

[4] Hutchins, E. Cognition in the wild. MIT Press, Cambridge, 1995.

[5] Loke, S.W. and Ling, S. Analyzing Observable Behaviours of Device Ecology Workflows. In Proc ICEIS (2004), 78-83.

[6] Rogers, Y. HCI Theory: Classical, Modern, and Contemporary. Synthesis lectures on human-centered informatics. Morgan & Claypool, San Francisco, 2012.

[7] Valanides, N. and Angeli, C. Distributed cognition in a sixth-grade classroom: An attempt to overcome alternative conceptions about light and color. Journal of

Research on Technology in Education 40, 3 (2008), 309–336.

[8] Vasiliou, C., Ioannou, A. and Zaphiris, P. Technology Enhanced PBL in HCI Education: A Case Study. In Proc Human-Computer Interaction–INTERACT (2013), 643-650.

[9] Vasiliou, C., Ioannou, A. and Zaphiris, P. Measuring Students' Flow Experience in a Multimodal Learning Environment: A Case Study. In Learning and Collaboration Technologies. Designing and Developing Novel Learning Experiences (2014), 346-357.

[10] Vasiliou, C., Ioannou, A. and Zaphiris, P. Understanding collaborative learning activities in an information ecology: A distributed cognition account. Computers in Human Behavior, 41 (2014), 544-553.

Supporting the Meeting Journey: Understanding and Designing Collaborative Device Ecologies

Aurélien Ammeloot
Centre for Interaction Design
Edinburgh Napier University
Edinburgh EH10 5DT, UK
a.ammeloot@napier.ac.uk

ITS'15, November 15-18, 2015, Funchal, Portugal
ACM 978-1-4503-3899-8/15/11.
http://dx.doi.org/10.1145/2817721.2820988

Abstract
The combination of personal and mobile technologies (*Bring Your Own Device*) with technology-augmented spaces designed for collaboration offers new design challenges for the HCI community. This paper is a summary of a doctoral work-in-progress aiming to further understand the design of multi-screen device ecologies for collaboration: understanding the activities, i.e. the *Meeting Journey*, and understanding the best design principles applicable to support this journey. In order to achieve this, a number of methodologies have been used: ethnographic observations, semi-structured interviews, and focus groups. The journey and design principles are established with an analysis method informed by Grounded Theory. Future work will include the development and evaluation of a software assistant supporting meeting journey activities using a *hybrid* approach.

Author Keywords
Design Principles, BYOD, Device Ecologies

ACM Classification Keywords
H.5.m [Information interfaces and presentation (e.g., HCI)]: Miscellaneous

Introduction
Recent years have been the stage of a significant change in form factors and everyday usage of portable and per-

Figure 1: The ICE, aka the future meeting room, as envisioned in 2010. The initial focus was multitouch surfaces rather than BYOD.

sonal technologies. Workplaces are currently witnessing a shift from a workstation-centric approach to the era of *Bring Your Own Device* (BYOD), letting users use more and more mobile devices, such as tablets and smartphones. In the meantime, the market for wearables is growing, with platforms such as Apple's WatchOS™or Android Wear™.

The *Future Interactions Group* (http://www.futureinteractions.net/) has a good experience with the *Interactive Collaborative Environment* (ICE, Figure 1) [3] and other meeting rooms. The feedback generated by their users triggered an investigation of the interaction design and user experience issues presented by these spaces, with a focus on BYOD integration.

This document is a summary of the my doctoral work within the group, as part of Edinburgh Napier University's *Centre for Interaction Design*. It introduces a quick overview of the background literature and existing work, a summary of the work achieved and its methodology, and a plan for the following steps of this project.

Background

Device Ecologies are defined by Loke & Ling [7] as "collections of devices interacting synergistically with one another, with users, and with the Internet". Later on, the term was re-employed by Tim Coughlan et al. [5], in a study of the focus and transitions in environments including BYOD devices and larger scale screens. Terrenghi et al. prefer the term "multi-person-display ecosystem" [11], although their definition encompasses ecologies going beyond the scale of a few users working together in a meeting room.

Meeting rooms have been the subject of a number of studies in the past years. Early works such as Roomware [10] offered a vision of the future where bespoke furniture would be the norm. This vision is interesting, however it comes from an era of HCI before the widespread existence of mobile devices as we know today. A few years ago, studies have started to include BYOD technologies to the meeting room [4, 12, 2]. Two approaches need to be highlighted. The one used by the *Future Interactions Group* when designing the ICE was to leave access to a standard Windows environment with standard productivity applications. Another approach is one of a bespoke cross-device user interface. This approach is the one used more notably by ReticularSpaces [2]. A side-effect of this approach is to remove access to industry-standard productivity software and imposing a process radically different from the ones people can be used to. More recently, additional research took place in the domain of cross-device interaction, offering novel ideas using different techniques such as video-capture [8] or a UI distribution engine [6].

The literature presents a range of theoretical frameworks, based on empirical and systematic studies. Yuill & Rogers [13] wrote a paper studying the mechanisms of collaboration on multi-user interfaces, more precisely in the domain of Natural User Interfaces or Tangibles. Benyon & Mival [3] provide a more theoretical and pragmatic framework, TACIT, applied to technologically-enhanced spaces. Bardram [1], with Activity-Based Computing (ABC), looks at the longitudinal support of activities in Ubicomp by offering an additional activity-centric layer above the traditional applications. The latter offers an interesting approach for the analysis of longitudinal activities that inspired in part the *meeting journey*. However, in terms of user-interaction, it does not permit the use of standard applications, in favour of an activity-centric user interface.

Issues Investigated

This project aims to produce a set of practical design principles for collaborative device ecologies. Previous case studies of device ecologies and smart meeting rooms have had different design rationale. The aim of this project is to inform design decisions surrounding the interconnection of various devices, in the context of a device ecologies and collaborative work. It has the following three main research objectives:

- Map out the variety of devices, configurations, and scenarios relevant to the use of collaborative device ecologies, in order to get an understanding of the different phases and generic activities involved in a meeting - or a longitudinal set of meetings. We called this *The Meeting Journey*.
- To draft design guidelines for the support of the Meeting Journey.
- To evaluate existing solutions against the guidelines, and offer alternatives.

First Study: The Meeting Journey

Following a short, exploratory ethnographic study of different meetings, the first main phase of work was a set of

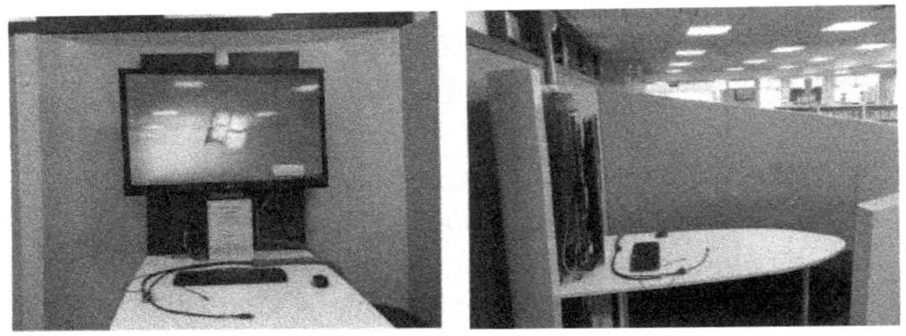

Figure 2: Self service study pods, where students were interviewed. The large screen can be used with a PC or accommodate own devices via a set of cables.

semi-structured interviews of groups of students and senior academic members of staff at Edinburgh Napier University. The undergraduate students were working as groups in self-service study pods (Figure 2), which are small spaces equipped with a large screen and enabling multi-device collaboration. They were approached spontaneously and although some groups were not willing to spare time for the interview, the responses were generally positive.The members of staff were chosen among regular users of the ICE meeting room, working on different projects and scenarios.

The interviews lasted 10 to 15 minutes and the interview protocol was divided into two parts: the first part was informed by ABC [1] and included questions about the activities, scheduling, participants, and assets. The second part was inspired by TACIT [3] and asked questions about participants' territorial issues, awareness of others' work, among other things. The details of the interviews are shown in Table 1 and Table 2.

The interviews were coded with a methodology inspired by Grounded Theory (GT) [9]. The Body of data led to the creation of 27 themes, which can be split into 3 broader themes:

Subject	Size of Group	Project Type
Computing	3	Longitudinal Project
Creative Industries	4	Presentation
Life Sciences	3	Presentation
Engineering	4 (2 Present)	Presentation
Engineering	3	Longitudinal Project

Table 1: Details of the student interviews.

Position	Subject	Project
Professor	English	Teleconference
Associate Professor	Computing	Business Meeting
Business Consultant	Computing	Business Meeting
Lecturer	Computing	Business Meeting

Table 2: Details of the staff interviews.

- Activities: the activities undertaken whilst the meeting is taking place. (9 sources, 103 references)
- Scheduling: the activities undertaken whilst the meeting is being organised. (9 sources, 37 references)
- Tools: tools supporting the Activities taking place in the previous themes. (9 sources, 82 references)

From the previous data, it is possible to establish a meeting journey. Its representation in the form of a mind-map (Figure 3) is based on the broader and narrower themes uncovered by the GT-based analysis described previously. The hierarchy of branches is the following:

- Main level: the broad themes, matching different high-level steps of the journey.
- Secondary level: the generic activities undertaken in each step.
- Third level: the tools and technologies involved (e.g. wifi, BYOD, cloud drives etc).

The meeting journey will be used as a basis to inform the following study, involving focus group probes on more specific user-interface ideas that can be used to facilitate the different steps of the journey.

Focus Groups and Draft Design Principles

A couple of hour-long sessions with targeted focus groups helped generate draft design principles. The groups consisted of Master students in HCI. The sessions were open discussions around screenshots of different functionalities matching the generic activities of the mapping journey: locating content, locating other devices, transferring files etc. The sessions were transcribed and the data was coded three times using a methodology similar to the one used for the interviews. Each pass narrowing down the number of categories. until each category helped inform a design principle.

The following points are examples of draft design principles (hypotheses) applicable to the design of systems supporting mixed ecologies arising from the focus group sessions:

- The ecology should enable a session making the configuration easier, restricting access to the network, assets, applications and devices accordingly.
- The UI should be designed at an appropriate abstraction level.
- If there is supporting software, it needs to be deployable to most major platforms. Alternatively, it should offer a web entry point.
- The system should provide for user accountability, providing a history of cross-device exchanges, as well as the possibility to rollback accidental interactions.

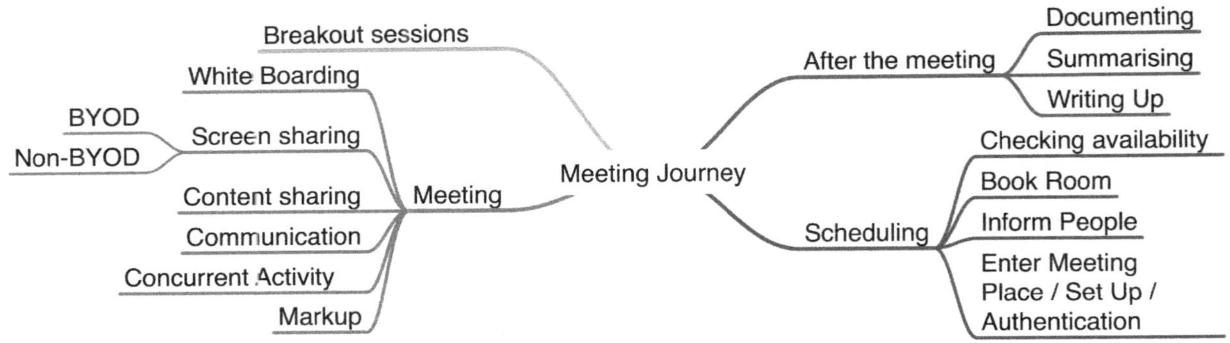

Figure 3: The Meeting Journey, rendered as a mind-map. Branches represent different steps and generic activities of the journey. Sub-branches, representing the tools used to perform the activities, are not reproduced on this figure.

- Users need to be aware of the usefulness, the possibilities, and the robustness of the system.

Upcoming Work and Expected Contribution

Follow-Up work will include the evaluation and validation of the design principles. The current phase consists in evaluations of existing commercial solutions, including a gap analysis of their shortcomings (currently). The final phase of the project will be the design, prototyping and evaluation of alternative solutions. This will take the form of a *hybrid* software assistant where cross-device interactions identified from the journey (e.g. screen-sharing, content sharing) will be led by a task-oriented user interface, whilst an access to standard applications will be retained. Several user-interface metaphors will be tested (menus, visual, touch, gestural).

Research in HCI already covers some issues related to collaboration in device ecologies in general [3, 5, 13]. The expected contribution of this project is twofold: at first, it will consist in a deeper understanding of activities and a formalisation of the meeting journey, in the context of collaborative activities with multiple devices; then, it will offer of a set of informed and tested design guidelines that cover challenges more specific to the integration of BYOD in technology enhanced-spaces, e.g. their integration, their configuration, and the interface challenges revolving around the generic activities identified in the meeting journey.

Acknowledgements

I would like to thank my two supervisors, Prof. David Benyon and Dr. Oli Mival, for their support, as well as Edinburgh Napier University's *Institute for Informatics and Digital Innovation*, for funding my PhD project since 2013. Many thanks to the people who took part in the studies so far.

REFERENCES

1. Jakob Bardram. 2005. Activity-based computing: support for mobility and collaboration in ubiquitous computing. *Personal and Ubiquitous Computing* 9, 5 (Sept. 2005).
2. Jakob Bardram, Sofiane Gueddana, Steven Houben, and Søren Nielsen. 2012. ReticularSpaces: activity-based computing support for physically distributed and collaborative smart spaces. *CHI '12: Proceedings of the SIGCHI Conference on Human Factors in Computing Systems* (May 2012), 2845.
3. D Benyon and O Mival. 2015. Blended Spaces for Collaboration. *Computer Supported Cooperative Work (CSCW)* (2015).
4. Andrew Bragdon, Rob DeLine, Ken Hinckley, and Meredith Ringel Morris. 2011. Code space: touch + air gesture hybrid interactions for supporting developer meetings. *ITS '11: Proceedings of the ACM International Conference on Interactive Tabletops and Surfaces* (Nov. 2011), 212.
5. Tim Coughlan, Trevor D Collins, Anne Adams, Yvonne Rogers, Pablo A Haya, and EstefaníA MartíN. 2012. The conceptual framing, design and evaluation of device ecologies for collaborative activities. *International Journal of Human-Computer Studies* 70, 10 (Oct. 2012).
6. Luca Frosini and Fabio Paternò. 2014. User interface distribution in multi-device and multi-user environments with dynamically migrating engines. *EICS* (2014), 55–64.
7. S W Loke and S Ling. 2004. Analyzing Observable Behaviours of Device Ecology Workflows. *ICEIS (4)* (2004).
8. Roman Rädle, Hans-Christian Jetter, Nicolai Marquardt, Harald Reiterer, and Yvonne Rogers. 2014. HuddleLamp: Spatially-Aware Mobile Displays for Ad-hoc Around-the-Table Collaboration. *ITS* (2014), 45–54.
9. A Strauss and J Corbin. 1998. *Basics of Qualitative Research: Techniques and Procedures for Developing Grounded Theory*. Sage Publications, Thousand Oaks, CA.
10. Norbert A Streitz, Jörg Geißler, and Torsten Holmer. 1998. Roomware for Cooperative Buildings: Integrated Design of Architectural Spaces and Information Spaces. *CoBuild* (1998), 4–21.
11. Lucia Terrenghi, Aaron J Quigley, and Alan J Dix. 2009. A taxonomy for and analysis of multi-person-display ecosystems. *Personal and Ubiquitous Computing* 13, 8 (2009), 583–598.
12. Daniel Wigdor, Hao Jiang, Clifton Forlines, Michelle Borkin, and Chia Shen. 2009. WeSpace: the design development and deployment of a walk-up and share multi-surface visual collaboration system. *CHI* (2009), 1237–1246.
13. Nicola Yuill and Yvonne Rogers. 2012. Mechanisms for collaboration. *ACM Transactions on Computer-Human Interaction* 19, 1 (March 2012), 1–25.

Supporting Interactive Graph Analysis Using Adjustable Magic Lenses

Ulrike Kister
Interactive Media Lab
Technische Universität Dresden
Dresden, Germany
ukister@acm.org

Figure 1: Magic lenses can be used to explore and edit graphs. Their adjustment with natural user interfaces is part of this work.

ITS 2015, November 15–18, 2015, Funchal/Madeira, Portugal.
ACM 978-1-4503-3899-8/15/11.
http://dx.doi.org/10.1145/2817721.2820989

Abstract
Magic lenses are important tools for visualization and can be used to explore and edit graphs. Here, large displays can be beneficial for both their visualization space and possibility for multi-user analysis. With this work, we contribute the enhancement of graph lens functionality by allowing the user to switch lens functions, adjust function parameters, and combine lenses. Further, we investigate the application of various interaction modalities for magic lenses, such as multi-touch, tangibles, and body-centric interaction, to support interactive graph exploration and manipulation.

Author Keywords
Magic lenses; information visualization; multi-touch; embodied interaction; graphs; territoriality.

ACM Classification Keywords
H.5.2. [Information Interfaces and Presentation (e.g. HCI)]: User Interfaces

Introduction
Graph data is essential in various domains, e.g., biology, computer science, or communication technology. There it is important to explore and edit graph data, their nodes, edges and individual attributes. Magic lenses are user interface tools that apply a function to data in a region of interest changing the view [2]. They have been used for diverse

tasks and data types in visualization [17] and can also be applied to graph representations (e.g., [16]). Most of these implementations have been designed for the desktop environment. However, novel large display environments provide tremendous benefits. The display space alone allows for more visualization space, so that larger sets of nodes or alternative representation of the data can be presented at once. Furthermore, these setups allow multiple users to explore and manipulate graphs collaboratively or in-parallel. In these scenarios, natural user interfaces are required as they support direct interaction while moving in front of the display. Here, both interaction *on* and *in front of* the display can be used to manipulate the visualization.

In my thesis, I investigate interactive exploration and manipulation of graphs and the use of magic lenses for this purpose (Figure 1). Within this topic, I plan to address various interaction modalities, e.g., multi-touch, tangibles, body-centric interaction, mobile device gestures, and gaze. I specifically focus on the individual properties, functions and function parameters of magic lenses and how they can be fluently adjusted by the user with appropriate interaction modalities and gestures.

The following section presents a selection of existing research and background on magic lenses. Afterwards, our prior work and the on-going research for this thesis are described. Finally, the future research plan and next steps are presented.

Background and Existing Research

This section aims at giving a short summary of the basic principles and properties of magic lenses and existing interaction approaches. A thorough overview is given in our state-of-the-art report [17] of which the following can only address few selected points.

For user interfaces, magic lenses were first defined by Bier et al. [2] and change the view within a region of interest. Their properties position, size and shape, and orientation make up their main geometry [17]. The lens' shape is fixed or changes dynamically. Fixed shape are the most commonly used and are often elliptical [11, 16]. Dynamic shapes are either defined by the content [12] or by the user, e.g., by sketching the region of interest in advance [3].

The most important aspect of the lens is its function. There have been more than 40 lens functions presented in literature for various tasks and data types [17], also for graph data (e.g., [13, 16]). However, they are presented as lenses with a single function. An exception is the Composite Lens [16] where a fixed combination of three functions is presented as a new lens. Additionally, to adjust the individual lens function (if at all possible) additional GUI dialogs are used. In the simple case of magnification the zoom factor is such a parameter to adjust. For more advanced lens functions, parameters such as degree of adjacency for Bring Neighbors Lenses [16] or filter parameters may need to be set. These parameters can be of various type (continuous, discrete, multiple-selections) and their adjustment can have an essential influence on the resulting outcome of the lens.

There has been research using magic lenses on interactive surfaces. As a first touch-enabled graph lens, the Push-Lens [13] declutters the region of interest by pushing edges from the lens. Butscher et al. [5] use magnification lenses for collaborative image exploration. In a demo, Lander et al. [10] present a map exploration with magnification lenses. However, while all these lenses can be dragged (and often resized) to adjust their selected region of interest, they cannot be adjusted further in selecting other appropriate lens function(s) or even setting individual parameters of the function.

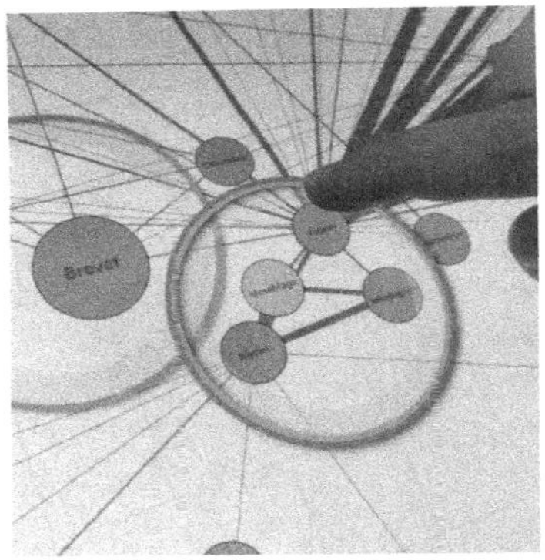

Figure 2: Multi-touch enabled magic lenses with various lens functions for graph exploration [8].

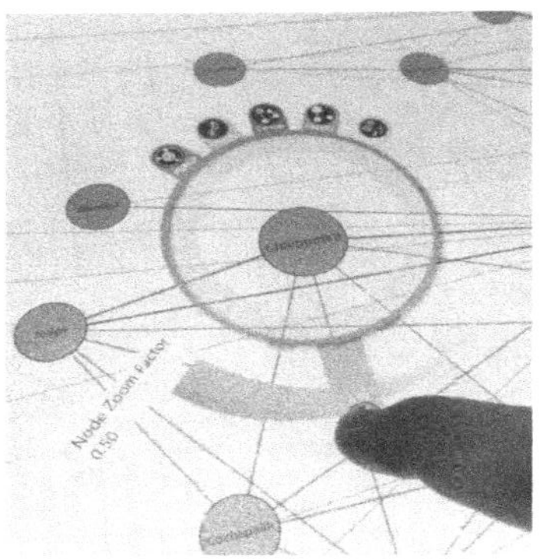

Figure 3: Parametrizing and adjusting multi-touch lenses in place [8].

Making magic lenses graspable, Kim and Elmqvist [7] use thin transparencies on tabletops and this way allow stacking of lenses. Even more so, Spindler et al. [15] use spatial interaction with magic lenses for information visualization. Among other applications, they use the distance to a tabletop surface to expand hierarchical nodes in a graph. They present an overview of a possible interaction vocabulary with tangible magic lenses above tabletops, which is likely to be adaptable to vertical displays. In front of a vertical display, Lehmann et al. [11] use head tracking to visualize a lens at the user's view point. However, again this lens is fixed in its shape and function and cannot be adjusted further by the user.

Goals and Expected Contributions

The main goal of this work will be to improve interaction with magic lenses using graph exploration and editing as the main application case. However, the developed concepts will also be generalized and made usable for other data exploration and editing tasks. In enhancing magic lenses, we aim at the following research goals:

(G1) Developing the magic lens as a tool with more than one lens function, that can be interchanged, parametrized and adjusted by the user.

(G2) Finding and combining appropriate interaction modalities to adjust the lens (in various degrees of granularity) within the user's workflow on and in front of large, interactive vertical displays.

(G3) Extending the magic lens from a view onto the data to a personal territory with individual tools supporting collaborative work.

Completed and On-going Work

Our approach to address this research started with an analysis of magic lenses, existing lens functions and especially the various interaction modalities that have been applied to implement interactive magic lenses in existing works [17]. We identified open research questions and found that especially the combination and parametrization of lenses has been neglected in research so far. As a consequence, we investigate various modalities, their appropriateness for magic lenses, and the possibilities to adjust and adapt the lens, its function(s), and parameters.

Investigating Function Parameter Adjustment using Multi-touch
To address our goals G1 and G2, we designed touch-enabled magic lenses that differ from previous work in that i) they allow flexible switches of lens functions within one lens, ii) lenses can be combined to include multiple lens functions, and iii) they allow explicit adjustment of the lens function parameters [8].

The lenses can be positioned and resized using multi-touch gestures (Figure 2), similar to previous work. However, we designed various novel ways of manipulating lens function and parameters. For externalizing the various possible graph lens functions that can be triggered within the lens, we have menus at the top along the border. Tapping or sliding these menu icons switches the lens function. Further, for each graph lens function, we identified its parameters. These can be adjusted in-place at the lower border of the lens (Figure 3). We implemented discrete and continuous widgets to adjust these parameters in place along the border. In the design process, we enforced use of spatial memory as menu items are always placed in the same location, and relative adjustment of values, as the slider adapts its position to the current value. For expert users, we also developed continuous gestures that allow fluent adjustment of both lens function and one primary parameter without lifting the fingers [8]. Further, we allow flexible combination of multiple lenses as dragging the lenses on top of each other

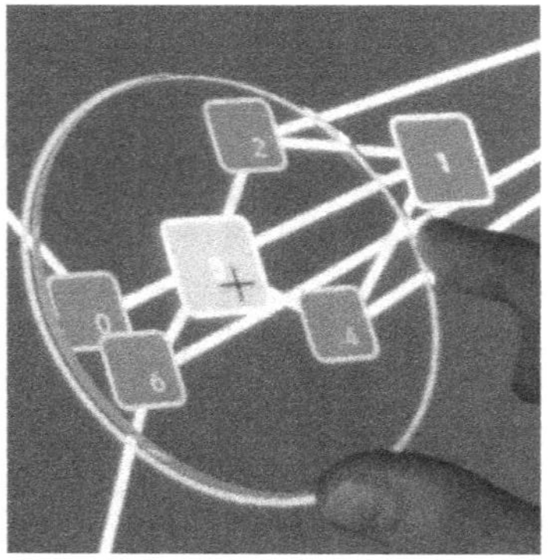

Figure 4: Transparent tangibles support use as magic lenses [4, 6].

Figure 5: Coupling the lens' position with the user's body can expand the lens' capabilities to a personal territory and embodied tool [9].

unites them to form one lens with multiple functions. We conducted a small pilot study to confirm usability. However, further work is required to understand long-term use of the tool by domain experts.

Addressing the Benefits of Graspable Magic Lenses
To improve use of multiple lenses by a single user, we examined the possibilities of making lenses tangible and thereby easier to grasp than touch-enabled virtual lenses. As by definition the lens' content is the main focus of the user, we looked at *transparent* tangibles as possible magic lenses [6] addressing our goal G2 (Figure 4). To first understand the properties of transparent tangibles, we reviewed the related work and defined a design space focusing on various properties, such as form factors, materials, role and function, and visualization space [4]. We identified potential benefits, e.g., precise positioning, that can be relevant for the application as magic lenses and investigated various application cases for transparent tangibles.

Using an interaction vocabulary similar to Spindler et al. [15], tangible lenses can be translated, rotated, flipped and interacted upon, as well as stacked. For transparent tangibles, we found that depending on tracking technology touch on the lens is possible. This is essential for magic lenses for graph exploration and editing as the data not the lens should be explored. In contrast to thin transparencies [7], thicker plates are better graspable. However, stacking of these lenses for combination is quite limited (in our setup: three tangibles) and requires additional tracking capabilities to be improved to still allow touch through the stack.

Thus far, we investigated magic lens functions, their combination and adjustment. However, we plan to further enhance the lens to be more than a tool for visualization but a collection of personal appliances and an all around analysis and editing tool.

Transforming Magic Lenses to Embodied, Personal Territories
The focus of our current work is the embodiment of magic lenses on large display walls, addressing goals G2 and G3. In our *BodyLens* concept [9], the user's body is tracked and is applied as input for lens adjustment. The lens' position is coupled to the user's movement. Thereby, the lens is always placed in front of the user to ensure that its region of interest coincides with where the user is working. Thereby the lens becomes more than a tool, but a personal work territory. In a multi-user scenario, the lens visualizes the user's position and other user's are made aware of which nodes and edges are currently handled by the user (Figure 5). Further, we apply the principles of proxemic interactions [1] and use dimensions such as position, distance, and orientation to adjust lens parameters.

As the user's body is tracked using the Kinect One, this input can also be used to influence the shape of the lens. Different stages of mapping the user's body form to the lens shape are possible. While presenting a human-shadow shape [14] makes the personalization of the lens obvious, this does not seem convenient for graph exploration and manipulation. Furthermore, we found that shapes that constantly react to the user's movement, e.g., when being coupled with hand positions, will take focus away from the data to be explored. We tested various stages of embodiment for the lens shapes and found the reduction of movement by not mapping very active extremities convenient. We hypothesize that a bullet shape (see Figure 6) shadowing the user but being convex and leaving a large center for observation and manipulation of the data, is most suitable. However, this has still to be confirmed in a user study.

Looking at the proxemic dimensions, the lens can further be influenced by the user's distance to the display. This distance can be used for lens properties, such as shape

Figure 6: When the user's body is tracked, dynamic, user-dependent lens shapes and contents are possible [9].

Figure 7: In the future, we want to develop mobile magic lenses that allow even more personalized views.

or size, e.g., the lens gets larger as the user steps toward the display as he/she occludes and occupies the data to work on. Further, the distance can be used to change a lens function parameter, similar to the sliders presented for multi-touch, a user can continuously change a value. For magnification this means the content is zoomed more (or less) when the user steps toward the content. An interesting aspect in this context is the interaction granularity when changing values. Depending on the context the user might want to casually stroll changing values in coarse grained steps to explore the data set. In other situations, precision might be key and transitions between both are necessary. These differences have yet to be investigated and the appropriate interaction modalities and gestures selected.

Future Research Plans

As a next step, we will design studies to further investigate the individual adjustment of parameters and specifically the collaborative aspects of using embodied magic lenses with the presented interaction modalities.

Moreover, we want to address the possible personal extension of magic lenses and use the benefits of graspable magic lenses as previously discussed for transparent tangibles. However, with the increase of personal mobile devices, we plan to enhance previous work (e.g., [15]) in making magic lenses mobile and using device interaction to parametrize and switch lens functions. Figure 7 shows a first setup with a lens on a mobile phone which is tracked using Optitrack IR-cameras. For this scenario, we want to combine proxemic principles with device sensor data to adjust the lens parameters and further develop our concept of personalizing magic lenses by using the properties and preferences saved on the user's personal mobile or tablet.

Additionally, further modalities should be considered for magic lenses. We could also use eye tracking to determine where the user is working and what he/she is interested to place the lens. Even more important, we plan to investigate the combination of these various interaction modalities using their individual benefits to form a coherent data exploration and manipulation setup for graphs on interactive display walls.

Conclusion

Magic lenses are an important tool in visualization. We investigate interactive graph exploration and editing and focus on magic lenses as a tool to support graph analysis on interactive display walls. A thorough analysis of the state-of-the-art resulted in open problems that we address by investigating various novel features, e.g., combination of lens functions and aspects of personalization, as well as exploring and combining diverse interaction modalities, e.g., multi-touch, tangible and body-centric interaction.

Acknowledgements

I would like to thank my supervisor Raimund Dachselt for his continuous support. Further, I thank the members of the IMLD for all their feedback and discussions during this work, especially my co-authors. The project in which this work is created is funded by the DFG (DA 1319/3-1).

REFERENCES

1. T. Ballendat, N. Marquardt, and S. Greenberg. 2010. Proxemic Interaction: Designing for a Proximity and Orientation-aware Environment. In *Proc. ITS '10*. ACM, 121–130. DOI: http://dx.doi.org/10.1145/1936652.1936676

2. E. A. Bier, M. C. Stone, K. Pier, W. Buxton, and T. D. DeRose. 1993. Toolglass and magic lenses: the see-through interface. In *Proc. SIGGRAPH '93*. ACM, 73–80. DOI: http://dx.doi.org/10.1145/166117.166126

3. J. Brosz, M. A. Nacenta, R. Pusch, S. Carpendale, and C. Hurter. 2013. Transmogrification: Causal Manipulation of Visualizations. In *Proc. UIST '13*. ACM, 97–106. DOI: http://dx.doi.org/10.1145/2501988.2502046

4. W. Büschel, U. Kister, M. Frisch, and R. Dachselt. 2014. T4 - Transparent and Translucent Tangibles on Tabletops. In *Proc. AVI '14*. ACM, 81–88. DOI: http://dx.doi.org/10.1145/2598153.2598179

5. S. Butscher, K. Hornbæk, and H. Reiterer. 2014. SpaceFold and PhysicLenses: Simultaneous Multifocus Navigation on Touch Surfaces. In *Proc. AVI '14*. ACM, 209–216. DOI: http://dx.doi.org/10.1145/2598153.2598177

6. M. Frisch, U. Kister, W. Büschel, R. Langner, and R. Dachselt. 2013. Translucent Tangibles on Tabletops: Exploring the Design Space. In *CHI 2013 Workshop on Blended Interaction*.

7. K. Kim and N. Elmqvist. 2012. Embodied Lenses for Collaborative Visual Queries on Tabletop Displays. *Information Visualization* 11, 4 (Oct. 2012), 319–338. DOI: http://dx.doi.org/10.1177/1473871612441874

8. U. Kister, P. Reipschläger, and R. Dachselt. 2014. Multi-Touch Manipulation of Magic Lenses for Information Visualization. In *Proc. ITS '14*. ACM, 431–434. DOI: http://dx.doi.org/10.1145/2669485.2669528

9. U. Kister, P. Reipschläger, F. Matulic, and R. Dachselt. 2015. BodyLenses - Embodied Magic Lenses and Personal Territories for Wall Displays. In *Proc. ITS '15*. ACM, 10. DOI: http://dx.doi.org/10.1145/2817721.2817726

10. C. Lander and S. Gehring. 2014. ClothLens Demo: Simultaneous Multi-User Interaction with Shared Content on a Tabletop. In *Proc. ITS '14*. ACM, New York, NY, USA, 415–418. DOI: http://dx.doi.org/10.1145/2669485.2669524

11. A. Lehmann, H. Schumann, O. Staadt, and C. Tominski. 2011. Physical Navigation to Support Graph Exploration on a Large High-Resolution Display. In *Advances in Visual Computing*. Lecture Notes in Computer Science, Vol. 6938. Springer Berlin Heidelberg, 496–507. DOI: http://dx.doi.org/10.1007/978-3-642-24028-7_46

12. C. Pindat, E. Pietriga, O. Chapuis, and C. Puech. 2012. JellyLens: content-aware adaptive lenses. In *Proc. UIST '12*. ACM, 261–270. DOI: http://dx.doi.org/10.1145/2380116.2380150

13. S. Schmidt, M. A. Nacenta, R. Dachselt, and S. Carpendale. 2010. A Set of Multi-touch Graph Interaction Techniques. In *Proc. ITS '10*. ACM, 113–116. DOI: http://dx.doi.org/10.1145/1936652.1936673

14. G. Shoemaker, T. Tsukitani, Y. Kitamura, and K. S. Booth. 2010. Body-centric Interaction Techniques for Very Large Wall Displays. In *Proc. NordiCHI '10*. ACM, 463–472. DOI: http://dx.doi.org/10.1145/1868914.1868967

15. M. Spindler, C. Tominski, H. Schumann, and R. Dachselt. 2010. Tangible Views for Information Visualization. In *Proc. ITS '10*. ACM, 157–166. DOI: http://dx.doi.org/10.1145/1936652.1936684

16. C. Tominski, J. Abello, F. van Ham, and H. Schumann. 2006. Fisheye Tree Views and Lenses for Graph Visualization. In *Proc. IV '06*. IEEE Computer Society, 17–24. DOI: http://dx.doi.org/10.1109/IV.2006.54

17. C. Tominski, S. Gladisch, U. Kister, R. Dachselt, and H. Schumann. 2014. A Survey on Interactive Lenses in Visualization. In *EuroVis - STARs*. The Eurographics Association. DOI: http://dx.doi.org/10.2312/eurovisstar.20141172

Architecting Collaborative Learning Places

Edward Tse
SMART Technologies
3636 Research Road NW
Calgary, AB, Canada T2L1Y1
edwardtse@smarttech.com

Ahmed Kharrufa
Newcastle University
Culture Lab
Newcastle, UK NE1 7RU
ahmed.kharrufa@ncl.ac.uk

Emma Mercier
University of Illinois at Urbana-Champaign
1310 S. 6th St. Champaign,
Illinois 61820
mercier@illinois.edu

Cresencia Fong
University of Toronto &
SMART Technologies
3636 Research Road NW
Calgary, AB, Canada T2L1Y1
cresenciafong@smarttech.com

ITS '15, November 15-18, 2015, Funchal, Portugal
ACM 978-1-4503-3899-8/15/11.
http://dx.doi.org/10.1145/2817721.2835065

Abstract
Over the years we have seen the proliferation of mobile internet connected devices. This growth is challenging the traditional notions of education being bound to a single time and place. At the same time teachers are asked to develop 21st century competencies such as creativity, collaboration, and technological literacy. The variety of technologies in today's Collaborative Learning Places present new opportunities for learning and new challenges in device orchestration. This is driving the need for design that considers the pedagogical, practical, and technical aspects of Architecting Collaborative Learning Places.

This workshop aims to connect the expertise of the ITS community with the domains of educational pedagogy and practice. The goal is to identify and explore challenges in Architecting Collaborative Learning Places. We aim to explore topics such as skills for a knowledge society, equity of participation, orchestration, collaboration, and practical challenges.

Author Keywords
Architecting, Places, Education, Practice, Pedagogy, Collaboration, Orchestration

ACM Classification Keywords
H.5.m. Information interfaces and presentation (e.g., HCI): Miscellaneous.

Introduction

Research indicates that engaging in collaborative activities leads to better learning, increased transfer and increased persistence in Science Technology English and Mathematics (STEM) fields [1], however, we rarely see this form of pedagogy being used in classrooms [2]. Despite advances in technology that provides new opportunities for students to benefit from this type of learning, a lack of integration in Collaborative Learning Places, and limited attention to the design of orchestration tools and the implementation of learning tools in Collaborative Learning Places hinders their adoption.

Knowledge is being democratized through the proliferation of internet connected devices. Strategy Analytics reported that in 2014 there were 1.4 internet connected devices per person in the world, and they predict that there will be 4.3 devices/person in 2020 [4]. This trend is particularly strong among young children, with 38% of children 0-8 years of age in the US using smartphones and tablets in 2011 .Only 2 years later, that number had risen to 72% [17]. As access to information and knowledge is democratized, pedagogical shifts become necessary – bringing about new practices through digital content, MOOCs, and collaborative inquiry. Coupled with new developments in digital fabrication, wearables, and ever more powerful mobile devices; educational decision makers face ever growing possibilities for their Collaborative Learning Places.

When considering architecture, it is important to understand not only the dimensions and infrastructure of a location but also the behavioural norms and cultural expectations. For this reason, we were connected with Harrison and Dourish's notion of places [7] as a venue for action. In this case the action that we are interested in exploring is collaborative learning. Classrooms and museums have different social norms with a similar objective of learning using different mediums.

Collaborative Learning Places encompass a broad range of expertise including environmental design, challenges of practice, shifting pedagogical needs, mobile proliferation and new demands for equity. We cover a few key themes below:

21st Century Skills: Schleicher from OECD argued that we need 21st century skills because curriculum that is "easy to teach and easy to test are also easiest to digitize, automate, and outsource." [15] He recognized that 21st century skills such as critical thinking, collaboration, and creativity were difficult to teach but argued that they are the key to competitive and economic success. The international student assessment, PISA, has begun to release questions related to 21st century skills in the form of computer simulation-based questions [12].

Equity of Participation: Equity of participation explores the democratization of knowledge [14], where learners are empowered to innovate on ideas as legitimate contributors to a knowledge community. As such, learners need to be provided with a means to publicly share their privately-held ideas, and a means by which to innovate on their peers' publicly-shared ideas – thereby collectively improving upon the community's shared knowledge base. To support learners as they traverse back-and-forth between public and private knowledge spaces, Designers need to consider not only the means by which learners contribute their ideas, but also the local Internet infrastructure, setup time, preparation time, and time for monitoring. Additionally, learners need a means to engage both inside and outside of class time.

Orchestration: A Collaborative Learning Place is a multi-layered environment and often has multiple constrains. For example, orchestration is a term used to describe how a teacher manages a classroom's multi-layered activities in real-time, which can be pedagogically driven and technologically supported [5]. For example, in a Collaborative Learning Place with many displays to pay attention to, it can be difficult to capture the attention of everyone for instruction. Interactive surfaces provide new opportunities for controlling mobile devices to gain learner attention, and for interactive visualizations that the instructor may use to monitor the learning; enabling the instructor to identify struggling learners so that s/he can provide timely support.

Scaffolding Collaborative Learning: The increased user mobility that mobile devices offer students in Learning Places offers new possibilities in the spatial distribution of classroom activities. For example, students can walk around different stations in a classroom or museum and engage with exhibits in small groups on their mobile devices. Collaborative Learning Architects can consider ways to promote small group discussion around an artefact or space in the room.

The types of tech-supported social interactions (e.g., whole class, small group, individual) offered by large displays and handheld devices supports learners as they traverse back-and-forth between public and private knowledge spaces. Collaboration needs to go beyond the contents and activities to also consider how the different devices affect the workspaces in the Collaborative Learning Place [6]. For example, a classroom of iPads could leverage spatial mobility for capturing images of plant life outdoors for discussion mediated by a teacher over a large display.

Architecting Learning Places: The Third Teacher book suggests that designers consider learner's sensitivity to colour, light and texture in Collaborative Learning Places [16]. Also, research from UK schools suggests that the quality of the built environment has an influence on students' scores on standardized tests [3]. In addition, research on the placement of technology in Collaborative Learning Places indicates that it influences the way students interact with each other, and their learning outcomes [9]. Collaborative Learning Places could benefit from the learnings of those from the ITS community working in formal (e.g., classroom) and informal (e.g., museums) learning environments. Researchers are also actively designing interactive surfaces to support learning in Collaborative Learning Places [8, 11]. This new design area offers opportunities to immerse and engage learners in ways that are not possible with any single technology or device.

Practice: If we desire to have an impact on Collaborative Learning Places we need to align with existing instruction and learning practices. By co-designing [15] with instructors and learners we ensure that our solutions fit within the available technology infrastructure, and learning objectives of the instructor and the learners.

To ensure broad impact we need to consider the purchase decision makers and their needs, values, and problems. We can look at industry trends such as mobile adoption to understand how our solutions will scale to meet the needs of a broader audience.

We also need to consider technical challenges such as mobile device computing power and limited Internet bandwidth to see how best to coordinate the activities of learners.

References

[1] B. Barron and L. Darling-Hammond, "How can we teach for meaningful learning?," in Powerful Learning: What we know about teaching for understanding, L. Darling-Hammond, Ed. San Francisco, CA: Jossey-Bass, 2008, pp. 11–70.

[2] P. Blatchford, P. Kutnick, E. Baines, and M. Galton, "Toward a social pedagogy of classroom group work," Int. J. Educ. Res., vol. 39, no. 1–2, pp. 153–172, 2003.

[3] P. Barrett, Y. Zhang, J. Moffat, and K. Kobbacy, "A holistic, multi-level analysis identifying the impact of classroom design on pupils' learning," *Build. Environ.*, vol. 59, pp. 678–689, Jan. 2013.

[4] Connected World: The Internet of Things and Connected Devices in 2020. (2014) Strategy Analytics, http://bit.ly/1EVm5AG.

[5] Dillenbourg, P. (2013). "Design for Classroom Orchestration", position paper. In In P. Dillenbourg, M. Nussbaum, Y. Dimitriadis, & J. Roschelle (Eds.), Design for Classroom Orchestration. Computers & Education (1-8). Elsevier.

[6] Fisher, B., Lucas, T., & Galstyan, A. (2013). The role of iPads in constructing collaborative learning spaces. Technology, Knowledge and Learning, 18(3), 165-178.

[7] Harrison, S., & Dourish, P. (1996, November). Re-place-ing space: the roles of place and space in collaborative systems. In Proceedings of the 1996 ACM conference on Computer supported cooperative work (pp. 67-76). ACM.

[8] Higgins, S. E., Mercier, E., Burd, E., & Hatch, A. (2011). Multi-touch tables and the relationship with collaborative classroom pedagogies: A synthetic review. International Journal of Computer-Supported Collaborative Learning, 6(4), 515-538.

[9] E. M. Mercier, S. E. Higgins, and A. Joyce-Gibbons, "The effects of room design on computer-supported collaborative learning in a multi-touch classroom," Interact. Learn. Environ., 2014.

[10] Microsoft Attention Spans (2015) Microsoft Canada, http://bit.ly/1dZdpnn

[11] Moher, T., Uphoff, B., Bhatt, D., López Silva, B., & Malcolm, P. (2008). WallCology: Designing interaction affordances for learner engagement in authentic science inquiry. In Proc. CHI 2008, pp. 163-172. ACM Press.

[12] PISA 2015 Release Field Trial Cognitive Items, (2015) OECD, http://bit.ly/1Edsgnn

[13] Roschelle, J., & Penuel, W. R. (2006). Co-design of Innovations With Teachers: Definition and Dynamics. Proceedings of the 7th international conference on Learning sciences. Bloomington, Indiana.

[14] Scardamalia, M. (2002). Collective cognitive responsibility for the advancement of knowledge. Liberal education in a knowledge society, 97, 67-98.

[15] Schleicher, A. (2015) The case for 21st-century learning. OECD, http://www.oecd.org/edu/Directorate-for-education-and-skills-brochure.pdf

[16] The Third Teacher (2010) Petersen, O. and Mau, B., Abrams Publishing, ISBN 978-0810989986.

[17] Zero to Eight: Children's Media Use in America 2013. (2013) Common Sense Media, http://bit.ly/1rzzmKS.

Collaboration Meets Interactive Surfaces (CMIS): Walls, Tables, Mobiles, and Wearables

Craig Anslow
Department of Computer Science
Middlesex University
London, UK
c.anslow@mdx.ac.uk

Pedro Campos
Madeira Interative Technologies Institute
University of Madeira
Madeira, Portugal
pcampos@uma.pt

Laurent Grisoni
Computer Science Laboratory
University of Lille
Lille, France
laurent.grisoni@univ-lille1.fr

Andrés Lucero
Mads Clausen Institute
University of Southern Denmark
Kolding, Denmark
lucero@acm.org

ITS '15, November 15-18, 2015, Funchal, Portugal
ACM 978-1-4503-3899-8/15/11.
http://dx.doi.org/10.1145/2817721.2835066

Abstract
This workshop proposes to bring together researchers who are interested in improving collaborative experiences through the combination of multiple interaction surfaces with diverse sizes and formats, ranging from large-scale walls, to tables, mobiles, and wearables. The opportunities for innovation exist, but the ITS, CHI, CSCW, and other HCI communities have not yet thoroughly addressed the problem of bringing effective collaboration activities together using multiple interactive surfaces, especially in complex work domains. Of particular interest is the potential synergy that one can obtain by effectively combining different-sized surfaces and sharing information between devices.

Author Keywords
Collaboration, interactive surfaces, large display walls, tabletops, mobile, multi-touch interaction, wearables.

ACM Classification Keywords
H.5.m [Information interfaces and presentation (HCI)]: Miscellaneous.

General Terms
Design; Human Factors

Figure 1: Eery Space: a remote user controls the wall, two users in different physical spaces engage in a collaborative activity (indicated by the same color of their auras) and a fourth user looks at them through a virtual window.

Figure 2: Bancada: multiple users collaboratively exploring geospatial information space with an overview map displayed on a tabletop.

Introduction

Large scale displays and interactive surfaces offer a unique visualization environment favorable to both individual and collaborative design tasks [6, 8]. During the last decade these devices have become both affordable and easier to setup, providing highly interactive environments with high resolution and support for stereoscopic images. Combined with emerging input devices, these provide new ways to interact with content as well as enabling new applications to support collaborative engineering tasks as well as many other activities, which involve communication, coordination, and cooperation [7].

Additionally, new devices have become available to enhance these interactions, including tablets combining several sensors [4], non-intrusive tracking solutions based on depth cameras, wearable devices, and other equipment. Despite this rapid technological advance, however, it still remains an unsolved problem how to bring effective collaboration capabilities to this myriad of heterogeneous interactive surfaces. This workshop aims at bringing together the most advanced techniques, user interfaces, and technological issues that are crucial in fostering co-located collaboration and remote communication between users across different facilities simultaneously [9].

Following the success of the workshop on Collaboration Meets Interactive Surfaces (CMIS) co-located at ITS 2014 and 2013 [1, 3], we propose to host another workshop at ITS 2015 in Madeira, Portugal. In the 2014 edition of the workshop, a total of 21 participants attended and in 2013, 27 participants attended. Participants exchanged experiences regarding collaborative user interface design and evaluation techniques involving interactive surfaces, in both remote and co-located settings. Some previous CMIS workshop papers discussed issues focusing on collaborative design space with proxemics [11] (see Figure 1), geospatial interaction on tabletops [13] (see Figure 2), collaborative medical visualization on tabletops [14] (see Figure 3), multi-user presentation software on large high resolution touch walls [12] (see Figure 4), mid-air gestures to support disabled users on tabletops [5] (see Figure 5), and software visualization on tabletops [2] (see Figure 6).

Relevance to ITS Community

The vast screen real estate, which is provided in large-scale interaction environments presents novel ways to visualize and interact with data-rich models. In parallel to this technological revolution, interactive surfaces have also become widespread in different sizes and devices, from large-scale walls to small tablets. Indeed, the ITS, CHI, CSCW and MobileHCI communities witnessed, in recent years, an increased usage of large display walls, interactive tabletops, tablet-sized surfaces, mobile phones, and wearables [10].

Topics of Workshop

Topics of the workshop to include (but not limited to):

- Design and evaluation of collaborative environments with interactive surfaces, either remotely or co-located;
- Collaborative applications on interactive surfaces for different domains (e.g. meeting rooms, 3D visualization, mechanical engineering, medical visualizations, emergency response scenarios, criminal intelligence);
- Communication, cooperation and coordination as well as social protocols;
- Interactive surfaces to enhance spatial perception of content and/or support navigation during collaboration activities;

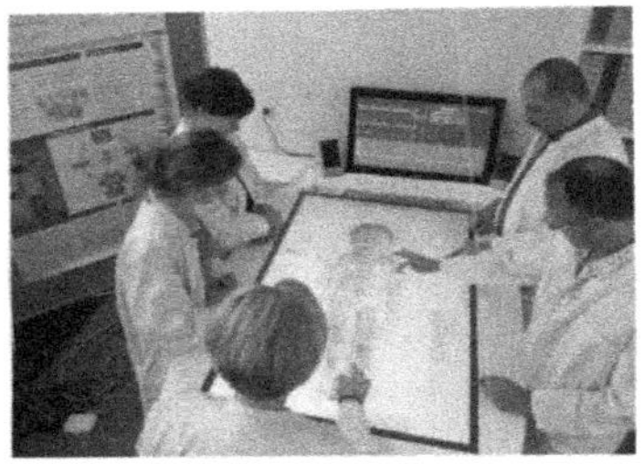

Figure 3: SimMed: multiple students collaborating around a tabletop for medical training.

Figure 4: The Cube: running CubIT a large scale multi-user presentation and collaboration platform.

- Issues when moving from desktop-based collaboration to large-scale walls, tabletops, touch-based mobile devices, and wearables;
- Integration of different devices and surfaces (Walls, Tables, Mobiles, Wearables) for collaboration;
- Physical navigation between different devices;
- Collaboration paradigms and user interface designs that address enhancement of collaborative activities using interactive surfaces and tabletops;
- Collaborative sense making and visual analytics with different interactive surfaces and devices;
- Theories and applications of social science for interactive surfaces and devices.

Organizing Committee

The following people form the organizing committee:

Craig Anslow is a Senior Postdoctoral Research Fellow at Middlesex University, UK. His research interests include multi-surface environments for emergency management and criminal intelligence as well as engineering novel visual analytics applications.

Pedro Campos is an Assistant Professor at the University of Madeira, Portugal. His research interests include interaction design, augmented reality, natural interaction for modelling, and museums and cultural heritage.

Laurent Grisoni Laurent Grisoni is a Professor in computer science at university of Lille (France), also associated to CNRS and INRIA (MINT research group). His research interest deal with tactile and gesture-based interaction, in the fields of virtual reality and HCI. He is also interested in the art-science relation.

Andrés Lucero is an Associate Professor at the University of Southern Denmark in Kolding. His interests lie in the areas of mobile human-computer interaction, co-design, and design research.

Program Committee

The Program Committee (PC) for the workshop will review papers and help promote the workshop in the ITS, CHI, CSCW, MobileHCI, and other HCI communities. The following people have agreed to serve on the PC:

Jason Alexander - Lancaster University, UK
Mirjam Augstein - University of Applied Sciences Upper Austria, Austria
Robert Biddle - Carleton University, Canada
Jacob Biehl - FX PAL, USA
Rachel Blagojevic - Massey University, New Zealand
Raimund Dachselt - TU Dresden, Germany
Andreas Dippon - TU Munich, Germany
Alfredo Ferreira - TU Lisbon, Portugal
Nick Graham - Queens University, Canada
Petra Isenberg - INRIA, France
Judy Kay - University of Sydney, Australia
Kris Luyten - Hasselt University, Belgium
Frank Maurer - University of Calgary, Canada
Alexander Nolte - University of Bochum, Germany
Harald Reiterer - University of Konstanz, Germany
Stacey Scott - University of Waterloo, Canada
Tony Tang - University of Calgary, Canada
Theophanis Tsandilas - INRIA, France

Figure 5: Disabled users performing mid-air gestures via a Leap Motion device to interact with a tabletop.

Figure 6: SourceVis: multiple users collaborating with multiple software visualizations being displayed on a tabletop.

Time	Activity
0900–0930	Welcome and introductions
0930–1030	Invited talk by Joaquim Jorrge (Technical University of Lisbon)
1030–1100	*Morning Break*
1100–1230	Presentation of workshop papers (lightning talks)
1230–1400	*Lunch Break*
1400–1530	Split into groups based on themes: from the workshop and discuss
1530–1600	*Afternoon Break*
1600–1730	Group design activity Closing remarks from OC

Table 1: Workshop Planned Activities

Planned Activities and Format

Table 1 outlines the proposed planned activities of the one-day workshop. In the first session we will have welcome and introductions by all attendees, followed by an invited talk by Joaquim Jorge from the Technical University of Lisbon. After the morning break the second session will have lightning talks of workshop papers from attendees. Lunch will follow to allow attendees to meet and mingle. In the third session attendees will split into groups based on themes related to the goals of the workshop. Once the groups have been formed discussions will happen amongst attendees and the groups will report back about this discussions. The fourth session will involve a group design activity based on the discussions from the previous session. Finally there will be some closing remarks from the organizing committee as well as feedback from attendees.

REFERENCES

1. C. Anslow, P. Campos, and A. Ferreira. 2014. Collaboration Meets Interactive Surfaces (CMIS): Walls, Tables, Tablets, and Phones. In *Proc. of International Conference on Interactive Tabletops and Surfaces (ITS)*. ACM, 495–498.
2. C. Anslow, S. Marshall, J. Noble, and R. Biddle. 2013. SourceVis: Collaborative Software Visualization for Co-located Environments. In *Proc. of Working Conference on Software Visualization (VISSOFT)*. IEEE, 1–10.
3. P. Campos, A. Ferreira, and A. Lucero. 2013. Collaboration Meets Interactive Surfaces (CMIS): Walls, Tables, Tablets, and Phones. In *Proc. of International Conference on Interactive Tabletops and Surfaces (ITS)*. ACM, 481–482.
4. K. Cheng, J. Li, and C. Müller-Tomfelde. 2012. Supporting Interaction and Collaboration on Large Displays Using Tablet Devices. In *Proc. of International Working Conference on Advanced Visual Interfaces (AVI)*. ACM, 774–775.
5. J. Creed, C. Sear and R. Beale. 2013. Using Mid-Air Gestures To Enhance Collaborative Experiences For Disabled Users On Multi-Touch Tables. In *Proc. of Workshop on CMIS at ITS*. ACM.
6. R. Jota, J. Pereira, and J. Jorge. 2009. A Comparative Study of Interaction Metaphors for Large-scale Displays. In *Proc. of Extended Abstracts on Human Factors in Computing Systems (CHI EA)*. ACM, 4135–4140.

7. J. Klimke and J. Döllner. 2010. Combining Synchronous and Asynchronous Collaboration Within 3D City Models. In *Proc. of International Conference on Geographic Information Science (GIScience)*. Springer-Verlag, 115–129.

8. E. Lantz. 2007. A Survey of Large-scale Immersive Displays. In *Proc. of Workshop on Emerging Displays Technologies: Images and Beyond: The Future of Displays and Interacton (EDT)*. ACM, Article 1.

9. A. Lucero, J. Holopainen, and T. Jokela. 2012. MobiComics: Collaborative Use of Mobile Phones and Large Displays for Public Expression. In *Proc. of International Conference on Human-computer Interaction with Mobile Devices and Services (MobileHCI)*. ACM, 383–392.

10. A. Lucero, M. Jones, T. Jokela, and S. Robinson. 2013. Mobile Collocated Interactions: Taking an Offline Break Together. *Interactions* 20, 2 (March 2013), 26–32.

11. D. Mendes, M. Sousa, J. Pereira, A. Ferreira, and J. Jorge. 2014. Enabling Remote Proxemics through Multiple Surfaces. In *Proc. of Workshop on CMIS at ITS*. ACM.

12. M. Rittenbruch, A. Sorensen, J. Donovan, D. Polson, M. Docherty, and J. Jones. 2013. The Cube: A Very Large-scale Interactive Engagement Space. In *Proc. of International Conference on Interactive Tabletops and Surfaces (ITS)*. ACM, 1–10.

13. F. Rodrigues, T. Seyed, F. Maurer, and S. Carpendale. 2014. Bancada: Using Mobile Zoomable Lenses for Geospatial Exploration. In *Proc. of International Conference on Interactive Tabletops and Surfaces (ITS)*. ACM, 409–414.

14. U. von Zadow, R. Martinez-Maldonado, and R. Dachselt. 2014. Tabletop Territoriality and Social Context: Examining Medical Simulation. In *Proc. of Workshop on CMIS at ITS*. ACM.

Cross-Surface: Workshop on Interacting with Multi-Device Ecologies in the Wild

Steven Houben
University College London
UCL Interaction Centre / ICRI Cities
s.houben@ucl.ac.uk

Nicolai Marquardt
University College London
UCL Interaction Centre / ICRI Cities
n.marquardt@ucl.ac.uk

Jo Vermeulen
HCI Centre
University of Birmingham
j.vermeulen@cs.bham.ac.uk

Johannes Schöning
Expertise centre for Digital Media,
Hasselt University - tUL - iMinds
johannes.schoening@uhasselt.be

Clemens Klokmose
Department of Computer Science
Aarhus University
clemens@cs.au.dk

Harald Reiterer
HCI Group,
University of Konstanz
harald.reiterer@uni-konstanz.de

ITS '15, November 15-18, 2015, Funchal, Portugal
ACM 978-1-4503-3899-8/15/11.
http://dx.doi.org/10.1145/2817721.2835067

Abstract

In this workshop, we will review and discuss opportunities, technical challenges and problems with cross-device interactions in interactive multi-surface and multi-device ecologies. We aim to bring together researchers and practitioners currently working on novel techniques for cross-surface interactions, focusing both on technical as well as interaction challenges for introducing these technologies *into the wild*, and highlighting opportunities for further research. The workshop will help to facilitate knowledge exchange on the inherent challenges of building robust and intuitive cross-surface interactions, identify application domains and enabling technologies for cross-surface interactions in the wild, and establish a research community to develop effective strategies for successful design of cross-device interactions.

Keywords

Cross-surface interaction, ubicomp ecologies, multi-surface interactions, multi-device interactions, spatial reconfigurations of displays, spatially distributed interfaces, multi-screen workplaces, wearable devices.

ACM Classification Keywords

H.5.m. Information interfaces and presentation (e.g., HCI): Miscellaneous.

Introduction
People are increasingly interacting with their personal information through different types of devices, ranging from large interactive surfaces, tablets, smartphones to wearable technologies such as smartwatches and head-mounted displays. This *device multiplicity* has led to situations in which users are employing multiple devices at the same time. The choice of which set of devices to use is governed by the affordances, capabilities, and properties of these devices and the context of use. To support this device multiplicity, prior work has introduced a wide range of techniques and infrastructures to facilitate cross-surface[1] interaction. These include sensing of nearby devices [7, 11] device pairing [3, 5, 10, 11], information exchange [9, 11] and configuration of cross-device ecologies [4].

Despite the success of these approaches, many cross-surface interaction techniques and systems require advanced sensing and infrastructure, which are impractical in real-world scenarios outside of the lab. There are still fundamental challenges that prevent the full potential of cross-surface interactions in the wild. Workplace and field studies (e.g., [1,5]) highlight these issues, revealing how users struggle with how devices can communicate, what content can be exchanged, how to opt-out from connecting devices together [2], and how to configure devices to cooperate in one seamless workspace. We need a better understanding of how to move cross-surface and spatial interaction techniques and systems into the wild, in terms of technologies, real-world use cases, and making sense of the available interactions and their impact on human activities.

[1] Also referred to as multi-device, multi-surface or cross-device.

Objectives
The *Cross-Surface* workshop aims to provide a practical, creative and structured forum for designers, practitioners and researchers to discuss the opportunities for and challenges of *in the wild* cross-surface interactions. The objective of the workshop is to *map out a design space* and *describe an interaction vocabulary* for cross-surface interactions outside of lab settings. These include multi-surface techniques and applications, spatially distributed interfaces and displays, multi-screen workspaces and wearable displays and interfaces. The workshop is structured around three topics:

1. **Use cases in the real world**
   What are the use cases and application domains for cross-surface interactions? Which concrete challenges do these pose (e.g., public vs. private settings) and which types of device and spatial configurations do they provide (e.g., opportunistic vs. fixed device ecologies)?
2. **From lab technologies to real-world solutions**
   Which enabling technologies can allow users to interact with complex device ecologies in the wild? How can these technologies be deployed, democratized and shared with a broader audience?
3. **Beyond interaction techniques**
   How do people make sense of cross-surface ecologies? How can we support discoverability and learnability of interactions, inform users of action possibilities and provide feedback about cross-surface connections? How can users configure cross-surface setups that support their activities?

Participants

We aim to bring together 15–20 participants from academia and industry that are working on cross-surface systems and related areas. In addition to an open Call for Participation, the organizers will personally invite researchers to submit their work and participate in the workshop. Participants will be selected by the organizers based on the submitted position papers and their relevance to the scope and goal of the workshop. We aim to gather a multi-disciplinary group of participants consisting of academic researchers, designers and practitioners from industry. Accepted workshop papers will be distributed among participants before the workshop and published on the workshop website.

Workshop Format and Activities

Before the workshop

We will setup a website and distribute a call for position papers in all relevant communities. In addition to being listed on the ITS 2015 website, we will announce the Call for Participation at popular mailing lists and calendars (e.g., ACM, CHI-announcements, Interaction-Design.org, WikiCFP) and social media (e.g., Twitter, Facebook). Workshop flyers will be distributed at related conferences and workshops that take place before ITS 2015. The calls will be posted on the workshop website, along with other details about the workshop. Furthermore, we will directly contact researchers and practitioners who are likely to be interested in the workshop and write to relevant institutions, projects or activities. We will continue our efforts of promoting the workshop and getting in touch with potential participants during the period leading up to the workshop deadline.

At the workshop

We propose a one-day, 8-hour workshop. The workshop will be a combination of brainstorming, discussions and design activities in groups of 4 or 5 people.

1. Preparation before the workshop

To reduce cold start problems, we will ask each participant to read and synthesize an assigned position paper before the workshop into research insights and design patterns, based on Kolko's method [8]. The collection of ideas gathered from this will seed into the brainstorming activities during the workshop.

2. Kick-off madness and keynote

We will kick off the workshop by asking all participants to introduce themselves and their position paper in a 1-minute madness presentation. We will also ask each participant to end with a bold, controversial or forward-looking statement about their work or the state of the field. After the kick-off, Professor Yvonne Rogers will give a keynote on cross-device interaction in the wild.

3. *Design solution*

Participants will select one of three subgroups based on the three workshop objectives (use cases, real-world technologies and making sense of cross-surface interactions). We will facilitate idea generation within each subgroup with a brainstorming exercise to generate ideas from random combinations of seed insights and design patterns from the pre-workshop activity. In follow-up break-out sessions, subgroups will select their top ideas, and discuss and work out these ideas using sketching, storyboarding or paper prototyping techniques. To limit the solution and brainstorm space, we will provide a design brief detailing a specific problem space and potential application domains.

4. Mapping out problem and design space

After lunch, each group will present their ideas, after which we move towards in-depth discussions of specific challenges of designing cross-surface interactions, and identify common themes from the earlier breakout sessions. As a group activity, we intend to use the generated ideas and prototypes to map out the design space of application domains, enabling technologies as well as cross-surface interaction techniques that can be deployed in the wild. For these discussions, we will switch between focused breakout groups and whole group discussions (and also adapt these activities depending on the size of the group).

5. Group reflections

As a final outcome, we will create a large collage/map visualizing the scope, overlap, and relations between different groups to allow for broader reflection and topical conclusions.

Time	*Activity*
09:00	Madness session
09:30	Keynote by Professor Yvonne Rogers
10:00	Brainstorm in 3 subgroups + design brief
10:30	Coffee break
11:00	Continue brainstorm Sketch/storyboard/prototype designs
13:00	Lunch
14:00	Present ideas + map out design space
16:00	Coffee break
16:30	Group reflections
17:30	Close

Table 1. Timeline of the workshop day

After the Workshop

Materials produced during the workshop will be posted on the workshop web site (http://www.cross-surface.io/). We will continue to maintain the site to serve both the participants and the broader community developing around this topic.

Soliciting Submissions

We will solicit position papers of up to 4 pages in the ACM SIGCHI Extended Abstract format that describe original research and outline a person's interest and experience in the topic of the workshop. Selected papers will serve as introductions for discussions and will be made available to the participants on the workshop website. Submissions will be juried by the organizing committee based on originality and relevance.

Publication Venue

The results of the workshop will be communicated to the larger HCI community by submitting an article to a magazine (e.g., *ACM interactions*). In this article, we hope to define future design spaces for cross-surface interactions in Ubicomp ecologies based on the collage of topics discussed and challenges identified in the different breakout groups.

We will also invite all workshop participants to submit an extended article of their submission for a special issue on "*Interaction with Device Ecologies in the Wild*" in the Personal and Ubiquitous Computing journal that will appear mid-2016. This information and call for papers will also be shared on the http://www.cross-surface.io/ website and will be open to other interested researchers in the community.

Organizers and Program Committee

Steven Houben *is a Research Associate at University College London. He works at the Intel Collaborative Research Institute on Sustainable and Connected Cities (ICRI-Cities) and UCL Interaction Centre on projects related to multi-device environments, physical computing and sensor-based systems.*

Jo Vermeulen *is a Research Fellow at the HCI Centre of the University of Birmingham. He is interested in addressing interaction challenges within ubicomp spaces, including providing intelligibility, discoverability, feedback and feedforward for cross-device interactions.*

Clemens Klokmose *is a Post Doc at the Computer Science department at Aarhus University and is associated with the center for Participatory Information Technology. His main interest is human-computer interaction that goes beyond personal computing.*

Nicolai Marquardt *is a Lecturer (Assistant Professor) in Physical Computing at the University College London. At the UCL Interaction Centre he works on projects in the research areas of ubiquitous computing, interactive surfaces, sensor-based systems, prototyping toolkits, and physical user interfaces.*

Johannes Schöning *is Professor of computer science at Hasselt University working at the Expertise centre for Digital Media (EDM). His main research interests lie at the intersection between human-computer interaction (HCI), geographic information science and ubiquitous interface technologies.*

Harald Reiterer *is Professor at the Computer and Information Science Department of the University of Konstanz. His main research interests include different fields of Human-Computer Interaction, like Interaction Design, Usability Engineering, and Information Visualization.*

References

1. Dearman, David, and Jeffery S. Pierce. "It's on my other computer!: computing with multiple devices." *Proc. of CHI'08.* ACM.
2. Greenberg, Saul, Boring, Sebastian, Vermeulen, Jo and Dostal, Jakub. "Dark Patterns in Proxemic Interactions: A Critical Perspective." *Proc. of DIS '14*. ACM.
3. Hinckley, Ken. "Synchronous gestures for multiple persons and computers." *Proc. UIST '03*. ACM.
4. Houben, Steven, Paolo Tell, and Jakob E. Bardram. "ActivitySpace: Managing Device Ecologies in an Activity-Centric Configuration Space." *Proc. ITS '14*. ACM.
5. Houben, Steven, and Nicolai Marquardt. "WatchConnect: A Toolkit for Prototyping Smartwatch-Centric Cross-Device Applications." *Proc. CHI'15.* ACM, 2015.
6. Jokela, Tero, Jarno Ojala, and Thomas Olsson. "A Diary Study on Combining Multiple Information Devices in Everyday Activities and Tasks." *Proc. CHI '15*. ACM, 2015.
7. Kortuem, Gerd, Christian Kray, and Hans Gellersen. "Sensing and visualizing spatial relations of mobile devices." *Proc UIST '05*. ACM.
8. Kolko, Jon. Methods of design synthesis: moving from data to innovation. *Proc. CHI '14*. ACM.
9. Marquardt, Nicolai, Till Ballendat, Sebastian Boring, Saul Greenberg, and Ken Hinckley "Gradual engagement: facilitating information exchange between digital devices as a function of proximity." *Proc. ITS '12*. ACM.
10. Mayrhofer, Rene, and Hans Gellersen. "Shake well before use: Authentication based on accelerometer data." Pervasive computing. Springer Berlin Heidelberg, 2007. pp. 144-161.
11. Rädle, Roman, Hans-Christian Jetter, Nicolai Marquardt, Harald Reiterer, and Yvonne Roger. "HuddleLamp: Spatially-Aware Mobile Displays for Ad-hoc Around-the-Table Collaboration." *Proc. ITS '14*. ACM.
12. Schmidt, Dominik, Julian Seifert, Enrico Rukzio, and Hans Gellersen. "A cross-device interaction style for mobiles and surfaces." *Proc. DIS '12*. ACM.

ITS Workshop DEXIS 2015: Visual Data Exploration on Interactive Surfaces

Petra Isenberg
Inria
Bât 660, Université Paris Sud
91405 Orsay Cedex, France
petra.isenberg@inria.fr

Alark Joshi
University of San Francisco
2130 Fulton Street
San Francisco, CA 94117, USA
apjoshi@usfca.edu

Bongshin Lee
Microsoft Research
One Microsoft Way
Redmond, WA 98052, USA
bongshin@microsoft.com

Tobias Isenberg
Inria
Bât 660, Université Paris Sud
91405 Orsay Cedex, France
tobias.isenberg@inria.fr

ITS 2015, November 15–18, 2015, Funchal/Madeira, Portugal.
ACM 978-1-4503-3899-8/15/11.
http://dx.doi.org/10.1145/2817721.2835068.

Topic of the Workshop

We focus on the use of interactive surfaces for visual data exploration. The workshop topics are situated at the intersection of Interaction and Visualization research, and we ask for contributions from members of one or both communities. Our main goal is to call for the development of more dedicated research on visualization systems for interactive surfaces ranging from small screen smartphones to medium-size tables to large wall-size displays. The workshop is meant to provide a space for visualization and interaction researchers to meet, discuss, advance the state-of-the-art, and refine research agendas.

Author Keywords

Visualization; Data Exploration; Interactive Surfaces.

Relevance to ITS

This workshop is motivated by the fact that visualization systems are, by design, well-suited candidates for deployment on interactive surfaces. In information visualization, scientific visualization, and visual analytics, useful insights primarily emerge from an interactive data manipulation experience. Nevertheless, interaction research to date in these domains has largely focused on mouse-based interaction and the research community still has not paid enough attention to how interactive data exploration can benefit from interactive surfaces [2]. Yet, we assert several apparent benefits of interactive surfaces for visualization systems:

1. As interactive displays become more ubiquitous, data can be accessed and analyzed anywhere and at any time (e. g., on phones and tablets, in meeting rooms, or on public displays);
2. Interactive surfaces offer research opportunities on novel interaction paradigms that can encourage alternative forms of data exploration;
3. Novel visualization designs and interaction experiences promote visualization use even for non-experts;
4. Large interactive surfaces offer the possibility of depicting and interacting with much larger visualization spaces than previously possible; and
5. As data analysis is increasingly turning into a collaborative process, interactive surfaces offer novel research possibilities on dedicated collaborative visualization platforms.

While many benefits exist to combining interactive surface and visualization research, much remains to be learned about the effects of providing a visual data exploration experience on interactive surfaces. For example, we need to learn more about (a) how to re-design desktop- and mouse-based systems for alternative forms of input, (b) when people would conduct data exploration in novel vs. traditional interfaces, and (c) how novel input modalities, on a higher-level, change the ability of viewers to understand data and draw insights from it. In addition, interactive surfaces often come in the forms of larger screens, smaller screens, more screens, higher pixel counts, and multiple simultaneous inputs, all of which create additional challenges for visualization designers.

In an effort to explore this research space, we would like to organize this workshop to give researchers and practitioners with a dual interest in interactive surfaces and visualization a chance to exchange ideas and perspectives on these challenges and to discuss how emerging devices can be used as new platforms for visualization research, data analysis, and data exploration. The workshop will be the second iteration of the first DEXIS workshop held at ITS 2011 [1, 3].

Topics Covered in the Workshop

We concentrate on discussing issues pertaining to the design of information visualization, scientific visualization, and visual analytics systems on interactive surfaces. Topics of interest include, but are not limited to:

- the design of information visualization, scientific visualization, or visual analytics interfaces and environments for interactive surfaces,
- the design of interactive visual representations for collaborative work on interactive surfaces,
- the design of multi-display environments for data analysis,
- the use of interactive surfaces to visualize and interact with information and data,
- guidelines and best practices for visualization and analysis environments on interactive surfaces,
- visual analysis and exploration for a wider range of audiences using emerging display technology,
- aspects of cognition in interactive visualization and visual analysis environments,
- evaluation of interaction in single- or multi-user visualization systems on interactive surfaces,
- collaborative visualization and visual analytics systems with interactive surfaces,
- collaborative sensemaking and its connection to interactive displays, and
- comparative experiences of visualization on desktop and on interactive surfaces.

Time	Event
09:00–09:10	Introduction & overview of the workshop structure
09:10–09:30	Minute Madness
09:30–10:00	Open Discussion
10:00–11:00	Design space characterization
11:00–12:00	Breakout sessions based on specialized topics such as multimodal interaction, varying requirements for information visualization, scientific visualization, and visual analytics, etc.
12:00-13:00	Consolidate workshop discussion and identify research agenda to address identified research challenges

Table 1: Proposed schedule.

Nature of the Workshop

The main goal of the workshop is to bring together researchers with shared interests on the topics named above. Together, we will identify and discuss challenges in the field, exchange experiences about ongoing research and best practices, and gather ideas about how interactive surfaces can be combined best with visualization systems.

We will follow the general contextual frame of "Past, Present, and Future"—we will discuss past research on visualization for interactive surfaces (presented by the participants), define the present design space with its technical characteristics and design options, and develop a future research agenda. The main focus of the covered topics in these discussions will depend on the submissions received.

As outcomes of the workshop, we expect

- to discuss success stories of using touch-enabled surfaces for practical visualization applications and to perhaps jointly collect these in a website—as already started here: http://goo.gl/5a0zH .
- to identify open challenges for information visualization, scientific visualization, and visual analytics applications using interactive surfaces with a focus on one joint topic (e. g., mobile visualization, touch interaction, increasing or reducing pixel counts, visualization redesign, . . .),
- to extract ideas for novel input modalities for visualization tools, and thus,
- to shape a research agenda for the use of surface computing and novel input paradigms in the visualization domains for the next years.

A first research agenda for visualization on interactive surfaces was published by participants and organizers of the DEXIS 2011 workshop [3]. This workshop should also to lead to a publication that, however, will be more focused on a highlighted topic. For example, visualization for mobile devices is an extremely interesting and promising area which could (pending interested by workshop attendees) be a focus topic.

The outcome of the breakout groups will be published along with the workshop papers in a technical report format to make it more widely available.

Format of the Workshop

Position Statements

We will invite position papers of up to four pages in length which will be reviewed by the program committee (PC). Accepted papers will be published on the workshop web site prior to the event after authors' finalization. Position papers can discuss past research in the area, provide a discussion of the design space for a specific subfield of visualization for interactive surfaces, or define a preliminary research agenda.

Agenda

The workshop will be structured as follows (Table 1).

We will start with a short overview of the day and give an introduction to the workshop topic. This introduction will be followed by a minute madness session in which participants will quickly present their position statement followed by a short open discussion. The next hour will be devoted to intense discussion of the design space of visualization systems for interactive surfaces.

We will break out into several smaller groups to draft the design space for specific topic areas. In addition to investigating the different requirements of information visualization, scientific visualization, and visual analytics, we will look at common aspects. Specifically, we will discuss how to support not only the most common interactions that are essential to the given visualization domain but also less common ones.

This design space and focus on one main topic of interest. The goal is to develop a clear view on this topic and how visualization and surfaces meet (e. g., with respect to mobile devices). We will use the discussion to identify the role of visualization systems, discuss what is missing from current types of systems, what visualizations can offer, and how to build and deploy useful data exploration environments. The outcome of this discussion should provide us with a refined research agenda along with pressing research challenges.

Participants and Workshop Attraction

To achieve a diversity of participants, we will actively advertise the workshop to people with backgrounds in the relevant fields. The target size of the workshop is about 20 participants (including organizers) in order to assure at least three breakout groups while making a plenary discussion feasible. We will select participants according to a number of criteria, which include:

- originality and controversy of position paper,
- complimentary nature of research background, and
- quality of previous publications related to the workshop.

Program Committee

We will ask a mixture of HCI and visualization researchers from the three areas (InfoVis, SciVis, and Visual Analytics) to join our PC and review 2–3 position papers. Our potential candidates are:

Mehdi Ammi, *CNRS (France)*
Craig Anslow, *Middlesex University (UK)*
Anastasia Bezerianos, *Univ. Paris Sud (France)*
Raimund Dachselt, *University of Dresden (Germany)*
Steven Drucker, *Microsoft Research (United States)*
Niklas Elmqvist, *University of Maryland (United States)*
Chi-Wing (Philip) Fu, *Nanyang Tech. Univ. (Singapore)*
Michael Haller, *Upper Austria Univ. of Applied Sciences (Austria)*
Daniel F. Keefe, *Univ. Minnesota (United States)*
Narges Mahyar, *University of British Columbia (Canada)*
Stacey Scott, *University of Waterloo (Canada)*
Chia Shen, *Harvard (United States)*
John Stasko, *Georgia Tech (United States)*
Christian Tominski, *University of Rostock (Germany)*
Melanie Tory, *University of Victoria (Canada)*
Wesley Willett, *University of Calgary (Canada)*
Anders Ynnermann, *Linköping University (Sweden)*

References

[1] Isenberg, P., Carpendale, S., Hesselmann, T., Isenberg, T., and Lee, B., Eds. *Proc. DEXIS (November 13, 2011, Kobe, Japan)*, INRIA (France, 2012).

[2] Isenberg, P., and Isenberg, T. Visualization on interactive surfaces: A research overview. *i-com 12*, 3 (Nov. 2013), 10–17. doi> 10.1524/icom.2013.0020

[3] Isenberg, P., Isenberg, T., Hesselmann, T., Lee, B., von Zadow, U., and Tang, A. Data visualization on interactive surfaces: A research agenda. *IEEE Computer Graphics and Applications 33*, 2 (Mar./Apr. 2013), 16–24. doi> 10.1109/MCG.2013.24

Workshop: MULTIsensory Interaction and Assistive Technology: Feasibility and Effectiveness (MULTI-AT)

Luca Brayda
Istituto Italiano di Tecnologia, Genoa, Italy
luca.brayda@iit.it

Andrea Serino
EPFL, Lausanne, Switzerland
andrea.serino@epfl.ch

Elisabeth Wilhelm
Imperial College London, United Kingdom
e.wilhelm@imperial.ac.uk

Marc Macé
Institut de Recherche en Informatique de Toulouse, France
marc.mace@irit.fr

ITS '15, November 15-18, 2015, Funchal, Portugal.
ACM 978-1-4503-3899-8/15/11.
http://dx.doi.org/10.1145/2817721.2835069

Abstract

The wide availability of human-computer interfaces which stimulate our senses (vision, hearing and touch) does not equally serve all categories of end users: people with sensory and/or motor disabilities cannot access information as the majority does, because solutions for the wider public are implicitly designed for persons with average sensory abilities. Assistive technologies exploit alternative stimulation methodologies complementing the residual sensory channels. [1, 2] Successful implementations would give people with disabilities the possibility of using everybody's human-computer interfaces [3] or the possibility of developing new interfaces for therapeutic and rehabilitation purposes.

However, many assistive devices, which look promising at a superficial level, do not go beyond initial curiosity. The most common sources of failure are, at the design stage, the lack of serious clinical tests proving the effectiveness of the stimulation methods. At the end user level, instead, failure comes from the interference of this new signal with the residual sensory channels and/or the negative impact in the social life of the person. For these reasons the joint effort of researchers and experts in the rehabilitation field is a mandatory step to design well-targeted, useful, socially acceptable novel devices [4].

The goal of this workshop is to attract contributions from scientists working on multisensory perception and related methodologies, to technologists and engineers interested in investigating alternative solutions for multisensory stimulation and to clinicians interested in developing new therapeutic strategies based on novel interfaces.

The ultimate purpose of this workshop is to integrate common interests in an interdisciplinary fashion from experts of different fields, which stem from the needs of end users and span up to technological solutions.

Author Keywords
Human machine interfaces, multisensory perception, haptic and tactile displays, acoustic feedback, sensory impairment, cognition, robotics, neuroprosthetics, rehabilitation.

ACM Classification Keywords
H.5.m. Information interfaces and presentation (e.g., HCI): Miscellaneous; K.4.2. Computers and society: Social issues

Audience

Topics include, but are not limited to, multisensory perception and integration, interaction through visual, acoustic and tactile feedback for disabled individuals (novel interfaces and studies about people with visual, acoustic or neuropathic impairment), learning methods for the rehabilitation of sensory and cognitive impairment, haptics and robotics for diagnostic and therapeutic applications, design of rehabilitation devices and protocols.

Program Committee

- Caterina Bertini, Università di Bologna, Italy
- Jaume Esteve Tintó, IMB-CNM (CSIC), Spain
- Alessandro Farne – INSERM, France
- Simon Gallo, Ecole Polytechnique Fédérale de Lausanne, Switzerland
- Franck Gonzalez, Imperial College London, United Kingdom
- Christophe Jouffrais, Institut de Recherche en Informatique de Toulouse, France
- Miguel Nacenta, University of St. Andrews, Scotland
- Francesco Pavani - University of Trento, Italy
- Bastian E. Rapp, Karlsruhe Institute of Technology, Germany
- Giulio Rognini, Ecole Polytechnique Fédérale de Lausanne, Switzerland
- Alice Roy - CNRS, France
- Giulio Sandini, Istituto Italiano di Tecnologia, Italy
- Rainer Stiefelhagen, Karlsruhe Institute of Technology, Germany

- Carla Tinti, Università di Torino, Italy
- Gerhard Weber, University of Dresden, Germany
- Limin Zeng, University of Dresden, Germany

Relevance to Tabletop and Interactive Surface community

The workshop will involve research projects involving experimental setups and prototypes, which put the end users in direct or indirect interaction with surfaces. We will consider as "surface" an object, external to the end user or wearable, which provides multisensory stimulations. We will also consider the human skin and body as an alternative surface where targeted stimuli can be projected to provide information or guide neural plasticity.

The interaction will be focused on tasks, which are relevant for assistive applications, specifically focusing on education, serious gaming, assessment of learning and personal spaces, visualization and attention, rehabilitation.

Topics covered in the workshop and planned activities

- Construction of cognitive maps
- Information visualization on unconventional surfaces
- Tactile graphics
- Virtual reality
- Assistive devices for visually impaired people
- Assistive devices for hearing impaired people
- Haptic and tactile displays
- Rehabilitation robots

Research questions to be addressed

How can we enforce knowledge transfer between scientists working in multisensory perception, engineers developing assistive devices and clinicians potentially applying the devices to rehabilitation contexts?

How will an accessible tool for displaying information to a broader community look like?

How can we design assistive devices and rehabilitation robots that address multiple sensory modalities?

What can we learn from former projects that addressed the development of assistive and rehabilitation devices but failed during the attempt?

What is the potential of a display that is able to address other sensory modalities than vision?

Acknowledgements

The organization of this workshop is supported by the FP7 EU STREP project BLINDPAD (www.blindpad.eu) One of the organizers is supported by a fellowship within the Postdoc-Program of the German Academic Exchange Service (DAAD).

References

[1] Chouvardas, V.G., Miliou, A.N. and Hatalis, M.K.: Tactile displays: Overview and recent advances. In: *Displays 29* (2008), 185-194

[2] Vidal-Verdu, F., & Hafez, M. (2007). Graphical tactile displays for visually-impaired people. *Neural Systems and Rehabilitation Engineering, IEEE Transactions on*, *15*(1), 119-130.

[3] Maidenbaum, S., Abboud, S., Amedi, A., (2014). Sensory substitution: Closing the gap between basic research and widespread practical visual rehabilitation. Neuroscience & Biobehavioral Reviews, Multisensory integration, sensory substitution and visual rehabilitation 41, 3–15. doi:10.1016/j.neubiorev.2013.11.007

[4] Brayda, L., Campus, C. ,Memeo, M., Lucagrossi, L. (2015), The importance of visual experience, gender and emotion in the assessment of an assistive tactile mouse. *in Haptics, IEEE Transactions on* PP, 1–1. doi:10.1109/TOH.2015.2426692

Shared Infrastructures for Tangible Tabletops & Interactive Surfaces

Martin Kaltenbrunner
University of Art and Design, Linz
4020 Linz, Austria
martin.kaltenbrunner@ufg.at

Florian Echtler
Bauhaus-Universität Weimar
93324 Weimar, Germany
florian.echtler@uni-weimar.de

Abstract

Although interactive surfaces have been a constant topic of research during the last decades, there is still little agreement on shared infrastructures for their conception and development. While the mainstream industry has already partially integrated basic multi-touch functionality in most mobile and some desktop platforms, any further attempts of introducing commercial table-tops have been largely abandoned since. Therefore our research community that seeks to conceive and implement novel interactive tabletop concepts, often relies on the prototyping of individualized solutions or the integration and extension of openly shared community solutions.

One example of such a shared ecosystem is the TUIO protocol [1] which has been designed to encode and transport a low-level interface abstraction within a wide variety of settings, from tangible user interfaces to multi-touch tabletops. However, our community also needs further implementations of common middle-ware solutions such as gesture-recognition or object classification as well as their integration into high-level development frameworks. Furthermore it would be also desirable to establish a shared collection of building-blocks at the hardware-level. Such a common ecosystem may not only accelerate the development efforts of our community, but should also ensure the scientific quality control through reproducible and comparable results.

ITS '15, November 15-18, 2015, Funchal, Portugal
ACM 978-1-4503-3899-8/15/11.
http://dx.doi.org/10.1145/2817721.2835070

Author Keywords
Protocols & APIs; Standardization; Open Source; Tangible Interfaces; Multitouch Surfaces; Programming Frameworks

ACM Classification Keywords
H.5.2 [User Interfaces]: Input devices and strategies; D.2.2 [Design Tools and Techniques]: User Interfaces; D.2.12 [Interoperability]: Interface definition languages

Objectives
The goal for this workshop is to gather researchers and practitioners who work on standardizing and streamlining development for software and hardware interfaces in the ITS context, learn about their ongoing efforts and identify possible roadblocks to a wider adoption. We hope to initiate a small developer community in which future efforts can be planned, discussed and collaboratively developed, with a strong focus on shared standards, open source software as well as open design hardware implementations.

Call for Participation
We invite researchers & practitioners who work on protocols, frameworks, APIs and similar efforts in the realm of interactive surfaces and tangible interaction to submit position papers describing their ongoing work on these topics. Position papers should be between 2 and 4 pages in length and follow the ACM SIGCHI Extended Abstract format. A jury will select the submissions based on their connection to the workshop topic as well as their suitability for stimulating discussion and ideas for future collaboration. Accepted papers will be archived on the workshop homepage.

Workshop Structure
This workshop intends to allow the detailed presentation, demonstration and discussion of the selected projects. After a general introduction and the following individual presentations in the morning, there will be the opportunity to show-case and experiment with all software and hardware projects in a hands-on session in the afternoon. A concluding panel will discuss the future goals for the shared development efforts. In addition to the actual presenters this workshop is also open to an interested audience.

10:00 - 11:00 Introduction
11:00 - 13:00 Presentations
13:00 - 14:00 Lunch
14:00 - 16:00 Code & Demo
16:00 - 17:00 Discussion

Biographies
Martin Kaltenbrunner is professor at the Interface Culture Lab at the University of Art and Design in Linz. He has been responsible for the interaction design of the Reactable - an electronic musical instrument with a tabletop user interface. In this context he developed the open source tangible interaction framework reacTIVision and the related TUIO protocol, which have been since widely employed for the realization of tangible tabletop applications.

Florian Echtler is junior professor at the Faculty of Media at Bauhaus-Universität Weimar. His research interests focus on formal languages for gesture descriptions and design of multimodal development frameworks. Additional topics covered by his research include computer vision for HCI applications, sensor technology and rapid prototyping.

REFERENCES

1. M. Kaltenbrunner, T. Bovermann, R. Bencina, and E. Costanza. 2005. TUIO - A Protocol for Table Based Tangible User Interfaces. In *Proceedings of the 6th International Workshop on Gesture in Human Computer Interaction and Simulation.* Vannes, France.

Interaction Techniques for Wall-Sized Screens

Lars Lischke
HCI Lab, VIS
University of Stuttgart
Stuttgart, Germany
lars.lischke@vis.uni-stuttgart.de

Albrecht Schmidt
HCI Lab, VIS
University of Stuttgart
Stuttgart, Germany
albrecht.schmidt@vis.uni-stuttgart.de

Jürgen Grüninger
Intel Visual Computing Institute
Saarland University
Saarbrücken, Germany
juergen.grueninger@dfki.de

Philipp Slusallek
German research center for Artificial Intelligence (DFKI)
Saarbrücken, Germany
philipp.slusallek@dfki.de

Khalil Klouche
Helsinki Institute for Information Technology HIIT, Department of Computer Science, University of Helsinki, Finland
khalil.klouche@helsinki.fi

Giulio Jacucci
Helsinki Institute for Information Technology HIIT, Department of Computer Science, University of Helsinki, Finland
giulio.jacucci@helsinki.fi

ITS '15, November 15-18, 2015, Funchal, Portugal
ACM 978-1-4503-3899-8/15/11.
http://dx.doi.org/10.1145/2817721.2835071

Abstract
Large screen displays are part of many future visions, such as i-LAND [11] that describes the possible workspace of the future. Research showed that wall-sized screens provide clear benefits for data exploration, collaboration and organizing work in office environments. With the increase of computational power and falling display prices wall-sized screens currently make the step out of research labs and specific settings into office environments and private life. Today, there is no standard set of interaction techniques for interacting with wall-sized displays and it is even unclear if a single mode of input is suitable for all potential applications. In this workshop, we will bring together researchers from academia and industry who work on large screens. Together, we will survey current research directions, review promising interaction techniques, and identify the underlying fundamental research challenges.

Author Keywords
Large displays, wall-sized displays, public displays, interaction

ACM Classification Keywords
H.5.2 [User Interfaces]: Graphical user interfaces (GUI).

Background

Marc Weiser's vision "Computing for the 21st century" [14] introduces three classes of devices to interact with digital content: "tabs", "pads" and "boards". "Tabs" and "pads" have already become commonplace with smartphones and tablet computers. In contrast, digital "boards" are still rarely used. However, there is a good chance that wall-sized display-"boards" will become commonplace within the next decade, like smartphones and tables did in the last decade. This development is in particular supported by software innovations. One example of software innovation is "Display as a Service" (DaaS) [7] which allows to display content from different sources across multiple single monitors without special synchronization hardware. By replacing specialized hardware with software like this, wall-sized displays and multi-display environments become significantly easier to set up.

Today, wall-sized displays are mainly used to visualize large and complex data. This is in particular beneficial, because humans are able to scan large areas quickly for objects and visual cues [5]. However, wall-sized public displays are becoming ubiquitous and are often used either for media installations or as information boards. Thereby, they do not only offer information to the user but can also help people to get in touch with each other [9].

In general, the success of wall-sized display installations depends highly on the interaction technique used in the particular setup. Already in 2006, Baudisch called for new user interfaces for wall-sized displays and tabletops [1]. In the future, wall-sized displays will not only be used in the context of professional visualizations and public displays, they will also become commonplace in office and some home environments. The large variety of interaction techniques and device form-factors we will use, need 1) a clear understanding of advantages and disadvantages of interaction techniques, and 2) an abstraction layer for software applications to map different interaction techniques in accordance to the specific given hardware setup of the user.

Workshop Goals and Themes

The goal of this workshop is to bring researchers together, who are focusing on interaction with wall-sized displays and multi-display environments, and to discuss challenges we are facing as research community. The results of the workshop will inspire work in the areas outlined below. As outcome of the workshop, we aim for a set of methods, challenges and topics in the field of wall-sized displays for possible joined publications and collaborations.

Appropriate input techniques depending on context of use
We see multiple approaches to interact with wall-sized displays. Kuikkaniemi et al. [4] propose a system using direct touch for presentations in public settings. In contrast, Liu et al. [6] used a remote touch pad for data manipulation. Zadow et al. [13] proposed to use a touch display mounted to user's arm in addition to direct touch. Morris [8] argued for using gestures for interacting with large displays in private homes. Seyed et al. [10] designed a gesture set for interacting in multi-device environments. In such environments, wall-sized screens, tabletops and mobile devices are connected. The variety of areas of applications and interaction techniques indicate that there might not be one standard interaction technique for wall-sized displays. We need to design categories for areas of applications and interaction techniques.

Content Representation on Wall-Sized Screens
When using abundant display space, organizing visual content, such as application windows, becomes a challenging task. Grudin [2] discovered the issue of focal and peripheral awareness for multi-monitor users. We as humans are used to map locations to information and tools [3]. Additionally, large display space enables uses to switch between tasks without hiding other information. These findings indicate a high importance of arranging content on wall-sized displays. For wall-sized displays in office environments, we assume that there are different areas on screen for different tasks. The classical approaches used by common window management, are not sufficient for wall-sized displays. We need to design new concepts to assist users to arrange visual content.

Novel Interaction Techniques
There are multiple sensors, which seem to be underexplored as sensors to interact with wall-sized displays. On body sensors like EMG or brain computer interfaces (BCI) promise to measure cognitive load. This technology could be used to adjust visual content on wall-sized display in accordance to the mental state of the users. This could lead to less information overload and thereby to a deeper engagement with the data set. In addition, BCIs are becoming smaller and less pricey. Turner et al. [12] proposes gaze in combination with touch to manipulate content on wall-sized displays. All these us to determine the user's mental state when interacting. Thereby the content can be adjusted to user's needs.

Towards standards for input techniques
The large number of different interaction techniques is challenging the design and implementation of successful applications. For example, there will be situations where, it might be interesting to use a wall-sized display without touch input, to give a presentation designed for a wall-sized display with touch input. To enable successful application development we need to design an abstraction model, which maps virtual actions to interaction techniques with specific input devices. There is also a need for mapping applications to a huge variety of screen sizes and screen resolutions. In an optimal case, this would not only cover different setups of wall-sized displays, but also desktop setups and mobile devices.

Organizers
Lars Lischke is a second year PhD-Student at the University of Stuttgart. Before he studied computer science in Stuttgart, Germany and Gothenburg, Sweden. In his PhD he focuses on new technologies for data exploration and interaction with large displays.
Jürgen Grüninger is a Researcher and PhD-Student at the Intel Visual Computing Institute and German Research Center for Artificial Intelligence (DFKI) in Saarbrücken. Before, he studied computer science in Reutlingen, Germany. His research focuses on exchangeable interaction metaphors, devices and graphical interfaces and the combination of those for various application areas, including large displays.
Khalil Klouche is a PhD-Student at the Aalto School of Arts, Design and Architecture and a researcher at the Helsinki Institute for Information Technology (HIIT). He received a Master of Arts in Media Design at the Geneva University of Art and Design in 2013. His research focuses on designing interfaces supporting information exploration.
Albrecht Schmidt holds the chair for HCI at the University of Stuttgart. He is co-founder of the ACM conference on Tangible and Embedded Interaction (TEI) and initiated the conference on Automotive User Interfaces. Albrecht is an associate editor in chief of the IEEE Pervasive Computing Magazine and edits a column

on invisible Computing in the IEEE Computer Magazine.

Philipp Slusallek is Scientific Director at the DFKI, where he heads the research area Agents and Simulated Reality. He is also Director for Research at the Intel Visual Computing Institute. His research interests are focused on novel service-oriented architectures for 3D-Internet technology, integrating research in areas such as real-time realistic graphics, artificial intelligence, high-performance computing as well as security by design for creating distributed, immersive, collaborative environments for simulation, analysis, visualization, and training.

Giulio Jacucci is Professor at the Department of Computer Science and director of the Network Society Programme at the HIIT. His research field is in HCI including: mobile interaction, mediated social interaction, multimodal and implicit interaction, haptics and tangible computing, mixed reality, and persuasive technologies. He co-authored Design Things by MIT press. He is also co-founder and member of the board of directors of MultiTaction.com. MultiTouch Ltd. is a spin-off from a EU FET and leader in modular interactive screens.

Acknowledgment: This work is partially funded by the European Community's H2020 Program under the funding scheme "FETPROACT-1-2014: Global Systems Science (GSS)", grant agreement # 641191 CIMPLEX.

References

[1] Baudisch, P. Interacting with Large Displays. *Computer 39*, 4 (2006), 96–97.

[2] Grudin, J. Partitioning digital worlds. In *Proc. CHI* (2001), 458–465.

[3] Kirsh, D. The intelligent use of space. *Artificial Intelligence 73*, 1-2 (1995), 31–68.

[4] Kuikkaniemi, K., Vilkki, M., Ojala, J., Nelimarkka, M., and Jacucci, G. Introducing Kupla UI : A Generic Interactive Wall User Interface Based on Spherical Widgets. In *Proc. ITS* (2013), 301–304.

[5] Lischke, L., Mayer, S., Wolf, K., Henze, N., Schmidt, A., Leifert, S., and Reiterer, H. Using Space: Effect of Display Size on Users' Search Performance. In *Proc. CHI EA* (2015), 1845–1850.

[6] Liu, C., Chapuis, O., Beaudouin-Lafon, M., Lecolinet, E., and Mackay, W. E. Effects of display size and navigation type on a classification task. In *Proc. CHI* (2014), 4147–4156.

[7] Löffler, A., Pica, L., Hoffmann, H., and Slusallek, P. Networked Displays for VR Applications: Display as a Service. In *ICAT/EGVE/EuroVR* (2012), 37–44.

[8] Morris, M. R. Web on the wall. In *Proc. ITS*, ACM Press (2012), 95.

[9] Peltonen, P., Kurvinen, E., Salovaara, A., Jacucci, G., Ilmonen, T., Evans, J., Oulasvirta, A., and Saarikko, P. It's Mine, Don't Touch! In *Proc. CHI* (2008), 1285.

[10] Seyed, T., Burns, C., Costa Sousa, M., Maurer, F., and Tang, A. Eliciting usable gestures for multi-display environments. In *Proc. ITS* (2012), 41.

[11] Streitz, N. A., Geiß ler, J., Holmer, T., Konomi, S., Müller-Tomfelde, C., Reischl, W., Rexroth, P., Seitz, P., and Steinmetz, R. i-LAND: an interactive landscape for creativity and innovation. In *Proc. CHI* (1999), 120–127.

[12] Turner, J., Alexander, J., Bulling, A., and Gellersen, H. Gaze+RST: Integrating Gaze and Multitouch for Remote Rotate-Scale-Translate Tasks. In *Proc. CHI* (2015), 4179–4188.

[13] von Zadow, U., Büschel, W., Langner, R., and Dachselt, R. SleeD: Using a Sleeve Display to Interact with Touch-sensitive Display Walls. In *Proc. ITS* (2014), 129–138.

[14] Weiser, M. The Computer for the 21st Century. *Scientific American 265*, 3 (1991), 94–104.

Author Index

www.ingramcontent.com/pod-product-compliance
Lightning Source LLC
LaVergne TN
LVHW082022200926
848481LV00010B/2907